The Larger Hope

John Murray (1741-1815), founder of American Universalism

THE LARGER HOPE

The First Century of the Universalist Church in America 1770-1870

Russell E. Miller

UNITARIAN UNIVERSALIST ASSOCIATION BOSTON

Printed in the United States of America

Library of Congress Cataloging in Publication Data

Miller, Russell E., 1916-
The Larger Hope.

Includes bibliographical references and index.
CONTENTS: v. 1. The first century of the Universalist Church America, 1770-1870.
1. Universalist Church of America—History.
2. Universalism—History. I. Title.
BX9933.M54 289.1'73 79-13789
ISBN 0-93340-00-4 (v.1)

ERRATA

The sequence of pages 107 — 110 is incorrect
The proper order is 106, 109, 110, 107, 108
Page 374, line 17. Sentence ends after the word "year"

First Printing, May 1979

CONTENTS

ILLUSTRATIONS

PAGE

FOREWORD

"What has a Universalist, who really and sincerely believes that doctrine, to fear?" asked the early 19th century Methodist circuit-riding preacher Peter Cartwright. "Just nothing at all; for this flesh-pleasing, conscience soothing doctrine will not only justify him in his neglect of God and man, but gives fallen nature an unlimited license to serve the devil with greediness in any and every possible way that his degenerate fallen soul requires or desires."—*Autobiography of Peter Cartwright,* originally published in 1856.

As this book chronicles, Universalists, freed from fear of damnation, gave themselves to humanitarian service not depraved wickedness. No wonder their doctrines spread so far and fast. The idea of human worth and divine love fitted the pioneer spirit of initiative and opportunity. In its first hundred years, the Universalist Church grew to become a large and influential denomination in America. Yet that story has not in our time been adequately told. No comprehensive history has existed since the 1880s. Ten years ago the Universalist Historical Society pledged all its financial assets to fill the vacuum. Taking its accumulated funds and raising additional money, it commissioned Russell E. Miller to research and relate the largely untold tale.

Some feared, with the 1961 merger with the then larger Unitarians, that Universalism would die. The second century of the Universalist Church is a story of decline and disappointment. (That history, also by Dr. Miller, is under way as a companion volume.)

But Universalism did not die. Its teachings of love leavened the loaf of American Protestantism. Its institutions of education and service enlightened many persons and communities. Its churches and denominational agencies strengthened the new Unitarian Universalist Association. Its people cherish the tradition, as the extraordinary response to financial appeals to help publish this work testify. (A complete list of contributing organizations, churches, and individuals follows this foreword.)

Universalism lives in the hearts and minds not only of old-line members but also of Unitarians who with merger adopted its traditions, and of thousands who have joined since 1961. "Unitarian Universalist" is too long a label and thus is often abbreviated "UU" or simply "Unitarian," but its contemporary religious expressions are warmer, more inclusive, more hopeful . . . . more Universalist than is readily recognized. The publication of this history ought help enlarge that awareness.

Christopher Gist Raible
President, Universalist Historical Society
June, 1978

ACKNOWLEDGMENTS

These individuals and organizations helped to make publication of this book possible. We are most grateful to them for their encouragement and support.

Conventions and Organizations

Central Midwest District, U.U.A.

Georgia Universalist Convention

Meadville Theological School (Unitarian) of Lombard College (Universalist)

New York State Convention of Universalists

North Carolina Universalist Convention

Northeast District, U.U.A.

Ohio-Meadville District, U.U.A.

Ontario Universalist Convention

Pennsylvania Universalist Convention

Prairie Star District, Unitarian Universalist

St. Lawrence University

Starr King School for Religious Leadership

Vermont & Quebec Unitarian Universalist Convention

Tufts University

Unitarian Universalist Association

Churches and Groups

Universalist Church, Santa Paula, California

First Universalist Society, New Haven, Connecticut

Rockwell Universalist Church (Grace House Memorial Fund) Hoschton, Georgia

Unitarian Universalist Society of Black Hawk County, Cedar Falls, Iowa

Ladies Aid of Unitarian Universalist Church, Caribou, Maine

First Parish Church of Berlin (Massachusetts)

Benevolent Fraternity of Unitarian Universalist Churches, Boston, Massachusetts

Kings Chapel, Boston, Massachusetts

First Parish Unitarian Universalist, Canton, Massachusetts

First Universalist Society, Franklin, Massachusetts

Independent Christian Church, Gloucester, Massachusetts

Ladies Circle Unitarian Universalist, Haverhill, Massachusetts

Unitarian Universalist Church (In memory of Mary and Fred McGregor, Edward Chesley and Aurola Pickard), Haverhill, Massachusetts

Unitarian Sunday School Society, Hudson, Massachusetts

First Universalist Society, Rockport, Massachusetts

Charities Committee, Trustees Spinney Fund, Unitarian Universalist Church of Greater Lynn, Swampscott, Massachusetts

First Universalist Church, Clark Lake, Michigan

Unitarian Universalist Women's Federation, Ellisville, Mississippi

Red Hill Universalist Church, Rose Hill, North Carolina

Federated Church of Marlborough, New Hampshire

Unitarian Universalist Church, Manchester, New Hampshire

Unitarian Circle, Wilton, New Hampshire

Unitarian Universalist Fellowship, Murray Grove, New Jersey

"The Pull Togethers" - Pullman Memorial Universalist Church, Albion, New York

Pullman Memorial Universalist Church, Albion, New York

"The Murray Class" group (Universalist Women), Unitarian Universalist Church, Auburn, New York

Unitarian Universalist Church, Canton, New York

St. Paul's Universalist Church, Little Falls, New York

Association Universalist Women, First Universalist Church, Syracuse, New York

First Universalist Society, First Universalist Church, Syracuse, New York

Association Universalist Women, Clinton, North Carolina

Association Universalist Women, Kinston, North Carolina

Judith Murray League of Unitarian Universalist Church, Akron, Ohio

Clayton Memorial Church, Newberry, South Carolina

Unitarian Universalist Church, Springfield, Vermont

West Bequest Trustees, Universalist Historical Church, Halifax, Nova Scotia

Individuals

Abdu, Mrs. Cyanne (Youngstown, Ohio)

Achenbach, Rev. and Mrs. Lyman (Oneonta, New York)

Adams, Rev. Eugene H. (Medford, Massachusetts)

Armbruster, Mr. and Mrs. Edward (Massapequa, New York)

Artman, Elinor (Cincinnati, Ohio)

Baker, Mr. and Mrs. Woody (Western Springs, Illinois)

Bakker, Rev. and Mrs. Cornelis J. (Gardner, Massachusetts)

Bialas, Jr., Mr. and Mrs. Michael E. (Chicago, Illinois)

Bowering, Rev. Vinton B. and Rev. Janet Hartzell (Haverhill, Massachusetts)

Brayton, Allison (Medford, Massachusetts)

Brooks, Rev. Seth R. (Washington, D.C.)

Campbell, Rev. Fred F. (Grosse Pointe, Michigan)

Carpenter, Rev. Frank W. (Wilton, New Hampshire)

Chandler, Prof. B.J. (Kingsville, Texas)

Christenson, Mr. and Mrs. Carl O. (Newtonville, Massachusetts)

Cleary, Rev. Maryell (North Olmsted, Ohio)

Cole, Mrs. Barbara S. (Wilmington, Vermont)

Corlett, Mrs. Webster D. (River Forest, Illinois)

Croom, Mrs. George H. (Kinston, North Carolina)

Crosby, Mrs. J.W. (Moravia, New York)

Davies, Mr. and Mrs. Francis M. (Maywood, Illinois)

Davies, Mrs. Mildred H. (Raleigh, North Carolina)

Dick, Rev. and Mrs. Robert T. (Elkhart, Indiana)

Donovan, William A. (South Weymouth, Massachusetts)

Erichsen, Mr. and Mrs. Frank P. (Ft. Worth, Texas)

Folsom, Rev. Ida M. (Dover-Foxcroft, Maine)

Gaines, Rev. and Mrs. Charles A. (Framingham Centre, Massachusetts)

Gardner, Rev. William E. (Wilmington, Delaware)

Graney, Mrs. Harold (Auburn, New York)

Greene, Mr. and Mrs. Nicholas H. (Lanoka Harbor, New Jersey)

Greve, Mr. and Mrs. Russell T. (Hopkinton, Massachusetts)
Haight, Mrs. Lyndon (Auburn, New York)
Harmon, Mr. and Mrs. Lindsey R. (Arlington, Massachusetts)
Hawkes, Rev. Kenneth C. (Falmouth, Maine)
Herzog, Mrs. Marion Rawls (Oak Park, Illinois)
Hobbs, Mr. and Mrs. Clinton H. (Kent, Ohio)
Holman, Sherwood (North Olmsted, Ohio)
Hough, Ms. Elizabeth B. (Gloucester, Massachusetts)
Houser, Rev. and Mrs. Argyl E. (Ann Arbor, Michigan)
Hunting, Mr. and Mrs. Everett C. (Berkeley, California)
Johnson, Kenneth M. (Bangor, Maine)
Joslyn, Jr., Clyde F. (Framingham, Massachusetts)
Kapp, Rev. Max A. (Vineyard Haven, Massachusetts)
King, Mrs. Charles R. (Oak Park, Illinois)
King, Miss Fannie (Auburn, New York)
Lavan, Rev. Spencer (Lexington, Massachusetts)
Leaming, Rev. Marjorie N. (Santa Paula, California)
Loomis, Mr. and Mrs. Ralph A. (Ann Arbor, Michigan)
Lovejoy, Rev. and Mrs. Warren B. (Rochester, New Hampshire)
MacDonald, Mrs. Earl L. (Hendersonville, North Carolina)
MacPherson, Rev. and Mrs. David H. (Richmond, Virginia)
Masdam, Mr. and Mrs. Oscar J. (Auburn, New York)
McKeeman, Rev. and Mrs. Gordon B. (Akron, Ohio)
Miller, Rev. and Mrs. David J. (Holden, Massachusetts)
Needham, Robert F. (Concord, Mass.)
Nieuwejaar, Rev. Olav F. (Milford, New Hampshire)
Smith, Rev. and Mrs. Donald (Addison, Michigan)
Spire, Mrs. Lyman J. (Wausau, Wis.)
Thurlow, Mrs. Cora (King) (Weedsport, New York)
Wait, Cleon G. (Sarasota, Florida)
Wallace, Mrs. Fremont S. (DeWitt, New York)
Webb, Mr. and Mrs. Hartwell M. (Washington, D.C.)
Webb, Rev. Theodore A. (Sacramento, California)
White, Mr. and Mrs. Marvin H. (Columbia, Maryland)
Williams, Carl H. (Hopkinsville, Kentucky)
Wintle, Rev. Thomas D. (Lancaster, Massachusetts)
Woodis, Miss Ruth G. (Worcester, Massachusetts)
Parmelee, Miss Elizabeth (New York, New York)
Parsons, Herman A. (Waltham, Mass.)
Peterson, Mrs. Agnes (Medford, Mass.)
Rabe, Mr. and Mrs. Valentin H. (Geneseo, New York)
Raible, Rev. Christopher Gist (Worcester, Massachusetts)
Reamon, Dr. and Mrs. Ellsworth C. (Brattleboro, Vermont)
Robertson, Martha Jones (Winchester, Massachusetts)
Robinson, Rev. Philip H. (Ontario, Canada)
Seaburg, Rev. Alan L. (Medford, Massachusetts)
Seaburg, Rev. Carl G. (Medford, Massachusetts)
Shepard, Jr., William H. (Quincy, Massachusetts)
Sleeper, Mrs. Donald, Sr. (Burlington, Massachusetts)
Smadbeck, Mrs. Warren (New York, New York)

PREFACE

This is basically an institutional study, tracing the development of Universalism in organized form, and stressing its interaction with various aspects of American society as well as its internal development as a denomination. One of the principal goals has been to place Universalism on record, in as comprehensive and as accurate a manner as possible, as part of the religious landscape of the nation. The fact that the author is not a member of the denomination about which he has written presumably lends an air of objectivity, but as to that the reader must serve as the best judge.

There is the inevitable problem of what to select or omit, emphasize or minimize, in a work of this magnitude, and the author realizes his vulnerability. Sources contemporaneous with the events, movements, and personalities being discussed have been used wherever possible, among them the denominational press in particular. Documentation has been provided in chapter notes at the end of the volume. The greatest single resource has been the library of the Universalist Historical Society. This collection, which had been located at Tufts University since 1869, was donated by the Society to the Andover-Harvard Theological Library of the Harvard Divinity School (where the basic Unitarian collection is) in 1975 and has been integrated into its collection.

This work was undertaken at the request of the Universalist Historical Society, which committed a large proportion of its treasury to finance the research and writing. It was this same organization which, exactly 100 years ago, first suggested the writing of a history of the denomination prepared by Richard Eddy, a Universalist clergyman. He produced, in a two-volume work published in the 1880s, the most ambitious history written up to that time, and still an important reference work. The Society gave the present author not only generous material support, but an absolutely free hand. Errors of omission or commission, and of either fact or interpretation, rest solely with the author.

> "He who expects a faultless work to see,
> Expects what never was, and what may never be."

In a work of this scope it would be an impossibility to acknowledge properly the indebtedness of the author to the host of organizations, institutions, and individuals who have contributed in some way to its preparation. Courtesies and assistance of all kinds have been rendered by libraries and historical societies in over a dozen states, and by

Universalist organizations and individuals from Maine and Vermont to North Carolina and Georgia. Among those persons to whom special thanks are due are the officers and executive boards of the Universalist Historical Society since 1970, especially Presidents Theodore A. Webb, Carl Seaburg, and Christopher Gist Raible; Alan Seaburg, Curator of Manuscripts in the Andover-Harvard Theological Library; and Joseph S. Komidar, Librarian of Tufts University, and his staff.

January 1979

Russell E. Miller
Dickson Professor of English and
American History, Tufts University

INTRODUCTION

This is the first volume of a study tracing the evolution of the Universalist Church of America, which was merged in 1961 with the American Unitarian Association to form the Unitarian Universalist Association. One of the smaller Protestant denominations during its separate existence of almost 200 years, the Universalist Church celebrated in 1870 its centennial anniversary in Gloucester, Massachusetts, where its first church was organized in 1779. The individual considered its founder in America was John Murray, an Englishman and convert from Methodism, who landed accidentally, or as late-eighteenth and early nineteenth-century Universalists believed, providentially, on the coast of New Jersey in September 1770. It is from this date that American Universalists trace their beginnings, and it is with the period 1770-1870 that this volume is primary concerned.

During the early stages of its growth it had to contend against much opposition—legal, religious, and popular—but spread throughout New England, where it was concentrated, and eventually across the nation, following the westward migrations. By the time of its 100th anniversary it had spread, in more or less organized form, into every state and every territory, with almost 1,000 parishes. By the end of the nineteenth century it had established missions in Scotland and Japan. By 1870 it was operating or had in the planning stage five colleges or universities, nine academies and other secondary schools, and two theological schools. It operated two publishing houses, one in Boston and one in Chicago, which between them published twelve periodicals.

Theologically, the Universalists rejected the predestinarianism of Puritan Calvinism and held to the distinguishing principle of the ultimate salvation of all humanity, a concept which had recurred in European Christian teachings over a span of centuries. Firmly rooted in Biblical authority and largely unitarian rather than trinitarian from the early nineteenth century onward, Universalism conceived of a God of love who would "finally restore the whole family of mankind to holiness and happiness." Out of this belief evolved the ethos of "the fatherhood of God and the brotherhood of man" which Universalists sought to practice as well as to preach. Eschewing the revivalism and emotional fervor which characterized so much of nineteenth-century Protestantism, Universalists combined reason and Christian faith to propagate their version of revealed religion.

Organizationally, Universalists were committed to what at times became an extreme form of congregational autonomy. The denomination was a loosely organized confederation of believers who feared and abhorred centralization and frequently failed as a consequence to become an effective religious force in an era of sometimes fierce denominational competition.

Universalists saw as their mission the leavening and softening of the harshness of what they conceived to be a traditional orthodoxy, at variance with the teachings of Christ. As one Universalist expressed it in 1875, they "do not expect that their church will swallow all other churches . . . but they do expect that its distinguishing doctrine will prevail before long in all Protestant Churches, and that it will stand in the very front rank of power as an evangelizing agency."* Universalists rejected the idea of a physical hell but believed, like the majority of their fellow Christians in the nineteenth century, in the immortality of the human soul.

Lacking much of the intellectual leadership and social respectability of the Unitarians with whom they shared many theological beliefs and a commitment to religious liberalism, Universalists stressed such principles as freedom of conscience, individual interpretation of the Scriptures, separation of church and state, the inherent worth and dignity of humanity, and the democratic faith and optimism of nineteenth-century America. They became deeply involved in all of the major reform movements of their day, including the abolition of slavery, temperance, prison reform, world peace, and women's rights, although their role has not been as well known as that of many other denominations. Most Universalists were proud of the fact that their church produced the first woman minister regularly ordained by a national denomination in America and provided much of the leadership in the suffrage agitation that resulted in the Nineteenth Amendment.

*E.C. Sweetser, pastor of the Bleecker Street Universalist Church in New York City; *Universalist* 57 (7 August 1875): [2].

A NOTE ON TERMINOLOGY

It is necessary at the outset to make several distinctions in order to clarify terminology and to avoid confusion; namely, to define the various meanings and connotations of the word "universalism." Spelled without capitalization, the term stands for an ancient philosophical concept reflecting the age-old attempt to discover basic elements, characteristics, and uniformities in both natural and human phenomena. This was most certainly an effort made long before Christianity posited its own system of universals.

Theologically, the concept—and again spelled with a small "u"—is associated with Christianity and embodies belief in human deliverance, in either or both body and soul, from the penalties of sin; in short, salvation as the end-product of human destiny by redemption in some form and by some mechanism, and within some time-span. More specifically, and integrally within the Christian framework and context, the term also refers to the doctrine of salvation for all which, at least in historic times, means that God would finally save all from sin and death through the mediation of Jesus Christ. This was, in brief, the basic belief of that religious grouping denoted Universalist which took organized form in England about 1750 and in the American colonies toward the end of the eighteenth century.

One of the continuing tasks of denominational Universalist spokesmen in America from the very beginning was to convince the skeptical, the ignorant, or the unbelieving that, however recent Universalism was as a Christian denomination of the Protestant persuasion, the concept or idea of universalism was at least as old as Christianity itself. Before Universalism as a distinct and legally recognized religious body in America was half a century old, one of its leading early scholars, Hosea Ballou 2d, amassed historical evidence that belief in the ultimate salvation of all was not only prevalent among early Christians, but that it was virtually unchallenged until the third century A.D.; and the very fact that universalism was declared a heresy (and then by strictly human authority) in the fifth century, testified to its existence.

Although driven largely underground until the sixteenth-century Reformation destroyed the unity of Western Christendom, the universalist idea persisted, and after 1500 appeared with renewed vigor in spite of the fact that there was no identifiable organization or specific designation for its adherents. The concept of universalism took root especially in France and the Germanies among the innumerable Protestant sects and sub-groups which surfaced or were created *de novo* as part of the great religious upheaval of the sixteenth century.

In England, where a combination of political maneuverings, nationalistic strivings, and personal considerations had resulted in the beginning of the Reformation in 1534 under Henry VIII, professed believers in universal salvation found themselves briefly in the heretical camp when the so-called Forty-two Articles of Religion, adopted in 1552, condemned universalism. But this prohibition was not to last long, for when the Thirty-nine Articles were adopted in 1563, and represented the completion of the establishment of the Anglican Church, those articles placing universalism beyond the pale were omitted. With the exception of a brief period in the mid-seventeenth century when the Presbyterian Parliament of 1648 attempted to outlaw universalist belief, adherents of the doctrine that all shall be saved were at least legally tolerated under the commodious umbrella of the Anglican Church and were numbered among the dissenters or nonconformists acceptable to the State so long as they did not deny the doctrine of the Trinity. It was out of this inheritance that the predominant universalist strain responsible for the establishment of American Universalism emerged, through the efforts of John Murray, whose spiritual pilgrimage from Anglicanism to universalism by way of Methodism becomes the early focus of this work.

American Universalism can also be traced, albeit as a subordinate but important strain, through the welter of German, and to a lesser degree French, mystical and pietistic sects which appeared in post-Reformation continental Europe and joined with their English counterparts in swelling the numbers that comprised the outposts of European civilization planted in the New World, particularly in the eighteenth century. However, the Germans who contributed to American Universalism differed from their English contemporaries in at least three respects. Unlike the majority of English Protestants, they permitted a wide range of individual beliefs, which could and did include universalism. Further, universalism among the German sects was usually implicit rather than explicit, and did not represent an overriding tenet. Hence they tended to retain their formal allegiance to other creeds and membership in other sects or denominations, and seldom, if ever, publicly professed the universalist sentiments they might have held. Finally, as Clinton Lee Scott, an historian of the Universalist Church of America, has pointed out, the German sects "were less interested in creating a denominational structure than in cultivating their interior religious insights." [*The Universalist Church of America: A Short History* (Boston: Universalist Historical Society, 1957), p. 3.] Universalists, on the other hand, put the matter of salvation of all at the top of their priority list, and eventually developed a denominational framework closely akin to those of most other American Protestant religious bodies.

A distinction must therefore be borne in mind between those who implicity or explicitly expressed universalist ideas but who, for one reason or another, remained within other organized religious groupings; and those who not only avowed their universalism but became members of a distinct body denominated Universalist. It is this latter (and much smaller) group with which this study is primarily concerned, although efforts to bring "outside" believers in universal salvation formally into the Universalist fold were made, and often with some success. The evidence is also abundant, not only that the generic concept of universalism has been held and/or expressed in some form—usually within a Christian nexus—for centuries, but that, in terms of immediate origins, the idea was sufficiently current in the seventeenth and eighteenth centuries to make its introduction into the American colonies a matter of no great surprise.

A group known as the Philadelphian Society was advocating universalism (universal restoration) in England by the end of the seventeenth century. [Geoffrey Rowell, "The Origins and History of Universalist Societies in Britain, 1750-1850," *Journal of Ecclesiastical History* 22 (January 1971): 36.] However, they described their doctrine as 'The Everlasting Gospel' (borrowed from the Book of Revelation) rather than "Universalism." The word "Universalist" was apparently first used in mid-eighteenth-century England in reference to a separate group worshipping on distinct principles; namely, those of James Relly and his followers. [Richard Eddy, *Universalism in America: A History* 2 vols. (Boston: Universalist Publishing House, 1884-1886), 2: 344.] John Murray, as one of his disciples, adopted the term. However, it was several decades before any real degree of uniformity was to be found in the nomenclature used either by Universalists or others, particularly at the local level. Believers in eventual salvation were variously known as "Universalians," "Hell Redemptionists," "Restorationists" (or "Universal Restorationists"), "Restitutionists," and even "Universelers." [William McLoughlin, *New England Dissent, 1630-1833.* 2 vols. (Cambridge: Harvard University Press, 1971), 2: 721n.] The names, both official and unofficial, of early Universalist societies reflected a similarly wide variation.

Likewise, there was no uniformity in the reasoning or evidence used to arrive at universalist belief. Aside from general agreement on the ultimate goal, there was, at least in the eighteenth century, no coherent or consistently agreed-upon body of precepts that could be called a Universalist theology. Many an idea was discarded, modified, or questioned before something approximating a set of "articles of faith" was adopted in 1803 by American Universalists; and even that required only minimal commitment compared to the creeds adopted by other denominations. Further, the so-called Winchester Profession of Faith of 1803 underwent many a modification and reinterpretation even before another century had passed, although its official wording was never changed. No one could rightly accuse early Universalists in America of adhering blindly or unquestioningly to a static credo. The failure to establish anything approaching absolutism theologically, coupled with emphasis on individual interpretation and a reluctance to develop anything resembling a hierarchal organization, admirable as this all might be to the religious libertarian, was a chronic weakness that plagued the denomination from the beginning.

The Larger Hope

SECTION I

John Murray and the Establishment of Universalism in America

Chapter 1

ENGLISH BACKGROUNDS AND AMERICAN BEGINNINGS

From Anglicanism to Universalism

On 30 September 1770 a young Englishman pursued his solitary way through the woods of the Jersey coast of the New World in search of provisions for the crew of a sloop anchored nearby. Little did he realize that he was to be the instrument by which a new and unique religious body was to be created, denominated Universalism, which was to challenge the grim Calvinism inherited from sixteenth-century Europe. Neither was he aware that the denomination which he would eventually help to found in America was to offer the hope of a spiritual democracy for a new nation.

John Murray (1741-1815) was born in England of what appears to have been the equivalent of upper middle class ancestry, probably of Scottish paternal antecedents, on 10 December 1741.[1] His birthplace was the country village of Alton, in Hampshire, some fifty miles southwest of London. He was the oldest of nine children (four sons and five daughters) "who were multiplied with uncommon rapidity." His father, a stern Calvinistic Anglican, was held in awe and fear by his offspring; the son "was studious to avoid his presence, and . . . richly enjoyed his absence." His mother, a gentler soul, was a Presbyterian; however, religious differences caused no disharmony in the household during Murray's youth. He was promptly baptized into the Anglican Church in a private service when a temporary ailment of infancy presumably made his parents apprehensive about his survival. Their fears about his future physical welfare were unfounded, for he lived, according to his account, a normal childhood in robust health, and was a model youngster. He was publicly received into the local church at the time his oldest sister was baptized. According to family tradition, his first audible (and understandable) word was an "Amen" at the conclusion of the ceremony. In contrast to many of his contemporaries, he did receive some formal schooling, and at the age of six could read, although admittedly with some stumbling, a chapter in the Bible.

Long before he was ten years old, the young Murray had been warned by his father about the anticipated terrors of the damned and the horrors of "endless misery" which "threw a cloud over every innocent enjoyment." The son also made it clear that during his youth frequent use was made of the rod "as a sovereign panacea." Because he was the oldest, he was frequently singled out for special chastisement, and hence was used as an example for his brothers and sisters. The head of the household took his religious obligations for himself and his family so seriously on Sundays that the day came to be dreaded by the younger generation. Extended family prayers, Bible reading, attendance at two church services (the first at 5:00 A.M.) winter and summer, and rigorous self-examination were borne with mixed feelings. Murray was frank to admit that he was "not always in a praying frame."

Murray's father, who had received "a good education" and was apparently successfully engaged in business, moved his family to the vicinity of Cork in Ireland in 1751, when Murray was ten years old. His paternal grandmother was at the time a resident of that city. Many years before, she had been sent to England by her father from her native France to be educated, and had not only become "a zealous Protestant," but had married one. In so doing, she had become a self-imposed exile and had thereby renounced a large share of what had been a substantial inheritance; even then, "the remains of affluence were still visible" and she lived "in easy circumstances." It was she who rescued the Murray family financially when they lost their home by fire when Murray was twelve.

The refusal of his father to allow him to leave the family circle prevented Murray from taking advantage of an offer by an Anglican clergyman for academic preparation which would have eventually provided a college education. Shortly afterward, the elder Murray did determine that the time had come for his son to "engage in some business," by which the youth could "secure the necessaries of life." This was particularly advisable, for declining health had required the retirement of the father from his own secular pursuits, and family income was correspondingly reduced. Murray reluctantly undertook a business career (unspecified) and disliked it.

While in Ireland the Murray family became acquainted with Methodism being spread by itinerant preachers, and the father became an enthusiastic follower and joined the local society, although he refused to become a preacher. The young Murray was attracted to Methodism also, principally because of the groups organized for young people, the frequent hymn-singing (at which he was adept), and the general sociability. Murray's father became well acquainted with John Wesley, the Methodist leader, who was a "great admirer" of the stern old man. The youthful Murray found himself in charge of a class of forty boys whose attendance he supervised; he also led the hymn-singing and prayer, and even was given the responsibility of examining the class as to their religiosity. He made such a favorable impression that he began to feel that he was to be among the Elect when Judgment

Day came; needless to say, he was a source of great pride to his devout parents. At the same time, his father cautioned him about the dangers of self-righteousness and the virtues of humility.

Murray's religious triumph seemed to be complete when he was soon admitted to the inner sanctums of the local Methodist society during its evening meetings. But the level of enthusiasm eventually waned. The class over which he presided began to disintegrate—weary in well-doing—with differences within the ranks. He found his own "devotional ecstasies" also diminished by what he considered an excessive literary diet of religious works which were almost the only books permitted by his father. Murray's passion for reading, particularly other than devotional books, was whetted by the sight, in his father's hands, of such works (for adults only) as *Tom Jones* and *Clarissa Harlow.* The works of Milton were available, but Murray was not enthusiastic about reading blank verse. By good fortune, he was able to broaden his intellectual horizons at the home of a neighbor, where he was introduced to the works of such writers as Addison, Pope, and Shakespeare. He did, however, with paternal permission, keep his religious interests alive with frequent attendance at Methodist meetings in nearby villages.

After embarrassing the local Anglican priest with pointed questions asked during the so-called instruction period, Murray was duly confirmed by the visiting bishop and became a full-fledged Anglican communicant, although with distinct sentiments in favor of the Methodists, who still considered themselves then part of the Established Church. One matter particularly bothered the ebullient new Anglican: it appeared that "glooms and melancholy were considered as infallible signs of a gracious disposition." Unfortunately for his religious standing, his sadness "was not uniform," and he found his cheerfulness becoming too obvious. So he restored his "respectability" to such an extent that even his pious father became concerned; although only sixteen years old then, the young Murray wrote that he felt old enough to be twenty.

He also experienced his first recorded romance, with a young lady visiting in the neighborhood. It was brought to a prompt conclusion, however, when the lady in question turned the first love letter Murray had ever written over to his father, who shamed him in the presence of his assembled family. Murray's ardor for the object of his affection cooled noticeably within a matter of hours after the nature of the missive was divulged. No more such epistles were written until he addressed the lady whom he first married.

The religious melancholy which promptly returned was almost as soon dissipated, although briefly. Murray experienced for the first time the mysteries and sorrows of death, when his closest friend succumbed to fever; Murray survived what appeared to have been the same illness.

Shortly thereafter, his father, who had been an invalid for almost twenty years, also died. Murray had the satisfaction of having, for the first time, established meaningful communication with the austere elder Murray during the last six months of the latter's life.

At the senior Murray's request, the eldest son became head of the family—a task made no easier by the awareness by his younger brothers and sisters that he was not the father; as a consequence, his continued liberal use of the rod brought revolt rather than submission to authority. In the realm of family finances, Murray was more successful. He regained, by pleading his own case, several houses which had been deeded fraudulently to others after the death of his maternal grandmother's second husband. The Murrays promptly moved into one and received rental income from the remaining property.

Murray's fortunes were further enhanced by an offer to become the manager of the business affairs of an elderly (and wealthy) couple who had been life-long friends, and both of whose sons had been casualties of the illness which Murray had also experienced; one of the sons had been his closest friend. The young man who had so recently become head of his own family household now moved to a new home, where he served not only as a family confidant but in effect as a liberally financed adopted son and heir. The nephews of Mr. Little, the gentleman who had suggested the arrangement and had become Murray's patron, were understandably far from happy.

Meanwhile, Murray took advantage of opportunities to preach, and made various trips to Cork and vicinity which gave him an increasingly wider audience for his speaking talents. His preoccupation with preaching, which required much absence from his adopted home, brought complaints. He resolved to be more attentive, but was convinced that God had appointed him "for a life of wandering." A fixed routine he found distasteful. So the lure of variety won out, and he set off for London, after having received unsolicited funds from his benefactor, which money he offered to his mother; she considered herself sufficiently well provided for, so he departed for London with a pocket handkerchief full of gold guineas. He declined requests to stay in Cork or to preach Methodism in Limerick. While staying over in Cork, he heard George Whitefield, with whom he was greatly impressed—the first Calvinistic Methodist he had ever heard who served as an itinerant minister claiming allegiance to no particular sect. Thereupon he resolved to abandon Wesleyanism and join the Whitefield adherents; Murray "cherished *liberty* to act myself without restraint."

Debarking in England, where he had no relatives or even many acquaintances, he soon made friends among the Methodists in Bristol and Bath; in the latter place he renewed acquaintance with a preacher who had known his father in Ireland. It was at this point that Murray expressed concern regarding his religious beliefs. He could not, he told the preacher, "with a good conscience, reprobate doctrines which, as [he] firmly believed, originated with God, nor advocate sentiments diametrically opposite to what [he] considered as truth." It was for this reason that he parted company with Wesley and his preachers. Murray still believed firmly in the doctrine of Election and Predestination at this time, and hence found himself suspect among the Methodists when he arrived in London. Religious matters were not, however, of consistently paramount concern at all times; by his own interpretation, he lived a "life of dissipation" in the city for about a year before his resources came to an end. He reported that he gave his last half-penny to a mendicant asking alms, and even contemplated suicide (not for the only time in his life).

Whitefield's famous "Tabernacle" became a religious refuge in London, while various good-hearted acquaintances kept him from debtor's prison. He obtained a position as an aide to an inspector in a textile factory in which broadcloth was made. He was employed briefly in the counting-room of a merchant, but found the position uncongenial and gave it up to return to his former employment. He had no success in finding a position in the business in which he had been engaged in Ireland (the exact nature of which Murray never specified). He reiterated the conviction that he "was never designed for a man of business."

His spiritual life, however, remained a continuing concern. In spite of occasional backslidings, he had long since become assured in his own mind that he was among the Elect. His religious zeal was manifested in the eclectic approach he took. He supplemented attendance at Whitefield's services by visiting a chapel in Tottenham Court, where Communion was available on alternate Sundays to "the Elect of God from every denomination." He visited services all over the city. Wherever he heard of an outstanding preacher, he made a point of attending. He obtained "great satisfaction," for example, from the meetings in a Baptist church, and participated in the services. He thoroughly approved of Whitefield's interdenominational approach and his insistence "that a difference respecting non-essentials was utterly inconsistent with the Christian character."

Murray's outgoing personality, religious background and experience, and piety were sufficiently attractive to result in several offers to become a public preacher. But he felt that he was not yet prepared to take on such responsibilities. "As the eternal well-being of the many was supposed to rest with the preacher, an error in judgment would consequently be fatal to his hearers; and as I had now learned that I was not perfect in knowledge, I could not be assured I should not lead the people astray; in which tremendous event they would, to all eternity, be imprecating curses on my head."

He did, however, become more and more deeply involved in

religious activities, and often delivered the prayers at public meetings. He managed also to combine church-going with romance, for he met Eliza Neale, sister of one of his numerous friends who attended meetings with him. It might be added that the young lady's grandfather, opposed to Whitefield and his teachings, was sufficiently convinced that Murray was merely a fortune-hunter as to cut her out of a will which would have furnished her a patrimony of £1,000 sterling. After a largely surreptitious courtship lasting over a year, they were married, Murray being probably no more than eighteen at the time.[2] They experienced generally happy years until her death in 1769.

The next stage in Murray's life involved another event in his religious development. He had heard of one James Relly, "a conscientious and zealous preacher in the city of London," for some time before he actually heard him speak. However, Murray was commissioned by the Methodist church of which he was a member to bring a young lady back from her erring religious ways; she had become "a firm and unwavering believer of universal redemption." Accompanied by two or three other members of the church, Murray acted as spokesman. He found himself bested by her logic and felt that her remarks were "*unanswerable*." His embarrassment was such that he determined to avoid thereafter "every Universalist, and most *cordially did I hate them.*" He took some comfort at the time from the fact that, at least among his friends, Relly was thoroughly maligned; but after "many months" he was persuaded to hear the controversial preacher. However, Murray's prejudices were such that he paid little attention to the speaker and congratulated himself that he was still among the Elect.

A greater opportunity to become acquainted with so-called "Rellyism" came when a Dr. Mason, a physician who conducted a Bible study group which Murray attended, requested that Murray read a manuscript the doctor had prepared opposing Relly's major work, *Union: or a Treatise of the Consanguinity and Affinity between Christ and His Church.*[3] Murray read and re-read the material, and was greatly disturbed by a quotation from Relly which Mason had not refuted to Murray's satisfaction; Relly's argument led inescapably to the conclusion that "all men must finally be saved." In spite of the fact that "what every religious denomination united to condemn must be false," Murray was much disturbed by what he had read. He received no satisfaction from Mason, and the pamphlet was published unchanged.

Some months later, while visiting one of his wife's relatives, Murray ran across Relly's work in a bookcase. He was given permission to take it with him. After seeking divine guidance in the interpretation of the work, still convinced that "the Elect were safe," yet nagged by the realization that he had judged and condemned a work without even having given the author a hearing, Murray and his wife studied Relly's writings. After checking the Scriptures against the references given in the *Union*, Murray wondered how it was possible that "discoveries so important should never until now have been made, and now only by this man." God apparently worked in mysterious and wonderful ways.

It seemed that many passages of Scripture had previously escaped his attention, or that he had misunderstood them. He re-read Mason's work and became less and less convinced of the doctor's criticism of Relly. Still, Murray was not completely sure. He re-studied the Scriptures, he prayed, and in the absence of his own pastor from the pulpit one Sunday, got up his courage to go, with his wife, to the former Quaker meeting house (Coachman's Hall) where Relly was preaching.

Murray paid close attention. Aside from the fact that the congregation "did not appear very religious; that is, they were not melancholy," everything impressed Murray positively. He was "captivated" by the sermon, humbled by the knowledge, so convincingly presented, that there was no such body as "the Elect." No one could claim to be uniformly good, to the exclusion of others. He told his wife that Relly's was "the first consistent sermon I have ever heard." Murray immediately re-read the *Union* and began to attend Relly's services frequently. Murray's own pastor sounded "more inconsistent than ever." Mrs. Murray informed her husband that it was he who had changed—not the minister. They decided to have the best of both worlds. They could attend Relly's services on one half of every Sunday, and Mr. Hitchens' the other half, in that way "hearing the truth, without running the risk of losing our reputation."

James Relly, who had made such an impression on Murray and whose disciple the latter became, was a Welshman, born in 1722, who had been converted to Methodism under the influence of George Whitefield in 1741, at the time of Whitefield's first visit to Wales.[4]

After serving as an evangelist for Whitefield in Wales, Relly moved to London and about 1750 broke with Whitefield, probably over the matter of universal salvation. He preached his version of universalism until his death (25 April 1778) at the age of fifty-six. The congregation to which he had been preaching was taken over by Elhanan Winchester, who had come over from America in 1787, but it soon disappeared.

After having first heard Relly preach in 1757, Murray still had many questions, so he consulted Mr. Hitchens about "election" and "final reprobation" and was comforted to be told that Jesus had died for all and that every one for whom Christ died would finally be saved. He had by 1760 become a complete convert to Rellyism and was ready to proclaim it to "the whole world." Relly became sufficiently well acquainted with Murray to have given him a volume comprising outlines of his sermons which Murray brought with him to America in 1770.[5] Murray and his wife had had "a taste of heaven below." But he immediately ran into the sobering fact that a so-called friend had informed the Whitefield congregation of his apostasy. The inevitable happened. He was voted out of his Methodist society, although by a narrow margin.

Events in the mundane world soon followed which brought Murray's spirits still lower. Although the details were not given, he was ostensibly arrested for debt from which he somehow managed to extricate himself. Then followed the death of his only son, aged one year, and the decline of his wife's health. The added expenses, and the desertion of his erstwhile "religious friends," and conflicts with his two brothers-in-law brought his morale even lower. His wife's death profoundly affected him. Debts, declining health (including impaired eyesight), and loneliness, produced temporarily another urge to take his own life.

To make matters worse, word was received from a brother that death had also come to one of Murray's brothers, and three of his sisters. Soon after, he secured a house, and his mother and remaining brothers came to England to live with him. The eldest sister had married some time before, and then also the other surviving sister, whom he never saw again. Under the circumstances, Murray found more and more consolation in religion; it was a disappointment to him, though, that the brother to whom he was closest (James) and his mother remained "inveterate opposers" of universalism.

After his brother-in-law, William Neale, rescued him from what would have been an indefinite term in Newgate debtors' prison, Murray reluctantly accepted a post in a mercantile house in order to repay his obligations. Even with that accomplished, he remained depressed and "sick of the world and all which it could bestow." His friendship with James Relly was what seemed to sustain him. However, Relly's urging that Murray become a public advocate of universalism fell on deaf ears. Murray preferred at this point in time "to pass through life, unheard, unseen, unknown to all, as though I ne'er had been." It was at this stage in his life, and in this frame of mind, that Murray "accidentally met a gentleman from America." What he heard about the New World intrigued him, and he determined to bury himself in the wilderness across the Atlantic.

Early American Experiences

John Murray's decision to come to America was an essentially negative one—to avoid further misery rather than to seek happiness. He even refused offers of letters of introduction from his "few friends," and the importuning of his mother had no effect on his decision. Short of suicide, travelling across the sea seemed the most effective way of "quitting the world." On a Saturday evening (21 July 1770) he sailed from Gravesend on board the brig *Hand-in-Hand,* with money, clothes, a Bible, a bundle of his late wife's letters, and other papers. He experienced neither anticipation nor apprehension, but recorded his state of mind as "suspended between two worlds."

His lethargy was somewhat diminished, however, by the impingement of affairs of this world. When approximately three days from New York, a vessel bound for England informed the captain of the ship on which Murray was a passenger that the non-importation agreement entered into by the American colonials opposing the policies of the Mother Country were in effect at New York, but not at Philadelphia. Being naturally concerned because he had goods on board that would be involved, the captain headed for Philadelphia, but upon arrival discovered that he had been misinformed. New York should have been his destination after all.

While waiting for final arrangements to be made, Murray temporarily debarked in Philadelphia, where the other passengers remained, and was much impressed by what he saw. The next morning, the captain, with Murray as the only remaining passenger, set sail for New York but the ship grounded on a sandbar off Cranberry Inlet in Barnegat Bay on the southern New Jersey coast.[6] Murray found himself in charge of part of the cargo which had been transferred to a sloop to lighten the load and enable the refloating of the brig. A change of wind the next day left the sloop stranded, and once again Murray went ashore in the New World—this time in search of provisions. The result was the acquisition of an interesting new friend, a significant turn in Murray's life, and the beginnings of what Universalists called "the Great Pilgrimage" of their church as they celebrated in 1920 the 150th anniversary of Murray's arrival because of that providential change of wind.[7]

The young Englishman landed on what was probably the bank of Cedar Creek, near a place dubbed Good-Luck Point. Good Luck became indissolubly associated with denominational tradition, and came to be a sort of shrine to be visited by scores of Universalists in later days. A poetic rendition of Murray's arrival in America was furnished in the early twentieth century by Henry Nehemiah Dodge, who composed a romantic epic comprising over 200 pages of small "memory book" size.[8]

Murray was welcomed by an unlettered but deeply religious man with mystical tendencies named Thomas Potter, who had carved a sizeable estate out of the pine wilderness and had built a meeting house for the use of itinerant preachers.[9] Potter was the fourth generation of a family which had migrated from Rhode Island. They had been Quakers but became affiliated with the Baptists after establishing residence in what became Ocean County, New Jersey. Among the Baptists with whom Potter grew to manhood was a group known as the Rogerines, or

Imaginative reconstruction of the first meeting of John Murray and Thomas Potter, September 1770

Quaker Baptists, followers of one John Rogers of Rhode Island. This small sect, holding that Christ had died for all men, was led in eastern New Jersey by John Culver, whose services Potter probably attended, and with whom he is known to have conversed. The group held fellowship with the German Baptist community at Ephrata (Lancaster County), Pennsylvania, which openly taught universalism. Mary Hulet, whom Potter married, had grown up in the same neighborhood as her husband, and also held universalist views. With all of this as part of his background and association, it was no wonder that Potter found Murray's ideas congenial. Potter became convinced that Murray had been heaven-sent to fill the pulpit, and begged him to stay as God's appointed messenger. Had God chosen Murray as his messenger?

A year after Potter's death in 1782, Murray made a nostalgic visit to Good Luck, where he viewed Potter's late home and grave. Murray was at the time visiting Philadelphia, where he had his first meeting with Elhanan Winchester. According to an account by Abel C. Thomas of Philadelphia of a visit in 1832 to the community where Potter had lived, several persons corroborated Murray's testimony that both men believed that Murray's arrival had been divinely foreordained.[10] In that year the Philadelphia Association of Universalists, which Thomas attended, met in Hightstown, New Jersey. He not only visited Potter's grave but preached in the original church and claimed to have been the first Universalist clergyman to have viewed the area since Murray's visit.[11] A conference of Universalists was held at the spot in May 1833, at which time a marble tombstone was erected to mark Potter's grave.

Sebastian Streeter, in an address delivered on the occasion of the removal of Murray's remains from the Granary Burying Ground in Boston to the Mt. Auburn Cemetery in Cambridge, Massachusetts, in 1837, realized that some individuals felt the Potter story partook "too much of the marvellous" but he did not consider the account left by Murray "at all incredible." Potter was "an eccentrick man" and Murray "believed himself to be under the special guardianship and direction of Providence." So he naturally "described things precisely as they appeared to himself."[12]

Murray, as Streeter pointed out, was indeed a firm and consistent believer in the operation of Divine Providence in all human affairs, and especially his own; so he naturally concluded that he eventually was destined to preach universalism publicly. His greatest fear was that he would be anathema to many of his hearers, and that he would bring the wrath of the orthodox clergy down on his head. Nonetheless, he decided that it was necessary that he preach, and did so in Potter's meeting house on Sunday, 30 September 1770.[13]

After receiving entreaties from Potter to return, Murray embarked for New York with the intention of complying as soon as possible with the wishes of his devout friend in New Jersey. Murray duly delivered the sloop and its contents to the captain, and after having retrieved his baggage from the brig, returned to what he hoped would be an idyllic permanent retirement in the New Jersey wilderness.

Word of Murray and his preaching was spread in New York by boatmen from the sloop, and he agreed to deliver a discourse in the Baptist meeting house in return for transportation back to New Jersey. Delay in departure arrangements resulted in several more public appearances; Murray was sure that the continued hospitality of the Baptists would not have been granted if they had really been aware of what kind of ideas he was expressing.

The return to New Jersey brought the promise of peace, yet an increasing realization that he was called upon to preach the Gospel as he saw it. He would take no pay for his services in Potter's meeting house, but would live out his days in quietude. But this life of serenity was not to be. His preaching became more and more popular, and people came from as far as twenty miles around to hear his message. Urgent requests for his services came from Philadelphia and New York. He went first to the latter city in 1771, where enthusiasm was so great that subscription papers were circulated to finance the construction of a meeting house for his use. He declined this gesture of confidence and good will, and for a few weeks used instead the Baptist meeting house where he had first spoken.

Upon his return to New Jersey, Murray was urged to join a Baptist church but declined, and continued to preach universalism. As his fame spread, so did the opposition which he had long anticipated; however, it was not sufficient to deter him from visiting Philadelphia. But he found every church there closed to him. Murray makes it clear that he was sensitive to criticism, and many of the obloquies cast at him wounded deeply. In his travelling ministry in the towns and villages near Potter's home, Murray did take some comfort from the fact that, although the clergy were much opposed, his lay hearers received him with enthusiasm. But it was at a meeting in Upper Freehold, New Jersey, that he was first seriously challenged for lacking official credentials for any kind of preaching. It was not until many years later that this deficiency was remedied.

Unpleasant as the opposition to him may have been, it failed to deter him from preaching. Beginning in the fall of 1772, he extended his field of activity to Newport, Rhode Island, and beyond.[14] He spoke to "very large congregations" in Milford, Guilford, and Norwich, Connecticut. Enroute to the last-named town, Murray found himself involved in an argument over salvation and future punishment with Samuel Hopkins of Newport, who in 1783 published a work attacking Rellyan universalism.[15]

While in Newport, Murray preached in Ezra Stiles' pulpit at the request of some of the latter's congregation, while Stiles was out of town. If the man who in 1778 was to become president of Yale College had been present, he would undoubtedly have refused the use of his church. For approximately two weeks, Murray delivered discourses every evening, so that "laboring persons . . . could . . . attend without loss of time." Evening meetings in the church represented a personal victory for Murray, for he had persuaded the parish to reverse an earlier vote prohibiting them—a consequence of Whitefield's last visit there.

Murray did meet Stiles, who received him "with cool civility" and explained that he could not invite the young universalist to assist him in the Sunday services the next day because Murray had no credentials. Stiles had become convinced by 1773 that Murray was preaching universal salvation and was shocked to be told that Murray had said that the Lord's Supper could be administered anywhere and at any time. Stiles hoped that those who heard Murray preach would realize that his ideas were "founded in delusion and insanity."[16]

After having been accused by a visiting preacher of such calumnies as having formerly labored for his living, of being currently a married man with children, of having been a "stage-player" and a song-singer, Murray vindicated himself regarding all but the last, and triumphantly presented by popular demand a final evening discourse in Dr. Stiles' meeting house. The visiting preacher who attacked Murray's character appears to have confused him with a Calvinist preacher of the same name, so a case of mistaken identity developed and again complicated

Murray's life later. In 1772, when both Murrays were in New York, they were distinguished as "Damnation" Murray and "Salvation" Murray.[17] It was said that 'The Universalist, little John Murray, had much of the primitive about him.'

Armed for the first time with a letter of introduction furnished by one of his listeners sympathetic to his views, Murray then departed for Providence, Rhode Island, to see one N. Brown, through whose good offices a meeting house was obtained. After having returned to New Jersey in the winter of 1772, he continued to preach, simultaneously increasing the number of both friends and enemies.

Early in 1773, he again visited Philadelphia, then Maryland, where he spent several weeks preaching, using the home of a wealthy retired physician as a headquarters. As at other places, Murray declined offers to settle, feeling that he "was sent *out* to preach the gospel." This meant no loitering by the wayside. There were brief stops in Newark and Wilmington, Delaware, on the return to Philadelphia. Until the fall of 1773, he divided his time also among the Jerseys and New York, making friends "among every class of people, from the highest to the most humble." Even some of the leading Anglican and Congregational clergy were among his friends, although they did not agree with his religious views.

In October, he returned to Newport where his fame had spread sufficiently to draw "crowded and attentive" congregations. In one instance he preached in the State House (Newport being the capital of the colony at the time) and no less a person than the governor was in attendance. An ecumenical spirit seemed to pervade the city, for many of the numerous Jewish community came to hear; there was consistency here, for Murray believed and taught that Jesus was the saviour of *all* men, eventually "making of Jew and Gentile ONE new man, so making peace."

Murray's travels next took him to East Greenwich, Rhode Island, where he preached to "a crowded audience" in the court house. Because the Superior Court was in session, the judges and lawyers were among his hearers. After visits to other communities in Rhode Island, he arrived in Boston on 26 October 1773, where he found friends and admirers in the family of Thomas Handasyde Peck, a Boston businessman (a hatter by occupation).

Murray preached his first sermon in Boston the evening of Sunday, 30 October, in the hall of a large building in the center of town. The congregation the next evening was even larger than the first. He spoke next in Newburyport; even though he had no official credentials, he was permitted to use the local Presbyterian church. Having had considerable experience earlier with opposition from many quarters, Murray circumspectly stuck very closely to the language of the

Scriptures in his several discourses, "leaving to my hearers deductions, comments, and applications." His deliberate obliqueness was more than once a source of irritation to his critics.

Portsmouth, New Hampshire, was the northernmost point in Murray's travels up and down the Atlantic seaboard. In November 1773 he spoke from several pulpits in Portsmouth, including that of Samuel Langdon, later president of Harvard College. On his way back to Philadelphia, Murray continued his preaching in Newburyport and Boston. In the latter place, he spent some time defending the authenticity of the Scriptures to a number of Deists who attended his services. On this particular visit, he preached not only in the hall in which he had first appeared, and in Faneuil Hall, but in Andrew Croswell's church. Croswell, originally from Groton, Connecticut, was pastor of the Eleventh Congregational Society from its organization in February 1748 until his death in 1785.[18] It was one of the numerous "New Light" congregations which arose as part of the Great Awakening, the religious revivalism which began about 1725 and which swept over the colonies following the arrival of George Whitefield.[19] Croswell's group occupied what had formerly been a French Protestant (Huguenot) church. There was a certain irony in Murray's use of Croswell's pulpit, for in 1773 the latter had marked Murray out as "a dangerous man."

Throughout his travels, Murray was requested to remain at various places; in April 1774 he received an invitation to settle in Portsmouth, New Hampshire, but declined on the ground that he was not yet ready to give up his itinerant life. In the early fall of 1774, while again preaching in Boston, he received an invitation to visit Gloucester from a leading citizen, Winthrop Sargent. Shortly after Murray arrived there (3 November), he was surprised and gratified to learn that knowledge of James Relly and his ideas had preceded him by some four years—the first such instance in Murray's American ministry. He therefore had a prospective audience who could more clearly comprehend what he had to say than could previous listeners. Murray spoke to appreciative groups for over a week. On a brief reappearance in Boston, Murray found the environment less congenial; his congregation was drenched with water and he became the intended target of an egg which missed its mark.

Meanwhile, an epistolary debate between Murray and Croswell in a Boston paper was climaxed by a confrontation in Croswell's church, whose pulpit Murray had been using. Murray found himself accused of "preaching damnable doctrines" by a man who had never heard him preach. The assembled throng was told that not only was Murray's mentor, Relly, a blasphemer but that Murray was himself a deist, with dangerous ideas. As the situation grew more tense, Murray undertook to defend Relly from his detractor.

Feelings were running so high by the time of Murray's third public appearance after his return to Boston that, after surmounting the all-pervading odor of asafoetida liberally sprinkled throughout the church, he and his hearers had to dodge stones thrown through the windows. Disregarding pleas to depart in the interest of his personal safety, Murray insisted on making his presentation. With a sense of the dramatic which he undoubtedly had learned from Wesley and Whitefield, and which often stood him in good stead as an accomplished speaker, Murray recorded the utterance of the following challenge: "not all the stones in Boston, except they stop my breath, shall shut my mouth, or arrest my testimony." These were not idle words, for at subsequent meetings he was similarly attacked. But it could have been worse, he wrote; he could be thankful "for the religious liberty of the country of my adoption." In a less tolerant country, he might well have been destroyed as a heretic. As it was, he relied on reason and Scripture, and no man ever silenced him.

In mid-December 1774, Murray made a second trip to Gloucester, where he resided at the home of Winthrop Sargent. The Sargent family, who were among Murray's staunchest supporters, became members of an informal group who worshipped in various private homes. Although he was given the use of the pulpits of some churches, Murray found more and more of them closed against him as he travelled again to Newburyport and Portsmouth (the opening to him of the Anglican church there was a notable exception). One of his most signal accomplishments while in New Hampshire was the conversion of Noah Parker, who became one of the first Universalist preachers in America.

It was in Gloucester that Murray faced the best organized and most effective opposition. He was accused (among other things) of being a "papist," sent out by the British government (specifically, Lord North) to help establish an Anglican episcopate. The use of Samuel Chandler's meeting house, previously granted him, was denied in January 1775, and word was spread that Murray treated the ordinance of the Eucharist (the Lord's Supper) "in a ludicrous manner." Two attempts were made to have him banished, the first by declaring him a vagrant under a provincial law; but Sargent came to the rescue and deeded him sufficient property to make Murray a freeholder.

After returning to Gloucester following visits to Boston and various places in Rhode Island in the late spring of 1775, Murray was invited by the officers of the Rhode Island Brigade, then stationed with the army besieging Boston, to become their chaplain. Among the many friends Murray had made in Rhode Island was General James Mitchel Varnum, who had offered him the chaplaincy.[20]

Nathaniel Greene was another friend with whom Murray carried on an extensive correspondence for several years. Greene, in May 1775, was placed in charge of three regiments authorized by the Rhode Island

General Assembly, and in the following month was made a brigadier general in the Continental Army. On 3 July Murray was among the detachment of the Rhode Island Brigade who paid their respects to Commander-in-Chief George Washington after he arrived in Cambridge to take charge of the Revolutionary forces.

Murray's activities as an army chaplain were rather short-lived. He did preach on several occasions (e.g., at Jamaica Plain and at Prospect Hill), and almost immediately other chaplains sought his removal. But Washington confirmed Murray's appointment as chaplain of the three Rhode Island regiments and furnished him with a commission as such. Murray's military career was cut short by illness after about eight months, necessitating his retirement to Gloucester. He thereupon set out to alleviate the economic distress precipitated by the war-time disruption of the commerce on which a high proportion of the Gloucesterians depended for their livelihood and prosperity. A personal plea to officers in the Revolutionary army brought money which Murray converted into much-needed food in the winter of 1776. Washington led the list of contributors with £10.[21] The provisions were sufficient to assist "upwards of a thousand individuals." However, patriotic feelings ran high in some parts of the community, and in spite of his humane efforts, Murray found himself, as a native-born Englishman, under suspicion. He was called in 1777 before the local Committee of Public Safety.

Murray defended himself and his friends against the imputation of disloyalty to the Colonial cause, pointing out to the committee that he was "a staunch friend to liberty, genuine liberty. It is well known that I have labored to promote the cause of this country, and I rejoice that I have not labored in vain." He cited his commission as an army chaplain among his credentials. But he was again ordered to depart. He wrote glumly to a friend that he was being subjected to "much persecution;" he was aghast at the action taken against him, being considered "an entire stranger" in spite of his relatively long residence in Gloucester and his efforts in making collections for the poor.[22]

There is no indication that any attempt was made to enforce the decision of the committee. Perhaps the town fathers were influenced by knowledge of a letter dated 27 May 1777 from (then) Major General Nathaniel Greene testifying to Murray's good character. Mrs. Murray later asserted that her husband "was in heart an AMERICAN . . . . He was decidedly and uniformly opposed to the oppression of the British ministry, and he would have embraced any upright measures to have procured redress; yet, perhaps, he would have been as well pleased had England and America been united upon terms of equality and reciprocal benefit." Murray's sentiments sounded much more like those of Benjamin Franklin than of Samuel Adams.

It would have been quite understandable if Murray, a native-born

Englishman, had suffered the pangs of divided loyalty during the excitement of the Colonial drive for independence. One individual recalled many years after the Revolution that Murray kept a box of earth in his study. It had contained two mulberry trees which Murray had brought over from England in 1770 but which had long since died. But he kept the box, and explained that when he was treated less kindly than he wished to be and felt out of spirits and downcast, he loved "to stand upon the earth in that box and . . . think I am on British ground."[23] As if to vindicate Murray and remove any lingering doubts as to his enthusiasm for the Colonial cause, as well as to emphasize the elevated social circles in which Murray moved, Thomas Whittemore proudly reminded the readers of the *Trumpet* many years later of an historical fact. Murray had been "an intimate friend and frequent visitor at the home of the illustrious John Hancock, whose name stands at the head of the signers of the Declaration of Independence, who was Governor of Massachusetts, and resided in Boston, while Mr. Murray was pastor here."[24]

In his lengthy Thanksgiving sermon delivered at the Universalist meeting house in Boston on 19 February 1795, Murray laid the entire burden for the coming of the Revolution on England.[25] According to his interpretation, it was envy of the "growing greatness" of the colonies that led England to take measures to perpetuate their subservience. Fortunately, "the encroachments of arbitrary power" and "the artful devices of designing men" were frustrated by those of exceptional wisdom and heroism. Murray contributed his mite to the near-deification of the Founding Fathers in his paean of praise; his friend George Washington was singled out for special tribute, as was the federal system of government established for the new nation.

One of the first indications that trouble over religious affairs might be brewing in Gloucester came in the form of a letter written in the spring of 1776, addressed to one Eli Forbes, pastor of the Congregational society, and signed by twenty-four persons, ten of whom were later among the organizers of the first Universalist society in America.[26] Forbes had been invited to assume the pastorate of the First Parish in 1775, following the death of its pastor. The letter, the first signatory of which was Winthrop Sargent, discouraged Forbes from coming to Gloucester, ostensibly because of the economic plight of the town—a situation which might jeopardize payment of a regular salary. There was, however, a hint in the letter that his appearance would disrupt the harmony of the parish. Although no formal opposition was expressed up to the time of his installation in June 1776, when Forbes arrived, several of the signatories to the letter immediately absented themselves from church, and listened instead to Murray.

One result was an attack on Murray's character as well as on his religious ideas. In answer to an inquiry about Murray addressed to Ezra

Stiles, Forbes was informed that the self-proclaimed preacher of universal salvation was "one of those ostentatious, obstinate, but subtle, delusory characters, with which it is best to have little to do."[27] Murray was described as "one of the most unprincipled of all men . . . a consummate hypocrite . . . and an unprincipled adventurer." Murray was given a true copy of the long letter. He was reported to have been "much offended" by it. The English immigrant who had landed almost unnoticed on the Jersey shore less than a decade earlier could certainly no longer bask in the obscurity which he had professed to seek. He was about to be involved in even more turmoil before the next decade passed.

Chapter 2

THE CREATION OF THE FIRST RELIGIOUS SOCIETIES

In February 1777, sixteen members of the First Church of Christ in Gloucester were called upon to give reason why they had absented themselves from services. They had, in fact, been listening to John Murray in various homes. An exchange of correspondence between church officials and the dissenters, lasting for over a year, resulted in their suspension.[1] Four of the signatories of the letter of veiled warning to Pastor Eli Forbes were among them; together with their wives, they comprised half of those on the list of delinquents compiled by the First Parish. The list included not only Winthrop Sargent but his wife and daughter (Judith) who was to become Murray's second wife.

The result of the suspension was a decision to create their own religious body and to set about providing their own meeting house. The building was constructed on Sargent's property; however, the society did not obtain title to the land on which it stood until 1799 when the sum of £100 was paid to the Sargent estate. Thirteen of the thirty box pews in the simple frame structure were assigned to Sargent and his family. The organ installed in the new edifice had been captured from an English merchantman by one Captain John Somes, a successful privateer during the Revolution.

Murray, who had disregarded all demands that he leave town, preached for the first time in the new meeting house when it was dedicated on 25 December 1780. This, the first Universalist church building in America built specifically for the purpose, was the outgrowth of an action taken on 1 January 1779, when the followers of Murray (including those suspended from the First Parish church) organized themselves into an Independent Church of Christ by covenant signed by the thirty-one men and thirty women comprising the congregation.[2]

John Murray was appointed minister of the new church in the covenant, and assumed the responsibilities of a full-time pastor. But almost immediately he and his church found themselves in serious difficulty. The assessors of the First Parish Church claimed that members of the dissenting group were still obligated to contribute to the support of the established church. The Universalists denied such an obligation, using as their authority the provisions of the recently

The first Universalist Meeting House in America, dedicated on Christmas Day, 1780

adopted Bill of Rights prefixed to the constitution of the state of Massachusetts in 1780. Articles II and III provided that:

> . . . no subject shall be hurt, molested, or restrained, in his person, liberty, or estate, for worshipping God in the manner and season most agreeable to the dictates of his own conscience; or for his religious profession or sentiments; provided he doth not disturb the public peace, or obstruct others in their religious worship . . . . religious societies shall, at all times, have the exclusive right of electing their public teachers, and of contracting with them for their support and maintenance. And all moneys paid by the subject to the support of public worship, and of the public teachers aforesaid, shall, if he require it, be uniformly applied to the support of the public teacher or teachers of his own religious sect or denomination, provided there be any on whose instructions he attends . . . And no subordination of any one sect or denomination to another shall ever be established by law.

These guarantees of religious liberty had not been adopted without a struggle. At the time the Gloucester covenant was signed in 1779, many of the members of the state constitutional convention in session in Boston were attempting to maintain religious orthodoxy and to prevent successful challenge of such dissenting groups as the Universalists. This effort was reflected in the original draft of Article III of the Bill of Rights. "Good morals being necessary to the preservation of civil society; and the knowledge and belief of the being of a God, his providential government of the world, *and of a future state of rewards and punishments,* being the only true foundation of morality. . . ." The italicized clause was rejected, but not before "a very long and severe debate."[3]

For three years (1781-1783) the members of the Universalist society refused to pay the taxes levied on them for the support of the First Parish. No concrete action was taken against them until 1782, when certain possessions of members of the group were seized and sold at auction to pay the delinquent taxes. This included articles of silver plate, various English goods, and the anchor of a vessel about to sail. One convert to Universalism (William Pearce) found himself temporarily lodged in the Salem jail for refusing to pay the tax. A suit filed by the Universalists to recover the property was withdrawn because of a legal technicality.

It was clear by 1783 that if the Universalists were to vindicate their status they would be forced to file suit and engage in lengthy court proceedings. For some three years the contending parties accumulated their verbal and legal ammunition, embodied in two pamphlets published in 1785. The first to appear, prepared by Epes Sargent, comprised thirty-nine pages of Universalist arguments (including an elaborate historical introduction), under the title *An Appeal to the Impartial Public by the Society of Christian Independents congregating in Glocester* [*sic*]. The First Parish's reply, *An Answer to a piece entitled "An Appeal to the Impartial Publick by an Association" calling themselves "Christian Independents in Gloucester,"* was a twenty-three page pamphlet prepared by Samuel Whittemore.[4]

The officers of the First Parish in Gloucester made it abundantly clear in 1785 that the Universalist society organized six years earlier represented an unwelcome and disruptive influence. Since 1779 the town had had not only Murray to contend with; it had been "infested" with "strolling mendicants" of the Universalist persuasion. All of this had kept the community "in one continual hubbub, to the obstructing [of] business, the corrupting of the morals of youth especially, and the total destruction of peace and harmony." Among the offenders who had appeared from outside and were listed (by last name only) were John Tyler, Matthew Wright, Shippie Townsend, Adams Streeter, Noah Parker, and Elhanan and Moses Winchester (referred to in the *Appeal* as "a duplicate of Winchesters"); all but Townsend were clergymen.[5]

The First Parish argued that the Universalists had failed to support the established church; that they were not a regularly constituted church or religious society, never having been incorporated. The Universalists were "but a mere jumble of detached members," including even individuals from other parishes. It was "the highest dishonour to the church of Christ for such a heterogeneous body to call themselves a church." They did not even pay their unordained minister and had never formally presented any reasons why they should be exempt from

The Gloucester Church as it appeared in the 1970s

paying taxes. Above all, they were being led by a "false and dangerous man" who was preaching all kinds of heretical ideas. How, it was asked, could "a man who publickly discards the doctrines of God's moral government—of future rewards and punishments—urge, with a good face, or with any hope of success, the practice of morality"? A group of members of the First Parish, in a manifesto to the citizenry, went even farther. They alleged that Gloucester was "moddling on the brink of ruin, owing chiefly, if not entirely, to this Association [of Universalists], headed by this foreigner [Murray] . . . . this man and his pernicious doctrines have been more damage to this town than the late war." Murray wrote a broadside in reply.[6]

Attacks on Murray came from all sides. In 1783 James Manning wrote to a friend in London portraying him in most unflattering terms. Murray was described as "a fugitive from justice in Great Britain [who was] all too successful in propagating the error of universal salvation which 'greatly contributed to the decline of the morals of the people, and to unsettle the minds of professors.' "[7]

The Independent Church of Christ in Gloucester believed it was on strong legal ground in challenging the seizures of property and in vindicating its own status under the Massachusetts Bill of Rights. The Universalists argued their case from the basic premise that they were a distinct sect, differing from other groups in theological belief, form of church discipline, and administration of ordinances. In short, they were "Independents," and as such they qualified for recognition as a separate religious body, not subject to the jurisdiction of the First Parish.

Yet there were certain embarrassments and complications to be met. For one thing, at least technically the Universalists were not supporting their pastor. Murray had consistently refused to accept money for his services, and suing for what seemed to be a material reward he had never sought was repugnant to him and would, he thought, be a reflection on his character and integrity. More bluntly, it appears that Murray just did not want to become involved in a complex and undoubtedly unpleasant controversy which was likely to last for months at least. It was only after repeated pleas, and reminders that the future of the Gloucester society, if not the whole cause of Universalism, would be jeopardized if he did not agree to have the case brought in his name, that he grudgingly consented. As it was, he played a minimal part, leaving to others the prosecution of the case. Murray was no doubt relieved when seven members of the Universalist society agreed by contract in February 1784 to shoulder the expenses of the suit against the First Parish.[8] Whittemore, in his account of the controversy, noted rather pointedly that, after victory was won, Murray was quite willing to admit that he had been "the happy instrument" that had brought it about, although Mrs. Murray recorded that Murray's permission to have his name used "was to him a permanent subject of regret."[9]

The case came to trial in 1783 and was not completed until 1786 because of various legal complications. A decision was handed down in the summer of 1785 by the Supreme Judicial Court, sitting at Ipswich, but was reviewed on order of the judges. The final decision, favorable to the Universalists, was handed down a year later. Although exemption from payment of taxes to the established church had been granted earlier by the colonial legislature to other dissenting groups (the Quakers in 1728 and the Anabaptists in 1729), this was the first instance in which the courts had extended exemption to any Protestant (Christian) denomination or sect regardless of whether or not it was incorporated.[10] Thus the state constitutional guarantees for such religious bodies were successfully tested by the Universalists for the first time, and Murray was found to have met the specifications for a public teacher of "piety, religion, and morality." As frequently emphasized, this court decision was important to other religious bodies which did not subscribe to the tenets of the established church.[11] The conflict which had precipitated the court decision in 1786 was settled by a legislative act in 1800 which authorized the paying over of taxes to dissident religious groups which presented certified lists of members.[12]

The Universalists thus joined forces with the Baptists as champions of individual religious liberty.[13] The Universalists, too, became unrelenting enemies of church and state alliances, and took a leading role in final disestablishment in Massachusetts in 1833, as will be indicated later.[14] In their *Appeal,* the Universalists stressed the fact that their challenge had broader ramifications than that of one religious group "so small and inconsiderable as ours." The decision would affect "every citizen of the Commonwealth" and every religious order "who in this State have been called Sectaries." The guarantees of religious liberty were strengthened, and the concept of an established church was weakened, as a consequence of the Universalist court action. An early step had been taken to encourage the religious pluralism which became a distinguishing characteristic of American civilization.

Murray was in Connecticut when the good news came by letter that the Universalists had, in June 1786, won their case. Almost a year earlier, he had journeyed to the village of Oxford, Massachusetts, to carry out a plan he had outlined to Noah Parker in February 1783, whereby Universalists "could have an opportunity of seeing and conversing one with another at least once every year . . . . wherever it may be most convenient." Because the Gloucester case was still undecided at the time, Murray, in all probability fearful of the outcome, wrote Parker that the meeting was "for the purpose of deliberating upon some plan to defeat the designs of our enemies, who aim at robbing us of the liberty wherewith the constitution has made us free." At the Oxford meeting, so important to the history of the denomination, Murray participated in the discussions and delivered the closing sermon. By this time he had already become concerned at the widening divergence of theological views between himself and such fellow Universalists as Elhanan Winchester, who presided at the Oxford session. Murray's widow noted, in her continuation of the *Life,* that even by 1785 "a root of bitterness sprang up, which destroyed his pleasure in the association," and he later regretted not having attended other meetings of the annual conventions decided upon at Oxford. After 1791 he attended only two in New England: Bennington, Vermont, 1795; and Sturbridge, Massachusetts, 1804, besides the Philadelphia Convention in 1793.[15]

Among the other difficulties which Murray had to face while in Gloucester was his legal competency to perform marriage ceremonies, an activity in which he had been busily engaged. For such allegedly illegal carryings-on, he was fined £50, but refused to pay it until his status was clarified. His conviction that he was commissioned by God to preach the Gospel and the fact of his election by the congregation to whom he ministered were not considered sufficient by the authorities. Prudence seemed to dictate that he leave the country while the issue was being settled; this he promptly did, on 6 January 1788. He frankly admitted in his petition that he fled the country because of "his well-grounded fears that prosecutions would be multiplied upon him, by the zeal of his religious adversaries." His petition, which was duly presented to the state legislature in February, included the fact that he had been ordained by his Gloucester congregation in December 1780. In no instance had he preached anywhere, except by the consent of the people involved. Ordination, in his view and that of his congregation, was accomplished merely by his election by his constituency, without any formal ritual or ceremonies. If anything more were needed, Murray cited his recent victory in the courts which recognized him as a constituted minister with a legally organized congregation. Even if the mode of his ordination by the Gloucester church were not considered conventional by orthodox standards, Murray's petition insisted that it was nonetheless valid. Murray's congregation also filed a separate petition in his behalf. The petitions admirably served their purposes, for Murray was, in effect, ordained by resolution of the Massachusetts legislature.[16]

In the early fall of 1788, the Gloucester society took another step which complied with the letter as well as the spirit of the state constitution. They voted to tax themselves sufficiently to provide Murray with an annual salary of £100. An assessment on 103 persons was made in 1789, and on 121 persons in 1790. One further complication plagued the Gloucester Universalist society before its status was settled beyond question. In spite of the decision of 1786, a court case was threatened in 1790 because taxes were being diverted to an unincorporated group. The society, on petition, was duly recognized as a corporate body by the state legislature in 1792. This was undoubtedly a wise decision, for in 1810 Theophilus Parsons, chief justice of the Supreme Judicial Court of Massachusetts, construed the existing law very narrowly by interpreting "public" to apply only to incorporated religious societies.[17] The newly incorporated society bore the offical name of "Independent Christian Church in Gloucester."[18] Almost fifteen years of Universalist activity in Gloucester was finally made legitimate in all respects; thereafter, each group of Universalists wishing to organize a society was careful to file the necessary papers required by the states in whose jurisdiction it intended to operate.

Equipped with letters of recommendation, including one "signed by the most respectable members" of his Gloucester church, and another by three so-called elders (including Winthrop Sargent) which emphasized his status as an ordained minister, Murray landed at Falmouth, England in 1788, about February. After preaching there for several days, he departed for London, preaching at such places as Plymouth and Exeter en route. His reception everywhere was most gratifying to him; "for were I an angel descended from above, I could not be followed with more uniform attention." Although there was some criticism, he was undoubtedly pleased to be described in one instance as "the most popular preacher in the United States." A visit with his aging mother in London seemed to make his journey complete. His determination to return to the United States was not diminished by requests that he remain in England. The return voyage on the *Lucretia* in April 1788 was made more than routine by the presence of John Adams and his wife Abigail. Murray, one of the three "Gentleman passengers" besides Adams, conducted religious services on board.[19]

On Christmas Day, 1788, the Gloucester congregation renewed Murray's election and ordination as their pastor with great fanfare and publicity, being careful to see that it was duly reported in the newspapers. The vote of the church included the specific reminder that the procedure of election and ordination was not only "according to the institutions of the first churches in New England," but was "in perfect conformity to the third article of the declaration of rights" of the state constitution, which was paraphrased repeatedly in the vote of the church and faithfully reproduced.[20] The Gloucesterians were taking no chances that the unhappy chain of events precipitated in 1782 would be repeated.

In many ways, the next period in Murray's life was the happiest and most serene. He had been completely vindicated as a minister of the Gospel, his friends were increasing, as were the number of adherents to the Universalist faith. The day after his return to the United States, he had attended a "select party" at the home of the governor. There was no question now of his "respectability." In addition, he had married, on 6 October 1788, in Salem, Mrs. Judith Sargent Stevens. An "intelligent and gifted woman," of considerable literary ability, Mrs. Murray was socially ambitious, and moved easily in the circles of "the best society" in the Greater Boston area.[21]

Judith Sargent, born in Gloucester on 5 May 1751, the oldest of eight children, was the widowed daughter of Winthrop Sargent, Murray's close friend who had become so deeply involved in the Universalist cause. Sargent, who died in 1793, also left a son and namesake (1753-1820) who in 1788 became the first secretary of the government established for the Northwest Territory, and who in 1798 became the first governor of the Mississippi Territory. Judith was educated under the tutelage of a Harvard graduate (John Rogers) who served one of the local churches. In October 1769 she married one John Stevens of Gloucester, an unsuccessful merchant and trader who, in order to escape imprisonment for debt, fled in the winter of 1786 to the British West Indies where he died soon after. Mrs. Murray had met her future second husband in the fall of 1774, when Murray had made his first visit to Gloucester at the request of her father, who had by then become acquainted with James Relly's writings.

Mrs. Murray was a prolific writer (a cousin commented that "she wrote poetry by the acre"). Her work was published during the 1780s and 1790s in such journals as the *Boston Monthly Magazine* and the *Massachusetts Magazine*. In 1798, after encouragement by both Murray and numerous friends, her writings were published under the title of the *Gleaner*, in three volumes. Indicative of both her circle of acquaintances and the literary reputation she had by then acquired was the roster of distinguished names on the subscription list of over 750; among them were George and Martha Washington; David Ramsay, the physician and historian from South Carolina; and such public leaders in Massachusetts as Governor Increase Sumner, Harrison Gray Otis, Elbridge Gerry, and Fisher Ames. The work was dedicated to the man who headed the subscription list—President John Adams.

Mrs. Murray was both an independent soul and a person who was not prone to hide her light under a bushel. Much of her writing was either anonymous or pseudonymous, and she was not at all loathe to explain that she tried to give the impression that her writings emanated from a masculine pen; one of the reasons was to give freer rein to her views—including hints of Universalism—and another, to assert her independence as a writer. She very well realized the low opinion most of the male of the species had of feminine writing. She had earlier written an essay on "The Equality of the Sexes," supplemented by four more on the subject in the *Gleaner*, which anticipated most of the arguments of a later day on behalf of women's rights. She also made it clear that she wanted, by means of her literary efforts, not only to be "distinguished and respected" by her contemporaries, but to "descend with celebrity to posterity." She was not very happy to have had two of her dramatic productions (reproduced in the third volume of the *Gleaner*) severely criticized by reviewers after the plays had been staged in the Boston Federal Street Theatre in 1795 and 1796.

Mrs. Murray frequently accompanied her husband on his numerous trips, and was with him when, in 1790, he visited New York City and New Jersey and during the early summer spent considerable time in Philadelphia. Several offers, of increasing generosity, were made in an attempt to prevail upon him to settle there; among the promised inducements were a rent-free home and an annual salary of $1,067. He was given use of the largest hall at the "College, Academy, and Charity School of Philadelphia" (the University of Pennsylvania) and, on his first appearance there, was escorted to the pulpit by the president and faculty. As Dr. Benjamin Rush, the eminent physician and man of letters (and Universalist) pointed out to Mrs. Murray, no one would have dreamed of the revolution in the religious world taking place during their lifetimes when an unknown immigrant from England had spoken in Bachelor's Hall in the same city twenty years before. Certainly there was mounting evidence that "the sentiments of the Universalists" were "growing every day more respectable." It was with great satisfaction that Mrs. Murray reported that Benjamin Franklin's family were "among the foremost of our favorers." With equally great satisfaction, Murray, who was proud of his wife's literary abilities, sent to a friend in England the series of letters which she had written to her parents while in Philadelphia. While in New York, the Murrays visited President Washington and received a call from the First Lady. They were also entertained by Vice-President and Mrs. Adams, whom they had earlier visited at the Adams' home in Braintree, Massachusetts. Not many of Murray's Universalist successors moved in such prominent and exalted company.

The high point of Murray's visit to Philadelphia was the invitation to draft, with William Eugene Imley, an address to George Washington congratulating him on his accession to the presidency of the United States and, incidentally, informing him of the creation of the first independent church in the new nation professing Universalist principles. They received a cordial reply.[22] Murray and Imley were speaking on behalf of the so-called "Convention of the Universal Church, assembled in Philadelphia," generally known as the Philadelphia Convention. Plans for this first gathering of Universalists in the Middle Atlantic area had been laid in 1789, and it had convened for its organization meeting on 25 May 1790. Murray was the only delegate from New England, representing Boston and Gloucester. Imley was one of two representatives from Upper Freehold, New Jersey.[23]

In 1793 Murray accepted a call to become the "settled pastor" of the unorganized group of Universalists who lived in Boston. It was already a familiar scene to him. He had visited the town in the fall of

The first home (1793-1838) of John Murray's First Universalist Society in Boston

1773 and had preached in various places, including the so-called Factory which had been constructed by the colonial government to encourage textile production (spinning) and stood near the spot where the Park Street Church was later built.[24] He had also delivered sermons in Faneuil Hall and at the former French Protestant church in School Street. It was in that former Huguenot chapel that Murray reportedly had had a confrontation with one of his opposers that demonstrated his ready wit. At one service attended by John Bacon, pastor of the Old South Church (1771-1775), he challenged Murray; the latter's replies were so well received by the assemblage that some of Bacon's supporters disappeared long enough to purchase eggs from a shop nearby and returned to pelt Murray with them. His rejoinder: "These are moving arguments, but I must own at the same time, I have never been so fully treated to Bacon and eggs before in all my life."[25]

Boston Universalists had had only occasional sermons, including some by Murray himself, until his settlement. In the winter of 1785, after the death of its pastor, Samuel Mather, the Congregational society sold its meeting house at the corner of Hanover and Bennett Streets to the Universalists. The church building, "a homely wooden edifice," was removed in 1838, and a new brick structure was constructed on part of the same lot. During his appearances prior to 1793, Murray had been paid varying sums from voluntary contributions; after unanimous election by the "First Universalist Church and Congregation" he received £4 a week; by 1795 his salary had been set at $22 for each

Sabbath. The Lord's Supper was celebrated in the church for the first time in 1791, after one of Murray's discourses. Even though solicited to take up his residence at other places, the only firm commitment he made was to preach at the Gloucester church occasionally. This he faithfully carried out for some ten years. He could have done no less, for the congregation there was much upset at his decision to move to Boston; he had been among them for nineteen years, and had seen the society take shape and prosper. But the Boston society had no settled pastor, and he recognized its strategic location as a future center for Universalist activity.

After the Murrays moved in 1794 to No. 5 Franklin Place (Street) in Boston, the First Universalist Society, incorporated by the legislature in 1806, retained his services for the remainder of his life (until 1815). Throughout his long pastorate in Boston he made frequent appearances in widely scattered churches, but never without "the assenting voice" of the Boston society. Beginning in 1810, however, Murray, because of the state of his health, was assisted, first by Edward Mitchell (1810-1811), then by Paul Dean (1812-1815). Murray was fortunate to have been able to obtain the services of Thomas Jones, a native of Wales, as his successor in the Gloucester church. Until Jones' installation in 1804, the congregation struggled along without a regular minister. Jones, a convert from Methodism to Universalism in 1788, had come to America in 1796 on the urging of Murray, who was seeking a minister for the Universalists in Philadelphia. Jones enjoyed a pastorate of thirty-eight years in Gloucester (until 1841) and officiated at Murray's funeral in 1815.[26]

In her portion of the account of Murray's life at the Boston church, his widow made a great point of the devotion with which he ministered to his congregation; he "considered the interests of the people of his charge as *his own.*" She made an even greater point of the exceptional harmony that prevailed between him and his flock, although she did admit that political differences apparently resulted in occasional displays of temper on both sides. As to the ordinances which Murray performed as a part of church services during his various pastorates, and his attitude toward them, numerous eyebrows were raised outside the denomination and even by some members of his own congregations. He rejected completely the doctrine of transubstantiation and celebrated the Lord's Supper only as a memorial service, and only when requested. He did not believe in water baptism of infants, and instead substituted the ceremony of dedication—a practice thereafter followed by most Universalist clergy. Murray could find no Scriptural authority for infant baptism, considering the one baptism referred to in the Pauline Epistles and Ephesians IV: 5, 6 to have been sufficient.

A day in mid-October 1809 was a sad one for the Murray household. He suffered a paralytic stroke that left him an invalid for his remaining six years. His last preaching in his Boston church was done as he was seated in the pulpit, being unable to stand. When he was almost seventy, he participated in the dedication of the new Universalist meeting house in Salem, Massachusetts, in June 1809, where he offered the dedicatory prayer and gave the charge to the pastor-elect, Edward Turner. Murray was already "weak and feeble" then, and for the duration of his life had to be carried in to the services he sometimes attended; one of his last appearances was at the installation of Paul Dean in the Boston church in August 1813. The venerable founder of organized Universalism in America died on 3 September 1815, a few weeks short of his seventy-fifth birthday. Prominent among fellow Universalists who participated in the funeral services were Thomas Jones, of Murray's old church in Gloucester; Hosea Ballou, who had become his leading theological protagonist; and Edward Turner, also of Gloucester. Paul Dean, Murray's successor at the First Universalist Church in Boston, delivered a eulogy.

Murray was buried in the Sargent family tomb in the Granary Burying Ground in Boston, but without any stone or inscription. At a meeting of Universalists in 1835, it was recommended that his remains be removed to Mt. Auburn Cemetery in Cambridge and that a suitable monument be erected.[27] A lot was purchased near the center of the cemetery, where his coffin was re-buried in June 1837. The money needed to provide the lot, a monument, and an iron fence, was raised by voluntary contributions.[28] A total of $637.57 was collected, of which $625.58 was expended. The balance was appropriated for maintenance. Thirty-four societies and four individuals made contributions ranging from $1.00 to over $80 (from the First Universalist Society in Boston). A dramatic (and possibly gruesome) note was struck on the occasion when arrangements were made immediately prior to the re-interment for the display of the coffin. A special service in the church where Murray had served for so many years was conducted. Delegates to the annual meeting of the Massachusetts State Convention of Universalists had adjourned in nearby Malden only the previous day, and attended both the church services and the Mt. Auburn recommittal ceremonies. Hosea Ballou delivered the graveside address.

Murray left no lineal descendants in America to carry on the family name. A son born of his second marriage died in infancy in 1789. A daughter, born in 1791, was married to Adam Lewis Bingaman of Natchez, Mississippi, in 1812, immediately after his graduation from Harvard. Mrs. Bingaman died in 1822, leaving one son who lived in New York. Following her husband's death, Mrs. Murray lived with her daughter at Oak Point, near Natchez, where she died 6 June 1820.

Chapter 3

ESTABLISHING A THEOLOGICAL BASE

Murray's Universalist Predecessors and Contemporaries in America

Tracing the origins, spread, and impact of ideas is always more difficult than documenting the history of an organization or institution. This is certainly true when one attempts to search for the origins of the belief in universal salvation in American religious thought. There seems to have been a tendency to go to extremes respecting this. Clarence Skinner and Alfred S. Çole, twentieth-century Universalist writers, in their study of John Murray, gave up in despair and concluded that it was "a difficult and fruitless task to determine who first taught Universalist doctrines in America .... no one really knows."[1]

On the other hand, virtually every historian of American Universalism includes a lengthy list of individuals holding to or expressing universalist beliefs long before they were officially expressed at the end of the eighteenth century. Thomas Whittemore, an aggressive champion of Universalism, writing in the 1820s, in his eagerness to backdate the movement as far as possible, reported numerous instances of which he had heard or read. He did, however, wisely make a distinction between those who may have privately held universalist convictions and those who expressed them publicly.[2] Hosea Ballou 2d, a denominational historian writing in the 1840s, pointed out that it was unfair to make claims to religious fellowship that may not have existed at all or might be offensive or unwelcome unless the person to whom the beliefs were attributed was present to explain or defend himself.[3]

Half a century later, Richard Eddy, in his two-volume history of Universalism in America, devoted much of his "Introduction" in the first volume and a 92-page first chapter to examples of individuals both in Europe and America who held universalist views before John Murray arrived in 1770. Among the individuals or groups identified and discussed in varying detail by Eddy were Mystics (including the Rappites), certain Quakers, the Dunkers (German Baptists), Moravians, some Anglicans (Episcopalians), and selected Congregationalists. It should be pointed out in the interests of exactitude that several individuals discussed by Eddy did not come onto the religious scene or become professed universalists until well after 1770; this does not necessarily weaken his argument for a relatively wide dissemination of the idea of universalism before Murray, but does raise the question of how much universalism came by way of writings from Europe (including England), by colonial writings (which were numerous), or by independent thought and personal discovery. A high proportion of converts to universalism even before it emerged as a denomination claimed to have been converted solely by perusal of the Scriptures.

No matter how few or great in numbers, the various individuals already embracing universalism in America by the 1770s or 1780s undoubtedly paved the way for reception of John Murray and his ideas, and furnished something in the way of a pool or reservoir from which a coherent movement could be built; but the organizational efforts which resulted in a distinct body of believers are to be traced directly from Murray and especially from among the converts he made after his arrival. A further distinction should be made between those who contributed in some way to universalist thought and those who founded an organization.[4] It is the latter which is emphasized in this study.

The three persons generally acknowledged to have been the earliest contributors to American universalist thought were George de Benneville (1703-1793), Elhanan Winchester (1751-1797), and Benjamin Rush (1745-1813). The life and ideas of each of these men, as well as the contributions of such early exponents of universalism as Charles Chauncy and Jonathan Mayhew, have been thoroughly studied and abundantly documented, and are considered in no great detail here.[5]

George de Benneville was considered by Thomas Whittemore to have been the first to preach universalism in America. He was born in London, where his French Huguenot parents had sought refuge from religious persecution on the continent. After almost twenty years in Holland, France, and the Germanies, where he was associated with a pietist group in Berleburg (Wittgenstein) and preached universalism, he emigrated to America, where he settled among German pietists in the Philadelphia area. He devoted the remainder of an exceptionally long life to practicing medicine and preaching universalism with a strong mystical flavor. He is credited with arranging for the American publication in 1753 of *The Everlasting Gospel.* This work, written by Georg Klein-Nicolai of Friessdorf, under the pseudonym "Paul Siegvolck," apparently had great influence on the shaping of American Universalist ideas, at least in the mid-Atlantic area. It was through Elhanan Winchester that de Benneville became known to most early Universalists. The two became acquainted and it was Winchester who made available to American and English readers de Benneville's autobiography. The autobiography, translated from the French by Winchester, was first published in London in 1791 and in the colonies in 1800 and 1804, with a preface by Winchester.

The actual influence of de Benneville on American Universalism is difficult to determine. No one has claimed that he should be considered a founding father of the denomination, for he never established a religious society or church. His association with the pietism and mysticism of the German immigrants to Pennsylvania, many of whom were acknowledged universalists, certainly contributed to that stream of American religious development.[6] Many pietist beliefs and practices, including the use of lay preachers, the emphasis on the authority of the Bible rather than later formulations of dogma and creeds, and millenialism were shared by Universalists long after Hosea Ballou had modified Universalist beliefs.

The German Baptists (Dunkers), who began arriving in 1719, were among the most important groups who believed in universal restoration. Many of them and their descendants in Pennsylvania, the Carolinas, and Georgia joined Universalist societies, and Universalists in Pennsylvania published a German-language newspaper for their benefit. Elhanan Winchester and de Benneville found each other's ideas congenial, and Winchester thought sufficiently highly of his contemporary to have thanked the Diety for having had the opportunity to become acquainted with "such an humble, pious, loving man [as] I have scarcely ever seen in my pilgrimage through life."

Winchester, whose contributions to early American Universalism were probably greater and more direct than de Benneville's, was born in Brookline (then Muddy River Village), Massachusetts, in 1751, the son of a farmer and shoemaker, and a deacon in the local established (Congregational) church. Although never receiving more than a common school education, the young Winchester had a facility in language and an unusual memory; these enabled him later in life to master Latin, Biblical Greek and Hebrew, and some French. His religious career began early; he started preaching in his father's home at the age of nineteen, having been influenced, together with his father, by the "New Light" Congregational revivalist movement of the 1750s and 1760s. In 1770 he became a Baptist following attendance at a revival meeting, and was ordained in Rehoboth, Massachusetts by the same preacher who had converted him. For the next few years he held several brief pastorates and served as an itinerant preacher. In the fall of 1775 he took charge of a Baptist church at Welch Neck, on the Great Pee Dee River in South Carolina, where, with the exception of brief trips to Massachusetts and Virginia, he remained until the fall of 1779. Although he intended to return, circumstances changed his plans; on his way back from a visit in the North, he stopped in Philadelphia in October 1780, found the Baptist church without a minister, preached to overflow congregations, and decided to stay. Between 1781 and 1785, after being ousted because of his universalist views, he and approximately 100 of the church members who had been excommunicated held services in the original hall of what became the University of

Elhanan Winchester (1751-1797), pioneer preacher of Universalism

Pennsylvania. Out of this group grew the "Society of Universal Baptists."

In 1787 he journeyed to England, where he lived until the spring of 1794. While there he preached to numerous congregations, most notably to a society which welcomed all Christians and ignored all attachments "to Party or Denomination."[7] In 1788, while in England, he published an attack on slavery which he had delivered earlier in Virginia, and his *Dialogues on Universal Salvation,* which was widely distributed in America. Winchester's views on slavery, which were formulated while he resided in South Carolina, were often cited and quoted by Universalists after they became seriously concerned about slavery in the 1830s. After returning to America in 1794, penniless and in ill health, he preached in various parts of New England and briefly in Philadelphia. He presided at the meeting of the New England Convention in Oxford, Massachusetts, in 1795, and died in Hartford, Connecticut, on 18 April 1797 at the age of forty-six.

Much of Winchester's personal life was marked by tragedy as well as religious doubt as he slowly made his way from Calvinism to universalism. Four wives predeceased him; all but one of his eight children (by three wives) were stillborn, and the remaining one (a daughter) died before the age of two years. His fifth wife, a widow when he married her and who outlived him, was apparently unbalanced mentally and made life miserable for him.

The long transition from Calvinist Baptist belief to universalism began in 1778, while he was in the South and had occasion to read Siegvolck's *Everlasting Gospel* while visiting in Virginia. The idea of the possible restitution (restoration) of all intrigued him, and set in motion a whole train of doubts about Predestination. He described his conversion to universalism in the preface to his edition of the *Everlasting Gospel,* published in 1792. By the time he had arrived in Philadelphia in 1780, he considered himself "half a convert." His next step was to read *The Restitution of All Things* by Sir George Stonehouse, an English divine educated at Oxford who had at one time been Charles Wesley's vicar. Stonehouse had supported the universalist position in three works published between 1760 and 1773. Judging from Winchester's own statement, he was familiar with most or all of Stonehouse's works, including *Universal Restitution, A Scripture Doctrine,* published in 1761.[8]

Like Murray, Winchester preached a version of universalism for several months without identifying it as such—probably for fear of being labelled a heretic and losing important friends. But an intensive reading of the Scriptures seemed to confirm "the truth of the Universal Restoration," and in 1781 he publicly admitted his new convictions and found himself the center of a bitter struggle which divided the Baptist congregation in Philadelphia. He could take some comfort, however, from the fact that he had a few of the most prominent Philadelphians in the new Society of Universal Baptists that was organized. Among them was Dr. Benjamin Rush, a signer of the Declaration of Independence and the man who was to word the first official statement of Universalist belief at a meeting in Philadelphia in 1790.

Winchester was also heartened by the presence in nearby Germantown of Dr. de Benneville, whose acquaintance he had first made in 1781 and whom he visited frequently thereafter. During his brief return to Philadelphia in 1796, Winchester also shared his pulpit with Joseph Priestley, the eminent Unitarian scientist whom he had met while in England. In 1783, two years after he had publicly avowed universalism, Winchester met for the first time John Murray, destined to be even better known to American Universalists.

Benjamin Rush, the versatile and distinguished Philadelphian—physican, writer, and humanitarian—not only articulated universalist ideas but translated them into a course of action in the world of man. Almost every Universalist social reform impulse from anti-slavery, temperance, and prison reform in the pre-Civil War era to participation in the Social Gospel movement of the late nineteenth century can be traced to Rush's influence. In both word and deed he was a convinced universalist.

Rush was exposed to the preaching of many of the evangelists associated with the Great Awakening, including Gilbert Tennent, Samuel Finley, and Samuel Davis, and was well acquainted with Elhanan Winchester and his ideas.[9] Like some of his contemporaries, Rush travelled the spiritual road from Calvinism to universalism. In his autobiography and correspondence he acknowledged the influence of Winchester as well as Stonehouse, Nicolai (Paul Siegvolck) and Chauncy in arriving at his universalist convictions.

Rush and Winchester corresponded frequently between 1788 and 1791, while Winchester was in England.[10] By 1787 Rush had already, as he wrote another friend, "embraced the doctrines of universal salvation and final restitution."[11] Rush had found Winchester, in his Sunday evening discourses in Philadelphia, "as usual, eloquent, Scriptural, and irresistible in his reasonings upon all subjects."[12] Rush, like Winchester, was able to equate universalism with Christian republicanism as opposed to the monarchism and absolutism of Old World Calvinism. The American Revolution was, in Rush's mind, but one step in the working out of the divine millenial plan for the new nation about to be born. Universalism was thus to be a major vehicle for establishing both religious and political equality under the aegis of a benevolent deity. Rush, like many later Universalists with broad vision, saw a system incorporating both the revealed faith in Christianity and the rational religion of humanity, a harmonious combination of the spiritual and the worldly.

Murray's Version of Universalism

John Murray had very little to say about his theological views in his autobiography, although Mrs. Murray made some attempt to summarize them in the concluding pages of the *Life*. However, the sources and characteristics of his thought in the area of religion may be ascertained readily from numerous other sources, and virtually no disagreement seems to exist among explicators and commentators, either among Murray's contemporaries or later interpreters.[13] His published *Letters and Sketches* are the major resource, and Richard Eddy undertook to pull the various strands together when he wrote a brief history of the denomination which became part of Volume X of the American Church History series in 1894.[14]

Basically, after Murray adopted James Relly's ideas, expressed in the latter's *Treatise on Union* and the sermons which Murray heard in England, he followed them with no significant deviation throughout his life. His religious beliefs, in short, went through no real evolution after he had accepted universalist ideas. The major change in Murray's approach over the years was in his technique of presentation rather than in the substance of his sermons. Until after his settlement in Gloucester, where he achieved a security unknown earlier, Murray tended to be oblique and somewhat defensive about his beliefs, possibly not being sure what the reaction would be. Particularly after the legitimacy of the Gloucester church, and his role in it, were assured after 1786, and after his return from England in 1788, Murray became more positive and aggressive in the expression of his ideas and less hesitant about propagating his version of human destiny.

Murray never abandoned completely the Calvinism in which he had been reared, nor did he ever waver in the generally accepted Christian beliefs in one great and indivisible First Cause; an omnipotent, omnipresent, and omniscient God; an overriding Divine Unity manifested in a Trinity; man as a creation of Divine Purpose, an imperfect and fallen creature after Adam; vicarious atonement through Christ; and the inspired nature of the Scriptures. Throughout his life he was adamant about the divinity of Christ. On one occasion, he wrote: "As I believe Jesus Christ to be the only wise God, our Savior, I know no other God in whom to trust, or of whom to be afraid. I am a Unitarian. I believe in one God over all blessed forever, and I am persuaded that it is this one God, who is the Savior of all men."[15]

He thought more favorably of professed deists than of Dr. Priestley, who spoke so irreverently of Christ and yet alleged to be a Christian. At least the deists were open about their beliefs (or lack of them). In the same letter in which these ideas were expressed, he explained his conception of the relationship between Trinity and Unity, in which the latter is emphasized. In other instances, he reversed the emphasis; he frequently drew the analogy between a triune God and the three elements of man—body, soul, and spirit.

Murray discarded the basic Calvinist tenet of the Elect; instead, he broadened the concept to include "the whole family of man" before Adam's fall, through a mysterious union of Christ and man (Relly's principal teaching). But this by no means assured salvation. Only those who, while on earth, believed in Christ would be saved; all others were damned. There was a Final Judgment beyond mortal life; and some would, for an undetermined period, suffer until eventually all ("universal humanity") would be redeemed and reconciled after the "Book of Life" in which a record of every human was kept, was opened by the Creator. What Murray (and Relly) held out to all men was "their indissoluble union with Christ"—a privilege not restricted to the Calvinist elect only—a hope that could be realized on earth by all, to assure them a place on the right hand of God, seated with Christ, when the ultimate reckoning took place—"the restitution of all things." It was not for his sins that a man was punished in a future life—for this had already been borne and suffered by Christ—but for his unbelief. Man's debts for his sins had already been paid.

Murray mined the Bible for every possible passage that pointed somehow to the ultimate salvation of all men, and triumphantly reaffirmed time after time that reason and the Scriptures were his only sources. His methodology, by which he cited literally dozens of chapters and verses, led him to conclude that every prophet from Moses through Christ himself taught universalism. Even a superficial review of those of his sermons which he wrote down, usually after delivery, and which are extant, indicate that the majority consisted of strings of Scriptural citations or paraphrases held together by a minimum of commentary by Murray.

There seems to be consensus that Murray was in no sense an original thinker, nor did he ever claim to be. Instead, he was the propagator of a core idea which held out the hope of something besides inexorable doom for all but a mere handful of humans. Moving frequently in the presence of the great and the near-great, Murray attracted an ever-expanding body of believers from all ranks of life; they, in turn, could and did spread Universalism in the new nation. The optimism implicit in the teachings of Murray and his followers was quite in tune with the aspirations of a burgeoning new civilization that believed with increasing certainty in the inevitability of progress of individual and nation alike.

Murray was, if nothing else, a powerful and effective speaker, with an ability to make friends and influence people to a remarkable degree. One of his major contributions was to pioneer in the organization of

Universalism as a denomination, or at least to pave the way for others to do so. Organization *per se* was never his major goal. Even though his theological concepts might not endure in the form, or according to the reasoning, with which he presented them, Murray did, as his wife very rightly indicated, lay a foundation to be built upon by his successors.

As has been emphasized earlier, throughout his life Murray held steadfastly to his version of Universalist truth. Mrs. Murray confirmed this when she wrote that in all of her almost forty years with her husband, she "never knew his testimony to vary in the smallest degree." It could be expected that others might come along to challenge his unswerving testimony, either with new approaches, interpretations, or different emphases; or, as the consequence of new insights which might (and did) result from the evolution of an individual's ideas through various stages. Mrs. Murray, writing within the year of Murray's death, regretfully admitted that, excepting John Tyler of Norwich, Connecticut (who retained his Anglicanism-Episcopalianism throughout), and Edward Mitchell of New York, she did not know of a single Universalist preacher in America who was "*exactly* in unison" with her late husband.

Caleb Rich, a native of western Massachusetts and a contemporary of Murray, came to his universalist beliefs by 1773 quite independently of Murray, and spread his ideas in several areas of New England.[16] Rich once made a pilgrimage to Boston to meet Murray toward the end of the latter's career. Murray had a less than cordial conversation with Rich after Murray discovered that his contemporary had arrived at his universalism by a somewhat different route than had Murray. As a result, Rich departed from Boston "with less reverence for human, and more for divine wisdom." As William S. Balch pointed out in his biography of Rich, Murray "was sometimes a little too sensitive, in his latter years, upon the peculiarities of his doctrine . . . . [and] spoke decidedly against any innovation upon his views." Murray also alluded to doctrinal differences with Rich in his correspondence.

Although Murray had been "completely won over" by Elhanan Winchester's personality, described by Murray as replete with "unassuming gentleness and warm Christian sympathy," Murray was apparently somewhat jealous of Winchester's success, and considered him something of a rival. But there were theological differences also that separated the two men, although Murray's ambivalence frequently blurred their conclusiveness. Despite the fact that they had arrived at the same ultimate universalist position, they, like Rich and Murray, had travelled there by different routes, and independently.

James Relly had been the primary influence on Murray, while Siegvolck and Stonehouse seem to have shaped the basic theology of Winchester. Both Murray and Winchester held to Trinitarian views, but

Murray's thinking, if carried out all the way, led to the denial of all future punishment. Winchester argued for a final apocalyptic cataclysm which would result in the purgation (at the end of some 50,000 years) of all sins of those who had erred; they would then join those who had already achieved spiritual purity to effect a union with Christ and God. In effect, they would be "restored" to eternal happiness. Murray found that man had already been saved (providing he met certain specifications) and would not be punished in the afterlife for sins committed on earth, but for lack of belief. Winchester found salvation by stages in a somewhat indefinite future, with punishment for earthly sins yet to come. One saw human salvation through an event accomplished in the past; the other looked forward to something not yet achieved but ultimately possible.

Even before Hosea Ballou's unitarian Universalism became well known after 1795, many of Murray's basic ideas were being questioned by other Universalists; this fact caused him great sorrow and unhappiness. Some, long before Murray's death in 1815, had raised doubts about his version of man's lack of personal responsibility for his sins, and of the existence, nature, and duration of sinfulness itself. They had come to the conclusion that the sins were not only of man's own doing, but the consequences were confined to mortal life, for which Christ's sufferings might have not been relevant at all. Others, while retaining the doctrine of the Trinity, rejected the theory of vicarious atonement and even of future judgment. Murray blamed "the works, or rather the ravings," of one Richard Coppin for this state of affairs. Coppin, a seventeenth-century dissenter during the Cromwellian era in England, not only argued in behalf of universalism, but insisted that all rewards and punishments were confined to this life. Murray was not able to go that far in his own thinking; for, among other things, it obviated the need for a Day of Judgment in which he firmly believed.

At the same time, "the general tendency of thought among Universalists was in the direction of the Unitarian view of the divine nature."[17] Murray wrote to a friend that he suffered "much from different descriptions of Universalists." It was to him a "source of inquietude, but the evil, as I fear, is a growing evil, and it is mine to lament its progress." He expressed fear that the result might be "the establishment of Deism." In *Some Hints Relative to the Forming of a Christian Church,* first published in 1791 and republished in the *Letters and Sketches,* Murray elaborated what he already perceived to be the varieties of Universalists. By that date he had identified no less than seven. Writing earlier, he discerned five, making a distinction between generic universalism and Christian Universalists.

A major variation came to the surface in his own church less than a decade after he wrote the aforementioned article. In the fall of 1798, because of absence from Boston on a trip to Philadelphia, Murray invited the ex-Baptist Hosea Ballou to fill his pulpit. The sermon, with strong unitarian overtones, provoked from Mrs. Murray an often-cited statement delivered from the pulpit at her request before the services had been concluded; namely, "that the views presented by the occupant of the pulpit of this church to-day, are not those that are usually promulgated here, and they are not in accordance with those entertained by Mr. Murray." Ballou undoubtedly realized the rift that was developing between Murray and an increasing number of Universalists, but out of deference to the older man he refused to accept an offer to move to Boston and form a new society which would obviously compete with Murray's and result in a divided congregation.[18]

Less threatening to the Universalist cause but of concern nonetheless, were apparent inconsistencies, faulty reasoning, and even contradictions in Murray's ideas and their expression. One of his failures was to make clear a distinction (on which he was equivocal) between "salvation" and "redemption." Andrew Croswell of Boston, who never took kindly to Murray or his ideas, categorically stated in a pamphlet published in 1775, entitled *Mr. Murray Unmask'd,* that Murray had even denied that he held to the doctrine of universal salvation, but argued only for universal redemption. Apparently Mrs. Murray felt constrained to explain something that her husband had never made clear, for she devoted several pages in the *Life* to attempting to make the distinction and thereby defend her departed husband, who had frequently ignored any distinction at all.

Long before the course of Murray's life had been run—in fact even before a single Universalist church had been established in America—his promise of ultimate universal salvation had been attacked. John Cleaveland, pastor of the Second Church in Ipswich, warned against Murray as a "false teacher" in a pamphlet published in 1776 with the prescient title, *An Attempt to Nip in the Bud, the Unscriptural Doctrine of Universal Salvation.* Cleaveland's pioneer attempt to perform theological surgery was fruitless. Religious polemics involving Universalism became the order of the day for over half a century to follow.

The Winchester Profession

There was no doubt that "some diversities of opinion concerning some points of doctrine" had come to exist among Universalists themselves by 1803. John Murray was still preaching the Rellyan theory that all souls would be saved through a mystical union of Christ with humanity. Elhanan Winchester and a sizeable majority of followers believed in the eventual restoration of all souls to holiness after long periods of suffering for sin. Caleb Rich was teaching that all punishment for sin was confined to earthly life, and Hosea Ballou was wavering toward that belief. He and Abel Sarjent, an early Universalist leader in Pennsylvania, had already challenged the concept of the Trinity.[19] The author of the *Circular Letter of the New England Convention of Universalists* in 1796 had acknowledged that "different professors of the Abrahamic faith have dissimilar views," and recommended that those who professed Universalism concentrate on the goal of ultimate salvation, and not "give themselves over to vain disputation" as to the means by which it was to be achieved or the nature and duration of an interim period.

It was this state of affairs that prompted the same convention at its 1802 meeting to appoint a committee to formulate some kind of a statement, and when one was produced in 1803, to preface it with the explanation that its purpose was "to prevent confusion and misunderstanding." The statement was called for because of "some diversities of opinion concerning some points of doctrine and modes of practice." The so-called "Winchester Profession" was intended therefore to serve as a broad statement of faith generally agreed upon, but at the same time would allow for differences of opinion and interpretation. Individual convictions on particular points could in this way be protected. According to Hosea Ballou, one of the "excellencies" of the Profession after it had been adopted was its very ambiguity; it could be accepted by all believers in universal salvation without requiring any distinction between belief in future punishment or no punishment at all.[20]

The Profession, a short document of only three brief paragraphs, became the formal basis of Universalist belief, with some emendation and interpretation, for the remainder of the nineteenth century. The status of the Profession can be determined a century after its adoption from the records of the commemorative services held in various parts of the United States on the 100th anniversary of its formulation.[21] When the Profession was originally drawn up, it was stipulated that although the Plan of Association for the denomination adopted at the same time could be changed as circumstances required, there was to be "*no alteration* in any part of the three articles, that contain the *profession* of our *beliefs* ever to be made at any future period."[22] Later generations thought otherwise, as will be noted in the restatement of Universalist faith in 1899 and again in 1935.

The original Profession read as follows:

Article I. We believe that the Holy Scriptures of the Old and New Testament contain a revelation of the character of God, and of the duty, interest and final destination of mankind.

Article II. We believe that there is one God, whose nature is Love, revealed in one Lord Jesus Christ, by one Holy Spirit of Grace, who will finally restore the whole family of mankind to holiness and happiness.

Article III. We believe that holiness and true happiness are inseparably connected, and that believers ought to be careful to maintain order and practise good works; for these things are good and profitable unto men.

The foundation on which the Profession was built was the "Rule of Faith" adopted at the Philadelphia Convention of Universalists in 1790 and in turn adopted by the New England Convention four years later.

[1] *Of the Holy Scriptures.* We believe the scriptures of the old and new testament to contain a revelation of the perfections and will of God, and the rule of faith and practice.

[2] *Of the Supreme Being.* We believe in one God, infinite in all his perfections, and that these perfections are all modifications of infinite, adorable, incomprehensible, and unchangeable love.

[3] *Of the Mediator.* We believe that there is one Mediator between God and men, the man Christ Jesus, in whom dwelleth all the fullness of the Godhead bodily, who by giving himself a ransom for all, hath redeemed them to God by his blood; and who, by the merit of his death, and the efficacy of his spirit, will finally restore the whole human race to happiness.

[4] *Of the Holy Ghost.* We believe in the Holy Ghost, whose office it is to make known to sinners the truth of this salvation, through the medium of the holy scriptures, and to reconcile the hearts of the children of men to God, and thereby to dispose them to genuine holiness.

[5] *Of Good Works.* We believe in the obligation of the moral law as to the rule of life; and we hold, that the love of God manifested to man in a redeemer, is the best means of producing obedience to that law, and promoting a holy, active, and useful life.

It will be noted that, of the three articles comprising the Winchester Profession, the first two are little more than paraphrases of the 1790 statement. The emphasis in the latter document on Jesus as the Mediator, and references to the Holy Ghost (the second and third articles) were omitted, and the statements about "good works" in the final article were incorporated into Article III of the 1803 Profession.

Appended to the Winchester Profession was the following:

Yet while we adopt a general profession of belief . . . we leave it to the several churches and societies or to smaller associations of churches, if such should be formed, within the limits of our General Association, to continue or adopt within themselves, such more articles of faith . . . as may appear to them best under their particular circumstances, provided they do not disagree with our general profession or plan.

This statement came to be known within the denomination as the "liberty clause." It was not only the formal recognition of the crucial Universalist stress on individual rights but was a recognition of the realities of the situation, both earlier and at the time it was adopted—"that where the brethren cannot see alike, they may agree to differ." The "liberty clause" remained attached to the Winchester Profession until 1870; it was reinstated in 1899.

Although the authorship of the Profession was not indicated in the convention records, the wording of the statement was the work of Walter Ferriss of Charlotte, Vermont. He had been appointed, together with Zebulon Streeter, George Richards, Hosea Ballou, and Zebulon Lathe, as a committee in 1802 to draft such a document.[23] It was Ferriss who had made the original motion in 1802 that a statement be prepared, and it was he who presented it on the floor for discussion. Several years after the Profession had been adopted, there was considerable interest in who had been responsible for composing it. Russell Streeter, in 1833, was the first person known to have mentioned Ferriss as the possible author.[24] The Profession was "said to have been penned by the venerable Ferriss," who had died in 1806 at the age of thirty-eight. In 1836 Hosea Ballou, who had served on the committee to draft the Profession, stated unequivocally that Ferriss had written it.[25]

The New England Convention did its best under the circumstances to publicize the Winchester Profession and to urge its adoption, or some statement similar to it. The point was made that the Profession had been adopted unanimously, and without change from what the committee had presented. The convention authorized the printing of 300 copies of the newly adopted Profession "for the information of all the churches and societies." Many Universalist newspaper editors, after a denominational press had been established, printed the Profession in their publications from time to time. For many years, John C. Burruss, editor of the *Universalist Herald* in Alabama, published the Profession on the first page of every issue.

Yet the adoption of any statement of faith at all went against the grain of numerous Universalists. When it was offered in the convention in 1803, it provoked much discussion and debate not reflected in the official minutes of the meeting. Noah Murray, from northern Pennsylvania, who had never before attended a Universalist convention, was joined by Solomon Glover of Connecticut and others in opposing the adoption of any written statement.[26] One young clergyman who was present (Nathaniel Stacy) reported that the proposal to adopt the statement caused "no little sensation among the brethren;" and the motion to adopt it resulted in "probably the longest and warmest debate . . . that had ever been known in that deliberative body."[27]

Noah Murray predicted future difficulty if the statement were adopted, and in colorful and homely language compared it to a calf: "It is harmless now . . . and its horns will grow, and then it will begin to hook." The supporters of the Profession countered by pointing out that

Universalists had already suffered for having lacked "an evidence to the world that they were, as a christian people, actually agreed in something essential both as to fact and practice."[28] They needed "some document to evince that they belonged to a denomination of christians distinct from the standing order of congregationalists." These arguments prevailed, and after Murray and Glover had left the convention early to make the long journey home, the remaining opposition yielded in the interests of harmony in order to provide a unanimous vote.

In subsequent years, many churches and societies (although probably only a minority) ignored the matter completely. Even in 1785, when the Gloucester Universalists had been struggling to achieve legal recognition, they had been opposed to establishing Articles of Faith.[29] Hence, when their society was organized, no statement was adopted, on the ground that it would limit individual freedom and leave the impression that men believed they were infallible. In 1793 the same society, when called upon for a statement of uniform belief by the New England Convention, was so independent-minded and so reluctant to be bound by any such statement that it refrained from participation in Convention activities for some twenty years.

The Universalist church of Charleston, South Carolina, doggedly Trinitarian in the face of overwhelming unitarianism in the denomination by 1830, reminded other Universalists that it had not been the practice to form creeds and articles of faith.[30] "Their creed is the Bible, their articles of Faith are the doctrines therein laid down . . . . creeds have always been an evil."[31] The official name of the society organized in 1829 was the "Association of the Primitive Apostolic Church of Trinitarian Universalists in the City of Charleston." When the schismatic Restorationists in 1833 adopted a Confession of Faith, William S. Balch, editor of the *Impartialist,* raised the question of whether Jesus imposed a creed on his disciples. "If not, why do his followers?"[32] The revised constitution of the short-lived Southern General Convention organized in Baltimore in 1835 stipulated that "no profession of faith shall be required or adopted either by the members of this body or any convention in fellowship with this."[33] The Pennsylvania Convention, in 1848, regretted any efforts to require assent "to even the vestige of a creed in our denomination, or any other test of Christian fellowship, but that of belief in the Bible, according to each individual judgement, accompanied by a pure life in an honest and independent seeking after truth for oneself."[34]

Those societies and churches which adopted a statement of faith frequently took advantage of the "liberty clause" and formulated their own. For example, the First Universalist Society of Albany, New York, adopted the following summary declaration in 1822:

We believe in one God, the Creator, Preserver, Benefactor, and final Savior of

> all men—whose infinite wisdom, power, and goodness, are displayed in the visible work of his hands—and especially in the revelation of his never-ending goodness to man in the sacred scriptures, through the man Christ Jesus, who hath abolished death, and brought life and immortality to light through the gospel.[35]

Occasionally a state convention or other official group would see fit to reaffirm the Winchester Profession, but would hasten to add (as did the Vermont Convention in 1854 and 1857) its own interpretation:

> Resolved, that as Universalists we hold to the right of private judgment, that every man is to decide for himself what is right and that we are not authorized to withhold our denominational fellowship from any person whose belief corresponds to the above named profession of faith and whose works also are in harmony therewith. [1854] .... We regard all as Universalists who believe in the final salvation of all men through divine grace, however they may differ in opinion as to punishment or discipline extending into the future state and as to progressive improvement and different degrees of happiness in the future world. [1857]

Such flexibility and permissiveness obviously had perils built into it, and sometimes Universalists did not practice what they professed in this regard. In fact, the Vermont Convention revised its constitution in 1864 to require that clergymen, as a condition of fellowship, signify a belief that the Bible was an all-sufficient guide to faith and practice. This was immediately interpreted by the editors of the *Universalist* as an unjustified addition to the Winchester Profession.[36] The Profession, they said, had acquired "a historical value, the prestige of years," and was a statement on which Universalists could "better unite, than any other that could be framed .... we think it unwise to contend for anything in addition to it."

When a new constitution was adopted by the General Convention in 1865, it was provided that the required assent to the Winchester Profession could be "implied" instead of expressed. It would have been difficult to envisage much more theological permissiveness than that. Most nineteenth-century Universalists probably agreed with Alonzo A. Miner, who delivered the Centennial Sermon in 1870 at the services celebrating the progress of the denomination, and remarked that the Winchester Profession had "providentially saved us from all the evils of a long-drawn creed, and yet has firmly anchored us to the word of God."[37]

SECTION II

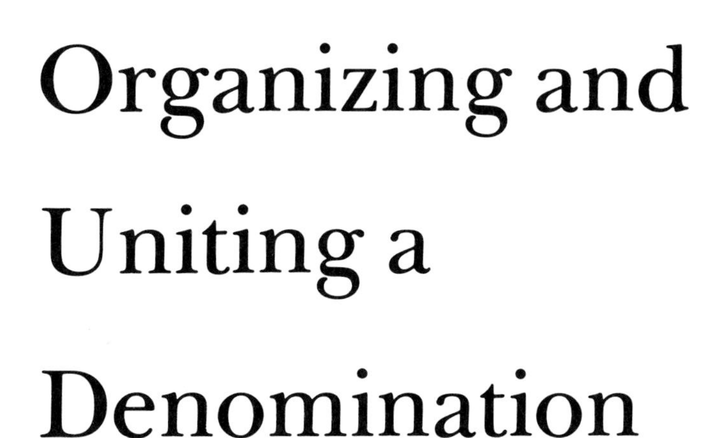

Organizing and Uniting a Denomination

Chapter 4

EVOLUTION OF A STRUCTURE

Preliminary Considerations

Two clarifications are advisable regarding the organization and structure of the Universalist church in America before proceeding with a more detailed consideration of its history. One has to do with its status within the general configuration of American religious groupings. The other, of more particular relevance to Universalist church history itself, is concerned with the internal evolution of a formal entity which was recognized, in varying degrees, as the executive body and general spokesman for Universalism when called for, and which furnished the continuity, corporate or otherwise, and conducted the business of the denomination. Whatever its designation at a given time or place, this entity has usually been known as the Universalist General Convention (although it began as a New England-centered organization) and existed from 1793 through 1960.

The exact time at which Universalism became a distinct sect, and when it became a denomination, depends largely on the matter of definition; this, in turn, can involve rather fine distinctions of a somewhat technical nature. If commonly accepted dictionary definitions of each term are used, and attention is paid to how the Universalists themselves used the terms in the context of their own day and their own interpretation, the year 1785 can be used as a date for their first appearance as a "sect," and 1793 as the date for their designation as a "denomination," confirmed and elaborated ten years later at an assembly in Winchester, New Hampshire. In 1785 they could be considered—and certainly conceived themselves as—"a schismatic body," or a "small faction united by common interests or beliefs," or "a group of people forming a distinct unit within a larger group by virtue of certain refinements or distinctions of belief or practice."

In the fall of 1785, in Oxford, Massachusetts, four preachers and nine laymen from nine communities representing three New England states met pursuant to a call issued by a group of Universalists a few weeks earlier, suggesting some form of cooperation among co-religionists in the area. They recommended not only a distinct name—"Independent Christian Society, commonly called 'Universalists' "—for a particular body of believers, but submitted to the religious societies they represented a proposal "to be cemented in one

The meeting house in Winchester, New Hampshire, where the Profession of Belief was adopted in 1803

body, consequently bound by the ties of love to assist each other at any and all times when occasion shall require."

The delegates also adopted a "Charter of Compact" which was intended to serve as a model for organization of Universalist societies, and was subsequently adopted by several, with many local variations. However, beyond voting to meet annually (beginning in Boston, in 1786), the representatives adopted neither a formal statement of belief nor a plan of government or organization for either the constituent societies acting as a group, or even rules for the conduct of such meetings.

It was at another session in Oxford—in 1794—that Universalists had become "an organized group of religious congregations," with legally recognized components (societies), and a profession of faith. In that year, approximately thirty delegates representing "Churches and Societies in General Convention" from the five New England states and New York State adopted the so-called "Philadelphia Platform." This document had been drawn up by Universalists meeting in that Pennsylvania city in 1790, before any legally recognized body had been created. This provided Universalists in the Northeast as well as elsewhere with both a set of "Articles of Faith" (five in number) and a "Plan of Church Government" (usually referred to as a "Plan of General

The Universalist Church in Oxford, Massachusetts, built in 1792 and used also for commercial purposes

Association" by the New England body). The latter contained guidelines both for organizing individual societies and for annual conventions attended by "deputies or messengers" from churches desiring to be represented. This periodic "communion of churches" was "for the purpose of more effectually spreading the gospel, and of assisting and of edifying each other." But no machinery was suggested for organizing the convention, providing formal representation of churches or societies in it, or even for giving them a corporate existence. If either the Philadelphia Convention had had a continuous existence, or any of its constituent societies had been recognized by law, the achievement of denominational status for Universalists might have been dated from 1790 instead of 1793.

During the next few years, as Universalism continued to spread, particularly in New England, both differences in theology and weaknesses in structure began to be evident. The result was further confirmation and refinement of denominational status by a series of recommendations and actions initiated in 1802 with the appointment of a committee "to form a plan of fellowship in faith and practice, for the edifying of the body, and the building it up together." Out of this came, at the meeting in 1803 of representatives of the denomination, the Winchester Profession of Faith, so called from the name of the New Hampshire village where the meeting took place.

It was this Profession that became the official core of Universalist religious belief throughout the denomination's history as an independent body. Appended to the three-article Profession were certain explanatory and supplementary paragraphs. One (in which the word "sect" had been stricken out of the original draft) was a declaration that Universalists considered themselves and their associates in fellowship "a denomination of Christians distinct and separate" from those who did not approve the entire Profession. In two other instances there were references to Universalists continuing to claim rights and privileges accorded to "every denomination."

The second document of importance adopted in 1803 was a "Plan of General Association" which spelled out for the first time in one place the composition, organization, and functions of what, under one of numerous designations over the years and many internal changes, became the executive agency of the Universalist Church of America. It was this latter body which, by consolidation with its Unitarian counterpart, the American Unitarian Association (organized in 1825), formed the Unitarian Universalist Association in 1961. It was then that the two groups ceased to exist officially as separate denominations.

Universalism as a separate denomination developed in a casual, uncoordinated, and almost accidental way, reflecting the individualism and suspicion of centralized organization shared by most Universalists who felt sufficiently strong in their religious convictions to join a distinctive group. It should always be remembered that scores of Universalists came to their religious beliefs independently of any proselytizing agency—by reading the Scriptures, or as a result of discussions with friends and neighbors, and often without benefit of any clerical direction, guidance, or even suggestion. Almost every step in the erratic evolution of a coherent and identifiable organization came quite pragmatically. Very little advance planning was evident, particularly in the early years; solutions to problems of organization and cooperation were arrived at on an *ad hoc* basis, forced by specific exigencies.

Convention Book

Which Contains the Minutes and Transactions of the Convention Holding and Believeing the salvation of all Men, in and throu our Lord Jesus Christ, met in Philadelphia, May 25th, 1790 &c as likewise some Circumstances that Brought About such Meeting.—

In the year of our Lord 1789, in A Conference between Some persons Who Resided in Philadelphia, and others from Jersey State holding said faith, it was lamented that altho we were Well Aquainted with many Christians in Different parts of this Continent who do hold and Injoy this Glorious Doctrine, yet for the Want of A more Social Union and Communion together our Groth Establishment and Consolation Was much Impeaded.— It was therefore Agreed that there should be A Meeting in Philadelphia on the 6th of Septbr 1789 there to Consult on the most Expedient Ways to bring this Desired object about. Accordingly at said Meeting there was A Committee of four appointed to Draw up and send out A Circular Letter to Various parts Inviteing, Such as held like faith with them to meet in A Conference on the Subject this was done and is as follows.—

A page from the records of the Philadelphia Universalist Convention (1790-1807)

Ecclesiastical terminology associated with Universalist affairs was, for many decades, very loosely used, and some designations were interchangeable; some were so vague at times as to create confusion and even misunderstanding. Some meanings and connotations achieved a degree of precision, or at least clarification, only with the passage of time and continued usage. Some distinctions were assumed but seldom spelled out. For example, a "preacher" in the eighteenth century and a good part of the nineteenth century was one licensed to expound the Scriptures and conduct religious services; a "minister" was a preacher who had been ordained, and could administer the two "ordinances" (sacraments) recognized by most Universalists: Baptism and the Lord's Supper (Communion). The term "pastor" began to be used in the 1840s to identify clergymen who had been settled for a considerable time with one society or church. Occasionally (and especially in the South, where Universalists were few in number and widely scattered), a clergyman held the dual title and served in the dual role of "pastor" and of "travelling preacher," "evangelist," "circuit rider," or "missionary."

Universalists were expected to refer to each other as "Brother" or "Sister," as appropriate, with emphasis on the concept of brotherhood, fellowship, and democratic simplicity.[1] In the early days of American Universalism, the term "Reverend" was seldom used in reference to the clergy, "Brother" being preferred; for the Universalists considered their ministering brethren "not a superior order of beings, nor more godly than the primitive heralds of salvation."[2] Linus S. Everett, a Universalist clergyman, editor, and newspaperman, went even further. In the 1830s, while editor of the *Southern Pioneer*, he deliberately abandoned the use of the term "Brother" as invidious and as maintaining a distinction which he considered unjustified.[3] He disliked titles of any kind, and preferred not to use even the title of "Reverend;" but as long as it was "known to signify nothing more than that a man is a preacher," he grudgingly agreed to use it when appropriate.

One Universalist complained in the 1830s that some clergy in the denomination were calling themselves "evangelists" and encouraging use of the title.[4] This was considered presumptuous, for the term, said the complainant, was properly limited to four of Jesus' apostles. Universalists should return to the historic simplicity of the Gospels and get rid of all titles, even "Reverend," and use "Brother" or "Preacher." The complaint was aimed specifically at Abel C. Thomas of Philadelphia, who had been a Quaker by upbringing and education, until his conversion to Universalism, and of all people, should never have recommended such usage. However, such a literal rendering of the word was exceptional, and "evangelist" or one of its variants was used extensively in the denomination, especially in the nineteenth century. The word "Evangelical" or "Evangelist" appeared in the titles of at least twelve of the numerous denominational periodicals during that century. When the first issue of the *Evangelical Universalist* appeared (in Macon, Georgia) in 1838, the editor explained that the Universalists rather than the "orthodox" or the "partialists" were "the only truly Evangelical Christians of the present age;" for they were the only ones who applied the true meaning of the terms "good message" and "good news" to *all* mankind rather than to some portion of it.[5] The words "glad tidings" appeared in the titles of four Universalist papers.

Most Universalists who gave the matter any thought made the commonly accepted application of "evangelist" to any individual fellowshipped or ordained but not settled with any particular society or church; i.e., a travelling clergyman.[6] The salutation of "Father" was a token of special respect usually reserved for those Universalists, such as Hosea Ballou, who had served the cause for many decades and had made special contributions to the denomination. Those who adhered to other faiths or doctrines, or who belonged to other religious groupings, were referred to either by their denominational designation, or as "Partialists" or "Limitarians" because they refused to acknowledge the possibility that *all* would eventually be saved. Thomas Whittemore, editor of the *Trumpet and Universalist Magazine* and an early historian of the denomination, credited Joseph Huntington with first using the term "Partialists" in the sense so extensively employed by nineteenth-century Universalists. Dr. Huntington was a Yale graduate and Congregational clergyman who wrote a defense of Universalism entitled *Calvinism Improved* which was published in 1796, two years after his death.[7] Members of the Congregational church were almost invariably referred to as "orthodox," even after that denomination had been disestablished. Buildings constructed for religious purposes were usually "meeting houses" rather than "churches." When shared with, or open to, more than one denomination, such edifices were usually referred to as "union houses" or, in the case of the South, often as "republican houses."

The terms "society" and "church" were frequently used to refer to the same group, although an important legal, ecclesiastical, and even social distinction did exist which became a matter of concern to many Universalists. A "congregation," at least as the term was used in the early days of Universalism in New York State, was any religious gathering which had not yet been organized.[8] Local usage was an important factor. The term "society" was widely used in New England but was seldom heard or used in the South, the term "church" being preferred there. After 1865, the term "parish," an ancient administrative division familiar to English colonials, began to be increasingly used by Universalists as a rough equivalent of a "society," or the jurisdiction which it embraced. The ambivalence was well illustrated as early as 1816, when the Universalists in one Massachusetts community organized under the legal title "First Universalist Parish or Society in Westminister."[9] The terms "association" and "convention," which came to have special meanings, were often used at first in their generic sense to signify almost any gathering of Universalists.

There is no better illustration of lack of precision in nomenclature than the history of what was popularly referred to until 1833 as either the "New England Convention" or even the "General Convention," although the latter term was not adopted until that year, when the organization became officially the "General Convention of Universalists in the United States." In 1866 that body became the "Universalist General Convention," when chartered under the laws of New York State. From 1942 until its dissolution in 1960, the official designation was the "Universalist Church of America." When the organization met initially (in 1793) it had no name at all. It was merely the "Ministers, Elders, and Messengers appointed by the Universal [*sic*] Churches and Societies" in Massachusetts, Rhode Island, New Hampshire, Vermont, Connecticut, and New York "to represent said Churches and Societies in General Convention." By 1803 it had become a meeting of "ministers and delegates" to the "General Convention of the Universal[ist] Churches and Societies of the New England States." In the following year, when a species of structuring occurred and an official title was adopted for the first time, the organization became the "Universal[ist] Convention of the New England States, and Others." In spite of this, at least six variations were recorded between 1804 and 1833, ranging from the "Universalian Convention" to "the meeting of Universal Churches and Societies." The terminology used depended on the vagaries of temporary clerks, errors of transcription, or just plain disregard for exactitude.

It was not until 1811 that a Standing Clerk (Abner Kneeland) was first appointed. One of his tasks was "to collect, if possible, all the proceedings of the Convention since that body has existed." Two years later, he was authorized to spend $13.75 for record books.[10] The result was a ledger labelled "General Convention of Universalists" in which he transcribed, in chronological order, those records he could find, leaving blank pages for those missing. The records for each meeting ordinarily consisted of minutes of the proceedings and a Circular Letter or Epistle which was often printed and distributed separately. Hosea Ballou 2d, who served as Standing Clerk from 1824 through 1838, obtained copies of all the missing earlier records except the minutes for the 1793 meeting and the minutes and Circular Letter of 1798, and dutifully transcribed them in the ledger. Beginning in 1819, the minutes or proceedings of each convention were usually reprinted in one or more denominational newspapers, but were sometimes edited beforehand.

It was not until American Universalism was almost half a century old that even an approximate denominational structure appeared, with a roughly ascending pyramidal arrangement emerging by the early 1830s; but in terms of allocation and distribution of power, it remained truncated until almost 1870—a full century after Universalism had been introduced.

The local societies and churches were the basic unit; representatives of these, in turn, met periodically and often informally in loosely-knit associations which were created as needed, often with vague or overlapping boundaries (and jurisdictions) which frequently ignored state lines. This rather inchoate situation was a source of chronic frustration for those who tried to compile statistics or describe with some degree of accuracy the state of the denomination at any given place or time.[11] Associations were almost constantly in the process of reorganization as the denomination expanded.

Intermediate organizations, regional in nature and broader in geographical base than the associations, were also created as circumstances seemed to warrant. Like the associations, they often included more than one state. State conventions also evolved, to which associations sent representatives. The state conventions, the first of which became operative in 1827, began in 1833 to meet annually, again on a representative basis, as the General Convention of Universalists.

Societies and Churches

The first group efforts were at the strictly local level, and were no more than small gatherings in private homes. Although hundreds of Universalists failed to take even the first step toward formal organization, the majority, after much prodding, eventually created recognized societies, organized according to the laws of the state or locality in which they resided. As Clinton Lee Scott has pointed out, "the people who identified themselves with the Universalist movement were, on the whole, extremely individualistic. They had come out of other churches that were not to their liking, and were reluctant to commit themselves to any form of organization."[12] However, if they were to enjoy the advantages of formal association, transact business, collect and disburse money, and enjoy any benefits that might accrue from legal recognition as religious bodies, it was expedient to organize.

The requirements for organizing a society were minimal, both by Universalist standards and by most state or local laws or by the customs of the community where there were no legal regulations on the subject. In 1828, in reply to several inquiries as to how to go about organizing a society, the editor of the *Christian Intelligencer* in Maine outlined the formalities.[13] In most cases, there was no need to petition the state legislature for an act of incorporation. The procedure was to request a local justice of the peace to issue a warrant in the name of one person.

The petitioners would then assemble, after appropriate notice (usually seven days), elect necessary officers (a moderator, a clerk, and a treasurer), and proceed with their business. The incorporated society could raise money so long as this was mentioned in the warrant, ordinarily for the employment of a preacher. It was suggested that as many organizers as possible of the society should sign the original petition.

The issuance of a warrant by a justice of the peace for the organization meeting of a society was usually a formality, but in Wareham, Massachusetts, in 1829 the opposition to the Universalists was so great that four local justices refused to issue the required warrants. As a consequence, the Universalists obtained the services of a lawyer from the neighboring village of Rochester, New Hampshire, who not only notified the petitioners in the prescribed manner, but presided over the first meeting.[14] The Universalists had no minimum membership requirement for creating a society. Even a constitution and bylaws, although desirable, were not considered necessary. Throughout the history of the denomination, the principles laid down by Murray in organizing the Gloucester society were adhered to.

Whether or not John Murray had any intention of organizing or establishing a distinct denomination in America when he arrived, he was forced almost by circumstance to do so after the experiences of the Gloucester congregation in the 1780s. His supporters likewise saw the necessity, and he began to receive inquiries as to how to go about forming religious societies. Even so, Murray's reluctance to establish a complex structure or elaborate ritual was made very clear. In 1791, complying with a request, he outlined his ideas.[15] The procedure was quite simple. All of like mind

> should associate together in Church fellowship, state the articles of your faith in clear and concise language; and let all those who choose to subscribe thereto, mutually consent to have fellowship one with another. Let them meet together upon the first day of every week, for the purpose of worshipping God . . . . If they have no one to preach the word of the kingdom unto them, let them read a portion of the scriptures which, accompanied by the Spirit of God, is sufficient to make them wise unto salvation.

Prayer could be offered by any member of the group who felt its need. The singing of hymns was quite appropriate. If ordinances were observed, Baptism and the Lord's Supper were sufficient, and optional even then. Observance of the latter ordinance was low on Murray's list of requisites. He argued that "the exercise of charity" was more important as a Christian duty than ceremonial acts. He would probably have been more amused than concerned to have witnessed the almost constant exhortation by Universalist ecclesiastical bodies a quarter of a century after his death to celebrate the Lord's Supper more frequently than most societies were wont to do. Any "difference of mind or manners" respecting the use or disuse of that ordinance "or any other ordinance," should "never intercept the gentle flow of . . . christian affection toward each other."[16] In this instance, Murray was following his mentor Relly's insistence that rites (ordinances and sacraments) were superfluous because salvation had already been procured for the believer.[17]

All that was necessary to assemble "as a church of Christ, meet together in his name, [was] two or three . . . thus met together . . . whether blessed with the public preaching of the word or not."[18] In 1831 the editor of the *Universalist Watchman* published a model constitution for a society, with the comment that "no reasonable excuse . . . can be offered for not forming Societies where eight or ten brethren of the Abrahamic Faith reside near each other."[19] In 1857 the Georgia State Convention of Universalists was faithfully following Murray's advice by recommending that whenever two or more Universalists were available, they should meet every Sabbath "without waiting for the presence of a preacher."[20] Denominational papers often reproduced model constitutions for prospective societies. The one most widely used in New Hampshire was drawn up in 1832 by William S. Balch and printed in the *Impartialist* (Claremont, New Hampshire), of which he was editor.[21]

In reply to an inquiry in 1832 from a convert to Universalism in Alabama as to how to go about organizing a society, he was told by the editor of the *Trumpet* that there were no general rules for forming such groups.[22] Interested individuals could "subscribe to any form of compact they may please to draw up which is consistent with the gospel of Christ, and the laws of the commonwealth in which they reside." An individual wishing to join a society had few hurdles put in his way. The requirements of the Second Universalist Society in Belpre, Ohio, may be taken as typical. Any person of "good moral character" could join through any pastor or any member by applying and by signing the society's constitution.[23]

The vast majority of societies were small and isolated, often consisting of no more than a dozen or so members, or even less. In the nineteenth century, societies of over 100 were exceptions rather than the rule, except in some metropolitan areas or centers of Universalist activity. Such was the society in Camp Hill, Alabama, probably the largest in the South during that century, with at one time 250 members.[24]

Scores of societies were formed without the assistance of a preacher. Even after organization, because dozens of societies had no settled pastor or even enjoyed occasional preaching, they were urged in season and out to meet each Sunday, study and discuss the Scriptures, or read to each other sermons which had been reduced to writing and appeared with great frequency in denominational newspapers, or were published in pamphlet form. Keeping many societies active or even alive was a perennial problem. Many did not seem to realize the purposes for which they had been created. In 1833 W.S. Balch undertook to outline their responsibilities, while at the same time chiding them for inactivity.[25] Their primary task was "to obtain religious instruction, and afford it to others." State statutes provided societies with the corporate powers to do this; it was their duty to employ preachers and to build meeting houses. "Societies have something more to do than merely to meet once a year and choose their officers, half of whom do not know the duties of their appointment, and then disperse until another year comes round." They could enlarge their scope of action, and thereby enhance their worth, by creating libraries of religious materials, by collecting and distributing Universalist sermons and tracts, and by sending delegates to denominational meetings, A.B. Grosh, editor of the *Universalist Register* for several years, was constantly urging his co-religionists to bring dormant societies to life by meeting in homes, whether a preacher was available or not, and to "do *something*–almost anything that is not inconsistent with reason and duty."[26]

Wary as most Universalists were of ecclesiastical organization, and as cavalierly as terms were used, bodies identifiable as churches in the technical sense had appeared in considerable numbers by the 1830s, one of the decades of greatest growth of the denomination. Churches were sufficiently numerous to justify a distinction from societies when the annual statistics of the denomination were published in 1840. In virtually all cases, the number of church members was much smaller than the number of society members within a given community. For the most part, churches were formed within existing societies and represented the most formal expression of fellowship. A church was said to exist when a group of believers adopted a set of rules for religious discipline or a profession of faith and when the ordinances of Baptism and the Lord's Supper were administered, although individual participation was optional. The plan adopted at Philadelphia in 1790 defined "churches" rather than "societies" by requiring subscription to its articles of faith and providing (optionally) for the administration of ordinances. It also specified marriage as an ordinance, although most later Universalists did not; i.e., marriages could be performed by licensed preachers as well as by ordained ministers.

There are numerous instances in the records urging societies to regularize their proceedings by adopting some statement of faith, which after 1803 was usually the Winchester Profession or some minor variation of it. The minutes of the Vermont State Convention and those of the Eastern Association (Maine) and the Maine State Convention are full of such recommendations. Even then, the line between a society and a church was often difficult to determine. When Calvin Gardner undertook an inventory of Universalism in Maine in 1836 for its state convention, he was unable to discern "whether there exist many churches in connection with societies, or what qualifications are necessary in order to obtain membership."[27] In some communities churches rather than societies were organized; in 1846 the Piscataquis Association (Maine) amended its constitution to provide that where such was the case within its jurisdiction, churches were to have the same privileges in the association as societies.[28] In Maine, if both a church and a society existed in the same community, the lay delegates to the state convention were to be elected at a joint meeting.

Organization of churches within societies was sometimes urged in order to bring Universalists into closer fellowship and to strengthen spiritual life. This seemed to be especially evident in Maine, where in numerous instances associations urged that "churches ought to be formed in connexion with our Societies."[29] Nevertheless, unanimity seldom prevailed about the advisability of taking such a step. In a protracted and earnest discussion at a meeting of the Somerset Association (Maine) in 1848 one preacher "cared not what a religious body is called, whether a church, a society, or a body of believers."[30] If covenanting together and adopting rules of discipline characteristic of a church was desired by a society, well and good; but it was not required. As late as 1872, when a resolution was offered in the Maine State Convention urging every society to organize a church which would observe Christian ordinances and hold weekly services, it failed for lack of support.[31] There was considerable opposition within the society in Washington, New Hampshire, when the majority decided in 1828 to organize a church.[32]

When a decision was made to form a church, the customary procedure was to have a public "service of recognition." This consisted of a regular service with one or more sermons, the observance of the ordinances of Baptism and the Lord's Supper, and the reading of a "uniting Compact and Profession of Faith" which included agreement to abide by the laws of the church. Those were usually embodied in a constitution and/or bylaws which provided for regular services, machinery for conducting routine business, and provision for the repair and upkeep of the church building.

Among the earliest Universalist churches (as distinct from societies) organized in Massachusetts were those in Gloucester (1806); Watertown (1828); Roxbury (1828); and Marlborough (1831), which started with forty members.[33] Apparently all of the earliest societies in central New York State (beginning in 1804) were immediately organized as churches, complete with constitutions, professions of faith, and the celebration of ordinances.[34] The same held true for the majority of the societies organized in the South. This was done at least in part to show skeptical neighbors that Universalists were not irreligious infidels outside the pale of Christianity.

The organization of churches, as distinct from societies, met with considerable opposition from within the denomination. Sufficient churches had been created by New England Universalists by the early 1830s to provoke an objection from Thomas Whittemore, outspoken editor of the *Trumpet.* He saw no reason for making any distinction between a society and a church.[35] He found no such distinction in apostolic times, and saw no reason why the ordinance of the Lord's Supper could not as well be administered to societies as to churches. As between alternatives, he preferred societies. Churches tended to create and promote artificial and unjustified divisions. Members of churches were likely to have "a high conceit of themselves [and] to suppose that they possess peculiar privileges over the rest of the believers in Christ."

The formation of churches and their relationship to societies was the principal topic of conversation at a meeting of Universalist ministers in Lebanon, New Hampshire, in 1835. Much opposition was expressed to organizing churches, and particularly to requiring subscription to any kind of a creed as a requisite for membership. This seemed "to imply that they consider themselves much better and holier than their brethren and sisters."[36] There was "something *aristocratical,*" in appearances at least, about such a practice. If a covenant had to be required at all, the clergy at Lebanon suggested that it do no more than "adopt the New Testament as the rule of our faith and practice" and invite to fellowship in the church "any person desirous of leading a christian life." The same fear of religious snobbery was reflected in complaints in some communities that some who were members of the church refused to unite with the local society.[37] Such coexistence of organizations also raised practical problems about employing and supporting clergy; building, using, and maintaining meeting houses; and furnishing delegates to denominational gatherings.

Opposition to the organization of churches was even expressed on the floor of the General Convention. In 1844 a resolution was offered which would have abolished the distinction between a society and a church, on the ground that such a division was "unauthorized by Apostolic usage and the word of God," and was "injurious to the cause of Christ."[38] The committee appointed to consider this matter was unable to agree; after discussing the problem at the next convention, the subject was dropped when the majority of the committee reported that, although there was not any evidence that the Apostles had followed the practice of organizing societies, neither had they prohibited it. Even unbelievers should be allowed to join societies (as distinct from churches), participate in their deliberations, and support the preacher. After all, that was the principal means by which to Christianize such wayward souls.

After 1865, as part of an accelerating trend toward Universalist unity, some state conventions tried to encourage greater uniformity at the grass-roots level. The Pennsylvania Convention in 1868 expressed its preference for using churches exclusively as the basis for local organization, and in 1871 urged reassessment of the bewildering conglomeration of churches, societies, and parishes that had evolved.[39]

Whether organized in societies or in churches, Universalists took an almost perverse pride in expressing their independence and localism. It was a matter of great satisfaction to the majority that the denomination used a strictly congregational form of ecclesiastical polity, in which "each congregation governs itself. It is amenable [*sic*] to nobody in regard to its choice, settlement, or dismissal of a pastor, the matter being regulated altogether by a contract between the parties."[40] The merits of this arrangement, great as they might have been, often became a serious obstacle to cooperation, coordination, and unity required by denominational identity. This weakness was sometimes recognized and articulated. What was considered unsatisfactory progress in the growth of one association in Maine was attributed to "the peculiar views of religious *liberty* entertained by a large portion of its friends. They imagine *organization* an encroachment upon this right, and therefore have opposed it."[41]

The first Universalist society, considered as such, was apparently organized in 1774 by Caleb Rich in Warwick, western Massachusetts, at the opposite end of the province from Gloucester, where John Murray's followers were responsible for later establishing the first Universalist society legally recognized by legislative action. Rich, his brother Nathaniel, and a friend, Joseph Goodell, having been refused membership in the Baptist church in Warwick, formed their own society after following accepted procedures, including issuance of a warrant.[42] Three years later, Rich, who by then had become a firm believer in Universalism although he had never met or communicated with Murray, began to preach. His efforts extended not only to Warwick but to the neighboring communities of Richmond and Jaffrey, New Hampshire, where societies were also organized after a fashion.

Almost simultaneously, but apparently quite independently, the fifteen members ousted from the First Parish Church in Gloucester organized themselves in 1779 under "Articles of Association." This is the first actual religious compact among American Universalists of which there is a complete record. It has been widely reproduced in Universalist literature. It was, however, only a "declaration of intention" and made no provision whatever for organizing the society or transacting business.[43] In 1785 the Gloucester congregation finally made provision for regular meetings, finances, the creation of committees, the admission of new members, and other operative matters by adopting a "Charter of Compact" which was also intended to serve as a model for other societies.[44] Societies which had been organized in 1785 in Oxford and Milford, Massachusetts, through the influence of Isaac Davis, Caleb Rich, and Adam Streeter, adopted the Gloucester charter, but many others, including the society in Boston, used their own.[45]

As to official titles for societies, the Gloucester document recommended the rather cumbersome designation of "Independent Christian Society in __________, commonly called *Universalists*." Universalists in Providence, Rhode Island, who presumably had no organization at the time, received a copy of the charter, and announced that they were designating themselves, at least temporarily, as "The Providence Universalists." There was not for a considerable time any uniformity whatever in official designation among societies, although the words "Universal," "Independent," or "Liberty" appeared in most, either as part of the corporate name or by popular usage. The original Gloucester society existed under four variant names between the date of its establishment (1779) and incorporation (1792); the word "Independent" appeared in all four. The congregation organized by Elhanan Winchester after their enforced departure from the First Baptist Church in Philadelphia in 1781 for believing in universal salvation were known as the "Society of Universal Baptists." The exact date of the founding of the society there is not known, but it was in existence in 1785.[46] About 1789 it was combined with Murray's group as the "First Independent Church of Christ, commonly called Universalists." A group of Methodists under the leadership of Edward Turner, believing in universal salvation, seceded from the parent group in New York City and organized themselves in 1796 officially as "United Christian Friends." They also called themselves "Christian Universalists."[47]

George Richards organized in 1812 in Philadelphia the "Church of the Restitution" which lasted only one year.[48] The "First Universalist Parish or Society" was created in 1816 in Westminster, Massachusetts and was listed as "Restorationist" by its pastor, Charles Hudson, in 1824.[49] The society of "United Christian Friends," comprising communicants from three towns in Connecticut (Norwich, Preston, and Groton) was admitted to fellowship in the New England Convention in 1821.[50] The "First Restorationist Society of Troy" was organized in 1823 in New York State, and in the same state the "First Society of Christian Friends, called Restorationists" appeared at Saratoga Springs in 1825.[51] The use of the term "Restorationist" reflected a theological difference of opinion which came to a climax after 1830 and for a brief time threatened to create a schism in the denomination in southern New England.

There were great numbers of churches in the South with the word "Liberty" included in the title. This, according to one nineteenth-century Universalist clergyman, was a reaction to what southern Universalists perceived to be the "ecclesiastical tyranny" of the so-called orthodox churches.[52] There was a short-lived Universalist group in Canterbury, Connecticut about 1800 which organized themselves into the "Independent Catholic Christian Society."[53] Early Universalists certainly could never be accused of deadly standardization of terminology.

Associations

The creation of the association as a second type of Universalist organization (beyond the society or church) was a logical outgrowth of a desire for some kind of communication and fellowship with other Universalists in neighboring towns, communities, or states. By the 1820s associations had become an accepted and increasingly used vehicle for cooperation, and had assumed a certain degree of authority. At first, they were strictly *ad hoc* bodies, their outlines only dimly discernible. Some merely faded away after having served some temporary purpose. The largest number, however, eventually took on formal activities and responsibilities and became the nuclei of other associations. In many cases they were the groups that took the initiative in organizing state conventions. In a few instances, as in Maine, the original association itself became the state convention, and created associations within its boundaries. In the Deep South, the first association included parts of Georgia and Alabama and preceded the organization of their state conventions.

Associations were creatures of the societies and churches, which tenaciously held onto their "sovereign and independent" character. The associations were considered, as late as the mid-1830s, as "but for social purposes, and to promote unity and harmony among and with each other."[54] They usually met at least annually, and organized as a council, comprising at first any number of delegates that societies saw fit to send to meetings, plus "the ministering brethren residing within the bounds of the Association." Visitation from clergy outside the jurisdiction claimed by any one association was encouraged, and they were usually admitted as members of the council, or at least invited to attend its deliberations.

The greatest authority, assumed piecemeal by associations, had to do with ministerial discipline. When first organized, they merely exercised the same function as societies in fellowshipping, ordaining, and disciplining ministers. However, by the 1820s associations began to take over more and more of these functions, and within a decade several had undertaken to suspend or even expel clergy within their jurisdictions who were found guilty of "gross offenses." Even then, however, association authority extended no further than withdrawal of fellowship. In all other matters, the associations were expected merely to advise or recommend, "leaving to societies and individuals the privilege of acting, or not, as circumstances or their own judgments may dictate and require."[55]

The first gathering that can properly be called an association was a very modest and impromptu affair. It was organized in Richmond, New Hampshire about 1780 by the first three Universalist societies known to have been created in New England. Universalists in Warwick, Massachusetts, and Richmond and Jaffrey, New Hampshire, almost immediately after having assembled in their respective communities, created a so-called "general" or "united" society, with one deacon from each of the three groups. Annual meetings were decided upon, at which preachers would be licensed and ministers ordained, as required. Caleb Rich was apparently the first to receive public ordination (1781) through that body, the service having been conducted by Adam Streeter, an ordained Baptist minister who had developed universalist tendencies and soon thereafter declared himself a Universalist.

The second such group that functioned in most respects as an association, although it met originally to confront a specific emergency situation, was that assembled at Oxford, Massachusetts, in 1785. It represented a conscious effort at inter-society cooperation. There was possibly a similar meeting held there the previous year, but no record of it exists.[56] Until 1816, when the Southern Association was created in New England, the group organized at Oxford, even though possibly not meeting regularly, served as the equivalent of an association for societies in the Greater Boston area and southern New England. There is no evidence, however, that it ever licensed preachers or ordained ministers. That was considered at the time the prerogative of the local societies.

The plans for the Oxford meeting took shape when the Second Religious Society in that Massachusetts village issued an invitation to the handful of societies then existing in New England to meet on 14 September. The invitation to the Gloucester society, dated 28 August 1785, probably the first sent out, made the purpose quite clear; it was to organize "in one united body," with a distinctive name, "in order to anticipate any embarrassment of our constitutional rights."[57] Murray, who was the only representative from Gloucester, had previously visited the Oxford society. In anticipation of the meeting, the Gloucester congregation drew up a "Charter of Compact" which served the double purpose of affirming that they were an organized religious body, and of serving as a possible model for other groups of Universalists who might wish to create societies. The charter was, after minor changes suggested at the Oxford meeting, signed by eighty-five male members of the Gloucester society.

Twelve men, representing five societies in Massachusetts and one in Rhode Island, met with the Oxford society and determined on the name "Independent Christian Societies, commonly called Universalists." Each of the societies represented was to "consider the propriety of . . . agreeing not only to be called by one name, but to be cemented in one body; consequently bound by the ties of love to assist each other, at any and at all times when occasion shall require"—a measure described by Murray as "being united in our common defence." The societies were also requested to react to the proposal that the first annual meeting of the new group be held in Boston in September 1786. Within three months each society was, through "committees of correspondence" reminiscent of those which had preceded the American Revolution, and a circular letter, to have informed the other societies of what means they had adopted.

Some historians of the denomination have attempted to backdate what became in turn the New England Convention and the United States (General) Convention to the meeting in 1785. Neither nineteenth- nor twentieth-century Universalists seemed able to agree on what might appear on the surface to be mere quibbling over a minor technical point. But it was a particularly vital one to the denomination in its younger days, when it was still in the process of establishing itself and defining its organization. The older and more continuous its existence could be demonstrated, the more likely it could command allegiance and support. Thomas Whittemore steadfastly insisted that the Oxford meeting in 1785 "may truly be stiled [*sic*] the parent of the General Convention of Universalists."[58] According to him, the (erroneous) dating of the origin of the General Convention in 1793 rather than the earlier (proper) date of 1785, was the result of the historical accident of record-keeping. When Abner Kneeland collected the scattered documents and commenced the book of records, he found nothing before 1793; so it was at this point that he began and from which the first General Convention was dated.[59] Kneeland's records were actually of the New England Convention, which *was* organized in 1793. When he inserted notices in the *Trumpet* for the meeting of the New England Convention of 1832, Whittemore emphasized (by italics) that it would be the forty-sixth annual session.[60] The editor of the *Universalist Register and Almanac* cautiously pointed out that if the organization of the so-called "United States Convention" in 1833 "be reckoned from the formation of the 'General Convention of the New England States and others,' which it superseded, then the session in September 1835 was its Jubilee or Fiftieth Anniversary."[61] Abel C. Thomas of Philadelphia had no doubts in 1835. He recommended that because it would be the fiftieth anniversary of the organization of the General Convention and therefore a special occasion with an unusually large attendance anticipated, the meeting that year should be scheduled for six or seven days instead of the customary two-day session.[62] (His recommendation was not adopted.) However, the printed report of the

1835 General Convention listed it as the "Fiftieth Anniversary" meeting.

The majority of Universalists, however, agreed with Richard Eddy, who considered the association formed at Oxford in 1785 as "purely local in its aim, and temporary in its purpose."[63] Edward Turner, who preached his first sermon in 1798 and was a member of a committee appointed in 1816 to prepare a history of American Universalism, dated the General Convention from 1793.[64] In a chronological table of Universalist historical highlights in the *Universalist Register* for 1865, the meeting at Oxford is quite properly described as the first association of Universalists in America and nothing more. In 1969 Elmo A. Robinson, a Universalist clergyman with the perspective of over fifty years in the ministry, asserted unequivocally that, regardless of title, the General Convention dated from the meeting in 1793—even though, it might be pointed out—the Philadelphia Convention had been organized three years earlier.[65]

There is no conclusive evidence that the series of annual meetings called for by the Oxford assembly in 1785 actually convened every year. However, it can be assumed that most of them were held although complete records do not exist. A.B. Grosh, the knowledgeable editor of the *Universalist Register,* made the statement in 1844 that after the first session was held in Boston in 1786 as scheduled, the association "met annually thereafter."[66] Whittemore presumed that meetings were held, for in 1832 he requested readers of the *Trumpet* to send in copies of the records for the years 1786 through 1792 if in their possession, so that they could be published; in his autobiography (most of which was written over a decade later) he still had "no doubt" that its meetings had been continued every year since 1785, even though the records were still missing.[67] Correspondence available to him indicated that the Gloucester society was expecting to send representatives in 1786. The Oxford society did choose four delegates for the 1787 meeting, which was held in Milford.[68] Hosea Ballou is known to have attended in 1791.[69] Eddy, on the other hand, stated categorically that no session was held after 1787.[70] Regardless of whether the meetings begun at Oxford met regularly or not, the efforts that had prompted the first meeting in 1785 had, by 1792, achieved their purpose. By that date the Gloucester congregation had finally achieved complete legal recognition.

By 1805 three organizations functioned as associations in New England, and one had been created in New York State. Although the organization created in 1793 bore the title of "Convention," it served association functions for several years, including the fellowshipping and ordaining of ministers. The second organization which, like the others, carried the word "association" in its title, was the Eastern Association, organized in Maine in 1799 while that territory was still a District of

Massachusetts. This association became the Maine State Convention after statehood was achieved in 1820. The Northern Association, organized at Jericho, Vermont, in the summer of 1804, included, besides that state, parts of eastern New York State as well as southern Canada. The Western Association was organized by three clergymen at Burlington, in Otsego County, New York, in the summer of 1805. In 1816 a Southern Association, meeting first in the Boston area, and then elsewhere in southern Massachusetts or Connecticut, was organized. Universalists in the Middle Atlantic area experimented briefly with a regional organization known as the "New York and Philadelphia Association," organized in the former city in 1829.[71] After holding two more meetings, it was decided that the joint arrangement was impractical. After separating, the Philadelphia Association continued to exist, but largely as a social and missionary body. In 1834 a similar association was organized in Reading, Pennsylvania, and in 1850 the two were joined as the "Philadelphia Union Association." In the course of the nineteenth century, associations by the dozens appeared as Universalism expanded in New England and spread into the then-frontier areas of the Middle West and the South.

Regional Organizations and State Conventions

Logical progression and orderly development would seem to require that the next step in Universalist organization beyond associations should have been state conventions. Such was not always the case. Before most of the twenty-one state conventions existing in 1870 had been created, regional organizations had appeared. Usually designated as "conventions," such bodies were defined as "sectional, as one or more states were included within their boundaries."[72] By this definition, and by designation, the Philadelphia Convention organized in 1790 and the New England Convention created three years later became the two pioneer efforts. Five other regional conventions had come into being before 1865, and another by 1872. However, the lifespan of most of them was short, and neither the extent of their powers nor the area of their jurisdictions was always clear.

An informal organization referred to as the "Western Convention," comprising portions of Ohio and Indiana, began to meet in 1827, and in 1833 was christened the "General Convention of Universalists of the Western States."[73] It consisted originally of three associations and any societies or churches "in the Western States" not connected with an association, and was intended to serve as an interim body until state conventions could be created. After this was accomplished in Indiana in 1837, the "General Convention" became the Ohio State Convention the same year.

The "Southern Convention of Universalists" was organized in North Carolina under the leadership of Jacob Frieze in 1827, but apparently met only once thereafter. Another regional organization with the identical name was organized in Baltimore in 1835, on the initiative of Otis A. Skinner.[74] Invitations were extended to Universalists in southern Pennsylvania, and as far south as Edenton, North Carolina, as well as to those in Virginia and Maryland.[75] According to its constitution, the principal purpose was to arrange for circuit preaching, particularly in Maryland and Virginia. Upon organization, it promptly received fellowship in the General Convention. The Southern Convention was organized with the expectation that state conventions would soon follow in Maryland and Virginia; this was accomplished in the latter state in 1835.

When news of the creation of the Southern Convention at a meeting in Baltimore reached Universalists in Alabama and South Carolina, the appropriateness of the name was questioned, for co-religionists in states farther south (the Carolinas, Georgia, and Alabama) were not represented at all, and in fact had never received an invitation to attend.[76] Skinner belatedly explained to Allen Fuller of South Carolina that the Southern Convention was intended to serve the entire South, and hence the choice of name.[77] He hoped that the time would come "when the Carolinas shall become members of it, yea, all the Southern States." He thereupon extended an invitation to Fuller to attend the second session, to be held in Portsmouth, Virginia, and see if the "grand object" could not be achieved. At the Portsmouth meeting (which was apparently the last), the constitution was revised and the organization was redesignated as the "Southern General Convention."[78]

Farther south, the organization of associations cutting across state lines, or state conventions, preceded the appearance of a comprehensive regional organization. It was not until 1858 that Universalists there organized on a regional basis, their places of meeting in crossroads country churches reflecting the predominantly rural character of pre-Civil War southern civilization. The formation of what became the "General Southern Convention" grew out of a recommendation made at the Georgia State Convention in 1857 that such a body be created, mainly "to exercise jurisdiction over our preachers of the South."[79] The organization meeting took place in August 1858 in Liberty Church, Feasterville, Fairfield District (County), South Carolina, and was attended by representatives from five states—Alabama, Georgia, Mississippi, and North and South Carolina. Two more annual meetings were held, but the outbreak of war in 1861 brought the fledgling and struggling organization to an abrupt end.

A regional convention to serve the Midwest was created in Chicago in 1860 as the Northwestern Conference, and included seven states. It had no powers beyond those already exercised by the state conventions or the General Convention, and confined its activities to "general denominational advancement."[80] It lasted only a decade. A Mississippi Valley Convention was organized in Oakland, Kentucky, in 1872, with delegates from five states, but apparently held no more than two sessions.[81]

It was not until the mid-1820s that any serious effort was made to organize state conventions. The impetus came from a combination of local and regional influences. Such conventions were based on representation from associations, with significantly large lay participation through the system of delegates. In spite of their alleged superiority over the so-called "minor Associations," the state conventions did not have a whit more power than the jurisdictions they represented. Except for the occasional granting of fellowship and the bestowing of ordination, the suspension of clergy, and the withdrawal of fellowship from them, state convention activities were no more than "recommendatory and advisory."

Because of the jealousy of local prerogative and the chronic suspicion of organization *per se,* the initial effort to organize a state convention met with time-consuming debate and much delay. The first such attempt took place in New York State in the summer of 1825, and almost came to grief. At a meeting of the Western Association it was voted to organize a state convention, and the draft of a constitution was prepared.[82] A plan to hold the first meeting the next year came to nothing, and a meeting in 1827 of representatives of the five associations in the state again considered the feasibility of creating a statewide organization.

The reason for the failure of the other four associations to heed the call of the Western Association in 1826 had been a provision in the draft constitution that the two delegates from each association were to be clergymen. This was interpreted as an attempt at "clerical domination."[83] In fact, suspicion of what might turn out to be "higher authority" was so widespread that the majority of delegates at the 1827 meeting had been instructed by their constituents to vote against forming any convention at all. Even after the convention was organized, the Genesee Association, which had been organized in 1814 as an offshoot of the original Western Association, refused to recognize the jurisdiction of the convention.[84]

The original practice of the New York State Convention of granting letters of fellowship and conferring ordination was successfully challenged in 1835 by several of the associations, which insisted on exercising those prerogatives on behalf of societies and churches.[85] In spite of suspicion and reluctance to create anything resembling a superstructure, the movement to establish and maintain state conventions gained momentum. After the General Convention was organized in 1833, one was created in almost every state.

Chapter 5

TOWARDS A NATIONAL ORGANIZATION

The Philadelphia Convention

While the Universalists in Massachusetts were struggling to remove the disabilities that had hampered their recognition as a distinctive religious body in the 1780s, another movement that had a somewhat broader base and a more ambitious goal came into being in Pennsylvania. The culmination was the Philadelphia Convention of Universalists, created in 1790, as the first national organization attempted by Universalists in America. It not only endeavored to draw together Christians "in different parts of this continent" who believed in the salvation of all men, but adopted a statement of faith and a plan of government intended both for local religious bodies and cooperation among them. A list of "sundry recommendations" dealing with relations between church and state and social attitudes was also addressed "to the Churches in the United States, believing in the same doctrine."[1]

The groundwork for the Philadelphia Convention was laid in September 1789, when a group of individuals from New Jersey and Philadelphia met in the latter city and lamented that, although they knew of persons holding similar views elsewhere, no effort had ever been made to call them together. It was then agreed that a meeting should be held in Philadelphia later that year "to consult on the most expedient ways to bring this desired object about." The meeting took place during the same month, and a committee of four was appointed to draw up and send out a circular letter "to various parts inviting such as held like faith with them to meet in a Conference on the Subject." The ultimate purpose, according to the circular, was to unite "in one General Church in bands of love and uniformity." The response to the circular being "very satisfactory," the meeting was scheduled for 25 May 1790. Quite appropriately, the sessions were held in the meeting house which had been purchased in 1785 for the use of Elhanan Winchester's Society of Universal Baptists.[2] Seventeen individuals (seven preachers and ten laymen) were present: five from Philadelphia, two from elsewhere in Pennsylvania; eight from New Jersey; one from Virginia; and one from Massachusetts. John Murray, from the latter state, was considered a delegate from both the Boston and Gloucester societies. The group, after meeting until 8 June, adjourned with the understanding that a "Convention" would meet exactly a year later, also in Philadelphia.[3]

It was during the two weeks of deliberation that were hammered out a five-point "Rule of Faith" and a "Plan of Church Government" that served the convention and most of the societies associated with it during its brief history. It was these documents that were also adopted by the New England Convention of Universalists in 1794 (although following them in spirit rather than in letter), and became the basis for both the Winchester Profession of faith and the "Plan of General Association" adopted in 1803. At the request of the Philadelphia group in 1790, both the Articles of Faith and Plan of Government were submitted to Dr. Benjamin Rush, the eminent physician and believer in universalism, for correction and arrangement.[4] It was at this time that Murray met Rush, and continued his contact with the doctor on his various trips to Philadelphia. Murray engaged in a considerable correspondence with Rush regarding the state of Murray's health; it appears that the New England Universalist suffered at least a mild case of hypochondria.[5]

The Plan of Government defined a church as "a number of believers, united by a covenant for the purpose of maintaining the public worship of God, the preaching of the gospel, ordaining officers, preserving peace and order among its members, and relieving the poor." Two sets of officers were provided: bishops and deacons. The first, in turn, was considered synonymous with "elder, minister, pastor and teacher," depending on the capacity in which individuals served. They were to be ordained by the churches in which they were found acceptable, such ordinations to be recognized in other churches professing the same faith. Deacons, likewise to be ordained, were to attend to the business affairs of the church and maintain its records. Actually, very few of the Universalist societies or churches ever used the term "bishop" or "deacon;" they probably smacked too much of ecclesiastical hierarchy and establishmentarianism. The term "preacher" (not listed in the Philadelphia document) was most commonly used in the early days.

The manner of conduct of religious services was left to the discretion of the local churches, except that they were to "meet statedly one day in seven, for the worship of God, and the preaching of the Gospel." Self-government of the individual churches was affirmed repeatedly. The provision for annual conventions of churches meeting as a group specified that no acts of those bodies were "to invade the freedom or sovereignty of a particular church. Each church reserves to itself full and exclusive power to judge of all matters relating to faith and practice (as established by our articles) among its own members."

The explanatory note accompanying the pamphlet in which the actions of the 1790 convention were printed described the plan of government as "nearly that of the Congregational Church."

Throughout its twenty-year history, the Philadelphia Convention remained a small and struggling body, although it tried to accomplish the purposes for which it was intended. At its meeting in 1791, with fifteen delegates present (eight from Philadelphia and vicinity, six from New Jersey, and one from Maryland), the convention immediately had a theological problem presented to it for determination. The clerical delegate from Maryland (William Hawkins) attended for the specific purpose of ascertaining, on request from a fellow-clergyman, the views of the convention regarding future punishment. Another delegate prepared a written reply, approved by the convention, which furnished ammunition, by argument and citation, to support belief in the existence of same. A year later, the convention was called upon to try to settle another "speculative point in doctrine"—the relationship between divine sovereignty and free will—which threatened to divide a church in Maryland. The convention counseled mutual forbearance and deplored any difference of opinion that might result in an attempt to exclude part of the membership of a church. Universalists had to "agree to disagree." Further, it was asserted that it was not within the province of the convention to "attempt to establish any rule of orthodoxy."

The convention tried, with only indifferent success, to establish and maintain communication with Universalists wherever they were known. In 1795 the delegates voted to send a report of the state of their affairs to their New England counterparts. They also solicited reactions to the idea of holding a triennial convention of delegates from these two organizations and a convention which had been established by then in western Pennsylvania. Nothing is known to have been done to carry this out. Occasional communications were received from isolated societies (e.g., Sharon, Connecticut and Egremont, Massachusetts), and in 1801 a circular letter from New England was read to the Philadelphia Convention "with great satisfaction." The Pennsylvania organization did its best to contact all Universalist groups by publishing circular letters, 100 of which were ordered printed for 1807. But Universalists were still too few and too scattered to make the efforts of the Philadelphia Convention effective.

The high point in the size of the convention came in 1792, when fifteen societies were in fellowship with it. Sixteen individuals representing eleven of these, from four states, attended. One was Abel Sarjent, who served as the delegate from three societies in western Pennsylvania. It was he who was responsible for editing the first Universalist newspaper in the United States. But distance posed such a great obstacle that in 1972 two groups of Universalists requested permission (which was readily granted) to organize their own conventions.

Three societies in southern and western Pennsylvania and western Virginia held their own meetings in 1793 and 1794, but these apparently then disbanded. The Boston society, which by 1792 had signed the Philadelphia Articles of Faith and could boast of almost eighty members, took the initiative in the Northeast. The result was the New England Convention of Universalists, destined to supplant the Pennsylvania-based organization and to assume the leadership of the entire denomination.

Between 1795 and its final meeting in 1809, the Philadelphia Convention was never able to muster even ten delegates to any meeting, in spite of circular letters urging societies to send representatives. Only three societies sent delegates in 1798, and in 1800 no meeting at all was held. Murray was present in 1805, when only three churches were represented, and in the following year he was one of the five individuals (all from the Philadelphia church) in attendance. Eight of the ten churches then in fellowship with the convention failed even to send letters and reports. Records for neither the 1808 nor 1809 meetings are know to exist, although it apparently met the latter year for the last time.[6]

Several reasons can be offered for the decline and eventual disappearance of the Philadelphia Convention.[7] Universalist societies in fellowship between 1790 and 1809 were small, weak, and lacked financial resources. With the exception of the Philadelphia church, the largest had only fifteen members and one had only six. Even the Philadelphia church had insufficient money to complete its first meeting house. Most of the societies in New Jersey, and many in rural Pennsylvania, were at isolated crossroads in sparsely inhabited areas, and did not even survive the dissolution of the convention.

Geography was always a consideration, and lack of adequate transportation and communication facilities was a major factor in the failure of the convention to continue. It was this circumstance that prompted the creation of both the short-lived western convention in Pennsylvania and the New England Convention. This action, in turn, automatically reduced the potential membership and strength of the Philadelphia Convention. Except for occasional attendance by John Murray when he happened to be in the Philadelphia area, New England sent delegates to only the first meeting. The practice of meeting in but one location rather than rotating meetings among several communities undoubtedly militated against a successful convention.

Perpetual shortage of clergy was an overriding consideration. Societies often went without even a visiting preacher for months at a time, and many had no settled pastor for more than a year or so. Only one society—at New Britain, Bucks County, Pennsylvania—had the equivalent of a settled clergyman; even then, David Evans, a faithful delegate who had been present at the first meeting in 1790, probably had to depend for most of his livelihood on his farm.[8] A review of the changing personnel on those lists of delegates available in the records testifies to the high degree of itineracy among the clergy. It was natural, therefore, that societies failed to meet regularly, and that they abandoned any attempt to send delegates regularly to a convention. The Lombard Street church in Philadelphia gloomily reported at the 1796 session that not only had they been "long without a minister" but that the general decline in religious interest at the time had decimated their congregation.

The turnover of clergy in the Philadelphia church in its early years must have been discouraging. Shortly after the 1796 report was made, the society obtained the services of Thomas Jones, who had just arrived from England at the behest of John Murray. But in 1804 they lost Jones to the Gloucester society in Massachusetts, where he remained until his death in 1846. After three years with no settled pastor, the Philadelphia church obtained the services of Noah Murray, but for only one year, and for some of that time on a part-time basis. After a second solicitation, George Richards became the pastor (from 1809 until his death in 1814). However, he led a secession movement in 1812-1813 which greatly weakened the parent church. The Church of the Restitution which he organized disappeared after his death, and the Lombard Street church was closed until 1816.[9] They lamented "the cold and lifeless state of Christianity in general, in this day of falling away." Then there was also the discouragement that came with opposition to Universalists, as well as apathy and indifference. The "reviling by our neighbors," as well as closed meeting houses and various legal obstacles adversely affected societies, and in turn the convention. Universalists, at least in the Philadelphia area, discovered by experience that religious conviction alone was a sandy foundation on which to build an effective organization.

The New England Convention

After the Gloucester society had achieved legal respectability in 1792, the next step was to see the plea to all Universalists for "our being cemented together in one united body" brought to reality. The opportunity to achieve this goal, at least for New England Universalists, was afforded in 1792 when a request to the Philadelphia Convention that year that a separate convention be organized for the (then) four New England states met with "hearty approbation." It was as a result of this that the meeting of 1793 took place, again in Oxford, Massachusetts, and that New England Universalists dated their first denominational organization.

The reasons which had induced the Universalist society in Boston to request that New Englanders be allowed to organize their own convention were eminently practical. The region was too far removed from Philadelphia to send delegates regularly, and limited resources imposed too great a strain on the infant societies and their clergy.[10] Intended originally to be no more than an extension of the Philadelphia Convention, by accident and by force of circumstances (rather than by design) the New England Convention gradually and haltingly engaged in more and more activity and assumed more and more responsibilities as the Philadelphia Convention correspondingly declined steadily and finally ceased to exist after 1809.

The New England Convention met annually, and without interruption, from 1793 until it became the United States Convention in 1833. Minutes of the proceedings were seldom kept, or at least not recorded, although for all but one session (1798) at least, a circular letter is extant which summarized what business was transacted. The circulars, of which John Murray wrote the first, were usually devoted more to earnest exhortation to live Christian lives than to accounts of proceedings as such. Calls for the first two meetings were ambitiously addressed to every town or community in which there were known or assumed to be Universalists. The circular of the 1793 meeting was addressed to all "Brethren in the faith of the Gospel" residing in thirty-seven towns (listed by name), with an "et cetera" for any that might have been missed in the tabulation. The circular for 1794 listed no less than seventy-one communities; this rather awkward system was abandoned the following year. In 1799, the circular was addressed not only to Universalist societies or churches but "to every individual of the human family whithersoever this Epistle may come." This was certainly universalism writ large.

Attendance was usually by a handful of clergy, one of whom served as moderator and another as clerk during business sessions, and a group of laymen representing the various societies. In 1799 there were only three preachers present at the session in Woodstock, Vermont.[11] Private homes were usually used for business meetings, although public services, which were an integral part of all convention meetings, were held in nearby meeting houses (if permission could be obtained), or in public halls of one kind or another. Much of the time at the early meetings was spent in checking credentials of the delegates ("messengers"). Annual meetings were rotated among various communities in all the New England states, and New York. Universalists in Hoosick Falls, New York, first played host to the convention in that state in 1806.

The authority claimed and practiced by local societies over the employment, fellowship, ordination, discipline, and dismissal of their pastors, embedded in congregational practice and affirmed by the Philadelphia Convention in 1790, led from the beginning to difficulties, embarrassments, and even misunderstandings both inside and outside the denomination. Most states had laws requiring licensing and ordination by some recognized or authorized body or agency professing a more or less uniform creed. In the call for the meeting of the New England Convention for 1798, delegates selected by societies and travelling to places where they were not known were cautioned to carry with them evidence "that they are received by us as Preachers of the Gospel, and persons of good moral character."[12] Every area had its share of "irregular" itinerant preachers who had no authority beyond their own assertion that they could conduct religious services or perform marriages. Vermont was one state which required evidence of ordination within its boundaries. As a consequence, several Universalist clergymen found it necessary to be re-ordained when they moved into the state.[13] There was also sufficient suspicion of Universalist clergymen by some state authorities to have their right to perform marriages challenged. This was the case with Walter Ferriss at the time he was pastor of three societies in Vermont and had already been properly ordained in the state. It was the attempt to straighten out matters respecting the status of Universalist clergymen that was largely responsible for the gradual growth in the strength and influence of the New England Convention.

It was not until 1800 that the convention undertook to fellowship or ordain clergymen officially, although in 1794 Hosea Ballou had received at least its equivalent from Elhanan Winchester in a completely spontaneous ceremony at the Oxford convention. Ballou was re-ordained in 1803 in Vermont in the name of the convention. This second ordination was considered advisable because the legality of marriages he might perform in that state might otherwise have been called into question.[14] At the meeting in 1800, four individuals were licensed to preach, three preachers were admitted to fellowship, and a standing Committee on Ordination was created. Miles Treadwell Wooley was to be the committee's first candidate, as soon as testimonials had been received from the Connecticut societies for which he served as pastor. All of these actions in 1800 were taken in complete disregard of the Philadelphia "Plan of Association" which had been adopted by the New England Convention in 1794 and which had provided that the fellowshipping and ordination of ministers was the exclusive privilege of the local societies or churches.

In 1801 the New England Convention established another precedent involving the clergy. Besides licensing and fellowshipping three preachers, on formal recommendation of the Committee on Ordination, for the first time ministers were ordained at the convention itself. One, Miles T. Wooley, had applied at the previous session. The second was Edwin Ferriss. Also for the first time, committees were appointed by the convention and authorized to ordain ministers between meetings. The candidates were Thomas Barnes of Poland,

Maine, and Solomon Glover of Connecticut.

By the time the convention of 1803 was adjourned, one more ordination had been authorized, and five more had been ordained by the convention itself. That year, for the first time, certificates of both ordination and fellowship were copied into the minutes, in case there should be any question about the status of the individuals involved. The standing Committee on Ordination was also enlarged to five; the ceremony could be performed by any three. It was at this same convention that ministerial discipline was first applied by that body to any of its clergymen. The fellowship of one William Thomas, who had claimed for a short time to be a Universalist preacher, was suspended because he had "not walked circumspectly as became his profession." At a public meeting during the convention of 1801, he was excommunicated for "various irregularities of life and conversation" and a warning was issued in case any other preacher might be found to "walk disorderly." In 1800 an ad hoc committee on discipline had also been appointed to investigate and take action if necessary regarding complaints about the pastor of the society in New Marlboro, Massachusetts.

The convention in 1800 also undertook the tasks of establishing lines of communication with Universalist bodies by instructing the moderator to "correspond with the societies to the southward" and with the Eastern Association recently organized in Maine. Societies within its boundaries also received considerable attention, by way of various suggestions and recommendations. They were urged to send delegates to the next convention, to report on the condition of each society, and to "pay peculiar solemnized attention to regularity and discipline."

At the convention the following year, for the first time an inventory was taken of Universalist clergymen in New England, and a list of "approved Ministers and Elders" was drawn up and recorded in the minutes. There were twenty-two in all: nine in Massachusetts, four in New Hampshire, three in Vermont, three in Connecticut, two in New York, and one in the District of Maine.[15] It was ascertained that the "far greater part" had received ordination; only a few were settled over one or more societies; most were without any "special engagements" and therefore comprised part of the great band of itinerant preachers who roamed over an impressively large territory and made immeasurable contributions to the growth and spread of the denomination, particularly in its early years.

For almost the first decade of the convention's history, no systematic attempt was made to finance its activities. Clerical and lay delegates to its meetings and travelling preachers seldom expected reimbursement for their expenses, depending instead on whatever resources they themselves possessed, or on the hospitality of others.

Special needs were met by taking up collections on the spot. At the 1801 convention, the first effort was made to establish a fund to be used "to supply the wants of Brethren, sent forth to preach; to aid in the printing of any useful works; and to answer all such charitable purposes as the convention may judge proper." To that end, the first treasurer (David Ballou of Richmond, New Hampshire) was optimistically appointed. Between 1801 and 1885, there was a forty-year gap (1824-1864) when apparently no one held the office.[16]

The immediate justification for authorizing such a fund seemed obvious: "our brethren, altho rich in faith, are poor in the things of this world." The recommendation for the establishment of a fund was put into more concrete form at the next year's meeting, the convention in 1801 having suggested merely that each society or church contribute the equivalent of one day's earnings each year, "according to the several abilities of every man."[17] It was anticipated that a total of between $50 and $60 could be raised by the approximately forty societies then in fellowship with the convention. But so many objections were promptly raised to the entire idea that the convention in 1802 prepared a circular reemphasizing the good work that could be done, including the relief of widows and fatherless children of deceased Universalist clergymen. The circular also reassured those who were suspicious that the convention was planning to enter the banking business that such was emphatically not the case, and that every effort would be made to prevent the appearance of opportunists who might be attracted by ecclesiastical revenue. There would be strict accountability.

But in spite of all efforts, money trickled in with agonizing slowness, and proved grossly inadequate. By the time the 1803 convention met, a total of less than $33 had been received from thirteen societies. The amounts ranged from $1.00 to $9.00 (contributed by the Newtown, Connecticut, society).[18] In 1802 George Richards had been authorized to arrange for placing a monument on the grave of Elhanan Winchester in Hartford, Connecticut, the expense to be borne by the convention.[19] The cost ($35) was defrayed by a special collection in 1803, the feeling being that the project was not a proper use of the newly established fund.[20] At the convention in 1810, it was also made clear that its funds were not to be used by delegates; they had to come at their own expense, or that of their societies. The society in the community where the meeting was held each year was obligated to provide only for those preachers who conducted public religious services in connection with the convention.[21]

By far the most significant action taken by the thirty delegates at the convention which met at Strafford, Vermont, in 1802, was the appointment of a five-man committee headed by Walter Ferriss, pastor of three societies in Vermont, "to form a plan of fellowship in faith and practice, for the edifying of the body, and building it up together."

They were directed to report at the next convention. The result was the adoption in 1803 by the delegates representing thirty-eight societies, at Winchester, New Hampshire, of a Profession of Faith and a "Plan of General Association." Ferriss drew up both documents, on behalf of the committee, and each was transcribed in the records of the convention.

The Plan of General Association was the first systematic and comprehensive attempt to regularize practice and achieve some measure of uniformity for New England Universalists, as well as to establish some rules for the membership and conduct of convention meetings. Whether or not the adoption of a Profession of Faith and a Plan of General Association at this particular time was precipitated by legal difficulties then being encountered by Universalists in New Hampshire and Vermont is a moot question, but the circumstances surrounding their adoption bear some resemblance to the actions taken by Massachusetts Universalists at Oxford and in Gloucester in the 1780s to obtain recognition as a distinct sect.

Eddy stoutly maintained that, Universalist tradition to the contrary, there was no visible connection between the events in New Hampshire and the activities of the convention that year.[22] He used negative evidence to make his point; i.e., that there was no reference in the records of any of the deliberations in 1803 to the disabilities under which Universalists were operating. On the other hand, Nathaniel Stacy, who attended the convention, clearly linked the adoption of the Winchester Profession to the legal status of the denomination. He asserted that a written creed or confession of faith was "absolutely necessary to save Universalists in New England, and particularly in New Hampshire, from clerical oppression."[23] As already pointed out, growing divergencies of belief among Universalists themselves was certainly also a factor necessitating the adoption of at least a minimal creed.

The disadvantaged position of Universalists in Vermont at the time of the Winchester meeting could very well have been related to the principal topics on its agenda. Until 1801 a person in Vermont wishing exemption from taxation for the support of religious societies other than one's own had merely to provide a certificate to that effect from an officer of his society.[24] However, beginning in that year, an individual seeking exemption was required to file with the clerk of the town or parish a signed declaration specifying that "I do not agree in religious opinion with a majority of the inhabitants of this town (or parish, as the case may be)."[25] A specific declaration of faith was required in order to comply with the law. Similarly, a Vermont enactment of 1800 required expressed denominational provision for ordaining ministers so that they could perform marriage ceremonies.[26] It was therefore quite logical that Ferriss should have drawn up the Plan of Association which included the procedure for ordination. The situation in New Hampshire made the need for establishing an official position even more pressing.

Originally, New Hampshire towns, as those in Vermont, were organized as parishes for the support of the ministry established by the majority, which was Congregational. Consequently, members of other religious groups were taxed for the support of those who had created the parishes. Relief was obtainable only by legislative action for each denomination, on appeal. At least one unsuccessful attempt had been made in the 1790s on behalf of Universalists, but a more amply documented case, settled in 1802, was that of one Christopher Erskine of Claremont, New Hampshire. He claimed to have been a member of a Universalist society in Charlestown, New Hampshire since 1796. Although no official record of such a society at that time is known to exist, one had probably been created in an informal manner by William Farwell, an early itinerant Universalist who had been ordained in 1791 by Caleb Rich and Zebulon Streeter, and who was living in Charlestown.[27] It was Farwell who furnished a certificate that Erskine belonged to "the Universalist Society and contributes to that order."[28] Erskine therefore refused to pay his share of the parish assessment ($4.49) in Claremont, on the certified ground that he belonged to a separate sect.[29]

Upon being arrested, and having been compelled to pay the tax (and legal expenses), Erskine appealed his case, which eventually reached the state supreme court. The court, by a very narrow interpretation of the state constitution, upheld Erskine's liability to pay the assessment. It declared in 1801 "that persons called Universalists are not such a sect, persuasion or denomination, as by the Constitution of New Hampshire are exempt from the payment of taxes for the support of a regularly settled minister of a Congregational Society in the town where such person lives."[30] Even though they might differ theologically, Congregationalists and Universalists, according to the court, were not different sects because they agreed on externals; i.e., organization and discipline. The Winchester Profession, which dealt only with religious belief and not with ecclesiastical organization, was therefore irrelevant in the eyes of the court; Universalists were hence obliged to pay taxes to the Congregationalists.

Erskine's case was a subject of great discussion at the 1802 Universalist convention, which directed George Richards to memorialize the court to reconsider.[31] Delegates were told that the judicial decision was a threat to the very existence of Universalism, and might result in the confinement of hapless individuals in "damp and unwholesome prisons." They were also reminded that all other non-Congregational groups faced the same problem.

There were, however, exceptions. In 1803, two years after the

Erskine decision, a Presbyterian was relieved by the same court of paying the Congregational assessment on the ground that he was a member of a separate sect because the Presbyterians differed as to church government and discipline, but not as to doctrine.[32] The greater numbers and influence of the Presbyterians, as compared with the Universalists, may have paid dividends, at least for the more Calvinist-minded.

Hope for a resolution of the difficulty was raised in 1804, for in that year the Free-will Baptists in the state who used, like the Universalists, a congregational type of church organization, were exempted from the parish assessment. After some delay, Universalists in New Hampshire achieved similar recognition as a distinct denomination by legislative action in 1805. Two years later, after satisfactorily proving their distinctiveness, New Hampshire Methodists likewise received legal recognition. All official support of an established religion was removed in New Hampshire by the Toleration Act of 1819.[33]

The "Plan of General Association" adopted by the convention in 1803 provided that each society approving the Profession of Faith was entitled to send one or more lay delegates to the convention. Each ordained minister and licensed preacher who had received fellowship in the denomination was to be considered a member of the convention. Consent of the majority of the convention, acting through a council, was required for admission of individuals who were neither ministers nor licensed preachers, nor delegates. Beginning with the 1800 convention, all clergy in attendance automatically comprised the council of each such meeting. Each member of the convention was to have one vote; each society was likewise to have one vote when business required such a vote. No person could in any case cast more than one vote or represent more than one society.

The attempt to create an over-all supervisory agency within the jurisdiction of the convention was evident in certain areas from the provisions for overview of societies, and fellowship, ordination, and discipline of clergy. The convention was not only to determine eligibility of societies, churches, and associations for fellowship but was to "look over the conduct" of Universalist clergy, and could "rebuke" as well as approve or deny fellowship.

The convention was also authorized "to examine into the qualifications" of clerical candidates for fellowship. A provision in the original draft to require unanimous consent of the convention for initial applications for fellowship by either individual clergy or organized groups was stricken, as was a provision that a three-fourths vote of the convention was to be required to approve withdrawal of a society or clergyman from fellowship. Ordinations were to continue to be conducted at conventions, as was the practice of appointing committees to conduct them between conventions.

On balance, the Plan of General Association assumed very little plenary power for the convention. The general principle of congregational form of religious polity, expressed in the Philadelphia Plan of 1790, was recognized and left unchanged. Therefore the right of self-government for societies and churches was stressed. Hope was expressed that each group of Universalists would look with Christian charity and forbearance on those within their ranks who had "different modes of faith or practice; that where the brethren cannot seek alike, they may agree to differ." The "General Association" disclaimed any authority over any constituent body or individual beyond "the mere withdrawing of fellowship." Its functions, mentioned repeatedly from then on, were to be no more than advisory at most.

It would appear on the face of things that there was no deliberate intent among the Universalists who met at Winchester, New Hampshire in 1803 to assume the organizational leadership of the entire denomination or to become its official spokesman. If the language of the various deliberative bodies is followed, the New England Convention was still only a "General Association," meeting in "General Convention." It was no more than a regional gathering of Universalists in the New England states, organized in a loose confederation. The Philadelphia Convention was, although in decline in 1803 and destined to last only six more years, still in existence and had it in its power, at least theoretically, to do exactly what the New England Convention had done. In fact, it was on the foundations laid in Philadelphia less than two decades before that the New Englanders built their structure. The various other associations and conventions that evolved over the next several years still exercised powers equal to, and quite separate from, those claimed by the New England Convention. Even the societies and churches, following both the letter and spirit of congregationalism, tended to go their own way.

Yet the fact remains that New England contained, by the first decade of the nineteenth century, the greatest concentration of Universalist laymen, clergy, and individual leadership in the country, and the second oldest regional organization, and certainly the most active. Unlike any other group in the denomination, it was being more and more widely referred to as the "General Convention," implying representation for all Universalists, and was being looked to more and more for counsel and advice. When the Western Association was created in 1805 in New York State, it was "recognized" by the New England Convention the same year, and in subsequent years the New England body almost always appointed delegates to attend association meetings, some of them hundreds of miles distant. When Hosea Ballou 2d sketched in the history of the denomination in 1848, he noted that in 1805 there were three "branches" of the "General Convention" then in existence—the Northern, Western, and Eastern—central and upstate

Vermont, central New York, and Maine, respectively.[34] The growing role of the convention as a national organization was exhibited when it admitted both the First and Second Universalist Societies of Philadelphia into fellowship in 1830.

There is no question about the broad intent of the Winchester Profession. Although leaving the addition of other articles of faith to the option of the several churches and societies "within the limits of our General Association," they were not to disagree with the general profession or diverge from its basic principles. Further, the Universalists who adopted the Winchester Profession claimed to be "a denomination of Christians, distinct and separate from those who do not approve the whole of this profession and belief." The New England Convention was clearly speaking here on behalf of all Universalists in the United States, wherever they might be. Even allowing for characteristic imprecision in designation, the evolution of the label attached to the organization within a thirty-year span clearly indicated its widening area of activity. In 1803 it was designated "The General Association of Universalists of the New England States." At the meeting in 1804 it became the "Universal[ist] Convention of the New-England States, and Others," and by 1833 was known as the "General Convention of the New England States and Others."

Between 1805 and 1820, the annual conventions were concerned primarily with examining the credentials of delegates, reading or hearing reports from those societies represented, and acting on applications for fellowship or ordination, and the admission of societies to membership. During this period, thirteen individuals were ordained (two as "travelling preachers"), three were granted licenses to preach, and thirty-two were given letters of fellowship, making a total of sixty given some kind of official standing by the convention. Meanwhile, the associations scattered across several states were engaged in the same activities.

During the same fifteen years (1805-1820), the convention admonished (and suspended for one year) only one preacher, and disfellowshipped one more. Preachers in fellowship with the convention who had migratory tendencies (as a large number did) had to be reminded in 1814 that it was their duty to inform that body when they changed their official status. This request was prompted by the actions of Abner Kneeland, whose involved relationships (and non-relationships) with the denomination had a long and stormy history. After having assumed charge of the First Universalist Society in Charlestown, Massachusetts, in 1811, with the blessing of the convention, he had, three years later, without consulting with or even informing the convention, left his pastorate to devote himself "to mercantile pursuits." He made his peace with the convention in 1816 by "returning to the work of the ministry."[35]

The convention also broadened its concerns by discussing or acting on such matters as preparation of hymnals, and launching the Universalists' first venture into secular education (Nichols Academy, discussed below). In 1819 the convention welcomed the appearance of the *Universalist Magazine* as a denominational newspaper, particularly because it was to carry the accounts of convention meetings and thereby reach a wider audience than the printed pamphlets which were used occasionally to relay its proceedings.

The practice of issuing pamphlets containing accounts of activities was continued erratically even after Universalist papers multiplied and printed the minutes and circular letter or "general epistle" which usually accompanied them. The proceedings of the 1819 convention were the first to be published in a newspaper.[36] The minutes of the 1821 convention were printed in an eight-page pamphlet, but none was published again until 1835 (to celebrate the "Jubilee" session). In that year the complete record was printed for the first time, including the reports of committees and the Occasional Sermon, as well as the minutes of the business sessions.

For many years, before the General Convention had a treasury, its publishing expenses, like most others, were defrayed by a special collection taken up at meetings. After the proceedings of the 1836 and 1837 conventions were published and a deficit incurred (met by a special on-the-spot collection at the 1838 convention), the practice of printing the proceedings was abandoned and not resumed until 1858. The issuance of a circular letter was discontinued after the 1850 session. Even in 1858 there were no funds provided for publication. When a new constitution and bylaws were adopted in 1855 and 1856 respectively, they were not published until 1858, together with the proceedings for that year; even then, a special collection had to be taken up to pay the printing expenses. Any surplus was to go to the Universalist Historical Society which had been created in 1834 and likewise had to depend on special collections for its financial sustenance.[37] Universalists had to depend on their newspapers for information about the doings of their convention and for transcriptions of sermons delivered on such occasions. If the minutes and other materials were reproduced at all in the press, they were likely to be spread over several issues because of space limitations or the whims of editors. The convention in 1838, which met in Portland, Maine, voted to publish the minutes that year in one newspaper only (the *Gospel Banner,* Augusta, Maine), with the hope that they would be copied by other papers.[38]

In 1821 the New England Convention took another step intended to strengthen and enforce ministerial discipline which also enhanced its power. It created, for the first time, a standing committee "to review complaints, call councils, and suspend the public labours of such brethren as may walk disorderly during the recess of the Convention."[39] Three years later, the convention crystallized certain practices which had crept in which were intended to regularize ministerial affairs and the conduct of convention business. It provided for the reprinting of the Winchester Profession and the Plan of Association of 1803, but voted to add to the latter three usages that had grown up in the meantime. The first of these, actually begun in 1814, provided that all clergy in fellowship with the convention were to inform it when they assumed a pastorate or changed locations. A practice instituted in 1820 to facilitate communication was made official policy by the provision that three copies of the proceedings of each convention were to be sent to three clergymen representing different associations. The third addition was a recommendation that differences among clergy or between them and their societies be settled by a council selected by the parties involved.[40]

Lines of authority and chains of command had become sufficiently unclear and bothersome by the mid-1820s to necessitate a review of the entire structure of the New England Convention. Relationships between societies and associations were vague, and the relationship of both of these to the convention were in need of restatement and clarification. A rather thorough reorganization seemed to be called for, if nothing else than by "the multiplication of Associations in fellowship with this Convention claiming the same powers, composed of the same members, and extending over the same territory."[41] It was time, according to the author of the circular letter for 1827, to clarify the role of the General Convention of New England States, and Others; it must establish "in *fact,* what it has ever been in *name.*"

The result, at the convention held that year in Saratoga Springs, New York, with twenty-two clergy and thirty lay delegates present, was more a hope still unfulfilled than a promise carried out. A slightly revised plan of government was adopted and sent to the various societies for their guidance. The basically confederate form of organization—a chronic source of difficulty from an organizational point of view—was not only retained but reaffirmed. Fear of anything resembling dictation from above resulted in the continued guarantee of virtual autonomy for the societies, without which the structure (such as it was) would not have existed at all.

There was no effort to define the word "society" or distinguish it from a "church," beyond stating that a society comprised individuals believing "in the final salvation of all mankind, by the mediation of Jesus Christ." Societies could choose to "be perfectly independent" of all other societies or bodies of believers. They were "to judge for themselves" in matters of faith and practice, which meant choosing their own form and time of worship, and calling, settling, and dismissing their own ministers. If they wished—and they were encouraged to do so—societies could join into associations, in order to extend their fellowship and communicate in this fashion with fellow-believers. Societies could withdraw from the associations at any time they saw fit. If they elected to join such a body, they were to send their pastors and two lay delegates each, as representatives.

The associations, to meet at least annually, in rotation at societies in their fellowship, were, like the societies, given complete freedom to adopt their own regulations, but also to adopt guidelines for the government of the societies within their jurisdiction. The associations were also to provide public worship services and the administration of the Lord's Supper as part of their meetings.

As the next step in the loosely hierarchal organization, the state conventions were to provide for two to four delegates (all clergy) from the associations, together with all ordained and licensed Universalist preachers in each state. The state conventions were to provide from four to eight clerical delegates to the annual meetings of the New England Convention, open also to any ordained or licensed ministers in the denomination who wished to attend. The state conventions were to adopt, if they had not already done so, and retain, the Profession of Faith adopted by the New England Convention. The hands-off policy regarding disputes among clergy and/or their societies, beyond mere guidance, enunciated in 1824 was reaffirmed. No association or convention was to hear complaints. All situations involving judicial determinations were to be settled by "a mutual council chosen by the parties."

The over-all plan designed for "the better government of the Convention, the Associations, and Societies in its fellowship" met with general approval among the societies, except for one provision. They balked at the exclusion of lay delegates, who from the beginning had been voting members when business was transacted.[42] At the 1828 convention the entire plan was shelved as "inexpedient." However, the convention that year did take another step which gave it broader jurisdiction than ever before. The hands-off policy regarding the settlement of disputes was significantly modified. The rule adopted in 1824 and repeated in the 1827 proposal was repealed. If settlement by a mutual council was not possible as between contending parties, a committee of discipline appointed annually at the convention would investigate and make a report; hence, final judgment would rest with that body.

Although the convention in 1828 had failed to act, there was too great a need to indicate more clearly the composition and relationship of the various components of the denomination to let the matter drop. In 1830 committees were appointed to visit the state conventions in Maine and New York and attempt to clarify their relations with the New England Convention. The replies made it abundantly clear that, so far as they were concerned, the state conventions would continue to follow their own policies. Desire for harmony and Christian fellowship was expressed by both, but that was as far as either would go. The Maine Convention conceived itself as "a *distinct* and *independent* religious body, having a right to transact its own business without the intervention of any other religious body whatever."[43] Its stance was "complete independency." To the New York Convention, the New England Convention was no more than a "sister ecclesiastical body." Each was "independent of the other so far as is consistent with strict and mutual fellowship."[44]

There was no clearer illustration that the New England Convention was considered superior to the associations in name only, than during the so-called Restorationist controversy. One of the results was the disbanding of the Providence Association in Rhode Island. It had been organized in 1828, and in 1831 joined with sympathizers in southern Massachusetts to form the Massachusetts Association of Universal Restorationists. All that the New England Convention could do was minimize this disruption of denominational harmony as best it could, meanwhile attempting to show the wayward brethren the error of their ways. However distasteful it might have been to the majority, theologically or otherwise, there was nothing in the structure or discipline of the denomination to prevent the New England Convention in 1825 from admitting to fellowship three Restorationist societies.[45] Were the practicing of religious liberalism and the building of a viable organization incompatible? This was one of the questions which the New England Convention had to attempt to answer.

The Creation of the General Convention in 1833

The New England Convention was in no wise daunted by the expressions of independence of other conventions and associations at previous meetings. Sensing the need for some agency that would tie the scattered threads of Universalism together, it began to lay the groundwork at its meeting in 1831 for what, two years later, became officially the "General Convention of Universalists in the United States." At previous sessions, especially in 1827 and 1828, much more attention had been paid to the status of societies and the relations of associations with the convention than to the potential value of state conventions. The first of these had been organized in New York (1825) and Maine (1828). The suggestion was made in 1831 that a coherent stair-step arrangement would be desirable, whereby associations (representing societies) would send delegates to state conventions, which in turn would send delegates to a general convention. The Rockingham Association (New Hampshire) suggested that Maine's organization, which followed this pattern, be used as a model.[46]

If state conventions could be created (and educated) so that a recognition of a central body could be provided, then the term "General Convention" would have real meaning. If state conventions were organized, this would provide a uniform organizational base throughout the United States and might provide a more balanced and better representation of the entire denomination at convention meetings. At the 1829 sessions in Winchester, New Hampshire, although nearly forty clergymen attended, there were no delegates from either Maine or New York, nor from any states south or west of New England.[47] Furthermore, all other denominations had a general headquarters or at least a central organization of some kind. Why should the Universalists lag behind?

More important, those state conventions already established had grown up in rather unplanned fashion, with no real guidance and ill-defined jurisdictions and prerogatives beyond the ambiguous statement that they were "in fellowship with the Convention in New England;" or, as an article in the constitution of the Maine Convention adopted in 1829 provided, "fellowship with the General Convention." The circular letter accompanying the printed minutes of the 1831 meeting referred to an Ohio Convention, as well as the ones in Maine and New York. The Ohio Convention was actually not organized until 1837.[48]

The New England Convention moved a step closer in 1831 to a more broadly-based organization when it voted that state conventions be organized where they did not already exist and invited them to send delegates to the next meeting "to consult on measures whereby a General Convention may be organized which shall extend its jurisdiction over the several Conventions of our order in the United States."[49] By 1832 the New England Convention was ready to act. Forty-nine clergymen, representing five states, met at Concord, New Hampshire in September, together with "an unusual number" of lay delegates. This was the largest assemblage of "ministering brethren" that had yet met. The occasion was also made notable by the presence of Colonel William Pierce, the only surviving member of the society organized by John Murray in Gloucester. Even more noteworthy was the appointment of a committee consisting of two representatives from states within the jurisdiction of the convention, "to consider the project for a General Convention of our denomination in the United States." The committee was to confer with delegates present from other conventions and make a report.

The urging by the New England Convention that state organizations be created bore fruit. By the time it convened in 1832, South Carolina, Connecticut, New Hampshire, Pennsylvania, and Vermont had joined Maine, New York, and the western states in either organizing state conventions or seriously contemplating the possibility. A regional convention had been somewhat prematurely organized in North Carolina in 1827, but had apparently held no more than one session thereafter. However, the rapid organization of state conventions that might be subservient to a central organization was by no means a certainty.

Differences of opinion were immediately expressed about the desirability of organizing an over-all body, and the debate was spirited and prolonged.[50] The majority of the delegates were "decidedly of the opinion, that a general bond of union in our denomination, was both desirable and practicable" and therefore voted to recommend action at the next annual meeting through representatives from the existing state conventions and any others that might be created in the meantime. The measure was finally adopted, but "contrary to the wishes of a very respectable minority."[51]

Those in favor of a central organization argued that its creation was necessary to provide "a common bond of union throughout the country." Such an agency would extend the acquaintance of both clergy and laity, bring Universalists in different parts of the country into communication, and provide a means by which information on the state of the cause could be gathered and disseminated. It was clear that the New England Convention was a general convention in name only; the existing state conventions refused to acknowledge its leadership or grant it any special status. It was argued, on the other hand, that the project of a United States Convention was chimerical and impractical. Even if appointed, delegates from the state conventions would refuse to meet as a group. Distance and expense were additional deterrents. There were already a "thousand and one" publications to provide and spread denominational information. Further, if the powers of the proposed general convention were advisory only—and it would be unacceptable otherwise—there would be nothing for it to do. There would be no justification for calling the delegates together in the first place.

The tentative composition of the convention proposed in 1832 was to be eight delegates (four clerical and four lay) from each state convention. The committee made haste to specify that it would "neither claim or exercise authority to make laws, or to prescribe regulations for the government or discipline of any of the State Conventions or Associations." The deliberations of the general convention were to be "*advisory only,* and for the purpose of communicating general information, and of promoting the general union and prosperity of the Order."

Even from a regional standpoint, the move to create a United States Convention was based on very incomplete and imperfect representation of the denomination at the Concord meeting. Only three New England states (Massachusetts, New Hampshire, and Vermont) were represented on the committee to consider the proposal. Clerical delegates from Massachusetts alone comprised almost one-half of the ministers present. There were no delegates at all from either Rhode Island or Connecticut, and the convention rules had to be suspended to allow the lone delegate from New York and the six delegates from Maine to have seats on the council, where they agreed to the proposed changes only if the general convention's functions were limited to "counsel and encouragement," and lay representation was provided. The total clergy present, in turn, comprised little more than one-third of those in New England who were in fellowship with the convention. According to Thomas Whittemore's computation, there were at the time 115 Universalist clergymen in fellowship, 42 of whom were from Massachusetts; of the latter, over half were in attendance in 1832.[52]

A partially successful effort had been made prior to the 1832 meeting to contact the existing state conventions to solicit their reactions, preferable by sending delegates. Nothing at all was heard from Connecticut at the time, although when its state convention voted in the fall of 1833 to join the General Convention, it considered such an organization "highly useful"—but only as "a kind of centre for information respecting the progress of our cause in all the United States."[53] The Pennsylvania Convention sent a letter expressing approval of the principle of a United States Convention, providing its powers were strictly limited.[54] At its meeting in 1832, the South Carolina Convention followed the wording of their Pennsylvania colleagues in approving the creation of the new organization, "provided the powers in it vested are only advisory."[55] The South Carolina body appointed two delegates "in person or by letter" to the 1832 meeting. When the Maine Convention met to appoint two delegates, it was expressly provided that they would attend "as an expression of fellowship" but were instructed "not to take any measures which should infringe the independence" of the state convention.[56]

The annual meeting in Strafford, Vermont, duly convened in September 1833, unanimously adopted, "after free discussion and mature deliberation," a revised constitution. The New England Convention thereby became officially the General Convention of Universalists in the United States. This landmark step in the organizational history of the denomination was taken by a much smaller gathering than the one the previous year. Only twenty-six clergy attended, representing five states. As might have been expected, the host state furnished the largest contingent—thirteen. Connecticut, not represented in 1832, sent one delegate (Charles Spear, of Granby), but there were no representatives from either Maine or Rhode Island. The three state conventions of New Hampshire, Vermont, and New York all sent at least one delegate, and the South Carolina Convention conveyed its sentiments by letter.

The new constitution reflected the general character and spirit of the recommendations made in 1832. The sixth article disclaimed "all authority over or right of interference with the regulations of any State Convention or Minor Association." The convention would "only exercise the privilege of *advising* the adoption of such measures and regulations as in their opinion shall be best adapted to the promotion of the general good of the cause." The purposes of the convention were reiterated; namely, "to concentrate the interests of the denomination in the United States; communicate useful information on all subjects connected with such interests; to promote ministerial intercourse and fellowship among the brethren; and to subserve the great interests of the cause of gospel truth at large." The most significant change from the recommendations of the previous year was to increase the number of lay delegates from each state convention from four to six. The number of clerical delegates was established at four, thus assuring lay preponderance, at least on paper, and giving to each state convention equal voice, regardless of the numbers or strength of the denomination in each.

Each state convention was to determine whether or not it wished to join the General Convention, by approving the newly adopted constitution. Structurally, the Universalists had been consistent in their distrust of centralization; they had retained the concept of loose confederation, with the societies and churches represented through associations, and the latter through the state conventions. As Thomas Whittemore, who had served as one of the three delegates from Massachusetts and as moderator of the convention, emphasized in his unofficial report, the General Convention was to have "no authority whatsoever" over other units in the denomination, and had not even a right—only a privilege—"of advising what is for the general good."[57] The creation of a really strong central authority had to await another day.

But no matter how tentative the step taken at the Vermont meeting toward a more comprehensive and tightly-knit organization, veteran Universalists could look with great satisfaction on the progress made since the first general meeting to cut across state boundaries that had been held in Oxford, Massachusetts, less than half a century earlier. The circular letter accompanying the minutes of the Vermont meeting exuded optimism and confidence for the future as well as a call for renewed and continued efforts. Using the often-expressed analogies of the fields, vineyards, and harvests, Universalists were exhorted to "strengthen our stakes, as well as lengthen our cords . . . . with SALVATION inscribed on our banners, our march will continue to be onward, and the victory sure." Only time would tell whether such exhilarating and heady rhetoric would be justified.

Chapter 6

MODIFYING AND REFINING THE THEOLOGICAL BASE

The Emergence of Unitarian Universalism

Only two years after the Winchester Profession had been adopted (in 1803) another significant milestone was reached in the evolution of Universalist theology. The man most responsible was Hosea Ballou, probably the best-known Universalist leader both in his own day and to later generations, and considered by many as the most original thinker and greatest theologian of the Universalist movement.[1] He made at least three major (and related) contributions to the religious thought of the denomination: the transition from a trinitarian to a unitarian belief regarding the nature of God and Christ; the finiteness of sin, which led eventually to the belief that all of man's sins would be punished on earth; and a new conception of the doctrine of the atonement.

Conclusions regarding these theological matters were, however, only means to a greater end, and for a larger purpose. For most Universalists, questions concerning the Trinity, vicarious atonement, and future punishment were almost always subordinate to the distinguishing tenet of the salvation of all men.[2] In the preface to his *Treatise on Atonement,* first published in 1805 and generally considered Ballou's major work, he explained that "what I have written on the subject of the Trinity, is mainly to show the reader in what light I view the Mediator, that my general ideas of atonement may be easier understood." It was not his intention "to attend to a full refutation of those ideas [concerning the Trinity], as I think that has frequently been done and well done."

Hosea Ballou 2d, writing almost half a century after the *Treatise* had appeared, pointed out that dissent from the doctrine of the Trinity had been expressed by Universalists even before 1805, but that it was only after the publication of Ballou's *Treatise* that the unitarian view had been "generally held, and openly maintained."[3] Likewise, Hosea Ballou had argued against the doctrine of vicarious atonement in a sermon delivered in Sturbridge, Massachusetts, in 1795, and his views had been generally accepted soon thereafter. He had not elaborated his ideas on either unitarianism or atonement before 1805, but a careful

Hosea Ballou (1772-1852), "Father of American Universalism"

reading of his *Notes on the Parables,* first published in 1804, would indicate that Christ was pictured as "merely the son of God, and his death as a necessary means only in the process of his enterprise."[4]

After the publication of the *Treatise on Atonement,* Ballou's arguments, "addressed so directly to the common-sense of mankind," had rapidly become "the common property of the Denomination." But unitarianism and a new conception of the atonement were still not Ballou's primary consideration; "the chief attention was devoted to the doctrines of 'the grace of God which bringeth salvation to all men.' " It was Ballou who offered not only an effective argument for unitarianism and opposed the traditional view of atonement, but who fitted them into a pattern that gave Universalists for the first time a reasonably coherent theological system.

Hosea Ballou was born in Richmond, New Hampshire, on 30 April 1771, the youngest of eleven children. His father, Maturin, was an industrious farmer and unpaid Baptist preacher who had migrated from his native Rhode Island in 1768 and tried to wrest a living from the inhospitable New England soil. The youngest son grew up with a good acquaintance with Calvinist teachings, and heard much in his early days of "predestination, election, reprobation, the fall of man, the penal suffering of Christ for the elect, the justice of reprobation, and many other particulars."[5]

When Ballou was nineteen, a religious revival occurred in the vicinity of his home, and as a result he and several of his friends joined the Baptist church of which his father had been ordained pastor in 1770. From 1789 until his death in Boston in 1852 at the age of eighty-one, Ballou was a "constant student" of theology. While a teen-ager, Ballou was exposed to the ideas of Caleb Rich and other itinerant preachers of Universalism, and he began to have doubts about the doctrine of eternal reprobation about which he had been taught. He then turned to the Scriptures and found sufficient passages favoring universal salvation to convince him that indeed God would "finally have mercy on all men." Ballou's career as a Baptist was brief. He became a Universalist later in the same year that he had joined his father's church.

For his efforts, the young Ballou was promptly excommunicated, but took comfort from the fact that an older brother, David, not only became a Universalist but began to preach. After attending briefly a Quaker-operated school in the community, and a nearby academy, Ballou's limited formal education came to an end, and in 1791 he too began preaching Universalism. He insisted many years later that he had come to accept the general principles of Universalism with the assistance of "no author, or writer," and used no resources but the Bible and his own reasoning ability. However, as to important specifics, his indebtedness to others has been demonstrated, and he himself made

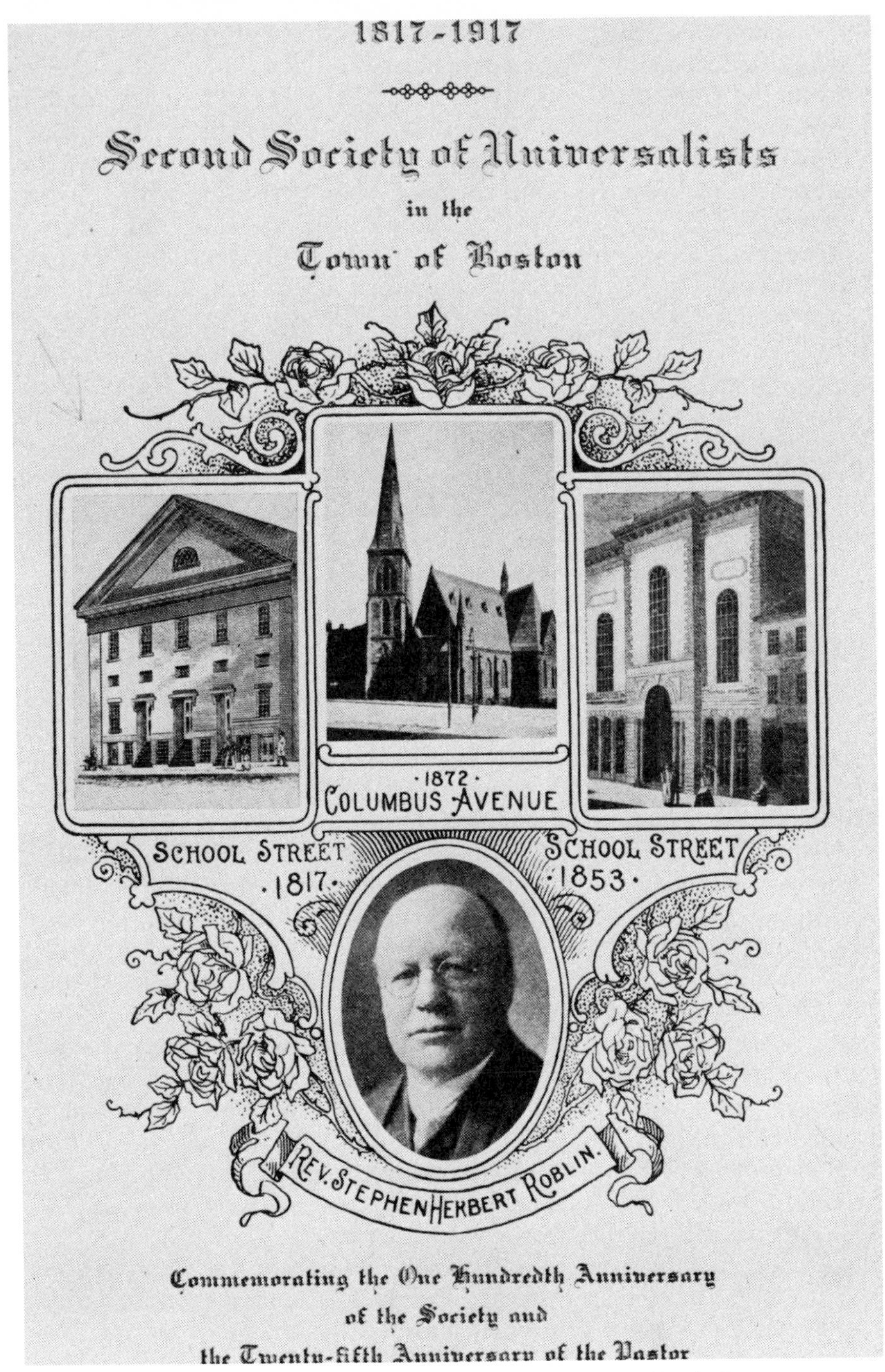

The School Street Church of the Second Society of Universalists in Boston of which Hosea Ballou was pastor from 1817 until 1852

some acknowledgement of this fact. He admitted that he had read "some deistical writings," and was clearly influenced by Ethan Allen's *Reason the Only Oracle of Man* (completed in 1782 and published in 1784).[6]

By 1792 Ballou seems to have committed himself to a ministerial career. In that year he supplemented school teaching with itinerant preaching, and in 1794 was spontaneously ordained by Elhanan Winchester at a meeting of the New England Convention in Oxford, Massachusetts. In 1803 he was re-ordained at Barnard, Vermont. Until he moved to Vermont that year, he lived at various places in Massachusetts, and was active on several fronts. He began an extended correspondence in the fall of 1797 with Joel Foster, minister of the Congregational society in New Salem, which resulted in Ballou's first published writing, part of a sixty-four page pamphlet.[7] He also preached for over two months in 1798 to John Murray's society in Boston, where he upset Mrs. Murray, and presumably some others present, by preaching a unitarian conception of Universalism which he had presented publicly for the first time in 1795.

For six years he ministered to several societies in Vermont, played an important part in the New England Convention, engaged in a series of doctrinal controversies, and published two of his most important works–*Notes on the Parables* (1804) and *A Treatise on Atonement* (1805). Between 1809 and mid-1815 he preached in Portsmouth, New Hampshire, operated a small private school there, published new editions of his two books, engaged in a variety of religious controversies, and as a good nationalist, supported the War of 1812.

Massachusetts remained his base of operations from mid-1815 to the end of his long and busy life. After a brief pastorate in Salem, he was installed as the first pastor of the Second Universalist Society in Boston, on Christmas Day, 1817. Immediately he plunged into other Universalist affairs. He served as the first editor, beginning in 1819, of the *Universalist Magazine* which became, under various names, the leading denominational newspaper. Later, in 1830, he became editor with his great-nephew, Hosea Ballou 2d, of the *Universalist Expositor,* a scholarly journal. Reluctantly but actively he became involved in the Restorationist controversy. With Edward Turner he cooperated in the compilation of a hymn book (1821), and found time for numerous preaching tours which included Philadelphia and New York. In 1834 Ballou produced another major work, *An Examination of the Doctrine of Future Retribution,* an outgrowth in part of the Restorationist controversy. In the meantime, he had attended denominational conventions almost without end, delivered the charge or sermon at the installation of innumerable new ministers, attended meetings of Unitarian clergy, and regretfully declined to visit Universalists in the South because time, energy, money, and other commitments would not allow it.

The weight of years and many obligations finally required that pulpit assistance be obtained. The Second Universalist Society in Boston had, by 1845, been organized for some twenty-eight years. Father Ballou, as he was by then affectionately known by hundreds of Universalists, had been its sole pastor, with only brief interludes, for the entire time. So it was quite in accord with his wishes that he be relieved of part of his arduous duties, and Edwin H. Chapin, pastor in neighboring Charlestown, arrived in 1846 as Ballou's associate. Two years later, Alonzo A. Miner resigned his pastorate in Lowell to replace Chapin.

In the fall of 1850 the elder statesman of the denomination delivered a valedictory discourse in his beloved School Street church, and on 7 June 1852 a long and fruitful career came to an end. He left a wife (who died less than a year later) and nine children, and his body joined John Murray's in Mount Auburn cemetery in Cambridge. In 1859 a monumental statue was erected over Ballou's grave, executed by E.A. Brackett of Boston, and financed by contributions from Universalists all over the nation.[8] Thus closed the career of a man who had, according to most Universalists, an influence "greater on the religious mind than that of any other clergyman of the age."[9]

Ballou had been a largely self-taught man. His formal education had lasted less than three years, his pulpit presentations were almost exclusively doctrinally centered and Bible-oriented, and his writings lacked polish. As a contemporary put it, Ballou's sermons were "always and entirely argumentative . . . . So addicted is he to the argumentative, that even his prayers are characterized by it . . . . The scriptures are his sword and shield . . . . In point of mere literary merit, Mr. Ballou's published and oral discourses are very far from deserving encomiums . . . . truth–plain, simple, and unadorned, constitutes with him the all and the everything."[10] His sermons were not only likely to be "of a controversial character," but he spoke extemporaneously, "without note or scrip before him."[11]

Suspicious of formal theological training, skeptical about the new emphasis on moral and social reform swirling about him in his later days, to the detriment of doctrinal Universalism, Ballou held fast to the religious verities he had come to accept early in life. In so doing, he furnished Universalists and Universalism with the undergirding that had previously been lacking. Alonzo A. Miner, in his centenary sermon in 1870, paid tribute to this giant in the denomination when he said that Ballou had "undoubtedly accomplished more for the kingdom of God than any other man of the century."[12]

Ballou's *Treatise on Atonement,* written in the winter of 1804-1805, was unquestionably his most influential work. In it, he recast much of the theology Universalists had inherited from James Relly and which was still being taught by John Murray, whom Ballou had met for the first time in 1791. Ballou's major purpose was "to prove the doctrine of *universal holiness and happiness*."[13] His more particular interest was to demonstrate, by the application of reason and examination of the Scriptures, the falsity of "the ideas, that sin is infinite, and that it deserves an infinite punishment; that the law transgressed is infinite, and inflicts an infinite penalty; and that the great Jehovah took on himself a natural body of flesh and blood, and actually suffered death on a cross, to satisfy his infinite justice, and thereby save his creatures from endless misery."[14] Ballou was ambivalent about the nature and duration of future punishment after physical death and devoted only a few sentences to the subject (e.g., p. 189). He hinted that he would develop his ideas on this topic more fully at some later time.[15] He did, however, categorically deny that the Scriptures proved "the *endless misery* of a *moral being,*" and went on to argue that Scriptural authority for belief in universal holiness and happiness was much more convincing than any that his opposers might offer for "the *endless* duration of sin and misery."

His principal aim was to prove that God was not a wrathful deity seeking justice, but a benevolent being full of infinite love. Christ was sent to earth not to atone for man's sins (which, according to Ballou, were very real and led to all kinds of misery), but to lead men to divine love. Christ had suffered for men, not instead of them. The atonement was "the *effect,* and not *cause,* of God's love to man." Hence Ballou rejected the traditional doctrine of vicarious atonement and argued that it was man who needed to be reconciled to God—not the reverse—and that Christ was the means by which divine love was revealed and demonstrated, as a living example on earth. The Creator of an harmonious (not depraved) world had, further, given man the power to reason and to discover for himself, basically through the Scriptures, the "Great Design." And, most important of all, the love God had for man could and should be shared by all, not reserved for a select few. Here was the core of universal salvation, much more clearly and logically stated than by either Relly or Murray.

Ballou's treatment of the doctrine of the Trinity was brief and explicit. He denied its validity, and could find no Scriptural justification for it. He posited Christ as "a *created dependent* being" who acknowledged God as father, and served as His representative to man, but deferred to His wisdom; God and Christ were not co-equal, although Christ was exalted above mere man. Christ the mediator had the power of performing "the great work of the atonement, which is the reconciliation of the world to God," but he did so as the special emissary of a superior agency.

Ballou argued that if the Godhead consisted, as trinitarians believed, of three distinct persons—Father, Son, and Holy Spirit—equal in power and glory, eternally and essentially one, that an impossible contradiction developed if logically applied. How could Christ be simultaneously the son of God and God himself? If Christ were really God, then did not God really die? "Again, if the Godhead consists of *three distinct* persons, and each of those *persons* is *infinite,* the *whole Godhead* amounts to the amazing sum of infinity, multiplied by three!" It was this sort of reasoning, spiced with a touch of humor now and then, that helped make Ballou's ideas so appealing and his influence so great. Many a Universalist gave credit to Ballou not only for confirming and strengthening their unitarian belief, but in converting them from "orthodoxy" or even from "infidelity."[16]

Ballou's unitarianism found a generally receptive audience among Universalists, clerical as well as lay. By 1805 his views of both the nature of God and of the atonement "pervaded the Universalist ministry, with but few exceptions."[17] John Murray and Edward Mitchell were the most strenuously opposed, and many of their congregations probably supported them. The only Universalist periodical which supported the Relly-Murray version of the Trinity and the atonement was the *Berean,* published in Boston at irregular intervals in eight issues between 1802 and 1810. After Murray's death in 1815 the only clergy known to be preaching trinitarian Universalism were Paul Dean of Boston and Mitchell in New York—and he was never in formal fellowship.[18] Hosea Ballou 2d considered unitarianism a settled question in the denomination by 1820, noting that "another and far more learned body of divines had taken the lead in defending the simple unity of God and the rational doctrine of atonement."[19] This contribution by the Unitarians relieved the Universalists "from the call to labor on the secondary points," and allowed them to concentrate on "the distinguishing tenet of their profession"—universal salvation.

Thomas Whittemore, frequently given to broad and sweeping statements, asserted that as early as 1800, "the doctrines of the Trinity and Atonement, with all kindred notions, were discarded by the denomination, with a very few exceptions."[20] In order to ascertain the views of the constituency, in 1829 Whittemore sent a questionnaire to the "principal Universalist clergy" soliciting their views on various theological matters. The overwhelming majority of the eleven replies he recorded indicated that trinitarian conceptions had disappeared from Universalist thought. He credited Ballou with being "one of the principal means of this change." This may very well have been true, but it should not be forgotten that the unitarian concept of God, particularly in the New England area and, more specifically, in Boston, had been long held in America and, like universalism, had deep European roots.[21]

Historically, both in early modern Europe and in colonial America, unitarianism and universalism, before assuming denominational form, also shared certain general characteristics. Each idea was recurrent and persistent. Both had been visible during the Reformation, and were openly professed by contemporaries of Martin Luther; e.g., Cellarius for unitarianism in the Germanies. Both ideas were put on the defensive because of the so-called "heresies" they represented, and both individuals and groups suffered as a consequence. The classic example was Servetus, burned at the stake in Geneva in 1553 for his unitarianism. Unitarians, experiencing various degrees of legal disability, were to be found in the Italies, the Germanies, Poland, southeastern Europe, Holland, and England in the sixteenth century and thereafter. Both unitarians and universalists frequently claimed the same persons as adherents to their views; such was the case with Joseph Priestley (1733-1804), the English clergyman, scientist, and philosopher; and Jonathan Mayhew (1720-1766), pastor of the West Church in Boston and an outspoken supporter of the colonial cause before the American Revolution.

Most nineteenth-century Universalists who were concerned about both the origins of their denomination and the historic relationship between unitarianism and universalism probably shared the views of Thomas Whittemore, one of the earliest historians of the denomination. He contended, with considerable evidence, that the Universalists were the first in America to assert and propagate unitarianism openly.[22] Whittemore went so far as to claim that even by the time of Ballou's treatise, Universalists "may be said to have become a Unitarian denomination," in spite of occasional exceptions such as John Murray. In 1755 Jonathan Mayhew had attacked the doctrine of the Trinity and had endeared himself to later Universalists by "plainly" proclaiming his belief in universal salvation in two sermons preached in 1762.[23] Charles Chauncy (1705-1787), with whose writings Ballou was familiar, had not only laid the foundations for American Unitarianism in his *Seasonable Thoughts on the State of Religion in New England* (1743) but by the 1780s had carried his religious liberalism to the point of advocating universal salvation.[24]

In the case of both unitarianism and universalism, however, it appears that belief was more widespread than open avowal. Most of unitarian persuasion before the organization of the Universalist denomination were hesitant or unwilling to express their views before the American Revolution. For almost a decade after his arrival in America (1770), John Murray was accused by his universalist-minded contemporaries of such obliqueness as to cause confusion and misunderstanding. And long after 1779, when the Universalists organized their first society (in Gloucester, Massachusetts), identifying and organizing those holding universalist beliefs into a coherent group of co-religionists were persistent problems.

The society worshipping in King's Chapel in Boston initially took a negative approach in professing their unitarianism. When they adopted

dissenting minorities as the Baptists, Methodists and Quakers, and German pietistic sects. Others who could claim a Congregational ancestry lost whatever approval was associated with their religious origins when they cast their lot with the Universalist denomination.

Although the shift from trinitarian to unitarian Universalism may not have been as swift and painless as Whittemore implied, it was never a really serious denominational issue. Another theological problem did arise, however, early in the nineteenth century, which exercised the more doctrinally-minded Universalists for almost thirty years and threatened to disrupt the denomination within its basically New England center. This was the debate over future punishment, the so-called Restorationist controversy. It had no visible effect on either the status of the Winchester Profession or the turn to unitarianism, in spite of the turmoil it created, particularly in Massachusetts.

Many Universalist clergymen, especially those who had ready means of communication at their disposal, undertook on their own initiative to review from time to time the theology of the denomination. They wanted to be sure that Universalists understood their own basic beliefs and were free of errors and misconceptions that developed both among communicants and among non-Universalists (the majority of the American population). Aaron B. Grosh of Utica, New York, long-time editor (1838-1864) of the *Universalist Register and Almanac,* was one such person. He varied the format, organization, and wording "in order that the careful reader may not be wearied" by repetition, but wrote literally dozens of articles which all boiled down to the same theological fundamentals. They were usually accompanied by abundant Scriptural references. In an article written for the 1844 *Register,* in order to clarify what he considered the five basics of Universalist belief, he cited over eighty Biblical proofs. In 1839 he used the device of refuting ten supposedly "common errors" about Universalism as a means of clarifying doctrine. The article which he wrote for the 1842 *Register,* after the Restorationist controversy had subsided, can be taken as a representative summary statement of where Universalists stood in the mid-nineteenth century, and for a considerable period thereafter.

Grosh emphasized the completely Christian framework within which Universalism operated, albeit with some divergencies within that structure and within the denomination itself. All Universalists believed in the existence of God; acknowledged Jesus as his Son, and of the Scriptures as divine revelation; recognized "limited rewards and punishments under the moral government of God and Jesus;" and "the final salvation of all intelligences from sin and suffering, to a state of endless holiness and happiness." The first two beliefs were shared by all Christians; the third by many; and the last by "a small but rapidly increasing number of Christians in various denominations," and by all Universalists, regardless of formal religious affiliation. The last point was the key one. Whether one believed in the unity or trinity of God, in total or partial depravity, in the real existence of devils as fallen angels or as merely symbolic personifications of man's sinfulness, in limited punishment after death or in the termination of all punishment at death was really beside the point. It was the belief in the final holiness and happiness of all men that really mattered, and made Universalism a distinctive doctrine.

Grosh reiterated Universalist rejection of "all traditions, creeds, and commandments of men" and denial of "all human authority in matters of faith and conscience." Universalists claimed the right, accorded to all others as well, to interpret the Scriptures for themselves, and to advocate beliefs according to the dictates of both mind and conscience. He would have been less than honest and woefully inconsistent if he had not also pointed out that, as to the nature of Jesus, "nearly every variety of opinion obtains among us that exists among our opposing brethren." As to the nature and location of the Holy Spirit, the same differences of opinion prevailed among Universalists, although they generally denied its separate existence or personality, as they did the existence of a personal devil. Grosh pointed out that although the latter belief was to be found in Milton's *Paradise Lost,* it was not revealed in the Bible. In conclusion, Grosh stressed the belief in man as a free agent—as a "moral actor," with a knowledge of good and evil, and accountable for his actions, but only so far as his finite knowledge and finite capacity carried him. Man, in short, was a responsible as well as a spiritual being.

These "basic beliefs" expressed by Grosh and many other articulate Universalists were to remain unchallenged by the majority for the remainder of the nineteenth century, and even then would be further explained and interpreted rather than repudiated by most Universalists. Murray's trinitarianism may have been abandoned and Winchester's mysticism may have been marked down as the religious idiosyncracy of an earlier day, but the unswerving belief of these two men in ultimate salvation for all, through revealed religion, remained the fundamental tenet of American Universalism. This is not to say that no questions were raised or no doubts expressed. The Restorationist controversy reached serious proportions in the 1830s. A second potential theological crisis developed in the 1840s. Although considered an aberration and quickly side-tracked at the time by the majority of old-line Universalists and not attracting much attention, it raised even more fundamental issues than did Restorationism. It called into question the creditability of Biblical accounts of Christ and reflected a small but growing rationalist movement which was later to become a major element in Universalist thought.

an amended liturgy in 1785, they merely excluded trinitarian sentiments; they waited two years to make an open and positive declaration of unitarianism, when in 1787 it became the first Unitarian church in America. Over a decade later (in a letter written in 1796), James Freeman (1759-1835), of King's Chapel, in commenting on the clergy in the neighborhood of Boston, chided those who believed in unitarianism for being too timid to let their views be known. When Dr. Priestley came to America in 1794, he apparently had hopes of promoting the unitarian cause, but met with no lasting success in the Philadelphia area where most of his efforts were concentrated.

The opening gun of what became the great "Unitarian Controversy" which lasted at least until 1820, was fired by the orthodox Jedidiah Morse in the same year that Ballou's *Treatise on Atonement* was published (1805). About the same time, John Sherman, pastor of a church in Mansfield, Connecticut, did avow himself a unitarian in a work entitled *One God One Person Only,* which naturally provoked the hostility of trinitarians. It was within the next decade that William Ellery Channing was to make explicit and public the dimensions of "Unitarian Christianity." Unitarianism was, in short, very much in evidence. But it was probably Ballou's rendering of unitarian thought that had the most immediate influence among Universalists. By 1805 he had achieved a considerable reputation among Universalists, the majority of whom could claim the same kind of humble background from which he had come.

While unitarianism was becoming a prevailing part of Universalist theology, those who professed unitarian ideas but were unwilling or unable to accept also the idea of universal salvation followed a course which set them increasingly apart from the Universalists in the early nineteenth century. Their historical experience even prior to their emergence as a separate denomination helps explain the failure of the two groups to unite until after the middle of the twentieth century.

Although both Unitarians and Universalists became involved in controversy with each other, theological and otherwise, in the early nineteenth century, the locus and intensity were basically different. Until 1815 unitarianism seldom became an issue, at least in the Boston area, and the subject was seldom introduced into the pulpit; in fact, the term itself was not at first widely used. Most believers in unitarianism were at first called Liberal Christians—a designation used early in the nineteenth century by Universalists also, to describe their own position. Even by the mid-1750s anti-trinitarianism had appeared, and even more was to do so within the next few decades.[25] According to Thomas Whittemore, who devoted much of his energies while a member of the Massachusetts legislature to securing repeal of that portion of the state constitution providing for compulsory support of religion, the long delay in obtaining such repeal was due to the fact that most of the

Unitarian Congregationalists joined forces with their more Calvinistic fellow-Congregationalists (who comprised the majority) in upholding the status quo.[26] One of the few controversies before 1815 involved the appointment of Henry Ware, of unitarian persuasion, to the Hollis Professorship of Divinity at Harvard in 1805.

The controversy which led to the formation of a Unitarian denomination can be said to have started in 1815, with the publication in Boston that year of a work published in England in 1812 by Thomas Belsham, in which he included a chapter on American unitarianism. The intent of the American editor in republishing the work was to warn against the spread of such views. A spirited defense of American unitarianism, by William Ellery Channing, precipitated a prolonged debate, climaxed by his challenge to trinitarianism and Calvinism in a sermon delivered in Baltimore in 1819 on the occasion of the ordination of Jared Sparks.

Between 1815 and 1819, a distinct line was drawn within Congregationalism over the issue. There was growing advocacy of a separation "in worship and communion from Unitarians," and the division between the Orthodox (conservative) majority and the Unitarian (liberal) minority became serious. Pulpit exchanges among clergy of the "contending parties" virtually ceased; arguments, both verbal and on paper, for one side or the other, were matched by rejoinders. The result was the establishment in 1825 of the American Unitarian Association in Boston, an organization of individuals representing some 125 churches. After the problem of the respective rights of parishes and churches to the division of property and the settlement of pastors was solved after a fashion, more or less peaceful coexistence was established. The division had frequently resulted in victories for Unitarian minorities as well as the subsequent establishment of new Orthodox churches.

But in spite of the fact that a new denomination had been created, the Unitarians had an important advantage over their Universalist contemporaries. The fight over trinitarianism and Calvinism had been an "in-house" affair—a squabble within the historic Congregational church in the Boston area. The Unitarians had had their origins in the so-called Standing Order; hence they could claim a background of religious respectability, being for the most part the descendants of the old Congregational families of New England. In fact, Unitarians acknowledged not only their church polity and organization but their historic ties by frequently retaining their original designation, and describing themselves as "Unitarian Congregationalists."

Universalists, as a denomination, had neither a set of beliefs acceptable to the majority of church-goers nor a "respectable" origin. Further, they had to struggle to win legal recognition; they had never been part of the Establishment. The vast majority came out of such

The Restorationist Controversy

Early nineteenth-century Universalist clergy, like their colleagues in other denominations, had a great propensity for theological argumentation and debate which often took up endless hours, not to mention column after column in the religious press. There is little reason to doubt the seriousness or sincerity of most of the participants, for the finer points of Universalist theology were still in the formative stage in the 1820s and 1830s, and honest differences of opinion were to be expected. The search for religious truth was especially complex for Universalists because of their emphasis on the right of individual interpretation and private judgment. It was therefore to be expected that a welter of interpretations would appear. Regardless of who claimed victory (and almost everyone did), tempers frequently ran high, and what would begin as personal disagreements on more than one occasion led eventually to polarization, with supporters lined up on each side of an issue.

Thus arose the so-called Restorationist controversy which came to a climax in 1831 with the secession of a handful of clergy and a scattering of laymen, and had organizational as well as theological implications and repercussions. The debate began innocently enough in 1811, when Thomas Jones, Hosea Ballou, Abner Kneeland, and Edward Turner met in Gloucester to organize a conference "for religious discussion and mutual edification." The controversy is related in the greatest detail by Richard Eddy and is at least mentioned in every other historical sketch of Universalism.[27] In order to do full justice to the subject, Eddy departed from the otherwise strictly chronological and annalistic approach he used, and devoted a lengthy chapter to it. The only other topical treatment which he provided was a chapter on Universalist educational efforts.

The plan of those who met in Gloucester was to hold a discussion annually, open to all interested members of the Universalist ministry. Meanwhile, the organizers of the conference agreed to meet as often as desirable to propose questions and circulate comments. One or more persons were to be responsible for initiating discussion on each topic. Between meetings, the members of the conference were to exchange observations in writing, with a clerk to keep a record. At the first meeting, five questions were decided upon, four of which were assigned. At a meeting some five months later, the group voted to publish the answers in the *Gospel Visitant,* a journal created for the purpose of discussing theological questions. In order to make this medium of communication as effective as possible in disseminating Universalist ideas, it was to be issued quarterly, and 1,000 copies were to be printed.

There is no evidence that all members of the original group ever assembled again, although at the three subsequent meetings in 1811 and 1812, two or three of them were usually present, together with other clergy including Richard Carrique and Sebastian Streeter. The *Gospel Visitant* (published in Charlestown, Massachusetts) ceased publication after the first volume, and from all appearances anything approaching a systematic attempt to discuss Universalist theology had been aborted. Such, however, was not to be the case. It turned out that both the *Gospel Visitant* and more or less formal disputation were merely dormant.

In 1817 Edward Turner, who had served as clerk of the Gloucester conference, and Hosea Ballou decided to revive the *Gospel Visitant* as a vehicle for furnishing "original tracts on moral and religious subjects."[28] Their intent was probably to continue the broadly based discussions of 1811 and 1812, continuing consideration of such questions as whether the observance of the Lord's Supper at Universalist services should be open to non-Universalists "provided their morals are generally good" (one of the questions proposed in 1811) or how to reconcile promise of salvation with man's works.

The discussions actually came to center around the problem of future punishment. The clergyman apparently responsible for sparking what resulted in a vigorous and prolonged debate was Jacob Wood, who reported to Ballou that Turner was anxious to discuss the subject. Ballou thought this a sufficiently fundamental question to deserve serious consideration, but saw no reason, at least in 1817, to provoke any antagonisms. Ballou was quite willing to engage in a friendly discussion with Turner, for the two agreed basically "on the general system of the gospel." The discussion might, however, help them to clarify their own thinking and thereby benefit Universalists at large. Ballou left it to Turner to choose the side he wished; the latter admitted a leaning toward belief in future punishment, and Ballou the reverse. But both made it clear that their ideas had not crystallized into convictions; in fact, Ballou expressed his willingness to have taken the other side if Turner's choice had been different.

The question of future punishment had been raised sporadically in earlier years and some disagreements had already been expressed. John Murray, an unquestioned believer in retribution after physical death, had, after the Philadelphia meeting in 1790, reported with chagrin that in the course of his return trip to New England, he had encountered, especially in Connecticut and Massachusetts, "some dangerous errors creeping in among the people, and I am afraid they will prevail. They teach that the day of the Lord is past, that there is no future sorrow to be apprehended."[29]

The Philadelphia Convention in 1791 saw fit to deny the allegation that Universalists did not believe in future punishment, although the degree or duration of chastisement after death was not known. In a paper prepared for discussion and publication in the first volume of the *Gospel Visitant* (1811), Hosea Ballou used the same example of Christ's preaching to the spirits in prison that had been approved by the Philadelphia Convention as evidence of future retribution and reward. In 1792 the moderator of the same convention, James Moore, acknowledged the existence of differences of view regarding future punishment and made a plea that disputation over "the mode of salvation" not result in a fatal division within the ranks. A correspondent in Abel Sarjent's *Free Universal Magazine* (June 1793) likewise alluded to some who denied future punishment, and Sarjent himself denied the doctrine. There were other occasional references to the subject before 1818.

The discussion launched by Ballou and Turner in 1817 and 1818 apparently represents the first formal consideration of the subject by Universalists. Ballou was admittedly ambivalent on the matter at first. Between 1797 and 1799 he had engaged in extended correspondence and conversation with Joel Foster, pastor of the Congregational society in New Salem, New Hampshire, over the question of future punishment. The correspondence was published in pamphlet form in 1799. When Ballou was first asked whether he believed "in any punishment at all after this life," his answer was "No." But after reconsideration he explained that his reply was negative because he had not yet made up his mind. On further reflection, he was "satisfied in the idea of a future state of discipline, in which the impenitent will be miserable." He had not discussed it in detail in either his *Notes on the Parables,* published in 1804, or in his *Treatise on Atonement,* published the following year, and did not investigate it closely until after 1816. Little had been said about "a future state of retribution" during Ballou's youth.[30] There had been no need, for Universalists had already determined to their satisfaction that "none of the human race would suffer endless punishment." That was sufficient unto itself. It was the exchanges with Turner that finally convinced Ballou that there was no ground for any belief in punishment in a future state. Man's sins on earth were punishable on earth and not in any other state—heaven, hell, purgatory, or otherwise.

The Ballou-Turner debate, which filled most of the columns of the two volumes of the revived *Gospel Visitant* (1817-1818) before it closed shop for the last time, eventually snowballed beyond anyone's expectations. One major contributor was Jacob Wood, who in 1817 had published a 32-page pamphlet in which he took an intermediate stand for limited punishment beyond death for sin. It was not only Wood's stance that heightened controversy but the strong language with which he attacked those who denied future punishment entirely. Wood also added fuel to the growing fire by appending extracts of letters from various Universalist ministers which indicated "with but *very few* exceptions" a belief in future punishment. Hosea Ballou 2d, who became one of Wood's most effective protagonists, readily admitted his belief in that doctrine, but resented the fact that the extracts from the letters of nine of the eleven clergymen quoted, including Hosea Ballou 2d himself, were published with neither their knowledge nor permission.[31]

Between 1819 and 1821, there was a temporary lull in the controversy, partly because there were so few Universalist publications available in which the debate might have been aired. When Hosea Ballou began the publication of the *Universalist Magazine* in 1819, he was apparently unwilling to make his new paper a means for imposing his own views. At first, he was reluctant to pay much attention to the debate, but soon opened its columns to discussion, and almost immediately brought down on his head the wrath of the Unitarian editor of the *Boston Kaleidoscope.* He placed Universalism in the same camp as Roman Catholicism, Calvinism, and Deism in their opposition to "rational and liberal Christianity."[32] Ballou obviously could not let that go by in silence. He defended Universalism as neither unreasonable nor illiberal, but refused to become embroiled in further controversy over future punishment beyond stating that "we cannot prove that sin and misery will exist in a future state of being."

For a period in 1821 and 1822, after Ballou had temporarily relinquished the editorship of the *Universalist Magazine* because of the state of his health, the controversy over future punishment waxed again in the columns of the paper. When he returned as co-editor later in 1822, with Hosea Ballou 2d and Thomas Whittemore, the floodgates were opened. Again it was Jacob Wood who was responsible for exacerbating the situation. To the already overcrowded columns, in which contributors were showing less and less of a tendency to produce Scriptural evidence and more and more of a propensity merely to call on the other side for proof, Wood proposed adding yet another dimension. He suggested that each side prepare argumentation and proofs independently, deposit them with the editors, and publish them (presumably simultaneously) so that the public could "draw their own conclusions." This was all well and good, except that Wood, who wrote variously under the pseudonyms of "Reason" and "Restorationist," added the gratitutious remark that if the believers in "*no* future misery" refused to meet on these grounds, there was a question of not only their sincerity but of their honor.

Hosea Ballou abandoned whatever restraint he had exercised up to this point, and entered unabashedly into the fray, either signing his own name or using his initials to identify himself. When he, Hosea Ballou 2d, and Whittemore assumed the joint editorship in May 1822, they made it clear that they objected to the aspersions and insinuations contained in Wood's various communications, and announced that the columns of their paper would continue to be open, as before, to materials dealing with the doctrine of future punishment. However, it was expected that Wood would reveal his real name, particularly if he were going to continue to engage in personal attacks as well as religious polemics. In August 1822 the editors announced that they would publish no further communications on the subject "unless they be composed of arguments directly for, or objections directly against one side or the other."

By the winter of 1822-23 the controversy had generated so much bitterness and animosity that the editors of the *Universalist Magazine* attempted to close debate completely. Tempers ran high, and some extreme language was used. One co-religionist sarcastically referred to his brethren who believed in the doctrine of restoration as "mongrel Universalists," while those who denied punishment beyond death came to be known as "Ultra Universalists."[33] The latter term was probably coined by Adin Ballou, a leading Restorationist.[34]

The contentious Wood, not satisfied with the progress of the controversy, kept the argumentation going by writing under yet another pseudonym—"Lover of Truth." Bad matters were made worse when he complained that one of his numerous communications had been subjected to editorial comment before it was presented to the public. This, and the oft-repeated hint by the editors that the controversy be brought to an end, were interpreted by Wood and his supporters as attempts to suppress dissent. He next carried the controversy beyond the boundaries of the *Universalist Magazine* by requesting that a series of his communications also be published in other Universalist papers which by then had come into existence, including the *Christian Repository* (Woodstock, Vermont). Its editor, Samuel C. Loveland, complied with the request.[35] Included in an explanatory remark appended to one of the documents already published in the *Universalist Magazine* was a thinly veiled threat by Wood that the Restorationists might be driven to a separation from the main body of Universalists.

The identity of those clergymen who were alleged at the time to be Restorationists was finally made known to the public by Hosea Ballou 2d, who as a co-editor of the *Universalist Magazine* had unsuccessfully tried to mediate the dispute. They were—besides Jacob Wood—Edward Turner, Paul Dean, Barzillai Streeter, Charles Hudson, and Levi Briggs. They had all attended a meeting in Shirley, Massachusetts, at which it was decided that Wood would write an "Appeal to the Public" and a "Declaration of Facts." It was these documents which appeared in the *Christian Repository*. All but Hudson were present at a second meeting which approved the documents as printed.

The scholarly and mild-mannered Hosea Ballou 2d, obviously upset by the controversy and the way it was being conducted, in a lengthy article in the *Universalist Magazine*, pointed out the inconsistencies, contradictions, and unsupportable innuendos in Wood's actions and writings. Among other things, Wood had refused over a period of several years to have a confrontation with the elder Ballou, although he had not been at all averse to talking "much against" him to others, including making the assertion that believers in no future punishment were "infidels." It was Wood who had deliberately provoked the discussion between Ballou and Turner on a subject that had not been seriously raised in Universalist circles. At the New England Convention in 1817, Wood had tried privately to persuade a number of ministers to join him in a separate (Restorationist) association, after having lobbied unsuccessfully the previous year to have the convention take an unequivocal stand in favor of the doctrine of future punishment. Hosea Ballou 2d went to the nub of the matter in his review of the whole controversy. It was not, he told the readers of the *Universalist Magazine,* in reality a *bona fide* theological rift between those who believed in future punishment and those who did not, but an unpleasantness deliberately instigated and aggravated by Wood, Dean, and Turner to "put down" the elder Ballou, whom they envied because of his dominant position among Universalists.

Hosea Ballou 2d's forthright statements were sufficiently impressive to receive overwhelming support from the readers of the *Universalist Magazine* and to produce clarifications as to the various parts played by the six men involved in the authorship of the "Appeal." Briggs almost immediately disassociated himself from it, followed by Streeter and Hudson. All six, however, had subscribed to the more theologically oriented "Declaration" written by Wood. Unfortunately for Universalist harmony, personal recriminations continued to be involved for several more months, especially after an attempt at settlement between the contending parties failed to come off. The long-standing friendship of the elder Ballou and Turner was seriously threatened. The Southern Association in Massachusetts in 1823 censured the Restorationist minority for their allegedly disruptive actions. Charges were even made against specific clergymen at the New England Convention the same year, although all concerned were exonerated. But by 1825 the various breaches had been at least patched over. Restorationist Paul Dean, for example, had been restored to the fellowship of the New England Convention, from which he had resigned. Even the outspoken Thomas Whittemore, who had no use for the Restorationists, was persuaded by the elder Ballou to temper his opposition sufficiently to make the vote readmitting Dean unanimous.

Even though the theological issue which had been involved in the first few years of the Restorationist controversy had been pushed to the rear by personal animosities, it was far from forgotten in the 1820s. In 1824 Abner Kneeland participated in Philadelphia, at his First Independent Church of Christ, in a ten-hour public debate with W.L.

Paul Dean (1783-1860), a leader in the Restorationist Controversy

McCalla over eternal punishment.[36] Kneeland used his half of the time (in alternate thirty-minute speeches, according to rules agreed upon in advance) to deny categorically the existence of any kind of punishment after death. According to the *Universalist Magazine* at least, he won the debate. Within the next five years, Charles Hudson, Whittemore, and Walter Balfour had, among them, published no less than ten books, pamphlets, and "Replies" to one or the other, detailing the pros and cons of the subject. Hudson challenged the elder Ballou; Balfour and Whittemore defended Ballou.

It was next to impossible to determine precisely how either Universalist clergy or laity lined up on the issue in the 1820s. In 1827 Samuel Loveland, editor of the *Christian Repository*, challenged a statement made in a non-Universalist paper that 'nearly all the Universalists' had renounced the doctrine of future retribution.[37] Loveland countered with the assertion that Universalist preachers believing in future punishment were "never more numerous than they are now." Whittemore came to quite different conclusions. As has been pointed out, in the course of preparing his *Modern History of Universalism*, which first appeared in 1829, he undertook to ascertain where sentiment lay regarding several theological matters by using the technique of a questionnaire to selected Universalist clergy.[38] Included was a question regarding the proportion of Universalists of their acquaintance who believed "in the doctrine of punishment in the future state of existence." If the eleven replies could be taken as representative, the overwhelming evidence indicated that only a miniscule fraction of Universalists, both clerical and lay, believed in such a doctrine if they thought about it at all; and if they did, they were likely to believe in punishment of limited duration.

William A. Drew, the Universalist newspaper editor in Augusta, Maine, found that even ministers who believed in the doctrine did "not seem to be strenuous about it," and the remainder were "studiously silent on the question." Such evidence—and possibly his own predilections—led Whittemore to inform his readers that "the doctrine of a *limited future punishment*, as a distinct question, has never excited a very general interest."[39] He went on to say that, although a difference of opinion on the question had existed for some twenty years, the difference "in itself" had not been the cause of alienation of feeling, or disruption of fellowship. A year later (in 1830) Whittemore was still minimizing any serious division, although he admitted there had always been a "*little* difficulty" among Universalists. Events were about to prove him wrong.

What appeared to be a real separatist movement was taking place not far from Boston. In 1827 Universalist clergy in Rhode Island, southern Massachusetts, and eastern Connecticut, led by David Pickering of Providence, decided to create an association. There seemed to be nothing unusual in this, for the clergy in those areas had been meeting informally on a quarterly basis for several years, and in 1826 the New England Convention had recommended such organizations to Universalists at large. The "Providence Association of Universalists" was duly organized and met periodically; it consisted mainly of Restorationists.[40]

After Pickering tendered his resignation from membership in the New England Convention in 1829, immediately after the Providence Association had adopted a constitution, the feeling began to grow that it might mean the beginning of an actual separatist movement. The Southern Association at least interpreted events that way, and chided the Providence group for creating divisiveness among Universalists. The Southern Association then undertook to set forth its conception of what the terms of fellowship were in the New England Convention. Restorationists in general considered this an unwarranted interference on the part of the Southern Association. At its 1830 meeting, the New England Convention adopted a resolution declaring simultaneous membership in two bodies claiming equal power to be "inconsistent with ecclesiastical order," especially if the bodies were pursuing policies in opposition. This was interpreted by the Restorationists in the Providence Association to mean that continued membership in their organization meant forced withdrawal from the New England Convention. A choice had to be made, so they chose to separate from the latter.

In August 1831 eight ministers and several laymen met at Mendon, in the southern part of Massachusetts, following adjournment of the meeting of the Providence Association, and formed themselves into "a religious community for the defence and promulgation of the doctrines of the Revelation in their original purity, and the promotion of their own improvement."[41] The Restorationist statement was widely disseminated among New England newspapers, and the Providence Association disbanded after a meeting in 1836.

The new group assumed the name of "Massachusetts Association of Universal Restorationists," although two of the clergy in the group, Philomon R. Russell and David Pickering, resided elsewhere—Russell in Winchester, New Hampshire, and Pickering in Providence, Rhode Island. Their announced reason for establishing an independent sect was the alleged departure of the majority of the New England Convention from what the Restorationists conceived to be the religious beliefs of the founding fathers of American Universalism—Murray, Winchester, and Chauncy—as well as "the ancient Authors who have written upon this subject." In brief, the Restorationists argued "that Regeneration—a general Judgment, Future Rewards and Punishments, to be followed by the Final Restoration of all mankind to holiness and happiness, are fundamental articles of Christian faith, and that the modern sentiments of no-future accountability, connected with materialism, are unfriendly to pure religion, and subversive of the best interests of society." The Restorationist manifesto further declared that the New England Convention, instead of providing a forum for "fair, manly controversy," had ridden roughshod over the minority by excluding them from ecclesiastical councils, and then by finally expelling them.

The seceding clergymen—besides Russell and Pickering—were Paul Dean, Charles Hudson, Lyman Maynard, Nathaniel Wright, Seth Chandler, and Adin Ballou. The latter had become a public spokesman for the Restorationists by launching a weekly paper, the *Independent Messenger,* on 1 January 1831. The paper lasted until 1839 under various editors; in 1836 the subtitle *Restorationist Advocate* was added. Beginning with its first issue, Adin Ballou had expressed the desirability of separation from the main body of Universalists. Whittemore was just as vehemently opposed to such a move. Soon after Ballou's paper appeared, Whittemore expressed his unhappiness with both its contents and its editor, but announced that he refused to get into a debate with Ballou over future punishment.[42] Such a policy would merely increase divisiveness in Universalism by advertising differences. Further, a debate would serve to give more ammunition to the *Boston Recorder,* an orthodox paper which had already tried to capitalize on the controversy.

Before the actual separation took place, Whittemore simultaneously tried to warn Universalists about the threat of the Restorationists to religious unity, and to recognize their right to exist within the fold. In May 1831 he cautioned the Universalist societies in the two New Hampshire communities of Winchester and Chesterfield that they were about to install a pastor (Philemon R. Russell) who was a Restorationist and an opponent of Ultra Universalism.[43] When they replied that they were fully aware of Russell's sentiments, Whittemore was forced to recognize that they had a perfect right to the Restorationist's services, but he still expressed fear that their new minister was unfriendly to Universalism in general. When it became evident by June that the Providence Association was going to pursue an independent course, he hoped that it meant it would still be within the larger Universalist family. If so, he wished them well.[44]

Whittemore continued throughout the controversy the self-appointed task of challenging the views of the Restorationists and in so doing engaged in an almost endless series of acrimonious debates which often involved personal attacks through the medium of his newspaper. On one occasion Whittemore accused Paul Dean, editor of the *Independent Messenger* between 1835 and 1838, of being "one of the most bitter, unreasonable, strife-stirring enemies of Universalists which the State of Massachusetts contains."[45] Whittemore himself was not conspicuous in pouring oil on troubled waters.

Public notice of the Restorationist action in creating their own sect elicited a prompt and peppery rejoinder from Whittemore.[46] Their allegations, he wrote, ranged from misinterpretation to misrepresentation and even falsehood. As to theological matters, Whittemore argued that the Restorationists had themselves departed in several respects as widely from early Universalist preachers as had other members of the denomination. A case in point was belief in the doctrine of the Trinity. Further, said Whittemore, the Restorationists' conception of both regeneration and the General Judgment were not the same as Murray's. In fact, Murray differed from Winchester about future punishment, arguing that it was only those who would not or could not see the promise of the Gospels that would suffer. The New England Convention had never attempted to legislate or dictate any particular view regarding future punishment; that was left to individual interpretation. The accusation that the Universalist majority did not hold to future accountability, and were materialistic, Whittemore dismissed as additional examples of misrepresentation.

Whittemore considered quite untrue the Restorationist statement that their ideas had brought about not only "exclusion from ecclesiastical councils" but "final expulsion" from the New England Convention. Two of them, Adin Ballou and David Pickering, made their resignations public and in writing. Neither Seth Chandler nor Philemon R. Russell were even acknowledged Universalists. So, whatever "expulsion" took place, was by the action of the aggrieved parties themselves.

It was mandatory when the New England Convention met in the fall of 1831 at Barre, Vermont, that some official reaction be recorded regarding the Restorationist statement. It was in fact, the first major item of business, and the five resolutions unanimously adopted represented a spirited vindication of the convention's position. In the first place, there had never been a departure "in the least" from the Winchester Profession of 1803, which included in Article II the statement that "the whole family of mankind" would eventually be restored "to holiness and happiness." All who believed in the final reconciliation of all men to the aforementioned "holiness and happiness" were considered Universalists. The convention had never treated the Restorationists except "with christian candor and kindness" and had never interfered in any way with the controversy. None of the five Restorationist clergy who held fellowship in the convention had, prior to the 1831 session and the adoption of the resolutions, been expelled from it. However, now that they had become, by their own declaration, part of another religious body, their membership in the convention was annulled. They could go their own way.

The newly organized Restorationists met annually for ten years (1832-1841). At their second meeting, in 1833, they adopted a constitution and Declaration of Faith. The localized and clerical character of the association was underlined by the constitutional provision (Article 3) that it would consist of "such clergymen within the State, as shall apply for membership, and consent to the subjoined Confession of Faith." The first two articles of the latter were identical with the corresponding articles of the Winchester Profession. The third article of the 1803 document was replaced by the following: "We believe in a retribution beyond death, and in the necessity of faith & repentance; and that believers ought to be careful to maintain order, and practice good works, for these things are good and profitable to men."[47]

Twelve ministers were added formally to the association during the decade, and about ten others were known either to be sufficiently sympathetic to have at some time been in fellowship, or to have attended association meetings.[48] One by one the Restorationist clergy drifted out of the association, and when the remnants convened in Westminster, Massachusetts, in 1841, it was decided not to continue the organization. As the convener of the last meeting, Adin Ballou, expressed it, the association "fell quietly asleep to wake no more."[49]

Even though no formal conventions were held after 1841, when I. Daniel Rupp of Lancaster, Pennsylvania, determined in the following year to compile a history of religious groups in the United States and to request members of the denominations themselves to write the articles, he apparently considered the Restorationist splinter group of sufficient importance to deserve separate treatment.[50] The nineteen-page article was written by Charles Hudson, probably the most scholarly of the group. He indicated that, between the time of the formal separation in 1831, and 1835, there were known to be about a dozen Restorationist societies, with an organized church connected with most of them. The largest societies were in Boston and Providence.

Hudson, in his explication (and defense) of Restorationism, noted that the early Universalists were firm believers in the doctrine that "the effects of sin and the means of grace extended into a future life." Restorationists admittedly differed but little from Universalists except over future retribution. Their main concern, said Hudson, was not only that the lack of retribution in a future world would weaken the moral fibre of men on earth, but that the promise of heaven, as held by the majority of Universalists, meant that men were saved by death, not by Christ. Hence a fundamental tenet of revealed religion was being abandoned, and the Atonement was made superfluous if not irrelevant. However, finding themselves more and more in the minority, the Restorationists resolved "to obey the apostolic injunction, by coming out from among them [the majority]" and forming their own organization.

A.B. Grosh, who wrote the article on Universalism for Rupp's compilation, minimized the separate character claimed by the Restorationists and argued that "the denomination itself, though composed of all classes thus attempted to be distinguished and divided off, claims for itself the sole name of UNIVERSALIST and disclaims any other distinctive title by which to be designated."[51] The concept of Universalism was large enough and flexible enough to claim the allegiance of many diverse views and groups. It was not so much the process and method as the claimed fact of ultimate salvation of all men that was most important.

It should be emphasized that scores of Universalists held to Restorationist views, if not the majority, and especially to limited future punishment, without feeling either the necessity or the desirability of renouncing their Universalist ties. As a definable and organized movement, Restorationism was a minority phenomenon, and was quite clearly motivated by other than purely theological considerations. Further, the Restorationist controversy, so far as it threatened a division within Universalism, was a largely localized affair. There is little evidence that it was agitated extensively outside the eastern New England area, although it attracted the attention of Universalists elsewhere and caused concern to Otis A. Skinner as far away as Baltimore. He was, in the early 1830s, pastor of the society there, and served also as principal editor of the *Southern Pioneer.*[52] The lone instance of a clergyman who withdrew from fellowship in New York State was Edwin Ferriss of the Western Association in 1856, ostensibly because belief in future limited punishment was not made a stipulation for the Universalist ministry.[53] He was admitted to another New York fellowship (the Chenango Association) four years later.

The debate within the denomination over future punishment continued to reappear from time to time, and in isolated instances became a matter for action. In 1843 a debate between a Universalist minister, Eben Francis of Dover, New Hampshire, and a Methodist clergyman in Maine over the Scriptural authority for future retribution was reproduced in pamphlet form.[54] Between 1851 and 1854 the controversy was carried on between T.J. Sawyer, J.M. Austin, and Thomas Starr King, all of whom advocated the doctrine of future punishment, and Isaac D. Williamson and Thomas Whittemore, who denied that evidence existed in the Scriptures for the extension of punishment into the future state.[55] In two successive years (1871 and 1872), the Vermont State Convention refused to seat a delegate from a Restorationist society and recognized instead a representative from another society.[56] In 1878 the Universalist ministers in the Boston area, after discussing the subject of future punishment extensively, approved a nine-point declaration, the burden of which was that punishment for sin, repentance, and salvation was not confined to earthly life, and that death in itself had "no saving power."[57]

Adin Ballou and Thomas Whittemore remained adamant in their opposing views to the end of their lives. Shortly before Ballou's publication, the *Practical Christian,* ceased publication in 1860, it carried an article referring to Whittemore's *Trumpet* and to the old antagonism between the two men. Ballou admitted that Whittemore and his supporters "triumphed ecclesiastically over our Restorationist secessional movement; but theologically and morally we believe the victory was on our side, and that ultra-Universalism has lost ground ever since."[58] Ballou admitted in 1859 that he dissented from Whittemore as inflexibly as ever, but that the two men respected each other and maintained the friendliest of relations.

Whittemore responded in like fashion. Unyielding as he remained on the theological points over which they differed, Whittemore, shortly before his death in 1861, admitted that during the heat of controversy he probably had not always been prudent, was "easily excited," and perhaps said some things rashly. But he never held any long-lasting hatred. His "great object was to do all I could to save the denomination as a unit." When Whittemore heard in 1860 that the *Practical Christian* was to be suspended, he had nothing but praise for not only the paper but for Ballou and the Hopedale community which he had founded (but which Whittemore had never visited).[59] The old bitterness between them had long since subsided, and Ballou saw fit to reproduce his old protagonist's "generous, whole-souled tribute" in the very last number of the *Practical Christian* as well as in his autobiography.[60]

In 1871, thirty years after the Restorationists had met for the last time as an organized group, Adin Ballou offered three explanations for the suspension and eventual extinction of their association.[61] In the first place, they were welcomed by many of the Unitarian clergy, who broke a long silence and finally admitted their own Restorationist beliefs. As a result the previously separate Restorationists appeared in Unitarian pulpits and parishes and "became to a considerable extent fused into their denomination." In addition, the battle with the main body of Universalists was virtually over by 1835, and by 1841 the tide was turning within Universalism to the Restorationist position. Hence there was no need for a sect "between the Unitarians and Universalists." Finally, other concerns—"the great moral reforms, temperance, anti-slavery, &c., &c."—had thrust theological interests into the background. On balance, wrote Ballou, the secession movement had been "a moral necessity." It had served its purpose and had vindicated itself. The attempt of the Ultra Universalists to impose their own orthodoxy had failed; by 1870, Ballou asserted triumphantly, nine-tenths of the denomination were Restorationists. Clinton Lee Scott, a prominent Universalist clergyman, and Benjamin B. Hersey, then dean of the Crane Theological School (Universalist), writing in the 1950s, both came to the same conclusion expressed by Adin Ballou—that

Universalists in general who were living at the time of the controversy eventually came around to the position held by the Restorationists.[62] Hersey pointed out that even after the Restorationists had disappeared as a separate sect, in matters of belief "they won the field completely." In 1899 the statement that "We believe in the certainty of just retribution for sin" was officially adopted as one of the five principles of the Universalist faith.

Not all of the members of the Restorationist Association returned to the Universalist denomination during the controversy or after the secessionists suspended their organization in 1841. Adin Ballou, probably the best known individual in the group, was himself a case in point. He had, in his early years, been successively a Baptist and a member of the Christian Connexion. Although introduced to Universalist ideas about 1818, he had not formally become a Universalist (of Restorationist belief) until 1822, after reading Elhanan Winchester's *Dialogues.* After ordination the following year, Ballou had become pastor of the Universalist society in Milford, Massachusetts and then briefly of the Prince Street society in New York City. A return to the Milford society in 1828 lasted only three years, for he had by then become involved in the Restorationist controversy and was dismissed in 1831 by the Ultra Universalists in the congregation.[63] This coincided with his resignation from the New England Convention. He immediately accepted the pastorate of the First Parish Congregational (Unitarian) church in Mendon, Massachusetts, which he served for eleven years. From 1842 until 1880 he preached in Hopedale, Massachusetts, and served "at large" thereafter, until his death in 1890.

It seems somewhat ironical that his reputation as an advocate of temperance, anti-slavery, the peace movement, and other reforms—all championed to some degree by socially conscious Universalists—was established after he had severed his official association with the Universalist denomination. However, as the author of one of Ballou's obituaries pointed out, the social reformer was not only a good man but "a firm believer in, and eloquent defender of, the doctrines set forth in the Winchester Profession of Faith."[64] Even though a Universalist by official ties for less than a decade, Ballou continued throughout his long and active life to represent, at least in broad outline, the precepts of the denomination to which he had once belonged. He is still claimed as a Universalist by the vast majority of the group to which he once professed formal allegiance.

As Ballou noted, many of the members of the Restorationist Association, like himself, became Unitarians. In 1856 T.J. Greenwood wrote a series of articles entitled "Liberal Christianity" which appeared in the *Trumpet,* in which he reviewed the generally unhappy fate of those who had embraced the Restorationist position. He also implied that many who changed their allegiance to Unitarianism had found themselves in a spiritual wasteland.[65] Greenwood was also convinced that the argument over future limited punishment had been only an excuse for most of the defectors. He was persuaded that the "real cause of the secession . . . was an aspiration for leadership in the minds of a few" who were jealous of the leadership of Hosea Ballou. They desired, by Greenwood's reckoning, to establish a new sect "which would swallow up at once the whole denomination of Unitarians, and draw to its support the thousands of *'liberal'* minds among the Orthodox."

Greenwood, with his Universalist bias showing clearly, noted that Paul Dean, occupying the Unitarian pulpit in a church in Boston built by the Universalists, had eventually been dismissed and, "passing through a sea of troubles, retired broken in hopes, in spirit, in mind, and in health, from the Christian ministry." Charles Hudson likewise abandoned the ministry and turned politician. According to Greenwood, Adin Ballou had isolated himself with his Unitarian congregation and the Hopedale community. Jacob Wood, who had been one of the instigators of the original controversy, was plagued by numerous personal misfortunes, including intemperance, flirted with infidelity, and eked out a living as a shoemaker, but did return to Universalism near the end of his life. Charles L. Cook, another Restorationist sympathizer, abandoned the ministry and stooped so low as to have been sentenced as a felon to seven years' confinement in the state prison in Charlestown, Massachusetts. Edward Turner, who had been drawn into the dispute long before the Restorationist Association had been organized, was lured to Charlton, Massachusetts, from his Universalist pastorate in Portland, Maine. When the Unitarian society was organized in Charlton, he was induced to become its minister with the proviso that he drop the designation "Universalist." After a few years of "indifferent success," he had moved to New York State, where he preached to a small Unitarian society and died in 1856, after a career described by Greenwood as one of disappointment and frustration following his defection from the Universalist mainstream. A scattering of other Restorationists were absorbed into the Christian (Free Will Baptist) denomination.[66]

It can be assumed, however, that the majority rejoined those who, regardless of their beliefs about future punishment, had remained with the parent body. Even though a more religiously sophisticated generation of a later day might be somewhat amused at the whole controversy, and even though it brought no fundamental or earth-shaking changes in the denomination, the Restorationist episode illustrates the seriousness with which nineteenth-century Universalists took their theology. It was probably an unavoidable step in the evolution of a denomination still suffering very much from growing pains.

Christian Universalism

The second problem of theological concern to some pre-Civil War Universalists arose in the 1840s and although it created considerably less stir than had the debate over Restorationism, it involved a much more basic challenge to the Christian Universalist orthodoxy which had come to prevail. It involved, in the last analysis, the position of the Bible in the whole Universalist schema. The question emerged out of the attempt of both the General Convention and various subordinate bodies to achieve some measure of uniformity in the practice of fellowshipping and ordaining clergy and raising ministerial standards, but it had even wider implications.

In 1847 the New York Convention revised its constitution to provide explicitly that no minister would receive or retain fellowship within its jurisdiction unless he subscribed to a declaration that he believed the Bible contained "a special and sufficient revelation from God, which is the rule of Christian faith and practice."[67] This addition to the constitution produced some discussion, but it was adopted without difficulty.

When the Boston Association attempted to achieve the same result during the same year, the story was quite different. One of the principal reasons for the unexpected difficulty encountered by the committee which had been given the responsibility of drawing up a statement was the very specific commitment it entailed. It was stipulated that a Christian minister "must believe in the Bible account of the life, teachings, miracles, death and resurrection of the Lord Jesus Christ."[68] The resolution was supported by such well-known and well-established leaders as Hosea Ballou, Hosea Ballou 2d, Lucius R. Paige, Sylvanus Cobb, and Thomas Whittemore.

Immediately a substitute motion was introduced and supported by younger members of the clergy, to the effect that the Profession of Faith adopted in 1803 was "sufficient for all practical purposes, as it respects Christian belief." To them, its very ambiguity was one of its merits; a few others voted against the original resolution because they considered it unnecessary. The resolution offered by the committee was overwhelmingly adopted by both clerical and lay delegates (34 to 8, and 42 to 8, respectively), but only after prolonged debate and the unsettling discovery that five of the eight clerical delegates who voted in the negative did so because they were unwilling to subscribe totally to the Biblical account of Christ.[69] It appeared that Universalism was spawning its own heretics.

The action of the Boston Association did result in the defection of a scattering of dissidents. B.H. Clark, pastor of the society in Annisquam, resigned in 1848 because he did not believe either in the divine inspiration of the Scriptures or in revealed religion.[70] Another was Woodbury M. Fernald, who in 1848 commenced publication in Boston of the *Christian Rationalist and Theological Reformer.*[71] He rejected the credibility of miracles and considered many of both the Old and New Testament accounts to be a compound of mythology and superstition. Fernald had by then become interested in the ideas of the Swedish religious leader, Emanuel Swedenborg (1688-1772) and wrote several tracts on his ideas. Fernald was ordained as a minister in the Swedenborgian Church of the New Jerusalem.[72] Clark and Fernald were, however, exceptions to the rule. Both clergymen and laymen overwhelmingly supported the resolution adopted by the Boston Association, and the Massachusetts Convention "cordially approved" the resolution.[73] Writing some thirty years after the debate, John Greenleaf Adams believed that the action of the Boston Association was "an exceedingly proper one" and had been "the conviction of by far the greater part of our churches and congregations of professed Universalists to this hour. It was a wise, timely, honest, and faithful utterance on their part against the loose German Rationalism and speculative free-thinking and doubting then so rife in New England and elsewhere."[74]

When the General Convention in 1848 agreed upon a statement of faith to which clergy were to subscribe, it followed the pattern of the New York Convention resolution of generalized wording rather than the explicitness regarding Christ included in the controversial statement adopted by the Boston Association. State conventions and associations were to require of candidates for the ministry "the recognition and acknowledgment of the Bible as containing a special revelation from God, sufficient for faith and practice."[75]

The vast majority of Universalists, both individually and collectively, accepted the General Convention's rendition of their faith, and remained steadfast in their belief in a divinely inspired set of Scriptures and a Christ with special endowments and a special mission. Dozens of clergymen in all sections of the country continued to refer to themselves for decades as "Bible Universalists" or "Christian Universalists." The ostensible departure of a few Universalist clergymen "from the recognized standards of Christian faith" at the Boston Association meeting had prompted Horace Greeley, an acknowledged Christian Universalist but admittedly no theologian, to write an article on the subject.[76] He supported the majority, arguing that he saw no way in which those rejecting the authority of the Bible could be accommodated within the Universalist family. He considered himself a traditional Universalist, although he believed that "the proper test of Christian discipleship [was] not so much belief in the letter of the Scriptures—even in Christ's changing water into wine, or sending devils into a drove of swine—as faith in him as the real and effectual Redeemer and Savior of Mankind." At the grassroots level, a less sophisticated recognition of the importance of Scriptural authority had been reported in 1840. In the course of his travels in Michigan, a Universalist had conversed with a woman (an Episcopalian) who told him that her husband "pretended to be a Universalist" but could not become a true convert.[77] The reason, she said, was that "he won't study the Scriptures, and I find they have to understand all about the Scriptures in order to support their doctrine."

Official pronouncements of various Universalist groups continued not only to give primacy to the position of the Bible in theology but to reflect the unquestioned Christology that had permeated the thinking of such Universalist pioneers as Relly, Murray, and Winchester. The Mohawk Association (New York) refused fellowship to one D.C. O'Daniels because he admitted his lack of faith in the Bible as taught by the Protestant Christian churches, and considered it in the same light as did Voltaire, Rousseau, and Thomas Paine.[78] The Bible was, by O'Daniel's interpretation, merely the sacred book of a particular body of believers. As Sylvanus Cobb pointedly remarked, in concurring emphatically with the decision to refuse fellowship, O'Daniels was placing the Bible, the Koran, and the Veda on equal footings "as authoritative references for religious faith." This obviously would not do. The Vermont Convention specified in 1860 that all ministers fellowshipped with it had to assent in writing to a declaration that "as a denomination of professing Christians, we accept the Scriptures of the Old and New Testaments as our sufficient rule of faith and practice."[79] A quarter of a century later, the Ohio Convention unanimously adopted a resolution recognizing "the religion of the Bible, as illustrated by the teachings and life of the Lord Jesus Christ, as completely meeting the intellectual and spiritual needs of humanity."[80]

In 1848 Hosea Ballou 2d undertook to review the theological history of American Universalism up to that point.[81] He identified three periods or eras in its development, each with certain distinctive features. In the first, the foundations had been laid prior to 1805 by Winchester and Murray, based on the conception of a trinitarian deity, the vicarious character of Christ's death, and Antinomianism. The second era had been marked by the replacement or modification of previous ideas by unitarian views and by the growing acceptance of the belief that sin and its consequences were confined to mortal life. These ideas had been embodied in Hosea Ballou's landmark *Treatise on Atonement* and had been argued out in part during the Restorationist controversy. The third step in the evolution of Universalist theology emerged after 1825 and was intensified during the next few years. It was a new emphasis on "a moral connection of the present life with the future," accompanied by a general softening and dulling of the once-sharp outlines of doctrinal debate. Hosea Ballou 2d also called attention to another consideration. Parallel to these internal developments he discerned the growing influence, from outside the denomination, of "rationalistic and transcendental tendencies" to which Universalists were obliged to respond. Their reaction was negative.

Hosea Ballou 2d himself was seriously concerned about the growing popularity of German rationalism in the United States. It was, in his estimation, an attempt "to transmute Christianity from a Revelation into a merely philosophical hypothesis" and to turn Deism into Christianity.[82] This was completely unacceptable to Ballou, for it destroyed the distinctive character of Christianity as a revealed religion. Among the "tendencies" to which he alluded was the Transcendentalist movement of the 1830s and 1840s which caught the imagination of New England intellectuals (mostly Unitarian). The transcendental concept emphasized the role of intuition in the perception of reality, minimized or denied the importance of external authority and tradition, and stressed the basic divinity of man as part of a World Over-soul. Theodore Parker, a Unitarian clergyman active in the Transcendental Club organized in 1836 by George Ripley, another Unitarian clergyman, created a stir with his unorthodox religious ideas. He posited a system of theism, first publicly expressed in a sermon entitled "The Transient and Permanent in Christianity" in 1841.[83] He rejected the plenary inspiration of the Scriptures and even the necessity for church organization, and stressed the individual's capability to achieve an intuitive awareness of God.

Most Universalist clergy in the Northeast who addressed themselves to theological questions, and some laymen, unreservedly condemned both Transcendentalism and Parker's theistic-deistic views. According to Sylvanus Cobb, editor of the *Christian Freeman*, "the whole Universalist denomination . . . are behind none in their reprehension of Mr. P[arker]'s sermon as rank deism."[84] Parker's "capital offense" was "his assumption that the Christian Scriptures are *not* an authoritative *revelation* of God's truth for us." T.J. Sawyer referred sarcastically to a few Universalist clergy among the younger generation who had "precipitated themselves into the bottomless profundities of American Transcendentalism."[85] Thomas Whittemore considered Transcendentalism and "Parkerism" as "decidedly hostile to revealed religion" and averred that they were placing the Unitarians "on the high road to infidelity."[86] He continued to be upset by the "new rationalism" which seemed to be gaining a foothold. It was, he wrote in 1846, "a sad feature of our times, this falling away in reverence for the Bible . . . . We are seeking to be literary Christians, fashionable Christians, but we are not seeking to be *Bible* Christians."[87] Hosea Ballou delivered a sermon in 1847 at the General Convention which received the complete approval of the older generation of Universalists for which he had by then become the spokesman. William A. Drew, editor of the *Gospel Banner*, who heard the discourse, described it as

Thomas Baldwin Thayer (1813-1886), a leading theologian of Universalism

one of Ballou's best productions. It was "a true *Gospel* sermon—utterly annihilating all the gossamer webs that transcendentalism and other 'reform' notions have attempted to weave around the body of old-fashioned Universalism."[88]

One of the staunch defenders of Parker among Universalists was Mary A. Livermore, herself deeply involved in such reform movements as abolition, temperance, and women's rights. Recalling in the 1890s several of Parker's addresses which she had heard half a century before, she denied that he was, as claimed by many of her acquaintances at the time, "an atheist, a dishonest man, a menace to Christianity and civilization, a man of bad manners and worse morals."[89] Even though considered a religious radical and an iconoclast in his own day, he still held to "the great essentials of the Christian religion, as he regarded them." Hence no one who had actually heard him, as she had, should have been shocked. She attributed much of the odium heaped upon Parker to "his unflinching opposition to slavery, and his scathing criticism of our proslavery public men."

But Mary Livermore's was not the pevailing view among Universalists in the 1840s. Otis A. Skinner rejected Parker's ideas and held firmly to Christianity as "a supernatural revelation."[90] He could not understand how Parker could continue to be fellowshipped as a Christian minister. The Union Association of Universalists, meeting in Hardwick, Massachusetts in 1846, adopted a series of resolutions to the same effect, and declared that it would withhold fellowship from any clergyman who denied "the divine authority of Jesus Christ, and the truth of his miracles."[91]

Having presumably laid to rest any doubts about the supernatural character of the Christian drama, mid-nineteenth century Universalists turned to other matters. The emphasis in the 1840s and 1850s and for many decades to follow was placed not so much on theological speculation as on the practical and moral side of Universalism, and the translation of its principles into social action. However, the Christian basis of reform was assumed throughout. The Universalist General Reform Association, organized in 1846, recognized the word of God "and especially the New Testament Scriptures, as the basis of all genuine reforms."[92] In the strictly theological realm, explication and clarification took precedence over novel ideas.

Typical of the publications widely read by Universalists in the 1840s, and with titles indicative of major concerns, were Thomas Whittemore's *Plain Guide to Universalism* (1840), John Greenleaf Adams' *Practical Hints to Believers in the Gospel of Universal Grace and Salvation* (1840), and Henry Bacon's *Practical and Experimental Religion; or the Teachings and Tendencies of Universalism* (1842), which was explicitly advertised by the author as "not a controversial work."[93] A popular manual published in 1844 was E.E. Guild's

Universalist Book of Reference. The author, without himself engaging in polemics, outlined in tabular form the "Pro and Con, on the Great Controversy between Limitarians and Universalists."

The most thorough and systematic treatment of Universalist theology before the Civil War was Thomas Baldwin Thayer's *Theology of Universalism,* published in 1862.[94] Although he included "liberal quotations from Fathers of the early Church" to demonstrate the antiquity of universalism, Thayer, unlike Hosea Ballou 2d in his earlier *Ancient History of Universalism* (1829), devoted the bulk of his 432-page treatise to Scriptural rather than historical foundations of denominational belief.[95] Most important, the "Universalist Christian" could claim that his faith had "all the characteristics of a divinely authenticated religion; that it is, in a word, identical with the Gospel as taught by the Savior and his chosen disciples" (p. 14).

Christian Universalism received no clearer expression than in 1866, when the newly incorporated Board of Trustees of the General Convention adopted an official seal. It bore the device of a Bible, surmounted by a cross, over which was the legend "Christ will Conquer."[96] The seal was first displayed in the official records of the denomination in 1870, as part of the title page of the printed minutes of the General Convention for 1869. Such was the confidence, conviction, and comfort, the hope and faith, of nineteenth-century Universalism.

Chapter 7

BECOMING A CHURCH: THE UNIVERSALIST GENERAL CONVENTION

Much of the time spent in annual meetings of the General Convention between its establishment in 1833 and the Civil War was devoted to systematizing the internal operations of that body, the setting up of machinery for improved communication, and the gathering of denominational statistics. The amount of activity and the number of delegates and visitors at convention meetings had become sufficiently great by the mid-1830s to raise the possibility of extending meetings beyond the customary two-day period. Some felt that there were too many sermons (an average of six each session) and too few opportunities to transact business; a plea was made "to repress this desire for preaching" which seemed to prevail among the clergy.[1]

There was also concern that convention meetings were becoming little more than social occasions. At the 1838 session, described by a participant as one of the most "exhilarating & glorious occasions" yet attended, there were only 24 clerical delegates but over 120 clergymen present, with over 800 people at public services. It seemed to some that so little was being accomplished by 1846 that a proposal was made to amend the convention constitution to provide biennial rather than annual meetings.[2] It was clear that the majority of the convention did not agree, for the motion was tabled indefinitely.[3] In 1850 another complaint was registered about insufficient time to deliberate. By that date, the practice of introducing resolutions had become widespread, and many were either tabled or hastily passed without adequate discussion.[4] The following year, a standing Committee on Resolutions was created to prepare subjects for consideration, to be published at least three months in advance of each meeting. It was finally determined to leave the length of annual sessions open, and not to adjourn until the necessary business had been considered.[5]

One of the recurring difficulties faced by the convention was poor attendance and inadequate representation. In 1836 only forty-three of the seventy authorized delegates were present.[6] Time and expense were considered the chief deterrents to satisfactory attendance, and state conventions and associations were urged to make arrangements to defray all or part of the expenses of delegates. A "denominational fund," to be administered by the General Convention, was proposed in 1857, part of it to be collected and expended for this purpose, but in the end the responsibility was shifted to the local societies. In 1837 only five state conventions sent delegates to the meeting in Philadelphia, and there was a full complement from only two. This prompted the General Convention to assure the state organizations that even though they were unable to send the number of clerical delegates (four) authorized for each state convention, those that did attend would have all the rights of membership (including voting) provided in the constitution.[7]

The legal status of delegates often provoked discussion and debate. When a code of bylaws had been adopted in 1834 under the "new organization," a provision was included that neither clerical nor lay delegates could serve as proxies for the other.[8] The convention the following year also prohibited persons from serving as delegates from one state if they resided in another, or resided in a state in which no convention had been organized.[9] This policy raised the particular ire of L.F.W. Andrews of Alabama, the only clergyman who attended that year from the South. He considered such rulings undesirable; they made for "too much exclusiveness."[10] He was also incensed because non-delegates like himself were required to obtain special permission by a vote of the Council in order to speak from the floor. The convention in 1838 finally ruled that clergymen from states with no convention were to be admitted automatically as "honorary" members of the Council, but whether or not that carried voting privileges as well as the automatic right to speak, remained a moot question.[11]

Most of these and other questions regarding the status of delegates had to be raised on many subsequent occasions, for the constitution adopted in 1855 provided merely that the Council of the General Convention would be the judge of the qualifications of its own members. In 1858 it denied the request of a preacher from Kentucky to be seated on the Council; he claimed the right by virtue of election as a delegate the previous year. The convention denied itself any constitutional power to elect its own delegates; that power belonged "strictly" to the several state conventions.[12] If they neglected to attend to their duty, they would perforce go unrepresented.

Although some progress had been made by the General Convention in conducting its internal affairs and attending to other matters that fell within its limited province, a much more fundamental difficulty had to be faced and overcome. Universalism had grown sufficiently in numbers, strength, and complexity by the 1840s and 1850s to reveal the inadequacy of the church polity that had been established in 1833. In fact, the principal organizational problem faced between that date and 1865 was to prevent the centrifugal tendencies that had always been present from overwhelming the denomination and threatening its very identity and cohesion as a religious body.

Those most concerned considered the strengthening of the General Convention the heart of the matter, and devoted their efforts to that end. The task of shifting the locus of power to a central authority was a slow and difficult process, and even after a revised constitution was adopted in 1855 which did make the General Convention somewhat more than a name, the denomination was reluctant to advance much beyond the concept of confederation in its organization. It was not until 1865 that the transition to federalism and beyond was completed by means of significant amendments to the "fundamental law" of what was by then coming to be more and more identified with the term "Church" as conventionally used. Universalism seemed to be losing whatever distinctiveness it might have possessed organizationally as a working example of congregational church polity carried to its logical conclusion.

The General Convention, equipped with nothing more than advisory powers, made no effort to exercise even that restricted function until 1838. The only real business transacted that year was a request that state conventions "respect the official acts of discipline of each sister Convention."[13] In order to get some sort of guidance, as well as to achieve some measure of uniformity, the Miami Association (Ohio) took the initiative. In 1841 it prepared and distributed a circular to all conventions and associations requesting that they instruct their delegates to the General Convention to provide a model constitution, plan of church compact, and "course of discipline" for the use of conventions, associations, and societies.[14] The Ohio Convention, at its meeting in 1842, repeated the request, and reiterated in a strongly worded set of resolutions, the need for establishing and enforcing rules of "strict discipline" over ministers, especially in regard to fellowshipping.[15]

Between 1803, when the New England Convention first dealt with a case involving clerical discipline, and 1833, when the General Convention turned over the bulk of such cases to the associations and state conventions, the New England Convention found itself faced with numerous instances of departure from accepted behavior which required some kind of action.[16] In the interim period, all jurisdictions interchangeably exercised disciplinary powers, with no clear line of demarcation. In 1820 an individual's letter of fellowship was summarily rejected by the New England Convention on grounds of "immoral deportment."[17] More precisely, he had failed to pay his debts, and had been deceitful regarding his religious views; he pretended to be a Universalist but all the while actually believed in "endless misery." A decade later, the Southern Association (New England) at first found it necessary to disavow any connection with one George W. Brooks, who had been fellowshipped originally by the New England Convention (1822) but became a source of contention among several associations.[18] He was accused (among other things) of passing counterfeit money, but in spite of that was given provisional candidacy for full fellowship by the Southern Association (New England) in 1831. The explanation for this somewhat unusual action derived from the fact that the society in New Marlboro, Massachusetts, expressed a desire for his presumably religious ministrations.[19]

After 1833 most of the recorded cases of ministerial discipline were to be found at the state convention level. Some bodies, such as the Vermont Convention, used the devices of "censure" and "disapprobation" as weapons, usually accompanied by a probationary period of six to twelve months to allow the guilty parties an opportunity to mend their ways. One individual who had been charged on several counts of "unministerial and unchristian conduct" had, after six months, not only given "no evidence of his penitence or reformation," but had treated the committee on discipline "with silent contempt."[20] He was consequently both disfellowshipped and read out of the denomination. Another preacher operating in Vermont, who received a note of "disapprobation," was charged "with setting at defiance the laws of the State by marrying a woman in Northfield, while he had a wife living in the State of New York from whom he had not been legally divorced."[21] The accused declined to appear before the convention to answer the allegations because in the meantime he had moved to Massachusetts, where actions were already pending as to his ministerial respectability. A preacher was disfellowshipped by the St. Lawrence Association (New York) for "disgraceful behavior" which turned out to have been the practice of forgery. But the action of the association against him was only an empty gesture, for it was discovered that he had left not only the state but the country.[22]

Of all the temptations which beset clergymen (as well as laymen) in rural areas, excessive use of alcoholic beverages seems to have been the most prevalent. There were dozens of preachers like the one fellowshipped by the Western Association (New York) who lost standing because "the proofs sustaining the charge of *intemperance,* were abundant and conclusive."[23] For the most part, disciplinary action reflected sympathy and forbearing, and provision was made for a probationary period before fellowship was withdrawn. Such was the case of one J.A. Bartlett, suspended from the fellowship of the Maine Convention for one year, with the promise of restoration if he abstained from the use of "alcoholic and narcotic stimulants" for that length of time.[24] In some instances other complications entered into the picture. The Genesee Association (New York) suspended a preacher for "intoxication and intemperance" but voted not to withdraw fellowship when he promised to reform.[25] Many Universalists in

Fredonia (where the case had originated) refused to accept the association's decision to suspend, on the grounds that it was too harsh a penalty under the known circumstances, and that the accused had never been notified that his case would be considered; he was therefore not present to defend himself.[26] The objections were sufficiently convincing to result in a cancelling of the suspension and a public admission of error on the part of the association.[27]

Unfortunate as the publicity might have been for the parties concerned, there was a sincere attempt by Universalist organizations to mete out justice. One New Hampshire preacher was accused of having "a pernicious and uncontrolled propensity to run into debt," one of eight counts brought against him.[28] But the charges were dismissed because they were not sufficiently substantiated. Further, the special "ecclesiastical council" which handled the case added the consoling footnote that running into debt was "no crime in itself."

Jurisdictional disputes regarding discipline took up an almost disproportionate part of some Universalist gatherings. The Maine Convention in 1844 declared that the ordination of a minister by the Penobscot Association was "null and void" because only the state convention exercised such power.[29] In the same state two years later two preachers were publicly censured by the convention for having conferred ordination on two others without consulting anyone. The Universalist society in Bangor was "severely reprimanded" in 1851 for ordaining a clergyman on their own initiative; he was not even in fellowship with the state convention. The propensity of preachers disfellowshipped in one jurisdiction—or never fellowshipped at all—to claim such was a chronic problem. The Genesee Association (New York) seemed to have been especially plagued with this sort of clerical waywardness. It repudiated one individual for "unministerial conduct" after it was discovered that he had "by some unaccountable means," been fellowshipped by the Northern Association (Vermont).[30] That association had withdrawn fellowship (for reasons unspecified) but had neglected either to request the return of the letter of fellowship or to inform New York Universalists of his lack of ministerial good standing when he migrated to that state. It was situations such as these that the Ohio Convention hoped to avoid with its call for uniformity of standards among the conventions and associations.

A related problem for which there were no uniform procedures was the handling of voluntary withdrawals from the ministry by individuals who still remained Universalists. The lack of any systematic communication within the denomination often created misunderstandings and sometimes did serious disservice to individuals who left the ministry for quite legitimate personal reasons—health, family commitments, financial difficulty, or decision to engage in a secular occupation. Other Universalists (and particularly newspaper editors) immediately started to speculate on the "real" reasons and created all kinds of doubts and suspicions.

Sometimes the clergy themselves were at fault in leaving incorrect impressions. Such was the case of Daniel D. Smith, who had sent in his resignation to the clerk of the Massachusetts Convention with the request that it not be published. Because he continued to preach in the state, and because he was the brother of the controversial Matthew Hale Smith, so many rumors began to circulate that Daniel Smith's resignation was finally made public.[31] Smith had served briefly in 1835 as editor of the *Universalist and Ladies' Repository,* published in Boston, and in 1842 moved to Richmond, Virginia, where he edited the first two volumes of the *Christian Warrior* (1842-1844). It seemed clear that some system needed to be agreed upon for informing the denomination at large of such withdrawals, of the reasons therefor, and of the character of those concerned; this was particularly important if they decided at some later date (as many of them did) to return to the ministry and to seek fellowship in another jurisdiction than the one in which they had previously served.

A case originating in the 1830s and extending into the next decade, although admittedly extreme, rather dramatically illustrated the difficulties faced by Universalists in enforcing discipline and in maintaining communication. It had, in fact, precipitated the request of the Ohio Convention in 1842 for uniform rules. The problem centered around a Robert Smith who, as one contemporary expressed it, "caused not a little trouble for several years past."[32] In 1834 Smith had had charges brought against him by the Connecticut State Convention alleging "falsehood, deception, and hypocrisy utterly incompatible with the principles of the Gospel."[33] His fellowship had been suspended until his case could be settled; a decision was postponed the next year because he failed to appear. It turned out that he had meanwhile moved west as a travelling preacher, claimed to have been fellowshippped by the Miami Association (Ohio), and had been employed by Samuel Tizzard, an editor of the denominational *Sentinel and Star in the West,* who knew nothing of the charges brought against Smith.[34]

When Smith returned to Connecticut to defend himself at the state convention in 1836, he was found guilty of the charges and his fellowship was withdrawn by a unanimous vote.[35] It appeared that the principal count against him was having passed himself off as a bachelor when in fact he had a wife and at least two children.[36] He had considered his grounds for separation from his family quite justified, and saw no reason to take the trouble of legalizing his action. In addition to his domestic complications, Smith was involved in a series of questionable business transactions in the newspaper field. After having lost his position with the *Sentinel,* he appeared in Baltimore and became a partner in the operation of the *Southern Pioneer and Gospel*

Visitor. After the paper went bankrupt in 1836, due in part to his mismanagement, Smith tried to collect subscriptions for the defunct paper and allegedly pocketed them for "his own private purposes."[37]

In spite of all this unconventional behavior, Smith challenged the decision to disfellowship him; although he admitted "impropriety and indiscretion" in his actions, he denied any criminal conduct sufficient to remove him from the ministry, and in 1836 appealed to Universalists in general through the press to disregard the decision and to allow him a fair hearing.[38] He also filed a complaint with the General Convention in 1836, but was told that it had no jurisdiction and no authority to hear cases from state conventions.[39]

The Ohio Convention then took up Smith's case, inasmuch as he was still a resident of that state. After a most thorough and prolonged investigation, the convention disfellowshipped him in 1841.[40] But he challenged that action at the convention meeting the following year, on jurisdictional grounds. He argued that in Ohio, only the associations had the right to grant or withdraw fellowship, and in this he was technically correct.[41] His claim to have been fellowshipped at various times by both the Miami Association and the Western Union Association could not be substantiated, but all the Ohio Convention could do under the circumstances was to make the declaration that Smith, as of 1842, was not in fellowship with the denomination in Ohio, as a minister, and that he was "acting on his own responsibility." They had no authority to withdraw fellowship.[42]

It was probably cases like Smith's that prompted the Pennsylvania Convention that same year to warn its constituency against imposters claiming to be Universalist preachers.[43] The Susquehanna Association (Pennsylvania) amended its constitution in 1843 to require the committee on fellowship and ordination to make a thorough investigation of the soundness of faith and requisite qualifications of all candidates.[44] This was necessary because so many persons desirous of entering the Universalist ministry were coming from other denominations, "some of whom prove to be imposters, or destitute of the vital principles and knowledge of our faith, and whose influence is sickly and deleterious to our prosperity."

Almost every association or state convention had one or more such cases brought to its attention. In 1843 the Illinois Convention was forced to deny any denominational connection with one Levi Chase who, after gaining an unsavory reputation as a peddler in southeastern Massachusetts, deserted his family, migrated to Illinois, and set himself up as an "Independent Universalist."[45] Without any authorization whatever, he established societies, attended meetings (at one of which he was even chosen moderator), and palmed off the sermons of others as his own. As William S. Balch, who attended the convention as a guest from the East put it, it was "a pity that some precaution cannot be exercised to spare our infant denomination from the odium brought upon it by unworthy and unqualified men;" there was too much "looseness in our mode of discipline."

It was clear that growing pressure was being put on the General Convention to do something to regularize denominational affairs. As the author of the Circular Letter in 1842 pointed out, the lack even of guidelines—let alone uniform rules—made a denomination with 12 state conventions, 59 associations, and over 500 clergy "an anomaly in the religious world."[46] Such casualness about so vital a matter as organization ought not be tolerated. Nothing was accomplished, however, until 1843, when the General Convention met for the first time in the Midwest (Akron, Ohio). It was a tumultuous meeting. There were such large gatherings and such "confusion, delay, and unnecessary waste of time" that the business sessions were spread over five days. It was estimated that total attendance at public services was 5,000; in order to accommodate the crowds, the windows on one side of the church being used had to be removed, and the listening area extended with a tent cloth.[47]

Thomas J. Sawyer was given the monumental responsibility of drafting "a plan of organization for the Universalist denomination" to be presented at the next meeting.[48] He approached his task with great determination and prepared his recommendations with equally great thoroughness. He indicated when he presented his lengthy report in 1844, that the relationship between the General Convention and its constituencies, and the exact powers of the local units, had to be clarified and decided before model constitutions or even rules and regulations for the conduct of General Convention business could be considered. Sawyer expressed his own long-felt conviction, which was shared by at least some other members of the denomination in positions of responsibility, that a better organization was needed, "and especially . . . a more uniform and more wholesome Discipline" than it then possessed. At the same time, he foresaw the probable difficulties "in introducing and carrying out any new measures involving considerable changes, however important and just."[49]

In a long historical preface to his recommendations, Sawyer pointed out several matters of which he thought Universalists should be reminded. First, unlike most other denominations, Universalism in America had not been transplanted as a well-defined organization from the Old World. It was not a branch or extension of an existing body. In some ways, Universalists were fortunate not to have had a "Mother church;" it was, as it had developed over the years, "of native, rather than foreign origin." Murray was neither the originator nor sole leader, as was the case with John Wesley among the Methodists or George Fox among the Quakers. Murray had been neither the first to preach Universalism in America, nor the systematizer of its faith. His great contribution, said Sawyer, had been to call attention to the subject and to create an awareness that Christ had died for all, not for a select few. Only a few traces of Murray's specific teachings were recognized by mid-nineteenth-century Universalists, and he had not "the slightest influence" on the organization and government of the denomination.[50]

Sawyer put much stress on the fact that, because of historic circumstances, Universalists had been left free to develop their own faith and polity, neither of which was the product of any single individual. Further, what had developed was the result of a felt need or "some exigency of the times." As Sawyer put it, "our fathers have wisely seemed willing to defer to the future what the future might require, and were satisfied if they could perform what was called for by the present." Hence it was to be expected that the first societies would be not only local in character but independent of all other groups. When the first association was organized in Oxford, Massachusetts, it was to meet an emergency, and exercised no powers in such important areas as fellowshipping and ordaining ministers, establishing an ecclesiastical structure, or enforcing religious discipline. It was, for example, the local society in Gloucester rather than some other higher echelon which had re-ordained Murray in 1788. When associations did develop, out of which some state conventions had emerged, they exercised powers coordinate with the New England Convention, while at the same time expressing a vague feeling of deference—"a kind of parental relation"—for what was then the central body.

Sawyer considered the roughly stair-step arrangement, pragmatically arrived at over the years, as "a beautiful organization" which could not be improved "by any outward modification." The "regular gradation" from the society or church up to the General Convention, "from the individual to the whole," could scarcely be improved upon. But it was "mere form" on the outside. Internally, there were serious difficulties besetting this outwardly symmetrical structure. When the relationships of these various strata of organization were examined closely, at the operational level, matters were actually in a "chaotic state." There was no real bond of union among the state conventions; no court of appeal for them in case differences arose; no means by which the actions of one were respected by the others. Preachers disfellowshipped or otherwise subjected to discipline by one convention turned up in another—as had been graphically illustrated by the Smith case in Ohio.

Ironically, the General Convention, as Sawyer insistently emphasized, had the least power of any organized group within the denomination—in fact, no powers at all beyond giving advice. This was also the prerogative of any individual Universalist. The General Convention, in Sawyer's view, was "a sad approximation to a mere nullity." Adopting measures for the "general welfare" was an exercise in futility so long as no one felt bound to observe them. Of all the problems, the lack of uniformity in the rules and regulations for fellowshipping and ordaining clergy was the most obvious and the most damaging to the Universalist cause. There were almost as many practices as there were state conventions and associations. The qualifications required for each therefore tended to drop to the lowest denominator. This had an obvious negative effect on the reputation that Universalism enjoyed in the community at large.

Sawyer's solution was to give to the General Convention the sole authority to issue licenses to preach and to ordain ministers. After all, Universalist clergy represented the entire denomination, not one church or a single locality. Sawyer hoped that the almost pathological fear of centralization and even of organization that had prevailed when the General Convention had been created had dissipated sufficiently by the 1840s to allow Universalists to "talk like rational beings who suppose that a social existence is possible." Perhaps they could each relinquish at least a little of their "absolute independence" in the interests of denominational order and progress. So the solution was not complete reorganization but the reassessment of the power and jurisdiction of each level of the structure, with mutual concessions along the line. A coherent chain of command was indispensable.

Sawyer was also dissatisfied with the basis of representation in the General Convention. Each state convention was entitled to the same number of delegates and an equal voice in its deliberations, regardless of how many Universalists or how many societies, churches, or associations existed within its boundaries. This might be of no great moment as long as the General Convention had no real powers, but it was still "unequal and unjust." In 1843, for example, Massachusetts had roughly four times as many societies and ministers as Pennsylvania, yet had the same number of seats in the General Convention. The cases of Rhode Island and New York were similar; the proportion as between them was twenty-two to one. A more equitable system of representation was obviously a desideratum to Sawyer.

The proposals Sawyer offered for delimiting the powers of the various levels were based on the assumption that the General Convention "ought to represent *the whole denomination* of Universalists" and because of this should have "exclusive jurisdiction" over all matters of common concern. Universalists could not continue to suppose that a society, an association, or a state convention had "a right to do what it pleases" and still claim to belong to a distinctive body of believers; otherwise, there was no such thing as a denomination. Sawyer's recommendations were consistent with his conception of a pyramidal structure with a General Convention at the top exercising real power over subordinate parts for the general good. Original jurisdiction, according to his plan, would have been placed in the General Convention regarding fellowshipping and ordaining, including the establishment of the qualifications required. That body could then delegate the actual process to state conventions and associations, but under its ultimate control. The General Convention would also have temporary jurisdiction over all societies and associations in states or territories (including "foreign states or provinces") where conventions had not yet been created, and which sought its fellowship. The supreme body was also to be given power to determine its own basis of representation.

Finally, the General Convention was to be the "ultimate tribunal" to which all disputes between or among state conventions would be brought, and which would receive and take final action on all appeals from decisions of state conventions, including cases involving withdrawal of fellowship. Similarly, state conventions were to have jurisdiction over associations within their boundaries, and have such supervisory power over fellowship and ordination, as well as general religious discipline, as provided by the General Convention. Conventions would also be the proper tribunals to which to bring disputes within their respective jurisdictions, with final judgment except where appeal to the General Convention was provided. The ratio of representation in the associations was to be determined by the appropriate state conventions. The same general chain of authority was provided for associations in their relations with societies, churches, and ministers, including the fellowshipping and ordaining of ministers in accordance with prescriptions laid down at higher levels. The authority to disfellowship was given to the associations, with the right of appeal by the aggrieved party. To societies were left all the powers of an independent body, including appointment and dismissal of their own pastors.

Neither the General Convention in 1844 nor most Universalists in general (or at least those who expressed their views on the subject) were ready to take up the challenge offered by Sawyer. The Massachusetts Convention was one of the very few bodies which attempted to take action within the next two years. In order to remedy the basic defect of its lack of power over fellowshipping and discipline and of the lack of any organic connection between the local associations and the state convention, a proposal was offered in 1844 to revise the constitution. The new version would have provided that no association was to admit to fellowship any minister or society rejected by any other association in the state, except with the concurrence of the state convention.[51] However, no further action was taken at the time.

The General Convention in 1845 went no further than to adopt the first of Sawyer's recommendations—a generalized statement that "the United States Convention has jurisdiction over the several State Conventions," including the right to enact rules governing relations among conventions. But the statement carried little force, for it was hedged about by such tentative words as "may" and "might." Universalists had to wait almost a decade before the General Convention attempted to implement the bulk of Sawyer's recommendations, and even then with some compromises and modifications which fell short of his goal of true power for what he conceived to be a desirable central authority.

The most outspoken opposition to Sawyer's proposal, couched in the most extreme language, came from Jonathan Kidwell, who was busy at the time publishing a newspaper in Philomath, Indiana, and expressing his Jacksonian democracy vociferously. Sawyer's plan, to Kidwell, was all part of a conspiracy—a device for creating a "religious aristocracy" by the high-handed and unscrupulous tactics of a few power-hungry ecclesiastics.[52] The plan was "a child of iniquity" which made "a perfect mockery" of religious liberty. Any attempt, according to Kidwell, to force uniformity was "an open violation of the order of nature, and the sacred religious rights of man." If only half a dozen individuals organized a society and called themselves Universalists, they had "an inherent right to establish that kind of government which meets their own interests and convenience, and no other organized body of men have a right to hunt them out and put a yoke upon their necks."

Kidwell's fierce and uncompromising independence was obviously shared by other Universalists in Indiana. The Montgomery Association vigorously resolved to oppose Sawyer's plan, or any other that would strengthen the General Convention at the expense of local units.[53] The association instructed its three delegates to the state convention in 1845 to act accordingly, and to make sure there would be no misunderstanding, a copy of the resolution was appended to the certificate of each delegate. The Western Union Association adopted resolutions the same year opposing any strengthening of the General Convention. The clerk of the association triumphantly reported that it had done much "in knocking the horns off of the calf we have been called upon to worship . . . . not a Universalist belonging to this Association will bow the knee to Baal."[54]

The Indiana Convention, which had been organized in 1837, was not even fellowshipped by the General Convention until 1848. Every attempt made by various members of the state convention even to request fellowship before then had been defeated. A motion at the 1844 state convention to do so had been "thrown *under* the table" in spite of an amendment offered by Kidwell that the convention would in no way relinquish any of its rights of self-government.[55] There was so much fear of "religious aristocracy" at any level that an attempt was made at the same time even to exclude all clerical participants whatsoever in the state convention. This would have meant that laymen would have been required to deliver all the sermons as well as conduct convention business, and even a pronounced democrat like Kidwell would not go that far.

At the Indiana Convention in 1845, which met a month before the General Convention, Kidwell had presented a set of resolutions unequivocally opposing Sawyer's proposal for a strengthened General Convention. Although they were tabled, the resolutions were pointedly made a part of the state convention record at Kidwell's request.[56] They denied absolutely the power of the General Convention or any other ecclesiastical body to assume any jurisdiction whatsoever over faith or conscience, "inasmuch as every individual is accountable to God, in these matters, in his own proper person, and not by proxy." No convention of any kind anywhere had "the right to legislate, prescribe, or proscribe in matters of faith and conscience." Any attempt "to establish and enforce any uniform church compact is injudicious, unwise, and an open violation of our religious and moral rights." The last of Kidwell's nine resolutions on the subject provided that no delegates would be sent to the General Convention from Indiana unless and until proper safeguards for self-government "and all other rights belonging to christians" were guaranteed.

The fact that the Indiana Convention had not yet applied for fellowship in the General Convention and sent no delegates anyway did little to strengthen Kidwell's case, and apparently failed to create consternation in the ranks of the General Convention. At the local level, his threat did have the desired result; even though his resolutions were not officially adopted, the state convention again refused to appoint delegates to the General Convention or request fellowship. If by any mischance delegates had been appointed, Kidwell had in readiness an amendment which would have given the state convention power to nullify any action of the General Convention which was not to the liking of the Indiana Convention.

Kidwell's language became even more intemperate after he had read the minutes of the 1845 General Convention and discovered that it had actually adopted part of Sawyer's plan. Kidwell considered it an "iniquitous presumption and barefaced deception . . . an outrage upon the liberty and good sense of the Universalist community!"[57] He called upon Universalists in the South and West to declare their independence from such an affront to their "right of self-government." Regardless of who won, it was the eastern Universalists, in Kidwell's estimation, who were the real schismatics—"the innovators . . . determined to establish a new order of things." It was Universalists who believed as did Kidwell that occupied "the original ground." They were the preservators of true Universalism according to his reading of denominational history. And it was precisely the kind of blatant and unrestrained Universalism that Kidwell expressed that Sawyer was trying to modify in the interests of denominational order and progress.

Between 1845 and 1855 the General Convention continued to struggle, in sporadic fashion, with the knotty problem of its own authority as well as with the discipline within the denomination as a whole. That body had, several years before, given up the practice of fellowshipping and ordaining directly, leaving it to state conventions and associations. The General Convention in 1853 denied a request by an individual for fellowship on the grounds that it had no power to grant such. Yet the General Convention continued to decline to establish rules regarding either ordination or fellowshipping.

In 1846, at the same time that an unsuccessful attempt was made to repeal the amendment giving the General Convention jurisdiction over state conventions, a committee was appointed to draft rules governing these matters and to provide a model constitution for societies and churches, but it failed to report. The General Convention in 1847 saw fit only to caution conventions and associations not to accept as preachers any individuals "unfitted by their principles or their conduct" for clerical responsibilities.[58] Some progress was made in 1848, when the General Convention adopted rules that provided at least minimum uniform requirements for fellowship and the issuing of licenses to preach. Every such candidate was to acknowledge the Bible "as containing a special revelation from God, sufficient for faith and practice" and declare his intention "to devote himself to the works of the ministry."[59] A penalty was also attached for any convention or association which refused to acknowledge these rules as a requirement: They were not to be entitled to "the fellowship or privileges of this Convention." Ministers in good standing who transferred from one jurisdiction to another were also to be given certificates to that effect.

The handling of cases of clergy accused of immoral or unministerial conduct was more complicated, and in 1848 Hosea Ballou 2d, who four years before had delivered a widely reprinted sermon on the need for tighter church organization, found himself appointed as a one-man committee to recommend proper judicial procedures; they were adopted the following year. However, the problem of what to do in cases where state conventions and/or associations disagreed among themselves remained unresolved. In 1848 one such disagreement arose between the Pennsylvania and New Jersey Conventions over a disciplinary case which had originated in the Philadelphia Association. The General Convention, to which the case was appealed, recommended merely that the two state conventions resolve the dispute with a special joint committee. Two years later, the case was still not settled, and the General Convention again declined to accept direct jurisdiction.[60]

By 1853 so many amendments to the constitution and bylaws of the General Convention had been suggested, and so many jurisdictional problems regarding fellowship and ministerial discipline had arisen, that a committee was appointed to present an omnibus plan "for the more perfect organization of the denomination."[61] The committee, on reviewing the events of the previous decade, was as firmly convinced as Sawyer had been that there was still a lamentable lack of uniformity in authority and practice among and within the state conventions, and that something had to be done.[62] The committee reported that the traditional independence of thought and action among Universalists had to be modified for the common good; this could still be done without sacrificing the historic American idea of personal rights or religious liberty or relinquishing the congregational polity historically practiced by Universalists. The best the General Convention seemed able to do (in 1852) was to affirm the desirability of a policy whereby the actions of one convention should be considered binding on all others. The General Convention scrupulously avoided taking any action "which should interfere with the exercise of all the powers invested in the several State Conventions."[63]

The new constitution proposed in 1854 and adopted unanimously in 1855, followed the recommendations made a decade earlier by Sawyer in spirit only. It was a brief document and not the elaborate and detailed spelling out of relationships among the various components which he had suggested. As might have been predicted, the greatest discussion was over the powers to be exercised by the General Convention. The net effect was to reaffirm the general jurisdiction of that body over the state conventions and to make it a court of final appeal in cases of conflict. After a three-year delay, the General Convention finally adopted two sets of regulations, "enacted" in accordance with its new constitutional powers. One regulated "the jurisdiction of the several State Conventions in matters of Discipline" and the other established "a uniform system of Appeals from the Decisions of State Conventions to this body in cases of Discipline."[64] In 1859 the first act was amended to include associations.[65] A year later, the General Convention handed down a series of rulings to untangle the jurisdictional knot which had developed in New Jersey between the state convention and the Philadelphia and New York Associations which claimed overlapping jurisdiction over various societies.[66]

An explicit disclaimer over interfering with matters of religious faith was included in the new constitution, and the Winchester Profession of 1803 was repeated. The basis of representation was also made more equitable, so that state conventions were entitled to delegates roughly in proportion to the number of societies and clergymen within their boundaries; the two-to-one ratio of laymen to clergymen was retained. The new constitution was declared in force when adopted by the General Convention in 1855, an article requiring the ratification by at least ten state conventions having been stricken out in 1854. A new set of bylaws was adopted in 1856, the first in over twenty years. The new "Rules of Order" did include one important innovation: Standing committees on the State of the Church, Education, Sunday Schools, and Complaints and Appeals were created. The need for the first committee was made evident by the growth of the denomination; the second and third bore witness to expanded fields of concern and commitment; and the fourth was an acknowledgement that the General Convention had taken on a new set of judicial responsibilities.

One provision in the new constitution extended the jurisdiction of the General Convention (if requested) to associations, preachers, or societies "in foreign States or Provinces" where no convention had been organized. The wording following that suggested by Sawyer in 1844, and reflected the fact that some Universalists in Canada were already members of at least one state convention and that there might be others who desired affiliation with their neighbors in the United States. The Universalist Convention of Vermont and the Province of Quebec had been organized in 1833 and was incorporated in 1888; in 1937 it was redesignated as "The Vermont and Quebec Universalist Unitarian Convention." A proposal had, in fact, been made in 1843 to change the official title of the General Convention to "The General Convention of Universalists in North America," but it was never acted on.[67]

Dissatisfaction continued to exist at General Convention meetings in the late 1850s over the lack of "cohesive power" in the denomination. I.D. Williamson, chairman of the newly created standing committee on the State of the Church, told the convention in 1858 that the situation called more "for prayer than thanksgiving."[68] From the societies and churches, "loose and imperfect in their organization," up through the General Convention, the framework was "sadly defective, . . . lacking an efficient denominational unity." He recognized that earnest efforts had been made in recent years "to gather up the scattered fragments of our fraternity, and mould them into one body," but the result had been failure. Perhaps, said Williamson, the problem was insoluble, given "the great Protestant principle of the right of private judgment, and the individual responsibility of each and every man to God, and to God alone" which Universalists espoused. Possibly the only solution was to abandon the entire attempt to operate through associations and conventions, and return to "the purely Congregational basis" from which Universalists had departed in theory but insisted in maintaining in practice. Could the denomination have it both ways? Williamson much preferred to see the existing church bodies invested with greater authority, and the General Convention especially, "elevated to the dignity of the head of the denomination." On behalf of his committee, he therefore rejected a series of proposed "declaratory resolutions" offered in 1857 by a delegate from the Maine Convention which would, in effect, have returned all power to individual societies, which would be held together only by common Christian fellowship. Williamson believed that such extreme congregationalism would mean the end of the denomination.

A resolution was offered at the same General Convention meeting to sound out the entire Universalist body on the path it should take: "Is it desirable to continue our existing system of Organization, or abolish it entirely, and adopt the plan of simple Congregationalism in our future religious operations?"[69] The committee on the State of the Church took up the challenge and presented a comprehensive report that in turn was commended to the attention of the entire denomination. Ministers were requested to read the report "at an early day" to their congregations, and another committee was appointed "to correspond with the several state conventions with regard to the matter of a more complete organization" as set forth in the report.[70] In order to assure wide distribution, provision was made to print and publish extra copies of the convention proceedings, and a collection was taken up for the purpose.

Elbridge Gerry Brooks, who made the report for the committee, went over much the same retrospective ground covered by Sawyer fifteen years earlier, and came to the conclusion that the denomination had fallen somehow between the two stools of "complete congregationalism" and a "systematic and effective organization."[71] It had adopted "the name and some of the forms of organization, but nothing of the thing itself." It was time to move from heterogeneity to homogeneity, reflecting the growing maturity of Universalism, which was described as "the advance party of Protestantism." The committee came down unequivocally on the side of "organization." The convention was told that any other course would be dangerous, if not fatal.

Brooks was very upset in 1860 when he heard that Universalists in the Chicago area were contemplating the establishment of a Northwest Conference. The result, he feared, would be the separation of eastern and western Universalists and the creation of "a double-headed and double-hearted denomination."[72] He was positive that the General Convention and the proposed midwestern organization would "inevitably" become rivals and pose a threat to denominational unity and strength. The General Convention, Brooks argued, should be able to hold funds and accept bequests; have a central publishing facility; and be "a live central body" and not merely a court of appeal. He called for a reorganization that would make the state conventions as well as the General Convention more than "names and shadows."

Brooks called for more positive action in other areas as well, citing the accomplishments of other denominations in record-keeping, support of Sunday Schools (considered "incidental, as a mere side-interest" by most Universalists), and the organization of churches, as distinct from societies. He noted with approval the organizational success of the Methodists, particularly in the field of ecclesiastical administration; and the attention given by the Roman Catholics and Episcopalians to the intimate and inseparable relation of their children to the church. He called very forthrightly for a plan to organize "the Universalist Church," fully as institutionalized as other religious bodies, and as frankly sectarian as they. The aggressive "denominational public spirit" to be found among "the so-called evangelical sects" was so lacking among Universalists as "to shame us for our short-comings." The rampant individualism and haphazardness of an earlier day had to give way to a new "social necessity and obligation." Disciplined organization, "the orderly exercise of liberty," was the key to success.

The theme of denominational distinctiveness emphasized by Brooks was echoed in the 1861 report of the committee on the State of the Church, of which John Greenleaf Adams was chairman. A "family interest" binding Universalists together was more effective in promoting the cause than attempting to enroll everyone under the banner of religious liberalism and attempting to embrace every idea current at the moment, from "an improved orthodoxy as the one extreme, and the speculations of German rationalism and modern 'Spiritualism' as the other."[73] The same spirit of religious solidarity had been reflected the previous year, in a report by a special committee to prepare a uniform constitution for individual Universalist churches. It recommended that societies should be completely abolished, that churches only should be recognized as the local religious unit, and that both the state conventions and the General Convention be given new and broadened powers.[74] A new mood was beginning to appear. Perhaps it was no mere accident of typography that the published minutes of the General Conventions of 1860 and 1861 carried the title "United States General Convention of Universalists."

So many proposals, counter-proposals, resolutions, reports, and committees had been generated by the question of denominational structure by 1860 that the General Convention finally gave to a single committee on Organization the responsibility of serving as a clearing house; in 1861 it was instructed "to prepare a detailed plan for the Organization of the Denomination."[75] It had to digest great quantities of material and somehow strike a balance among the divergencies that inevitably appeared. In 1860 the committee on the State of the Church, headed by Alonzo A. Miner, had backed off from too great a commitment to consolidation, and had denied that comparisons with the practices of other denominations served any useful purpose. Nevertheless, the committee on organization, under the dynamic leadership of Brooks, pushed for greater centralization and uniformity. By the mid-1850s a new word—"national"—began to be used to describe some of the organizations within the denomination. A.B.

Grosh referred in 1854, for the first time, to "a national organization called the United States Convention—to which is attached a national Historical Society." It was Brooks who used for the first time in official records the term "national body" in referring to the role that the General Convention should play. In urging its incorporation as a legal entity, he recommended the name "American Convention of Universalists."

The committee on organization, which solicited reactions and suggestions from the state conventions in 1859, had received incomplete and diverse responses, although several were favorably inclined to the idea of having both themselves and the General Convention incorporated in order to handle funds and property. The Ohio Convention had already taken such a step in 1855.[76] The Vermont Convention referred the entire matter of organization to its associations, believing that any basic change had to originate with them. The Massachusetts Convention, reorganized and incorporated in 1859, was offered as an example of what could be done to strengthen organization and to authorize funding for its activities. Its history was taken as typical of the rather unsystematic evolution that had prevailed through the state convention system.[77]

The Massachusetts Convention, which had been organized in 1834, originally exercised the same power of fellowship and discipline as the associations within its boundaries. In 1842 the state convention relinquished these functions to the associations and exercised no real power at all; it served "simply as a Mass Meeting of Ministers and Delegates for the purpose of social and religious communion." There had been attempts, beginning in 1845, to draft a new constitution which would have given "greater unity and a more positive power," but nothing concrete was accomplished for over a decade.

In the meantime, various organizations had grown up outside the Massachusetts Convention and independent of it. A Sabbath School Association had been formed, at the suggestion of the Convention, in 1837. Missionary work in communities without regular pastoral service was started by the Boston Association ten years later, and after other associations had done likewise, the Massachusetts Home Missionary Society had been incorporated in 1851. The first effort to centralize these fragmented attempts had been taken by the Sabbath School Association in 1856, which proposed that their activities be a responsibility of the state convention and that a Sabbath School secretary be appointed. The plan was shelved because there was no provision for direct representation of the Sabbath Schools themselves. Repeated attempts in the next three years to involve the state convention more closely in local affairs finally resulted, in 1859, in the incorporation of the convention under state law, the dissolution of the Missionary Society and the Sabbath School Association, and the creation of a "unitary organization." The Missionary Society agreed to the arrangement with the understanding that its funds, to be administered through the new organization, would be "forever set apart for missionary purposes."[78] In 1859 the Missionary Society had a permanent fund of $2,286. and an operating balance of slightly over $400.

The council of the reconstituted convention consisted of all the clergy in fellowship, one lay delegate from each society and one from each Sabbath School. An executive committee, with standing subcommittees, was also provided, together with a Committee on Ordination, Fellowship, and Discipline. Bylaws adopted in 1859 rounded out the organizational details. There was no provision in the convention constitution for the intermediate associations which had created so many chronic jurisdictional problems in the past. It was assumed that they would continue to exist, but they were requested to relinquish their practice of fellowshipping and ordination. To emphasize the point, the restructured convention immediately appointed a standing committee on fellowship, ordination, and discipline, as provided by its new bylaws.

The urging in 1860 by the General Convention that state conventions incorporate and reorganize brought only a scattered positive response, partly because the Civil War had intruded and had taken priority over many denominational concerns, and partly because there was reluctance to accept the recommendation of the Committee on Denominational Organization that "all State bodies should become, *de facto,* subordinate to the United States Convention."[79] A. St. John Chambré, chairman of the committee, did little to please the opponents of centralism by considering "rigid organization indispensable, all notions of congregationalism to the contrary notwithstanding—organization that shall centre somewhere."

The Committee on Organization did not make a final report until 1863, the delay being due not only to the exigencies of wartime but to the complexity of the whole subject of organization and "the diversity of opinion which has been found to prevail."[80] The detailed report, comprising twenty closely printed pages, included a plan for organization at each level: churches, associations, state conventions, and the General Convention.[81] The plan for the latter body was offered in the form of a constitution. There was, in the committee's view, "just enough of radicalism in the instrument to preserve it from stagnation, and just enough of conservatism to keep it within bounds." The committee hoped that the plan of government proposed would relieve the denomination "of the nightmare which has paralyzed our efforts." The key question raised by the committee on the State of the Church was whether Universalists could adopt "some form of organization that shall give us system, unity and harmony as a Christian body."[82]

The reaction to the plan of organization submitted to the state conventions after the General Convention of 1863 was mixed, to say the least. Ohio, Indiana, Pennsylvania, and New York approved it; Rhode Island, Iowa, and Illinois rejected it; and action was deferred by the remaining states.[83] It was ignored completely by the independent-minded Vermont Convention; it was not even on their council agenda, nor was there a printed copy available.[84] There was a certain consistency in attitude here, for the Vermont Convention had opposed the adoption of Sawyer's plan of denominational organization in 1846.[85] It had likewise suggested in 1864 that the General Convention should meet no more frequently than triennially; it considered annual meetings "inconvenient, unnecessary, and inexpedient."[86]

The plan of organization, which was not to take effect until a majority of state conventions had approved it, failed to win the necessary approval and had to await still further review and revision by a special committee on bylaws. The general tenor of the communications received from state conventions was favorable to the plan as a whole, but there were two sets of specific objections: the amount of detail was considered excessive, and it did not leave sufficient discretion to the state conventions and associations. The strategy then used was to submit a new constitution in the form of an amended document. This time the effort was successful. At the General Convention in 1865, Richard Eddy, the recording secretary, was able to report that ten state conventions had approved the new constitution, and it was declared "the fundamental law" of the convention on the spot.[87] Among those missing from the count were Vermont and Rhode Island, and all of the southern and border states.

The preamble to the new constitution of the "General Convention of Universalists in the United States of America," like earlier versions, was modelled on that of the Constitution of the United States:

> In order to form a more perfect bond of union, promote a more intimate fellowship, establish a more efficient organization, enforce a more uniform system of government, and secure the ends contemplated in the existence of a religious denomination, we ordain and establish the following Constitution for the Universalists in the United States of America.

The most significant provisions of the constitution proper were the establishment of the offices of permanent secretary and treasurer (to be compensated for their services), the inclusion of the president and secretary of each state convention in the General Convention membership, and the creation of a Board of Trustees which would serve as an executive commmittee comprising the five principal officers of the convention and four elected members. Each state convention was entitled to a minimum of one clerical and two lay delegates to the General Convention, with additional representation in the same proportion for each fifty legally existing societies or churches. Sawyer's recommendation for an equitable basis of delegate representation made some twenty years before had finally been adopted. The General Convention was made "the ultimate tribunal" for adjudication of disputes among state conventions and a court of final appeal in cases involving discipline.

One of the most important provisions of the 1865 constitution was the authority provided to raise, hold, manage, and disburse funds. To this end the bylaws, adopted at the same time, provided that the Board of Trustees was to act as a finance committee as well as to manage convention affairs between meetings. The board members were to receive travel expenses as a reward for their efforts. Besides specifying in some detail the organization of the convention and the order of business, the bylaws also provided for five annually appointed standing committees, required to make annual reports. Convention activities were to be financed by a one-per-cent assessment based on the annual budget of each church or society. Provision of annual statistics from both state conventions and clergymen was also made. If completely and accurately submitted, it was hoped that the information would give a reasonably precise profile of the denomination at any given time.

The General Convention in 1865 also approved, after many years of delay and disagreement, comprehensive and detailed rules for "securing a uniform system of denominational organization" (churches, associations, and state conventions), and a uniform system of fellowship and discipline which plugged most of the loopholes that had previously caused such difficulty. These two sets of regulations were finally adopted a year later (1866), the culmination of over a quarter of a century of effort. The final step in rounding out the General Convention and giving it the necessary legal authority to handle funds was the incorporation of the Board of Trustees in 1866 under the laws of New York State. The new corporation was given the right to hold real and personal estate to the value of $500,000, "to be devoted exclusively to the diffusion of Christian knowledge, by means of missionaries, publications, and other agencies."[88]

The final step in the institutionalizing of American Universalism in the nineteenth century was taken in 1870, when yet another constitution was adopted at the meeting in Gloucester, Massachusetts, celebrating the centennial of John Murray's arrival on American shores. From that year forward, the religious body of which he was acknowledged to be the principal founder, was to be known as a "church" and not as a "denomination," and its governing body was to be known as the "Universalist General Convention."[89] Although this designation was to be changed to the "Universalist Church of America" in 1942, when another charter was adopted, the real organizational transformation had been effected by 1870. It was most clearly articulated that year by Israel Washburn, Jr., who "possessed an admirable faculty for . . . describing, in most expressive words, the principles and theories which convinced his judgment and were in accord with his moral sense."[90] A member of the committee appointed by the General Convention to arrange for the observance of the centennial, Washburn told his colleagues that "I hope we shall drop that word 'denomination.' We are more than a mere 'collection of individuals called by the same name;' we are a church, an organized power, and we stand for the intellectual, moral and spiritual force which has wrought marvellous changes in the old theology . . . . It is the Universalist Church which has made this possible. So let us call ourselves, and hope that the Universalist Church will do something worthy of its name and privilege."[91] The Universalists had travelled a long way since a dozen or so who professed belief in the salvation of all men had met in Oxford, Massachusetts, in 1785, as part of their struggle to have themselves recognized as a distinctive sect.

SECTION III

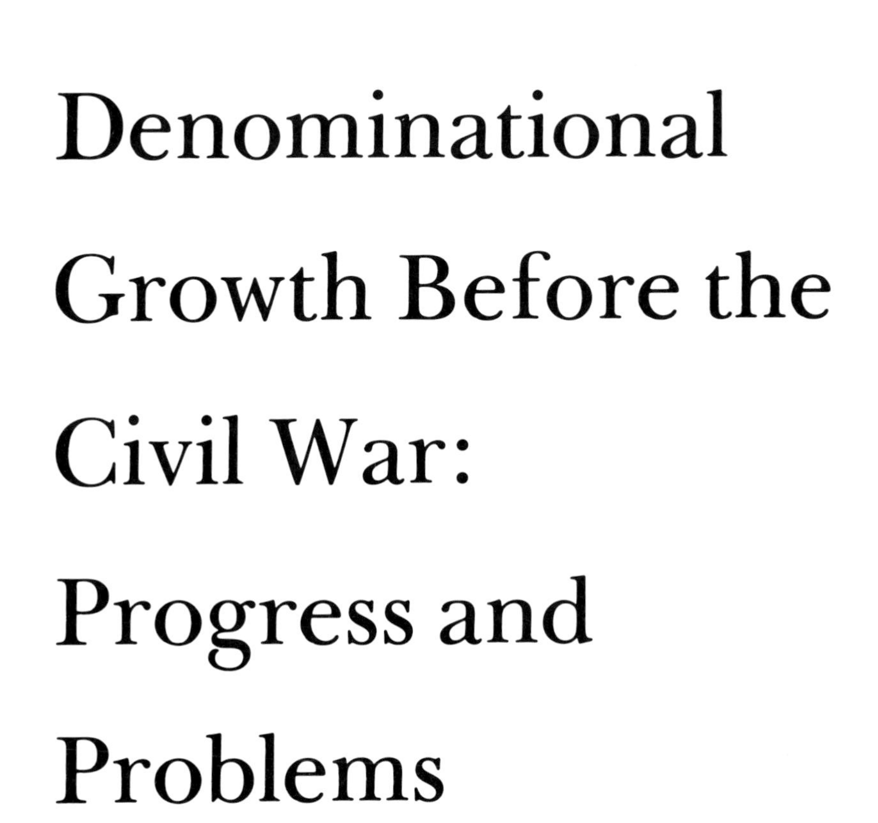

Denominational Growth Before the Civil War: Progress and Problems

Chapter 8

"THE PROMINENT HERESY OF OUR TIMES"

The Statistics of Growth

In the circular letter accompanying the minutes of the annual meeting of the General Convention for 1834, the clerk, Thomas Jefferson Sawyer of New York, reminded his readers that the denomination would be celebrating during the next year the semi-centennial of "the old General Convention" which had met in Oxford, Massachusetts. Organized Universalism had come a long way since that meeting in 1785, when there were only eight known preachers of that faith in America, and only about six organized societies.[1]

On the eve of the so-called "Jubilee" in 1835, the *Boston Recorder* (an orthodox journal) had asserted that "Universalism is the reigning heresy of the day. It is spreading itself far and wide. It is poisoning more minds, and ruining more souls, than any, if not all other heresies amongst us."[2] The editor of the *Christian Advocate and Journal* (Methodist) was dismayed to find, in travels in the North and East in 1843, that "this destructive heresy had obtained a footing in the country through which we passed, for which we were wholly unprepared."[3] These far from complimentary statements gave at the same time some indication of the growing attention being paid to the denomination that had had such apparently unauspicious beginnings less than two generations earlier.

How much had it grown? Collecting reasonably accurate and up-to-date statistics was a problem for Universalists that was never solved in the nineteenth century. Hence a precise accounting of growth in the half-century ending in 1835, and even for the decades beyond, is impossible to obtain. Systematic record-keeping never existed, in spite of efforts by the General Convention. It was not until 1834 that a concerned effort was made, through the state conventions, to collect statistics, and when they were reported thereafter, they were never complete and not always accurate. It was not very revealing to be informed, as were the delegates to the General Convention in 1835, that in some areas of Connecticut there were "more or less Universalists."[4]

The first systematic attempt to review "the state of the doctrine and denomination of Universalists" in the United States in the 1830s was made by Thomas Whittemore, editor of the *Trumpet,* in two articles which appeared in the *Expositor and Universalist Review* in 1833.[5] The original plan was to review the state of the cause every six months, but only one more article in the series was ever published. In 1836 there appeared the first publication intended to present facts about the entire denomination on an annual basis, in the form of a Register and Almanac, issued from Utica, New York, and usually reflecting information gathered the previous year. Even its information was frequently inaccurate, in spite of valiant efforts over the years by many editors to obtain correct information. At no time was there a serious attempt to gather information on the number of individual members in societies; even after the Civil War, membership was listed by number of families only.

When reports on the state of Universalism in various areas were made at all to the General Convention, they were likely to be verbal and did not become a matter of record at all. In 1834 Massachusetts was the only state which reported in writing.[6] Lack of concern and/or failure to cooperate was usually to be blamed on the subordinate associations and societies, but the state conventions were seldom sufficiently sensitive to the requests of the General Convention to obtain the desired information. Publication of the official proceedings of the 1838 General Convention in denominational papers was delayed for over two months in the futile hope that returns would be received.[7] Despite the fact that the convention voted in 1848 to receive no more reports unless they were in writing, two years later the delegates listened to fourteen verbal reports.[8] A rather drastic proposal in 1851 (never acted on) would have deprived state conventions of voting privileges at General Convention meetings if they failed to send in statistical reports.[9]

By 1800 the number of Universalist preachers in the United States had risen to at least twenty-two, by a conservative estimate.[10] In 1813 the number of preachers had risen to forty.[11] The number of meeting houses owned exclusively by the Universalists at this time was much smaller, for they frequently shared facilities with other denominations in proportion to their contribution to acquisition, construction, and upkeep, or met in other buildings such as town halls, courthouses, or in the church buildings of other religious groups if the latter saw fit to allow such use.

It has been a long-standing and often-repeated assumption which has achieved the status of a generalization that, historically, organized Universalism has been an almost uniquely frontier, rural, and small-town phenomenon; while its liberal religious counterpart, Unitarianism, has been an almost exclusively urban movement, confined in the American colonial period to the Atlantic seaboard, especially New

England, and thereafter seldom found in any strength except in towns and cities.[12] It would probably be easier to document the second half of the generalization than the first.

Organized Universalism was, in fact, confined at first largely to urban centers, and did not spread to the interior until after 1820 as part of general westward migration. At the beginning of the nineteenth century, the concentrations were in Boston and Gloucester, Massachusetts; Philadelphia; New York City; Providence, Rhode Island; Portsmouth, New Hampshire; and the vicinity of Bennington, Vermont.[13] John Murray had preached in towns rather than rural areas, and Elhanan Winchester had labored in Hartford, Connecticut. Except for small concentrations in southwestern New Hampshire and southern Vermont and along the northwestern border of Massachusetts, early Universalism was limited to the eastern urban areas of most states. It had not yet extended into central or western New York State, and in the middle and upper South was confined to Baltimore.

Likewise, most publications before 1820 written or edited by Universalists had emanated from metropolitan centers where both printing facilities and readership were most likely to be found; and when a denominational press was established, the leading papers were published out of urban centers. Long before the General Convention was organized in 1833, Boston and its immediate environs had become the unofficial but recognized headquarters of the denomination rather than some hamlet in rural New England or upstate New York. It should also be remembered that, in any case, America was a rural nation before it was an urban one.[14]

The years between 1820 and 1840 have been considered the most active and aggressive in denominational history, at least before the Civil War. Richard Eddy, the most scholarly historian of the denomination in the late nineteenth century, came to this conclusion after his own thorough research.[15] By 1820 Universalists had organized approximately 200 societies and/or churches.[16] Although this was a far cry from the 2,700 churches then claimed by each of the two largest Protestant denominations (Methodists and Baptists), there were fifty more Universalist than Unitarian churches by 1820.

The greatest Universalist expansion occurring during the period was in New England and upstate New York. Stephen R. Smith, whose labors were concentrated in the latter area, estimated that by 1822 there were 120 preachers in fellowship with the New England Convention, with over 200 societies, of which no less than 70 were in New York State.[17] The size of Universalist societies, he reported, was impossible to ascertain, for they ranged from fifteen or twenty members in most societies to several hundred in others. Although only three states were represented among a group of Universalist clergymen who had met in Gloucester in 1824 to commemorate the semi-centennial of Murray's first preaching there, it could be proudly reported that in 1829 alone, seventy-nine new societies had been organized in no less than eleven states and one territory (Michigan), twenty-six men had been licensed to preach, and twenty-one meeting houses had been erected.[18]

The prospects appeared so bright by 1832 that the suggestion was made to set aside a Sunday in November "as a day of public Thanksgiving by the denomination of Universalists throughout the United States, in view of the rapid spread of the doctrine of Universalism, and the consequent happy change in the moral condition of society."[19] The time had arrived, wrote Thomas F. King of Charlestown, Massachusetts, for Universalists to cease being so defensive about their faith and to emphasize the positive character of their beliefs. Universalism was "not a mere system of negatives. It does not consist in opposition to orthodoxy, so called . . . . The basis of Universalism is the nature of the blessed God. It recognizes the impartial and unchangeable love of our heavenly Father, and its grand moral design is, *to assimilate man to the likeness of his Maker*."[20]

Although many of the statistics were obviously faulty, and overly enthusiastic Universalists were prone to exaggerate, figures for the 1830s, so far as they can be determined, seemed to justify the satisfaction and optimism expressed at the General Convention at mid-point in the decade that "a more auspicious day has dawned upon our denomination."[21] In the years 1831 and 1832, seventy-eight new preachers were added to Universalist rolls, including twenty-one who had been clergymen in other denominations.[22] The *American Almanac,* published in Boston, listed Universalism as the sixth largest denomination in 1832, with approximately 500,000 members.[23] Even though this was probably a greatly inflated figure, A.B. Grosh insisted that the number was probably much greater in actuality, and that the Universalists belonged in fifth place, with the Episcopalians in sixth place. There were about 300 clergy and approximately 600 societies by 1833, and even by the most conservative estimates, the number of both preachers and societies had increased by one-third between 1833 and 1839.[24]

But consensus ended whenever an attempt was made to translate figures for societies into individual membership or even to estimate the number who held to Universalist ideas but did not have formal church membership. In a Thanksgiving sermon delivered in West Rumney, New Hampshire, in 1833, John Greenleaf Adams calculated "the number of believers in Universalism within the borders of our own land" to be 300,000.[25] The same year, Whittemore threw caution to the winds and claimed a Universalist population of "upwards of 1,000,000," not including a "vast number" unconnected with any society.[26] Less than six months earlier, Whittemore had admitted that the total number of

Universalists in the United States was unknown.[27] In 1834 Bicknell's *Geographical Chart* indicated 550,000 Universalists.[28]

In 1836 John Hayward of Boston began a series of publications of religious statistics, with brief notes on the history and beliefs of each denomination. He estimated the Universalist population at 500,000 that year.[29] Whittemore considered the account of the Universalists to be "the best that has appeared in any book of this kind."[30] It should have been, for he and Lucius R. Paige of Cambridgeport, Massachusetts, had written it.[31] According to statistics compiled from "official publications" in the same year, Universalists were the seventh largest denomination in the United States, with approximately 600,000 members.[32] Hosea Ballou 2d was more cautious than either Whittemore or Price about the numerical strength of Universalism. In a review of the state of the denomination in 1839, he considered the figure of 500,000 made in 1836 "on conjecture" to have been an exaggeration if only those formally connected with societies were counted, but considered that figure to have been a reasonably accurate estimate for 1839.[33] The annual figures for societies, churches, and clergy compiled by the editor of the *Universalist Register,* beginning in 1835, although far from complete and sometimes of questionable accuracy, gave some indication of the extent to which the denomination was growing. In the five-year period, 1835-40, the number of societies increased from 653 to 853 and the number of clergy from 308 to 512 (still considered far short of the 500 additional preachers thought to be needed).[34] Throughout the nineteenth century, the ratio of societies to clergy was about two to one.

The rise and fall of the economic barometer was usually reflected in the number and prosperity of societies. The economic depression following the collapse of land speculation in 1837, accompanied by crop failures, unemployment, bank closings, scarcities, and high prices, perceptibly slowed the momentum of Universalist growth. "The pressure of the times," when "every thing has been counted in dollars and cents," meant postponement in the building or repair of meeting houses or inability to pay preachers; "great pecuniary embarrassments" and the need for retrenchment had an adverse effect on many societies.[35] Despite such temporary setbacks, however, numerical growth was still registered in other indices besides the number of preachers and societies. Twelve state conventions had been organized, as well as fifty-five associations, by the end of the 1830s; and for the first time, the number of meeting houses owned wholly or in part by Universalists equalled roughly the number of clergymen. New England remained the point of concentration of American Universalism, and more particularly Massachusetts and the Greater Boston area. In 1840, almost one quarter (109) of the clergy in the entire denomination were located in that state.[36] By 1833 there were three Universalist clergymen and five societies in Gloucester alone, and within three years the same number of societies in the city of Boston.[37]

The denomination continued to expand in numbers and strength in every direction, except in the South, in the 1840s and simultaneously to broaden or intensify its activities in social reform, education, and publication. Net gains were reported almost every year in the number of societies and churches, clergy, and meeting houses, which were now being often called "houses of worship." When Robert Baird published his history of religion in America in 1844, he noted that the Universalists (for whom he had little but contempt) claimed "600,000 of the population under their influence"—a figure he considered "much too high."[38] Three years later, Hosea Ballou 2d, in studiously ambiguous language, estimated that "probably 700,000 people nominally belong to our Connexion."[39] The year 1847 or 1848 was probably the high-point of denominational strength measured in comparative terms. While this rather dramatic increase took place over the thirty-year period from 1820 through 1850, it should be pointed out that the population of the United States almost doubled between 1820 and 1840 (from 9,600,000 to over 17,000,000) and had exceeded 23,000,000 by 1850. Thus, the Universalists were about 3 per cent of the total population.

The rapid growth into the 1840s was a source of great pride among many Universalist leaders, notably if it was compared with other denominations. Unlike most of these, Universalist organizational efforts were minimal at first; the idea of establishing home missionary societies did not become widely accepted until *after* accessions to Universalism had increased substantially. Universalists in the 1840s had established not a single college or theological school. They could boast of few men of learning, and as a group they had no great wealth. Whittemore, himself a self-made man, pointed out in 1844 that "it is well known that Universalists are poor and they are not ashamed to acknowledge it."[40] Then how was the unparalleled growth to be explained? The secret, said Whittemore, was the "internal power" and logic of Universalism itself.

According to the Seventh United States Census (1850), the Universalists were among the twenty-one "major sects" for which information was given. Universalists were reported to have a total of 529 churches in twenty-two states, possessing religious property valued at $1,752,316, and accommodations for 214,115 individuals.[41]

The denomination may have increased in an absolute sense, but in relation to national population growth the high-point of Universalism before the Civil War, estimated numerically, seems to have peaked shortly before 1850. In that year, A.B. Grosh, the denominational statistician, pointed out that in 1849, for the first time in his recollection, the rate of growth of Universalism had not exceeded the annual increase of total population.[42] It appeared that, proportionately to the general population, the denomination had reached a plateau—that a sort of equilibrium had been achieved. Increases in the number of churches continued to be posted for many years after 1850 but they were in no sense as striking as those between 1830 and 1850. In fact, the denomination apparently lost ground after 1850 in relation to other denominations and total population growth. Religious statistics compiled for 1855 placed Universalism tenth among the Protestant denominations, which claimed a total membership of 4,100,000.[43] In the Eighth United States Census (1860), the Universalists were still listed as a "major sect," with 664 churches in 24 states, with religious property valued at $2,856,095, and with accommodations for 235,219 individuals.[44]

The total population of the United States (whites, free colored, and slaves) in the intervening decade had risen from 23,191,876 to 31,443,321. While the number of churches of all denominations had increased by over 49 per cent, according to the census reports, the number of Universalist churches had increased less than 23 per cent. As had been the case a decade earlier, there was a glaring discrepancy between official census figures and denominationally-gathered statistics. According to the *Universalist Register,* by 1860 organized bodies of believers existed in thirty-two of the thirty-three states then comprising the Union (Arkansas was the single exception) and in two of its territories (Kansas and Washington).[45] There were said to be 1,264 separate societies or churches, excluding churches organized within existing societies.

Even if the denomination was growing at a more modest pace than others, and even if its own momentum was beginning to slow down in relative quantitative terms, the record was still impressive for a religious body that had never attracted more than a minority of the American population to formal membership. It was even more impressive if other yardsticks were used besides the numbers of societies and clergy. Universalists on the eve of the Civil War could still look with a measure of gratification on how far they had travelled in the ninety years since the arrival of John Murray. The majority of Universalist churches in 1860 had Sunday Schools and/or Bible classes connected with them. Universalists owned or reportedly had an interest in over 950 houses of worship. There were 86 ecclesiastical associations representing locally various groups of societies and/or churches, these associations in turn sponsoring tract, home missionary, and Sunday School organizations. At the next level, there were conventions in twenty-two of the thirty-three states which also sponsored tract, educational, home missionary societies, ministerial relief funds, and even denominational newspapers, as was the case in New York State. Three regional organizations existed in 1860: a Southern Convention (five states), a home missionary society (three states), and a Northwest Conference (seven states). At the national level, and representing the entire denomination, was the United States (General) Convention.

In addition, the Universalists had two specialized organizations of national dimensions—a general reform association and an historical society. Universalists were also actively publishing. In the year 1860 alone, they were responsible for maintaining seventeen periodicals and had published twenty new books, besides reprints of former works, and had issued numerous tracts and sermons. Universalists by that date had launched a full-scale effort to enter the field of education at both the secondary and college level. As of 1860 they had established one college (Tufts) which had been in successful operation for six years; two universities (Lombard and St. Lawrence), a theological school (at Canton, New York), over a dozen academies and preparatory schools, of which six were still in operation in 1860, and had a controlling interest in one industrial reform school (in Pennsylvania). The tangible evidences of the Universalist presence were indeed noteworthy for a denomination that had had such modest beginnings only a relatively short time before.

Almost every Universalist greeted the spurt of denominational expansion before 1860 with great satisfaction, but there were those who restrained their enthusiasm and warned against self-complacency. Hosea Ballou 2d was one of these. After assuring himself that the "trunk" of Universalism (the older established societies in the East) was not decaying while the "branches" (the newer societies in the Midwest) were flourishing, Ballou acknowledged that outward progress was in fact occurring.[46] However, he offered some sobering considerations concerning "the internal condition" of Universalism. He suggested that the tone and spirit of opposition and combativeness which still prevailed in some Universalist quarters needed to be replaced by positive expression of religious truths; in this he was offering the same advice as Thomas F. King had proffered almost a decade earlier. Theological warfare *per se* was no longer appropriate or necessary.

Further, Universalists should overcome (where it existed) their historic aversion to church organization and ceremony; casually operated societies had no real permanence. Such religious observances as celebration of the Lord's Supper, even though no more than symbolic, were necessarily a part of "social religion." Many Universalists, Ballou argued, in their attempt to preserve simplicity in their religious practices, had gone to the other extreme by discarding all usage and forms associated with conventional Christianity. After he had paid some attention to the desirability of "conference meetings" to involve the laity, but without the excesses of revivalism, and had stressed the importance of religious instruction for children, which he considered to be woefully neglected, Ballou chastised Universalists for their failure to realize the value and importance of formal education for both clergy and laity.

These were some of the deficiencies that Ballou believed should be the concern of every thoughtful Universalist, who should not develop a false sense of well-being about the prosperity of the denomination. Half a century later, Universalist historian Richard Eddy was echoing many of Ballou's cautionary remarks. A review of Universalism during the Jacksonian era convinced Eddy that the surface expansion after 1820 did not necessarily signify a gain of real strength. The aggressiveness of Universalists had been dictated primarily by the unusually large amount of opposition which had been encountered. To him, steady institutional growth through "organized power" in all areas was needed to insure denominational permanence as well as prosperity, which he believed was basically lacking in the sporadic and atomistic development characterizing the growth of Universalism, at least to the middle of the nineteenth century.[47]

Some of the Perils of Dissent

The rapid numerical growth of the denomination after 1820 took place in spite of numerous handicaps under which the Universalists were forced to operate. They were, in the first place, a denomination of "come outers" who challenged prevailing religious orthodoxies. They were on the defensive from the outset, and found themselves subject to all kinds of attack, although usually short of physical abuse. They were lumped together with the deists, athiests, and all breeds of heretics. They were assaulted verbally from dozens of pulpits, were made the subject of innumerable written polemics, found their right to give testimony under oath challenged. They were accused of licentiousness and general immorality, and were often characterized as the dregs of society. They frequently found the doors of churches and public buildings locked against them. Many were excommunicated from orthodox churches.

Both Universalist clergy and laity had, of course, found themselves religiously *persona non grata* long before a denominational press had been created through which to publicize the disabilities under which Universalists labored. Aside from the difficulties of the Universalists in Gloucester and elsewhere which had received a fair amount of attention, there had been at least seven recorded instances before the end of the eighteenth century of clergymen dismissed from their churches for advocating Universalism.[48] Almost as soon as such papers as the *Christian Repository* and the *Universalist Magazine* began publication, they regularly carried detailed accounts of not only current but past cases of excommunication for which records existed.

One of the first such episodes, with complete transcripts of the proceedings and accompanying correspondence, all of which occupied several columns of fine print, appeared in 1822.[49] This particular controversy, which resulted eventually in the excommunication of two individuals from the Congregational church in Plymouth, Vermont, lasted for a full decade (1810-21). A deacon of the Baptist Church of Christ in Whiting, Vermont, had been excommunicated by an ecclesiastical council in 1819 on four charges of heresy, to wit: "for denying the doctrine of endless punishment of the wicked; for holding the doctrine that all rational intelligence will finally be eternally happy; for denying the existence of fallen angels; for not acknowledging the doctrine of the general judgment after the resurrection."[50] To make matters worse, the erring deacon was accused of being "exceedingly evasive, during his examination."

The seriousness of the offense which called for excommunication was well illustrated by the case of an eighty-four-year-old gentleman who was ousted by the Congregational Church of Christ in Wrentham, Massachusetts. He had not only "embraced the doctrine of Universal Salvation" [but] had attempted to propagate it among the brethren of the Church and others."[51] His unorthodox belief was considered "subversive of the peace and well being of the Church, injurious to morals, and to the spiritual and eternal interest of immortal souls."

Some individuals whose orthodoxy was questioned received an "admonition" prior to consideration for excommunication, as a warning if a retraction were not forthcoming. Others who never claimed to be Universalists at all were found guilty by association. A printer in Portland, Maine, found himself excommunicated by the Third Parish (Congregational) church in 1834 because he had contracted to produce the *Christian Pilot,* a short-lived Universalist weekly.[52] There was at least one instance when the tables were turned. A convert from Presbyterianism to Universalism in Hartford township, Pennsylvania, announced that "I do solemnly eject and excommunicate the society above named, from all fellowship or connexion with me in religious sentiment; and do hereby avow my honest disbelief in the doctrines professed by its members."[53] There is no record of how the Presbyterian Society of Hartford responded to this challenge.

For many years the editor of the *Trumpet* routinely published a column recording excommunications brought to his attention, but during the period of denominational expansion in the 1820s and 1830s the number of instances had become so great that he stopped publishing all but the most unusual or interesting cases. Excommunications had become so common that they ceased to attract much attention out of their immediate neighborhoods.

Even allowing for exaggeration, and a certain martyr-like tone which sometimes crept into their accounts of their difficulties, there is little doubt that many Universalists did find themselves "put upon" and that they found themselves outside the pale of religious respectability. Typical of the treatment the Universalists received in religious encyclopedias and other compendia in the 1840s was the account in *Religion in America.* This substantial volume, originally published in 1843 in Great Britain, and written by Robert Baird, an American Presbyterian clergyman, appeared in a United States edition in 1844. The author, who had visited Europe several times between 1835 and 1843, had written in 1837 a slender volume on the history of American Unitarianism, published in Paris under the title *L'Union de l'Eglise et de l'Etat dans la Nouvelle Angleterre.* His major work, *Religion in America,* was an outgrowth of this book, and was written for the information of Europeans. Universalists were relegated to a short section in the rear of his 338-page, double-columned publication, and were listed with other "unevangelical" denominations. This classification included all those religious groups, so classified by "Orthodox Protestants," which "either renounce, or fail faithfully to exhibit . . . the fundamental and saving truths of the Gospel." This included a curious combination of Roman Catholicism, Unitarianism (which received over fifteen columns), the "Christian Connection," the Swedenborgians, the Tunkers (Dunkers), the Jews, the Mormons, and the Universalists.

The Universalists (who were discussed in less than two columns), were treated with the greatest disdain. Hosea Ballou, although acknowledged by Baird to be a Universalist, was discussed in the context of Unitarianism. The basic Universalist belief that all men would be saved was described as a doctrine "favoured by a few men of considerable learning and respectable morals; but its chief success has been among the ignorant, the vulgar, and the vicious, not one of whom was ever known to be reformed by it." Baird made the unsupported and simplistic declaration that the majority of Unitarians had "embraced the doctrine of the final salvation of all men," and hence there was no doctrinal distinction between the two groups. In fact, he wrote, Universalists were tempted to change their name and call themselves Unitarians because "Unitarianism is esteemed the more genteel religion of the two."

Baird had no kind words for the Universalist clergy; most of them were "men of little learning" who exerted their unholy influence by concentrating on only one point and becoming "wonderfully skilful in wielding their sophistry, so as to seduce such as want to find an easier way to heaven than can be found in the Scriptures." The only Universalists whose preaching seemed to have had "any moral influence" were the "handful of Restorationists." The rest were "heard with delight chiefly by the irreligious, the profane, Sabbath-breakers, drunkards, and all haters of evangelical religion. Their preaching positively exercises no reforming influence on the wicked, and what worse can be said of it?"[54]

The columns of the Universalist newspapers, naturally prone to be biased, were full of "horror stories" of all kinds involving the treatment that Universalists received at the hands of their religious enemies. Copious extracts from "partialist" publications (with direct quotations generally reproduced with accuracy, based on a spot-check of the original sources), make it very clear that Universalists and all that they stood for made popular targets for denunciation.[55] Universalists were not loathe, of course, to counterattack where possible, and the belligerence of some of the Universalist polemicists was deplored both by contemporaries and later co-religionists.[56]

Two of the areas of Universalist thought and action in the nineteenth century seldom mentioned by denominational historians and generally neglected by others were the outspoken advocacy of separation of church and state, and untrammeled freedom of conscience, often against firm opposition; and the challenge to the legal disabilities which Universalists suffered because of their "heretical" religious beliefs. Part of their attitude was undoubtedly conditioned by and accounted for by their own historical experience, and hence they had a vested interest in opposing what did not serve or promote their personal or denominational welfare. Yet at the time they argued on the basis of principle and conviction as well as expediency.

John Murray, in 1779, had laid down the basic precepts to be followed by Universalists regarding church-state relations. There was, he said, no guide in spiritual matters but Christ. "As dwellers in the world, though not of it, we hold ourselves bound to yield obedience to every ordinance of men, for God's sake, and we will be peaceable and obedient subjects to the powers that are ordained of God in all civil cases."[57] But as subjects of the divine kingdom, "we cannot acknowledge the right of any human authority to make laws for the regulating of our consciences in any spiritual matter." The same principles were affirmed when Universalists met in Philadelphia in 1790 and adopted a Plan of Government, under the heading "Of Submission to Government."

Universalists argued against so-called sectarian education supported by the state, and were driven by necessity to establish their own schools until a system of public education could be established that was presumably free of ecclesiastical control. In the interim, however, they found themselves accepting the same public aid offered to the educational institutions of other denominations; the Universalist rationale was that no religious doctrines of any kind would be forced on the students, and that their schoolroom doors were open to all who were otherwise qualified. So far as can be determined, they practiced in their schools what they preached in regard to liberality and permissiveness in the religious realm. The charter of the Clinton Liberal Institute prohibited the teaching of religion in any form during regularly scheduled school hours. Similarly the charter of Tufts College, obtained in 1852, expressly forbade a religious test or interference with the religious opinions of either faculty or students.

When Daniel Webster recommended support of Christianity by law in 1821, Thomas Whittemore, one of the more vigorous Universalist defenders of civil liberties, immediately pointed out that under those circumstances clergymen would automatically become "as much the public officers of the State, as those who are in the military or civil department."[58] If a state should undertake to support a religion, there was the need for a constitutional provision "which should tolerate the people in professing and supporting any kind of religion they might choose, at their own expense." Whittemore considered that if this route were taken, the most workable system was the one to be found in England whereby the Anglican Church was supported as the religion of the Crown, but liberty was given to individuals to support "the doctrine in which they believe."

But this was by no means the ideal solution; the guarantee established by the First Amendment to the Federal Constitution was far superior to the British system, providing the constitutional guarantee were vigilantly guarded. When Jedediah Morse, well-known author of geography texts, was reported to have lamented the lack of an established religion in the United States comparable to that in England or Scotland, Whittemore gave thanks to the Founding Fathers for establishing the principle of religious liberty. As he put it, "no two things ought to be kept farther asunder than RELIGION and LEGISLATION."[59] Whittemore objected strongly to a Congressional attempt in 1828-29 to forbid the carrying of mail on Sunday. He considered such legislative efforts as "meddling . . . with things that belong to the conscience alone," and as a device for breaking down the wall of separation between church and state.[60] He likewise disapproved of the prosecution of Abner Kneeland for blasphemy on grounds of broad principle. "The religion of Jesus Christ has no need of the secular arm to support it. It will stand by its own strength . . . . We have vastly more confidence in the Christian religion to support itself, than we have in any human law to support it."[61]

It was in Massachusetts that the last battle at the state level for relief of compulsory support of religion had to be fought and won. Universalists found themselves faced very early in their history with overcoming the obstacles they faced as religious dissenters from the inherited tradition and practice of a system in which both control and supervision of religion in all its manifestations was a prerogative of the state. It was the challenge to this tradition that had occupied the Universalists in Gloucester for so many years at the end of the eighteenth century. They had been forced by circumstances to "go to law"—an expedient deplored by Universalists in Philadelphia who had drawn up their Plan of Government in 1790.

For more than a quarter of a century after the Universalists had been recognized as a distinct denomination in Massachusetts and had received, as a result of court litigation, the right to support their own pastors under the constitution of 1780, religion in the state continued to be supported by law.[62] The tradition of compulsory support could be traced back at least to 1654, when the Massachusetts Court of Sessions was authorized to levy a tax for the support of religion in the various towns whenever the people did not voluntarily make suitable provision. Similar acts were passed in 1692 and 1703, except that in the latter year, Quakers and Baptists were excused from the obligation, under certain circumstances; in 1728 they were given specific exemption. The right and obligation of the people to support religion was reaffirmed in 1760, and again was written into the third article of the state Bill of Rights in 1780. It was under this article that Murray and his supporters in Gloucester had brought suit.[63]

Although the General Court consolidated all of the laws respecting ecclesiastical matters into one statute in 1800, the principle of establishment still stood. As a consequence, Thomas Barnes, a Universalist preacher in Maine, lost a tax suit against the First Parish in Falmouth in 1807. Theophilus Parsons, who had been one of Murray's major judicial opponents in the Gloucester case, was at the time of Barnes' suit the Chief Justice of the Massachusetts Supreme Judicial Court, and had in no degree modified his opposition to Universalism and its theology.

An unsuccessful attempt was made to modify Article III at a constitutional convention assembled in 1820 for the purpose of amending the 1780 document. Two Universalist clergymen, Thomas Whittemore and Paul Dean, were among the delegates, and Dean spoke in favor of separation of church and state.[64] The modification would have eliminated the provision confining the responsibility for maintenance of public worship to Protestant teachers by extending it to all Christian denominations. There was also a move to annul the clause which invested the legislature with power to compel attendance at public worship, as well as to liberalize Article III in other respects, if not annul it completely. The end-result was to leave the provisions for religious support unchanged, regardless of whether or not they were enforced. The people were still compelled to support religion and the legislature retained the power to compel attendance at public worship.[65]

This was met, as was to be expected, with disapproval from Universalists. They interpreted the failure to act as an effort by the established (Congregational) church to seek artificial support for their threatened hegemony. This included the Unitarian churches organized within Congregationalism; they wished to maintain existing practice which sometimes gave them advantages in the allocation of parish property when they separated from the parent body. Universalists pointed out that "those sects which have left the congregational order have increased wonderfully in this country for half a century without the aid of the law."[66] They seemed, in fact, to have actually flourished under persecution.

Public discussion of the subject of drastically modifying existing constitutional provisions relating to support of religion was renewed after 1830, and Universalists were active participants. Editor Whittemore laid the groundwork for the readers of the *Trumpet* with a series of articles, in one of which he quoted extensively from the constitution of every state to point up the fact that not a one had "the same *offensive* provisions for the support of religion" as was to be found in the constitution of Massachusetts. He argued further that its so-called "Bill of Rights" which contained the offending provision about religion was misnamed.[67]

His efforts to bring about a change in church-state relations in Massachusetts were not confined to newspaper rhetoric. He was elected as a representative from Cambridge to the state legislature in 1831, where he served for five years. He was instrumental in effecting the desired constitutional changes, and was responsible for presenting a petition in 1831, signed by sixty-four other individuals, calling for repeal of Article III. He served for three successive terms as chairman of a special committee to receive the petitions in favor of modification with which the legislature was bombarded. Over 200 such documents were received in 1831 and 1832 from all over the state, from churches of many denominations, and with some 12,000 signatures.[68] Judging from the similarity in the wording of many of the petitions, the Universalists, with Whittemore as their principal spokesman, played a key part in this stage of the movement for disestablishment. Whittemore also addressed the state House of Representatives on the subject.[69]

After an attempt failed to expunge the entire Article III the first concrete step to effect a constitutional change was taken in the lower house in 1831. An amendment was passed removing all state responsibility regarding religion, and providing only that "the people of this commonwealth have a right to make suitable provision at their own expense for the institution of public worship of God, and for the support and maintenance thereof." The amendment passed (272 to 78) with much more than the two-thirds required.[70] The Massachusetts Senate temporarily defeated the measure by indefinite postponement, but by a very close vote. Whittemore listed in his newspaper by name and by county all senators who had voted against the amendment to disestablish.[71] The next tactic was a vote by the House of Representatives to annul Article III of the Bill of Rights. Whittemore's chronic dislike and distrust of Unitarians was only heightened by the fact that the opposition was led by members of that denomination, including Samuel Hoar and Leverett Saltonstall, who were members of the Senate committee that reported against the amendment.

In 1832 the amendment was passed by both houses of the legislature (347 to 90 in the House and 25 to 13 in the Senate), and the following year received the second vote of approval required (431 to 75 and 28 to 9). Whittemore was chairman of the special House committee which reported favorably on the amendment. This final step was the adoption of what became the eleventh amendment to the state constitution by popular referendum. The majority for it was almost ten to one (32,234 to 3,273). After enabling legislation was passed in 1834, Massachusetts and its inhabitants finally achieved legal religious freedom and Whittemore witnessed the triumph of his conviction that "no civil government has a right to compel the citizens to support any system of religion whatsoever."[72]

The story of disestablishment in Massachusetts was extremely complex, with roots extending back well into the seventeenth century. Although a series of modifications had taken place over the decades in legislative and judicial halls, and in practical application, both the tradition and the principle had remained embedded in the fundamental law of the state. It was the goal of the religious dissenters to remove those last vestiges of Puritanism. And it was the Universalists who were largely responsible for taking the final steps. The Baptists, long the leaders in the movement to separate church and state, had lost their momentum. Whittemore accused them not only of having abandoned their zeal for religious liberty but of having even joined the establishment that was opposing change.[73] Instead, "the most sustained and vigorous political effort for disestablishment between 1830 and 1833 was not by purveyors of evangelical truth but by the Universalists."[74]

Universalists, of course, in no sense carried the struggle to a successful conclusion single-handedly; they were neither strong and respectable enough denominationally nor politically powerful enough to gain a legislative victory. Furthermore, other important factors were at work. Part of the explanation for the failure to retain beyond 1833 the principle of compulsory support of religion in Massachusetts is to be found in the religious division (and its political consequences) which had developed within the old "standing order." The orthodox Congregational church had been badly divided and greatly weakened by the rift which had appeared between its trinitarian (orthodox) and unitarian dissenting wings and had repercussions that extended well beyond narrowly religious concerns. The Universalist effort represented one of the many elements of a larger thrust against aristocracy and privilege called for by the intensified democratic stirrings that were appearing more and more prominently in American political and social thought.

There were other areas of church-state concern in New England and in Massachusetts in particular which involved Universalists, although they did not represent such fundamental issues as disestablishment. The setting aside of "Fast Day" by gubernatorial proclamation in New England each year was looked upon with special dislike. The practice can be traced back to 1622 in the Plymouth colony when, after a period of drought and the ordering of a fast by religious authorities, the rains came, and a day of thanksgiving was ordered, first publicly observed on 22 February 1631. Legislative sanction was soon obtained to enforce church attendance on periodic celebrations of days of "fasting, humiliation, and prayer," and secular pursuits were suspended. The dates for both fasting and thanksgiving varied, but were usually scheduled in the spring and fall respectively.

Whittemore considered religious holidays such as these, decreed by civil officials, a relic of the historic union of church and state, and most inappropriate. Public officers had no right to "appoint days of devotion for other people."[75] Originally a religious observance, fast day had become a secular holiday by the 1830s, particularly treasured by schoolchildren, and lasted into the 1880s. By then, it was being observed on the first Thursday of April.[76]

Fast Day also was considered an occasion for special sermons in all churches. On the appropriate day in 1829, Warren Skinner, pastor of the Universalist societies in Cavendish and Plymouth, Vermont, and Thomas G. Farnsworth, pastor of the First Universalist Society in Haverhill, Massachusetts, devoted their sermons to the alleged threats to separation of church and state. They singled out for particular criticism the activities of the American Sabbath School Union, the American Bible Society, and the American Board of Commissioners for Foreign Missions, which were allegedly attempting in various ways "to amalgamate religion and politics" by imposing their "orthodox" views.[77] When the threat of cholera reached near-disaster proportions in New York City in 1832, the Dutch Reformed Church requested President Andrew Jackson to declare a national day of fasting. His refusal to do so met with Whittemore's hearty endorsement. To have complied would, in the Universalist editor's view, have been an intermeddling of civil authority in religious affairs.[78]

Another tradition inherited from the colonial period in New England that came in for sharp rebuke by Universalists was the delivery of an annual "election sermon" before the state legislature. A clergyman selected for the purpose was expected to deliver a religiously oriented inspirational discourse to the incoming and outgoing officials, for which purpose the legislature was adjourned. The clergymen so chosen sometimes served also as chaplains while the legislature was in session. Whittemore, who himself sat in the Massachusetts legislature for several terms, felt that by the 1830s the tradition of the election sermon had become an expensive anachronism which served no good purpose and might even do harm. He estimated that every such sermon cost $2,000, $1,500 of which was the equivalent of valuable time lost in balloting for choice of a clergyman and "in consequence of the three branches leaving business and attending church."[79]

Further, according to Whittemore, the sermons over the years had become either increasingly politicized or sectarian in character, or were not at all appropriate to the occasion. Professor Moses Stuart, of the very orthodox Andover Theological Seminary, dropped a strong hint in his 1827 election sermon that Universalists should be deprived of the right of making oaths in judicial proceedings. Another clergyman, a Methodist named Wilbur Fisk, predicted in his election sermon the eventual destruction of the material universe—a topic of dubious relevance to matters before the legislature at the time.

Several Universalists were chosen to deliver election sermons before the Massachusetts legislature. Paul Dean was chosen for the 1831-32 session after a stalemate almost developed in balloting, his chief competitor being another Universalist, Linus S. Everett. The *Boston Transcript* blamed the delay on internal feuding among Universalists.[80] Such was actually the case, for Dean was one of the leaders of the Restorationist controversy which divided New England Universalists for several years. One of the last election sermons delivered before the Massachusetts legislature was that of Alonzo Ames Miner, in 1884. Miner, a leading temperance advocate among Universalists, devoted his discourse to a strong attack on the use of alcholic beverages in general and the "liquor traffic" in particular.

Election sermons were also delivered occasionally by Universalist clergymen in other state legislatures. The choice of Robert Bartlett by the Vermont legislature in 1824 provoked a sharp controversy over allowing such heretical personages to appear before august legislative bodies, and a decade later, Warren Skinner served in the same capacity before the same body but with apparently less repercussion. Even though Skinner was a fellow Universalist and had used the opportunity to make a plea for separation of church and state, Whittemore was less than enthusiastic about the whole tradition of election sermons. He considered them merely a device in "a struggle for sectarian pre-eminence."[81] When the Connecticut legislature in 1830 abolished the practice of election sermons, Whittemore greeted the news with great satisfaction; they would no longer be vehicles for propagating "orthodox theology, and high toned church-and-state principles."[82]

Many Universalist spokesmen put religious liberty in a much larger context. William A. Drew, editor of the *Christian Intelligencer* in Maine, equated religious freedom and pluralism with the spirit of the American republic. In 1833 Constantine Pise, a Roman Catholic priest, was elected chaplain of the United States Senate. There was much alarm among Protestant clergy over his selection. Like many laity of the time, they interpreted this as part of a "popish plot" to take over the nation. Drew viewed Pise's election with favor, not because Drew subscribed to Roman Catholicism, but because he saw in the Senate's choice "the evidence of a republican and liberal spirit . . . which would treat all sects with equal courtesy and exclude none on account of its peculiar religious sentiments."[83] It was "in this spirit of liberality only that our institutions can be preserved." In 1853 the Maine State Convention of Universalists officially endorsed a movement to secure, in treaties between the United States and foreign countries, "reciprocal rights and privileges of conscience & worship."[84]

There was a more negative and more localized aspect of church-state relations to which Universalists had also to address themselves. They were at a distinct legal disadvantage in several areas of citizenship. Many were debarred from giving sworn testimony, serving as witnesses, taking the oaths prescribed as part of the judicial process, or even from holding office in some states. They had been counselled by the Universalists at their meeting in Philadelphia in 1790 to use "simple affirmation" and to avoid the necessity of swearing oaths. But they found their right to follow either course frequently blocked in courts of law. They often found themselves lumped together with all unbelievers and penalized by the common law inherited from England which disqualified persons from participating in judicial proceedings unless they believed in a Supreme Being and in a system of rewards and punishments in a future life.

It was the second proviso that worked to the disadvantage of most Universalists in the nineteenth century, rather than any question about belief in God. These principles were embodied in the Judiciary Act of 1789 at the national level and followed by the states, and were applied in a variety of ways.[85] The determination of the competency of a witness to testify was left up to the states, and as recently as the 1960s there were still seven which had not specifically modified the common law restrictions regarding nonbelievers.

The number of cases involving Universalists in the nineteenth century was legion, with the greatest number to be found in the pre-Civil War period. There was no uniformity in application or interpretation of the state laws, and in some instances Universalists were able to avoid disqualification if they encountered a sympathetic or liberal-minded judge, or made a particularly convincing argument. The opposite was, however, more likely to occur. In a trial being conducted in Albany, New York, in 1827, a Universalist witness was challenged because he did not believe in a future state of rewards and punishments.[86] He was allowed to testify when he told the court that he believed the Deity would punish sin in this world.

The decision went otherwise for Universalists in the same year in the United States Circuit Court in Providence, Rhode Island. Judge Joseph Story, later to sit on the Supreme Court of the United States, rejected a witness on the ground that he was a Universalist. Story, a Unitarian, thus supported the contention by Moses Stuart of the Andover Theological School that Universalists should be excluded from giving testimony.[87] Stuart went so far as to argue that Universalists should be excluded from all public offices.

In 1828 Whittemore ran a series of articles in the *Trumpet* reviewing dozens of such cases, and came to the optimistic conclusion that there was an increasing disposition to grant the right of Universalists to make oaths.[88] Although he did not mention it, Whittemore was no doubt aware of and heartened by a pamphlet published in Boston in 1828 "by a member of the bar" entitled *The Right of Universalists to Testify in a Court of Justice Vindicated.*[89] Whittemore considered the practice of requiring a civil officer to check on a person's religious views to be a violation of the principle of separation of church and state.[90] Disabilities for Universalists and other dissenters were not removed in Connecticut until 1830, when a so-called "Religious Freedom" bill was enacted which allowed individuals to affirm rather than swear to their belief in the existence of God; furthermore, every individual was given the right to take an oath without being interrogated as to religious beliefs.[91] Only two years earlier, the state supreme court had ruled that 'if a person believes in a God, the avenger of falsehood, and in a future state of rewards and punishments, he may be a witness, and not otherwise.'[92] It was through the efforts of such Universalists as Menzies Rayner, pastor of the society in Hartford, that the 1828 decision was changed by legislative action.[93] As late as 1836, Universalists in Massachusetts were still not considered credible witnesses; a bill was defeated that year prohibiting inquiry into the religious beliefs of witnesses.[94]

Disabilities experienced by Universalists were limited neither to northern states nor to the matter of competency as witnesses. Abel C. Thomas of Philadelphia drafted and presented to the constitutional convention in Pennsylvania in 1837 a petition asking for abolition of all religious tests for exercise of civil rights, including office-holding.[95] The effort failed. Jacob Grosh, father of the Universalist clergyman and publisher A.B. Grosh, was nominated by Governor Porter of Pennsylvania in 1840 to fill a vacancy in a judgeship in Lancaster. Twenty-six persons objected to his appointment because he was a Universalist, and the state senate refused to confirm him.[96] This proscription based on religious opinion evoked a letter of vigorous protest from the elder

Grosh, who wrote to one of the state senators warning against setting a dangerous precedent by turning the legislative body "into a religious inquisition to try presumed Heretics."[97] His name was re-submitted in 1842 and this time he was confirmed. He served on the bench until retirement in 1851.[98]

At least one attempt was recorded in each of the states of Georgia, North Carolina, and South Carolina to deprive Universalists of the right to testify in court because of their disbelief in the doctrine of future endless punishment.[99] In North Carolina a judgment that Universalists were not competent to testify was overturned by the state supreme court in 1856.[100] A case occurred in South Carolina as late as 1887 in which a ruling of ineligibility was likewise overturned by the state supreme court. In 1841 two witnesses to a murder in Georgia were disqualified from testifying by a judge in Oglethorpe County because they were Universalists. The case was the main topic of discussion at the Georgia Universalist Convention that year.[101] After a mistrial was declared because of the disqualification of the Universalist witnesses, the alleged murderer broke out of jail and disappeared. At the next session of the legislature, a bill was passed stipulating that no person thereafter was to be debarred from giving testimony because of religious faith or opinions.[102]

The draft of the new constitution in Tennessee in 1834 not only prohibited clerical membership in either house of the state legislature, but left unchanged the statement that 'No person who denies the being of a God, or a future state of rewards and punishments, shall hold any office in the civil department of this State.'[103] This provoked an angry edited by L.F.W. Andrews, fiery Universalist editor of the *Southern Evangelist,* after the Tennessee document had been approved by the state constitutional convention.[104] Otis A. Skinner, senior editor of the *Southern Pioneer,* who also quoted the Tennessee constitutional provision, was quick to point out the contradiction in the new document. It also provided that 'No human authority can in any case whatever, control or interfere with the rights of conscience . . . . no religious test shall ever be required, as a qualification to any office or public trust under this State.'[105]

Such were the complexities with which Universalists (and others) had to deal in the tangled web of church-state relations. But there were other problems also facing the denomination in the first half of the nineteenth century. Among them were the challenges posed by the threat or actuality of infidelity, both from within and outside the Universalist family.

Chapter 9

UNIVERSALISM AND INFIDELITY: DENOMINATIONAL DEFECTIONS

Like other religious bodies, the Universalists in the nineteenth century had their share of defectors, apostates, and wayward souls, both clerical and lay. Although even rough statistics are impossible to obtain, the very nature of the religious liberalism and individualism preached (and usually practiced) by Universalists, the lack of cohesive organization, and the difficulty or reluctance in enforcing religious discipline, may have resulted in a higher denominational mortality rate than might be found in other groups. Personal motivations are difficult to gauge at best, but it is certain that Universalism turned out to be a convenient way-station for hundreds making their spiritual pilgrimages. Undoubtedly the denomination embraced, at one time or another, a goodly number of non-believers, opportunists, and even charlatans as well as individuals sincerely seeking and finding a congenial religious home. Others suffered from chronic intellectual restlessness, while still others were mentally and/or emotionally unstable or were at least thought to be so.

Some—probably the majority—who were lost to the denomination merely disappeared, virtually or totally unnoticed by clerks and other ostensible record-keepers. Many clergymen dropped out of the ministry to pursue other occupations and were seldom or never heard of again. Some migrated quietly to other denominations, while still others turned on Universalism, for a variety of reasons, and made a noisy departure which caused varying degrees of concern and excitement among the faithful. Staunch and loyal Universalists almost always tried to put a positive reading on such departures, arguing that it was for the good of the cause in the last analysis; in a few cases, when clergymen departed with a round of attacks on Universalists or Universalism, the occasion provided an opportunity for public rebuttal and attendant publicity when return salvos were fired. This presumably had the advantage not only of setting the record straight but of providing the opportunity for educating the non-Universalist public.

However, the answers to attacks had built into them calculated risks, and could very easily backfire by merely confirming in the minds of the skeptic or opposer the falsity or even danger of Universalist teachings. But there were few alternatives; certainly, silence in the face of attacks—some of them vitriolic—was usually not the better part of wisdom. In some instances, other denominations were accused of fomenting discord among Universalists or of attempting to capitalize on situations that might weaken or embarrass the denomination. In a few cases, there was nothing for Universalists to do but accept the reality of the situation and to make the best of it.

Probably the two best-known cases of defection from Universalism in the nineteenth century were those of Orestes A. Brownson (1803-1876) and Abner Kneeland (1774-1844), who represented the two extremes within the religious spectrum. Of the two, Kneeland attracted more attention within the denomination and caused greater concern. Brownson eventually found satisfactory accommodation within Roman Catholicism, after temporarily abandoning Christianity, while Kneeland rejected the entire Christian ethos.

Brownson, a convert to Universalism in 1824 at the age of twenty-one, was born in Stockbridge, Vermont, and between the ages of six and fourteen was left by his parents in the care of an elderly couple in the village of Royalston. From them, and from what few books were available, he acquired a vague Protestant background, and attended local Methodist and Christian church meetings.[1] According to his autobiography, he was a seeker after spiritual satisfaction from his early youth, and determined to be "a minister of religion" from the very beginning. At the age of nineteen, while residing in Saratoga County, New York, he unenthusiastically joined the Presbyterian church, feeling that submission to some kind of religious authority was his best recourse. He found what he considered the excessively harsh Calvinistic discipline completely uncongenial and found no justification for Presbyterian claims to be the true church of Christ.[2]

Brownson next turned from orthodox to liberal Christianity. After two years as a Presbyterian he became a Universalist, and was fellowshipped by the New England Convention at Hartland, Vermont, in 1825, and was ordained the following year at Jaffrey, New Hampshire.[3] His introduction to the denomination had come by way of a maternal aunt who, in her youth, had listened to the preaching of Elhanan Winchester, and by way of Universalist books which she furnished him while he was in his early teens and which he had read before becoming a Presbyterian. Brownson had come to the conclusion that even though preceded by John Murray—"that eccentric Irishman"—Winchester had been the real founder of American Universalism. Brownson had been unsettled by what he read, including the London edition of Charles Chauncy on universal salvation, Joseph Huntington's *Calvinism Improved,* and Hosea Ballou's *Treatise on Atonement.* Brownson, who became personally acquainted with Ballou after entering the Universalist ministry, recalled him with respect, remembering him as "the patriarich of American Universalism" who in the 1820s was "its oracle, very nearly its pope." Ballou was, to his knowledge, the first American writer who combined "the doctrines of modern Unitarianism with Universalism."

Brownson reluctantly admitted that both Ballou and his writings had impressed him greatly during his early years, and considered the *Treatise* "a most remarkable production" in view of the educational and literary handicaps under which Ballou had written. The work exhibited "wonderful acuteness and power, in language, clear, simple, forcible, and at times beautiful and eloquent." In fact, wrote Brownson, Ballou's *Treatise* "certainly entitled him to rank among the most original thinkers of our times." Unfortunately, added Brownson (with the wisdom of hindsight), "a book fuller of heresies, and heresies of the most deadly character, not excepting Theodore Parker's *Discourse of Matters pertaining to Religion,* has probably never issued from the American press, or one better calculated to carry away a large class of young, ingenuous, and unformed minds." It was, in fact, the pernicious Universalist writings that had so unsettled Brownson's thinking that he was driven to become a Presbyterian in despair. He confessed, however, that he agreed with Universalists to the extent that they denied the doctrine of eternal punishment of the wicked. So he put aside the qualms he had as to the final authority of the Scriptures which the majority of Universalists claimed, and joined the denomination. At least they preached a more rational doctrine, in his estimation, than did the orthodox.

Between 1826 and 1829 Brownson preached in New Hampshire and northern New York State as well as in his native Vermont. While pastor of the society in Auburn, New York, he edited the last two volumes of the *Gospel Advocate and Impartial Investigator* (1827-29).[4] It was while editing the paper that Brownson's doubts about Universalism began to assume serious proportions. He satisfied himself that, when forced to study the Scriptures closely in order to defend Universalism against its detractors, the Bible (if literally interpreted) did not teach the final salvation of all men. He was left with the unhappy alternative of rejecting the Scriptures "as authority for reason" or accepting the doctrine of endless punishment. He chose the first. He could find no half-way house so far as reconciling the authority of the Scriptures with their authenticity and divine inspiration were concerned. He could not convince himself that the Bible was the infallible word of God. And there were other difficulties.

He was not clear in his own mind about what Jesus really taught, and he failed to find definitive answers in Universalism. He became convinced that the entire Universalist theological structure, with its conception of a God of love, failed to provide moral accountability, and blurred, if it did not destroy completely, any objective distinction between virtue and vice, between good and evil. What assurance was there that good would ever triumph?

With his thinking in such a snarl, Brownson saw no solution by 1829 but to renounce Christianity. He had by then assured himself "that Universalists generally had no belief in revelation, and were really deists or sceptics, and professed to be Christians only because they could combat all religion more successfully under a nominally Christian banner, than under the banner of open, avowed infidelity." He went so far as to acknowledge that "the most anti-Christian period of my life was the last two years that I was a Universalist preacher."

As Brownson interpreted Universalism, he had no challenge or obstacle to overcome; if man's fate in a future world were already guaranteed, whether he exerted himself or not, why bother? So his principal task seemed to be negative—merely to combat orthodoxy—and gave Brownson no sense of purpose in his ministerial career. The only reality for him was to "take my stand on the solid earth, and devote myself to the material order, to the virtue and happiness of mankind in this earthly life."

Just before abandoning Universalism, Brownson published "half in mockery" his "creed" in the *Gospel Advocate.*[5] In it he "rejected heaven for earth, and God for man, [and] eternity for time." Universalism had been "only a stage in my transition from the religion of my childhood to socialism." That was to be the new dispensation. His first opportunity to try a new direction came with Robert Owen's attempt to create a model community in the New World, the Harmony experiment in Indiana.

Brownson's reform-mindedness, especially his support of the socialistic ideas of Robert Owen and his followers, and his advocacy of the rights of the working man, estranged Brownson from many Universalists. Thomas Whittemore was greatly perturbed in 1829 when it was announced that Brownson had joined the staff of the *Free Inquirer* and had become associated with a group of radical social reformers who had allegedly renounced Christianity altogether.[6] Whittemore and other Universalists had been caught by surprise, for Brownson had just preached, by invitation, in two Universalist churches in Boston and had made it known that he would either assist Menzies Rayner in editing the denominational *Religious Inquirer* in Hartford or return to upstate New York and secure another pastorate. As Brownson preached in New York State, New Hampshire, and Massachusetts he became more and more critical of some aspects of institutional Christianity, including Universalism, and in 1830 was disfellowshipped by the New England Convention.[7]

Whittemore, long suspicious of Brownson and his ideas, accused him in 1831 of currying favor with Unitarians by casting aspersions on Universalists. Brownson suggested, among other things, that Universalists "pay less attention to polemics, and more to the improvement of the heart."[8] Whatever his motives, Brownson did become a Unitarian in 1832 and held Unitarian pastorates. Adin Ballou recalled many years later that he had participated in Brownson's installation at the First Congregational Church (Unitarian) in Canton, Massachusetts, in 1834. George Ripley of Boston had delivered the sermon.[9] Ripley was afterwards to be the leader of the widely-heralded Brook Farm community and thereafter to serve as literary editor of the *New York Tribune.* Ballou recognized Brownson's merits as "a ripe scholar, an able preacher, and a writer of rare ability. But in theology, metaphysics, ethics, and ecclesiasticism, his convictions, positions, and associations underwent strange vicissitudes."

Brownson continued to criticize Universalism after he changed his denominational allegiance. In his *New Views of Christianity, Society, and the Church,* published in 1836, Brownson argued that Universalism lacked a coherent philosophy.[10] The outspoken Whittemore considered Brownson's departure from Universalism as good riddance. The fact that Brownson "soon sunk down to the level of Unitarianism" was, said he, quite predictable.[11] Brownson had never been a sincere Universalist, in Whittemore's estimation, in spite of professions to the contrary, and "it was a matter of congratulation to us that the connexion was dissolved."

Almost no mention was made in the Universalist press either of the transcendentalism which Brownson expressed in his *Boston Quarterly Review* or of his rather dramatic conversion to Roman Catholicism in 1844. Sylvanus Cobb, editor of the *Christian Freeman,* inserted a notice of Brownson's baptism and confirmation two months after the events took place. Cobb disposed of the whole matter in a few sentences, commenting that Brownson had seemingly become weary of seeking the truth for himself and would now depend on the Pope to do his thinking for him.[12] Another Universalist dispensed with Brownson by referring to him as "the perpetual motion politico-religionist."[13] Whittemore had noted in 1831 that Brownson had already "in his religious professions . . . fairly *boxed the compass.*"[14]

Four years after Brownson's conversion to Catholicism, Whittemore rather flippantly remarked that in his "circuit of all the sects," Brownson might next journey to Constantinople and become a Mohammedan.[15] Whittemore even went so far as to associate Brownson with Benedict Arnold, saying that the former deserved a place in religion comparable to that held by Arnold in affairs of state—with the latter possibly the better of the two men.[16] The Vermont-based *Watchman and Christian Repository,* edited by Universalist Eli Ballou, described Brownson in 1854 as "that boasting, swaggering, brow-beating bundle of inconsistencies."[17]

The ill feeling between Brownson and his former Universalist colleagues was apparently reciprocal. When his autobiography was published in 1857, it carried most unflattering portraits of individual clergymen as well as Universalists in general. Charles Hudson, Paul Dean, and Edward Turner had all participated in Brownson's ordination in 1826. Hudson was described as "very conceited, very disputatious, with moderate learning, fair logical ability, and no fancy or imagination—a dry, hard man, and an exceedingly dull and uninteresting preacher." Dean came off somewhat better, partly because he deserted Universalism to become a Unitarian. Brownson admitted that Turner was "the best sermonizer I ever knew among Universalists. But he had too refined and cultivated a taste to be a popular Universalist preacher." He, like Brownson (according to the latter's interpretation) had the good sense to leave the denomination and associate with Unitarians.

Brownson, after noting the Restorationist schism among some New England Universalists and Adin Ballou's part in the movement, dismissed him in 1857 as "a spiritualist, spiritist, or devil-worshipper, conversing with spirits." Brownson referred contemptuously to Linus S. Everett as "originally . . . a house and sign-painter, a man of little learning, but a good deal of mother-wit [who] had little religious belief, and not much moral principle." Everett's redeeming features were his "popular address and engaging manners," and the fact that he was "a philanthropist, and talked well."

Perhaps one explanation for the failure of Universalists to say much about Brownson's apostasy is to be found in his support of religious liberty, the desirability of separation of church and state, the importance of lay involvement in church affairs, and the accommodation of Catholicism to American principles of democracy—all Universalist precepts.[18]

The case of Abner Kneeland was in sharp contrast to that of Brownson. His formal association with Universalism lasted much longer and was more intimate than Brownson's; and Kneeland's rejection of Christian Universalism was so frequently and so bluntly stated that his attacks could not be ignored and had to be answered in some fashion. There is no question that his rejection of Universalism caused concern, particularly when the denomination was linked in the popular mind with his succession of trials, and his subsequent conviction and imprisonment for blasphemy.

Abner Kneeland (1774-1844) was born in Gardner, Massachusetts, on 6 April 1774 and started his secular career as a carpenter, and his ministerial career in Dummerston, Vermont, as a part-time preacher among the Baptists while serving also as a schoolteacher.[19] He became familiar with Universalism through Elhanan Winchester's writings and decided to apply for fellowship at the New England Convention meeting in Winchester, New Hampshire, in 1803. Once accepted, he functioned as an itinerant preacher in the state until ordained in the fall of 1804 by the New England Convention and installed as pastor of the Universalist society in Langdon, New Hampshire. The sermon was delivered by Hosea Ballou.

Kneeland made himself visible to the Universalist community immediately by publishing a sermon delivered prior to his ordination. A second published sermon had been delivered at the meeting of the Northern Association (Vermont). In 1807 he served as clerk of the New England Convention and again from 1811 to 1815. He was appointed to a committee, along with Hosea Ballou, to prepare a hymn book. Kneeland contributed over 130 hymns to the collection. Writing long after Kneeland had abandoned Universalism, Thomas Whittemore made the acid comment that most of Kneeland's contributions were "weak, and insipid, and unpoetical."[20]

After six years in Langdon, Kneeland was installed as the first pastor of the Charlestown, Massachusetts, society, beginning in 1811, at a salary of $10 a week. Hosea Ballou again delivered the principal sermon.[21] Kneeland promptly became involved in the series of discussions on theology published in the *Gospel Visitant* which became associated with the later Restorationist controversy. While at Charlestown, Kneeland, whose first wife and a young child had died while he was in New Hampshire, remarried. His matrimonial choice, a wealthy widow named Osborn, operated a retail business establishment in Salem, Massachusetts, in which Kneeland saw a great financial future. So he abruptly left the ministry in 1814. There was so much adverse comment about his precipitate action that he felt called upon to vindicate himself in print two years later.[22] Being called upon to justify his sometimes erratic and unpredictable behavior became a lifelong avocation with Kneeland. In any case, the store, which specialized in bonnets, had gone bankrupt by the time Kneeland returned to the ministry in 1816 at New Hartford (Whitestown, Oneida County), New York, where he remained less than two years.

The Lombard Street society in Philadelphia was Kneeland's next post, where he spent seven busy years (until 1825) engaged in preaching a distinctly unitarian Universalism, editing and publishing sermons and tracts, engaging in public religious debates, assisting his wife in another retail establishment, and serving as a government inspector of imported hats.[23] A series of sermons on "universal benevolence" which he delivered in the Lombard Street church was published in 1818, and republished in 1824 with "additional notes." In 1824 he proclaimed himself the inventor of a system of "Phonotypy," described in his *American Pronouncing Spelling Book* as "a phonetic system of orthography." He set the type for the book himself. Kneeland found time to prepare his own translation of the New Testament, in which he left all references to future punishment, hell, and damnation in the original Greek.[24] He also had a four-day debate with one W.L. McCalla, "the battle-axe of sternest Orthodoxy," in Philadelphia the same year; it was published as a 336-page book.[25]

Kneeland's interest in hymnology was again expressed by his compilation of the *Philadelphia Hymn Book* in 1819. His selections, made while he was still at least outwardly a Universalist, were a far cry from those which he published under the title *National Hymns* in 1832, after he had abandoned Christianity. His desire to engage in religious journalism was achieved when he assumed the editorship of the weekly *Christian Messenger,* a Presbyterian journal established in Philadelphia in 1819. After two years, Kneeland transformed the paper into the *Philadelphia Universalist Magazine and Christian Messenger* (a monthly), of which two volumes were published. He also tried his hand at secular journalism with the *Gazeteer.* Publication was suspended in 1824, after less than a year's existence, when Kneeland decided to change his location.

After a brief visit to North Carolina in 1825, Kneeland resigned his pastorate in Philadelphia and moved to New York City, where he became a controversial figure among Universalists because of his growing religious skepticism. This had been induced, at least in part, by reading the works of Joseph Priestley, and by personal acquaintance with Robert Owen, the Welsh communitarian. Kneeland's decision to move to New York had arisen out of a three-month pulpit exchange in 1825 with Nehemiah Dodge, pastor of the Second Society of United Christian Friends, known as the Prince Street church, which had been organized in New York in 1824. Kneeland's connection with the Second Society lasted less than two years. Charges and countercharges were made about his alleged infidelity, extending possibly even to atheism.

Early in 1827 he abandoned the society and set up his own, populated by a number of individuals attracted by his questioning of some of the basic tenets of Christianity, or possibly by his convincing performances. The splinter group met at various locations, including Tammany Hall, for several months, and in 1828 Kneeland shocked more conventional Universalists by inviting Miss Frances Wright to lecture to his congregation, meeting at the time in the Masonic Hall on Broadway.

Miss Wright, a social reformer and colleague of Owen, caused no end of excitement and consternation with her ideas about marriage and her agnostic religious attitude, not to mention her plans for the benefit of emancipated slaves in Memphis, Tennessee. Even the more liberal Universalists looked askance at her "advanced views" and the result was still another secession movement in Kneeland's group. Many of his followers left his society and the remaining minority organized the "Moral Philanthropists" in 1830 and began the publication of the *Free Inquirer.* This was the heart of the so-called Freethought Movement with which Kneeland became associated.[26]

Kneeland made his break with Universalism in 1829 and soon thereafter with Christianity in general, but only after much confusion and premature action by various Universalist bodies and an earlier history of difficulties with the New England Convention under whose general jurisdiction he had originally preached. He had received a vote of "disapprobation" in 1814, when he had suddenly left his pastorate in Charlestown, Massachusetts, to enter secular business and had failed to notify the convention of his action. According to its records, he had "disconnected himself" with the Charlestown society and was considered at least temporarily disfellowshipped.[27] Kneeland objected to this rendition of his status and requested that the record be changed to indicate that the separation from the society had been mutual and not unilateral, and had been considered "expedient" by both parties. The convention then requested him to reconsider and to resume his ministerial career. This he did, much to the gratification of the convention.[28]

After his removal to New York State in 1816, he had attended the meeting of the Western Association, within whose jurisdiction his ministry was then located. Stephen R. Smith recalled that Kneeland's preaching at the time was "a matter of pride and benefit to the denomination."[29] Smith had only two reservations: Kneeland's pulpit discourses were "too dry and metaphysical to secure continued interest and attention," and he was given overmuch to religious speculation in his sermons. In 1827 Kneeland, who was then in New York City, had found himself in the bad graces of the Hudson River Association which included the New York City area. Charges were brought against him for leaving his society in Prince Street without warning—constituting a breach of contract—and for giving his parishioners reason to doubt his belief in the divine authenticity of the Scriptures.[30] He denied the second charge.

Kneeland's utterances and actions seemed to raise so many doubts that the Kennebec Association in Maine, which could claim no jurisdiction whatever over him, precipitately withdrew fellowship early in 1829. Several other Universalist groups in the state took the same action, including the Penobscot and Washington Associations.[31] Their reasoning was that Kneeland had left doubt in people's minds that he believed in the existence of God and the divine inspiration of the Bible—two basic Universalist tenets. The Penobscot Association justified its action out of "a sense of duty to the cause of Christianity."[32] Thomas Whittemore, who was watching Kneeland with growing apprehension because of the effect his pronouncements might have on the denomination and its public image, at the same time objected strenuously to what he considered the premature and irregular actions of the associations in Maine. Kneeland should first have been "admonished and labored with in private," then given a fair hearing.[33]

Kneeland, thinking he had found a sympathetic ear, wrote Whittemore to lodge a complaint that the Kennebec Association had drummed him out of that body without either a hearing or having been apprised of the specific complaints against him.[34] Kneeland further asserted that he still believed in a Supreme Being and the resurrection of Christ, but that he did doubt the authenticity and historicity of some books in the Bible. Furthermore, he believed and made public his conviction that all had the right to construe Scriptures as they wished. When he had accepted the pastorate of the Philadelphia church in 1825, he had done so with the clear understanding that he reserved the right to interpret for himself the Articles of Faith recently adopted by that church.[35] Kneeland then appeared at the Southern Association (New England) meeting in Hartford, Connecticut, and had his wish granted that he be suspended from fellowship until he could show conclusively that he was "a real believer and defender of the christian religion."[36]

There was so much controversy regarding his beliefs and his status within the denomination that during the same year (1829) Kneeland issued in pamphlet form a sworn statement in which he insisted that he was still a Christian but simultaneously dissolved his connection with Universalism.[37] At this point Whittemore was thoroughly exasperated. There was, to him, no half-way house in the matter of Universalist faith. "If he [Kneeland] fully believes in the resurrection of the Saviour, if he holds to the future immortality of man, and the restoration of the whole human family to holiness and happiness, through the grace of our Lord Jesus Christ, he is a Universalist, whether he has fellowship with the whole world, or with no person whatsoever."[38]

Kneeland completed his break with Christianity by the fall of 1829, when he informed the public at large in an article in the *Free Inquirer* that he did not believe either in the existence of God or in man's consciousness in any form after physical death.[39] By the logic of his conclusions, presumably arrived at after some thirty years of arduous study and more than twenty-five years in the ministry, Kneeland likewise expressed his disbelief in the resurrection of Christ. These basic elements in Christian belief were not, according to Kneeland, susceptible of proof, but he would continue to search for answers satisfactory to him.

There was probably no Universalist more upset by Kneeland's defection than Hosea Ballou, who had known him almost from the day he had joined the denomination and had served as his friend and adviser. When Kneeland had his doubts about the authenticity of the Scriptures as early as 1804, he had sought help and had received comfort and assurance from Ballou.[40] After Ballou's *Treatise on Atonement* had appeared the following year, Kneeland had accepted its entire contents without question.[41] In 1829 Ballou attempted to show Kneeland where he was in error in an exchange published in the denominational press, but all to no avail. Kneeland remained unconvinced, and requested Ballou to cease addressing him as "Reverend."[42] Ballou challenged Kneeland's own claims to complete disbelief by pointing to the latter's *Appeal,* published in 1829 and containing theistic views. Ballou's advice to Kneeland was not to believe in any God at all rather than to leave room for a deity that the orthodox conceived as cruel and vengeful.

The cases of both Kneeland and Brownson were a subject for discussion at the New England Convention when it met in Lebanon, New Hampshire, in 1830. A committee headed by Hosea Ballou 2d reported that there was "full proof" that each man had renounced his faith in the Christian religion.[43] This renunciation was considered sufficient justification for "a dissolution of their fellowship with this body." After the relationship of Kneeland and Brownson with the New England Convention had been dissolved, the author of the circular letter accompanying the minutes considered it timely to exhort fellow Universalists about exercising care in admitting candidates into their ministry. There were some who joined for purposes of personal aggrandizement or "to gain favor or applause of the world."

Involvement of the Universalists with Abner Kneeland was far from over in 1830. He continued to debate as well as defend himself through the press, and commenced operations in the very stronghold of Universalism. In 1831 he moved from New York City to Boston, where he became a lecturer for the Free Inquirer's Society. After having been ejected from one public hall in 1834, he conducted, according to Universalists, "infidel meetings" in the Federal Street theater.[44] The society had been organized in 1830 as a non-sectarian forum of opinion, and lasted for a decade.

Kneeland also became the editor of the *Boston Investigator,* a weekly paper sponsored by the Freethought movement. The paper was devoted to social reform in behalf of such causes as a national educational system, abolition of slavery and imprisonment for debt, women's rights, and the betterment of the "laboring classes," and lasted until 1904. Kneeland travelled over much of New England and upstate New York on behalf of the movement. Part of his energies were also devoted to replying to attacks by Universalist journalists who accused him, among other things, of conspiring with Fanny Wright and others to "overthrow society," and of using the Free Inquirer societies as agencies for subverting law and order.[45]

Linus S. Everett, controversy-minded newspaperman and at the time pastor of the Universalist society in Charlestown, Massachusetts, who carried on an extended debate in the press with Robert Owen over social reform, labelled Kneeland a super-egotist who had been led astray by his own pretensions to omniscience. "The world of mankind are fools because they do not know that he knows more than other people."[46] Whittemore had nothing but contempt and pity for Kneeland, considering him an "unfortunate individual" with "absurd and visionary notions" who had "boxed the compass" religiously.[47] Whittemore was particularly outraged when he received a letter in 1833 from Kneeland (which Whittemore published) declaring himself an athiest.[48] God, wrote Kneeland, was "nothing more than a chimera of . . . imagination," and the story of Christ and his resurrection was "as much a fable and fiction as that of the god Prometheus." This was especially offensive to Whittemore in view of the fact that just a few months before, Kneeland, while lecturing in New Hampshire, had written a long letter to Whittemore outlining his "philosophical creed," in which he had declared that Nature and God were synonymous; hence he was a pantheist and not an atheist at all.[49]

Early in 1834 Kneeland replied to his Universalist critics in an article in the *Boston Investigator* entitled "Universalist Intolerance," in which Hosea Ballou was one of the principal targets. For his efforts, Kneeland was characterized by Whittemore as "pedantic, unsound in mind, and superficially informed on almost every subject."[50] But then events took a new turn. Kneeland was indicted for blasphemy by the Suffolk County (Massachusetts) Grand Jury. After four years of litigation, appeals through various state courts, three hung juries, and an impassioned plea in his own defense, Kneeland was found guilty and was sentenced to imprisonment for sixty days.[51] He became the last individual to be jailed by the state for the crime of blasphemy. The indictment was based on a Massachusetts statute originally enacted in 1782 which provided a series of alternative punishments, including up to twelve months' imprisonment, for anyone found guilty of blaspheming or denying "the holy name of God" in various ways.[52] Substantially the same ordinance was reenacted as part of the General Laws of Massachusetts in 1920.[53]

The complaint resulting in Kneeland's indictment had been filed by a Boston lawyer, Lucius M. Sargent (an Episcopalian, and not a Universalist, as Whittemore carefully pointed out). The indictment was based on three publications involving Kneeland, all of which appeared in the issue of the *Boston Investigator* of 20 December 1833: an allegedly obscene essay reprinted from the *Free Inquirer*; a letter signed "A Skeptic" which called into question the efficacy of public prayer;

and extracts from a letter written by Kneeland to Whittemore in 1833 and published in the *Trumpet.* The key document, on which Kneeland's conviction was based, was the third.

Kneeland had explained that he still considered himself a Universalist so far as he believed in "universal philanthropy, universal benevolence and universal charity" and rejected the idea of punishment after death. As to the other "religious notions" of the Universalists, he did "not believe in any of them."

> 1. Universalists believe in a god which I do not; but believe that their god, with all his moral attributes, (aside from nature itself), is nothing more than a chimera of their own imagination.
>
> 2. Universalists believe in Christ, which I do not; but believe that the whole story concerning him is as much a fable and a fiction, as that of the god Prometheus, the tragedy of whose death is said to have been acted on the stage at Athens, 500 years before the christian era.
>
> 3. Universalists believe in miracles, which I do not; but believe that every pretension to them can either be accounted for on natural principles or else is to be attributed to mere trick and imposture.
>
> 4. Universalists believe in the resurrection of the dead, in immortality and eternal life, which I do not; but believe that all life is mortal, that death is an external extinction of life to the individual who possesses it, and that no individual life is, ever was, or ever will be eternal.

The declaration crucial to Kneeland's case was the very first one.

Until Judge Lemuel Shaw of Boston, the Chief Justice of the state Supreme Judicial Court, handed down the majority opinion in March 1838 upholding Kneeland's guilt, the case was covered in detail in both the secular and religious press. Kneeland, not to be silenced by anyone, and with support from the most diverse quarters, published a series of tracts in his own defense. After Kneeland's conviction had been upheld, a group of distinguished citizens petitioned the governor for an unconditional pardon for Kneeland, but the governor declined to comply. The petition, written by William Ellery Channing and Ellis Gray Loring, was signed by over 150 persons, including such eminent men as Ralph Waldo Emerson, Theodore Parker, William Lloyd Garrison, George Ripley, and Bronson Alcott.[54] The document was an eloquent statement on behalf of freedom of speech and of the press, and of Kneeland's constitutional right to express himself, however "pernicious and degrading" his ideas might be. Public reaction to Kneeland's conviction was mixed, although criticism of the court decision seems to have outweighed support for it.[55]

Universalists joined with their erstwhile religious protagonists, the Moral Philanthropist Society of Philadelphia, and the various other Freethought groups, in roundly condemning the court decision. While repeatedly denying that Universalists had any sympathy for Kneeland's atheistic ideas, Whittemore just as vociferously expressed indignation that the indictment had ever been brought, and called the whole procedure an unwarranted interference of the state in religious affairs.[56] "Civil prosecutions for the mere expression of opinion on the subject of religion, are productive of no good." Even though Kneeland was, in Whittemore's estimation, a "poor, miserable, deluded fellow mortal," the entire case was a violation of both the spirit and intent of the second article of the Massachusetts Bill of Rights which provided that no one was to be molested in any way for his religious profession or sentiments. Universalists lamented "most deeply" the course Kneeland had pursued, but no more so than the course followed by the government in "this invasion of his natural rights."[57]

S.J. McMorris, making his rounds as a Universalist preacher in Alabama, was "mortified" at the treatment accorded Kneeland in some southern papers.[58] The *Southern Times and State Gazette* (Columbia, South Carolina) had greeted Kneeland's conviction with approval, and advocated that a "hardened Atheist" like Kneeland, and especially those who rejected the doctrine of future rewards and punishments, should be excluded from testifying in court. McMorris stood firmly on the ground that every individual was entitled to his own opinions, and the expression of them, no matter how "absurd" they might be. Abel C. Thomas, prominent in Philadelphia Universalism, considered the treatment accorded Kneeland at the hands of the courts "one of the most barbarian as well as impolitic expedients of the nineteenth century."[59]

Hosea Ballou visited his one-time friend while Kneeland was in jail because Ballou felt it was part of his "Christian duty," and tried to reason with him.[60] But communication between the two men had already broken down. By 1838 they were poles apart on their religious thinking. Ballou was frank to admit that Kneeland, whom he found in good spirits, was apparently prospering from the "persecution" which had brought him notoriety and had made him something of a martyr. The likelihood that this might happen had been pointed out in the Channing-Loring petition only a short time earlier, and was made even more evident by Theodore Parker, who wrote that even though "Abner was jugged for sixty days . . . he will come out as beer from a bottle, all foaming, and will make others foam. . . ."[61] After Kneeland had served his prison term, he and Ballou engaged in another brief round of debates through the columns of the *Trumpet,* but the end-product was, predictably, a stalemate.[62]

Kneeland, eternally restless and seeking new outlets for his energies and ideas, and frustrated by the opposition which had been climaxed by his trials and conviction, departed in 1839 for the frontier community of Salubria, Iowa. This settlement, which had been planned by Kneeland and others since 1836, but for which no location was decided upon until 1839, was intended to be a center of freethought in the West.[63] There he died on 27 August 1844, at the age of 71. Before leaving Boston, he had delivered a "Valedictory Address" to his First Society of Free Inquirers and gave them some rather cynical advice. If they were unable to continue as a group, "just go to some Unitarian meeting, for the sake of being in the fashion. The Unitarians are nothing more than a fashionable kind of Deists . . . ."[64]

No one who has even a superficial familiarity with Abner Kneeland and his ideas can deny that he was a complex and contradictory person and that his constant search for personal fulfillment and his quest for religious satisfaction resulted in inconsistencies, mistakes, and misunderstandings for which Kneeland himself was often responsible. The reactions and assessments by his Universalist contemporaries must be treated with great caution, for their evaluations were inevitably skewed by some degree of bias. Most of the estimates of Kneeland by Universalists were made under circumstances unfavorable to him—either after he had defected from not only the denomination but from Christianity in general, or during the heat of some controversy of which he was the center, when tempers on both sides were likely to flare.

Setting aside the dimensions and implications of Kneeland's religious quest, there were some traits of character which seemed to appear with great regularity and were critically observed, and usually documented, by his contemporaries. The first was his propensity to flit from one enthusiasm to another, the most recent in his experience seeming to be the best—until superseded by another. Nathaniel Stacy left a most unflattering picture of Kneeland in this respect. It must be pointed out, however, that Stacy's personal contact with Kneeland (whom he actually saw in action on only two occasions) was limited, and his most vivid impression of Kneeland was the latter's performance as a brash young man.[65] Stacy heard Kneeland deliver "the least interesting and instructive" discourse he had ever heard from a Universalist minister who did not even have a Bible with him to verify the text from which he preached. Stacy stressed the fact that Kneeland "never possessed the faculty of original thought—he never originated a single idea; it was all borrowed; and he was generally the echo of the last author read."

This did sometimes lead Kneeland dangerously close to the brink of plagiarism when he appropriated someone else's ideas as his own without attribution. On departing from his pastorate in Langdon, New Hampshire, in 1811, he had delivered not one but two "farewell sermons." After he arranged to have them published, he acknowledged that they were originally a single sermon delivered by Hosea Ballou five years before.[66] Kneeland was successively enamored of the doctrine of materialism (via Joseph Priestley), Robert Owen's theory and practice of "social community," and other unconventional plans and programs.

Stacy also implied a tendency on Kneeland's part to dissimulation; for example, Stacy was convinced that Kneeland had become a confirmed religious skeptic by the time he assumed his first pastorate in New York in 1825 and had become "tinctured with [Owen's] Atheistical sentiments," yet continued to use a Christian Universalist pulpit from which to spread his ideas.[67]

Kneeland was also, and with some justification, considered "a visionary man," showing a "want of judgment."[68] Abel C. Thomas drew up a balance-sheet on Kneeland in the early 1850s. Although Thomas considered him "a man of excellent moral character, of amiable spirit and imperturbable calmness . . . and commanding presence," he saw basic faults. Among them were "errors of judgment, . . . liability to deception, and a morbid seeking after new things."[69] It is indisputable that Kneeland had very little business acumen, and was frequently victimized by various schemes. He was apparently fascinated with all kinds of social experiments. He expressed great enthusiasm in 1826 for the possibilities of a plan for a model town, the Franklin Community, based on the principles advocated by Robert Owen, and to be located near Haverstraw, New York, on the Hudson River.[70] While in New York, he was also involved in organizing a company to seek Captain Kidd's treasure, reputedly located forty miles north of the city according to the divining capabilities of a young girl. He spent $9,000 of his second wife's inheritance of $14,000 in buying merchandise for a business venture which failed. He spent $100 paid him by the Universalist society in Shirley, Massachusetts, on what turned out to be a worthless cure for cancer. He also borrowed several hundred dollars to invest in an invention to demonstrate the principle of perpetual motion.[71]

Kneeland's impact on the fortunes of Universalism in his own day is difficult to determine. Russell Streeter, who had just accepted the pastorate of the society in Watertown, Massachusetts, after many years in Portland, Maine, had expressed great concern when Kneeland's defection became known in 1829. He hoped that Kneeland's action would not have an adverse effect on young men entering the Universalist ministry.[72] There is no statistical evidence that his concern was justified. Twenty-six new preachers were licensed in 1829; during the last year of Kneeland's trial (1838), eighty were added to the rolls.[73]

There was, of course, the other side of the coin. Universalism appeared to be, simultaneously, the nursery and seed-bed of infidelity and even of heresy in the minds of many. Was not Kneeland a typical product of its pernicious influence? The term "infidel," used indiscriminately and loosely, was often made synonymous with "Universalist," particularly before 1850, and the two were almost invariably associated in the religious press.[74] The clerical-journalistic leaders among Universalists did their best to disabuse the general public of the error of such linkage. During the 1830s at least half a dozen major works had been published by Universalist clergymen stoutly defending not only their denomination but Christianity as well. Hosea Ballou 2d, writing in 1839, pointed out that no one could "overlook the fact that, if any denomination is doing its part to uproot infidelity, it is the denomination of Universalists."[75] He cited as examples recent books by David Pickering (*Lectures in Defence of Divine Revelation,* 1830), Isaac D. Williamson (*An Argument for the Truth of Christianity,* 1836), and Stephen R. Smith (*The Causes of Infidelity Removed,* 1839), which Ballou reviewed. The denomination thus gained at least one indirect benefit from the Kneeland episode: his very attacks on Universalism as a benighted Christian sect, and the vigorous defenses which they elicited, gave the lie to the popular notion that it stood beyond the pale of Christianity.

Scarcely had the reverberations of the Kneeland blasphemy trials died down when Universalists were faced with two more defections widely publicized at the time, and accompanied by spirited attacks on the denomination. The first touched off a controversy which filled the columns of Universalist newspapers off and on for almost ten years and involved one Matthew Hale Smith. The first public airing of his prolonged feud with Universalism occurred in the spring of 1839 when Smith, apparently to avoid the discipline of the Massachusetts Convention on a charge of forgery and "deceitful behavior," withdrew for the second time from fellowship.[76] He alleged unwarranted interference of that body in clerical affairs and argued that a minister was accountable to his local society only and could not be directed by any higher authority. Several months later, after having been dismissed by his society in Salem, Massachusetts, he resigned from the denomination for the third and final time.[77]

Not content with this step alone, he published what turned out to be grossly inaccurate lists of preachers who had renounced Universalism, and of Universalist societies which had purportedly ceased to exist. According to Universalist intelligence, he had left the denomination because of a dislike for its overly rigid discipline, and had sold his services to other denominations for the express purpose of vilifying Universalists for their laxity in morals, their faulty organization, and their unseemly zeal.[78] He was described as one of the "hired slanderers and revivalists [who] have foamed out their own shame . . . in unprincipled attempts to injure Universalism."[79]

The consensus among Universalists at the time was that Smith was suffering from inherited mental instability, and the evidence seems to have borne out this conclusion. Smith's father, Elias, who had joined the Baptists at the age of sixteen, had been one of the founders of the "Christian Connexion" in northern New England about 1802.[80] The elder Smith had been considered by his friends and associates to have been "naturally unstable," and had wavered constantly in his religious beliefs from the time he had been ordained as a Baptist preacher in 1792. He had proclaimed himself a Universalist in 1801, withdrew a few months later, joined again in 1817, then again renounced his allegiance in 1826. In 1842, four years before his death, he swung back toward Universalism, and was finally reconverted in 1843.[81]

His son Matthew's religious itinerary seemed to have been an exaggerated version of his father's experience, although his early career was not unusual. He had started out as a Free-will Baptist in Vermont, became a convert to Universalism as a teenager, preached his first sermon at the age of eighteen, and settled briefly in southern Vermont, where he preached in Brattleboro and Guilford. He studied theology briefly under Hosea Ballou 2d in 1829–a fact which Smith's mentor lived to regret.[82] In 1830 Smith had been fellowshipped by the Southern Association (Connecticut) and two years later had been invited to take charge of the society in Hartford.[83]

Trouble did not begin to brew until mid-1835, half way through Smith's fourth year at Hartford. He suddenly renounced Universalism, changed his mind in a matter of days and recanted, but finally resigned his pastorate for reasons of ill health some three months later. He gave as the explanation for his erratic and unpredictable behavior "an affection of the head," which later generations would probably describe as temporary insanity.[84] Before the end of his life, he had not only renounced his Universalist connection three times, but professed on two separate occasions to have been a Presbyterian, and briefly to have been a Unitarian. He had embraced "orthdoxy" by becoming a Congregational pastor in Connecticut in 1841, and then held a series of brief pastorates in New Hampshire, Washington, D.C., and Massachusetts. In all, he had changed his religious affiliation at least seven times up to 1850.

He decided that year to read law in the office of Judge Rufus Choate in Boston.[85] After three months' study he was admitted to the Massachusetts bar and then resigned his post at the Church of the Pilgrims (Congregational) in Boston.[86]

Smith took a temporary position as a part-time preacher in the Episcopal church in Chelsea, Massachusetts, in 1851, and spent the rest of his time engaged in secular journalism.[87] He became editor of the *Morning Chronicle* in Boston in 1852 and continued to provoke the ire of Universalists–particularly those who were temperance-minded–by advocating repeal of the "Maine Law" of 1851 which forbade the manufacture and sale of alcoholic beverages of all kinds within the state.[88] In 1854 Smith applied for readmission to the ranks of the Congregational clergy, but his request was unanimously denied.[89] There was an unconfirmed report that he had met a similar fate at the hands of the Baptists.

After a second brief flirtation with the Episcopal church—this time in New York State—he next appeared in New York City as one half of the law firm of Richardson and Smith.[90] At the time of his death in 1879 at the age of sixty-nine, he professed to be a Presbyterian.[91] As one Universalist editor noted, it was extremely difficult "to keep up a journal of the tergiversations of this erratic comet."[92] Smith's unpredictable and quixotic career extended beyond religious matters and dabbling in the law. In 1853 he claimed to be a native of New Hampshire when he attended a "Sons of Portsmouth" 4th of July celebation.[93] When the "Sons of Maine" arranged a festival in Boston later the same year, he appeared as a native of the Pine Tree State.

Of the three extended written attacks on Universalism which Smith produced, probably the one that attracted the most attention appeared in 1842. It bore a typically lengthy nineteenth-century title: *Universalism Examined, Renounced, Exposed; in a series of Lectures, embracing the experience of the author during a ministry of twelve years, and the testimony of Universalist ministers to the dreadful moral tendency of their faith.* It was reprinted several times, and the American Tract Society continued to circulate the work as late as 1859.[94] In this polemic he attacked the denomination as corrupt and rapidly declining, and charged its ministry, by personal references, with deception, mercenary motives, ignorance, "looseness of taste and morals, and bitterness of spirit." One of his targets was his former teacher, Hosea Ballou 2d, who, with other Universalists, considered Smith's book "unworthy of notice."[95]

Universalists became convinced that hitherto competing denominations had somehow united in sponsoring Smith in his campaign to discredit them, but evidence of an actual conspiracy is impossible to come by. Whether such a combination had ever been effected or not, A.B. Grosh put the best possible reading on the entire matter by interpreting Smith's attacks on Universalism as acts of desperation and despair over its rapid spread.[96] He found something else to be cheerful about in the Smith case: to his knowledge, not a single Universalist had been converted to "partialism" as a result of Smith's apostasy.

Grosh's optimism was by no means shared by other Universalists. Lewis C. Browne, a clergyman in New York State, felt that Smith's misrepresentations had done so much damage to Universalism that a rebuttal was in order. The title of Browne's reply, published in 1847, almost matched that of Smith's major work in length: *Review of the Life and Writings of M. Hale Smith; with a Vindication of the Moral Tendency of Universalism, and the Moral Character of Universalists.* Smith's own brother, Daniel D. Smith, a Universalist clergyman who did not defect, documented Matthew Hale Smith's periods of insanity, due apparently to a brain tumor, and considered the *Universalism Examined* as "without any exception [the] greatest tissue of nonsense and misrepresentation that ever was issued from the press."[97] The known fact of M.H. Smith's mental instability did not diminish his presumed threat to the integrity of Universalism and the reputation of individual Universalists.

The second defection which caused much less excitement in Universalist circles than Smith's, but which nonetheless attracted some attention, occurred in August 1840. William Whittaker, pastor of the Fourth Universalist Society in New York City, dramatically renounced his belief from the pulpit one Sunday. The "renunciation sermon" was widely reprinted in Universalist publications and elicited sharp rebukes from the faithful. A.B. Grosh attributed Whittaker's abrupt action to "the influence of mortified vanity."[98] Whittaker, originally an Episcopalian, had begun preaching Universalism in 1832.[99] After a six-year pastorate in Hudson, New York, he had moved to New York City, where he had organized his own congregation without any formal invitation to do so. The ad hoc society lasted until mid-1840, when, faced with financial difficulties and dissatisfied with Whittaker's services, it urged him to resign. This he refused to do, hoping instead to remain until he received a call either to Salem, Massachusetts, to fill the vacancy caused by Matthew Hale Smith's departure, or to the Bleecker Street church in New York City, which also lacked a pastor. His overtures there having been rejected, he apparently withdrew from the denomination in a fit of pique.

Whittaker was then installed as the pastor of a Congregational church in the same city, after having been rejected by the Presbyterians. Following this action, E.F. Hatfield, a Presbyterian clergyman, published a book entitled *Universalism As It Is,* warning his denomination about such men as Whittaker. By allegedly taking scraps and parts of paragraphs and sentences from Universalist writings out of their context, "dovetailed and glued together with artful comments," the author was accused by Universalists of distorting and misrepresenting their views "in the worst possible manner." T.J. Sawyer, then also in New York, promptly undertook a bit of missionary work. In an extended series of exchanges in the religious press (later published in book form) he tried not only to correct Hatfield's errors but to set Whittaker, the misguided ex-Universalist clergyman, on the right path.[100] By the time a new and enlarged edition of Thomas B. Thayer's *Christianity against Infidelity* appeared in 1849, Hosea Ballou 2d, then editor of the *Universalist Quarterly,* believed that most of the "downright" infidels had been removed from the ministry of the denomination, although a few were still being listed as Universalists in the *Register*.[101]

Universalist thought and action during the 1830s and 1840s was by no means all negative or defensive. There was considerable feeling that they were responding positively and constructively to the challenges they faced both from outside and from within the denomination and were gaining influence and respectability as well as strength. In 1841, when A.B. Grosh, editor of the *Register,* took inventory, he liked what he found. Even the character and extent of the chronic opposition to Universalism, represented by the defection of the previous year of Matthew Hale Smith and William Whittaker, and their attacks on the faith, failed to dim Grosh's optimism. He expressed satisfaction in the softened attitude taken by authors of Universalist books, periodicals, and sermons toward opponents (with the notable exception of Smith). Polemics seemed to have become more restrained, there was "less severity of judgment, less censoriousness toward opposers generally—less caustic sarcasm and irony in discussing doctrines—and more manifested compassion and godly sorrow over the sins, and follies, and errors of our opposers." This hint of self-righteousness was tempered by Grosh's observation that perhaps this change had been brought about at least in part by the influence of their own doctrines on Universalists, who were finally being brought to conform to the principles of their own faith—including charity and "the spirit of Christ." There were signs of growing maturity within the denomination itself.

Further, Grosh detected a growing positive influence of Universalism on other denominations. Its spread as manifested by the increase in its own numbers and strength was "but trifling compared with its actual but unseen spread in the very ranks of Partialism." He offered the recent division in the ranks of the Presbyterian church over the issue of revivalism as an example; it had resulted in the secession of the so-called "new school" Presbyterians which, in turn, had spawned a group of Perfectionists, "many of the most rational of whom [were] believers in man's ultimate salvation from sin and torment." Many of the new school Presbyterians of liberal persuasion had, according to Grosh, secretly embraced Universalist ideas.

Grosh found the Methodists travelling down the same road toward liberal Christianity. They too had recently experienced a schism, when a group organizing themselves as Protestant Methodists, had rebelled against an overly authoritarian church government which gave "all the property and power to the clergy, and none to the people." Grosh attributed Universalist leanings or sentiments to several of the seceding group, including some who did not hesitate "to preach and publicly avow" their faith in universal salvation. Universalists could take comfort from the fact that almost every division or other crisis within other denominations, and every change made in their doctrines, brought them "nearer to our faith, if not quite into it."

It is, of course, impossible to ascertain how much of this actually happened, and how much was self-fulfilling, wishful thinking on the part of Universalists. But men like Grosh were positive that Universalism was sufficiently sturdy in the 1840s to withstand the onslaughts of such men as Whittaker and Smith, and to prosper while other denominations faltered or even suffered disaffection and actual disunity in their ranks.

Chapter 10

UNIVERSALISM AND THE CHALLENGE OF SOCIAL AND RELIGIOUS UNORTHODOXY

Blueprinting Ideal Societies

Deviant religious behavior by individuals within the denomination was only one of the many challenges which mid-nineteenth-century Universalists had to face. There was still the larger problem of how to react to that part of the great ferment of social reformism characterizing the Jacksonian era which emphasized rationalism, secularism, free-thought and attacks on inherited (and usually sacrosanct) social institutions—attacks which horrified some Americans and at least attracted the attention of others.

A fractional minority of Universalists or those who held to Universalist principles in general, defended radical social change and some even tried their hands at social experimentation. One such was Adin Ballou, founder of the Hopedale Community in Massachusetts. However, his venture, unlike many intentional communities of the time, was firmly grounded on Christian principles and did not partake of the secularism or anti-clericalism evident elsewhere. The great majority of Universalists, like many of their compatriots, greeted radical change—or the threat of radical change—with fear and trepidation, or at least with hesitation and serious reservations.

A second set of challenges centered about the appearance of new "isms"—or old "isms" in new guises—which had, in variant forms, the redemption of American society as their core. They ranged from the Adventism of William Miller, with his Biblically-centered, cataclysmic view of history, to the millennialism implied or expressed in Mesmerism, phrenology, Swedenborgianism, and spiritualism, all of which dealt in some fashion with the relationship of the natural and the supernatural.[1]

For Millerism, the overwhelming majority of thoughtful Universalists had no use. But for some of the other theories about human destiny, including the ephemeral as well as the more enduring, there were champions or supporters among Universalists. Many of the arguments they offered expressed clearly the "supernatural rationalism" which had characterized much of Hosea Ballou's thinking. Simultaneously, they attempted to fit scientific (or pseudo-scientific) discoveries into the larger framework of the divine plan. Some Universalists even abandoned the denomination in favor of such movements as spiritualism, finding in them new paths for the reunion of souls and happiness in a future state.

Of particular interest were the dozens of blueprints for ideal societies, many based on some form of communitarianism, which flourished and fell between 1830 and 1860, and which became associated with unconventional ideas about religion, marriage and the family, and private property. For most Universalists who were articulate on such subjects, the attacks on tradition which were associated with attempts at radical reconstitution of society gave them an excellent opportunity to defend revealed religion, reject infidelity, and support in general what was conceived to be "the American way of life."

Among the numerous plans for recasting society which attracted much attention in the United States in the 1830s and 1840s were those of Francois Charles Marie Fourier (1772-1837). Fourier, a French reformer and utopian, offered a proposal for the organization of associations or communities ("phalanxes") of approximately 1,800 persons, based on units of about 400 families each, which were to operate as virtually self-sufficient producing and laboring units. Albert Brisbane and Horace Greeley were among his more prominent American devotees, and such colonies as Brook Farm and Hopedale were attempts to incorporate some of Fourier's economic principles and to achieve ideal societies. Fourier and his disciples were not content with reforming what they saw as specific abuses in society, such as the exploitation of the laboring man, but wished to restructure it completely. Cooperation was to be substituted for competition, and private property was to be abolished for the common good. By various devices, including education, human nature would somehow be revolutionized and perfected, and the ideal of happiness for all would be achieved.

Some Universalists, like Hosea Ballou 2d, were skeptical. In fact, the whole scheme of "Associationism" sounded to him like a chimera—"a dream of the most fantastic kind." He used the occasion of the publication of two works on the subject of social reform to express his own ideas at some length.[2] Even assuming that human nature could be reconstituted, there were difficulties in the schemes of Fourier and others which Ballou found completely insurmountable. The destruction of individuality by submergence in the group was only one of the many faults he had to find with plans for social regeneration.

Ballou's rather caustic treatment provoked a long reply from fellow-Universalist Horace Greeley, who defended the principle of

Associationism and argued that Fourier himself never claimed or expected "universal perfection."[3] Greeley quite correctly pointed out that Fourier's scheme was only one among many, and to condemn out of hand not only his but similar ones was unfair and did but poorly serve those, like himself, who were sincerely interested in finding some way to ameliorate the lot of the less fortunate in society. Ballou, however, continued to take a dim view of the possibility of man's ultimate perfection. In a short article entitled "The Millenium; or the Golden Age to Come," he made the categorical statement that he looked for "no such state of things ever to take place, here on earth, and among mortal men."[4]

Ballou broadened his attack on Fourierism to include such "fads" as phrenology, transcendentalism, rationalism, and Mesmerism. He noted, in an extended review of Andrew Jackson Davis' *The Great Harmonia, concerning the Seven Mental States,* published in 1852, that Universalists seemed particularly prone to be fascinated with such aberrations.[5] He accounted for this tendency in two ways, both characteristic of the denomination. One was an overly loose and permissive organization which not only allowed but encouraged many individuals to "find a way into our ministry apparently from other than religious motives, especially from ambition to make a noise in the world; and whose principal qualifications . . . for making a noise . . . are an unfurnished head, a voluble tongue, and a cockerel smartness." The other unfortunate denominational trait was "the great want of systematic mental discipline" which resulted in temporary enthusiasms for wild-eyed schemes of dubious character. Some led to no less than infidelity.

Early in 1831 there appeared in the columns of the *Trumpet* a series of seven articles entitled "Rise and Progress of Infidelity in America."[6] On publication of the last article, the author, who had signed them previously simply as "A Universalist," identified himself as Linus S. Everett, of Charlestown, Massachusetts. A person cursorily glancing at the title of the series would probably assume that the articles were merely another in an apparently endless outpouring of religious polemics. The actuality was quite the contrary. The author, who in 1829 had been installed as pastor of the Universalist society in Charlestown, and who in 1833 prepared one of the numerous editions of John Murray's autobiography, had a broader purpose in mind than fending off attacks on traditional Christian beliefs in the Jacksonian era. He undertook a critique of the whole pattern and tendency of social reform and experimentation as expressed by the leaders of a loosely structured group known as the Free Inquirers.[7]

Everett, like so many of his contemporaries, saw his era in general in the rosiest of colors. He lived in "an age of improvement," in a nation which had no equal in the rapidity of its progress, which was on the road to "obtaining the highest and best blessings that man is capable of enjoying." Advances were evident in every field. But unfortunately, there were evils intermixed with the blessings, dangers lurking in the American Eden which could eventually "sap the foundations of every institution in America, and poison every source of rational enjoyment." The culprits were the atheists who had set themselves up as "self-styled reformers." Education and enlightenment of the public as to these persons and exposure of their dangerous ideas was what was needed. Universalists had a special stake in setting the record straight because many of these unbelievers had "pretended to wish well to the cause of Universalism–they have approached us with arms extended to receive us–[and] hailed us as brethren." Everett wished to assure his readers that Universalists had by no means flocked to the atheistic banner; "so far from being infidels in disguise, we look upon their principles with unqualified disgust, and deep abhorrence."

The author did not hesitate to name names. The villains were Robert Owen; Frances Wright; Robert Dale Owen, the son of Robert Owen; Robert L. Jennings; and Abner Kneeland, who had just recently deserted Universalism. Everett considered Robert Owen "the projector of the whole Infidel scheme," and devoted three of his seven articles to this immigrant who had selected America for the social experiment which resulted in an ill-fated but well-advertised community at New Harmony, Indiana.[8] Two of the articles were concerned with Frances ("Fanny") Wright, the Scottish-born critic of American institutions, pioneer agitator for women's rights, co-editor (with Owen) of the *Free Inquirer,* and founder of Nashoba, a utopian community for Negroes near Memphis, Tennessee. Much of the space devoted to these two individuals was taken up with extended quotations from their writings. Everett felt that the views of Robert Dale Owen and Abner Kneeland, being "of the same stamp, with those of Miss Wright," needed no explication.[9]

Robert Dale Owen availed himself of the opportunity given to him by the editor of the *Trumpet* to reply publicly to the allegations made by Everett in his series of articles, and to correct any presumed errors.[10] In two lengthy communications addressed to Editor Whittemore, Owen stood firm in his views regarding God. "I have taxed my human reason in vain for evidence of that which is superhuman . . . . I affirm, I deny, nothing regarding a Being whom I know not." As to the historicity of Jesus, Owen had no doubt, but he saw "not a shadow of rational evidence that he was more divine than other equally wise men, nor to substantiate all the wonderful stories respecting his superhuman powers."

Everett's series of articles on the "Rise and Progress of Infidelity in America" produced a protracted and sometimes acrimonious controversy with various champions of Robert Dale Owen's ideas. Among the charges and counter-charges that were hurled back and forth between Everett and those whose views he criticized was the accusation that Everett himself was actually an infidel, or at least a skeptic, but hypocritically took refuge behind a Universalist facade.[11] Everett's two-part article in the *Trumpet* was subtitled "Slander Exposed and Refuted." He was certainly not above using similar language himself. He described Abner Kneeland as "too far beneath contempt to be found without the aid of *fortune-tellers,* and a *diving-bell,* and too self-satisfied to heed the castigation which he once merited."

Probably one of the reasons for the attacks on Everett—aside from natural sensitivity to his sometimes biting criticism—derived from his own interest in social experimentation. His attacks on the Owenites, and particularly those known as the Free Inquirers, were apparently considered somehow a betrayal of their ideas. Everett had, in fact, been interested in some of the numerous communitarian societies that flourished and languished in the Jacksonian period. He was, among other things, admittedly a reader of the *New Harmony Gazette,* and was sufficiently interested in one community in which Universalists were involved to consider joining the group and publishing a liberal paper in association with it.

The so-called Kendall Company was established briefly in Ohio in the 1820s. It originated with Universalists in Portage County and at its inception, at least, the majority of the members were "professed Universalists," including one E. Williams, a clergyman, and A. Bailey (Bayley), a layman. They purchased an extensive tract of land and proposed to try to "live together on the principle of 'co-operative labor,' and in the bonds of good will," according to Everett. He denied that it was an "infidel" community. Regardless of its religious proclivities, the experiment apparently failed after a rapid accumulation of indebtedness, and disaffection in the ranks. In Everett's view, a principal villain had been one S.S. Underhill, an "infidel" who had joined the community "in the garb of a Quaker." His attempt to turn it into an Owenite project "created disturbances, which finally led to the dissolution of the company."

While pastor of the Universalist society in Buffalo, New York, Everett and his congregation had talked in the 1820s of purchasing an estate at nearby Williamsville where a community might be established which followed in general Owenite principles of "political economy and cooperative labor" but only insofar as they were "congenial with the genius and spirit of pure Christianity."[12] Apparently, nothing came of the proposal. Many Universalists did, however, participate in several of the six Fourierist colonies (phalanxes) which flourished briefly in the mid-1840s in the vicinity of Rochester and Watertown, New York. Part of the explanation for their greater popularity among Universalists, as compared to the Owenism about which Everett complained at such length, was probably less emphasis on religious skepticism.[13]

Jonathan Kidwell's Frontier Community

Robert Owen did find at least one defender and champion among Universalists, in the person of the controversial and iconoclastic midwestern preacher and newspaperman, Jonathan Kidwell (1779-1849).[14] He announced in 1837 that he would publish an extended analysis of Owen's ideas, to appear in several installments in his paper, and that he would demonstrate much more sympathy for Owen than had Everett and others. The series appeared, as announced in Kidwell's *Philomath Encyclopedia,* in 1837.[15] He used as the basis of his discussion the published version of a celebrated public debate in Cincinnati in 1829 between Owen and Alexander Campbell (1788-1866), ex-Baptist founder in 1830 of the sect known as the Disciples of Christ. Kidwell considered the "wordy conflict" between the two men inconclusive, although he believed Owen to have been the more capable of the two.[16] Kidwell attributed the failure of the clergy in general to have made a thorough and systematic study of Owen's religious views to the fact that he was an "infidel" and hence not worthy of serious consideration. Kidwell thought otherwise, and linked himself with Owen as "a fellow infidel."

However, Kidwell's promised in-depth study of Owen was much more a series of disquisitions in which he outlined his own interpretations of Scripture than an analysis of Owen's views. Kidwell's own ideas coincidentally agreed with most of Owen's. Kidwell dispensed with Owen by accepting most of the latter's views about Christianity, and criticized him mainly on the ground that he erred "in bringing into his conclusions more than is embraced in his premises" and in leaning too heavily on other men's commentaries instead of turning to the Bible itself.[17] A proper understanding of Scriptures, said Kidwell, indicated that Christ was "simply a man;" turning him into part of the Godhead was "a gross corruption of primitive christianity."

Kidwell had a second affinity with Owen besides generally similar views regarding Christianity. He too was the founder of a community (Philomath, Indiana), although it was more of a real estate venture than an ideologically oriented utopian experiment. Kidwell, a denominational maverick who refused to break his ties with Universalism but caused no end of consternation among his eastern brethren, was born in Mt. Sterling, Kentucky. A convert first from Methodism to the Christian sect and then to Universalism by 1815, he became a travelling preacher.[18]

His circuits in the 1820s extended into nine western counties in Ohio and seven eastern counties in Indiana as well as Louisville, Kentucky, and environs.[19] Full of ambition and all kinds of plans, distrustful of the East, and determined to put Universalism on the western map, he started, and abandoned, a whole series of newspapers, and challenged most of the religious principles dear to the hearts of more orthodox Universalists, often in colorful and pungent language. Until his death in 1849 at the age of seventy-six, he was a thorn in the side of "respectable" Universalists everywhere.

Kidwell started his journalistic career in 1827 with the publication of the monthly *Star in the West* in Eaton, Ohio. Two years later the paper became a weekly as the *Sentinel and Star in the West,* with three editors, including Kidwell, and was published in Cincinnati. Between 1833 and 1836 the paper was located in Philomath, Indiana. After several changes of editorship and location, the *Star in the West* became the leading Universalist paper in that area, comparable to the *Trumpet* in the East, and retained its identity until 1880. Not content with sharing editorial responsibility with others, Kidwell abandoned the *Star in the West* in 1836 and for ten years (1836-1846) published the *Philomath Encyclopedia* as a monthly. The cost was $2.00 (in advance) for twelve issues; the purpose of the publication was "to facilitate the spirit of reform" by imparting "the elementary principles of knowledge, free from a false prejudice of preconceived opinions."[20] It was intended for "ordinary minds"—particularly those of youth—and was to be a specimen of democracy personified. It was to be a vehicle for disseminating the findings of science (including cosmogony and phrenology), and for pricking the balloons of purportedly infallible theological dogmas.

Publication of the *Philomath Encyclopedia* was also strictly a bootstrap operation. Kidwell started with less than 200 subscribers, a creaking second-hand press, badly worn type, and not even a journeyman printer.[21] The necessity of using printers' apprentices, poor quality paper, and wornout type produced such an illegible sheet that in 1844 Kidwell reprinted a series of articles from the first volume so that they could be more easily read.[22] Significantly, they comprised Kidwell's essays on Owenism. The paper had to be suspended in two instances for several months because of lack of funds (in 1839-40 and in 1842).[23] Kidwell estimated that he had already lost $1,000 by 1840, despite the fact that he had obtained agents for his paper in eight states. In that year he secured the services of a person to do job printing; among the publications emanating from Kidwell's establishment was a political paper, the *Genius of Liberty,* which supported William Henry Harrison for the presidency.[24]

Kidwell also provided another, and presumably unrelated, service to those who visited his newspaper office. He offered for sale all kinds of drugs and medicines for such ailments as rheumatism and toothache.[25] His nerve and bone liniment was especially recommended. The *Encyclopedia* was succeeded by the *Independent Universalist,* a weekly published jointly by Kidwell and E.M. Knapp in Terre Haute, Indiana, where the latter resided. The paper lasted only a year beyond Kidwell's death, after Knapp himself died in 1850.

The word "Independent" in the title of the last paper in which Kidwell was involved aptly characterized his entire career. He was a born controversialist who took on all comers, bowed to none, and expressed his views, whether solicited or not, in direct and home-spun language. He participated in a four-day debate in 1841 with John Reynolds, a Presbyterian clergyman, at Miami University in Oxford, Ohio. No less than the president of the institution, George Junkin, served as co-moderator, with George McCune, a Universalist preacher, as his partner. Kidwell had no hesitation in doing verbal battle, in spite of the fact that he, by his own admission and in sharp contrast to his learned opponent, was "an unpolished son of the forest . . . raised in the back-woods of Kentucky, under the hooting of the owl, and the war-whoop of the red man, without even a common education!"[26] He modestly reported that the well-attended debate created as much excitement as did an election day.

Fellow Universalists were as likely to be the objects of Kidwell's verbal shafts as individuals outside the denomination. He accused Thomas Whittemore, editor of the *Trumpet,* and other Universalists in the East, of trying to dictate to western Universalists.[27] A case in point was his opposition to eastern efforts to strengthen the General Convention. Kidwell delighted also in shocking eastern Universalist religious sensibilities. He greatly upset Whittemore by claiming that the Pentateuch of the Old Testament was not written by Moses under divine inspiration, but was nothing more than "a heterogeneous mass of vague traditions combined with Jewish history."[28] Kidwell completely discarded the story of the creation of the world as portrayed in the Biblical account because it conflicted with the findings of geology which by then dated the age of the world as at least 60,000 years. He campaigned against observation of Sunday as a special religious day, denied the divine inspiration of all of the Scriptures, and rejected all supernatural revelation. He told his readers that "Nothing is more completely calculated to deceive the ignorant and unwary, than the false superstitious notion that preachers of the gospel are divinely inspired to teach the mysteries of God and another world."[29] Celebration of the Lord's Supper, even as only a symbolic memorial gesture, as it was to most Universalists, was too much for Kidwell. He described it as "nothing but a mock-supper; the mere relic of Papal ignorance and superstition . . . a piece of Catholic mummery."[30]

Reactions of more traditionally-oriented Universalists were predictable. When A.B. Grosh listed Kidwell in his directory of preachers in the 1849 issue of the *Universalist Register,* he added a warning footnote. "It is but justice to state, that Mr. Kidwell's views are very generally condemned by Universalists, as *skeptical* and unsound." One of the counts against a Universalist preacher disfellowshipped by the Western Union Association was the fact that he patronized Kidwell's newspaper, "that infidel work."[31] Sylvanus Cobb, editor of the *Christian Freeman* in Boston, considered Kidwell's "manifest infidelity" as "disgracing our religious body, and paralyzing its influence."[32]

But such condemnations did nothing to deter Kidwell. He had earlier taken up cudgels in behalf of George C. McCune, who had been disfellowshipped by the Montgomery Association (Ohio) for aggravated assault with a cane on an individual with whom he was having a heated verbal exchange.[33] Much to Kidwell's delight, McCune's fellowship was soon restored.[34]

When Kidwell was criticized—as he often was—for his outspoken religious views, he usually managed to produce a sharp and biting rejoinder or even to detect a conspiracy for "putting him down."[35] He was positive that Erasmus Manford, a prominent Universalist publisher in the Midwest and a newspaper competitor, was one of the "conspirators" who, in season and out, were trying to dominate Universalist affairs and drive him out. Kidwell referred to his erstwhile colleague as "this little excuse of a man" and as "our little Erasmus."[36] Kidwell characterized an attack by another Universalist on his *Encyclopedia* for being "an infidel work" as "one of the most contemptible pieces of jargon nonsense" he had ever seen and as an example of "zigzag balderdash."[37]

A democrat and egalitarian to the core, Kidwell had nothing but contempt for church forms, ritual, and ecclesiastical officialdom. He labelled those who challenged him for denying the plenary inspiration of the scriptures as "bishops" or "little bishops," depending on the magnitude and intensity of their strictures against him. He was truly, as Whittemore said of him in another context, "a host of himself, and . . . the terror of the adversaries of truth."[38] He was also the terror of other Universalists.

Jonathan Kidwell was more than an upsetter of religious tradition. He was a dreamer of dreams, and a planner and organizer of projects on a large scale. In the 1830s he turned an ambitious plan to establish a seminary of learning in the Midwest into an even more ambitious plan to create a community which would become a center for Universalism and a rival to the unofficial headquarters of the denomination in the East. Like dozens of his fellow-Americans, Kidwell saw the American

West as the future hope of the nation, abounding in illimitable opportunities for a burgeoning new civilization as well as a fruitful field for Universalism.

The impetus for what became the town of Philomath, Indiana, came from the decision of the Western Union Association (Indiana) in May 1832 to establish an academy under denominational auspices. Kidwell was appointed as agent both to obtain subscriptions and to find a suitable location. The idea of establishing a seminary of learning on the frontier was, at first, sufficiently attractive to the General Convention of Universalists of the Western States (Ohio, Indiana, and Kentucky) to become its sponsor. They retained Kidwell's services, and agreed to pay him a commission of 20 per cent for his efforts.[39]

Kidwell went searching for a site, and came upon the remains of what had been the village of Bethlehem in Union County, in the southeastern part of the state and a few miles south of the town of Richmond. Only a few deserted log cabins bore witness to the earlier settlement.[40] Kidwell immediately saw larger possibilities than merely an academy, and determined to plant an entire community, complete with a printing office for the entire Midwest, and a non-sectarian college or university to meet western Universalist educational needs. Approximately fifty acres were acquired "by donation," with Kidwell and one Joseph Adams as joint proprietors. The projected community was christened Philomath ("lover of learning") by Kidwell, who was also appointed one of the nine trustees of the school. The monthly periodical *Philomath Encyclopedia* (with the alternate title of *Circle of Science* added in 1845) was to be published for the benefit of the seminary.[41]

Kidwell drew up a detailed plan for the new community, allocating ten acres for the proposed college. A grist mill was to be erected on one corner of this college lot and other land was marked out for garden plots, shops, and boarding houses; part of the remaining acreage was "first-rate timbered land," and the rest was to be sold to future inhabitants. It was estimated that the property was worth from $6.00 to $15.00 an acre.[42] Kidwell promptly started an extensive advertising campaign to recruit prospective inhabitants with a variety of skills. Although much of the advertising appeared in the *Sentinel and Star in the West,* the denominational journal published in Cincinnati, the community was to be open to all. "Strangers" (presumably non-Universalists) were required to produce certificates of good moral character.

How many people were attracted by Kidwell's efforts is not known. The community was sufficiently well established by 1837 to have acquired a post office, with Kidwell in charge.[43] There was much difficulty in placing the academy on a firm foundation, and it appears to have lasted less than ten years. Kidwell did move his publishing operations to Philomath in 1833, where they remained until his death. No matter what his expectations might have been, the entire operation was an unmitigated personal financial disaster for the Universalist entrepreneur. Within an eight-year period, he lost $2,000 in unpaid subscriptions to his paper, lost an equal amount on a steam mill, sank over $1,000 in the ill-fated academy, and had to pay out another $1,000 in "security money" for loans he had obtained for himself or others.[44]

Throughout his residence in Philomath, Kidwell was listed in the *Universalist Register* as the preacher in the community, and a society had been organized by 1845 and fellowshipped by the Western Union Association.[45] A church building was not constructed until 1854, and there appears to have been no regular pastor after Kidwell's death in 1849.[46] Most of the inhabitants of the settlement seem to have drifted away after 1850, and some thirty years later there was only a "little cluster of houses" to mark the community. There were still a few Universalists remaining in the settlement as late as 1884; they heard preaching by Miss Mary T. Clark of Dublin, who served as a missionary operating out of Richmond on behalf of the state convention. She was also secretary of the Women's Aid Association.[47] Philomath had met the fate of many another settlement on the rapidly moving western frontier of the pre-Civil War period. Whatever the reasons for the failure of this particular one—a combination of inadequate support, unwise management, opposition to Kidwell's unorthodox theological ideas, personality conflicts, and unrealistic expectations—neither the plans for the academy nor the town of which it was a part was permanently realized.[48]

The Communitarianism of Adin Ballou

> That there are evils existing in the present organization of Society few will deny; that something may be done to correct them there is reason to hope. To whom does this work of correction more properly belong than to Universalists? We have the best theory that can be devised—universal benevolence—justice, mercy, equality, peace, holiness, happiness, for all men. What can be better? But of how much worth is the doctrine without its application? . . . . how can it be accomplished? Ah, that HOW is the difficult word, and you have hit it at last. My answer is, by a re-organization of society—by forming an Association, colony, or community, upon the christian plan, where the countervailing and overpowering influence of evil shall be taken away, and the great and positive ends of human life pursued in concert.[49]

It was William S. Balch who wrote these words, but it was an ex-Universalist clergyman, Adin Ballou, who attempted to make them an actuality. Ballou had long been convinced that the original precepts of Christianity had been misinterpreted over the centuries, and set out to do something about it.[50] In 1870 he criticized both the Universalists and Unitarians for departing from the original conception of the church as projected by Christ.[51] Ballou established in 1841, near Milford, Massachusetts, the community of Hopedale which lasted until 1859, and which was to have been a model for others. He presided over the Hopedale Community until 1856. After it disintegrated, the remnants were absorbed into the Hopedale Parish (Unitarian) of which Ballou was pastor until 1880.[52]

Although he had formally left the Universalist denomination in 1831 when he helped organize the Massachusetts Society of Universal Restorationists as a splinter group, what Ballou attempted to do was to carry out what he conceived to be Universalist principles to their logical conclusions. Because he was "a firm believer in, and eloquent defender of, the doctrines set forth in the Winchester Profession of Faith, and was a man of consecrated life and of unwearied and successful effort in doing good," Ballou at the time of his death was included along with other deceased Universalist ministers in the necrology section of the *Universalist Register.*[53]

Adin Ballou was born in Cumberland, Rhode Island, on 23 April 1803, the son of a farmer and sawmill operator. Ballou died in Hopedale, Massachusetts, on 5 August 1890. He attended a series of local schools, but his wish to attend Brown University in Providence was thwarted by lack of money. His last exposure to formal education was attendance at an academy in Franklin, Massachusetts, in 1818-19.

He first attended the local "Six Principle" Baptist church dominated by various branches of the Ballou family in the neighborhood. Ballou, with the rest of his family, then joined a church of the "Christian Connexion" during a religious revival. At the age of eighteen he preached in the village church and announced his intention of entering the ministry, supposedly as the result of a dream. He was first introduced to Universalism about 1818, when sixteen years of age. After initially rejecting its ideas, in 1822 he read Elhanan Winchester's *Dialogues on Universal Restoration;* attended the meeting of the Southern Association (Massachusetts); and met and corresponded with Hosea Ballou. He became a Universalist by the end of the year, probably influenced also by Abby Sayler whom he married in 1822, and by her parents, who were Universalists of the Restorationist stamp. After his wife's death in 1829 he married Lucy Hunt in 1830. Ballou, after preaching in several communities in southern Massachusetts, was ordained by the Southern Association and became pastor of the Universalist society in Milford in 1824. After a brief pastorate in New York City (1827-28) he returned to Milford where he remained until 1831. He accepted the pastorate of the First Church and Parish

(Unitarian Congregational) in Mendon, Massachusetts, where he remained until 1841.

Ballou had, by the end of the 1830s, become committed to pacifism, the abolition of slavery, women's rights, and temperance. He had also re-thought his earlier belief that the New Testament was concerned chiefly with man's future beyond earthly life.

> . . . I had come to see that the teachings of the Master were essential to human well-being in this world as well as in the world to come; that it was one of the declared objects of Christ's labors to inaugurate the kingdom of heaven *on the earth;* and that it was the imperative duty of his disciples to pray and to work earnestly for that sublime end, as one of the best preliminaries to immortal blessedness. The supreme, universal, unchangeable Fatherhood of God and the universal Brotherhood of Man had become settled articles of my faith, and whatever contradicted either of them, in theory or in practice, I was certain must be false and wrong.[54]

Out of these convictions was born the Hopedale Community.

The *Practical Christian,* a semi-monthly, was established in 1840 as an organ for the "promulgation of Primitive Christianity" and as a vehicle for Adin Ballou's ideas in particular. He was chief editor throughout its history, and from 1857 until it ceased publication in 1860, was also the sole proprietor.[55] He outlined in the very first issue the philosophy behind and the plans for his proposed community. The theoretical bases had been formulated at a series of meetings of Restorationist clergy in 1839, out of which came a "Standard of Practical Christianity."[56] In the declaration the five ministers and two laymen who signed it pledged to live Christian lives akin to their conception of the "primitive purity" of Christ and his apostles. This meant a policy of abstention from "the government of this world," excepting for payment of taxes. Universal charity and forbearance were to be the principles applied to all human relations. War, slavery, intemperance, licentiousness, covetousness, and worldly ambition were to be abhorred in any form. All told, the declaration established a set of personal and social standards of the highest imaginable level. None of the five clerical editors and contributors to the *Practical Christian,* all of whom had signed the declaration, expected such goals to be popular, but they remained ideals to be realized.

Adin Ballou outlined in September 1840 his proposal for the establishment of "practical Christian communities" roughly comparable to those maintained by the Shakers and the Moravians, but differing in significant details.[57] He rejected the celibacy and principle of communal property practiced by the former and the excessive detail and complexity of the government of the latter. Ballou called for "a compact neighborhood or village of practical christians, dwelling together by families in love and peace, insuring to themselves the comforts of life by agricultural and mechanical industry, and devoting the entire residue of their intellectual, moral and physical resources to the christianization and general welfare of the human race."

For the particular community he had in mind, Ballou would require assent to the document known as the "Standard of Practical Christianity." A tract of land on which the community would be created was to be acquired by subscription to shares (at $50) in a joint stock fund and divided among the proprietors in proportion to the amount of their subscriptions. Ballou did not rule out the holding of all property in common, provided "all were perfectly agreed." He did not consider this likely, and preferred the principle of private property. In 1843 he made even more emphatic his preference for private property-holding. When the constitution of the Hopedale Community was amended to provide this, it reflected Ballou's conviction that "the theory of common property Communities [was] false to nature, destructive of true personal freedom, and wholly impracticable except by the junction of despotism and slavery."[58] Even though there might be a decline in membership with the application of this principle, individuals had to "depend on their own capabilities, industry, and frugal economy, rather than on the . . . magic economies of an associated mass." Ballou thus anticipated and answered one of the main objections usually raised against socialism; namely, that it relieved the individual of any responsibility for his or her own welfare.[59]

The location of the proposed community was immaterial, provided the land was good, the water supply adequate, the environment healthy, and a market for garden produce and other items was available. He recommended a place "a little retired from the bustle of the world." The maximum population should be 150 families, with a minimum of 50. A very simple compact or agreement should be drawn up, providing for a "fraternal communion" to be governed by elected "official servants." Dismissal or withdrawal from the community was to be provided for, and first preference in acquiring vacated land and/or shares was to be given to other members of the community. Individual rights, including that of conscience, were to be guaranteed. The community would not only afford a haven and refuge from a corrupt church and an oppressive world, but would be a basis for missionary activity. If such communities could be multiplied indefinitely, "the reign of ignorance, selfishness, pride and violence would be terminated among men and the whole great brotherhood of our race dwell together in unspeakable peace."

The outgrowth of this tentative and idealistic plan was the Hopedale Community which first took organized form in January 1841. Plans were first discussed at a conference in Mendon. Consisting largely of Restorationist clergy and laity, these meetings were held for worship and to discuss such problems as the evil of covetousness,

Adin Ballou (1803-1890), Utopian reformer and practical Christian

slavery, and intemperance, and the desirability of non-resistance. Most of the January meeting was devoted to discussing and acting on "the Community question." The result was the adoption of a constitution of an association to be known as "The Fraternal Communion," and the organization of "Fraternal Community No. 1."[60]

The constitution provided for the creation of independent, numbered "Christian commonwealths" which would be organized in a loose confederation, the members of which would meet as occasion warranted, but would have no plenary power. Membership required assent to "a religious and moral test—a sort of Confession and

Covenant" which was based on the previously mentioned Standard, and embodied the following precepts and practices: To do no harm to anyone in any way; to practice such Christian virtues as humility and truthfulness; to refrain from gambling in any form, and from any connection whatever with intoxicating liquor as a beverage; to refuse to take or administer any oaths, or to serve in the military in any capacity; to refuse to participate in any way "in any case involving a final authorized resort to physical violence" (including the bringing of legal action, voting, holding office, or requesting governmental interposition). There was to be complete personal equality, "irrespective of sex, colour, occupation, wealth, rank, or any other natural or adventitious peculiarity." No artificial or man-made "middle walls of distinction" were to be built up, recognized, or maintained, on any ground whatever. Individuals came into the community with no more advantage than whatever talents God had seen fit to bestow. With a variety of skills and interests expected in any given group, there would be work for all. The community was just as willing to license and send out women preachers and missionaries as men.[61]

Full membership was provided for those eighteen or over. Ballou recognized that this was three years under the generally recognized age of legal majority, but that should cause no concern, for parental consent was still to be required for those under twenty-one. More important, the educational system to be established in each community would be of such excellence that eighteen-year-olds would be more competent to act the part and bear the responsibilities of members than persons generally were at twenty-one. Members were free to resign from communities at any time, and were not required to give any reason. When voting was necessary, all decisions were to be by a two-thirds majority of those present; this included the disowning of any member who was deemed unworthy or proved incorrigible. Elected officers, chosen annually for each community, were to be a president, secretary, auditor, and six "intendants"—one for each aspect of community activity, such as agriculture, education, and missionary activity. The latter was the responsibility of the "intendant of Religion, Morals, and Missions," who was to conduct the "Sixth Department." One of the functions of this subdivision was to organize "Inductive Conferences" of interested individuals who might become nuclei of future communities. The officers were to comprise an executive council.

Members of communities were to be housed in "habitations," each with accommodations for at least 100 persons. These and all group public boarding and other facilities were to be provided by the community; however, separate private arrangements could be made, and basic necessities obtained through the community. Large-scale purchases at wholesale were to keep expenses to a minimum. Settlement of accounts was to take place at least once a year. Ballou had thought originally in terms of completely separate dwellings for each family, but modified this in favor of some group living, in the interests of simplicity and economy.

The stockholding plan Ballou projected in his preliminary outline was incorporated into the constitution of the Fraternal Communion. The bulk of the funds for each community was to be expended on real estate, and the remaining sum was to be set aside as a "floating fund" to pay for community-wide operating expenses such as public taxes. Special assessments were authorized for extraordinary expenses. Any profits were to be distributed on the basis of the amount of capital invested and labor performed by each participant. Financial assistance was to be provided to any members of the community who became destitute through no fault of their own.

Each person was expected "to perform a reasonable amount of productive labor, either corporeal, mental or mixed, in some department of useful industry." Adults were to receive a uniform wage not exceeding 50 cents for every eight hours of service, based on a forty-eight-hour work week. Those under eighteen, beginning at age five, were to be paid at reduced rates, depending on age. Ballou emphasized that women were to receive exactly the same wages as men. He pointed out that women had too long suffered from discrimination in this respect, and in his scheme would "be placed on a footing of equality with male labor." Women were also to be eligible for any office in the community, although Ballou expected the majority to be filled by men because of the nature of the responsibilities they entailed. All teachers who went out into "the surrounding world" were expected to work on the same basis as those employed within the community, and were strictly accountable for any monies received for their services.

Comprehensive educational facilities were to be provided, beginning with nursery and infant classes and extending through the equivalent of secondary school, up to age eighteen. The emphasis was to be on the practical, "conducted on the manual labor principle" and aimed to qualify all youth "for the actual business of life." There would be a balance of physical, moral, and intellectual education. The goal was strong and healthy children, manually dexterous, with "minds well stored with useful knowledge, their hearts filled with divine principles, and their moral characters unblemished. Health, knowledge and goodness are necessary to the free idea we entertain of a well educated youth." Corporal punishment was ruled out; "apple-tree sticks, birch switches, rattans, raw-hides, ferulas, and that sort of apparatus" were not among the "resources for the maintenance of good order."[62]

The constitution of the Fraternal Communion was published in the *Practical Christian,* and 500 additional copies were printed for general distribution. The constitution was accompanied by a detailed "Exposition" written by Ballou which set out the purposes of the new communities. He had no illusions about the skepticism or even the opposition likely to be faced, or the probability that mistakes would be made. But the attempt "to illustrate the virtues, and promote the ends of pure religion, morality, and philanthropy" would be worth the effort. The kingdom of God on earth would thus be achieved. The communities would be living examples of reform and models for the future. "War, oppression, intemperance, debauchery, and ten thousand hateful vices now prevalent will gradually disappear, and man returns to his primeval Eden."

Neither the communities nor their inhabitants were in any sense to be isolated from society at large. Individuals were not going to withdraw from the world and seclude themselves like monks and nuns from the rest of mankind. "We are not going to retire into mountain glens and desolate places of the earth . . . but . . . locate . . . in the midst of the general population." There would be constant interchange with "relatives, friends and neighbors for any and every christian purpose." Missionaries would always be abroad, and the communities would be "public demonstrations of the excellency, safety and advantages of true righteousness."

Fraternal Community No. 1, the first of the contemplated series, was immediately organized in January 1841, with a seven-man provisional committee in charge. Between thirty and forty adult members who had committed themselves were supposed to be joined by at least that many more who seemed on the verge of joining.[63] A full roster of "official servants" had been completed by the fall of 1841, with Ballou as president. A 258-acre farm, with a main house and several outbuildings, was selected by Ballou, who assumed complete responsibility for acquiring it; possession was to take place in April 1842.

The property was located in the western part of the town of Milford, adjacent to Mendon, and some two miles from the center of population. The "estate," as the farm was called, was formerly referred to as "the Dale," subsequently the Jones farm, and then the Hastings Daniels place. At the time it was acquired for the new community, it had been recently purchased by Cyrus Ballou, with whom the proprietors conducted their negotiations. The community immediately christened it "Hope Dale" (which soon became a single word), as an expression of "their present reigning sentiment." The community undertook at the outset to raise $6,000 by subscription, although that figure had to be increased almost immediately. The executive council was authorized to prepare the buildings and provide livestock and farming implements, as well as a school, a library, and a printing office.[64]

The first annual meeting of the community was held in January 1842, when eight new members were admitted to full membership and three others on probation, none of the latter being known to the members present.[65] The *Practical Christian,* which had a subscription list in excess of 400 and was virtually self-supporting, became the property of the community and the means of disseminating information about it. The total price of the property was $3,800, with $641.50 committed in addition for supplies and crops on hand. It was estimated in 1842 that a total of $7,500 was needed to pay off obligations and commence operations.

By April 1842 the community, which up to that time had existed only on paper, actually began to function. Almost thirty individuals moved into the main building, including Ballou and his family. He resigned his pastorate in nearby Mendon, and delivered his farewell sermon in June.[66] By then there were forty-five individuals in residence (thirteen men, twelve women, and twenty children), all being boarded in one "general family."[67] Twenty acres were under cultivation, and a mechanics' shop was under construction to house machinery to be operated by water power. A printing office was included in a new multi-purpose building, from which the *Practical Christian* was published. Religious services were conducted, open to anyone in the vicinity, and generally harmonious relations were enjoyed with residents of neighboring towns. Even the inhabitants of the community itself seemed to be getting on well with each other. Gifts of cash, farm implements, and even paper on which to print the *Practical Christian* were numerous, gratefully received, and immediately put to use.

Less than a year's experience dictated certain changes in the constitution of the Fraternal Communion, in most cases to spell out details. The general blueprint for the community which Ballou had worked out in advance in such detail was altered in surprisingly few respects. Most changes were procedural rather than substantive, and the basic structure of the community remained as he had projected it. The intent of most amendments was to assure greater individuality and equity, while at the same time assuring the stability and prosperity of the whole enterprise. Property bought from the community by members was to revert to it when it ceased to be owned within the membership. Maximum compensation to be paid for all activities was set at $1.00 a day, and $300 a year. Economic self-sufficiency was also emphasized, with the furnishing of necessities to be at cost. Any profits of the community up to 4 per cent per annum on capital were to be divided among the stockholders according to the amount of their investment. Profits in excess of 4 per cent were to be devoted to community purposes.[68]

The main body of Universalists seemed to have paid scant attention to Ballou's efforts to establish a Christian commonwealth. Thomas Whittemore ignored it almost completely in the columns of the *Trumpet.* Sylvanus Cobb made passing reference to Hopedale in the

Christian Freeman. In 1846 he commented that the community had started in a shabby old house, with a few decayed outbuildings, and was handicapped by "much prejudice from without, and many misgivings from within."[69] He expressed some surprise that it had lasted so long, but noted that by 1846 it had expanded its holdings to 400 acres, had constructed a chapel, and in general was allowing more individual freedom than most Fourierist societies which it resembled in some respects. The Hopedale experiment had also made labor more attractive than customary.

Reactions from outside the denomination were generally favorable, according to Ballou, although there were minor criticisms. The *Dial* and the *Transcendentalist,* social reform journals, objected to the restrictions imposed regarding temperance, abolition, and non-resistance as contrary to the freedom which should be enjoyed by "universal man."[70] Ballou sent a copy of the constitution and plan of the community to William Ellery Channing for his reactions. Ballou received a warm letter of approval, although Channing doubted that the unity and harmony that Ballou anticipated would ever come about, and predicted conflict between the individual members and the community.[71] Lydia Maria Child, editor of the *Anti-Slavery Standard,* objected to the principle of non-resistance as a test of membership and called Ballou's attention to the fact that the Brook Farm community in West Roxbury, not far from Hopedale, had no religious or moral test for membership.[72] Ballou repeatedly underlined the two characteristics which he believed distinguished Hopedale from other social experiments: It was based explicitly on religious principles, including a profession of Christian faith; and it required a strict morality, severer than the ethical rules generally recognized by even the Christian world.[73]

The Hopedale Community, which reached a population peak of 300 residents in 1856 (of whom only 110 were actually members) consisted, according to Ballou, of "men and women belonging to the more substantial self-respecting middle class of American society—the rank and file of the American people."[74] As a whole, they were "in no proper sense such a set of visionary dreamers, deluded fanatics, restless impracticables, and thriftless incompetents" as to require an autocratic mastermind at the top. There were selfish and unworthy individuals associated with the community, but by and large the members were "only such as Jesus Christ and his Apostles were and taught us to be."

The event which signalled the end of the community as Ballou had originally conceived it was the withdrawal from membership in 1856 of Ebenezer D. and George Draper, brothers who owned approximately three-fourths of the joint stock. Seeking enlarged profits, they invested in the Hopedale Manufacturing Company, which made textile machinery. This move, in effect, turned the community into an industrial town. Great as was the blow to Ballou, he refused to censure them for their action; it was their right, regrettable as it might have been.[75] He was confident that if they had not withdrawn most of the capital on which the community had depended, it would have continued to prosper. Fourteen residents who had been members remained in 1876.

Ballou wrote, in reviewing his life, and many years after the collapse of the Hopedale experiment, that he had "not been a man of much popular success, but in several respects a failure."[76] His hopes were "too urgent and sanguine; my standard and aim were set too high for immediate realization." He felt that his importance lay in the future rather than in his own lifetime. He had lived for coming generations rather than for his contemporaries.

From Adventism to Spiritualism

In 1833 William Miller (1782-1849), a recently licensed Baptist preacher, produced a pamphlet based on a series of lectures in which he predicted with complete certainty the second physical coming of Christ "about the year 1843." He had first announced the imminence of the event in 1831, and immediately started relaying his message in upstate New York, northern New England, and western Massachusetts. In 1838 an enlarged edition was published in book form.[77]

Although he did not argue the physical destruction of the world, Miller did predict the end of time, to be followed by Christ's "personal reign of 1,000 years." His computations were based on a thorough and literal examination of the Scriptures. By the early 1840s Miller's ideas had spread as far east as Boston and a relatively elaborate organization had been developed to propagate his ideas.

Universalists roundly condemned Miller and all that he predicted. He and his ideas were obviously used to further revivalist activities, including protracted meetings, and to raise religious excitement to a fever pitch. Given the dim view that the majority of Universalists took of revivalism in general (see below), it was understandable that his ideas, especially for the fate of the unregenerate, were discounted and even ridiculed. Such men as Thomas Whittemore, Abel Thomas, Otis Skinner, and John Austin attempted to demolish Miller with both tongue and pen.[78] All that Miller's theories did, in their eyes, was foster irrationalism and hysteria, spread delusion, and raise false hopes among the credulous. Whittemore called the whole movement "humbug" and Miller a charlatan.[79] Austin, pastor at the time in Danvers, Massachusetts, devoted an address in 1840 attempting to discredit Miller and his ideas. Otis Skinner delivered a series of five lectures that were published that year, in which he claimed to have "utterly exploded" Millerism.

Sylvanus Cobb delivered a series of discourses in his church in Waltham, Massachusetts, entitled "The Miller Mania" and referred to him as "Millenian Miller."[80] Charles Spear, busy with such social betterment projects as prison reform and rehabilitation of the criminal, was falsely accused of being a Millerite. He vehemently denied any connection with "that wild delusion."[81]

By 1842 news of Miller and his ideas had spread to the Midwest. Jonathan Kidwell considered Miller and his followers to be "visionary fanatics" and "deluded dupes."[82] When someone suggested that the government take a hand and try to control the movement, when it seemed to be getting out of hand, Kidwell vetoed the suggestion. "Let them alone:—men have a right to be as religiously crazy as they please." When a series of dates predicted by Miller failed to produce the anticipated event, his movement collapsed, but not before an estimated 50,000 people had joined the ranks and probably a million more were "skeptically expectant."[83] Among the by-products of Millerism was the establishment in 1846 of what became the Seventh-Day Adventist Church, and paralleling Millerism were several varieties of spiritualism.

A Universalist editor, in the course of noting the publication of Andrew Jackson Davis' *The Great Harmonia, concerning the Seven Mental States* (1852), complained that there was "rather a disproportionate number in our Connection" who became attracted to the fads and novelties of thought then current.[84] First there had been Mesmerism (animal magnetism). Then there had been phrenology; "one could hardly enter a Universalist minister's study, but there hung the chart, or stood the bust, like the guardian angel of the place, with the 'organs' all marked out and numbered on the cranium . . . . but this freak, of a harmless sort, betrayed a shallowness, that soon came out in broader symptoms." Other popular fancies had successively come into vogue, and "the heads of several of our ministers were turned at once." The latest rage was spiritualism, represented by Davis' work. "Taking them together, what a brood of Mesmerists, Rationalists, Biologists, Fourierists, and Necromantists, we have hatched from our maw!"

The propensity of some Universalists to entertain such notions, or at least to inquire into them, has been frequently noted by later scholars as well as by nineteenth-century commentators. The leading early twentieth-century historian of spiritualism, Frank Podmore, found this tendency especially noticeable among religious groups such as the Society of Friends (Quakers), Unitarians, and Universalists, which all "held some liberal or attenuated form of Christian doctrine."[85] In fact, he asserts that "no religious body gave a larger contingent to the new faith [of spiritualism] than the Universalists." Winthrop Hudson, writing in the 1960s, commented that the Universalist denomination provided not only the greatest number of recruits for spiritualism, but never completely recovered from the experience.[86]

Mesmerism, or belief in animal magnetism, which laid the foundations for the modern practice of hypnotism, had been associated with Franz Anton Mesmer (1734-1815), an Austrian physician, and developed by a pupil, Count Maxime de Puységur, in the late eighteenth century. By the time that popular interest in the subject had begun to appear in the United States after a series of lectures delivered in Boston by a Frenchman, Charles Poyen, in 1836, animal magnetism had become associated with both medical healing and clairvoyant powers. By the 1840s the theory and practice of animal magnetism had not only spread over New England, New York State, and much of the Midwest, but had been linked with the pseudo-science of phrenology in an uneasy alliance known as "phrenomagnetism."

Phrenology had been invented by Franz Joseph Gall (1758-1828), a German physician, whose ideas were spread to America by an associate, Johann Kaspar Spurzheim (1776-1832), who actually coined the term; and a Scottish lecturer, George Combe. Phrenologists taught that the brain was divided into a number of separate sections or "organs" (thirty-seven, as originally announced by Gall and Spurzheim), each representing various individual traits or tendencies. An inspection of the topography of the skull would presumably enable one to determine the predominant and recessive traits of an individual and therefore not only determine character but indicate which "organs" needed development or restraint. Hence the diagramming of the brain became a widespread phenomenon, the literature on the subject became overwhelming, and discourses and demonstrations by the dozens became the order of the day. George Sumner Weaver, prominent midwestern Universalist clergyman and educator, took time out in the fall of 1851 from a busy schedule as principal of the Western Liberal Institute in Marietta, Ohio, to deliver a series of *Lectures on Mental Science, according to the Principles of Phrenology,* published the following year.

Probably the best known Universalist clergyman associated with both Mesmerism and phrenology was J.B. Dods, who in 1847 published *Six Lectures on the Philosophy of Mesmerism.* Dods was at first a preacher in Maine in the early 1830s, and travelled also in the South.[87] In 1848 he was disfellowshipped by the Massachusetts Convention and read out of the denomination for reasons not given.[88] He next wrote *Etherology and the Phreno-Philosophy of Mesmerism and Magic Eloquence,* the second edition of which appeared in 1850. In this work he attributed seance manifestations, which by then had become very popular, to "vital electricity." By the mid-1850s, he had become a spiritualist, and had published a major work on the subject.

Claims of communication with the spirits of the dead (mental spiritualism), rappings, trances, and the moving of objects propelled by no observed motive force (physical spiritualism), and "spirit healing," all of these usually accomplished by the intervention of a medium, and numerous other alleged manifestations beyond ordinary explanation, were in a general way related to the earlier claims of Mesmerists and phrenologists. However, spiritualism as an identifiable body of thought in nineteenth-century America, particularly as developed in the 1850s, was a much more complex and sophisticated phenomenon, and made a much more permanent impression on those with a mystical bent than did either Mesmerism or phrenology.[89]

Among the Universalist clergy who embraced spiritualism in some form or in some degree were Thomas Lake Harris, William Fishbough, S.B. Brittan, Woodbury M. Fernald, John Murray Spear, S.C. Hewitt, R.P. Ambler, J.B. Dods, and Charles Hammond. Adin Ballou, who had formally left the denomination prior to the upsurge of interest in spiritualism but who continued to be identified with Universalist thought, was a believer in "spirit manifestations" and wrote on the subject.[90] His conviction that it was possible to communicate with the dead was quite consistent with belief in the universal restoration of souls.[91] He held steadfastly to this idea, as did many Universalists, throughout his life. He also welcomed mediums to his community at Hopedale, Massachusetts, and several spiritualists, including J.M. Spear, delivered lectures there. Some Universalists, like Woodbury Fernald, claimed to have had their horizons so enlarged by spiritualism that, while remaining Christian ministers, they declared their independence of "any sectarian or ecclesiastical authorities."[92] Others remained within Universalism but expressed at the same time a wide range of attitudes toward their original Christian inheritance, from continued unquestioning adherence to its theology, to a vague sort of pantheism.

Among the varieties of spiritualism in which some Universalists were caught up in the later Jacksonian period was Swedenborgianism. The ideas of Emanuel Swedenborg (1688-1772), a Swedish scientist, religious philosopher and mystic, were first brought to America by James Glen, who made efforts to establish reading circles in Philadelphia in 1784.[93] Swedenborg had never intended to establish a church in the conventional sense, and the spread of his ideas to America depended at first on small bands of followers who met for discussion. However, a New Church Society was organized in Baltimore in 1792 and the General Convention of the New Jerusalem in the United States was formed in 1817. With the burst of interest in spiritualism, particularly in the 1840s and 1850s, Swedenborg's writings, originally in Latin, achieved new popularity and several editions of his works appeared; they were first made available to American readers in English translation. One of the most widely sold was a *Compendium of the Theological and Spiritual Writings of Emanuel Swedenborg,* a selection published in 1853 from over thirty of the author's works, together with a fairly detailed biography. Although appearing anonymously, the volume was known to have been the work of Fernald.[94]

Swedenborg claimed a unique divine dispensation and insight which enabled him to live simultaneously, via trances and other extraordinary phenomena, in both the physical and spiritual world. He taught the immortality of the soul, claimed powers of clairvoyance, and communication with spirits. Although he believed in both heaven and hell, with an intermediate state, and warned against the attempts of others to communicate with spirits, some modifications of his ideas were made. Universalists who believed in Swedenborgianism were among those who made or accepted the modifications or failed to heed his admonitions about communicating with spirits. For those Universalists who rejected the concept of a physical hell in the afterlife, and who argued for punishment before death and eternal glory thereafter, it was relatively easy to reject the Swedenborgian belief in a physical hell while retaining his other basic ideas. Aside from the appeal of the idea of a future life, cogently presented by Swedenborg, his use of Scriptural authority to support his teachings appealed to many.[95]

However, it should be emphasized that not all Universalists of spiritualist persuasion were necessarily strict Swedenborgians in their orientation. There were too many variations and permutations to allow neat classification. The number of laymen who turned to spiritualism is even more difficult to ascertain than the number of clergy who became involved. There are only scattered and generalized references in Universalist literature on the extent of the appeal of spiritualism to the rank-and-file Universalist. The searcher for such information must be content with such ambiguous leads as that provided by Abel C. Thomas, who noted, for example, only that after the closing in 1850 of the Universalist church in Kensington, a suburb of Philadelphia, "several" members organized a circle of spiritualists.[96]

The work which made spiritualism close to a household word in American homes in the 1850s was the product of one Andrew Jackson Davis (1826-1910), by way of a book published in 1847, entitled *The Principles of Nature, Her Divine Revelations and a Voice to Mankind.* It had purportedly been dictated by the author who, at the age of nineteen, was in a mesmerized state. By the year prior to his revelations, Davis had already achieved a reputation as a medical clairvoyant. This came about at least in part by the propagandizing of Gibson Smith, a Universalist clergyman who had a mysterious chronic illness correctly diagnosed by Davis, and wrote of his experiences.[97] For over thirty years Davis, who came to be known as "the seer of Poughkeepsie," continued to write all kinds of works on various aspects of spiritualism. Among the more than twenty books he wrote or edited was an autobiography (*The Magic Staff,* published simultaneously in New York and Boston in 1857) which he updated in 1885 under the title *Beyond the Valley*. His most ambitious work, published after his

Principles of Nature brought him to public attention, was *The Great Harmonia: being a philosophical revelation of the natural, spiritual, and celestial universe,* eventually totalling five volumes (1850-66). Some went through numerous editions and printings; e.g., the first volume (*The Physician*) had gone through ten editions by 1880.

Universalist clergyman William Fishbough of New Haven, Connecticut, who had been pastor of the society in Taunton, Massachusetts, served as scribe for Davis' first book. Fishbough also wrote the introduction, in which he described the trances in which Davis was placed by one S. Silas Lyon, a physician. It may have been Fishbough who was responsible for Davis' emphasis on the Universalist concept of the eventual regeneration of mankind.[98] The question has been raised of how much of Davis' work was actually attributable to Fishbough who, "like so many other Universalist ministers of his time, . . . was well read in various fields of knowledge." Davis had had only a few months of formal schooling. In 1852 Fishbough himself published *The Macrocosm and Microcosm; or, the Universe Without and the Universe Within* which dealt with many of the same subjects as did Davis' work.

Another Universalist clergyman who knew Davis and supported many of his ideas was S.B. Brittan, brother-in-law of Dr. Lyon. Brittan, who wrote four major works on spiritualism as well as numerous pamphlets and reviews on the subject, defended the credibility of Davis' trances and the circumstances under which *The Principles of Nature* had been composed. Brittan was also known to Universalists through several tracts, including one published in 1845 attacking the Baptist revivalist Jacob Knapp for having in turn attacked Universalists. Brittan was also the author of a series of discourses defending "Universalism as an Idea," published the same year that Davis' first work appeared (1847). In 1847 there also appeared the first issue of the *Univercoelum,* edited by Brittan. Its columns were to be devoted to such topics as dreams, somnambulism, clairvoyance, prophecy, and trances, as well as to serve as a medium of communication for Davis.[99] Most of the contributions had a distinctly socialist flavor, emphasizing such institutions as trade unions and trade associations, and cooperative organizations of all kinds.

By mid-1849 the *Univercoelum* was replaced by *The Present Day,* edited by W.M. Channing. The *Univercoelum* was, in effect, a vehicle for a whole bevy of Universalists, or ex-Universalists. Besides Brittan, who served as the chief editor, and Fishbough, Fernald, J.K. Ingalls, and Thomas Lake Harris (born in England) were among his associates. Joshua Ingalls had been ordained in 1840 and had served a pastorate in Southold, Long Island (New York).[100] Harris, shortly before the first issue of the new journal appeared, had withdrawn from the Universalist ministry to become a lecturer on behalf of spiritualism, and later became associated with other social and religious experiments. In 1848, the *Univercoelum* had absorbed both Fernald and his short-lived *Christian Rationalist.*

Spiritualism entered the popular imagination beginning in 1848, after a series of mysterious rappings in the home of John D. Fox, in Hydesville, western New York State, involving his two young daughters. By 1852 "spirit manifestations" of all kinds had appeared all over the northeastern part of the United States, mediums appeared in astonishing numbers, and seances became too numerous to record. Adin Ballou, who attended such meetings, started investigating spiritualism about 1850 and two years later published his *Spirit Manifestations,* including reports of physical spiritualism of which he had heard but not personally experienced. J.B. Dods, who had become a lecturer and writer on Mesmerism, published in 1854 *Spirit Manifestations Examined and Explained,* in which he attributed rappings to electro-magnetic discharge from the medium. Horace Greeley, a well-known Universalist layman and publisher of the *New York Tribune,* became interested in spiritualism and devoted many columns of his widely-read paper to all aspects of the subject.

The individual claiming spiritualist powers who came closest to home for most Universalists interested in such matters in the 1850s was John Murray Spear (1804-1887) who, with his older brother Charles, became well-known as a supporter of almost every reform movement then abroad in the land, including abolition and prison reform. J.M. Spear first became aware of his extraordinary powers in 1851 and immediately put them into practice with both words and actions. His first success came as a spirit healer the following year, when, on instructions from the spirit world, he presumably cured one David Vining of chronic neuralgia by a laying on of hands. Spear claimed also at one time or another to have "conversed" with many American and British notables who had long since passed off the scene.[101]

Spear worked closely with another Universalist clergyman, S.C. Hewitt of Cambridgeport, Massachusetts, who in 1852 published a work dramatically entitled *Messages from the Superior State; communicated by John Murray, through John M. Spear, in the summer of 1852. . . .* This 167-page book, of small physical dimensions, was divided into three roughly equal parts: a biography of Spear, emphasizing his spiritual experiences; a sketch of the life of John Murray; and twelve "messages" presumably relayed by the founder of American Universalism to the aforesaid Spear. Hewitt also edited the *New Era,* published in Boston to promote spiritualism. Part of what became his book on Murray appeared serially in the *Christian Freeman,* under the heading, "Letters on the New Era; or, Heaven opened to man."[102]

Spear attracted even more attention with the construction of a table-top machine known as The New Motive Power located in a cottage atop High Rock, an eminence overlooking the city of Lynn, Massachusetts. The machine, completed in 1854, was intended to provide new energy for man and his new world, and was to somehow pave the way for an ideal social order in the creation of which Spear was told by the spirits he would play a leading part. Breathing life into the machine was to be accompanied by the animal magnetism provided by selected individuals; thereupon it would provide inexhaustible energy for man's use. However, the only movements of the machine discernible to the human eye were apparently caused by the liberal use of magnets in its construction. In any case, the results were disappointing. The machine was dissembled and shipped to Randolph, New York, where it disappeared.[103]

As interest in Mesmerism, phrenology, spiritualism, and kindred phenomena swept over the northeastern United States in the 1840s and 1850s it was inevitable that the denominational press would take cognizance of the various "enthusiasms." As might be expected, the columns of all of the leading Universalist papers were full of discussions and comments by both correspondents and editors. The clear majority of the latter were cautious if not completely skeptical about the claims and counterclaims of the "strange doings" that were attracting so much attention. Whittemore, conspicuously not a convert to the new passion for phrenology, informed his readers in 1842 that, much to his delight, an expert in the field, not identified, had come to the conclusion that Universalists had a large share of benevolence in their makeup.[104] The previous year he had himself submitted to examination by two phrenologists and, as he perceptively noted, was told exactly what he wanted to hear—his "benevolence" and "reverence" were well-developed, and he had "large philoprogentiveness."[105] He was no doubt amused to be told of his "small combativeness" and "small acquisitiveness," in view of his often-demonstrated fighting spirit on behalf of Universalism and his considerable worldly wealth derived from railroads, banking, real estate, and publishing interests.

When Andrew Jackson Davis' supposed revelations were reported, Whittemore expressed the hope that "the time will come when the Universalist denomination will not be the receptacle of every strange thing under heaven."[106] He emphatically denied the credibility of spirit-rappings. When one individual of whom he heard claimed to be a medium, the unbelieving newspaper editor suggested that "the rappings he ought to have, are raps on the head, though not hard enough to deprive him of any portion of his brains, of which he has none to spare."[107] Whittemore promised that if such phenomena appeared in his own home, they would "be accommodated in the best room in our house, if they do not break the furniture."[108] It was all a mystery to him—part of the "occult sciences" which he professed not to understand.[109]

Sylvanus Cobb shared the skepticism about spiritualist doings expressed by Whittemore. Cobb, who had attended one of the lectures included in Spear's volume on John Murray, as reported by Hewitt, found in the lecture and book "nothing . . . which affords the least evidence to our mind that the immortal John Murray was their author."[110] Cobb did produce an elaborate history of spiritualism which appeared serially in his paper in 1861. He planned to publish it in book form, provided he could obtain 1,000 subscribers. The work was to have been entitled "Spiritualism and Kindred Topics."[111] But the project was dropped. By the 1860s the excitement over spiritualism seems to have subsided, and with the imminence of civil war, there was no market for such a work.

That some variety of spiritualism appealed to some Universalists, especially in the mid-nineteenth century, cannot be denied. Neither can it be denied that many of the "isms" of that era seemed to undermine revealed religion, sometimes by attributing to the human mind characteristics and powers that seemed to threaten belief in traditional supernaturalism. One British scholar, in noting the large number of Owenites attracted to spiritualism, pointed out that many of its adherents rejected, like the Universalists, religious orthodoxy and sought a rational, non-creedal substitute which could be reconciled with an interest in science.[112] It was this same seeking after newer and broader explanations of man's nature and his role and spiritual destiny as well as his relation to the world of nature around him, that prompted Whittemore to see some merit in Fishbough's *Macrocosm and Microcosm,* published in 1852. The editor considered it a worthy effort "to harmonize the present aspects of natural science with spiritual faith, and blend Swedenborg and [Auguste] Comte into a new cosmogony."[113]

Most nineteenth-century Universalists who expressed themselves on the subject of spiritualism did their best to reconcile that phenomenon with traditional Christianity. There were historical precedents already, so far as a thread of mysticism was concerned, if one considers the visions of de Benneville, the speculations of Murray, and even the blend of rationalism and supernaturalism in Hosea Ballou's religious conceptions. There was, however, a persistent and growing tendency to minimize or even eliminate the divine element, at least as expressed in or inferred from the Bible, and to stress more and more the power of the human mind and its achievements as the ultimate reality; in short, traces and of what was to become the philosophy of humanism could be found in the mid-nineteenth century urge to add larger dimensions to man's never-ending quest for wider spiritual horizons.

But the search was not to be achieved without a struggle which created and perpetuated serious differences within Universalism well into the twentieth century. A portent of theological difficulties and doubts yet to come was expressed after the Civil War, when some Universalist organizations felt obliged to warn against any modern spiritualism that rejected the Bible as a divinely-inspired authority. Illustrative was a resolution offered in the Vermont State Convention in 1871 to that effect. It was recommended that Universalist churches not be opened for the dissemination of spiritualist teachings which failed to acknowledge the unique primacy of the Scriptures as an indispensable element in historic Universalism.[114] It should be added that the resolution was tabled indefinitely in 1872, and the decision about access to spiritualist teachings was left up to each church. The Christian version of man's ultimate destiny was still firmly entrenched, but so also was the right of individual interpretation so dear to every Universalist.

Chapter 11

"ONE SADDLE AND BAGS:" THE PREACHER ON THE ROAD AND AT HOME

"Sept. 22nd, 1786, then departed this life our Beloved Elder and Brother, Adams Streeter, to the great lamentation of all his hearers."[1] Among the items mentioned in the inventory of his modest estate (valued at approximately $200 by modern reckoning) were 'one saddle and bags'—the trade-marks of the travelling preacher who played such a key role in the spreading of religion to almost every nook and cranny of America.

Traditionally, this interesting phenomenon of the itinerant clergyman in American religious history has been associated with certain Protestant denominations, and particularly with the Methodists. The term "circuit rider" has, more specifically, been historically identified with such men as John Wesley, Robert Strawbridge, Peter Cartwright, and Francis Asbury. The term "pioneer preacher" used here is a broader and more generalized designation, intended to include not only those who had scheduled itineraries to which they devoted their full time and for which they were supported by the various "stations" on their routes, but also any preacher who may or may not have been settled in one pastorate but travelled far and wide in the courses of his ministrations.

There is no doubt that the Methodists and the Baptists, who used the device of the circuit rider extensively, gained the highest proportion of adherents in the rapidly expanding population west of the Alleghenies after 1800.[2] One may be tempted, as a consequence, to minimize, or even overlook, the participation of other denominations in the process of carrying organized religion to the frontier, wherever that frontier might exist. Most church historians do pay some attention to the activities of the older established groups such as the Congregationalists, the Presbyterians, and the Episcopalians in the outposts of settlement, and to the existence of smaller and lesser-known sects such as the United Brethren and other predominantly German groups, the "Christian Connexion," the Campbellites, and the whole spectrum of the various "Disciples" movements, usually associated with the cutting edge of westward settlement.

It is also true that some denominations, such as the Unitarian, made no concerted effort to exploit frontier possibilities, or did so belatedly. The Unitarians tended to cling to the Atlantic seaboard and to their New England origins; or, if they ventured beyond, to settle in urban rather than rural environments. The Universalists, on the other hand, although also associated historically with New England, were much more inclined to venture onto the frontier. However, their activities as itinerant preachers have seldom been noted or their contributions in this area acknowledged. Sydney E. Ahlstrom, a prominent historian of American religion, does point out in passing that the Universalist denomination "was far more evangelical than is generally realized . . . . On the frontier their views frequently found favor."[3] But he did not elaborate.

The identification of Universalism with itinerant and circuit preaching can of course be made, as in the case of all religious bodies, with its very origins. To all sects and denominations seeking a footing, all efforts were pioneer efforts, and all geographical areas were frontiers to be conquered. There was not a single Universalist preacher in the formative days who did not "itinerate" sometime during his life, whether to a community next door to his own town or village, or to locations hundreds of miles distant. John Murray made his entrance into America as a religious wanderer.

If a composite Universalist clergyman were created for the period up through the mid-nineteenth century, whether settled in a pastorate or living on the road as an itinerant, what would his character and prospects probably have been? Allowing for inevitable exceptions, he might be described in the following fashion. He would be a farmer or mechanic in background, with not much more than a "common school" education, and would be likely to serve in the ministry on a part-time basis. His origins would be rural rather than urban (sharing this background with the majority of his countrymen), and his commitment to Universalism would have come at a relatively early age—in his teens or early twenties. He would have been licensed to preach without any very exhaustive inquiry into his background or qualifications, and he would not have expected much material compensation, if any, for his efforts. If seriously devoted to the denomination, he would be more likely at first to travel than to settle for any length of time in one community, and would be expected to meet opposition from "orthodox" clergy; his reputation might be based, in fact, on how well he could handle himself in public debate, usually arranged extemporaneously. He would depend on the generosity of both friends and strangers in his travels, as well as on a dependable horse and a sturdy pair of boots. He would be willing to countenance rebuffs as well as to welcome hospitality, and hope that when adversity struck, his family would somehow be provided for. In spite of discouragements, he would be an optimist, buoyed by his religious convictions, and would be likely to exaggerate his successes and to minimize his failures. He was not likely to be an "original thinker," but the greater his knowledge of the Bible, the better. Besides the Bible, he would probably have at hand a well-thumbed copy of three or four works on Universalism, such as Hosea Ballou's *Treatise on Atonement,* or one of Walter Balfour's disquisitions, or a sermon or two by Paul Dean or Edward Turner. There would, perhaps, be a copy of Streeter's hymnal available, as well as a few dog-eared issues of the *Trumpet* or its predecessor, the *Universalist Magazine.*

The itinerant Universalist preacher was also likely to be young. The tendency was for those societies which could afford a settled pastor to draw on older and more experienced clergy. This was pointed out by Stephen R. Smith, who, with his extensive experience on the upstate and western New York frontier in the early nineteenth century, could generalize with authority.[4] Hence, with some exceptions, those under about twenty-five were required by force of circumstances to itinerate. There was also an advantage for their hearers; relatively inexperienced preachers could be obtained at little or no expense, and were more likely to be mobile and more willing to travel (and therefore be more readily available) than their older colleagues who had acquired sizeable families and other commitments which made it either inadvisable or actually impossible to operate far from home.

The Pioneer Preacher

The early itinerant Universalist preachers shared some characteristics with their religious counterparts in other denominations. They travelled usually on horseback over all kinds of terrain and in all kinds of weather, and during all seasons of the year. They suffered illness, fatigue, loneliness, and hardship of almost every conceivable sort. They "got up" congregations or at least listeners on the spot, and hoped that their visits would pay religious dividends. In many respects, however, the Universalists operated under distinct disadvantages. Representatives of other denominations did, occasionally, discover much to their disgust that Universalists had preceded them. But because they were neither as numerous nor as well-known as most of the other religious bodies represented in frontier areas, Universalist preachers roving about the back-country or even in some of the larger towns as late as the 1830s and 1840s found themselves the first of their faith to have made an appearance.

More often than not, Universalist preachers received rebuffs rather than welcomes from the communities in which they appeared, because of the doctrines they preached. Their arrival was often greeted by indifference if not hostility, and their influence ended with their departure. Yet they doggedly made their rounds, and occasionally planted religious seeds that later matured into societies and churches that made all the effort seem worthwhile. The majority of Universalist itinerants in the pre-Civil War period were obscure even in their own day, and completely unknown to later generations. Their names might have been mentioned momentarily in a local newspaper, or a notice of a meeting might have appeared on a hitching post or a random building. Appearances, particularly in the Midwest and South, were often unscheduled and the "discourses" strictly impromptu.

Above all, the Universalists in the pioneering days of the denomination were handicapped because they had no central or even regional headquarters to which to turn for material support. They had to depend on their own limited resources and ingenuity to a much larger extent than did other itinerant preachers—or so they thought. In the course of his travels in the Genesee country of northern New York about 1815, Stephen R. Smith found that "the Methodist circuit preacher and the missionary" had already arrived.[5] The explanation, he believed, was not far to seek: The Universalists had neither official backing nor support from the East, and were left to fend for themselves. The Civil War was over before the General Convention assumed any real responsibility for systematic domestic missionary activity, considering it meanwhile a strictly local affair and responsibility.

It is difficult to estimate how many early itinerants kept records of their travels, although a large enough number did furnish sufficient information by way of accounts in denominational papers or diaries or reminiscences in book or pamphlet form to enable one to obtain some sense of their life-styles, their frustrations, and their hopes. The experiences of one are included at this point as a case-study—not so much to rescue him from historical oblivion or to single him out in such a way as to do injustice to scores of others, as to shed some light on how Universalism was spread in the nineteenth century.

Other individuals who performed much the same tasks and met many of the same challenges will be considered in other contexts—men and women of both the nineteenth century and later who illustrated vividly the itinerant tradition, such as Nathaniel Stacy, Daniel Bragg Clayton, and John C. Burruss; Quillen Hamilton Shinn, Augusta J. Chapin, Caroline A. Soule, James A. Inman, Ada C. Bowles, Hannah Powell, and Charles H. Pennoyer, to mention only a few. There were scores of obscure individuals of the stamp of J. Edwin Churchill, who had travelled by horse and buggy from Michigan to Alabama in 1870, and made his living as a portrait painter and preached Universalism on the side.[6] Many a Universalist, especially in the rural areas of the nation, was still depending on the travelling clergyman, circuit-connected or not, long after the Civil War had come and gone.

George Rogers (1804-1846) was one of the most representative of the Universalist pioneer preachers in the South and in the border states of the Midwest during the Jacksonian era.[7] Diminutive in stature, with a thin and high-pitched voice, he did not in those respects at least seem to have all the assets presumed desirable for the rough-and-tumble life of a frontier preacher; yet he appeared to possess a constitution, a well-developed sense of humor, and an adaptability which stood him in good stead at all times and enabled him to survive all kinds of rigors. Disregarding all artificial political boundaries and surmounting all kinds of barriers, whether thrown up by Mother Nature or otherwise, he spread Universalist ideas far and wide.

Rogers arrived in 1818 from the British Isles as an orphan, in the charge of his maternal grandmother. By the age of sixteen he had developed a "propensity for roving" which he attributed to the prison-like atmosphere of several years in a Philadelphia orphanage. This was followed by an apprenticeship to some kind of trade (which he neither identified nor practiced). Somehow he managed along the way to acquire the basics of a common-school education, including proficiency in Latin, and became an omnivorous reader and a composer of both poetry and hymns.

Although confirmed as an Episcopalian, his eclecticism in regard to religion, which interested him very early in life, was demonstrated from the very beginning. He moved easily from one religious group to another, and during his late teens and early twenties, preferred to sample rather than commit himself to any one denomination. His approach was strictly ecumenical. He attended Methodist services, took part in the debates of the local Berean Society, composed principally of Universalists; and developed a "very sincere" opposition to that faith, which at the time he considered "a most dangerous delusion." He did, however, make a favorable impression on Abner Kneeland, who was then in Philadelphia, and who predicted that Rogers would "make a good Universalist preacher one of these days."

During the 1820s, Rogers roamed up and down the mid-Atlantic seaboard, preaching to all kinds of congregations. Without any kind of credentials, he avoided all denominational ties and claimed to be only "a christian minister." He disliked the emotionalism of much of the preaching he heard, and deplored the narrow sectarianism which seemed to be so popular among Protestant clergy. While serving briefly in 1827 as preacher to a Methodist group in Trenton, New Jersey, he admitted that the membership of the congregation would probably have been greater if he had "encouraged shouting, and paid less attention to grammatical precision." It appeared to him that "those who make the most noise are accounted the best christians."

The young preacher's transition to Universalism began about 1829, when a careful examination of the Bible revealed no authority for trinitarianism and convinced him that Jesus was literally the son of God and not coequal with the Deity. He also made the discovery that Christ's mission had been the reconciliation of the world to God rather than the reverse, and that the doctrine of total depravity was "absurd." Equipped with these new insights, Rogers became acquainted in 1830 with Abel C. Thomas, then pastor of the Lombard Street Universalist Church in Philadelphia. Thomas left an amusing description of Rogers when they first met. Rogers, who walked into Thomas' quarters unannounced one day, was described by his host as "short of stature, roughly dressed, having great metal buttons on a coat that might have fitted almost any other man as well—a sadly-worn white hat, 'run to seed'—the other extremity of his person bearing muddy shoes with the strings untied."[8]

Thomas told Rogers that Universalists had no rigid creed to which to conform and that each individual could, in effect, create his own, and promptly invited Rogers to preach in his church. With this assurance in hand, Rogers decided to be a Universalist, and found himself preaching not only in Thomas' church but to Zelotes Fuller's Callowhill Universalist congregation, also in Philadelphia. Between 1831 and 1835 the new convert preached to a Universalist congregation in Brooklyn, Pennsylvania, and wandered over a large area in the eastern and central parts of the state as well as western and upstate New York, preaching to any one who would listen. He finally obtained the credentials he had previously lacked, when he was fellowshipped by the Chenango Association (New York) in 1831, and was ordained the following year.

It appeared by 1834 that Rogers might actually settle in Pennsylvania. But the lure of far horizons was too strong to be resisted. He mounted his horse that winter and headed west, with Pittsburgh as his destination. As the first Universalist preacher to visit that bustling and rough-hewn city, still frontier-like in many respects, Rogers attracted large crowds of the curious and those opposed to his obvious religious unorthodoxy. He had missiles thrown at him (one of which broke a window of the courthouse in which he was speaking), but he persisted, and determined to return the next year to spread the Universalist message. On his second trip (in 1835), he organized a society and arranged for the purchase of a meeting house. He also acquired for them a preacher of his acquaintance from western Maryland.

Rogers never missed an opportunity to preach, no matter where he was or how unpropitious the circumstances. In fact, he created opportunities if they did not already exist. On his return to Philadelphia from his first visit to Pittsburgh he delivered seventeen sermons on the way, in a two-week period. He also detoured via Cincinnati, where he promised to revive a defunct society on his next trip. He remained in Pennsylvania only long enough to pack his wife, a two-year-old daughter, and his scant earthly possessions into a chaise. He later wrote that in 1835, when he headed west, he had all of $100 in cash in his pocket, and no debts. He was never to be so rich again.

From his arrival in the winter of 1836 until his death a decade later, Rogers used Cincinnati as his base of operations. But he was seldom home. During the first few months of 1836 he did reorganize the local society, as he had promised, and obtained a meeting house. But his interests and his inclinations lay far beyond the confines of one location. He organized a society in Patriot, Indiana; became an editor of the denominational *Sentinel and Star in the West* (published in Cincinnati for many years); went on the road throughout southern Ohio to get support for the paper; journeyed again to Pittsburgh, and preached in western Virginia. Upon his return to Cincinnati, destitute of funds, he found his neglected society in a shambles. He was forced to sell his horse and his books to pay the substitute preacher he had hired, and to provide for his own growing family, a second child having been born during his absence.

After resigning the pastorship of the Cincinnati society, which had no funds to pay his salary, he set off on the first of the extended trips that became a sort of personal trademark. For five months during the winter and spring of 1836-37, Rogers travelled some 2,000 miles (1,400 on horseback) through five states, from Kentucky to Alabama, preaching as he went, and regaling readers of Universalist papers, East and West, with his experiences transcribed from the detailed diary which he kept. He crossed over twenty major rivers, several more than once, under all kinds of conditions. He commented wryly on his discovery that "ferry-houses are *always* on the opposite shore of *all* rivers." He saw and heard Andrew Jackson as the latter made his triumphal return to Nashville in 1837 after completing his second term as President of the United States, and was much impressed by "Old Hickory."

The indefatigable Universalist preacher held forth in theaters, in barns, in forest clearings, in private homes, as well as in churches of other denominations. From time to time he ran across an isolated Universalist, but for the most part the religion he professed was unknown to Rogers' hearers. In Alabama, he found only one avowed Universalist in the town of Selma; however, he was impressed by the Universalist meeting house in Montgomery, which had not only a bell but an organ. The society here had been organized only three years at the time of his trip.

Rogers became totally convinced of how much work there was to be done. He remained in Cincinnati only a few weeks before he was itinerating again. After preaching, in company with Samuel Tizzard, fellow-editor of the *Sentinel,* in four counties in Indiana, Rogers set off again for the South. This time his destination was New Orleans. While there in 1838 he attended the services of the renowned Theodore Clapp, who preached Universalism without identifying it as such, and also spoke from Clapp's pulpit several times. After brief preaching excursions into Mississippi, Rogers returned home just in time to re-pack his bags and make a three-month trip over "a good portion of Ohio," including the Western Reserve in the northeastern part of the state; here he found many New Englanders and their descendants, some of whom had established Universalist societies. A third trip in the winter of 1838 took him south again. His purpose was an inventory of Universalist prospects in western and central Mississippi. He concluded that, at least in this part of the South, religious indifference was a greater obstacle than bigotry. In Natchez, as in so many other communities, Rogers was told that he was the first to have preached Universalism in the area. Lack of denominational publications and the fact that most of the population had emigrated from other southern states rather than from the East and North, were the reasons assigned by Rogers for this state of affairs. In the course of the 1838-39 journey south, Rogers revisited both Selma and Montgomery, Alabama. In the former he conducted services in a theater and administered the Lord's Supper to an all-female congregation—a most unusual occurrence, in his estimation.

Rogers' fourth tour of the South, begun in March 1840, had one unique feature. It took place by horse and buggy. The first had been endured on horseback; he used up two mounts on that trip. The second and third journeys had been made largely by steamboats, which he characterized as floating volcanoes; he had narrowly escaped death on one which blew up. But travelling on the fourth trip was no more pleasant than the others, for he was required to traverse roads that had not been repaired "since the fall of Adam." He considered himself fortunate to cover as much as forty miles in a long day, and often saw no more than one or two habitations or as many as half a dozen people. The area covered on the fourth journey included Kentucky, Tennessee, and northern Mississippi, and his vivid pen-pictures of what he saw in these states included the grubbiness, poverty, and isolation of frontier life as well as the amenities of plantation and city existence. He made the interesting observation that, in Tennessee, it was the Presbyterians rather than the Methodists who had originated camp meetings (of which he had a very low opinion).

The East was next on Rogers' seemingly endless itinerary. In 1840 and 1841 he visited up and down the Atlantic seaboard from Baltimore to Boston, where he met for the first time two leading Universalists he admired greatly: Hosea Ballou 2d and Thomas Whittemore. He also visited Thomas B. Thayer in Lowell, a city which he disliked, full as it was of the noise and the clamor of textile machinery and urban congestion. He preferred open country, rural quiet, and the spaciousness of the Midwest and South he had grown to love. En route home, increasingly crippled with rheumatism brought on by "improvident over-exertion and exposure," he insisted on preaching in the Hudson and Mohawk Valleys.

Scarcely had a new year begun when he was on his way to Louisiana via St. Louis, Missouri, where he lingered a month to preach. After two months in southern Louisiana in 1842, including a return appearance in Parson Clapp's pulpit in New Orleans, and side-trips into western Mississippi, he spent almost two years travelling all over Ohio, Pennsylvania, and western Virginia. He stopped long enough in one place to engage in a fifteen-hour debate spread over three days.

The next year (1844) found him again in Tennessee; in Robertson County he delivered no less than nineteen sermons in a sixteen-day period, finding his audiences as full of babies and dogs as of adults. He preached in a Methodist church in Princeton, Kentucky, until he was finally locked out, and in the Senate chamber of the state capitol in Jackson, Mississippi, with the governor present. Before the year was over, he had preached in Erie County, Pennsylvania, and had even ventured into Upper Canada (London and environs, Toronto, and Hamilton, among other places).

At Smithfield (Niagara District) he attended a meeting called to organize a Universalist Convention for Western Canada ("Canada West"). He found himself appointed a one-man committee to draw up a constitution for the new organization, which was adopted, and tarried sufficiently long to deliver three sermons.[9] After nearly two months in upstate and western New York, he returned home via Michigan where he preached eight times in Ann Arbor. Christmas Day, 1844, found him in Farmington, Illinois, assisting in the funeral exercises for the wife of a Universalist clergyman.

Scarcely a year before his own death, in 1846, in Cincinnati, Rogers set out on a typically lengthy trip which took him again to St. Louis, as far west as Burlington, Iowa, and as far north and east as Massachusetts, New Hampshire, and Maine. This was to be the last of his travels. Abel C. Thomas, who was pastor of the Cincinnati society at the time the wanderer returned, recalled that "the stamp of death" was upon Rogers, although the latter refused to admit it.[10] Rogers did tell Thomas that "he was tired of rambling all over the land," and was looking forward to building a home for his family, digging in his garden, and preaching on Sundays.

Rogers died of consumption at the age of forty-two, literally worn out. Yet he had defied the prediction made shortly after his arrival from London at the age of fourteen, that because he was so frail he would probably never attain adulthood.[11] He was interred in Delhi township, near Cincinnati, in accordance with his request that he be laid to rest "in the midst of my brethren . . . with the beauty of nature all around."[12] It was here that he had organized a society and dedicated a meeting house many years before. It was appropriate that Thomas, who had completed Rogers' conversion to Universalism, should preach the funeral sermon.[13] Memorial sermons were also preached from Universalist pulpits all over the Midwest and even in the East.[14]

Tributes to Rogers were paid both before and after his death. Abel Thomas, writing in the early 1850s, described him as "the most active, persevering, widely-operating missionary, ever connected with our denomination."[15] Over a decade earlier, Thomas Whittemore, in whose paper various installments of Rogers' journal appeared from time to time, had had nothing but praise for the intrepid traveller. Rogers was described in 1835 as "a faithful pioneer in the cause of truth . . . a real *working* preacher."[16]

Whittemore was at the same time struck by the forwardness and casualness of itinerants like Rogers. They operated in quite different fashion from their comparatively staid counterparts in the East. What preacher in New England would dare to appear in a community without prior notice or at least an invitation, and make it clear in advance that he would expect no compensation for his services?[17] That aside, Whittemore was sure that Rogers had "travelled more, suffered more, and encountered greater perils, in his efforts to spread the doctrine of universal grace, than any man now in active life. He is never still . . . ."[18]

Certainly but few Universalists could match Rogers' travel record. During his denominational ministry of less than twenty years he had preached in all but three states of the Union, (Vermont and the Carolinas), as well as in the territories of Wisconsin and Iowa, and in Upper Canada as well. He was more than once compared to John Murray as a fellow pioneer.[19] Whittemore went so far as to suggest that Rogers' autobiography (his *Memoranda*) be renamed "The Life of John Murray, 2d."[20]

There was yet another comparison with Murray, this time suggested by Hosea Ballou 2d, but in another context. The Massachusetts-based clergyman reviewed Rogers' autobiography shortly after it appeared in 1846, and commended the book for its readability, lightness of touch, and "wilderness of variety."[21] Ballou had read it straight through—a feat he could not accomplish with Murray's autobiography. Ballou admitted that he "never yet had the superhuman, or sub-human, patience" to read even one quarter of Murray's *Life* at one time.

Ballou's estimate of Rogers' facility with pen and language was applicable also to the only major theological work that the frontier preacher produced during his busy life—*The Pro and Con of Universalism.* This collection of essays, replete with the homespun, direct, and commonsensical language and down-to-earth examples that would appeal to frontier readers without sophisticated religious background or inclination, was begun in 1837 and published in book form a year later. He began to compose the essays after returning from his first trip south, his writing sandwiched in between serving simultaneously four societies within a twenty-five mile radius of Cincinnati. He had neither the time nor the money to write or to publish the entire work, so it originally appeared in sixteen installments. Rogers took to the road to solicit subscriptions and sold the first twelve issues for a total of $1.00.[22] Within three years after the essays were published in a single volume, Rogers had disposed of 3,000 copies in the course of his travels, and the work went into a fourth printing. Total sales were in the neighborhood of 5,000.[23]

George Rogers was in no sense a serious or profound thinker, nor did he ever claim to be. Some of his ministerial colleagues were, in fact, rather critical of his lack of intellectual depth. L.F.W. Andrews, active in southern Universalism, heard Rogers preach in Selma, and was not at all impressed.[24] Although the presentation was "clear and convincing," it was an old-fashioned "doctrinal sermon," the subject of which, wrote Andrews, had long since lost its novelty. Rogers was, in Andrews' estimation, behind the times.

But whether or not these strictures were deserved, Rogers undoubtedly felt that he was making a contribution to those who had never heard a Universalist or even knew that such a denomination as Universalism existed. His message was direct, and delivered in unadorned language, spiced with humor and good will. He conceived his mission to be the propagation of "useful truth . . . for practical purposes; for comfort under affliction; for encouragement amid the vicissitudes of life; for enlargement of the charities of the hearer; the elevation of their aims; and the increase of their confidence in God."[25] The special responsibility of Universalists was to lay "a foundation of love, gratitude, and trust toward a God who loves mankind." It was as simple as that. It was Rogers' obligation, as he saw his role, to bring a message of cheer and reconciliation, and to draw men into closer union with both God and fellow-man, regardless of "condition, nation, complexion, [or] creed." Such was the life, thought, and activities of one Universalist on the rapidly-changing American frontier.

Sources and Supply of Clergy

One of the major obstacles to denominational growth, especially in the early decades, was almost total dependence on conversion as a means of recruitment. Until households could produce at least one generation of Universalist children, and until Sunday Schools and religious discussion groups ("institutes") were first established on a continuing basis in the 1820s and 1830s, the denomination had to depend for both its laity and its clergy on its powers of persuasion. Additions to Universalist ranks came both by individual decision and by the conversion of entire congregations, such as occurred among some of the Dunker groups in the South, notably in South Carolina. In Massachusetts, thirteen Congregational churches organized prior to the creation of the first Universalist society in Gloucester in 1779, eventually became Universalist, as well as a scattering of others organized after that date.[26] Many of these, as well as other congregations which eventually became Universalist, lived an erratic or precarious existence and eventually closed. The number of Congregational churches that officially or formally became Universalist represented only a fraction of the total of what had been the established church in Massachusetts until 1833. A much higher proportion of those which abandoned orthodoxy became Unitarian rather than Universalist.

No statistics exist that can give a precise accounting of the sources of Universalist clergy who came by way of conversion in the nineteenth century. In 1824 a list of twenty-five still living and indicating their religious backgrounds was published.[27] Over half (thirteen) had been Baptists; seven had been Methodists; and the remainder had come from the Congregational, Episcopal, and Lutheran churches. Almost all had been preachers in their respective groups. Somewhat more than a decade later (1838), A.B. Grosh published a selected list indicating the denominational origins of prominent Universalist clergymen and laymen.[28] Of the thirty-one ministers listed, eleven were former Baptists and five were former Methodists. Other denominations represented were Congregational, Presbyterian, Episcopalian, Lutheran, and Christian. Among the latter (frequently hyphenated as "Christ-ian"), were Elias and C.C. Smith, associated with the founding of an anti-Calvinistic northern New England sect which eventually merged with others of the so-called "Christian Connexion" into Alexander Campbell's Disciples of Christ. One ex-Christian who was fellowshipped by the Northern Ohio Association in 1822 was described as a person who had finally "found his way through the fog."[29]

Seventeen of the twenty laymen that Grosh identified in 1838 were former Baptists or Methodists. The editor of the *Gospel Banner* (Maine) in 1842 identified twenty Universalist clergymen who had come from other sources within the preceding five years. Sixteen of the twenty had been either Baptist or Methodist preachers.[30] A review of approximately 100 Universalist clergymen whose religious backgrounds were known indicates that, at least before the Civil War, the highest proportions came from these two denominations, with the Baptists as the major source, particularly for the earlier converts. Elhanan Winchester, Hosea and Maturin Ballou, Caleb Rich, and Isaac Davis had all been Baptists at one time. The majority of the seventeen individuals attending the Philadelphia Convention of Universalists in 1790 were, or had been, Baptists.[31] According to the records of the Baptist churches between 1780 and 1810, the Universalists made great inroads into their membership—a fact recognized by Isaac Backus, a leading Baptist in New England.[32] Murray, who for a time had been associated with Methodism in England, was considered primarily responsible for bringing about the conversion of Baptists to the "damnable heresy" of Universalism. Backus felt constrained to write a tract entitled "The Doctrines of Universal Salvation Examined and Refuted" (1782) to counter the ideas of such men as Murray, Chauncy, and Relly.

If considered as a group, the early Universalist preachers were a grand mixture of "discordant materials," drawn from almost every Protestant denomination.[33] According to Stephen R. Smith, long-time Universalist clergyman in New York State, they represented the widest possible range, with no "common character and capability" except some degree of allegiance to Universalist principles. Some possessed "great talents" while others exhibited none at all. With disarming frankness and an obviously personal judgment, he compared former Baptist with former Methodist preachers, and found the latter wanting. The Baptists, according to Smith, gave the Universalists "*good* if not always *great* men."[34] On the other hand, of twenty clergy arriving from other denominations between 1805 and 1845 that in his estimation contributed nothing or were in fact liabilities, fourteen were ex-Methodists.[35] The typical convert "had lost either his influence, or character, or both, before his conversion." This was one reason, Smith thought, for the poor reputation suffered by Universalists, who were made scapegoats for other denominations.

Bringing the supply of clergy into balance with demand was a chronic problem in the denomination, and the General Convention was called upon more and more frequently to assist in supplying "destitute societies and places." That body was, however, slow to respond. A special committee was finally appointed in 1836 to investigate the matter, but came to the conclusion that the problem was not so much a shortage of preachers as indifference, "lack of pecuniary ability," and "deficiency of . . . Christian zeal."[36] The convention immediately turned the problem back to local organizations by recommending the creation by each state convention of a missionary fund, the appointment of one or more itinerants in each state, and the use of denominational periodicals as clearing-houses for requests for clergy.

The next effort to make the problem a national responsibility by way of the General Convention was not made until 1852, when a committee was appointed "to consider the subject of a General Missionary Union."[37] The idea was not so much to finance itinerant preachers by then as to create a fund by subscription to assist societies in maintaining public worship and in construction of meeting houses.

Nothing came of the proposal, for the committee reported that the time had not yet come for a national effort.[38] It was better to operate at the state and local level; furthermore, there were, in 1853, inadequate numbers of clergy for existing societies as it was, without attempting to organize new ones. J.G. Adams estimated that fifty clergymen were needed in New York State and Ohio alone.[39]

In 1853 Cyrus H. Fay, then pastor of the Orchard Street church in New York City, devoted a long article to the problems of the denominational ministry.[40] The most critical one, as he saw it, was the acute shortage—a cause for "much anxiety and alarm." He offered several explanations for this sad state of affairs. The vocation of the ministry had become more demanding than ever; increasing educational qualifications were needed which many young men were reluctant to acquire; and older clergy failed to encourage promising candidates. Those who had entered the ministry too hastily and had then withdrawn had often blamed the denomination rather than recognizing their own deficiencies, and had consequently exerted a negative influence. There was also the ever-present appeal of the secular life, and especially the inducements of the business world with its opportunities for both prestige and profit. He also detected a growing religious indifference and loss of missionary spirit on the part of both clergy and laity.

One of the major explanations which Fay offered for the crisis in the Universalist ministry was increasing mobility, with resulting instability. The denomination gave the impression "of a chess-board in the hands of unpractical players [with] our ministers the chess-men, constantly changing places." The same observation was made by others. One disgruntled layman complained of the constant changes of clergymen. "Ministers . . . just get established in one place, by gaining the confidence and hearts of the people of their charge, then forsooth, the first thing we know, they pull up stakes and off they go."[41] A comparative study of the post office addresses of Universalist clergymen in New York, New Hampshire, and Massachusetts in 1838 and 1843 revealed dramatically the extent to which preachers moved about within just one five-year period.[42] Of 148 in New York in 1838, only 29 had the same address in 1843; only 2 of the 38 in New Hampshire had remained in the same location; and the figures for Massachusetts revealed that only 18 out of 130 had retained the same address. The compiler of the statistics came to the conclusion that "pastors should have their dwelling houses set on wheels!"

Difficulties created by migratory clergy were not, however, to be blamed entirely on them. Many societies contracted on a year-to-year basis, but frequently waited until the very end of the year to inform the pastor of whether or not his services were desired the following year.[43] One device more and more frequently used to alleviate the problem of uncertainty and chronic turnover was the settlement of pastors for five-year periods. This practice was being used successfully by many societies in Maine, for example, in the mid-1840s.[44] It had become widespread by the time of the Civil War in both urban and many settled rural areas, although the itinerant preacher simultaneously remained a prominent fixture in the religious landscape almost everywhere.

Clerical Welfare

Whether at home or on the road, Universalist clergy in the nineteenth century found themselves inadequately compensated—if at all—and with little or no security for themselves or their families after they were forced to retire from the ministry for such reasons as health or age, or who died with no provision for those they might have left behind. Part of this situation derived from the long-standing tradition that preachers donated their services and were expected to depend on free-will offerings and the generosity of their constituents. This goes far to explain why so many Universalist preachers, notably in the early years of the denomination, considered their religious duties as avocations rather than as part of a full-time profession. A large number of preachers until well after the middle of the nineteenth century earned their livelihoods as farmers or shopkeepers, or in some other fashion. The institution of the "settled pastorate" evolved but slowly; one prime reason was the inability of the clergyman to support himself and/or his dependents on a full-time basis.

In 1840 A.B. Grosh drastically reduced the number of clergymen appearing on the rolls in the *Universalist Register.* He listed as "active" only those who made "preaching their business" and omitted those "who devote very little time to it."[45] So many in Vermont were conducting religious services on a part-time basis, or had dropped out of preaching in 1857, that the state convention ruled that any minister ceasing to be active for one year (except for illness, age, or "other justifiable causes") automatically forfeited fellowship.[46] The ruling was invoked the following year, and several other state conventions followed the same practice. In 1864 Abel C. Thomas investigated the status of the fifty clergymen who had attended the General Convention thirty years before, and found that only twenty were still in the ministry.[47] Allowing for the fact that twelve had died in the thirty-year period, eighteen had dropped out for one reason or another. Several had found more lucrative positions or had left the ministry temporarily; such a person was J.M. Austin, who was serving as paymaster of the Union Army during the Civil War.

The parlous state of ministerial finances can be illustrated copiously. Stephen R. Smith of upstate New York estimated that, in 1815, the typical Universalist preacher averaged less than $200 a year from all ministerial sources, and was forced to supplement his income by teaching, farming, or engaging in some handicraft.[48] He attributed the paucity of clerically-derived income not so much to the miserliness of societies as to the reluctance of clergymen to request or even accept larger salaries. He was himself a good example of his own generalizations. Fellowshipped in 1813, he started his career as a young schoolteacher, with preaching on weekends and vacation intervals. During a six-month period he received for his ministerial services one-half bushel of dry apples, several wagonloads of wood, and a total of $10 in cash.[49] As late as the 1850s, as a "country pastor," he never earned more than $600 a year, and seldom received as much as $500.[50] When Adin Ballou became pastor of the First Congregational Parish (Unitarian) in Mendon, Massachusetts, in 1831, and signed a five-year contract the following year, his annual salary of $400 was only $70 a year more than he had been receiving in another community almost a decade before.[51] T.J. Sawyer, of Clinton, New York, who was supposed to be receiving $400 a year in the 1840s, at least on paper, seldom collected more than $375 because pledges or subscriptions were not paid in as promised.[52]

Delegates from societies at the annual meeting of the Somerset Association (Maine) in 1848 were reminded that they should not expect their pastors to perform their duties for nothing. "They are men, and have wants like other men; and they depend upon their labors for the means to supply their wants."[53] Eliphalet Case, who served as a part-time pastor in Lowell, Massachusetts, in the 1830s (meanwhile editing a secular journal and serving as postmaster), migrated to New York State.[54] After a few years he returned to Massachusetts in disgust. He found the chronic shortage of clergy about which everyone seemed so concerned quite easy to explain. Most, like himself, were discouraged by the "miserable avarice and parsimony" of Universalist societies which refused to support the clergy adequately, yet demanded instant and unremitting service of all kinds, and at all times.[55] Preachers were fortunate if they received as much of a reward as "kind wishes and grateful smiles" for delivering a sermon, conducting a funeral, or writing a letter for a parishioner. When he resigned as pastor of the society in Geneva, New York, after two years, he was still owed $50, and had to borrow money to retrieve his mail from the post office (in the days before prepaid service had been introduced). Fellow-clergyman W.S. Balch castigated Case for making such harsh statements about the treatment he had allegedly received, but Case was defended by A.B. Grosh. The latter considered Case's criticisms unfortunate but based on fact; Grosh was ready to offer examples of even worse experiences of clergy at the hands of indifferent and unfeeling societies.

In 1853 the Boston-based "Society for the Relief of Aged and

Destitute Clergymen" appointed a committee of three ministers and three laymen to collect information concerning clerical salaries in New England; their report was published the following year.[56] A seven-point questionnaire was answered by some 1,500 individual clergymen representing all Protestant denominations in Massachusetts, and by numerous church officials, theological school personnel, and college presidents in other states. The replies were sifted and identified by denomination, although the names of individuals were not released. Several Universalist replies were included, and indicated responses typical of the majority. An analysis of the returns indicated what most clergymen, regardless of denomination, already knew: They were grossly underpaid and suffered accordingly from lack of financial and professional security and prestige. The small material rewards discouraged "many young men of talent and character" from entering the ministry; consequently, a high level of "Christian scholarship" and effectiveness was lacking. The only solution was "a thorough reform of public opinion" in the direction of more adequate support than then existed.

It was, of course, impossible to strike a meaningful average of ministerial salaries because of the wide individual range, but the overall median was about $600 a year in the 1850s, with rural areas paying distinctly lower salaries than urban centers. The average annual salaries for Universalists, based on incomplete returns, in urbanized Essex County, Massachusetts, was slightly over $700, as compared to $900 for Unitarians.[57] A local study made the same year by the Universalists of the salaries received by pastors in the Boston Association (Middlesex, Essex, and Suffolk Counties), also based on incomplete returns, indicated an average of slightly over $700.[58] The salaries ranged from $400 to $2,000 (paid by the Second Universalist Society in Boston). A follow-up study of forty-nine societies in the Boston Association in 1854 indicated a slight upward trend, an average of slightly over $780.[59] The average age of the clergy was 25, ministering to congregations with an average attendance of 216. One clergyman estimated that the average salary across the country for Universalist preachers in 1854 was "less than $400 a year."[60] To make matters worse, there were so many demands on their time and energy that they had no opportunity to supplement their totally inadequate incomes.

Beginning with the centennial year (1870) the *Universalist Register* carried the dollar value of the church properties of societies, when known, but carefully refrained from reporting pastoral salaries, which continued to lag far behind most other professions. Nearly half of the Universalist ministers in Vermont, a predominantly rural state, were receiving annual salaries of less than $650 as late as 1906.[61]

The Universalist clergyman acknowledged by the denomination to have been receiving the highest salary in 1853 was Edwin H. Chapin, pastor of the Fourth Universalist Society in New York City. His annual stipend was set at $4,500 that year, and by 1855 had risen to $5,000.[62] Almost all respondents to the New England questionnaire in 1853 agreed that, even where public sentiment had changed for the better over the previous twenty years, salaries lagged far behind the cost of living, and that when some increases were evident, it was only because no minister at all could be obtained otherwise, and not because of any conviction that the clergy should be more liberally supported. The Universalists reported "some improvement for the better," but salaries were still too low.

One Universalist wrote vehemently that "a man must have the spirit of self-sacrifice in no ordinary degree, and be willing to live the life of a hermit, if he enters the ministry now." He went on to say that "we must have the martyr-age back again, or there must be some change in the compensation of the clergy." Another was frank to say that the denomination should refuse to ordain young men when it was known that their salaries would not support them. The same clergyman suggested that salaries should be tied to the price of "common articles of living" at any given time; i.e., that a cost-of-living clause be written into every ministerial contract.

On occasion, pastors received fringe benefits not provided by formal agreements with their parishioners. Societies with very limited means or those which wished to recognize the loyal services of their clergy, made special gifts of food, clothing, or other items. Adin Ballou was presented with "a fine blue broadcloth cloak" by forty-five ladies in his parish in 1836 as a testimony to "his individual and pastoral character."[63] Universalists often held "donation parties" in which they would descend on a preacher's family and contribute "necessaries," which sometimes even included money.[64] Such occasions also served social purposes, and the tangible benefits were sometimes in doubt. Mrs. D.P. (Mary A.) Livermore experienced her first and last "donation party" while her husband was serving the Universalist society in Stafford, Connecticut. The interior of her home was left in a shambles because of the large crowd and the conviviality. She forbade her husband ever to allow another such event, and threatened to seek another parish where such traditions did not exist.[65]

But more often, emergency collections or pleas for help had to be made for destitute or impoverished preachers or their surviving families. The widow of one Universalist minister advertised in 1854 in the denominational press, seeking foster homes for her two destitute boys.[66] On-the-spot donations of all kinds were solicited at meetings when the need arose. A public plea was made in 1865 for the unfortunate Abraham Norwood, who had served as a preacher for thirty years and as the state missionary in Connecticut for a decade.[67] At the time he had been forced to retire because of failing health (1862), he had a large family to support, and an income of only $200 a year; his entire assets consisted of a homestead on which he still owed $500.

The plight of the families of departed clergymen was first recognized by the New England Convention in 1825, although nothing tangible was done by that body for many years. A committee was appointed to consider the feasibility of creating a "charitable society, for the purpose of raising a fund for the relief of widows and orphans of deceased brethren in the ministry . . . who may be left in indigent circumstances."[68] Two years later the committee was still wrestling with "the best method of raising a widow's fund."[69]

The Boston Association considered the problem in 1832 and during the following year created the "Society for the Relief of Destitute Families of Deceased Universalist Ministers" which evolved into the "Massachusetts Universalist Charitable Society" in 1833, complete with a constitution.[70] Any person paying $2.00 automatically became a member. These funds were to be supplemented by donations and "public contributions." The families of any Universalist minister who had lived in the state and had made contributions were eligible for assistance.

The Central Association in New York took the lead in that state in 1836 by creating a similar society, followed almost immediately by most of the other associations in the state.[71] The New York State Convention lent encouragement, but no actual financial support until 1845.[72] In that year it was announced by his son that Colonel Cornelius Harsen, a wealthy Universalist layman, had bequeathed $6,000 to the convention, the interest to be used to assist the families of deceased Universalist clergymen who had belonged to the state convention.[73] A board of trustees was appointed to administer the fund which, when first established, was estimated to provide only about $420 annually; this was to be supplemented by contributions by local associations. All requests for funds had to receive the concurrence of the convention.[74] The first recipients of aid from the Harsen bequest were the widows of three clergymen; each received $50.[75]

The long-range hope was to use the Harsen Fund as the nucleus of a mutual aid society treasury, with annual contributions of $6.00 from each clergyman. Thus was to be created the rough equivalent of both a contributory pension fund and benefits for widows and orphans (for which $1.00 was to be earmarked). A.B. Grosh, active in the lodge of Odd Fellows, suggested their mutual aid plan as a model, and devoted several pages of the *Universalist Register* to a detailing of the scheme. He also recommended the creation of a similar fund at the society level for the relief of indigent members. This, he believed, would be less repugnant than dependence on local public charity or residence in the county poor house. E.M. Locke of Newark, New York, announced in the same year that the Harsen bequest became available (1845) that he was single-handedly planning to embark on a campaign to raise a combined missionary and relief fund of no less than $100,000.[76] This ambitious plan, which was never carried out, was to have involved a visit to "every Universalist in the state that is able to give." The Harsen Fund did grow, however, and by 1885 amounted to $46,000.[77]

Other segments of the denomination had, by 1870, haltingly and rather belatedly made some provision for assistance for clergymen and their families. The deliberations of the Maine Convention were fairly typical. Assistance for "superannuated clergymen" was discussed from time to time, beginning in 1853, but it was not until 1867 that a "Fund for Aid of Aged and Indigent Ministers and their Families" was formerly established.[78] Meanwhile, the General Convention had paid scant attention to the problem of clerical welfare. It was not until 1863 that it took up the matter of assistance, by considering the creation of a "General Aid Association," one of whose five functions was "to aid aged infirm ministers and their families."[79] However, nothing concrete grew out of this recommendation, and the trustees of the General Convention concentrated their disposition of the limited missionary funds on such endeavors as supporting theological students and assisting in the financing of church construction.

When the Centenary Committee made its report at the General Convention in 1869, it included among the desired objectives of the denomination a generalized statement calling for support of "Relief Funds, wherever located or instituted."[80] No mention at all was made in the proposal to create the Murray Centenary Fund of using any of its resources for such purposes. However, the trustees were authorized to receive and disburse contributions "bestowed for specific purposes." In this way funds began to be accumulated. In 1870 the General Convention was notified that John G. Gunn, of Nyack, New York, had bequeathed the sum of $8,000 "in trust for the relief of disabled clergymen."[81] By 1900 the Gunn Ministerial Relief Fund, "for the relief, support and maintenance of needy clergymen, their widows and families," amounted to $18,000.[82] Economic security was a long time in coming for many who had suffered hardship and sacrificed much for the good of their denomination, and much yet remained to be done in this area by the time of the 100th anniversary of American Universalism.

Chapter 12

EXTENDING DENOMINATIONAL ACTIVITIES

From the point of view both of nineteenth-century Universalists concerned about the welfare of their denomination and later observers, several other obstacles to growth and prosperity could be identified besides those already discussed. Many of these handicaps were in the nature of limitations imposed within the religious body itself, either by principle or necessity, and not by outside pressures or agencies. One was the failure in a highly competitive religious world to develop a vigorous and successful home missionary movement until relatively late. A second closely related limitation was tardiness in entering the field of tract publication and distribution to which so many other denominations were committed and which presumably added to their ranks and strength.

Comparative lack of attention to either sending out regularly appointed missionaries or to attracting adherents by propagandistic publications resulted not so much from any inherent reluctance or opposition among Universalists to such policies as from lack of resources and the failure to develop an effective central administration. Coupled with this was a more or less naive assumption expressed by Thomas Whittemore in 1844 that the very nature of Universalist beliefs would be their own best salesmen. But the necessity of getting these beliefs before the American church-going public was not always realized. Universalism might have been a self-generating discovery for some, but something more tangible than reliance on unaided individual insight was needed.

A third factor militating against denominational prosperity was the refusal of the majority of Universalists either to approve or follow the practice so prevalent in other Protestant groups of holding revivals or camp meetings associated with vigorous evangelism, although a milder substitute was found. The majority of Universalists thus deliberately turned their backs on what could have been a major recruiting device. The decision to be an "unevangelical" denomination was a considered one, based on conviction and policy and not merely on expediency. John Coleman Adams, a leading Universalist clergyman, frankly recognized some of these denominational weaknesses when he delivered, on invitation, one of the King's Chapel public lectures in Boston in 1916. He told his listeners that Universalist "aversion to the emotional elements and factors of the religious nature, [and] their failure to grasp the new motive to missions" had been serious historic deficiencies in the strategy of spreading Universalism.[1]

One other weakness which was not remedied in any systematic way until American Universalism was almost half a century old was the lack of a coherent Sabbath School organization for the younger generation. Although sporadic and isolated attempts had been made to provide for the religious instruction of children as early as the 1790s, no real denominational responsibility was undertaken until the 1830s. Thereafter, rapid progress was made, and by the time the Universalists had completed their first century, an elaborate and generally successful Sunday School movement had gone far to remedy what some considered a major weakness.

A Belated Home Missionary Movement

Awareness of the need for Universalist outreach existed from the start, regardless of the labels or titles that were appended to the religious pioneers, or whether support was available. As early as 1794 the New England Convention had appointed Elders Michael Coffin and Joab Young as "missionaries, to go forth in a circuitous manner, and preach the Everlasting Gospel . . . for the space of one year."[2] Timothy Bigelow of western Massachusetts and Nathaniel Smith were ordained as "travelling preachers" by the same body in Barnard, Vermont, in 1809.[3] A Universalist in far-off Kingston (Roane County), Tennessee, requested a preacher in 1820 who would be willing to travel about the countryside and preach the Gospel as interpreted by Universalists.[4] Three years earlier, Stephen R. Smith had established his own circuit of some 250 miles, with headquarters in Buffalo, New York.[5] It took him one month to cover; he delivered between twenty and thirty "discourses" on each trip. Seth Stetson, operating first out of Plymouth, Massachusetts and later in Maine, periodically toured all of Cape Cod in 1823, speaking to all kinds of assemblies in all kinds of places.[6] Aylett Rains was preaching, in 1827, in Indiana, Kentucky, and Ohio.[7] The principal item on the agenda of the Southern Convention which met in Richlands (Onslow County), North Carolina, the same year, was to establish preaching stations for Jacob Frieze.[8] His circuit for 1828 was to include fifteen meeting-houses spread over four counties. No mention was made of remuneration.

The need for some kind of system and regularity in frontier preaching had become pressing by the 1830s, as the population spread westward and into the border areas of the South. A few Universalists recognized this, although the denomination was slow to do much about it. The editor of the *Universalist Register* issued a general plea in 1838 to provide circuit preaching "on a permanent foundation" because "hundreds of societies" were languishing for want of a settled pastor.[9] Religious facilities were not keeping pace with expansion. Even in the more settled areas there was an acknowledged lack; itineracy should be placed on some kind of an orderly basis, regardless of where the preachers operated. Walter Balfour of Massachusetts recommended in 1830 that Universalists in each state employ a clergyman to cover all the societies in its jurisdiction as a roving "ambassador" to stir up interest and help form new societies.[10]

But then, and for many years to come, travelling Universalists usually set up their own circuits, and had to depend on voluntary contributions. E.B. Mann, in Indiana, claimed to have journeyed more than 3,000 miles in 1829-30, and to have preached over 300 sermons within the space of little more than a year.[11] His total income for a period exceeding twelve months, according to his reckoning, was $40.31, although his expenses had amounted to $71.62. He believed that the good he had accomplished made up for the deficit. His reports for the next two years told the same grim financial story.[12]

Universalist preachers in both the East and the Midwest complained constantly that they found themselves at a distinct disadvantage because their denomination had no home missionary establishment, that they were too few in number, and that they were being inadequately supported at all levels.[13] S.J. Hillyer reported that in the eighty-one places he visited in 1832-33, embracing five states (including New York and New Jersey), he was the first to have preached Universalism in twenty-two of them.[14] Universalists in the then frontier community of Janesville, Wisconsin in 1851 deplored the absence of preachers of their faith. They noted that "partialist sects" seemed to be well provided for; every Norwegian settlement, for example, had its Lutheran pastor, and Roman Catholics had their priests.[15] Why were there no more Universalist preachers?

One explanation offered for the lack of clergy was the reluctance to endorse missionary activity on principle. Although by no means a frequently heard argument, it apparently carried some weight. One clergyman in Connecticut reported in 1842 that many Universalists were actually opposed to supporting missionary preachers because this type of activity was associated with the "orthodox" denominations, and that somehow Universalists would be tainted if linked with them in any way.[16] Another insisted that there was already "too much of a proselyting spirit among our Universalist brethren; they appear zealous after numbers, whether they have embraced the simplicity of the gospel or not."[17] Still another factor discouraging entrance into the missionary field was the uncertainty of compensation sufficient even to cover the needs of bare subsistence. Typical was a plea in the 1830s from Troy, New York, where a circuit preacher was needed to service four rural societies.[18] There was no guarantee of a stipend, although the hope was expressed that $100 could be subscribed in each of the four communities.

Despite all of the roadblocks and discouragements that seemed to face the missionary cause, the momentum to make some kind of provision began to accelerate by the end of the 1830s, and by the close of the next decade had become a major focus of attention at the regional as well as the state and local levels. Universalists in Maine were apparently the first to establish "an itinerant ministry" by action of a state convention (1834), after a series of efforts the preceding year.[19] When the Indiana State Convention was organized in 1837, one of its first acts was to attempt the establishment of "a general system of itineracy."[20] But the project proved "altogether ineffectual" because it depended entirely on voluntary subscriptions which failed to be paid. The Maine Convention was more systematic and more successful, at least on paper, for it actually put an agent in the field to solicit aid and promote the idea.[21] The agent himself became, as was frequently the case, the preacher as well.[22]

The experience of Maine prompted Isaac D. Williamson to report in 1836 that a similar effort in New York State had been unsuccessful because it was impossible to recruit preachers who were willing to spend the major portion of their lives on the road.[23] Jonathan Kidwell of Indiana, who spoke from wide experience, noted that many preachers "travelled months at a time, preached day and night without receiving as much as would pay for shoeing a horse."[24] This somewhat contradictory character almost simultaneously announced that "salary preaching" was an abomination, "making merchandise of the gospel."[25] Free will offerings were to be preferred over a regular stipend, for there was no reason that a preacher should not labor for his bread six days a week, like others—"is he any better than they are"? Almon Gage, about to undertake a trip through Alabama in 1850, had a quite realistic notion of what lay ahead after he had invested $150 in a horse and saddle. He asked his ministerial friend Otis A. Skinner to imagine him "on horseback, saddlebags on behind, wending my way over hills and plains, through swamps and streams, and over ferries, sometimes for ten miles through a barren pine region, then over a prairie of forty miles, mud knee deep."[26] It was not a life to be envied.

Nonetheless, tangible progress was made. The New York Universalist Missionary Society was created in 1839. When its constitution was revised three years later, the goals of the organization were made both broad and explicit: In order to promote Universalism both in New York City and beyond, the society was to sustain preaching, issue tracts, carry Universalism to destitute societies and "dark places," and encourage the formation of "auxiliary societies."[27] An annual membership fee of 50 cents (with a lifetime subscription of $10) was provided to fund the society's activities. Connecticut established a similar organization in 1842.[28] Various "agents" had visited nearly twenty communities within three months, and a goal of six missionaries was set for the state. It was never achieved. The Rockingham Association (New Hampshire) not only organized a missionary society in 1842 but immediately put Henry Jewell, who had resigned as pastor of the Lynn, Massachusetts, society, on the road. He had "covered" twenty-five of the thirty-five towns in the association's jurisdiction by the end of the year.[29]

The Boston Association, representing the most populous area within Massachusetts Universalism (over forty societies), advocated creation of a society in 1846 to sponsor a "gospel missionary" to serve thirty towns still known to have no ministers or societies.[30] The "Boston Association Home Missionary Society" was organized the following year.[31] By the end of 1847 the missionary who had been appointed was able to report that he had visited forty communities, preached in fourteen, and had travelled over 2,000 miles.[32] The society, incorporated by the state five years later, was authorized by its charter to hold funds totalling $45,000.[33] This was partly the result of the realization that Universalist growth in the Boston area seemed to have slowed perceptibly. The challenge of the future was not to deliver "doctrinal discourses" to those already informed, but to carry the message to those who had not yet heard it.[34] The effort brought results, at least in terms of financial support. The society by 1852 had 170 members paying dues of $2.00 a year. A resolution that year called for an aggressive campaign to recruit converts.[35]

Whatever reluctance Universalists had had, at least in Massachusetts, to engage in proselytizing activities seems to have disappeared by the 1850s. At the annual meeting of the Massachusetts Convention in 1854 the delegates officially avowed by resolution that seeking new members for the denomination was not only desirable but essential. G.H. Emerson called for an aggressive stance, for Christianity, he declared, could not by its very nature be neutral. "It is all for war. We must become soldiers of Jesus Christ. We must put on the armor of God. We must fight for the faith under the Captain of our salvation."[36] A new militancy was creeping into missionary efforts as Universalists everywhere created machinery to spread their faith. The Connecticut Universalist Missionary Society was not only incorporated in 1853 but claimed a paid-up membership of 675 that year.[37] Its agent, Abraham Norwood, reported that he had travelled over 3,000 miles that year in its behalf. Itineracy was by no means limited to the western or southern frontiers.

Universalist home missionary fervor had spread to every state by the late 1840s, and enthusiasm ran high. Even regional organizations, especially those in the Midwest, had begun to sponsor systems of travelling clergy. The Western Union Association in Ohio was one of the first such groups. It had authorized three circuits in 1834, covering eleven counties in Ohio and seven in Indiana.[38] However, enthusiasm alone was insufficient, and had to be tempered by harsh realities. Even the modest average stipend of $400 a year, pledged by local societies and collected and disbursed by the appropriate convention or association, was seldom collected in its entirety. Circuits planned for never came into being or had to be revived from time to time. Some of the circuits were intended to be temporary, to last only until societies could be firmly established. But many were unable to procure or support preachers at all, and struggled endlessly with the problem without success.

Such was the case in Vermont, where the state convention had created machinery in 1837 for establishing circuits for one or more preachers for "destitute societies."[39] A decade later, the Vermont Convention was engaged in repeating the process of attempting to establish "missionary labors." A missionary preacher was selected in 1850, and another joined him within the next two years, but that arrangement failed to produce the desired results. The two travelled through eight counties, "preaching as they went, and at the same time collecting funds for the cause." Contributions from 250 individuals averaged $1.00 each—far short of the $400 annual salary pledged to each by the state convention. But the "Universalist Home Missionary Enterprise" in Vermont was again seeking both personnel and funds in 1853. One of the two missionary-agents actually employed had "retired from the field" after only three months. J.S. Lee proposed in 1858 the creation of a missionary society independent of the state convention. That idea bore no fruit either, and in 1864 the original "Missionary Enterprise" was revived and two representatives were employed. But both left the state before any record of accomplishment was posted.

The situation looked gloomy indeed. There were fifty-seven societies known to exist in the state when an inventory of the denomination was reported at the 1866 state convention. But there were only thirty-five ministers listed, and some of these were retired. Only twelve of the societies had full-time pastors; the majority had to depend on part-time preaching or had no preaching at all. A burst of activity by the convention resulted in temporary success by 1868, but by then plans were under way for celebrating the centennial of Murray's arrival in America and missionary efforts lost their priority as energies were diverted elsewhere. The convention found it impossible to meet a pledge of $10,000 to the national Centenary Fund. But at least a partial solution had been worked out by the late 1860s, when a Committee on Parishes and Circuits was created to arrange "parish unions" of adjacent churches which would share one preacher. However, it was not until the 1880s that a state missionary was satisfactorily supported and showed tangible results, partly because a permanent convention fund had finally been created.

Most notably lacking during the expansion of Universalist missionary activity in the 1840s was financial support from the General Convention. There had been vague discussion in that body of the need for home missions as early as 1836, but no steps were taken for over twenty years. In the intervening period a campaign was launched to stir the convention into some kind of action. A writer in the *Universalist Quarterly* in 1849 presented an inventory of missionary organizations in other denominations and called attention to the complete failure of Universalists to organize any agency comparable to the American Home Missionary Society (a cooperative Congregational-Presbyterian venture) or the interdenominational American Bible Society.[40] It was pointed out that Congregational churches in New England supported or aided in some fashion more than 250 ministers in their missionary activities. Why could not the Universalists do likewise? Sylvanus Cobb suggested (also in 1849) that the denomination organize a "National Missionary Society" under the auspices of the General Convention, with a board to receive and disburse funds and coordinate state and local activities.[41] He speculated, in an expansive mood, that it could be part of a long-range plan "for evangelizing our country, and in due time the world."

The General Convention finally appointed a Board of Missions for the first time in 1858, but it failed even to meet during the year, and was discharged in 1859.[42] It was described sardonically by E.G. Brooks, in his annual report on the state of the church, as a "fruitless creation." The convention was not stirred to further action in the domestic missions field until 1865, and then on the initiative of the Indiana Convention. Its delegate to the General Convention was instructed that year "to urge, by all suitable and proper means, the immediate assumption of a general Missionary work by the Convention."[43] By good fortune, a special committee to take into consideration the means of raising funds for the convention "and especially for Missionary purposes" had been created during the same session, and to which the resolution from Indiana could be referred. The committee considered it not only expedient but necessary "to inaugurate a judicious missionary enterprise, operating in the name of the whole Church." The sum of $100,000 was called for, "to be immediately raised." The committee did not hesitate to acknowledge the beneficence of "evangelism" in general, as well as the desirability of aid to "feeble societies and churches," and the establishment of new congregations. Four trustees, all from New York State, were authorized to comprise, together with the officers of the General Convention, an executive board to manage the funds received.[44] One immediate practical result of furthering missionary efforts on the home front was that the General Convention was legally incorporated through its board of trustees.

Incorporating the central body of Universalists in 1866 turned out to be much easier than raising the funds to support the missionary activity to which the General Convention had committed itself. The board of trustees confronted a tangle of problems which made it appear that the whole project might die aborning. The report made to the convention in 1866 was a grim recounting of what lay ahead.[45] Committees of Correspondence had been created for each state to receive the appeal of the board, to make suggestions for suitable persons to serve as agents, and to suggest the best mode of proceeding. The board was far from subtle in making its appeal: "We are sure of your sympathy and your prayers, but we want also *your money.*"

The attempt to secure agents was singularly unsuccessful. The soliciting agent recommended for Maine, Giles Bailey, was unable to serve because of illness. No person had been selected for New Hampshire, although negotiations were under way. Vermont would probably share an agent with New Hampshire. In Massachusetts, A. St. John Chambré declined to serve because of the pressure of other duties, and no substitute had been found. Rhode Island was not yet ready to act. The agent for Connecticut, Charles H. Webster, became the representative of the state missionary society instead of the General Convention. There was no recommendation for an agent in Ohio, and the Indiana Convention was taking the whole matter under advisement. In Pennsylvania one agent was found only for the western part of the state. Universalists in Michigan preferred to employ their own agent, independent of the General Convention, and Illinois wanted to work on a regional rather than a national basis, as did Wisconsin. No one had been able to find "a competent man for the work" in Iowa. Minnesota was itself a missionary field, and reported "need of help, rather than an ability to help others." New Jersey failed to respond at all to the appeals of the board. Universalists in the South were presumed to be in such disarray following the end of the Civil War that no solicitation for agents was apparently even attempted in that section.

One of the major problems faced by the board in raising funds was conflict with local interests, priorities, and jurisdictions. Vermonters were involved in the establishment of the Green Mountain Central Institute in Barre and were still trying to raise the remaining $10,000 needed. They therefore considered it "inexpedient to attempt to do anything for the Missionary Fund." Furthermore, they considered the emphasis misplaced. When anything was attempted, "it had better be for the help of weak churches and societies already in existence, than for the opening of new fields." In Massachusetts the claims of denominationally-sponsored Dean Academy were being urged, and the board did not consider it "practicable to place our general work even in seeming rivalry to that enterprise."

Localism was even more evident in Connecticut. After the soliciting agent had raised about $250 on behalf of the General Convention, the state missionary society decided that his efforts should be expended in their behalf. The board could do little but accede, and withdrew after informing the state organization that it was inadvisable to "interfere" with any local missionary interests.

An even more serious problem of jurisdiction and the conflict of regional and national loyalties also had to be faced. Indiana, Michigan, Wisconsin, and Illinois all made it clear that they preferred to work through the Northwest Conference. This *ad hoc* body had been organized in Chicago in 1860 and had as one of its announced purposes the furthering of tract and missionary endeavors as well as improving denominational communication in general in the upper Midwest. It had already undertaken to raise $25,000 for missionary purposes. After communication with board members, Indiana Universalists agreed to submit the whole matter to the state convention to determine who should receive missionary funds. But the other states were adamant.

After a "mass meeting" of the Northwest Conference was held in Chicago in the fall of 1865, Michigan decided that all efforts would be carried out for the benefit of the conference rather than for the General Convention. Universalists elsewhere in the Middle West expressed the same sentiments. Illinois emphasized the point that the idea of a missionary fund had originated in the Northwest Conference in the first place. The conference was not only "an established organization" but had the confidence of the people and could "accomplish more for the West than it is at present possible for the Convention to do." The money raised by the conference was needed in the West and ought to be expended there. One solution suggested was to make the Northwest Conference a branch or "auxiliary" of the General Convention. The board was of the unanimous opinion, however, that this was impossible. There was no provision in the constitution of the General Convention for such an organization as the Northwest Conference; it fell into no existing category and had no representation in the General Convention. Therefore, said the board, the Northwest Conference could not be recognized as a branch.

The board underlined, by a resolution unanimously adopted, their feeling that all missionary affairs "should be wholly under one general head," namely the General Convention. This was the only way that "the interests of the whole church" could be well served. The board made haste to recognize the contributions of midwestern Universalists to various denominational interests, including education, but the matter did not rest there. The convention in 1866 refused to accept the board's interpretation of the status of the Northwest Conference. As soon as the board's report was accepted, an *ad hoc* committee was appointed "to take into consideration the relation of other working bodies to this Convention." The result was a resolution adopted the next day recognizing the Northwest Conference as "auxiliary to this Convention in its Educational and Missionary Work" and requiring it to make an annual report to the board of trustees. The tension between the Northwest Conference and the General Convention over the raising and disbursement of missionary funds was lessened, but it was not until 1870 that the conference surrendered its missionary work to the central authority. There was no provision for regional organizations or associations in the revised constitution adopted at the centennial observance that year, and the Northwest Conference came to an end as an official body.

Of the fourteen states on which a report was made in 1866, only one—New York—had carried out the mandate of the General Convention as outlined the previous year. D.C. Tomlinson, who served as agent, obtained subscriptions and bequests amounting to $17,000 and had almost finished his work. In addition, the widow of Pitt Morse had undertaken the task of obtaining subscriptions in Jefferson County. She was to become one of hundreds of Universalist women who were to make the raising of the Murray Centennial Fund established in 1870 such a phenomenal success.

The board of trustees in 1866 drew up a set of general rules for the conduct of their national missionary responsibilities, which they interpreted broadly but with due regard for local interests.[46] The intent of the board in the older sections of the country, where conventions and associations were already engaged in missionary work, was to supplement rather than supplant existing efforts. The board, with its unhappy experiences with "strong local feeling" during the first year fresh in mind, made it clear that it reserved the right to apportion funds wherever most urgently needed, regardless of location. Otherwise there would be no assistance available for new fields or new places which had little or no resources of their own. The board agreed to honor gifts with conditions attached, but obviously preferred unrestricted funds. Possibly with the Northwest Conference in mind, the board placed its top priorities on assistance to the West and Northwest; the South ranked second. The board, however, reminded Universalists that its solicitations and its constituency were national rather than local and that the welfare of the entire denomination was their basic responsibility.

Procedures were worked out in considerable detail and in such a way that there would be no misunderstanding. All applications were to come directly from the society or group directly involved; the assurance of prompt as well as permanent results was among the criteria to be used in the distribution of aid. Thorough investigation of each request was promised. If the purpose of a request was to establish a new parish or congregation, its ultimate aim had to be clearly the establishment of a formal church organization, complete with observance of religious ordinances; if the prospects appeared unpromising, then assistance would not be forthcoming. The time for informal and casual operation at the local level, reminiscent of the days of Murray and other founding fathers, had long since passed. Assistance was promised also in the construction of meeting houses. So far as the board had control over the selection and qualifications of missionary preachers, it would insist that ability to preach dogma alone would be insufficient. Preachers had to emphasize "the power of practical godliness" and refrain from "*mere* speculative or controversial preaching." More directly, the board deemed it "a proper department of missionary effort" to encourage and assist in maintaining students in theological training in the form of cash loans. The understanding was that such money was not to be paid back, but was to take the form of a free scholarship set initially at $180 per year. This was to apply only if the beneficiaries actually entered the ministry after completing their theological course. Their names were not to be made public.

Both the collection and distribution of funds by the General Convention for missionary purposes proved immediately to be a major problem. The missionary fund at the end of the first year of operation showed a deficit of over $500. Most of it was accounted for by the travelling expenses of state agents. The board had immediately decided not to create a permanent fund until contributions began to be given expressly for that purpose. The board discussed the possibility of reserving half of all collections for such a fund, but abandoned the idea because of the urgency of missionary work of all kinds, and the fact that "the people want to see results." Collections for general purposes had been taken up at public religious services held in conjunction with the 1866 General Convention and had produced only $291.40.

Hardly had money begun to trickle in when the board was deluged with applications for aid. By the end of the fiscal year 1866 final action had been approved on three requests: Assistance was granted to thirteen ministerial students; the sum of $4,000 was allocated for a new church building in Clinton, New York, in return for a mortgage to be held by the board; and $300 was appropriated to the Church of the Restoration in Newburgh, New York, toward the support of its ministry for one year. Fortunately for the missionary fund, the $4,000 was not to be paid until the church edifice had been completed, and its construction had not yet begun. The appropriation for the Newburgh church was payable in four quarterly installments. Applications for other assistance in 1866 were parcelled out among various committees of the convention for their investigation and recommendation.

On the surface the missionary fund looked more promising in 1867, for more than $5,000 had been received in cash and a balance of $8,000 remained. But a closer scrutiny indicated that about $5,000 in subscriptions still remained uncollected. The treasurer used strong language in his explanatory note that year. Until Universalists recognized the necessity of centralizing their fund-raising efforts, he saw no hope for the future. "So long as every State and Society are active in starting their own little local enterprises by themselves, and insist upon them to the entire exclusion of a centralized and general work by the head of the denomination, or, what should be the head, the General Convention, so long will our denomination possess no power or strength as a united National Organization."[47]

The general fund of the convention was faring even worse. The "One Per Cent Assessment Fund," to be derived from societies and churches, provided in the by-laws and effective in 1866, produced $578.60 the first year. All of $97.41 was contributed in 1867 by a grand total of eleven societies; the largest amount ($20) came from the First Universalist Society in Philadelphia. For a General Convention aspiring to be the viable head of an entire religious denomination, this was not a very impressive financial beginning.

The secretary of the board of trustees warned in 1867 that if the work of the General Convention were not provided for, it would have to be abandoned. He was obviously unhappy to learn that the efforts of the Northwest Conference that year had been devoted almost exclusively to raising $100,000 for the endowment of Lombard University in Illinois rather than for more closely related missionary activities. The situation seemed no more hopeful in 1868. With requests far exceeding resources, the newly elected trustees chided their predecessors for being overly generous. The treasurer, with his books showing a total of but $5,702.32 contributed during the entire year for missionary work, complained of the weakness of the "disjointed" denomination to which he belonged, and suggested that the only financial solution was to hire a group of national canvassers on a commission basis.[48]

With one exception, no special effort was made to raise money in 1869, pending the recommendations of the special Centenary Committee appointed that year to arrange for the observance of the first century of Universalism in America. The official goal of what was designated the Murray Centenary Fund was $200,000, part of the income of which was to be used for "the missionary cause." Until that materialized, one suggestion made in 1868 by D.L. Holden, a Universalist layman and banker in New York City, was translated into action. It took the form of "Family Missionary Boxes," to be distributed throughout the denomination. By the fall of 1869 over

3,000 had been distributed, with over 22,000 by 1870. While the average receipts were only slightly over $1.00 per box in the two-year period, they represented in the aggregate a substantial source of income and gave to Universalist families the opportunity to develop a sense of involvement which no other avenue might have afforded. Contributions, whatever the amount, source, or channel, were always welcomed by the General Convention. Such was the donation of three cents from "little Lizzie 'for Missionary tause [*sic*]' " duly recorded in the account book of E.G. Brooks, the general secretary, for the year 1867-68. The amount may not have been large, but the intent and spirit of the gift were unquestioned. The Universalists had long before learned to appreciate the value of small contributions; they were traditionally the principal source of income for a denomination which seemed to survive on almost nothing at all except determination for many periods in its history.

Closely associated with general missionary activity was the movement to publish religious tracts as a means of extending Universalist influence. The initiative that resulted in the establishment of denominational "tract societies," which had become widespread by the 1840s, came from the Eastern Association (Maine). In 1825 that body formed the "Christian Visitant Society" for the publication and free distribution of "interesting and useful articles in a pamphlet form."[49] Samuel C. Loveland was the author of the first of several tracts authorized by the Washington Association (New Hampshire) in 1828.[50] In 1829, the editor of the *Trumpet* pointed out the deficiencies of Universalists in respect to tract publication.[51] Other religious groups, he wrote, were engaging in a "conspiracy to extract money as well as obtain religious control." The best counterattack was "still wider spread of liberal periodicals." The publication of sermons and articles on doctrine in the *Universalist Register* and an occasional fugitive pamphlet was not enough.

The Central Association (New York) promptly took up Whittemore's challenge. That year they created a committee "to prepare, publish and distribute pamphlets and tracts, as an antidote to the poison of the thousands of orthodox tracts which are disseminated throughout the community."[52] The Universalists in Lowell, Massachusetts, were among the first actually to form a tract society. In 1840 they sponsored three publications to counter anti-Universalist literature. One, written in verse, was printed in 2,000 copies which were promptly disposed of, with the title "Universalism against Partialism."[53] It was in reply to an anti-Universalist tract written in doggerel.

The great decade of tract publication was the 1840s. Associations, state conventions, and even societies participated.[54] The Pennsylvania Convention in 1842 urged societies to form publishing organizations as auxiliaries to the central Universalist Publishing Society in Philadelphia.[55] The Rhode Island Convention in 1844 went so far as to dissolve its state missionary society and turn it into a tract society.[56] Subscriptions were solicited to defray costs "for the publication, purchase and distribution of tracts in advocacy and explanation of Universalism." Rhode Island had frequent difficulty in securing the services of a state missionary, so the tracts were a valuable supplement to the services of the five Universalist clergy active in the state in 1846. All were written by resident ministers such as Henry Bacon and J. Boyden, Jr.[57] The Rhode Island Convention made up for the paucity of ministers by distributing over 20,000 pages of tracts in 1846-47, financed by collections taken up at convention meetings and by societies.[58] By 1850, the state tract society had issued thirty-nine such pieces of literature, with up to 4,000 copies of some titles.[59] In 1855 the General Convention adopted a resolution favoring "a general and free distribution of tracts or pamphlets, written in defense and exposition of our system of faith."[60] Special collections were to be taken up by all societies to establish a Publications Fund administered by the convention. The plan was to begin with ten tracts, each written by a different clergyman on topics of their choice.

New York City became an important headquarters for Universalist publications, and as early as the 1820s a bookshop was opened with a circulating library which disseminated tracts.[61] The New York Missionary Society had put into circulation in the metropolitan area some 140,000 tracts by 1845.[62] Tracts averaged four pages and were sold for less than a cent each.

Universalists in the Midwest joined their eastern brethren in tract publication in the early 1840s. John A. Gurley, editor of the *Star in the West,* the leading denominational paper beyond the Appalachians, began to issue in 1841 "suitable tracts for circulation among friends and opposers."[63] Series of pamphlets such as George Rogers' *Pro and Con of Universalism* were often collected and republished in book form.

Lack of numbers and strength, and limited resources, handicapped Universalist tract publication in the South. Only one state convention before the Civil War undertook to sponsor tract publication. In 1860 the Georgia Convention voted to embark on tract production for free distribution, to be printed by John C. Burruss, publisher and editor of the *Universalist Herald.*[64] A committee was appointed to raise funds "to sustain the tractarian movement," but the outbreak of war apparently brought the project to a halt. Men like Burruss and C.F.R. Shehane were prolific writers of both tracts and books. Typical of Burruss' contribution was an eight-page pamphlet published in 1845, entitled "One Hundred and Ten Scriptural Reasons for being a Universalist." One of the most widely circulated of Shehane's writings was *A Key to Universalism,* published by the author in Griffin, Georgia, in 1854. Much of the responsibility for producing tracts for the denomination was taken over after 1860 by the central publishing house established in Boston. Like other denominations, the Universalists depended heavily on the printed word to relay their message to the general public.

Anti-Revivalism

When the Committee on the State of the Church made its report to the General Convention in 1870 it stressed the historical disposition of Universalists "to dread any large growth of emotional religion among our people, as leading away from a rational theology, and opening a door to pietism or priestcraft."[65] It may have been a basic belief among Universalists that "the relations of man to his Maker are essentially reasonable," but it tended to run counter to the much more widespread and compelling conviction among American Protestants that emotionalism was an integral part of the individual's personal religious experience, and revivalism an acceptable and appropriate means of achieving and expressing it.

Revivals also served to assure the continued existence as well as spread of Protestantism in the individualistic, fluid, and mobile society of America during the 18th and 19th centuries when a geographical frontier both beckoned and challenged. Further, from the viewpoint of many who promoted or conducted revivals, they were necessary to counter the disintegrating force of the frontier experience by bringing a semblance of order and stability, restoring or protecting "moral probity," reminding the individual of his religious responsibilities, and assuring salvation for the backslider.[66]

Among the features of revivals have been their cyclical and regional character and their relatively brief duration. William G. McLoughlin, a serious student of the phenomenon, identified only two revivals before 1865 which could be considered national in scope, and which lasted as long as a generation (1725-50, 1795-1835). However, there were literally hundreds of local revivals, often occurring quite independently of each other and involving sometimes only a single congregation. Others, starting in strictly local and spontaneous fashion, became part of much larger movements. Such were the famous camp meetings conducted by the Presbyterian frontier revivalist James McGready in Logan County, Kentucky, in 1800. The climax of his efforts came with the meeting conducted by Barton W. Stone at Cane Ridge (Bourbon County), Kentucky, in the summer of 1801. The phenomenon spread rapidly all over frontier America and contributed to what is known as the Second Great Awakening which affected thousands of individuals. It was in this context that revivalism often became equated with excesses of emotional behavior. Frontier religion, particularly as practiced by revivalist-minded Baptists and Methodists, became associated with periodic excitements which shocked and horrified more settled areas of the nation—especially the Northeast.

Until the appearance of Charles Grandison Finney (1792-1875) on the frontier scene in upstate New York in 1824, most of the revivalists were Calvinists at heart and used as their principal stock-in-trade the terrors of hellfire and eternal damnation to save souls and to recruit converts. Finney, himself a convert from Congregationalism to the Presbyterian ministry, used much the same arguments about the dangers and realities of perdition, and employed many of the techniques of fellow-revivalists. However, Finney added his own "New Measures" of religious persuasion (including the "anxious bench"), modified the Calvinistic doctrine of predestination, used an interdenominational approach, and argued that, within limits, salvation was within the reach of all.[67] He attained a national reputation with a four-year revival movement in western New York (1824-27) which left in its wake a "burned-over district" swept by the fires of his heady brand of evangelism.[68]

Finney had occasion to confront Universalists more than once on the tumultuous New York frontier.[69] Needless to say, he pictured them as troublemakers bent on disturbing the peace. According to Finney, in the village of Antwerp they tried to break up Presbyterian Sabbath meetings, even to the extent of taking the wheels off the carriage of one of the elders to prevent him from arriving to conduct services. Finney, of course, claimed ultimate victory in all bouts with Universalists. He conducted a revival in a schoolhouse in the midst of enemy territory in the same village, and succeeded in "a complete upturning of the very foundations of Universalism."[70]

Universalists had to make a decision about the role that revivalism should play in both their own lives and in their denominational activities. It was inevitable likewise that their attitudes toward, and relations with, other denominations would be colored by their own proclivities. The vast majority of Universalists firmly resisted the temptation to use revivalistic tactics and arguments. If for no other reason, they lacked one potential resource in their theological arsenal: They could not, as did most other Protestants, use the torments of hell and damnation to frighten the unconverted or unrepentent. If Universalists completely repudiated, as most did, the entire notion of future punishment, and argued for a benign rather than a vindictive God, the element of fear which played such a large part in most revivalist thinking, could not be exploited. Even more important, they were generally hostile to such devices as "protracted meetings" and the emotional outbursts which frequently accompanied them, because they ran counter to Universalist conceptions of the individual.

Universalist opposition to revivalism and all that it implied was not recorded with any frequency until the Second Great Awakening began to manifest itself in the 1820s. In a debate in 1824 between Charles Finney and an itinerant Universalist preacher in Adams, New York, differences that were expressed had to do more with theological points than with the conduct of revivals themselves. Finney and the unidentified Universalist agreed in opposing Calvinism, but Finney denied that Christ's death, as the Universalist argued, granted salvation automatically to all men.[71] Christ merely made possible "a universal amnesty," according to Finney. It was up to individuals to take advantage of the opportunity, and they would necessarily suffer damnation as a logical consequence of divine justice if not redeemed.

However, it was not so much on purely doctrinal grounds that Universalists opposed revivalism as on the methods used, including appeal to the irrational. The *Trumpet,* beginning in 1828, carried disparaging accounts of camp meetings, some of them based on eyewitnesses. Warren Skinner of Cavendish, Vermont, drew a most uncomplimentary picture of Finney, whom he heard several times. Skinner was revolted by the revivalist's "fanatical ravings" about the joys of regeneration and the horrors of hell.[72] Almost thirty years later, in the 1850s, Universalists were still complaining about Finney's artful "tampering with the emotions," and his adeptness "in the art of proselytism."[73] The occasion for these complaints was a series of revivalist-type lectures by Finney in 1857, delivered in the Park Street (Congregational) church in Boston. He purportedly made 1,000 converts to the church by graphically portraying the terrors of death and hellfire for the unconverted. Whittemore reacted by challenging Finney to find a single Scriptural justification for such a horrid end of man, and averred that Finney seemed "to delight in tormenting mankind."[74]

Theophilus Fisk was welcomed in Reading, Pennsylvania, as "a more rational Evangelist" than Finney, who had preceded him on a revival tour. Many people had been "disgusted with [Finney's] extravagent and abusive measures."[75] Jacob Frieze, editor of the *Liberalist* in Wilmington, North Carolina, in 1827 refused to use in his circuit preaching "those powerful excitements, technically termed 'revivals,' converting the passions, without informing the understanding."[76] Two years later, while in Pawtucket, Rhode Island, Frieze offered to debate the merits of revivalism with a Baptist preacher, who declined.[77] Having reported this fact, Frieze proceeded to tell the readers of the *Trumpet* that revival declamations were "without argument, without reason, without proof; and appeal to the passions, in which reason and judgment have no place."

Hosea Ballou 2d warned that to try to bring Universalists over to the idea of holding camp meetings would be a disservice to the denomination, for they furthered neither the cause of religion or morality, and they threatened good order.[78] I.D. Williamson thought that the energy and resources consumed in revivals could be better expended on caring for the destitute—"the suffering, shivering, and starving poor of the city."[79] Unfortunately, wrote another Universalist, most revivals were merely "animal exertions . . . . manifestly the effect of cunning and labor on the part of men," with the true divine spirit usually missing.[80] Otis A. Skinner produced a long list of individuals who had fallen victim to "religious insanity" induced by protracted meetings.[81] Some had become so emotionally unbalanced that they had committed suicide.

Thomas Whittemore, in his usual pungent fashion, expressed nothing but contempt for revivals, including one widely advertised in Hartford, Connecticut, in 1831. "The boobies did not look more earnestly for the late eclipse, than for this expected advent of Jehovah. Hell was opened, and sinners were invited to view its very bowels; damnation was threatened; the preachers screamed; the dupes cried; the hypocrites laughed in their sleeves."[82] Whittemore saw revivals also as "a species of sectarian warfare, in which the spirit of God has no more connexion, than it had with the march of Bonaparte into Russia."[83] He was referring here to what was described as a power struggle between Methodists and Congregationalists in a community in the Greater Boston area.

He also went carefully through the annual reports of the trustees of the state lunatic hospital in Worcester and triumphantly pounced on all cases reporting insanity attributed to "fanaticism," "religious excitement," "religious fanaticism," "dread of future punishment" (pronounced "incurable" according to the report).[84] In an analysis of the reasons for the commital of sixty-five patients to a lunatic asylum in Ohio, he found that by far the largest number were suffering from "religious excitement."[85] Jacob Knapp, one of the more flamboyant Baptist revivalists, who used Universalists as one of his favorite targets ("tools of the devil"), provoked Whittemore's wrath while on a revival tour in Boston in the winter of 1841-42.[86] The Universalist editor hinted darkly about "retribution in store for those pastors and churches who have been instrumental in bringing Mr. Knapp to Boston." It was Knapp's activities that prompted Otis Skinner to publish his *Letters . . . . on Modern Revivals* in 1842.

The revivalist activities and personalities of the 1830s and 1840s continued to generate protests from Universalist spokesmen. Both the theology and the form of expression were subjects of attack. Russell Streeter produced a scorching satire on "religious extravagance" stirred up by Calvinist preachers in his *Latest News from Three Worlds, Heaven, Earth, and Hell,* published in 1832 and provoked by a four-day meeting in Shirley, Massachusetts. In 1835 he singled out for special criticism Jedediah Burchard, who participated in a protracted meeting of no less than twenty-six days which took place in Woodstock, Vermont. Streeter called his 168-page production *Mirror of Calvinistic Fanaticism.* His brother, Sebastian Streeter, pastor of the First Universalist Society in Boston for forty years, entertained the same sentiments. He strongly opposed revivals as "these feverish excitements, these violent assaults upon the nerves and passions of the multitude" which resulted in "the utter prostration of reason."[87]

Universalists in the South and Midwest, the regions most frequently associated with revivalism, were just as outspoken against the practice as those in the North. The South Carolina Convention went on record in 1832 to condemn

> the excitements, falsely called 'Revivals of religion' produced by the leaders of the popular religious sects, together with the aid of their dupes, which have so generally prevailed the past year. [Revivals were] reprobated because, being founded on terror, they drive many to despair, insanity and suicide; disturb the peace of neighborhoods and families; promote self-righteousness, superstition and bigotry; and fill the professed church of Christ with time-serving hypocrites and slaves to the priesthood; besides profaning the name of God, and representing him in a most odious character.[88]

Philo Brownson, on the editorial staff of the *Evangelical Universalist* published in Macon, Georgia, considered revivals the bane of American religion. In referring to those parts of the nation that were "burnt over," as he expressed it, by the extravagances associated with revivalism, he found nothing in the "falling and groaning, and laughing and jumping, and dancing" but "moral desolation."[89] Likewise, S. J. McMorris of Alabama saw no value in "getting religion" by means of "distracted [*sic*] meetings."[90] L.F.W. Andrews, who roamed all over the South preaching and defending Universalism in most aggressive fashion in the 1830s, tarried long enough in one location (unspecified) to publish a pamphlet on the whole subject. He collected no less than 113 examples from both religious and secular papers and published them under the following self-explanatory title: *A Looking Glass for Fanatics, or, a collection of cases of cases of insanity, suicide, and murder, The result of 'four days,' 'protracted,' and other 'meetings,' and exhibiting in a condensed manner, the unhappy fate of more than ONE HUNDRED VICTIMS!!! to the dogma of 'Endless Misery.'*[91]

There were honest differences of opinion among some Universalists as to what the permissible limits of outward religious enthusiasm should be. Admittedly it was difficult to draw what might be considered a hairline distinction between the warmth and camaraderie of a religious gathering of congenial souls and the so-called excesses which so many Universalists deplored. Nonetheless, numerous attempts were made to articulate these distinctions. Lucius R. Paige was not averse to some warmth in the expression of one's religious feelings. Universalists, in his view, had to strike a balance between "iceberg" behavior and the use of camp-meeting tactics.[92] T.J. Sawyer disagreed. Religious excitements had no place at Universalist meetings. The two men engaged in a lengthy discussion of this matter in the denominational press and each had his supporters and defenders.

The provocation for the debate was the institution, beginning in the 1830s, of Universalist-sponsored "conference meetings," which were evening sessions of public worship in which both clergy and laity participated, and which became more and more vivacious and enthusiastic as they spread throughout the denomination. The meetings were also referred to as "concerts of praise"–an expression coined in the 1830s by Abel Thomas of Philadelphia.[93] Probably typical was the "social conference" which was part of a meeting of the Chautauqua Association (New York) in 1842. According to the records, "a good degree of piety and religious ardor was evinced in the course of the evening."[94]

Such goings-on were frowned upon by Sawyer, who considered them undignified and too much like the protracted meetings of other denominations. He singled out for particular criticism a Universalist meeting in Deerfield, New Hampshire, where entirely too much "religious excitement" was evident.[95] Christian Universalism, said Sawyer, should never become associated with "gross and temporary excitement produced by declamation and noise;" revivals tended "to fill our lunatic asylums with religious maniacs."[96] Zelotes Fuller, an editor of the *Southern Pioneer,* supported Sawyer by unequivocally opposing such meetings; they tended merely to "inflame the imagination and excite the passions, rather than to convince the judgment and instruct the mind."[97] Even in the rough-and-ready frontier environment of Indiana in the 1830s, Universalists like Jonathan Kidwell called for restraint rather than unbridled enthuasiasm. He was skeptical of the revivals that periodically swept over the Middle West, and believed that, far from doing permanent good, they were "an injury to the human family, and the promoters of them mere pests in society."[98]

Thomas Whittemore came down on the side of warmth rather than coldness, and attempted to make a distinction between "true" religious fervor and "revivalist-type rampaging." Abel Thomas also came to the defense of the supporters of "concerts of praise" and, like Whittemore, accused Sawyer of being "constitutionally cold."[99] Whittemore pointed out that conference meetings, no matter what they had been called in the past, had been held in the First Universalist Society in Boston ever since the days of John Murray, and served a very useful purpose. Murray was himself probably the first evangelistic Universalist, using revivalist tactics and appealing to emotion as well as to intellect.[100]

A great burst of "conference meetings" erupted in Boston-area churches in the winter of 1842-43. Judging from the newspaper reports, they were lively affairs, with much lay participation, including the giving of testimonials, the delivery of extemporaneous speeches, and the enthusiastic singing of hymns. Whittemore even compiled a book of "Conference Hymns" to be used on such occasions.[101] To those who raised their eyebrows about such meetings, Whittemore repeated a distinction he had often drawn between "revival of pure religion" and "merely animal excitement produced by false doctrines." It was not, it appeared, only the means that were used to achieve personal religious satisfaction, but also the end-product with which Whittemore was really concerned. And that end-product was the triumph of Universalism.

Whatever their protestations to the contrary, some Universalists were not immune from the infection of revivalist enthusiasm, and some were frank to admit their approval and practice of it. Abel Thomas, who held briefly a pastorate in the bustling frontier metropolis of Cincinnati in the 1840s, was struck by the vehemence and excitement surrounding all kinds of gatherings. He recollected that "every enterprize in Ohio [was] in motion on the high-pressure principle."[102] When he attended the Ohio Convention in Columbus in 1846, he "certainly heard more 'thunder' during that session, than I had ever heard elsewhere among Universalists in the same space." So he entered into the spirit of the occasion, and thundered also. "The only deficiency was in my lungs. Nevertheless, I did the best I could in that line." As long as reason was "kept in the ascendant," he had no objection to "the terrific style of preaching [by] revivalists of the fiery school . . . . The fault is in their *doctrine,* not in *them.*"

I.D. Williamson, who had moved to Mobile, Alabama, in the fall of 1843, commented that "I am, as you well know, no revivalist. Having no thunder and very little lightning at command, and little skill in creating an excitement, I do not anticipate any remarkable shaking among the 'dry bones' to result from my efforts."[103] George Rogers attended a Methodist protracted meeting in Indiana in 1843 and had nothing but contempt for the "wild rant" of the preachers.[104] One revivalist used the device of "maudlin sentimentalism about Jesus, which is usually resorted to by preachers of his class to make women weep." But Rogers had no hesitancy in conducting the same sort of protracted meetings if the circumstances called for them. He was "thus fighting error with its own weapons."[105]

There seems to be no question that resort to revivalistic measures was often purely a defense mechanism on the part of Universalists, who were often made favorite targets for other denominations.[106] During the great "spiritual resurrection" of 1800, the Presbyterian Assembly reported that among the hundreds who were received into the church were "infidels and Universalists."[107] Much to the irritation of other denominations, Universalists also frequently attracted large numbers of the curious until the orthodox clergy warned them away.[108] And it was the men rather than the women who usually had the courage to attend Universalist meetings in the early days.

But the aversion of Universalists to emotional extremism associated with religious enthusiasm had also a positive side. The rapid growth of Universalism in western New York in the 1830s has been attributed in part to the very fact that "people became satiated with protracted meetings and revivals," and turned to Universalism for relief.[109] Jabez Swan, a revivalist of the Baptist persuasion, travelled throughout upstate New York and New England, beginning in the 1830s, and told his delighted hearers that Unitarians, Universalists, deists, and Masons were to be abominated. It was Swan who referred to the Universalist church as 'the Fire Insurance Company' because "all its members were assured of a place in hell."[110] In some instances the technique of attacking Universalism seemed to backfire. One result of the general spirit of revivalism in Ohio, according to Universalist interpretation, was "making many converts *from* the faith of endless woe."[111] In Cincinnati, a Methodist revival resulted in adding approximately 200 members to the First Universalist Society there.

A surge of revivalism in the Universalist society in Hamilton (Madison County), New York, in 1817, cut across denominational lines. It appeared to non-Universalists that "there could be no religion, no true spiritual godliness among professors who were never warmed into newness of life by the power of a revival."[112] The Universalists were joined by a neighboring Presbyterian congregation in a spontaneous "festival of celebration." The affair was brought to an abrupt halt when Presbyterian authorities heard of it and declared that it was going too far to "recognize Universalists as fellow-christians." Even then, some 100 individuals joined the Universalist society in a four-year period; over half of them were baptized by immersion.

When non-Universalists expressed surprise at such enthusiasm manifested at Universalist meetings by a denomination not known to indulge in such excitement, Stephen R. Smith explained: Universalists tried to conduct their religious exercises with decorum, avoiding "those offensive and revolting peculiarities, for which more modern revivals are so remarkable." The language used, for example, was free from "outrageous bombast and blasphemous impertinence and arrogance" usually associated with revivalism. Smith did admit, however, "that in many instances, the passions were over-excited" and fervor was demonstrated that could not be maintained. From the perspective of a quarter of a century, Smith concluded in 1843 that the "great awakening" on the New York frontier in the early nineteenth century did no permanent good. Where revivalist enthusiasm had appeared among Universalists, it soon cooled, and some societies sank back into an apathy more obvious than before. Revivalism, he decided, was not a technique to be commended as denominational policy.

Sylvanus Cobb reacted very much the same way as did Smith. Looking back in 1857 to the "Union Conference Meetings" so popular among Universalists in the early 1840s, he admitted that they had been part of "the high and feverish state of religious excitement which raged all through the United States, among all denominations."[113] But it had been "an unnatural, a hot-bed state of things" which, fortunately in his estimation, had soon subsided. One of the numerous crests of the emotional brand of revivalism which had been reached by the late 1840s, seemed indeed to have receded, if orthodox journals were to be believed. This was greeted with relief in most Universalist circles. The hope was that one by-product would be the decline of "all the abusive and slanderous things that they have said against us."[114]

But the periodic outbursts of revivalistic activity were not to disappear. They seemed to be built into American Protestantism, and the Universalists continued to experience their share. Another round of evangelical fervor emerged in the late 1850s. The new "religious awakening" was greeted with approval in 1858 by the Maine Convention which had, the previous year, urged pastors to "give more attention to the subject of Prayer and Praise meetings."[115] William H. Ryder delivered a sermon on "Religion, and the Present Revival" before the First Universalist Society in Roxbury, Massachusetts, in 1858.

Ryder detected two characteristics of this revival which distinguished it from similar movements earlier in the century. One was its ecumenical character; individuals from all denominations were welcomed—even Universalists and Unitarians, who had been, by contrast, excluded when the Baptist revivalist Elder Knapp had conducted meetings in the Boston area. The other distinguishing feature was the general absence of the sectarian bitterness which had marred so many earlier revivals. Ryder accounted for this by noting that fewer professional revivalists, such as Burchard and Knapp, led them; hence the revivals of the 1850s were less "got up" as artificial creations and were more spontaneous than most of their predecessors.

Nonetheless, Ryder had words of caution for his listeners and readers. There was still bigotry and intolerance among Christians which had to be erased. There was, according to Ryder, still too much "excitement" connected with religion and too much attention devoted to frightening individuals and describing an "imaginary danger." Finally, much of revivalism, including its consequences, was superficial and spasmodic, and led to "effervescent excitement" which had no lasting value. Alonzo A. Miner, in a sermon delivered on the same subject the same year, emphasized the meretricious and distasteful character of revivals in general, and their appeal to fear rather than to love.[116]

After the Civil War, and noticeably in the 1870s, revivalism reached another peak.[117] D.B. Clayton and John C. Burruss held a three-day "pentecostal feast" at the Red Hill Universalist church in North Carolina in 1870.[118] There were similar religious events elsewhere among Universalists, but the preponderant attitude in the denomination still seemed to be resistance to this form of expression. Although the Washington Association (Ohio) recommended in 1875 "that revival meetings be held in all of our churches during the year," the resolution was adopted only after "much earnest discussion."[119] When Dwight L. Moody, one of the best known revivalistic evangelists of the post-Civil War era, attracted national attention in the 1870s and 1880s, he received a cool response from Universalists.[120] Most felt that there were more rational ways of propagating liberal religion than by way of the tumult of mass meetings and descent to the level of mass hysteria which brought permanent constructive results neither for the individual nor the denomination.

The Sunday School Movement

Universalists usually date their first Sunday School from 1816, opened in the Lombard Street Church in Philadelphia.[121] However, there were earlier precedents. The first Universalist sufficiently interested in the subject to publish—in 1787—a twenty-four page catechism for the religious instruction of children was Shippie Townsend (1722-1798), a native of Charlestown, Massachusetts, and a member of John Murray's society in Boston. When Murray attended the Philadelphia Convention of Universalists in 1790, he took copies of Townsend's catechism with him. One of the probable results was the provision for religious instruction included in the Plan of Church Government adopted by the convention. This in turn undoubtedly played a part in the creation, in 1791, of the first Sunday School society in Philadelphia, in which Benjamin Rush, an acknowledged Universalist, was much interested. It had been preceded in Pennsylvania only by the Sunday School established by the Dunkard sect in Ephrata (1740-1777).

The Philadelphia Sunday School was in reality a charity school which gave instruction to indigent youth in reading, writing, and arithmetic as well as in religion, as recommended by the 1790 Plan of

Government. There were three such schools, all non-sectarian in character, in Philadelphia by the time they ceased operation in 1816. The original Sunday School movement in Philadelphia had been, in actuality, an ecumenical venture, through the cooperative efforts of Benjamin Rush; Bishop White, the first Protestant Episcopal Bishop of Pennsylvania; and Matthew Carey, a prominent Roman Catholic.[122]

With the closing of the other schools, the women of the First Universalist Society then opened their own Sunday Schools the same year, the first one for females only; a male department was provided a few months later. The school was financed by a combination of membership fees, subscriptions, and voluntary donations, and provided material aid such as clothing as well as instruction.[123] Sunday Schools operated primarily for religious purposes and officially connected with Universalist churches in Philadelphia were opened in 1833 (Second Universalist Society) and 1834 (Lombard Street church).

A Universalist Sunday School appeared in Boston in 1791, almost simultaneously with the opening of the Philadelphia Sunday School.[124] It was operated by Oliver Wellington Lane (1752-1793), a deacon in John Murray's society who conducted a private school for many years. Lane had also participated in Murray's installation in 1793. Murray had declared himself in favor of religious education for youth, but never developed his thoughts on the matter.[125] Like the Philadelphia school, the Boston equivalent was open to both sexes.

The second Sunday School known to have been organized in Boston was conducted by Paul Dean, pastor of the First Universalist Society.[126] It was begun in 1817, but ceased to exist after Dean's departure in 1823. The Sunday School in the Gloucester church seems to have been the third one organized in New England. Established in 1820, it was the outgrowth of a series of short sermons for children delivered by the pastor, Thomas Jones, who had preached in Philadelphia prior to his arrival in New England in 1804. Children were expected to commit passages of the New Testament to memory. Beginning in 1821, the children were assigned Hosea Ballou's *Child's Scriptural Catechism,* the first edition of which had been published in Portsmouth, New Hampshire, in 1810.

The New England Convention first considered the subject of religious instruction for youth at its meeting in Oxford, Massachusetts, in 1794. A committee was appointed "to compose a short piece, simplifying a system of religion, adapted to the capacity of children; to instruct them in the first rudiments of the Gospel of Christ."[127] Nothing having come of that effort, the convention in 1797 issued a circular exhorting parents to bring up their children "in the nurture and admonition of the Lord;" to provide for their religious education; and to serve as models of Christian behavior by, among other things, shunning conversations which tended toward "profaneness or unchastity." The learning of the Epistle to the Ephesians was recommended for children as a good introduction to the Scriptures.[128]

During the 1820s Universalist associations and state conventions began to add their voices in encouraging the formation of Sunday Schools. Editorial approval of the growth of the movement also appeared in the denominational press, although the obtaining of qualified teachers was predicted to be the greatest problem.[129] Several Universalist clergy also undertook to prepare catechisms for Sunday School use, such as the one compiled by S. Brimblecom of the Maine Convention in 1831.[130] The same convention encouraged the formation of Bible classes and Young Men's Institutes to provide the younger generation with Universalist instruction. Sufficient interest had been generated in furthering the Sunday School movement in the Greater Boston area to justify the creation of the Universalist Sabbath School Association in 1837, with Lucius R. Paige of Cambridgeport as the first corresponding secretary.[131]

The relative decline in the numerical strength of Universalism as a denomination after 1850 became a source of worry to supporters of the Sunday School movement, and they found an explanation. Much of the onus was placed on parents who neglected the religious upbringing of their children because of indifference. So many Universalists were so fearful of sectarianism that, as one critic put it, the end-product was "nothingarianism."[132] The columns of the religious press as well as the records of deliberations of conventions and associations were replete with pleas to organize and support Sunday Schools. In the 1850s in particular, parents were urged to provide appropriate reading material for children in their own homes as a supplement to the Sunday School libraries, which were often lacking in printed materials suitable for children. There was also dissatisfaction with many of the existing Sunday Schools because of the allegedly low level of instruction provided and the failure of the men to offer their services as teachers.[133] A further complaint was the failure of Sunday School teachers to indoctrinate their pupils sufficiently with distinctively Universalist precepts, particularly "the Scriptural and rational bases" upon which the denomination rested.[134]

The first official encouragement from the General Convention for the establishment of Sunday Schools had come in 1840 "for the proper education of the young." In the same year, William S. Balch prepared a manual on how to conduct a Sunday School, part of which was published in the *Universalist Register.*[135] By 1842 at least two publications aimed at the Sunday School population had appeared—the *Light of Zion and Sabbath School Contributor* (which became the *Gospel Teacher and Sabbath School Contributor*), published in Boston, and the *Eastern Rose Bud* (Portland, Maine). The first appeared semi-weekly, the second semi-monthly. The *Youth's Cabinet* (which lasted only one year) appeared in 1844, published as a monthly in Concord, New Hampshire; it was intended also for Sunday School use.[136]

Other publications intended either for Sunday School use or for juveniles were the *Youth's Guide,* published in Boston in 1850; the *Youth's Monthly Magazine* (1850-51), published also in Boston and edited by John G. Adams; the *Youth's Friend* (1846-60), edited by Abel C. Thomas in Cincinnati; and the *Eastern Harp,* which was a widely-used Sunday School manual and service book, including music for hymns, compiled by John Boyden, and first printed in 1848. The *Myrtle,* described as "A Sunday School Paper," first appeared in 1851 and lasted over thirty years. Several of its editors or associate editors were women, including Mrs. P.A. Hanaford, Mrs. H.A. Bingham, and Mrs. E.M. Bruce. Another paper intended for Sunday School use was the *Guiding Star*, edited for eleven years by Caroline A. Soule. It was used in over one-half of the Universalist Sunday Schools in the 1860s, and in 1870 had a circulation of 10,000 copies.[137] One publication begun in the centennial year was the *Sunday School Helper* (often referred to as the *Universalist Helper*), a monthly magazine published successively in Chicago, New York City, and Boston, and intended to provide teachers with some degree of guidance in uniform lesson planning (which was stoutly resisted by many).

The recommendation that a set of graded textbooks for Sunday Schools be prepared was first made in 1861.[138] The rationale offered was that "the study of the Christian religion, in some sense . . . like the study of any science," should be reduced to a system. But the denomination contented itself until 1901 with the so-called Uniform Lesson Plan introduced in 1873, and intended for all Protestants and not exclusively for Universalists. It was not until after the turn of the century that the Universalist (Murray) Graded Lessons were made available.

By the 1840s statistics of Sunday Schools began to appear in denominational publications. Over forty such organizations were reported to exist in eastern Massachusetts alone in 1841, and three years later Universalists in the entire state reported over 6,500 pupils, with more than 1,100 teachers in fifty-eight communities.[139] The First Universalist Society in Boston boasted at the time of a Sunday School enrollment of almost 400. On a national scale, the decades of most rapid growth seemed to have been the 1850s and 1860s, although, as with other denominational statistics, precise figures were never compiled.

The Committee on Sabbath Schools of the General Convention presented grossly exaggerated estimated totals for 1861 by extrapolating statistics for the entire country by using one of the states most densely populated by Universalists as a base—Massachusetts. By this computation, there were about 1,100 Sunday Schools, 8,500 teachers and officers, 74,500 pupils, and 300,000 library books.[140] Nine years later, the same committee (but with entirely different personnel) estimated about 500 Sunday Schools, with approximately 40,000 pupils. Even though these figures were also only approximations, they were probably closer to reality than those of a decade earlier.

The information in the *Universalist Register,* the basic (but not always accurate) source for denominational statistics for these years, was not very revealing. The 1,279 churches or societies in 1861 were reported to have had "numerous Sunday Schools." There was no report at all for 1870, but the best estimate for 1871 was the figure cited here, although the reported total, admittedly underestimated, was 439; many of these were organized on the eve of the celebration of the denominational centennial.[141] One such "centenary school" was opened by Mrs. Julia E. Outlaw in Duplin County, in eastern North Carolina. With its forty pupils, it was the only one known to exist in the state at the time.[142] A century later, members of the same family were active Universalists in the same rural community in which she had conducted her school almost single-handedly.

Coordination of Sunday School organizations and activities, which had first been attempted on a local basis in the Boston area in 1837, was considered on a national basis in 1844 in the form of a "Sunday School Union." Such an organization, proposed at the General Convention, was at first considered "inexpedient." Anything smacking of central authority was still considered anathema by a large number of Universalists. Whatever organization there was seemed to go no further than the state level. The General Convention encouraged state conventions to form local Sunday School associations, of which there were seven by 1849.[143] The greatest progress made before 1870 was the creation of standing committees on Sunday Schools, at first by state conventions such as that of Maine in 1845.[144]

In that convention a portion of time was devoted to Sunday School matters at annual meetings, with a secretary to collect and disseminate information first appointed in 1848. In 1864 the constitution of the Maine Convention was amended so as to entitle each organized Sunday School within its jurisdiction to a delegate.[145] In several states, such as New Hampshire and Vermont, Sabbath School Associations, consisting of the pastors of all societies having such schools, and lay delegates from each, met simultaneously with the state convention.[146] The Vermont State Convention in 1869 authorized the creation of a separate "Universalist Sunday School Convention," to which clergy and laity from the Christian denomination as well as Universalists, were welcomed.[147] However, the impetus was lost, in spite of sporadic efforts like those of George W. Perry, editor of the *Universalist Helper,* who spoke at the state convention in 1873 and urged greater activity.[148]

Pressure continued to mount after 1840 to obtain official recognition of Sunday Schools by the General Convention, the initiative coming from Universalists in Rhode Island and New York City.[149] The General Convention was urged to create machinery to supervise all Sunday School activities, including choice of instructional materials. Resolutions for creating a national Sunday School Union under the auspices of the General Convention were offered in 1852, 1856, and 1858. In the latter year a proposal was made by supporters of Sunday Schools to hold a special meeting of teachers in 1859 to organize an independent Sunday School Union.[150] There is no evidence that the call was heeded, probably because a concession was finally made by the General Convention. The most that proponents of official recognition achieved was the creation of a standing committee on Sunday Schools in 1857. But this "slender provision" failed to produce positive results, for the committee, not completely constituted until 1859, did not even make a report for three years after its creation. When a report for 1860 was finally forthcoming, it was not received until after the convention had adjourned.[151]

A central organization was again called for, and the committee went so far in 1870 as to recommend to the centennial session that the constitution be amended at that very session so as to require that half of the trustees of the General Convention as well as half of the delegates from state conventions be actually engaged in Sunday School work and be so certified.[152] Instead, the proponents of formal Sunday School recognition had to be content with not even half a loaf. Sunday Schools were to be considred "simply one of the instrumentalities of the Parish," and were not to comprise "a distinct power;" they were, like Bible classes or conference meetings, merely auxiliary organizations.

From 1870 to 1913, the Sunday School movement operated in a hodgepodge of jurisdictions and with widely varying practices. There were, in the year the committee on Sunday Schools failed to achieve its goal, thirteen Sunday School Unions scattered about the country, three of which were state organizations. But a large number of Sunday Schools belonged to no chain of command at all, and were operated with a complete lack of uniformity in relationship to parishes and churches. In some locations, Sunday Schools existed independently of societies, and were in fact looked upon as rivals.[153] Even when the General Sunday School Association received official endorsement of the General Convention in 1913, the trustees still opposed the creation of a separate organization devoted to religious education.

One activity involving Universalist children which was more successful than administrative organization was Children's Day (known also as Children's Sunday, the Children's Church, Flower Sunday, Rose Sunday, or Lily Sunday). This observance, intended to serve as an occasion when the importance of young people to the church was publicly recognized with a dedication ceremony, was originally scheduled (in 1868) for the second Sunday in June to coincide with the height of the flower season.[154] The person to whom the credit for originating the observance is traditionally given is Charles H. Leonard, then pastor of the Universalist society in Chelsea, Massachusetts, and later dean of the Tufts Divinity School. He probably initiated the practice in 1856.[155]

In 1858 the first Universalist "Children's Festival" was held in Boston, in the School Street church. The program was so well received that in the following year a similar celebration took place in Tremont Temple, the largest public hall in the city. A children's choir of over 1,000 took part, and addresses were given by Leonard, A.A. Miner, and other leading clergymen.[156] This celebration was a clear testimony to the importance of the Sunday School movement, which had finally been recognized by the denomination.

Sunday School activities by the 1850s also included adult Bible classes. At its last meeting before it merged with other groups to form the incorporated Massachusetts Universalist Convention in 1859, the Sabbath School Association urged attention to the needs of others besides the younger generation.[157]

Retaining the religious allegiance of youth in the transition from childhood to adulthood was also a matter which received attention in the 1850s. The First Universalist Church of Norway, Maine, was one of the pioneers in creating the category of "junior member" in order to provide for continuation from Sunday School membership to full church membership. Beginning in 1859, any child who expressed a desire to do so could become a junior member, usually by baptism, from the age of about seven to the age of twelve.[158] They were not called upon to assent to any article of faith, nor were they eligible to take part in any business deliberations. But at the age of twelve they could become "adult members" if they expressed such a desire, and if they were elected by a majority of church members. There is no indication in the records that parental permission was required. Junior membership had to cease at age eighteen, presumably recognizing the fact that by then the individual was capable of exercising full religious responsibilities. It was by such devices as those discussed here that Universalists attempted to lessen their dependence on recruitment from other denominations in order to strengthen and maintain their ranks.

SECTION IV

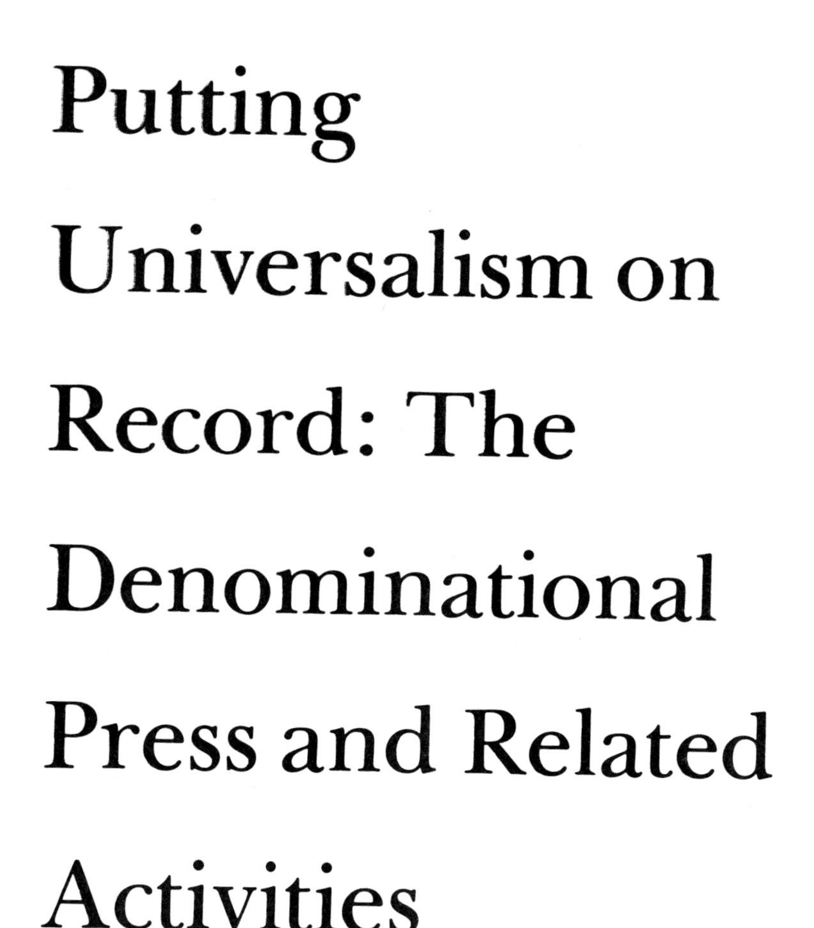

Putting Universalism on Record: The Denominational Press and Related Activities

Chapter 13

THE NEWSPAPER PRESS

The Denominational Press and Related Activities

For a religious denomination with comparatively meagre resources and claiming a clientele which represented only a fractional minority of the American people in both the nineteenth and twentieth centuries, the publication activity of the Universalists, particularly in the field of the periodical press, was little short of amazing. The multitude of newspapers and magazines under Universalist auspices of one kind or another became an indispensable arm and extension of the denomination, way out of proportion to either numbers or strength—in a sense a compensatory mechanism which made up at least in part for deficiencies in other areas. It was fortunate for both Universalists and their antagonists that paper, ink, and labor were cheap, for material of all kinds poured off the presses, especially in the nineteenth century, and bade fair to overwhelm the reader of a later day who attempts to find order, pattern, and significance in the welter of verbiage.

Richard Eddy, the leading nineteenth-century historian of Universalism, had accumulated a bibliography of no less than 2,096 books and pamphlets published in America alone on the subject of Universalism up to 1886.[1] They ranged from polemical and ephemeral works, theological treatises, hymnbooks, devotional manuals, and sermons, to biographies and historical discourses of various degrees of depth and sophistication. In addition, Universalists were responsible for no less than 182 periodicals, including weekly, monthly, and quarterly newspapers, with subscription lists ranging from a few hundred to over 5,000; an almanac and annual register beginning in 1836; magazines (both "family" and scholarly); and Sunday School papers.[2] The heyday of both book and pamphlet, and newspaper publication, occurred between 1820 and 1850, coinciding with a period of significant denominational expansion. In that period, books and pamphlets appeared at the rate of over thirty a year, and 138 periodicals were launched, although few survived for long.

Yet the millions of words written over roughly two centuries had, and have, their value. For the audience for which they were originally intended, they furnished information (and sometimes misinformation) about Universalism and its so-called opponents; inspiration and exhortation; to a lesser degree, news of the secular world; and, above all, an

Richard Eddy (1818-1906), historical scholar and denominational editor

outlet for those, both lay and clerical, who had, or thought they had, something to say about which the Universalist world should be apprised. The newspapers in particular served in the nineteenth century as a channel of communication, and oftimes comfort, for hundreds of readers who were Universalists in sentiment or sympathy as well as profession, who were scattered in the vastnesses of a still predominantly rural and isolated America. In dozens of hamlets, villages, and cross-roads settlements which did not possess organized religious societies or could not afford the luxury of a settled preacher, the newspaper was the only link to a larger religious world. To the reader of a later day, Universalist publications—notably the newspapers—offer a unique, and in some cases almost week-by-week account, of Universalist development, from the intricacies of theological controversy to the formation of new societies, the raising of meeting-houses, and the experiences of ministers in the field. Possibly most important of all, a careful reading of the newspapers will give some insight into the image the Universalists had of themselves and of others at any given point in time, as well as information about the state of the denomination. In short, periodical literature becomes an irreplaceable tool not only for reconstruction of a vital past but for shedding light on an important aspect of the Universalist heritage.

At first, all of the periodicals were intended to supply the needs of specific localities, as clusters of Universalists appeared in widely scattered locations. However, over the decades, as many newspapers ceased publication or were consolidated or merged, a few eventually took over leadership and their editors became, in effect, the spokesmen for the denomination. Whatever or wherever their origin or life expectancy, virtually all Universalist periodicals had certain characteristics in common. They were almost invariably edited by clergymen rather than by laymen. They had, as a rule, no firm financial base, and for approximately half a century carried no commercial or secular advertising. As a result, many editors, with more enthusiasm than business acumen, suffered serious financial losses. This was a principal explanation for the bewilderingly frequent changes of editors, printers, and titles, transfer of subscription lists, defunct publications, and combinations of papers. The high mortality rate of periodicals was a reflection of the atomistic, individualistic, and uncoordinated character of not only the denomination but of American life in general during much of the nineteenth century. Universalist editors (much to the delight of students of Universalist history) copied copiously and indiscriminately from each other; one result has been that at least part of the contents of papers of which no traces have remained have been preserved for later generations.

Two illustrations are offered as random but pertinent samples of how Universalists viewed their press in the middle of the nineteenth century, when the high-point of denominational newspaper publication occurred. One reviews in capsule form the peripatetic newspaper career of a single individual; the other, the reaction of a critic of press proliferation and the response he received.

The editorial career of Linus S. Everett may be taken as typical of many Universalist clergymen with journalistic aspirations.[3] His first newspaper venture had started in 1825, when he began to publish the *Gospel Advocate* in Buffalo, New York. Three years later, he disposed of his interest in that publication and moved to Charlestown, Massachusetts, where he became an associate editor of the *Universalist Expositor.* When that journal was suspended, he assumed responsibilities as an editor of the *Universalist* (Boston). This tour of journalistic duty lasted seven months. That came to an end when he encountered opposition from fellow-editors who objected to the entrance of yet another publication onto an already cluttered field. He then tried his hand at the political press with the *Independent Chronicle and Boston Reformer.* He discovered that he could not be "an honest man and a Christian, and a politician at the same time." He then returned to religious journalism by acquiring Otis A. Skinner's *Southern Pioneer and Gospel Visiter* [*sic*] in Baltimore, and tried to combine newspaper operation with a full-time pastorate there. Ill health forced him to sell the paper in 1836 to L.F.W. Andrews, but things went so badly with the paper that Everett bought it back and immediately handed it over to Philo Price, proprietor of the *Universalist Union* (New York City). Everett became an associate editor of that publication for one year, after having vowed the previous year that he would never return to the newspaper business. He did agree to serve as a correspondent for the *Union*; but his resolve to abandon the life of a clerical newspaperman was soon reversed. In 1839 he became editor and proprietor of the *Connecticut Universalist,* published initially in Middletown. His commitment to that publication extended over only two volumes. In 1842 John Moore, who had been the corresponding editor, assumed control of the paper and moved its headquarters to Hartford, where it lasted but one year; it was merged with the *Trumpet* in 1844.

Still persisting in his efforts as a newspaperman, in 1846 Everett began editing the *Western Evangelist* (Buffalo, New York) which in its two-year history, absorbed the *Western Luminary* (Rochester, New York) and the *Ohio Universalist and Literary Companion* (Cleveland). After all these maneuvers, Everett claimed 3,000 subscribers.[4] The *Evangelist,* in turn, was merged into the *Star in the West* in Cincinnati in 1847; while the transition was being made, Everett published in Buffalo (for less than a year), a journal called the *Ambassador,* made up of material extracted from the *Evangelist.* While in Buffalo he was suspended from fellowship by the Buffalo Association of Universalists (for reasons unspecified); he retaliated by dissolving his connection with this and all similar bodies, and disappeared from sight.[5]

Another Universalist who, however, remained in the good graces of the denomination was Thomas J. Sawyer. He took a very critical view of his colleagues who had created such a plethora of newspapers by the 1840s. In a lengthy article he made his sentiments abundantly clear.[6] He recognized not only the need for but the merit of some of the papers (without mentioning them by name) but saw no justification for some twenty-five or thirty. There were so many congesting the field that aspiring editors seemed to be hard-pressed even to find sensible names for them all. He decided that "dire necessity" was the only explanation for such titles as *Balm of Gilead, Primitive Expounder, Light of Zion, Genius of Truth, Banner of Love,* and *Western Luminary*. What compelled clergymen to enter a field in which they were likely to suffer heavy financial loss was a mystery to Sawyer. Some may have had "the spirit of martyrs;" praiseworthy as that might be, he believed they would do both themselves and the cause a much greater service "if instead of wasting their time with these periodicals, they would study Greek and Hebrew, or even write better sermons." He had no use for those would-be editors whose egotistic inclinations compelled them to "have a medium of communication with the public." It seemed all that was needed to set oneself up as a proprietor and/or editor of a paper was "pen, ink and paper, a pair of scissors, and credit with his friends or the printer to the amount of fifty dollars federal money."

What was the solution to needless proliferation? Combine the talents of twenty-five papers into five, strategically located about the country, and with a subscription list of about 5,000 each. The saving would, within ten years, be sufficient to support one of Sawyer's favorite projects: a theological seminary. With five well-edited and well-patronized weeklies, one Sunday School journal, one monthly "for the ladies," and a scholarly quarterly, Universalists would be most adequately served. It was high time, he thought, "that the denomination should come to a stand and look about itself, and seriously inquire what it needs, and what it wishes, and how it shall go about accomplishing its mission." Less than a month after Sawyer's commentary on excessive publications appeared, the *Gospel Messenger* (Providence, Rhode Island) was suspended for lack of patronage, and the *Genius of Truth* (Zanesville, Ohio), to which he had alluded in not very complimentary terms, was merged with the *Star in the West.*

It was not to be expected that Sawyer's strictures would go unanswered. Charles Hammond, editor of the *Western Luminary,* which had also been one of Sawyer's targets, countered by informing Sawyer that Universalists had a right to "publish just as many papers as they please, and of just the size they please, and as long as they please."[7]

Hammond resented the implication that newspapers should be "privileged monopolies" and had seen no proof that fewer papers would automatically mean better papers. Competition was just as much the life of the journalistic trade as it was of the economic. Less than four years after Hammond wrote his reply to Sawyer, the *Western Luminary* came to an end, absorbed by the short-lived *Western Evangelist* of Buffalo, New York.

It would clearly serve no constructive purpose to detail the sometimes dull and often tortuous histories of each Universalist newspaper, and would pose a task next to impossible to achieve even if it were worthwhile. Instead, the histories of only a few are included here—because they were unusually influential or had especially interesting histories or outstanding editors. Many of the papers have been either described briefly or alluded to in other contexts. Separate treatment has been accorded denominational journalism in the South, partly because it has never received either systematic or relatively detailed attention, and partly because it illustrated important aspects of both Universalist journalism in general and southern Universalism in particular.

The first Universalist periodical published in America was the *Free Universal Magazine,* four issues of which were published in 1793 and 1794. It was intended as "a display of the mind of Jesus as manifested to his servants, the members of the New and Free Church," and was edited by Abel Sarjent, a Universalist preacher in the Middle Atlantic area.[8] The first two issues, the initial one of which appeared 7 June 1793, were printed in New York City, the remaining two in Baltimore. The last issue appeared in March 1794, although there was an announced proposal for a second volume. The publication, totalling some 200 pages, gave the first rough inventory of Universalism. There were five churches in New Jersey; four in Pennsylvania; three in Maryland, and three in Virginia. According to the editor's information, there were "many" in New England; and the cause was "prospering" in Kentucky, through the efforts of two former Baptist preachers. Among those listed in various locations were John Murray (New England), three in Maryland (not including "one Methodist minister, who thinks not proper to declare himself"), and most of the preachers in Pennsylvania and New Jersey who participated in the organization of the Philadelphia Convention of Universalists in 1790. Notices of the annual meeting of this body through the one scheduled to meet in Philadelphia in 1794, were included.

There were six attempts to publish Universalist periodicals between 1802 and 1819, only one of which survived. The *Berean; or Scripture Searcher* appeared irregularly in Boston in a total of eight issues between 1802 and 1809; the first six were reprinted in 1804. The Western Association (New York) undertook to publish the *Religious*

Inquirer in 1810 as a quarterly, but only one issue appeared. The next effort was the *Gospel Visitant,* published in two volumes (1811-12, 1817) by a group of New England clergy. Intended to be principally a vehicle for "original tracts on Moral and Religious Subjects," it became associated with the early phrases of what became the Restorationist controversy of the 1830s and early 1840s. Another attempt at early religious journalism was the *Herald of Life and Immortality,* a quarterly which first appeared in 1819 in Boston, edited by Elias Smith, but was suspended in 1820 after only eight issues. The *Christian Messenger,* published in Philadelphia between 1819 and 1821, had been founded by one Jonathan Gardner, a Presbyterian, and was acquired by Abner Kneeland, whose checkered career as a Universalist has already been related.

The Evolution of the "Trumpet"

The year 1819 was a significant one in Universalist journalism, for a newspaper was begun that, under various names, lasted as long as the separate denomination which bore the name Universalist. The *Universalist Magazine,* which appeared in the summer of that year in Boston, became one of the oldest continuously published denominational newspapers (as distinct from monthly or quarterly magazines) in American religious history. The first regularly published religious paper had been the *Herald of Gospel Liberty,* established in 1808 and originally published in Portsmouth, New Hampshire every fortnight by the same Elias Smith who had later published the short-lived *Herald of Life and Immortality.* The *Herald,* which lasted until 1817, had originally no connection with any denomination.[9] However, Smith helped to organize a sect known as the "Christian Connexion" and professed to be a Universalist twice during his lifetime. On the first occasion (1818) the *Herald of Gospel Liberty* was taken over by one Robert Foster, and was renamed the *Christian Herald,* under the auspices of the New Hampshire and Maine Christian Conference.[10] In the early 1820s other religious papers appeared in rapid succession: The *Christian Register* (Unitarian, 1821), the *Christian Watchman* (Baptist, 1823), and *Zion's Herald* (Methodist, 1823).

In its 142-year history the *Universalist Magazine* (1819-28) became, successively, the *Trumpet and Universalist Magazine* (1828-61), the *Trumpet and Christian Freeman* (1862-64), the *Universalist* (1864-78), the *Christian Leader* (1879-97), the *Universalist Leader* (1897-1924), again the *Christian Leader* (1926-52), and finally (again) the *Universalist Leader* (1953-61). In April 1961 the last issue of the *Universalist Leader* was published, after having adopted a new and sprightly format the previous December, and appeared in May 1961 as the joint

Universalist Magazine.

PUBLISHED EVERY SATURDAY, BY HENRY BOWEN, CONGRESS-STREET............PRICE $2,50 PER ANNUM, PAYABLE IN ADVANCE.

VOL. I. BOSTON, SATURDAY, JULY 3, 1819. NO. 1.

TO THE PATRONS

OF THE UNIVERSALIST MAGAZINE.

As it may reasonably be expected that the first number of our paper may contain something of an address to its Patrons and the Public, we think proper in this communication to signify to the reader the general objects which are to be embraced in the following numbers that will be published.

The great and momentous subjects of DOCTRINE, RELIGION, and MORALITY have been already presented to the public in the Proposals which were issued for this paper; and whatever may be communicated calculated to promote a growth in these essential concerns will be gratefully received, and duly inserted in the Magazine. Nor is it the intention of the Editor to exclude from this paper the views of those who may differ from him in opinion, if such should be kind enough to contribute to enrich its columns with such communications as they may think honorable to the Divine character, promotive of the religion of Jesus, and wholesome to that genuine morality which adorns the doctrine of God our Saviour; retaining the right, at the same time, of suggesting, by way of question or examination any errors which may be thought to be of dangerous tendency.

It is confidently believed that, if the lovers of Christianity of different creeds should exercise that charity and condescencion toward each other, as to state with candor and undisguising frankness their different tenets accompanied with those evidences and arguments on which they rest their respective opinions, it could not fail to produce an increase of divine knowledge. A better understanding of each others sentiments would in this way be obtained, than is generally gained by the reports of those who are opposed to the sentiments which they represent to others. There are many reasons for apprehending that the greatest differences among religious people of different denominations owe their existence to a want of the knowledge of each other's views and arguments.

Pursuant to these considerations, the Universalist Magazine invites the sentiments of different denominations to expose themselves to the best advantage, clothed in their most simple light and shining in their purest lustre, that the mind of the reader may be able to know where to bestow a justifiable preference.

Objections no doubt will arise in the minds of many against the bringing into contact different sentiments, because writings of this kind sometimes partake of acrimony, and manifest more of asperity than of christian meekness and forbearance. To this objection we reply, that it frequently happens that neighbours lose for a time the exercise of due regard for each other, which imbitters their condition and renders their proximity to each other an infelicity rather than a blessing. And it sometimes happens that the domestic circle is disturbed by incautious indulgencies of those passions which ever ought to be kept in due subjection to the dictates of reason, and permitted to act only in conformity to the safe directions of that wisdom which is profitable to direct. But to infer from these known facts that it would be better to exclude ourselves from society, and relinquish all our dear interests in family connections would evince as great a folly as for man to put out his eyes that he might never more be troubled with motes which sometimes irritate them.

Further, it may be that some would object to any thing like controversy on points of Doctrine, because it requires more writing to vindicate a point of doctrine, and to answer objections brought against it, than could with convenience find a place in so small a paper. To this objection we reply, by acknowledging that there is some weight in it, but which may be in a great measure, at least, removed by the writer habituating himself to studied conciseness. And as a further inducement to a laconic manner, it may be urged that the common mind will more readily comprehend that which is expressed in a few words, than those subjects on which prolixity spends her profusion of language.

On the subjects of Religion and Morality, christian people, of different persuasions, would do well to interchange their views, freely commune with each other and give and receive liberally and gratefully. By such means that improper distance of feeling, so injurious to the christian traveller, would soon lessen, unfriendly feelings wear off, and all parties find themselves united in the great interests of human happiness. That so much may reasonably be expected from such means seems evident when we consider how near alike all denominations are on what they call pure religion and genuine morality.

But, why, says the reader, do you denominate your paper the Universalist Magazine if you invite all denominations to contribute freely of their views to its columns?

Reply, this is what makes it the true Universalist. The Universalist is no sectarian, the moment he excludes any denomination from any privilege he enjoys, he is no longer what he pretends to be. He keeps his eye on the divine Master, who is the same to all nations, to all sects, and to all denominations. In Christ Jesus "there is neither Greek nor Jew, circumcision nor uncircumcision, Barbarian, Scythian, bond nor free; but Christ is all and in all."

The Editor would humbly solicit of his brethren, in the labours of the gospel, any Communications, Questions or Arguments, which they may deem worthy of public consideration. The progress of truth, revivals of attention to divine things, the formation of new Societies, &c. &c. are subjects which must be interesting to our readers.

Minds of either males or females, labouring under difficulties and doubts, occasioned by a want of understanding in any portion of the divine testimony, may freely cast their burdens, by way of query, into the Universalist Magazine, and hope that from some quarter it may please God to give them an answer of peace.

How often is it the case with private Christians that they find in reading the scriptures certain passages, which, though they have a great desire to understand, yet their meaning is out of sight? In such cases let the passage be presented to our readers, and let every one feel an interest in contributing to the benefit of others, and in very many instances no doubt, difficulties may be removed and light caused to shine.

It is deemed proper further to observe, that all Communications for this paper must be free from asperity; and that though controversy is not only admissible, but solicited, in order to be acceptable it must appear in the ornament of a meek and a quiet spirit.

Selected, or original pieces, either in prose or verse, calculated to elevate the mind to the contemplation of divine things, to reduce haughtiness, to humble pride, to exalt the Divine Being, to endear the Saviour, to cultivate piety, to admonish, to warn or to rebuke, to administer comfort and consolation will be gratefully received, and as speedily as convenient communicated to the public, that their utility may be enjoyed.

As the Universalist Magazine will be published on Saturdays, it will seasonably call the attention of its Patrons to the contemplation of those religious subjects which are consistent with the joyful and solemn duties of the Sabbath; and pious parents may realize a rational enjoyment in seeing, in the hands of their children, on the morning of the Lord's day, something designed to instruct them in the knowledge of him to whose worship the day is and ought to be devoted. *EDITOR.*

DOCTRINE.

FOR THE MAGAZINE.

BY Doctrine we mean a system of Divine Truth, founded on the nature and attributes of the Supreme Being. No tenet, no opinion can be true, however generally it may be imbibed, however long the time may be that it passes for orthodoxy, unless it be in harmony with th[illegible] attributes.

If, for instance, an opinion be incorporated into our belief, which, in any way denies the infinity of Divine Wisdom, that opinion is false. And though we may have been taught it from our infancy, and adhered to it unto old age; and though we can cite the authority of learned divines, and the consent of the schools in support of this opinion, it is false.

If an opinion or sentiment have all the advantages above mentioned, and as many more as general consent, learning, and eloquence could bestow upon it, should either directly or by implication deny the Divine Omnipotency, that sentiment is false.

Any tenet, though it be considered as a most essential article of faith, which necessarily leads to a denial [illegible] omnisciency or infinite knowledge of our Creator, is false.

On a careful examination of the tenets of our faith, should we find one which opposes the impartial justice of the Supreme Governor of the Universe, though this tenet may seem as dear to us as the apple of our eye, it is false, and we are bound to reject it.

If an examination of our sentiments should lead us to discover any thing in our doctrine, that does not acknowledge that our heavenly Father is as infinitely good as he is wise, powerful, omniscient and just, it must be rejected as erroneous.

It is evidently consistent with the foregoing observations further to remark, that whatever doctrine so explains any one of the Divine attributes, or applies it in any way by which it is made to operate in opposition to any other attribute of the Divine Being, proves itself thereby to be false, and of dangerous tendency.

What we have here stated is a compendium of the first unalterable principles of true doctrine: And it is confidently believed that there is no denomination of Christians who would disagree with us in this foundation of all truth.

The first page of the first issue of the *Universalist Magazine,* which lasted under variant titles from 1819 to 1961

publication of the American Unitarian Association and the Universalist Publishing House under the combined name, *Unitarian Register and the Universalist Leader* (1961-62). Beginning with the October 1962 issue, the only slightly less awkward and less cumbersome title of *Unitarian-Universalist Register-Leader* (1962-68) was adopted. After a period of readjustment and settling in during which the interim *UUA Now* appeared (1968-69), the *Unitarian Universalist World*, a bimonthly newspaper first published on 1 March 1970, became the journal of the Unitarian Universalist Association. On the Unitarian side, it represented the successor to the *Christian Register*, and on the Universalist side, to the *Universalist Leader*. The new publication was not only one of the many tangible evidences that the newly created denomination did in fact exist but that both Unitarian and Universalist journalism had had a long history.

What started out as the *Universalist Magazine* and by the time of the Civil War had become the *Trumpet and Universalist Magazine* and the leading denominational paper and eventually the only Universalist paper, began as modestly as all other periodicals under their auspices. It was also the first Universalist newspaper (designated as such) published in the United States. It began on 3 July 1819 as a weekly sheet of four pages, about nine by twelve inches, and for the first two years was edited by Hosea Ballou, who was already the best known and most active Universalist in New England. He resigned the editorship when the publisher, Henry Bowen, made "a very injudicious appointment"—a person who not only knew nothing of Universalism but lacked "good character."[11] He was removed before the third volume was completed, and was replaced in 1822 by three editors—Hosea Ballou (Boston); his great-nephew, Hosea Ballou 2d (Roxbury); and Thomas Whittemore (Cambridgeport). Each received the munificent salary of $1.00 a week. In 1823 Henry Bowen's brother Abel joined the publishing firm in downtown Boston. Three years later, Hosea Ballou 2d resigned in order to devote a greater proportion of his time and energy to the preparation of what became the *Ancient History of Universalism*, published in 1829. The senior Ballou and Whittemore continued as editors, the latter still in his mid-twenties and already becoming a veteran in the newspaper business. He made a visit to Cincinnati in 1827 with the expectation of settling there, and the publisher of the *Magazine* set about making new arrangements for the paper.

Bowen decided to double the size of the pages of the *Magazine* without increasing the price ($2.50 per year, or $2.00 if paid in advance) and to employ Eliphalet Case, Jr., as Whittemore's replacement. But both Whittemore and Case changed their plans, and still another arrangement was required. Case accepted the pastorate of what became the First Universalist Society in Lowell, and Whittemore decided to return to his native Massachusetts. He became convinced

Thomas Whittemore (1800-1861), newspaper editor, writer, and religious controversialist

that Case's departure would probably mark the end of the newspaper, so in 1828 he suggested to Russell Streeter, then pastor in Watertown, that the two of them launch a new and enlarged paper to be called the *Trumpet.* A prospectus duly appeared, just as Bowen announced that Hosea Ballou, Sebastian Streeter, and Hosea Ballou 2d would serve as editors of the next volume (the tenth) of the *Magazine.* Bowen, quite understandably, received the news of a possible rival newspaper on his very doorstep with "no small regret."[12] Wasteful duplication of effort and resources was avoided when Whittemore and Russell Streeter purchased the subscription list of the *Magazine* for $1,250. The actual paid-up subscriptions amounted at the time to approximately 700, to which Streeter had added over 500 names when the first number of the combined papers, under the title of the *Trumpet and Universalist Magazine,* appeared on 5 July 1828. Three months after the *Trumpet* appeared, Streeter retired from the arrangement, with the understanding that he would not become associated with another newspaper.[13] Whittemore, who assumed all of the debts (mostly to Bowen), mortgaged all of his real estate to pay off the obligations, and immediately undertook a major advertising campaign to bring the paper to public attention. The effort produced results. Whittemore's name and that of the *Trumpet* became synonymous until his long editorship came to an end with his death in 1861.

Thomas Whittemore (1800-1861) was, at least by his own account, the epitome of the self-made heroes later to be made popular by the one-time Unitarian clergyman Horatio Alger, Jr. (1834-1899). Whittemore, in his autobiography published in 1859, told the story of "how I was obliged to struggle against honest poverty, which was never a reproach to any man . . . and how I laid the foundation, by habits of industry and economy, of all the worldly prosperity I have since enjoyed."[14]

Whittemore was born in Boston, Massachusetts, in the section then known as Copp's Hill, on 1 January 1800. He was descended from an old New England family which traced its ancestry back to a man of the same name who emigrated from England and settled in that part of Charlestown known as Mystic North Side, which in 1649 was incorporated as Malden. Whittemore, the fourth of ten children, was baptized as an infant in the Brattle Street Church (Congregational) in Boston, presided over by Jedidiah Morse. When he was five years old, Whittemore's family moved to Charlestown, where the father established himself as a baker. At the time of the father's death in 1814, he left a widow, seven children, and a failing business. With the exception of a few months of evening school and private tutoring, the young Whittemore received only a common school education, and was apprenticed at the age of fourteen to a dresser of morocco leather. But his restless temperament—he was described as a "not over quiet boy" from the very beginning—resulted in a series of short-lived attempts to train him for a variety of trades. He was apprenticed briefly in a brass foundry, but he soon wearied of that and ran away twice. He then tried shoemaking in Lynn, with no more success. He was then bound over by his widowed mother to a Boston bootmaker with whom he served an apprenticeship which lasted until Whittemore reached the legal age of freedom at twenty-one.

Whittemore's religious development as a youth took place within the stern confines of Calvinism which so revolted him that he, like many adolescents, lost all reverence for the Bible and verged on "infidelity." His church attendance continued to be regular, but this was due to his love of music rather than to his religiosity. He sang for a time in the choir of the Universalist church in Charlestown, of which Edward Turner was the pastor, and then became a salaried employee of the First Baptist Church in Boston, where he played the bass viol. His acquaintance with Hosea Ballou, beginning in 1819, which resulted in Whittemore's conversion to Universalism, was made possible because Ballou was at the time occupying part of the house in which Whittemore and his master resided. The initiative which prompted the apprentice to meet Ballou came not from a religious impulse but from a desire to improve his command of English grammar. Whittemore submitted a piece of poetry ("Reflections over the Grave of an Infant") for inspection, and after receiving advice about his writing, shortly thereafter found his literary effort printed in the *Universalist Magazine,* of which Ballou was then the chief editor.

In order to hear Ballou preach, Whittemore resigned his position in the Baptist church and was employed by the Second Universalist Society, of which Ballou was pastor. With a new and more positive interpretation of the Bible offered by Ballou, Whittemore's faith in it was not only rekindled but Ballou's suggestion that he prepare for the ministry was taken seriously. So he diligently studied the Scriptures, and delivered his first sermon at the age of twenty in the Universalist church in Roxbury. With financial assistance from members of Ballou's society, Whittemore studied for the ministry for a few months under his mentor, and accepted an invitation to settle with the Universalist society in Milford, Massachusetts, in 1821. He was ordained by the Southern Association (Massachusetts) in Stoughton the same year.[15] After one year at Milford he took charge of the society in Cambridgeport, where he remained for nine years, until the pressure of other activities necessitated his resignation.

Throughout his early life he lectured and preached in almost every community in the Greater Boston area. His first public appearance as an orator took place on 4 July 1821, when he addressed "the Republican citizens of Milford, Mass., and the adjacent towns." He sent a copy to Thomas Jefferson at his home at Monticello and was thanked in the following words: 'It is always a matter of great satisfaction . . . to see the principles of the Revolution avowed, and cherished by those now charged with their preservation . . . . [to be] handed down, in all their purity, from generation to generation.'[16]

Whittemore also began his career as an author of religious works at an early age. In 1821 he prepared a twenty-two page *Epitome of Scripture Doctrine, comprised in a Catechism, for the use of children.* At the suggestion of Hosea Ballou 2d in 1823 Whittemore agreed to prepare the second half of a two-part history of Universalism, of which Ballou would write the first ("ancient") half, and Whittemore the "modern," using the Reformation of the sixteenth century as the dividing line. Whittemore promptly undertook to master the French language in order to prepare himself for his part of the proposed task, which represented the most ambitious historical project yet to be undertaken by any member of the denomination. As he admitted, "to arrange a mass of materials possessing so great a variety, has been found no easy task."[17]

Between 1823 and 1830, when the first edition of Whittemore's *Modern History of Universalism* appeared, he was involved in a series of other projects.[18] He engaged in an extended written controversy concerning the doctrines of Universalism with a Methodist clergyman in Charlestown which extended for over six months in the *Universalist Magazine.* Regarding the trip he made to Cincinnati in 1827, he recalled later (1852) that it was nothing but restlessness and boredom that drove him there in search of a larger field of operation. "I had not half enough to do. To prepare two sermons a week . . . and take care of the parish, did not occupy one-third of my time." In the spring of 1828, when he established the *Trumpet,* at least part of his remaining free time was occupied. For the first few years of his editorship he answered all of the correspondence personally and kept all of the accounts without assistance.[19] It was this regimen that finally forced him to resign his Cambridgeport pastorate in 1831.

Not content merely with running a newspaper and preaching on occasion, Whittemore plunged into secular affairs. He ran successfully for the Massachusetts legislature in 1831 as a representative from Cambridge, and during his five years' service in that body was the leading force in amending the third article of the state Bill of Rights so as to bring about complete legal freedom of religion in 1833.[20] Among his other activities in the legislature, he secured reservoirs scattered about Cambridge to assist in fire-fighting, and was instrumental in securing a charter when it became a city.[21] In the midst of his crusade to bring about separation of church and state in Massachusetts, he published *Notes and Illustrations of the Parables* (1832), with a revised and enlarged edition appearing two years later. Besides continuing to indulge in a favorite pastime of public debate with religious opponents, he lectured frequently on temperance, and delivered sermons at denominational state and national conventions. In 1838 he prepared a *Plain Guide to Universalism,* a helpful handbook of which over 10,000 copies were sold. His interest in music was illustrated by his membership in the local Handel and Haydn Society as a youth and by his *Songs of Zion* (1836), a collection of hymns to which he made several original contributions of both words and music. He was responsible for a second book of church music, the *Gospel Harmonist,* published in 1841. By 1844 he had published three more collections of hymns, including one intended for Sabbath School use. He also took time to compile the first history of hymnology in the denomination, published in the *Trumpet.*

A strong supporter of the denomination's educational efforts and an enthusiastic advocate of serious scholarship, in 1834 he was instrumental in founding the Universalist Historical Society, of which he was the first treasurer. It was fitting that Tufts College, for which he had been an outspoken champion, conferred upon him its first honorary degree (Doctor of Divinity) in 1858. Even a prolonged bout of ill health in 1845 and 1846 had failed to slow him down. He wrote constantly for both the paper he edited for thirty-four years, and for other denominational publications such as the *Universalist Quarterly.* He also produced numerous other theological works besides those already mentioned, including an *Exposition of the Book of Revelation* (1848). In secular affairs, he was a selectman when Cambridge was a town and an alderman after it became a city. He also served for many years, beginning in the 1840s, as president of the Vermont and Massachusetts Railroad. He was likewise president of the Cambridge Bank, and felt constrained to assure everyone that he had, in spite of multifarious activities outside the denomination, "never permitted any thing to interfere with my duty to the cause of Universalism." He was sufficiently denomination-conscious to list in 1852 the religious affiliation of each of the other six directors of the bank. Two others besides himself (including Lucius R. Paige) were Universalists.

Short, stocky, and as pugnacious in his appearance as in his behavior, Whittemore was described by a contemporary as one who "rushes on with the impetuosity of a war horse."[22] A great believer in a systematic schedule for everything, he retired regularly between 10 and 11 P.M. and rose at 4 A.M., winter and summer, and found mornings his best time for writing. He believed wholeheartedly in exercising, and refused to use the public transportation provided between Cambridge and Boston. He walked the five-mile round trip from home to office almost every day of his active life. He married Lovice Corbett in 1821, while pastor of the Milford society, and was the father of eight children.

Whittemore's writing was as blunt and direct as his personality. As

Thomas J. Sawyer expressed it, Whittemore's style was "distinguished rather by force than elegance," and always went straight to the point, whatever it might be. If lacking in refinement and grace, and sometimes bolder and more plain-spoken than necessary, even his enemies respected him for his frankness and honesty. He lived at a time, and was engaged in causes when "paper hats and silk gloves" were out of place. Whittemore was in no sense an intellectual or philosopher, and all of his preaching was soundly based on an intimate knowledge of and respect for the Scriptures. He was, above all else, a "doctrinal preacher" who never wrote out his sermons in advance and only occasionally preached from notes, usually pinned to the leaf of a Bible. He was, he admitted, seldom at a loss for words. With "a frame of iron, and lungs of brass," he relayed his religious messages with a vehemence, as one acquaintance put it, not even exceeded by Edward Everett, one of the foremost orators of his day.[23]

As Whittemore grew older, he became more and more conservative in his religious ideas, and when "the specious guise of New England transcendentalism [and] the arrogant pretensions of clairvoyance" caught the imagination of some Universalists, he stood firm and unyielding in his Biblically-centered Christian belief.[24] As one of the most aggressive and uncompromising of Universalists, the very name of Whittemore's newspaper was selected to reflect his conviction of his mission "of blowing the gospel trumpet under the walls of [the] spiritual Jericho" of the orthodox.[25] He would have none of the "progressive Christianity" much talked about by religious liberals toward the end of his life. Christianity was, to him, perfect when first announced, and he saw no reason to try to improve it. It was, rather, the duty of men to improve themselves and not their religion.[26]

Throughout its long history the *Trumpet* was Whittemore's main concern as an instrument for promoting and defending Universalism, and he insisted on running it single-handedly. After Russell Streeter transferred his interest to Whittemore in 1828, Whittemore was not only the sole editor but the paper's owner and chief clerk. In order to emphasize the continuity of the denomination as well as to provide publicity for the word "Universalism," he numbered the volumes consecutively from the beginning of the *Universalist Magazine* and put the name of the former publication in large type on the masthead.[27] He immediately made the paper a lively arena for religious controversy, in which he insisted on playing a major part. He eschewed all mention of politics, and told his readers repeatedly and from the very beginning not to expect either news items or editorials on the subject.[28] "We have enemies enough *without* to contend with."[29] For several years (in the 1830s) he carried on a feud with the editor of the orthodox *Boston Recorder* and with editors within his own denomination. John M. Austin, long-time editor of the *Christian Ambassador* (New York) was accused by Whittemore of being too sympathetic to the Unitarians.

Whittemore broadened the scope of the *Trumpet* in the 1840s sufficiently to put on its masthead: "Devoted to Religion, Miscellany, Agriculture, and General Intelligence." Words like "Morality," "Literature," and "Education" also appeared from time to time. He also increased the space devoted to advertising, but he always limited it to part of the third page of the four-page weekly sheet. Between 1840 and the end of his editorship the paper remained substantially the same in format, with only minor changes in columning and typography. The price ($2.50 per year) remained the same until the paper came under new management after 1861.

The energetic editor had his share of difficulties with his *Trumpet.* Within a few months after the paper was established, three attempts (according to his interpretation) were made to burn down the office on Cornhill Street.[30] He came reluctantly to the conclusion that "sectarian hatred" had been the provocation. The building in which Whittemore's office was located was destroyed by fire in 1839, but the account books and other valuable papers were saved, thanks to the installation shortly before of a new safe.[31] An issue of the *Trumpet* was in press at the time of the fire.[32] It was the only issue never published.

The editor of the *Trumpet* received numerous complaints in the early years of the paper from mail subscribers that copies arrived late (or not at all), dirty, torn, and sometimes with candle drippings adorning one or more pages. Whittemore did some sleuthing and discovered that several postmasters were lending out copies to friends before delivery, including orthodox clergymen.[33] He soon abandoned the practice of using pseudonyms in signing his own writing, and made it abundantly clear to his readers that journalistic responsibility required that correspondents attach their real names to all communications.[34] Another source of irritation to the editor was the excessively lengthy and verbose communications which he received. He had no hesitation in naming names. Kittredge Haven of Vermont was chastised for not being "a little more brief."[35] Lucius R. Paige was another offender. When he sent in an extended commentary on a Biblical passage and Whittemore refused to print it because of the amount of space it would consume, Paige merely broke up his long communication into parts, and fed them to the frustrated editor on the installment plan.[36] This was not what Whittemore had in mind.

Then there was the perennial problem of delinquent subscribers that plagued every newspaper editor. Time after time he grumbled about patrons who never paid their bills or who moved (with accounts usually in arrears) without leaving forwarding addresses. He usually listed such miscreants by name in the *Trumpet,* and for many years published a "Black List," with the amount owed. Occasionally Whittemore was criticized for presenting only one side of a religious issue. It took some self-control on his part, but when this occurred, he usually complied and included more of "the other side." Thriving as he did on opposition and controversy, Whittemore did not hesitate to publish the views of opponents and detractors (usually by extended quotations). This he did with great relish, for it gave him an opportunity to blast away at his religious enemies, the doctrine of endless misery ("the great abomination of the age"), priestcraft, and other assorted evils. Ever determined to spread Universalism far and wide, Whittemore distributed complimentary copies of the *Trumpet* by the dozens. When a student group ("The Society of Inquiry") at Lane Theological Seminary in Ohio requested copies, he promptly sent them, but wrote an open letter that the paper was to be available to all, not limited to a select group.[37] He followed the common practice of requesting exchanges from fellow-editors, but frequently failed to receive them. He was comforted by the fact that the *Trumpet,* at least, might find new readers.

One by one, in the course of the *Trumpet's* history, small denominational papers disappeared into its pages. By 1843 no less than seven had been absorbed.[38] Cobb's *Christian Freeman* had an even more impressive record; it absorbed what at one time had been nine separate papers. Other editors began to raise eyebrows at the continuing absorption of papers by the *Trumpet,* and several made reference to the analogy with little fish being swallowed by larger ones until the *Trumpet* would 'probably have the whole ocean to itself.'[39] The *Trumpet* also served as the denominational paper for Connecticut Universalists. In 1851 the state convention discussed the possibility of establishing a Universalist paper to take the place of one absorbed by the *Trumpet* in 1843, but abandoned the idea after arrangements were made with Whittemore, beginning in 1842, to carry a "Connecticut Department."[40]

The subscription list of the *Trumpet* went up steadily, due in part of course to the absorption of other papers. But before it had been in existence for a year the press run had gone up to 2,800—more than double the 1,200 with which it had been started.[41] By 1831 the list had grown to 3,900, and the *Trumpet* had the largest circulation of any Boston-based religious newspaper, including the *Boston Recorder* and the *Christian Watchman* (Baptist).[42] A year later Whittemore boasted that, of the fourteen papers then being published by the denomination, only the *Evangelical Magazine and Gospel Advocate* (Utica, New York), exceeded the *Trumpet,* with 5,500 subscribers as compared with 4,700 of the Boston paper.[43] By 1836 Whittemore had 5,000 subscribers.[44]

Most fellow-editors in the denomination admired and respected Whittemore even though they were not reluctant to disagree with him on many issues, such as his vociferous criticism of Unitarians. Sylvanus Cobb noted with some distaste that his journalistic colleague was so fiercely loyal and militant about Universalism that Whittemore seemed incessantly to engage in a species of "Christian warfare."[45] Henry Bacon, editor of the *Ladies' Repository* in the 1840s, characterized the *Trumpet* as "probably the most conservative" of Universalist papers, but "foremost and reliable for denominational news."[46] He believed that if Editor Whittemore could devote his full time to his paper, he would "do the world more good" than any of his careers in railroading and banking.

Whittemore's most powerful and closest competitior in the newspaper business after 1838 was Sylvanus Cobb, whose *Christian Freeman* by the 1850s was largely paralleling the coverage of the *Trumpet*. Except for reporting of social reform activities which Whittemore tried more or less inconsistently to avoid, the two papers were almost identical. Both papers were published in the midst of the unofficial denominational headquarters on Cornhill Street. James M. Usher, a Universalist clergyman who for several years operated the bookstore and publishing office connected with Whittemore's establishment, was located in the same building with him. Abel Tompkins also ran a publishing business and bookstore across the street, and produced a Sabbath School paper as well as the *Ladies' Repository* and the *Rose of Sharon*. Nearby, fellow-Universalist B.B. Mussey was likewise engaged in publishing activities. The *Christian Freeman* and the *Trumpet* were published within a day of each other (Friday and Saturday, respectively) and went to press simultaneously. They were even serviced by the same denominational printer, George Bazin. In his thirty years in that occupation he had probably "put in type more arguments in vindication and illustration of our faith than any other man that ever lived."[47] The proximity of the two papers resulted in much wasteful overlapping and duplication of communications and notices.

Whittemore stuck to his editorial tasks to almost the very end of his life. When he suffered serious illness in 1857 and a rumor circulated that he was about to abandon the paper and sell out, he vigorously denied such a possibility and declared that he would "go on with the *Trumpet* as long as we shall be able to handle a pen."[48] But a few weeks before his death in 1861 the state of his health was such that he had to relinquish both the editorship and ownership of his beloved *Trumpet* to others. A significant era in Universalist publishing history had come to an end.

The "Christian Freeman"

Of all the Universalist social reformers before the Civil War, Sylvanus Cobb was probably the best known and most influential. One of his special goals was the abolition of slavery wherever it might exist, and to this end he not only became a pivotal figure in Universalist anti-slavery organizations, but in 1839 established a newspaper which would be "more decidedly committed to the moral reforms of the day, such as Anti-Slavery and Temperance," than any weekly paper then under Universalist auspices.[49] The only paper in any way associated with liberal religion up to that time that had taken a strong anti-slavery stand had been the *Independent Messenger,* edited by Adin Ballou, who had left the denomination officially in 1831. But his paper, begun that year as an organ of the Restorationist splinter group, had never had a wide circulation among Universalists, and came to an end in the same year that Cobb began his paper. In the prospectus for what came to be the *Christian Freeman and Family Visiter* [*sic*] Cobb announced that one of his purposes was "the loosening of the bonds of our brethren in slavery."[50] This was but part of the carrying out of Universalist principles, particularly of "universal *active* benevolence." It was his aim to make the word Universalism synonymous with social reform.

The publication of the new paper, the first issue of which appeared on 19 April 1839, took considerable courage and fortitude on Cobb's part, both personally and professionally. Although he had been associate editor of the short-lived *Gospel Sun and News Register* (1835-37) in Haverhill, Massachusetts, in 1836, he had had no business experience whatever in conducting a paper, and had very little capital with which to undertake such a project. He followed the widespread practice of allowing individuals to receive the paper on credit; before the end of the second year over $1,000 was due him from delinquent subscribers, and he was forced to borrow in order to meet his obligations.[51]

Furthermore, Cobb was enlisting in causes, notably anti-slavery, which had little or no popular appeal at the time among Universalists. One friend expressed his sorrow that Cobb could not publish "a good Universalist paper without *meddling with Rum and Niggers!*"[52] In fact, he immediately raised the hackles of several of his fellow editors and friends in the denomination. The reaction of Philo Price, editor of the *Universalist Union* in New York City, was one of dismay. He considered the prospectus for the paper too aggressive, and the subject of abolitionism too sensitive for treatment by Universalist editors. He felt that its public discussion would inevitably stir up dissension.[53] Price changed his mind after the *Christian Freeman* had been published for three years. He admitted in 1842 that his earlier apprehension had been unjustified; the paper was much less objectionable and more moderate than he had anticipated.[54]

Linus S. Everett, who had already tried his hand at newspaper editing and was destined to fail several times, was notably unenthusiastic about the entire abolitionist cause, and greeted Cobb's new venture with displeasure. Everett was no militant defender of slavery,

Sylvanus Cobb (1788-1866), minister, newspaper editor, and social reformer

but neither was he a confirmed abolitionist. He considered a hands-off policy the best one to follow, and withdrew from the Boston Association in 1838 "because it meddled with the slavery question."[55] He believed Cobb had "embarked in a sort of half-way advocacy of the mad schemes of the abolitionists."[56] They were "hair-brained fanatics, who have made a business of meddling with what they do not understand." Further, their motives were suspect; they were governed, Everett thought, more by political considerations than by any real concern for the welfare of the black man. Deplorable as slavery was, it should not be touched until the slaveholders themselves took the initiative to do away with it. Cobb's reply was to label Everett "our pro-slavery brother."

William A. Drew, editor of the *Gospel Banner* (Maine), was another colleague who gave Cobb "the cold shoulder."[57] Thomas Whittemore, Cobb's long-time friend and journalistic rival, opposed his new paper at great length and with great decisiveness.[58] Whittemore took umbrage at the implication that existing papers were lacking in adequate coverage of material of interest and relevance to Universalists. One feature which Cobb did introduce, and which was not included in Whittemore's paper (although he did not acknowledge it) was a section addressed to "the younger members" of Universalist families. This was part of the justification for Cobb's choice of the second half of the title of his new paper—the *Family Visiter.* But Whittemore's principal objections were on other grounds. Cobb was appearing to set up a competitor to the *Trumpet,* and there were already four Universalist periodicals being published in Massachusetts. Were so many really necessary? But above all, Whittemore looked on Cobb's paper with a jaundiced eye because the new editor and proprietor insisted on becoming involved in such potentially explosive issues as temperance and especially abolition. There was no room for such controversial subjects in the denominational press. Whittemore insisted that he would not "mingle in any of the party strifes of the day." He conveniently forgot the thousands of words he had published in the *Trumpet* on the church-state issue only a few years earlier; and he overlooked completely his strong and continuing editorial support of the temperance movement and the various attempts to abolish capital punishment, both of which were lively public and political issues. Fortunately for Cobb's morale, and the cause of reform, he received words of encouragement and enthusiastic support as well as of criticism and rebuke. He published in his paper sufficient numbers of letters of endorsement to show that his was not a solitary voice crying in the reform wilderness.

For its first two years the *Christian Freeman* was printed and published in Waltham, Massachusetts, and thereafter in Boston. Between 1838 and 1841 Cobb lived in Waltham, where he had built a home and served as pastor of the local Universalist society on a part-time basis. In 1841 he accepted the pastorate in East Boston and moved to that community. He found the then semi-rural settlement on the outskirts of the city a very pleasant place in which to live. Its serenity was marred only by the opening of the Suffolk Downs race track in 1842 which, according to Cobb, encouraged gambling and the consumption of liquor, and attracted "the meaner sort."[59] The East Boston society, which met originally in what had once been a bath house connected with a neighboring resort hotel, prospered under Cobb's ministrations.[60] But in 1844 he resigned his pastorate in order to devote more attention to his newspaper and to allow the society to secure a full-time minister.[61] The paper did very well, but the society did not. When the latter was on the verge of dissolution, Cobb resumed his pastoral duties in 1846 and strengthened the Sabbath School which he had organized soon after his arrival in East Boston and in which his family was continuously active. His second term lasted only two years, when the old bath house was moved by its owners in 1848 and the Universalists found themselves without a place to hold services. Cobb resigned and the society became moribund for a time.

The *Christian Freeman* served as the principal organ for reform-minded Universalists, and was an acknowledged influence in creating and extending enthusiasm for reform. J.M. Spear, who for many years preached against slavery and was active in other reform efforts, said that by 1840 he was compelled more than ever after reading the *Christian Freeman,* to favor "the entire abolition of all capital punishments, of all war, of all monopolies, of all intemperance, and of all slavery."[62] Zephaniah Baker, while editor of the *Gospel Messenger* in Providence, Rhode Island, credited Cobb's paper with a wholesale conversion of clergymen in Massachusetts to the abolitionist cause. He noted that when the *Christian Freeman* began publication in 1839, only nine Universalist ministers out of over 125 in that state were willing to state publicly that slavery was a sin and should be abolished.[63] By the time the fifth volume was begun in 1843, it would have been difficult to have found nine who were opposed to abolition.

Cobb opened the columns of his paper to all sides of reform questions, and often carried controversies which lasted for months on end. J.B. Dods, a Universalist clergyman, participated in an extended debate with Luther Lee, an orthodox clergyman, in the columns of the *Christian Freeman* in 1840. After about a dozen exchanges which began in June, the controversy was brought to a halt in December by Editor Cobb, who felt that the debate had degenerated merely into a controversy over how to conduct it, and that readers had understandably lost interest.[64] Dods not only insisted that the matter of slavery should be left to the several states, but actually defended the institution on Scriptural grounds.

Cobb's well-edited paper grew rapidly in popularity. He had begun with only 300 subscribers in 1839; by the time the seventh volume was started in 1845, there were almost 3,000 subscribers, with an estimated readership of at least 12,000.[65] The paper was to be found in all the New England states, and Drew in Maine even accused Cobb of poaching on the territory covered by his *Gospel Banner.*[66] The influence of the *Christian Freeman* was enhanced by acquisition of two other papers. The first was the *Gospel Messenger,* published in Providence, Rhode Island. This paper had been started in the fall of 1840 by Zephaniah Baker, but it had only a slender subscription list; an attempt in 1842 to increase circulation by arranging simultaneous publication in Worcester, Massachusetts, and adding S.P. Landers of that city as assistant editor failed to produce the desired result. Another clergyman, Asher A. Davis, had then acquired the paper. But after only eight months he had exhausted both his money and his health, and in 1843 he sold the subscription list to Cobb.[67] Four years later, Cobb acquired the *Gospel Fountain* (Lowell, Massachusetts, and Nashua, New Hampshire), another struggling denominational paper which had itself replaced two others in 1846.

Cobb's paper was always more than an abolitionist and reform sheet. Although it carried extracts from abolitionist writers such as Sarah M. Grimké and Theodore Dwight Weld, as well as proceedings of anti-slavery and other reform societies both denominational and otherwise, much space was devoted to other subjects, particularly after other papers were merged with it. There were doctrinal expositions, sermons, religious and secular news columns of general interest, and transcripts of the proceedings of numerous Universalist societies, associations, and conventions. Some readers, in fact, complained that it was much more of a general family paper than the "organ of reform" which it was originally intended to be.[68] Throughout its relatively long history, Cobb saw to it that the paper faithfully carried out the promise of its prospectus issued in 1838—to be devoted to "religion, literature, news, and universal freedom."

William Lloyd Garrison, the radical and single-minded abolitionist, had a very low opinion of Cobb's paper. In 1848 he informed the readers of his *Liberator* that the *Christian Freeman* had 'woefully disappointed the expectations that were raised in regard to its reformatory spirit. A more dull, conservative, milk-and-water sheet is hardly to be found in the land.'[69] Cobb defended himself in his usual mild-mannered and straightforward way. Even though he lived through an age of excitement, turmoil, and division, he managed to remain throughout his career a moderate, reasonable, and compassionate person. He seldom replied in kind when subjected to attack, and throughout his busy life he kept a balance between his desire to reform and improve society without attempting to destroy it, and his commitment as a clergyman and practicing Universalist.

The *Christian Freeman* lasted as an independent paper until 1862. In the spring of that year, after the outbreak of the Civil War that finally brought to an end the slavery against which Cobb had struggled so valiantly, the paper was merged with the *Trumpet.* It was a complex and rather confusing transition. In April 1861 Cobb informed the readers of his *Freeman* of several plans being discussed by the General Convention to establish a denominational publishing house under its control. Cobb also decided that he could no longer continue the responsibilities of his own paper. Meanwhile, Whittemore had determined to relinquish the *Trumpet.* He obtained the editorial services of George W. Quinby, then of Middletown, Connecticut, who had been briefly in the 1850s the editor of the *Star in the West* (Cincinnati, Ohio), the most prominent Universalist paper in the Midwest.[70] Whittemore then sold the *Trumpet* to James Usher. After Whittemore's death in March 1861, John Stetson Barry was appointed editor by the new proprietor.[71]

There was much discussion in the General Convention about the best path to pursue in view of the fact that two of the major papers in the denomination were in a state of uncertainty or under probably temporary new management. The union of the *Trumpet* and the *Christian Freeman* was considered by the trustees of the New England Universalist Publishing House, which in 1861 and early 1862 was itself still in the process of formation. It was estimated that at least $12,000 would be needed if the merger of the papers were accomplished and placed under the supervision of the publishing house.[72] It was tentatively decided "to drop the whole matter." Rumors then began to multiply as to the fate of the two papers. The editor of the *Gospel Banner* in Maine reported that still another denominational paper was about to be born in Boston, and that both the *Banner* and the *Christian Repository* in Vermont would probably be next on the list to be swallowed up.[73]

The newspaper tangle seemed to be somewhat simplified when agreement was reached by 1862 that the time had come to consolidate the two Boston papers and to have the entire operation, in the interests of economy and greater efficiency, become the responsibility of the General Convention. The interim plan was to create a joint stock company to purchase both papers until the net profits repaid the stockholders' investments, plus six per cent. The combined paper would then be given to the convention and be operated through the publishing house. But the new proprietor of the *Trumpet* (Usher) demurred when he was unable at first to arrange satisfactory terms with Cobb regarding the *Freeman.* Cobb then proposed that his paper be put in the same category as it would have been under the joint stock company; namely, a valuation would be placed on Cobb's publishing company. When its net earnings had equalled the capital, plus six per cent, Cobb would give his paper to the convention.[74] A satisfactory arrangement was worked out, and Quinby and Usher formed a partnership and acquired the *Freeman.* The last issue of that venerable paper was published on 18 April 1862 and the first issue of the *Trumpet and Christian Freeman* appeared less than ten days later. Beginning in mid-1864 the name was changed, in the interest of simplicity and euphony, to the *Universalist.* Whittemore would probably have approved the new title, but would have been even more gratified if he had known that the cumulated volume numbering of his old *Trumpet* was the one continued in the new publication in spite of an occasional confusing use of "new series" and "old series" numbering. The *Trumpet* and its predecessor, the *Universalist Magazine,* had endured through forty-two volumes.

Cobb served briefly as the senior editor of the new paper, until the transfer to the newly created New England Universalist Publishing House was completed in the fall of 1862. He then held the post of theological editor from which he resigned in 1864. The veteran newspaper editor and reformer was not happy in his less independent and more constricted position. Although his relations with his colleagues on the paper and with the directors of the publishing house were generally harmonious, he was no longer his own master. He was also deeply involved in preparing a commentary on the New Testament for publication.[75] Both before and after leaving the editorial chair, he also wrote frequently for Boston secular journals on issues of the day. He treasured a warm letter of thanks from President Lincoln for supporting his plan for emancipation.[76] Until his death in 1866, Cobb maintained an office near the one from which the *Trumpet and Christian Freeman* was published. His office served as a depository for his *New Testament with Notes* and other books.[77] A new generation was beginning to appear to replace such successful personalities as Whittemore and Cobb in maintaining the traditions of a strong denominational newspaper press. But the personal touch that had marked their papers was somehow lost in the successors to the old *Trumpet* and the *Christian Freeman.* A policy of editorial anonymity was announced in the very first issue of the paper that in 1864 bore the simple name *Universalist.* The heroic age of a receding past began to fade.

Southern Denominational Journalism

Universalist newspapers published in the nineteenth-century South followed very much the same pattern as elsewhere, both in physical format and contents, and in their individual histories. Every single paper in that century was published and/or edited by one or more clergymen. After very short lives, most of the papers either disappeared or were consolidated with others, usually after economic difficulties and lack of sufficient paid-up patronage made their continuance impractical or impossible. By 1861 only one paper, the *Universalist Herald*, was being published in the South, and even it was forced to suspend publication until 1867. It served not only as a channel of information and a platform for opinion but, like its predecessors, as an invaluable and sometimes sole source for the record of some aspects of southern Universalist activity. Southern papers, as their counterparts elsewhere, carried the minutes and reports of proceedings of state conventions and other organizations in their area. In the case of the North and South Carolina, Georgia, Alabama, and Mississippi Conventions, no original records of their official proceedings before the Civil War have survived. The newspapers therefore comprise the only source in these instances.

Newspapers were often the only means available for communication among Universalists, and were frequently the only tangible evidence to the majority of the population that the denomination existed at all. Sometimes, travelling preachers found that the newspapers (as well as a scattering of other denominational publications) had preceded them when they went into places where Universalism had never before been preached. Occasionally a Universalist attributed his or her conversion to a chance reading of such a paper. Many a Universalist who migrated to another state or section took great pains, as did one South Carolinian who moved to Texas in the late 1850s, to see to it that his Universalist paper went with him.[78]

The first Universalist paper known to have been edited in the South appeared in 1826 in Milledgeville, Georgia. The editor, Michael Smith, had begun preaching in that community the previous year.[79] The paper, entitled *Star of the South,* was a small quarto monthly which, in spite of thirty-one agents spread over seven southern states, apparently did not prosper, and lasted only one year.[80] The paper was printed in Hartford, Connecticut, at the office of the *Religious Inquirer* which was edited that year by John Bisbe, Jr. The *Star of the South* was actually a reprint of the Connecticut newspaper, with an "editorial department" devoted to news from the South. This arrangement was undoubtedly made to save expense. In 1830 Smith, then living in Bainbridge, Georgia, published a Universalist paper called the *Southern Spy*. How long it lasted is not known. The editor of the *Universalist Herald,* who probably wrote a series of unsigned articles on the history of the denomination in Georgia which appeared in that paper, assumed that because the religious ideas expressed in the *Southern Spy* were too advanced for the time, Smith's second venture into journalism failed to obtain sufficient patronage.[81]

The first Universalist paper both edited and published in the South was the *Liberalist* in Wilmington, North Carolina. Three volumes appeared between February 1827 and 1830. The editor, who was originally from New England, and was then residing in Wilmington, was the first Universalist minister to locate in North Carolina and was responsible for organizing the first Universalist societies there. Plans for the paper were announced in the summer of 1826, but publication was delayed because the editor made an extended trip to Boston.[82] The first volume appeared semi-monthly, but the paper received such "rapid increase in patronage after small beginnings" that it became a weekly. Unfortunately for its prosperity and continued existence, Frieze decided to return to his native Rhode Island, although he did make two subsequent trips to North Carolina. Alexander McRae, a Universalist layman, served as acting editor of the third volume after Frieze's departure. The plan was to continue publication, with another Universalist minister, Spencer J. McMorris, as editor. McMorris, who had been a contributor to the *Liberalist,* was then preaching in South Carolina. His editorship was contingent upon acquiring 500 additional subscriptions. It was to have been a semi-monthly, beginning with the fourth volume (March 1830), but the plan failed to materialize, and for four years there was no newspaper devoted to the interests of Universalism in the Carolinas, Georgia, or Alabama. Universalists had to depend on papers such as the *Trumpet* in faraway Boston and elsewhere to carry notices of their meetings and to report their activities.

The next attempts to establish southern papers were more successful, although none covered the entire area as originally planned. Two newspapers, both ostensibly to be devoted to southern Universalism, appeared almost simultaneously, but neither cooperated with the other. Both went through confusing changes of title, editorship, and experienced varying fortunes. The first began as the *Southern Pioneer* in Baltimore and lasted from 1831 until 1837; the second was started as the *Southern Evangelist* in 1834 and eventually expired (under another name) in 1842. Their only linkage, tenuous at best, was L.F.W. Andrews, whose peripatetic career as a newspaperman illustrated the unstable state of Universalist journalism in the nineteenth century as well as the restless temperament of one of the denomination's more aggressive and abrasive editors.

The *Southern Pioneer* was launched in 1831 by Otis A. Skinner, a Vermonter who had moved to Baltimore after brief pastorates in New England. The paper was originally to have been called the *Gospel Visitor,* but Skinner changed the name to please Universalists in Virginia who were on the verge of starting a paper entitled the *Southern Pioneer.*[83] It therefore became the *Southern Pioneer and Gospel Visiter* [*sic*].[84] The paper, issued originally as a monthly by "an Association of Gentlemen," was published simultaneously in Baltimore and Richmond, although printed in Baltimore throughout its history. The expressed intent was to serve Universalists in Maryland and Virginia. It was not until 1833 that the editors were identified as Skinner, his brother Samuel, J.B. Pitkin of Richmond, and L.F.W. Andrews.

Andrews had already accumulated considerable newspaper experience. He had for a short time conducted the theological department of the *Herald of Freedom,* published in 1832 by Phineas T. Barnum in Bethel, Connecticut, after Andrews' *Gospel Witness* (Hartford, Connecticut) merged with it after less than a year's existence. After a few months, Andrews resigned his associate editorship of the *Southern Pioneer* and undertook to publish his own newspaper farther south.

Otis Skinner, who served also as pastor of the Universalist society in Baltimore, remained as senior editor of the *Southern Pioneer* until he returned to New England in 1835 to assume a pastorate in Haverhill, Massachusetts. During his editorship, he itinerated extensively in Maryland and parts of Virginia, turned his paper into a weekly, and increased the subscription list from 1,000 to 2,500. In 1835 the *Southern Pioneer* absorbed the *Philadelphia Liberalist* which had been started in 1832, edited and published by Zeolotes Fuller. Fuller continued to reside in Philadelphia and served as associate editor of the combined paper for another year. On Skinner's recommendation, the *Southern Pioneer and Philadelphia Liberalist* was then issued under the auspices of the Southern Convention, which had been organized in Baltimore in 1835. The paper's name caused no end of confusion among postmasters, and communications were frequently sent to Philadelphia by mistake. For this reason, the name of the paper was arbitrarily changed to *Southern Pioneer and Evangelical Liberalist* in the middle of the fifth volume in 1836 by Linus S. Everett, formerly of Charlestown, Massachusetts, who had taken over the paper following Skinner's return to the North.

Everett, finding the labors of editing a paper and simultaneously serving the Baltimore society too great a strain on his health, in 1836 turned the *Southern Pioneer* over to Andrews. The latter had carried out his plan to edit his own paper but decided in 1836 to move to Baltimore and take up Everett's offer. The results were disastrous for the paper. Without Everett's knowledge or permission, Andrews formed a partnership with George C. McCune, a Universalist preacher in Virginia, and Robert Smith, who had been disfellowshipped by the Connecticut State Convention for various irregular activities and had engaged in several brief newspaper enterprises. Because of mismanagement, the partnership went bankrupt and was dissolved.

To make matters worse, Andrews, with his outspokenly southern sympathies, used the columns of the *Southern Pioneer* to accuse various Universalist editors of abolitionist proclivities. He, in turn, was accused of provoking discord between northern and southern Universalists.[85] Everett, much distressed by the turn of events, resumed the responsibility for the paper but did not have the resources to continue it. He therefore transferred the subscription list to the *Universalist Union,* published by Philo Price in New York City; Price was one of the targets of Andrews' editorial attacks. Everett became one of the *Union's* associate editors, and the *Southern Pioneer* came to an end in 1837.[86] The merger was greeted with general relief; in that year the Pennsylvania Convention made a point of expressing its satisfaction with the new arrangement, considering it the best way "to promote and secure . . . unity and harmony."[87]

The disappearance of the *Southern Pioneer* left only one newspaper devoted primarily to southern Universalism, and again L.F.W. Andrews was directly involved. After the South Carolina Convention in 1832 had pointed to the lack of a newspaper for that section of the South, at its meeting the next year it was announced that Andrews, then living in Alabama, and Allen Fuller, whose services as a circuit preacher for South Carolina had been secured in 1831, would supply the deficiency. The result was the *Southern Evangelist,* the first two volumes of which (1834, 1835) were published in Montgomery under the editorship of Andrews, with Willis Atkins of Georgia as associate editor.[88]

When the editor "entered upon the doubtful experiment of publishing a Southern Universalist periodical" he started with a subscription list of 200.[89] The experiment was successful, at least from that point of view, for by the fall of 1835 there were almost 1,000 subscribers. However, the editor found himself barely able to pay current expenses for a publication which began as a monthly at the modest charge of $1.00 a year, and which he had threatened to close down during the first year if it were not more generously supported.[90] In the fall of 1835, nearly one-half of the subscribers were delinquent. Andrews had high hopes of turning the paper into a weekly after the first volume, but patronage was not sufficient, and except for two issues in mid-1835, it remained a monthly. When Otis Skinner, editor of the *Southern Pioneer* in Baltimore, proposed turning his paper from a semi-monthly into a weekly and charging only $1.50 a year, Andrews warned him that it could be done only at "severe personal sacrifice," and unless Skinner planned to "work for nothing."[91]

Andrews, like most Universalist newspapermen, never received a cent for his services; all he obtained from the state conventions was moral support. Although intended to be the denominational organ for the entire South, two-thirds of the subscribers to the *Southern Evangelist* were in Georgia and South Carolina, and almost no news was reported from elsewhere in the South. There was probably very little to report from some states, such as North Carolina, and for very good reason. Although there were six agents for the paper scattered about that state, there was not a single resident preacher, and a state convention had not yet been organized among the widely dispersed and struggling societies.

The third and fourth volumes of the *Southern Evangelist* were published in Charleston, South Carolina, where Andrews served briefly as corresponding editor and as pastor of the Universalist society until forced to resign because of ill health in his family.[92] The paper was for a short time under the editorship of Theophilus Fisk, who was much more interested in secular politics and in the labor reform movements of the Jacksonian era than in conducting a denominational paper. He filled its columns not only with his political and economic ideas but with attacks on his fellow clergymen, including Thomas Whittemore, George Rogers, and T.J. Sawyer.[93] Further, he was accused of appropriating Universalist materials wholesale from other papers and passing them off as his own. He was in sufficient disgrace within the denomination by 1838 to prompt the preparation of a paper by several clergy "stating his disqualification for the ministry" which was not published because he promised to leave the ministry altogether.[94] Much to their relief, he withdrew from both the ministry and the denomination that same year.[95]

Andrews, after his brief and unfortunate association with the *Southern Pioneer* in 1836-37, retrieved the editorship of the *Southern Evangelist*; thereafter, the paper underwent a rather confusing metamorphosis. During the period of the *Evangelist's* location in Charleston, one John Gregory of Macon, Georgia, undertook to publish another paper, the *Southern Universalist,* which was intended to serve the interior. Andrews had earlier realized the need for such a paper, and while the *Evangelist* was being published in Charleston, he had had a plan to publish the paper simultaneously in Augusta, Georgia, but that never came to pass.

Andrews decided to consolidate the two papers, for it was more desirable to publish one paper "in the central city of the Southern States" than to have two papers "languishing for want of support and encouragement." Thus was born the *Evangelical Universalist,* the first number of which appeared in the spring of 1838 in Macon.[96] The second issue appeared as soon as the fourth (and final) volume of the *Southern Evangelist* was completed. The *Evangelical Universalist,* which was intended to serve specifically the needs of the three states of Georgia, Alabama, and South Carolina, was launched with ambitious plans. Andrews hoped for 1,500 subscribers, the number to be doubled within six months, and by the end of 1838 actually had 140 agents in five states as far north as Virginia and as far south and west as Louisiana.[97] But the paper was destined to last little more than a year, with the final issue in the spring of 1840, after several changes of editorship and proprietorship, but with Andrews always in the key position.

In 1839 Andrews moved temporarily to Pittsburgh, Pennsylvania, and Philo Brownson, a Methodist turned Universalist, who had been associate editor when the new publication was begun in 1838, took over the paper and saw the second volume to completion. After the Civil War, Andrews ventured once more into religious journalism. While residing in Georgia (where he died in 1875), he edited the *Christian Crucible,* published in Macon. The paper lasted less than two years (1871-72) and was merged with the *Star in the West,* published in Cincinnati, Ohio.

After having acquired the *Evangelical Universalist,* Brownson rechristened it the *Southern Universalist,* and continued to serve both as editor and proprietor. He was assisted by Albert Case, who had resigned his pastorate in Plymouth, Massachusetts, and had settled in Charleston in 1838, and served briefly as associate editor.[98] When the paper was renamed and its publication commenced in 1840, Brownson included secular news for the first time. He also announced that it would be "a fearless advocate for our Southern institutions," as against the "fanatics" who were attempting to destroy "Southern Rights."[99] In 1842 he and the paper moved to Columbus, Georgia, where it appears to have finally ceased publication under that name the same year.[100]

Between 1842 and 1844, S.J. McMorris and C.F.R. Shehane, one of the more colorful figures in ante-bellum Universalist history, tried their hands alternately at publishing the *Messenger of Glad Tidings* as a weekly, first at Wetumpka, Alabama (1842-43), and then in Columbus, Georgia (1843-44).[101] Its closest neighbor in the South at the time was the *Christian Warrior,* a weekly published in Richmond, Virginia, between 1842 and 1845.[102] The *Messenger of Glad Tidings* was intended to replace the defunct *Southern Universalist.*[103] The paper lasted only one year (1842-43) under McMorris' editorship. After the publication of one volume, Shehane took it over and transferred it to Columbus, Georgia.

In 1845 McMorris started another paper in Wetumpka—the *Gospel Messenger*—with Isaac D. Williamson of Mobile as associate editor. Williamson, a native Vermonter who held numerous pastorates in both the North and the South, spent two winters in Mobile for the sake of his health, and became a staunch defender of the South. The *Gospel Messenger,* too, had but a short life. McMorris lost his newspaper office and equipment in a fire which devastated two-thirds of the business area of Wetumpka shortly after his paper was begun.[104] He resolutely acquired new facilities, but was forced to close out the paper in 1846 because of lack of patronage. The paper was merged that year with the *Star in the West,* published in Cincinnati.[105] Thomas Whittemore, editor of the *Trumpet* in Boston, in wishing McMorris well when he had first heard of the publication of the *Messenger of Glad Tidings,* had made it clear that this did not mean that he was approving in any way "any

John Crenshaw Burruss (1821-1910), denominational publisher and champion of Southern Universalism

defense or justification of slavery."[106] On being informed of the collapse of the *Gospel Messenger* in 1846, Whittemore made no mention of the slavery issue, but instead described McMorris as "a faithful and unrequited laborer" who was "among the pioneers of Universalism at the South," and had sacrificed money, ease, comfort, and his health to the cause.[107]

In 1847 Shehane was responsible for beginning another Alabama-based Universalist paper, the *Religious Reformer,* a small monthly at first published in Montgomery and then moved to Wetumpka in 1848 and to Notasulga in 1849, by which time its name had been changed to the *Religious Investigator.* It was out of this newspaper that came the most important and long-lived of all Universalist newspapers in the South both before and after the Civil War—the *Universalist Herald.*[108]

In 1849 John C. Burruss purchased the *Investigator* from Shehane and changed the name briefly to the *Investigator and Universalist Herald.*[109] Burruss then settled on the name *Universalist Herald* and assumed responsibility as both editor and proprietor on 1 January 1850. Shehane became the associate editor.[110] Burruss, determined to make the *Herald* not only a financial success but the single voice of Universalism in the South, enlarged the paper to folio, turned it into a weekly, and secured the part-time services of other clergymen in the South as assistant editors, including S.J. McMorris, D.B. Clayton, and Almon Gage. Marmeduke Gardner, who had moved to Texas in the 1850s, was later added. Burruss had a subscription list of 800 within a year, reported to be "increasing very fast."[111]

In 1857 discord developed in the ranks of the *Herald.* Shehane, apparently resentful of his demotion from associate editor to merely one of the assistant editors, and suffering from "hypochondriasis, which at times, bordered on insanity," attempted to operate a rival newspaper, the *Southern Progressionist.* According to a contemporary, Shehane "imagined his best friends his worst enemies, and imagined and said things concerning them which otherwise he would not have uttered."[112] Ostensibly the new paper was established to further the spread of southern Universalism, but Burruss was convinced that the real purpose was to injure him.[113] Although living in Alabama at the time, Shehane had his paper published at the office of the *Independent Blade* in Newnan, Georgia.[114] The Georgia Convention in 1857 had no choice but to recommend to their constituency the patronage of both the *Herald* and the *Progressionist,* but in any case "in preference to Northern Periodicals."[115]

Shehane died in 1857, at the age of fifty-four, and J.M.H. Smith, who had been ordained at the Georgia Convention the same year, decided to continue the publication, but "on his own individual responsibility."[116] Smith was described as a person with an "irascible and petulant disposition [which] rendered him wholly unfit for his calling as a christian teacher" and quite probably "retarded the cause he sought to advance."[117] He soon found the paper "a losing business" and after a few months turned the subscription list over to Burruss and his *Herald.*[118] At this juncture, Daniel Bragg Clayton decided to launch a new paper, to be called the *Banner of Love,* to be published in Macon, Georgia.[119] But when this was made known at the Georgia Convention meeting in 1859, the reaction was so negative that he abandoned the idea. Southern Universalists were told to unite behind one paper and not to "divide up their patronage into small pieces." McMorris supported this argument from his own experience; he had come out the loser by some $500 in his efforts in the newspaper business.[120]

Burruss closed the fourteenth volume of his paper on 1 March 1861, with every intention of publishing the next one.[121] But the outbreak of the Civil War made that impossible. The last two issues in 1861 carried the Constitution of the Southern Confederacy and Jefferson Davis' Inaugural Address, respectively. Nothing daunted, after the conflict was over, Burruss revived his newspaper, with a capital of $100, beginning 1 March 1867. The originial printing office and fixtures, located in a small shed at the rear of the lot on which Burruss' residence stood in Notasulga, Alabama, were destroyed by fire in the fall of 1870, but were replaced and continued to be used for almost thirty years.[122] Burruss continued to publish the paper until he sold it to the *Georgia Universalist,* edited by John M. Bowers in Canon, Georgia, in 1896. The name *Universalist Herald* was retained, however, and it continued to be published from that post office in the 1970s, with Mr. Haynie Summers of Turin, Georgia, as the first layman to serve as editor in the long history of the paper.

After the Civil War, Burruss acquired, by merger, the *Atlanta Universalist.* This paper, begun in 1879 by W.C. Bowman, had been taken over by D.B. Clayton as it was verging on collapse after only a year.[123] Bowman had presumably been more effective as a clergyman than as a businessman. After temporary suspension late in 1880, publication was resumed in 1881 with the assistance of R.E. Neeld. Clayton changed the paper from a weekly to a semi-monthly to save money, and for the next two years it appeared in alternate weeks with the *Universalist Herald.* The *Atlanta Universalist* came to an end in 1884, after Clayton moved to South Carolina, where he had earlier resided, and sold the subscription list to Burruss in 1883.[124]

There can be no doubt that the *Herald* was of great importance in keeping Universalism alive in the South in the nineteenth century. As B.F. Strain in Georgia pointed out after the war, "we have but few preachers—they cannot go and preach everywhere, but the *Herald* CAN," provided it were adequately supported.[125] Burruss' contributions to Alabama journalism were also recognized when, in 1975 at a ceremony at Auburn University, he was inducted posthumously into the Alabama Press Association's Hall of Honor in recognition of forty-six years of newspaper publishing and editing.[126]

During his long editorship of the *Herald,* Burruss used his paper not only as a collection and distribution point for Universalist news, but as a vehicle for reporting local secular affairs and supporting southern institutions (including slavery) and southern rights. He included items from every section of the country of presumed interest to Universalists, and dutifully reported the meetings of the General Convention, although in summary form only. In reference to the 1857 meeting, he saw no point in reproducing in full the lengthy proceedings; it would have been, he wrote, a waste of print. "Like the most of Conventions, they pass a great many resolutions, and do a great deal of talking, and there it ends."[127] He condensed the convention report into three short paragraphs.

No exact circulation figures were published before the Civil War but, judging from those subscription lists and reports of agents which do exist, the press runs in the nineteenth century probably exceeded 1,000, and the total readership was probably much greater. At its height, the *Herald* had a subscription list in excess of 1,300. Copies of the paper were sent to subscribers in every southern state in the 1850s and again in the late 1860s, when publication had been resumed. The *Trumpet* and the *Christian Freeman* in Boston occasionally printed excerpts from the *Herald,* so that northern Universalists could have at least a partial idea of what was going on in the South. Even then, those in each section might have sometimes felt that they lived in different worlds.

Chapter 14

HYMNOLOGY, LITERARY CULTURE, AND SCHOLARSHIP

Sacred Words and Music

Like the vast majority of other Protestants in the nineteenth century, Universalists honored Sunday as the Lord's Day and were constantly exhorted to consider it a time of "rest from all secular pursuits and business, as a day set apart for religious and moral instruction, and the special worship of Almighty God."[1] In instances too numerous to record, Universalist conventions, associations, and societies adopted resolutions deploring what they perceived to be tendencies to turn the Christian Sabbath into a day of amusement and secular labor. Readers of Thomas Whittemore's *Trumpet* were frequently reminded that it was neither morally nor religiously right to perform other than "works of necessity and mercy" on the Sabbath.[2] The Ohio Convention was strongly opposed to having the World Columbia Exposition in Chicago in 1892-93 open on Sundays.[3] The Franklin Association (Maine), at the very end of the century, viewed "with alarm the increasing and widespread desecration of the Lord's Day."[4] In a similar vein, families were urged, as were Universalists in Ohio, to set up family altars and to offer daily prayers.[5] If church services were not available, Universalists everywhere were encouraged to observe the Sabbath in their own homes with appropriate devotions, or to gather in the homes of neighbors for group worship.

When services were held in meeting houses, proper decorum was naturally expected. At times protocol was discussed at great length, as at the meeting of the Northern Association in Vermont in 1848. Societies were urged to adopt some uniform practice of posture while at prayer. Some stood, some sat, and others kneeled. Careful research indicated no Scriptural authority or precedent for sitting, so either of the other postures was considered acceptable, but not both at the same service. This resolution of the problem was arrived at only after "a spirited debate."[6]

Universalists intended their church services to be dignified, but at the same time to be spiritually joyful occasions, not marked by the austerity and gloom-saying that seemed to pervade other denominations, especially those that preached the stern Calvinism of Puritan days which Universalists rejected. The services in the early days may have been numerous (as many as three each Sunday) and the sermon may have been long (up to three hours in some instances), but there was variety even then, for both vocal and instrumental music were used from the beginning. Murray's Boston congregation, for instance, had a fifteen-year-old blind organist who "performs in a style very rarely to be met with," according to a notice in the *Columbian Centinel* for 2 May 1792.

Manuals for the conduct of church services had begun to appear by the late 1830s. One of the first, published in 1839 and designed for public as well as private worship, was prepared by Menzies Rayner (1770-1850). He advised that "in no case should the services be burdensome and tedious; so as to induce weariness, or render the worshipper impatient or uneasy." Of all the parts of a religious service, he considered singing indispensable.

Universalists found in the New Testament no "particular and express directions as to the external manner in which Christian worship shall be celebrated." Consequently there were many variations in both the order and conduct of worship services, a practice considered quite acceptable. However, a general pattern was evident in the nineteenth century. Rayner recommended the following sequence: The reading of a passage or chapter of the Scriptures; the "first singing;" the Lord's Prayer (in unison); a responsive reading; the sermon; singing; "closing supplication" and benediction, with an "Amen" and/or "Praise the Lord," to conclude the service. Abel C. Thomas outlined eight different "formulas" in his *Gospel Liturgy* in 1857, to be used interchangably for morning, afternoon, or evening services. He added such refinements as silent prayer, and an exhortation by the pastor, accompanied by selected passages from Scripture.[7]

Celebration of holidays on the Christian calendar was common by the 1830s. As early as 1789 there were newspaper accounts of celebrations of "the Birth of our Saviour" in the Boston meeting house.[8] Christmas was observed as a symbolic gesture. Whether 25 December was the proper historical date or not, it was the day chosen on which to make an appropriate gesture.[9] On that occasion, it was customary to decorate the church with evergreens and candles. Mary Livermore noted that Universalists made much more of Christmas in the 1840s then most other Protestant groups, and never showed the hostility to that observance that was to be found in many other denominations. While in Duxbury, Massachusetts, before she became a Universalist, she usually attended the local Methodist or Unitarian church. But in 1844 she went to her first Christmas service in the Universalist church, and found the religious spirit and warmth of fellowship so much to her liking that she became a regular worshipper and within a year had married the clergyman who had conducted the Christmas service.[10] Decorated Christmas trees and exchanges of gifts were part of many Universalist household traditions by the mid-nineteenth century.[11] Easter was celebrated as early as 1790 by Universalists in Boston, complete with hymns and organ accompaniment.[12] The congregation of George Richards' society in Boston sang an original hymn which he had composed for the occasion.

Universalist were just as willing to celebrate civil and semi-religious holidays, such as Thanksgiving, and faithfully adhered to the governors' proclamations of Fast Days at which special services and sermons were arranged. Independence Day was uniformly recognized by Universalists with appropriate patriotic ceremonies. A special program celebrating American independence was held in 1793 in John Murray's Boston church, in which an ode was presented, again from the pen of the prolific hymn-writer Richards. There was some objection to the "hilarity and intemperate mirth" displayed at Fourth of July celebrations. In 1821 Henry Bowen, publisher of the *Universalist Magazine,* suggested that instead of the roar of cannon, the holiday ought to be commemorated "as one of Thanksgiving and praise," and all churches thrown open for worship.[13] In 1845 Hosea Ballou suggested that the celebration of Thanksgiving and Christmas be combined on the same day; this would dispose of the problem of having two separate holidays coming so close together.[14]

The first Universalist meeting houses were simple boxlike frame structures with simple exteriors. The interiors of the early churches were equally unadorned, and a pulpit or platform was the only special furniture usually found, aside from the pews, which were more likely to be backless benches than enclosed family box pews. The first *logos* of record, representing the word of God pictorially in a Universalist church, was designed in 1830. A young lady in Boston portrayed in a painting a pair of balanced scales, with the inscription 'As in Adam all die / even so in Christ shall all be made alive.'[15] It attracted the attention of Abel C. Thomas, who had it lithographed. An enlarged painting was made by an artist whom he employed, and the canvas (four feet by six feet) was installed behind the pulpit of the Lombard Street Church in Philadelphia, of which he was then pastor. Thomas arranged to have added to the painting an all-seeing eye, a hand pushing forward into the light from clouds, and an inscription reading "A just God and a Savior." The painting, formally presented in 1831, became the theme for a series of sermons which Thomas delivered. A copy of the painting was also made, at their request, for the Universalist society in Reading, Pennsylvania.

Because Universalists welcomed music as part of their services, almost all churches organized choirs as soon as possible, and some created departments of music with their own budgets. Galleries were often constructed for choir purposes in new churches or added to old ones. A church organ was considered a prized possession, and a meeting house which boasted one ranked along with one with a tower and one or more church bells. The First Unitarian Universalist Society of Montgomery, Alabama, was notably proud of its organ, donated in 1834. When the society adopted its constitution that year, Article 16 read as follows:

> As the anthem and the sacred song are appropriate and delightful parts of public worship, it shall be the duty of the Board of Trustees, as convenient, to provide an organ for this Church and obtain the services of an organist and such other assistance in the department of music as may be expedient.[16]

Some Universalists, like Thomas Whittemore, were particularly interested in music and displayed their talents at church services or in composing hymns by the dozens. Whittemore was both a vocalist and instrumentalist. In 1836 he undertook formal training in musicology.[17] He prepared a book of church music, *Songs of Zion,* in which he included some of his own compositions, and in 1841 published the *Gospel Harmonist,* which he considered an improvement over the earlier work.[18] He also played the violincello, bass viol, flute, and violin.

Congregational singing, often "lined out" by the minister, was an integral part of the religious services of American Universalists, even before they achieved denominational status. Collections of hymns which had "the restitution of all men" as their major theme had appeared before the end of the eighteenth century.[19]

At first American Universalists used the hymns of other denominations, including the psalms and hymns of Isaac Watts (1674-1748), the English theologian.[20] Even after they had started composing their own, Universalists tended to be eclectic in their choices, and to draw upon a wide variety of hymn writers, regardless of denomination. The first Universalist hymn book to be used in America was *Christian Hymns, Poems and Spiritual Songs Sacred to the Praise of God our Savior,* published originally in London by James and John Relly, for the use of James Relly's congregation. When John Murray visited Philadelphia in the summer of 1776, six years after his arrival in America, he arranged for the publication of the first American edition of the Relly hymnal.[21] Over 200 subscribers bought more than 450 copies.[22] It was reprinted in 1782 in Portsmouth, New Hampshire, with the addition of five hymns by Murray.

In 1786 Shippie Townsend published *A Collection of Songs designed for Entertainment and Edification,* but there is no record that it was ever used in public worship. Silas Ballou (1753-1837), a distant relative of Hosea Ballou, was a Universalist layman and poet who lived most of his life in Richmond, New Hampshire. He published *New Hymns on Various Subjects* in Worcester, Massachusetts, in 1785, and in Newbury, Vermont in 1797. Thirty-five of his hymns were published in the first officially commissioned Universalist hymn book, compiled by a committee authorized in 1791 by the Philadelphia Convention.[23] The collection, entitled *Evangelical Psalms, Hymns, and Spiritual Songs, selected from Various Authors,* was published in 1792.[24] The 192 selections were arranged according to authors, in eleven chapters; those by James and John Relly comprised the first two. There were also hymns by Murray, Winchester, and Isaac Watts. In 1795 Winchester published in Philadelphia a small collection of *Hymns on the Universal Restitution,* probably a reprint of a 1784 London edition.

The attempt of the Philadelphia Convention to publish a collection of hymns acceptable to all Universalists was unsuccessful, in spite of the fact that nine individuals had been appointed to carry out the project.[25] Universalists in Boston insisted that the collection be one of praise rather than one emphasizing Universalist doctrine, the latter preferred by the Philadelphia Convention. Boston Universalists then proceeded to prepare their own hymnal, known for many years as the "Boston Collection." It appeared in 1792, compiled under the auspices of the First Universalist Society and was entitled *Psalms, Hymns and Spiritual Songs: Selected and Original, designed for the Use of the Church Universal, in Public and Private Devotion,* and comprised 415 hymns.[26] Oliver Wellington Lane and George Richards served as the committee to prepare the collection, and Richards himself contributed no less than fifty-two original hymns. His compositions were apparently better remembered for their quantity than for their quality. Although Richards was known as "the principal poet of the Universalist denomination," he was not considered, at least by Whittemore, as a good poet, and very few of his hymns were in use by the 1840s.[27] When the work was reprinted in 1802, all of Richard's hymns were quietly omitted, but were restored in 1808 and placed in an appendix.

The Boston congregation had used the Relly hymnal but had decided not only to revise it but to include hymns from other denominations. There was also a theological as well as literary reason for both updating the Relly hymn book and subordinating Richards' hymns after 1805. They included not only trinitarian references but allusions to the vicarious sufferings of Christ and the Atonement. As Whittemore expressed it, many of the hymns were "too argumentative in character."[28] Richards did publish his own hymn book, *A Collection of Hymns,* in Dover, New Hampshire, in 1801, which included six more of his own. An enlarged edition, with twenty-six more of Richard's creations, was published in 1806.

The New England Convention was the next group to sponsor a hymn book. A committee consisting of Hosea Ballou and Abner

Kneeland was appointed in 1805 to provide a collection "suitable for public worship on all occasions." At the meeting in 1806 they were instructed to prepare a work of not less than 500 hymns, to be sold at not more than 75 cents. In 1807 Edward Turner was added to the committee.[29] They were further instructed to avoid all "limited views of the great salvation . . . and also Calvinistic views of the atonement and all recognition of the doctrine of the Trinity."[30] The plan was to have made a selection mostly from other works, with only a few original hymns. Instead, the creative urge became overwhelming, and the entire collection of 410 hymns, totalling 360 pages, consisted of originals. Of the total, 193 were by Hosea Ballou, 138 by Kneeland, 48 by Sebastian Streeter, 23 by Silas Ballou, and 10 by Turner. The collection, entitled *Hymns Composed by Different Authors, by Order of the General Convention of Universalists of the New England States and Others,* was published in 1808. The copyright was granted to the committee, and the convention assumed no financial responsibility.

Even though widely publicized, the 1808 hymn book was not popular, for it still failed to serve the purpose originally intended. Only one other edition was published, in Charlestown, Massachusetts, shortly after Kneeland began a brief pastorate there.[31] The second edition included some original hymns by Samuel Thompson. The Charlestown society promptly ceased to use it after Kneeland's departure for Philadelphia, where, in 1819, he published his own. He attempted to do the impossible by announcing that it would "equally answer for all denominations of Christians, without being particularly objectionable to any." The collection included selections from "the best European standard authors." Most of the Universalists represented, including Hosea Ballou, Sebastian Streeter, Turner, Silas Ballou, and Kneeland himself, were relegated to an appendix.

Until 1821 Universalists got along as best they could with existing hymn books, none of which seemed satisfactory. The initiative for a new one came from Hosea Ballou, who was still using the Boston Collection in his own church. But he did not like the allusions to the Trinity or recognition of the Atonement in some of the hymns. So he suggested to Edward Turner of Charlestown that the two prepare another collection. The idea was followed up in 1817, when Ballou, Turner, and Paul Dean were authorized by the New England Convention to prepare a new hymn book which could be recommended by the convention.[32] The manuscript was to be ready for inspection at the next meeting. The new hymn book was indeed prepared, but it was not published until 1821, and without Dean's collaboration. It was entitled *The Universalists' Hymn Book: Being a New Collection of Psalms and Hymns for the Use of Universalist Societies.*[33] It was considered the best collection yet published, and went through many editions. Most of the hymns, organized in no discernible way, were from other

325. S. M. *H. BALLOU.

The Same.

1 IN God's eternity
There shall a day arise,
When all the race of man shall be
With Jesus in the skies.

2 As night before the rays
Of morning flees away,
Sin shall retire before the blaze
Of God's eternal day.

3 As music fills the grove
When stormy clouds are past,
Sweet anthems of redeeming love
Shall all employ at last.

4 Redeemed from death and sin,
Shall Adam's numerous race
A ceaseless song of praise begin,
And shout redeeming grace.

A hymn proclaiming the salvation of all, by Hosea Ballou, from an 1839 Universalist collection

collections; those from the Boston Collection which had been considered doctrinally inappropriate were omitted.[34]

David Pickering published, in 1822, *Psalms and Hymns, for Social and Private Worship; carefully Selected from the Best Authors.*[35] A second edition was published in 1832.[36] The hymns were arranged alphabetically according to the first letter of the first stanza of each, and their use required therefore considerable familiarity with their exact wording. This hymnal was "but little used."[37]

In 1823 a committee of the Central (Third) Universalist Society on Bulfinch Street in Boston, headed by Samuel Gray, published their own hymn book, *Christian Hymns adapted to the Worship of God our Savior.*[38] There is no indication that it was used elsewhere. The collection included selections from a wide variety of sources. The Rellys, Murray, and Richards were the Universalists represented, suggesting that theological differences from the majority had a part in both the choice of hymns and the decision to publish a separate hymn book.

A notice appeared in 1829 that Sebastian and Russell Streeter were about to publish a new denominational hymn book. One of its advertised merits was that no hymn was to consist of more than six stanzas, so that they could be sung "without fatigue to the singers or hearers."[39] It appeared under the title *The New Hymn Book, designed for Universalist Societies.*[40] Another of the merits of the new collection was that the hymns were arranged by subject. The hymnal was so popular that by 1834 it had appeared in a pocket edition.[41] By 1837 the hymnal (in both editions) had gone through twenty printings, and by 1845, thirty-five. The hymns were from "approved authors, with variations and additions." Among the "variations" was the rather free editing of some of the hymns, and some of the stanzas were omitted.[42] This was done presumably to keep all hymns to a reasonable length.

A hymnal to have been edited by G.W. Montgomery and William Queal of New York City was announced in 1836, but apparently never appeared.[43] Hosea Ballou 2d was responsible for the next hymnal, *A Collection of Psalms and Hymns for the Use of Universalist Societies and Families,* usually referred to as the "Universalist Collection." It was published in 1837.[44] It was compiled at the request of the Boston Universalist publisher B.B. Mussey, who held the copyright. This book contained the greatest number of hymns that had yet appeared, arranged by subject.[45] The hymnal was widely used, although some criticized the collection for being too stiff and formal, lacking "fervid hymns, without which a Hymn Book is a body without a living spirit."

Manuals for devotional use often contained hymns. Typical was the *Universalist Manual, or Book of Prayers and other Religious Exercises . . .,* compiled by Menzies Rayner and first published in 1839.[46] Rayner included selected verses from 121 hymns. He edited existing hymns with considerable freedom when they were "thought to be longer than necessary; and when the sentiment, in some of the verses, was considered exceptionable."

The first hymnal to provide tunes was published in Philadelphia in 1839, edited by Abel C. Thomas. The copyright originally belonged to him, but was transferred to Gihon, Fairchild & Co. of Philadelphia. The collection, entitled *Hymns of Zion,* which went through numerous printings, was designed primarily for conference meetings and contained 216 pages.

Universalists along the Atlantic seaboard had no monopoly on hymn publishing. A "Western Universalist hymn book" was announced in 1837, to be prepared especially for use in the Midwest and more particularly in Ohio.[47] It was published in 1842 and was compiled by George Rogers.[48] The 1845 and 1848 editions carried the following discursive title:*Universalist Hymn Book, Comprising a Great Variety of Sacred Effusions, Original and Selected, Suitable to the Livelier as well as Graver Purposes of Devotion.*[49] Of the 660 selections, arranged according to subject in forty-five sections, twenty-six were his own. Rogers found the compiling of the hymnal "the severest literary drudgery in which I ever was engaged."[50]

The most widely used Universalist hymnal published in the nineteenth century was *Hymns for Christian Devotion; especially adapted to the Universalist Denomination,* and was also referred to as "Universalist Hymns," which first appeared in 1845.[51] Prepared by J.G. Adams and E.H. Chapin, it was intended for all who claimed allegiance to "a *liberal* and *progressive* Christianity." The hymns were selected for their "devotional tendency, rather than . . . chiefly commendable for their poetical excellence." Users had 1,008, indexed by subject, from which to choose. The hymnal continued to be popular for many decades; its publication was continued by James M. Usher, beginning in 1861. In 1863 a congregational hymn and tune book was prepared by J.S. Barry and B.F. Tweed, entitled *The Musical Supplement and Congregational Melodist,* published by Abel Tompkins two years before his business interests were acquired by the (New England) Universalist Publishing House in Boston. This work was intended to accompany the *Hymns for Christian Devotion,* which was described as "the standard Hymn Book of the Universalist denomination."[52] The two books, taken together, gave Universalists a choice of almost 1,200 hymns.

After 1850 hymns for all kinds of audiences and occasions poured off the presses. Adin Ballou had edited in 1849 *The Hopedale Collection of Hymns and Songs, for the Use of Practical Christians,* but there is no indication that it was used by Universalist congregations. In 1850 Henry Bacon published *A Service Book, with a Selection of Tunes and Hymns for Sabbath Schools.*[53] Abel C. Thomas compiled a *Gospel Liturgy* in 1857 by direction of the General Convention. Within a year

9,000 copies had been sold.[54] It was often used in conjunction with his earlier work, *Hymns of Zion,* which was sometimes referred to also as "Hymns of Devotion."

A committee was appointed by the General Convention in 1860 to prepare a book of hymns and tunes, but a year earlier two of the three members of the committee had already made arrangements with James M. Usher of Boston to prepare such a work.[55] They had not been apprised of their appointment to the committee until the book had already come off the press in the summer of 1861. So the *Gospel Psalmist, a Collection of Hymns and Tunes,* edited by J.G. Adams and S.B. Ball, appeared without any connection with the General Convention. Adams published a smaller collection in 1868, entitled *Vestry Harmonies.*[56]

Sunday School, devotional books, and family hymnals were not neglected in the 1860s. Typical was *The Manual and the Harp,* prepared by L.J. Fletcher and published in 1861 as a 345-page work intended for Sunday School use.[57] Sylvanus Cobb compiled in 1848 a *Primary Hymn and Tune Book* which in 1861 was published in a pocket size and sold for 25 cents.[58] It consisted of 358 selections from many sources, and 82 tunes. J.G. Adams also prepared *The Sabbath School Melodist* in 1866, designed for children from seven to ten years of age. In the following year J.G. Bartholomew compiled a collection also intended for Sunday Schools, entitled *The Altar,* in which all of the hymns were set to music. Thomas W. Silloway, better known as a designer of Universalist academy and college buildings than for his musical contributions, prepared in 1867 *Cantica Sacra: An Aid to Devotion,* with music arranged by Leonard Marshall.

After 1862 hymnals usually bore the imprint of the denominational publishing house, including *Hymns for the Church and the Home,* which appeared in 1865. This collection grew out of a need expressed by the First Universalist Society in Portland, Maine, and was edited by the pastor, E.C. Bolles, with assistance from members of the congregation, including Israel Washburn, Jr.[59] It was available with a liturgy in 1866, under the title *Prayers and Hymns for the Church and Home.* A variant edition was also published in 1866, entitled *A Book of Prayer for the Church and the Home, with Selections from the Psalms, and a Collection of Hymns.*[60] In 1867 a 116-page *Gloria Patri* was published, consisting of "prayers, chants, and responses for public worship," and including "about 100 choice pieces of music."[61]

The 100th anniversary of American Universalism in 1870 brought forth five "centenary hymns" used at the Gloucester celebration. During the same year, of the titles carried in stock by the Universalist Publishing House, nine were hymn books. Between that date and 1937, when *Hymns of the Spirit for Use in the Free Churches of America* was published as a collaborative venture by editorial committees from both the Universalist and Unitarian denominations, several other major collections were published in various editions: *Church Harmonies* (1837); *Church Harmonies New and Old, a Book of Spiritual Songs for Christian Worshippers* (1895); and *Hymns of the Church, with Services and Chants* (1907). Universalists indeed belonged to a music-minded denomination, even though their hymn-writers were not well known outside its limits, and their productions seldom if ever appeared in collections other than their own. This was attributed not to poor quality but to the fact that Universalists were neither as numerous nor as popular as others in the public mind.[62]

General Magazines

Among the most popular forms of "polite literature," especially before the Civil War, were the monthly literary journal, the annual, and the gift-book. The contents, frequently sentimental and romantic in character, and often with religious overtones, were intended to appeal primarily to women, whose names often appeared among the lists of authors of the poetry, short stories, anecdotes, and other "literary effusions," as they were commonly called. Typical of the small gift-books produced by Universalists in 1845 were *Hours of Communion,* by E.H. Chapin; *Sacred Flora, or Flowers from the Grave of a Child,* by Henry Bacon; *Language of Gems,* by Miss Henrietta J. Woodman; and *Fables of Flora* by Miss Sarah C. Edgarton (later Mrs. Mayo). All four were described as "not particularly denominational in their characters."[63] Periodical publications often included steel engravings or even mezzotints of pastoral scenes, classical subjects, or chaste young ladies in demure poses. Women likewise edited many of these volumes, which sometimes included items not only of considerable literary merit but by prominent writers.[64] Such publications provided an outlet for both the literary talents and the social aspirations and frustrations of those concerned with the "woman question" which agitated much of America in the nineteenth century.

For Universalists, their literary productions, usually of a "mild religious character," also did much to remove prejudice against the denomination and to promote the growing respectability which Universalism seemed to be enjoying by the 1830s and 1840s.[65] The literary reputation of American Universalists, and particularly of the women, was also enhanced by the conversion to Universalist ranks of such individuals abroad as Mrs. Mary Martha Sherwood (1775-1851), "the well-known English authoress of numerous religious works for children." Booksellers were finally losing their fear of offering Universalist publications for sale.

Universalists contributed several titles to the vast outpouring of literary periodicals in the nineteenth century. Most representative of this genre was the *Rose of Sharon: A Religious Souvenir,* which first appeared in 1839 and lasted until 1858. In its history there were only two editors, Mrs. Sarah C. Edgarton Mayo, who served from 1839 until her death in 1848; and Mrs. Carolina M. Sawyer, who continued to edit the publication until 1858. Both were wives of clergymen (A.D. Mayo and T.J. Sawyer, respectively). The *Rose of Sharon* was published by the Boston firm of Abel Tompkins and B.B. Mussey, associated for many years with the production of Universalist materials. The magazine, bound in red buckram with elaborate gold scroll work on the covers, had an initial press run of 2,000.[66] The contents of each volume were faithfully listed, as they appeared, in the major denominational papers, usually with highly complimentary remarks to encourage readership.

The *Rose of Sharon,* judging at least from the not overly objective comments of Universalists, was a popular publication, and objections were few and far between. One disgruntled critic (male) did complain that publications such as the *Rose of Sharon* appeared to have overdone one particular theme. "We have become sick and tired of the constant use of one sentiment as the plot of so many stories. We allude to the passion of love–sexual love."[67] There were surely "other sentiments of the human heart" that could be exploited by those writing for such magazines.

One other publication intended to appeal particularly to women appeared the same year as the first issue of the *Rose of Sharon,* but had a shorter history. In 1839 five clergymen edited the *Christian Palladium and Ladies' Amulet,* a semi-monthly published in Portland, Maine. It lasted only until 1842, when it was merged with the *Star of Salvation,* published in Lowell, Massachusetts.

A new annual appeared in 1851 under the title *Lily of the Valley,* edited at first by Mrs. Mary A. Livermore, then residing in Strafford, Connecticut. Published by J.M. Usher of Boston, it was considered a potential rival to the *Rose of Sharon,* and likewise started with 2,000 copies.[68] Described as "a religious and literary gift-book," the *Lily of the Valley* was intended to represent no "sect or society."[69] However, an examination of its contents would indicate that most of the contributors were Universalists. Mrs. Livermore edited the *Lily of the Valley* only two years, and was replaced by Miss Elizabeth Doten. A total of eight volumes appeared (1851-58).

The Universalist-sponsored publication of general literary interest with the longest history and the largest audience was the *Ladies' Repository,* published between 1832 and 1874, under a bewildering array of changing titles and sub-titles.[70] The *Ladies' Repository* had a confusing history. It started as the *Universalist* in May 1832, a monthly sponsored by "an Association of Universalist clergymen," with

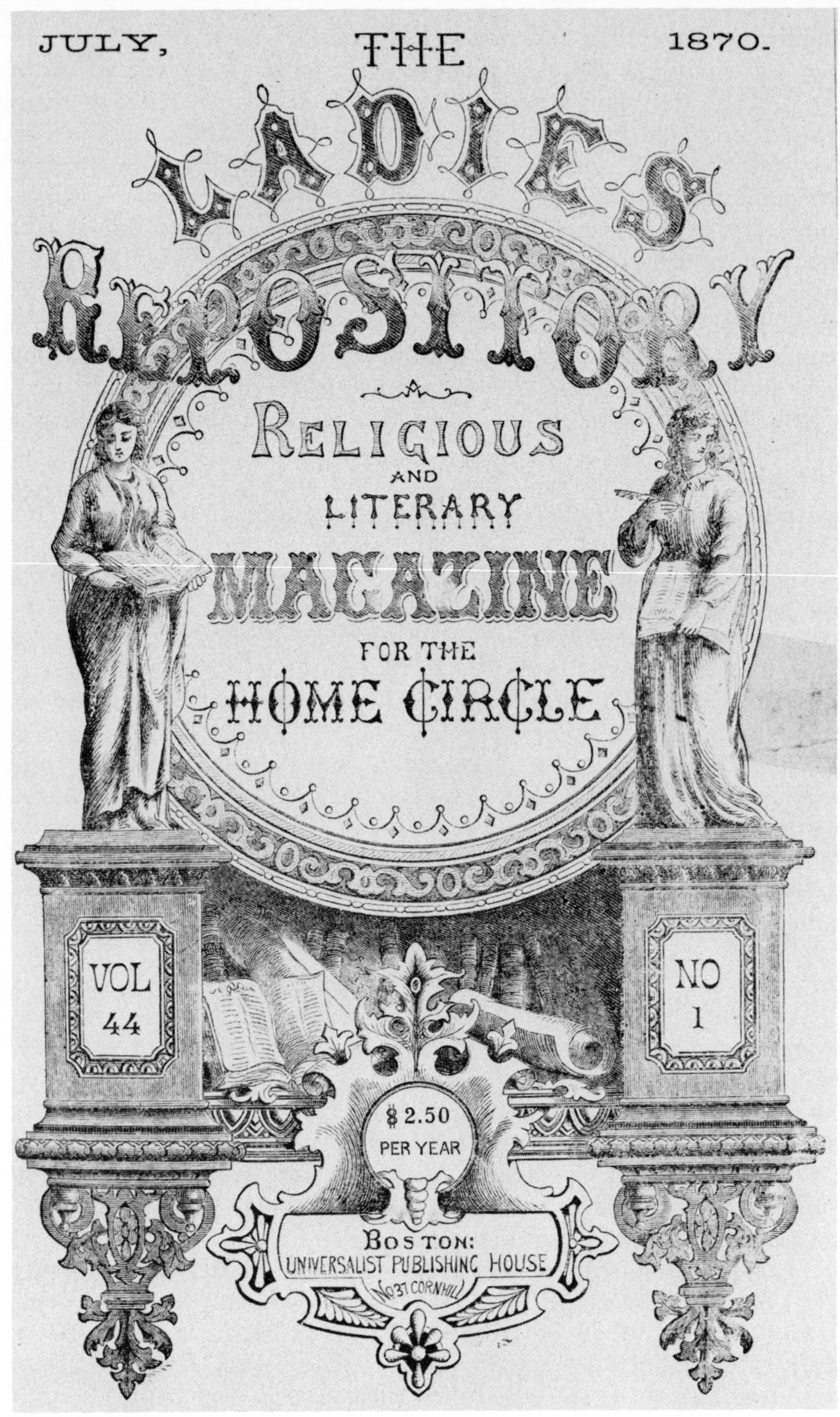

A typical cover of the *Ladies' Repository* (1870)

Sebastian Streeter as principal editor, and was published in Boston by B.B. Mussey. The other original editors were Benjamin Whittemore (Boston), Calvin Gardner (Lowell), J.N. Bugbee (Plymouth), and L.S. Everett (Charlestown). For its first four years the new journal was edited for short periods by a whole series of clergymen. It was Daniel D. Smith who added "Ladies' Repository" to the title in 1834. If any profits accrued from the journal (which evolved from a weekly into a monthly and which originally cost $1.00 a year), they were to be deposited either in a fund for the benefit of the widows and orphans of deceased ministers, or to assist in establishing a literary institution. The younger generation was encouraged "to improve their talents by furnishing brief essays;" many did, particularly, young ladies.

The publication was originally to have been called the *Age of Inquiry*, but the name *Universalist* was selected to promote "a more extensive and general circulation than was originally anticipated." The journal carried, besides "moral essays and doctrinal discussions," sermons and local religious notices, "poetic effusions," and sentimental offerings heavily weighted with religious themes. Included also were articles on such topics as the necessity for separation of church and state, the evils of the "excitements and excesses" of camp-meeting revivalism, and "the importance and influence of female character." When it was decided to broaden the scope of the publication and to appeal particularly to women, Streeter and Otis A. Skinner abandoned in 1833 their plan to publish yet another journal, to have been called the *Ladies' Christian Advocate*.[71] The attention given to feminine interests was reflected not only in the addition of "Ladies' Repository" to the title of the *Universalist* but the appearance in a few issues in 1836 of a subtitle: "Devoted to the Defense and Illustration of Universalism and the Rights of Females."

Henry Bacon, a clergyman, assumed the editorship of the new magazine in 1836 and remained in that position until his death twenty years later. He announced that the publication would be "the constant advocate of female education, and the proper dignity of women," and that its pages were to be intended for "the especial benefit of the softer sex."[72] Many of his editorials were devoted to strong arguments in favor of women's rights in all fields of endeavor.

The *Ladies' Repository* fared reasonably well under Bacon's editorship, with 2,000 subscribers.[73] After his death in 1856 his widow, Eliza A. Bacon, served as editor, assisted by Mrs. N.T. Munroe and Mrs. Caroline A. Soule. But troubles began to brew when the magazine lost over 200 subscribers in 1857-58. Complaints were registered that there were no illustrations; that the magazine (by then a monthly) was overpriced at $2.00 a year; and that the contents were too narrowly feminine and too sentimental. Some readers immediately came to the defense. It was not only the sole literary/religious monthly published by the denomination, but was "totally unlike" other magazines addressed to the ladies.[74] They were "based on the idea that woman is inferior, and therefore are filled with silly novelettes and small talk, scarcely a remove above the juvenile trash designed for little boys and misses just learning to read."

But declining readership had economic implications which the publisher, Abel Tompkins, could not overlook. He had taken over the business management and publication of the magazine in 1836, so had the perspective of several years' acquaintance with the market for such publications. He brought sufficient pressure on Mrs. Bacon and her assistants to force their resignation in 1861. He insisted on less emphasis on "the higher literature and religious thought" and more attention to lighter and more secular material.[75] In her last year as editor, Mrs. Bacon did make the format more legible, introduced a "Child's Department," and started a new series of volume numbering; but these cosmetic changes were in no way sufficient to halt declining popularity. She and her cohorts were replaced by Mrs. Caroline M. Sawyer, assisted by Mrs. Caroline A. Soule, and Miss Minnie S. Davis. A succession of women edited the publication thereafter.[76] The Universalist Publishing House purchased the Tompkins interests in 1865, and the *Ladies' Repository* therefore became one of its responsibilities.

As time passed, both the denominational emphasis in the title and/or sub-title of the magazine lessened and the designation became more and more generalized. When the final volume was issued, the publication had become simply the *Repository*. The word "Ladies" was dropped to avoid confusion with a Methodist journal of similar character and identical title, and because the Universalist publication was neither written exclusively by nor for women.[77] When the magazine came to an end with the December 1874 issue, the editor explained that its mission had been largely accomplished and that general-interest magazines such as the *Atlantic* and *Scribner's* were fulfilling the purpose originally served by the *Ladies' Repository*.[79]

Readers of the *Ladies' Repository* were treated to a varied literary fare, and much besides. There was poetry, although a high proportion of the contributions were prose pieces. Aside from tales from many countries (translated from the French and German, the latter by Mrs. Sawyer), short stories, "literary and romantic musings" which abounded, and inspirational passages with various messages and themes (death being a favorite), there were reports of travels, sketches of famous historical personages, and columns devoted to the works of contemporary literature and the arts, both in the form of book reviews and news notes. One of the most valuable features was a series of biographical sketches of Universalist personalities, many drawn from personal acquaintance and with information unavailable elsewhere.

A final Universalist contribution to popular literature in the mid-nineteenth century was made by Abel C. Thomas (1807-1880), a clergyman who founded and served briefly as editor of a unique publication, the *Lowell Offering.* A native of Pennsylvania, Thomas had a varied career as a printer and as a preacher in a number of states. He accepted the pastorate of the Second Universalist Society in Lowell, Massachusetts, in 1839 after two visits to "that city of spindles" in 1835 and 1838.[79] It was a bustling industrial city which, ten years after its incorporation in 1826, boasted over 17,000 inhabitants and over 20,000 by the time Thomas arrived. It was a leading center of textile manufacturing, staffed predominantly by young men and women who flocked in from both urban and rural areas to tend the machines.[80] There were large numbers of Universalists in the young and growing city, and both Thomas' congregation and that of Thomas B. Thayer, pastor of the First Universalist Society, were made up largely of young men and women who worked in the mills.[81]

A group of young women from one of the mills organized in 1837 an "Improvement Circle" in which they discussed topics of current interest and read to each other various literary pieces which they had composed. Thomas and Thayer saw the value of such activities, and in 1839 established similar circles in their respective churches. The group organized by Thomas met every two weeks. He encouraged "intellectual culture" and the development of writing skills; both he and Thayer spent considerable time correcting compositions and listening to both poetic and prose literary efforts.[82] When Thomas arrived in Lowell in 1839, he and Thayer, together with George W. Gage, edited for two years a weekly newspaper, the *Star of Bethlehem,* in which they published some of the work of the young women.[83] Thomas then conceived the idea of putting into magazine form the best of the writings, and in the fall of 1840 issued a pamphlet entitled "The *Lowell Offering,* a Repository of Original articles written by Females employed in the Mills." After three more numbers were published, the pamphlets became so popular that a new series was started, on a monthly basis. There were sufficient contributions to comprise a complete volume by December 1841. In 1842 *The Operatives' Magazine,* written, edited, and published beginning in 1841 by women members of an Improvement Circle organized at the First Congregational Church, was merged with Thomas' publication.[84] Financed at first by sales and by local advertising, and then by a list of regular subscribers, the first two volumes of the *Lowell Offering* were both published and edited by Thomas. As a "model publisher," whenever there were profits from any issue, he shared them with the contributors.[85] In all, five volumes appeared (1840-1845). The *Lowell Offering* was succeeded in 1847 by the *New England Offering,* published erratically until 1852.

Thomas followed a policy of rigidly excluding all articles or poetry of a sectarian character. For that policy, and because he was a Universalist, he was frequently attacked in the local press and had to explain that the magazine was not a Universalist publication.[86] Mrs. Harriet Hanson Robinson, who worked in the mills from age ten to twenty-three (1835-48), commented in her reminiscences that the good work the Universalists tried to do was "hindered in more than one direction by . . . unchristian persecution."[87] Mrs. Robinson's mother, who ran a boarding house for mill employees for a few years, was a Universalist who had attended Paul Dean's church in Boston. Mrs. Robinson herself eventually became an Episcopalian, but during her youth had been excommunicated from the orthodox Congregational Church because she could not subscribe to the idea of eternal damnation for part of the human race.

Thomas kept very much in the background of the *Lowell Offering,* and his name appears only once in the publication—at the end of the second volume. When two of the young women active in the Improvement Circle movement took over the publishing, editing, and co-proprietorship of the magazine in 1842, it was Thomas who arranged for a public endorsement by prominent local citizens.[88] This was considered necessary because of the prejudice then existing against female editors and publishers. Thomas anticipated the question of whether or not the young ladies actually wrote the material appearing in the *Lowell Offering.* He assured prospective readers, in the unsigned preface to the first volume, that "The articles are all written by factory-girls, and *we do not* revise or re-write them. We have taken less liberty with them than editors usually take with other than the most inexperienced writers."[89]

Thomas did remain quite visible in other respects during his three years in Lowell, for he cooperated with other churches in numerous social-service projects, including the delivery of a series of Sunday evening temperance lectures in the city hall. While there he also had a verbal encounter with Elder Jacob Knapp, a virulent anti-Universalist and Baptist revivalist who spread the word that Thomas, while in Lowell, had dragged his wife by the hair from a revival meeting. Thomas was a bachelor at the time, not marrying until his return to Pennsylvania in 1843.[90]

The *Lowell Offering,* in spite of qualms about its female editorship beginning in 1842, did attract considerable favorable attention. It was endorsed by the *North American Review* and in England was reviewed in the *London Atheneum.*[91] Charles Dickens, who visited the United States in 1842, met Thomas, who sent him a bound volume of the *Lowell Offering.* After his return to London, Dickens, in his *American Notes,* commented that the *Lowell Offering* compared 'advantageously with a great many English annuals.'[92] Harriet Martineau was responsible for a selection from the first two volumes (those edited by Thomas), published in book form in England under the title of *Mind Amongst the Spindles.*[93] Thomas was very proud of the *Lowell Offering,* and in the preface to the first volume called attention to the fact that it was "not only the first work written by factory-girls, but also the first magazine or journal written exclusively by women in all the world."

After his brief sojourn in Lowell, Thomas continued an active life as a pastor, publisher, and editor. While serving in Cincinnati he edited a denominational periodical known as the *Youth's Friend.* During the year 1852 he served as a missionary in England and Scotland. Until his resignation in 1863, in the course of his life he was three times the pastor of the First Universalist Church in Philadelphia, totalling nearly twenty-five years. Besides serving other churches, he was an editor or co-editor of several Universalist papers, a corresponding secretary for the Universalist Historical Society, and a prolific writer. His *Century of Universalism* has been cited frequently in this study.

Universalists made only one more attempt to publish a literary or scholarly magazine after the *Ladies' Repository* came to an end in 1874 and the *Universalist Quarterly* ceased publication in 1891 for financial reasons. The latter was carried at a loss for twenty-seven years by the Universalist Publishing House, which had been responsible for it since 1865.[94] Beginning in 1894, Frederick A. Bisbee published and edited in Philadelphia a monthly known as *To-Day.* It was an interesting hybrid, combining general-interest articles, poetry, and scholarly essays with matters of denominational concern. Most of the contributors were Universalists, and the publication was advertised as "the voice of Universalism," intended to be "helpful to our church." However, individuals outside the denomination were also represented. The lead article in the first issue was a discussion of "The Immigration Question" by Senator Henry Cabot Lodge of Massachusetts.

To-Day was a hybrid in another respect. In its brief history (1894-96), three other publications were united with it—*Manford's Magazine,* the *Non-Sectarian,* and the *Nationalist.*[95] *Manford's Magazine* (1856-96) was a monthly published first in Chicago and then in St. Louis by Erasmus Manford, a Universalist clergyman, and his wife Mrs. Hannah B. Manford. The *Non-Sectarian* (1891-95), a monthly devoted to the cause of liberal religion edited by H.R. Whitmore and W.S. Crowe, was published in St. Louis.[96] The *Nationalist* (1889-91) was a by-product of a utopian non-Marxist socialist novel, *Looking Backward,* published in 1888 by Edward Bellamy. He argued that "the entire capital and labor of nations should be nationalized, and administered by their people, through their chosen agents, for the equal benefit of all."[97] Over 150 Nationalist clubs sprang up all over America, and their first official publication had been the *Nationalist,* a monthly published in Boston and edited by Henry Willard Austin. When Bellamy started his own periodical (the *New Nation*), Bisbee acquired the original publication and united it with *To-Day*.

In spite of all attempts to keep it alive, *To-Day* faltered and died. The publication had entered the highly competitive field of cheap periodicals (it sold for 10 ¢ per issue, $1.00 a year) which were greatly dependent on advertising. Even this source of income was insufficient to sustain the journal. It lasted less than three years (January 1894-March 1896) although its literary quality was high and it contained a wide range of material besides denominational news and comment.

Scholarly Journals: The "Universalist Quarterly" and Its Predecessors

In the spring of 1830 there appeared in the denominational press a prospectus for a new publication which would, it was said, in no way compete with the numerous serials that already dotted the Universalist journalistic landscape. There was, according to the advertisment, a pressing need for a periodical which, unlike newspapers which contained much transient material, would serve "as a safe depository for the more labored essays, for systematic disquisition on doctrine, and for occasional reviews of such works as are peculiarly interesting to Universalists."[98] It was designed to be "a work of investigation, rather than warfare, and of deep search and criticism."[99] The journal thus described was the *Universalist Expositor,* the first issue of which appeared (after some delay) in July, coedited by Hosea Ballou and his great nephew, Hosea Ballou 2d, and published by the Boston firm of Marsh, Capen, and Lyon.

The idea for such a publication had come from Hosea Ballou 2d, whose *Ancient History of Universalism* had just appeared, and who felt strongly that the denomination lacked a serious journal intended particularly for young men planning to enter the ministry and for whom no formal theological training was yet available. The younger Ballou, who wrote over one-third of the articles in the two volumes that were published, presented such intellectual treats as "A Dissertation on the Phrase, Kingdom of Heaven, as used in the New Testament" (with copious documentation), and "Observance of Sunday among the Primitive Christians," as well as poetry based on various Biblical passages.

The *Universalist Expositor,* which was published in alternate months, had begun with only 500 subscribers, and even though a third editor (Linus S. Everett) had been added, and newspapermen like Thomas Whittemore had enthusiastically endorsed the journal, it had only 300 subscribers at the end of the second year and had to be suspended.[100] The proprietors of the *Universalist,* also published in Boston, and established just as the *Expositor* was on the verge of collapse, bought the subscription list for $50 and announced that their weekly semi-popular publication would serve as a substitute for the *Expositor* until sufficient support could be found to reestablish it.

The second effort to establish a scholarly journal was scarcely more successful. Hosea Ballou 2d teamed up with Whittemore to publish the *Expositor and Universalist Review* in 1833, after a concerted advertising campaign which included endorsements from half a dozen Universalist papers and an official vote of encouragement by the Vermont State Convention at its very first meeting as an organization that year.[101] A.B. Grosh, editor at the time of the *Evangelical Magazine and Gospel Advocate* (Utica, New York), like other Universalist spokesmen, was afraid that the scholarly tone of the new journal would frighten prospective readers away, so he reassured them that it would not be of such a "learned cast, filled with Greek and Hebrew words, so as to be unintelligible to common readers."[102] But insufficient patronage continued to plague the editors; it was estimated that 1,000 subscribers were needed to sustain the journal, yet there were only 350 in 1833, in spite of pledges by several individuals to buy five or even ten copies to keep it solvent.[103] There was no alternative but to suspend publication after only one year.

For the next four years a persistent minority endeavored to stir up sufficient interest and support to revive the defunct publication. The General Convention urged in 1836 that the *Expositor* be resurrected, and several associations and state conventions added their voices in support. Universalists were told that their highly respected Hosea Ballou 2d had agreed to edit it if it could be brought to life again. Thomas B. Thayer assured Universalist newspaper readers that even one of Ballou's articles would be worth the modest annual subscription rate of $2.00, and that they should not "be afraid of being strangled with Hebrew, or Greek, or Latin."[104] J.H. Gihon, then living in Berlin, Connecticut, and later to become a prominent Universalist publisher in Philadelphia, volunteered in 1837 to resume publication of the *Expositor* if 650 subscribers could be obtained, and if someone of the caliber and reputation of Hosea Ballou 2d would serve as editor.[105]

The combined efforts of friends of the project in the Boston area finally brought results, for in 1838 the *Expositor* reappeared, with Ballou as editor as promised. The publication was financed this time by the sale of fifty shares (at $5.00 each), with a five-man "Committee of Publication."[106] But the results were no more successful than the earlier attempt, although the life-span of the journal this time was three years; the last issue was published in November 1840. Lack of patronage was again the villain, in spite of diligent efforts on the part of newspaper editors and others to encourage readership. Otis A. Skinner tried the tactic of shaming Universalist preachers by pointing out that only about 150 clergy had subscribed to the *Expositor* out of almost 500 in the denomination, at the very time there was agitation for a better-educated and more knowledgeable ministry.[107] Philo Price, editor of the *Universalist Union* in New York City, refused to carry excerpts or articles from the *Expositor,* on the ground that it might decrease sales, but all of this was to no avail.

With the second demise of the *Expositor,* still another attempt was made to revive it, but the effort was marred by a squabble which erupted among various potential proprietors. J.H. Gihon had in the meantime moved to Philadelphia; operating through the publishing firm of Gihon, Fairchild & Co., he renewed the offer he had made in 1837 to publish the journal. Whereupon New York Universalists countered with a plan to establish their own magazine, to be known as the "Universalist Quarterly Review, and Theological and Literary Magazine." They promised broader appeal than its predecessor had made to the reading public, and announced that Thomas J. Sawyer would be the editor and Philo Price of the *Universalist Union* would be the probable publisher.[108] Meanwhile, Gihon had progressed sufficiently in his planning to solicit subscriptions. Whittemore of the Boston-based *Trumpet* considered the announcement from New York as unfair and unsportsmanlike. He argued that if the journal were revived (and he hoped it would be), it ought to be published by the previous owners, who still had the subscription list, or by Gihon in Philadelphia. Whittemore was immediately criticized by the editor of the *Universalist Union* and accused of having a financial interest in the *Expositor* and of selfishly attempting to keep the defunct publication headquartered in Boston.[109] Whittemore expended considerable energy in vigorously denying all such allegations, and for the next two years continued to urge his readers to make possible the revival of the *Expositor* for the good of the denomination, regardless of where it was published.

The eventual result was the launching of the *Universalist Quarterly and General Review,* which had a continuous history from 1844 through 1891. Published in Boston, it was edited until 1858 by Hosea Ballou 2d, except for a brief interval beginning in 1851 when he requested relief from the ardors of the task and was assisted by Thomas Starr King.[110] George H. Emerson edited the publication between 1858 and 1862 and remained on the staff until a new series was begun in 1864. Emerson's successor, Thomas B. Thayer, held the chief editorial post for more than twenty years—until his death in 1886. He was succeeded by Richard Eddy, who served until the *Quarterly* ceased publication in 1891.

Throughout its existence of almost half a century the *Quarterly* was competently edited and was unquestionably "the most scholarly work of the Universalist Church."[111] Another factor making for success besides a high level of editorial talent was the policy announced in the first volume and consistently followed of including "such departments of general literature, both secular and religious, as shall be deemed of popular interest." But even though its readership extended considerably beyond the confines of the denomination, like most scholarly productions it appealed in the last analysis to only a limited audience which provided only limited support. When the new series began in 1864, the circulation was only 600.[112] It was published at a loss for much of its history; even the reduction of the price from $3.00 to $2.00, beginning in 1883, did but little to increase patronage. Time after time, appeals were made in its columns to both clergy and interested laymen to support the journal in sufficient numbers so that it could be self-sustaining. But for most of its history after 1864 it was a deficit operation under the wing of the Universalist Publishing House.[113] It was not until 1959 that a comparable publication was again sponsored by Universalists—the *Journal of the Universalist Historical Society*—and its appearance had itself represented an effort which had extended over a generation.

The Universalist Publishing House

For almost a century after their appearance as a denomination, Universalists had no central printing, publication, or editorial agency to make their views known or to meet their own needs. The task of making available periodicals, pamphlets, sermons, hymnals, books, and other publications was "a merely personal enterprise" until the 1860s.[114] Universalists depended on such laymen as Henry Bowen, George W. Bazin, James Usher, and Abel Tompkins who operated printing establishments and often conducted bookstores on the side, such as the one on "publishers' row" on Cornhill Street in Boston; or made their own arrangements with whatever printers and publishers were obtainable at any given time or place. The need for facilities under denominational control had become so pressing by the late 1850s that the General Convention took cognizance of the problem and proceeded, over a period of several years, to attempt to provide a central agency.

The first step in establishing a publishing house was taken in 1859, when the *ad hoc* Committee on Publications which was customarily responsible for collecting sufficient funds at convention meetings to cover costs and was expected to have convention proceedings printed and distributed, was enlarged and instructed "to initiate measures for the establishment of one or more religious newspapers to be under the direction of the General Convention."[115] It was out of this very limited and tentative beginning that was to arise the Universalist Publishing House.

The first effort of the committee to carry out its mandate met with no success at all. They entered into negotiations with the proprietors of the *Christian Ambassador,* one of the more successful and influential denominational newspapers, published at the time in Auburn, New York (1851-63), and subsequently moved to New York City (1863-75) and then Utica, New York (1876-78). It was then consolidated with the *Universalist* under the name of the *Christian Leader* in 1879. The *Christian Ambassador* itself had originated in New York City in 1850-51 out of the merger of the *Christian Messenger* (1831-50) and the *Ambassador,* published between 1847 and 1850 by Linus S. Everett in Buffalo. There were five editors of the combined paper—"four too many," in the eyes of Henry Bacon, himself a magazine editor.[116]

The proposal of the committee in 1859 was to take over the New York paper and made it the nucleus of the proposed convention-sponsored publication. However, some of the proprietors of the *Christian Ambassador* were not present when the arrangements were discussed, and they objected. One of the complications was that separate negotiations were under way which resulted in having the New York State Convention take over the *Ambassador.* Having been apprised of this, the committee of the General Convention approached the New York Convention at its meeting in 1859 and offered to take over the paper, assume its responsibilities, and distribute its assets among state conventions in proportion to their patronage of the paper. In spite of the obvious advantages which would have accrued to the New York Convention because of the concentration of subscriptions in its jurisdiction, the convention flatly refused to accept the proposal. It would not agree to lose its identity unless all of the numerous denominational papers would in turn agree to merge "in the *Ambassador* establishments." The General Convention committee quite logically came to the conclusion that "to attempt so much at the outset is to fail altogether." After much debate as to how next to proceed, the General Convention voted that it was "expedient and desirable to establish a publishing house" under its control. The next task was to devise a plan of operation.

At the 1860 convention, nine trustees were appointed to obtain an act of incorporation so that it could receive and disburse funds for the project. The initial treasury was to come from annual contributions from societies for a three-year period. Trustees were to be elected by the state conventions, with one vote for each $100 contributed.[117] The necessity for such an organization was underlined by the authors of the report of the Committee on Sunday Schools that same year. The point was stressed that Universalists had been forced to depend on the sectarian publications of others for their Sunday School materials, and even if usable were expensive to obtain. It was also hoped that one of the functions of the proposed publishing house would be the sponsorship of a Sabbath School journal.

The furthering of the proposal for a national publishing house was delayed by "the disturbed state of our country" between 1861 and 1865. No action was taken at the 1864 General Convention when the matter was discussed, the feeling being that first priority had to be given to the support of educational efforts.[118]

The movement that resulted in the publishing house was actually initiated in New England rather than in New York, when the possibility was explored of acquiring control of the two leading Universalist papers in Boston—the *Trumpet* and the *Christian Freeman.* This seemed particularly timely since Whittemore, editor of the *Trumpet,* had died in 1861 and the paper had consequently changed hands. But complications arose regarding the other paper, because Sylvanus Cobb, editor of the *Christian Freeman,* had been approached prior to Whittemore's death to ascertain the terms on which he would sell his publication. He was not at the time disposed to relinquish it, so he deliberately set the asking price too high to be negotiated.[119] The hurdle was overcome in 1862, when "some friends of the enterprise in New England" formed a joint stock company and combined the two publications as the *Trumpet and Christian Freeman,* an arrangement which lasted for three years. Cobb agreed to take an appointment on the staff of the consolidated papers.

The men who sponsored the plan were all members of the Massachusetts State Convention. It was, therefore, no surprise that it voted to establish "a denominational paper, to be the organ of the Universalists of Massachusetts, and of such other States as shall elect."[120] It was "to become the organ of the New England Universalist Conventions" and proprietors of the several papers in the six-state area were contacted, with offers to purchase their interests. But the response was unencouraging, and the plan was abandoned as too ambitious. So the combined *Trumpet and Christian Freeman,* and the *Myrtle,* a Sunday School paper also published in Boston, became the only publications at first.[121]

In addition all of the publishing and bookstore interests of the firm of Usher and Quinby, and of James M. Usher on Cornhill Street, were acquired. A company was organized as the "New England Universalist Publishing House," on the basis of 250 shares held by stockholders organized in the spring of 1862. After the stock had been paid in, the original plan had been to transfer the company to the denomination and have the profits divided among the states according to the number of subscribers in each. But this plan was modified so that the state convention would take over the business directly, as soon as sufficient numbers of fifteen-year subscriptions (at $20 each) were obtained to cover the original outlay. Two years was the anticipated time necessary. Russell A. Ballou, who had edited the *Gospel Banner* in Augusta, Maine, became the agent of the publishing venture in 1864, in the same year that G.H. Emerson began a long service as editor of the *Universalist,* the successor to the *Trumpet and Christian Freeman.*[122]

One by one the publishing enterprises of individual Universalists were acquired by the new publishing house. The interests of Tompkins and Co. (Boston) were purchased in 1865, and two years later the name of the new organization was changed to the "Universalist Publishing House" in order to indicate that it was intended to be more than a purely regional activity. In 1870 the *Christian Repository,* long published in Vermont, was added, and its list of subscribers was transferred to the *Universalist.* A year later the company had paid all of its expenses and obligations to stockholders, and became an organization with its own trustees. In spite of the intention to make it a truly national enterprise, all of the original board were from New England, with fourteen of the twenty-one trustees from Massachusetts.

Even before it was incorporated in 1872, the publishing house had become a flourishing business. In the year of the denominational centennial observance (1870) it was responsible for five periodicals, carried 150 titles on its book sales list, and had assets of $40,000.[123] If Horace Greeley, prominent Universalist layman, founder of the influential *New York Tribune* (1841) and its editor until his death in 1872, and a delegate to the 1870 convention, had had his way, the publishing house would have been even more substantially supported. He made an unsuccessful effort to divert exclusively to publishing activities the entire Murray Fund of $200,000, the raising of which the General Convention had approved in 1869 as a "special memorial offering" in honor of the centennial.[124]

According to his plan, the publishing house would produce books and tracts on a grand scale. He was positive that at least half of the large Methodist denomination had been recruited as a result of their efficient tract and book business. A similar facility operated by Universalists would, according to Greeley, bring their views "more distinctly and more generally before the public than I think they have yet been brought." He was quite specific in outlining his ambitious plan to blanket the American nation with Universalist writings. He envisioned the subsidized publication of thousands of copies of Hosea Ballou's *Treatise on Atonement* at 50 cents each; the autobiography of John Murray at 25 cents; 100,000 volumes of "standard works;" and 1,000,000 tracts per year.

But the committee to which his proposal was submitted reported unfavorably, on the ground that such a use of the Murray Fund would have been contrary to its purposes and spirit, and would have committed resources to too narrow an object. Furthermore, the General Convention had, in 1869, already approved the establishment of a publication fund "divorced from private enterprise and interest, and conducted for the pecuniary benefit of the Church," and steps had already been taken to create and finance it. A publication fund was established in 1873, with slightly over $2,500 in hand. Mrs. Mary Goddard added $10,000, and by 1886 trust funds amounted to $17,000.[125] Income allowed the publication of denominational materials at or below cost.

The Universalist Publishing House gradually but steadily acquired other papers, although a few, such as the *Universalist Herald* published in Alabama, remained outside of the Boston organization. The *Sunday School Helper* was added to the list of Publishing House imprints in 1873, and in 1879 the *Christian Leader* (Utica, New York) was acquired. The *Universalist* thereupon was renamed the *Christian Leader.* Between 1897 and consolidation of the Universalist Church of America with the American Unitarian Association in 1961, the title of the paper alternated, in rather confusing fashion, between *Christian Leader* (1879-97, 1926-52) and *Universalist Leader* (1898-1925, 1953-61). The genealogy of the paper, traced back to the *Universalist Magazine* (1819), comprised a grand total of 143 volumes.

In the meantime, the publishing house continued to add other Universalist publications to its roster, including several outside of New England and New York State. By 1880 it was responsible for the publication of eleven periodicals in the interest of the church, and possessed the printing plates of 140 volumes of all kinds.[126] In 1881 it purchased most of the publications of the firm of Williamson & Cantwell in Cincinnati, and in 1883 acquired the *Star and Covenant* of Chicago, which in turn had represented an earlier consolidation of papers. It also acquired, in 1884, the *Universalist* published in Chicago; this city became the headquarters of the western branch of the publishing house. The holdings and resources of the Boston-based organization were most impressive by 1886. Its net assets were $65,000, and it either published or owned title to 150 volumes and six periodicals.[127] A business of over $70,000 was conducted that year. The publishing house was to function until the mid-twentieth century, when its activities were merged into the publication activities of the combined Unitarian-Universalist Association.

The Universalist Historical Society

By the early 1830s, as the Universalists became more firmly established, the need was expressed for some systematic means of preserving the evidence of their past. Credit for establishing what became the Universalist Historical Society in 1834 was shared by Thomas J. Sawyer of New York, and Thomas Whittemore, editor of the *Trumpet* in Boston. According to Whittemore, it was Sawyer who originally conceived the idea.[128] The desire to supplement and update Hosea Ballou 2d's *Ancient History of Universalism* (1829) and Whittemore's *Modern History of Universalism* (1830) was, according to Sawyer, the principal reason for creating the organization. It was Whittemore, in any case, who took the initiative.[129] He not only gave the proposal his enthusiastic endorsement, but outlined an ambitious program for it. As to the value of such an enterprise, he had no doubt. Every person ought to be "somewhat acquainted with the history of the religious denomination to which he happens to belong." This was particularly important for Universalists, for "no christians have so great cause for strong attachment to their sect, . . . few greater reason to study the history of their predecessors, or to make themselves familiar with their present circumstances of prosperity."

The following activities and functions were suggested for the proposed society: The collection and preservation of all the historical facts related to the denomination, both ancient and modern; the compilation of statistics for both contemporary use and for future generations; the conduct of correspondence with Universalists in Europe; the collection of all printed materials on the subject of Universalism, including the writings of those who opposed it, and the solicitation of copies from authors and publishers; and the issuance of an annual report of the society's researches, the state of the denomination, and information received from Europe. Whittemore urged that such a society be organized at the next session of the General Convention, which was to meet at Albany, New York, in the fall of 1834, and that thereafter it meet annually at the same time and place as the convention.

At the outset, plans were carried out largely as Whittemore had suggested, although in later days the dates and places of meeting departed widely from his original plans. The organization meeting, attended by "a respectable number of brethren" and chaired by Whittemore, was duly convened on 18 September 1834. A constitution was adopted which provided for a president, vice-president, secretary, treasurer, and as many corresponding secretaries "as it may be deemed expedient from time to time to appoint."[130] The purpose of the Society, as stated in its constitution, was "to collect and preserve facts pertaining to the history and condition of the doctrine of Universalism, together with books and papers having reference to the same subject." The first officers (to be elected annually) were Hosea Ballou 2d, president; Pitt Morse, vice-president; Thomas J. Sawyer, secretary; and Thomas Whittemore, treasurer. Twenty corresponding secretaries were selected, representing eighteen states and Lower Canada; New York and Pennsylvania originally had two secretaries each.

The constitution provided that "any Universalist in good standing" might become a member by signing the document. At least nineteen recorded their signatures in 1834, led by Hosea Ballou. The names of 397 members had been inscribed by 1912.[131] Frank A. Hawes, the secretary in 1912, identified 145 other individuals who had been mentioned in the minutes up to that date, but whose membership status was not certain. Among them was Phineas T. Barnum, the famous showman.

At the annual meeting in 1835, the original officers were reelected and the list of corresponding secretaries was greatly enlarged to include twenty-two states, as well as three Canadian provinces and England. Whittemore became president in 1836 and served for three consecutive years, and again in 1847 and 1848. Hosea Ballou 2d also served a second term (1846). Dolphus Skinner replaced him as treasurer. One is struck by the high proportion of Universalist leadership represented by the charter members. Five had already become, or soon would become, prominent authors in the denomination and five were editors of Universalist periodicals.

The new Society immediately set out to fulfill its self-imposed responsibilities, although it soon abandoned some of the extensive activities originally outlined by Whittemore. The original plan to collect information on the state of the denomination was never carried out, for the *Universalist Register and Almanac,* begun in 1836, served that purpose, and efforts by the Society would have been wasteful duplication. One of the first steps taken was to build up an inventory of material dealing with early Universalism, particularly before 1825. Each member of the Society was requested to furnish a list of all items in his personal library so that the secretary could compile a catalogue. In order to establish contacts abroad, John Relly Beard of Manchester, England, was made a corresponding secretary, and communication was opened with David Thom of Liverpool and with any other individuals either in the British Isles or on the Continent who might assist. Thom became a second corresponding secretary in England in 1836, Richard Roe for Ireland, and William Scott for Scotland. In 1838 Roe declined to serve in an official capacity, but offered his informal services; the difficulty was that he could not subscribe to the unitarian brand of Universalism.[132]

Immediately after the Society had been created, Whittemore enthusiastically reported that it marked "the beginning of one of the most valuable institutions connected with our denomination."[133] Judging from the response, however, Universalists thought otherwise. At no time in its history did more than a fraction of the denomination express any interest in its concerns, participate in its work, or contribute in any way to its efforts. In this respect, it shared the same fate as the scholarly *Universalist Expositor* and its successor, the *Universalist Quarterly and General Review.* The Society remained the province of a small but faithful group, and was never able to complete or even inaugurate some of its major projects. Typical was the unsuccessful effort of Sawyer to have the Society sponsor a scholarly historical journal, first made in 1844. Well over a century elapsed before this was accomplished, when the first volume of the *Annual Journal of the Universalist Historical Society* came off the press in 1959.

The most persistent difficulty over the years was the failure of most of the corresponding secretaries and of the membership in general to show sufficient zeal in collecting both information and publications, which by the constitution were to be deposited with the secretary. The system of appointing corresponding secretaries, although continued until 1848 and resumed in 1901, brought only scattered responses. Allen Green in Georgia sent in valuable recollections of early Universalism there, and W.S. Balch, a resident of New Hampshire at the time he was appointed corresponding secretary for that state, wrote a series of articles entitled "Random Sketches of the Early History of Universalists in New England," published serially in the *Universalist Union* beginning in 1839. Among the most valuable of his efforts was a study of Caleb Rich, one of the important early Universalists who influenced Hosea Ballou, and based largely on interviews with Rich's family and descendants.[134]

Sawyer carried on an active correspondence with David Thom, the leading English Universalist, and persuaded him to write his autobiography which was published in various periodicals.[135] In 1839, corresponding secretaries were requested to solicit autobiographies and reminiscences from every clergyman over fifty years old in their state, but they apparently failed to comply. Sawyer reported in disgust in 1844 that Thom, the corresponding secretary in England, had contributed more than all those in the United States put together. The practice of appointing corresponding secretaries was abandoned after 1913 as a fruitless endeavor. In that year, of the twenty-four appointed, only two agreed to serve, and there was no response at all from most of the others.

Time after time the Society sought to obtain information and records from various groups within the denomination, and almost invariably the requests were ignored. Sawyer had almost no response to a plea to state conventions that they send copies of their proceedings so that they could abstract them and thereby preserve "a correct and continuous history of our denomination." State conventions were asked in 1882 to furnish histories of their parishes, but the returns were disappointing.

The collection of historical materials grew very slowly and unevenly in the early years. There was no provision for dues in the original constitution, so the Society had to depend on gifts of books and on voluntary contributions. In order to obtain money to purchase "rare foreign works," it was decided to depend on collections taken during public religious services at General Convention meetings. The first such collection (in 1838) brought $52. Collections averaged about $50, although one was only $16. The decade of the 1840s, during the presidencies of Stephen R. Smith (1839-42) and W.S. Balch (1843-45), then also from New York State, was a period of rapid growth of the Society's library. It totalled between 150 and 200 volumes in 1840, and had reached 300 by the end of the next year; almost half had been purchased by a library committee which was created early in the Society's history. The bulk of the purchases were foreign-language publications, including several imported from Berlin, and averaged less than $1.00 per volume. Much of this accomplishment was due to the indefatigable secretary, Thomas J. Sawyer, who for many years doubled informally as librarian. He scoured second-hand bookshops in New York City and attended all the auctions he could manage.

For much of the nineteenth century, the Society library was almost a one-man operation in the hands of Sawyer. He served as secretary and chief spokesman for the library and the Society for no less than sixty-five years (1834-1899) until failing eyesight, then death, put an end to his labors. He was not only an ardent Universalist but a knowledgeable bibliophile with scholarly interests that ranged widely. It was he who was primarily responsible for obtaining books from Europe (including the multi-volumed complete works of Origen) and for maintaining correspondence with Universalists abroad. He planned for several years to update Hosea Ballou 2d's *Ancient History,* and to write a history of Universalism in Germany, but other commitments prevented the realization of this life-long ambition.

There were nearly 500 volumes in the library by the time Sawyer made his customarily detailed (and discursive) report at the meeting in 1843. A year later, there were nearly 600 volumes. Besides these, there were dozens of tracts, pamphlets, sermons, and other miscellaneous matter. He considered it of sufficient value by 1844 to take out $500 in fire insurance. The rapidly growing bulk of the library also caused Sawyer increasing concern, for it was in his charge. He resided in New York City at the time the Society had been organized, and the library went wherever he might go. When he moved to upstate New York in 1845 to take charge of Clinton Liberal Institute near Utica, the library went with him, and was used by students in the theological course which he conducted independently of the school. Upon his return to New York at the close of 1852, the library had to be moved a second time—and again at his own expense.

Financing the activities of the Society in the building up of a library continued to be uncertain at best, dependent as it was on the technique of "passing the hat" at Convention meetings. Between September 1844 and September 1845, 110 books were added, and the funds were exhausted. In fact, a deficit occurred which was not made up until a record-breaking collection of $100 was taken up at the 1847 Convention.[136] By then, a total of 443 volumes had been purchased for a library comprising nearly 800 volumes. The collection had become so sizeable by 1847, and so many duplicates had been accumulated, that Sawyer decided to start a second collection to be located elsewhere than at Clinton, New York, where he was then living. He was concerned "in case an accident should occur from a conflagration."[137] Sawyer approached Hosea Ballou 2d, who had moved to Medford, Massachusetts in 1838; the latter readily agreed to receive all duplicate material and to serve as "a kind of joint librarian."

In his constant search for every scrap of information about Universalism, Sawyer encountered the greatest difficulty of all in acquiring copies of the dozens of newspapers published by Universalists. He was fearful that many would be "lost forever" if not collected as promptly as possible. Unfortunately, his fear was well grounded, as any student of Universalist history can testify. One of Sawyer's few triumphs in collecting old newspapers was the acquisition in 1843 of a complete set of the *Christian Repository* (1820-29) donated by Samuel C. Loveland of Vermont. One of Sawyer's chronic frustrations was obtaining complete runs of newspapers—a problem that was never solved by either him or the Society. Whittemore, through the *Trumpet,* issued frequent pleas for assistance in filling out sets, but they brought few results. He did advertise successfully for a complete set of his own newspaper, which was donated to the Harvard Library.[138] Ironically, the Society itself did not have a set at the time; as the result of a special appeal, a complete set was finally pieced together in 1846.[139]

The Society's activities were never considered part of the annual General Convention programs, although it had been provided in its original constitution that Society meetings would take place at the same time and place as the Convention. The Society constitution was amended in 1840 to provide for meetings "without reference to the sessions of the United States Convention," which meant for all practical purposes that it would meet whenever a sufficient number could be assembled during recesses or intermissions, or after adjournment of scheduled Convention sessions. This rather unsatisfactory arrangement resulted in the failure of the Society to meet at all between 1849 and

1873.[140] Sawyer wrote a tart letter to the newspapers in 1852 complaining that no one paid any attention to the Society, and that it was impossible to assemble a quorum at Convention meetings to do business because insufficient time—or no time at all—was allotted to it.[141] He was ready at all times to report, but there was no one to listen to him.

The Society may have ceased to meet for some twenty-six years, but it continued to exist. A collection in its behalf was taken up at the 1855 Convention.[142] Three years later, Sawyer was given permission to speak to the Convention for a few minutes prior to taking up a collection, and reported that the library consisted of 1,200 volumes, of which approximately 800 had been purchased.[143] When the decision was made at the 1874 Convention by a small group of interested individuals to revive the Society, Sawyer was at the forefront. He explained that, notwithstanding the "long period of apparent inactivity," contributions of books and other material had continued to be received. The official evidence of the resurrection of the Society came with the election of a full slate of officers, with Abel C. Thomas of Philadelphia as president and Sawyer as secretary, and the announcement that it would meet in 1875 in conjunction with the General Convention to be held in Lynn, Massachusetts.

The library, meanwhile, had changed location and continued to grow. It had remained in Sawyer's possession during most of the period when no meetings were held, but by the 1850s he had considered more and more seriously the possibility of locating it at Tufts College. The institution had been chartered by Universalists and had opened in 1854. It was Sawyer who had written a circular calling for a special Educational Convention which had met in 1847 and had resulted in Tufts' establishment. He was closely involved in the affairs of the new institution, and had been a long-time associate and friend of Hosea Ballou 2d, its first president. In fact, Sawyer had declined the presidency of the newly chartered institution when it had been offered to him in 1852. He did accept the first professorship at the Tufts Divinity School in 1869 and served as its dean from 1882 until his retirement ten years later.

In 1861 Sawyer had sounded out the possibility that the Society library might be moved to Tufts. President Ballou had been receptive to the idea and had even offered to serve as its librarian.[144] He offered space adjacent to his office on the second floor of the main college building. He also suggested that the Society library be kept separate from the college library, at least until a full-time librarian was provided. Ballou himself served as the college librarian until just prior to his death in 1861; a full-time librarian was not appointed until 1884, and his responsibility was not primarily the Society's collection.

When Sawyer was appointed to the Tufts faculty in 1869, he

brought the library with him. It was housed initially in the same room as the college library, but on separate shelves, and was made available to both faculty and students. When the college library was moved to another building in 1887, the Society library was also relocated there. The bulk of it was stored on the top floor, and was hence separated from the main college collection. Part of the Society library remained in that same building (Middle, later renamed Packard Hall) until 1928, while the remainder, including periodicals and other items not frequently used, were placed in the stacks of Eaton Library which had been opened in 1908.

The Society library had increased to over 2,700 volumes by 1885, and the number of miscellaneous unbound items had risen into the hundreds. So many duplicates had been acquired by that date (including those assembled earlier by Hosea Ballou 2d), and space had become so limited that Sawyer recommended donation of extra copies to the Ryder Divinity School of Lombard University, a Universalist-sponsored institution. At the suggestion of Anson Titus, one of the more active members of the Society, the practice of exchanging duplicates with other religious historical societies was begun on a limited scale. After Lee S. McCollester became the librarian in 1912, the practice was followed for many years of giving duplicates to students in the theological school at Tufts.

After the decision had been made in 1874 to rebuild the Society, Charles H. Fay (then of Washington, D.C.) was elected president the following year, and Sawyer (as might have been expected) was chosen as the combined secretary and librarian. The Society took a very business-like attitude toward its rebirth. It decided to incorporate under Massachusetts law. Necessary legal steps were taken in 1876, and on 1 January 1877 the rejuvenated organization received its new charter. It was incorporated as an entity with headquarters in Boston, and with no capital stock. Membership, as provided at the organization meeting in 1876, was open to any persons interested in the objects of the Society who signed the bylaws which had been adopted at the same time. The object of the Society remained the same as it had been in 1834: ". . . to collect and preserve Books, Periodicals, Pamphlets, and whatever relates to the history of the doctrine of Universal Salvation." Officers were to be a president, vice-president, secretary, treasurer, and a board of five directors, including all the officers except the vice-president; two additional directors were therefore to be elected each year.

In practice, however, no more than minimum attention was paid to the niceties of constitutional and bylaw provisions among the small group that kept the Society going over the years. The board of directors had increased to seven members by 1933, and included all the officers in spite of the original provision in the constitution. It was realized by 1942 that discrepancies such as this had developed over the years, and a committee was appointed to recommend revisions that would bring the rules and the actual practice into harmony. This was accomplished when the Society was reorganized in 1954 and a new constitution was adopted placing the officers on the board.

According to the Articles of Incorporation drawn up in 1876, the annual meetings of the Society were to be held at the same time and place as the General Convention unless otherwise ordered by the board of directors (which was referred to interchangeably as the "executive committee" in the records). The Society had no more success in finding a place in General Convention proceedings after 1875 than it had before 1850. A formal request was made in 1878 and again in 1886 that time and facilities for a public meeting be provided, and a place reserved for it on the program, but to no avail. The expressed hope that Society business would eventually become "a feature of our annual Conventions" remained only a hope. On more than one occasion the Society found time at Conventions to do no more than hurry through an election of officers and adjourn. The effort to have Society meetings coincide with Conventions was finally abandoned in 1904; the constitution was amended to provide that thereafter the Society would meet in Boston in May of each year. Meetings were held at various churches in the area, and often at Ballou Hall in the then headquarters of the Universalist Publishing House on Boylston Street. After the library had been moved to Tufts, and particularly after 1930, when new facilities become available there, the annual meetings usually took place on the Medford campus.

After its incorporation in 1877, the Society entered a period of stability and steady, if not spectacular, growth for over a decade. Richard Eddy, already busy collecting material for his monumental two-volume *Universalism in America,* was elected president in 1876 and held that office for thirty years. Sawyer continued his labor of love as secretary and librarian, and a number of prominent clergymen and laymen held the posts of vice-president and treasurer, and served on the board of directors. Such was Llewellyn D. Seaver of Cambridge, Massachusetts, who was vice-president of the First National Bank of Boston, and who served as treasurer of the Society for twenty years until his death in 1936.

The Society reached a low point in its vitality in the early 1890s. In 1893 there were only eight members (one more than the minimum for a quorum) present at the annual meeting, and both the treasurer and secretary were absent. The Society lost the services of Sawyer from that year onward because of the infirmities of age, and the office of assistant secretary was created to carry on his work. The man who served in that capacity (Charles F. Potter) died only three years later. George T. Knight, of the Tufts Divinity School, who became secretary in 1899, also served as acting treasurer for the two succeeding years. After a period of personnel readjustments, the Society then went through a phase of revival and expansion. Hosea Starr Ballou replaced Richard Eddy in the presidency in 1907 and served through 1941. If his terms on the board of directors and as vice-president are included, Ballou served the Society in an official capacity for forty-two years. Another individual having a long association with the Society was Theodore A. Fischer, who served in various capacities (including the vice-presidency) for a total of twenty-seven years (1912-1938). By the time of the First World War, the Society's activities had expanded to such an extent that five committees were in operation, concerned with the library, membership, necrology, marking historical sites, and collection of manuscripts.

The Society received its first bequest in 1900, a gift of approximately $1,700 from the estate of John J. Low. He had been a Boston jeweler whose business was carried on under the firm name of Shreve, Crump, and Low. Low, who lived in Jamaica Plain and had originally attended the local Unitarian church, was attracted to the Universalist church by the preaching of Charles H. Leonard, and after 1864 became a strong supporter of Universalism and a benefactor of the church. The Society also became the beneficiary of the Sawyer Memorial Fund which had been established by the Universalist Club of Boston following Sawyer's death in 1899. By 1937 the original fund of $61 had grown to $210.91 by accumulation of interest.

The assets of the Society grew steadily after 1908, although the sources of capital for its investments in stocks and bonds were not clear from either the minutes or the treasurer's reports. They were presumably derived from gifts and bequests and judicious investments on behalf of the Society by Hosea Starr Ballou, Jr. through the Boston firm of Ballou, Adams & Company. The Society, even up through the 1940s, was careful not to use its principal for any expenditure. Society assets were listed as over $2,800 in 1913, and had risen to over $5,700 by 1926. Assets were almost $8,000 in 1934, and in spite of the Great Depression, the market value that year was listed as greater than the book value by some $400. By 1946 the assets were in excess of $13,700, with an operating budget slightly in excess of $3,200.

Between the time of Sawyer's death in 1899 and the year 1910, the library did not have a custodian to make it available for use. For many years after that date, when the offices of secretary and librarian were separated, Prof. George T. Knight, Sawyer's son-in-law, served in the latter office. In 1910 Librarian Knight was authorized to purchase a bookplate and to impress the seal of the Society on the title page and page 100 of each book. He was also instructed to secure an estimate of the cost of cataloguing the collection. When Lee S. McCollester became dean of the Crane Theological School in 1912, he also became the Society's librarian and served for twenty-seven years. He was elected president in 1942 and served until his death two years later. Because of the press of administrative and teaching duties, Dean McCollester was unable to devote much time to the library, so Miss Ethel Munroe Hayes served as assistant librarian. Miss Hayes, the Tufts librarian from 1907 until 1928 and reference librarian until her retirement in 1943, began her services for the Society in 1912.

The problem of keeping the library intact was a serious one for many years. When the outbreak of the First World War resulted in the transfer of the headquarters of the Crane Theological School, together with its library, to Packard Hall in 1914 (where it remained through 1927), the Society library continued to be divided between that building and Eaton Library, with the understanding that materials most frequently used by theological students would remain in Packard and the remainder would be stored in Eaton. McCollester recognized the practicality of this arrangement, although he did not like it. Ideally, he believed that the entire collection should have been consolidated in the main library, and that a continuous inventory should have been established so that materials would not be lost or misplaced. His often-repeated recommendation that manuscripts, photographs, and other Universalist memorabilia possessed by the Society be placed on permanent display finally bore fruit. The College, on authority of President John A. Cousens (himself an active Universalist layman), set aside a room in Miner Hall for the purpose in 1933. The dean also had the satisfaction of seeing some of the prized possessions of the Society displayed in a special exhibit in 1941, when the School of Religion and Tufts College played host to the General Convention.

When the theological school was returned to its former location in Miner Hall in 1928, that portion of the Society's library which had been located in Packard Hall was also transferred until space could be found for it in Paige Hall (adjoining Miner) which was in the process of renovation. By then, the holdings of the Crane theological library and those of the Society had become almost hopelessly intermixed, for many items had been stamped as belonging to both. According to McCollester, even new acquisitions of current materials intended for the use of Crane students had been assigned to the Society even though not paid for out of the latter's funds. The failure to distinguish between the two collections could be traced all the way back to Sawyer's tenure in the 1870s. The interchange of materials was continued for many years in spite of McCollester's concern; after all, his own theological students were benefitting from the presence of the Society's library.

The librarian of the Society also faced another dilemma which had become acute by the late 1920s. The college library was being more and more pressed for space for its collections and needed that taken up by the Society's library. The situation was made even more embarrassing by the fact that, since 1908, the Tufts library had borne, with the exception of a cataloguing project in 1917, the entire cost and overhead of housing and maintaining the Society's library. The only solution seemed to be the removal of the entire library either to Miner or Paige Hall. What did happen was that the books and manuscripts were moved out of Eaton Library, but the bound periodicals and a few miscellaneous items were not. The material in Eaton was not sorted out and separated until the 1950s.

Only one catalogue of the library holdings was ever printed and distributed to the membership (in 1839), despite frequently announced plans to publish periodic inventories. Whittemore, editor of the *Trumpet,* occasionally printed lists of acquisitions in his paper, as did Philo Price, editor of the *Universalist Union,* but they gave no systematic overview of the contents of the collection. Secretary Sawyer had been authorized in 1844 to publish a catalogue, but his removal from New York City to Clinton, New York, the following year prevented it. He was requested again in 1847 to prepare one, but it was never completed. Thirty-one years elapsed before the request was repeated. In 1941 the secretary called attention to the fact that the request made in 1878 had never been carried out. Sawyer had, in 1886, announced that a catalogue was almost ready, but there were no funds to publish it. A card catalogue was finally compiled and took the place of a separately printed listing.

It was not until 1916 that money was appropriated to begin cataloguing the library. A student was employed during the summer of 1917 under the direction of Miss Hayes and consisted of a listing by author and title only, and only of books then on the shelves. Neither periodicals nor a subject catalogue was included, although the latter had been planned. Another cataloguing project was undertaken in 1938 (at no cost to the Society) by a work crew sponsored by the depression-born National Youth Administration, and again in 1947, by a student in the School of Religion.

The library remained in Miner Hall until 1938, when it was transferred to Paige Hall and was stored for several years in an unheated basement area known as the "crypt." Meanwhile, Alfred S. Cole joined Miss Hayes as a second assistant librarian in 1932, a year after he was appointed to the faculty of the theological school. Until his departure from Tufts in 1955, he served the Society in many capacities—as librarian between 1939 and 1943, and as president in 1944 and again in 1947. He was succeeded as librarian by Miss Blanche H. Hooper who, like Miss Hayes, was an alumna of Tufts. Miss Hooper served on the college library staff in various capacities for forty-eight years.

It was largely through Cole's efforts that the Society's collection was protected and sustained through very trying years. One of his major projects was to collect photographs and portraits of every Universalist clergyman and clergywoman and to write brief biographical sketches to accompany each. It was he who worked with the officials of the Work Projects Administration, beginning in 1939, to furnish information and assistance on behalf of the denomination for their comprehensive history and inventory of church records in the United States. The *Inventory of Universalist Archives in Massachusetts* was the first one published by the Historical Records Survey in the state and one of the few of the projected series actually completed and published by 1942 when the Second World War intervened.

One of the activities in keeping with the spirit of the Society's purposes was the delivery of papers on historical subjects. The scholarly tone of many of its meetings had been set in 1835, when Abel C. Thomas of Philadelphia read a paper on Universalist books published prior to 1800 which were in his personal library. He prepared descriptive bibliographies of these works which were published in the *Universalist Union* from time to time.[145] Hosea Ballou 2d delivered a learned discourse in 1836 on universalism in the Greek Orthodox Church. After the practice of preparing papers fell into disuse for many decades, it was revived in the early twentieth century with the addition of poetry readings. Typical of the "literary exercises" were the following: E.W. Whitney, "History of Universalism in Milford, Mass." (1904); Anson Titus, "Religious Life in New England before the Revolution," and a poem composed and read by David L. Maulsby of the Tufts faculty (1905). In 1911 Mrs. Gertrude Rugg Field read several original poems written for various denominational occasions.

Part of the Society treasury after 1940 was used to assist in the publication of various Universalist works. Over $200 was contributed in 1941 to defray the costs of producing *Hell's Ramparts Fell,* a biography of John Murray by Clarence R. Skinner, then dean of the Tufts School of Religion, and Alfred S. Cole, under the imprint of the Universalist Publishing House. The Society also contributed $250 toward the publication of Dean Skinner's collection of essays, *A Religion for Greatness,* which appeared in 1945 after considerable delay caused by the Second World War.

The period between the Second World War and the mid-1950s was an uncertain one for the Society. It failed to meet for seven years after 1947 and the meeting scheduled for May 1953 was not held because of the lack of a quorum. The directors finally resorted to a mail ballot of the membership "to determine whether or not the Society shall continue its existence or that, after a long and beneficial career, its usefulness as a separate organization has now ceased." With the strong possibility that the decision would be to dissolve the Society, the directors prepared a plan by which they would be authorized to transfer both the library and the net balance of the treasury to the Trustees of Tufts College.

Another attempt was made to convene the Society in June 1953, and those present, after much discussion, voted to continue the organization as then constituted.[146] Alfred S. Cole, who had previously served in that capacity, was elected president; E. Louise Jewell, secretary; Thomas S. Knight, treasurer; and Richard B. Coolidge, director.

The determination of a handful of interested individuals in 1953 to keep the Society alive was reinforced by an address delivered to the General Assembly of the Universalist Church of America at its meeting in Andover, Massachusetts, in August. The person who delivered a forceful plea for the revitalization of the Society was Robert Cummins, outgoing General Superintendent, and a member of the Society since 1941. The immediate result was a burst of enthusiasm which rescued the Society from continued decline and probable demise, and brought new life and blood into the organization. Applications for membership poured in, and at the 120th annual meeting of the Society, held in the Crane Library of the School of Religion on the Tufts campus in 1954, seventy-seven new members were added.[147]

The annual meeting in 1955 was an historic occasion for the Society. It was held in Detroit, in conjunction with the meeting of the General Assembly of the Universalist Church and the first biennial meeting of the Council of Liberal Churches which had been organized in 1953 in Andover, Massachusetts, at a joint meeting of the Unitarian and Universalist denominations. The Society's meeting in 1955 was the first in over half a century held in conjunction with its "parent organization," the Universalist Church of America. As the secretary emphasized, the Society had become again the denomination-wide organization it was intended to be, and was no longer limited to the Boston area, as had been provided in 1904. It was no longer "an orphan . . . handicapped by a small provincial membership." Its treasury was well-filled, it had broadened its spheres of activity, and had dramatically increased its membership.

Several changes were made in the organization and internal operation of the Society after its rejuvenation in 1954. An almost completely new slate of officers was elected, with Albert F. Ziegler as president (who resigned after less than a year and was succeeded by Emerson H. Lalone). Melvin C. Van de Workeen served as secretary, and Robert Cummins as treasurer.

The momentum of the Society's activities was temporarily slowed in 1956 by the simultaneous resignation of the president, the vice-president, and the treasurer, because of the pressure of other commitments, and in the case of President Lalone, of illness. But the Society vigorously continued its expanded programs, and by 1959 had 145 members on its rolls.

The financial state of the Society was a matter of congratulation in the 1950s and 1960s. A balance often exceeding $1,000 was maintained annually to cover operating expenses. Principal, in the form of stock investments in public utilities, industrials, investment trusts, and trust funds (such as the Sarah P. Blake Fund) held by the Universalist Church of America for the Society, amounted to over $24,000 in 1954. As Treasurer Cummins had pointed out in his annual report in 1955, one motive behind the effort to reinvigorate the declining Society the previous year had been "to save for and preserve to our Universalist cause the . . . rather substantial treasury."

The investment assets of the Society grew rapidly in the late 1950s. In 1959 they had a market value of almost $40,000, a gain of some $15,000 above cost in one year only. In 1963 the management of invested funds was turned over to the Unitarian Universalist Fund (investment pool) of the Association, with the proviso that the Society continue to maintain ultimate control of its funds. Investment funds alone exceeded $59,000 in 1965 and 1966, and when a decision was made in 1969 to subsidize a major research and publication project which would use capital funds, the general investments had a market value in excess of $50,000. However, sharp fluctuations and a precipitate drop in the stock market after 1970 cut deeply into general fund investment assets. In 1974 the market value of the securities held in the name of the Society had fallen to less than $17,000–some $5,000 below book value. There was increasing concern expressed by the directors about meeting the commitments the Society had made by that time.

It was not until the 1930s that any official recommendation was made that a new history of the denomination should be written. Richard Eddy's *Universalism in America,* the second volume of which had appeared in 1886, was the only reasonably systematic and comprehensive work that had been published. Dean Lee S. McCollester at Tufts had frequently suggested that Eddy's history be updated, and had Alfred Cole in mind as a possible author. However, it was not until 1944 that any actual step was taken in this regard. In that year, Dean Clarence Skinner was appointed chairman of a committee to oversee a project to update Eddy's work and carry the story to 1940. It was to have been written by a Universalist layman (to be selected). It was agreed that the capital funds of the Society would not be touched, and that the author would receive no more than $200 for his efforts; an additional $50 was authorized for student assistance. After one "report of progress," the undertaking was temporarily abandoned following the retirement of Dean Skinner in 1945. The idea was revived less than a decade later, when Clinton Lee Scott was commissioned by the Department of Education of the Universalist Church of America to write a history.

The librarian, who in 1954 had been designated as the Society's publication representative, had been requested to confer with Scott regarding his proposed history. The possibility was to be explored of having his history of the denomination sponsored solely by the Society rather than by the Department of Education. Negotiations between Scott and the Society finally produced concrete results in 1957, when the directors of the Society were authorized at its annual meeting to proceed with publication plans. Scott's work appeared later in 1957, and was entitled *The Universalist Church of America: A Short History*. It was actually only a brief sketch of less than 125 pages, and was put into print so hurriedly that numerous errors in proofreading slipped by.[148] Scott's work was considered primarily an introduction to the denomination for new members. It was published in part on the urging of the Department of Education and the Board of Trustees of the Universalist Church.[149]

One of the visible evidences of the renewed vitality of the Society in the late 1950s and early 1960s was the appearance in 1959 of the first volume of the *Annual Journal of the Universalist Historical Society*. The new publication was intended to be not only a means of preserving in permanent form "selected materials from the past," but "to publish original materials of historical interest to Universalism," and to encourage further research and writing. It actually served very much the same purposes as had the earlier *Expositor* and its successor, the *Universalist Quarterly*. By 1976 ten volumes had been published.[150]

The need for continued research and publication of studies of Universalism continued to be expressed by members of the board of directors. In 1968 Theodore Webb, newly elected to the board, suggested the establishment of a special Fund for Universalist Studies, with possible assistance from several churches in the Boston area possessing substantial resources. A committee was appointed to solicit funds, and over a three-year period ending in 1972 had secured $4,500. The original purpose of the special fund had been a very broad one. However, by 1969 the committee appointed to raise money decided to concentrate whatever resources could be obtained on one major project: The preparation of a comprehensive institutional history of the denomination which had been discussed since the 1930s and even planned, but which had yet to be written. The ambitious project was undertaken, beginning in the fall of 1970, with the great bulk of the Society's assets on hand or anticipated, pledged to its support.

The Universalist Historical Society library, in many ways the heart of its operation, received considerable attention in the 1950s, after the revival of the Society.[151] In 1968 an event occurred at Tufts which was to have a profound effect on the future of the Society's library. By vote of the Tufts trustees, the Crane School was closed, effective at the end of that academic year. The Society library, occupying what the university librarian referred to as "prime space" adjacent to the Crane library collection, had been assigned to its location "entirely because of the relationship with the Crane Library." With the School of Religion closed, its library was broken up, some of it being incorporated into the Tufts library, and other parts donated to various institutional libraries, including those related to Unitarian Universalism. By 1972 the rapid growth of the Tufts library holdings, in spite of the expanded facilities provided in 1965, had made provision of additional space a matter of growing importance. As the university librarian pointed out to the Society in 1972, every effort would be made to find suitable quarters for its library elsewhere on the campus. But diligent search for a suitable alternate location at Tufts having proved fruitless, the university librarian made the tentative suggestion that the Society might consider relinquishing its library.

The Society responded to the librarian's suggestion by appointing a study committee in 1972 to review the situation and to suggest ways to somehow preserve its collection. The directors were divided as to the best location for the Society library, some suggesting that it remain permanently as Tufts under arrangements to be worked out; others felt that the Harvard Divinity School library (the Andover-Harvard Theological Library) was the logical place, particularly in view of the fact that much of the Unitarian historical material was already there. Other suggested locations discussed between 1973 and 1975 were the Massachusetts Historical Society, the library of the Meadville/Lombard Theological School at the University of Chicago, and even the Library of Congress. There seemed to be no way by which the Society could itself provide either a suitable location or the necessary servicing of the collection.

The disposition of the library became the principal item on the agenda of the annual meeting of the Society, held in New York in 1974. A motion, prepared by the board, provided that the ownership of the collection be transferred to the Andover-Harvard Theological Library, effective on or after 1 September 1974. This proposal was in response to the questionnaire sent out to the membership earlier that year, in which an overwhelming majority of the seventy-five replying, indicated a preference for the Harvard location. However, a final decision was again postponed, there being considerable sentiment at the annual meeting for yet another review of the entire matter. No further progress having been made in renewed negotiations with Tufts, the Society gave its formal notice to terminate the agreement of 1967, and the transfer of the library to Harvard was approved by vote of the membership of the Society at its annual meeting in 1975. On 31 December of that year, the move was completed. The end of an era had come for the library, which had been on the Tufts campus for 106 years, and a new chapter was ready to be written as the collection so painstakingly accumulated by Thomas J. Sawyer and his contemporaries over a century before, and augmented over the years, was established in a new home.

A new chapter in the history of the Society as well as its library was written in 1978. At meetings during the annual General Assembly of the Unitarian Universalist Association in Boston the Universalist Historical Society and the Unitarian Historical Society, organized in 1901, agreed to merge as the Unitarian Universalist Historical Society. The possibility of union of the two groups had been discussed as early as the spring of 1960, over a year before the official consolidation of the two denominations. Eventual merger of the two historical societies seemed to have been taken for granted by a majority of the directors of the Universalist society at the time, although there had been but few formal joint endeavors before 1960. A step toward closer cooperation between the two societies had been taken, beginning in 1961, with the holding of joint sessions at the annual meeting of the denomination, with alternate sponsorship of a speaker.

The Unitarian group at first maintained no library of its own, but utilized the collection which was owned, housed, and serviced by the American Unitarian Association at its Boston headquarters. The material that in fact belonged to the society was considered to be on deposit at Unitarian headquarters, and a library committee was appointed from time to time. By the mid-1970s most of the collection was transferred, by gradual stages, to the library of the Harvard Divinity School. Like their Universalist counterparts, the Unitarian society published a scholarly journal (*Proceedings*) which was started in 1925 as part of the celebration of the centennial of the denomination, and appeared on an occasional basis and often in several installments.

The consolidated Universalist and Unitarian historical libraries, combined with other material from the headquarters of the once-separate denominations, strengthened the already rich resources of the Andover-Harvard Theological Library. Together, they created a collection of unique breadth and depth for the study of liberal religion on a world-wide scale.

SECTION V

Universalist Educational Efforts

Chapter 15

NON-SECTARIAN EDUCATION IN THEORY AND PRACTICE: ACADEMIES AND SEMINARIES

When the Committee on Education of the General Convention of Universalists in the United States made its annual report at the centennial session in 1870, it pointed with pride to the accomplishments of the denomination in the field of education. In that year, Universalists had either in operation or on the drawing boards no less than five institutions of higher learning, seven preparatory schools, and two theological schools. The grand total represented assets of nearly $2,000,000 and an enrollment of some 2,000 students.[1] Only half a century before, Universalists were operating but one school—an academy—and had just completed a struggle to raise $1,000 to support it. The record in 1870 was indeed an impressive one, but the bare enumeration of numbers by no means told the whole story. Between 1819 and the date of the great celebration at Gloucester, the denomination had actually sponsored, often in hit-or-miss fashion, no less than twenty secondary schools, and had placed their stamp of approval on more than two dozen seminaries and academies which had in some way been associated with Universalism or Universalists.

Probably no one could have foreseen in 1870 that of the five colleges and universities in operation or proposed in that year, only two would survive as independent institutions bearing their original names; and that the last theological school with Universalist origins would have its doors closed on its ninety-ninth birthday.

The story of Universalist educational efforts is, like that of most other denominations, a mixed one, ranging from triumphal successes to abysmal failures. All too many were inadequately planned, unfortunately located, poorly financed, or insufficiently patronized. As Henry L. Canfield, a well known clergyman, ruefully expressed it, "We builded a castle in the air and called it a Universalist academy."[2] But some members of the denomination perceived a need, and did what their limited resources and small numbers could muster to meet that need. Given all the circumstances, it was "a stupendous undertaking."[3]

Universalist educational institutions fell under one or more of four categories. The first were academies or seminaries (secondary schools) officially sponsored and/or supported by some denominational body, such as a local, or regional association, or state convention. In such schools, all or a majority of the personnel on the governing boards were Universalist clergymen or laymen, at least when the institutions were initially organized and opened. The second group consisted of secondary schools privately operated and financed, but conducted either by Universalists or by individuals whose academic policies and religious proclivities were acceptable to Universalists. No attempt is made here to identify or relate the history of all of the schools in this category. Some were operated briefly by Universalist clergy as adjuncts to pastorates which they served, often for no more than a year or so; many private schools changed hands with bewildering rapidity, and left no known impress outside their immediate localities; still others were too transient in character to have left any record at all beyond a single mention in a denominational publication.

A third group comprised colleges or universities, all of which had official denominational sponsorship of some kind when they were begun, and which often operated preparatory departments or had themselves been founded as secondary schools and later became institutions of collegiate grade. A fourth category included theological schools or departments which were operated with some type or degree of relationship, affiliation, or personal connection with other denominationally-connected educational enterprises. Within the half-century in which Universalist academies and seminaries were established (1819-1871), by far the greatest number were opened in the 1830's and 1840's—decades which coincided with the period of greatest expansion of the denomination. Only four were established after the Civil War, reflecting the rapid spread of the public school system and denominational concentration on support of its colleges and universities which had been established between 1852 and 1870. Universalist secondary schools were established in nine states, with the greatest number in the New England area.

The motives which prompted the establishment of institutions of learning at all levels by the denomination can be simply stated. It was to offer educational opportunity supposedly free from the sectarian bias and religious proselytizing that Universalists professed to find almost everywhere, especially before public education had become widespread. It was, at first, not so much the historic association of religion, education, and the state to which they objected as the kind of religion that was taught. After all, the idea that the provision of educational facilities was a joint responsibility of church and state was part of the inheritance from the colonial period.[4] It was therefore not surprising that public aid to private institutions was taken for granted early in the nation's history, as was also the inclusion of religious instruction in the education of youth.

Universalists never objected in principle to state aid to private institutions. In fact, many of their academies, seminaries, and colleges benefitted from public largesse. It was the fact that so much of such aid went to sectarian institutions or was not, they thought, equitably distributed, that sparked their dissatisfaction. In a sense, Universalists themselves had but little cause for complaint on this score, for their first college did indeed receive substantial state aid before the school was a decade old. As to the relation between academic training and the church, Universalists themselves, in their Plan of Government adopted in Philadelphia in 1790, had urged the establishment of schools "under the direction of every church" to teach "reading, writing, arithmetic, and psalmody."[5]

However, by the 1820's and the 1830's, with the growing popularity of the concept of tax-supported education, especially in New England, and increasing evidence of sectarian teaching in private schools (which Universalists vigilantly monitored), denominational spokesmen argued with increasing vehemence that religious instruction in the schools was inappropriate. As champions of complete separation of church and state, and of freedom of conscience, Universalists in Massachusetts strongly supported the efforts of Horace Mann to establish free, non-sectarian education in that state. They also greeted with enthusiastic approval the achievement in 1833 of complete separation of church and state in Massachusetts—the last state to take this step. It was Universalist Thomas Whittemore who helped make this a reality through his influence as a legislator (see above). That battle won, the next challenge was to eradicate if possible the widespread practice of using educational institutions "merely as sectarian engines."[6] Those schools operated under "orthodox" or "partialist" auspices were particularly subject to condemnation. Even though a teacher might be a Universalist, if he were found indoctrinating students "he would be dismissed from the district at once, and we certainly think he ought to be."[7]

Universalists overwhelmingly supported the concept of public school education, as free as possible from religious influence. They conceived their own academies to be the closest approximation to that ideal until tax-supported schools became widespread. Even though the growth of the public school system meant the eventual doom of most Universalist secondary schools, the denomination seldom considered public schools their enemies or even their competitors. The numerous Universalist academies which rose and fell were seen as serving a transitional role towards completely unsectarian education.[8] Time after time, Universalist leaders such as Thomas Whittemore and Edwin H. Chapin expressed their pride in the New England common school system, recognizing that region's contributions to American educational development.[9] Linus S. Everett suggested that the best course for Universalists to follow was not to dilute their energies and resources in establishing numerous poverty-stricken and struggling schools of their own, but to drive sectarianism out of existing schools.[10] Universalists, he believed, were obligated, as responsible citizens, thus to work for the public good. He felt this course of action was far superior to isolating Universalist children by withdrawing them from existing schools. The potential advantages of public schooling far outweighed the establishment of additional private, church-related facilities.

Not all Universalists, however, agreed with this argument. J.S. Barry (who succeeded Whittemore as editor of the *Trumpet* after the latter's death in 1861), argued that Universalist parents as well as those of other denominations should have the option of sending their children to schools teaching the Christian heritage rather than exposing them to the "infidelity" which might lurk in public schools which rejected all religious teaching.[11] *The Christian Repository* (Vermont) ran a series of articles so strongly opposed to denominational schools of any kind that the editor of the *Gospel Herald* (Maine) came to their defense. The public school system by the 1850's had not yet become sufficiently non-sectarian to permit Universalists to abandon their own schools. Freedom of choice, said some Universalist spokesmen, was part of the larger area of freedom of conscience. It was for such a reason that T.J. Sawyer sympathized completely with Roman Catholics in New York City and Philadelphia who objected to having the Protestant (King James) version of the Bible read in public schools.[12]

Numerous state conventions went on record in support of public schools. The Pennsylvania Convention, in 1853, endorsed the establishment of such a system in that state. Universalists there never established or sponsored a single denominational school. Vermont Universalists considered tax-supported schools as "the strength and glory of our country," and called on every denomination "to unite in support of our free common school system."[13] Children should be educated in the same schools "in order to fit them for the intelligent and safe exercise of the elective franchise . . . . without fear of tyrannical dominance of any one denomination or of the ignorant, wicked misrule of irreligion."

Moral training was an indispensable task of the schools, but not religious training as such. As Edward Turner, in 1819, told the students of the first academy sponsored by Universalists, it would be the task of schools established by the denomination not to turn out "captious and wrangling politicians" or religious zealots, but youth prepared for responsible citizenship.[14] Schools should be "nurseries of sound sense, sound morality, and sound learning. Sectarianism should be banished from them."[15] The public schools had to be kept free of such influence, whether it was Romanism, Calvinism, Unitarianism or Universalism.[16] In order to underline their non-sectarian character, of all the institutions of learning established by the denomination, only one even bore the word "Universalist" in its name (the ill-fated Universalist Institute of Ohio City). Instead, the word "liberal" appeared in the official designation of almost half of their schools.

Universalists also participated extensively in public school affairs, and dozens of them served on local school boards or in other related capacities. In 1847 New Hampshire created the post of State Commissioner of the Common Schools to supervise and report on the status of public education. County commissioners were appointed to carry out the responsibility. Of those serving between 1847 and 1854, Universalists were the most numerous of any denomination.[17]

As might have been expected, Universalists found a disturbing proportion of schools, both public and private, operated with a religious bias unacceptable to them. Typical of such were Phillips Academy and the Abbott Female Seminary in Andover, Massachusetts, under stern Calvinist Congregational control. The teachers were expected to warn their pupils against such heretics as "Jews, Papists, Mahametans, Arians, Pelageans, Antinomians, Arminians, Socinians, Sabellians, Unitarians, and Universalists."[18] It was reported that students at the Abbott Female Seminary who expressed Universalist ideas were discriminated against because of their unorthodox religious ideas. The same story was to be told, with local variations, for schools operated or controlled by almost every denomination. Some schools were accused of "manufacturing Baptists," and Methodists were charged with making their so-called literary institutions "the nursery bed of sectarian zealots."[19] Universalists objected vigorously to the holding of revivals ("protracted meetings") while schools were in session. They confused and upset the students and interfered with the learning process.[20] A Universalist student at Chester Academy (Vermont) complained that students were "being continuously tormented" with solicitations to attend such meetings, where they heard lectures "upon the wrath of God" instead of pursuing their academic activities.[21] Sylvanus Cobb lodged a formal protest with the Boston School Committee because a teacher had offered to excuse pupils from recitations if they would attend Charles G. Finney's revivalist prayer meetings.[22]

Non-Universalist academies were commended to Universalist patronage only if the teachers "kept aloof from those theologico-sectarian entanglements, which are calculated to fetter the minds of our youth in the rusty iron of human creeds."[23] Not a single New England college between 1830 and 1850 escaped Universalist censure of some kind or degree for their alleged sectarianism. Universalists did not hesitate to claim that many "literary" institutions such as Colby, Dartmouth, Brown, Williams, and Amherst were nothing more than theological schools in disguise. When a charter for Holy Cross College

(Roman Catholic) was denied by the Massachusetts legislature in 1849 on the ground that it would be sectarian, Whittemore noted that colleges founded by Protestants were just as sectarian in their own way.[24] He suggested that, in the interests of consistency, the legislature should either force such institutions as Harvard, Amherst, and Williams to abandon their sectarian exclusiveness or grant Holy Cross its charter. Complaints by Universalist about the sectarian character of education were easily made. Remedying the deficiencies they observed, and translating their own ideals into reality, were another matter. The challenges were there; could they be successfully met?

The Northeast

Massachusetts. In view of the concentration of Universalists in Massachusetts, and more specifically in the Greater Boston area, in the early and mid-nineteenth century it would be logical to assume that the educational achievements of the denomination would reflect its strength there. After all, Boston was the acknowledged headquarters of Universalist activity, embracing most of its publishing efforts, much of its leadership, and many of its largest societies and churches. Yet such was not to be the case. True, the first attempt in the entire denomination to operate a school took place in the state, but it failed, as such, in less than five years. Between 1825 and 1850, Universalists in Massachusetts, either as individuals or collectively, attempted to establish and operate six educational facilities including a theological school. Yet only one had survived by the mid-nineteenth century, at the time of the most significant expansion of Universalism in other respects. When the Reading Seminary was opened in the community of that name in 1843, it remained for over twenty years the only secondary school in the state with even an informal denominational association. It was not until 1852 that a college was chartered under Universalist auspices, and not until 1865 that an officially sponsored successful Universalist academy was established in Massachusetts. It was Universalists elsewhere, notably in upstate New York and in Maine, who were the first successful educational pioneers in establishing denominational schools.

But a small group of Universalists concentrated in the Boston area did take the initiative early in the nineteenth century to do something about sectarian education. Their efforts were, in perspective, in no sense an unalloyed success, but at least a start was made. Six individuals—four clergymen, including Hosea Ballou, and two laymen—issued a Circular Letter in 1814 "setting forth the outlines of a Seminary embracing the united interests of Religion and Literature."[25]

The circular was presented to the New England Convention, meeting that year in Westmoreland, New Hampshire, and was "accompanied with significations of acceptance and strong intimations of patronage from many societies and individuals." The convention thereupon voted to take the proposed institution under its wing and appointed a committee of twelve to promote it "with all the means with which they may be furnished."

The committee duly reported in 1815 that it was "expedient" to raise money for such a project, and proposed that an attempt be made to raise $5,000. Subscriptions were to be divided into 200 shares of $25 each; the interest on this endowment was to help support the institution.[26] A committee of five was appointed "to obtain the subscription of said shares." Nothing was reported for the next two years, but in 1817 the fund-raising committee was doubled in size and charged with making whatever arrangements they deemed necessary. Again nothing happened; the committee reported "no success" in 1818, but yet another committee, this time consisting of only three individuals, was given "discretionary powers, to devise the plan of a Seminary of Science." This effort bore greater fruit: Nichols Academy was established in Dudley, Massachusetts, in 1819, the first educational institution under Universalist sponsorship.

The individual with whom the new school was to become most intimately associated, and after whom it was named, was Amasa Nichols, a wealthy merchant and Universalist layman of Dudley. He had long been interested in opening a school under liberal (Universalist) auspices and in 1815 had provided $10,000 for an academic building in the community. But almost immediately after the school had opened under the direction of Barton Ballou, a Universalist clergyman, it had been destroyed by fire. The determination to rebuild was reflected in the decision of the New England Convention to obtain funds for such a school. But because only $1,000 of the goal of $5,000 was subscribed, Nichols financed the rebuilding himself. The academy opened late in 1818 and was incorporated the following year with fifteen trustees. Nichols, who was one of the incorporators, deeded the land and building to the trustees, with the understanding that not only would they keep the school open on a regular basis but that it be "respectable"—a term synonymous in his mind with the word "Universalist."[27] The New England Convention in 1819 reaffirmed its sponsorship of the academy and stipulated that the trustees were to be members of the convention or of societies in fellowship with it. This provision was also to apply in the filling of all vacancies that might occur on the board.[28] If any surplus income were produced by the school, it was to be used for "free education of young men, of indigent circumstances, but moral and pious habits, designing to enter the gospel ministry." There was immediate objection to this provision for subsidizing ministerial training, on the ground that it might attract opportunists rather than *bona fide* candidates.

One of the first acts of the trustees was to urge the New England Convention "to exert their influence with their friends to procure Scholars and funds for the School."[29] Providing scholars turned out to be a much easier task than securing funds: there were over sixty students when the fall term opened in 1819.[30] It was one of the very few Universalist-sponsored schools that was not coeducational when it opened. The curriculum included English grammar, arithmetic, geometry, "and the learned languages." The trustees selected a committee to examine the pupils "at or near the close of each quarter," and took turns in addressing their charges with inspirational and didactic messages.[31] A gentleman named Wildes was employed as the "Preceptor" at an annual salary of $400.

On the less positive side, when the school opened it had virtually no operating funds, the interior of the frame building in which it was housed will still only partially completed, and the exterior was already in need of paint to protect the structure.[32] The trustees paid for basic repairs and paint out of their own pockets. Apprehension was quite appropriately expressed in 1820 that societies initially pledging support for the academy would promptly forget their promises as soon as it was in actual operation.[33] An attempt to obtain state aid was made in 1823, and was successful after a drive for subscriptions was undertaken to raise the required minimum of $2,000. On the basis of these subscriptions and $2,500 from the sale of a half-township of unimproved land in Maine under a grant from the Massachusetts legislature which still had jurisdiction over that territory, the struggling academy managed to complete and improve its physical plant. But economic rescue was not alone sufficient to maintain the school under Universalist control. Beginning in 1823, the school passed into other hands as a result of trustee action.

The trustees, disregarding the mandate of the New England Convention, decided to fill two vacancies with non-Universalists. The intent seemed to have been based on a number of considerations—to emphasize the non-sectarian character of the school (in which there was no provision at all for religious instruction), to broaden the base of support, and to recognize the financial aid of members of other denominations, who had contributed some $800 to the subscription drive in 1823. But the trustees had not reckoned on Amasa Nichols' reaction to their unauthorized decision. He had intended to support an exclusively Universalist-sponsored school which could itself provide the necessary "encouragement of freedom of opinion" without the involvement of other denominations. As he told the students in 1820, "each and every one here resorting, will be equally respected and derive every advantage which may be afforded, without the least regard to sentiment."[34] But he was outvoted by his fellow trustees. He severed all connections with the school. With the withdrawal of his support also went Universalist responsibility for the school. Although some Universalist families continued to send their children to Nichols Academy as late as the 1840's, it had by then fallen prey, in Universalist eyes, to "Partialist" (Orthodox Congregational) indoctrination and "sectarian maneuvering."[35] The school was not even mentioned in the records of the New England Convention after 1823. Nichols Academy lasted until 1911. In 1931 it was reopened as a new non-denominational junior college for men; after closing briefly during the Second World War, it was reopened in 1946. In 1958 it became a four-year college emphasizing business administration, and in 1970 became coeducational.

For twenty years after Nichols Academy had fallen into other hands, Universalist educational activity in the state was confined to the conduct of numerous privately operated academies, most of which were short-lived; some never developed beyond the planning stage. In 1825 Barton Ballou, who had been the principal of what had become Nichols Academy, announced the opening of Wrentham Academy in that community south of Boston. It was advertised as a "private seminary . . . for the instruction of youth, in the several branches of an Academical education . . . to fit young gentlemen for Business, for College, and for the study of a Profession."[36] But there is no evidence that the school lasted for any length of time, for Ballou soon moved to Rhode Island. A proposal to establish an academy in Woburn in 1829 fared no better. Plans were announced to conduct a school "on truly liberal principles" in the basement of a new Universalist meeting house under construction. It was intended to counterbalance the existing school operated by the "orthodox" Deacon Warren, and would have presumably protected the local youth from "the dangerous influence of Calvinism."[37] The idea of a school to be conducted by the First Universalist Society in Woburn received the blessing of the New England Convention and the enthusiastic editorial endorsement of the *Trumpet.*[38] But after the meeting house was completed, the Woburn society found that it did not have the requisite $600 to finish the interior of the basement. An attempt to raise money by subscription came to nothing, as did an offer to lease the basement for ten years to anyone willing to operate the school.[39]

The next attempt to establish an academy did succeed temporarily and was located this time north of Boston. It was an outgrowth of a meeting called in Andover in 1838 to organize "an American, or Massachusetts Universalist Educational Society." The Boston Association immediately urged an "onward course" for establishing a literary institution.[40] The coeducational school did open, as Methuen

Liberal Institute, but shortly after classes began in 1839 the academy was moved from Methuen to Gloucester. It occupied a two-story building built for the purpose on the grounds of the Independent (Universalist) Christian Church.[41] Bearing the name "Murray Institute," the school was made possible by a subscription of $3,500, with an endowment goal of $6,000.[42] It was advertised as "the first school of importance that owes its origin to the most liberal christians of this commonwealth." All twelve of the original board of trustees were members of the denomination.[43] Universalists in Massachusetts were challenged to make the school as prosperous as had their New York brethren with Clinton Liberal Institute (opened in 1831).[44] It seemed at first as though the challenge could be met, for Murray Institute had 180 students enrolled in its first year. An ambitious plan to have a library of 2,000 volumes was announced, and a complete secondary school curriculum was planned, including such "ornamental" subjects as piano, voice, and organ.[45] Even a "juvenile school" was added in 1840.[46] But the entire school was abandoned later the same year, for

Samuel P. Skinner, a native Vermonter who in his twenty-eight year ministry held pastorates in four states and was involved briefly in newspaper publishing, announced in 1844 the opening of Newton Seminary southwest of Boston; but it seems never to have opened.[47] A year later, Miss Louise M. Barker, who had served for a time as supervisor of the female department of Clinton Liberal Institute, announced the opening of a "female boarding school" to be known as Whittemore Hall in West Cambridge; but no further mention is made of it in denominational records.[48] A community north of Boston became the original locale of the next Universalist school of importance, which lasted over twenty years.

Reading Academy (Seminary), established in 1843, was unique in two respects: It was a cooperative effort with other proponents of liberal religion (in this case, the Unitarians), and in its own day stood as the only Universalist-operated school in the state. The first public announcement of the proposed school appeared in the denominational press in May 1843. One of the sponsors and original trustees, Otis A. Skinner, told the readers of the *Trumpet* that "Br. W.B. Wait has made arrangements to open a Male and Female Seminary in Reading." Skinner had so much faith in the project that he made arrangements to send his own daughter there.[49] Mrs. Wait (*née* Hannah A. Hoyt) had been in charge of the "female department" of Murray Institute until it closed; she married Windsor B. Wait (1812-1884) in 1840, the year the school had ceased to operate. Wait was at the time a Universalist preacher who had started his career as a mechanic. After preparing for the ministry he held brief pastorates in West Newbury, Massachusetts (1839) and Freeport, Maine (1841).[50]

Only one week after Skinner had paved the way for the school by assuring prospective students and their parents that "a more delightful situation could not be selected, or one offering better accommodations" than in the "healthy and beautiful town" of Reading, Wait added his own endorsement. It was situated, he wrote, "in the very centre of a great body of liberal Christians; in a town so beautiful, and so congenial to health; amid a people of sober and temperate habits, possessing a high tone of moral and intellectual feeling, why should we fear a want of patronage sufficient to ensure success?"[51]

A Universalist society had been organized in South Reading (Wakefield) in 1813 in a private home, and Universalists had become the dominant group by 1833 in what had been the original Congregational church in North Reading. Sufficient Universalists had also settled in Reading proper by 1838 to attempt the creation of the "Second Universalists Society" (the first having been organized in North Reading). But probably because there were already Universalist societies in both neighboring communities at the time, the Second Society had only a brief history, and merged with the then-faltering Unitarian group which had been organized in 1827 as the "Third Congregational Society."

There was no problem in providing housing for the new school, for a building had already been constructed by the Unitarians. The lower floor was fitted up for the academy, and the upstairs was equipped with pews ("slips") and used for religious services—a very common practice in the nineteenth century. The school was duly opened in the summer of 1843, with Wait serving also as the minister of the combined societies and conducting services in the same building.[52] Four sessions of the school were scheduled during the year, beginning in June, September, December, and April. Instruction was offered "in the various English branches usually taught," with tuition at $4.00 per term. In addition, "languages, drawing, &c." were offered at $1.50 extra. Board was advertised as available "in respectable families with superior accommodations, at $1.50 per week, including washing."[53] For those who wanted to inquire regarding the respectability of the school, they were referred to what amounted to a roll-call of the leading Universalists in New England, including Hosea Ballou and his great-nephew, Hosea Ballou 2d, who was one of the original trustees of the institution. Although the school was to be operated under private auspices, it was more than the responsibility of a single individual. It received the endorsement of the Massachusetts State Convention, and therefore obtained official denominational approval and encouragement.[54]

In the fall of 1843 Trustee Skinner made a glowing report on both the school and the town, indicating that twenty-four pupils were in attendance.[55] A year later it was reported that the school was "patronized chiefly by Universalists."[56] In order to attract patronage,

Skinner extolled the virtues of the community, pointing among its advantages to the fact that the citizens "have done what many New England villages have not—closed all their tippling shops."[57] Another leading Universalist, John Greenleaf Adams, also commended the school, noting that twice as many students could be accommodated as were then attending. By the spring term of 1844, enrollment had increased sufficiently to justify the addition to the staff of John Batchelder, a local resident and Harvard graduate.[58]

There was every indication that the school would prosper. In 1844 it had broadened its activities to include a one-year program leading to a certificate in teaching, and gave assistance in job placement. It also offered special reading courses for those planning to enter the ministry. In the same year, a "large and convenient house . . . neatly fitted up for the accommodation of pupils" was also provided. Parents were assured that "a proper restraint and influence" was exerted.

The state convention continued to pass resolutions urging support of the school.[59] Wait was authorized by its seven trustees to visit Universalist societies throughout the state to lecture on education and to solicit funds to purchase teaching equipment and build up a library.[60] The results of his efforts were modest at best. He began his money-raising tour in Medford, where he collected only $85, but with the promise of gifts of "some handsome pieces of apparatus" from the ladies of the local Universalist society.[61] By June 1846, he had obtained subscriptions in nine towns totalling $294.[62]

The original board of trustees was also enlarged in 1846 to fifteen.[63] Among them was Alonzo A. Miner, who was to become the second president of Tufts College. In addition to attempting to broaden the base of the school and hence obtain enhanced support, the suggestion was made that a female seminary in Whittemore Hall, a school opened in 1845 in West Cambridge by Miss Louisa M. Barker, be merged with the Reading Seminary. However, nothing apparently came of this proposal.

The merits of the school continued to be advertised. When the term for the fall of 1846 was announced, there was a concerted effort to attract commuters. It was pointed out that the school was only a thirty-minute train ride from Boston. Furthermore, students could take advantage of a "package deal" whereby the total fare and tuition for the "England branches" would amount to only $12 per term.[64] A campaign was also launched to raise $800 to purchase additional teaching equipment.

The school had become sufficiently large by 1848 to require new quarters. The result was a decision by Wait to move it to another community. The Reading Seminary was therefore closed after the end of the spring term that year, and in July 1848 opened as the Melrose Academy in Greenwood Village, a community which became part of

Wakefield in 1868. The school was advertised as housed in two buildings–one a boarding house. Both quarters were described as "new and elegant."[65] The Waits, after only a year, tried their hands at operating still another school. Leaving Melrose Academy temporarily in the charge of Josiah W. Talbot, who was the first Universalist pastor in Melrose (1849-1853), the Waits opened the Lexington Academy in that community, in the fall of 1849.[66] One D.C. Quimby was placed in charge.[67] The Waits then returned to the South Reading (Wakefield) area and in 1853 reopened their school as the "Greenwood Seminary," housed in a new three-story building.[68] By then, Wait had apparently ceased his ministerial activities completely, for no mention was made in the advertising of any Universalist connection; he identified himself only as "Mr." Wait. However, Abel Tompkins, a prominent Boston Universalist layman and publisher of denominational books and newspapers, continued to be listed as the general agent.

The school lasted until after the Civil War, and remained under Wait's supervision until about 1868, when he retired from teaching and resumed his first occupation as a mechanic.[69] After the building ceased to house the seminary, it was used briefly (1872-1874) as a home for inebriates, operated by Dr. Albert A. Day of Boston, who founded the Washingtonian Home there for the reformation of alcoholics. The old seminary building was destroyed by fire in 1878, after having remained vacant for several years.[70] By the mid-1860s, Universalists in the state had already arranged for another secondary school more directly under denominational auspices than the institution in Reading and Wakefield.

Between 1840 and 1865, Massachusetts Universalists made three attempts to establish their own schools, each intended to serve different but related purposes; two of the three were successful. The first was an abortive attempt in the 1840s to establish a theological school in the Boston area. The second (which did succeed) was the establishment of an exclusively collegiate level institution (Tufts College, chartered in 1852 and opened in 1854). The third was the provision of a preparatory school, the main (but not exclusive) function of which was to serve as a feeder for the college.

The steps which resulted in the chartering of Dean Academy in Franklin in 1865 were first taken two years earlier, when the state convention met in Gloucester. The Secretary, John S. Barry, called attention in his report that year to the vital need of "a first class Academy in this State, to be under the charge of the Universalist denomination." He presented a battery of reasons centering around three themes: Existing academies were "generally under objectionable religious auspices" and sent their graduates to colleges in sympathy with them; public high schools were accessible only in the cities and larger towns, and tended to favor the "older colleges;" and the denomination's own college, although "eminently encouraging" in its prospects, was being insufficiently patronized. Given this background and the discussions which took place at the 1864 convention, a committee chaired by Thomas A. Goddard was appointed to consider the subject "of establishing a denominational school of a grade between the Common schools and Colleges."[71] Their recommendation being positive, a sixteen-man board of trustees, with A. St. John Chambré at its head, was appointed by the convention to make the necessary arrangements. A public meeting was held in Boston in the fall of 1864, and several offers of location followed from various communities, including neighboring Stoughton. After "protracted and careful consultation" the board accepted the offer of Dr. Oliver Dean of Franklin.

Tufts President Alonzo A. Miner's often-reiterated plea for "more and better preparatory schools" was at least partially met in 1865, at least so far as Universalists in the state were concerned, when a charter was obtained for an institution to be known as Dean Academy.[72] The creation of the school would not have been possible without the financial support and encouragement of Oliver Dean, "a noble-hearted friend of education." He was a prominent and wealthy physician and Universalist laymen who had already served as president of the trustees of the Walnut Hill Evangelical Seminary (which never came into being), and had been also a member of the original Tufts board of trustees in 1851, as well as the first president of that body. He was also a business agent for the Amoskeag Manufacturing Company, a textile firm located in Manchester, New Hampshire. It was Dean who arranged for Sylvanus Cobb to preach in the chapel provided for the company's employees.[73] Dean had offered twenty acres of land and the sum of $20,000 if Tufts College had been located in Franklin, but had indicated his willingness to support the institution wherever it was located; in fact he became one of its most generous early benefactors.

In order to provide an endowment for the new "State Denominational School" in Franklin, Dean secured the estate of Nathaniel Emmons, for many years the Congregational minister of that town. The value of the estate was to comprise the nucleus of a permanent fund of $50,000. Dean also donated some fifteen acres of land (worth $5,000) and also offered $10,000 toward the construction of a suitable building, the total cost of which was projected at $50,000. Altogether, Dean contributed in excess of $130,000 toward the establishment and maintenance of the institution.[74] This, together with contributions from other sources, made the academy the best endowed institution of its kind in the denomination. Citizens of Franklin also promised upwards of $10,000 if the academy were located there—no small inducement in those times. It was made the "imperative duty" of Massachusetts Universalists to raise the remaining funds needed (estimated at $40,000). The school was designed to be coeducational from the start, although its primary purpose was to prepare young men for college. It was intended also for those preparing "for business and social life."

The decision of the board of trustees under the leadership of A. St. John Chambré was made to open the school immediately, although only students in advanced classes were accepted because over a year would elapse before the main building could be constructed. The basement of the local Universalist church was used in the meantime.[75] Within a year, three-fourths of the needed funds had been pledged. The principal involvement of the state convention was to educate its constituency to the needs of the school. The convention itself had no funds to contribute, and had to be content with periodic urgings to pastors, parishes, and congregations to contribute to the academy. It was forced, in fact, to put aside its own plans to raise money for missionary purposes in order that funds for the academy could be secured.

Dean Academy seemed to be a success from the start, even though the main building, a structure of "magnificent proportions" costing $175,000 and with accommodations for 200, was not ready until 1868. The delay was explained by the difficulty in raising the $40,000 required to supplement the Dean gift. The problem at first was not lack of patronage but inability to provide sufficient facilities. The school opened in the fall of 1866 with a staff of four and with eighty students, but this number so taxed the church's available space that the number of students in 1867 was limited to seventy. When the principal structure was completed, the number of students immediately rose to 150. Resources for the new institution were provided with great rapidity after 1868, with funds donated by several generous Universalists, including Thomas A. Goddard. Even with an indebtedness of $35,000 in 1869, net assets amounted to almost a quarter of a million dollars.[76]

The staff had been increased to ten by 1871, presiding over three thirteen-week terms, and all seemed to be in order.[77] Then disaster struck a year later. The main building was totally destroyed by fire in mid-summer of 1872, as renovations were being made to ready it for the fall term. The decision was made immediately to rebuild; meanwhile, the ninety students then enrolled were provided with temporary accommodations. A new fund-raising drive had to be organized, as none of the endowment could be used for building purposes. The building destroyed in 1872 was replaced in 1874 with an even more elaborate Gothic structure than its predecessor. With the destructiveness of fire very much in mind, the architect provided brick fire walls extending from foundation to roof, dividing the building into six distinct parts. The boilers were also, as a safety precaution, installed in a separate building.

The curriculum at the academy was considerably broader than at

Dean Academy on the eve of a fire in 1872 which required a new structure

most other Universalist schools, and was revised periodically to meet not only what were perceived to be student and societal needs, but the changing character of the school itself. Two courses of study had been originally provided: an "academic" and a college preparatory. In 1871 a "common English" (grammar school) curriculum was added to the three-year academic course and the four-year college preparatory program. The latter two were offered at the reasonable tuition charge of $10 per term. A "scientific" course of study was offered, in 1872 and a "philosophical" curriculum was added in 1876.

An exciting announcement for those interested in denominational higher education had been made at the Massachusetts Universalist Convention in 1870. The trustees of Dean Academy had indicated their intention of establishing a college for women in conjunction with the academy. It was to make the same academic demands on women as did first-class male institutions on men. With high standards of both admission and curriculum, the women's college would "be an opportunity for demonstrating the validity of the claim that women are not intellectually inferior to men." Authority to grant the customary degrees would be sought from the legislature, and the course of study would possibly be in operation by the fall of 1870. But all of these hopes were dashed, for funds were not forthcoming in sufficient amount, and less than two years later with the main academy building destroyed by fire, all resources had to be concentrated on rebuilding. It was left to Tufts College to furnish denominational collegiate education for women in the East, beginning in 1892.

However, the trustees of the academy did try the experiment of turning it into a boarding and day school for women exclusively, beginning in the fall of 1877. For a brief period, Dean was the only exclusively female school supported by Universalists.[78] The curriculum was correspondingly revamped to offer a one-year English preparatory course, and "Higher English," "academic," and "classical" curricula of three years each. "Ornamental branches" such as drawing, painting, and music were extra offerings, advertised as "reasonable" in price. The minimum age of students accepted was set at thirteen. The "new departure," as the decision to admit only women was called, lasted but two years. In 1879 the school again became coeducational and most of the regular curriculum was reinstituted, emphasizing college preparatory subjects.

With a substantial physical plant, a comfortable endowment, undiminished enrollments, competent academic and administrative leadership, and an excellent reputation, Dean Academy retained its Universalist affiliation as a secondary school longer into the twentieth century than any similar educational facility established by the denomination. Between 1898 and 1934 its head was Arthur Peirce, formerly principal of another denominational school (Goddard Seminary). Dean became an independent two-year junior college in 1941 after over seventy years of Universalist sponsorship. In 1957 the old academy ceased to exist after having been operated concurrently with the junior college for some fifteen years.

New York. Of the numerous secondary schools established under Universalist sponsorship in the nineteenth century, Clinton Liberal Institute was the second to be founded (preceded by Nichols Academy), and enjoyed one of the longest continuous histories—a seventy-year span extending from 1831 to 1900. The school, located for most of its life in the upstate New York village of Clinton (Oneida County) near Utica, was the outgrowth of efforts articulated early in 1831 by Dolphus Skinner, editor of the *Evangelical Magazine and Gospel Advocate,* published in Utica.[79] Within a month after Skinner called for a Universalist-operated school, the idea of establishing such an academy was broached at the annual meeting of the state convention and promptly and favorably acted upon by a series of resolutions. The editor of the *Trumpet* in Boston was skeptical about the results. No such institution, he told his readers, would ever "rise by the aid of *resolves* only."[80] But the Universalists of New York State went far beyond a mere declaration of intent. They acted.

A committee consisting of Skinner, Stephen R. Smith, and A.B. Grosh was appointed by the convention to prepare a circular "on the subject of establishing a literary institution in this State, for general purposes of science and literature, but with a particular view of

The Male and Female Departments of Clinton Liberal Institute, Clinton, New York, in 1860

furnishing, with an education, young men designed for the ministry of reconciliation."[81] The Central Association was the first group to respond. It not only unanimously approved the convention's recommendations, but settled on a location. It suggested that the school be established in or near Clinton. The association went even further and appointed a fifteen-member "Board of Trust" to oversee the institution. An executive committee was also appointed and instructed to proceed "with as little delay as possible." This reflected the sense of urgency expressed by Grosh when he declared that "something *must immediately* be done."

The convention-appointed committee had appealed for support for such an institution from the "liberal portion of the community" in general, as well as from Universalists in particular. A tangible result was the appointment of one non-Universalist to the original board—a Quaker.[82] Most of the vacancies, at least in the next decade, were filled by Universalists, although occasionally representatives of other denominations were appointed, including Episcopalians. The Central Association also went a step beyond the original recommendation and provided that the school be opened "for the mutual instruction of males and females in the respective sciences." Coeducation, as it turned out, however, did not mean complete academic or social togetherness. After the institute was actually opened, the males were located in the northern part of the village and the females in the southern, half a mile apart, the latter facing Hamilton College, an institution under Presbyterian auspices.

Other associations in the state promptly endorsed the enterprise, and a fund-raising drive brought in $5,000. Each subscriber to the permanent funds who paid at least $10 became a shareholder and was entitled to one vote in the election of trustees.[83] The new academy opened its doors in the fall of 1831, in temporary quarters, with forty pupils. In May 1832, John W. Hale, a member of the executive committee, arranged for the construction, at his own expense, of a frame building for the use of the female department, which served for almost twenty years. A "new, spacious building for the Female Department" was provided in 1851.[84] A site for the main building which was to serve as the headquarters of the school, and a dormitory for the males, were donated by a Universalist layman (Judge Sweeting). The building, of stone and four stories high, surmounted by a cupola and with a large basement, was erected at a cost of $9,300 and was opened in December. Besides teaching facilities, there were forty-five rooms designed to accommodate ninety students. No room rent was to be charged, but the students were required to furnish and maintain their own quarters. They had free access to the library, which by 1836 comprised about 1,000 volumes. Board and tuition amounted to less than $100 for the academic year, which was originally divided into three terms. George R. Perkins and Miss Jane M. Burr were in charge of the male and female departments, respectively, and classes for the young men and young women were held separately. A German immigrant, one C.B. Thummel, who held a master's degree and had been trained in linguistics, was secured prior to the opening of the school to serve as principal.

Meanwhile, Stephen R. Smith became the most active supporter of the new educational venture. Smith was described as "virtually the parent of the Institute."[85] He served as its agent until he moved to Albany in 1837, and travelled hundreds of miles, from Buffalo to Philadelphia, attempting to stir up enthusiasm and obtain financial support.[86] It was Smith who recruited the first faculty and students, and who superintended the construction of the first building. He was responsible for raising a total of about $6,000 in the course of years of effort. Among his original goals (never realized) was the obtaining of at least $10 from every Universalist clergyman in the state.[86] Much of the early financing for the school, including assistance in construction of the main building, came from the treasurer, Joseph Stebbins.

From all indications, the school, begun with great enthusiasm, seemed to have a bright future in store. There were almost 100 students by 1833, with about equal representation of males and females.[88] Two years later the school was reported to be in a "highly prosperous state;" enrollment had climbed to over 150.[89] Legal recognition was accorded in 1834, when the school was chartered by the Board of Regents of the University of the State of New York. Under the system then in operation each school so recognized was to receive state aid, but it was slow in coming. By 1836 plans were under way to expedite matters; it was thought that the best way would be to turn the school into a collegiate institution by revising the charter so that the institute could offer both the bachelor's and master's degrees.[90] It appears that the sponsors of the school had entertained such a plan from the beginning, at least for the male department. Even before the original charter had been obtained, the proposed course of instruction had been described as including "every branch of education usually taught in our American Colleges."[91] George Rogers had visited Clinton in 1835 on his way west and had referred to the fact that the Universalists had a "college there for male students . . . and a neat academy for females."[92]

The non-creedal, non-sectarian educational philosophy professed by Universalists was carried out to the letter in the early history of Clinton Liberal Institute. When the Central Association had taken up the challenge offered by the state convention in 1831 to establish a school, they had made no mention at all of any provision for theological training, which had been hinted as a possibility in the convention resolutions. It was made clear, furthermore, that the school was quite unlike existing "literary institutions" in the country. There was no "inculcation of the peculiar doctrines of some sect . . . The Institute admits of no interference with the doctrinal opinions of the students—nor will it suffer its officers to dictate when, or where they shall attend church. Youth from the families of every sect in our land, may here receive the best literary instruction without censure because they, or their fathers, believe in a particular creed."[93] For this reason, Thomas Whittemore commended the school as "a blessing to the land."[94] Its supporters insisted that it was "strictly unsectarian rather than Universalist" and therefore merited the support of "the Liberal public of every denomination."[95] Grosh kept insisting that "the Institute is *not a Universalist School*" but was completely without sectarian characteristics.[96]

When a constitution and bylaws for the Institute were adopted in 1836, the principle of religious permissiveness attained almost anti-clerical proportions.[97] It was specified that no students were to be required to abandon their studies to attend religious exercises. "And no minister, of any denomination, shall have liberty to perform the services of public worship within the Institute, on any occasion whatever." It was specified that this article of the constitution was never to be altered. There was no requirement that the board of trustees (enlarged from fifteen to eighteen) be Universalists. The establishment of a professorship of theology was specifically prohibited by Article XVI. Public worship was required only for pupils "whose tender age renders it proper that some one should decide for them."[98] Even then, students had a choice of three churches besides the Universalist to attend in Clinton in 1841: Baptist, Methodist, and Presbyterian. The closest approximation to religious instruction allowed was the occasional reading of a passage from the Bible or the offering of a prayer when academic exercises began for the day (and that was limited to the female department).[99] The non-sectarian policy was also reflected in the makeup of the faculty. The first principal (Thummel) was a Lutheran minister, and the first teacher in the female department was a Presbyterian. Another was an Episcopalian. The editor of the *Universalist Register* in 1840 quite properly described the Clinton School as "an unsectarian English and Classical Seminary of education for both sexes."

Nothing had come of the proposal made in 1836 to turn the academy into a college, or even to provide a collegiate department, but the school had become solidly enough established and sufficiently well patronized by 1840 to make another attempt. By that year there were 228 students and a faculty of five under the leadership of Thomas Clowes, a former Episcopal clergyman who had become a Universalist in 1838.[100] Clowes resigned in 1843 to become principal of a grammar school in Philadelphia to which post he had been unanimously elected by the city board of school directors. He was precipitately replaced when it became known that he was a Universalist.[101]

The initiative for again considering collegiate status for the school was taken in 1841 by the New York State Convention which voted to turn the institution into a college "equal in grade to the highest and best in the United States."[102] It was to be under the patronage of the denomination and would offer both collegiate and preparatory courses. Nothing happened; so a resolution with the same intent was unanimously adopted the following year.[103] In order to achieve this goal and secure a proper charter, it was necessary to raise the endowment to $100,000. Inducements were offered to prospective subscribers in the form of tuition entitlement for one student, or both board and tuition for one student, depending on the size of the individual contribution. This was the greatest challenge yet offered to Universalists in the state, who over the past decade of the school's history had, according to its agent, Stephen R. Smith, been chronically apathetic toward the whole enterprise. He estimated that the school had really been supported by only about 100 families, with the "unwilling countenance" of about 200 more.[104] Less than $12,000 had been received in support of the school in its first ten years, all from private sources. There would be no glimmer of a chance to achieve the $100,000 if Universalists refused to mend their ways and contented themselves merely by passing resolutions or waiting for others to complete the work.

Nothing had yet been done to alter the character of the school by 1844, although limited public funds had by then been made available to assist in supporting its operations. The financing and control of the school continued to be in an ambivalent state, "as far under the influence of the Universalist denomination as it can be and receive its share of the literature funds from the State."[105] The Institute had continued to prosper, with 236 students enrolled in 1844, a faculty of six, and with a "military department" in operation.[106] Arrangements were also made so that lectures in Hamilton College were made available to Institute students.

After stockholders in the Universalist enterprise had requested the state convention to take over the school, that body finally decided to clarify the ambiguous status of the Institute, feeling that it ought to be either a *bona fide* public school or a frankly denominational institution.[107] Sentiment leaned clearly toward the latter choice, and a committee was appointed to confer with the trustees to see what could be done to give the school "a more elevated position and a more commanding general influence; also of identifying it more effectually with the interests of our denomination." Funds were also needed to pay off the indebtedness that had accumulated, and the buildings needed repair.

Clinton Liberal Institute became officially a Universalist school in 1845. A revised charter was secured and the board of trustees was reconstituted, consisting entirely of Universalists. A new constitution also reduced the number of trustees from eighteen to twelve.[108] The new charter also gave the school "collegiate privileges," although they were never exercised because the institution was unable to raise the $100,000 endowment required by the New York Regents. The new authority to grant degrees prompted several suggestions for a new name—including "Clinton Collegiate Institute" and "Murray College."[109] Philo Price, editor of the *Universalist Union*, suggested that it be renamed "Clinton Universalist Institute," but most Universalists continued to prefer the word "liberal" in the names of their educational institutions. There were also other significant changes. T.J. Sawyer of New York City, who had served churches there for over fifteen years, assumed the direction of the institution and announced simultaneously the opening of a theological school, to be operated independently of the Institute but also under his control.

Clinton Liberal Institute was now the complete responsibility of Universalists, "a strictly denominational school."[110] Could the challenge be met? A general agent, D.S. Morey of Clinton, was immediately appointed by the trustees and promptly distributed a circular soliciting funds for the liquidation of the $1,600 debt which existed in 1845. Every Universalist clergyman in the state was, in effect, to be an agent to raise funds for the reconstituted school.[111] Whittemore, an enthusiastic supporter of education, called for support of Clinton by all Universalists, wherever they might be located.[112] Even the General Convention took a hand by voting in 1846 to appoint agents to solicit subscriptions totalling $50,000 "for the purpose of erecting it into a College or University."[113] The attempt to raise $50,000 was a complete failure; even by 1849 the state convention had been unable to raise all of the minimum of $10,000 considered necessary to provide new facilities for the young women.[114]

Sawyer was so discouraged that he threatened to resign if the school were not properly supported, and wrote rather bitterly that four years of his life had been wasted in trying to keep the school alive.[115] There was even a rumor circulated in the Boston area that Sawyer had actually resigned because of a difference of opinion with some of the trustees.[116] Whittemore (who had been instrumental in spreading the rumor) recommended that the school be abandoned entirely and relocated elsewhere—preferably in the vicinity of Boston. He pointed out, quite realistically, that the Clinton school would never prosper as an institution of higher learning as long as Hamilton College existed in the same community. Sawyer admitted that there had been "local differences," which at times had "threatened the very existence of the Institute," but he was determined to see it survive, even as only a secondary school. When the news reached New York that Massachusetts Universalists were contemplating the opening of a college, Sawyer assured eastern Universalists that Clinton Liberal Institute was in no sense to be considered a rival. By 1849 he had become reconciled to the idea that the Institute would never become a college, and in fact suggested that it could logically become a preparatory school for the proposed Massachusetts institution. He recovered his spirits sufficiently to suggest facetiously that his coeducational school could furnish wives for the graduates of what was being planned as an all-male college.[117] With the possibility that the eastern school might actually become a reality, Sawyer revised the Clinton curriculum, providing a three-year terminal course of study and introducing a two-year college preparatory program.[118]

It was not until 1850 that the goal of $10,000 set earlier was reached, thanks to subscriptions by some of the trustees. A new three-story wooden building for the female department was completed in 1851, and there was sufficient money to provide badly needed scientific apparatus.[119] Sawyer was still disappointed with the results of the fund drive, noting that only twenty-six of the more than 200 societies in the state had contributed at all.[120] But he could take comfort in the fact that in the 1850-51 school year the enrollment had risen to almost 250, with a faculty of eight, and to almost 300 a year later.[121] The interior of the building housing the male department, in continuous service since 1832, had become so shabby and worn after twenty years of hard use that Sawyer labelled it more suited as a factory than as an academic building, and in 1852 called for money to refurbish the structure.[122] One result was the creation that year of the Universalist State Educational Society, with Sawyer as its first president. It met in conjunction with the state convention, and was intended to raise funds for both the Institute and Sawyer's theological school.[123]

The 1850s were not happy ones for the Institute. Indebtedness continued to increase, and in 1852 it lost the valuable asset of Sawyer's leadership and devotion. After seeing a fund drive to strengthen his theological school collapse in failure, he decided to give up the struggle in Clinton and returned to New York City where, after preaching for the Fourth Universalist Society for a year, he resumed the original pastorate in the Orchard Street Church which he had held, beginning in 1830. The principalship remained vacant for three years, until another Universalist clergyman, J.A. Aspinwall, secretary of the state convention, assumed the post in 1855.[124] Even then, there were two vacancies in the male department, and Aspinwall remained only two years, leaving because of ill health which resulted shortly in death.

Despite the fact that the school was entirely under the control of the state convention, a high proportion of the efforts of the state educational society was by then being devoted to establishing a theological department in St. Lawrence University in Canton, chartered in 1856. The male department of the Institute was forced to close temporarily in 1858, "owing to embarrassments and debts, and the want of a principal."[125] E.H. Chapin, one of the strongest supporters of Universalist educational efforts and well known in New York City, prevailed upon Henry Ward Beecher, an even better known clergyman (Congregational), author, and public speaker, to deliver a lecture in support of the Institute.[126] The proceeds were assigned to help pay off the debt. In 1858 all but $2,500 of the $14,500 thought to be necessary to "redeem" the closed department had been subscribed. The only other ingredient necessary for success for the school, which by then represented an investment of almost $40,000, was "a permanent and liberal patronage of the school by Universalists and other liberal families having sons and daughters to educate."

Effort was rewarded, for the male department was reopened in 1859, thanks to the "great exertions" of Dolphus Skinner as principal fundraiser. He and Sawyer personally subscribed a total of $1,200.[127] Sufficient money had finally been raised to pay off the debt which had been "so long oppressing and crippling the Institute."[128] The male department was "now prepared to prosper" under the leadership of a new principal, Heman A. Dearborn, a member of the first class to graduate from Tufts College (in 1857). Ninety-nine male students were enrolled in 1859, with over 170 in the women's department.[129] The latter was under the coequal principalship of Miss H.M. Parkhurst, who remained in that position throughout the uncertain years of the school in the 1850s and who retired in 1862.

Dearborn resigned in 1864 to accept a faculty position at his alma mater. He was replaced by another Tufts graduate, Wyman C. Fickett, and from that time on, one or more Tufts alumni were likely to be found on the Institute faculty almost every year. Likewise, as many as half of a typical graduating class attended Tufts. Even while the Civil

War was being fought, the Institute's enrollment continued to increase, as did the school's assets. During the academic year 1864-65, enrollment approached 400, and the school remained narrowly in the black with income exceeding expenditures by $100, with total assets of $50,000.[130] The Institute furnished, in proportion to the number of students, more teachers in the 1860s than any comparable school in New York State.[131]

Throughout its relatively long history, Clinton Liberal Institute remained under the aegis of the state convention. Ties with the school became even closer when its charter was amended in 1868 to require the convention to fill all vacancies on the board of trustees. Although separate academic departments continued to be maintained for men and women, by 1871 some of the advanced classes had become coeducational, and several of the women on the faculty taught in both departments. The separate corps of teachers for the historically separate "Gentlemen's and Ladies' Departments" were consolidated in 1874 under the supervision of the principal (redesignated as "president" in 1880), although a woman continued to serve as preceptress.

In 1869 the school year was divided into two terms, replacing the traditional three-semester arrangement which had included a summer term. The enrollment for several years stabilized at about 150 students each semester. The curriculum was revised and expanded to include greater emphasis on modern foreign languages, and a business (commercial) course was introduced. Even though the Institute never became the college once dreamed of, a three-year collegiate program for women was introduced in 1876.

As early as 1867 the recommendation was made that a new building for the men be constructed adjacent to the women's quarters, which had been separated by half a mile since the school had opened. This new arrangement was thought to promote both "economy and good discipline."[132] A fund-raising drive was begun in 1875, with a goal of $80,000. Before two years had elapsed, the canvass was reported to be "a complete success," with the full amount subscribed.[133] Then a new development changed the plans. An opportunity arose to acquire title to the buildings and grounds of what had been the Fort Plain Seminary and Collegiate Institute in nearby Montgomery County. The educational plant at Clinton had become not only inadequate but obsolete, so the offer was accepted by the Clinton trustees and reaffirmed by the state convention. After the legality of the move was established by the state supreme court, the new quarters were occupied in 1879 after arrangements had been made for the modernization of the existing buildings. Accommodations were provided for 200 students.

The Institute then entered its most successful and prosperous period for about a decade. Assets were estimated in 1879 to be $100,000, and the $26,000 in liabilities were easily liquidated by funds from the earlier subscription. Resources were available to expand the curriculum to six courses of study, which sufficiently broadened the appeal of the school to attract students from other denominations. Such students were even offered the inducement of lowered tuition. However, the separate collegiate course for women was abandoned beginning in 1881. Both physical facilities and teaching personnel continued to expand, with the construction of a men's gymnasium and the provision of working laboratories for chemistry and physics; the number of faculty eventually reached nineteen. Among the most popular programs were the business course, for which the Institute achieved a wide reputation; and the music curriculum which in the 1880s attracted as many as 125 students. For many years, piano instruction was offered by Carl Bodell, a graduate of the Royal Conservatory of Music in Stockholm.[134]

The character of the school underwent a significant change in 1892, when the men's department was organized "on a military basis," with an officer of the United States Army as commandant. A brick armory was constructed and equipment was furnished by the War Department. The change was recognized in 1895, when the name of the school became "Clinton Liberal Institute and Military Academy," and the male students were officially referred to as cadets. For two years, an army colonel (Charles E. Burbank) served as president of the institution. When a civilian again became president (1897), an army captain continued to teach the courses in military science and tactics.

The Institute came to an abrupt end in March 1900. The main building was gutted by fire. The estimated cost of replacement was $100,000, and insurance coverage was inadequate. Several alternatives were considered by the trustees. One was to rebuild on the same premises, but that idea was discarded because of the expense involved. Another was to move the school to Canton and reopen it. That also being considered impractical, the decision was finally made, on the advice of the executive board of the state convention, to merge the Institute, with its remaining resources (including the remnant of the library), with St. Lawrence University.[135]

With the wisdom of hindsight, it might appear that the school would eventually have been closed in the normal course of events. Enrollment had begun to decline after 1890, and shortly before the fire the trustees had discussed the possibility of closing the women's department. Total enrollment dropped from 275 in 1891-92 to 189 in 1893-94; meanwhile, tuition and other academic costs had to be increased sharply to keep the school solvent. Annual costs to the students had risen from $220 in 1890 to $300 four years later, and to $400 for the academic year 1899-1900. The steady expansion of the public school system was beginning to take its toll in the private sector, and the Institute had only limited funds for scholarship aid.

Even though the Institute had come to an unplanned end, it had served its purpose well and had survived its many vicissitudes of earlier decades. As the secretary of the Committee on Education of the General Convention had noted, in a retrospective mood some thirty-five years after the Institute had opened, it had even by 1866 lived a career of "singular usefulness" as an educational facility, and as a pioneer denominational effort.[136] In sharp contrast to the policies followed by Universalists in some other states (such as Maine and Vermont), New York Universalists concentrated almost all of their efforts on maintaining one major academy.

Two others besides Clinton were operated by Universalists in New York State before the Civil War for at least part of their histories. However, neither received official denominational support. One was Southold Academy on Long Island. Founded probably in the 1830s, it had passed through several hands before being taken over in 1844 by Daniel M. Knapen, who also served as pastor of the local Universalist society. A graduate of Middlebury College, he had served briefly as the principal of Newton Academy in Shoreham, Vermont.[137] The other New York academy was located at Cooperstown, and was headed for several years by Orren Perkins, who had previously served in the New Hampshire legislature and had been state superintendent of schools in that state for ten years.[138]

Maine. The initiative for the establishment of the first Universalist academy in Maine came from the Kennebec Association at its annual meeting in September, 1830. With the support of the Penobscot Association, within a month a meeting of interested individuals was held in the Universalist chapel in Stevens Plains, Westbrook, a suburb three miles from Portland and later incorporated into that city. The first of the nine resolutions adopted called for the creation of a school "in whose teachers liberality of sentiment shall so far prevail, as to form no check upon the religious opinions of persons as may apply for instruction."[139] It was intended, from the beginning, that the academy would be coeducational, it was to appeal to "the religious sentiments of all orders of Christians" of liberal persuasion; and, although to be controlled by Universalists, was to be conducted with any others disposed to unite with them. It was further hoped that the school would serve all of New England and not Maine alone. After considering several possible locations, including Waterville and Winthrop, Westbrook was chosen because of its presumed accessibility to prospective students from New Hampshire and Massachusetts.

Eleven individuals were granted a charter for Westbrook Seminary early in 1831, and the state convention promptly took over the responsibility for soliciting funds. An application for aid from the state was likewise made, in order to place the school "on an equal footing

Westbrook Seminary (Maine) in 1863

with others which have enjoyed its fostering care."[140] Two local residents donated eight acres of land, and within less than two years $3,000 had been raised by subscriptions and gifts, and $1,000 was appropriated by the state legislature in 1832. Building plans were drawn up, although it was estimated that an additional $2,000 would be needed to put the institution into actual operation.[141] The state provided an additional $1,000 in 1833.

The seminary opened in the summer of 1834, in a two-story brick building, and with high hopes. The school was described proudly as "the only institution of its kind in all New England," and was intended to serve the same purpose as Clinton Liberal Institute in New York State. Samuel Brimblecom, a clergyman, served as the first principal, remaining for two years. But the school almost immediately fell upon hard times, and was temporarily closed at the end of the 1838-39 academic year. The unfortunate event was blamed on the "total destitution of spirit and energy on the part of the trustees."[142] They were blamed not only for inactivity but for "an injudicious use of the funds of the institution."[143] Although they were cleared of the latter charges, they had already incurred an indebtedness of $1,200 before the school had been in operation five years. Enrollment had also not come up to expectations—blamed in part on the fact that the institution was too far removed from the center of Universalism in eastern Massachusetts. Undoubtedly, another explanation for the near-collapse of the school was the opening in 1836 of another Universalist academy in Waterville.

The Maine Convention in 1840 refused to take up an emergency collection to aid the ailing seminary but did create the Universalist Educational Association which was able to raise sufficient funds to reopen the institution late in 1840. However, it was not until 1843 that sufficient patronage was obtained to assure that continuation of the school; 120 students were enrolled that year, with year-round operation under a quarter system.[144] Just as the school appeared to be afloat, the Educational Association became moribund. The continuous precarious financial condition of the school required renewed measures for support. So in 1849 the Maine Universalist Educational Society was organized and incorporated in 1853.

The goal was the creation of a fund of at least $20,000, to be raised in part by selling life memberships at $10. Besides the support of "a permanently established male and female seminary of a high character," the fund was intended to assist indigent young men of good reputation and promise, who may be desirous of entering the ministry." One of the incorporators and leaders in the move to establish the educational society was Israel Washburn, Jr., later governor of Maine and a United States Congressman. By agreement with the trustees of the seminary, the educational society was to select its trustees (all to be Universalists) and nominate candidates for both the principalship and instructional staff. No more than one-fourth of the thirteen trustees could be clergymen.

The educational society, at least for a few years, greatly enhanced the fortunes of the seminary and put it on a surer footing than it had yet enjoyed. The school was freed of debt, and the society undertook to raise money to add a men's dormitory, to endow a department of languages and another in natural science, and to provide scholarships for students intending to enter Tufts College. Worthy and ambitious as all of these aims might have been, few were actually realized. The agents appointed to solicit funds were also expected to raise money on behalf of the state convention for the use of its missionary and tract societies, so financial solicitations tended to be diffused. From 1856 to 1860, when it disappeared, the business of the educational society was confined largely to keeping its own roster of officers intact, and in nominating trustees for the seminary when vacancies occurred. The momentum for supporting Westbrook had seemingly been lost, for by 1858 a "relief fund" had to be created by the state convention to pay off an indebtedness which had risen to $7,000.

The prospects were so discouraging that J.P. Weston, principal at the time, was on the verge of resigning but was induced to remain until 1860.[145] He was paid no regular salary, depending instead on a share of uncertain tuition fees. Sufficient money was raised by 1859 to reduce the indebtedness by more than half, and enrollment had exceeded 250. Even with the full use of the two boarding houses which by then had been provided, student accommodations were inadequate. Then enrollment declined again and the "flourishing condition" described in 1859 had so far deteriorated that the school closed briefly in 1861 for a second time. The raising of $5,500 made possible its reopening the following year.[146]

Westbrook Seminary, in the winter of 1862, embarked on the same experiment with the higher education of women that Clinton Liberal Institute undertook. Westbrook was authorized by a change in its charter to offer "a course of study for young ladies, equivalent to that of any female college in New England." For a time the school offered the degree of L.L.L. (Lady of Liberal Learning) and L.E.L. (Lady of English Learning) which, together, became the L.A. (Laureate of Arts). An L.S. (Laureate of Science) degree was later added.[147] The school therefore offered a terminal education for women but continued to serve as a college preparatory school for men.

Having surmounted the difficulties of its early years, the seminary prospered by the mid-1860s, with annual enrollments exceeding 400. The school received, besides the income from timber lands, benefactions from several individuals, including Mrs. Thomas Goddard and General Samuel F. Hersey, after whom buildings were named. A Universalist church, which had been lacking at first in the community, was finally provided, owned jointly and shared by the school and the parish. Ties with the state convention remained close, and in 1868 the trustees of the seminary were made *ex officio* members of the Maine Convention by an amendment to the latter's constitution.[148]

When the Committee on Education made its report to the centennial meeting of the General Convention in 1870, it could report for Westbrook a permanent fund of $30,000 and grounds and buildings worth $80,000. The school continued under Universalist sponsorship well into the twentieth century, and in 1925 became a women's school and eventually a junior college for women, as an independent non-sectarian institution. Nineteenth-century Universalists had thus made a distinct contribution to the educational history of upstate New England.

Universalists in Maine had considerably less success with the second academy they established than with their first. Waterville Liberal Institute was chartered in 1835 as a counterbalance to the preparatory school which the Baptists had established in the community as a feeder for their institution of higher education, Waterville (later Colby) College. The trustees of the Universalist academy, all from the vicinity, purchased a lot and arranged for the construction of a two-story building, the lower floor of which was originally used to house the coeducational school. The new facility seemed to have served the purpose intended, for it opened in 1836 with fifty-four students and had an enrollment of 134 by the opening of the second year.[149] An arrangement was made with the town to use the academy's facilities for advanced students; hence it served a quasi-public function. It also provided a college preparatory education for such institutions as

Harvard and Bowdoin as well as a training ground for "young gentlemen and ladies for the profession of school keeping."[150] It reached in 1850 a maximum of 305 students. But the school's success was brief, for in 1854 the town provided expanded public school facilities and withdrew its patronage of the Institute. The Maine Convention, called upon to aid the faltering school, was already devoting as much money and effort as possible to keep Westbrook Seminary alive. So the decision was made to close the school in 1857 and to rent the property as a private stock venture. But that "very questionable mode of procedure" failed, and the building was sold and the proceeds divided among the stockholders.[151] Thereafter, only one Universalist school was operated in the state.

Vermont. Failures as well as successes were part of Universalist educational experiences, as the history of Nichols Academy in Massachusetts had indicated. The aborted plan to turn a military academy in Norwich, Vermont, into a denominational school in the early 1830s was another such example. It should be pointed out that the inclusion of an institution with the word "university" in its official title in a discussion of seminaries and academies would seem to represent a misclassification or to be out of place. It is abundantly clear from the extant records that those Universalists interested in acquiring control of the school had an academy (secondary school) in mind rather than a degree-granting institution of higher education. Further, their concept of a "university" should not be confused with the contemporary definition. To them, the term was associated with the historic and generic meaning of "a society or community of masters and students," following the medieval precedent. Norwich did indeed become a collegiate institution when it was rechartered in 1834, but it was at this very point that the Universalists ceased to have any official connection with the school.

The opportunity to acquire the "American Literary, Scientific, and Military Academy" came suddenly in the winter of 1833. Universalists in Vermont received two letters from Captain Alden Partridge, who offered to sell the land, buildings, and equipment of the school which he headed.[152] After an enthusiastic reception of the idea by Universalists in Vermont and New Hampshire in 1834, the rechartering of the institution, and the election of a board of trustees, the practical problems of raising the necessary funds, internecine conflict over the institution itself among Universalists, and growing doubts over the feasibility of the entire project, brought the arrangement to an abrupt end within a year. Although official Universalist involvement with Norwich was brief, it had a lesson to convey. It demonstrated clearly that both the will and the resources had to be found before an educational institution could be successfully operated, and that a clear conception of what functions it should perform had to be developed before commitments were made. At the least, it was an interesting episode in educational history.

The person who made the unexpected offer of the school was a native of Norwich who had entered Dartmouth College in 1802 but interrupted his course to accept an appointment to the United States Military Academy in West Point, New York, established the same year Partridge had entered Dartmouth.[153] After graduating in 1806, Partridge was associated with West Point for twelve years, ten of them as a professor of mathematics and civil engineering, and for two years as its superintendent. He was a strong advocate of military schools and opened his first academy in his native community in 1819: he later established military schools in other sections of the country. The academy in Vermont was an immediate success, and drew students from all over the United States, particularly from the South. In 1825 Partridge was induced to move his school to Middletown, Connecticut. After having been unsuccessful in 1828 obtaining a charter which would have turned the institution into a degree-granting college, he moved the school back to Vermont the following year. Meanwhile, Partridge had continued to operate a preparatory school at the Vermont location, intended to prepare young men for admission to his military school in Middletown or for West Point.

The return to Norwich came at a most inopportune time, for it coincided with a reaction against military education in the North and resulted in a sharp decline in enrollment. In desperation, Partridge leased the school to a group of Methodists until September 1834. He had hoped they would continue to operate the school; instead, they decided to build their own in another community.[154] Partridge's plight seemed to be the opportunity for Universalists in New Hampshire and Vermont who had, for several years, expressed a desire to establish "a Seminary of learning in this part of the Union that shall be free from the influence of sectarianism."[155] Existing Universalist schools, such as those at Clinton, New York, Philomath, Indiana, and Westbrook, Maine, were too far away. Some Universalists in Vermont and New Hampshire were already familiar with the military academy and had sent their sons there.

The facilities which Partridge offered consisted of two brick buildings which could accommodate almost 200 students; approximately four acres of land; a 600-volume library; and such teaching equipment as maps, globes, and surveying instruments which he offered to donate.[156] He also expressed an interest in being connected in some way with the institution, and offered one year's services free of charge. He claimed that the original cost of the school had been approximately $15,000, but that he would sell it for $11,000, with a small down payment. Partridge's offer was discussed at a hastily called meeting of

Vermont Universalists at South Woodstock on Christmas day in 1833, and a committee was appointed to explore the possibilities and report to an open meeting in Norwich in February, 1834. Partridge, in the meantime, suggested that funds could be raised by offering one tuition-free place for four years to every individual who subscribed at least $100.[157] Three days before the meeting was to take place at Norwich, a small group of Universalists in Claremont, New Hampshire, met, endorsed the idea of establishing a school, and selected three delegates to attend the forthcoming meeting.[158] William S. Balch, who had chaired the *ad hoc* meeting and was at the time the senior editor of the *Impartialist* (published in Claremont), prefaced the published report of the Vermont meeting with the remark that the delegates had been instructed to be "very cautious" about accepting Partridge's offer until it could be investigated thoroughly. Balch was particularly concerned about the actual value of the buildings, which he considered no more than "*half the amount* asked for them."

Representatives from Vermont and New Hampshire, and one Universalist from Massachusetts, duly met and decided that it was expedient to establish a Universalist school. Committees were created to confer with Partridge and to examine the property. The captain was also appointed as the agent to solicit funds. After the facilities had been inspected, the enthusiasm of several individuals cooled perceptibly. Balch was particularly dubious. He considered the oldest structure, built in 1819, "just ready to tumble to the ground" and not worth repairing, and the second building "unnecessary." A minute examination of the original building by another member of the committee disclosed no less than six cracks, running from top to bottom; one was between two and three inches wide. In addition, one end of the building was buckled outward. It was no wonder, he wrote, that the owner wished to get rid of it.

There were other problems also, according to Balch. The school was too close to Dartmouth College (across the Connecticut River), and there was no Universalist meeting house available for the students. He was convinced that Universalists were being forced into an unwise purchase by high-pressure tactics. He insisted that the original committee had voted to establish *a* school, not necessarily acquire Captain Partridge's. It was also pointed out that the "General Committee" of ten appointed at the Norwich meeting to investigate the possibility of acquiring the school was overbalanced in favor of Vermont, with seven representatives. Kittredge Haven, one of the delegates from that state, stoutly defended the desirability of obtaining the Norwich property and added the note that the walls of the aforesaid building had been fractured in only one place (not six) and that the crack had appeared immediately after construction and had not enlarged since.[159] Balch vigorously defended himself against Haven's allegation that opposition to the Norwich location was at base Balch's desire that the school be situated on the New Hampshire side of the river.[160]

In any case, the majority of the special committee had their way. After a series of further meetings they voted to acquire the Partridge school, to seek an act of incorporation for "The Norwich University," to select a board of trustees, and to raise the $8,600 (reduced from $11,000) which was finally agreed upon as a fair price.[161] Resolutions favoring the plan were adopted by both the New Hampshire and Vermont Conventions.[162] A proviso attached to the resolution of the New Hampshire Convention that the charter was to give complete control to the Universalists "forever" was not carried out; nor was the stipulation voted at the meeting to establish the university that the act of incorporation provide for Universalist control of the property.[163] The charter, approved by the General Assembly of Vermont on 6 November 1834, nowhere mentioned the Universalists.[164] It did provide, however, that "no rules, laws, or regulations of a sectarian character, either in religion or politics, shall be adopted or imposed, nor shall any student ever be questioned or controlled on account of his religious or political belief."

Only fourteen of the twenty-five-man board of trustees provided in the charter, with representatives to be selected from all six New England states, had been appointed when the charter was approved. There was not a single Universalist clergyman among them. The denomination had abandoned the entire project. Before the act of incorporation had been obtained, Balch had predicted the eventual failure of Universalist efforts to take over the school. The buildings were in too decrepit a state to be used without major expenditure; the final appraisal of $8,600 was still unrealistically high; the village of Norwich had pledged no money—only the equivalent of $300 in labor and services; and, most important, there was no guarantee to the subscribers that the institution would ever open under Universalist auspices.[165]

To make matters worse, Theophilus Fisk, who had been appointed general agent for the new university, departed from New England and in 1838 resigned from both the Universalist ministry and from the denomination.[166] In 1839, a year after he renounced his religious allegiance, he was unanimously elected by the Norwich University cadets to deliver the annual commencement address.[167] Even though the group which had committed the Universalists to acquire the institution passed a vote of confidence in Captain Partridge's "liberality and integrity" and had immediately appointed him as president of the university before the charter had even been approved, some suspicion still lingered concerning his motives and qualifications for other activities than teaching military science.[168] But the prime fact was that the Universalists in the area had undertaken too much. They did not have the resources to fulfill the commitments they had undertaken, and were too badly divided among themselves to have made the venture successful.

The failure of the Universalists to acquire control of Norwich University meant neither the end of the institution nor of Universalist support of it. The university opened in the fall of 1834 with eighty students.[169] By the end of the 1835 academic year, 107 students were enrolled, approximately half of them in the preparatory academy attached to the university.[170] During the same year, a seminary for young ladies was opened in Norwich, undoubtedly a reflection of Universalist influence in providing education for women. Although the seminary was operated independently of the university, its students had access to its library and lectures, and in some of its classes (including foreign languages) they recited with the cadets. The female seminary ceased to exist when a fire destroyed part of the university in 1866, at which time the latter was relocated in Northfield, Vermont.

Thomas Whittemore, influential editor of the *Trumpet,* strongly supported Norwich University as a nonsectarian institution, although he underplayed the importance of the military instruction required by the charter.[171] He explained to his readers that, although the school was not under Universalist sponsorship, its nonsectarian character attracted many students who belonged to the denomination.[172] Several students who later became Universalist or Unitarian clergymen attended the school. Among them were Cyrus H. Fay and Josiah Marvin.[173] Fay, a nephew of Captain Partridge, graduated in 1837 as the class valedictorian and in later years returned twice to deliver commencement addresses. Marvin entered in 1835 and remained three years. Another Universalist minister, Isaac D. Williamson, received an honorary D.D. in 1850.[174] Paul R. Kendall, a layman prominent in Universalist educational circles, graduated in 1847. Among the many positions he held was the first presidency of Lombard University.

In 1836, two years after the collapse of the plans to take over the academy at Norwich and turn it into a university, the Vermont Convention created a committee to report on the expediency of having Universalist associations establish academies throughout the state.[175] This idealistic plan remained completely unrealized. It was not until 1847 that a Universalist academy was actually opened in Vermont, and it was destined to have but a short life. Melrose Academy was built on the foundation laid half a century earlier, when a school operated "under Orthodox auspices" had been opened. Having no other convenient educational institution to attend, Universalists patronized the school. But their experience, as at other schools operated by other denominations, was reported to be an unfortunate one. So two liberally-minded brothers (the Goodenoughs) fitted up a building in the community of West Brattleboro for Universalist use after a principal acceptable to them had operated the school, beginning in 1845.[176]

The opening of the academy in the fall of 1847 was duly announced in denominational papers, and the school was put in charge of J.S. Lee, who for one year had served as principal of the Mt. Caesar-Swanzey Academy in New Hampshire.[177] He brought two former students with him as assistants. Lee was to have been succeeded by one N.D. Putnam, a graduate of Williams College, who apparently found greener academic pastures elsewhere. The coeducational school opened with 100 students and with the primary purpose of training teachers for the common schools.[178] The enrollment increased to over 200 in 1848, about equally divided between young men and young women.[179]

But the entire operation had come to an end by 1852 in spite of a sizable student body. There was not a cent of endowment; and the village was too small to provide adequate living accommodations. And all that the state convention could do was exhort Universalists, as their "imperious duty," to patronize the school.[180] No tangible aid was ever forthcoming from that body. Furthermore, another Universalist institution (Green Mountain Institute) opened in 1848 and probably siphoned off prospective students. Melrose Academy quietly faded into oblivion.

The Green Mountain Association was responsible for establishing a Universalist academy which had a considerably longer history than the school operated in West Brattleboro. The educational venture in South Woodstock (Windsor County) was planned in 1845, but did not open until the fall of 1848. Funds for constructing a building were provided by local citizens under the leadership of Ammi Willard, who served as the first president of the board of trustees.[181] It opened auspiciously with 112 students, but after three years had to be suspended until a suitable principal could be found. J.S. Lee took over the supervision of the new school in the fall, after Melrose Academy closed in 1852. He had great hopes that the academy would become a preparatory school for Tufts College, which had been chartered in Massachusetts the same year.[182] His hopes materialized, for ten of the first twenty students at Tufts were graduates of the school.

The academy became sufficiently well known by 1853 to attract students from ten states as well as from Canada East (Quebec).[183] The enrollment rose that year to a healthy 250, divided about equally between young men and women. Besides its function as an important source for Tufts, the academy operated a successful teacher-training program. Of the 140 enrolled in the fall of 1854, eighty were engaged to teach in district schools during the winter.[184] J.S. Lee, during his five years in South Woodstock, followed the prevalent practice (as did

Sawyer at Clinton Liberal Institute) of conducting theological training as a voluntary separate duty. In 1855-56 Lee supervised the ministerial preparation of six students.[185]

The financial stability of the school, as was the case with other institutions with no endowment, had become a grave problem by 1859. The academy was found to be in a "prostrate and hopeless condition," and there was serious doubt that it could be continued.[186] Through the frantic and last-minute efforts of Nathan Lamb of Bridgewater, president of the trustees, sufficient funds were raised to keep the school open and an endowment campaign to raise $10,000 was announced. But the prospects of the school appeared so dim, and the news of the fund drive so belatedly known, that enrollment plummeted. Under the aggressive leadership of William R. Shipman, an exceptionally capable money raiser as well as principal, the school finally regained its footing and its debts were paid.

The academy experienced two changes of name during its history. The word "Liberal" was dropped in 1860—not because the Universalists had changed the character of the academy, but to distinguish it from a school operated by a group of Spiritualists in the community of Plymouth Union.[187] The Universalist academy underwent a second change of name in 1870 and became "Green Mountain Perkins Academy" in honor of Gaius Perkins, a local tanner and shoemaker who bequeathed a United States bond of $1,000 toward the endowment. But over-dependence on tuition and donations was still a basic weakness which plagued the school periodically. Its whole future was in question by 1865, when there was talk of establishing another academy in the state, to be under the direct sponsorship of the state convention.[188] Nonetheless, the academy continued to operate, and even to expand its physical plant. A neighboring farm of 100 acres was acquired, and the main building was used as a boarding house. The trustees also acquired the village hotel in 1867 for the same purpose.[189] The modest goal of a $10,000 endowment was finally achieved in 1866. The total resources never exceeded $15,000 during the life of the school, and when it closed its value was listed as a mere $6,500.

Green Mountain Perkins Academy, which had served the educational needs of Universalists in Vermont and western New Hampshire for more than half a century, unobtrusively closed its doors in 1893, a victim of economic stringency, public school expansion, and the opening of Goddard Seminary in Barre which diverted many of its potential students. In the 1970s the original building, just a few feet from a main highway, was being cared for by people in the neighborhood, and was opened during summers as a museum and testament to a bygone era.

When Massena Goodrich, on behalf of the Committee on Education of the General Convention, made the annual report in 1865, he called attention to the propensity of Universalists to pass high-sounding resolutions urging the establishment of educational institutions which they "utterly failed to endow."[190] The truth of his complaint was documented too many times to require repetition here. But Orleans Liberal Institute, located in the village of Glover, was a typical example. The academy was opened in the fall of 1852 and struggled to survive for twenty years. It was largely the result of efforts of the Northern Association, which appointed the trustees.[191]

The building erected to house the school was after 1867, jointly owned by the trustees and by the school district in which it was located; hence it had a semi-public character almost from the outset. The academy was launched with great expectations, and the state convention met there in 1852 to celebrate its opening.[192] In its relatively brief history, the school was served by no less than six principals between 1852 and 1872. It appears to have reached its greatest prosperity under Isaac A. Parker, the second person to assume charge (1854-59). Like many of his peers in similar positions, he was himself the product of a Universalist academy (Green Mountain Liberal Institute) and held other positions at Universalist-sponsored institutions—in this case, Lombard University in Illinois.

The Orleans Liberal Institute, never more than "slenderly endowed," seldom had more than fifty students enrolled at any one time in either of its two terms.[194] With a permanent fund of less than $500 derived from the sale of half the school building to the local school district, it "shared the fate of all moneyless institutions."[194]

The school gradually faded out of denominational records. When the centennial meeting of the General Convention was held in 1870, the Committee on Education reported that the institution was assumed to be "still under the patronage of Universalists," but no notice of it had been received.[195] Its last principal, Albert B. Ruggles, a layman, was the sole teacher when the school closed in 1872.

The initiative for establishing an academy in central Vermont came from the state convention and resulted in the only educational institution officially sponsored by that body. At its session in 1863, the movement was begun by John Stebbins Lee, long active in Universalist educational enterprises, and at the time, principal of the collegiate and preparatory department of St. Lawrence University. He called for the creation of a committee to consider plans "for establishing a denominational academical school in this State."[196] The two-man committee reported that it was expedient to do so, but failed to suggest a location beyond the specification that it should be "in some part of the state." An enlarged committee was thereupon established to provide concrete plans, and a separate committee to recommend a specific location was appointed. The fact that none of the three men who served was from Vermont presumably assured an objective decision.[197] The larger committee was given three responsibilities: to confer with the trustees of the two existing denominational schools in the state (Green Mountain Institute at South Woodstock, and the Orleans Liberal Institute at Glover), "for the purpose of making a satisfactory arrangement for the future of these schools;" to appoint an agent to secure funds; and to obtain an act of incorporation.

The charter for the "Green Mountain Central Institute" was promptly secured from the state legislature in the fall of 1863. There was provision for coeducation, and the committee on location appointed by the convention in 1863 was empowered by the charter to select a site. They received proposals from five Vermont communities (including South Woodstock) but decided on a sixth: Barre (Washington County), in the center of the state. An initial goal of $30,000 was set to get the new school under way, and William R. Shipman was designated as the agent to raise funds. His attempts at first brought discouraging results, for by the end of 1864 he had secured commitments for only $16,000.[198] J. Jay Lewis, principal of Green Mountain Institute and a graduate of Tufts College, was appointed agent in the spring of 1865 to complete the task of raising funds, the minimum considered necessary by then having been set at $50,000.[199] The greatest encouragement came from Thomas A. Goddard of Boston, who offered to give $5,000 toward the $50,000, or one tenth of whatever sum would be required. In all, Goddard contributed $10,000. Two years after his death (1868), and before the institution had been opened a year, its charter had been amended to change the name to Goddard Seminary in his honor. Sufficient money had been raised in 1866 to finance construction of a building which was completed in the spring of 1870 at a cost of $72,000.[200] The new school opened with an indebtedness of $10,000 which, after rising to $12,000, was finally paid off in 1874, when a permanent fund was started.[201]

The edifice, a sturdy structure of five stories graced with two towers, was designed by T.W. Silloway of Boston, and was constructed of brick manufactured on the spot from clay taken from the hill on the nine-and-one-half acres purchased for the seminary.[202] Roads were constructed and the grounds were prepared by the people of the village at a cost of approximately $3,000. The building was considered one of the most modern in its day, with steam heat and hot and cold (spring-fed) water in the bathrooms.

The new school, built to accommodate over 150 students, with a chapel to seat up to 350, was presided over at first by L.L. Burrington and Miss Mary A. Bryant, with three other faculty members. The institution was originally in the hands of twenty-one trustees (later enlarged to twenty-five), five of whom lived in other states. Eli Ballou of Montpelier, Vermont, and William R. Shipman, a native Vermonter then on the faculty of Tufts College in Medford, Massachusetts, were among the most prominent. Shipman served for over twenty years as president of the Goddard trustees, beginning in 1876 while on the Tufts faculty, and acted as a self-appointed financial agent for the Vermont institution. Goddard Seminary at first provided a three-year college preparatory ("classical") course for men and an "English" curriculum of equal duration, in four six-week terms each year; and a four-year "female" (later changed to "ladies") collegiate curriculum. The latter provided a much broader course of study than for the men, and with numerous electives in such fields as music, painting, and drawing. The Ladies Collegiate Course was "especially recommended to young ladies of limited means as an excellent substitute and in many respects the equivalent of a course in college." The young men were told that none who had completed the college preparatory course "need fear the entrance examinations of any college." A "thorough drill in the English branches, Latin, and Greek" was therefore included in their curriculum. There was also considerable emphasis on science, including physics and astronomy. A fourth course of study—a two-year college "scientific" preparatory course for men—was added in 1871 (without a foreign language requirement) but was abandoned five years later. In 1873 the three-year English course of study was opened to women.

The total enrollment never reached 200 in any one term, from the opening of the academy in 1870 until its reorganization during the depths of the Great Depression of the 1930s. The school population tended to stabilize at about 140 in any given term, with a maximum annual enrollment below 400. As was customary in many nineteenth-century schools, outside boards of examiners checked the proficiency of students at the end of the academic year. For much of its history, Goddard annually played host to three examiners on behalf of the trustees and a like number for the state convention. By the time of the First World War, the linkage of the school with the state convention became more and more tenuous, and by 1931, when the institution temporarily became the "Goddard School for Girls (with a two-year junior college curriculum added in 1935), almost all formal connection with the Vermont Convention had come to an end, although Universalists continued to patronize the school. In 1938, two years after the institution had become "Goddard Seminary and Junior College," the school was closed. Its assets were transferred to a new corporation and a new institution known as Goddard College, opened in Plainfield on a country estate about ten miles from Barre. The new school was established as an innovative educational experiment, without official Universalist affiliation although with some denominational patronage. Royce Pitkin, president of Goddard College at this time, was prominent in Universalist endeavors in the state and was head of the Vermont-Quebec Convention for a number of years. The new institution bore little resemblance to the traditional seminary opened by Universalists over sixty years earlier.

New Hampshire. The three academies sponsored by Universalists in New Hampshire (Unity School, Lebanon Liberal Institute, and Mount Caesar Seminary-Swanzey Academy) shared several characteristics in common. They were for the most part strictly local in both establishment and clientele; they were founded within a short span of time (in the 1830s and 1840s); and they had but brief histories. The first of these, offically designated as the "Unity Scientific and Military Academy" in the village of that name, was opened in 1835, with Alonzo A. Miner at its head. It, like most other Universalist secondary schools, was coeducational from the time it opened. Universalists in Unity and vicinity financed the construction of a building and considered the institution a community enterprise; its courses were advertised as open to all, including lectures on natural philosophy, astronomy, chemistry, and school-keeping.[203] It claimed to have reached a maximum enrollment of 135 in 1838.[204] But enthusiasm for supporting the school appears to have waned after Miner's departure in 1839. There is record of only one more principal. In the 1840s the school building was sold and moved to Claremont, New Hampshire.[205]

The brief history of Lebanon Liberal Institute in New Hampshire clearly illustrated the transitional and fragile nature of so many Universalist educational efforts. This academy, originally a cooperative venture, lasted only fifteen years. In 1835 a substantial two-story brick edifice had been erected in the village of Lebanon to serve as a secondary school. Known at first as Lebanon Academy, located on Seminary Hill, at least two-thirds of the initial cost of the building and equipment ($2,500) was borne by local Universalists.[206] The institution was incorporated under a nonsectarian board of trustees and opened with encouraging community support. By the end of the first year, over 150 students were enrolled, with 100 in the "female department."[207] Although the students were expected to attend religious services on the Sabbath, they were left free to choose from among the three local churches available—Methodist, Congregational, and Universalist.[208]

The school's prosperity was short-lived. Like so many comparable academies, it had no endowment originally and almost immediately went into debt and ceased operation. In 1840 local Universalists, acting through the Grafton (New Hampshire) Association, proposed to revive the school under their auspices, and agreed to assume the indebtedness of $637.50 and to operate it at least three quarters during the year.[209] A new act of incorporation was acquired and a new board of trustees was constituted which included five Universalist clergymen from the area. The academy was rechristened "Lebanon Liberal Institute" and opened with only a female department in the spring of 1841. Later in the year, a department for young men was added and by the end of 1841 the school had a total enrollment of seventy-five, some of them recruited from Vermont.[210] J.C.C. Hoskins had been graduated from Dartmouth College in time to take over as principal that summer, and the students organized the "Lebanon Philomathic Fraternity," a "society for mutual improvement."[211]

An effort was made to obtain sufficient endowment, by voluntary contributions, to furnish the modest annual income of $300.[212] Meanwhile, Universalists in the area were solicited to furnish a total of $200 a year for operating expenses, including part of the salary of the principal.[213] Efforts "to place the Institution on a permanent foundation" were not at all successful in 1842, and the Universalist trustees were unable to liquidate any of the debt they had assumed.[214] Sufficient money was raised at a public meeting to keep the school in operation for a few more quarters, but lack of sufficient patronage threatened to close its doors from one term to the next.[215] Only 81 students were enrolled in 1842, but the situation had improved by the end of the next two years, when the student body exceeded 100. This was due in part to the addition of a boarding house.[216] In 1846, at which time the property was estimated to be worth $5,000, the school received its first substantial endowment. James Willis of Lebanon donated $2,500, the interest to be used to help support the school.[217] The fund was to go to the local Universalist society if the school ever passed out of denominational control.

The school managed to survive until 1850, when it ceased operation permanently. The death of one of the turstees who was in the process of securing another endowment was one factor.[218] In addition, student boarding facilities in the village were impossible to obtain during the construction of what was then known as the Northern Railroad. The rapid turnover of principals also weakened the school. Among the better-known men who headed the academy was John P. Marshall, a Yale graduate who served for two years, beginning in 1846, and who became a member of the original faculty of Tufts College when it opened as a Universalist institution in 1854. John Stebbins Lee of Vermont, the last principal of the Institute (1849-50), was associated with three other Universalist academies at various times, and was the first president of St. Lawrence University (1859-1868), the second institution of higher learning established by the Universalists.

Mount Caesar Seminary-Swanzey Academy, a coeducational school located in the New Hampshire community of Swanzey, was the outgrowth of efforts by the Cheshire Association in 1842 to establish a "liberal" school.[219] Friends in Swanzey offered to erect the necessary buildings at their own expense, and the institution was opened in September 1843 with sixty-six students. L.J. Fletcher, a Universalist clergyman, served as the first principal, with Miss Fidelia Loveland as supervisor of the "female department." Students had a choice of attending Sunday religious services in the local Congregational or Universalist churches. Considerable stress was placed on science, particularly applied mathematics, for the young men, who were given field experience in such subjects as surveying.

The school had no endowment and struggled for survival on donations and on tuition of $3 per term for the "common English branches" and $3.50 for the "higher English branches," with extra charges for such academic luxuries as classical and modern languages; penmanship, drawing, and painting; and music (piano or organ). Funds were solicited through societies in the Cheshire Association to furnish necessary teaching equipment, which became the property of the Association and was used by the school as long as it was supported by the denomination.[220] In 1847 all connection with the Cheshire Association was dissolved because it was "impracticable" to continue its support.[221] As a consequence, the school almost collapsed, but was rescued by Sullivan H. McCollester, who also served until 1856 as pastor of the Swanzey society.[222] In that year he resigned his position as principal because of the burden it imposed on him, and the school lingered on for three more years. In 1859 the seminary was closed and the main building became a public school and later the village library.[223] Of the six men who served as principals, J.S. Lee and S.H. McCollester were among the best known.

One effort among New Hampshire Universalists to establish an academy in the village of Plymouth in 1855 came to naught. When a local private school closed in that community, Universalists saw an opportunity to open their own. J.H. Shephard undertook to raise funds for the purpose, and even an engraving of the building was distributed as a part of an advertising campaign.[224] The institution was to have been known as "Ballou Seminary" and was to have offered both a business course and a preparatory curriculum specifically intended for those planning to attend Tufts College. But there is no evidence that the school ever opened.

The Midwest

Indiana. The Universalists of southeastern Indiana were responsible for establishing their only denominationally-sponsored academy in that state. The seminary, located in the community of Philomath, which had been created on the site of the deserted village of Mechanicsburg (Union County), lasted less than a decade, but in its short life embodied some rather unusual educational features and deserves at least brief mention as part of the educational record. The school was originally sponsored by the Western Union Association in 1832, and Jonathan Kidwell was appointed its special agent to get the institution under way. Nine trustees were appointed, including Kidwell, and the seminary was duly incorporated by the state legislature in 1833.[225] The school was opened the same year in temporary quarters, but suffered one setback after another and ceased operations in 1841.

It was to be a manual training school for young men, "purely scientific" in its emphasis, and was to provide no religious instruction of any kind. The charter expressly provided that the seminary was to be "entirely free from sectarian influence [and] no religious creed, catechism, dogmas, or confession of faith, shall ever be taught in said seminary, but simply the arts and sciences. . . . [E]very student shall enjoy the free exercise of his own religious opinions . . . without molestation." It was also provided that, when not being occupied by the school, the main building could be used for public worship "free for any christian denomination whatever, without favor or partiality."

The curriculum was to include "the mechanical arts, also the science of agriculture . . . .[T]his will enable young men who are not in affluent circumstances, to obtain an education by their own exertions."[226] The students were to pay their tuition and other expenses by working in shops and gardens which were to be provided; they were to receive a thoroughly practical and useful education in this way, with a minimum of outlay.[227] The philosophy back of this experiment in strictly secular and vocational education was expressed by Kidwell, the leading spokesman for the school. He argued that "the clergy are the last class of the community who should have the management and control of our seminaries of learning," for they were "hostile to civil and religious liberty and a free investigation of natural science."[228] He spoke from some knowledge, for Marietta College in Ohio had dismissed a student for subscribing to Kidwell's free-wheeling and science-oriented *Philomath Encyclopedia* which showed more than a trace of "infidelity." When the same student was then admitted to Kenyon College, he was threatened with expulsion, together with others in the student body who subscribed to the journal. Kidwell offered an entire volume (twelve issues) free to any student who would resign from Kenyon in protest against abridgement of his intellectual freedom.

At first, enthusiasm for the projected school was great. In less than a year, $11,000 had been pledged, and construction of the first permanent building was under way.[229] New England Universalists greeted the news with great pleasure and hoped that they could demonstrate the same zeal in establishing nonsectarian schools.[230] The prospects for the school appeared so bright late in 1833 that the General Convention of Universalists of the Western States agreed to take control of the seminary.[231] But it was all a false hope. The first head of the school (Jacob S. David) was unsatisfactory and was dismissed.[232] Then came delays and financial difficulties which plagued the school throughout its brief history. Pledges of support were not honored, and no person could be found to direct the school until 1836. The "manual labor" system was not yet in operation that year because insufficient funds had been collected. The entire donations for 1836 amounted to $68.80.[233] Neither the main building nor the boarding house had been completed by 1836; prospective students who were mechanically inclined were encouraged to assist in the construction, and were promised credit towards school expenses in exchange for their labor.[234] If they had their own financial resources, students were "privileged to start shops of their own."[235]

In 1836 Kidwell finally managed to obtain the services of Henry Houseworth. He had been an itinerant schoolteacher in Kentucky and Ohio, and had neither training nor practical experience in the subjects to be taught in the Western Union Seminary.[236] He was, instead, a "professor of polite English literature, and the Latin and Greek Languages," and agreed to take charge of the school as soon as there was sufficient enrollment.[237] In the meantime, he offered such diverse subjects as basic reading, writing, and arithmetic; astronomy; chemistry; and elocution, at tuition ranging from $2.50 to $5.00 per quarter, depending on the subjects selected. He and his wife supplemented their income by taking in boarders. He also served for a time as clerk of the Western Union Association and in the same capacity for the school's board of trustees. While at Philomath, Houseworth prepared and sold several thousand copies of primers or "reading books," consisting largely of patriotic selections in support of "pure republicanism."[238] Among the most popular of his readers was *Federubian, or United States Lessons,* of which 6,000 copies were printed.

In 1837 a decision was made to find another head for the school, although Houseworth was to continue to serve on the faculty. The additional teacher was to receive an annual stipend of $100 in addition to whatever "tuition money" he could collect.[239]

Difficulties continued to face both the administration and financing of the school. The General Convention of the Western States, which had taken over the supervision of the seminary in 1834, had decided by 1837 that its optimism was premature. The convention (which became the Ohio State Convention that year) had no resources to carry out its commitment, and was forced to borrow $225 to help support the school. It was unable to repay the loan, and decided to divest itself of all further responsibility for the seminary and return it to the Western Union Association.[240] It was also agreed that the association was to hold its meetings in Philomath so that the institution could be under its "immediate inspection."

The involvement of what became the Ohio State Convention in the affairs of the school had caused nothing but difficulty from the very beginning. Many of the members of the convention had been reluctant to become involved with the seminary in the first place, and an effort was made by others to relocate the institution in Ohio. A campaign was begun to discredit the seminary. Neither its location in Indiana nor its management was considered satisfactory. One correspondent in the *Star in the West* averred that the school "probably put back the cause of education among us for a quarter of a century, or more."[241]

Kidwell, who had consistently opposed the transfer of the school to the Ohio Convention, argued that the convention had no legal power over the school in any case, because it had been chartered in Indiana and not in Ohio. It had, he said, been illegally transferred to the Ohio Convention after he had earlier agreed to be responsibile for the debts of the school (about $1,000) but had been unable to bear the financial burden. He defended the trustees against the allegations of mismanagement and insisted in 1841 that the school could survive. But after announcing the commencement in May 1841 of a new school term, the record of the seminary came to an end and Kidwell published its obituary in January, 1842.[242]

Ohio. Of the secondary schools projected or established by Universalists in Ohio before the Civil War, Madison Liberal Institute was the first. It was another of the numerous examples of unsuccessful attempts to finance education by selling stock; each shareholder was to have a voice in whatever organization was being so created. This particular school was proposed in 1835 by Universalists in Madisonville, near Cincinnati. The institution was incorporated in 1836 and a building was constructed on what had been the foundations intended for a church. It apparently never became operative, even though an announcement of its opening was made for the fall of 1837.[243]

The same fate befell an attempt to open a Universalist academy in northern Ohio, bordering on Lake Erie and near Cleveland. A piece of land valued at $3,000 was donated in 1837 by Richard Lord of Ohio City and James S. Clarke of Cleveland for the purpose of establishing a school.[244] In addition, the two men pledged $350 each, to be used toward construction of a building.[245] Alvin Dinsmore was employed as the principal, and a notice of opening in June, 1838 appeared in the denominational press.[246] However, the "Universalist Institute of Ohio City," sponsored by the society in that community, had a short life. It disappeared in 1839, probably the victim of the financial crisis of 1837-38, one of the many economic upheavals associated with frontier land speculation. Dinsmore then became principal of another school patronized by Universalists, Sharon Academy near Cincinnati, where substantial numbers of Universalists were to be found.[247]

Universalist dissatisfaction with the sectarian character of education being furnished by the Presbyterians in the college and academy which they operated in Marietta, Ohio, was the occasion for the next educational venture of Universalists in the state. Western Liberal Institute was established in 1849. Although a charter had been obtained in 1840, nothing was done for almost a decade. George S. Weaver (1818-1908), who had accepted the pastorate in Marietta the previous year, was largely responsible for bringing the school into being. Soon after his arrival he canvassed his parishioners and other Universalists in the vicinity and determined that there was sufficient interest to support an academy of their own.[248]

The services of T.C. Eaton, whose place Weaver had taken when Eaton had moved to western New York, were immediately obtained as financial agent to raise $6,000. Within a year the requisite sum had been pledged, and a two-story brick building erected, adjoining the Universalist church. Weaver secured the services of his brother-in-law, Paul R. Kendall, as principal and his wife, Abby A. Weaver Kendall, as assistant. The coeducational school seems to have met a real need, for enrollment soon reached 125. Weaver himself taught the classes in "mental and moral science" in which he followed the phrenological principles so popular at the time. At the urging of students, Weaver delivered a series of public lectures on the subject which were printed by the Phrenological Publishing House under the title of *Mental Science.*

The academy was, at first, so successful that the possibility of creating a rival to Marietta College was considered. Additional property was acquired for that purpose in 1851, but the new academy had no endowment, and the principal had not only to teach the courses in classics, natural science, and mathematics, but to recruit students, collect tuition, and obtain (and retain) a staff.[249] The academy did become so well known that it attracted the attention of Universalists elsewhere, including C.P. West of Galesburg, Illinois, who decided to establish a similar school in that state. The result was Illinois Liberal Institute, later to become Lombard College. Kendall resigned from the headship of Western Liberal Institute to take charge of the new school in Illinois and left the Ohio academy in the hands of his brother Nathan and their sister Sarah, who in 1853 married Weaver, by then a widower. After Nathan Kendall's resignation because of ill health, the school declined, and "unfortunate changes" thereafter, including the installation of a new pastor not basically interested in education, resulted in its closing in 1853 after the trustees refused to assume financial responsibility.

Several years after the academy ceased to exist, the Ohio State Convention explored the possibility that the school might be reopened, but found the building being used as a woolen factory and hence quite unsuitable.[250] It was the determination of the convention to have a school somewhere in the state that produced Buchtel College.

Wisconsin. The one Universalist academy in Wisconsin operated under official sponsorship was Jefferson Liberal Institute. The individual largely responsible for its existence was B.F. Rogers, who in 1865 was serving as pastor of the Universalist society in the shire town of Jefferson (Jefferson County), midway between Madison and Milwaukee. An act of incorporation was obtained from the state legislature for the coeducational school in the spring of 1866. It immediately opened under the pastor's direction in the local Universalist church and then in the county courthouse, with fifty students. The state convention promptly took the academy under its wing, and when the school opened for the fall term in 1866 it had sufficient patronage (seventy-five students) to require the full-time services of a principal. The individual who headed the institution, Elmore Chase, was a graduate of Lombard College in Illinois; the new high school was intended as a feeder for it.[251] Chase's wife supervised the "female part" of the academy. An ambitious five-track curriculum was offered, including both college preparatory and business. The school was particularly proud of its courses in the natural sciences, on which special emphasis was placed in almost every Universalist-operated school.[252]

A fund-raising drive produced $13,000 in pledges and gifts, and a three-story brick edifice was erected in 1869 on a four-acre site purchased in 1866. The expenditure for the building ($32,000) brought inevitable indebtedness ($10,000).[253] As was customary at the time, gifts were supplemented by selling shares of stock at $25. However, the amount raised was never sufficient to cover either current operating expenses or provide an endowment. The school was encumbered by one or more mortgages from the day it opened. Prospects looked brighter by 1872, and the trustees were able to take advantage of two offers of substantial sums provided previous obligations were discharged. With this spur to activity, the indebtedness, totalling $17,000 by 1872, was paid off within one year.[254] But the financial panic and depression of 1873 dealt a death blow to the struggling institution, and in 1877 its property had to be sold to satisfy creditors. The building was eventually sold to public authorities in 1879, who turned it into a community high school.

Iowa. Mitchell Seminary, located in the frontier community of Mitchellville (Polk County), near Des Moines, Iowa, was the last general-purpose academy to be established by Universalists in the nineteenth century.[255] It was the outgrowth of discussions in the Iowa State Convention in 1870, after Thomas Mitchell made two offers of land for educational purposes. Eighty acres of town lots worth $10,000 were offered, together with twenty additional acres for a site; part of this allocation was owned by J.R. Sage, the Universalist pastor.[256] The convention readily accepted the Mitchell offer, and the school was incorporated early in 1872, with a board of trustees elected by the state convention at a special session. Plans were made to erect a building, with the school to be opened in the fall of 1872. Sage served as financial agent and Mitchell as president of the board of trustees.

The three-story combined brick and stone edifice, standing tall and isolated on the Iowa prairie, was completed and furnished in the fall of 1873, with seventy-five entering students. The building was to have been one of three projected structures, but the master plan was never carried out. There were so many delays in construction that the local Universalist church had to be used for the first year to house the coeducational student body which in 1872-73 numbered slightly over sixty. Even though headed by a man of the cloth (Sage) and still under the control of the state convention in 1875, the school, as emphatically pointed out, was "not a theological school, nor is it designed to propagate the doctrine of a sect."[257] A "good practical education" was the basic aim of the institution. A conscious attempt was also made to serve the sons and daughters of the large number of inhabitants of German immigrant background in the area, by employing a teacher whose entire academic responsibility was offering instruction in German language and literature.

The school was saddled with debt from the beginning. The construction of the main building required a loan of $5,000, and the estimated initial cost soared from $15,000 to $28,000 in actuality. Although the property of the seminary was valued at $35,000, there was already an indebtedness of $9,000 in 1872. Five years later, the results of a special fund drive proved inadequate and in 1880 the trustees sold the building to the state, which used it as an industrial school for girls. The $20,000 obtained from the sale was still insufficient to pay off the total indebtedness, including accumulated unpaid interest, and Mitchell and other members of the board of trustees assumed responsibility for the balance.[258] Elmore Chase, who had succeeded Sage as principal in 1876, and had been employed on a five-year contract, was undoubtedly an unhappy man. He had just watched his previous employment at Jefferson Liberal Institute come to an end a short time before, when that institution was forced to close. Mitchell Seminary came to an end in 1879, the victim of financial difficulty and changing times.

Although only five Universalist academies remained in 1880, the denomination could take satisfaction in the fact that it was also sponsoring four colleges and universities that year, as well as two theological schools. Universalists could also derive a measure of satisfaction from the fact that their seminaries and academies had fulfilled a vital function in American educational history in a period of rapid change and often uncertain transition to a greatly broadened public school system in which traditional sectarian control was playing a diminishing role.

Chapter 16

THE HIGHER LEARNING: THEOLOGICAL OR LITERARY?

In the perspective of the first century of American Universalism, four broad (and overlapping) generations of clergy can be identified, so far as their preparation for the ministry was concerned. The first comprised the pioneer preachers—usually equipped with little more than an ungraded common-school education, seasonally acquired, often interrupted or uncompleted, and frequently offered by individuals with little more education than the pupils themselves were receiving. Building on this slim foundation, most preachers provided their own theological education out of personal investigation, more or less random reading, and plain experience. It was men such as Caleb Rich and Hosea Ballou who "reasoned their own way into Universalism, and proceeded to spread the word."[1] These were the "doctrinal" preachers, with knowledge of the Bible as their main stock-in-trade, who were better at defending the faith from the stump than serving as settled parish ministers.[2] They lacked both the social graces and intellectual sophistication of those of a later day, and seldom had credentials of any kind. Even those who obtained the minimum that was expected (formal fellowship) were often inexperienced, and were accepted on no more than their own recognizance or were able in some instances to produce someone who would vouch for them. As T.J. Sawyer, one of the most accomplished individuals in the denomination in the nineteenth century expressed it, in the days before formal theological training was available, "young men often went from the plow to the pulpit in the course of six weeks."[3]

A second generation of preachers who appeared in the 1820s and 1830s obtained their skills by apprenticeship and study under someone more experienced than they. The clerical teachers operated what were somewhat pretentiously called "schools," although this might have meant no more than two students at any one time. Typical were those conducted by Samuel Loveland in Vermont and Hosea Ballou 2d in Massachusetts. Although Sawyer did possess a college degree before he decided upon the ministry as a career, and even though he had briefer exposure to an apprenticeship than many of his generation, his general description of this stage of ministerial preparation filled the experiences of dozens of both his contemporaries and of many who came later. If a young man decided upon the ministry,

> it was customary for him to seek a place in some clergyman's family for a longer or shorter time—frequently shorter—read such book or books as were put into his hands, which were generally such as the clergyman chanced to have, and in a familiar and not seldom desultory way, converse on matters of faith, or perhaps discuss points of doctrine. The clergyman, on his side, endeavored to assist his pupil, as far as he was able, in the art and mystery of sermon-making . . . . Finally the young man was afforded early opportunity to try his wings in the pulpit, and as soon as possible hurried into the field, and left to find in actual service the range of his powers, his faults and his needs, and succeed or fail as the chance might be.[4]

With the exceptions noted above, Sawyer's own experience can be taken as typical. He delivered his first sermon in the neighborhood of Reading, Vermont, only a week after his graduation from Middlebury College in 1829 and then decided to prepare for the ministry. He studied for less than two months with W.S. Balch, who was two years his junior and lacked a college education. On the suggestion of Balch, Sawyer accompanied him to a meeting of the Franklin Association, where Sawyer was promptly fellowshipped on the recommendation of his mentor. Less than a week later, Sawyer was ordained (without examination of any kind) at the New England Convention which met in Winchester, New Hampshire. A few weeks later Balch accepted a pastorate in Albany, New York, and left Sawyer to fend for himself. He had accomplished in little more than six weeks what usually required a minimum of three years not many decades later. It was, needless to say, with rather limited preparation that Sawyer took over a full-time pastorate in New York City in 1830.

By the 1830s and into the 1840s, a transitional stage had been developed in ministerial training, running parallel to the old apprenticeship system but by no means supplanting it. Facilities for clerical preparation were often attached to Universalist academies, such as those conducted by J.S. Lee at the Green Mountain Perkins Institute in Vermont and by Sawyer at Clinton Liberal Institute in New York State. The final stage, comprising formal academic and professional training in theological departments or separate theological schools, came with the establishment of the Canton Theological School as an independently administered part of St. Lawrence University; the Divinity School (later the Crane Theological School) at Tufts College; and the theological department (later the Ryder Divinity School) of Lombard College. Regardless of the exact relationship between the theological school or department and the parent institution, it was, with one exception, the college or university that was created first and the theological school which followed. The first attempt in the denomination was to establish a completely independent theological seminary, and it failed.

A False Start: The Walnut Hill Evangelical Seminary

Almost half a century was to elapse between the first mention in the records of the desirability of formal ministerial training of some kind (1814) and the actual opening of a regular theological school (1858). When Universalists once determined to establish schools of any kind under their auspices, they divided at once over what the nature and purposes of such schools should be. The vast majority who favored education in general, balked completely when theological education as such was mentioned; or they assumed that an academy or a college would automatically furnish all of the preparation necessary without separate instruction. The first mention of the possibility of preparing clergymen by means of formal schooling also created a dilemma. Universalists had inveighed against sectarian education so long and so loudly that the recommendation that any schools they might establish should also provide clerical training seemed like the grossest inconsistency. And would not the provision of theological training be an insult to those preachers of Universalism who, while lacking the refinements of formal education, were doing great service for the cause? Above all, there was fear and suspicion of theological education *per se* as somehow promoting an artificial aristocracy not in keeping with the simplicity and democracy of Universalism. These and many other arguments had to be met and countered before advocates of an educated clergy could prevail.

The first step in the long and controversial debate over providing theological education came in 1814, when the New England Convention issued a circular calling for the establishment of a seminary "embracing the united interests of Literature and Religion." The seminary referred to was what became Nichols Academy when chartered in 1819, but which remained under Universalist supervision less than five years. The important point here is that, although it was intended as basically "a Seminary of Science" with literary purposes, there was also the possibility that, if surplus income were accumulated, it would "be expended in the free education of young men, of indigent circumstances but moral and pious habits, designing to enter the gospel ministry."[5]

Some modification in the original plans for the school appears to have taken place, for in the circular drawn up in 1814 there was a clear indication that theological training was to be part of the curriculum. Paul Dean, one of the sponsors of the proposed school, had in 1815 visited Universalists in New England and New York State to acquaint them with the idea of establishing a theological school. Among other visits was one to the Western Association (New York). Nathaniel Stacy, then a preacher in that jurisdiction, had already received a copy of the 1814 circular "soliciting subscriptions for the establishment of a theological seminary in Massachusetts."[6] The understanding was that if any of the New York associations made contributions to the proposed school, they would be refunded if New York Universalists decided to establish their own school. Stacy himself was much in favor of a better-educated ministry, but felt that an exclusively "literary" institution would serve the purpose. If students wanted to become preachers, they had only to go to the Bible for their preparation, and not "to human, theological institutions." Further, gratuitous instruction for "indigent young men," as proposed, would attract "idle and unprincipled youngsters" who would "make a profession" for the sake of getting an education; and acquire "a living without labor." Stacy's argument against free theological instruction was so convincing that Dean did not introduce the subject at all to the Western Association. In any event, nothing came of the rather vague plan to use Nichols Academy even in part for systematic theological instruction.

The next expression of the need for a better educated clergy came at the 1826 meeting of the New England Convention. It took the form of a resolution "that no candidate for the ministry shall be entitled to a letter of fellowship, from any association in this connexion, until he shall have obtained a competent knowledge of the common branches of English Literature, and devoted, at least one year, exclusively, to the study of Theology."[7] Hosea Ballou 2d headed a committee to establish requirements for ordination, which reported in 1827. The convention not only authorized the committee to examine candidates "in secular and sacred learning" but instructed it to explore "the most practicable plan for establishing a Theological Seminary."[8] But no progress was made, and in 1828 the committee to which the task had been assigned reported only "an interesting discussion" and no action.

Between 1828 and 1835, when the subject next appeared on the agenda of what had (in 1833) become the General Convention, Universalists began a discussion about the pros and cons of theological education which agitated the denomination for well over a decade. Just as Clinton Liberal Institute, the second academy to be opened under Universalist sponsorship, was getting under way in 1831, Linus S. Everett urged that no time should be lost in establishing a theological school separate from the literary institution.[9] Thomas Whittemore, an outspoken supporter of education throughout his long career as editor of the *Trumpet,* added his voice in favor of such a plan. He suggested that the Greater Boston area would be a good location.[10] He estimated that at least $20,000 would be needed, one-half of which would be needed for physical plant. If forty persons could be found to supply the funds, he was willing to be one. He recommended that tuition be charged and that "an academical department" might also be opened to help meet expenses.

But the opposition at first drowned out the supporters. The Connecticut State Convention in 1833 vigorously opposed any such proposal as both unnecessary and "diametrically opposed to the simplicity of the Gospel of Christ."[11] Calvin Gardner in Maine, in favor of a theological school which would provide more systematic and thorough training than apprenticeship alone, was immediately attacked for advocating "minister factories."[12] A proposal offered in 1836 in the Hudson River Association (New York) that the state convention establish a theological seminary was completely unacceptable.[13] Another negative vote was recorded in 1836.[14] L.F.W. Andrews, editor of the *Southern Evangelist,* identified forty individuals who had become Universalist preachers in the first eight months of 1834, all without the aid of "Theological 'factories' where young men are manufactured into priests."[15]

The question came up again at the General Convention in 1835. After a "spirited debate" a resolution offered by T.J. Sawyer was adopted that "said subject be recommended to the consideration of the members of our denomination."[16] It was indeed considered, and it fared badly. The council of the New York Convention disapproved, by a vote of 11 to 9, but did agree to recommend at least that the proposal be considered by Universalists in the state.[17] The New York Association disapproved the whole notion while Sawyer, who was present, listened with chagrin.[18] The idea met with "the decided *disapprobation*" of the Susquehanna Association (Pennsylvania).[19] A Universalist Institute in Philadelphia argued that formally trained clergy would not sufficiently resemble the Twelve Apostles to be acceptable, and that preachers should continue to come "from the work-shops and the fields."[20] Theophilus Fisk offered a resolution in May 1836 at the Maryland State Convention strongly opposing theological schools. The six clergymen present were at first evenly divided; then the resolution was adopted, then it was rescinded.[21] Fisk had better luck at the Southern Convention held in Portsmouth, Virginia, a month later. His resolution that theological seminaries were "dangerous, and inconsistent, and inexpedient" was unanimously passed.[22] He added an aside in the circular letter which accompanied the minutes that theological schools were "a trick of the priesthood to obtain power" and maintain themselves as a privileged class.[23] Sawyer was much upset, and hoped that responsible members of the Southern Convention would repudiate Fisk's statement.

But the supporters of a theological school would not be stilled. The question was brought up again at the General Convention in 1836.

Asher Moore, who prepared the circular following the meeting, made it clear that the denomination needed "not only a virtuous, but an enlightened and educated ministry."[24] The Connecticut Association favored a theological school "without a dissenting vote."[25] Discussion in the Old Colony Association (Massachusetts) resulted in a tie vote. A substitute resolution recommended merely that "a greater attention be paid to the subject of ministerial qualifications."[26] In 1837 the Boston Association produced, after prolonged discussion, a general endorsement of theological institutions, but indicated that the circumstances were not yet propitious.[27] The debate was so vigorous at the Steuben Association (New York) that "all persons present, both *ladies* and *gentlemen,*" were allowed to vote on the resolution "disapprobating the establishment of a theological seminary."[28]

Thus the controversy continued. Philo Price, editor of the *Universalist Union,* personally opposed to the idea of an officially sponsored theological school, was probably right when he stated that "a respectable portion, if not a large majority," of both clergy and laity, as of 1838, were opposed to a seminary.[29] All kinds of alternative suggestions were made for solving the problem short of establishing a school. Why not endow a professorship of theology at an existing academy? Or, said one Universalist, why not have ministerial students attend the theological school of another denomination? The Harvard Divinity School (Unitarian) was available, as was the Andover Theological School (orthodox Congregational). They had good libraries and good faculties. If Universalists could not withstand the "partialism" taught at such institutions, they were not sufficiently committed to their faith to be good clergy anyway.[30] Furthermore, they would eventually be required to deal with the ministers and theologies of other denominations, and they might as well include this exposure as part of their education.

But there were objections to exposing Universalists to a Harvard Divinity School education. It lacked "a definite system of theology" and insufficient attention was paid to the Bible.[31] Students were "too much tinctured with rationalism." Still another suggested that, for Universalists in Massachusetts at least, a suitable person might be located near Harvard to receive ministerial candidates who could, by arrangement, use its libraries and be enrolled as special students for particular courses.[32] Hosea Ballou 2d in Medford, would be a logical choice, for he was already offering instruction to students in his home. By 1840 he had so many applications that he was forced to set up stated times during the year when students could be received, and had to offer classes as well as individualized instruction.[33] The previous year he had prepared a syllabus, complete with bibliographies, for a three-year theological course.[34]

Whittemore, never noted for his patience, had by 1838 become completely exasperated by the do-nothing policy of the denomination. Getting Universalists to pursue an enlightened policy and commit themselves to supporting a theological school was "almost altogether an *uphill* business."[35] The age of miracles had passed, he wrote somewhat sarcastically, when men were prepared for the ministry solely "by immediate communication from heaven." Something more was needed than divine inspiration alone; namely, some human effort. Piety alone was insufficient; the dignity of scholarship had to be added to ministerial qualifications.[36] He was stung to the quick by an article which appeared in the *Boston Recorder* and described, in contemptuous language, the unfortunate Universalists who possessed "no colleges or schools of theology, or any literary institutions other than second rate academies," and had to fill their pulpits "largely from the bench and the shop, . . . with little culture, in manners or in mind."[37] Hosea Ballou 2d, just as much in favor of theological education as Whittemore, but with more sensitivity and finesse, urged supporters to recognize the right of others to disagree, and warned Universalists not to push too far too fast. Otherwise, the issue might become a serious divisive force in the denomination.[38]

Even at the risk of creating a rift in the ranks, Sawyer, anxious to keep the subject before the Universalist public, published a whole series of articles in 1839 stressing the importance of systematic training for an educated ministry.[39] Calvin Gardner thought enough had been written and said by 1839 that the time had come to be "up and doing."[40]

Then the log jam broke. The Massachusetts Convention, which had been reluctant to take any kind of concrete action, unanimously adopted a resolution in 1839 endorsing the idea of a theological school, to be located in the state; and a five-man committee was appointed to draw up plans.[41] The next year it was voted "to proceed forthwith" to establish a seminary, and a board of trustees was authorized to secure a site, erect a suitable building, and do whatever else was necessary to bring the institution into existence. Whether the promise of a site was primarily responsible for bringing about such a complete shift in attitude and finally stirring the convention to action cannot be stated with certainty; but an offer of ten acres of land by a wealthy Universalist in Charlestown probably influenced the decision. The offer of a site was known before the trustees had even been nominated.[42] Charles Tufts owned some 200 acres of land straddling the communities of Medford and Somerville, about seven miles northwest of Boston, and including the highest hilltop north of the city. The offer of the land on what was known as Walnut Hill was promptly accepted, and the committee appointed to nominate trustees agreed to name the proposed institution the "Walnut Hill Evangelical Seminary."[43] The board, which could reach a maximum of twenty-five members, was to consist exclusively of individuals who subscribed to the Winchester

Profession, the denominational profession of faith, but there was no requirement that they be clergymen. Membership on the board was to be for life, except in cases of "voluntary resignation, immoral conduct, mental imbecility, or want of belief or interest" in universal salvation. The rules for the governance of the trustees which were prepared in the fall of 1840 were in all likelihood drawn up by Hosea Ballou 2d.

The nine men originally designated as trustees were all from eastern Massachusetts and their names were familiar to most Universalists: Hosea Ballou (Boston), Thomas Whittemore (Cambridge), Oliver Dean (Framingham), Charles Tufts (Charlestown), Lemuel Willis (Lynn), James Bartlett (Plymouth), Timothy Cotting (Medford), Sylvanus Cobb (Waltham), and Benjamin Mussey (Boston). Only four were clergymen. Oliver Dean, a prominent physician, was to serve as the president of the trustees. The intent of the original board when it organized in January 1841 was to appeal to as broad a constituency as possible, and for that reason provided that each New England state was to be represented by at least one trustee, and New York by two. However, only two more were actually elected, and both were from Massachusetts (Samuel Bugbee of Wrentham and Sebastian Streeter, from Boston).

Sawyer, who was to have been one of the representatives from New York, declined to serve. He announced that his time and energy would be fully employed because he was "about to embark on a grand enterprise in our own state—the establishment of a College or University that will successfully compete with any institution in this Empire State." It could very well be that Sawyer was also disappointed that New York State had not been considered as a location for the school, and that he resented the fact that he had not been appointed as a charter trustee. Sawyer may have had in mind Clinton Liberal Institute, which he had visited in 1833, when discussions had already taken place about the possibility of turning it into a college.[44] Rivalry between Massachusetts and New York over the location of Universalist schools in which Sawyer was involved was later to surface more than once. Others were nominated from various states, but there is no indication that they met as a group after May 1841. Both Hosea Ballou and his great-nephew and namesake were on the original nominating committee, of which Hosea Ballou 2d was the clerk, but there is nc clear evidence that he ever served as a trustee despite his active involvement in the entire project.

The goal of the trustees was an ambitious one. They committed themselves to raise $50,000 by scubscription. Calvin Gardner of Waterville, Maine, although inexperienced in such matters, agreed to serve as the fund-raising agent at an annual salary of $600, plus travelling expenses. Compensation from any preaching he might do along the way was to be credited to the fund. His services lasted less than a year, for he had taken a leave of absence as pastor of his society and returned, discouraged with his almost total failure to raise money. The trustees fared no better in their efforts. Four pledged $1,000 each, but some tied strings to theirs beyond the cutomary provision that none would be called in until the entire sum had been subscribed. Both Whittemore of the *Trumpet* and Cobb of the *Christian Freeman* conditioned their pledges on acquiring additional subscribers for their newspapers.[45]

A circular letter setting forth the plan for the seminary[46] was issued in the summer of 1841. The burden of the call for assistance was that Universalists had fallen behind other denominations in providing an educated ministry, and the days of inertia and apathy had to come to an end. One response was a pledge of $100 from a young man in Philadelphia.[47] A series of meetings was held in various communities in Massachusetts, including Boston and Worcester, to drum up support, and continued into the fall of 1841.[48] Edwin H. Chapin spoke in Boston in favor of the school "with great eloquence." At a sparsely attended meeting in Worcester, with about twenty clergymen and a few laymen present, $700 was raised in pledges.[49] Hosea Ballou 2d obtained about $1,200 from his own society in Medford, in addition to the $1,000 promised by Timothy Cotting, a member of his congregation and a trustee.[50] There was moral support from the Pennsylvania Convention, and a sermon at the Massachusetts Convention strongly advocating the seminary.[51] But only $5,325 was ever pledged—scarcely more than one-tenth of the total required. So the projected school never became more than a name that soon faded from memory.

The General Convention, meeting in New York City in September 1841, went no further than recommending that "institutions be established for the purpose of assisting young men, who contemplate entering the gospel ministry."[52] No other aid was forthcoming. It was at this point that Calvin Gardner resigned as finaincial agent. Hosea Ballou 2d continued to advertise that he would offer instruction for the ministry.

The utter failure to even approach the target of $50,000 was reason enough to explain the collapse of plans for the seminary. But there were other factors at work as well. Gardner had recognized that his efforts were premature, the denomination was not yet ready to take such a step. Another consideration needs likewise to be taken into account. Many of the pioneer generation of Universalist preachers were still active and still unconvinced that formal education of any kind was necessary for ministerial preparation.

The appointment of Hosea Ballou as a trustee of the ill-fated seminary was without question motivated by deference to his stature in the denomination, but it was a serious tactical error so far as the potential success of the theological school was involved. He was far from enthusiastic about the idea of theological schools at all. A call to preach the Word and determination to succeed were all that was needed.[53] He, as much as any individual on the board, sabotaged the entire effort by marshalling every argument as his command. Times were hard, and the climate was unfavorable for establishing a theological school.[54] He saw no reason why a young man had to leave home to gain an understanding of the Scriptures or even seek the help of an experienced preacher.[55] Beginning in the late summer of 1841 he wrote a long series of articles published in the *Trumpet* expressing doubt about theological education. Gardner immediately challenged Ballou, and the debate continued for weeks. Gardner forthrightly (if not diplomatically) told Ballou that the Universalist community could no longer be satisfied with the type of ministry acceptable fifty years earlier.[56] It certainly did the cause little good to have a trustee of the project engage in a debate with the very individual hired to raise the funds. Four years were to elapse before another proposal was made to establish a theological school.

Educational Leadership: Thomas Jefferson Sawyer and Hosea Ballou 2d

Whether theological schools, academies, or colleges were being discussed by Universalists between 1830 and 1860, the names of T.J. Sawyer and Hosea Ballou 2d were invariably invoked. The two men were indissolubly associated with every educational effort made by the denomination during their lifetimes. It was they, above all others, who, in season and out, and each in his own way, urged their denomination to recognize the value and even the necessity of formal education. Of the two, Ballou was probably more concerned with and interested in promoting higher learning in the tradition of the liberal arts, while Sawyer tended to concentrate his efforts on promoting the professional training of the clergy. It was Ballou who, without an earned college degree, became the president of the first institution of higher learning founded by the Universalists. It was Sawyer, himself lacking professional theological training but with a college degree, who, after Ballou's death, became the first head of the divinity school in that same institution. In an address the year before his death in 1899, Sawyer singled out the establishment of the first theological school in the denomination as his greatest contribution. Although the two were in many ways a study in contrasts, no other team did more to further the cause of denominational education as their paths paralleled as well as crossed for almost thirty years.

Thomas Jefferson Sawyer (1804-1899), born in Reading, Vermont, on 9 January 1804, followed in his early years the educational pattern of many of his contemporaries.[57] He attended the local district school

Thomas Jefferson Sawyer (1804-1899), minister, teacher, and denominational historian

during the winter months and at age eighteen alternated as both teacher and student. After attending Chester Academy he was admitted to Middlebury College, from which he received a Bachelor of Arts degree in 1829 and a Master of Arts in 1833. He did not have an easy time, for limited resources bordering on poverty forced him to interrupt his education frequently until school teaching or other temporary employment replenished his treasury.

He decided to enter the Universalist ministry upon graduation and began an apprenticeship under W.S. Balch that lasted less than two months because of Balch's departure for another pastorate. In spite of completely inadequate preparation, Sawyer was both fellowshipped and ordained in a matter of weeks, and he found himself a year later in charge of a small and struggling society in New York City. After fifteen years of sustained effort he built a strong Universalist base in the city and took charge of the Clinton Liberal Institute located upstate. It was, when he assumed control in 1845, the only Universalist-sponsored educational institution in the state and was in serious financial difficulty. Until 1852 he not only strengthened the faltering school but conducted separate training for theological students. He resigned to return to the Orchard Street church in New York City and remained until 1861. The fact that he was receiving an annual salary of $2,500 by 1853 undoubtedly entered into his decision to decline successive offers of the presidencies of three Universalist institutions during the decade of the 1850s (Tufts College, St. Lawrence University, and Lombard University).

After his departure from New York City in 1861 Sawyer lived in semi-retirement on the twenty-acre farm near Clinton he had purchased in 1846 and had subsequently enlarged to forty acres. He again returned to New York City in 1863, where for three years he edited the *Christian Ambassador.* After another brief retirement, this time in New Jersey, he became in 1869 the first faculty member of the newly-created divinity school of Tufts College. He remained at that post until 1890, when failing eyesight impaired his work sufficiently to force retirement. He died at his home at the college at the age of ninety-five, the oldest member of the denomination at the time. He was venerated by all and left behind him a long and varied career in the service of Universalism.[58]

Sawyer first publicly discussed the value of formal education, and particularly the necessity of theological training, in 1832. At a meeting of the Hudson River Association (New York) he outlined a course of study for young men preparing for the ministry, and his listeners were so impressed that they unanimously passed a resolution requiring candidates for fellowship not only to produce evidence of having studied theology under an accredited preacher for at least six months but to be able to pass an examination in "the principles of the English language, rhetoric, and logic," and to write an essay on "some moral or doctrinal subject."[59] The reaction outside the association was far from enthusiastic, however; one critic considered the requirement of competency in English grammar "absurd" for ministerial candidates.

In 1833, three years after he had begun the first pastorate of his career in New York City, Sawyer visited Clinton Liberal Institute. He was much impressed with its potential as an instrument for educational advancement only two years after it had opened, and published a detailed report of his impressions. He emphatically declared that the school was a "scientific and literary" institution, having for its object "not to inculcate religion, but to afford opportunities for the acquisition of learning."[60] He was to reiterate time and time again the necessity of keeping secular and theological education in two separate and independent tracks. When he offered theological training, after taking over the supervision of Clinton Liberal Institute in 1845, Sawyer did not even use the school building at first; he rented an attic room in a private residence for his ministerial classes.[61]

Devoted almost single-mindedly to education and scholarship, Sawyer was the prime mover in the establishment of the Universalist Historical Society in 1834 and, as already noted, served as its secretary and librarian for well over half a century. The very last article which he wrote, published in the *Universalist Leader* in 1899, dealt with the library to which he had devoted so much of his life. It was he who, in 1844, had drafted the plan for the organization of the General Convention which was eventually adopted many years later. And it was he who issued the call for an educational convention in 1847 out of which Tufts College was born and in the destiny of which he was intimately involved. The institution recognized his services to education and to the denomination by conferring upon him the honorary degree of LL.D. in 1895.

Hosea Ballou 2d (1796-1861), born in Guilford, Vermont, on 18 October 1796, demonstrated a love of learning as a youth when he studied Latin both with a neighboring clergyman and in the district school which he attended between the ages of four and fourteen.[62] After teaching in local schools for three seasons and being informed that college was inadvisable because virtually all New England colleges were under the control of proselytizing Congregationalists whom Universalists distrusted, Ballou was forced to continue his education by his own efforts. He became an aide in 1813 in a private school operated by his great-uncle and namesake, Hosea Ballou, in Portsmouth, New Hampshire. It was under his great-uncle's guidance that he trained for the ministry. By the close of 1816 he had delivered over forty sermons, many in western Massachusetts and southern New Hampshire.

Ballou's first regular pastorate was in Stafford, Connecticut, which at the time had the only Universalist meeting house in the state. He also

Hosea Ballou 2nd (1796-1861), Universalist scholar and first President of Tufts College (1853-1861)

preached in surrounding communities. From the time of his first regular preaching in 1817 until his death in 1861 Ballou was deeply involved in denominational affairs; he delivered sermons, served on numerous committees, drafted reports, and from time to time was moderator, clerk, and secretary for the New England Convention (General Convention after 1833). In 1819 he was appointed one of a committee of visitors to the Eastern Association (Maine), an important assignment for a young man of only twenty-three.

A year after his marriage to Clarissa Hatch, whom he had known since childhood in Vermont, Ballou, in 1821, became the first pastor of a new Universalist society in Roxbury, Massachusetts, where he served for seventeen years. While there he perfected his knowledge of Latin, learned to read French, German, and Greek, and began the study of Hebrew. He was therefore admirably equipped linguistically for the scholarly work he was later to produce. The books in his extensive private library which he had collected by the time of his death were carefully annotated in the language in which they were written.[63] Ballou also operated a private school for boys between 1826 and 1836, in which his brother Levi assisted. Ballou also served on the local school board which by 1838 was overseeing a rapidly growing school system with 1,000 students enrolled.

Ballou's third (and final) pastorate was in Medford, Massachusetts (1838-53). Meanwhile, he had become a contributor to the *Universalist Magazine,* and for four years, beginning in 1822, was one of its editors. One of his first responsibilities was to serve as editorial peacemaker among the contenders in the Restorationist controversy which, after 1822, threatened to create a schism among New England Universalists. He continued to play the same role in various crises that faced the New England (General) Convention during his service as its standing clerk for fifteen years (1824-39). He counseled "union and peace" time after time, as he served at dedications, installations, and other denominational functions.

Judging from the record left by his contemporaries and acquaintances, Ballou's greatest strength was as a scholar, writer, and thinker, rather than in the pulpit. He was considered by one historian of the denomination who knew him well as "probably the most learned theologian in the ranks of self-educated men in the country."[64] Modest and unassuming to the point of self-effacement, Ballou devoted every spare hour to scholarly pursuits. His first major work was the *Ancient History of Universalism,* an outgrowth of a suggestion he made in 1823 to Thomas Whittemore, his colleague in editing the *Universalist Magazine,* that the two prepare a comprehensive history of Universalism.

Up to that time, such a study had never been undertaken, although several times considered.[65] The first such suggestion had been made in

1812 by a group of preachers meeting in Gloucester who decided to start a publication known as the *Gospel Visitant* which became associated with the Restorationist controversy. They requested one of their number (Edward Turner) to prepare for publication in the *Gospel Visitant* a history of the doctrine of universal salvation in America.[66] Nothing having come of that, the New England Convention in 1816 appointed a three-man committee, including the elder Hosea Ballou, to prepare such a history.[67] At the next meeting the committee reported "no success" and in 1818, in spite of the reconstitution of the committee, the result was the same. A "General Epistle" soliciting material accompanied the proceedings of the 1819 session. Turner had actually composed about twenty pages, and the committee saw fit to issue a prospectus in 1820 announcing plans to publish by subscription at least 1,000 copies of a history covering both Europe and America.[68] It was to comprise approximately 250 pages and sell for $1.00, "handsomely bound." That was as far as the project went.

There had been, shortly after the decision of Ballou and Whittemore to write a history, only one other attempt known, and it was far from serving the intended purpose. An ex-Shaker of Quaker background, who later claimed to be a Universalist, one Thomas Brown, M.E., published in 1826 *A History of the Origin and Progress of the Doctrine of Universal Salvation* in Albany, New York. A copy came to the attention of W.A. Drew, editor of the *Christian Intelligencer* (Maine), who had a very low opinion of both the book and its author.[69] Drew considered it a poorly written apologetic rather than a true history, and was irked by the pretentiousness of the author's addition of the initials "M.E." to his name; they stood for "Medical Electrician." The author later published a work entitled *The Ethereal Physician, or Medical Electricity Revived.*[70] Sawyer, like Ballou a meticulous scholar, noted that Brown's work had little value as history.[71] It was almost entirely lacking in references, and even the quotations were so carelessly cited that it was impossible to distinguish the author's statements from those of his presumed authorities.

Ballou and Whittemore therefore had a wide-open field in which to operate. As pointed out earlier, they divided the task, with Ballou carrying the story up to the Reformation of the sixteenth century, and Whittemore continuing the history beyond that point.[72] Ballou worked assiduously on his share of the history in his spare time, over a period of over five years. He visited the Harvard College library at least once a week to do the necessary research. The *Ancient History of Universalism* was published in 1829, an impressive contribution to original scholarship using primary sources. It covered exhaustively the first six centuries of the Christian era, and an appendix dealt in briefer fashion with the period from the condemnation of universalism in 553 A.D. to the era of the Reformation.[73] The principal theme of the work, as implied by the title, was the antiquity of universalism as a religious concept and that it was not at all a doctrine originating in America.

Like many scholarly books, this one sold very slowly. It had gone out of print in 1839, but largely because part of the press run had been lost in a conflagration in Boston.[74] When Ballou's work appeared in a second edition in 1842, with some editorial changes but no substantive revisions, Ballou (in the preface) expressed dissatisfaction with part of his own book because he did not consider his research sufficiently thorough. A third edition was published in 1871, a decade after his death, and was reprinted in 1885. In 1833 Ballou edited an English translation of J.C.L. Simonde's *History of the Crusades against the Albigenses in the Thirteenth Century,* which Ballou considered a continuation of his own book.

It was only fitting, as his biographer pointed out, that Ballou was elected as the first president of the Universalist Historical Society when it was organized in 1834. It was Ballou who was responsible for providing the denomination, beginning in 1830, with a scholarly journal intended primarily to strengthen the educational background of Universalist ministers, few of whom had ever had formal theological instruction, even under the tutelage of experienced clergy.[75]

He had become sufficiently well known in the Boston area by 1843 to be nominated for the Board of Overseers of Harvard University with six other candidates, to fill the vacancy created by the death of William Ellery Channing the previous year. He was nominated in part to comply with the requirement that, because the institution received public funds, representatives of more than one denomination had to be on the board.[76] It might also be added that Ballou was well acquainted with Josiah Quincy, who was president of Harvard at the time. Ballou won the election and was also reelected, serving a total of fifteen years, until 1858. In 1844 Ballou received an honorary Master of Arts degree from Harvard at the same time that a similar degree was awarded to Asa Gray, the eminent botanist. Only a year later the same institution conferred on Ballou an honorary Doctor of Divinity degree, the first such honor ever bestowed on a Universalist. Ballou also served for four years (1854-58) on the state board of education.

In the absence of a denominational theological school, Ballou, like many other clergymen, accepted students who wished to prepare for the ministry. While serving his pastorates in Roxbury and in Medford he offered such instruction, and in 1839 developed a three-year course of study, complete with extensive bibliographies.[77] Two of Ballou's younger brothers, Levi and William Starr, were among his theological students in Roxbury. Probably the best known of Ballou's students was Thomas Starr King.[78]

Ballou's involvement with the educational efforts of the denomination had begun early in his life. In 1817, at the age of twenty-one, he was appointed to serve on a committee to solicit subscriptions for the Universalists' first school, Nichols Academy. He served in 1827 and again in 1836 on committees to explore the possibility of establishing a theological seminary. He issued his first call for denominationally-sponsored schools in an article published in 1839 and widely copied.[79] It was largely out of Ballou's plea that had come the decision of the Massachusetts State Convention in 1840 to establish the ill-fated Walnut Hill Evangelical Seminary. Between 1840 and his death on 27 May 1861 of a kidney ailment at the age of sixty-four, while serving as the first president of Tufts College, Ballou was associated with every movement that had to do with denominational education.

Establishing Educational Priorities

The General Convention of Universalists met in New York City in 1841. The theme of the keynote sermon, delivered by Sawyer, was education, and Hosea Ballou 2d was there to hear the appeal for founding and endowing "at least one university, to be a monument to the coming age of our zeal for education." With the encouragement of a vote of approval, Sawyer called a special meeting of "the friends of education" immediately following the adjournment of the convention and invited all who favored immediate action to attend.[80] After endorsing the resolution passed at the convention favoring theological education, and stressing the need for Universalist-sponsored schools, in a burst of enthusiasm those present created an eleven-man committee representing Universalists in that many states to devise and submit a "plan of operations." All six New England states, New York, Pennsylvania, Ohio, Illinois, and South Carolina were represented on the committee. Another committee (all from New York State) was created to serve as a channel of communication. No clear distinction was made as to whether the proposed school was to provide theological training exclusively or instruction "in the higher branches of literature and science." The ambiguity was never resolved, for the report to have been prepared and circulated by the committee was never made, and the entire idea evaporated as suddenly as it had appeared.

Nothing might ever have been done despite the persistent efforts of Sawyer and Ballou if a crisis had not occurred in 1845 at Clinton Liberal Institute. It was in danger of closing for lack of adequate patronage and financial support; the female department, in fact, had been suspended that year. An urgent appeal went out to the New York Convention to salvage the institution by assuming responsibility for it, and Sawyer answered the call in 1845 to head the Institute. He found himself not only elected to the reconstituted board of trustees but to the principalship of the struggling school as well. The announcement was immediately made that a theological department would be attached to the Institute, to be conducted by Sawyer.

Ballou was delighted to hear the news, although he warned Sawyer that the double task would be "a very laborious one for a while, demanding much patience and forbearance as well as activity."[81] Ballou was especially worried over the availability of funds; something more substantial than hand-to-mouth contributions on a temporary basis had to be provided. He urged Sawyer to bring the matter of financing to the attention of the next General Convention, together with definite plans for conducting each part of the operation. Sawyer followed Ballou's advice, although no commitment of any kind was made for financial support. The resolutions adopted by the convention expressing pleasure at Sawyer's dual appointment at Clinton were drafted by Ballou.[82]

The "Universalist Theological Seminary," the first in the denomination, was about to be opened.[83] It appeared that a new era in Universalist educational history was about to begin. Sawyer was forced, however, to make one important clarification. He vigorously objected to the implication in the minutes of the 1845 convention that the institute at Clinton was about to be turned into a theological school. At the 1846 meeting of the General Convention he had the minutes of the previous year corrected to read that the theological school was to be "a distinct institution of itself, and not a department of the other" even though both would be conducted by the same person.[84]

There was further encouragement for Sawyer following the 1845 convention. A mass meeting was held at which a resolution was adopted "by a loud and unanimous response" that it was "the duty of Universalists to sustain the Literary Institutions of their denomination." This was immediately followed by two related resolutions to the effect that "the circimstances of the present age require that we have a ministry of high literary and theological attainments; and that great care is essential in introducing any person into the ministry." A committee was appointed to prepare an "Address to the Universalist public" on the subject. The next resolution was an enthusiastic endorsement of the theological program established at Clinton under Sawyer's supervision. He was to receive $500 a year for five years for his services; twenty subscriptions at $5 each were obtained on the spot.

The choice of Sawyer to head the institute was a wise one, for the school immediately began to prosper, and he announced that he was prepared to devote two hours a day, as an additional and voluntary duty, to the instruction of those who wished to study theology. He was assisted on a part-time basis by four other clergymen, including Stephen R. Smith, who had played a leading part in establishing the institute.[85] He also expressed the hope in 1846 that the institute might be turned into a college if sufficient money could be raised to comply with state requirements for a charter. With this as a possibility, a committee headed by Ballou made a report at the 1846 General Convention recommending that agents be appointed in every state where there was a convention to solicit subscriptions totalling $50,000 to turn Clinton Liberal Institute into a college or university.

By the time the New York Convention met in 1846, Sawyer had undertaken to supervise the ministerial preparation of sixteen young men in a fourteen-week course. With many more candidates needed, additional formal support of Sawyer's efforts seemed to be warranted. It was time, as Philo Price observed editorially, to lend Sawyer a helping hand. The New York Convention thereupon aided Sawyer's bootstrap attempt to train clergymen by creating the "Clinton Theological School."[86] A fourteen-man board of trustees (seven clergymen and seven laymen) was appointed to raise funds, acquire books, and establish the school on a permanent basis. It was decided to obtain 100 subscriptions at $25 each, payable over a five-year period, to provide Sawyer with an annual salary of $500. The goal was a fund of $10,000, the annual interest from which was to defray expenses. Instruction was to be provided to students without charge.

There were, however, some ominous signs from the very beginning which boded ill for the future of the school. The decision to establish it was made by only a minority. With sixteen associations in the state, each entitled to four delegates (two clerical and two lay), less than half of those eligible to vote had attended the meeting. Further, all of the trustees were from New York. Sawyer made haste to explain the reasons. Aside from the purely practical problem of assembling trustees from a distance, New England Universalists had expressed no real interest in the proposed theological school in New York State and were not supporting it in any visible way.[87] He undoubtedly remembered that all of the original trustees of the proposed Walnut Hill Seminary had been from Massachusetts and considered their decision to nominate trustees from other states, including New York, as a mere token gesture and an afterthought.

There was also the matter of who should head the institution. It was an obvious impossibility for one individual to operate both the institute and a full-fledged theological school. In addition, Sawyer served as pastor of the local Universalist society, with two sermons to deliver every Sunday. Even if he had had the time and energy, conducting both educational operations did not keep the two schools truly separated, as Sawyer himself had insisted. He submitted his resignation from the theological school at the first meeting of the trustees.[88] So the General Convention took a hand when it met in Troy, New York, a few weeks after the state convention had voted to establish the theological school. The convention appointed Hosea Ballou 2d to take charge of it. He was requested "to enter upon the duties of his office as soon as possible" and his annual salary was set at $800. But Ballou could not be induced to take the proffered position, although he waited for over a year before declining, in order to provide time to raise the necessary funds. By 1847 the $10,000 endowment remained unprovided; and there was not even sufficient money to pay Ballou's salary.

Ballou continued to urge Sawyer to stay at his post at Clinton in spite of the sacrifice it entailed, even if he had to abandon the theological training and concentrate on the possibility of turning the institute into a college.[89] Ballou took a dim view of Sawyer's proposal to hold a special convention on the subject of education, feeling that only "magniloquent votes and resolutions on paper" would come out of it.

The proposed theological school sponsored by New York Universalists seemed doomed to fail for lack of financial support. So, with the idea of making Clinton into a college still in mind, Sawyer made one more attempt on a grand scale, in spite of Ballou's advice, to get the support of Universalists at large for both a theological school and a college. He called for an educational convention to be held in New York City in 1847 in advance of the General Convention about to meet there.[90] The letter of invitation was addressed "to the Universalists of the United States," and not merely to those in New York State.

Sawyer suggested four questions for discussion: Was there a need for a well-endowed college and a similarly supported theological seminary? Should the effort be delayed any longer? Where should the schools be located? What methods were to be adopted to raise the necessary funds? The answers to the first two questions were self-evident to Sawyer: a firm "yes" to the first and an equally firm "no" to the second. As to the remaining two questions, he was careful not to be overly specific. He made no mention of Clinton, New York, as a possible site for either school but acknowledged that the question was "of no little delicacy and difficulty" and that local prejudices and preferences had to give way to what was best, "whether it suits our individual interests or local feelings or not." He did not offer any plan for money-raising except to state that Universalists had the means to accomplish "the great work." If the denomination refused to accept the challenge, it surrendered itself once and for all "to hopeless ignorance and stupidity for another generation."

The meeting was held as scheduled, in the Orchard Street church in New York City, but the attendance was grievously disappointing. No one appeared from Pennsylvania, Ohio, or any of the southern states. Of the New England states, only Massachusetts and Connecticut were represented. But two highly significant resolutions came out of the deliberations, voted unanimously and without debate.[91] The first provided that means be immediately devised for establishing a college; and the second recommended the establishment of a permanent theological school. They were to be separate institutions.

The college was to be established in either the Hudson or Mohawk valleys, but its "definite location" was to be determined by a board of trustees to be appointed. A committee which included Hosea Ballou 2d, Sawyer, and Otis A. Skinner, was given the responsibility of making the nominations, which were approved. As originally constituted, the fifteen-man board was drawn from eight states—those in New England; (except Rhode Island); New York, which had the largest representation (six); Pennsylvania, and Ohio. It was evident from the composition of the original board that the new institution was to be a denominational enterprise, and not under the control of any one state; it was equally clear that New York State was intended to be the eventual location. Three agents (Otis A. and Dolphus Skinner, and W.S. Balch) were originally appointed as agents to solicit funds, with a target of $100,000 (set by Ballou) to be raised within two years. When the educational convention met in conjunction with the General Convention in 1847, the decision was made that one full-time agent would be more successful than a committee, so Otis A. Skinner was selected.

The location of the theological school was to be determined by a committee of seven selected from among those attending the convention. It was also left to them to determine the best method of raising funds. If one reviews the makeup of the committee it is easy to see that New England was assumed to be the future site for the theological school. Five of the seven trustees were from the Greater Boston area and two were from Connecticut. There was no representation from New York State.

Hosea Ballou 2d delivered the principal sermon at the General Convention in 1847, which met immediately following the assembly of the educational convention. He chose as his theme "the responsibilities of Universalists."[92] He expressed himself with unusual force and intensity, and many who heard it considered it "the most powerful discourse ever delivered by that distinguished man."[93] He "seemed to possess an energy altogether beyond himself in some parts of it, especially towards the conclusion." His final remarks indeed were a blunt and straightforward appeal to pay more attention to education. "I once indulged the confident expectation that I should live to see Universalists doing their duty in this cause—founding well-endowed academies, and at least one college, placed on a permanent basis." He hoped to share in the work, but had almost given up hope. He was ashamed that a rapidly growing denomination, with eighteen state conventions, eighty associations, some 700 preachers, more than 1,000 societies, and probably at least 700,000 nominal communicants, had been so lacking in concern for "the pursuit of general knowledge and the cultivation of mind."

The General Convention listened sympathetically to the pleas for establishing a college and a theological school and left it up to the members of the educational convention to carry their recommendations into action. It was to the founding of a liberal arts college rather than an independent theological school to which Universalists first committed themselves. The original proposals at the educational convention in 1847 had been based on the assumption that Sawyer would head Clinton Liberal Institute (to be turned into a college) in New York State, and that Hosea Ballou 2d would take charge of the theological school which was to be located in Massachusetts. But the plans underwent an interesting reversal when an actual attempt was made to carry them out. The college was chartered in 1852 as a strictly literary institution, and in Massachusetts; and the theological school, when it finally materialized in 1858, was located in New York State, after a struggle of many years and the passage of so many resolutions that some kind of a record must have been set.

Chapter 17

THE HIGHER LEARNING: COLLEGES AND UNIVERSITIES

Tufts College

When Tufts College (which became a university in 1955 by a change in its charter) was created in 1852, it was a unique institution in several respects. It was the first collegiate facility to be opened under Universalist auspices. Although it was the fourth institution of higher learning chartered in Massachusetts, it was the first to be founded by a denomination other than the Congregational church. And it was the only educational enterprise established by Universalists that was not coeducational when it opened; it was not until forty years after the college was chartered that women were admitted. Tufts was the only Universalist college that did not have a general preparatory school attached to it when it opened, although it did operate one for its engineering department for several years, beginning in 1893. Tufts also represented the largest financial commitment of any school yet operated by Universalists and by 1870 had by far the largest assets of any. Of the five colleges established by Universalists in the nineteenth century, only Tufts and St. Lawrence continued to exist as identifiable institutions beyond the period of the Second World War.[1]

The immediate origins of the college can be traced back to the Educational Convention of 1847 held in the Orchard Street Universalist church in New York City, at which time it was voted to establish a liberal arts college and a theological school as two separate entities. In 1848 Otis A. Skinner, who had been selected as the financial agent, agreed to the stipulation that he would receive no compensation for his fund-raising services unless the full amount of $100,000 were subscribed; his inducement was a commission of 10 per cent. He immediately set out on his mission and less than three years later he had secured commitments of $81,000, including an individual pledge of $20,000 and the donation of twenty acres of land worth $20,000. The bulk of the subscriptions came from New England, but there were some from New York, Pennsylvania, and Maryland. The very first remittance received ($100) came from Ohio.[2] In the interval between 1848 and the meeting of the subscribers in Skinner's church in Boston in 1851, when the announcement was made that the goal had been reached,

Tufts College in the 1860s

Ballou and Sawyer corresponded frequently, alternating between hope and despair. Whittemore, meanwhile, bombarded the readers of the *Trumpet* with pleas and exhortations to contribute.

As many of the subscribers as could attend met in Boston in September 1851, during the same week as the General Convention, at which the good news of the successful campaign was announced. The subscribers immediately appointed a board of trustees to replace the one appointed in 1847, and made arrangements to secure a charter. The twenty-three candidates for the board were duly elected, of whom nine were clergymen. The most familiar names among the latter were Ballou, Sawyer, Whittemore, and Skinner. The most prominent laymen were Silvanus Packard, the chief early benefactor who had made the largest single pledge ($20,000), to be followed by much more; Oliver Dean, a wealthy physician and another substantial contributor; Phineas T. Barnum, already nationally known as a showman; and Israel Washburn, Jr., governor of Maine. Nine states were represented, with Massachusetts and New York having the largest numbers (eight and five, respectively).

The problem of a location for the college produced much discussion, and a large number of possible sites were brought forward. The original plan had been to give one vote to every person who subscribed $10 for the college.[3] But that rather cumbersome proposal was abandoned. Instead, the trustees appointed a five-man committee on location of which Ballou and Skinner were members. The location that had been recommended at the 1847 educational convention had been either Mohawk or Hudson valleys, but by 1848 Skinner had decided, probably because his solicitation of subscriptions had been concentrated in New England, that a site farther east would be more appealing. When Ballou informed Sawyer of this possible change of location, the latter was greatly disappointed; he thought that the original plan should have been followed.[4]

Ballou at first professed indifference as to what site would be selected, but by 1849 was alarmed to hear that Walnut Hill, shared by Medford and Somerville, was being considered. It was entirely too close to Cambridge. The new college "would be exposed to the disadvantage of competition, at least comparison, with old, richly endowed Harvard, right before its face."[5] Ballou was concerned not only because the new institution would be overshadowed by Harvard but because the students would be subjected to the questionable influence of the Unitarians, who at the time controlled the school in Cambridge.[6] Ballou was not alone in objecting to the Medford/Somerville location. Kittredge Haven and J.S. Lee of Vermont not only voiced the same concern about proximity to Harvard but had qualms about the high cost of academic living in a metropolitan area.[7] There was always the argument, likewise, about the diversions and temptations of nearness to the wicked city.

Ballou had no objection to establishing a rival theological school near Harvard, but another literary institution was quite out of the question, and would probably result in failure. He felt so strongly about the matter that he was willing to go so far as to sacrifice the donation of land which Charles Tufts offered, and select another site. It was one of the ironies of his life that Ballou cast the lone dissenting vote when the decision was finally made to accept the Tufts offer, and that he became the first president of the institution that he was confident would not survive under such circumstances.

Besides the Boston area, there were three other possibilities considered for locating the college—Brattleboro, Vermont; and Worcester or Springfield, Massachusetts. Brattleboro offered $3,766, $2,000 of which could be used to acquire a desirable twenty-acre site.[8] However, attention was called to the fact that Silvanus Packard's pledge would be made good only if the institution were located in Massachusetts. The field had been narrowed even further by two offers from the eastern part of the state. Oliver Dean was willing to donate twenty acres of land and $20,000 in Franklin, about twenty-five miles south of Boston. The most attractive possibility of all had come from Charles Tufts, who eleven years before had offered ten acres of land for the Walnut Hill Evangelical Seminary. He had not only renewed the offer but had doubled the acreage to be given, provided the college would be located there. Besides, a total of $1,000 in cash had been pledged by various donors in Somerville, and individuals stood ready to buy up ten acres of the Tufts gift at $2,000 an acre, leaving a ten-acre square for the college proper. Altogether, the combined Tufts and Somerville offer would be worth $24,000, plus land for the college buildings.

A new committee was empowered to make the final decision as between Franklin and Medford/Somerville. Ballou, who served also on this committee, was among those who visited Franklin and found the site most acceptable; when he made his report and recommended that site, he was outvoted by a motion made by Packard that the college be located on Walnut Hill. The Tufts gift was too tempting to resist. Charles Tufts (1781-1876), a farmer, brickmaker, and owner of over 200 acres of land northwest of Boston, was a resident of Charlestown and a member of the First Universalist Society, to which both his grandfather and his father had belonged. The land, inherited by Tufts in 1840, had been acquired by the first generation of the family in Ameria. Tufts had already committed himself on three separate occasions to establish a school of some kind on what was the highest hill northwest of Boston. He was said to have told a relative, when asked what he would do with "that bleak hill over in Medford," that "I will put a light on it."

The chartering of the institution, incorporated under the name of "The Trustees of Tufts College," was routinely accomplished on 21 April 1852.[9] A previous attempt, in 1850, to create the "Tufts Institution of Learning" had failed; although a charter had been obtained, it had lapsed because the incorporation authorized under it had not taken place. There had been insufficient funds and inadequate planning to carry out a proposal made by three Universalist laymen—Benjamin B. Mussey, Timothy Cotting, and Richard Frothingham, Jr.[10] These same incorporators were listed in the 1852 charter which also referred to the earlier attempt.[11] Because the charter applied only to the Medford part of the Tufts grant and because part of the property was located in Somerville, an "Act in Addition" had to be obtained to make the charter applicable to both communities. The 1852 charter contained some interesting provisions. As long as the corporate name remained unchanged, the charter was to remain in effect "forever." No religious requirements of any kind were to be imposed on the board of trustees (which was self-perpetuating), on the faculty, or on the students. The trustees were also prohibited from establishing a medical school; the prohibition was removed by a charter change in 1867.

Of the twenty-three members of the provisional board of trustees selected in 1851, fourteen were retained under the new charter. Cotting and Frothingham, two of the incorporators, were new. The trustees began their work in 1852 by facing a formidable series of disappointments and obstacles. In July they unanimously chose Sawyer as the first president. He not only refused to serve at the salary that was offered, but resigned from the board. He and Ballou had discussed by letter the matter of the presidency as early as 1848, when the college was only in the preliminary planning stage, and long before a location had been decided upon. Ballou had strongly urged him to take the position if offered. "We must have you for president, for want of anybody else who is at all qualified for the office . . . . of all who are now on the stage, you are the only one who can be seriously thought of for that office—no matter how poorly qualified you may think yourself."[12]

Ballou was a member of the committee appointed to confer with Sawyer, who agreed to accept the appointment only if he could receive a salary of $2,500. This was the stipend which he had been offered (and had accepted) upon his return to the pastorate of the Orchard Street church in New York City after he had decided in 1852 to give up the running of the Clinton Liberal Institute. In May 1853 the Tufts trustees, completely unable to match such a salary, declared the presidency vacant. Two days later, Ballou was unanimously elected to the position. He accepted reluctantly, asking only that his annual salary be no less than the $800 he was receiving from his pastorate; the trustees concurred, and in 1855 raised his salary to $1,000.

With the presidency settled, the trustees next had to face the problem of providing one or more buildings. In 1852 a committee had been placed in charge of arranging for the erection of a main structure, at a cost not to exceed $20,000, with the foundation to be in before winter. But almost everything went wrong. The building was not started until mid-November; work had to be suspended not only because of the onset of the rigors of winter, but because the money was rapidly running out. The building committee was forced to request an additional $50,000, which was supposed to provide also for boarding facilities and the laying out of the grounds. The cornerstone of the "college edifice" was laid with appropriate ceremonies on 19 July 1853. In 1896 Hosea Starr Ballou, Ballou's biographer, attempted to obtain a copy of the original hymn prepared for the occasion by Mrs. Mary T. Goddard, one of Tufts' benefactors, but was informed that the only one available had been safely housed in the cornerstone.[13]

Ballou had already (in 1852) been appointed to a committee to prepare "a system of instruction." After his election to the presidency he found himself not only the chairman of the committee but responsible for recruiting a teaching staff. He received permission for a year of preparation in which he visited all of the New England colleges and some preparatory schools to study their curricula first-hand, and toured Europe briefly before undertaking his combined administrative and instructional duties in the fall of 1854. When he returned late in September he discovered that the college had already been unofficially opened, with one full-time faculty member and two serving part-time, with seven students. The majority of the trustees had decided to delay the official opening until a boarding house could be provided, but Trustees Mussey and Skinner thought it was inadvisable to wait any longer, and opened in August. Rooms in the main college building were made available to students, with the institution offering to furnish the bedsteads.[14] Ballou was formally inaugurated and the faculty officially installed a year later, in August 1855. In reporting in detail the formal opening and dedication of the college, Sylvanus Cobb wrote ecstatically about the "glorious day for Universalists . . . . the great event in our denominational history."[15]

In 1857 the first class, consisting of three young men, was graduated from the four-year "classical" program which had been adopted. Two of the graduates had been admitted with sophomore standing. By 1859 there were seventy students enrolled, and the number increased slowly but steadily thereafter. In that year the Committee on Education of the General Convention called attention proudly to the growing enrollment and to the fact that the existence of the institution demonstrated that the denomination possessed "the will and the means to carry on enterprises of moment and magnitude."[16] The college by that year had assets totalling $172,000. However, behind that statistic lay five years of struggle to keep the institution from collapsing.

Financial woes plagued the college from the day it opened, and more than once there was a serious question of whether it could continue. Even with the aid of the Tufts College Educational Association which began to function in 1855, the college was far from self-supporting, and deficits appeared almost every year during Ballou's administration in spite of stringent economies. The main building had cost $38,000; a boarding house, $9,700; and a residence for the president, $3,600.[17] Total operating expenses in 1856 were $5,000, of which $4,000 was paid out in salaries. The indebtedness was over $10,000 when the panic of 1857 struck. The appropriation in 1859 of $50,000 by the state from the proceeds of the sale of the Back Bay lands in Boston, matched to private subscriptions, probably saved the college from extinction. Oliver Dean contributed the largest single amount ($10,000). Forty-seven acres of additional land were also donated by Charles and Hannah Tufts (1856) and ten acres by Timothy Cotting, a member of Ballou's former congregation in Medford. There were also sizeable bequests to the college in its early years (e.g., $50,000 by John Wade in 1858; and over $300,000 by William J. Walker) but these funds were not available for many years. The most pressing need was operating income, only a fraction of which came from the annual tuition (two terms) of $35, raised to $60 in 1870. Student bills were also frequently in arrears. Thomas A. Goddard, for many years the treasurer of the corporation, quietly gave money from his own pocket to help make up losses.

From the fall of 1854 until his death in 1861, Ballou attended not only to his presidential duties but conducted Sunday services, taught two courses as Professor of History and Intellectual Philosophy, and served as the college librarian. He collected, by soliciting donations, a working library of over 6,000 volumes at almost no expense to the institution. It was he, with three colleagues comprising the original faculty, who laid the academic foundations of the institution, and it was one of these colleagues, John P. Marshall, who served for over a year as Acting President (1861-62) until a permanent successor to Ballou could be found. Marshall, who taught the natural sciences, had been principal of Lebanon Liberal Institute (New Hampshire) and held other positions in New England schools.

The trustees had a discouraging amount of difficulty in finding an individual willing to serve in the presidency. Sawyer was approached and declined for the second time, partly because he was in semi-retirement and engaged in farming, and partly because the college was in such dire financial straits in 1861 that it could not even afford to pay the modest salary of $1,200 which he requested (less than half of what he had asked for in 1853). James P. Weston, president of Lombard University, also declined, among others, to be considered. The office was finally filled by Alonzo Ames Miner, pastor of the Second (School Street) Universalist Society in Boston, and a Tufts trustee since 1855. He had attended many of the meetings in Boston at which Skinner had made reports on the progress of fund-raising. Miner had also headed the subscription list at his church when funds were being sought. Silvanus Packard, the most generous early benefactor of the college, was a member of Miner's congregation. Miner's first official contact with the college had been made when he delivered the principal address at the cornerstone-laying ceremony in May 1853.

Alonzo Ames Miner (1814-1895) was born in Lempster, New Hampshire, on 17 August 1814. After attending schools in Hopkinton, Lebanon, and Franklin, New Hampshire, and Cavendish, Vermont, he became a schoolmaster in Hanover at the age of sixteen.[18] After further study in Cavendish, he became an assistant in, and for one year, principal of, Cavendish Academy. He served for almost five years (1835-39) as head of the Unity (New Hampshire) Scientific and Military Academy from the time it opened. A cousin (Amasa Gleason), a graduate of Norwich University in 1836, was an instructor in military drill and tactics, and mathematics. While at Unity, Miner, in 1836, married Maria S. Perley of Lempster, who served as preceptress and co-worker in the academy. They had no children.

The young schoolteacher was fellowshipped in 1838, the year he preached his first sermon (in Chester, Vermont). He also preached part-time in Unity and neighboring villages, and was ordained in 1839 in Nashua, New Hampshire. Immediately before his ordination Miner, together with a woman in the process of becoming a Universalist, were baptised by immersion in a nearby stream.[19] W.S. Balch performed the ceremony. Miner served his first full-time pastorate in Methuen, Massachusetts (1839-42). In 1842 he was called to Lowell, Massachusetts, where he served for six years (1842-48). In 1846 he succeeded

Phineas Taylor Barnum (1810-1891), Impresario and Universalist benefactor

Alonzo Ames Miner (1814-1895), long-time pastor of the Columbus Avenue Universalist Church in Boston, temperance leader, and second president of Tufts College (1862-1875)

E.H. Chapin as junior pastor on a part-time basis at the Boston church of which the elder Ballou was pastor, and in 1848 took over the position full-time. Miner continued in that post until his death on 14 June 1895.

Much to the delight of his fellow-trustees Miner agreed to accept the presidency (at first with no salary), which he was to hold for almost thirteen years. During this extra busy period in an unusually active life he continued to minister to his church in Boston, assisted from time to time by junior clergymen. He resigned from the presidency in 1875 to devote full time to his church duties but remained a trustee until his death. Miner was also a benefactor of considerable importance. Besides bequests to Westbrook Seminary, Goddard Seminary, and Dean Academy, he left $43,000 to the college, most of which was used to construct the building which bore his name and was the headquarters at Tufts for the theological school until it was closed in 1968.

During his long career Miner was prominent both in denominational and community affairs and took active stands on national issues. Within the denomination he was a founder and officer of the Universalist Publishing House, as well as president of the trustees of the Bromfield School in Harvard, Massachusetts, and of Dean Academy. Before moving to Boston in 1848 he had served on school boards in Methuen and Lowell; he was not only on the Boston School Board, but was a member of the Massachusetts State Board of Education for twenty-four years. Always interested in education, and like Ballou without an earned college degree, he was the recipient of honorary degrees: a Master of Arts from Tufts (1861); a Doctor of Sacred Theology from Harvard (1863); and an LL.D. from Tufts (1875), the latter in recognition of his services as president. Miner was also elected an honorary member of Phi Beta Kappa in 1893, near the end of his life. It was largely through his influence that the State Normal Art School was established; he served as chairman of its board of visitors for some twenty years.

Miner was also active in the social reform movements of his day, and spoke out against slavery, advocated the settlement of international disputes by arbitration, and was for a time on the executive committee of the American Peace Society. He was best known in the Boston community for his activities on behalf of the temperance movement. According to one biographer, Miner wrote more lectures on that subject than he did sermons.[20] Although Miner delivered innumerable lectures, sermons, and addresses, and wrote a few articles, including a brief history of Universalism which appeared in Justin Winsor's multi-volume *Memorial History of Boston,* and prepared some materials for church and Sunday School use, he was not a prolific writer. Much of what he said that appeared in print consisted of transcriptions by others, for he seldom wrote his materials out in full, and kept neither a diary nor a scrapbook.

The college was barely surviving when Miner assumed the presidency in 1862. The small student body had been made even smaller by the outbreak of the Civil War because of the departure of so many students who volunteered for military service. There were only forty in attendance when Miner became president. The main college building, a frame boarding house, and two brick buildings, one a combined library and dormitory, and the other a dormitory made possible by the grant from the state, comprised the academic plant in 1862. A frame structure built for President Ballou's use was the only other building on the campus; Miner did not occupy it, commuting instead from Boston.

Aside from the meagre receipts from tuition and fees, the only operating funds available consisted of the $1,000 interest from the bond donated by Packard. To make matters more serious, the institution was already $18,000 in debt. President Miner, with first-hand knowledge of the plight of the institution, immediately set out to broaden the financial base. For three and one-half years his Boston church supported him while he served the college without salary. It was in his church that the Tufts College Educational Society had been organized in 1855 to raise funds, and Miner tapped every other resource at his command during a most trying period in the college's history. Over half of the $700,000 which was added to the funds of the institution by the close of his administration in 1875 came from members of his church.[21] In a period of less than three years (1863-65), over half ($225,000) of the donations, bequests, and subscriptions to the eight educational institutions then being operated by Universalists, went to Tufts.[22]

Miner concentrated his efforts on building up an endowment rather than on expansion of the physical plant. Only one building was added to the campus during his administration—a much-needed dormitory. Instead, he focused on strengthening academic facilities and offerings. The first three endowed faculty chairs were created during his administration. Like his predecessor, Miner also served as a member of the teaching staff, offering courses in ethics and political economy. As an administrator, Miner showed exceptional executive ability. After obtaining funds, he turned to curricular improvements, largely with an eye to making the institution serve a larger clientele than it had attracted at first. He estimated that the college could serve a population of 150,000 Universalists in New England alone.

It was during his presidency that a three-year "Philosophical" course of study was introduced in 1863, leading to the degree of Bachelor of Philosophy as an alternative to the traditional four-year classical curriculum. In 1865 a three-year combined liberal arts and professional program was introduced, leading to the degree of "Civil

Engineer." This became the nucleus of the engineering department (later, school) established in 1869. It was Miner who made numerous personal appearances before the state legislature in 1866 and 1867 to bring about the removal of the provision written into the college charter prohibiting the granting of medical degrees.[23] Although the college did not take advantage of the new opportunity to establish a medical school until 1893, it was a victory won over the vigorous opposition of Harvard.

Another important development during the Miner administration, in which the president took a special interest, was the creation of a divinity school. This was, it will be recalled, an old idea. The original assumption had been that the theological school voted by the educational convention in 1847 was to be located in New England. Whittemore, himself a Tufts trustee in 1855, in answer to an inquiry as to why no theological school had yet been established, replied: "It has always been supposed by the trustees that a Theological Department would at once be established in it. It was the original design."[24] But a combination of circumstances had turned the situation around, and the theological school planned in 1847 had opened in New York State instead.

It is clear that many students who entered Tufts College intended to enter the ministry. Such students even organized a "Theological Association" in 1857 to foster "a professional enthusiasm," held frequent meetings, and prepared and delivered sermons which they evaluated.[25] President Ballou had encouraged such activity. A goodly proportion of the early graduates did indeed enter the ministry. One of the three members of the first class of the "College of Letters" (Harvey Hersey) did so, as did three members of the nine-member Class of 1858. Of the seventy who had been graduated between 1857 and 1865, eleven entered the ministry and eight non-graduates had done likewise.[26] The other popular professions were teaching or educational administration, medicine, and law. One Universalist expressed great disappointment that there was no graduate in 1866 planning to enter the ministry.[27] Actually, one of the thirteen, Edwin C. Sweetser, did become a clergyman.

Very few Universalists made any sharp distinction between a college and a theological school. Many who made pledges to the college when it was in the process of establishment did so on the presumption that one of its tasks was to educate ministers. This was a correct assumption; at a meeting of the trustees in 1852, Otis A. Skinner, the principal fund-raiser, had explained that the proposed school was intended to "meet the wants of the agriculturist, the manufacturer and the merchant, as well as of the minister, the lawyer and the physician."[28] In short, it was to offer the liberal arts background thought essential for any educated person, regardless of vocational or professional choice.

The college was intended to appeal, in terms of social class configuration, to "what may be called the Middle Million, as in contradistinction to the Upper and Under Ten Thousand."[29] By the same token, it was to be of "a more simple, republican character, free from the encumbrance of aristocracy" than such institutions as Harvard.[30]

The decision to open a divinity school grew out of a bequest of Silvanus Packard, who died in 1866. His will provided that a Professorship of Christian Theology be established in the institution. This created a dilemma for the trustees, for they had consistently adhered to the principle that theology as such was not to be part of the curriculum. T.J. Sawyer had followed the same principle by insisting that the theological instruction which he offered while head of Clinton Liberal Institute be kept separate from the regular program. The same policy was followed at St. Lawrence University and at Lombard University, where separate theological departments were also established. So, in order to be consistent, and at the same time to honor Packard's bequest, the Tufts trustees decided to create a separate school, still to be "in connection with Tufts College," but with its own faculty, curriculum, and library.

After the trustees established the Packard Professorship in 1867 they offered the position to Sawyer. He at first declined, but when the offer was renewed in 1869 he accepted it, but with doubt and hesitation, at a salary of $2,500. In his inaugural address that same year he stressed the fact that the school was to be grounded strictly on Christianity as a revealed religion and would in no sense be a school of "natural theology" based on human or speculative philosophy.[31] He considered himself a representative of the third generation of Universalist ministers, making the transition to the completely professional training which he had found lacking in his own apprenticeship.

A second faculty member was obtained before the school opened, in the person of Charles H. Leonard, who was appointed Goddard Professor of Sacred Rhetoric and Pastoral Theology. It was financed from part of the estate of Thomas A. Goddard who had died in 1868 and who, with Mrs. Mary Goddard, provided $43,000 to the college.

Charles H. Leonard (1822-1918), who had prepared for the ministry in Sawyer's theological program at Clinton Liberal Institute, for twenty-three years had held a pastorate in Chelsea, Massachusetts. It was while there that Leonard introduced in 1858 the denominational custom of celebrating "Children's Sunday."[32] The school opened with four students who were provided with a flexible program of three or four years, depending on the extent and type of previous preparation. The school, the relationship of which (including financing) to the main body of the college was often closer than the trustees had originally intended, remained associated with Tufts until it was closed in the spring of 1968 for basically financial reasons. Until after 1890, when the first of two separate buildings was provided for the school, it used the existing facilities of the college.

One of Miner's special interests besides the divinity school was the provision of feeder schools for the college. Clinton Liberal Institute, Westbrook Seminary, and Green Mountain (Perkins) Liberal Institute were already serving that purpose. But Miner felt strongly that one should be provided in Massachusetts, nearer the college than the other Universalist-sponsored institutions. So it was Miner who approached Oliver Dean and urged him to contribute to the denominational educational cause by endowing an academy. With this possibility in mind, Miner brought the matter of establishing a preparatory school to the Massachusetts Convention in 1864. After endorsement of his proposal was obtained, Dean agreed, and contributed both property and a substantial amount of money by direct gift and by bequest. Dean Academy, opened in 1866, served precisely the purpose Miner had intended, furnishing dozens of students to Tufts over the years.

Miner also had a hand in the establishment of Goddard Seminary in Vermont. One of the principal donors who made the school possible was Thomas A. Goddard who, like Dean, was a member of Miner's Boston congregation. Miner served on the committee which chose a site for the school; he also raised funds, and in other ways assisted in establishing the academy which opened in 1870. It was quite in keeping with Miner's longstanding interest in education that he devoted a portion of his major address (the "centenary sermon") to the subject at the Gloucester festivities in 1870.

The college over which Miner had presided between 1862 and 1875 had indeed, as his principal biographer pointed out, "taken on the proportions of a university" by the end of the nineteenth century.[33] It finally became coeducational (in 1892), and to its theological school had added both a medical and dental school (1893 and 1899, respectively), to be followed later by a graduate school and numerous professional schools. By the time the centennial of its chartering had been celebrated in 1952 it had become, in the words of the eighth president, "a small university of high quality." Even greater aspirations for its future were outlined by Jean Mayer, who was inaugurated in September 1976 as its tenth president. Long before then, Tufts' Universalist origins and associations had been forgotten or were never known; it had, many decades earlier, truly become the non-sectarian institution that its founding fathers had planned it to be.

St. Lawrence University

For its first seventeen years (until 1869) Tufts College was an exclusively literary institution, with no theological department. The school represented the carrying out of the first of the two votes passed at the educational convention in 1847: the establishment of a college or university. The second institution of higher learning established by the Universalists, St. Lawrence University, was the long-delayed result of efforts to make into a reality the second vote at the 1847 convention: the establishment of a theological school on a permanent basis.

Between 1847 and the chartering of Tufts, the denomination had had to depend for its formal theological training on the volunteer services of Sawyer at Clinton Liberal Institute. Even that service had come to an end when he returned in 1852 to New York City to resume his pastorate at the Orchard Street church. When it came into being in 1856, the liberal arts college which comprised part of St. Lawrence University was actually an appendage to the theological school and depended on it for both staff and financing despite the fact that the charter provided for separate funding and administration. It did, however, except for one brief period, share the same board of trustees until 1910, when a separate board was created for the theological school.[34] St. Lawrence University was not only a school with a dual program when it opened, but almost immediately was forced by the inadequate academic background of many of its first applicants to add a third branch, a preparatory school which lasted for ten years. All three parts of the school shared with Tufts in their first years a financial struggle which more than once almost closed down the institution. Like Tufts, it was rescued by timely state aid as well as by private donations, and was staffed by men sufficiently dedicated to the tasks before them to subordinate their personal welfare to the cause for which they labored.

Nothing at the time had come out of the effort of the educational convention in 1847 to establish a theological school under the auspices of the General Convention. But in 1849 it refused to establish a permanent fund in view of the demands already being made on New York Universalists to rescue Clinton Liberal Institute.[35] Sawyer was so discouraged that he temporarily abandoned the training program that he had been conducting at Clinton. He had a change of heart in 1850, when the state convention voted that year to make an appeal to every society in the state for special collections, due within a year, with annual pledges thereafter.[36] Tuition was to be charged at an annual rate of $30. That proposal made no more headway than all of the previous attempts. Only eight societies in the state responded, and appeals to Universalists outside New York brought almost no response even though the editors of both the *Trumpet* and the *Christian Freeman* in Boston urged support.[37] Whittemore called attention to the critical shortage of clergymen in the Middle West, notably in Ohio, and estimated that at least fifty were needed in New York State alone.[38]

Supporters of education in the state convention then tried another

Richardson Hall (1857), the original building of St. Lawrence University, Canton, New York

approach. In 1851 a committee was appointed to "take into consideration the entire educational interests of the denomination in this State, both literary and theological." By then the Universalists in Massachusetts, backed strongly by their state convention, were on the verge of chartering their own literary institution. The incipient rivalry which had already appeared between Universalists in the two states now became fully visible. At the next meeting of the New York Convention, in 1852, the committee appointed the preceding year recommended the formation of an organization to promote education, including facilities to prepare students for the ministry. Out of it came the "New York Universalist Education Society," complete with a constitution and board of trustees. It was surprising to no one that Sawyer was selected as president of the board. Membership required an annual contribution of $1.00; life memberships were $15.

Until 1852 Sawyer continued to do double duty, and even then at scarcely half of the salary voted by the state convention. He continued to struggle with his extra load until forced by health and constant discouragement to give it up and return to New York City. Even though he had conducted a part-time and inadequately financed theological program, he had trained thirty-eight young men, of whom twenty-nine actually entered the ministry.

When the newly created board of the Education Society met later in 1852 it resolved that the theological school conducted by Sawyer be continued under its supervision, but that idea was abandoned when it was discovered that the subscription for the continued support of the theological school, solicited in 1851, amounted to only $396.78. Instead, a public meeting was called in New York City in the summer of 1853, at which it was determined to cancel the plan to continue to operate the theological school at Clinton and instead to throw the question of location open to any community that would house it. An agent, Eben Francis, was appointed in 1853, to collect funds, but he resigned before the year was out. He was replaced by J.T. Goodrich who remained at his post for several years and met with "encouraging success." At the meeting in 1853 it was reported that $2,094 had been raised and at about the same time the Education Society received from Mrs. Magdalene Ritter Halsted a bequest of $1,000 which was invested in bonds of the Erie Railroad.

Through the efforts of agents Francis and Goodrich, about $16,000 had been subscribed by the time the state convention met in the fall of 1854. At another meeting of the Education Society held in New York City in the fall of 1854, the amount of money pledged had risen to more than $25,000. Official encouragement (but no other support) came from the General Convention. The efforts of the Education Society to establish a theological school were commended in 1853 and a plea for support was routinely included in the resolutions of every General Convention thereafter.

Continuing editorial backing also came from Universalist publications in Boston. Henry Bacon used the report of the Education Society in 1854 as a basis for a detailed review of the relation between "ministerial culture and theological school," and came out strongly in favor of the latter.[39] The time to put the school into operation seemed to have come, and a Committee on Location solicited possibilities in 1855 while W.S. Balch took over the task of fund-raising. The goal was a $30,000 endowment, with the proceeds to support two professorships.[40] By the spring of 1855, $26,000 had been pledged. Balch recommended, in order to make the school more than a New York operation, that trustees be elected from all state conventions which contributed at least $1,000. In 1856 he raised the goal of the permanent fund to $40,000.[41]

Inducements to locate the theological school were received from twelve communities, although no formal proposal came from the village of Clinton. At a meeting in Utica in the late summer of 1855, it appeared that Canton would be the most advantageous location. The final decision to place the school there was made some six months later. The offer which settled the matter was the donation of twenty acres of land and pledges of $15,000 toward the construction of a three-story brick building to accommodate seventy-five students. Although the original goal had been to provide facilities for ministerial training only, it occurred to "the friends of the enterprise" that no institution of collegiate grade existed in the region. The idea was favorably received to establish such a college in connection with the theological school, and an act of incorporation was obtained on 3 April 1856. Hence it was the citizens of Canton who made the establishment of a college a condition of raising the promised $15,000. Such had not been the intention of the Universalists, and Sawyer as well as others in the denomination immediately began to worry about the commitment to support two colleges at once, at a time when even the first one (Tufts) had not yet become firmly established. The citizens of Canton had also stipulated that each student was to perform manual labor for two hours each working day as part of the curriculum.[42] There is no evidence that this provision was carried out.

The act of incorporation authorized the creation of a college and a theological school, to be known collectively as St. Lawrence University, named after the nearby river. Although the new institution was to have a single board of trustees, the funds and administration of each part of the university were to be kept separate. The original bylaws provided that the College of Letters and Science was to be unsectarian, but that the theological school was to prepare students for the Universalist ministry.[43] A board for the university corporation was organized in November 1856, with Sawyer as its president. He held the post until his resignation in 1867.

The cornerstone of the substantial brick building which was at first to house both parts of the school was laid on 16 June 1856, with addresses by W.S. Balch, Sawyer, and E.H. Chapin.[44] By the summer of 1857 the structure was completed. A year later, on 15 April 1858, the long-awaited theological school was formally opened. The prospects were not auspicious when the inaugural ceremonies were held for what in 1855 (and for many years thereafter) was designated as the "Canton Theological School." The festivities took place in the local Universalist church in the midst of a late spring snowstorm and the newly-appointed principal, Ebenezer Fisher, was downcast to discover that only four young men constituted the student body. Sawyer tried to cheer him by pointing out that the new school had more students than when he had begun his own in Clinton many years before. Fisher, who was to be associated with the school for twenty-one years, could take courage, for the student body had risen to seventeen by the end of the second year.[45] None came from Massachusetts until the following academic year, when two were enrolled from that state.

Those responsible for and interested in the Canton Theological School tried their best to impress on the denomination the fact that, while most of the funds of the school were derived from New York Universalists, the institution was intended to be more than local in character and influence. By 1860, eight states were represented and applications had been received from candidates in several others.[46] Only eight of the twenty-five students in 1861 were from New England.[47] Nonetheless, the Canton Theological School continued to be thought of as a primarily New York institution, and many prospective students chose Tufts, even though it had no theological department. The isolated location of the small farming community of Canton in extreme northern New York, only a short distance from the St. Lawrence River and the Canadian border, was also probably a factor in the choice of Tufts over St. Lawrence.

A concerted effort was made for many years to highlight the attractiveness of the institution at Canton by advertising the merits of its location.[48] St. Lawrence, it was emphasized, commanded the field of higher education in northern New York State. Canton was "a beautiful, flourishing village, easily accessible by rail from all points, and is soon to be the focus of two or three new railroads." It was the shiretown (county seat) of St. Lawrence County; and the community was only eighteen miles from the city of Ogdensburg. Whether such a list of advantages attracted additions to the student body is not known, but many Universalists in New England heeded Thomas Whittemore's advice to patronize Tufts, insisting that it was intended to train future clergymen as well as laymen. He quite correctly pointed out that several of the first students were serving neighboring churches on a part-time basis while pursuing their studies.[49]

Tufts students who had no intention of entering the ministry were irked to hear their college referred to frequently as a theological school. This problem of the public image of the institution was aggravated when a divinity school was actually opened in 1869. Supporters of Tufts had not been at all pleased when, at the General Convention in 1856, a special plea was made to raise money for the projected theological school at Canton.[50] The possibility that much-needed funds for both Tufts and St. Lawrence would be diverted to one, to the detriment of the other, became a constant source of tension in the early history of both institutions.

Ebenezer Fisher (1815-1879), who was associated with the theological school at St. Lawrence from its very beginning, was a largely self-educated clergyman who had been born in Charlotte, Maine, on 6 February 1815 in what was then frontier country.[51] Except for one term in the Kent's Hill Academy in Readville, he received only a common school education. Of Baptist heritage, he became a Universalist about the age of sixteen and was fellowshipped by the Maine State Convention in 1840 and preached his first sermon that year. He was ordained in 1841 and for six years preached at Addison Point, Maine, and then at Salem, Massachusetts, between 1847 and 1853. While there he began writing articles for the *Universalist Quarterly*. Between 1853 and 1858 he held a pastorate in South Dedham

(Norwood), Massachusetts. It was Balch who was to a great extent responsible for persuading Fisher to become the head of the new theological school and for two years its only faculty member. He worked faithfully under the most discouraging handicaps throughout his career at St. Lawrence until a heart attack brought a sudden end to his work on 21 February 1879. In all, 103 students were graduated during his long tenure. He received an honorary Master of Arts degree from Tufts College in 1861, and in 1862 Lombard University bestowed on him an honorary Doctor of Divinity degree.

The need for a second professor to lighten the load carried by Fisher was painfully obvious by the spring of 1860. It was determined from analysis of the census reports that in the forty-four theological schools then in existence in the nation, there was one faculty member for each ten students, and an average of three faculty per school.[52] The Universalist school fell far short of this, for there were twenty-two students, divided into two classes, being taught by one faculty member who also preached every Sunday.[53] Adding a third class made additional personnel an absolute necessity, but there was no money available, and at least $18,000 was needed. Five students completed the full three-year course in 1861; four who would normally have been graduated had to delay receipt of their diplomas because they had been forced, largely by economic necessity, to take only a partial course.[54] This happened even though there was no charge for tuition.

Massena Goodrich was appointed to the Professorship of Theology late in 1860, but he remained less than two years because insufficient funds were raised to pay his salary. In 1862 Fisher made a personal visit to Boston to raise the $400 needed, but was unsuccessful.[55] Goodrich returned to his former pastorate in Pawtucket, Rhode Island. The outbreak of the Civil War had a near-disastrous effect on the school, with an abrupt decline in enrollment and an accumulation of unpaid pledges.

The plight of Canton Theological School had become nothing short of desperate by the fall of 1864. With $45,000 already invested in land and a building, it produced only three graduates that year. One, Herman Bisbee, was later to be charged with heresy and disfellowshipped. At Commencement he read a paper on "The True Church" in which he rejected all dogmas and creeds and argued in favor of only "the spirit of Christ," and by 1870 had moved even farther left theologically.[56] In 1864 one student had dropped out to accept a pastorate in Canada, and one who was still enrolled was serving as chaplain of a Negro regiment at Port Hudson. In 1867 there were no graduates at all. The school had been in operation six years and had graduated, beginning in 1861, twenty-five young men. Another ten students had dropped out for one reason or another, but had nevertheless entered the ministry. Yet the school had been kept alive only by the self-sacrifice of a handful of clergy, most notably Fisher. The school was grossly understaffed; it had almost no resources on which to draw, particularly for student assistance, and its enrollment was pitifully small. Its future existence was very much in doubt, in the eyes of its beleaguered head.[57] After the resignation of Goodrich, Fisher had again undertaken to serve as the entire faculty. Fisher toiled alone, prepared his lessons for two classes, read (and re-read) 7,500 pages of theological materials, much of it "very dry," and continued to preach every Sunday.

What was needed? Everything. But Fisher would settle for three palliatives: another professor, a loan fund, and more students. The sum of $25,000 was needed to endow the professorship, but only $8,500 had been pledged by 1864. Fisher was harsh in his language and accused his fellow-Universalists of being "so sentimentally liberal, that we fail to be practically liberal, in our own work." A comparison of the impoverished and struggling Canton school with the prosperous Unitarian theological school which had been established in 1844 in Meadville, Pennsylvania, was deliberately made by Fisher to shame the lagging Universalists. A loan fund of even $1,000 would be a boon to needy students. Nearly all who attended the school were poor; Fisher reported that less than half of the students were financially able to complete the three-year course of study. He had only $350 available in 1864 for such assistance. Under the circumstances Fisher did not feel justified in recruiting students; hence a major reason for the small enrollment. If the other two deficiencies were remedied, the third would take care of itself. If indifference to the plight of the school meant that Universalists did not wish to sustain it, then neither did he. Even the indomitable Fisher became discouraged at times.

When the General Convention met in 1864 it issued a plea for support of the school, calling for an immediate sum of $25,000.[58] Five hundred circulars were mailed by Richard Eddy, secretary of the convention, and special sermons were called for.[59] The denomination was also warned not to establish any more theological schools until the one in Canton was on its feet.

It may not have added to the prestige of the school, but Fisher, when he did attempt to recruit students, emphasized not only the constant need of ministers, especially in rural churches, but the fact that the school's admission standards were quite flexible. During his lifetime (until 1879), the requirements were "a good English education" and a professed intention of the applicants "to devote their lives to the Gospel ministry." Certificates of good moral and religious character were also required. Belief "in the Holy Scriptures" was added in 1869.[60] Fisher admitted that most of those accepted had "only a fair English education."[61] But three years of training prepared them adequately, in his estimation, and it was much cheaper than preparatory school, followed by four years of college and at least two years of theological school. He calculated in 1865 that, with the free tuition available, the expenses for a year were only $170.

College graduates could complete the course in two years, as did Olympia Brown, the first woman in any denomination to be regularly ordained who had completed a formal course of theological instruction. A graduate of Antioch College, she received her diploma from Canton Theological School in 1863 and was ordained the same month by the Northern (St. Lawrence) Association at Malone, New York.[62] Other women were to follow in her footsteps at the theological school.

After a second visit to Massachusetts, in 1863, including a plea for funds from the state convention, Fisher raised over $2,000 in cash and pledges of the $3,000 target which had been set to get the school out of its financial morass. As a result, it was able to employ an additional faculty member, Orello Cone, as Professor of Biblical Languages and Literature.[63] By the time of the denominational centennial in 1870, the theological school seemed finally to have emerged from its most critical period. Charles A. Ropes of Salem, Massachusetts, came to the rescue with a check for $1,000, with the promise of $5,000 more if $20,000 could be raised elsewhere. John Craig, a benefactor from Rochester, New York, pledged $50,000. In all, $85,000 came out of the combined efforts of money-raiser Balch and theology professor Fisher.

The school had received sufficient funds to endow Fisher's chair through a gift from George R. Dockstader, and to operate with a faculty of four, as well as a librarian. J.S. Lee, who had earlier served as the president of St. Lawrence and had returned from a year's leave abroad, became Professor of Ecclesiastical History and Archeology. Miss Edna J. Chaffee was Instructor in Elocution.

By the fall of 1859 the theological school had already acquired, by gift, two substantial private libraries purchased and then donated by Silas C. Herring of New York City.[64] One, comprising 2,500 volumes, had been the property of a German scholar, and the other, of 1,700 volumes, had belonged to Samuel C. Loveland of Vermont. By 1870 the library, with modest additions over the years, and shared with the rest of the institution, was housed in its own building.

Even in its earliest history, it had been the theological branch of the university that had to a significant extent made possible its survival, especially during its first decade. The other components of what became St. Lawrence University almost failed to come into existence at all. When it was decided to accept the offer of the Canton citizenry of land and $15,000, there were insufficient assets to meet the charter requirements of the New York State Board of Regents, so Balch had been required to apply directly to the state legislature for a charter.[65] Even before the main building had progressed much beyond the cornerstone stage, money had run out, and one-third of the funds collected by the committee responsible for establishing the theological school had to be borrowed. A matching grant of $25,000 from the state in 1857 was made on the assurance that an unsectarian college would be opened, in accordance with the bylaws. The institutions would probably never have opened without public assistance. The promise of support for the college from other denominations, somewhat naively expected by Balch, never came.[66]

The academic department did open in the fall of 1859, with sixty-five students, but it was not the exclusively college-level program that had been anticipated. J.S. Lee, a graduate of Amherst College who had for seven years served as the principal of Green Mountain (Perkins) Institute in Vermont and had been elected to head the College of Letters and Science as Acting President, found no applicants ready to enter a college-level program. So his only alternative was to establish a preparatory school which lasted until 1866. As a faculty member he taught Greek and Latin, and was joined in 1860 by John W. Clapp, a civil engineer who became Professor of Mathematics and the Natural Sciences, a post which he held for five years.

There was not only considerable interchange between the various faculties of the university but considerable confusion about the relationship between the collegiate and preparatory departments on the one hand, and the theological school on the other. Lee assisted Fisher in the theological school in offering language instruction, while Fisher served as Professor of Intellectual and Moral Philosophy in the collegiate program. After his resignation from the presidency in 1868 Lee became a full-time faculty member in the theological school, where he served for some thirty years.

Fisher jealously guarded the autonomy of the theological school throughout his long association with it. It even set its own academic calendar, which did not coincide with the rest of the university. In 1868 he turned to the New York Convention for assistance in supporting the school. Among its commitments the convention agreed, effective in 1868, to award $180 a year to "worthy and indigent students" in the theological school. The General Convention also assisted in this respect, beginning in 1865. In 1870 the trustees of the convention took over from the Northwest Conference its missionary projects, which included aid to divinity students, then amounting to five scholarships. The General Convention added fifteen more, at $180 per year per student, and by 1870 had granted forty-five such scholarships. Only one student had abandoned the ministry and twenty-nine were holding pastorates in 1870.[67] Scholarships were awarded to both Tufts and St. Lawrence students.

In return for assuming financial responsibility for St. Lawrence University, the New York Convention was given, by a change in the university charter, the authority to nominate its trustees and officers.

This arrangement lasted until the institution once more became independent in 1910. After Lee resigned in 1868, the convention selected Richmond Fisk as president. During his administration (1868-71), he tried without success to integrate the theological school into the university structure, but Fisher insisted on a separate status for his school. For a brief period (1868-69) the theological school had its own board of trustees; over half of the twenty-one individuals (including Fisher) served on both boards.[68] Sawyer, who had resigned from the university board in 1867, and was living in New Jersey, headed the short-lived board of the theological school. Until 1890 the description of the Canton Theological School in the *Register* was written up separately from that of St. Lawrence, although it was also listed as a department of the university. After 1900 it was still referred to occasionally as the Canton Theological School, a practice which gave the mistaken impression that it was a completely separate and independent institution.

The preparatory school, like the collegiate program, was coeducational from the start. There were forty-five students in the preparatory school when the academic year 1859-60 began, and the number increased gradually thereafter. In the college program, two students had met the requirements for the Bachelor of Science degree in 1865, and two women comprised the collegiate graduating class in 1866. During much of the 1860s even the residence facilities in the original college building were coeducational, a fact which undoubtedly raised some eyebrows. The financial margin was a slender one for the institution, but much to everyone's relief there was a surplus of income over expenditures in 1865, even though it amounted to only $20.

Building up the academic and other resources of the university was a slow and tedious process at first. Thanks to gifts and other acquisitions, the theological library, which at first was kept separate from that of the college, comprised 5,000 volumes by 1865, while the collegiate library had only 600 volumes.[69] The total assets of the university in 1865 were $60,000, exclusive of the theological school, of which $15,000 was owed to the latter.[70] But the hopeful sign was an increase in the student body which in 1865 totalled 103, slightly over half of whom were young women. The collegiate department by that year offered two courses of study: the "classical," leading to a Bachelor of Arts or Science; and a "scientific," leading to a Laureate of Arts or Science, intended for women.[71]

In 1869 a Law Department was added to the theological, classical, and scientific curricula, by a special act of the legislature in 1868.[72] The full course, leading to a Bachelor of Laws degree, consisted of three terms. The total cost was $75, less than at any other law school in the state.[73] It lasted but two years, and was discontinued when the law schools at Columbia University and Albany were given the exclusive right of qualifying students for the bar without examination. The charter authority was again used when the Brooklyn Law School became part of St. Lawrence in 1903 and remained so for exactly forty years. Beginning in 1907, St. Lawrence also operated and administered a state school of agriculture which after the Second World War became part of the New York State university system. The first faculty member of the agricultural school was a graduate of the theological school (James M. Payson).

The prospects of the university looked most promising as the centennial year of the denomination approached. However, the theological school continued to insist on its separate status, even though it did not obtain its own building until Fisher Hall was dedicated in 1883; it burned in 1951 and was replaced in 1955, ten years before the theological school was closed. The theological school continued to share in major gifts to the university in the nineteenth century, including a $25,000 bequest in 1869 from the Craig family of Rochester, New York; an identical bequest was made to the college. The total assets of the university (including unpaid subscriptions) in 1870 were $153,000, 60 per cent of which were in the name of the theological school.[74] The assets of Tufts College the same year were estimated at $800,000. The termination of the preparatory curriculum in 1866 had made St. Lawrence into a full-fledged university of collegiate grade. A second successful institution of higher education had been created under Universalist sponsorship.

Lombard University (College)

Like Tufts College and St. Lawrence University, what eventually became Lombard College had certain features which gave it a distinctive character despite the fact that the three institutions shared a common Universalist origin. Tufts College had begun as a liberal arts institution with a fairly standard classical collegiate curriculum leading to the Bachelor of Arts degree, and evolved into a university, complete with professional schools. St. Lawrence, although technically a university when it was chartered, had actually opened as a professional school of theology, and after having added temporarily a preparatory department, had finally emerged with an undergraduate liberal arts college as part of its structure. The third institution under Universalist sponsorship that eventually became both a college and a university started out as an academy, offering instruction only at the secondary school level.

After being incorporated in 1851 as Illinois Liberal Institute, located in Galesburg, the charter was changed in 1857 to Lombard University, four years after it had been authorized to offer college-level instruction. The institution's charter was changed in major respects on

The original building (1850-1851) of Illinois Liberal Institute, Galesburg, which became Lombard University (College)

several other occasions until the institution was merged with neighboring Knox College in 1930 after almost eighty years of service.[75] Lombard was the first Universalist college established in the Midwest. It was the only school remaining under denominational auspices for any considerable length of time that evolved from an academy into an institution of higher learning. And it was the first Universalist-sponsored college (and the second college in the United States) to award Bachelor of Arts degrees to women, earned through the regular curriculum.

There was sufficient numerical and organizational strength among Universalists in the semi-frontier area of central Illinois by 1850 to generate discussions about the possibility of establishing some kind of an educational institution to serve denominational needs. The impulse came from the Spoon River Association, which had been organized in 1841 in the first Universalist meeting house to be built at Farmington (Fulton County), in what was known as the "Military Tract." The initiative came from Amos Pierce of Greenbush, a layman, and C.P. West, a clergyman. At its meeting in 1850, the council of the association unanimously adopted a resolution presented by West that the Universalists of the state "ought immediately to adopt measures for the establishment of the seminary of learning" to be free from the sectarian influence prevalent in those schools "in the hands and under the control of our religious opponents."[76] The "sectarian influences" to which Universalists objected were "detrimental to the course of free inquiry after religious truth, injurious to the spread of Universalism, and sometimes ruinous to the peace and happiness of the students themselves." As was the case with all Universalist-sponsored schools, the academy was to be open to all of "the liberal portions of the community." It was also voted to establish the institution at Galesburg (Knox County) and to present the plan to the state convention so that it could be carried into effect. Clergy present were also requested to solicit the cooperation of other associations.

The financing of the proposed school was considered a speculative operation, like any other business. A joint stock company capitalized originally at $5,000 but later increased to $20,000 was organized in the fall of 1850. Taxable shares were originally $25 each. The tax was to support the school and dividends were to be declared if the institution's revenue exceeded its operating expenses (an eventuality which never took place). Fifteen stockholders who were also to serve as trustees were selected, to serve on a rotating basis. Work began immediately on a three-story brick building (with basement); the amount authorized was $6,000. The charter was duly secured on 15 February 1851 and by the summer of the next year $6,500 had been subscribed. Paul R. Kendall (1822-1897), who had already had teaching and administrative experience, including over three years as principal of Western Liberal Institute in Ohio, was chosen to head the new academy. Miss Caroline S. Woodbury was placed in charge of the "Ladies' Department" of the coeducational school.

Kendall, prominent throughout his life in denominational education, was a graduate of Norwich University (1847) and for two years conducted an academy in Sharpsburg, Kentucky. Although ordained in the ministry while in Ohio, he never held a pastorate. After serving in Galesburg he became a recruiter for the Union Army and helped raise several military units during the Civil War. He became the principal of Clinton Liberal Institute in 1868, and in 1870 accepted the presidency of Smithson College, where he served until 1874. Between 1875 and 1880 he was again the head of Clinton Liberal Institute; it was he who made the arrangements for the relocation of that school at Fort Plain, New York. After a year as a teacher of mathematics, he retired to private life. He became a semi-invalid in 1894 after a paralytic stroke, and died in Canton, New York, on 4 April 1897.

The Illinois Liberal Institute opened in the fall of 1852 with sixty students "of all grades of education," and offered a choice of three curricula: "academic," "scientific," and "collegiate," although this program had not yet been authorized by the state legislature. Women were allowed to substitute German for mathematics. No residence or boarding facilities for students were provided on the campus for over twenty years, and students were scattered about the community. In 1873 a boarding hall for women, under private operation, was opened near the campus. It was not until 1881 that a residence hall with dining facilities was built for women by the school. Complete living requirements (room, board, and fuel) could be obtained in 1870 for $4.00 a week.[77] Tuition at the same time ranged from $3.75 to $8.25 for a ten-week term, the amount depending on the course of study pursued.

Kendall had aspirations from the very beginning to turn the institute into a college, and received strong backing from the Spoon River Association. The combined stockholder-trustees reluctantly agreed to follow his recommendation. Kendall had, in fact, organized college classes when the school opened in 1852, some of the students having come from Knox College in the same community.[78] This institution, operated by the Presbyterians, had been chartered in 1837, at the same time the town had been founded, and was Lombard's local rival throughout the latter's history. Through Kendall's efforts the charter was amended in 1853 to provide a college as well as a preparatory department. At the same time, the school was authorized to increase its capital stock, exclusive of legacies and donations, to $50,000, which Kendall was required by the stockholders to raise within two months. About $60,000 was subscribed for the purpose, largely by the sale of scholarships. After the institute had opened, C.P. West served as financial agent, and sold $2,500 in stock at $100 a share. A scholarship system was then substituted, whereby certificates worth $100 in tuition were issued, of which the school received $50 in cash or notes at 10 per cent. Approximately $75,000 in such notes was obtained, worth $150,000 in tuition.

The institute had a promising beginning. In 1853 there were 134 students enrolled, 39 in the collegiate division (25 men and 14 women), and 95 (59 men and 36 women) in the preparatory and scientific departments, the latter emphasizing vocational education.[79] There were 170 students by 1854, some from Indiana and Iowa; by contrast, all of the college officers were from New England. The institution was considered "well manned and womaned [*sic*]."[80] The faculty, including the president, had been increased to seven by 1866; two were women.[81] The academic year was originally divided into four ten-week terms but after 1870 was modified to three terms of uneven length.

Just as the school seemed to be on the road to success and Kendall had announced a fund drive of $175,000 to establish the college, disaster struck in the form of a fire which in 1855 almost totally destroyed the main building; to make matters worse, the insurance had lapsed. But the institution continued to operate in temporary quarters, including the local Lutheran church. In no way deterred, the stockholders authorized a new building of Gothic design which was under construction by mid-1856 on a new campus on the outskirts of town, southeast of the center. Although the completion of the new building was delayed until sufficient funds could be secured, and classes had to be held in unfinished rooms, without light, heat, or other amenities, sufficient money was raised to pay for the new structure, known to alumni as "Old Main." The graduation of the first "college class" (four men and two women) took place in 1856 in the unfinished building.

Kendall, more determined than ever to carry out his plans for creating a college, decided to go on the road and become his own financial agent. So, leaving John Van Ness Standish, a member of the faculty, as Acting President, Kendall resigned and undertook to raise money. He was assisted by George S. Weaver, who had been a prime mover in founding Western Liberal Institute in Marietta, Ohio and was itinerating in the Midwest.[82] By mid-1856 Kendall had raised $37,000 for buildings and $39,000 for endowment.[83] The largest single donation was $20,000, partly in cash and partly in eighty acres of prairie land, from Benjamin Lombard, Sr., of Henry, Illinois. The institute charter was amended in February 1857, rechristening the school "Lombard University."

After the brief presidency of Otis A. Skinner (1857-59), James P. Weston served from 1860 until 1872. At the time he was elected, the net assets of the institution were approximately $100,000, of which over $75,000 was available for immediate use. The Northwest Conference of Universalists undertook the responsibility of creating an endowment fund, of which $82,000 had been secured by 1866.[84]

Several curricular changes were made during Weston's administration. The preparatory program was set at two years for college entrance; a four-year course of study was established for Bachelor of Arts candidates; and a three-year program, extended in 1860 to four years, was provided for the Bachelor of Science. Lombard followed the common nineteenth century practice of awarding the Master of Arts degree to graduates of three years' standing, the first in 1859. A three-year "Ladies' Collegiate Course" offering the Laureate of Arts degree, was also established (1861) for those not wishing to become candidates for a Bachelor's degree.

Enrollments in the collegiate course remained smaller than those of the other departments throughout most of Lombard's history. There were only nineteen in 1859 and twenty-one in 1861, when enlistments in the Union Army decimated almost completely the male portion of the student body.[85] The total number of college alumni/alumnae was only 198 by 1886.[86] In sharp contrast to the experiences of Tufts College and St. Lawrence University, very few graduates of Lombard entered the ministry; only five had done so by 1863, ten years after the collegiate program had been authorized.[87]

President Weston had to make a personal plea at the General Convention in 1861 to prevent the university from closing.[88] In 1863 there was no sophomore class at all in the arts or scientific departments. Because there were no Universalist academies in that section of the Midwest, the preparatory department continued for many years to be the most largely populated part of the institution, averaging close to 300 a year during the Civil War period. Out of the more than 250 students enrolled in the university in 1865, almost all in the preparatory department, only 20 were from outside Illinois.[89] When Erasmus Manford attended the General Convention which met in Galesburg in 1866, he commented that the term "university" was an overly pretentious title for the school, but added that the Midwest was "fond of high sounding names."[90] The official designation of the institution was in fact changed from "University" to "College" on 12 April 1900.

There was no question by 1864 that "the permanent establishment of the University, by adequate endowment" was the most urgent need.[91] There were 300 students enrolled that year, all but thirty-six in the preparatory department. An effort was made to raise $100,000 in endowment, but by the fall of 1864 only $10,000 had been raised, and had to be applied to the liquidation of indebtedness. The institution was still clearly a deficit operation.[92] One step to bolster the financial base of the school was taken in 1865 when a new charter was issued. The institution was given tax-free status, and the board of stockholders was also dissolved and replaced by a conventional board of trustees consisting of twenty individuals serving staggered five-year terms. It was provided also that Lombard was to be officially a church-related and church-supported school, which it had been in actuality from the time it opened. The trustees were to be elected by Universalists according to the new charter. The university in 1865 was also authorized, through its board, to establish law, medical, and divinity schools in addition to its existing College of Arts and Sciences, preparatory school, and special programs such as music and art. All diploma and degree programs were set at four years in 1869, although that of the preparatory school varied from time to time.

Support for the university began to trickle in from Universalist organizations outside the state after the new charter was obtained. The Washington Association (Ohio) pledged nearly $1,500 toward the endowment in 1866.[93] The Northwestern Conference pledged its assistance in 1865 in raising $20,000 to endow a chair of theology.[94]

The institution continued to live a precarious existence, with inadequate endowment and an even more inadequate enrollment. The financial panic and depression of 1873 brought a sudden decline in the number of students, and the expansion of the public school system in Knox County severely affected the preparatory school. Enrollment in all branches had slipped below 100 by 1875, and in 1877 was down to 71, with only 18 in the college division. Two years later the enrollment of the entire institution had declined to fifty-eight. When the school opened in the fall of 1884 there were only three degree candidates in other than the scientific course. Invested funds from which income was available amounted to only $123,000 in 1886; the property was valued at $200,000 that year.[95] Yet the institution continued not only to exist, but to expand in other directions.

The idea of establishing a theological school or department was first suggested by Otis A. Skinner in 1861.[96] He had hoped that such a step could be taken as soon as the Civil War was over, but it was not until 1881 that the possibility was actually realized. In that year William H. Ryder provided an endowment of $20,000 to establish such a school. The divinity school opened in the fall of 1881 with an ideal faculty-student ratio. President Nehemiah White, John V.N. Standish, and Isaac Parker comprised the faculty and an equal number of students constituted the first class. C.W. Tomlinson, pastor of the Galesburg church, also served as a lecturer on a part-time basis, as did Ryder for six years (1881-85). Only two of the original student body completed the three-year course in 1884 and only four had graduated by 1886. White resigned the presidency of Lombard in 1892 to head the divinity school, where he served until his retirement in 1905. The school was officially designated the Ryder Divinity School in 1889, in recognition of Ryder's gifts, which totalled $50,000. At the same time, the school received a $20,000 gift from Amos Throop of Pasadena, California.

Ryder Divinity School was transferred to Chicago in 1912 and affiliated with the complex of the University of Chicago Divinity Schools. L.B. Fisher, who had served as president of Lombard since 1905, became Dean of Ryder when it moved. In 1917-18, a structure known as Ryder Divinity House was built as a unit of Divinity Quadrangle. But enrollment declined steadily in the mid-1920s, so the building was sold to the University of Chicago in 1928. The divinity school was transferred to the Meadville Theological School (Unitarian) which had moved from Pennsylvania to Chicago, and the Ryder Chair of Parish Administration was established. The arrangement to join forces with the Unitarian school was part of a larger plan for Universalist-Unitarian cooperation for educational and social service purposes, as one of the steps toward proposed union of the two denominations.

From the closing years of the nineteenth century until the stock market crash of 1929 and the onset of the Great Depression and other factors put an end to the institution, Lombard put more and more emphasis on pre-professional and professional education and less and less emphasis on the collegiate liberal arts curriculum. It drew decreasing numbers of students as enrollment in most of the other parts of the college increased. In 1889 the preparatory school, which lasted until the reorganization of the college took place in 1912, extended its curricula to include training of elementary school teachers and employees of business concerns. Both pre-medical and pre-agricultural courses were introduced in 1902-1903, and three years later a domestic science department was created. By 1912 nearly twenty such vocationally oriented programs were available. A graduate program leading to the Master of Arts was begun in 1894. Although a doctoral program was announced at the same time, the college was not equipped to offer all that was needed for the Ph.D., so candidates had to have taken most of their course work elsewhere. The total assets on the eve of the transfer of the Ryder Divinity School were less than $350,000. The institution, in short, attempted to operate too many programs without the necessary resources.

After surviving the period of the First World War, the college started a $500,000 endowment campaign, and the enrollment (in 1923-24) exceeded 500, the highest in the history of the institution. But full-time enrollments continued to decline as more and more students registered in two-year "certificate" programs in such fields as agriculture, home economics, and music, and in extension courses. By the late 1920s the financial plight of the college was so critical that few believed it could survive much longer. In desperation, a businessman (G.D. Davis) was selected in 1929 to head the institution, of which the Unitarians had taken control the previous year as part of the proposed Universalist-Unitarian merger. But inadequate endowment, deficit financing over a period of years, the loss of income because of the stock market crash, the inability to raise capital funds, and the failure of the contemplated denominational union, all played a part in bringing Lombard College to an end.[97]

The possibility of merger of Lombard with Knox College had been considered off and on for many years, the first serious consideration of which had taken place beginning in 1907. A faculty committee interested some of the trustees in such a proposal. They, in turn, consulted with representatives of the Rockefeller and Carnegie Foundations. Officials of the two foundations arranged a meeting in Chicago in 1912 with trustees of both Lombard and Knox. Although the idea was favorably considered, nothing came of the discussions. The proposal was again revived after the First World War, and had become a certainty by 1929-30. On 3 June 1930, two months after the announcement had been made that the institution would be merged with Knox College, the Lombard Class of 1930, forty in number, became the last to graduate. Students still enrolled in Lombard desiring to do so were transferred to Knox without loss of academic standing, and members of the Class of 1931 were able to complete their degree requirements at Knox under the original Lombard requirements. All students' records were transferred, and three members of the Lombard staff accepted positions at Knox. Lombard alumni were invited to consider themselves part of the Knox alumni association. Some equipment, and part of the library, were also transferred. The campus was eventually sold to Galesburg and became part of the property of the public school system and the site of Lombard Junior High School. The various buildings were remodelled or removed. "Old Main," the structure built in 1856, the year after the original building had been destroyed by fire, was razed in spite of efforts to save it.

Thus closed the institution which Universalists had started seventy-nine years before, first as an academy on the Midwestern prairie, and then as their third institution of higher learning. But Lombard did not disappear completely. Legally, the board of trustees still exists, for the charter was never revoked; it continues to be held by the Meadville Theological School in Chicago, now officially called Meadville/Lombard Theological School.

Lombard was an educational pioneer in several ways. From the day it opened it admitted young women to all of its departments on a completely equal basis with young men. They attended the same classes and were eligible for the same diplomas, degrees, and honors. Many of the literary clubs and social organizations which were traditionally thought to be the exclusive domain of the men were coeducational. Two of the six recipients of Bachelor of Arts degrees, first awarded in 1856, were women. Supporters of Lombard were quick to point out that Knox College nearby did not admit women until 1870. They likewise noted that coeducation on the collegiate level was not yet even an experiment on the conservative eastern seaboard, where all-women or coordinate but separate colleges for men and women was the dominant pattern.[98] Just a year prior to the time that this observation was made by the Committee on Education of the General Convention, Vassar College, exclusively for women, had been opened in New York State.

Women's rights were frequently the subject of lectures and even of official exercises. In 1868 President Weston devoted his baccalaureate address to the subject, making a "moderate plea" for equality of the sexes.[99] During the same Commencement weekend, Augusta Jane Chapin, the second woman to be ordained in the Universalist ministry, delivered an address on the liberal education of women. The first recipient (in 1881) of a Master of Science degree by a graduate of Lombard of at least three years' standing, was a woman. Miss M. Agnes Hathaway, later to serve as a Universalist missionary in Japan, served at

Lombard, beginning in 1900, as one of the first Dean of Women in the history of American educational administration.[100]

Lombard was an innovator in other respects besides women's education. Beginning in 1854, only a year after it was authorized to award college degrees, students were allowed to offer modern foreign languages (a choice from French, German, and Italian) instead of Greek and Latin which were the staples of the prescribed classical curriculum at most institutions. Students at Lombard were also among the first in the nation to be given a responsible share in conducting not only their own affairs but in the governance of the institution. In 1895-96 the "Septemvorate" was formed, a board of control consisting of three faculty, three students, and the college president. A self-government association was formed by dormitory residents in 1896-97. There seems to be no doubt that during its lifetime the institution served as best it could both denominational and societal needs.

Buchtel College

There was a growing feeling among Ohio Universalists in the 1860s that an educational institution under their control should exist somewhere in the state. No denominational academy had been in operation in Ohio since Western Liberal Institute in Marietta had closed in 1853. For several years the state convention had contributed funds to both St. Lawrence and Lombard, and it was thought that a locally supported school should receive such money. At the state convention meeting in 1867 the Committee on Education was instructed to report on the desirability of establishing a coeducational seminary. The proposal to create one was approved in 1868, with the provision that $50,000 was to be raised among Universalists in the state, the school to be located in a town or city offering at least $10,000. The following year the convention reconsidered its earlier action and authorized its trustees and Committee on Education to take the necessary steps to provide a college instead of an academy. The change of direction came about because it was realized that Akron was a promising possible location and that an excellent public high school already existed there; another secondary school in Akron would have been superfluous.

Thus was born Buchtel College, which opened in September 1872 and remained under denominational control until 1907.[101] Between 1907 and 1967 the institution had a varied history. After six years as a private, independent school, it became, in 1913, the liberal arts division of the Municipal University of Akron. Between 1963 and 1967 it was a state-assisted university, and after 1967 became part of the state university system.

Henry F. Miller, then living in Dublin, Indiana, was appointed financial secretary in 1869, having served in a similar capacity for raising funds for Smithson College. Proposals were solicited for locating the new college, which was designated as the Ohio Universalists' special contribution to the denominational centennial celebration in 1870. Several sites were considered for the "Universalist Centenary School of Ohio," including Oxford, Kent, Woodstock, Mt. Gilead, and Akron (Summit County). After a motion to locate in Mt. Gilead was defeated, Akron, which had made the most attractive offer (a desirable site and $25,000 already pledged), was selected in February 1870 under certain conditions. At least $60,000 had to be subscribed within thirty days, and the money was to be raised within the county. The financial agent sent up a prayer that "God will raise up to this school a friend, who, with ample means, . . . will leave his name in a monument more lasting than the chiseled marble."[102] The man who met the specifications was at hand, in the person of John R. Buchtel (1820-1892).

Buchtel was a wealthy and philanthropically-inclined manufacturer, president of the Buckeye Mower and Reaper Works in Akron. With only a limited formal education, he had become successively a prosperous farmer and businessman, and profitably exploited rich mineral lands in southern Ohio. He was engaged throughout his life in public affairs and contributed thousands of dollars to numerous endeavors. Among his many other activities he served on the original board of trustees of the state's land-grant institution which became Ohio State University. When he was approached in 1869 for a contribution to the proposed Universalist college he was in the process of assisting in the financing of a free public library for the city of Akron. Miller, responsible for fund-raising for the projected college, prevailed on George Messenger, a retired Universalist minister from Springfield, Ohio, to persuade Buchtel to subscribe. So the public library received its benefactions from Buchtel at a later time.

More than the initial $60,000 required to establish the school was actually pledged. The total by 1870 amounted to $62,000, contributed by 100 individuals and 13 business firms. The largest sum came from Buchtel. He subscribed $25,000 toward the endowment and $6,000 to the building fund. When the institution was chartered he served on the building committee and became the first president of its board of trustees, a position which he held until his death in 1892. Buchtel repeatedly made donations to the college, which struggled in its early years with annual deficits. In addition to his original gift of $31,000, in 1882 he gave $100,000 in securities as a contribution toward the permanent endowment. Five years later, after having been stricken with paralysis, he donated (on Commencement Day) $100,000 in bonds and his life insurance of $74,000. The college was also his residuary legatee. Except for small donations, and provisions for his widow, his entire

Buchtel College, Akron, Ohio, a monument to collegiate Gothic architecture (1871)

fortune went to the college, amounting in all to more than half a million dollars.

At the time the college was chartered in 1870, John Buchtel had been formally a Universalist for only a short time. He had originally been a Methodist, although in religious sentiment he claimed to have been a Universalist for a quarter of a century.[103] There was no organized Universalism in Akron in 1870, the society established many years earlier having succumbed to internal dissension. Buchtel and his wife (they had no children) had joined Andrew Willson's Universalist society in nearby Kent early in 1870. The Akron church was reconstituted by George S. Weaver in 1873, and Buchtel served as its moderator for several years.

It was to be expected that the college would bear Buchtel's name, as its principal donor, and such was the case. Nonetheless, several alternatives were considered, among them "Murray College," and "Murray Centennial College." After considering "Buchtel Universalist College," the trustees finally settled on "Buchtel College" by a unanimous vote. Four of the original trustees were clergymen, including

Henry L. Canfield, who had been a visiting minister in Akron in 1870 before the church was reorganized, and had helped stir up enthusiasm for establishing the college; and Everett L. Rexford, who was destined to be a president of the institution. Seven of the original trustees were prominent local businessmen. The school was to be not only of a "high order" but was to provide education "on equal terms, of both sexes, and for the preparation of teachers for our Common Schools."

The site donated for the college, consisting of less than three acres originally, and later enlarged to about six, was on an eminence overlooking the city, and was described erroneously in the *Universalist Register* and in some newspaper accounts as "the highest point of land in Ohio."[104] Ground was broken for the main building in March 1871, with ceremonies for the laying of the cornerstone according to Masonic rites taking place on 4 July. Thus, several purposes were achieved: the celebration of the anniversary of American independence; recognition of the centenary year of Universalism; and the establishment of the college. Horace Greeley, the nationally-known Universalist editor of the *New York Tribune* which he had founded in 1841, delivered the main address, entitled "Human Concepts of God as They Affect the Moral Education of our Race."

The building constructed in 1871-72 was as elaborate as its cornerstone-laying ceremony had been. It was a massive, heavily ornamented five-story structure, complete with towers, and combining Doric, Gothic, and Norman architectural features.[105] Designed by Thomas W. Silloway of Boston who was responsible for the plans for several other Universalist school buildings, Buchtel Hall cost over $40,000 more than the original estimate of $125,000. It was, like most other such buildings used for educational purposes in the nineteenth century, constructed as a self-contained unit intended to house all operations. There were accommodations for 150 students, the young men residing in one end of the building and the young women in the other (with proper supervision, of course). Universalists were encouraged to be financially responsible for furnishing one or more rooms. The church in McConnellsville, Ohio, contributed $60 for the purpose.[106]

After Thomas B. Thayer, then pastor in Salem, Massachusetts, declined the presidency, Sullivan H. McCollester (1826-1921) became the first head of the institution, and served until his resignation in 1878. McCollester, born in Marlborough, New Hampshire, and a graduate of Norwich University and Harvard Divinity School, had served as principal of several Universalist academies and for three years as State Commissioner of Education in his native state. The school, operating on a three-term academic year until 1900, originally offered two college-level curricula: a four-year classical course leading to the Bachelor of

Arts degree and elected by only a small number of students throughout the history of the school; and a two-year philosophical course which in 1875 was extended to four years and led to a Bachelor of Philosophy degree. A four-year scientific course (Bachelor of Science) was also added in 1875. Buchtel, like St. Lawrence, found it necessary to provide a preparatory department from the very beginning; it was at first combined with a two-year "normal" course to prepare elementary school teachers for certification. The preparatory course, geared for each of the three collegiate curricula, was later extended to three years, and in 1903 to four.

Of the 217 students enrolled when the college opened in 1872, 171 were in the preparatory department; 93 of the total student body were young women. Tuition was originally $30 a year, room $10 a year, and board $5 a week. Even at those rates some students found it difficult to finance their education, and ten scholarships of $60 each had been established by 1872. Annual expenses were estimated at $250 in 1873. At no time were all of the student rooms occupied, thus contributing to a perpetual deficit. Use of the building for residential purposes did not come to an end until 1899.

The first commencement was held in 1873, with four graduates of the philosophical course (two men and two women), and the first Bachelor of Arts degree was awarded to one student in 1875. A total of 103 students had been graduated from the collegiate divisions by 1886, in which year there were 369 students enrolled, a high proportion of them commuters taking courses on a part-time basis. By then there were fifty "perpetual" scholarships of $60 available, endowed at $1,000 each. A total of 465 students were awarded Bachelor's degrees by 1913, 217 of them women.

The college opened with a faculty of seven, including the president who, in addition to his administrative duties, taught reading to the preparatory school students and, until Weaver's arrival in Akron to take charge of the local Universalist church, conducted services in the college chapel.[107] In 1873 Mrs. Buchtel offered to endow a professorship for women to the extent of $20,000, provided the Universalist women of Ohio and western Pennsylvania would raise an equal sum for a second such professorship.[108] The project was to be supervised by the Women's Centenary Association, and Mrs. Caroline Soule, its president, immediately went into action. The campaign which she led at both the Ohio and Pennsylvania conventions garnered $16,000 in a matter of weeks and was so successful that the two professorships were both established as planned. The second of the two, which became an actuality in 1875, was made possible by a $10,000 gift from Mrs. Chloe Pierce, widow of one of the incorporators of the institution. She had promised the money at the time of the state convention meetings in 1873. The

Buchtel and Pierce professorships were among the first of their kind in the nation.

John Buchtel, a blunt advocate of women's rights, pointedly requested in 1892 that, in view of the fact that the college was a coeducational institution, there should be at least one woman on its board of trustees. The state convention promptly complied, and before the end of the year Mrs. Abby S. Schumacher of Akron was elected to the board. Mrs. Henrietta G. Moore of Springfield, ordained as a Universalist minister in 1891, became the second woman on the board in 1893.

The college had its share of difficulties and failures in its early years. The indebtedness of the institution had already exceeded $29,000 by 1874, exacerbated by the Panic of 1873, and had reached $50,000 by 1870 when a special money-raising campaign was necessary to pay off the obligations. A request by the Ohio Convention in 1876 that a theological school be established could not be honored because it was completely beyond the resources of the college. When the convention expressed disappointment several years later that so few of the Buchtel graduates went into the ministry it had to be contented with the hope that a theological school might sometime be established somewhere in the state—a hope never fulfilled.

By 1878 there was increasing dissatisfaction with McCollester's administration, to which was added a rift in the Akron church in which he was involved. Sixty students also called for his resignation. Weaver, who had been pastor of the Akron church, moved to Galesburg, Illinois, in 1877. A daughter and a son enrolled in Buchtel at the time withdrew; the daughter re-enrolled in St. Lawrence and the son transferred to Tufts. Everett L. Rexford succeeded McCollester as president (on the latter's recommendation) in 1878. Rexford also replaced Weaver as pastor in Akron. Rexford, a graduate of St. Lawrence, had held several pastorates and had served on the Committee on Education of the state convention and had been an incorporator and was a trustee of Buchtel. He too resigned the presidency, after only three years, to take charge of a new church in Detroit in 1880. Like McCollester, he had become a center of controversy. Simultaneously holding the Akron pastorate and serving as a college president made his position rather awkward, and it became evident that he was more interested in the ministry than in the presidency. He was not as successful in this respect as Alonzo A. Miner had been when in a similar situation earlier at Tufts.

A third clergyman, Orello Cone, assumed the presidency of Buchtel in 1880 and remained until 1896. Preeminently a scholar rather than an administrator, he published some of his major works on Biblical criticism (1891, 1893) while serving as president, and was a co-editor in 1892 of the *New World*, a quarterly replacing the *Unitarian Review*. He had been lured from the theological school at St. Lawrence, where he had served since 1865 as Professor of Biblical Languages and Literature. He faced a multitude of problems in his new post, and made no rash promises. He was undoubtedly aware that the indebtedness of the institution stood at over $60,000 when his predecessor resigned, and that one year after his own inauguration, $13,000 was still needed, in spite of the efforts of the Ohio Convention and an on-the-spot canvass of Akron in 1881 to raise funds. The student body that year dropped to less than 180 and the total capital assets were less than $300,000.[109]

President Cone selected his faculty very carefully, on the basis of their professional competence rather than their religious affiliation, and resisted pressure from the state convention to stress the denominational character of the school by giving preference to Universalists for all positions. The student body was still predominantly Universalist when he assumed office, but like other denominational schools was admitting a larger and larger number of students from other faiths, reflecting the changing composition of the population. By the end of the nineteenth century students from Universalist families ceased to comprise the majority of the student population at Buchtel, a development which occurred later at that institution than at Tufts, which was admitting Roman Catholics early in the 1880s, as well as numerous students from various Protestant backgrounds, and Jewish students who found the medical and dental schools attractive when they were opened in the decade of the 1890s. The bulk of the non-Universalists at Buchtel came from native white evangelical Protestant families. Foreign students were relatively few, reflecting in part the fact that denominational foreign missionary work (except in Scotland) was not officially undertaken until 1890.

One explanation for the difference in the Tufts and Buchtel student bodies, besides demography, was probably the fact that the legal status of the schools differed so far as their relations with the denomination were involved. Tufts was under the direct control of no single Universalist body, while Buchtel was officially under the supervision of the Ohio Convention and was required by its charter to make annual reports to it. In the 1880s the financial agent of the state convention was responsible for raising funds for both Buchtel and the permanent missionary fund. It was also the Ohio Convention which nominated the trustees. Visting committees, beginning in 1885, were required to report to the state convention annually. The convention records usually referred to Buchtel as "our college." When A.B. Tinker made his final report in 1891 as long-time secretary of the convention trustees, he commented that Buchtel had always been "a hopeful institution [with] . . . the faith of a true Universalist. It expects to be *saved,* and has no idea of being lost."[110]

The institution in fact was almost lost at the very end of the nineteenth century. Between 1893 and 1895 there was growing dissatisfaction with Cone's presidency. He had been reluctant to take the position in the first place, and only John Buchtel, in a personal visit to the eastern seaboard in 1880 to interview him, had persuaded Cone to take the position. A consensus developed after 1892 that he was a poor politician, diplomat, and fund-raiser, and was emphasizing scholarship to the detriment of the college's obligations to the denomination and to the community. He also had difficulties with Ellwood Nash, pastor of the Akron church, and with the state convention. The president also lost a strong supporter with the death of John Buchtel in 1892.

A year before his resignation in 1896, Cone wrote an article in which he attempted to accentuate the positive aspects of the college.[111] Additional benefactions by 1895 totalled $250,000, bringing the total assets to about $860,000. Many of the contributions had come from outside the denomination, notably from Akron businessmen. Besides these gifts, other benefactions helped by 1895 to provide a science building, $35,000 for scholarships at $1,000 each, and the construction and equipment of a gymnasium which Cone described as "the finest College structure of its kind in the West."

The institution by the mid-1890s was in fact suffering from extreme financial stringency, especially after the Panic of 1893, and it lost many of its faculty who were not replaced at the very time that it had over-extended itself with an expanded elective system. The situation was so critical by 1896, with enrollment dropping precipitately, that one trustee recommended that the college be closed for a year. Cone resigned in 1896, and after two years as pastor in Lawrence, Kansas, returned to St. Lawrence, where he served on the theological school faculty until his death in 1905. After Charles M. Knight, a faculty member, served briefly as Acting President (1896-97), Ira Priest assumed the presidency. He had graduated from Goddard Seminary and Tufts College and received a degree from its divinity school in 1887. After serving churches in Massachusetts he had become pastor of the Akron church in 1896 and was also chaplain and an instructor in the college. He worked valiantly but not very successfully to raise money, and had the unhappy experience of watching the main building go up in flames in December 1899. A new Buchtel Hall, with much more modest dimensions than the original, was built in 1901. That building too, the last one constructed during the period of Universalist control, was destroyed by fire in 1971; its rebuilding was financed with public funds.

By the best estimate, $293,000 was the minimum necessary to rebuild that portion of the physical plant which had been lost in 1899, and to raise the endowment required to make the institution both solvent and self-supporting. President Priest was relieved of many of his duties so that he could devote time to fund-raising. The college managed to reopen in January 1900 after the unscheduled event of the previous December. The fire, however, represented a turning-point in the history of the college, for the Universalists were unable to sustain it any longer. The Ohio Convention was unsuccessful in raising the $100,000 it had pledged after the fire, and the citizens of Akron took more and more of the responsibility for financing the institution. It became after 1900 a community rather than a Universalist enterprise.

Priest resigned from the presidency in 1901, largely because of alumni dissatisfaction, left the ministry, and became a businessman in Akron. Augustus P. Church, who had replaced Priest as pastor of the Akron church in 1897, served also as an instructor in the college and in 1898 was elected to its board of trustees, on which he served until his death in 1912. He became Acting President and then president of Buchtel, beginning in 1901. He was a graduate of both St. Lawrence and its theological school and had held pastorates in New England. During his administration, services to the community became increasingly a part of the college's activities, including the conduct of basic research in rubber chemistry, the operation of a short-lived commercial school, and the offering of evening extension courses. But the potential of this and other programs was not fully realized until the college became a public institution and more adequate financing was available.

Buchtel College severed its official ties with Universalism in 1907, when it became a private, independent school in order to make its faculty eligible for pensions administered by the Carnegie Foundation. All denominational connections, including the sponsorship by the Ohio State Convention, were required to come to an end.[112] However, all Universalists who were members of the trustees and staff remained and filled out their terms; there was no wholesale reshuffling of personnel. By 1907 the connection between the Universalists and the college had become largely an "inoperative technicality," for Universalist patronage in both students and money had almost come to an end. Only 16 of the 180 students in the collegiate courses in 1913 were from Universalist families. In 1908 the productive endowment was only $100,000, half of the minimum required for membership in the Ohio College Association. The board of trustees became a self-perpetuating body, and Buchtel assumed the same independent status that St. Lawrence was to achieve in 1910, and for the same reason.

President Church considered leaving the presidency in 1908 and actually submitted his resignation in 1911; but he was persuaded to continue, and died in office in 1912. He made one desperate attempt that year to salvage Buchtel for the denomination by recommending its merger with Lombard College in Galesburg, Illinois, but the Lombard trustees, already struggling with their own serious financial problems, elected not to follow that course of action. In 1913, a year after

Church's death, the college which the Universalists had opened forty-one years before became the Municipal University of Akron, with the Buchtel College of Liberal Arts as one of its components. The ordinance creating the new public university out of the old Universalist college was countersigned, no doubt with mixed feelings, by Ira Priest, clerk of the city council and one-time president of what had been Buchtel College.

Smithson College

The denominationally-sponsored institution of higher education, chartered at almost the same time as Buchtel College but with the shortest life of all, was Smithson College in Logansport, Indiana. It was named in honor of Joshua Smithson who, although not its largest donor, was its first. He was born in Randolph County, North Carolina, in 1792 and died in Vevay (Switzerland County), Indiana, on 24 June 1867. After living in Hillsboro, Ohio, as a youth, he moved in 1816 to Vevay, where he remained for the rest of his life.[113] Vevay, located on the Ohio River in the southeastern corner of the state, was at the time of Smithson's arrival a flourishing town with many economic opportunities. He started the first coal business in the community and was briefly a cabinet maker. He then erected a carding machine and cotton gin. He was one of the first in the area to convert from horse power to steam power, and his business prospered.[114] Smithson eventually sold out, receiving land in exchange. He built an imposing brick residence about 1850, and became one of the town's leading citizens.[115]

Smithson was first a Methodist, then joined the Christian Church, and finally became a Universalist. He was one of the first members of the Universalist church when it was organized in Vevay in 1852 and became one of its trustees and most generous supporters. He bequeathed all of his property to his wife, Sarah Goddard Smithson, whom he had married in Flemingsburg, Kentucky, in 1816. They had no children. After her death one-third of his estate was to go to the church, the interest to be used for the support of preaching. The remaining two-thirds was bequeathed to the Northwestern Conference for the establishment of a denominational school in the state. Smithson also left money for the construction of a new church in Vevay, with the proviso that if it had to be sold, the proceeds were to be turned over to the school. The church used when Smithson died had been constructed in 1862; it was replaced in 1894, but the school disappeared before the church did.

As soon as the $8,000 bequest (to which Mrs. Smithson later added $2,000) was made known, plans were under way to establish Smithson

Smithson College, designed in 1871; the wings were never constructed

Academy, to be located in Muncie. The school was incorporated in 1867, and Henry F. Miller was appointed as financial agent. But Universalists in the state refused to subscribe, on the ground that the academy could offer no service that was not already obtainable in the numerous public high schools which already existed.[116] Less than $7,000 was raised in 1867.[117] Then Mrs. Elizabeth Pollard, widow of Philip Pollard, came to the rescue, with an offer of $20,000 in land and money, subject to two important stipulations. The proposed institution was to be a college, and it had to be located in Logansport. The offer was immediately accepted, and the state convention assumed the sponsorship, taking over the trust funds held by the Northwestern Conference in 1868.[118] Mrs. Pollard then deeded slightly over ten acres of land as a site for the school, on a 150-foot bluff overlooking the Wabash River and the city of some 12,000. The land was thought to be worth about $10,000 at the time, and hence constituted one-half of Mrs. Pollard's gift.[119] Donations totalling $15,000 were also made by other citizens of Logansport in order "to secure its location."[120]

By the fall of 1869 a total of $50,000 had been raised, including Mrs. Pollard's gift of $10,000 for endowment.[121] It was confidently expected that $100,000 could be raised by the end of 1870, so plans were promptly drawn up to construct a four-story brick building while Paul R. Kendall took over from Miller the canvass for additional funds. The foundations of the building were laid in the fall of 1870 but the cornerstone was not in place until May 1871, the same year in which the institution was incorporated. The structure, with auxiliary utility buildings, was completed in the fall of 1871 at a cost of nearly $80,000, more than twice the amount pledged. Smithson College opened on 2 January 1872 as a coeducational school with 90 students, but with boarding accommodations for 120. The original plans had called for a building with two wings that would have housed a total of 200 students, but they were never built. If the entire structure had been completed as planned, the estimated cost would have been $150,000.[122] Even without the wings, the building was described as having "all the conveniences of a first-class hotel."[123] All of the faculty, including the president, lodged and boarded in the same building as the students.

The same emphasis on the equality of coeducational opportunity for young men and women that was found at Lombard University and Buchtel College was repeated at Smithson, extending as far as coeducational living facilities. "Believing that the happiness of the sexes requires them to live together in the companionship of equals, this College opens its doors to them on the same terms."[124] The relative standing of the students was to be determined by "individual merit and attainment," not by sex. It was noted also that the "lady principal," who was a faculty member, served at exactly the same rank and salary as other members of the staff. There were numerous regulations at Smithson, as at other comparable institutions, governing student conduct. A list entitled "Strict Prohibitions" (fourteen in number) included use of ardent spirits, tobacco in any form, profane or obscene language, card playing or other games of chance, and visiting between the sexes without permission.[125]

James Hervey Cravens, a United States Congressman from Indiana and a state judge, served as president of the board of trustees.[126] The original faculty consisted of Kendall, the first president; Mrs. Carolina S. Kendall as "lady principal;" and Howard R. Burrington, Professor of Ancient Lanaguages and Literature. The faculty eventually reached a maximum of ten. Five different curricula were offered: the "college" (four years), "academic" (three years), "philosophical" (two years), college preparatory (three years), and a commercial course (one year) for those wishing to prepare for a business career.[127] The college operated on a quarter system, with the academic calendar comprising three thirteen-week terms. Elective courses were also available in music, drawing, oil painting, and wax work. Tuition was $12 for the "college" course, with extra charges for elective courses, including modern foreign languages. The maximum total expenses for a year were estimated at $277.50.

Smithson College opened with bright hopes and great enthusiasm, and little else. It carried from the first a crushing burden of indebtedness impossible to liquidate. The cost of construction of the main building had far exceeded the funds available, so the property of the institution was mortgaged even before a student body appeared. The endowment was negligible to begin with, amounting to only $16,000 at its highest point, and was swallowed up by operating expenses. Total assets, exclusive of the land and buildings, were estimated in 1870 at $55,000, including subscriptions not collected, pledges unfulfilled, and bequests not yet available.[128] Even an arrangement made in 1874 for joint sponsorship of the institution by the state conventions of Indiana and Michigan did little to brighten the financial picture. The indebtedness in 1875 stood at $25,000.[129] The estimated value of the land donated by Mrs. Pollard was by 1870 not the $10,000 originally assumed, but closer to $5,000. The financial panic and depression of 1873 did nothing but damage by further depreciating property values.

The college lost the leadership of Kendall and his wife after only two years, when in 1874 he moved back to Clinton Liberal Institute. George S. Weaver, at the time the pastor of the Universalist church in Akron, Ohio, was offered the presidency but declined to serve after inspecting the institution.[130] He found it encumbered with debt, and very much doubted that it would survive for long, especially with two other Universalist colleges (Lombard and Buchtel) already competing for students in the Midwest. His skepticism was well-grounded. Richmond Fisk, Jr., assumed the presidency in 1874 but stayed only one year. He was succeeded by R.H. John, who was the last head of the institution. All of the presidents faced declining enrollments, which never came close to expectations. The total student body (all departments) dropped from the initial ninety to eighty by the beginning of the second year. Three students were graduated from the college course in 1874.[131] The number of students plummeted to forty-two in 1875, and was down to forty the following year.

Any effort to keep the college in operation any longer was obviously futile. It closed in the spring of 1878 and its property was turned over to the Phoenix Insurance Company. The buildings of the defunct school were leased to the American Normal College, a privately operated teacher training institution which opened in 1883.[132] Some of the Smithson faculty continued in the new school. As if to add an extra note of finality to the demise of Smithson, the main building so optimistically constructed in 1870-71 and lost to the denomination in 1878 was destroyed by fire in the 1890s.[133]

If any lesson was to be learned from the Smithson and Buchtel experiences, it was that "a great educational institution cannot be built up without large endowment funds."[134] It might be added that, neither can even an institution without aspirations to greatness but only a will to survive. In the case of Smithson College, the Indiana Universalists had completely disregarded the warning of the Committee on Education of the General Convention at the centennial assembly in 1870 not to establish any new institutions without firm commitment to support them.[135] It was further pointed out that Universalism was weaker in Indiana than in any other state in which a college had been established or projected. The denominational statistics for 1870 completely supported the committee's argument. Indiana had less than half as many parishes, meeting houses, and ministers as did Illinois.[136]

It was not until 1891 that another school under the patronage and control of Universalists was opened (Throop Polytechnic Institute in Pasadena, California), and its direct association with the denomination lasted but three years. Like Throop, the Southern Industrial College, established at Camp Hill, Alabama, under the auspices of the denomination in 1899, was a special-purpose institution which also passed out of Universalist hands. Yet, in historical perspective, while the denominational centennial celebrations of 1870-71 were taking place, Universalists were operating no less than fifteen educational institutions—five colleges or universities; three professional schools (two for theology and one for law); and seven academies, with almost 100 teachers and assets approaching two million dollars.[137] It was indeed an impressive record, all things considered.

SECTION VI

Universalism and a Social Ethic

Chapter 18

BETTERING THE LOT OF HUMANITY

The Universalist General Reform Assocation

There has probably been no epoch in American history more replete with reform enthusiasm and humanitarian crusades than the years from about 1830 to 1860.[1] This was the period, sometimes broadly defined as the Jacksonian Era, when American institutions were analyzed as never before, when old ideas were reexamined and new ideas put forth. There were plans for almost every conceivable human activity, from dietary reform to land distribution. Some basic reform impulses marked their start in this period, while others gained momentum and intensity. Change—usually considered synonymous with "progress"—was in the air. This was the era of agitation to abolish slavery, to reform the drunkard and rehabilitate the prisoner, to bring about world peace; this was the era, as previously indicated, of millenialism and spiritualism in religion; and the launching of what became a major indigenous religious denomination (Mormonism). This was the era of search for new ways of constituting society, as illustrated by the enthusiasm for Fourierism in which some Universalists became involved. Universalists, in fact, could no more be impervious to the reform excitement around them than could other Americans. Many a Universalist pitched in with a will—if not always a way—to bring about the social amelioration which they conceived to be not only necessary for a better America but imposed by the religious principles they believed and professed.

"Active benevolence is the characteristic of a good man, and a christian. And there is no duty of our holy religion that is more earnestly enjoined, and to the performance of which there is attached a most lasting reward, than that of benevolence." These were the opening words of a discourse delivered by Henry Bacon, pastor of the Second Universalist Society in Cambridge, Massachusetts, on behalf of the Universalist Female Charitable Institute of Boston, at an open meeting in 1836.[2]

If Universalists needed a theoretical, philosophic, and religious rationale for their reform efforts, they could readily find it within their denomination in the lectures and discourses of Edwin Hubbell Chapin (1814-1880), unquestionably one of the leading clergymen of the nineteenth century. An impressive orator, his services were in constant demand on speaking circuits spread over many states. In a series of lectures delivered in various New York churches in 1843, Chapin presented a generalized, rhetorical, and inspirational defense of moderate reformism, halfway on the continuum between the conservatism which "holds on to all things" and refuses to move at all, and radicalism, which "would destroy all things" and move too fast.[3] In all of the numerous benevolent and philanthropic movements he found a hopeful common denominator which might lead to both peace and union among competing Christians. Like Cobb and other socially-minded Universalists, however, he saw the ultimate secret of enduring change for the better in the inner reformation of each person. No renovation of society was possible without the renovation of the individual. All of this was to be achieved within a broad Christian framework expressed in a spirit of universal love.

"Benevolence," broadly defined, could and did take many forms among Universalists, and came to a climax with the organization in the 1840s of a general reform association which lasted almost twenty years and embraced almost every social institution and/or problem known to man. Until 1846 Universalists expended most of their reform efforts—from the abolition of slavery and capital punishment to prison reform and temperance—either with fragmented and uncoordinated organizations, or with no organization at all, and in virtually every instance with a determination to work independently of similar organizations outside the denomination. The first major organized effort among Universalists to bring about social change and to take an official stand on the issues of the day came in attempts to abolish slavery in the South. But, in spite of some attempts at organization, the majority of reform energies continued to be expended on an individual level.

This is one reason for the difficulty in gauging the actual influence that Universalists exerted in bringing about—or at least attempting to bring about—reforms in which other Americans were interested as well. Part of the explanation for the comparative lack of attention to organization among Universalists can be found in their traditional fear and suspicion of authority and centralization, whether imposed or otherwise, which characterized the denomination. Part was due to a firm and long-held conviction by many leading Universalists that secular problems were not the proper domain of basically ecclesiastical bodies, as the debate over abolition made abundantly clear. As William A. Drew, veteran editor of Universalist newspapers told his readers, he disliked when attending religious meetings, being "placed in an attitude that shall oblige us to legislate for State or Nation."[4] He therefore welcomed the creation of an umbrella organization as an outlet, for "all the contentious subjects foreign from our *religious* Associations, may be poured in, for debate."[5]

A channel and focus for reform enthusiasm within the denomination was provided when the "New England Universalist General Reform Association" was organized on the initiative of the Massachusetts Convention in 1846.[6] The Association, which met annually in Boston until 1862, had for its original object "the collection of such statistical information, relative to the various reform movements of the age, as illustrates not only the progress of Christianity . . . but the best means of prompting and applying it." The twelve-man committee charged with carrying into effect this ambitious undertaking represented the current denominational leadership in the Boston area, and was sponsored by Cyrus H. Fay. In an emotionally charged burst of humanitarian fervor which characterized the 1846 meeting of the state convention, the assemblage came close to adopting a blanket resolution which would have carried out literally the Biblical injunction to love one's enemies. Russell Tomlinson, who presented the resolution, was finally successful in having it adopted at the next annual meeting, but only after much debate; its tangible results are not easy to determine.[7]

At the first business meeting of the Association in May 1847, clergymen were present from all of the New England states and New York. The scope of the organization was broadened when the words "New England" were dropped from the title at a meeting in which a constitution was adopted. It was provided that any person interested in the objects of the Association could become a member merely by signing the constitution. Each New England state was represented by a vice-president. Addresses were delivered on peace, criminal reform, temperance, and human freedom in general, followed by appropriate resolutions.

By long-established custom extending back into the colonial period, the various religious and benevolent societies in New England met annually during the last week of May, and combined social as well as philanthropic activities. When the Universalists joined other denominations in "Anniversary Week," among the Universalist groups which met were the Sabbath School Union, the Sabbath School Teachers Union, and the Home Missionary Society, as well as the Reform Association. In 1859 an *ad hoc* "New England Conference of the Churches" was added, intended to provide for interchange of information and experiences among Universalist clergymen present during Anniversary Week.[8] Because of scheduling so many meetings simultaneously, Universalists could attend only a fraction of the many events in progress, and complained accordingly. The Reform Association customarily concluded its two-day meetings with a "breakfast party" held in downtown Boston (usually in Faneuil Hall), with speakers, hymn-singing, toasts (non-alcoholic), and a generally festive atmosphere. At the first meeting, attended by some 200 persons, Richard Frothingham of Charlestown presided.[9] Much rhetoric was generated and expended by such individuals as C.H. Fay (Roxbury), Alonzo A. Miner (Lowell), Henry Bacon (Providence, Rhode Island), Edwin H. Chapin (Boston), and Sylvanus Cobb (Malden), who spoke at length on the cheering fact that no intoxicating beverages were in evidence at the festival. The peak attendance at Reform Association meetings was reached in 1853, with over 500 present. There was usually extended reportage in the local secular press as well as denominational papers.

The magnitude and diversity of social problems that the Reform Association announced it would tackle boggled the mind and constituted projects that, if all were completed, would have taken several lifetimes. At its eleventh annual meeting (in 1857), the following categories of activities were decided on, totalling no less than forty subjects:

1. *Economic and Domestic Relations.* Slavery and the Colored Race; Domestic Slave Trade; Service; Wages; Marriage; Women's Rights; Parental Relations; Rights in the Soil.
2. *International Relations.* War; Non-Resistance; Diplomacy; Commerce; Seamen; Foreign Slave Trade; Colonization; Indians; Foreign Relations; Conflict of Races.
3. *Social Institutions and Habits.* Temperance; Education; the Pulpit; the Sabbath; the Press; Politics and Laws; Amusements; the Poor; Dress; Food.
4. *Offenders, Irresponsible and Unfortunate Persons.* Capital Punishment; Prison Discipline; Juvenile Offenders; Imprisonment for Debt; Dueling; Gambling; Courts; Trials; Idiots: Insane; Deaf and Dumb.

The corresponding secretaries of the Association (one for each state represented) were expected, with one assistant each, to collect and digest the facts pertaining to each subject.[10] Most of the findings (only a fraction of the total listed) were published as part of the annual report prepared by a secretary, the costs of printing defrayed by a fifty-cent assessment on each member of the Association. Many of the reports that were actually prepared were also carried in the two leading denominational papers in Boston—the *Trumpet* and the *Christian Freeman.* Resolutions were occasionally adopted on subjects not specifically included even in the comprehensive listing above. In 1852 the use of tobacco was condemned in no uncertain terms as "pernicious, . . . expensive in point of cost, injurious to health and mental vigor, and likely to lead to practices of a decidedly immoral character."

Until 1861, when all but the Universalist Sabbath School Union meetings were cancelled because of "the unsettled state of the nation," the May meetings provided not only fellowship and numerous platforms from which to discuss current issues in both the religious and secular spheres, but promoted a denominational solidarity in New

England that undoubtedly helped to strengthen the Universalists. But by the late 1850s the momentum of reform had visibly slowed and the increasing tension between North and South over the slavery issue and fear for continuation of the Union had resulted in a sharp decline in Reform Association vigor. At the sparsely attended business meeting held in 1861, an animated discussion took place over whether to continue the organization at all. Some thought that its work had been accomplished, and that "the spirit of reform" had finally permeated the denomination.[11]

There seemed to be some evidence to support this view. At its annual meeting in 1858 the General Convention adopted a lengthy report recommending the establishment of a Board of Missions, and created such a board, with one clergyman and one layman representing each of the twelve state conventions which had sent delegates. The purposes of the board, according to Judge John Galbraith of Pennsylvania who presented the plan, were much broader than the word "missions" might imply. Anything that could be done to promote "social and religious culture" was included in the mandate given to the board, ranging from the establishment of newspapers and Sunday School journals to "such other works as may be recommended . . . or best calculated to promote the cause of truth and disseminate the principles of Christian righteousness." The latter included benevolences for the destitute such as the establishment of "schools of labor and reform," one of the purposes of which was to work for the abolition of capital, corporal, or vindictive punishments in the administration of criminal justice.[12] The entire plan, amorphous as it seemed to be, reflected the tenor and philosophy of the Reform Association; but it was too ambitious and too imprecise to accomplish what was intended. After the board failed to report at either of the next two convention meetings, it ceased to exist.

The positive view prevailed at the Reform Association meeting in 1861, and the vote was to continue the organization. There was much work yet to be done, so a slate of officers was elected for the next year. The directors were authorized to call a meeting whenever advisable, but the event never took place and the organization came to an end. There was a certain note of finality about the 1861 meeting, for it was reported at the time that the record book of the organization had been lost. But the spirit which had resulted in the Universalist General Reform Association had not only not been lost, but had been present in the minds and hearts of Universalists long before 1846.

"The Prisoners' Friend": Charles Spear

In an address delivered in the Hollis Street Unitarian church in Boston in 1856, Thomas Starr King described a man he considered one of the "walking publications to the community of prominent deficiencies in our civilization . . . . a travelling placard" of needed reforms.[13] The person to whom he was referring was Charles Spear (1801-1863), who had given up his Universalist parish ministry to devote his life to social reform. His concerns ranged from ridding the world of war to the abolition of slavery, and in the course of his life he became involved in almost every reform movement that blossomed and faded in pre-Civil War America. But his particular interests centered around penal reform in all of its aspects. He fought against the death penalty, the harsh treatment of prisoners, the conditions of jails, and for a change from the prevailing philosophy of punishment to rehabilitation. His goal was to encourage and apply "the spirit of charity to all outcasts" and to eliminate "the barbarities of the penal code," no matter what form it might take. In short, Spear had, according to King, "grown gray in the service of a great principle that belongs to Christianity," the reformation and uplifting of society. King's plea was for support of Spear and what he stood for.

Charles Spear was born in Boston in 1801 and, together with his younger brother, was dedicated (as an alternative to baptism) in the Universalist church by no less a person that the founder of the denomination in America. It was understandable that, at their father's request, the younger brother was named John Murray.[14] The latter, often confused in the public mind with his brother, followed an erratic path in a variety of occupations, including the Universalist ministry, and was so vociferously radical in his abolitionist views that in 1844 he was assaulted and seriously injured while making a speech in Portland, Maine.[15] While recuperating he decided to join forces with his brother Charles and to devote all of his time to the many reform movements in which the latter was interested. For a short time John Murray Spear pitched in with a will to help in promotiing penal reforms. In 1850 he assisted more than 300 individuals who had been discharged from prison, delivered approximately fifty lectures on crime and its treatment, and made numerous visits to prisons.[16] He, with his brother, also edited *Voices from Prison: Being a selection of poetry from various prisoners, written within the cell,* published in Boston in 1847. He was for about five years a partner with Charles in publishing a reform journal, the *Prisoners' Friend,* but in the midst of this John Murray Spear became enamored of spiritualism and was involved briefly in Adin Ballou's Hopedale community. But he lost his enthusiasm for prison reform.[17] Charles Spear was much disappointed at his brother's propensity for flitting from one enthusiasm to another, and more than once had to explain that he was in no way connected with the spiritualist movement in which John Murray Spear was involved.[18]

After receiving a common school education Charles Spear became a printer, a skill which he found very useful later in life. He then decided to become a Universalist preacher and was fellowshipped by the Northern Association in Vermont in 1827. After brief pastorates, one on Cape Cod and one in Boston, he decided upon a career as a reformer and single-mindedly devoted the remainder of his life to that end, living always on the ragged edge of poverty. During the Civil War he served for a few months as a chaplain in St. Elizabeth Hospital in Washington, D.C., where he died on 13 April 1863.[19]

Spear entered the field of prison reform at a time when it had become a topic of considerable interest, sparked in part by the wave of humanitarian enthusiasm which swept the country. The American nation had inherited from England a system characterized by much physical brutality, of which both corporal and capital punishment were integral parts. At the end of the eighteenth century the statutes in England still provided the death penalty for 160 offenses, although the ex-colonies had departed significantly from British practice in this regard by the time of independence.[20]

Only in Pennsylvania was there in the colonial period a relatively humane system, emphasizing clemency, useful prison labor, and rehabilitation, and retaining the death penalty only in the case of homicide. This colony's exception to the general rule had been the work of the Quaker William Penn, who had himself served six months in Newgate Prison in London for refusing to take an oath on grounds of conscience. Universalists could also recall that John Murray had spent time in debtor's prison in London before his arrival in America. Although many of the punitive laws and practices so commonplace in the nineteenth century were restored in Pennsylvania after the founder's death, the first prison reform society in America had been formed in Philadelphia in 1776 and was revived in 1787 after ceasing to exist during the Revolution. It became the prototype for many others founded throughout the nation. Pennsylvania, largely through the efforts of the Quakers, also operated the first state prison in the United States, beginning in 1790. It was also in that state and about the same time that Benjamin Rush, associated with early Universalism in Philadelphia, outlined in an address given in Benjamin Franklin's home in 1787, a theory of penal reform that included most of the basic principles of a later day: reformation as well as punishment; deterrence from crime; and protection of society from those manifestly unfit to live in that society.[21] Spear cited Rush's ideas extensively in numerous writings.

The state prison system with which Spear became most familiar was the one in Massachusetts.[22] Prison life was a grim affiar, judging from the records, with many punishments retained from the colonial period, including use of irons, stocks, and the pillory. A legislative committee in 1817 had found conditions intolerable, including congestion and the indiscriminate mixing of men, women, and juveniles, with as many as eight to twelve prisoners housed in the same room. The conditions at the Charlestown prison had attracted sufficient attention by the mid-1820s to result in the organization of the Prison Discipline Society in 1826, which led the struggle to improve prison conditions and which drew up architectural plans for a new and enlarged building in 1829. The prison administration followed the "Auburn Plan" introduced into the New York prison in that community. This plan was based on the ideas of silence, separate cells, and productive prison labor, with group association in the daytime and separation at night for those not doomed to solitary confinement. The architecture called for several tiers of open cells. The first such construction at Auburn had taken place in 1821, in a new wing added to the existing structure, and was widely copied throughout the United States.

The situation in Boston was much improved after the construction of the new prison. Women were separated from the other prisoners and lodged at first in county jails and later at reformatories such as the one established at Framingham. Juveniles were, beginning in 1826, sent to the House of Correction in South Boston. Corporal punishment was reduced and there was a marked decrease in recidivism and recommitment. Moral and religious instruction was introduced in the late 1820s and a resident chaplain was provided. A Sunday School was organized in 1829, out of which also evolved a semblance of instruction in elementray school subjects.

One of the recommendations made by the legislative committee which investigated the state prison in Charlestown in 1817 had been the provision of after-care for released prisoners, the first such proposal in American penal history.[23] The committee suggested that a wooden building be erected outside the prison where discharged prisoners could be temporarily lodged if they were completely destitute. They would have been able to secure meals from the prison at a reduced rate and could practice whatever trade they had learned until they could find other employment. But the recommendation fell on deaf ears. The establishment of an asylum for discharged convicts had again been considered in 1829 but a board of inspectors had recommended against it. In 1845 a state agent was appointed to counsel released prisoners and to assist in finding employment. A voluntary association, patterned on one established in New York State in 1844, was organized in 1845, known as the "Boston Society in Aid of Discharged Convicts." It cooperated with the state agent, who also served as the agent of the private organization.

It was to the task of aiding the discharged prisoners that Charles Spear devoted his main efforts, although he also taught Sunday School classes in both the state prison and Charles Street jail in Boston until he was prohibited from doing so because he was a Universalist. For many years Spear and his wife expended not only their energies but their meagre resources on travelling up and down the Atlantic seaboard and into the interior as far west as Michigan. They addressed church and other groups, visited reform schools and prisons, and lectured on the treatment of criminals, the causes of crime, and "reformatory institutions." In 1846 Spear delivered over 150 lectures on these subjects.[24] He and his wife made innumerable requests to appear in churches of almost all denominations (Roman Catholic and Episcopal excepted), and were frequently refused permission to use the premises.[25]

Mrs. Spear frequently addressed audiences on the need for asylums for inebriates, on temperance, and on slavery. She also appeared before a committee of the Massachusetts legislature on her favorite subjects.[26] Spear himself also addressed state legislatures whenever the opportunity arose; in 1852 he was urging penal reform before that body in New Hampshire.[27] He often spoke from the same platform as nationally-known reformers like Lucretia Mott, with whom he was greatly impressed. He described her as "interested in every reform, and . . . long a devoted friend of the prisoner."

In 1851 Spear was authorized by the governor of Massachusetts to visit England to report on American legislation relating to capital punishment. The trip was probably the high point in Spear's life, for his great hero was John Howard, who had been the foremost prison reformer in that country in the eighteenth century. While in England, Spear also visited numerous prisons and "ragged schools" for vagrant and outcast children.[28] While abroad he visited Paris and, after some delay, obtained permission to visit prisons there.

One of the means by which Spear sought to bring about the reformation of society was a publication of which he was the editor and proprietor for many years. He also operated a bookstore in Boston from which interested individuals could obtain literature on such subjects as capital punishment, world peace, anti-slavery, hydropathy (the "water cure," which Spear himself used), and phrenology. His periodical started with the unfeliticous title of the *Hangman,* the first issue of which appeared on 1 January 1845. The name had been suggested by John Pierpont, a Unitarian clergyman also interested in social reform. Spear frequently found Unitarians more supportive of his activities than his fellow Universalists. The original plan had been merely to publish, over a three-month period, a series of pamphlets intended only to oppose capital punishment.[29] Thirteen issues were to appear in 1844-45 while the Massachusetts legislature, which had the issue of capital punishment on its agenda, was in session.[30] But the idea was so well received that some 3,000 persons became subscribers and the publication was continued "under the same obnoxious name" (to quote Spear) for the remainder of 1845.

Encouraged by the apparent interest in prison reform, the Spear brothers organized the Prisoners' Friend Association in 1845 and changed the name of the publication to the *Prisoners' Friend,* beginning in 1846. Some of the earlier articles were published in Boston in 1846 under the title *A Plea for Discharged Convicts.* Even the new title of the magazine was unacceptable to some, who objected that prisoners did not need or deserve friends. Simultaneously, the number of subjects dealt with in the journal was increased to include prison reform and the treatment of discharged convicts, and when it became a monthly instead of a weekly in 1848, its title page promised coverage also of "criminal reform, philosophy, literature, science, and art." The publication was also intended, starting in 1848, to serve as a substitute for the reports of the Boston Prison Discipline Society (1826-54) which were no longer being published.[31] Its editor and proprietor claimed the *Prisoners' Friend* to be "the only journal known in the world that is wholly devoted to the Abolition of Capital Punishment and the Reformation of the Criminal."

The periodical (which changed size three times, reduced from newspaper to pamphlet dimensions) lasted until 1861, and from 1857 until its demise, appeared quarterly because it was in chronic financial difficulty. The subscription rate was, for the time, at the rather high rate of $2.00 a year. The paper had no fixed place of abode, for Spear and his wife opened their successive dwellings in Boston to discharged convicts. For that reason they had much difficulty in obtaining and retaining residences, and were constantly on the move.[32] For most of the time he conducted the business of his paper from wherever his home might be, for he could not afford a separate office, and often set the type himself. The number of subscribers in 1848 was 1,700, with a maximum prior to that of 2,000. It carried no advertising, and almost ceased publication several times because there were insufficient funds; somehow, Spear managed to keep it alive. The paper lost about one-third of its potential revenue in 1852 because of unpaid subscriptions.[33] The magazine carried short articles, statistics on crimes and prisons, and a considerable amount of poetry, most with a social message of some kind. Among the authors published in its columns, besides Universalists (the majority of them clergymen), were such Unitarian leaders as William Ellery Channing, Henry Bellows, and Theodore Parker.

Pleas for funds were inveterate parts of Spear's activities. All kinds of money-raising devices were used. In 1847 a fair was held in Boston to promote his efforts to hire a missionary to visit the various prisons in the state.[34] Spear spent over $1,800 in 1849 providing bail; furnishing discharged prisoners with food, clothing, and housing; reuniting families; and in attempting to find employment for ex-convicts.[35] He visited P.T. Barnum at the latter's Oriental villa "Iranistan" in Connecticut in 1849 and probably secured financial assistance from the showman who, among his other interests, professed to be a promoter of prison reform.[36] Among the financial supporters of Spear's efforts was Jenny Lind (1820-1887), "the Swedish nightingale," who performed in the United States between 1850 and 1852 under Barnum's management. After an interview with Spear she donated $225.[37]

Spear received only minimal official assistance from the denomination, and almost none in the form of the money which he so sorely needed. After debating whether it was an appropriate topic for an ecclesiastical body to discuss, a committee at the General Convention in 1835 had decided that consideration of the evils of capital punishment was permissible in view of the fact that it involved a subject "deeply affecting the public morals."[38] A resolution to that effect was then tabled. The Massachusetts Convention recognized the importance of penal reform, but called for linking it to other reform movements. In 1850 the convention resolved that "the subject of prison discipline, the prevention of crime, the reform of the criminal, and the abolition of the gallows, are worthy of the attention and encouragement of abolitionists."[39] Universalists were told by the General Convention in 1854 that "we should take a deeper interest in the subject of Prison Reform, and the abolition of Capital Punishment" and allowed a collection to be taken up during the meeting to assist Spear; the amount received was not recorded.[40]

Four years later the denomination was admonished "to take a deeper interest in . . . Abolition of Capital Punishment, the Visiting of Prisoners, the aiding of Discharged Convicts." The convention then refused to take up a collection in Spear's behalf.[41] Vermont Universalists were likewise told that it was their duty "to take a deeper interest in . . . the mission of Prison Reform," but no mention of Spear or of specific support for his efforts was made.[42] The Universalist General Reform Association saw fit to resolve in 1858 "that whilst we look upon the prisoner as an object alike demanding our interest and commiseration, we also regard our faith with increased confidence as an instrumentality for his reformation and redemption."[43] Both Spear and his wife were present and spoke in support. A collection garnered $16.

Spear argued day in and day out for a policy of rehabilitation for prisoners, and was often discouraged by what he saw. After visiting the state prison in Maine he decided that society seemed much readier "to build the cold, damp dungeon [than] to find modes of reformation."[44] Besides his attention to the problems of discharged prisoners, Spear campaigned for a state inspector of prisons in Massachusetts; matrons for female prisoners; prison libraries; full-time chaplains for all prisons, local as well as state; counselors for criminals; expanded educational facilities; and crime prevention by means of better housing, the practice of temperance, and greater employment opportunities in the outside world.[45] He was much concerned about the problem of juvenile delinquency and advocated and supported the then novel idea of placing young offenders in the hands of responsible adults under a parole system rather than imprisoning juveniles for "trifling offenses." It would be "much cheaper to prevent crime in this way than to punish it. Instead of building institutions on purpose, society itself should be the institution."[46] If there had to be incarceration for delinquent youth, it ought to take place in reform schools rather than in conventional prisons.[47]

Charles Spear and his ideas about, and contributions to, prison reform went largely unheralded both in his own day and among later generations. His was an unpopular cause and he belonged to an unpopular denomination. In spite of his high visibility as a penal reformer for most of his life, he and his efforts were seldom mentioned outside of denominational circles. His work was virtually ignored in the reports of the Prison Discipline Society prepared for many years by its militantly reformist leader, Louis Dwight. This neglect was attributed to the fact that Dwight was a stern Calvinist Congregational clergyman who had no use for Universalists.[48] Spear was inadequately supported for promoting a cause that the majority of Americans professed to know little about and to care even less about.

Yet Spear could and did take some comfort from the fact that some tangible progress was made in some aspects of penal reform by the mid-1850s. In 1833 over 1,300 individuals had been jailed for debt in Massachusetts, over 600 in Suffolk County (Boston) alone.[49] Less than twenty-five years later, there was only one debtor in a Boston prison, and he was there only because he "endeavored to cheat his creditors by concealing his property." Spear took part of the credit for bringing about the abolition of imprisonment for debt in Connecticut, accomplished in 1842. He had labored for this while living briefly in Hartford in the 1830s, where he had published *Essays on Imprisonment for Debt.*[50] He greeted with great satisfaction the opening of a state reform school for boys in Westboro, Massachusetts, in 1849.[51] Similar institutions had been established earlier in other states, but were privately endowed. The Massachusetts school was financed by a combination of private benefactions from Theodore Lyman of Boston and state aid, and hence was the first to have a public character. An industrial school for girls had also been opened in Lancaster, Massachusetts, by 1859.

Much remained to be done in the field of penal reform after Spear's death in 1863, and only a start had been made in some areas. It was not until 1876 that state reformatories, so called, began to be established, with the one at Elmira, New York, heading the list. Even then, their success was far from unalloyed, and debates over what should be the proper treatment and disposition of prisoners continued unabated. If other Universalists did not become as deeply immersed as Spear in the movements for penal reform, some of them at least lent a sympathetic ear. The organization of the Prison Association of New York in 1844 had received the enthusiastic endorsement of Philo Price, editor of the *Universalist Union,* who reproduced the constitution of the new association in his paper.[52] Otis A. Skinner wrote an article in 1847 entitled "The Duty of Society to Reformed Persons" in which he called for tolerance, sympathy, and assistance rather than revenge for discharged convicts.[53]

Another Universalist clergyman, George W. Quinby (1811-1884) of Maine, although not as deeply involved as Spear in actual reform activities, was nonetheless an influential newspaper publisher, editor, and writer. After beginning a preaching career in 1835 which extended intermittently throughout his life, he purchased the *Star in the West* in Cincinnati, where he had served as pastor of the First Universalist Society since 1851. He edited the paper until 1857 and for almost thirty years thereafter was associated with newspaper work. In 1862 he became part owner of the combined *Trumpet and Christian Freeman* in Boston, and two years later acquired the *Gospel Banner* in Augusta, Maine, which he published and edited until shortly before his death in 1884. While in Cincinnati, Quinby published *The Gallows, the Prison, and the Poor-House: A Plea for Humanity; showing the demands of Christianity in behalf of the criminal and perishing classes.*[54] In this work he applied Christian Universalist precepts to the plight of the unfortunate and argued strongly against capital punishment.

Capital Punishment

The problem of capital punishment is by its very nature inseparable from prison reform in general, and was so considered in the nineteenth century. And every Universalist associated with prison reform, notably Charles Spear, disapproved of the death penalty for one or more crimes and in most instances called for its complete abolition. One scholar has observed that "Universalists . . . unquestionably provided more anti-gallows reformers than any other denomination."[55] The cast of characters opposing capital punishment included many whose names appeared on the rosters of other reform movements, for the death penalty was considered but one part of a pernicious system that blocked the attainment of human happiness. The name as well as the objectives of the Universalist General Reform Association, organized in 1847, reflected the determination to attack the ills of society on all fronts.

As was the case with the abolition of slavery, prison reform and other movements to ameliorate and/or improve the lot of man, nineteenth-century Universalists opposed to capital punishment could find supporters in their eighteenth-century predecessors.[56] Benjamin

Rush had opposed the death penalty, and Elhanan Winchester, in *A Plain Political Catechism* (1795) had argued that capital punishment should be limited to only the crimes of murder and treason.[57] Rush had published in 1787 *An Inquiry into the Effects of Public Punishments Upon Criminals and Upon Society,* in which he stressed rehabilitation as the goal of punishment. He also offered "the first reasoned argument in America favoring the abolition of capital punishment."[58] Rush provoked sufficient controversy over this to result in his *Considerations on the Injustice and Impolity of Punishing Murder by Death* (1792).

The movement among Universalists to abolish the practice first got under way in Massachusetts in the late 1820s, but that state was by no means the only one in which efforts were made and opinions were aired. Those who devoted their talents and resources to this reform had a long and arduous road to traverse, with many turns, twists, and excursions into blind alleys and against stone walls. But their devotion to the principle of the sanctity of human life bolstered their determination to succeed. The core of Universalist arguments against capital punishment was offered in 1830 by Abel C. Thomas, then in Philadelphia, in the course of announcing his intention to publish a newspaper to be called the *Messenger of Peace.* His proposal was never carried out, although another denominational paper with the same name had appeared in Hudson, New York, and had lasted one year (1824-25), edited by Richard Carrique. One of the purposes of Thomas' paper was to have been to demonstrate that the practice of punishment by death was inhumane and "wholly opposed to the genius of Christianity, and entirely subversive of the legitimate ends of justice."[59] Many other variations and repetitions of this argument were offered in later years, and others were added. Capital punishment was nothing but "legal murder;" it was not a sufficient deterrent to crime to be justified; it was a waste of human resources as long as reformation of the criminal remained a possibility; it smacked too much of vengeance. Capital punishment was, above all, contrary to Universalist teachings, for "if God's punishments were remedial and reformatory in their nature, so likewise should be the punishments inflicted by man upon his fellow-man."[60]

The first real attempt to stir the Massachusetts legislature to action came in 1828.[61] At the time, nine offenses were punishable by death under the United States code, and of these, seven were technically in force in Massachusetts although not all were actually invoked. Like most subsequent attempts to abolish the death penalty in the state, the bill introduced in 1828 was never reported out of committee. Three years later, in 1831, another effort was made, largely through Robert Rantoul of Beverly, a strong supporter of Spear's reform journal, the *Prisoners' Friend,* for which Rantoul had more than once advanced funds to keep it alive. A study committee recommended that the application of the death penalty be limited to murder, but the only result was a series of indefinite postponements or rejections.

Thomas Whittemore was the first Universalist editor to express himself on the subject. In 1830 he seriously questioned whether punishment by death was justifiable for any crime except murder.[62] Both he and Sylvanus Cobb lent support to the abolition of the death penalty. Cobb absolutely opposed "the judicial taking of human life."[63] Whittemore warmly supported a speech delivered in the legislature recommending that capital punishment be abolished for all crimes except murder, and reproduced the entire speech in his paper.[64] He was greatly disappointed when a bill to substitute life imprisonment in cases involving treason, highway robbery, burglary, and rape was defeated in the state senate in 1836.[65] Public executions were abolished in 1835, and the death penalty for highway robbery and burglary were not invoked after 1839. Between 1780, when the state constitution was adopted, and 1847, there had been, according to Spear's statistics, sixty-one executions, none for rape.[66] In Connecticut, in 1847, only treason and murder were capital crimes. Most Universalists strongly backed the attempt of the governor in 1843 to eliminate capital punishment completely, and E.H. Chapin was among those who participated in legislative hearings.[67] In 1847 the legislature considered it "inexpedient to legislate upon the subject." It was not until 1852, after numerous petitions by Spear and others, that the laws were modified at all.

Universalists elsewhere in the nation were also expressing their opposition to capital punishment in the 1830s and 1840s. Warren Skinner, appointed to deliver the election sermon to the Vermont legislature in 1834, chose capital punishment as his theme, and spoke in complete opposition to it on both civil and religious grounds.[68] In the South, when L.F.W. Andrews was informed, in 1833, that a Methodist preacher had been hanged in Milledgeville, Georgia, for murdering his sister-in-law, the outspoken Universalist preacher announced that capital punishment was not only barbarous but "subverted the great design of punishment—the reformation of the offender."[69] When Alabama voters were considering in 1834 whether to establish a penitentiary system, Andrews suggested that at the same time they should abolish capital punishment for all offenses, "wilful murder not excepted."[70] Requiring the death penalty should "be left to the exclusive practice of Pagans and Savages."

In the Midwest, Erasmus Manford, a Universalist newspaperman, went so far as to raise the question of whether even murderers should be treated as criminals at all, but as "morally insane."[71] He disliked the unchristian idea of seeking vengeance, and believed that convicted persons should be regenerated if possible, although he agreed that chronic offenders had to be taken out of circulation. Jonathan Kidwell in Indiana referred to capital punishment as "a barbarous relick [*sic*] of savage ignorance and cruelty."[72] The Spoon River Association (Illinois), at its organizational meeting in 1841, made the adoption of a resolution opposing capital punishment the first item of business after adopting a constitution.[73] The Northern Association of Indiana expressed itself in the same way in 1842.[74] By the mid-to-late 1840s, other Universalist groups by the scores had included condemnations of capital punishment among their reform resolutions.

The subject of the death penalty first came to the floor of the General Convention in 1835, when a resolution was introduced asserting "that Capital Punishment is the relic of a barbarous age, and decidedly anti-Christian; that it violates the social compact; engenders a spirit of cruelty, and is highly dangerous."[75] Universalists were asked to petition their legislatures for repeal or modification of statutes authorizing it. But even after a committee appointed to consider the resolution had roundly condemned capital punishment on about every conceivable ground, the resolution was tabled, contrary to the hopes and expectations of many.

When the resolution came up for discussion in 1836, it passed, but with completely different language. It called upon Universalists only "to use their exertions" to form and direct public opinion. Even more significantly, the toned-down resolution was prefaced by the statement that it was offered "although we deem an interference with the legislation of our State or of the United States, by ecclesiastical bodies improper."[76] The convention thus ran into exactly the same roadblock that it encountered when anti-slavery resolutions were presented. Some Universalists at least were very much aware of their own pronouncements about the desirability of separation of church and state.

Some local groups were much less hesitant than the centrol body about jumping into the fray. At the Old Colony (Massachusetts) Quarterly Conference in 1840, ministers were urged to preach on the subject of capital punishment, "with a view of showing its evils, its inconsistency with the spirit of Christianity, and the propriety of its speedy abolition."[77] In 1847 the Grafton Association (New Hampshire), in somewhat contradictory fashion, refused to recommend that each clergyman devote a sermon to the subject, on the grounds that it was a political question, then at the same meeting circulated petitions to the state legislature calling for abolition of the death penalty.[78] The Maine Convention eschewed all political involvement and merely condemned the practice as "without support in the instructions of Jesus Christ."[79] The Ohio Convention also opposed capital punishment on Biblical grounds, arguing that the references in the Old Testament that could be construed as condoning capital punishment had been superseded by the New Testament.[80]

The resolutions of most Universalist organizations, following

Spear's philosophy, called for the abolition of the death penalty regardless of the crime involved. However, individual Universalists were frequently in disagreement over this. D.P. Livermore published a pamphlet in 1846 denying the right of government to take life under any circumstances.[81] But the editors of the *Universalist Miscellany* at the time (Otis A. Skinner and E.H. Chapin) disagreed. Skinner wrote a series of three articles on capital punishment which appeared in the *Miscellany* in which he considered the death penalty appropriate in certain circumstances, such as first-degree (premeditated) murder.

Charles Spear was the unquestioned Universalist leader for some thirty years in agitating for abolition of the death penalty. He had first become interested in the problem about 1830, and joined or helped to found almost any organization that would further his determination to get rid of the practice. He had announced in 1836 that he was "one of the most unwavering, unflinching advocates for the abolishment of Capital Punishment that exists on the face of the whole earth," and had gone on to invite all Universalists to discuss the subject.[82] He had first taken an active role himself when he was living in Connecticut in the early 1830s. As a delegate to the state convention there in 1833, he offered a resolution in favor of abolishing capital punishment and of circulating petitions to that effect.[83] His proposal precipitated a heated debate, not over whether the infliction of the death penalty was a moral wrong, but over whether the convention might be attempting "a mingling of politics and religion" by taking a stand on the issue. The convention finally approved his resolution but added the note that it had no intention of establishing "anti-hanging parties;" it had for its only aim getting rid of a law which was "a relic of a dark, cruel, and barbarous age."

Spear served as the first recording secretary and then as agent of the Massachusetts Society for the Abolition of Capital Punishment which was organized in 1845 as an outgrowth of a meeting held the previous year at his home in Boston.[84] The occasion of the meeting, attended by two women and four men, including the Unitarian clergyman John Pierpont, and the orator and reformer Wendell Phillips, had been an effort, which was unsuccessful, to prevent the execution of one Thomas Barrett of Worcester. The society made a great effort in 1849 to save a Negro sailor, Washington Goode, from the gallows. They considered the evidence of his alleged murder of a white man only circumstantial.[85] Protest meetings were held all over the state, and Alonzo A. Miner, who had just become junior pastor of the Second Universalist Society in Boston, was one of the speakers on Goode's behalf. But the governor and council refused to commute the death sentence.[86] Among Universalists active in Spear's organization was E.H. Chapin, who used his oratorical skills for the benefit of many reform movements, including the promotion of world peace.

Spear wrote extensively on the death penalty, and his major work opposing capital punishment, *Essays on the Punishment of Death,* was published in Boston in January 1844. It also appeared in a London edition. Over 1,000 copies of the American edition were sold in a few weeks and by 1850 had gone through twelve printings.[87] Spear included in the thirteenth printing in 1851 an updated section on all legislation dealing with capital punishment. His only hesitation about opposing the death penalty was the realization that life imprisonment would be the only likely alternative. His humanitarian instincts revolted at the conditions existing in many prisons which he knew from personal observation, and he was reluctant to condemn prisoners to such experiences. But his determination to abolish what he referred to constantly as a form of legal murder overbalanced that consideration. So he sponsored one petition after another in the Massachusetts legislature. He even prepared printed forms to be signed.[88]

In 1851 Spear went on a mission to England to report, in answer to inquiries from Parliament, on American legislation dealing with capital punishment. In order to prepare for the trip, and to obtain a passport as an official representative of the United States, he spent some time in Washington, D.C. He had some difficulty in securing his passport, and finally obtained certification of his American citizenship from Horace Mann, the well-known educator, who was then serving as a Congressman from Massachusetts.[89] He also obtained a letter of introduction from Senator Daniel Webster to expedite his labors in England, and a letter of introduction from Edward Everett to Abbott Lawrence, then the American Minister in London. Spear addressed the House of Representatives while in Washington, and conducted interviews with numerous individuals. Everett did not concur with Spear's contention that all capital punishment be abolished; Henry Clay held out little hope that criminals could ever be reformed.

Spear accomplished the task which he had undertaken in England, and while in London and Paris visited prisons and poorhouses. He was widely criticized at home for making the trip, which coincided with the great Crystal Palace international industrial exhibition. He was accused of spending for a six-month vacation the $1,000 raised in donations to finance his trip. He assured the public that he had made the journey solely for humanitarian reasons. He observed in passing, as a good temperance man, that he was astounded at the great quantity of beer and wine consumed by Britishers.[90]

The decades of the 1840s and 1850s were marked by a concerted effort to lobby for the abolition of capital punishment in several state legislatures. An attempt in Vermont almost succeeded in 1842, due in all probability to the work of Warren Skinner, a long-standing enemy of the death penalty.[91] It was erroneously reported that such a law had actually been enacted in Vermont and the mistaken news was greeted with great satisfaction among Universalists.[92] In actuality, abolition of the death penalty for first-degree murder was not accomplished in Vermont until 1965. Universalists in that state continued after 1842 to urge substitution of life imprisonment for capital punishment, and resolutions to that effect were adopted time after time.[93]

In New York, John Louis O'Sullivan, a young assemblyman from New York City, attempted unsuccessfully in both 1841 and 1842 to remove the death penalty for murder. He was blocked to a large extent by George B. Cheever, an influential Presbyterian clergyman with whom he had an extended public debate in New York City.[94] Two Universalist clergymen then in the New York City area, W.S. Balch and Abel C. Thomas, also challenged Cheever and another supporter of capital punishment to a debate, but it never took place. Balch was impressed by O'Sullivan's anti-gallows arguments and delivered at least one sermon on the subject.[95] Spear also met Cheever in New York City and of course the two men disagreed.

Almost all Universalists who left a record of their views supported O'Sullivan and his efforts in the New York legislature. The Chenango Association (New York) urged petitions and any other means they thought advisable to erase from the statutes "the odious law which inflicts the punishment of death."[96] Only one letter from a Universalist (Henry Fitz of Baltimore) supporting Cheever and capital punishment ever appeared in the *Universalist Union,* published in New York City.[97] The Chautauqua Association (New York) went so far in 1844 as to sponsor and forward to the legislature a petition signed by 600 voters.[98] An organization had been started in New York City in 1844 as the "American Society for the Collection of Information in Relation to the Death Punishment."[99] In 1845 it became the New York Society for the Abolition of Capital Punishment and published a newspaper, *Spirit of the Age.* Several Universalists were associated with the organization, which was formed basically to present memorials to the state legislature. Horace Greeley and Jacob Harsen served on the executive committee. W.S. Balch was the corresponding secretary.[100]

In the 1850s anti-gallows Universalists concentrated their efforts on Massachusetts. In 1850 there were still seven crimes punishable by death on the statute books although not all were enforced.[101] The citizens of the state had become very much aware of their anachronistic penal code in 1849 when George Parkman, on the faculty of the Boston Medical College and brother of the historian, Francis Parkman, was murdered by John W. Webster, Professor of Chemistry at Harvard. After a controversial trial, Webster was executed nine months after the murder, to which he had confessed. Charles Spear took an active part in the debates over the nature of Webster's fate.[102] It was not Webster's guilt that agitated Spear. He was among those who tried without success to have the sentence commuted to life imprisonment, and appeared before the governor and council, but to no avail. Spear wrote bitterly that Webster was another unfortunate example of the application of "the barbarous law which has again disgraced our State." Petitions flooded into the legislature "to substitute some more humane method of correcting crime" than the death penalty.[103]

Hearings were held on capital punishment in the 1851-52 session of the state legislature, and Spear testified before a joint committee, together with such other reformers as William Lloyd Garrison and Wendell Phillips.[104] Several important enactments came out of the hearings. The legislature, in 1852, abolished the death penalty for treason, rape, and arson. Although it retained the death penalty for murder, it modified its application by making a provision similar to one enacted by Maine in 1836. It mandated a one-year delay between sentencing and execution, and that could not be carried out except on direct order from the governor.[105] The law was amended in 1853 to provide that those sentenced to imprisonment and awaiting the carrying out of the death penalty could be confined in the county jail or house of correction rather than in the state prison. The reason for this change was to provide housing for women under sentence of death; they were not allowed to be sent to the state prison.

A crisis developed in Massachusetts in 1853 when Governor John H. Clifford, acting under the 1852 law, ordered the execution of a convicted murderer, to be effective in 1854.[106] The governor's decision brought a renewed campaign to abolish capital punishment and in 1854 was one of the principal topics of conversation among penal reformers. Alonzo A. Miner and Spear were among those who presented the case against the death penalty in the four days of open hearings provided by the legislature. Miner argued that the existence of the death penalty, so far as he could determine, failed to deter such crimes as murder.[107] Attempts to stay the convicted murderer's execution were fruitless, and he was hanged on schedule in April 1854. The 1852 law providing a one-year delay in execution was revoked in 1857. The Universalist General Reform Association reacted "with pain" to this "retrograde movement in Massachusetts" and announced that it would continue to oppose capital punishment until it was "better convinced of the infallibility of the courts or the good results of executions."[108]

By 1856 three states had abolished capital punishment, and Massachusetts was not among them. They were Michigan (1847), Rhode Island (1852), and Wisconsin (1853). Maine had virtually abolished the practice by retaining its one-year delay provision; several other states, including New Hampshire, made similar provisions.[109] But victory was far from won by the opponents of the death penalty. Although Maine had pioneered in at least reducing the incidence of executions, the authority was retained, and the Maine Universalist Convention continued (e.g., in 1864, 1867, and 1875) to reiterate its

Horace Greeley (1811-1872), prominent newspaperman, Universalist social reformer, and presidential candidate in 1872

opposition to the death penalty, as did numerous other Universalists both individually and collectively. Spear and his fellow reformers had long since been gathered to their fathers before the Supreme Court of the United States, in 1972, outlawed the death penalty as a cruel and unusual punishment. Even then, the debate did not cease.

Peace Movements

Although a defensive war may be considered lawful, yet we believe there is a time coming, when the light and universal love of the gospel shall put an end to all wars. We recommend, therefore, to all churches in our communion, to cultivate the spirit of peace and brotherly love, which shall lead them to consider all mankind as brethren, and to strive to spread amongst them the knowledge of their Saviour and Redeemer, who came into the world "not to destroy men's lives but to save them."

* * * * * * * * * *

The sober truth about war is, that it will never cease till the nations become thoroughly imbued with the genuine principles and spirit of Universalism.

These two statements were written by Universalists ninety-nine years apart. The first was adopted in Philadelphia in 1790 and the second was written by Daniel Bragg Clayton, an itinerant preacher in the South who had served briefly in the Army of the Confederacy during the Civil War. Both represented an ideal which has been expressed throughout history and which Universalists not only alluded to from time to time but attempted to bring about by invoking their principle of human brotherhood. Their ideas ranged from condemnation of war as an instrument of national policy to pacifism and conscientious objection as a matter of personal conviction. William Farwell, pioneer Universalist preacher in northern New England, refused to bear arms during the Revolution and spent several weeks in the Charlestown, New Hampshire, jail as a consequence.[110] He was finally liberated by payment of a fine.

Three American organizations to promote peace had appeared when Universalists began to discuss the subject of peace and war in the 1830s and 1840s. The New York Peace Society, the Warren County (Ohio) Peace Society, and the Massachusetts Peace Society had all appeared in 1815, independently of each other.[111] They were, in part, reactions to the French Revolution and Napoleonic wars in Europe, and to the not very popular War of 1812. More importantly, they also reflected the idea that war as a human institution should be abolished and that if properly educated, individuals and nations could be convinced of its futility and its evils. This, in turn, was another facet of the burst of humanitarian enthusiasm associated with the idea of progress in the late eighteenth century and extended well into the nineteenth. Of the three societies, the Massachusetts organization, founded in the Boston home of William Ellery Channing, was the most influential. Branches were immediately formed, and a journal, the *Friend of Peace,* was published. The most important group of all, the American Peace Society, was organized in New York City in 1828 under the leadership of William Ladd of Maine. The Massachusetts Peace Society, with its membership declining, had been merged with it by 1845.

Although the editor of the *Universalist Magazine* had made a passing reference in 1822 to the evils of war, very few Universalists left a record of their ideas about peace until after 1830.[112] In 1834 the corresponding secretary of the Massachusetts Peace Society requested clergymen of all denominations "to preach, at least, one sermon, on the great christian topic of permanent and universal peace." Benjamin Whittemore was one of those who complied.[113] He immediately linked doctrinal Universalism and the promotion of world peace, arguing forcefully that belief in peace and in endless misery were incompatible. Every Universalist society was really a peace society in miniature. "Every Universalist is commanded, by the religion which he professes, to pursue the things that make for *peace,* and to overcome evil with good. He is opposed to the spirit of war, and war is opposed to the spirit of christian religion." Abolition of war had to be accomplished "by common consent of nations" and could not be brought about unilaterally. A "court of nations" was the best device to settle international disputes.

So far as can be determined, the General Convention did not adopt a single resolution dealing with peace between the date of its organization under that name in 1833, and 1870. At its meeting during the centennial year, Eli Ballou of Vermont introduced a series of resolutions referring to the evils of war and the importance of solving international difficulties by arbitration or a congress of nations.[114] They were presented at the very last business session of the convention and action on them was postponed because the Committee on Resolutions had had no opportunity to formulate them. So it was left up to state conventions and other groups to make official statements and to individual Universalists to do what they could.

The Somerset Association (Maine) was one of the first to express itself by rejoicing in 1843 in all the efforts being made "to suppress the spirit of war."[115] The resolution may very well have been suggested by the London Peace Society which had held the first international peace convention earlier in that year, on the suggestion of the American Peace Society.[116] The Old Colony Association (Massachusetts) adopted in 1843 a resolution which amounted to an ultimatum: "As believers in Christianity, we deprecate *war,* with our whole souls, and we will not

Edwin Hubbell Chapin (1814-1880), prolific Universalist writer and pastor of the Church of the Divine Paternity, New York City (1866-1880)

give it our countenance, by officiating as Chaplains, or becoming members of any Military company; and furthermore, we urge *all men*, especially *Universalists,* to carry out peace principles." The Strafford Quarterly Conference in New Hampshire adopted a similar resolution in 1844.[117] There was a certain irony in the fact that in 1845 N.C. Fletcher became the first Universalist to serve as a naval chaplain, on board the *Vincennes.*[118] Sylvanus Cobb was delighted when he learned that Fletcher had almost immediately resigned. Cobb was responsible for a resolution adopted by the Connecticut Convention in 1845 declaring war to be "a great sin against God."[119] Charles Spear, a spokesman for peace as well as prison and other reforms, addressed the eighth session of the American Peace Society in 1843.[120]

The war between the United States and Mexico (1846-1848) was, like the War of 1812, fought with Americans much divided. Universalists who spoke against it had difficulty at first in getting a hearing in their official meetings. A resolution opposing the conflict was tabled by the Massachusetts Convention in 1846, ostensibly for lack of time to discuss it, and the same fate befell a similar resolution in the Boston Association.[121] The moderator broke a 12-12 tie by moving for adjournment. The Norfolk Association (Massachusetts) did adopt resolutions declaring war to be repugnant to Christian teachings and condemning the war with Mexico as one of "invasion and conquest . . . wrong and iniquitous in the extreme."[122] The Massachusetts Convention finally adopted anti-war resolutions in 1848, one specifically condemning the Mexican war.[123]

In 1847 the American Peace Society offered a $500 prize for the best essay on the Mexican war. The winning essay, published in 1850, was reviewed by Hosea Ballou 2d, who completely agreed with the author's sharp criticism of American involvement.[124] Ballou considered the war "a very black page in our history" and called on Americans to take a long, hard look at their "world-renowned self-glorification."[125] The United States, in his view, had become just as much the aggressor as any European nation about which America had complained.

Individual Universalists continued to be active in peace movements in the 1850s. E.H. Chapin, who attended the World Peace Convention in Frankfort, Germany, in 1850, and was one of the speakers, had already delivered lectures objecting to war as unjust.[126] Charles Spear and Alonzo A. Miner were among the thirty American delegates to the international Congress of the Friends of Universal Peace which met for three days in London in connection with the Crystal Palace Exhibition in 1851.[127]

The Universalist General Reform Association, which had the promotion of peace as one of its many reform objectives, passed resolutions on the subject at almost all of its meetings. Any related developments thought to be of interest were included in the extensive annual reports from the corresponding secretary. E.G. Brooks, who was serving in 1852, called attention to the fact that Maine and New Hampshire had both abolished their militia systems, and with them "those annual pests, 'general musters.' "[128] Universalists were told by the Association in 1853 that it was their Christian duty to support all efforts at peaceful negotiation of international difficulties and to condemn "all war and warlike operations."[129] The outbreak of the Crimean War in 1854 brought forth a further anti-war resolution from the Association which provoked considerable debate because it included a statement that war was never to be engaged in "save in the last necessity."[130] An unsuccessful attempt was made to strike out this clause.

It was the question of what the limits of pacifism should be that split the American Peace Society in 1838 and resulted in the creation of a splinter group, the New England Non-Resistance Society. The organization represented the radical wing of the peace movement and refused either to condone or justify even defensive war, on the ground that all war was inconsistent with Christianity. With the exception of the debate in the Universalist General Reform Association mentioned above, there is nothing to indicate that any Universalists desired to go beyond the statement in the 1790 Philadelphia declaration which had justified defensive warfare. The individual who was perhaps the "most philosophical and able advocate" of non-resistance and who published "the most thorough exposition of non-resistance made in the pre-Civil War period" was, however, a former Universalist, Adin Ballou.[131] Ballou, who became president of the Non-Resistance Society in 1843, a year after he had founded the Hopedale Community, published in 1846 *Christian Non-Resistance in all its Important Bearings, Illustrated and Defended.*[132] He had expressed his views earlier in *Non-resistance in Relation to Human Governments,* a twenty-four page pamphlet.[133]

Ballou had severed his formal connection with the Universalists in 1831 when he withdrew his fellowship letter and resigned from his pastorate of the Universalist society in Milford, Massachusetts.[134] He had little or no contact with members of the denomination thereafter, although he sometimes wrote for Universalist publications. Thomas Whittemore in 1849 went out of his way to compliment Ballou in his efforts to apply the principles of Christianity and lauded him for defending the basic precepts of Universalism although no longer officially affiliated.[135] Ballou had become interested in the non-resistance movement in the 1830s and was undoubtedly influenced by William Lloyd Garrison and others responsible for organizing the Non-Resistance Society, which Ballou did not immediately join.[136] By 1839 Ballou had completely renounced his earlier life-style and ideas about war and had become a radical pacifist. He admitted that he had once been chaplain of a contingent of the Massachusetts militia (1825-37); had delivered patriotic addresses on Independence Day; and had seen no inconsistency between support of civil government, backed if necessary by "deadly force," and genuine Christianity.[137]

The heart of Ballou's theory of non-resistance was to be found in his rendition of the life of Christ and his apostles. The living of a true Christian life meant a policy of abstention from "the government of this world" by refusing to vote, hold office, serve in the military, seek redress in the courts, or obey "unrighteous" laws, although there would be no forcible resistance to public ordinances.[138] War was to be abhorred in any form because it threatened the sanctity of human life. The term "non-resistance," used in the sense employed by Ballou and most of his colleagues, was derived from Christ's words: "Resist not evil." (Matthew 5:39).[139] Evil meant to Ballou the infliction of injury of any kind. Hence no true Christian could kill even in self-defense or defense of others. "Christianity forbids its disciples ever to retaliate, resist or oppose evil in their fellow human beings with evil."[140] It followed that one could not support government by voting or holding office, for it was governments that authorized the waging of war and required the death penalty. Practitioners of non-resistance, said Ballou, would eventually evoke a similar reaction in others, and all would be well. Like begets like.

After the Non-Resistance Society fell apart in the years following 1849, Ballou continued to advocate his version of non-resistance through his *Practical Christian* (1840-1860) and other publications. On the eve of his death in 1890, he corresponded with Tolstoy, the Russian Christian anarchist and apostle of non-resistance.[141] Ballou's name was invoked on many occasions by pacifists, but few Universalists of his generation seemed to have acknowledged his ideas or even his existence. To them, he lived in a world of his own.

Chapter 19

FROM TEMPERANCE TO TOTAL ABSTINENCE

The temperance movement, in which Universalists played a prominent part, was possibly the most widely advertised social reform effort in the nineteenth century, reaching one of its several periods of intensity in the 1840s and 1850s, and extending into the Civil War period.[1] Several basic points need to be made in discussing the temperance movement, including matters of definition. First of all, it had an evolutionary or at least sequential character, from sporadic local and atomistic origins to a highly disciplined, well organized, and powerful crusade which became statewide and eventually national. It was at first literally a temperance movement, not one calling for the complete prohibition of the manufacture, sale, and use of alcoholic beverages. It began by making a distinction between use and abuse, and evolved for many supporters into an uncompromising opposition to alochohic beverages in all forms and degrees. A distinction was originally made between naturally fermented liquors, such as beer and wine, which could be used in moderation, and distilled products, artificially made, which were to be avoided. At first, when abstinence was called for, the reference was to distilled liquors only. But then this distinction broke down and became one of degree rather than quality; whether naturally or artificially produced, it was recognized that both types of liquor were alcoholic and led to some degree of intoxication.

The next step in the development of attitudes toward consumable alcohol was to discard any idea that it conduced to health or well-being. Then it was unreservedly condemned as a deleterious beverage in every way; hence total abstinence from all intoxicants, which was being widely advocated by the mid-1830s, was the only path to be followed. And finally, because it was considered injurious, regardless of whether consumed by healthy individuals or not, calls were issued for a total end to its manufacture and sale. Thus, thought on the subject had moved from "approved moderation" to complete opposition to the use of any beverage that might inebriate. Hence, long before the Civil War, the term "temperance" had become to a large extent a misnomer. To many it actually meant total prohibition of the use of all beverages with alcoholic content and inebriating properties.

The temperance movement went through a period of change in another important respect. When it began in earnest the intention was to avoid legislative action if possible. Moral suasion and voluntary compliance were thought to be all that was necessary or desirable to control the liquor traffic and to regulate consumption in the interests of both individual and public welfare. Appeals to reason, conscience, and emotion were considered far superior to the invocation of the law and its penalties. The drunkard seems to have received, by and large, a more sympathetic hearing than the convict or even the pauper. However, the ideal of achieving reform and regeneration without the involvement of government was never more than that; liquor regulation of all kinds abounded in the colonial period, and the authority of the federal government to control both traffic and consumption was invoked as early as 1790.

As one attempt after another failed at the private level, legislative bodies had to be called in to remedy a situation in which, according to one nineteenth-century Universalist clergyman, George H. Emerson, "the existence of civilization itself was threatened. The women and better class of the community were stricken with terror."[2] Restriction by statute increased in frequency and severity, so that the unlicensed sale of alcoholic beverages was being made punishable by imprisonment as well as fines. The climax before the Civil War in the legislative realm came in 1851, with the passage of the so-called "Maine Law" which became the archetype for almost every attempt at similar legislation in other states, and remained on that state's statute books in one form or another until 1934.

During the entire colonial period of American history, extending for over 170 years, alcoholic beverages were a staple part of the diet. In the colony of Massachusetts, by 1750 the distilling of rum had become a major manufacturing activity; that beverage produced in the village of Medford, beginning in 1735, achieved particular fame. There had been no real objection to the consumption of alcoholic liquor in moderation, and the medical effects of such consumption had not been seriously questioned or even investigated. The only semblance of a temperance movement had been aimed at excessive use of intoxicants by Indians (largely the white man's contribution in the first place); regulation of use by servants and apprentices (more in the self-interest of the master than for humanitarian motives); and attempts to control drunkedness when community peace and order were disturbed or threatened. The use of wine and rum at funeral services had not been forbidden in Massachusetts until 1742.[3] Occasional voices had been raised during the colonial period objecting to excessive use of alcohol and even calling for total abstinence by members of such diverse religious groups as the Puritans, the Quakers, and the Methodists. But nothing approaching concerted action appeared until after American independence had been achieved.

Much to the delight of temperance-minded Universalists, it was Benjamin Rush of Philadelphia, one of their number, who is given the credit for pioneering in the temperance movement. It was he who laid the foundations for a systematic attempt to control both the consumption of and traffic in distilled liquor, and was the first to call attention to the potentially dangerous medical consequences of over-indulgence. In 1772 he had written *Sermons to Gentlemen upon Temperance and Exercise,* and in 1777 prepared a statement advising against the use of distilled spirits by soldiers while on active duty during the Revolution; the pamphlet was circulated among the troops by the Continental Congress. In 1784 he published his *Enquiry into the Effects of Spirituous Liquors on the Human Body,* almost immediately published also in England, and in several American editions with slightly variant titles. In 1794 Rush expanded his original work into a book published as *Medical Enquiries into the Effect of Ardent Spirits on the Body and Mind,* which created considerable controversy among physicians. The burden of his argument was that an excessive amount of alcohol was injurious both physically and mentally.

Rush, a personal friend of Bishop Francis Asbury and other Methodist leaders, had appeared before the General Conference of the Methodist Episcopal Church in 1788 to urge that body to use its influence to promote total abstinence as well as to prevent abuse of the consumption of ardent spirits.[4] In 1790 he had recommended the establishment of a special hospital for inebriates. In the same year a volume of sermons on the evils of intemperance was published anonymously, and attributed to Rush. He also appeared before the General Assembly of the Presbyterian Church, meeting in Philadelphia in 1811, where he distributed copies of his treatise.

John Murray wrote Rush from Newburyport, Massachusetts, in 1791 complimenting him on his "excellent publication against intemperance."[5] Murray wrote that the growth of "that ruinous vice in these parts is very alarming." Almost 100 years later, Richard Eddy, Universalist clergyman and scholar, and himself a committed temperance man who wrote a major work on the subject, was mystified that Rush, when assisting in the drawing up of the Articles of Faith and Plan of Church Government adopted by the Universalists in Philadelphia in 1790, had made no mention of temperance in either document.[6] Rush, in his "Letters, Facts & Observations," made it clear that under certain circumstances (medical) the use of distilled liquor was acceptable. "Avoid drinking spirits except you should be *wet* as well as cold. In that case you may drink them freely. They are the best antidotes to fever from riding in the rain." Whether Rush wrote this undated memorandum ("Directions relative to the conveniences of life founded on experience") before or after his pamphlet of 1784 is not known.[7]

The evidence points overwhelmingly to the widespread use of intoxicating beverages all over the nation when the Universalists issued their first official pronouncements on the subject, beginning in 1800. In 1792 there were over 2,500 distilleries in the United States, with annual per capita consumption estimated at two-and-one-half gallons, a figure greatly exceeded in later years.[8] Liquors distilled domestically for consumption totalled over five million gallons that year, with imported spirits amounting to over four million gallons, and imported wines at over one million gallons. Alcoholic beverages had become an important source of tax revenue, and rations of spirits (rum, brandy, or whiskey) for the armed forces were still being authorized by the federal government; they were not discontinued until 1830 for the army and 1862 for the navy.

The retailing of distilled liquor had achieved such proportions by 1800 and was considered productive of so many evils that the General Conference of the Methodist Church felt constrained to reiterate and supplement resolutions against both the traffic and the consumption of ardent spirits passed as early as 1780. It was in 1789 that John Wesley had issued his call for total abstinence from distilled spirits. By 1800 several other church bodies had made generally-worded official pronouncements condemning the use of distilled liquor, including the General Assembly of the Presbyterian Church (1789), the Quakers (1794), and the Seventh Day Baptists (1797). However, it should be emphasized that all of these calls for temperance, control of the liquor traffic, and total abstinence, were beamed at their own memberships and in no sense constituted attempts to impose restrictions on the generality of Americans.

The same holds true for the first temperance group generally acknowledged to have appeared in the United States. It was an informal association of farmers in Litchfield County, Connecticut, created in 1789, and was strictly local in purpose and had no formal organization. Conscious efforts to influence individuals beyond denominational boundaries were not to come until the temperance movement had achieved organized proportions, beginning in 1826 with the American Society for the Promotion of Temperance and the host of local and regional temperance societies that followed. The high point came with a wave of attempts to achieve statewide prohibition in the 1850s and 1860s.

When the Universalists became actively involved in the organized temperance movement after 1830 they never exhibited as much reluctance to speak publicly about the issue in their own pulpits and deliberative bodies as they did in handling the controversies over the abolition of slavery. The basic reason was the fact that the American churches themselves took the leadership in making use of alcohol into a moral rather than a political issue at first. The initial subordination of politics to morality avoided the agonizing debates over the appropriateness of preaching about or discussing temperance. The opposition to temperance agitation came not from church organizations but from those engaged in the lucrative liquor traffic; from those (the majority of Americans) ignorant of or oblivious to what were eventually considered the dangerous effects of alcohol; and from those who considered temperance or intemperance a personal and private matter and not the proper province of preachers and reformers. The overthrowing of long-standing prejudices, habits, and customs was no small challenge.

Aside from their willingness to discuss temperance within their own ranks, Universalists also played a much more prominent part in the mainstream of temperance and prohibition movements both locally and nationally than was the case with many other reforms. There seemed to be less fear of joining forces with those of other denominations in a common effort than was true of anti-slavery agitation. Rubbing elbows with "partialists" was not a major obstacle to cooperation with Congregationalists or Presbyterians or others where the curbing of the use of alcohol or reform of the drunkard was involved. Consequently, the names of Universalists appeared with considerable frequency on the rosters of many temperance organizations. Some Universalists also made significant contributions to the serious literature of the subject that transcended denominational affiliation.

Richard Eddy (1828-1906) was commissioned in the early 1880s by a committee of the National Temperance Society and Publication House, founded in 1865 and based in New York City, to prepare two of the three parts of what was intended to be the most complete treatment of temperance yet to appear. In 1873 a prize competition had been established and a committee appointed to review manuscripts. Two of the members were Neal Dow, whose name had been closely associated with the enactment of the Maine prohibition law of 1851; and Alonzo A. Miner, prominently associated with other advocates of complete prohibition, although not as well known outside denominational circles as a leading Universalist clergyman and educator.

The first of the three-part work had been completed by William Hargreaves, a physician from Philadelphia, who dealt with the medical aspects of alcohol, published under the title *Alcohol and Science.* After no acceptable manuscripts were received for the sections dealing with the historical and social aspects of temperance, Eddy was selected to complete the project, which appeared under the imprint of the society as *Alcohol in History.* A work of almost 500 pages, it covered the subject on a worldwide basis. At the time the book was published Eddy was editor of the *Universalist Quarterly,* for which he wrote all of the book reviews. He elected to write one for his own work, and told his readers that it was extensively documented and that they could be assured of its accuracy.[9] Eddy also mined out of Universalist records every resolution that he could find that dealt with the temperance question and presented his findings in a paper read at the Centennial Temperance Conference in Philadelphia in 1885.[10]

Universalists at first shared the same fondness for alcoholic beverages and the same attitudes toward their consumption that were to be found among Americans everywhere. Liquor was freely available at Universalist meetings in the late eighteenth century, as at those of many other denominations, and was particularly visible at cornerstone-layings, dedications of meeting houses, and even at ordination ceremonies. Stephen R. Smith observed that in upstate New York, the habit of drinking intoxicating liquors on every conceivable occasion was "nearly universal."[11] Clergymen seemed especially vulnerable because they were exposed to liquor so often. Local visits "always brought out the *bottle*, at every place, at which they called." It was an habitual and expected token of hospitality. The fact that no liquor was consumed at the raising of the Universalist meeting house in Halifax, Massachusetts, in 1828, was considered of sufficient importance to have been noted in the denominational press.[12] In the following year the same phenomenon was reported in connection with the construction of the meeting house in Norway, Maine: "No ardent spirits were used, not so much as 'a little wine for the stomach's sake.' "[13]

Sometimes Universalists were subjected to unusual amounts of temptation. In one instance a Universalist preacher, unable to obtain more appropriate facilities for a service conducted in a community on the New York-Pennsylvania line, was forced to deliver his message in the second-floor storeroom of a distillery in full operation.[14] It was not indulgence that was criticized, but intemperance carried to the point of drunkedness, visible in speech and behavior. When preachers were at first disciplined or disfellowshipped by Universalist conventions, associations, or societies for use of intoxicating drinks, it was for excessive consumption, not for drinking as such.

Even in its early days, the New England Convention found private homes too small to house its annual meetings, so they were often scheduled in public taverns, which usually had the most commodious facilities in the community as well as a convenient public bar. The convention had experienced so much difficulty with the intemperate use of alcohol at such meetings that in 1800 it uttered its first *ex cathedra* statement on the matter. It recommended thereafter that the council meet in private homes if possible, "as it becometh us to abstain from the appearance of evil." In 1814 the convention requested societies not to furnish liquor when they played host to denominational meetings. The first resolution "designed to discountenance the improper use of ardent spirits" was offered in 1829 but action was postponed until the next year because of the question of the propriety of discussing such subjects. Even then, the resolution did not come up for a vote in 1830.[15] The next consideration of the subject took place in 1835.

Meanwhile, the first formally organized temperance society in the United States had appeared in 1808 in Moreau (Saratoga County), New York, complete with a constitution.[16] It was instigated by B.J. ("Billy") Clark, a local physician, who had become convinced that "we shall all become a community of drunkards in this town" if something were not done. With the support of the local Congregational minister the society was organized with forty-three male members. No women ever attended its meetings, which convened for several years. This was a true temperance society, for the prohibitions were confined to distilled spirits and the constitution permitted the use of wine at public dinners. A fine was imposed on members who became intoxicated.

A somewhat broader step was taken in 1813 with the organization in Boston of the Massachusetts Society for the Suppression of Intemperance.[17] It was not only the first such society organized on the state level but was created through the cooperation of the Congregational and Presbyterian churches. Its primary goal was the curbing of the use of ardent spirits only; it even provided a recipe for making currant wine.[18] Between its founding and 1818, about forty local auxiliary societies were formed. In 1833 it was reorganized as the Massachusetts Temperance Society and was incorporated in 1845. It was never an effective organization. Its principal contribution was to set in motion a whole host of other temperance societies, some of which had modest success. Thomas Whittemore, suspicious as usual of any reform organization not controlled by Universalists, opposed the Boston-based temperance society because he was positive that it was only a scheme to extend "orthodox" influence.[19] He preferred to have Universalists become examples of proper conduct, even to the point of total abstinence if necessary, rather than to join organizations sponsored by other denominations.[20]

The American Temperance Society (later known also as the American Society for the Promotion of Temperance) was the first such organization on a national scale. Founded in Boston in 1826, its pledge called for total abstinence from ardent spirits. At the first national temperance convention, held in Philadelphia in 1833, a consolidation of all temperance organizations was proposed and in 1836 the American Temperance Union was created, composed of the members of the American Temperance Society and officers of state temperance conventions. When the American Temperance Society was originally organized it attempted to wean away users of distilled liquors by encouraging the drinking of beer. To that end, some friends of the cause invested $20,000 in a brewery in Roxbury, Massachusetts, in

1828, but it failed.[21] Consumers apparently wanted more potent beverages.

But the organization of the national society brought positive results, for it prompted the formation within a year of four state societies, not to mention over 200 local auxiliaries. It was estimated that there were 5,000 temperance groups in existence by 1833, including one organized by United States Congressmen. By 1840 the number had increased significantly. An important step was taken in 1838, when total abstinence was extended by the American Temperance Society to include all intoxicants, fermented as well as distilled. Hundreds of local societies immediately rewrote their constitutions and bylaws accordingly.

The Maine Convention of Universalists became, in 1830, the first such body in the denomination to adopt a statement dealing with temperance. Mild and ambiguous as the resolution was, it was a start. Because "the excessive use of ardent spirits has become alarming to the community, and degrading to human nature; and . . . the means that have been taken by various religionists to suppress it, have tended to defeat, in some instances, the benevolent object . . . [we] will use our best endeavors, by precept and example, to suppress the injurious practice as far as our influence will extend."[22] In 1830 thirteen distilleries were operating in the state, with an annual output of one million gallons of rum, while three hundred thousand gallons of rum, cider, and fermented liquors were imported.[23] These statistics probably help explain why the Maine Temperance Society was organized in 1832; William A. Drew, Universalist clergyman and newspaper editor, was the first recording secretary.[24] The Maine Convention in the 1830s and 1840s continued to adopt temperance resolutions, most of them more emphatically worded than their first. In 1834 they declared that the use of ardent spirits was "one of the worst plagues of a sinful world" and called for total abstinence (except for medical purposes) as the only "safe principle."

The temperance movement was beginning to make noticeable headway among Universalists by the 1830s. Sylvanus Cobb delivered in 1828 the first of many sermons on the subject to his congregation in Malden, Massachusetts, in which he called for total abstinence.[25] He circulated the constitution of the local temperance society and the majority of his congregation signed it, pledging themselves to total abstention from all alcoholic beverages. "Taking the pledge" had originated in Virginia in 1800, where the first total abstinence society had been organized in 1804; in 1818 the term "T-totaler" had been coined.[26] In Gloucester, Massachusetts, the town authorities made their first formal statement against intemperance in 1831. Local Universalists not only supported this action but were among the leaders in organizing the first temperance society in the community that year.[27] Adin

Ballou, in 1832 pastor of the First Church and Parish (Unitarian Congregational) in Mendon, Massachusetts, and himself a "moderate drinker," cautiously joined forces with the pastor of the local orthodox Congregational church to organize a temperance society.[28] He was soon transformed into a total abstainer and took to the lecture platform accordingly.

Universalist papers in the 1830s began to carry notices of local temperance meetings and advertisements soliciting information about the number of taverns in each town and the number of gallons of ardent spirits sold each year. Thomas Savary, a Universalist who operated a tavern in Wareham, Massachusetts, delivered a temperance address in 1833 in his own place of business, and posted a sign reading "No Ardent Spirits sold in this House."[29] A reference to Benjamin Rush's contributions to temperance was included in a resolution against the use of ardent spirits adopted by the New Hampshire Convention in 1833.[30]

More and more Universalists followed the lead of Sylvanus Cobb after 1830 and called for total abstinence, one argument being that "cautious drinkers" invariably ended as drunkards.[31] Linus S. Everett delivered an address to the Haverhill Temperance Society (Massachusetts) in 1833 calling for abstention from malt beverages and wine as well as distilled liquor.[32] He told his listeners that "He who gets drunk on wine or beer, instead of New England Rum, is not the less a drunkard on that account."[33] The Universalist pastor in Meredith, New Hampshire, in calling for total abstinence in a speech to the local temperance society, announced that "Universalists will be second to no part of the Christian church in their endeavors to aid this reformation."

In their attempt to impress upon Universalists the contributions the denomination had made to the temperance movement, there began to be circulated in 1833 the idea that the New England Convention had been the first ecclesiastical body in America, representing an entire denomination, to pass resolutions in behalf of temperance. William A. Drew, editor of the *Christian Intelligencer* (Maine) was one of the first to make the claim.[34] It was picked up immediately by half a dozen other newspaper editors who (without documentation) circulated the idea.[35] Universalists were either unaware at the time of the early resolutions of such groups as the Methodists, Quakers, Congregationalists, Presbyterians, and United Brethren, or if they were, they made no acknowledgment of it. In 1830, three years before Drew made his statement about the pioneer role of Universalists in the temperance movement, the Methodist Protestant Church was organized and had included in its constitution a statement opposing the manufacture, sale, or use of liquor as a beverage.[36] Eddy, after his investigation of the history of temperance resolutions among Universalists, made no claim to a denominational "first," much as he might have liked to do so. Even in 1835, when the General Convention of Universalists adopted a series of resolutions calling for "the suppression of intemperance in all its forms," they were addressed specifically to the Universalist state conventions and through them to the denomination. Of course, resolutions by any group dealing with temperance implicitly carried the expectation or hope that others could be dissuaded from use of intoxicating drink.[37]

Universalists engaged in temperance activity were to be found almost everywhere in the 1830s, and state conventions were adopting resolutions so rapidly (and repetitiously) that it was difficult to keep up with them. In some cases temperance resolutions were presented to entire congregations for action during public services. This occurred in churches in the Quinnebaug Association (Connecticut) in 1836, when voting privileges were extended to all adults present.[38] On the return trip to Boston from the sessions of the General Convention in New York City in 1841, an impromptu temperance meeting was held on board ship, complete with resolutions on the subject.[39]

While William S. Balch was on the temperance circuit in New Hampshire and Vermont, Otis A. Skinner was alternating between delivering sermons and lecturing on temperance all over Maryland.[40] Edwin Thompson, another Universalist clergyman, was appointed as the agent of the Massachusetts Temperance Society in 1833 and later served in the same capacity for the Massachusetts branch of the Washingtonian Movement, the Massachusetts Temperance Alliance, and the Massachusetts Total Abstinence Society.[41] L.F.W. Andrews, editor of the *Southern Evangelist,* delivered temperance lectures in 1834 at the request of the Montgomery County Temperance Society in Alabama.[42] He called for temperance in the use of language and food, and in politics, as well as in the use of alcohol. S.J. McMorris assisted at the same time in organizing a temperance society in Chambersville, Alabama.[43] Allen Fuller reported from South Carolina that the temperance cause there was progressing much more rapidly than denominational interests.[44]

Russell Streeter was among those participating in the activities of an inner-denominational temperance society in Shirley, Massachusetts.[45] In Ohio, where the first woman's temperance society had been organized in 1828, the Ohio Convention condemned the use of ardent spirits in 1834 and made the same declaration many times thereafter. Erasmus Manford, a life-long teetotaler, devoted much effort to the temperance cause in Ohio, and lectured frequently.[46] A Young Men's Temperance Society was organized in Claremont, New Hampshire, in 1834, at which Balch spoke frequently.[47] Between 1834 and 1836 the Vermont Convention moved from condemnation of intemperance to approval of total abstinence.[48] The same transition was recorded in the resolutions of numerous other state conventions in the 1830s and

1840s. The Boston Association voted unanimously in favor of total abstinence in 1836.[49]

Universalists sometimes found themselves in difficulty in advocating temperance. The issue caused rifts in societies, as in Woburn, Massachusetts, in the 1830s. Much to the discomfiture of Thomas Whittemore, John Gregory, the pastor of the Woburn society, published in 1836 an anti-total abstinence pamphlet entitled *The Bramble: An Exposé of Temperance Societies, formed on the Plan of Total Abstinence.*[50] Whittemore was heartened to learn that a member of the Boston Young Men's Universalist Institute had prepared a rejoinder entitled *The Hoe, designed to uproot the 'Bramble' of John Gregory, of Woburn, Mass.*[51] Allegations about excessive alcoholic consumption by Universalists were favorite devices used by opponents in attempting to discredit the denomination. A Methodist preacher in South Carolina accused Hosea Ballou of being a drunkard.[52] Affidavits were collected and published to show the falsity of such a charge. The New York Association came to the unhappy conclusion in 1841, after passing a temperance resolution, that Universalist ideas were not treated with respect, and that societies favoring temperance should establish their own organizations, independent of outsiders.[53]

Members of the denomination became increasingly involved with temperance organizations other than their own in the 1830s. They were well represented among the delegates at a statewide temperance meeting held in Boston in 1835 and "were all on the right side," namely in favor of total abstinence.[54] Sylvanus Cobb was probably, except for Alonzo A. Miner, the best known temperance man among Universalists in nineteenth-century Massachusetts. He was an unwavering believer in total abstinence both in principle and in inclination long before the movement became popular. According to his son and biographer, Cobb only once ever tasted distilled spirits unless prescribed by a physician. His first and last experience on his own initiative occurred when he was ten years of age; he tried a tumblerful of "pure old New England rum" (undiluted).[55] As a newspaperman, one of his principal motives in establishing the *Christian Freeman* in 1839 was to aid the temperance cause as well as the abolition of slavery, prison reform, and other crusades to build a better society. His sermon on total abstinence delivered to his Malden congregation on Fast Day in April 1828 was both an early such presentation and the first of hundreds of discourses which he delivered on the subject during his lifetime. Beginning in 1836 he was employed as a lecturer for the Middlesex County Temperance Society, and for three years delivered a total of over 450 lengthy addresses, both day and night, on behalf of total abstinence. He did not deliver "little thirty minute essays" but prerorations which averaged over an hour apiece.[56] Such length was required, he recalled, because there was so much ignorance, prejudice, and hostility to be overcome. He was committed, he said, to changing and molding public opinion rather than supporting it, by trying to uproot the generally accepted and cherished social habits of alcoholic consumption. He noted in passing that it was women as well as men who prided themselves on offering the best "in spirituous hospitality."[57]

Cobb circulated "teetotal" pledges at the close of every lecture, and claimed that "thousands of names were won, and many new societies were organized." He even reformed some existing societies to the extent that they abandoned the "partial pledge" (avoidance of distilled spirits only) in favor of "the thorough pledge." He called on tavern-keepers and grocers all over Middlesex County to abandon the liquor traffic voluntarily. When the state legislature enacted the "fifteen gallon law" in 1838 which prohibited the sale of ardent spirits in lesser quantities, Cobb was one of those who assisted in enforcing it.[58] He did not leave any reaction for the record when the law was repealed in 1840. One of his greatest local triumphs came in 1842, when the citizens of Malden voted unanimously in town meeting that the selectmen be instructed to grant no licenses for the sale of intoxicating drinks. He had earlier conducted a house-to-house canvass and had obtained the signatures of almost fifty heads of household to the abstinence pledge of the local temperance society.

Cobb tried to avoid the devices of exaggeration, vituperation and personal attack, and to handle the subject of alcohol with rationality, deliberation, and a thoughtfulness which, he was convinced, protected him from making rash statements which he might later feel compelled to modify or retract. His low-keyed approach was probably responsible for the fact that, although he was more than once threatened with physical harm, he was never actually attacked; nor was his speaking seriously disrupted.

The decades of the 1840s and 1850s witnessed the founding of the greatest number of temperance organizations that had yet appeared. The Washingtonian Movement was organized in 1840; branches soon appeared elsewhere; and a women's auxiliary was organized. In 1842 the first local society of the Sons of Temperance was created; in 1843 its first state organization (in New York) came into being. The Order of Templars of Honor and Temperance went into operation in 1845. The Society of Good Samaritans appeared in the following year, and the "Father Mathew" movement began in 1849. Of all the organizations, the Sons of Temperance and its various subsidiary groups were the most extensive during the 1840s. Most of these organizations, supported by dues, required a pledge of total abstinence as part of the initiation ceremonies. The Independent Order of Good Templars, organized in 1851, exceeded even the Sons of Temperance in membership and influence before the Civil War. Out of it came much of the leadership of the National Temperance Society (1865) and the Prohibition Party (1869).

The "Washington Society," as it was originally called, was organized in Baltimore, Maryland, in 1840, by six tradesmen who repented of their alcoholic ways through the influence of a temperance lecturer. They took a total abstinence pledge, adopted a constitution, and set out to reform drunkards, and with astounding success. They claimed to have brought more than one hundred thousand to sign the pledge by the end of their first year of operation, which included missionary effort in New England, upstate New York, and the Midwest. Although the Washingtonian Movement never had a formal national organization, branches were organized all over America.[59] A women's auxiliary, the Martha Washington Society, was organized in 1841 to assist reformed alcoholics. One of the most important reasons for the dramatic early success of the movement was the fact that the six founders could and did speak from personal experience. The novelty and excitement of hearing ex-drunkards give testimonials eventually wore off, and some church leaders opposed the movement because it was not under religious auspices, but it remained an important influence for many years.

The very fact that the movement was non-sectarian appealed to Universalists, and denominational spokesmen for temperance enthusiastically endorsed it. They noted with satisfaction that none of the founders had been a Universalist. Numerous state conventions specifically endorsed the Washingtonian Movement, including that of Connecticut, which pledged to support it as long as it remained non-sectarian.[60] Universalist relations with the Washingtonians were always cordial. James Shrigley, pastor of the First Universalist Society in Baltimore, corresponded with five of the six original Washingtonians.[61] A Boston branch, the "Parent Washington Total Abstinence Society," was organized in 1841 and by 1860 claimed that over seventy thousand individuals had signed their pledge.

What became the Washingtonian Home was opened in Boston in 1857 as an asylum for inebriates. The person largely responsible for establishing the institution was Mrs. Charles Spear. In her labors with her husband to reform discharged convicts she concluded that the greatest obstacle to rehabilitation was the widespread use of alcohol.[62] She therefore circulated a petition to the state legislature on which she obtained 6,000 signatures. Although the proposal to charter and establish a home for drunkards was reported favorably by a special legislative committee, the bill was never acted on because of the expectation that the governor would veto it. So a group of humanitarian-minded community leaders headed by Judge Joseph Story took the matter into their own hands and temporary quarters were obtained in downtown Boston. The "Home for the Fallen," as it was first called, began operations under an organization created in the fall of 1857 at a meeting in Faneuil Hall. A board of directors, of which Alonzo A. Miner was a member, was selected, and in 1858 enlarged quarters were obtained. But the demand for the services of the institution were so great that new facilities were obtained the same year. The home was established on a firm basis by Albert Day, a Congregational layman who served as superintendent for many years.

The Home for the Fallen was incorporated as the Washington Home in 1859, assisted by a $3,000 grant from the legislature. Judging from numerous recorded testimonials, the institution met an obvious need and was considered a great success. The anonymity of those who gave testimonials was carefully preserved, including one ex-Universalist clergyman from central New York State who was completely reformed and became an effective temperance lecturer.[63] A Universalist layman who was identified (Samuel Gowen of Danvers, Massachusetts) was reformed by way of the Washingtonian program, and became a lecturer for the cause.[64]

Temperance advocates were greatly encouraged when Father Theobald Mathew, an Irish priest known as the "Apostle of Temperance," visited the United States in 1849. He was enthusiastically received, given a banquet by President John Tyler, and administered the total abstinence pledge in New England to thousands (the statistics vary widely). Sylvanus Cobb had nothing but praise for Father Mathew and his work when the priest visited Boston and Cobb had an opportunity to talk with him.[65]

Temperance seems to have become an all-engrossing topic among Universalists in the 1840s and 1850s. According to Otis A. Skinner, intemperance was "the greatest evil of the land," possibly more important than even the slavery issue.[66] Resolutions favoring total abstinence continued to be ground out by Universalist state conventions and associations in record numbers after 1840. The Rhode Island Convention, after pledging its members to complete prohibition in 1841, supported attempts of the state temperance union to obtain signatures to a temperancy pledge in Sunday schools.[67] In some instances resolutions failed of adoption because they were too strongly worded to be acceptable. A resolution offered at the Washington Association (Ohio) in 1841 referred to "the crime of intemperance" and in effect indicted all Universalists who did not work for total abstinence.[68] The Indiana Convention adopted a temperance resolution the very year it was organized (1842) and in 1854 went to the length of calling on the state legislature to prohibit the manufacture, sale, and use of alcohol, and to provide the power of search, seizure, and destruction of all liquor unlawfully possessed or sold.[69]

Not all Universalists lent such whole-hearted support to the temperance cause. The Union Association (Pennsylvania) resolved in favor of temperance in 1842 but made a point of the fact that it was an individual matter, and refused to recommend any restrictive or compulsive measures.[70] Members refused, in response to a strong temperance resolution adopted by the General Convention that year, to submit to what they interpreted as "dictation" by that body, making "membership in an ultra temperance society . . . the test of fellowship in our denomination." The controversial resolution of the General Convention aimed primarily at the lay delegates, which precipitated this reaction, read in part as follows: "Persons engaged in manufacturing, vending or using intoxicating liquors as a beverage, though ever to be treated with christian kindness, are not in the opinion of this body, the proper persons to represent the religious interests of our denomination, as delegates in our public ecclesiastical bodies."[71] The circular letter which accompanied the minutes had emphatically declared that this resolution, like others passed by the General Convention, was not to be received "as dictation or command, but only as *advisory*."

At the 1843 meeting of the convention the resolutions of the previous year dealing with temperance were rescinded, on the initiative of the Pennsylvania Convention, and a milder and more generalized statement was substituted. Even that did not mollify the Union Association, for in 1844 it adopted resolutions to the effect that "any connexion between the Pennsylvania Convention and the U.S. Convention of Universalists is no longer essential to the harmony and peace of our order."[72] Whittemore tried to calm them down by reminding them that they had nothing to fear from the General Convention anyway, because it was "as utterly destitute of power over the denomination, as an individual."

Hosea Ballou delivered an address in Medford, Massachusetts, in 1843 advocating total abstinence. Conscious of the sensibilities of some members of the denomination, he apologized in advance to any that might be offended.[73] Sumner Ellis, junior pastor of the First Universalist Society in Boston, resigned in 1853 because some members of the congregation objected to his insistence on signing a memorial to the city of Boston requesting stricter enforcement of the laws for suppressing the liquor traffic. The reason was simple: They were themselves engaged in it.[74]

Individuals as well as organizations were active in the 1840s and 1850s in promoting temperance. Whittemore put aside his suspicions of Unitarians sufficiently in 1842 to give a temperance lecture in their church in Jamaica Plain, Massachusetts, after which 100 individuals signed a total abstinence pledge.[75] A.B. Manley of Stockbridge, Massachusetts, began publication of the *Temperance Samaritan* in 1842, but had to suspend it almost immediately for lack of patronage.[76] This might have been explained by the fact that by 1839 there were already fifteen successful temperance journals available in the United States, four of them in New England.[77] The field was too crowded for yet another one. Throughout the 1840s and beyond the Civil War, Horace Greeley continued to open the columns of his powerful *New York Tribune* in behalf of temperance, and wrote many editorials in its support. E.H. Chapin used his considerable oratorical powers in its behalf, although he found some churches closed to him because he was a Universalist. He delivered the keynote address at the Massachusetts temperance convention in 1853.[78] J.G. Adams wrote a hymn suitable for dedicating temperance halls.[79] The effects of temperance efforts are naturally impossible to measure, but now and then there were tangible results. Universalists in Plantersville, Ohio, closed out the last remaining liquor store in the town in 1850 by renting the premises and turning the building into a temperance hall.[80]

Mary A. Livermore, while conducting a school in Duxbury, Massachusetts, in the 1840s, found herself caught up in the temperance movement.[81] She worked with the "Cold Water Army" recruited from among children as part of the efforts of the local total abstinence society. She won a $50 prize for a story, based on fact, illustrative of the Washingtonian Movement. It was published in the form of a booklet, was republished in England, and was reprinted in the United States in 1876.[82] Her husband, D.P. Livermore, also a strong temperance advocate, assisted in the passage of a prohibitory law in Connecticut, but it was vetoed by the governor and replaced by less stringent legislation.

The decades of the 1840s and 1850s were marked by attempts to enact state prohibition laws, but none was successful until the so-called Maine Law, enacted after years of effort. The principal architect of the law was Neal Dow, elected mayor of Portland, Maine, in 1849, and a persistent and influential temperance man who campaigned widely for total abstinence. An ineffective prohibition law had been passed in 1846 and a stronger one in 1848 which had been vetoed by the governor. The "Neal Dow Bill," the most severe to date, had been lost by a tie vote in the state senate in 1850. But in the following year victory was won by a vote of 86 to 40 in the lower house and 18 to 10 in the senate.

The famous (or infamous) Maine law of 1851 prohibited, under severe penalties, the manufacture and sale of alcoholic liquors, cider alone excepted. The latter beverage, unadulterated, could be sold in quantities of five gallons or more. The penalty for convicted violators of the prohibitory portions of the law carried a two-months' imprisonment and a $100 fine, increased for subsequent offenses. It was further provided that anyone injured in any way (including property as well as person) could bring an action for damages against the seller and the owner or lessee of the building where the liquor was sold, if cognizant that such was taking place. There were also fines and imprisonment for intoxicated persons disturbing the peace either on the streets or within their own families. Liquors kept for sale, and the vessels containing them, were considered contraband and hence liable to seizure. A state commissioner was appointed to oversee the "necessary sale" of such liquors used for "medicinal, mechanical, and manufacturing purposes." The law was reenacted in 1855, repealed in 1856, and put back on the statute books in 1857, where it remained until 1934.

Prohibition advocates among Universalists all over the nation greeted the Maine law with jubilation, from the Boston Association in the East to the Fox River Association in Illinois.[83] Resolutions too numerous to mention were adopted at all levels in the denomination approving the aim and spirit, if not the specific provisions, of the landmark legislation. The prohibitory law in Massachusetts, modelled on the Maine law and enacted in 1852, was similarly greeted with enthusiasm. The Universalist General Reform Association included prohibitory legislation enacted in Rhode Island and Vermont in 1852 in its stamp of approval.[84] The General Convention endorsed the Maine law in 1853 with only one dissenting vote (identity not disclosed), and in 1854 went ever farther by announcing that the principle of prohibition as applied to the liquor traffic was "sanctioned by Divine Authority as truly as the prohibition of any other sin."[85]

The prohibitory laws enacted in fourteen states by 1855 encountered more or less difficulty in passage and operated with widely differing effectiveness. Many had to be submitted to public referenda because of constitutional complications or executive vetoes, or were repealed, rewritten, and reenacted (or defeated), or failed to be adequately enforced after passage. Vermont's prohibition law was ratified by direct vote in 1853; parts of the prohibitory law in Massachusetts were declared unconstitutional two years after it had been passed in 1852; a revised law in 1855 stayed in force until 1868. By the 1850s regulation of liquor had become as much a political question as slavery and even a party issue, a situation which divided the temperance forces and weakened the movement. It was John Pierpont of Boston, a Unitarian clergyman, who at a widely heralded temperance convention in 1853, issued an urgent call for political involvement.[86] But the prohibition forces failed to rally sufficiently to present a united front or to achieve anything approaching solidarity. The issues of the Civil War became paramount and overshadowed the "alcohol question."

When prohibitory statutes were once enacted, there was a noticeable decline in temperance activity. Apathy replaced enthusiasm when the less exciting problem of enforcement arose. Liquor consumption in both the military and on the home front seems to have increased notably during the war. Universalist organizations continued to adopt prohibition resolutions, and when peace came the number increased. There was mounting concern, expressed in countless resolutions, about the lack of enforcement and violation of existing laws. The Massachusetts Convention was worried in 1866 about the increase in wine drinking, especially by those of wealth and high position who helped set the tone of society.[87] Matters were made worse by a growing movement in the state to repeal the existing prohibition legislation; it came to a climax in 1867 with a protracted legislative debate which first brought to public notice Alonzo A. Miner, who became the most prominent Universalist associated with the state prohibition movement.

Miner had first attracted attention with his leadership in the Massachusetts Temperance Alliance, an inter-denominational group which attempted to retain the prohibitory legislation. He was president of the organization for ten years, and was its elected spokesman in the hearings in the state legislature.[88] He was an uncompromising enemy of alcoholic consumption of any kind and in any amount, and at any time in his life "would have blessed an opportunity to put his endorsement upon an imperial edict relentlessly and autocratically striking alcohol in all its combinations out of existence."[89] He and the prohibition forces faced a well-organized campaign to substitute a local-option license law. One of the most influential opponents of prohibition was ex-Governor John A. Andrew, a Unitarian.

A special joint legislative committee reviewed the entire matter in much detail, and a whole bevy of clergymen, teachers, and other citizens, including Miner, fought the license bill. Miner accused Andrew of allowing the liquor interests and the politicians to prevail, and delivered a highly-charged address in Tremont Temple under the auspices of the Sons of Temperance.[90] Although the movement to retain prohibition went down in defeat, Miner worked until his death in 1895 to have the prohibition law restored. He was one of the speakers in 1868 at the Massachusetts Temperance Alliance in Springfield, and called for unconditional repeal of all license legislation.[91] He was a candidate for the governorship of Massachusetts on the state Prohibition Party ticket. He had a later occasion to appear before the Massachusetts legislature when, in 1884, he delivered, on the invitation of Governor Benjamin F. Butler, the last annual election sermon ever heard by that body. Miner was so critical of the way the state government was being operated that the historic provision for election sermons inherited from the colonial period was repealed.[92]

An inevitable by-product of the Universalist temperance agitation which affected all church members in some degree was the question of using alcoholic beverages at celebrations of the Lord's Supper. This seems not to have been a subject of serious discussion until the 1840s, and when voices were heard on the subject they in no sense spoke in harmony. There was no uniformity whatsoever in either theory or practice. Thomas Whittemore was one of the first to speak out on the matter. The temperance movement had reached sufficient proportions in the orthodox Congregational church in Lowell, Massachusetts, in 1834, to result in substituting "Tamarind water" for wine at Communion. Whittemore considered this ridiculous, inasmuch as Christ himself had used and advocated wine for religious purposes, according to Whittemore's reading of the Scriptures.[93] After much soul-searching and Biblical research, he decided less than ten years later that the churches would do a great service to the temperance movement as well as to themselves if they abandoned all use of "intoxicating wines" in religious services.[94] The First Universalist Society in Lynn, Massachusetts, substituted plain water for wine in 1842.[95] Even Sylvanus Cobb, strong temperance supporter that he was, considered this step "an unnecessary extreme." After all, the Lord's Supper was only a symbolic gesture; hence it was immaterial what was used. Unfermented grape juice was his first choice. He was distressed to hear that Horace Greeley had refused to partake of the Lord's Supper because "alcoholic wine" was used.[96]

One argument occasionally raised against the use of wine was pragmatic rather than moral. Reformed inebriates might have their taste for alcohol revived. The story was widely circulated in 1868 that such had actually happened, and the unfortunate backslider had had to be expelled from the church (unidentified).[97] In 1870 T.H. Tabor wrote a two-part article opposing the use of wine for Communion purposes. He argued that the church was not likely to be successful in reforming drunkards if it allowed the use of alcohol in its own services. In the second article he attempted to prove that neither Christ nor his apostles used wine at Passover. He reasoned that if unleavened bread was required, it followed that unfermented "juice of the vine" was used likewise.[98]

No solution satisfactory to all had been found by any official Universalist body by 1870. In that year the Massachusetts Convention debated the subject at some length, and finally recommended the use of "pure water" only; there is no way of knowing whether that advice was followed. The General Convention was first heard on the subject when in 1842 it voted unanimously to recommend that Universalists "consider the expediency and practicability of substituting some other emblem, in place of those wines which contain the intoxicating quality."[99] The convention reaffirmed its stand many times afterward, usually recommending unfermented grape juice. But the matter was never settled definitively by that body in the nineteenth century. A resolution which would have prohibited the use of wine presented by Quillen Hamilton Shinn in 1882 was tabled. The most that can be said is that by 1885 the majority of Universalist state conventions had gone on record against using fermented beverages to celebrate the Lord's Supper.[100]

The Massachusetts Convention objected strenuously and repeatedly to the license law and recommended that every church and Sunday School form temperance societies where they did not already exist.[101] There was considerable disagreement in the Boston Association over whether to support a political party devoted exclusively to advocating prohibition, but finally they endorsed the idea.[102] Universalists almost everywhere continued to pass resolutions favoring prohibition, up through support of the Eighteenth Amendment in the 1920s.

Individual Universalists like Mary A. Livermore continued to be active in the cause in the 1870s in Ohio and in the 1880s in Massachusetts; and for a decade she was president of the Massachusetts Women's Christian Temperance Union, the parent organization of which had been formed in 1874. In 1885 she was one of the founders of the National League for the Suppression of the Liquor Traffic.[103] Richard Eddy was for many years the head of the Order of Good Templars in Massachusetts.[104] At the time of his death in 1904, Universalist Henry B. Metcalf was the gubernatorial candidate of the Prohibition Party in Rhode Island.[105] Whether they were successful or not, Universalists continued to crusade against what the Ohio Convention called "the fearful evils of intemperance . . . fraught with mischief to all the interests of humanity."[106]

Chapter 20

'GOD BLESS AND MAKE US GRATEFUL FOR OUR WOMEN!'

Universalism and Women: An Overview

If our women need no eulogy, we need the satisfaction of making a warm, explicit confession of our admiration of their attempt, and our gratitude for what they have done. They can well afford to dispense with this acknowledgment, but we cannot afford not to make it. It becomes us here to raise no question as to woman's fitness for certain employments and political prerogatives, hitherto the prerogatives of the rougher sex. But should we reach what some call "extreme views" on the several points, and should our zeal bring us onto the platform as a champion thereof, the sledge-hammer we should wield is, *the work of the Universalist women in their Centenary Year.* God bless and make us grateful our our women!

* * * * * *

Thus wrote George H. Emerson, editor of the *Christian Leader,* a Universalist newspaper published in New York City.[1] It was a tribute to the hundreds of women in the denomination who, as members of the Woman's Centenary Aid Association, had raised over $35,000 for the benefit of the Universalist Church at the time of its centennial in 1870. It was in the 1860s and 1870s that Universalist women first became truly visible in the denomination, although their participation in Universalist affairs and in other fields of activity, notably literature, prior to 1860, was at least partially recognized. Taken as a whole, in spite of all the legal, social, and political disabilities and prejudicial attitudes which women faced in nineteenth-century America, it may be safely said that Universalists in general took an advanced position regarding women's status and women's rights. Two Universalists were among the eighteenth-century pioneers. Enlarged educational opportunities for women were first called for by Judith Sargent Murray.[2]

Mrs. Murray believed in the complete equality of men and women and did not hesitate to say so.

> Our evidences tend to prove them [women] alike capable of enduring hardships; equally ingenious and fruitful in resources; their fortitude and heroism cannot be surpassed; they are equally brave; they are as patriotic, as influential, as energetic, and as eloquent; as faithful and as persevering in their

attachments; as capable of supporting with honor, the toils of government; and equally susceptible of every literary acquirement.[3]

Benjamin Rush had earlier called for more extensive educational opportunities for women. While serving on the all-male board of visitors of the Ladies' Academy in Philadelphia, he had published *Thoughts on Female Education* in 1787.[4]

In view of the relatively small number of Universalists compared with other denominations, there seems to have been an unusually large number of individuals, both men and women, who became champions of the rights of women and/or made significant social contributions. Some of the women achieved considerable prominence outside the denomination, including Olympia Brown, Clara Barton, and Mary A. Livermore. Toward the end of the nineteenth century a host of biographical dictionaries of women appeared and received wide circulation. One of these was compiled by Phebe A. Hanaford, an ordained Universalist minister.[5] Mrs. E.R. Hanson published in 1881 the first work dealing exclusively with Universalist women, containing biographical sketches of 146 individuals.[6] Mary A. Livermore was co-editor with Frances E. Willard of *A Woman of the Century* in 1893.[7]

As Universalism began to take organized form in the late eighteenth and early nineteenth centuries it was very much a man's world when it came to the legal status of women. In most states they were prohibited from signing papers organizing religious societies. A New York law of 1813 required that all incorporators of such organizations be "male persons."[8] So it was the Universalist men whose names appeared on the early records creating societies and organizing churches. When the Gloucester church in Massachusetts was created out of the existing society in 1806, the covenant and articles of faith were adopted by the male members.[9] The church organization thus created consisted originally of nine men and thirty-four women, but no women held an office until the church was reorganized in 1838. Thomas Jones, pastor when the church was first established out of the society, was opposed to having all the officers and activities in the hands of the men, but the women themselves preferred it that way, and Jones' protests went unheeded for over thirty years.

By the same token, the early Universalist congregations seemed to have been made up predominantly of men. The wives of many Universalists were not sure about the respectability of their religion, and were afraid they might lose caste with their neighbors and friends if they attended Universalist meetings.[10] It took courage not only to profess the faith but to participate. Calvin Gardner, compiling state denominational statistics in 1836 in Maine, was unable "to ascertain whether, as a general thing, females are admitted as members of societies."[11] Allen Fuller, clerk of the South Carolina Convention in

1833, noted that women were conspicuously present at Baptist gatherings, but at the public services of the Universalist convention the audience was "almost exclusively of men."[12] He hoped that this unbalance would be remedied eventually, and that "even the softer sex" would find Universalism appealing.

After preaching to an all-male audience in Alabama in 1837, George Rogers scolded his host for failing to invite women. Rogers did not "like to be treated as if I were a traveling philosopher, who taught matters too high for female comprehension or unconnected with female interests."[13] He even turned his pulpit over to women now and then when they told him they had received a call to preach. Most, he decided, had mistaken their vocation, but a full house was always assured when it was announced that a woman would occupy the pulpit.[14] There was visible progress in feminine attendance at the public services of the Rockingham Association (New Hampshire). In 1828 only one woman had appeared; at the services in 1836, when a new meeting house was dedicated in Epping, women filled almost every pew. Many had not dared before to appear in public to hear a Universalist preacher.[15]

Women had begun to appear as delegates to state conventions by the 1850s. The first woman to serve in Vermont was a representative from the Green Mountain Association in 1855.[16] The Otsego Association (New York) suggested in 1856 that one-half of the delegates (two out of every four) from each society be women; they could then participate as voting members of the council.[17] Universalist women first began to serve as officers in organizations operated by societies and churches, but not in the societies and churches themselves. During the 1830s, when "conference meetings" began to be popular, women were at first not even invited; so they organized and conducted their own.[18] Within a few years they became active participants in all conference meetings.

The Universalist Institute organized by the society in Cambridge, Massachusetts, tried in 1835 the "novel experiment" of making women eligible for office.[19] Two of the eight officers elected that year were women. Five of the fifteen charter members of the Universalist Publishing Society of Pennsylvania, organized in Philadelphia in 1841, were women, and they served on its committees.[20] Two women served as officers when the Universalist General Reform Association was organized in 1847. Mary A. Livermore was one of the five vice presidents and Eunice H. Cobb, wife of Sylvanus Cobb, was one of the five directors.[21] It was Mrs. Livermore who was later to become the first woman delegate to the General Convention. Voting privileges were extended in 1836 to "both *ladies* and *gentlemen*" at the Steuben Association (New York) when a resolution was adopted disapproving of the establishment of a denominational theological school in the state.[22]

Women found many champions and defenders among Universalist men. Warren Skinner of Cavendish, Vermont, delivered a sermon in 1833 on "The Importance and Influence of the Female Character" which was published in the denominational press.[23] He concluded that "the unwarrantable distinction between the male and female portions of the community is fast disappearing" and that women were "formed and intended by nature to be the help-mate, the associate, and the friend, not the slave of man." Women's best influence could be exerted "in the domestic circle" and in the church. When Daniel D. Smith, the editor of the literary journal, the *Universalist,* added the words "Ladies' Repository" to the title in 1833, he explained that the publication would "advocate the rights of FEMALES, and earnestly contend for FEMALE education."[24] William A. Drew, editor of the *Christian Intelligencer* (Maine) believed that women were entitled to acquire the same training as men in "the useful and practical sciences."[25] There was no reason at all, he wrote, why their education should be confined to drawing, dancing, music, and painting, and their training to keeping a house in order, "turning a spinning wheel, [or] making a pudding." Any deficiency that women exhibited in critically examining philosophical or metaphysical subjects, said Linus S. Everett, was due not to any inferiority to men, but to the way they had been treated by men, "self-styled lords of creation."[26] When he became editor of the *Southern Pioneer* in 1835, Everett introduced a "Ladies' Department" and announced his refusal to write down to women.

Erasmus Manford completely supported his wife's various activities as a lecturer on "temperance, the elevation of woman, and general education."[27] She also edited and published his newspaper while he was travelling in the Midwest in the 1840s and 1850s and found time to serve for several years as the president of the Illinois Woman's Association. Manford insisted that a woman should share fully all the rights of men. They should "sue and be sued, buy and sell, vote if she please, and be president too of these United States, if she can get votes enough."[28] England's best rulers, he said, had been queens rather than kings. Another prominent Universalist, Otis A. Skinner, wrote a series of essays on "The Influence of Christian Women," published in 1843.[29]

Probably not even the most militant Universalist woman would have gone as far as one correspondent to the *Trumpet* in 1850. In what appeared to be all seriousness, the writer pointed out that there was no law prohibiting women from learning such trades as shoemaking, carpentry, and blacksmithing. "What harm would follow if young ladies were to be instructed in military tactics—permitted to graduate at West Point, and to advance to the highest degree of discipline as scientific soldiers?"[30]

Charles Spear, active in many reform movements, together with his wife Sarah, urged women to enter social reform as a career, and welcomed contributions from women in the columns of his *Prisoners' Friend.*[31] Lucretia Mott, one of the nationally known advocates of women's rights, was among those whose articles appeared in his journal. Spear questioned the practice of limiting propertyholding by women and was also distressed by the exploitation of working women. He called for higher wages and a ten-hour day.[32] He had much to say about the causes of delinquency among women. In 1851 he wrote a series of articles on prostitution and reminded his readers that women were unjustly blamed for indulging in such an occupation while it was the men who demanded the service and were just as much to blame.[33] He was, in effect, challenging the traditional double standard of morality. Spear recognized the role that economic necessity played in driving women into prostitution. The problem could at least be alleviated, if not solved, by giving women enlarged opportunities in less reprehensible occupations. He suggested drygoods retailing, medicine, and law as possibilities. But he was sufficiently realistic to recognize that this would never happen until men relinquished their self-assumed monopoly over power and property.[34]

Henry Bacon, editor for many years of the *Ladies' Repository,* was a vigorous supporter of the women's rights movement. He applauded the conventions held in their behalf and warned that if men did not, by legislation and a change of attitude, allow women to enlarge their sphere of employment, then it was up to them to right such wrongs themselves.[35] He did not, however, provide any guidance in the way of proposed strategy or tactics. Women found a hearty supporter in E.H. Chapin, who spoke from the platform in favor of legal equality with men and greater access to education of all kinds.[36] He disagreed with those who believed gainful employment would somehow destroy "the work of the home and of the household." He did not foresee women as speculators in Wall Street or orators in Tammany Hall; but if they chose such careers, they would probably do well.

Some Universalists, even though they expressed "advanced ideas" about many issues, were hesitant about allowing women full participation in deliberations historically reserved for men. Sylvanus Cobb doubted whether the New England Anti-Slavery Convention which he attended in 1839 had taken a wise step in allowing women to participate in discussion and to vote. He finally decided that the cause of human freedom was too basic to allow such scruples to interfere.[37] After the first national women's rights convention had met in 1850 in Worcester, Massachusetts, Cobb approved, in a cautious way, several of the reforms that had been recommended.[38] He agreed that laws regarding property and inheritance should be liberalized; he opposed wage discrimination based on sex. But he was strongly opposed to feminine participation in politics in any way and at any level; he absolutely excluded the franchise and public office-holding. Cobb had lost by 1859 his doubts about the propriety of allowing women to speak in public. He defended their right to do so when T.J. Sawyer expressed strong opposition to allowing women to speak at religious meetings.[39] But much beyond that he would not go.

Thomas Whittemore reacted to the women's rights movement with very mixed feelings. In reference to the Worcester meeting in 1850, he acidly remarked that "some distinguished female talkers were there, whose husbands at home must have had a time of heavenly stillness during their absence."[40] That was the only good he could see coming out of the convention. The aggressive tone he detected displeased him greatly. Women were men's partners, not their rivals. To Whittemore, women had a separate sphere, superior to that of man. Women had charge of "all the higher destinies of our race."[41] They would be degraded by getting involved in public affairs, especially politics.

Charles Spear, preoccupied as he was with reforms of all sorts, wrote an article in 1853 entitled simply "Woman."[42] He recognized women's superiority only in the moral realm and in their "sensibilities." He saw no reason why they needed the franchise. The sphere of women was "to take a part in removing war, intemperance, slavery, licentiousness, ignorance, poverty, and crime." She could do all this without going to the polls.

Now and then a woman would support men opposed to feminine political involvement. One argued that it was "as absurd for a woman to make stump speeches, and crowd to the ballot box, as for men to make preserves and work embroidery."[43] There were still activities reserved exclusively for each sex. Tradition died hard.

Universalist organizations were very circumspect about officially endorsing the women's rights movement, which had taken on significant proportions by the 1850s. Very few of them had anything at all to say on the subject. The Quinnebaug Association (Connecticut) adopted a resolution in 1853 recognizing "the general agitation" for the elevation of women and considered it "a pleasing evidence of the progress of the age" but acknowledged that there were some who did not concur in all the means being used.[44] A resolution was offered at the General Convention in 1863 acknowledging the contributions of women, especially during the Civil War. The resolution might have been adopted if it had not also urged recognition of the social, intellectual, and political rights of women and had not called for the elimination of all manifestations of belief in the inferiority of women.[45]

The very fact that a resolution dealing with women had been introduced at all in the national body of the denomination gave some indication of how far the "Woman Question" had penetrated Universalist ranks on the eve of its centennial in 1870. It would have been difficult to imagine any mention at all of such a question seventy years before, when the New England Convention had been organized. By

1870 women had received degrees from Universalist and other colleges, had been ordained in the ministry, had made their mark in literature, and had participated actively in denominational affairs. They had also contributed significantly to the struggle to achieve rights for women on a national scale.

Women and Higher Learning

With only one notable exception, Universalists avoided a struggle within the denomination over educational rights for women in the nineteenth century, and that struggle resulted in a victory for the women. Every one of the academies, seminaries, colleges, and universities established by Universalists from 1819 to 1870 was coeducational from the day it opened, except Tufts College. In fact, Lombard College in Galesburg, Illinois, was the second institution of higher learning in the United States to have admitted women from the beginning. The first, Oberlin College in Ohio, had opened as a coeducational institution in 1833 and in 1841 awarded the first Bachelor of Arts degree received by any woman who had taken the same academic program required of men. There were variations in the administration of coeducation at Universalist schools. At some, like Clinton Liberal Institute in New York State, young men and women were at first taught in separate classes and had completely separate living facilities. In others like St. Lawrence University and Smithson College, not only were the classes coeducational but at times students of both sexes were housed in the same buildings.

Most Universalist spokesmen for education took what was, for the times, a forward position on opportunities for women. Sylvanus Cobb, in noting that Illinois Liberal Institute (which became Lombard University) had been authorized in 1853 to offer collegiate instruction, emphasized the fact that all departments, including the preparatory, were open to women on a basis of complete equality with men.[46] "We are decidedly opposed to that woman's rights partyism, which should break down all external distinctions between the sexes, and thus degrade women.—But in the culture of the mind and the pursuit and acquisition of knowledge, we see not why the sister, after having accompanied her brother in the Academic department, should have the door of the Collegiate shut against her."

After Tufts College had been chartered in 1852, but before it opened two years later, there was considerable discussion over whether women were to be admitted. The general expectation was that it would be coeducational, like all of the academies already operated by the denomination.[47] A resolution was offered at the Massachusetts Convention in 1853 "recommending the admission of females into the higher institutions of learning." However, after having been discussed "at length," no action was taken. A more explicit resolution in 1854 in favor of opening all Universalist institutions of learning to women (a thinly veiled reference to Tufts) met a similar fate. In 1855, after the college had opened, the same convention adopted almost unanimously an even more explicit resolution; namely, that those responsible for governing Tufts "consider the propriety of opening it to both sexes alike, and of awarding its honors according to proficiency in study, irrespective of sex."[48]

Denominational leaders like T.J. Sawyer strongly endorsed the idea of coeducation. At the celebration of the first anniversary of the opening of the college in 1856 he called "separation of the sexes . . . a relic of monastic institutions."[49] He held firmly to the belief that women, who had the same mental capacities as men, should have the opportunity to pursue the same studies as men. Cobb preferred coeducational institutions to either all-men or all-women colleges, and recommended that the Tufts trustees open a "female department." He made even clearer the distinction he had drawn earlier between the "Woman Rights" question and equal educational opportunity for women, the latter of which he thoroughly approved. He had no sympathy whatsoever for the extremists who wanted "the obliteration of all distinctions between the sexes in the sphere of life . . . prated about by a few female men and male women."[50] He was emphatically not in favor of seeing women serving on police forces or in the military, or engaging in "political warfare."[51]

In the summer of 1856 a young lady from South Reading (Wakefield), Massachusetts, applied for admission to Tufts. The faculty, not knowing how to reply, referred the request to the executive committee of the trustees, who took no action of record. The refusal of Tufts to admit women brought an angry letter from Amory Battles, pastor of the Universalist society in Bangor, Maine. He announced in 1857 that he would neither support the institution nor solicit funds for it from his society until the college was opened to women. His sister had been rebuffed by every institution in New England to which she had applied.[52] He reproached the trustees for being false to the principle of "a Universal Father and Universal Humanity" by refusing to open Tufts' doors to women. Neither sex nor color should be a bar to educational opportunity.

Throughout the controversy in the 1850s over coeducation at the new college, the Tufts trustees remained conspicuously silent, even after St. Lawrence University had been chartered in 1856 as a coeducational institution under Universalist control. According to Thomas Whittemore, himself a Tufts trustee, the subject of admitting women had never been discussed, and when preparations were made to open the institution no public statement had been made about the admission of women.[53] At least two explanations can be offered for the failure to admit women. It had been a struggle to raise the funds to establish Tufts, and provision for coeducational facilities would have stretched the slender resources beyond an acceptable limit. More important, the institution was to be a college and not an academy, and there was no precedent in all of New England for coeducation at that level. Further, there was still so much opposition to the very idea of coeducational colleges in the East that venturing onto such an untried path would probably have spelled disaster immediately.[54]

John G. Adams was among those who saw no reason why Tufts had to be coeducational.[55] There was no evidence that either Massachusetts or any other New England state was foreordained to take the lead, and Universalists certainly did not have any obligation to do so. Adams thought that the very fact that Tufts was to be "like other Colleges in New England" was one of its most attractive features.

Pressure continued to mount in the 1860s and 1870s to open Tufts to women, but the trustees stood fast. Universalist parents were told that coeducational denominational schools already existed, and should be patronized from the East as well as elsewhere. It was reported that in Lombard, women were proving themselves "fully equal to the gentlemen in the recitation room."[56] This applied to all subjects, including foreign languages, mathematics, and natural science. Universalists in New England countered by complaining that sending their daughters to such institutions as St. Lawrence and Lombard was not only inconvenient but often financially impossible.

The news in 1870 that Dean Academy, conducted by Universalists and located in Franklin, Massachusetts, was planning to establish a collegiate program for women, was greeted with mixed reactions, most of them negative. On the surface it might have sounded like an excellent idea, but there was opposition on several counts. Most Universalists preferred coeducational institutions, with which they were already familiar, to unisex schools. The question was immediately raised of why an existing college (Tufts) less than fifty miles away, and with much greater academic resources than could be established at Dean, could not serve the purpose.[57]

Richmond Fisk, president of St. Lawrence University, delivered the main address at the Founder's Day celebration at Dean Academy in 1871 and told his audience that Tufts should remain a men's college.[58] He took this stand not because he was opposed to coeducation, being himself the head of an institution open to both sexes, but because he was in favor of "the variety demanded by diversities of opinion." He was also more doubtful than his colleagues at Lombard about the academic success of the very few women enrolled in the classical course. At St. Lawrence a background was required in science and mathematics which women lacked. Fisk's ideas were not very warmly received. A writer in the *Christian Ambassador* (quoted in the *Trumpet*) commented that "this old, fossilized idea of herding only men together in college for educational purposes" had not always proved satisfactory. Further, men had "proved themselves far less proficient in pursuit of their studies than as if they had been stimulated by the presence and ambition of lady students." A faculty member at Dean presented President Miner of Tufts with the credentials of two young ladies at Dean pursuing a college preparatory course in 1873 and asked if they should take the entrance examinations.[59] Miner's reply is not known, but they were not admitted.

In the meantime, the trustees of Dean Academy had abandoned in 1871 the idea of establishing a women's college, and Universalists in the East still had no college facilities of their own for women. Those in favor of a coeducational Tufts continued to express their dissatisfaction with the status quo. The writer of an editorial in the *Ladies' Repository* aimed a barb directly at Tufts. "Unfortunately the one school of our own order which does not admit women to its privileges is in this same son-loving and daughter-forgetting New England."[60] The same writer complained about the inadequacy of education for women in general. They wanted greater opportunity than to obtain a "finished" education at an academy, "with nothing to do but go home and sit down."[61] And there was not a single public school in Boston, which boasted so loudly of its educational system, where women could even be prepared for college. Women's colleges outside the denomination were considered just as deficient. Their academic standards were too low, even those at Vassar which had been recently established.

The first full-dress discussion of the question of coeducation at Tufts took place at the Massachusetts Convention in 1873. It was sparked by four resolutions favoring the admission of women, offered by Mrs. E.M. Bruce and accompanied by a lengthy prefatory statement. The burden of the argument was as follows. At the Commencement festivities in 1872 no less a person than President Miner had stated publicly that the trustees had never opposed coeducation; the presence of women "would not be disagreeable to the students;" the faculty would be delighted to give them instruction. Therefore, the entire burden of responsibility for the exclusion of women rested on the shoulders of the people and "the backward state of public opinion."[62] Taking Miner at his word, Mrs. Bruce therefore proposed that the convention emphatically disclaim all responsibility for any backwardness or defect in the opinion of people outside of the denomination; that coeducation was a long-standing policy in Universalist schools; that denial of this "doctrine" would violate "the theories of our thinkers, the declarations of our press, and the convictions of our people;" and that, by opening its doors to women in the not-too-distant future, Tufts would cease to be an exception to the traditions of the denomination.

The future turned out to be somewhat more distant than Mrs. Bruce and her supporters had in mind, for when the resolutions were laid over until the next year, President Miner blocked their adoption.[63] He explained away his alleged statements reported the previous year as merely "sportive remarks which he had made at a commencement dinner," not enunciations of official policy. He had, he said, actually grown more and more dubious about the supposed advantages of coeducation. He wanted additional evidence before advocating it, and suggested that "separate schools for the sexes" might be a preferable route to follow. His remarks undoubtedly bore great weight, for the resolutions, preamble and all, went down to defeat by way of indefinite postponement. Universalists in favor of coeducation at Tufts had to wait almost twenty years to see their dream realized.

One of the most widely read and warmly debated books on the "woman question" in the 1870s was Edward H. Clarke's *Sex in Education; or, A Fair Chance for the Girls.*[64] Clarke, a physician, was concerned about the debilitating effects of educational effort on the physical and mental health of young women, and offered five case-studies to prove his point. Clarke, described as the "self-appointed guardian and champion" of women, brought their wrath down on his head for his patronizing and condescending tone as well as for his opposition to higher education for women. Henrietta A. Bingham, Universalist editor of the *Repository* in 1874, completely disagreed with his opposition to higher education for women.[65] They were not only completely capable, physically and mentally, of enjoying equal opportunity with young men, but should be placed in coeducational environments. This should extend, she said, throughout the school system, from the elementary grades on up, and should be reflected in female membership on school boards.

Julia Ward Howe, well-known advocate of women's rights, immediately collected reviews and other reactions to Clarke's book.[66] One of the many criticisms of Clarke was inadequate documentation for his generalizations about the experiences of women in various schools and colleges. So Mrs. Howe solicited information from several institutions where women were enrolled, including Vassar, Antioch, Oberlin, and Universalist-sponsored Lombard University. Sixty-nine men and forty-five women had been graduated from Lombard between 1868 and 1874.[67] Not a one had become an invalid, and of the twelve graduates who had died, only three were women. Twenty of the women were married and eleven had become mothers. The women were not only as healthy as the men but the health of some had visibly improved during their school years, partly because of the systematic regimen to which they had been exposed.

Olympia Brown, ordained as a Universalist minister after pursuing a regular college course at Antioch and theological training at St. Lawrence, was naturally cited by Universalists as a complete refutation of Clarke's findings.[68] It was she who had written the report on Antioch for Mrs. Howe's volume and had indicated that neither she nor the six other young women in her class had ever experienced unusual health problems while students.[69] In over ten years as a pastor, Brown "never yet was absent from an engagement or suspended labor on account of sickness." While travelling in Kansas from July to November 1867 on behalf of women's suffrage, she delivered no less than 205 discourses, and had experienced no ill effects. The author of a contemporary account of Brown's travels in Kansas called attention to the fact that she had "great physical power of endurance, lately speaking two or three times each day, in the hottest weather, travelling from twenty to fifty miles each day, with only an average of about four hours sleep, and her speeches from one to two hours in length, without apparently the least fatigue, and weighing only ninety-one pounds avoirdupois."[70] In 1874, fourteen years after her graduation from Antioch, she declared she was ready to "walk ten miles in a day with ease."[71] She considered Clarke's arguments about the precarious state of women's health in college to be "absurd." In fact, women who had graduated from college were "stronger in mind and body, able to endure more and work harder than the others."

Brown presented her ideas about higher education for women at some length in an article written in 1874.[72] She called for an ambitious program that, besides training for Christian character, would provide "an education which shall give them the executive ability of the business man, the intellectual acumen of the scholar, the comprehensive thought of the philosopher, the prophetic vision of the seer." This required "no modified course, prepared with special reference to the female mind," and no continuation of the female seminary, which was a "miserable farce," but complete equality with men in all branches of instruction. Women were likewise entitled to the franchise. "Not till women share in the responsibilities, and enjoy the privileges of the enfranchised citizen can it be expected that they will gain the highest excellence." Far from impairing the traditional positions as wife and mother, enlarged rights would strengthen them by broadening their horizons. There was no justification for confining a woman's knowledge or experience to "the half dozen or more rooms which she calls her home." It was arguments such as those offered by Brown that finally prevailed at Tufts College; the institution became coeducational in 1892 and created a coordinate college for women (Jackson College) in 1910.

Women and the Ministry

In 1838 L.F.W. Andrews, peripatetic preacher of Universalism in the South, stayed long enough in Macon, Georgia, to sit down with a copy of the *Universalist Register* at hand and count up the number of individuals who were listed as preachers in the denomination in the United States and Canada.[73] The total came to 434 men and one woman, Mrs. Mary Ann Church of Merrickville, Upper Canada. Thirty years later, there were seven women preaching Universalism; four of the seven attended the General Convention in 1868.[74] According to the editors of the *Universalist,* up to the centennial year of 1870, fifteen women had preached or were preaching under Universalist auspices.[75] They were not identified. When John G. Adams reviewed the state of the denomination in 1882, he identified nearly thirty women ministers in the *Universalist Register.*[76] By the time the Nineteenth Amendment had been ratified in 1920, eighty-eight Universalist women ministers had been ordained.[77] Taken by themselves, these statistics reveal what may seem neither very exciting nor very meaningful information. But behind them lay a very human story which sheds considerable light not only on the lives of the individuals involved but on the denomination to which they claimed allegiance.

Maria Cook (1779-1835), unmarried and about thirty years of age when she attracted the attention of Universalists, is generally considered to have been the first woman to have preached in Universalist pulpits.[78] She had held religious meetings in Sheshequin (Bradford County), Pennsylvania, about 1810, and appeared at the meeting of the Western Association (New York) in 1811 at Bainbridge (Chenango County) which convened in a newly-built barn.[79] She was escorted by "two gentlemen of the first respectability" and indicated a desire to deliver a discourse. There was much difference of opinion over whether she should be allowed to speak, but curiosity was so great about hearing a female preacher that she was permitted to do so, and apparently was a great success. A Universalist by intuition rather than knowledge, she was reported to have been "of genteel and commanding appearance, well educated, and certainly a very good speaker."[80] She was immediately tendered an "informal" letter of fellowship and invited to speak before societies elsewhere. She preached in at least five New York counties in 1811 and 1812, but she later destroyed her letter of fellowship because she believed it had not been sincerely proffered.

Opposition to her preaching because she was a woman was considerable, and her friends importuned her to give it up. They were "extremely averse to her assumption of the ministerial character; and probably not without grounds of apprehension that so extraordinary an undertaking was an evidence of *mental alienation.*" That apprehension about the tendency of women to step out of their traditional roles was to be expressed many times before the end of the nineteenth century and even after. Maria Cook was arrested as a vagrant and jailed in Cooperstown, New York, presumably by someone hoping to discredit the Universalists.[81] She was soon released and went into retirement. She was considered an "eccentric woman" by Nathaniel Stacy, who knew her. Judging from his account of her "visions and presentiments" she probably did not contribute in any substantial way to the progress of Universalism.

Sally Barnes Dunn (1783-1858), the youngest daughter of the eight children of the pioneer New England Universalist preacher, Thomas Barnes, was another woman who was considered an evangelist. She never had formal ministerial training or a pastorate, but preached frequently in Maine at conferences and other gatherings. According to George W. Quinby, Mrs. Dunn "could preach as good a sermon in ten minutes as most ministers could in an hour."[82] Thomas B. Thayer had the same reaction when he heard her speak at a meeting in Saco, Maine.[83]

The first woman to be regularly fellowshipped as a Universalist preacher was Lydia A. Jenkins of New York State. A convert from the Baptists, she began preaching in 1857; she and her husband, Edmund S. Jenkins, constituted a unique clerical team. The first record of her appearance, when she and her husband were living in Clyde (Wayne County), was at the Cayuga Association (New York) in 1857, when she offered a prayer at one service and preached at another.[84] She made a most favorable impression, although she was not considered sufficiently forceful in her delivery. This may have been accounted for by a spinal injury early in her life which left her partially crippled.[85] She was fellowshipped by the Ontario Association (New York) in 1858.[86] Mrs. Jenkins was especially active as a preacher for the next several years, and attracted so much attention that her husband, who usually accompanied her on her travels and also preached, was quite overshadowed. They moved frequently within New York State; this was probably no great hardship, for they had no children. In the spring of 1858 she attended a women's rights convention in New York City and while there delivered two sermons in T.J. Sawyer's Orchard Street church. Horace Greeley heard the first one and reported it in his *Tribune.* He called attention to the unusually large attendance, due in part to "the novelty of a woman occupying the sacred desk."[87] Greeley described her discourse as a "most interesting . . . well considered, calm, earnest presentation."

Mrs. Jenkins had become sufficiently well established and prominent as a preacher to be invited to deliver a sermon to a "great assembly" during public services at the New York Convention in 1868.[88] She also served several weeks as a supply pastor in 1858 in Williamsburg, New York, while the regular minister (Barnard Peters) was travelling in Europe.[89] In the fall of that year she visited New England and preached in Providence, Rhode Island, and extensively in the Greater Boston area.

It was no doubt Mrs. Jenkins who brought an eventual about-face in Thomas Whittemore's attitude toward women in the pulpit. After seeing Mrs. Jenkins in action at the Cayuga Association in 1857, a correspondent wrote that "if even the editor of the *Trumpet* had been present, his soul would have been moved and all opposition to female preaching would have departed."[90] It most certainly did, after Whittemore himself had seen and heard her. When he was first informed in 1857 that she was preaching, he vigorously disapproved. "It were better for her to remain at home, and attend to her domestic duties."[91] He knew of no Biblical authority for female preaching; Christ had appointed none; and none had been ordained by Christ's apostles. Whittemore considered it appropriate for women to speak at conference meetings, but no more. Then he heard Mrs. Jenkins deliver a sermon in Providence at the General Convention in 1858. He expressed cautious approval and admitted that she was "possessed of great talents."[92] After he accompanied her to Lawrence and heard her preach in that Massachusetts city a few weeks later, he went a step further. After granting that "the sermon, preached though it were by a woman, cannot possibly have done any harm," he conceded that it was one of the most effective and well-delivered sermons he had ever heard.[93]

Whittemore, like many others, was forced to admit that Mrs. Jenkins did not fit the stereotype of women who spoke in public. When she appeared in the pulpit in Erie, Pennsylvania, many in the assemblage expected to see a "large, bold and strong-bodied female, with about as much of the masculine as the feminine in her dress, and sporting, perhaps, a bloomer dress."[94] Instead, they saw a very feminine person, of delicate appearance, gentle and earnest. Mrs. Jenkins spoke to the largest audience that had yet heard her in Lowell. "The question whether a woman ought to preach, is not yet fully settled in all minds, but there is no longer any doubt that a woman *can* preach."[95] Whittemore admitted that "a woman can speak, can preach, can pray, in the pulpit, without throwing off her womanly dignity and modesty."[96]

But ordaining a woman and settling her in a pastorate was another matter. A correspondent in the *Religious Inquirer* (Unitarian) had noted in error that Mrs. Jenkins had been ordained, and wondered why Whittemore had not even mentioned it in his newspaper.[97] After all, the event should have been "hailed as an auspicious omen by . . . the friends of human rights and progressive thought in this country." Without verifying the rumor that she had actually been ordained, Whittemore replied that his silence had not meant approval. She had been ordained, he wrote, by only "a small part of the Universalist denomination . . . . The whole denomination would not like to be held accountable for it." A.B. Grosh took a middle ground by disagreeing with Whittemore about ordination. He recommended instead that, considering the state of denominational feeling, a woman should be discouraged unless she had exceptional talents and was willing to face up to "the opposition and cold frowns and doubts that must beset her pathway."[98]

Mrs. Jenkins received considerable support from Judge John Galbraith, a prominent Universalist layman in Erie, Pennsylvania, who was largely responsible for the establishment of the state industrial reform school for boys.[99] After he strongly endorsed her capabilities the constitution of the Lake Erie Association (Pennsylvania) was amended to provide that each society and church was entitled to send one woman delegate in addition to the two lay delegates already authorized.[100] As a delegate from Pennsylvania at the General Convention in 1858 he offered a resolution expressing pleasure that Mrs. Jenkins had been fellowshipped and recognizing "the right of women possessing high moral and religious attainments, and prompted to aid in the work of preaching the doctrine of Christian Universalism, to receive letters of fellowship, and engaging in the work of the ministry."[101] The resolution was indefinitely postponed.

Mrs. Jenkins was a groundbreaker in other respects than in her preaching. She was the first woman invited to deliver a Commencement address in the denomination, and possibly in the entire country.[102] The invitation was proffered by the students of Lombard University in 1859. She also set a precedent by being invited, with her husband, to hold a full-time pastorate in Clinton, New York, in 1860.[103] They actually remained in Clinton until 1862. Then they became itinerants about the state, and after a brief sojourn in New Jersey in 1864 they returned to New York State. Mrs. Jenkins preached in Cortland for one year.[104] For the remainder of their careers she and her husband resided in Binghamton and retired from the ministry. Until the time of her death she was a practicing physician, and with her husband conducted an hygienic institute.[105]

There were numerous other women both before and after 1870 who preached on a part-time basis and even obtained licenses, although they were never ordained or held regular pastorates. Many Universalist women intended to enter the ministry but never achieved their goal, for various reasons. Elsie A. Magoon of Bombay, New York, informed Thomas Whittemore in 1859 that she had done some preaching and hoped, after her four children were older, to prepare for the ministry.[106] Elvira J. Powers, who had been a nurse during the Civil War, and wrote of her experiences in a book entitled *Hospital Pencilings,* began to read theology in 1866 and was admitted to the Canton Theological School.[107] But she had to abandon her studies after

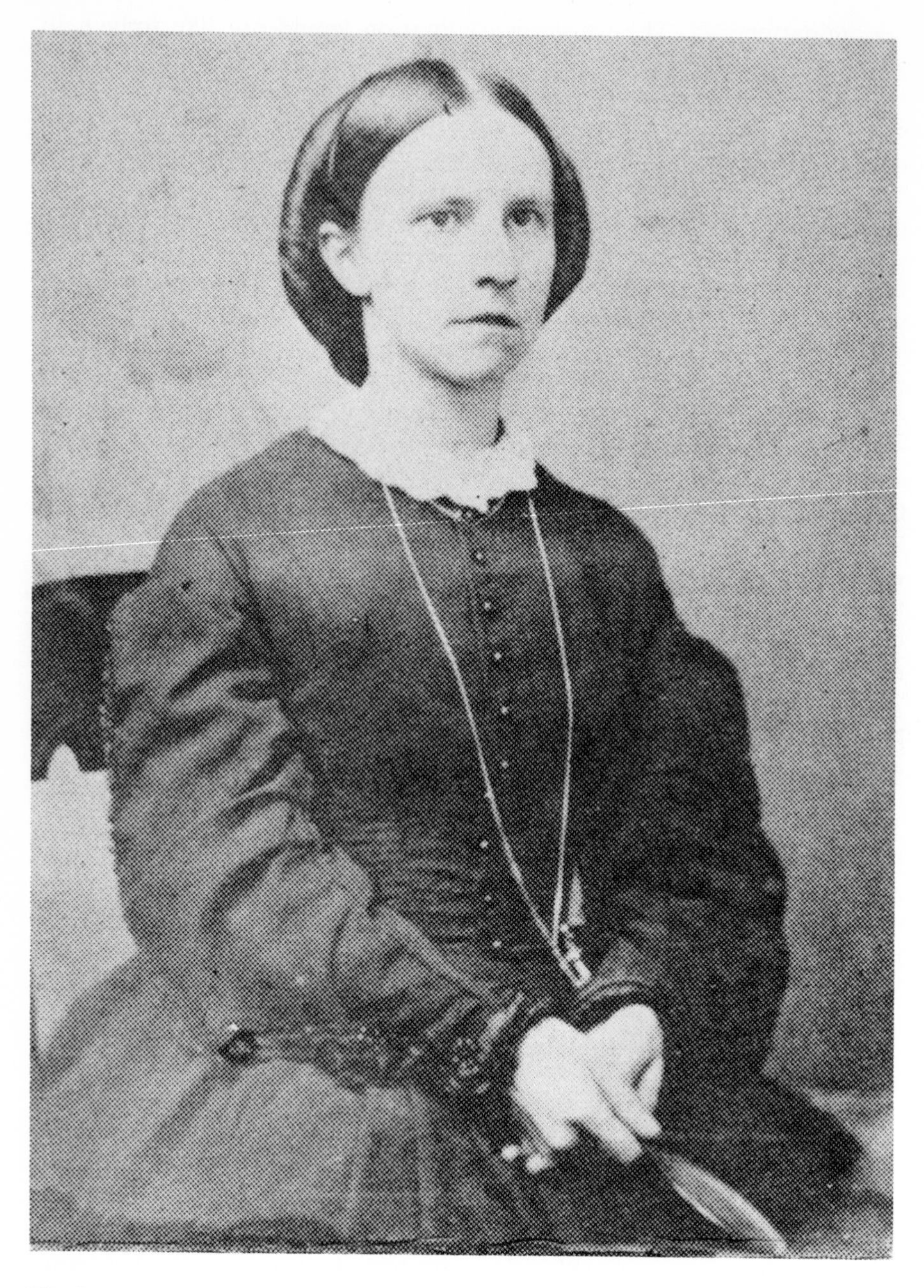

The Rev. Olympia Brown (1835-1926), the first woman to receive fully recognized ordination in America (1863)

six months because of poor health, and died in Worcester, Massachusetts, in 1871.

Some women might have been ministers but elected other careers. Harriott K. Hunt (1805-1875), one of the first women physicians in the United States, started out as a Universalist.[108] Her parents had been converted by John Murray.[109] Shortly after she was born she was dedicated by Murray, who presented her with a Bible in which he had inscribed her name.[110] After twenty-five years in the medical profession, in which she became quite wealthy, she became a missionary preacher in 1859 in New England.[111] In 1870, five years before her death, she became a member of the Swedenborgian church. She lived most of her life in Boston where she acquired her medical education through private instruction. After she acquired a fortune she paid her taxes under protest because women were denied the vote and had no direct representation.[112]

Mary A. Livermore, who delivered addresses and sermons in many churches, was asked repeatedly why she did not enter the ministry. With characteristic forthrightness she replied publicly in 1868. She had a basic responsibility to her husband (Daniel P. Livermore, himself a Universalist minister) and to her home. If one entered the ministry it had to be the primary commitment. Furthermore, she had no predeliction for such a career; her interests ran in other channels.[113] She confessed that early in her married life she was neither a good housekeeper nor cook. She strongly advocated training in these arts. Higher education for women was all very well, but "lower education" was equally important. "While the world stands, the majority of women will always be wives, mothers, mistresses of homes, and . . . for these positions they require thorough and special training."[114]

A milestone was reached when Olympia Brown became not onl, the first ordained woman minister in the denomination but the first in the United States to have been ordained with full denominational authority.[115] The first woman ordained in America, and the first to perform a marriage ceremony, was Antoinette Louisa Brown Blackwell (1825-1921). She was ordained in 1853 by the Congregational church in South Butler, New York, but without the concurrence of the Congregational General Conference, She preached as a Congregationalist for less than a year, and was later fellowshipped by the Unitarians.[116] When it was reported that (then) Antoinette Brown had resigned her pastorate in 1854, Sylvanus Cobb approved her decision. There were "certain branches of labor to which [women] are not, all things considered, naturally adapted."[117] Holding a pastoral office was one of these. It was Cobb who preached the sermon at Olympia Brown's installation as pastor of the society in Weymouth, Massachusetts, in 1864.

Olympia Brown (1835-1926) was born in Prairie Ronde (Kalamazoo

County), Michigan, on 5 January 1835, the eldest of four children of Universalist parents. She attended Mt. Holyoke Female Seminary in 1854-55 and Antioch College, from which she graduated in 1860 and received an honorary Master of Arts in 1867. She was influenced in her decision to become a minister after hearing Antoinette Brown Blackwell. Brown had invited her to speak at Antioch while an undergraduate. She was discouraged in her attempt to gain admission to several theological schools, including the Meadville Theological School (Unitarian) in Pennsylvania. The Canton Theological School at St. Lawrence University, headed by Ebenezer Fisher, reluctantly admitted her.[118] Her student days there were by no means easy ones, for she encountered prejudice from almost every quarter. She wrote several years afterward that she had come away "with every feeling outraged and my nervous system permanently shattered, through the persecutions which I had endured at that institution inflicted solely because I, a woman, was seeking a chance to do the work to which the Lord had called me."[119] She had expected no recommendation, and had received none.

After her ordination by the St. Lawrence Association in June 1863, Brown held a brief pastorate as a supply minister in Marshfield, Vermont, and in 1864 accepted a call to the Universalist society in Weymouth, Massachusetts. She had obtained the position on her own initiative, after Alonzo A. Miner was generous enough to inform her that a vacancy existed. It was not a very encouraging prospect. The society was small, "mostly rationalistic," had been without a regular minister or even a Sunday School for two years, and was heavily in debt. The meeting house was about to be leased as a public hall. Both Universalist and neighboring ministers had been uncooperative and had meddled with her pastoral work and had even tried to turn some of her congregation against her. All she had asked was a fair chance, not preferential treatment, and certainly not roadblocks.

Perhaps she felt she had given too gloomy or one-sided a picture of her experiences, for a few weeks later she was looking on the brighter side.[120] She acknowledged that while at St. Lawrence a few of the students and some of the faculty had supported her. There were, indeed, many faithful Universalists in her Weymouth congregation, and the debt which she had reported earlier had been paid off. When she wrote her autobiography in 1911 she considered her pastorate in Weymouth "perhaps the most enjoyable part of my ministerial career."[121]

There had been no outcry from the denominational press when Brown was ordained. The individual who had reported her ordination and installation in the *Universalist* in 1864 had taken the opportunity to comment that while she might have been "an exception to the majority of her sex" in the choice of a vocation, "every consideration

The Rev. Augusta Jane Chapin (1836-1905), the second Universalist woman to be ordained (1863) and the first woman in America to receive an honorary D.D. (1893)

of religious freedom requires that she should be allowed to go on in the way she has chosen."[122] After completing her first year in Weymouth the *Universalist* gave her honorable mention for her excellent work. "If all the ministers of the stronger sex had half the zeal and industry, the results would be apparent in prospering parishes."[123]

Brown served the Weymouth congregation for six years, and for the next six years, beginning in 1870, the society in Bridgeport, Connecticut. While residing in that state she delivered the occasional sermon at the Connecticut State Convention in 1872.[124] She was the first woman to be accorded that honor. In 1878 she was pastor in Racine, Wisconsin. Her parish complimented her by paying for a life membership in the Woman's Centenary Association.[125] After a nine-year pastorate she resigned in order to devote more time to the women's suffrage movement in which she had already become involved. She continued, however, to preach on an occasional basis. In 1873 she married John Henry Willis, a businessman and newspaper publisher. She elected for the rest of her life to use her maiden name. After his death in 1893 she supervised his business until 1900. She died in 1926 at the home of her daughter in Baltimore at the age of ninety-one.

The second woman to be ordained as a Universalist minister was Augusta Jane Chapin (1836-1905). She was born in Lakeville, New York, on 16 July 1836, the oldest of eleven children. She died in New York City on 30 June 1905. She grew up in Michigan, attended Olivet College and Michigan Female College (which closed), and received a Master of Arts degree from the University of Michigan which she attended between 1882 and 1884. She decided to become a Universalist minister while attending Olivet. She planned to obtain further education at Lombard University, even though it did not yet have a divinity school at the time. Instead, she became an itinerant preacher in Michigan. Many years later, Lombard, in recognition of her services, conferred on her the honorary Master of Arts degree (1868) and an honorary Doctor of Divinity degree (1893). She was the first woman in the United States to be awarded such a degree.[126]

Miss Chapin was fellowshipped in 1862 by the Michigan State Convention and was ordained in Lansing, Michigan, in December 1863, the same year as Olympia Brown. She was preeminent as a missionary preacher, and between 1864 and 1901 she served over a dozen pastorates and preaching stations spread over fifteen states, among them California. She was the first ordained woman minister to serve on the council of the General Convention (as a delegate from Iowa at the Centennial Convocation in 1870). She was also one of the organizers of the Woman's Centenary Association in 1871.

Phebe Ann Coffin Hanaford (1829-1921), the third woman ordained in the Universalist ministry, like most of the others, had many interests besides preaching and parish work. An author, lecturer for the

The Rev. Phebe Hanaford (1829-1921), writer, lecturer, and supporter of women's suffrage, ordained in 1868

temperance cause, peace advocate, magazine editor, and supporter of women's suffrage, Mrs. Hanaford was the epitomé of the active woman. She was born in Nantucket, Massachusetts, on 6 May 1829 and died in Rochester, New York, on 2 June 1921 at the age of ninety-two. Reared as a Quaker, she joined the Universalist society in Reading, Massachusetts in 1864. She had married Joseph Hibbard Hanaford, a physician, in 1849. She was ordained in Hingham, Massachusetts, in 1868 without having ever received formal theological training or even having graduated from any of the schools she attended on Nantucket Island.[127] She was one of the many women Brown had encouraged to go into the ministry. It was the latter who gave Mrs. Hanaford the right hand of fellowship at her ordination and delivered the sermon at the installation.[128] The six hymns rendered on the two occasions had all been written by women, among them the ordination hymn composed by Julia Ward Howe. Hymns at all of Mrs. Hanaford's installations were written by women.[129] Much to the disgust of Mrs. C.A. Winship, who wrote the account which appeared in the *Universalist,* the hymns were all "lined out" for singing by men.

Mrs. Hanaford had preached occasionally before her ordination, not only in Hingham in 1866 but in Gardiner, Maine, and in churches elsewhere. After preaching three sermons in one day in Maine in 1867 she reported the experience with enthusiasm. "The old prejudices all melted away" when people learned that a woman could preach as well as a man.[130] Between 1869 and 1891 she held pastorates in Waltham, Massachusetts; New Haven, Connecticut; Jersey City, New Jersey; and Newport, Rhode Island. She had the sad distinction of conducting two of the funeral services for co-workers in the women's suffrage movement–for Susan B. Anthony and Elizabeth Cady Stanton.

In her capacity as an ordained minister Mrs. Hanaford claimed an impressive number of "firsts" which she recorded in the writeup of herself in her *Daughters of America,* one of the fourteen books she wrote. She was, among other precedent-setters, the first woman regularly ordained in Massachusetts; the first to participate in the ordination of her own son (Howard Hanaford, who became a Congregational minister); the first to officiate at the marriage of her own daughter (Florence); the first regularly appointed woman chaplain to officiate in the Connecticut legislature, and was "the first woman in the world who ever officiated in such capacity in a legislative body of men;" the first woman to offer a dedicatory prayer at the dedication of a Universalist church (Waterbury, Connecticut, 1872); the first of her sex to give the charge at the ordination of a male minister (W.G. Haskell, Marblehead, Massachusetts).[131] Probably no other woman in the ministry could claim so many pioneering contributions.

No attempt has been made here to identify or chronicle the lives or indicate the accomplishments of all of the women ministers in the denomination in the nineteenth century, many of whom were still active well into the twentieth. By the time of the centennial in 1870, five had been ordained, many more preached on a part-time basis or were engaged in theological training or had obtained licenses to preach.[132] Some, like Lorenza Haynes (1820-1899), entered the ministry in middle age; she was ordained in 1875. Caroline Soule (1824-1903) was ordained in Glasgow, Scotland, in 1880, at the age of fifty-six. Many women who might not have entered the ministry at all did so through the encouragement of such pioneers as Brown, Chapin, Mrs. Hanaford, and Mrs. Soule.

Caroline Augusta White Soule, whose career rivalled that of Hanaford in scope and variety, was born into a Universalist family in Albany, New York, on 3 September 1824. She died in Scotland on 6 December 1903.[133] She graduated with high honors from the Albany Female Academy in 1841 and the next year became principal for a brief period of the young woman's department of Clinton Liberal Institute, where she met and married in 1843, Henry Soule. At the time she met him he was principal of the young men's department. Between 1844 and his premature death in 1852, he held pastorates in Massachusetts and Connecticut, and was about to move to New York State. When he died his widow was left with five small children and almost no resources. She supported her family with aid from friends and with her pen. After a decade of frontier living in Iowa (1853-63), she returned to the East.

Mrs. Soule was one of the founders of the Woman's Centenary Aid Association and its first president. After it became the Woman's Centenary Association she continued as its head for almost a decade. It was she who was largely responsible not only for fund-raising but for mailing out thousands of Universalist tracts. She became the first foreign missionary in the denomination, living most of her remaining life in Scotland between 1875 and 1903.

In 1874, after fifteen years of uninterrupted pulpit and parish activity which included rural neighborhoods in the West and familiarity with religious activities in over a dozen states, Augusta Chapin reviewed her career and took stock of the status of women in the Universalist ministry. She came to the conclusion that the "experimental stage" was long since over and that those in the ministry could carry on a multiplicity of activities with even less complaint than men.[134] The Universalists had more ordained women than any other branch of the Christian church. Most were married and none of them were "exceptional or peculiar in their temperament and disposition." All were earnest, devoted women who had vindicated their right to appear in Universalist pulpits.

While Universalist women were proving themselves in the ministry the men were still debating the entire question. One wrote that "I individually cannot countenance, and dislike to have cast up to me . . . this woman preaching feature."[135] Prejudice against Universalists was already great enough without making it any worse. The correspondent's indignation was heightened by a news item in the *Boston Traveller* reporting a marriage ceremony conducted by Mrs. Hanaford, assisted by Brown. "To make the affair complete, the bridegroom will hereafter be known by the family name of the bride." As the bridegroom himself pointed out a few weeks after the original article had been reproduced in a Philadelphia paper, the statement that he had assumed his wife's name was "editorial drollery descended into falsehood."[136] It had been only another way of calling attention to the vagaries of Universalists. The bridegroom had deliberately chosen Mrs. Hanaford to officiate because he wanted to emphasize his support of women's rights. He knew of no authority that had bestowed on men the right to define the sphere of women.

The inevitable debates took place over whether there was Scriptural precedent or authority for women ministers. For weeks this subject was discussed between two correspondents in the *Universalist* in 1870 until the editors brought the exchanges to a halt.[137] The editors of the *Universalist* resisted the whole idea of a "woman ministry." Even though there was an acknowledged critical shortage of clergy in the denomination, they refused to concede an official place for women. The majority would fail; it was "a waste of money and effort to engage in fitting young women for the duty of pastors and preachers."[138] Women would inevitably be measured by standards different from those applied to men and would make "the 'woman question' an eternal one."[139] If women were encouraged to become ministers as a matter of denominational policy the demand would soon exhaust existing educational facilities and resources. One-half to two-thirds of those women would marry and would (and should) retire from the ministry. So much for a costly and impractical experiment.

George S. Weaver, a long-time clergyman, was quite exasperated by all of the talk about establishing a "woman ministry." All that was needed was a "human ministry." Why should masculinity confer any divine right to the ministerial office? If women wanted to try their hand at it, and succeeded, "all the more honor to them . . . . whether they do better or worse, a church that has stood the failures and blunders of a man ministry as long as the Christian church, need not fear the experiment of a few women preachers. They may know themselves, better than we men, whether God calls them or not."[140] Erasmus Manford summed it up this way: "Some of our people are opposed to women being in the ministry, but those we have in the work are quite as successful as the best men. That is a pretty strong argument for the women!"[141] Even then, the debate was far from over.

The Rev. Caroline Augusta Soule (1824-1903), first President of the Woman's Centenary Association (1869-1880)

Women and Literature

If comparatively few Universalist women entered the ministry, the situation was quite otherwise in the field of literature. They wrote both prose and poetry by the ream, and much of it attracted attention outside the denomination. In 1853 Sarah Josepha Hale, author and poetess, champion of women's rights, co-editor of *Godey's Lady's Book* for forty years (1837-77), and largely responsible for making Thanksgiving a national holiday, edited a monumental biographical dictionary of famous women in history which went through many editions.[142] Six Universalist women were included in the 1860 edition, some of them in a separate section on "Young Writers," some of whose contributions had not yet been collected in book form, but who showed much promise. John G. Adams, in his review of the denomination in 1882, considered twenty-three women authors worthy of mention by name.[143] Some were little known in their own day, and the literary quality of some of their output possibly explained the obscurity which descended on them and their works.

Mrs. Hanaford, the third woman to be ordained in the Universalist ministry and one of the most prolific writers in the denomination, admitted that much of her writing was inferior, sandwiched as it was between pastoral, domestic, and other duties, and much of it commissioned and composed under pressure. She considered the hundreds of poetic pieces she had produced "for all sorts of occasions" not "equally worthy of publication."[144]

Some of the names associated with literature were not familiar even to Universalists, let alone to the outside literary world, but they left some kind of a record and deserve at least brief mention. Many wrote on a variety of topics that carried them far beyond sentimental poetry and romantic tales. And many, like Mrs. Hanaford and Mrs. Soule, were frank to say that they wrote in order to add to family coffers. Much, but by no means all, of the writings of the women appeared in Universalist publications such as the *Rose of Sharon* and the *Ladies' Repository,* some of which the women themselves edited. Their editorial work was usually considered above reproach. Only one had to be removed from her position by the publisher for failure to perform satisfactorily. The reason was simple; she had, by any standards, attempted to take on too much.

In 1866 Mrs. Hanaford was employed by the Universalist Publishing House to edit the *Ladies' Repository* and at the same time edit the *Myrtle,* a Sunday School paper. If that were not enough, she had charge of the children's department of the *Universalist,* which appeared weekly, and she proofread the *Universalist Quarterly.*[145] When word spread that Mrs. Hanaford had been forced to resign in 1868, the *New*

Covenant (Chicago) raised a hue and cry and alleged the real reason was that the Publishing House did "not believe in women ministers."[146] To make matters worse, Mrs. Hanaford had not been allowed to publish the customary "valedictory" on departing from the editorship. The *Star in the West* (Cincinnati), the leading denominational paper in the Midwest, also demanded an explanation.

The Publishing House, by way of the *Universalist,* replied to the "untrue allegations." Benton Smith, the business agent, had had to seek a replacement for Mrs. Hanaford because complaints had been made about the manner in which her work was being done; she was neglecting her obligations; other individuals had to cover for her, while she continued to receive her full salary ($600 a year).[147] She had been warned when she announced that she was entering the ministry in addition to all of her other activities (including domestic obligations and temperance lectures), that this new responsibility would seriously interfere with her work. But she went ahead with her plans. As to the alleged prejudice against women ministers, Smith had no objection whatsoever to such, and in fact had been, as himself an ordained clergyman, on the ordaining council of a woman. The claim that Mrs. Hanaford had not been given an opportunity to publish a farewell to her readers was easily explained. It was the policy of the Publishing House to edit their periodical publications "impersonally;" hence no names appeared. The interests of the denomination had to take priority over individual interests. The rule, approved by Sylvanus Cobb, George H. Emerson, and others when the Publishing House had been established in 1862, had worked admirably, and there was no reason to change it.

Mrs. Hanaford's hand was very visible, anonymity or not, during the three years she edited the *Ladies' Repository*. The number of articles and news notes dealing with women's rights, and particularly the suffrage agitation, went up sharply. In acknowledging a letter from Brown relating her experiences in 1867 in behalf of women's suffrage in Kansas, Mrs. Hanaford wrote that eventually, "as sure as Universalism is true, their cause . . . will triumph."[148] Mrs. Hanaford published in the *Ladies' Repository* several articles by Mercy B. Jackson, who favored the entrance of women into the professions. Mrs. Jackson, who died in 1877, was a homeopathic physician and member of the Shawmut Avenue Universalist church in Boston. After her husband's death she had attended the New England Female Medical College from which she graduated in 1860.[149] She conducted a successful practice in Boston and became a specialist in children's diseases.

Mrs. Hanaford cited Mrs. Jackson as evidence that the Universalists were "in advance of most all others in according to woman an open field for usefulness." She may also have had in mind her own installation in the ministry a few months before.[150] She probably shocked some of the readers of the *Ladies' Repository* when, in commenting on an article contributed by Mrs. Jackson arguing for greater opportunities for women in the medical profession, Mrs. Hanaford said she knew of no reason why women physicians could not treat men. After all, they had treated women for a long time.[151]

No attempt has been made here to catalogue all of the Universalist women who contributed to the tremendous outpouring of literature, good and bad, which would be an unprofitable exercise at best; only those have been included who were recognized outside the denomination, and those considered to have made substantial contributions to it. Literary efforts by women were always welcomed in Universalist periodicals, and an analysis of the contents of almost any would confirm this. There was no lack of opportunity to appear in print.

Three of the earliest women writers who achieved considerable prominence were Julia H. Kinney Scott, Sarah C. Edgarton Mayo, and Caroline M. Sawyer. Julia Scott (1809-1842), who attracted Mrs. Hale's attention in her biographical dictionary, was born in Sheshequin (Bradford County), Pennsylvania, and died in 1842 at the age of thirty-three. She began writing for Universalist papers at the age of sixteen and in 1835 was married to David L. Scott, a physician. She wrote "poetry of the household, full of gentle and feminine feeling and tender pathos."[152] A year after her death, a memoir of her was published by (then) Miss Sarah C. Edgarton, with samples of Mrs. Scott's poetry. However, the volume provoked a sharp controversy both among Mrs. Scott's family and her friends. The hastily assembled biography ignored the fact that she was a Universalist, and the author changed the titles of some of the poems and made other unauthorized editorial alterations.[153] A far superior treatment of Mrs. Scott and her writings was prepared by Caroline M. Sawyer in 1853.[154] A.B. Grosh, editor of the *Evangelical Magazine and Gospel Advocate* (Utica, New York), recognized her poetic talents, and her compositions appeared in the *Rose of Sharon* and other magazines.

Sarah C. Edgarton Mayo (1819-1848), a native of Massachusetts who for several years was responsible for editing the *Rose of Sharon,* had served earlier on the staff of the *Universalist* and the *Ladies' Repository.* She married A.D. Mayo, a Universalist clergyman, less than a year before her death at the age of twenty-nine. Her special interest was poetry, often with a religious cast; representative was a series of sonnets based on the Lord's Prayer, written jointly with Charlotte Fillebrown Jerauld (1820-1845).[155] Mrs. Mayo's *The Flower Vase,* a collection of poems published in 1843, was one of her most popular works. A reviewer (male) paid the author the compliment of saying that the poetry seemed "wholly free from the vapid nonsense and sickly sentimentality which frequently characterizes works of this description." Before the end of 1844 the book had gone through ten printings of 1,000 copies each.[156] The premature deaths of Mrs. Mayo and Mrs. Jerauld gave ample opportunity for expressing sentimentality.[157] After Mrs. Mayo's death in 1848 the General Convention, for the first time in its history, paid an official tribute to the contributions of women to the denomination. It adopted a "special resolution" recognizing by name Mrs. Mayo, Mrs. Scott, and Mrs. Jerauld, all of whom having "done so much to adorn our literature and elevate [their] sex."[158]

Caroline Mehitable Fisher Sawyer (1812-1894), one of the best known Universalist women in the nineteenth century, wrote extensively for denominational publications and led an active life in many other respects. While her husband, whom she had married in 1831, held a pastorate in New York City (1830-1845) she reared five children and conducted extensive charity work through the Dorcas Society, which she organized.[159] She had written considerable poetry by the time she was thirteen; studied Hebrew and German; and published a series of short stories and works for young people while editor of the Youth Department of the *Universalist Union* published in New York City. She also contributed to *Graham's Magazine* and the *Democratic Review,* the editor of which, John L. O'Sullivan, coined the expression "manifest destiny" in reference to American territorial expansionism. Horace Greeley, one of her husband's parishioners, discussed his plans to publish the *New York Tribune* at several of his visits to the Sawyer home in 1841. Greeley sought Mrs. Sawyer's reaction to the first issue before it was placed on newsstands.[160]

Sarah Josepha Hale, in her sketch of Mrs. Sawyer in her biographical dictionary, noted that the quality of her writings indicated a "thorough and extensive education" and that she possessed "a mind of much power."[161] Mrs. Hale was particularly impressed with Mrs. Sawyer's excellent translations of German folk tales, many of which appeared in the *Ladies' Repository* and the *Rose of Sharon,* both of which she edited for part of their history. Mrs. Sawyer's poetry was also included in several nineteenth-century anthologies, among them Carolina May's *American Female Poets* and T. Buchanan Read's *Female Poets.*[162] Her printed poetry was never collected, and she kept no written copies.[163]

If Mrs. Hale's judgment as to the importance of Universalist women writers is taken seriously (and it was in the nineteenth century), four more should be at least identified. They were the Cary sisters, Alice and Phoebe, Luella B. Case, and Mary Ann Hanmer Dodd. Alice and Phoebe Cary (1820-1871 and 1824-1871, respectively) rated five pages in Mrs. Hale's dictionary. Alice, who always overshadowed her younger sister, had her portrait reproduced in a pen-and-ink sketch, had ten of her short poems reproduced; four of Phoebe's were also included. Both sisters showed, according to Mrs. Hale, a lack of formal training in their poetic productions, but their work was "outstanding." Erasmus

Manford, a Universalist clergyman who lived in their home near Cincinnati for two years (1839-40), had known them when they were in their 'teens, and left an interesting comparative character sketch of the two sisters in his autobiography; he also possessed an oil portrait of each.[164]

Luella Juliette Bartlett Case (1807-1857), born in Kingston, New Hampshire, was the granddaughter of Governor Josiah Bartlett, a signer of the Declaration of Independence. She married a Universalist clergyman and newspaper editor, Eliphalet Case, in 1828. She contributed poetry to both Universalist literary journals and newspapers, among the latter the *Star of Bethlehem* (Lowell, Massachusetts) in which Thomas B. Thayer and Abel C. Thomas also published the writings of Lowell factory girls before Thomas began the *Lowell Offering.*

Mary Ann Hanmer Dodd, born in 1813 in Hartford, Connecticut, was probably the poet least known even among Universalists who were included in Mrs. Hale's biographical dictionary. She was described as "not as generally appreciated as she deserves to be," although some of her poems were "gems of thought and feeling."[165] Two of Mrs. Dodd's collections of poetry were published: *Poems,* and *Frederick Lee; or, the Christmas Present.*[166]

The decades preceding the Civil War seemed to have represented the heyday of feminine literary production in the denomination.[167] The talents of the women after 1865 were turned more and more into other channels.

Movers and Shapers: The Struggle for Women's Rights

The movement for the enlargement of the rights of women and the removal of historic restrictions achieved national dimensions before the Civil War. The precipitants were not only a growing awareness among women of their key role in shaping American society but the discovery that their effective participation in such vital reforms as the abolition of slavery and temperance was either seriously limited or completely blocked. They discovered that they were not welcome on the lecture platform or in the deliberations of reform organizations. They likewise became more conscious than ever before that their opportunities in education, employment, voting and office-holding, and their legal rights in marriage, property-holding and inheritance either did not exist or were drastically limited. They expressed mounting resentment at the widespread notion that they were mentally inferior; and they were increasingly irritated by the patronizing and condescending attitude reflected even among some of the men who sympathized with their drive for full participation in society.

Alice and Phoebe Cary (1820-1871, 1824-1871), two poetic sisters

The meeting called by Lucretia Mott and Elizabeth Cady Stanton in Seneca Falls, New York, in 1848, was but the first of many organized efforts to achieve women's rights. Susan B. Anthony, already active in the abolition and temperance agitation, contributed her leadership to the broadening of the movement, as did Lucy Stone, known for her oratorical abilities. Dramatic progress had been made by the time the Civil War had been fought. But there was unfinished business of all kinds, obstacles yet to be overcome, and victories yet to be won.

With the abolition of Negro slavery, accomplished in 1864 by constitutional amendment, there was still the temperance movement; the removal of remaining legal disabilities encountered by women; the problems of employment, wage discrimination, and child labor; and above all the matter of suffrage. Women had seen the Negro granted citizenship by the Fourteenth Amendment in 1868 and enfranchised in 1870 by the Fifteenth Amendment; many women had labored to bring these fundamental changes about. Yet they still found themselves excluded from voting rights even though they met the constitutional definition of citizenship. The great task that lay before the women was, in short, to bring to pass the Declaration of Independence which they had reworded in 1848 declaring the self-evident truth that all men *and women* were created equal. For the half-century after 1870 it was the gaining of the right to vote and hold public elective office to which the greatest attention was directed.

Universalist women were to be found in all of these reforms and more. They knew, worked closely with, and were identified with those women who had spearheaded the women's rights movement. They joined organizations to defend and promote the rights of women, and frequently served as officers. The first three women to be ordained in the Universalist ministry (Olympia Brown, Augusta Chapin, and Phebe Hanaford), while winning the right to enter that once all-male preserve, did battle on other fronts as well. A fourth (Mary A. Livermore), who became preeminent in almost every major reform cause both before and after 1870 and championed the cause of women throughout her life, was considered by her contemporaries to be "one of the most remarkable of the women of the nineteenth century."[168]

Brown, active in the women's suffrage movement beginning in the 1860s, lived to see the Nineteenth Amendment ratified in 1920, and to vote in a national election.[169] While pastor of the Weymouth society (1864-1869) she attended a suffrage convention in New York City and had become a charter member of the American Equal Rights Association in 1866 which had been organized to advance the interests of both Negroes and women. In this way she met the leaders of the suffrage movement, which became more and more important in her thinking. In 1867 the first political test for women's suffrage took place in Kansas by way of a referendum on taking the words "male" and

"Negro" out of voting requirements. With a leave of absence from the Weymouth society, Brown campaigned vigorously in Kansas for several weeks, together with Mrs. Stanton and Miss Anthony. She wrote Mrs. Hanaford about her efforts: "I must fight this campaign out if the world comes to an end as a consequence."[170]

The efforts were unsuccessful at the time, but the supporters of women's suffrage only intensified their efforts. In 1868 Brown became a member of the New England Woman's Suffrage Association, of which Julia Ward Howe was president.[171] Brown, after moving to Wisconsin, was elected president of the state Woman Suffrage Association in 1884, a position which she held for over a quarter of a century. She also served as vice president of the National Woman Suffrage Association organized by Mrs. Stanton and Miss Anthony in 1869.

Mrs. Hanaford was, like Brown, active in many reform movements, and they extended over an even wider field. She was active in the American Woman Suffrage Association organized in 1869 as a rival to the National Woman Suffrage Association. The two were merged as the National American Woman Suffrage Association in 1890. In 1874, a year after it was organized, Mrs. Hanaford served as one of the vice presidents of the Association for the Advancement of Women (Women's Congress). She was active also in the temperance movement, and was an officer of the Daughters of Temperance and women's auxiliary lodges of the Good Templars.[172] She was a vice president of the Woman's Peace Convention in 1870 called by Julia Ward Howe in New York City and delivered an address which was later published.[173] She opposed capital punishment so vociferously that she ran head-on into the opposition of the *Universalist.* In 1871, while she was living in Connecticut, a convicted murderer was hanged in the state. She delivered a sermon on the subject in which she flayed the state and the law, and called the execution a case of "judicial murder."[174] The *Universalist* considered her discourse "singularly intemperate" and criticized her for appealing to the passions of the moment. She replied by refusing to modify her position in any way.[175]

Augusta Chapin's activities outside the ministry and the denomination were both numerous and varied. Her particular interests in literature were reflected in lectureships at both Lombard University and the University of Chicago. Not as deeply involved as Brown or Mrs. Hanaford in the suffrage movement, she was nonetheless active as a member of the first executive committee of the Association for the Advancement of Women, and presented a paper at its first meeting in 1873 on "Women and the Ministry" which was published the following year.[176] She attended numerous meetings promoting both women's suffrage and temperance.

Of all the Universalist women active in nineteenth-century reform causes, it was Mary A. Livermore (1820-1905) whose name appeared

Mary A. Livermore (1820-1905), lecturer, organizer of soldiers' services during the Civil War, and leader in the women's rights movement

most frequently and over the longest time-span.[177] Born in Boston on 19 December 1820 near historic Old North Church, Mary Ashton Rice Livermore died in Melrose, Massachusetts, on 23 May 1905. After two years on the frontier in New York State where her father had moved when he caught the "western fever," she returned to Boston. She completed the four-year course in two years at the (Baptist) Female Seminary in Charlestown and was immediately placed on its staff. Between 1841 and 1843 she served as a tutor to the six children of James Henderson, owner of a large plantation in southern Virginia. It was here that she developed her life-long aversion to slavery and became a confirmed abolitionist.

After returning to New England she resided in Duxbury, Massachusetts, where in 1844 she met and married in 1845 Daniel Parker Livermore, the local Universalist clergyman. She had long before had doubts about belief in predestination and endless punishment which had been part of her Calvinistic Baptist upbringing. She had, in fact, learned sufficient Greek on her own initiative to read the New Testament in that language. She found no evidence of the doctrine of endless punishment. Her religious beliefs satisfactorily settled, she conducted a coeducational school in Duxbury between 1844 and 1847, where she introduced such educational innovations as student self-government, and assigned contemporary literature rather than conventional school readers. She had a facile pen and unusually well-developed verbal intelligence, demonstrated before she was in her 'teens. She spent much of her leisure time writing hymns, "poems for all sorts of occasions," essays, and sketches, many of which were published in local papers and magazines.

Her husband held several brief pastorates in Massachusetts, Connecticut, and New York, and then moved to Illinois. Between 1858 and 1869 he edited the *New Covenant,* the leading denominational newspaper in the Northwest, to which Mrs. Livermore frequently contributed as a writer as well as assistant in publication. At the same time, she wrote voluminously for other Universalist publications, and for three years edited the *Lily of the Valley*. Before she had been in Chicago for long, she plunged into philanthropic, charitable, and church work. She served on the board of directors of the Chicago Home for the Friendless; helped establish the Home for Aged Women, and a hospital for women and children; and was active in the Bible class and Sunday School of the Church of the Redeemer (Universalist). She was "the moving spirit" in the Northwestern Conference which assumed the responsibility for raising a $100,000 endowment for Lombard University, assisting churches to pay off debts, and in general aiding the Universalist cause in the Midwest.

Between 1862 and 1865 she was the agent for the United States Sanitary Commission in the Northwest and organized a huge fair which netted over $100,000 to assist in relief work for soldiers. Besides this, she travelled extensively, visiting military installations and hospitals. Mrs. Livermore used the columns of the *New Covenant* to keep readers abreast of her many activities, and in 1888 published *My Story of the War: A Woman's Narrative of Four Years' Personal Experience.*[178] The 700-page book had sold over 50,000 copies by 1896. Mrs. Livermore was a great admirer of Abraham Lincoln and twice had an opportunity to see and hear him.[179] She was present as a reporter for the *New Covenant* when he was nominated for the presidency in 1860; and was part of a delegation from Illinois during the war which had an audience with him.

By 1881 Mrs. Livermore was serving simultaneously as president of the Massachusetts Woman's Christian Temperance Union; as an officer of the Woman's Educational and Industrial Union, of which she became a life member; the Woman's Congress; and as a trustee of the New England Female Medical College in Boston. She also preached (although neither fellowshipped nor ordained) about half the Sundays in the year.[180] She travelled and lectured in Europe as well as in the United States. While abroad in 1876 she attended the preliminary sessions in Paris of the International Women's Rights Congress which she, Mrs. Stanton, and Julia Ward Howe had organized. Before the end of her life the number of organizations to which she belonged was legion. Among others, she served as president of the Massachusetts Woman Suffrage Association, and for over fifteen years was president of the Beneficent Society of the New England Conservatory of Music in Boston. This auxiliary organization assisted indigent young people to obtain a musical education. Several years after she had decided that political activism was one of the most effective avenues for achieving women's goals, she served as a delegate to the Massachusetts State Republican Convention, where she presented the temperance and women's suffrage resolutions incorporated into the party platform. This selected list of her organizational affiliations gives some indication of the directions in which her interests pointed.

Livermore took advantage of every opportunity to promote the women's rights movement, whether within the denomination or outside. She took Universalists to task constantly and sometimes with severe language for failing to enlist women in the full range of activities. They could do much more, she said in 1865, than holding tea parties to benefit Sunday Schools or operating fairs to help pay ministerial salaries.[181] She delivered one of the major addresses during the annual Anniversary Week in Boston in 1870. She chose as her topic "The Work of the Universalist Church" and developed at some length the theme that the denomination had failed miserably to utilize the resources of its women.[182] The women should be found everywhere—on boards of trustees of schools and colleges operated by the denomination, on the rosters of officers of Universalist conventions and associations, and in the General Convention itself.

Up to the time of her own experiences in the Civil War, Livermore had agitated, on the lecture platform and in the *New Covenant* and other Universalist publications, for the opening of all colleges and professional schools to women, and for enhanced employment opportunities. She took every occasion she could to call attention to the unhappy fact that Tufts College (until 1892) was closed to women. Before 1865 she felt that all of these goals could be reached without resort to the ballot by women. But by the end of the 1860s she had come to the realization that they had to enter the political world if they were ever to achieve equality with men; "without this legal equality, she is robbed of her natural rights." With this uppermost in her mind, she arranged for the first women's suffrage convention held in Chicago, to which she invited Mrs. Stanton, Miss Anthony, and other advocates of women's suffrage. She also helped to organize the Illinois Woman Suffrage Association, of which she was the first president.

She established while in Chicago, at her own "cost and risk," the *Agitator,* begun in January 1869. The periodical was devoted primarily to the suffrage cause, but also espoused the temperance movement. Mrs. Livermore conducted the paper for a year, with her husband as business manager. When she returned to the East she merged her paper with the *Woman's Journal* which had been founded by Lucy Stone in 1870, and which lasted until 1931. Mrs. Livermore was immediately invited to become editor-in-chief, a position which she held for almost three years. The paper, a weekly, was financed by way of a joint stock company with initial capital of $10,000 raised largely through the efforts of Lucy Stone and her husband, Henry B. Blackwell. Among its male contributing editors were Thomas Wentworth Higginson, William Lloyd Garrison, and Henry B. Blackwell.

The women's rights movement had split into two wings in 1869, with Mrs. Stanton's National Woman Suffrage Association representing the more radical segment. Their principal organ was the *Independent,* edited by Theodore Tilton. The *Woman's Journal* represented the more moderate American Woman Suffrage Association, to which Mrs. Livermore belonged.[183] She resigned from the editorship in 1873 in order to devote more time to lecturing.

Many of Mrs. Livermore's platform appearances were under the auspices of the Lyceum Bureau organized in 1868 by James Redpath, long associated with Horace Greeley's *New York Tribune.* She completely ignored Redpath's advice to avoid such controversial subjects as temperance and women's suffrage. One of her most popular presentations was entitled "What shall we do with our daughters?" She delivered this lecture over 800 times in a span of twenty-five years, from Maine to California. It was later published in book form, together with other popular lectures; among them was "Superfluous Women." In the first lecture mentioned, she outlined (in seventy pages of print) the contributions of women throughout history. The burden of the second was a defense of unmarried women who should receive all the training that was necessary, whatever the field, to become both self supporting and socially useful.

Mrs. Livermore received the unqualified support of her husband in her multitude of activities. He spoke and wrote constantly in behalf of the women's suffrage cause, and defended at length the right of women to enter the ministry. In the midst of the fund-raising which was part of Universalist activities during their centennial in 1870, he replied to an editorial in the *Universalist* expressing a general lack of confidence in women ministers. He strongly disagreed, and raised the question of why women should be excluded from the benefits to be made possible by the money the women were themselves raising.[184] He wrote two works arguing at length in favor of women's suffrage.[185] Mrs. Livermore also engaged in public debates over the suffrage issue. She reportedly demolished the arguments put forth by Miss Catherine E. Beecher in a confrontation in 1871.[186]

The cause of women's suffrage so vigorously espoused by Mrs. Livermore ran into some difficulty in her own denominational backyard. The editors of the *Universalist* took a very conservative and cautious view of the whole movement. They announced in 1868 that they were in favor of the franchise for women as a matter of principle, but refused to expect the miracles promised at most women's rights conventions.[187] Suffrage had to be requested by the majority of women and not imposed by a militant minority. The claims made for it had to be tested by experience. The editors detected a visible decline in the popularity of the women's rights agitation in 1870, shortly after the division in the suffrage ranks. They were immediately challenged.[188] In reply, they announced their conviction that the number of women in Massachusetts who really wanted the ballot and were willing to make sacrifices to achieve it was not sufficiently large to fill completely Tremont Temple in Boston.[189] One of their arguments was that extremists such as Victoria Claflin Woodhull were discrediting the movement and somehow had to be controlled. Mrs. Woodhull, an advocate of complete sexual freedom, had invaded the stock market, established with her sister a brokerage firm, had tried to take over the National Woman Suffrage Association, and had been the candidate of the Equal Rights Party for the presidency of the United States in 1872.[190]

The *Universalist* carried on a brief running battle in 1873 with the *Woman's Journal,* which had accused the *Universalist* of opposing both coeducation and women's suffrage. The editors of the latter paper replied that they had consistently supported coeducation and that criticism of the way the women's crusade was being conducted was not tantamount to opposition to women's suffrage.[191] Olympia Brown came to the defense of the *Universalist* in an article which appeared in the *Woman's Journal* in December 1873.[192] The errors the *Universalist* had fallen into, she wrote, had been honest ones, based on mistaken information. Further, they were entitled to their own opinions as long as the facts were accurately presented.

The editors of the *Universalist* were not always happy with Mrs. Livermore's sometimes outspoken language and ideas, and inadvertently or otherwise, did not always do her justice. There was some dissatisfaction because, when she spoke from various pulpits, she insisted on delivering addresses (to use her own words) that were "always unsectarian, and always ethical or religious." She did not sufficiently stress her denominational identity. In truth, her thinking went beyond denominational boundaries, and she never stressed Universalism *per se.* She was the only woman speaker at the Anniversary Week meetings of the denomination in 1872. The other speakers received almost no mention in the *Universalist,* but two columns were devoted to a critique of her address. Much was made of her twice-repeated statement that "provided the good aimed by it was done she did not care whether the Universalist church had a future or not." What she actually said was: "Whether the Universalist church is to be the church of the future or not, under the name of the Universalist church, I do not know—I do not care. I do know, just as surely as I know the sun is to rise tomorrow, that the blessed faith of the Universalist church is to be the faith of the church of the future. *That* I care for, but whether it is called the Universalist church I do not care."[193]

Mrs. Livermore's devotion to the Universalist cause was certainly as sincere and as wholehearted and as often demonstrated as was her allegiance to the cause of women's rights. According to Isaac M. Atwood she probably did more work and raised more money through the Woman's Centenary Association, which she helped to organize than any other individual in the denomination.[194]

In the 1890s, at the age of seventy-seven, Mrs. Livermore looked back on the period spanned by her full and active life up to that point. She liked what she saw. The world of 1897 was much different and much better than the one into which she had been born. "I congratulate women that their long struggle for freedom, knowledge, opportunity, and the rights of human nature is nearly ended, and that the day is close at hand when it shall be as good a thing to be born a girl as to be born a boy."[195] She did not live to see women's suffrage completely achieved, but she saw a promising future.

Chapter 21

"WE ARE ALL BRETHREN": UNIVERSALISTS AND THE ABOLITION OF SLAVERY

Given the premises from which Universalists operated, emphasizing as they did the fatherhood of God and the brotherhood of man, it might be expected that they would immediately condemn the institution of slavery, take appropriate action to further its abolition, speak as one voice, and become the pioneers in a great effort to further the cause of humanity. After all, as the editors of the *Universalist Miscellany* (Otis A. Skinner and Edwin H. Chapin) told their readers in 1846, belief in the brotherhood of man was "one of the distinguishing excellencies of Universalism."[1] The world was in reality one great family; "however remote we may live from each other, however different may be our complexions, we are all brethren." A special obligation was imposed on Universalists, built into their teachings—"to love man because he is a man"—an obligation which transcended national ties and national boundaries. These were fine words, and the idea was repeated time and again, and was sometimes even more eloquently and fervently expressed. But the historical fact is that Universalists were no more able than their contemporaries in other denominations to translate into immediate effective action an ideal by abolishing an institution that had become so inextricably interwoven into the fabric of the entire nation and which involved as many complexities and contradictions as slavery.

Nineteenth-century Universalists could claim anti-slavery champions and precedents from the preceding century of which they could later be proud. But for over a quarter of a century the past lay dormant, even in the minds and memories of those few who were concerned when the abolitionist movement took on the character of a crusade, after a slow and erratic start before 1830, and eventually swept over the consciousness of Americans and came to a tragic political and military climax after 1860. Universalists could take pride in the convictions and contributions of a small but determined handful of dedicated people who eventually made the abolition of slavery a central goal and set out to educate their fellow Universalists about the evils of the institution; but it was a halting and uncertain process, and defeats were at first more numerous than victories. Universalists, special obligation or not, encountered the same obstacles to the realization of the ideal of a free "brotherhood of man" as did other reformers of like mind outside the denomination.[2] There was not only apathy, ignorance, self-interest, and prejudice to be overcome, but opposition from numerous sources. Many leading Universalists, fully recognizing the sensitivity of the slavery question especially after 1830, and particularly when it became more and more a political issue after 1840, were reluctant to discuss it or become involved in debates over it for fear it would divide and disrupt the denomination.

Universalists could see with their own eyes the effects of differences over slavery within such religious bodies as the Methodists, the Lutherans, the Episcopalians, and the Presbyterians, some of which actually split asunder into sectional churches over the issue. Although southern Universalists were but a fractional minority of an admittedly small denomination, the reluctance to antagonize the South served as an important deterrent to anti-slavery agitation among some northern Universalists, although it never represented a complete block. There were also clergymen within northern Universalism itself such as Linus S. Everett and J.B. Dods who were so far from enthusiastic about interfering with the *status quo* that they came close to becoming apologists for slavery.

But even though debates over slavery occasionally seemed to threaten denominational unity, they never resulted in a constitutional crisis of serious proportions within Universalism. Like the Congregationalists and Unitarians, the major strength of the denomination lay outside the South; hence the majority of communicants were not as likely to be offended by anti-slavery agitation.[3] By the same token, a strong central authority to enforce obedience was lacking in Universalist organization; any attempt to impose a uniform discipline of thought would, even if attempted, have been anathema to most Universalists. Nonetheless, anti-slavery proponents among northern Universalists ran into a major obstacle in the refusal of their ecclesiastical bodies at first to allow the introduction of the subject of slavery into their deliberations. Hence the effectiveness of their efforts was blunted at the start, and they were forced to organize their own vehicles for arguing their case and disseminating their views.

Almost every major argument used by opponents of slavery of every stripe in the United States, no matter what their religious or political affiliation or status, from the end of the eighteenth century to the coming of the Civil War, was offered at one time or another by anti-slavery Universalists. They had little to say about the complex subject of the economics of slavery.[4] Regardless of differences of emphasis on particular points, the vast majority of Universalists opposed slavery on philosophical, moral, and religious grounds, and because of its effects on the individual, rather than on economic, political, or constitutional grounds.

The principles on which they opposed the institution were reiterated time and time again in their anti-slavery literature and pronouncements.[5] The entire argument was built on the assumption that mankind was "one great family" which would ultimately "share one common destiny . . . in the kingdom of immortal blessedness." Slavery was "a great sin against God, and a most grievous wrong to man;" it not only robbed the slaves of most or all of their essential rights as "God's intellectual and moral children" but it corrupted and endangered the free population wherever it existed; in this case, both the oppressed and the oppressors were objects of concern—the first for their freedom and the latter as objects for "redemption and elevation." The watchwords were love and brotherhood. Universalists were reminded that the slaves, too, even though treated as cattle, were "your brethren and sister, heirs of immortality." It was but natural and logical that one of the continuing concerns of anti-slavery Universalists which went beyond the immediate problem was the evil of racial prejudice and discrimination. In this area, they spoke to later generations as well as to their own.

There was among opponents of American slavery much more agreement as to ends than means. The latter ranged between two extreme poles, with many intermediate possibilities. Some advocated immediate, uncompromising, and complete abolition, single-minded devotion to the goal to the exclusion of other reforms, and disregard of consequences, condoning even the use of physical force if necessary, and the disruption of the Union. Others argued in behalf of various degrees of gradualism, cooperation with other reform efforts, and the use of peaceful and constitutional means.[6]

The overwhelming majority of Universalist leaders in the abolition movement were moderates rather than extremists. They almost unanimously rejected the militancy, immediatism, and radicalism of William Lloyd Garrison and his supporters and followers, and called for abolition by gradual and peaceable means based on moral suasion, example, and enlightenment through education. They pleaded for patience, forbearance, and tolerance while steady and unrelenting pressure was exerted to transform the American conscience. Universalists were exhorted to distinguish between slavery as a system and individual southern slaveholders, who had been victimized by historical circumstances.[7] Universalists were therefore warned not to brand all slaveholders as cutthroats and pirates, and not to call every man a time-server and hypocrite who did not happen to see the matter in the same light or who declined to support all of the measures advocated by the opponents of slavery. What constituted "moral influence"? It meant support of free discussion of the subject; reading and weighing of all the arguments, including those offered in Southern papers; and above all, the practice of benevolence called for by the social ethic built into Universalism and the Christian spirit as they interpreted it. But there was also more than what Philo Price, editor of the *Universalist Union,* called "the Law of Kindness." There was a very pragmatic consideration based on extensive experience. Universalists should be "the last people in the world to embark in a denunciatory warfare on this subject [slavery] or fan excited feelings. They knew, too well, the effect of denunciation upon themselves."[8]

In the early phases of their anti-slavery efforts, Universalists rejected political abolitionism out of hand, arguing that mere adherence to their religious principles would somehow bring about a reformation in the character of the Southern slaveholder which would in turn automatically bring about the desired result. The regeneration of the individual, Northerner as well as Southerner, was considered the key not only to the freeing of men from legal bondage but to the elevation of American society in all of its dimensions. Abolition of slavery, to most Universalist spokesmen, was but one of the many goals to be achieved in order to create a new and better world. But this goal was of paramount importance because it involved the destruction of the greatest obstacle of all to the creation of a common humanity. However, translating all of these noble ideals into reality was considerably more difficult and challenging than the enunciation of the principles themselves.

When Universalists opposed to slavery first undertook to launch a campaign to extirpate it, one of their first steps was to cast back over their own history to find support. They readily found early spokesmen. In particular they proudly offered "those eminent Universalists, Dr. Benjamin Rush, and Rev. Elhanan Winchester," who had been actively engaged in their day in efforts to do away with both slavery and the slave trade.[9] Rush had published in 1773 *An Address to the Inhabitants of the British Settlements in America, upon Slavekeeping.*[10] This was soon followed by another publication by Rush written as a reply to an attack by a West Indian planter on the first pamphlet. It was also Rush who, in 1784, had been an organizer and later one of the presidents of the revived anti-slavery society founded by Quakers in 1775 and after its incorporation by the state legislature in 1789, known as the Pennsylvania Society for Promoting the Abolition of Slavery, and Relief of Free Negroes Unlawfully Held in Bondage, and for Improving the Condition of the African Race.[11]

These and other contributions of Benjamin Rush to the anti-slavery movement were never spelled out by later Universalists, perhaps on the mistaken assumption that they were already well known in the denomination and that his influence could be naturally assumed. More attention was paid to the efforts of Elhanan Winchester. While preaching to a Baptist society at Welsh Neck, on the Pee Dee River in South Carolina in the 1770s and simultaneously making his way toward Universalism, he had spoken against slavery. He had visited in Fairfax, Virginia, where in December 1774 he had preached a discourse on the subject which was published "with several additions" in London in 1788. At that time, Winchester was in England and had already professed his Universalism openly. In his pamphlet, *The Reigning Abominations, especially the Slave Trade, considered as Causes of Lamentations,* Winchester made a strong plea for human freedom and castigated both slavetraders and slaveholders for the avarice and greed which he believed was responsible for the existence of the evils of both institutions in which they participated. Winchester also spent considerable time while in South Carolina preaching to slaves and baptizing them into the Christian faith.[12] They seemed to have had no prejudice against him, and showed more disposition to attend his ministry than had ever been shown by them to anyone else. Winchester's explanation was that he had "never had anything to do with slavery, but on the contrary, condemned it." In the summer of 1779 he addressed about thirty slaves from a nearby plantation, telling them that "Jesus Christ loved them, and died for them as well as for us white people, and that they might come and believe in him and welcome." Within three months he had baptized 100 men and women, all of whom had been either born in Africa or were "immediately descended from such."

It was with great satisfaction that John Murray Spear, a leading abolitionist in the denomination, could in 1840 call to Universalist attention the pioneer work of these two men. But it was also a source of great distress to him that in the intervening years almost nothing had been heard from Universalists on the subject. Where, he asked, was "the courageous spirit of Winchester"? He expressed regret that the contributions of Rush and Winchester had been neglected so long, and set out to do something about it. He called attention to Thomas Clarkson (1760-1846), a leading British abolitionist who had written extensively on the slave trade and slavery. Clarkson had been influential in bringing about emancipation in the British Empire by Parliament in 1833, and had paid tribute to both Rush and Winchester in his history of the abolition of the slave trade.[13] Clarkson had also noted Rush's anti-slavery publications and his part in the reorganization of the nation's oldest abolition society.

It was also Clarkson who, in noting Winchester's 1774 discourse, had credited him with having "turned the attention of many of his hearers to this subject, both by private interference and by preaching expressly upon it."[14] The author pointed out that Winchester had donated 100 copies of his discourse against the slave trade to the London Abolition Committee to aid its cause. There was no better illustration of the linkage between the efforts of Rush and Winchester in the late eighteenth-century and nineteenth-century Universalist interest in the subject of slavery than the circumstances surrounding the reprinting of Winchester's anti-slavery sermon. Spear determined to make it available again, but it was a scarce item by 1840. Only one copy was known to exist in America at the time, in the library of the late Benjamin Rush. Spear borrowed it from Rush's son James, and reprinted it in its entirety, with Winchester's annotations, in the *Christian Freeman.*[15]

Adin Ballou, founder of the Hopedale community in Massachusetts, called the attention of the readers of his *Practical Christian* to the Winchester sermon and requested 100 copies from Sylvanus Cobb, editor of the *Christian Freeman,* who had reprinted it in quantity.[16] However, very few Universalists probably had seen the excerpts that Ballou reprinted in his paper in 1841, for he had formally left the denomination a decade before and was associated with Unitarian Congregationalism. Ballou had been the first clergyman in Mendon, Massachusetts, to open his church to an anti-slavery lecturer (in 1832). Until then, "not a ripple of anti-slavery" had reached the town.[17] Even in 1832 there had been but a small audience and no visible reaction to the speech.

Universalists in the 1830s and 1840s, in their efforts to document early examples of their concern over slavery, the slave, and contact with the black man, overlooked several additional opportunities to strengthen their case. They neglected to inform Universalists that the first black man known to have been associated with the denomination was Gloster Dalton, an African brought to America as a slave. He was among the eighty-five signatories of the Charter of Compact of the Gloucester Society in 1785.[18] It was with reference to Dalton that Thomas Jones, long-time pastor of the Gloucester society and successor there to John Murray, had uttered the dramatic words: "There are no slaves. All men are born free!" It was that same pastor who, during the War of 1812, delivered a special sermon, the burden of which was that "the claim of Great Britain to the right of impressing seamen is as absurd and wicked as is the claim of the southern planter to ownership in man."[19] Nineteenth-century Universalists also failed to refresh their own memories with the fact that the first official challenge to slavery by "the sect calling themselves Universalists" had been adopted at their Philadelphia convention in 1790, in which Benjamin Rush had played an important part.

> *Of holding Slaves.*—We believe it to be inconsistent with the union of the human race in a common Saviour, and the obligations to mutual and universal love, which flow from that union, to hold any part of our fellow creatures in bondage. We therefore recommend a total refraining from the African trade

and the adoption of prudent measures for the gradual abolition of the slavery of the negroes in our country, and for the instruction and education of their children in English literature, and in the principles of the Gospel.

Universalists might also have noted that William Pitt Smith, author of a series of letters published in 1787 under the title of the *Universalist,* and elected to the New York State legislature in 1796, had been "a strenuous advocate" of a bill providing for the abolition of slavery.[20] Likewise, they could have called attention to the fact that a black woman, Amy Scott, was one of the incorporators in 1801 of the first Universalist society to be organized in Philadelphia (what became the Lombard Street church).[21] They apparently did not know that John Murray took an interest in the welfare of Blacks while he was pastor of the First Universalist society in Boston. His efforts at benevolences extended far beyond provision for the poor in his own congregation, when he not only sponsored quarterly charity lectures (at least one of which he delivered) in 1792, before he became the regular pastor, but took up collections to assist inhabitants of Philadelphia, which had been ravaged in 1793 by a yellow fever epidemic. There were notices in the Boston secular paper, the *Columbian Centinel,* of his scheduled appearances to speak to Blacks in Faneuil Hall.[22] Murray spoke also to the African Society which had been organized in 1796 by forty-four Blacks in Boston as a benevolent and self-improvement group.[23]

Mention might also have been made of John Kenrick, "well known as a Universalist," in Newton, Massachusetts, who was remembered for his many philanthropies at the time of his death in 1833.[24] He was a pioneer in the anti-slavery movement, and in 1816 had published at his own expense 3,000 copies of a small volume entitled *The Horrors of Slavery* which he distributed to members of Congress and state legislatures as well as to private individuals.[25] He had donated $600 to assist in getting the New England Anti-Slavery Society started the previous year, $250 of which was to support a "Manual Labor School for Colored Children" to be sponsored by the society. Kenrick was elected as the society's second president, but unfortunately for the abolitionist cause, he had died soon after at the age of seventy-seven and did not serve his one-year term.[26] He was a friend and correspondent of Garrison, and had supported the efforts of Benjamin Lundy (1789-1839), the Quaker abolitionist.

During the 1820s there were occasional references to slavery by Universalists, and all who are known to have left a record in that decade were opposed to the institution. In 1824 an unidentified correspondent in the *Universalist Magazine* asserted that it was "utterly impossible to reconcile Slavery with the pure doctrines of Christianity."[27] With the issues of the War of 1812 probably still in mind, the same correspondent expressed the hope that the time was near "when the government of the United States, which has so long and manfully contended, 'that *free ships* should make *free goods,*' will see the propriety of contending with no less ardor, 'that a *free Republic* shall make free citizens.' " The *Universalist Magazine* carried advertisements in the 1820s for Lundy's *Genius of Universal Emancipation,* an anti-slavery journal.[28]

References to slavery became much more frequent in Universalist publications in the 1830s as agitation over the question mounted, slave insurrections occurred, and anti-slavery societies were organized in increasing numbers. William S. Balch, Universalist editor of the *Impartialist* in New Hampshire, expressed horror at the harrassment (including imprisonment) of Miss Prudence Crandall, who attempted to open her private girls' school to Blacks in Canterbury, Connecticut in 1833.[29] This, he thought, was a demonstration of the most odious kind of race prejudice. The following year, Whittemore noted the publication by George W. Light of Boston of *The Memoirs and Poems of Phillis Wheatley* and invited anyone who was interested "in the cause of the oppressed race to which [she] belonged, or who pretend to doubt whether Africans have any souls, or belong to the human species," to purchase a copy of the book.[30] Phillis Wheatley (ca. 1753-1784) was a black slave brought from Africa at the age of seven or eight, purchased by John Wheatley of Boston, and taught to read and write by her mistress. The slave became a well-known poet in her day. The book was sponsored by abolitionists, who furnished the memoirs to accompany the poems.[31]

Universalists who expressed themselves in the 1830s on the subject of slavery continued to oppose it on principle, but at the same time advocated a generally hands-off policy. The slave rebellion in Virginia led by Nat Turner in 1831, which provoked national excitement, elicited from Thomas Whittemore, editor of the *Trumpet*, a cautionary note that although New Englanders were opposed to slavery and wished it abolished, they should not encourage slave uprisings.[32] It was impossible, he told his readers, to abolish the institution suddenly and violently; it must be "brought to an end eventually, in a safe and prudent manner." Meanwhile, Whittemore recommended that slaves "be treated with kindness, and thus be made kind and faithful to their masters." When Universalists were chided for not praying for "that portion of our fellow creatures who are in bondage," Whittemore replied that it was their duty "to pray for the oppressed of any name, color, or nature . . . . it is out duty also to pray for masters as well as slaves, that a sense of justice and humanity may distinguish them."[33]

At the end of the decade of the 1830s, Whittemore expressed himself somewhat more forcefully than earlier. In 1839, after Thomas F. Buxton, a British anti-slavery leader, had published a work on the

African slave trade, Whittemore took the opportunity to condemn slavery as well as the slave trade in unsparing language. "We claim to be considered an enlightened and a moral nation—and whatever difference of opinion may exist in relation to the subject of slavery in the Southern states, there can be none in respect of the impolicy and wickedness of slavery in the abstract—and above all, in respect to the injustice and atrocities of the slave trade."[34] John Moore, pastor of the society in Danvers, Massachusetts, in 1833, held that slavery in a free country was a paradox and "a stain upon our Constitution . . . but the southerners have their slaves, they were left to them by their fathers, and to turn them out at large would be both cruel and dangerous—and it requires more wisdom than I profess to devise a plan for the abolition of slavery at the south."[35] Moore shared his dilemma with many others. What could be done? One possible solution was to organize.

Growing Denominational Concern About Slavery

By the 1830s all kinds of organizations, many with state and local branches, had appeared which attempted to deal in some manner with the complicated problems posed by slavery and the status and fate of the black man in America. One was the American Colonization Society which had been established in 1817. It had been intended originally to better the plight of free Blacks, and was associated with a "back to Africa" movement which resulted in the creation of the state of Liberia in 1847.[36] Universalists, like their fellow Americans, differed as to the feasibility of this solution. Sebastian and Samuel F. Streeter, editors of the *Universalist* in 1833, carried extracts from the proceedings of the Massachusetts Colonization Society which had been organized in 1831. They thoroughly approved the "humanity and Christian benevolence" of both this and the parent organization.[37] In 1833 John Moore, pastor of the Universalist society in Danvers which was less than a decade later to adopt a strong anti-slavery resolution, thought "the project of colonizing the blacks will not be very likely to succeed, so long as the fashion of propagation [so-called slave breeding] is continued."[38] He, like others both inside and outside the denomination, considered the colonization of free Blacks no real solution to the problem of slavery itself, but only a palliative which did not get to the heart of the matter.

William S. Balch opposed the whole movement to resettle Blacks in Africa as impractical as well as unfair to them as human beings.[39] The eventual failure of the colonization project vindicated Balch's judgment. Sylvanus Cobb's views were in complete harmony with Balch's. Getting rid of slavery by transporting Blacks to Africa was completely unacceptable to the editor of the *Christian Freeman*. Driving the black man out was no way to treat a fellow human; he should be free, as other men, to choose his own place of residence. Mass enforced emigration seemed to Cobb to be merely a cowardly way "to get rid of a people whom we are too unchristian to treat as men and women."[40] He advocated instead any plan that would weaken slavery and improve "the condition of the colored race" by raising a fund to help slaves buy their freedom; i.e., compensated emancipation.[41]

Universalists were, however, sympathetic to those who elected to migrate to Africa. B. Bowzer, a Negro Universalist born in 1830 near Canton, Ohio, who had moved to Mt. Pleasant, Iowa, found his plans for a law career thwarted by his color.[42] So in 1860 he left for Africa, where he established himself in Cape Palmas, Liberia, and immediately issued a plea for Universalist publications so that he could establish a church and Sunday School. Cobb assisted in soliciting contributions. In 1861 one of the secretaries of the African Civilization Society in New York spoke to the General Convention meeting in the city that year, and requested assistance. The convention voted "to render all the aid in our power to return all such as desire it to their father-land."[43]

Organized opposition in Massachusetts to slavery took form in 1831, soon after William Lloyd Garrison had begun his famous abolitionist journal, the *Liberator*. The New England Anti-Slavery Society was created that year under his leadership. After a slow and unpromising start, its name was changed to the Massachusetts Anti-Slavery Society three years later, and by 1837 claimed 145 local societies.[44] In the fall of 1833 an attempt was made to bring together the dozens of scattered and sometimes competing abolitionist groups which had sprung up everywhere in the nation. The effort produced the American Anti-Slavery Society that year; by 1838 it claimed 1,350 societies, with a membership of about 250,000.[45] In that same year a rift developed between the militant Garrisonians who advocated immediate abolition and the use of physical force, and a more moderate wing led by Theodore Dwight Weld (1803-1895) who favored passive resistance, including non-compliance with laws requiring the return of fugitive slaves. Out of this division came the American and Foreign Anti-Slavery Society, organized in 1840, and a local equivalent organized the preceding year—the Massachusetts Abolition Society.[46] The latter society became an auxiliary of the new and larger organization, separate from the older Massachusetts Anti-Slavery Society organized by Garrison.

By the 1830s the anti-slavery movement, so far as it was organized, was as much a political as a religious phenomenon; it was largely Presbyterian and Congregational in makeup, although ostensibly inter-denominational.[47] Most Universalists refused to join any of these organizations on grounds of both their political orientation and of their domination by the "orthodox" denominations. So Universalists determined to create their own, beginning in 1840. With the exception of John Kenrick, no prominent Universalist layman is known to have been associated with any anti-slavery organization outside the denomination after 1830. At the time Kenrick was active in the movement which resulted in the organization of the New England Anti-Slavery Society in 1833, abolitionist agitation had not yet become either well-organized or well-known. Anti-slavery minded clergy in most major Protestant denominations, in fact, from the 1830s onward, tended to operate within their own religious groups, although they were sometimes forced to act separately at first because of opposition by the majority to anti-slavery agitation.[48]

One of Garrison's tactics was to urge abolitionists to leave those churches which either supported slavery or which did not take an official stand against it. He had himself left the Baptist church for this reason by 1836.[49] It appeared that very few Universalists followed his advice. One who did withdraw from the denomination was Mrs. S.R. Morris, who belonged to the First Universalist Church in Providence, Rhode Island.[50] She was not rejecting "the distinctive sentiments of Universalism," she explained, but was objecting to its failure to carry out its principles to their logical conclusion. And as long as the denomination maintained full fellowship with Southern Universalists who apparently supported slavery, such as the editor of the *Messenger of Glad Tidings* in Alabama; who were not overtly opposed to slavery; or who failed to denounce it by remaining silent, she could no longer remain a member. She felt that anti-slavery resolutions passed by Universalists were without significance unless carried into effect, and had come to the conclusion that the denomination, "like all the others," was really pro-slavery. Cobb replied that the churches were not, as Mrs. Morris and many other abolitionists argued, lagging behind the rest of society in attempting to get rid of slavery, but were mirror images of it. It was a problem for all, not just for churchmen who were being told by Garrison and others to be "come-outers." Leaving any church would accomplish no real good and would in fact weaken the entire movement if not defeat it outright. Cobb had no sympathy for Garrisonian policies; if he had followed them, he would have been forced to become an "anti-sabbath, anti-minister, and anti-church man." But, in or out of the church, the task of abolishing slavery had to go forward.

It was probably Universalist refusal to participate in what turned out to be the mainstream of the anti-slavery movement, and their determination to operate independently, that explains more than anything else the apparently limited influence that Universalists exerted on the general abolitionist movement. It probably explains, as well, the almost complete neglect by historical scholars of Universalist activities in this domain. Certainly the arguments used by Universalist abolitionists were as cogent and as well stated as those of any other group, and their concern was fully as sincere and genuine. Their insistence, at least on paper, that mankind included the black man, slave or free, was posited on a firmer and more consistent theological and interpretive base than that of many of their nineteenth-century contemporaries.

New England Universalists at first were hesitant to commit themselves at all on the slavery issue, so far as they acted in official capacities as members of societies, associations, or conventions. They backed off from the issue, using initially the argument that it was not a proper subject on which a position should be taken by ecclesiastical bodies, or on which discussion should even take place. The first known recorded consideration of the subject within the region occurred at the annual meeting of the Maine State Convention in 1836. There was no doubt as to the prevalence of anti-slavery sentiment in that body; it was assumed to be unanimous and was accepted without challenge. Slavery in "a land of freedom" was acknowledged to exist "to an alarming extent, & is forming an awful crisis, dangerous to the Union, holding in bondage one sixth part of the nation, whom we regard as brethren, forming a great barrier to the spread of the Gospel to this portion of the population; it becomes our duty as Christians and freemen, to repent before God, of this great wickedness."[51] Slavery was "a national disgrace . . . contrary to both our Declaration of Rights & a tremendous sin against high heaven, & therefore ought to be immediately abolished." It might have been instructive to know what the reaction of other Universalists would have been if this resolution regarding slavery had been adopted. But it was postponed indefinitely because it was considered "inexpedient to discuss the subject of slavery in our religious bodies." These words, or ones of similar import, were to be heard and read so frequently in the deliberations of Universalist gatherings in the next several years that they almost achieved the status of a set formula.

Until 1841 not a single resolution had been passed by an officially recognized association or convention in the entire denomination deprecating the existence of American slavery or expressing a desire for its abolition. The great majority of Universalist clergymen, at least in their professional capacities, maintained "the profoundest silence on this great moral subject."[52] It was again a group of Universalists in Maine who took the lead. Credit for having been the first duly constituted body within the denomination to adopt an official pronouncement opposing slavery went to the Hancock and Washington Association. At its annual meeting in September 1841 the association condemned slavery as a "direct contradiction of the Golden Rule . . . the law of God," and urged that slavery be "preached against, like other sins in proportion to its magnitude and prevalence."[53] This association, of which Andrew Pingree of Belfast was the standing clerk at the time, had been organized in 1838. It comprised the two counties named, and was in one of the more sparsely and newly settled parts of the state. According to the *Universalist Register* for 1840 it was an area "where little effort has been made on behalf of our cause, from the fact that it is extremely difficult to induce preachers to go there; it seems to them so much out of the world." Their action in 1841 made them, in denominational perspective, very much a part of the world in the 1840s.

The greatest debates over taking an official stand on slavery occurred in Massachusetts, where the concentration of Universalists and Universalist leadership was greatest. The first public airing of the question, on a strictly unofficial basis, came in 1836, when a panel of the Boston Young Men's Universalist Institute engaged in a debate on the subject. The institute was one of dozens of similar groups organized throughout the denomination, beginning in the 1830s, for the purpose of religious discussion, self-improvement, and general sociability, and attracted hundreds of young men (and eventually, young women, who were admitted to membership after due consideration). The topic for the fall meeting in 1836 of the Boston group raised the question of whether people in the non-slaveholding states were justified in attempting to sway public opinion against slavery, in view of the fact that it was "tolerated by the Constitution of the slave-holding States, and by the Constitution of the United States."[54] Unfortunately, the results of the debate were never reported, although the very choice of the subject indicated the growing interest in it.

Official concern among Massachusetts Universalists over slavery was first expressed the very next year. It became immediately such a matter of debate and disagreement that actual passage of resolutions on the subject came considerably later. At its annual session, held in Boston in 1837, the Massachusetts Convention of Universalists was thrown into turmoil when Benjamin B. Mussey, a lay delegate, introduced a resolution opposing slavery. It was indefinitely postponed, and a vote was taken that nothing should be published in the minutes concerning the discussion which had taken place regarding the resolution. This did not prevent Thomas Whittemore from editorializing on what had taken place. He reported that the tranquility of an otherwise happy meeting had been marred by "the unfortunate introduction of the subject of southern slavery [which] produced a very strong and dangerous excitement. There was not an individual present who was not heart and soul opposed to slavery. Of these some were decidedly opposed to the measures of the abolitionists also, but an overwhelming majority of the Convention, were decidedly of the opinion, that such a matter, should not be agitated in our ecclesiastical bodies."[55] He noted that the vote to postpone was taken only "after much bitter feeling."

Whittemore made it clear that he was himself "decidedly opposed to slavery, and . . . desirous it should be abolished, as speedily as it can be done, in a legal, peaceful, proper manner." But it was not an appropriate topic for discussion in Universalist religious meetings, and would "split asunder" the denomination if introduced. From that time on, he followed a policy not "to agitate this subject" in his newspaper.[56] He not only refused to admit discussion of slavery in the *Trumpet* but announced his intention not even to carry notices of anti-slavery meetings or to report in full the proceedings of Universalist organizations which included any discussion or action involving slavery. It was obviously impossible to carry out this unilateral policy completely, for he had always felt obligated, and had expressed his willingness, to make the proceedings of Universalist meetings available as a public service. In addition, he was placed in a dilemma when societies, associations, conventions, and other organizations formally voted to have their deliberations published in his paper. He would have been put in a most untenable position if he had refused. He did feel free to grumble occasionally about the amount of verbiage he felt obliged to print from various Universalist organizations, even though it took up valuable space that could have been better used in his estimation for other purposes. He also reminded his readers periodically that he did not agree with "*all* the resolutions of our ecclesiastical bodies" that he published.[57]

Whittemore's somewhat inconsistent policies regarding coverage of slavery endeared him to no one, and was partly responsible for the establishment of a rival paper. He accumulated an inheritance of ill will among his cohorts that lasted for many years. Whittemore's policy provoked accusations that he was afraid of offending his Southern subscribers and even that he had pro-slavery proclivities.[58] Henry Bacon, editor of the *Universalist and Ladies' Repository,* was but one of the many who disagreed with Whittemore's stand and called for free discussion of slavery.[59] But Cobb defended Whittemore's prerogative to follow his own policy, right or wrong.

Once introduced at the Massachusetts Convention, the subject of slavery could no longer be swept under the rug. At the 1838 meeting, Joseph O. Skinner presented the following resolution: "That slavery as it exists in this country, is a great moral evil, that we deprecate its existence, and earnestly desire its abolition."[60] An attempt to postpone action by referring it to a committee to report the next year was defeated. Instead, Walter Balfour offered an amendment acceptable to Skinner, which disclaimed support for any particular measure sponsored by an abolitionist or colonization society. After spirited discussion the whole subject was indefinitely postponed.

When the Massachusetts Convention met the next year, not one but a whole series of resolutions and petitions regarding slavery was offered. Nonetheless, the committee to which they were referred considered it "inexpedient to take any further action on the subject."[61] Indefinite postponement was the fate, after considerable debate, of a similar set of resolutions proposed at the 1840 convention by Sylvanus Cobb.[62] He was much upset when the convention not only refused to pass his resolutions but when the clerk omitted from the published minutes both the text of his resolutions and the lengthy preamble which accompanied them. The clerk had explained his action by reporting that some members of the convention council had objected to their inclusion.[63] So Cobb published them in full in his own paper. He had become convinced by then that those Universalists who opposed slavery would have to create their own organization, and that his establishment of a new denominational paper the previous year (*The Christian Freeman and Family Visiter* [*sic*]) had been a wise idea.

As soon as the *Christian Freeman* was under way, Cobb set forth his views regarding slavery. In the second issue of his new paper (10 May 1839), in an article entitled "What Can We Do?," he had announced as top priority the need "to vindicate and establish the principle of free discussion, and deliver a large portion of the community from the slavish fear of looking at a great moral subject." The second task was to educate and enlighten the Southern slaveholders so that they would be stirred to action to abolish the institution. Cobb was never as concerned as most other clergymen, regardless of denomination, about the fact that no clear-cut arguments either for or against slavery could be found in the Scriptures. Walter Balfour, a leading Universalist scholar and expert in Biblical exegesis, looked for guidance in the New Testament and was unhappy to find that Christians held slaves and were nowhere exhorted to free them or even authorized in apostolic times to discuss the subject in religious meetings.[64] This apparent failure to condemn slavery worried Cobb not at all. He categorically stated that slavery and Christianity were incompatible; the early Christians were a weak minority and were in no position to challenge arbitrary governments which set up the rules. But the existence of slavery did not make it moral. Further, said Cobb, the New Testament was to be used as a guide for moral action, to be applied in common-sense fashion, according to "the varying circumstances of different ages and countries." The times in America called for abolition of slavery as a great evil. It was as clear and simple as that.

Cobb was convinced that in the last analysis moral regeneration would be the solution to the slavery problem, although he was also willing to recommend peaceful and constitutional measures when appropriate. In 1839 he offered a three-part program—a compound of practicality and idealism: legislate slavery out of the District of Columbia and prevent its further spread in the territories under Congressional control; free all Blacks who had been kidnapped in the North and taken south to be enslaved; and bring about the moral reformation of the Southern slaveholders.[65] He even went so far in

1839 as to forecast what would happen in the South after emancipation was accomplished. The ex-slaveholders would admit that they had been wrong all along, and in a fit of remorse, buttressed by economic need, would promptly hire their ex-slaves; then all would be well.[66]

John Murray Spear, Cobb's reformist colleague, made an independent but largely unsuccessful attempt to test the actual power of Universalism to bring about the hoped-for reformation of the slaveholder. In 1843 he reviewed old denominational papers to find examples, but was disappointed to uncover but a single account of a slaveholder whose Universalism had demonstrably resulted in emancipation of his slaves.[67] John Winn, a former owner of five slaves, and a Baptist, became a Universalist and immediately liberated his Negroes. He moved with them to Ohio, where he not only posted bond to assure their good behavior but gave each of them eighty acres and farming implements. He and another Universalist then purchased three more slaves for $200 each and likewise established them as freemen.

Division in the Ranks

Cobb was strengthened in his resolve to see the creation of a separate anti-slavery organization within the denomination and to continue his reform-oriented newspaper by a series of occurrences in 1839 and 1840 which made uncomfortably clear the inability of Universalists to arrive at a consensus about slavery.[68] The first event took place at a meeting of the Old Colony Conference in southern Massachusetts in 1839. For many years prior to 1840, so-called "conferences" had been held periodically at various locations throughout the denomination, at which there were public religious services, discussions, and opportunities for clergy and laity to mingle on a more informal basis than when doing business at convention and association meetings. The conferences, which became popular particularly in the 1830s and 1840s, usually met every two or three months, and occasionally passed resolutions concerning local church matters. However, more and more attention was paid to expressing opinions on current social issues. At the Old Colony meeting in 1839, Elmer Hewitt of Hanson introduced a resolution expressing his opinion that slavery was an evil and an obstacle to "pure religion." After some discussion, action on the resolution he offered was postponed until the next meeting. Hewitt's proposal then became the occasion in the conference for acrimonious debate which lasted for almost a year, with reverberations throughout the denomination.

At the next meeting of the conference, held in Fall River in February 1840, a resolution urging ministers to preach against capital punishment was adopted with little discussion. Hewitt then reintroduced his resolution against slavery. It would have called only for a "sense of the meeting" that slavery was "a sin against God and man."[69] Again, action was postponed until the next meeting in August. By then, opinion had become badly divided. There was much debate over whether the subject should even be considered; by a vote of 28 to 25 it was decided to allow the resolution to be introduced. After "a somewhat protracted and rather unpleasant discussion," the anti-slavery resolution, which by then had been expanded into several parts, was adopted by a vote of 15 to 11, with many abstentions.[70]

But the matter was far from settled. There was the question of whether to publish the proceedings because they included the resolution. The vote to do so was 11 to 9. Almost immediately, five clergymen and nine laymen who had attended the meeting lodged a formal protest against publication. The discussion of such questions as slavery was not considered appropriate in such meetings; the subject was "political" in nature; and the meeting had been not only an unofficial gathering with inadequate representation, but had been improperly conducted. It was alleged that everyone present—men, women, and children—had been allowed both to take part in the discussions and to vote; and that almost all of those present were from the community of Hanson, where the conference had been held, and in no sense represented the denomination. The moderator stoutly denied the accuracy of this account, and accused the clerk who had prepared the minutes of distorting the whole record. The meeting, said the moderator, had in no way been a free-for-all, and there had been nothing reprehensible in the way it had been conducted.[71] It was true, however, that the clerk (Edward Y. Perry) had included in the minutes the editorial comment that it had been a good meeting except for "the unwise and injudicious introduction of the resolutions on Slavery."

Cobb and J.M. Spear, who were both at the meeting and defended the resolutions, rejected the argument that it might antagonize the South by somehow associating northern Universalists with the radical abolitionists. Their reply was that slavery constituted a moral rather than a political question, and even though there might be "some fretting and menacing for a season," eventually the denomination would be thanked for standing by the great principles of humanity. A correspondent in the *Christian Freeman* not only supported the stand taken by Cobb and Spear, but urged other Universalists to consider the question in their meetings. The action taken by the Old Colony Conference should show Southern slaveholders "that one Universalist body at least has no fellowship, or sympathy, with their legalized system of abominations."[72] Although the actions taken at this meeting in no sense comprised an official denominational declaration, another precedent had been set, besides the one in Maine, to which Universalists opposed to slavery could point.

Because conference resolutions had no official standing but were considered merely expressive of the views of those who happened to attend, J.M. Spear decided to introduce the subject of slavery at the next meeting of the Old Colony Association, a regularly constituted body, and secure an official statement. The theme of the meeting in 1841 was set by John Allen, who delivered a strongly-worded anti-slavery sermon in which he blamed slavery for the failure of Universalism to prosper in the South. He pointed out that of the approximately 800 Universalist societies then in the United States, no more than 30 were in slaveholding states, and they were weak and poorly supported.[73] Spear withdrew his proposed resolution in order to give another individual an opportunity to present an alternate: "Whereas, we believe the system of Southern American Slavery to be morally wrong, we do earnestly desire its abolition as far as it can be accomplished by moral suasion." It was voted to refer the resolution to the societies within the association, which were requested to instruct their delegates in the anticipation of a vote at the meeting the following year. As was customary, the clerk was instructed to prepare the proceedings for publication in the *Trumpet.*

Russell Tomlinson, clerk of the 1840 session, and the one who was responsible for the motion at the 1841 meeting to refer, was strongly opposed to the discussion of "the slavery question" in Universalist meetings, but had dutifully prepared the proceedings in 1840 and had forwarded them to the editor of the *Trumpet.* Whittemore's opposition to having the issue of slavery aired at all was so great that he condensed the proceedings (ostensibly because of pressure of space), omitted the resolution on slavery, and garbled the minutes in such a way that it appeared only that some kind of a resolution on slavery had been passed after the adjournment of the regular business session. Much as he personally opposed the introduction of the entire subject of slavery, Tomlinson had reported the proceedings as fully as possible, and was so upset by Whittemore's action that he prepared the minutes of the 1840 session in pamphlet form and in a long explanatory note attempted to set the record straight.[74]

Whittemore continued his policy of avoiding any mention of slavery whenever he could so far as the *Trumpet* was concerned, and continued to be criticized for lack of journalistic responsibility. When he reported the meeting of the Boston Association in Lynn in 1842, he omitted any mention of the resolution on slavery presented by John Prince of Essex. Prince had to turn to the *Christian Freeman* to give Universalists the content of the resolution. What Prince had done was to condemn the editor of the *Southern Universalist* (Philo Brownson) for carrying advertisements of slave auctions in his paper, a practice approved by the Georgia State Convention.[75] Whittemore was undoubtedly sincere in his desire to be "perfectly willing to be a peacemaker between the parties" when division threatened among Universlaists. But deliberately failing to report fully and accurately the disagreements that did exist, merely in order to avoid antagonizing one side or the other, was not considered an honorable way of doing business.

Supporters of the anti-slavery resolution in the Old Colony Association had no more success at the meeting in 1841 than in the previous year. It was defeated by a vote of 3 to 9.[76] This had been preceded by an unsuccessful parliamentary ploy by opponents of the resolution to block action by refusing to elect a moderator, so that no business could be transacted. To complicate matters, the two delegates from New Bedford filed a formal protest that they were not allowed to be heard in debate on the resolution. They had been instructed by their society to vote for it, but, on the strength of Tomlinson's objection from the floor, they were not allowed by the moderator to speak, on the ground that the resolution had already been debated fully the previous year.[77] When the frustrated delegates from New Bedford then attempted to obtain a report, to be entered on the record, on the instructions delegates had received from societies, they were ruled out of order. At least some members of the Old Colony Association were apparently in no mood to allow any public commitment on such a sensitive issue as slavery.

Two regularly constituted Universalist bodies in Massachusetts at the local level had taken an official stand on slavery by the fall of 1841. The New Bedford society, where J.M. Spear was then the pastor, had adopted resolutions opposing slavery, and the church connected with the society in Danvers had taken similar action. The wording of the latter's resolutions may be taken as typical of many to follow from within the denomination. "Slave-holding is not only a heinous sin against God, and an outrage on humanity, but is diametrically opposed to the best interest both of the master and the slave; and . . . it is our imperative duty as Patriots, as Philanthropists, and especially as Christians, to exert our utmost influence, at all times and under all circumstances, in accordance with the law of God and the dictates of our consciences; for the immediate and final overthrow of American Slavery."[78] As promising as resolutions such as this might have been, the anti-slaveryites wanted a broader base for their efforts than local congregations. Such a base had been established in 1840 and paralleled the actions of many societies.

Talk of creating a denominational anti-slavery organization had become widespread in Massachusetts by the winter of 1839-40. There seemed to be sufficient interested individuals to support such a movement. One layman who endorsed the idea thought also that the public should be shown that there were Universalists "whose practice is somewhat in accordance with their professions."[79] The first organized movement among Universalists for the express purpose of abolishing slavery took the form of the Universalist Anti-Slavery Convention, which held its initial meeting at the First Universalist Church in Lynn on a stormy November day in 1840, It resulted from a call signed by fourteen individuals, including Sylvanus Cobb, and J.M. Spear and his brother Charles. Its purpose was "to discuss the character of slavery (especially as viewed in the light of the religion, which we, as Universalists, profess), and the means of hastening its peaceful abolition."

A separate organization was considered necessary to accomplish these goals, for two reasons: "to explain and enforce" the distinguishing religious principles of Universalism which had a peculiar and unique bearing on the subject; and to counteract the opposition of many Universalists to having the subject discussed in ecclesiastical circles.[80] Thirty-four individuals attended. Whether the number would have been greater if weather had permitted is not known. However, two other considerations probably adversely affected attendance. Very few denominational papers carried advance notice of the meeting, and through a failure to coordinate, the Old Colony Conference, of which many of the clergy hoping to attend the anti-slvery meeting were members, met simultaneously. All present at the Lynn meeting were from Massachusetts. Among the leaders were Elmer Hewitt (Hanson); Charles Spear (Boston), and his brother J.M. Spear (New Bedford); Joseph O. Skinner (Framingham), who served as the clerk; Sylvanus Cobb (Waltham); and Edwin H. Lake (Lynn), who a decade later was to settle in North Carolina. Only one, A.A. Dawes, is known to have visited the South; he had travelled and preached briefly in the border state of Kentucky on a single visit, and found that anti-slavery sentiment was strongest in those areas in which Universalists were found in the greatest numbers.

The tone of the anti-slavery meeting in 1840 was set at the very beginning. Even before J.M. Spear delivered the principal address, a resolution was offered asserting that "no individual can be a consistent Universalist who refused to acknowledge the sinfulness of Slavery, and give his voice and influence in favor of its immediate abolition."[81] The resolution was tabled and never acted on officially, but the clerk hastened to explain that this was due to "an oversight" rather than to design, and that other resolutions that were passed carried out the intent of the mover (John Allen). The first resolution that was adopted (unanimously) declared that any holder of another in bondage was "in the sight of God guilty of theft and robbery." Lemuel Willis and others thought this language both too harsh and too sweeping, but an attempt to substitute milder wording ("guilty of great wrong to his fellow man") was defeated and the original resolution was adopted by "a small majority." The next resolution to be approved challenged the idea that slavery should be accepted because it was lawful in the South. The right to "reform error in practice and in law" by peaceful means was an acknowledged and legitimate course to pursue. Speaking in behalf of the resolution, Charles Spear used an argument often heard in Universalist circles: "Human laws do not make anything right—they are not a standard of truth . . . and when wrong we should labor to bring about a change in them."

In a lengthy five-point address J.M. Spear sketched in the Universalist efforts up to that time to advocate free discussion, promote temperance, and abolish capital punishment. After a review of the course pursued in Massachusetts respecting slavery, he summarized the leading arguments against the Southern institution, paying tribute to Elhanan Winchester and including a synopsis of Winchester's sermon of 1774. Spear then stressed the unique obligation of Universalists to involve themselves in the abolitionist movement, and concluded with several suggestions for action: prayer, preaching, passage of resolutions, discussion in the press, the breaking down of the prejudice that existed against "men of color . . . which is the offspring of slavery," petitions to legislatures, and material aid and comfort to escaped slaves. These were nothing more, Spear told his hearers, than the putting of Universalist principles into practice. Universalists, if true to their faith, should not only consider all men as brothers, but should "oppose all monopolies, despise all partiality, break down all unnatural distinctions, elevate the despised classes, and introduce a system of perfect equality."

Another resolution asserted that slavery obstructed the diffusion of the Gospel and therefore presented an impediment to the spread of Universalism in the South. Altogether, twelve resolutions dealing with slavery and Universalist responsibilities for its abolition were passed. The editors of denominational publications were chastised for remaining silent on the subject or displaying hostility toward attempts to discuss it in their columns. The editor of the *Christian Freeman* was commended for publishing the only newspaper that provided a forum for debate over slavery among Universalists. Societies were urged to open their meeting houses to "any subject connected with the moral and spiritual welfare of man," including anti-slavery. Several Universalist ministers had actually experienced difficulty in obtaining the use of their own meeting houses for such discussions. John Allen, pastor of the society in Watertown, Massachusetts, and a confirmed opponent of slavery, threatened to resign in 1839 if he were not permitted occasional use of his meeting house to lecture on the subject outside of church services.[82] Permission was granted by his society, although an attempt was made to reconsider the vote.

There was extended debate on resolutions involving the responsibility of Universalist clergy "to bear . . . pulpit testimony against the sin of slavery." The upshot was the adoption of a resolution in support, after the defeat of a much more strongly worded one which would, in effect, have proscribed any clergyman in the denomination who did not oppose the institution. As Cobb pointed out in calling for a less provocative resolution than the one originally offered by E.Y. Perry of Hanson, societies and churches could be led "the right way" but not driven. Education, not coercion, was the key to success. The convention voted to meet each fall "until American Slavery is abolished"—a pledge not quite carried out—and Cobb was chosen as the principal speaker for the next meeting.

The sparsely attended second meeting of the Universalist Anti-Slavery Convention took place, again in Lynn, in the fall of 1841. There were thirty-two who signed the convention roll, including six women, as well as several visitors. Only eight Massachusetts communities were represented, and there was one person present from Bath, Maine.[83] The initial action was to adopt unanimously, after long speeches, two resolutions. The first equated the anti-slavery movement with "the cause of truth, justice, and humanity" and made it the duty of all Christians to labor for its success. In the discussion which preceded its passage, E. Thompson made the sweeping declaration that "all believers in Universalism" acknowledged slavery to be wrong. The second resolution expressed the optimistic view that the anti-slavery cause was making "sure progress" among Massachusetts Universalists despite the fact that no association or convention had yet seen fit to adopt any statement expressing an opinion on the subject. Those present were unaware that the Maine Convention had already acted just a few days before. As soon as he heard of its anti-slavery resolution, Cobb inserted in his paper a notice of the fact, so that the anti-slavery convention minutes could be corrected accordingly.

J.M. Spear was not as sanguine as Thompson about the progress of the anti-slavery movement within the denomination. So far as he knew, most associations which had paid any attention to the subject were decidedly opposed to taking any action at all. The anti-slavery resolution adopted by the Old Colony Conference had barely passed, and only after great debate. John Allen agreed with Spear, and opposed the second resolution because it was contrary to the facts. He noted that the meeting was even more thinly attended than the one the previous year. He saw no sign of progress in the cause. But the optimists at the convention won the day, for a resolution was adopted acknowledging with great satifaction that two Universalist societies (in New Bedford and Danvers) as well as the Old Colony Conference had condemned slavery.

The greatest debate of all at the convention centered around four resolutions, eventually adopted, which did nothing to improve relations between Northern and Southern Universalists. Some in the South had already warned their Northern compatriots not to become involved in the controversy over slavery. At their most recent meeting (in 1841) the South Carolina Convention had adopted resolutions protesting what they considered to be unjustified interference with slavery by Northerners, including their fellow Universalists. The South Carolina resolution left no room for doubt: "We entirely disapprove of any interference with the subject of negro Slavery by the people of those States where it does not exist; and we *solemnly protest* against any action on that subject by the brethren of our order."[84] The identical resolution was presented by Allen Fuller, a Southern Universalist clergyman, and unanimously adopted by the Northern Association (Georgia). Fuller, who wrote the circular letter accompanying the minutes of the South Carolina Convention, urged Northern Universalists "to heed the admonition;" otherwise, the unity of the denomination would be disrupted and Universalist preachers in the South would be put in jeopardy.

The anti-slaveryites countered by asserting that no ecclesiastical body, Universalist or otherwise, would deter them from "acting, and acting earnestly and vigorously, for the entire overthrow of American Slavery in the South." When "universal right" was involved, Southern Universalists were obligated to *"obey God rather than man,"* and to practice what their religion taught them, even if it cost them "self-banishment, for safety, from the slave-holding borders." Speaking emphatically in support of the resolutions, Cobb argued that it was better that Universalists be driven from the South than, by remaining, give the impression that Universalism and slavery could coexist. If Southern Universalists thought so, they were betraying their religious and moral principles. There could be no compromise. This was the tenor also of Cobb's rhetorical and emotional keynote address, delivered during the two-day session. J.M. Spear was quick to point out that Northern Universalists found it easier, from their safer location, to speak out against slavery than their Southern brethren who were in a much more perilous position. However, in the last analysis, as both Spear and Cobb argued, "it would be better for our southern brethren to suffer 'persecution for righteousness sake,' than to connive at wickedness." Northern money and influence in the South also came in for a share of blame for sustaining slavery.

L.S. Everett opposed the resolutions on several grounds. What the Southern Universalists needed was support and encouragement in their religious efforts, not "holier than thou" pronouncements from the North. He considered the opposition to Universalism in the South to come not from the slaves or their owners but from orthodox clergy. The real enemy was "partialism," not slavery. Preaching the Gospel did not require preaching against slavery. Further, said Everett, there were other evils besides slavery that needed attention. The North had its own problems, such as exploitation of factory girls and imprisonment for debt—to cite only two instances. Why not concentrate on those? Everett argued that the wording of the resolutions implied that all Southern Universalists, especially clergymen, who did not mount the rostrum to attack slavery were somehow remiss in their duty. What about freedom of conscience of which Universalists were always talking? Were the words "abolitionism" and "virtue" synonymous? Everett went on to point out that the condition of the slaves was not as horrible as had been pictured by radical abolitionists and that the position of free Blacks in the North was, generally speaking, worse than that of the slave in the South. Race prejudice and discrimination in the North had recently been demonstrated by the policy of several railroads of requiring segregated facilities. Everett had completely supported the resolution unanimously passed by the convention during that same session censuring the Eastern Railroad Corporation and the New Bedford and Taunton Railroad Corporation for inflicting such "outrages."

Everett argued that the common brotherhood for which Universalists contended was not identical with literal equality; there were some distinctions among men, he said, that had been "set up by the Almighty." Granted this, the true obligation of Universalists was "to labor for the good of every member of the human family." Given the fact of the existence of slavery, the task was to see that the slave was treated kindly. Perhaps, Everett believed, the colonization of the Black somewhere—in another location besides the South or even in another country—might eventually be the best peaceful solution. If Blacks could be gradually emancipated from slave status but left temporarily under white tutelage and moved, perhaps somewhere west of the Mississippi River, then the problem might be solved. Blacks could then be "instructed, elevated, improved intellectually, and thus be fitted to enjoy liberty with us." Everett was suggesting here one of several proposals which were considered before the Civil War involving the relocation of the Blacks.

There was at least one "man of color" at the 1841 meeting, and he could no longer keep silent after listening to Everett. His name was Frederick Douglass of New Bedford, who had probably come on invitation of J.M. Spear, the pastor of the society there. Douglass, who became the best-known black abolitionist in America, was a native of the Eastern Shore of Maryland. He had escaped from bondage in 1838 and had located temporarily in Massachusetts.[85] Just a few months before attending the Universalist convention he had spoken about his experiences as a slave at an anti-slavery meeting in Nantucket. He had made such an impression that the Massachusetts Anti-Slavery Society promptly employed him as a lecturer. In this capacity he spoke and travelled widely for four years, and attracted international attention because of the power of his oratory and the publication of several autobiographical narratives, the first of which had appeared in Boston in 1845.

Before challenging some of Everett's assertions, Douglass pointed out that, unlike Everett, he knew of slavery from personal experience. He flatly contradicted Everett's statement that slavery was not "necessarily, a system of cruelty." Although Douglass had never had a day's formal schooling in his life, his common sense told him that the master-slave relation could not be sustained without harsh treatment. The fact that a few of the slaves were well treated did not justify the institution. He cited several instances of cruelty (reproduced in his autobiography), including one in which he had been a victim.[86] He had once, he told his audience, been handcuffed and dragged fifteen miles behind a horse, on his way to jail; he was suspected of having forged a pass to allow him to leave the plantation, and of having aided two other slaves to escape. Yet his master, Thomas Auld, was at the time a devout Methodist, having been converted at a revival in 1832. Whether or not slaves were well treated was not the issue in Douglass' view. The basic question was the right of one man to claim ownership of another—"the right to make a chattel of one, an intelligent, thinking being, to appropriate my earnings to himself, and to sell me in the market like a dumb beast." Everett presumably abstained when the votes in favor of the resolutions aimed at the South were adopted unanimously.

After the convention was over, the clerk, John Prince, was apparently concerned about the effect the resolutions might have on Southern Universalists. He published an "Appendix to the Minutes" in which he assured them that the intent was not to stir up animosities or to create division but to exert only a moral influence.[87] He called attention to the fact that Everett differed sharply from the majority of his colleagues in several of his ideas about slavery, but felt free at the same time to express his own convictions and was given liberty to do so. This was the way things should be—"Come now, and let us reason together."

There is no indication that such Southern Universalist clergymen as L.F.W. Andrews, Allen Fuller, Philo Brownson, Albert Case, John C. Burruss, or D.B. Clayton tempered their views or that Prince's attempt at conciliation lessened the assumed threat from the North to Southern institutions and Southern security. Although few in number, most Universalist clergymen in the South did not hesitate to speak their minds on slavery, and their views were frequently at complete odds with those of their Northern brethren. L.F.W. Andrews, editor of the *Southern Evangelist,* was among the most outspoken in his criticism of abolitionists in general and sometimes of anti-slavery Universalists in particular. While on a visit to the North in 1835 he prepared an editorial on the subject which he sent back to Montgomery, Alabama, to be published in his paper. Under the heading "Doings of Fanatics," he told his Southern readers of a "restless faction of *religionists* at the north, who are forever conjuring up some new subject of excitement, wherewith to inflame the public mind and keep the people in a whirl of emotion."[88] Their latest preoccupation was with "the *immediate emancipation* of all slaves in the United States." The South was justly indignant, said Andrews, at the conduct of "such madmen as [Arthur] Tappan, [William Lloyd] Garrison, [A.L.] Cox and [George] Thompson," who were producing "mischievous effects of that false and misdirected philanthropy." It was a new form of "partialism"—for the Blacks over the whites—and would result in no good.

Andrews offered the familiar argument that the laboring classes in the North were much worse off than "the whole race of blacks, in the whole South!" Northerns had better put their own house in order before interfering in someone else's business. He put his newspaper on record as "in every sense of the word an anti-Abolitionist journal [which] will ever, while under the control of its present conductor, who is a native of the South and a Southern[er] in feeling, oppose each and every one of those measures which have for their object the disorganization and ruin of the Southern portion of our beloved country."[89]

He was delighted when the Massachusetts Universalist Convention in 1838 postponed indefinitely an anti-slavery resolution, and thought it should have expelled "those factious spirits who are madly interfering with what does not concern them." He recommended that any incipient abolitionist movement within Universalism should be promptly "vetoed." Otherwise, the denomination would be threatened with the sort of schism that some other denominations were already facing. He requested that the proprietors of such "vile abolitionist prints" as the *Emancipator* (New York) and the *Independent Messenger* (the schismatic Restorationist paper in Boston) keep them "at home, as we have no use for such publications."[90] For a brief period in the 1830s when he was an editor of the *Southern Pioneer* in Baltimore, Andrews accused Everett of being an abolitionist (which he was not) and attacked other Universalist editors for supporting abolition merely because they did not speak on behalf of the South.[91] Andrews would admit of no compromise or accommodation.

When Universalism was attacked at a Methodist camp meeting in Monroe, Georgia, as "worse than Abolitionism," Andrews immediately rose to the challenge—but to defend Universalism and not abolitionism. In fact, he "positively and unequivocally" denied that Universalism and abolitionism had the least affinity.[92] On the contrary, he was prepared to prove that the principles advocated by Universalists were "the *only* principles upon which any *Southern* man can or does act, if he would hope to preserve his hearth-stone from blood and his country from devastation!" And what were the principles?—"prompt and certain punishment according to the deed, and in proportion to the magnitude of the offense committed . . . a present and prompt retribution is far more restraining in its influence than distant and uncertain punishment." This was a common-sense principle practiced by "every slave-holder in the South." A good cowhide promptly applied to recalcitrant slaves was much more effective "than all the *hells* ever heard of . . . . Every one can perceive, therefore, that it is *only* on the principles of the Universalist, to wit—a *just, prompt,* and *certain* punishment in this life, that he or any other man could retain his lawful power over his bondsmen." Thus reasoned the fiery Universalist editor who reminded his readers time and again that he was a Southerner "by birth and feeling, and an *anti-abolitionist* in heart and soul" who resented bitterly "those who would madly and wickedly interfere with the domestic policy and institutions of the South."

Andrews' reaction to Cobb's announcement that he planned to publish the *Christian Freeman,* to be devoted in part to opposing slavery, was vigorously negative. He was "deeply mortified" that a man of Cobb's stature in the denomination would embark on "such an unholy crusade against the rights and interests and feelings of his Southern brethren."[93] Cobb reminded the aggressive Southern editor that Universalism was a religion of love, and not of vindictiveness, and that its adherents could not stand by and see a part of the human race being deprived of "their rights and privileges as God's moral children."

Philo Brownson, who succeeded Andrews as editor of the *Evangelical Universalist* published in Macon, Georgia, made a plea for continued support of the paper. In announcing his editorial policy, he explained that he would advocate "the civil, and religious rights of every man to worship God as he pleases" and would oppose "ecclesiastical tyranny" of all kinds.[94] But simultaneously, he urged "every liberal minded man to support a paper which possesses some sympathy on the all absorbing question of slavery." His policy was made crystal clear: "We do not admit slavery to be an evil, but the greatest blessing that ever happened to the Negro race."[95] He opposed the giving of religious instruction to slaves and the policy of some denominations, such as the Methodists, of encouraging Blacks to preach. He was not even averse to carrying notices of slave auctions and of runaway slaves in his paper.[96] Brownson accused Whittemore of being an abolitionist and condemned the *Trumpet* for its anti-slavery bias.[97] Cobb in turn went so far as to raise the question in 1842 of whether Brownson's paper (by then renamed the *Southern Universalist*) should even be "fellowshipped" as a denominational paper.[98] No decision had to be made, for the paper went out of business that same year.

Another defender of slavery and the South among Universalist clergymen was Albert Case. While pastor of the society in Charleston,

South Carolina, in 1839 he greeted with great pleasure the news of the renunciation of Universalism by William Whiting of Abington, Massachusetts. After Whiting had been disfellowshipped by the Old Colony Association, Case announced that it was no great loss; after all, Whiting was "a raving abolitionist" who attacked the Southern way of life.[99] It is not known whether Case was aware of later developments concerning Whiting; if so, he was undoubtedly less than happy. In 1845 the Old Colony Association annulled its earlier action and restored Whiting to full fellowship.[100] Case could take comfort from the fact that a leading Northern Universalist like L.S. Everett condemned the "wild and fanatical schemes" of the radical abolitionists.[101] Case interpreted Everett's somewhat ambivalent stand on slavery as a "defense of the legal institutions of the South."

Spencer J. McMorris, Universalist clergyman and newspaper editor in Alabama, was at first equivocal about expressing his views on slavery, and apparently hesitated before informing Northern Universalists of where he stood. But by 1846 he made his pro-slavery commitment known. His situation was compounded at first by a series of misunderstandings from which he managed to extricate himself, but not before stirring up great excitement among Northern Universalist abolitionists. In 1841 John Allen, who had delivered a strong anti-slavery sermon to the Old Colony Association in Massachusetts, sent to McMorris a copy of the *Christian Freeman* in which the sermon had been published. McMorris was then living in Lafayette, Alabama. In due course the newspaper was returned, with postage unpaid, and with a note scrawled across one margin signed with McMorris' initials. It referred to Allen as "a Blackleg of the blackest kind" who would "instantly be put to death" if he preached such a sermon in the South.[102]

Nothing more was heard of the incident for almost two years. In the meantime Philo Brownson's pro-slavery *Southern Universalist* had ceased publication and McMorris undertook to replace it with the *Messenger of Glad Tidings.* The news was greeted with pleasure in the North, for Brownson's paper was considered "hostile to the spirit of Universalism."[103] The hope was expressed that McMorris' new paper would not be disfigured by "the stains of slavery."[104] But it appeared that this optimism was premature. One of the early issues of the *Messenger of Glad Tidings* carried the sad tidings of an escaped slave who had been jailed until his owner could retrieve him. McMorris then found himself roundly condemned by three Northern Universalist editors—Drew of the *Gospel Banner,* Cobb, and Whittemore.[105] McMorris admitted that his paper had carried the notice about the escaped slave, but insisted that it had been inserted, contrary to his instructions, by a printer from another paper who was temporarily assisting him.[106] McMorris belatedly denied that he was responsible for the return of Allen's sermon almost two years before, or for the uncomplimentary remarks accompanying it. He was, he said, in Mississippi at the time of the incident, and the unauthorized note had been written by the postmaster at Lafayette during McMorris' absence. McMorris reported that the postmaster had subsequently been discharged for indulging in such unauthorized activities. These explanations seemed to have restored confidence in McMorris among northern Universalists, but it was short-lived.

In 1845 McMorris issued an editorial plea for support of a new paper he had begun—the *Gospel Messenger*—after his earlier attempt with the *Messenger of Glad Tidings* had failed. The grounds on which McMorris argued were completely unacceptable to most Northern Universalists. He justified his paper on the premise that it was needed "to defend our views against the pernicious sentiments of Northern Abolitionists."[107] He informed his readers that Northern newspapers to which Universalists in the South subscribed were "apt to be tinctured with the poison of abolitionism." To make matters worse, the same issue in which this editorial appeared carried an advertisment of slaves available for hire from the estate of a deceased slaveholder for which McMorris was the administrator.

Tension between Northern and Southern Universalist newspaper editors reached even greater intensity after 1850, the year that John C. Burruss of Alabama established the *Universalist Herald.* This paper became not only the sole denominational paper in the South but the one with the longest continuous history. The policy of carrying advertisements for slaves which McMorris had followed and which had so upset Cobb was continued by Burruss and resulted in an acrimonious verbal duel which lasted virtually until the *Herald* was suspended in 1861. (Publication of the paper was resumed in 1867, under the same editorship). The controversy between the two men was precipitated in 1855 when Cobb told the readers of his *Christian Freeman* that there was no longer a Universalist paper in the South. He admitted the existence of the *Herald,* but denied that it could be considered a truly denominational paper as long as it made "part of its business to advertise colored people as articles of merchandise" and failed to acknowledge that all men were brothers.[108] J.M.H. Smith, a Universalist preacher who had lived in the South for ten years, and in 1864 moved to the North to avoid conscription in the Confederate army, was at the time of Cobb's attack residing in Huntsville, Alabama.[109] Smith came immediately to the defense of the *Universalist Herald* and its editor. He challenged Cobb's self-appointed task of casting the *Herald* out of the denomination merely because its editor was following Southern laws and customs.[110] Cobb's rejoinder was prompt and to the point. In the first place, he was speaking as an individual and in his editorial capacity and not *ex cathedra.* More important, Smith and Burruss were neglecting their responsibilities by abandoning the mission of Christianity as a "reformatory instrumentality." Cobb then lectured Smith at great length for supporting slavery and told him that taking such a position brought "shame to the denomination throughout the world" and retarded the progress of the Universalist cause everywhere.[111] Even though Smith accused Cobb of "*irrelevant* meandering," the exchanges between the two remained on a relatively civil level.

This was not the case when Burruss joined the dispute. Even the usually mild-mannered and temperate Cobb was stung to anger. Burruss' reply to Cobb's attack on the *Herald* comprised a series of banner headlines: "The South Again Insulted: More Abolition Insolence!" He lumped together all opponents of slavery, including Universalists, as "fanatical abolitionists at the North" who were engaged in the "filthy, contemptible work" of attacking Southern institutions. Burruss accused Cobb of having come forth "to snarl and snap at Southern men" and made the unqualified statement that "the Universalist papers at the North are the enemies of the South."[112] Cobb retorted by calling Burruss "a bar-room linguist" and accused him of deliberately distorting Cobb's language. Cobb finally announced that he would refuse any longer to publish Burruss' "rash invectives and reckless assertions and denials."[113] Tempers cooled somewhat and a species of truce was declared in 1856, when, in spite of all his fulminations, Burruss did promise to refrain from carrying slave-trading advertisements in his paper. This naturally pleased Cobb, who took the credit for this "great improvement;" however, he could not resist the comment that the style of the *Herald* sometimes resembled that of a partisan political journal rather than of a religious paper.[114]

Editorial relations did improve somewhat between Cobb and Burruss in the late 1850s, after Burruss retreated from his earlier aggressiveness. In 1858 Cobb found Burruss' paper "much improved" after the editor had apparently "resigned the guardianship of the 'peculiar institution' " and had devoted most of the columns of the *Herald* to other subjects.[115] But this in no sense meant that Burruss had changed his feelings about slavery or had become reconciled to Northern criticism; he had other editors to battle besides Cobb.

At least one Universalist clergyman in the South went a step beyond rhetorical pronouncements. After the Confederate States of America was formed in 1861, both the forty-year-old D.B. Clayton of Holly Springs, Mississippi, and his nineteen-year-old son enlisted in the Jeff Davis Rifles, a contingent of the Ninth Mississippi Regiment.[116] Clayton hoped that he would never be called upon to fight, but he felt constrained to enlist for two reasons: He refused to accept the sectional domination of the North, and he could never subscribe to the idea of Negro equality with the white man. He believed firmly in the "heritage of social superiority [of] the Anglo-Saxon race . . . over the flat-nosed, kinky haired sons and daughters of Africa." Cobb was greatly incensed by Clayton's remarks and hoped that the Southerner would "never dishonor the Universalist name by returning again to its ministry, unless he shall give satisfactory evidence of his hearty repentance of his apostasy." As if to defy the South in general and Clayton in particular, Cobb printed in the same issue in which Clayton's communication was reprinted, both the words and music of the "Star Spangled Banner."

Clayton actually served in the military less than a year because of ill health, and his place was taken by a younger volunteer. But he remained a loyal Confederate throughout the conflict, and when General Ulysses S. Grant's troops occupied the community where Clayton lived, his home was ransacked and burned.[117] For over twenty years after his brief military career, Clayton became one of the best-known and most widely-travelled preachers and newspaper editors among Southern Universalists. Cobb did not live to receive the evidence of Clayton's "hearty repentance of his apostasy," on which he had insisted, for the New England editor died in 1866. But many years later Clayton wrote that the Civil War had come out as it should have, and that "slavery, as an institution, was inherently wrong in principle . . . and, as such, was bound to perish." He held fast, however, to his views about the black man, and stressed the "civilizing influence" of the white on the semi-barbaric Negro; slavery, he insisted to the end, was worse for the whites than for those enslaved.

Pro-slavery pronouncements by Southern Universalists were a source of constant embarrassment to co-religionists in the North. To attempt to shut them up would have been completely contrary to Universalist principles. Instead, the Anti-Slavery Convention continued to use "sweet reason" to attempt to correct erring Southerners, and tried to find ways to paste over the cracks within the denomination caused by disagreement over slavery. Concern over the "southern question" was expressed in some manner at every Anti-Slavery Convention meeting, and by many other Universalist groups in the North.

Some Universalists above the Mason-Dixon line, particularly those who had some first-hand knowledge of the South, were worried about the spread of exaggerated and inaccurate conceptions of what went on in that part of the nation and undertook to correct such misapprehensions. One such Universalist was Samuel P. Skinner, who had lived for several years in the slave-holding border state of Maryland and was co-editor with his brother, Otis A. Skinner, of the *Southern Pioneer* in Baltimore. In the mid-1830s, Samuel Skinner had reassured readers that "the great body of the people of the North view with indignation and horror the incendiary effections of the abolitionists."[118] He likewise made the point that he was no advocate of slavery and would support "any lawful and expedient means" for getting rid of it.[119]

A correspondent in the *Christian Freeman* was convinced that Universalism could never be firmly established in the South because clergy there were not allowed to preach "the pure gospel" or to apply it to uproot slavery; or, if they tried, they would suffer martyrdom.[120] Skinner challenged all of these generalizations with concrete evidence. He considered these assertions false and unfounded, unjust to both the South and derogatory to Universalists residing there.[121] Skinner indicated that during his eight years in Maryland he was not molested or hindered a single time in expressing his ideas. Both his brother and Edwin H. Chapin had formerly lived in slaveholding states (Maryland and Virginia, respectively) and had retained the confidence and respect of Universalists both North and South. Visiting Universalists from the North were "uniformly well received" in the South.

Skinner pointed out that there were twenty-seven Universalist preachers in nine slaveholding states in 1844, and all but ten were formally fellowshipped. Their mission was to exert a moral rather than a political influence. He knew of no attempt by any Universalist clergy in the South either to interfere with existing political arrangements or to go to the barricades by demanding immediate and unconditional emancipation or otherwise inciting to rebellion. Skinner realized the sensitivity of the South regarding slavery and understood the resentment at "what they regard as improper interference with that which chiefly concerns themselves . . . by the action of Northern abolitionists." It was no wonder, he said, that Southerners tried to protect themselves, wrong as they might be. Skinner was sure that he spoke not for himself alone, but for "nearly all our ministers who are engaged in the anti-slavery movements." Accusations based on emotion and on incomplete or distorted information rather than on reason based in turn on truth could result only in "exciting embittered and angry feelings towards our Southern brethren."

One Universalist clergyman who saw slavery at first hand, albeit in a fragmentary and hurried way, was the much-travelled George Rogers. Using Cincinnati as a headquarters betweeen 1834 and his death in 1846, he made five extended tours into all the slaveholding states except the Carolinas. He kept Universalists abreast of his itinerant life with lively accounts published from time to time in Universalist periodicals and summarized in his autobiography, published the year before he died. Rogers, who grew up on the Middle Atlantic seaboard, made it known that he was in no sense an apologist for slavery. It was to him a "vice" and an "insufferable curse."[122] He hoped that somehow it could be abolished "in a way consistent with the happiness of the enslaved, and the rights and safety of their masters."[123] He believed the best solution to be compensated emancipation for which he was willing to be taxed. Young Blacks could serve as apprentices in various trades, and the money they earned could be set aside for the day they were prepared to establish their own businesses. Thus the freeman would be prepared not only for self-support but would "erase the reproach of natural incapacity which has long attached to the African race."[124] Rogers estimated that an initial investment of one million dollars was needed to get the proposal under way, with a pilot program involving 4,000 Blacks. If free Blacks could not be "colonized on a domain by themselves" to protect them from unscrupulous whites, and the two races had to coexist, Rogers would extend to Blacks "*every* civil and political right which we ourselves claim and exercise."[125]

A variation on the same proposal outlined by Rogers was offered in 1853, and reported by Sylvanus Cobb. Slaveholders were to be compensated for loss of investment and thereby encouraged to emancipate their slaves. Congress could provide that if and when a state agreed to abolish the institution within its borders, an inventory of every slave would be made, and a sum of money paid to the state by the United States Treasury for each. This plan would provide reimbursement to the ex-slaveholder without placing the entire burden on the state.[126] If a border state such as Kentucky took the lead, Cobb thought that others would follow, and liberty could be proclaimed throughout the land. This was, he believed, a better use of American resources than fighting wars such as the one recently concluded with Mexico.

Rogers found on personal inspection that the system of slavery was not nearly as horrible as portrayed in the Northern abolitionist press. He reported, after a trip through Tennessee, Kentucky, and Mississippi in 1840, that slavery was an easy-going and tolerant system, and that the enslaved Blacks were often happier and more relaxed than the free whites.[127] He talked to slaveholders wherever he could, and found that humanitarian considerations existed side-by-side with economic and social pressures. He reported one conversation with an Alabaman who wished to emancipate his remaining thirty slaves but could not afford to.[128] It was against the law to free them without removing them from the state, and the slaveholder was unwilling to send them North without resources or protection. Rogers uncovered one free black man and his family who were members of the Mt. Olympus Universalist society in Alabama.[129] They were "of industrious, prudent habits, and much respected," and were apparently also Americanized, at least by Southern standards. They were opposed to abolitionist agitation and considered slavery "a providential visitation upon them for their barbarous and unnatural conduct toward each other in the parent country [Africa]." The free Black also approved the policy of colonization in Africa, but was sufficiently Universalized to decline to go himself to Liberia because of the fear that the white-sponsored colony there was "strongly sectarian in its character [and] would not comport with his enjoyment of the rights of conscience."

Isaac D. Williamson reported much the same experience as did Rogers. Williamson, a native of Vermont who had held several pastorates in New England and elsewhere, moved to Baltimore in the late 1830s. He noted that "my education, my religious principles, and all my habits of thought and feeling are opposed to slavery. But I confess that my views have somewhat changed upon that subject since I have been here."[130] He was particularly concerned for the free Blacks, for whom emancipation had been largely a tragedy, and was much concerned about the plight of the whites. He had found in Baltimore (admittedly in a border state and not in the Deep South) many who considered slavery an evil. But they had inherited an institution they did not know how to eradicate "without inflicting a worse evil upon themselves and their slaves." Neither did Williamson have a solution to offer.

Eliphalet Case, who moved to Richmond, Virginia, and remained as firmly opposed to slavery as ever, was frank to admit that after actually having been in the South he realized that "the most extravagant views prevail at the North about slavery."[131] Henceforth he would "look with many grains of allowance on much that I hear on the subject from those who never crossed the dividing line between it and freedom." A northern Universalist (C.D. Stewart) made an extensive trip into the South in the winter of 1844-45, including Virginia, the Carolinas, Georgia, and Alabama, and reported his impressions of slavery.[132] He came to the conclusion that the lot of the slave was not nearly as bad as had been pictured, and that the stories about "scars and lashes" were "a thorough bugbear . . . . The meddling of the North . . . has done more to hinder emancipation than all else put together." Like many other observers, this traveller was sure that the whites were as much victimized as the Blacks. The white Southerners were living "over a quick-sand that may [over] whelm them . . . . The hour must come, and the South must rise, and rescue itself from lassitude and slumber, or perish in the mesh it has woven!" He was a firmer opponent of slavery than ever after he attended a slave auction in Montgomery. Alabama, and watched a woman being sold—"one poor soul unhappily disguised by a black skin." Most of the evidence presented by Universalists who travelled or lived in the South before the Civil War points to the prevalence of ignorance and misunderstanding about the circumstances prevailing in both North and South. When E.H. Lake, who established himself in North Carolina on the eve of the Civil War, visited Boston in 1858 and was asked "a thousand and one" questions about slavery, he decided that the North was as ignorant of the South "as the reverse."[133]

Northern Universalists who travelled in the South always ran the risk of criticism by their abolitionist-minded brethren when they recorded their impressions of slavery and failed to condemn it unreservedly. George Bates of Maine made a "flying tour" through the South—mainly to Georgia—and found the material condition of the slave to be not nearly so wretched and miserable as portrayed in the North.[134] Sylvanus Cobb did not deny the possibility, but was quick to reply that Bates had missed the point. Most slaves had no other alternative than to make the best of their situation. This in no way justified or excused the system. It was still an abomination to be wiped out, and Cobb was afraid that people failed to make the important distinction between the superficially acceptable practices of slaveholders and the evils of the system itself.

Universalists in the Midwest who expressed themselves on slavery were less aggressive in their opposition than their Eastern brethren; some even came to the defense of the South. Jonathan Kidwell, itinerant preacher, newspaper editor, and controversialist *par excellence* in Indiana, had been reared in the border state of Kentucky and was considerably more sympathetic to the slaveholder than his New England contemporaries. He admitted that slavery was a moral, social, and political evil, but until the federal constitution was amended (which he thought most unlikely), Southern slaveholders had rights which had to be protected.[135] He was an eyewitness in 1844 to an attempt by an "abolition mob" in Hamilton County, Indiana, to take by force six or seven Blacks who were in the custody of a state officer. This was nothing more than "an open hostility to the letter and spirit of our government."[136] He was convinced that the inflammatory attacks of the abolitionists would destroy the Union; the cure—the destruction of slavery—would be much worse than the disease. It was a system too deeply entrenched to be ended without violence and bloodshed. He pointedly asked Eastern Universalists: "Who made you and your abolition brethren guardians for the Southern states and their colored population?"[137] He was frank to admit that in his estimation " 'The Negro race' in regard to their mental and moral faculties, are naturally inferior to the whites." The best solution was to keep the Blacks in slavery and treat them well.

It is impossible to determine how many Universalists in the pre-Civil War South were slaveholders, but the fact that some existed is indisputable. There are numerous references in the denominational press, correspondence, and other sources to "our slaveholding brethren;" these references are unmistakeably to Universalists and do not refer to "brethren" in the generic sense.[138] Almon Gage, pastor of the society in Richmond, Virginia, in 1850, told the Universalist General Reform Association that he had slaveholders in his congregation.[139] William Bell, a Universalist clergyman from Lowell, Massachusetts, spent most of the winter of 1848-49 in eastern North Carolina as the guest of G.C. Marchant, a physician and active Universalist layman.[140] While there, Bell preached in four communities to congregations which included both slaveholders and slaves. He scrupulously avoided mentioning his own firm anti-slavery views for fear of stirring up trouble, but he was saddened to find himself preaching to white Universalists who, while "professing a belief in the impartial love of God to his children," were holding other men "in servile bondage" and treating them as property. Bell hoped to see slavery only "in its mildest form" while in North Carolina, for he could not "behold it in any other and *keep cool.*" His wish was gratified, but he found the entire system—benign or otherwise—completely objectionable. It was a curse and a "blighting influence over the people," both slave and free.

Another Universalist who saw slavery at first-hand, but for a much longer period and under different circumstances than the foregoing, was Mary A. Livermore, one of the most prominent women in the denomination in the nineteenth and early twentieth centuries. She spent three years (1841-43) in southern Virginia as a teacher for the six children of a wealthy planter, and her experience impressed her sufficiently to cause her to devote over one-third of her long autobiography to her sojourn in the South.[141] She returned to her native New England "a pronounced abolitionist, accepting from no one any apology for slavery," even though she had seen it "in its mildest form, . . . under its best administration, and in the most favorable part of the South." She had arrived in complete ignorance of slavery, and with only a vague feeling of "colorphobia." She departed with a wider knowledge of, and sympathy for, both the white Southern planter and the enslaved Black, caught as they were in the web of a vicious system. The slaveholder who was her employer was apparently among the more humane planters, operating an enterprise with a slave population of approximately 500. But Mrs. Livermore saw enough of slavery to recoil from it in every way. Upon return to the North, she became a subscriber to Garrison's *Liberator,* attended every anti-slavery meeting she could, and contributed funds to the abolitionist cause. She considered Harriet Beecher Stowe's rendition of slavery in *Uncle Tom's Cabin,* which she read serially before it was published in book form in 1852, to have been a realistic portrayal.

Chapter 22

BRETHREN ONCE MORE

Taking an Official Position

Eighteen clergymen and sixteen laymen and women signed the roll as members of the third annual meeting of the Universalist Anti-Slavery Convention, which was held in East Boston in the fall of 1842.[1] Others were present but did not vote, including Hosea Ballou, who alleged that he did not even know until the day that the convention met that the organization existed, although he was "heartily opposed to slavery." But he refused to sign the roll on the ground that the discussion of slavery was not a proper denominational question. It was a tumultuous meeting. The sessions were lengthy and active, the debates lively and protracted, and the convention itself remained in session an entire day longer than originally planned.

Members of the convention plunged into the subject of slavery without delay, and immediately divided over a resolution stating without equivocation that "perverted religion" was the strongest supporter of slavery, and that "reformation in the church" had to be the first step in the abolition of that Southern institution. Disagreement with this viewpoint was promptly registered. It was considered too strong and too sweeping a condemnation, and the resolution overlooked the other villains in sustaining slavery, such as the spirit of avarice (emphasized earlier by Elhanan Winchester), "the love of power," and political expediency. A resolution making "the prevailing corruption of the religion of the country from christian purity" *one* of the causes for the perpetuating of slavery rather than *the* effective hindrance to the abolition of slavery fared somewhat better. It was finally adopted "as the sentiment of the Convention" when debate was brought to a close.

The termination of discussion was brought about in part after the assemblage was addressed by a visitor who, after listening to the various arguments, came to the conclusion that the Universalists seemed "not to know where to begin, or how to approach the subject." The visitor was black abolitionist Lunsford Lane. Like Frederick Douglass, who had attended the convention the previous year, Lane had escaped from slavery. He was from Raleigh, North Carolina, and had spent eighteen of his thirty-two years purchasing freedom for himself, his wife, and seven children. He was employed as a lecturer on the abolitionist circuit by the New England Anti-Slavery Society after making a speech at an anti-slavery convention in New York City.[2]

Much time and effort was expended during the second day of the convention on a resolution (overwhelmingly but by no means unanimously defeated) which would have ruled out the consideration of slavery by any established Universalist religious bodies except those called specifically to discuss and act on the subject. This met with strenuous objection as a species of "gag rule." J.M. Spear argued that conventions, associations, and societies were the very place where slavery *should* be discussed, and expressed regret that separate anti-slavery conventions had to be held at all. Otis A. Skinner, who had introduced the resolution, took the opposite view, arguing that discussion of slavery would result in fatal division within Universalism, and accused his abolitionist colleagues of trying to "destroy the church in the madness of their zeal, and overturn all our religious societies and organizations." Skinner was, in turn, accused of gross exaggeration and of fostering a delusion. Nothing daunted, Skinner tried again, and this time his resolution passed in spite of much opposition. It condemned slavery in all of its aspects, but looked "with painful emotions" on the bitter and vindictive spirit manifested by some (unnamed) abolitionists who were using "reckless and disorganizing measures" to achieve their goal.

Before acknowledging by resolution that the year 1842 marked the fifth anniversary of emancipation in the British West Indies, the convention unanimously adopted a resolution expressing sympathy for an escaped slave, George Latimore, then imprisoned in the Leverett Street jail in Boston on orders from his master in Norfolk, Virginia. The convention, through Cobb's efforts, tried to steer a course which would both placate and reprimand Universalist clergy in the South. While deeply sympathizing with them, and attempting to appreciate the situation in which they found themselves, the convention scolded Southern Universalists for their "servility in the slave interest, and advocacy of the unchristian, oppressive, and alarming system of slavery." The "prostitution" of the *Southern Universalist,* the only denominational journal then in the region (1840-42), to the slave dealer by carrying advertisements for the sale of Negroes was likewise deprecated in very strong language. Cobb scoffed at the threat of disruption of either the denomination or of the American Union implied in the resolutions from the South. Even if secession of the South did take place, preservation of national unity was secondary to the maintenance of principle; "we had rather that ourselves and our children should be saved, than that our whole country should become like unto Sodom."[3] Even the creation of a separate South would not silence the voices of admonition from the North.

In 1842 several resolutions on slavery were introduced at the annual meeting of the Boston Association.[4] Feelings ran high. A resolution protesting the jailing of the runaway slave George Latimore was indefinitely postponed by a vote of 13 to 10 "after much discussion and excitement, and questioning about ecclesiastical bodies interfering with laws."[5] Only one resolution condemning slavery in general, worded in the vaguest of language, was passed, and even then there was much dissatisfaction with this action in view of the fact that a separate anti-slavery body already existed where the matter could be more appropriately considered. The Middlesex Quarterly Conference in Massachusetts unanimously passed two anti-slavery resolutions the same year.[6] However, another resolution criticizing Southern Universalists for objecting to the anti-slavery sentiments of their Northern brethren passed with only a slim majority. The Second Universalist Society in Lynn, Massachusetts, also adopted a series of resolutions in 1843 opposing slavery. They called for freedom for the slave by applying the principle of love of mankind rather than calling down "fire from heaven" on the heads of slaveholders, who would realize eventually that "we are all brethren."[7]

The Hancock and Washington Association (Maine), which had been the pioneer group in condemning slavery in 1841, carried the generalized ideas expressed by the Lynn society one step farther in 1842. The association completely repudiated the view of one of its number who had expressed reservations about whether universal salvation applied to Blacks. Such doubt was "iniquitous in itself . . . slanderous and subversive of our principles; and further was tending to foster that prejudice which already exists in the community, shutting out our colored brethren from the rights and privileges of society; and aiding to perpetuate that slavery which is *the curse* of the land."[8]

The action taken by the Vermont State Convention was the most heartening news in Universalist anti-slavery ranks for the year 1842. Eli Ballou, a leading Vermont Universalist and newspaper editor, introduced three resolutions which, after calling forth "spirited yet friendly remarks," were adopted. The first Universalist organization at the state level had expressed itself on the issue.[9] The third of the resolutions illustrates the circumspection with which the subject was handled: "Resolved that while we disclaim all intention of acting as political abolitionists in our denominational capacity, we cannot consistently neglect to bear a faithful testimony against the sin of slavery, and in the spirit of Christian fraternal kindness to warn those who hold slaves of the evils to which their sin exposes them, and to exhort them kindly to cease to do evil and learn to do well." Few if any Universalists probably realized, unless they had had access to the records, that a resolution to this same effect, although somewhat more vigorously worded, had been introduced into the Vermont Convention in 1838. It had been defeated by a resolution by the same person who had introduced the one four years later. Eli Ballou had in 1838 argued that it was "inexpedient to pass any resolution either for or against . . . or to agitate the subject of Southern slavery at all in our councils."[10] It was evident by 1842 that times and attitudes were changing. A few weeks after the Vermont Convention had acted, the state legislature adopted a series of resolutions protesting the admission to the Union of any state or territory which tolerated slavery, and called for a constitutional amendment to abolish it throughout the nation.[11]

Massachusetts Universalists were the second group to condemn slavery in a state convention. At their meeting in 1843 Charles Spear introduced a resolution which was passed ultimately by a unanimous vote, although the better part of a day was spent in debating it.[12] The resolution was in no sense a belligerent one; it stated in part that "as believers in the common brotherhood of man, we ought to do all we can, consistently with moral means, to remove the evil from the world."[13] Joseph O. Skinner echoed the same theme in the sermon which he delivered at the annual meeting of the Universalist Anti-Slavery Convention in 1843. He told the assemblage that it was not convened "to lay plans of political action, or to meditate forcible resistance to any institution whatever."[14]

Another Universalist meeting in 1843 attracted considerably more attention than that of the anti-slavery convention. The General Convention met in Akron, Ohio, that fall. It was an historic occasion in several respects. It marked the first time that the central body had met west of the Alleghenies; the sessions lasted for a record five days; and the public religious services attracted the largest number of people yet assembled at a Universalist gathering. The meeting was memorable also because the denomination, so far as it had an official body to speak for it at the national level, expressed itself for the first time on the slavery issue.

The subject had been introduced in the annual meeting the year before, but not in the form of an official resolution. Isaac D. Williamson had delivered the occasional sermon in 1842, the theme of which had been the mission of Universalists in promoting Christian progress. In it he had given "an overwhelming swoop" to the principle of anti-slavery.[15] Slavery had also been discussed by the council in connection with other reform movements, such as temperance, but no action had been taken. It was T.J. Sawyer of New York who presented the resolutions in 1843 which, "after an amicable discussion," were adopted with only one dissenting vote among the fifty delegates present (twenty-five clergymen and an equal number of laymen).[16] All the New England states except New Hampshire were represented, and New York State had the largest delegation.

The resolutions condemning slavery reflected the general tenor of

Universalist thinking, which had already been articulated on numerous other occasions. Slavery was considered inconsistent with the basic precepts of Universalism which regarded "the whole human family as in the largest sense our brethren . . . . contrary to the plainest dictates of natural justice and Christian love, and as in every way pernicious alike to the enslaver and the enslaved." It was the particular obligation of Universalists, "by duty and inclination," to be concerned for "the oppressed, the benighted, the downtrodden, of our own and other lands, and to labour for their restoration to the rights and blessings of Freedom, Light, and Truth."

More specifically, "the holding in bondage of our brethren for whom Christ died, or the treatment of any human being with obliquy, harshness, or any indignity on account of his color or race," was "contrary to righteousness, inconsistent with Christianity, and especially with that doctrine of Universal Grace and Love which we cherish as the most important of revealed truth." It was recognized that "many worthy and upright Christians" were slaveholders from either conviction or necessity; nonetheless, the institutions had to be abolished. The means were not to be "indiscriminate denunciation or proscription," which would not be countenanced, but a change of heart brought about by the slaveholders themselves. The resolutions entreated "all Christian and especially all Universalist slaveholders to consider prayerfully the nature and tendencies of the relation they sustain . . . appealing to the gospel, to humanity, and to their own consciences." If "the principles of Divine and Universal Love" were allowed to work, slavery would disappear.[17] Otis A. Skinner, who served as clerk of the convention, considered the resolutions "candid, fair, and plain," and thought they would meet with the approval of all except "the rabid abolitionists."[18]

The action taken by the General Convention caught many Universalists by surprise. Such reformers as Cobb and the Spear brothers were naturally delighted, for they had not really expected the resolutions to pass.[19] J.M. Spear had not anticipated "such strong and pointed resolutions" to be adopted so soon and with such great unanimity.[20] It was especially surprising in view of the opposition expressed even to discussion of the question in so many conferences, associations, and state conventions, not to mention societies. He was also immensely gratified to see that secular papers such as the *New York Tribune* had given the convention anti-slavery resolutions widespread publicity. The fact that its editor, Horace Greeley, was not only a Universalist but a committed reformer might have had something to do with the attention the resolutions received.

Spear quoted with great satisfaction and at length the reactions of the editor of the *Herkimer Journal* (New York) who, although "a decided abolitionist," was far from being a Universalist. The editor of that upstate New York paper commended the denomination for its stand, noting that "the Universalists have been very generally denounced and hated by other religious sects of the country, as a set of unmitigated reprobates, who richly deserved the damnation they so seriously doubted." Here was a relatively small denomination (of about 150,000 members, according to his estimate), but "embracing much eminent talent and moral worth," which had the courage to make its position known. He thanked heaven that "the Universalists have felt constrained to do something, however little . . . . We care not in what light their distinctive religious tenets may be regarded by those who fancy themselves a great deal more righteous than their neighbors; the stand taken by the Universalists in this matter is eminently honorable to them as men, as patriots, and as Christians."

The editor of the Herkimer paper pointedly called attention to the fact that not a single major Protestant denomination had yet taken a public stand on slavery. Instead, some, like the Methodists and Lutherans, were in the process of splintering over the issue. The editor asked if the various large Protestant denominations were not ashamed to be outdone "by those whom they have so long regarded as destitute of all just title to the Christian name." In 1844, the very next year after the Universalists had taken an official stand on slavery, the Methodists divided into nothern and southern wings, as did the Baptists in 1845.[21] The creation of the Methodist Episcopal Church, South, and the Southern Baptist Convention was duly noted by the Universalist press.[22] The denomination, largely because Universalism was so weak in the South, had been spared that disruptive experience, although tension between Universalists in the North and South at some points did reach a critical stage.

A similarly complimentary reaction to the Universalist resolutions came from the editor of the *New World,* a secular journal published in New York City. Universalist editors were so pleased by this that even Price, Whittemore, and Drew, three of Cobb's most articulate critics, reproduced in their papers this "honorable mention" which Cobb had reported in detail.[23] Even the orthodox author of the report of the American and Foreign Anti-Slavery Society in 1853 felt compelled to acknowledge that the Universalist denomination had "embraced anti-slavery truth with readiness, and fearlessly avowed their sentiments."[24]

Other Universalist bodies by the scores followed the lead of the General Convention in repudiating slavery. A local conference in Duxbury, Massachusetts, promptly endorsed the resolutions adopted at the Akron meeting. The Essex County (Massachusetts) Quarterly Conference "heartily concurred" with the resolutions, but only "after considerable discussion, in the course of which a good degree of energy [was] manifested." The Maine State Convention adopted the General Convention resolutions at its meeting in 1844.[25]

There were, of course, dissenting voices. One angry Universalist layman was "perfectly astonished" that the General Convention would dabble in public issues such as slavery.[26] He hoped that it would reconsider its hasty and ill-conceived action at its next session and would expunge the resolutions from the record. If it did not, and continued to intrude into matters outside its proper province, the convention ought to be dissolved. But other Universalists were critical on other grounds. Charles Spear, gratified as he was at the action taken, believed that the convention had not gone far enough. He made an unsuccessful attempt in the Massachusetts Convention in 1844 to read out of the denomination any Universalist "who willingly and wilfully appologizes for the enormous evil." This was too strong medicine to be acceptable, and instead Cobb substituted a much milder and more generalized resolution calling upon Universalists to use their influence to bring about a change of heart among Southern slaveholders which would remove "this mammoth evil from our land."[27] J.M. Spear "deeply regretted" that his brother Charles' resolution did not pass. Cobb disagreed: "Because one certain item in a man's conduct is *inconsistent* with Universalism, therefore he cannot be a Universalist, is neither logic nor philosophy."[28]

Other Universalist bodies followed Cobb's more moderate policy. The Connecticut Convention, in its anti-slavery resolutions adopted in 1844, attempted to strike a balance—on one hand, to "avoid that wild and extravagant fanaticism which looks for the accomplishment of an object without means, or time, and on the other hand, that coldness and indifference which refuses to act when duty prompts."[29] Cobb continued to chide in a gentle but firm way those who objected to denominational involvement with the anti-slavery cause. When the American Anti-Slavery Society held its anniversary meeting in the Second Universalist Church in Philadelphia in 1844, an agitated Universalist clergyman objected strenuously to this "desecration of the place of public worship."[30] He was in turn admonished by Cobb for taking such an uncharitable and un-Universalist attitude and for disclaiming any interest in the abolitionist movement.

The small group of Universalists who kept the anti-slavery agitation in motion continued to prod the denomination into taking further action. In 1845, almost two years after the General Convention had spoken on slavery, Joseph O. Skinner noted glumly that Universalists had been "slow and equivocal" in their response to the evil of slavery; they should have been foremost in the entire anti-slavery movement, and their failure to have been in the vanguard had done them "but little credit."[31] However, something was about to be done.

After the General Convention had completed its scheduled business and religious services in 1845 a large number of individuals remained an additional day "for the purpose of discussing certain important subjects closely connected with the welfare of the denomination." An agenda was hastily prepared which included education, theological schools, the role of the denominational press, and "the great principles of moral reform," including temperance, world peace, the abolition of capital punishment, and the slavery question. Most of these topics had been alluded to in one or more sermons preached during the convention, the majority of which competed with the business sessions of the council.[32]

After a blanket resolution urging effort to promote all moral reforms was unanimously adopted, it was voted overwhelmingly that a committee be appointed to prepare "a solemn, earnest and plain Protest against American Slavery." It was to be presented to every Universalist clergyman for signature; those not willing to sign it were to give their reasons in writing. After the committee had collected the replies, the names of those signing the resolution were to be published, together with the reasons of those declining to sign the documents. Henry Bacon of Rhode Island, Edwin H. Chapin, Lucius R. Paige, Sebastian Streeter, and Sylvanus Cobb, all of the Boston area, constituted the committee. The Protest, written by Bacon after consultation with other members of the committee, added no new arguments against slavery to those already offered by Universalists. Two of the nine reasons adduced to oppose the institution emphasized the moral and religious nature of the slaves, which was being suppressed and denied because of failure to recognize the existence and sanctity of human personality. The core of the objection to slavery was its failure to distinguish between man and property. The whole thrust of the protest was the violation of "moral sense" which slavery represented. There was no call for action other than the use of "all justifiable means" to promote abolition.

The text of the Protest was not published until early in 1846. Cobb printed it in February, together with a long and detailed objection by Isaac D. Williamson, who had recently moved to Mobile, Alabama.[33] Cobb had intended to delay publication until a list of signers could be reported. But Whittemore had forced his hand by publishing the Protest in the *Trumpet* almost a month earlier. Cobb was distressed at the slowness of the clergy to respond, for a similar protest had already been signed by 170 Unitarian ministers.[34] Eventually, 313 Universalist clergy signed their denomination's protest, the largest numbers in Massachusetts, New York, Maine, and Ohio.[35] Whittemore had estimated that at least 400 clergy would sign the petition.[36] There were, according to the *Universalist Register,* 696 preachers in the denomination, which included the Canadian provinces.

Stephen R. Smith of Buffalo, New York, objected at length to the Protest, using familiar arguments: There was an honest difference of opinion about slavery; it was a political and not a religious question and the Protest appeared to be uncalled-for meddling; the Protest required Universalist ministers to have their names published before the world, and hence was a violation of the right of privacy; the Protest would do great mischief to the unity of the denomination by polarizing the clergy, and would put Universalists in the same unenviable position as other religious bodies which were dividing over the issue.[37]

Whittemore himself had no objection to any of the ideas expressed in the Protest itself, and thought very few Universalists did. Bacon disagreed.[38] He was convinced that too many Universalists, as well as others, considered slavery a sacred institution not to be touched. Whittemore believed that many clergy did object to the manner in which the Protest was presented; being asked either to sign or to give reasons for declining, sounded dictatorial to some. One who demurred on such grounds was Dolphus Skinner. Kittredge Haven and Russell Streeter, both well-known Vermonters, also objected.[39] Whittemore's major complaint, like that of Streeter's, was that there was no concrete plan offered for getting rid of slavery. Bacon admitted that he had no simple solution to the problem, but contended that if sufficient will to abolish it were created, somehow a way would be found. He took refuge in the fact that the committee handling the protest was not instructed to propose a specific method—only to prepare a protest. He was sure that if a method had been proposed, it would have been attacked by someone, no matter what it was. He was probably right.

The reactions to the Protest were as varied as one could imagine. Altogether, thirty-seven different reasons were given by various clergymen for not signing. Many not only signed the Protest but gave reasons, more or less eloquent, for so doing, even though they were not solicited. G.H. Emerson announced in the *Ohio Universalist* that he would cheerfully sign any protest against any evil, whether existing in the North or the South.[40] John M. Austin signed his name "in characters large and distinct as this hand could well trace," wishing it were as worthy as the name of John Hancock, whose signature was affixed in bold letters to a more famous document—the Declaration of Independence. Several ministers sent their communications directly to newspaper editors rather than to the committee.[41] They apparently had no aversion either to expressing themselves or to receiving a bit of publicity.

George Messenger of Ravenna, Ohio, obviously did not take the Protest seriously. According to a communication he sent to the *Ohio Universalist,* he did not even read carefully the letter accompanying the Protest, for he referred to it as an official act of the General Convention, which it clearly was not. He considered "the anti-slavery movements in the free States of little consequence, and calculated to effect very little good in any way."[42] Benjamin Whittemore refused to sign for eight reasons, among them the fact that he "was not ordained to sign Protests, but to preach the Gospel."[43] That in itself was one way of "abolishing slavery in all its forms." William A. Drew, editor of the *Gospel Banner* (Maine) complained that the sentiments of the laity as well as the clergy should have been requested.[44]

Jonathan Kidwell of Indiana left no doubt in the minds of the readers of his *Philomath Encyclopedia* as to his stand on the Protest. He reprinted the circular and objected to almost every sentence in it.[45] The meeting out of which the Protest had arisen had no legal standing and no right "to meet in mass and meddle with political questions over which they have no control and . . . no legal participation." Slavery was an evil, but it was sanctioned by the constitution and neither Congress nor individuals had the right to interfere with it; attempts by unauthorized meetings to concern themselves with slavery were nothing less than treasonable. Attempting to array the Universalist ministry against the institution could be interpreted as nothing less than "a hostile attitude against our confederate union." The Universalist ministry was turning itself into "a phalanx of ecclesiastical politicians." The evils of slavery had been exaggerated, and attacks on Southern Universalists for holding slaves or sympathizing with slavery were "a libel on our brethren" based on ignorance.

All of the arguments Kidwell had used against the abolitionist movement two and three years before were repeated, and with the same vigor. He went even further in defending slavery. He found not only Biblical justification for it but numerous indications that Christ had exhorted his followers not to become involved in earthly (political) concerns. The authors of the Protest were therefore accused by Kidwell of inconsistency and contradiction as well as of dabbling in someone else's affairs. He pointedly suggested that the poverty-stricken inhabitants of the Eastern cities would make a more appropriate subject for Universalist benevolence than Southern slaves. It appeared to Kidwell that Eastern Universalists were not content "to dictate for their western brethren in ecclesiastical questions, but also in regard to political questions!" He interpreted the Protest to mean that the authors were "determined to get up *a christian* party in politics"—the worst thing that could happen. Universalists would then suffer the same schismatic fate as the Methodists and Baptists.

Most Universalists in the East disregarded Kidwell's strictures and fulminations and turned to other pressing problems associated with social reform, although slavery and abolition continued to lead the list of priorities. The Universalist Anti-Slavery Convention disappeared as a separate organization after 1845 and merged its efforts with the much broader-based Universalist General Reform Association, which had held its first meeting in 1847. The Reform Association, with most of the leadership of the old anti-slavery group included within it, passed largely repetitious but often strongly-worded abolitionist resolutions at most of its sessions as the tensions between North and South over the slavery issue continued to rise and reached one critical stage after another.

Northern Universalists also did what they could on an individual basis to keep the problems of the slave in the forefront, and at the same time to render direct assistance when they could. Many clergy, such as J.G. Forman, pastor of the Universalist society in West Bridgewater, Massachusetts, arranged to have fugitive slaves speak to their congregations. William Wells Brown, author of a widely read account of his experiences, and the first American black novelist, who had escaped from slavery in 1834, lectured to Forman's society in 1849 on the evils of slavery.[46]

The clergyman was much impressed with Brown's moderation and his attack on the institution of slavery itself rather than on individual slaveholders. Brown fled to England to escape capture under the Fugitive Slave Law of 1850. In 1851 J.M. Spear journeyed to England with two extra passengers in his party. At the request of Wendell Phillips, the well-known Boston reformer and orator, Spear took with him Brown's two young daughters, and safely reunited them with their father in London.[47] In order to transport them without detection, Spear listed them as his "servants." While on a trip to Paris, he later encountered the two girls at a school in Calais and was gratified to learn that their color was no bar to their acceptance.

Facing the Mounting Crisis

From 1844 onward, the problem of slavery became more and more entwined in political controversy and scarcely a move was made on the national scene that did not have reverberations boding ill for future peace and stability. The annexation of Texas was delayed until 1845 in part because of the opposition of anti-slavery forces. When annexation was finally accomplished, it was by joint resolution of Congress rather than by the more normal route of a treaty because a two-thirds majority in the Senate was thought to be too difficult to obtain; such an attempt had been blocked in 1844. Many Americans in the North felt, as did Sylvanus Cobb, that the slavery which already existed in Texas in spite of earlier Mexican attempts to abolish it, would be strengthened by annexation. He was positive that the campaign to attach Texas to the United States was part of a conspiracy among slaveholders to buttress their power.[48]

The conclusion of the war with Mexico (1846-48) brought under American control extensive territory which raised the question of whether it would be slave or free; this in turn became involved in the question of the future status of slavery in the Oregon territory. A series of attempts to prohibit slavery in all land acquired from Mexico precipitated a heated Congressional debate which lasted two years. Northern Universalists, like most of their neighbors, blamed the South for attempting to extend slavery, and warned against the dangers to free institutions which such extension might bring. Hosea Ballou 2d reminded Universalists that it was votes from the North in Congress that had already made possible the extension of slavery by legislative process to three times its area at the time the Constitution had been adopted.[49] Self-righteously blaming the South was both inaccurate and unfair. Not only the existence of slavery itself but tolerance of the slave trade in the nation's capital and among the various states was as much the responsibility of the North as the South.

Slavery—particularly its status in the territories and the question of Congressional power to regulate it—became the major issue in the presidential campaign of 1848-49, and sectional antagonism had reached alarming proportions by 1850. Henry Clay, in order to settle some of the most pressing questions agitating North and South, and in order to avert a national crisis, proposed a series of solutions which resulted in five laws referred to later in a collective sense as the "Compromise of 1850." California was admitted as a free state; New Mexico and Utah were organized as territories without reference to slavery, its status to depend on what provisions were written into their constitutions when statehood was achieved ("popular sovereignty"); and stringent provisions were made for the return of fugitive slaves, with heavy penalties for violation, including failure to cooperate with federal officers; the fifth law abolished the slave trade in the District of Columbia.

Like most compromises, Clay's proposals failed to satisfy everyone, and future crises were delayed rather than permanently averted. Many abolitionists in New England were unhappy when Daniel Webster supported Clay's resolutions and denied any need for legislative action restricting slavery in the territories. He offered what has often been called the "natural limits" theory, contending that in the long run climate and soil would prevent the spread of slavery and obviate the necessity for controlling it by law.

When the Universalist General Reform Association convened in Boston in 1850, the general atmosphere among the anti-slavery contingent was one of gloom. Disappointment was voiced at what was interpreted as Webster's concessions to "the slave power." A call was issued for Congress to prohibit slavery completely in the territories acquired from Mexico.[50] Cobb refused to accept the natural limits argument offered by Webster and saw no reason why Congress could not reassert the power it had exercised to prohibit slavery in the Northwest Ordinance of 1787.[51] Hosea Ballou 2d abandoned his customary scholarly aplomb long enough to express dismay and indignation at what he considered to be Webster's temporizing, short-sighted attitude, and his delaying tactics.[52] In Ballou's view, Webster was refusing to face up to reality and was merely seeking to postpone an inevitable conflict. Slavery had first to be contained, and then eliminated. T.B. Thayer was sufficiently concerned about talk of dissolution of the Union to write a sober article for the *Universalist Quarterly* calling attention to the fact that, far from abolishing slavery, the creation of an independent South might mean a reinvigorated slave empire which included Mexico and the Caribbean.[53]

At the Reform Association meeting in 1850, William H. Ryder voiced his concern about slavery, but on other grounds than its possible extension. He had just returned from abroad, and had come to the conclusion that race prejudice in the United States, as contrasted with the situation in free Europe, was exacerbated by slavery. He reiterated the often-expressed dictum that Universalist principles required that persons of another color be treated "with respect and kindness." In 1851 J.M. Spear, while in Europe to report on the progress of prison reform in the United States, made the same point that Ryder had emphasized. "The prejudice against color" in France as well as in England was "unknown." Spear found that "no one thinks of showing any disrespect to the color of a man's face any more than to the color of his coat."[54]

Of all the measures comprising the Compromise of 1850, it was the Fugitive Slave Law that produced the most dismay among Universalists. The irrepressible Whittemore, who had repeatedly announced that he would not discuss social reforms or political issues in his paper, could remain silent no longer. He wrote an indignant editorial opposing the act and informed his readers that he would neither support it nor be a party to its enforcement.[55] One after another, Universalist associations and state conventions adopted resolutions condemning the new legislation. The Old Colony Association (Massachusetts) pledged as representing "both Christians and citizens, . . . the abolishment of this detestable act."[56]

The law was the subject of innumerable sermons criticizing it unsparingly. Otis A. Skinner, of the Fifth Universalist Society in Boston, in a discourse on "Duty to Government and to God," called for passive resistance short of force.[57] The Boston Association called for the unconditional repeal of the law in the name of "outraged humanity."[58] Cobb reproduced the entire text of the Fugitive Slave Act on the front page of his paper, accompanied by an editorial on the shameless encroachments of the slave power upon the free states."[59] Elbridge Gerry Brooks called on Universalists to disobey the new law because it was morally wrong.[60] The Massachusetts State Convention called for both "no obedience" and immediate repeal.[61] A resolution was offered in the Rhode Island Convention in 1853 which declared the

Fugitive Slave Law contrary to both the laws of nature and the word of God; the law thus had no validity or authority, and should be treated accordingly.[62] This was considered too extreme a statement, and was tabled.

There were some New England Universalists who refused at first to go along with the majority in rejecting the fugitive slave legislation, or even in condemning slavery, but eventually most were swept along by the rising tide of anti-slavery sentiment. The Vermont Convention at first tabled a resolution "strongly condemning" the 1850 law. But two years later the same convention resolved that it was the "imperative duty" of Universalists to obey God rather than man, and to be prepared to suffer the penalties prescribed if they refused to comply with the law.[63] A resolution first offered in 1851 in the Maine Convention condemning the law was laid over for a year and was tabled indefinitely in 1852 by a tie vote. Calvin Gardner considered any discussion of slavery by the convention "unnecessary, impolitic, and inexpedient." E.G. Brooks of Massachusetts then admonished the Maine Convention publicly for refusing to condemn the law out of hand.[64] There is no way of knowing whether Brooks' criticism was responsible, but in 1853 the Maine Convention adopted a resolution "demurring to the spirit and intent of the Fugitive Slave Law."

Two events within a few weeks of each other in 1854—one in Boston and on in Washington, D.C.—reinforced the already tense situation over slavery and evoked from Universalists and others in New England fresh outbursts of indignation. Anthony Burns, a fugitive slave, was arrested in Boston and ordered returned to his master in Virginia by a local probate judge who was also a commissioner to enforce the Fugitive Slave Law. Business was disrupted, sullen and angry mobs found barricaded streets patrolled by soldiers with fixed bayonets and loaded muskets as the prisoner was marched to a waiting ship; rioting had already taken place at the Suffolk County court house where the decision had been handed down, and had resulted in one fatality.

Sylvanus Cobb had vivid first-hand knowledge of the Burns affair, for the fugitive slave had been employed in the same building where the *Christian Freeman* was published.[65] The application of the Fugitive Slave Law to Burns he considered "a measure of unequalled atrocity."[66] Thomas Whittemore, whose blood was "at the boiling point" over the incident, produced his own eyewitness account of the Boston scene in the *Trumpet.*[67] He had calmed down sufficiently a month later to engage in a spirited but friendly epistolary debate with Theodore Clapp over the Burns case.

Clapp, a religious independent but with both Unitarian and Universalist sympathies who had achieved a considerable reputation as a preacher in New Orleans, was visiting in Pittsfield, Massachusetts when Burns was arrested, and read Whittemore's account. Clapp argued for enforcement of law and the maintenance of order, while Whittemore voiced the opinion that such "outrages" as the capture of the fugitive slave in Boston, the very cradle of liberty, might call for the appliation of a "higher law" than Congressional enactments.[68] Clapp assured Whittemore that he was as strongly opposed to slavery as was the editor of the *Trumpet,* but that what was needed was patience. Clapp agreed with both John C. Calhoun, the great champion of Southern right (and "a decided Universalist"), and Henry Clay, the "great compromiser," that slavery would eventually die out.[69] Clapp, who reported that he had conversed at some length with both men on the subject, referred to Calhoun's prediction that slavery would "have run its race" in 100 or 150 years. Whether the nation could wait that long was another matter.

The second event in 1854 which made matters worse regarding slavery was the passage of the Kansas-Nebraska bill by Congress. The issue of extension of slavery into the territories had been reopened when Senator Stephen A. Douglas had presented a bill for organizing the territory of Nebraska (later divided into two parts). Whether slavery was to be permitted was to be left up to the inhabitants. The bill, as finally enacted after several months of bitter debate, specifically repealed the Missouri Compromise of 1820 which had excluded slavery north of the line 36° 30′. By reversing itself, Congress in 1854 established a policy of non-intervention in the territories and gave both the slavery and anti-slavery citizenry the opportunity to fight it out. Opponents of slavery immediately interpreted the new law as both a victory for slaveholders and as an abdication of Congressional authority and responsibility.

Anti-slavery Universalists found a political ally from within their own ranks in the 1850s in the person of Israel Washburn, Jr. (1813-1883). He was one of the leading laymen in the denomination, member of the United States House of Representatives during the critical decade between 1850 and 1860, governor of the state of Maine for two terms, and not only a founder of the Republican party but the person responsible for choosing its name.[70] Above all, he was an uncompromising foe of slavery. Washburn fought unsuccessfully to prevent the passage of the Kansas-Nebraska bill and any measure which might protect or extend slavery.[71] Thomas Starr King, who became prominent in California Unitarianism as well as in state politics, considered Washburn's speech against the bill the best summary yet presented of the issues at stake.[72]

Washburn was born in the town of Livermore, Maine, a community founded by a maternal ancestor.[73] He came of a family long active in public life. His paternal grandfather had been a member of the convention which drew up the first constitution of Massachusetts in 1780 and served several terms in the legislature. His father, who had moved in 1806 to the District of Maine from Massachusetts before

Maine achieved separate statehood in 1820, was active in town affairs. The son, after receiving private instruction and reading law, was admitted to the bar in 1834 and practiced law until 1851. He served one term in the state legislature (1842) and was elected in 1850 to Congress from Maine as a Whig in an otherwise Democratic stronghold. He served for five successive terms (until 1861), and had the unique distinction in 1852 of having been elected simultaneously with a brother, Elihu B. Washburn, who served as Representative from Illinois.[74] Washburn was merely carrying on the family tradition of public service, for two other brothers also served in Congress and several held, at various times, diplomatic and other official posts, and served as Union officers during the Civil War.

When Washburn took his seat in Congress, he had immediately plunged into the debates over the issue. He delivered a major speech in 1852 appealing for national unity and a firm stand against Southern demands. Fearful that the local option provided by the Kansas-Nebraska Act would mean a victory for slaveholders, Washburn called a meeting the day after the bill was passed attended by thirty Congressmen who had opposed the bill. Out of this was born the Republican party, cutting across existing political lines, and dedicated to blocking the further extension of slavery. Washburn abandoned his Whig allegiance, and for his remaining terms in Congress was active in organizing the new party. Washburn was on the losing side, so far as attempts to curb the extension of slavery were concerned, but he delivered such a powerful speech in Congress in 1860 outlining the ramifications of the Dred Scott decision that he was prevailed upon by his large constituency in Maine to become the gubernatorial candidate of the newly created Republican party. After a resounding success at the polls, and two years of strong leadership as "War Governor," Washburn was appointed in 1863 to the post of Collector of Customs in Portland, Maine, by President Lincoln; Washburn held the position until his retirement in 1877. A forceful speaker, with considerable oratorical ability and wide-ranging interests, Washburn was in constant demand as a speaker and writer. He also resumed his law practice, became involved in railroad expansion, and wrote on a variety of literary and historical subjects. One of his fields of special interest was education. He served on the board of trustees of Tufts College from the time of its chartering in 1852 until his death in 1883; for many years he also served as president of the board. The institution conferred on him the honorary degree of LL.D. in 1872, and three years later offered him the presidency, which he declined.

Excitement over the Kansas-Nebraska Act spread everywhere in 1854 and a new round of anti-slavery resolutions was voted by Universalists, this time with much hostility to Congress built in, and with frequent reference to the Burns case as well. The First Universalist

Church of Lynn, Massachusetts, called not only for the repeal of "the infamous statute" which had resulted in Burns' arrest, but after passage of the Kansas-Nebraska legislation urged brethren of all denominations to disassociate themselves from "the great sin of slaveholding;" at the same time they called upon Northerns to present a united front, regardless of religious affiliation, to voice their detestation of slavery.[75] The Massachusetts Convention protested "in the name of Almighty God" the opening of a vast territory "to the inroads of the vilest institution known to any land."[76] The Rhode Island Convention, which had tabled a resolution against the Fugitive Slave Law in 1853 as too extreme a statement, promptly passed it unanimously after the Kansas-Nebraska bill was enacted.[77] The Reform Association shunted aside its customary resolutions on peace, temperance, and capital punishment and adopted a whole series on the subject in 1854, one of which called for the defeat at the ballot box of every Congressman who had voted for "the iniquitous Nebraska bill;" such legislators were considered "traitors to the cause of freedom."[78] Even the General Convention renewed "its testimony against the evil and sin of American slavery, and would especially express its disapprobation of the act of Congress repealing the Missouri Compromise."[79]

Universalists in the Midwest were neither as vocal nor as uncompromising about their opposition to slavery as were the New Englanders. Typical of the reaction to the Kansas-Nebraska bill was a resolution adopted by the Spoon River Association (Illinois) which was couched in very general terms and placed the emphasis on preventing the further extension of slavery rather than on its extinction.[80] The Indiana Convention merely lumped slavery in with such "moral evils" as intemperance, aggressive war, and capital punishment, and warned "that preachers gain nothing, but lose much, by the introduction of partisan politics into the pulpit."[81] Erasmus Manford, prominent Universalist and newspaperman living in the slave-holding state of Missouri in the 1850s, was frank to recognize slavery as a great evil, but was more inclined to favor plans for gradual emancipation, such as those offered by Henry Clay, than to approve of the militancy expressed in the Northeast.[82]

Spokesmen for Southern Universalism who had grown increasingly irritated by the anti-slavery contingent of the denomination in the North up to 1850 became decidedly belligerent thereafter. The precipitant was an action by a group of New England Universalists. When members of the Old Colony Association (Massachusetts) were informed in 1850 that some Universalists in the Deep South were "manifestly guilty" of the sin of holding slaves, the association announced that it was severing "all Christian fellowship" with them which would not be restored until said slaveholders "shall truly repent of this their sin."[83] John C. Burruss reprinted the resolution in the

Universalist Herald with the contemptuous remark that he was "heartily sick of this insignificant grumbling–such *pseudo* philanthropy."[84]

So far as he could see, fellowship with Northern Universalists had brought no assistance to their confreres in the South anyway, and Northern abolitionists were merely "a tribe of busy bodies." Burruss had no use for the Universalist General Reform Association's attacks on slavery, and recommended that Southerners stop subscribing to Northern denominational papers.[85] He had no use either for Universalist newspapermen who were ambivalent about their stand on slavery, or did not have the courage of their convictions. John A. Gurley, long-time editor of the *Star in the West* (Cincinnati) and G.W. Quinby, editor of the *Gospel Banner* (Augusta, Maine) were among the guilty parties according to Burruss. When he resumed publication of his paper after the Civil War, Burruss staunchly defended his own pro-slavery position. "We believed it was right and *said* so."[86]

When friction was heightened by the passage of the Kansas-Nebraska Act and repeated passage of anti-slavery resolutions by Northern Universalists, the Georgia State Convention went so far as to "disclaim having any connection with the Universalists of the North, further than faith in an entire world's salvation."[87] They recommended to all Universalists in the South "the speedy organization of a distinct Body, to be known as the Southern Convention." Such a convention was actually organized in 1858 but a formal break with the rest of the denomination failed to take place, for the new convention's constitution provided that it was to be "subordinate to the General Convention." The resolution adopted by the Georgia Convention in 1854 that most angered other Universalists asserted that not only would no delegates be sent to any denominational meeting in the free states, but that they would refuse to receive any Universalists from the free states at their own meetings.

Isaac D. Williamson, who had spent many years in the South (mostly in Alabama) sought not to defend but to explain the action of the Georgia Convention. He interpreted it as a defense mechanism needed to answer allegations in the South that Universalism and abolitionism were synonymous.[88] It was, he believed, a step toward self-preservation, and Northern Universalists had inadvertently forced them to take their stand because of their constant anti-slavery utterances. But most Northern Universalists greeted the ultimatum of the Georgia Convention with silence. Some members of the Maine Convention were sufficiently incensed by the unilateral pronouncement from the South as to offer a resolution that it was "inexpedient to fellowship slaveholders as followers of Christ," but it was unanimously rejected.[89] At the North Carolina Convention in 1856, S.J. McMorris, visiting from Alabama, offered a resolution (unanimously adopted) to the effect that Northern Universalists, "in servile imitation of other religious denominations," were engaged in "officious inter-meddling with matters which do not, or ought not to concern them."[90] Such interference was "impertinent, unchristian, and uncharitable" and needlessly distracted and divided the denomination. Sylvanus Cobb's reply was that Northern Universalists had never attempted to dictate or officially censure any Southern Universalist, but attacked slavery only as a moral evil. Where to draw the distinction was a difficult one indeed.

There were so many vociferous expressions of opposition to government policies regarding slavery from Universalists that one layman expressed great dismay and fear that "insubordination, resistance and political demagogueism" had become substitutes for the preaching of peace and good will that were the supposed hallmarks of the denomination.[91] Universalist assemblies continued to pass resolutions, clergymen continued to preach against the "new barbarism," and after the Kansas territory became the frontier locale for battles between slaveholding settlers and their opposers, Universalists joined the migration westward. D.P. Livermore helped organize a group from Auburn, New York, which settled the town of Cayuga near Atkinson, in the northeastern part of the territory.[92]

The Reform Association in 1856 debated vigorously a report on peace which somewhat paradoxically included a call for support of the anti-slavery inhabitants of Kansas, even to the extent of sending them Sharps rifles ("Beecher's Bibles") to protect themselves against the "slave power." It was adopted after much discussion, but one speaker wanted even stronger language than that in the report. He wished to "lay on to these villains with the most biting and severe invectives of which the English language was capable." Another wanted every Universalist society to take up special collections "for the especial purpose of procuring Sharpe's [*sic*] rifles."[93] There was such excited and prolonged discussion that the association did not have time to adopt the usual anti-slavery resolutions prepared in advance by the Committee on Business.

While the fate of the Kansas territory was being debated in Washington and instances of bloodshed and violence were mounting in the territory, another episode added to the conflict. Senator Charles Sumner delivered a speech in 1856 which came to be titled "The Crime Against Kansas" because of its denunciation of the South. The intemperate language, including personal references, so angered Congressman Preston S. Brooks of South Carolina that he caned Sumner, who remained conspicuously absent from the Senate for over three years. The question of freedom of speech became an issue and Universalists spoke up immediately. They had for years carried on their own battles over freedom of speech in the pulpit, and their right to dissent from the religious majority. The closest to a consensus was probably offered by the Green Mountain Association (Vermont) in the same year that the Sumner-Brooks episode took place. The association voted that "any subject which has the direct tendency to promote the moral, spiritual, or physical happiness, and well-being of mankind, is suitable for the clergy to discuss in the pulpit."[94] Edwin H. Chapin devoted most of a sermon in his Broadway church in New York City to the assault on Sumner; after receiving some criticism for his forthrightness, a week later he averred that he would speak on any topic he thought appropriate and would "raise a voice against every sin and evil that threatened the public good."[95] No one could dictate what he was to preach. A.St. John Chambré told his congregation in Newark, New Jersey, substantially the same thing.[96] A special meeting of the Tufts College student body presided over by President Hosea Ballou 2d protested the caning of Sumner and adopted four resolutions condemning the act as an attempt to restrict freedom of speech, and demanded Brooks' expulsion from Congress (which did not take place).[97] Whittemore grimly observed that "Brooks's gutta-percha cane has done more for freedom in Kansas that Sharpe's (*sic*) rifles."[98]

While virtual civil war was raging in Kansas, the Supreme Court, in a divided decision (Dred Scott *v* Sandford in 1857), declared that neither Negro slaves nor their descendants were citizens and not entitled to sue in federal courts. Furthermore, the Missouri Compromise was declared unconstitutional (after having been in effect for over thirty years), and slaves were declared to be property and hence could be taken into any portion of the United States. Northern Universalist reaction to the decision was swift and predictable. The Massachusetts Convention called it a "perversion" of the judicial branch; the Reform Association considered it a means of "crushing of the colored race;" and the Maine Convention labelled it a clear violation of the Golden Rule.[99]

When talk was heard in 1858 of Southern attempts to reopen the slave trade, a Reform Association resolution was so belligerently hostile (calling for the use of naval forces to prevent it) that the resolution was withdrawn.[100] When John Brown conducted his raid on Harper's Ferry, Virginia, the following year, Cobb agreed with his antagonism to slavery but considered Brown's methods of violence thoroughly reprehensible.[101] But Cobb did suggest that the raid should be considered as a warning to the South of how Northerners felt, and an illustration of the extremes to which some of them were being driven by their antagonism toward the South and all it stood for.

When, in compliance with a call from President James Buchanan designating 4 January 1861 as a national day of humiliation, fasting, and prayer because of the "distracted and dangerous condition of our country," Cobb dutifully printed the proclamation. He accompanied it with the first of a series of six installments detailing the history of slavery and placing squarely on that institution the responsibility if full-scale war should break out.[102] Just as his series was completed, the dreaded event took place, with the firing on Fort Sumter. He, like many another Universalist, had "fought the good fight" on behalf of freedom, as he sadly recorded the death of Thomas Whittemore which had taken place scarcely more than three weeks before the fateful bombardment in far-off South Carolina.

How much of a contribution Universalists made to the abolitionist movement, particularly outside the denomination, is difficult to determine. But the record is clear that their efforts were extensive, and their willingness to commit themselves officially as a denomination, even at the risk of disunion, is testimony to their courage and their concern for freedom. The battle had been waged on two fronts: to win over the majority of Universalists to the cause; and to help persuade whoever would listen and read that slavery was a great moral blot on the national escutcheon. Even more, it was contrary to the basic teachings of the denomination and raised problems more enduring and more sensitive than legal bondage.

Universalists eager for the abolition of slavery repeatedly insisted that, whether accomplished by peaceful means or by resort to war, there was an even larger challenge to be met. As E.G. Brooks told the Reform Association in 1853, "the indignities and oppressions so wickedly heaped on the man of color"—whether slave or free—had to be removed.[103] Free Americans must see not only to the emancipation of the black man but providing him an opportunity to develop self-respect, "hastening the overthrow of caste, annulling social exclusiveness, and opening the way for him to take his stand as the equal and brother of the noblest." Universalist brotherhood had to be more than an abstract concept embroidered with rhetoric, and more than the monopoly of the white man. It would not be an easy task. John Greenleaf Adams, speaking to the Rhode Island Convention in the midst of war in 1864, reminded Universalists that emancipation from legal slavery, as great a step as it was, solved only part of the problem.[104] To make really meaningful the abolition of slavery for which so many Universalists of good will had struggled, "We must conquer our miserable prejudices." Only then could true social justice be achieved.

The Civil War and Its Aftermath

At 4:30 A.M. on 12 April 1861, Fort Sumter, in Charleston Harbor, South Carolina, was fired upon. Three days later President Abraham Lincoln declared that an insurrection existed against the government of the United States. The outbreak of hostilities that spring was to signal an internecine conflict that was to last for four long years and was to touch in some way almost every American. When the tragedy of civil war struck the nation, Northern Universalists almost to a man staunchly supported the Union cause. Even John C. Burruss, the best-known and most influential Universalist in the South, vociferously supporting slavery and the Southern way of life through his *Universalist Herald,* was "an unswerving opponent of secession."[105] J.M.H. Smith, manning his lonely Universalist outpost in Huntsville, Alabama, was sure that Burruss' unpopular stand "served to quicken the fate of [Burruss'] paper" when it closed up shop in the spring of 1861 for a six-year period. Burruss, in fact, had waited until after Lincoln's election in November 1860 to express his views on the mounting sectional crisis which had already led to serious talk of secession of some Southern states. He considered this alternative to be "suicidal" and the worst possible way to protect and preserve Southern interests.[106] The editor of the *Universalist Register* commented that Burruss' paper "to the last . . . declared that the South was *running away from its 'rights'* in leaving the Union.[107]

One denominational convention after the other went on record as supporters of the Union and of the goal of abolishing slavery. The Maine Convention resolved that the ends justified the means, which meant going to war.[108] After acknowledging that war of any kind was a great calamity, the Pennsylvania State Convention in 1862 affirmed that an even greater calamity might be the overthrow of liberty and the substitution of anarchy with which the nation was seriously menaced "by the rebellion now rampant in a portion of our common country."[109] The delay of the Pennsylvania Convention in expressing itself may have been due to the fact that the Philadelphia-Union Association had within its fellowshipped churches in Maryland members who were slaveholders. In pledging its complete support in prosecuting the war in a whole series of resolutions against "an unwarrantable and atrocious rebellion," the General Convention in 1861 warned that the success of the South "would jeopardize the cause of civil and religious freedom throughout the world."[110] A committee was appointed to present the resolutions to President Lincoln. In 1863 the General Convention adopted resolutions not only supporting Lincoln and his policies but approving the arming of freed Negroes to support the Union cause.[111]

To most Universalists the nature and causes of the conflict could be simply and unambiguously stated. The Civil War was a purely defensive effort to preserve the Union, and the South and slavery were entirely to blame for the hostilities. Slavery, wrote J.G. Adams many years later, was itself a form of war—"an outrage on the rights of human beings."[112] The South "could no longer bear to have their wrong-doings questioned, but claimed the right to multiply and perpetuate them." A sense of the inevitability of eventual conflict between North and South had been voiced by a Universalist newspaperman some fifteen years before war actually broke out. Eli Ballou, editor of the *Universalist Watchman and Repository* in Vermont, had come to the unhappy conclusion by 1846 that there would be no solution to the slavery problem "except by insurrection and extermination."[113] In pledging its support of a "civil war waged against the best government on earth by an ungodly set of men," the Vermont Convention recognized "slavery as the sole cause of this wicked rebellion, and the guilty author of all the miseries of the existing war." It appeared to the Maine Convention that the Civil War was "the natural & legitimate fruit of slavery."[114]

Universalists in the North were naturally proud of those who served in various capacities in the Union armies and the navy and their support units during the Civil War. Members of the denomination were to be found in every branch of service, and at every level. The editor of the *Universalist Register* did his best to provide information on who served where, from year to year. In 1865, E.G. Brooks, on behalf of the Committee on the State of the Church, presented to the General Convention as complete a list as could be compiled of Universalists who had served as chaplains and nurses, and of those who had served as officers and had died in battle or in hospitals. His list of chaplains totalled almost fifty, including such prominent names as A. St. John Chambré, Richard Eddy, William H. Ryder, and Charles Spear. Chambré, of the 1st New Jersey Militia (reorganized as the 8th New Jersey Volunteers) was reported to have been "the first regular Volunteer Chaplain of any Denomination, to go into the field."[115] Many clergymen, like William A. Start, who graduated from Tufts College in 1862 and later served on its staff as well as secretary of the Massachusetts Convention (1877-1894), began their war-time careers as privates and were subsequently appointed chaplains, while other clergymen served as officers or enlisted men in other capacities.

Universalists had the grim distinction of claiming the first casualty of the war on the Union side—Sumner Henry Needham (1828-1861) of Lawrence, Massachusetts. He was a member of the 6th Massachusetts Volunteer Regiment and was the first of four soldiers to lose their lives as a result of a riot on 19 April 1861 in Baltimore en route to defend the national capital.[116] George S. Weaver, Needham's pastor, became the first clergyman called upon to preach the first funeral sermon of the war.[117] The Universalist parish in Salem, Massachusetts, furnished over 250 men to the Union army and navy, and thereby probably set a record for percentage of participation. Among them was Seth S. Buxton, who raised a company of 100 men within six days, and became a major in the Massachusetts 1st Heavy Artillery. Of the eighty-five men who had attended or graduated from Tufts College by 1865, forty-three had served in the Union military forces; one (Seldon Connor) became a brigadier general. Seven lost their lives.[118] Theophilus Fisk in Washington, D.C., who sometimes preached to as many as 800, discontinued meetings of his society when all but three male members enrolled in the military to defend the nation's capital.[119] Although not serving in a military capacity, A. Bosserman, pastor of the Universalist church in Richmond, Virginia when the war began, attracted considerable attention because he was the only clergyman in the city who supported the Union.[120] The reward for his failure to support the Confederate cause was arrest, imprisonment, and a death threat.

Of all the activities of Universalists during the Civil War, those which involved the most contact with its participants and made the denomination most visible were associated with providing services and amenities to the soldiers. Caring for the sick and wounded, bolstering flagging morale, and meeting the spiritual as well as the material needs of the military off the battlefield was too great a task for the government to carry alone. There developed to fill this need both an elaborate network of voluntary civilian organizations and a lengthy roster of individuals who contributed their time, energy, talents, and even their personal resources to provide nursing care and other services. Best known was the United States Sanitary Commission headed by Henry W. Bellows, a prominent Unitarian clergyman. Frank B. Fay, a Universalist from Chelsea, Massachusetts, served as superintendent of the Sanitary Commission relief corps in hospitals. The commission was supported by contribution of goods and money collected in systematic fashion all over the North and Midwest through the device of "sanitary fairs." According to fellow-Universalist James Eastwood, it was Fay who originally suggested the idea of such fairs and organized the first one.[121]

Relief associations and "Soldiers' Missions" were other agencies created for similar purposes, and often operating through the Sanitary Commission. Several state conventions organized Soldiers' Missions and scores of Universalists participated. J.W. Hanson, representing the Massachusetts Convention, travelled 3,000 miles in 1864, as far south as Florida.[122] Like other clergymen, he distributed religious tracts by the hundreds, together with supplies for the sick and needy. James Eastwood armed himself with a typical assortment which included everything from hospital supplies and jars of blueberry syrup to copies of the *Universalist,* the leading denominational newspaper at the time. The Massachusetts Soldiers' Mission, which terminated its activities on 1 July 1865, worked particularly with the Army of the Potomac, which included contingents in the Shenandoah Valley.

Probably the best-known name among Universalists associated with the United States Sanitary Commission was that of Mrs. Mary A. Livermore who, at Bellows' request, served for four years as a coordinator of many of the organization's diverse activities. Her

Clara Barton (1821-1912), nurse and founder of the American National Red Cross

headquarters was in the Northwest branch of the commission in Chicago, but her relief work carried her far afield, including battlefields themselves. Between 1862 and 1865 she organized soldiers' aid societies, delivered public addresses to secure donations, wrote letters "by the thousand" for soldiers, visited hospitals and encampments, delivered wounded soldiers to their homes, planned and conducted innumerable "sanitary fairs," and assigned women to hospital posts as nurses.[123]

The most familiar name outside the Universalist community among those women who served as nurses during the Civil War was that of Clara Barton (1821-1912). Although not formally a Universalist by church membership, she had come of a Universalist family, was sympathetic to the tenets of the denomination, and has always been claimed by it.[124] Known as "the Florence Nightingale of our war" and as "the angel of the battlefield," she organized supply and nursing services in Washington when the war broke out in 1861. Most of her energies thereafter were devoted to duty in field hospitals, for which she served without compensation. For a brief period beginning in 1864, she was a superintendent of nurses, and after the cessation of hostilities was for almost five years in charge of the government-sponsored search for missing soldiers—a project she had initiated and President Lincoln had approved. One of the results was the establishment, partly through her efforts, of the national memorial cemetery at Andersonville, South Carolina, one of the more notorious of the Confederate prisons.

Clara Barton's relief work in Europe during the Franco-Prussian war in 1870-71 was to lead to the establishment, through her efforts, of the National Society of the Red Cross in the United States a decade later. She was introduced to the international Red Cross (conceived and founded by Jean Henri Dunant in 1863) during her stay of over three years in Europe. Building on the unsuccessful efforts of Bellows in the 1860s to obtain official American adherence to the organization, she saw her dream finally realized in 1882. She was the only woman delegate as the first American representative to the international convention of the Red Cross when it met in Geneva in 1884.[125]

Throughout the Civil War the General Convention urged the continuation of war until complete victory had been achieved over slavery. Bargaining or compromising with the enemy or arranging any kind of negotiated peace was out of the question.[126] But the termination of hostilities in the spring of 1865 was hailed by Universalists "with profound gratitude to God" when the convention met at Middletown, Connecticut, in the fall of 1865, and appropriate resolutions were unanimously adopted to herald peace. The "wondrous hand" of the Deity in the outcome of the conflict—"the death of slavery"—was unquestionably evident in the minds of those who framed and adopted the resolutions. The Providential interpretation of history was nowhere more clearly expressed, and Universalists were again reminded of their particular obligation "as the special representatives of the great doctrines of the universal Fatherhood of God and the universal Brotherhood of man."[127]

In fact, the outcome of the war was, according to E.G. Brooks, proof positive of the vindication of Universalism itself. The conflict had been waged officially to preserve the Union and to assert the authority of its government, according to Brooks, but that was "in form" only. The underlying goal had actually been to protect "the principle of human equality and the essential brotherhood of our race"—a religious precept he claimed to be unique to Universalism. Among the special obligations that rested on Universalists as well as on the victorious Union government was "to follow the evident indications of Providence and . . . accord all the rights of citizenship to loyal men without regard to color." The assassination of President Lincoln, "the loved and trusted head of our Republic," was greeted with dismay, as was the conflict between his successor (Andrew Johnson) and Congress over Reconstruction policies.

Concern for the Negro both during and after the war was frequently expressed by Universalists, and was based on first-hand experience as well as rhetorical pronouncements from the North. W.W. Lovejoy of Maine, who enlisted as a private in the 2d Maine Cavalry and subsequently served as a lieutenant in a colored regiment, became its chaplain.[128] One correspondent who had served in the military wrote to the editor of the *Universalist* that "those who deny the valor of our colored troops are either ignorant of the facts, or else strangely prejudiced."[129] James Eastwood, who travelled extensively in the South on behalf of the Soldiers' Mission, visited in 1864 a "colored hospital" operated by the Union army in Virginia. He was delighted to find that "Uncle Sam does not discriminate against the sick colored soldier here."[130] He had the same facilities and received the same medical attention as "those of Saxon blood."

Northern Universalists were as strongly supportive of efforts to reconstruct the shattered union after 1865 and to assure the rights of the Negro as they had been to prosecute the war itself. They supported every major piece of legislation enacted by Congress which seemed to further the welfare of the newly freed black man. Maine Universalists were urging in 1864 that the federal constitution be amended "to prohibit forever" the institution of slavery and urged that all states, in the meantime, should repeal laws recognizing or protecting slavery.[131] The ratification of the Thirteenth Amendment to the federal document in 1865 was greeted with joy among Universalists, for slavery had finally been legally abolished. The Civil Rights Act of 1866 drew approbation, as did the Fourteenth Amendment adopted in 1868 and ratified the same year, bestowing citizenship on the Negro. Universalists had been told by way of the General Convention in 1865 that colored men should have secured to them the full rights of citizenship, especially of equal suffrage. It was the "imperative duty" of the denominational press and pulpit to urge this course of action.

After the Freedmen's Bureau had been established by Congress in 1865 to assist in post-war readjustment in the conquered South, Universalists by the dozens volunteered their services. Agents were appointed by some state conventions, such as Maine and Vermont, to solicit and collect funds to aid the newly freed Negro. The Vermont Convention appointed a one-man "Freedmen's Committee" (F.S. Bliss, a clergyman) "to correspond with those laboring in the South and to render them such assistance as we are able."[132] W.N. Van de Mark of Wisconsin, who had been chaplain of the 92d U.S. Colored Infantry in 1864, served as agent of the Freedmen's Bureau Board of Education in Louisiana.[133] He served briefly as superintendent of all Negro schools in New Orleans, with some 14,000 pupils.

When it appeared that President Johnson was not sufficiently enthusiastic about enfranchising the freedman and otherwise assuring him of his rights, and was exhibiting too much leniency toward the South, some Universalists turned against him. The Maine Convention refused to give him a vote of confidence in 1866 and the General Convention the same year criticized him for not taking a hard line in treatment of the South, and requiring "sufficient security" that rebellion would be prevented in the future.[134] Mary Livermore, who greatly admired Lincoln, had nothing but derogatory remarks to make about Johnson, who she felt sure was betraying the Northern cause. She considered him an "incapable and inconsequential man."[135]

But Universalists did not speak with one voice about what stance the nation should take regarding the South. The editors of the *Universalist* called for a spirit of Christian charity and understanding rather than of revenge by a victorious North.[136] The sentiments of very few Southern Universalists regarding Reconstruction policy seemed to have been placed on record. However, the ideas of at least one articulate Southerner have survived—those of Henry Summer, a leading Universalist layman in Newberry, South Carolina, and one of the very few from that section of the country who ever attended a General Convention meeting. In 1867 he wrote a six-part essay that appeared in the *Universalist Herald,* which by then had resumed publication. This series of articles, addressed "To the Universalists of the South and North," was a thoughtful and temperate plea for an end to sectional strife and bitterness.[137] Proclaiming himself a champion of the rights of the freedman who was entitled to "fair and just compensation for his labors" and protection from unscrupulous exploiters, Summer called for a new era of cooperation between both black and white in the South and between North and South. He insisted that whites were *not* "the enemies of the colored race" but wanted to see the Negro prosper. It was, after all, a matter of self-interest to rebuild the shattered South, and every resource at hand should be utilized. Although smacking a bit of paternalism, Summer's argument was undoubtedly offered as a gesture of good will.

As to the recent armed conflict, Summer believed that both sides had been wrong, and both had suffered. Not until men had been brought "face to face with the influence of Love—the very essence of Christianity," would animosities and distrust be eradicated and men regard each other as brothers. One of the crucial starting-points, according to Summer, was the integrating of the freed Negro into American culture; and that was to be accomplished by means of formal education to fit him for mental as well as physical labor. The freedman should be given every opportunity to which he was entitled as a free human being. Admittedly, it could not be done in a day, but that was no reason to procrastinate or equivocate. Legal emancipation was but the first step, "only the beginning." But here was the great occasion for those Christians who talked repeatedly about "works of benevolence and charity" to translate their professions into actions. The opportunity was greatest for those who held "the enlarged faith" of Universalism. But Summer's call remained as an item of unfinished business as the denomination entered its second century.

SECTION VII

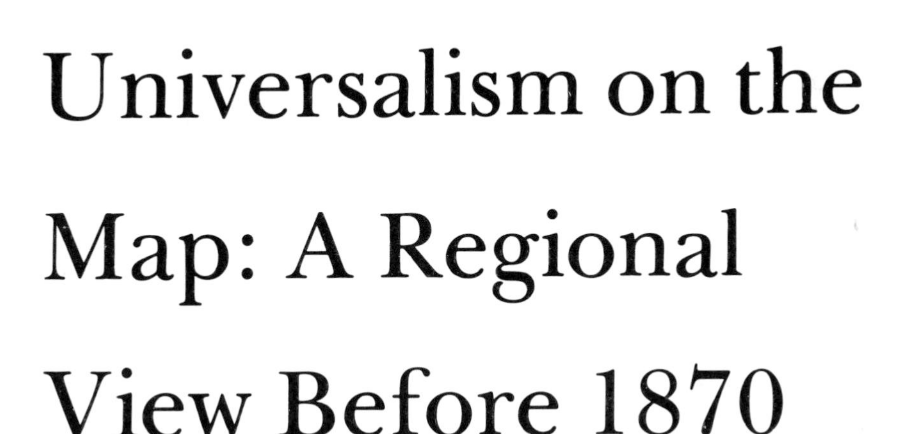

Universalism on the Map: A Regional View Before 1870

Chapter 23

THE HEART OF UNIVERSALISM: NEW ENGLAND AND NEW YORK

Historically, denominational Universalism has been associated with the six New England states and neighboring New York. It was in this northeastern area that the first societies were organized, that effective regional organizations first appeared, that what became the General Convention was born, and that the greatest early concentrations of adherents were to be found. It was in New England that the denominational headquarters for the nation evolved, that the first Universalist academy and the first institution of higher education under denominational auspices were chartered.

By 1845, in the middle of the peak decade of Universalist numerical strength, more than 100 societies or churches existed in each of the states of Maine, Massachusetts, New Hampshire, New York, and Vermont. The regional character of emerging Universalism was reflected even in the ordering of information in the annual *Universalist Register* begun in 1836. For the first thirty-five years that denominational statistics were reported, it was the New England states and New York that were listed first in the state-by-state inventory. It was not until 1871, a year after the centennial of the denomination was celebrated, that the states in which Universalism was eventually organized were listed in alphabetical order. In short, New England, even before the middle of the nineteenth century, had become the center of gravity for American Universalism.

In the twenty years following 1845, as Universalism became more of a national and less of a distinctively regional denomination, reflecting the westward movement of the American population in general, the momentum of Universalist growth in the Northeast slowed perceptibly. Although new societies continued to be organized in most New England states, many older local organizations ceased to exist or were combined with others. Maine reported less than half the number of societies in 1865 than in 1845. There was, with the notable exception of New York, a corresponding decrease of about one-third in Massachusetts, New Hampshire, and Vermont. In Connecticut and Rhode Island, where the total number of societies was proportionately much smaller than in other New England states in relation both to geographical extent and total population, there was a similar decline in the twenty-year interval. There was a roughly corresponding decrease in the number of preachers in the same period in all the states of the Northeast—again with the exception of New York.[1] Nonetheless, the six states comprising New England still contained, by the time of the Civil War, by far the largest share of Universalists in the United States and continued to reflect the general image of the denomination as a basically eastern and northeastern religious phenomenon in the pre-1870 period.

Massachusetts

Of all the states in which Universalism took root and flourished in the half-century before the Civil War, Massachusetts took the lead in the Northeast. By 1845 it could claim the greatest number of Universalists of any state in the region, and was not surpassed until almost twenty years later by New York State. It was in Massachusetts that the first legal victory had been won which gave organized Universalism a sure footing, and it was from the same state that many pioneer Universalists fanned out over the rest of New England and into New York as well as elsewhere. More specifically, it was in the Greater Boston area that the institutional manifestations of the denomination were most in evidence, from newspaper publishing to the organization of reform activities.

When John Murray died in 1815, twenty-two Universalist societies had already been organized in the state. Between that year and 1845, when a peak of 144 societies or churches had been established, an average of four were created annually. Although counterbalanced by a mounting number which ceased to exist, there was a steady increase for the next twenty years, resulting in an "organizational plateau," with an average of 140 societies newly created or reactivated between 1845 and 1865.[2]

When associations were organized among Massachusetts Universalists in the early nineteenth century, they were not only regional from the very beginning, but were tied in closely with the New England Convention. The first such organization was originally called the Southern Association, organized in 1816, and comprised five counties in central and western Massachusetts. In 1834 it was redesignated as the Union Association.[3] When the Southern Association was recognized in 1816 by the New England Convention it was intended to be a regional body, embracing all of Massachusetts, Connecticut, and Rhode Island.[4] Three years later the New England Convention divided all of the six-state area into four associations on a geographical basis, with a visiting committee to be appointed annually for each. The Northern Association was to have been based in Vermont; the Western

Association in western Massachusetts; the Southern Association in the eastern part of the state; and the Eastern Association in Maine. However, this arrangement, which might have appeared logical on paper, did not evolve as originally planned. The Southern Association actually met in the 1820's in the western as well as southeastern part of Massachusetts, and in Connecticut. The latter state was removed from the jurisdiction of the Southern Association when the Connecticut State Convention was organized in 1832.[5] The associations exercised fellowshipping and ordination functions from the start.

In spite of the extensive area first planned for the Southern Association, it was actually a very small and limited organization during the 1820s. It usually met in private homes and conducted religious services in whatever churches could be borrowed for the occasion. Typical were the meetings in 1821 and 1822. In the former year, at the meeting in Milford, only three clergymen were present (Hosea Ballou, Hosea Ballou 2d, and Thomas Whittemore, who had been ordained by the association earlier in the year). In 1822, after meeting at a home in Wrentham, when three preachers were fellowshipped, public services were conducted in the Baptist meeting house.[6] The Southern Association, as early as 1823, was threatened by division with the emergence of the Restorationist controversy, but the association managed to keep doctrinal disagreements from disrupting it until after 1830.[7]

In 1827 the Old Colony Association was organized, representing five counties on Cape Cod and offshore Nantucket Island. By 1830 this association claimed eleven preachers, twelve meeting houses, and twenty societies.[8] The Boston Association, organized in 1829, included Essex, Middlesex, Suffolk, and Norfolk counties, which included collectively the greatest number of Universalists of any four counties in the entire nation.[9]

The decades of the 1830s and 1840s were ones of noticeable expansion in the Universalist population of Massachusetts. In 1835 there were over thirty societies in the Union Association, the largest number of which were in Worcester County.[10] At the time, thirteen preachers operated within the jurisdiction of the association. Eighteen societies and twelve preachers were active in the Old Colony Association, although only seven societies had settled ministers. The greatest strength was in Barnstable County, which organized its own association in 1838 with headquarters in Brewster. Universalism was prospering sufficiently in western parts of the state by the 1830s to justify the division of the Union Association into two parts. The Winchester Association was created in 1839, using the Connecticut River as the dividing line. The areas west of the river were placed in the new organization, while the Union Association included those east of the river, and the strict county division originally followed was abandoned.

The Boston Association in 1836 reported fifty-one societies and thirty-seven preachers; less than half the societies had regular or full-time ministers. Between 1823 and 1836 the number of meeting houses used by Universalists had jumped from ten to thirty-two, seventeen of them erected by Universalists.[11] The number of Universalists and clergy in the four counties of the association by the end of the 1830s was considered so large that the association had become unwieldy.[12] The result was the creation of the Norfolk (County) Association in 1844.[13] Even with the reduction of one county, the Boston Association by 1853 comprised fifty-eight societies, twenty-two of which had churches organized in connection with them.[14] There were Sunday schools in all but two of the forty societies which provided detailed reports. However, only thirty-five societies had regular preaching.[15] Four of the associations organized between 1816 and 1844 were still in existence in 1870. However, with the strengthening of the state convention, associations tended to decline in both importance and scope of activities. The Norfolk Association had become an informal "Conference" in 1869 and the Union Association had all but disappeared.

The impetus for the organization of a state convention in Massachusetts came in 1832 from the most populous sector of Universalistm—the Boston Association. A committee was created that year to confer with the Old Colony Association as to the feasibility of forming such a body.[16] The expediency of creating a state convention "as soon as convenient" was affirmed by the neighboring association, but a special meeting in 1833 to effect such a goal brought very disappointing results; less than half of the fifty clergy expected were actually present at Gloucester in the winter of 1833 to vote on the proposal.[17]

The whole movement had been prompted by the organization of the General Convention in 1833, which provided for a chain of state conventions. As the Boston Association pointed out, "the business of forming a Convention should begin somewhere," so it took the initiative.[18] The state convention was duly constituted in the summer of 1834 and consisted of all regular clergy and one delegate from each society.[19] A constitution was adopted the following year, and clerical and lay delegates were appointed to the newly formed General Convention.[20] The state convention was neither very active nor important in denominational affairs for the first twenty-five years of its history. Its annual meetings were poorly attended, with seldom more than half to one-third of the clergy ever present.[21] In 1842 it relinquished to the associations all powers of fellowship and discipline, and an attempt to broaden its authority by a revised constitution in 1845 failed.

Meanwhile, other autonomous organizations had appeared or were about to appear, including the Massachusetts Sunday School Association (1837) and a Home Missionary Society (1851). The halting of this centrifugal tendency within the state finally came in 1859, when the Massachusetts Universalist Convention was chartered as an incorporated body, representing a merger of existing organizations. The newly invigorated state convention, among other things, eventually resumed its jurisdiction over fellowship, ordination, and discipline, and became in effect the denominational legislative body for the state. Provision was also made in the 1859 edition of the bylaws for the granting of licenses to candidates for the ministry, providing the applicant signed the Declaration of Faith represented by the Winchester Profession. Such licentiates, if approved by the council, received full fellowship. The maximum allowable time during which an unordained minister could hold a license was left unanswered when the question was discussed at the convention in 1865, but a recommendation that it be limited to two years was put into force in 1867.[22] Licentiates were permitted to serve as lay delegates from societies and Sunday schools. A recommendation in 1867 that licenses to preach be extended to laymen was defeated.

For the first time in its history the convention exercised real as well as theoretical powers, although the persistence of localism resulted in considerable delay in achieving the goal of a more effective state organization. Some Universalists in the state, notably those farthest removed from Boston, for a time refused to cooperate with the newly structured convention. The Winchester Association, embracing Universalists west of the Connecticut River, at first advised its societies and preachers to "stand aloof from the new organization," but within a year had accepted it.[23] But it was reported in 1861 that the Barnstable Association "still adheres to its position of independence." The independence of clergymen was also evident, especially in the 1860s. The convention's committee on fellowship, ordination, and discipline was kept busy with numerous cases of ministers who skipped over the licentiate state and arranged or requested of their societies ordaining councils without any authority of the convention.[24]

The streamlining of the state convention, which made it for the first time a reasonably effective administrative organization, sounded too secular and too business-oriented to some Universalists. Thomas Whittemore was positive that the consolidating of activities in a greatly strengthened state convention had been preceded by inadequate discussion and secret caucusing, and that somehow a conspiracy had taken place.[25] Regardless of Whittemore's reservations, the Massachusetts Convention served as a generally workable denominational agency long beyond 1870. The fact that it became actively involved in such reform movements as the abolitionist cause probably antagonized Whittemore—not because he was unsympathetic to such causes—but because he did not consider social reform as a legitimate activity for ecclesiastical organizations *per se.*

One of the first projects undertaken by the secretary of the Massachusetts State Convention after its reorganization in 1859 was an attempt to conduct a grand inventory of all societies in the state. But the results were far from encouraging, thanks to the failure of either pastors or their congregations to reply to repeated requests for information, or to keep even minimal records. The *Universalist Register* reported 168 societies, 158 meeting houses, and 126 preachers in 1860. Secretary Henry B. Metcalf received returns from only ninety-four societies, of which only seventy-six had settled pastors and held regular services. The numerous discrepancies and gaps in statistical reports of the denomination have been alluded to frequently in this work and no exhaustive attempt has been made to reconcile them. Typical of the differences were the figures given for Massachusetts in the *Universalist Register,* compared with those in the report of the secretary of the state convention for 1861. The former reported 169 societies and the latter, 118. The more conservative estimate was probably closer to actuality.

Even more discouraging to the convention was the fact that, with an average attendance of over 220, totalling slightly over 20,000 individuals, only 52 societies had church organizations; the aggregate membership was less than 3,000. Believers in Universalism and commitment to formal membership were obviously two different things. Of the seventy-six settled pastors, only thirteen had been located with the same society or church as long as five years. Metcalf, as secretary, could not refrain from calling attention to this obvious "instability of the relations between pastors and societies" and from commenting on the fact that in the majority of instances there had not even been opportunity "to become mutually acquainted."

Even the missionary effort to which the convention had pledged support failed to achieve the goals desired, largely because no machinery was at first established to coordinate efforts and to utilize fully the services of those who volunteered.[26] Only about forty societies, all supposed to be prosperous, had contributed less than $1,000 to the missionary cause in 1862. Local interests and demands on resources continued to take priority over statewide needs. Business depression, the onset of war, and the constant mobility of population were also contributing factors to the failure to achieve more than partial success.

During and immediately after the Civil War, the state convention made various attempts to establish a missionary system, but none was truly successful. Even the appointment of agents did not work out well. The most ambitious attempt to raise funds was made in 1866, but that too was thwarted the following year. The convention had determined, in support of the General Convention, to raise $20,000 within a year, two-thirds of which was to be earmarked for the use of the national body.[27] But that had to be temporarily abandoned when the board of trustees of the newly chartered state denominational school (Dean Academy) undertook their own solicitation among societies in the state; they completely bypassed the state convention, which itself had encouraged the establishment of the school. One of the provisions of a gift made by Oliver Dean was that $40,000 additional be raised. With this additional demand on societies, the only alternative left to the convention was to postpone its own fund-raising efforts for missionary purposes until the following year. The lack of coordination in setting up and carrying out priorities became a source of embarrassment and frustration to the convention.

Prospects appeared more encouraging, beginning in 1868, when J.H. Chapin, who had served with the Freedmen's Commission, was employed by the convention as a combined financial secretary and missionary agent at an annual salary of $2,000.[28] A thorough canvass of societies indicated that there were eighty among which the goal of $20,000 could be apportioned. By 1869 it seemed that the corner had been turned in raising missionary funds; in that year over $4,000 was raised—a most promising development.[29] Nonetheless, local needs continued to come first with most churches and societies. As the financial secretary wryly pointed out, when a solicitation for missionary purposes was made, societies suddenly discovered that they had debts which had somehow been overlooked—"a fact so old it had been forgotten by many of the members."[30] Assessments to meet the general expenses of the state convention met a similar fate; of the $10,000 allocated in 1871, little over half had been realized a year later.

Another undertaking of the state convention in behalf of the missionary effort was the holding of denominational gatherings ("conferences") in the state, under the auspices of various associations. In 1867, four were planned "for the purpose of awakening a practical interest in those measures most vitally connected with our denominational welfare."[31] The state was divided into four districts, and two conferences were actually scheduled—one in Lowell and one in East Boston. The first was declared a success, but the attendance at the second was so poor that the project was abandoned.[32] The scheduling had been such that the second conference conflicted directly with the activities of two Sunday school organizations, an association meeting, and the simultaneous convocation of two conventions in neighboring states. After the lapse of two years, the experiment was tried again, and with greater success. Six were scheduled in 1869 and all but one association participated.

There continued to be other demands on the limited resources of the state convention besides those from the missionary-minded. Until the convention had been reorganized in 1859, there had been no formal provision for creating a relief fund for clergy who were "infirm or destitute," or for their widows or children after their decease. When the desirability of establishing such a fund was recognized, it was provided that life memberships in the convention, at $20 each, be set aside for such purposes. Contributions could be made either by the clergymen themselves or by societies or churches in their behalf. One such life membership was bestowed on Mrs. Phebe A. Hanaford, one of the prominent women ministers in the denomination, by her society in Hingham.[33] By 1867 about $1,000 had been raised in this fashion, and there were fifty-three such memberships by 1869.

This system created an anomalous situation; the convention constitution provided that these life members had the same voting rights as fifty-three societies. Consideration was given to creating a category of honorary (non-voting) life memberships, but the plan was discarded, as was the whole idea of life memberships. Instead, clergy were urged to contribute at least $1 annually to the relief fund.[34] Thirty-five clergymen had contributed $54 by the end of the first year of the new system. Two other devices providing for ministerial welfare were recommended: collections at the annual convention meetings; and life insurance, the premiums to be paid by each parish. It was the latter practice that eventually became widespread.

Another request for funds came by way of the creation of the Murray Centenary Fund, and the financial secretary was directed in 1869 to devote his entire attention to that endeavor. Of the state quota of $50,000 for this purpose, $40,000 had been paid in or pledged by the fall of 1870. Within a year the full amount had been paid to the Treasurer of the General Convention.[35] A major financial challenge had been met, and it was now time to shore up other resources. Yet another demand on the convention was the securing of a fund of $50,000 for the strengthening of the denominational publishing house, which had been organized in 1862.

The meeting of the state convention in 1871 in Springfield signalled the end of one era and the beginning of another in the history of Massachusetts Universalism. The bylaws were extensively revised to bring them into harmony with the framework of government of the General Convention. The word "parish" was substituted for "society;" official representation of Sunday schools in the convention was ended; and the number of lay delegates was increased from one to two for each parish. In addition, the celebration of Children's Sunday was recognized officially; ministerial contributions to the relief fund became a requirement; and the status of licentiates was regularized and clarified. There were still financial obligations to be met and missionary work still undone. But the convention's existence had been more than justified. The secretary found a spirit of unity and loyalty of heartening dimensions. In no case had the actions of the convention been ignored or repudiated during the previous year. "We are," he reported confidently, "as never before, active, earnest and united as one church."

Maine

The establishment of Universalism in Maine was a slow and halting process. The denomination did not show signs of real life until the District of Maine was separated from Massachusetts and was elevated to statehood in 1820. As William A. Drew, editor of the Maine-based *Christian Intelligencer,* remarked, it was in that year that "the cause of Universalism in this State may be said to have been born."[36]

The early denominational records for Maine are as sparse as were the Universalists themselves. The first systematic attempt to piece the story together was made by Drew in a series of historical sketches in the newspaper of which he became editor in 1826.[37] Individual Universalists who were willing to identify themselves as such had appeared in Maine before the end of the American Revolution, but they were neither numerically important nor organized in any effective fashion for several decades. Most of the earliest Universalists were migrants from the then-parent colony of Massachusetts, of which Maine had been a part since its acquisition in 1677. Settlements were small and scattered at first, and what few Universalists had appeared by the 1780s suffered under the same legal disabilities as their contemporaries in Gloucester, Massachusetts and elsewhere.

The first Universalists known to have settled in Maine established the community of New Gloucester (Cumberland County). As the name implies, they had moved from the Massachusetts community of Gloucester farther south. Among them was Joseph Pearce, who became the lay leader in services conducted in private homes, and who was requested to secure the services of a preacher.[38] In 1783 the Universalists in New Gloucester joined forces with the Baptists in objecting to compulsory support of the "standing order" (Congregational) minister so that they could establish their own society. The Baptists, with the support of Universalists, obtained exemption from paying the required ministerial tax, but then refused to allow the Universalists to do the same. Ten Universalists finally, by petition to the town meeting in 1787, obtained exemption. Two years later an unsuccessful attempt was made to retrieve the money they had paid in to the town since 1786.[39] The suit, initiated by Thomas Barnes, the pioneer Universalist preacher in Maine, was carried on appeal to the Supreme Judicial Court of Massachusetts, and was lost in 1811 on the ground that the Universalist Church in the town was unincorporated at the time the case originated. They were therefore not entitled to recover.[40]

Universalists in Paris Hill and Norway (Oxford County), desirous of having a preacher, raised a subscription in 1798 to induce Thomas Barnes (1749-1816), then preaching in Gloucester, Massachusetts, to come to their area.[41] He is considered to have been the first public preacher of the faith in the state.[42] A native of New Hampshire, he had been converted from the Baptists after hearing Caleb Rich preach in the village of Richmond in 1782, and before arriving in Maine had preached in Vermont, southern Massachusetts, Rhode Island, and Connecticut. Provision of a house and other unspecified benefits were sufficient to lure him to Maine, where he spent the remainder of his life as a farmer and preacher.

The society organized in Norway in 1798 through his efforts was the first to be established in what became the state of Maine, and held its first meetings in 1799. The original society comprised ten members (all male) and by 1828 had grown to fifty.[43] It was also the first society in Maine to construct a meeting house. It was started in 1802 and the finishing touches were added two years later. The "First Independent Union Society of Norway and Paris," as the original society was called, organized a church in 1828, with eighteen members. When it was reorganized as the First Universalist Church of Norway in 1859, the new pastor and several other individuals were baptized by immersion. While he served the society, Barnes had used the village of Poland (Cumberland County) as his headquarters. He was evidently well thought of, for he served several terms as a representative to the General Court (legislature) in Boston.

In the fall of 1799 Barnes invited representatives from the three or four societies then probably in existence in the state to meet in the village of Gray. The records of the meeting are not known to exist, although the circular letter written by Barnes survived. It was not until the 1804 meeting that Barnes was even instructed to keep records; money to purchase a record book was provided at the time. The second meeting of what became known as the Eastern Association was also held in Gray in 1800, as were the next four. At the New England Convention held in Swanzey, New Hampshire, in 1801, Barnes was ordained at the request of the Maine societies, who also defrayed his expenses. He was installed at Gray in 1802. Judging from the circular letter of 1803, Universalists were still suffering from the application in Maine of the law requiring annual tax support of Congregational ministers by unincorporated societies. Petitions for incorporation were therefore filed and approved for the New Gloucester, Norway and Paris, and Turner societies in 1804 and 1805. A counter-petition objecting to the incorporation of the Turner society failed to override the fifty-five original petitioners.[44]

The Norway Universalist Church, the first meeting house built in Maine (1802)

There is no precise way of knowing how many individuals actually attended early Universalist meetings in Maine, but it can be assumed that the number was small enough to be accommodated in private homes. Besides Barnes there were three preachers present when the Eastern Association met in Turner in 1805: George Richards of Portsmouth, New Hampshire; Sebastian Streeter, then also preaching in New Hampshire; and Isaac Root. A convert, like Barnes, from the Baptists, Root had been fellowshipped in Vermont in 1802 and had preached in northeastern Massachusetts and southern New Hampshire. He had first appeared in Maine at the Eastern Association meeting in 1804, had settled in Livermore, and traversed much the same territory as Barnes. He also collaborated with Barnes in writing the early circular letters distributed by the association.

The practice of all Universalist associations of rotating their places of meeting was followed in Maine, usually where societies had recently been formed or were about to be organized. Such was the case at Livermore, where a society was created in 1807, and where the association met that year. William Farwell, the pioneer Universalist preacher in Vermont, was one of those present. Farmington served as the meeting place in 1808, and a society was organized there in 1811. At the 1809 meeting in Norway, the Winchester Profession of Faith was adopted, and Barnes was selected to represent the Eastern Association at the New England Convention, where it was admitted to fellowship. By the time of the 1813 meeting of the Eastern Association, only two preachers were present, Barnes and Root. The work of these two early Universalists then came to an end, Barnes retiring because of ill health and advancing age, and Root moving to New York State. The two men had contrasting personalities. Barnes was described as "a very apostolic man," while Root "was given to much levity even in the pulpit, which injured his usefulness."[45]

By 1819 four other clergymen had commenced preaching in Maine: Joseph Butterfield (Readfield), a one-time Baptist preacher who soon moved to Pennsylvania; D. Young (Avon); J. Hilton (New Portland); and Fayette Mace (Strong). In the following year the clerical ranks were augmented by Sylvanus Cobb, Jabez Woodman, William Frost, and William A. Drew, who by 1861 was the senior Universalist clergyman in the state in point of service. Between 1815 and 1820, no more than four preachers were present at any one session of the Eastern Association. At the 1818 meeting, however, a very important event occurred: It issued its first license to preach, to Mace. He continued in the Universalist ministry until 1832 and for a brief period joined a Shaker community. The 1820 meeting established a precedent by extending its deliberations to two days, necessitated no doubt by the expectation that every preacher would wish to deliver at least one sermon. In 1821, at Winthrop, an unprecedented number of preachers (eight) attended, including three men later to become prominent in the denomination: Sylvanus Cobb, William A. Drew, and Russell Streeter. The meeting at Winthrop was also memorable because a constitution was adopted, and Cobb became the first Universalist minister to be ordained in the state.

Universalism in Maine seems to have taken on a new lease on life by the 1820s. At the end of the decade there were upwards of eighty societies and some thirty preachers. Twenty of them had been licensed in Maine in the decade since Mace had received his certificate. The council of the association showed steady accretions to its membership, as it comprised all preachers who happened to be present, whether they resided in the area or not. Until 1828, when the Eastern Association was transformed into the state convention, the councils also included "messengers;" that is, laymen who might come from any community, whether societies had been organized or not. They were usually voted into the council on the spot. Delegates were first formally appointed in 1829.

The association meetings were as much social gatherings as religious convocations, and usually there was little business to transact. As Drew pointed out in his reminiscences of the early days, "there were no Universalists then in Portland or any other fashionable town—they were confined to the rural districts." The population of Maine, clustered along the seaboard, was thinly scattered elsewhere over a large territory. Most of the new arrivals were from other parts of New England, unacquainted with each other and lacking deep roots. Above all, most of them were poor in material possessions.

With the restoration of peace after the War of 1812 and the final determination of Maine's status as a full-fledged state, commercial and agricultural activities stabilized and increased. In the religious realm, the Universalists in Maine, as elsewhere, benefitted from the growing challenges to orthodoxy in the Boston area, and there was an increased stimulus to religious interest. Their numbers were augmented by increased migration from other parts of New England, and by 1830 Universalists had established firm enough foundations to develop rapidly in both numbers and strength. Eleven societies were organized during 1828, together with four new associations.[46] By the close of 1829, sixteen new societies had appeared, and eight preachers were converted to Universalism. Thomas Whittemore estimated in 1830, on the basis of adult males only, that membership in the denomination was "as large as any in the state," and that the societies averaged fifty members each.[47] He put the number of Universalists at the grossly exaggerated figure of 45,000.[48] The report made to the New England Convention in 1835 was unquestionably more accurate: 10,000 Universalists, with an average of 40 per society.[49]

One factor that undoubtedly accounted for the rapid growth was the relative lack of opposition. Walter Balfour made an extended preaching tour in Maine in 1830 and was greatly impressed by the liberality and good feelings shown by other denominations toward Universalists. This included extensive use of union meeting houses and attendance at each other's services.[50] This had to be a reciprocal matter. "I trust the day will never come, that Universalists will refuse to accommodate any other sect with the use of their meeting houses. Let them have them, even if the professed object is, to refute Universalism. If it cannot stand, by a fair appeal to scripture and arguments, down let it go." Charles Spear, who attended the Maine Convention in 1843, was impressed with the prevalence of Universalism in Maine, and concluded that "there seems to be a soil here congenial to liberal sentiments."[51]

By 1835 Universalists in Maine supported three periodicals, all weeklies: the *Christian Intelligencer,* the *Christian Pilot,* and the *Gospel Banner*, all of which had a subscription list in excess of 1,200.[52] Five years later, there were six associations, over 100 societies, and over 20 Sunday schools.[53] The meeting house in Portland had to be enlarged in 1841 by thirty-three additional seats.[54] Throughout the pre-1870 period the number of churches organized within societies lagged far behind, as did the membership. Of the 150 members of the Portland society reported in 1840, only 35 were actual church members.[55] In 1843 the editor of the *Gospel Banner* made a comparative estimate of the state of Universalism in Maine as described by Whittemore in 1830 and the situation thirteen years later, and claimed that one-sixth of the Universalists in the nation (600,000) resided in Maine.[56]

The rapid creation of associations in the late 1820s and 1830s reflected the mushrooming of the denomination. Four were organized in the one year of 1828, following roughly county lines at first, and later subdivided as the need arose (York, Cumberland, and Oxford; Penobscot; Kennebec; and Washington).[57] By 1838 several more had been added: Somerset; Lincoln and Waldo; Hancock and Washington. Each was entitled to nine lay delegates from societies, a more generous representation than in most associations elsewhere.[58] They comprised representatives from ten to over thirty societies each, claiming from less than 400 members within their jurisdictions to over 1,000.[59] Before 1870 the associations underwent several reorganizations as their boundaries shifted, and only one more association was created (Piscataquis, in 1844), representing the subdivision of an existing association (Penobscot). Ironically, the church and society in Dexter, where the organization meeting of the Piscataquis Association took place, at first refused to join the new organization.[60]

The greatest difficulties encountered by the association were failure of societies to send delegates to meetings, and a chronic shortage of preachers for the societies within their jurisdictions. Extra effort by laymen was called for to reach those who were Universalists in sympathy but were without ministerial services.[61] "Social prayer meetings" in the community were another device recommended.[62] After 1870 only one more association was added, the Franklin and Eastern Oxford, in 1880, as a result of a consolidation of jurisdictions.[63] Meanwhile, all but three of the original associations had disappeared. They lost the right of representation in the state convention when its constitution was revised in 1859.

The Maine State Convention, organized in the home of James Lowell in Lewiston in June 1828, was at first actually the Eastern Association writ large. At its annual meeting it was decided to divide the state into four ecclesiastical districts, with a "minor association" in each, responsible to the Eastern Association.[64] Before the meeting was over the name was changed to the "Maine Convention of Universalists," and provision was made for the associations to send seven delegates each. In 1862 the number of delegates from societies and churches was established at one each. By then, each Sunday school was also represented.

The first annual meeting of the new organization met in Readfield in 1829, attended by twenty-three clergy and twenty-one laymen. One of its first acts was to adopt a constitution, the last article of which emphasized its independent character. Although it considered itself in fellowship with the New England Convention, the Maine Convention announced that it would transact its business without any "interference" whatsoever.[65] When the state convention appointed two delegates to the New England Convention in 1832 they were instructed "not to take any means which infringe the independence of the Convention." The Maine Convention also reserved the right to act not only in fellowshipping and ordination, but on all withdrawals. When the Penobscot Association ordained a clergyman in 1844 without the permission of the convention, the action was declared null and void.[66]

There was no question that the state convention intended to exert its authority. It drew up a "stringent" system of discipline for both societies and ministers in 1851, and announced that non-conformity would result in "disapprobation and censure." It was the state convention that took the initiative within the state in creating a "missionary enterprise" in 1848. It also created separate missionary, tract, and educational societies, each with its own constitution. Calvin Gardner and Moses Goodrich were among those who served as general agents for the special societies in the 1850s. A charity fund organization was incorporated in 1857. The attempt to supervise societies closely was indicated by the provision that those employing clergy not in fellowship with the convention were subject to suspension.

The Maine Convention was reorganized, with a revised constitution, in 1859, and incorporated in 1861 as a legal body in order to hold and disburse funds and collect assessments. The missionary, tract, and educational societies lost their semi-autonomous existence and were merged into the convention. In taking this step the convention was following the same pattern as the convention in Massachusetts.[67] The treasuries of the three subsidiary organizations totalled less than $1,500 in 1859, and none had been notably active. The tract society had "rested quietly . . ., nothing having occurred to disturb its repose in the least." The missionary committee created in 1859 was slightly more active than the tract enterprise, but was still not very successful. A decade after the missionary committee had been created, the state convention recommended that societies without pastors raise $1,000 to secure the services of a missionary, but less than $500 had been obtained by 1870 and the committee was unable to find an individual willing to serve.[68] There was not even a vote in the convention in 1873 on a resolution to raise $1,000 to assist "feeble parishes and circuits."

The state convention consistently expressed, in its relations with the General Convention, the independent spirit it had shown when first organized. The executive committee of the Maine Convention voted to raise $10,000 for the Murray Fund for the centennial in 1870, and a state centenary committee was appointed and held a mass meeting in the Congress Square Universalist Church in Portland. But the payment of the full pledge was long in coming. The convention in 1871 considered the intent of the fund worthy but did not see the propriety of "sending more money abroad." Money raised by the convention "may as well be kept at home." As a consequence, the convention voted in 1871 to pay only the interest on the balance due. By that date the number of Universalist societies (parishes) had shrunk to seventy-four, there were twenty-nine church organizations, and only thirty-five clergy active in the state.[69] Although still numerically important and active by 1870, the strength of organized Universalism in Maine seemed to have passed its peak.

Vermont

The New England Convention held its third annual meeting in Bennington, Vermont, in 1795. John Murray, the founder of American Universalism, for that occasion made his only visit to the state. The location of the convention brought the existence of Universalism in Vermont to the attention of the denomination for the first time.[70] This was understandable in view of the paucity of early records and the migratory tendency of both preachers and laymen as Americans migrated northward by the hundreds following the Revolution. Vermont Universalists were relatively more fortunate than some of their coreligionists in other states respecting their legal status and the nature and intensity of the opposition they faced. Opposition there was, and sometimes it reached even political proportions in the first quarter of the nineteenth century. But the initial legal handicaps were soon overcome and opposition to their theology from members of orthodox denominations had lessened to a great extent by 1850.

Hosea Ballou, Caleb Rich, and Walter Ferriss all ran into difficulty with state laws relating to ministerial qualifications. The first two had to be re-ordained when they entered the state, and Ferriss' right to perform marriages was questioned. So far as guarantees of religious freedom were concerned, the Vermont constitition of 1793, at least on paper, assured freedom of conscience, established no state religion, required support of no one church, and prohibited the abridgement or denial of civil rights for reasons of religion. But that in no way protected Universalists from accusations of heresy and infidelity by others. When Universalists started arriving in the 1780s and came in steadily increasing numbers in the 1790s, orthodox Congregationalists were numerous and religiously aggressive, but were prevented from establishing their own church officially because other Protestant denominations, notably the Methodists and Baptists, also secured an early foothold. In some communities Universalists comprised the majority of the population in the late eighteenth and early nineteenth centuries.

At least seven Universalist preachers had appeared in Vermont before 1800: Thomas Barnes, who had moved to Newfane in 1786 and subsequently pioneered in Maine; William Farwell; Michael Coffin; Joab Young; Hosea Ballou and his older brother David; and Zebulon Streeter.[71] Seven preachers in Vermont were in fellowship with the New England Convention in 1813.[72] The first society to have been organized is not known; no less than fourteen were in existence in the state by 1800. That one existed in Rockingham in 1794 is a certainty. Between 1800 and 1833, when the Vermont Convention was organized, over 100 Universalist and Unitarian preachers had been, or were, active in the state. The Universalists outnumbered the Unitarians many times over. Some of the preachers even extended their activities into Lower Canada.

There were approximately twenty preachers and about eighty societies in 1833, and the number of both climbed steadily after that.[73] By 1840 there were some forty preachers and about ninety societies, six of which had organized churches. There was also a weekly newspaper, then known as the *Green Mountain Evangelist & Universalist Watchman,* published in Montpelier, with a circulation of 2,000.[74] The paper, tracing its ancestry back to the *Christian Repository* (1820), went through numerous changes of title and combinations, and lasted until 1870; the subscription list was sold that year to the *Universalist* in Boston.[75] The peak in the number of societies was reached in 1856, with over 100 reported. But the maximum number of clergy reported in any one year between 1856 and 1865 was forty-four. It is clear that many societies were actually moribund and that many had only occasional preaching. The ratio between the number of societies and clergy was almost exactly two to one during this period. Even allowing for discrepancies and inaccuracies, the downward trend in Universalist numerical strength in the state was obvious after 1861. At its height, however, it should be emphasized that Universalism was to be found in almost every town and hamlet of this predominantly rural state.

By the time of the centennial of the denomination in 1870 there were five associations, sixty societies (parishes), about forty Sunday schools with an attendance of 2,000, and thirty-four ministers.[76] There were fifty-four meeting houses, thirteen of them shared with other denominations. Behind these statistics were hidden the stories of dozens of societies which rose and fell, shifting not only with the fortunes of the denomination but with the social and economic changes in communities over time.

The general history of the Universalists in Shoreham may be taken as typical of the early development of the denomination in Vermont, although in some details it may also have been unique. Quite possibly there was, in the beginning, a larger number of Universalists as original settlers than in any other community in the state.[77] A high proportion of the town's Universalist population immigrated from communities in Worcester County, Massachusetts, including Warwick, Sutton, Oxford, and Hardwick. They had first heard Universalism preached by Caleb Rich, who had been born in Sutton in 1750 and who located in Warwick, where he started preaching about 1773. Some two years later he was joined by Thomas Barnes and Adam Streeter. Rich had been ordained as pastor of the Warwick society in 1781. Both Elhanan Winchester and Hosea Ballou had also preached in the area.

In 1787 Thomas Rich, a brother of Caleb, moved to Shoreham from Massachusetts, where he had served as a lieutenant in the Revolutionary army. His son Charles, one of his eight children, later held several offices, including a seat in the United States Congress. All of Thomas' children eventually joined him and they and their descendants were Universalists. Among the other Universalist families from Massachusetts was that of Levi Jenison, whose son Silas became governor of the state, and held that office for six years (1836-41). Between 1795 and 1806, Shoreham Universalists had the occasional services of Caleb Rich, William Farwell, and other itinerants. A society was organized in 1806 and Richard Carrique, an Englishman from Canada, served the society until about 1814.

Until 1810 the Universalists used district schoolhouses as places of worship. An academy was then built bordering on the Common in the center of the village, the initiative having been taken by Charles Rich.

The ground floor of the frame building was used as a school, and the second floor was built as a chapel where religious services were held by any denomination; the extent of use was determined by the number of shares owned by each. Of the fifty-six original stockholders, forty belonged to the Universalist society or attended its meetings. Of the seventy-one shares eventually sold, fifty-five were taken by Universalists. This entitled them to use of the chapel three-fourths of the time. "Free" seats were also provided for those who wished to attend, and both a pulpit and organ were added. A new and larger meeting house, this time of brick, was provided in 1852.

Between 1814 and 1827 the society was supplied "more or less" with preachers, among them Kittredge Haven who, beginning in 1828, became their resident pastor. During the first half-century of its existence, the society experienced the same changes—sometimes reverses—that befell similar groups. The last of the original settlers had died by the end of the 1850s. Their descendants, and those of others who had moved into the community before 1800, for the most part continued their membership. But emigration had greatly reduced the native population, and they had begun to be replaced by French Canadians and others who gave "no support to Protestant Societies." Another development changed the character of the village population and contributed to the slow but steady decline of the size of the community, and with it the size of the society. As small farms were merged into larger and larger units, the number of freeholders was reduced. Universalists lost their preeminent position and found themselves numerically, financially, and socially, in about the same position as their neighbors.

Antagonism to Universalists on theological grounds was still very visible in the early 1820s, and was most clearly apparent when a member of the denomination was nominated in the fall of 1824 to deliver the annual election sermon and serve as chaplain of the state legislature at its 1825 session. The individual who provoked a lively controversy was Samuel C. Loveland (1787-1858), one of the most active and influential of the early Universalists in the state. He had migrated from his native New Hampshire after having been ordained by the New England Convention in 1813. He held several pastorates in Vermont, the most important in Barnard and Reading (Windsor County) between 1819 and 1842. He operated private schools in both communities, out of which came such well-known Universalist clergymen as William S. Balch, Dolphus and Otis A. Skinner, and T.J. Sawyer.[78] Loveland who established in 1821 the first Universalist newspaper in Vermont, the *Christian Repository,* of which he was editor for five years and later for one year. A self-taught linguist, Loveland received, on the recommendation of T.J. Sawyer, an honorary degree from Middlebury College in 1829, in recognition of the Greek lexicon which he prepared. Loveland was the first Universalist clergyman in America to receive an honorary degree.[79]

In 1824, while serving in the state legislature, Loveland nominated a fellow Universalist, Robert Bartlett, to deliver the next election sermon and to serve as chaplain.[80] Bartlett (1793-1882), like Loveland a native of New Hampshire, had been ordained likewise by the New England Convention, and was an itinerant preacher in Vermont for much of his life. He succeeded Loveland as editor of the *Christian Repository* (1826-28).

Loveland recognized, in nominating Bartlett, the prejudice existing against Universalists but justified the nomination on denominational grounds. He pointed out that Universalists were both sufficiently numerous and well organized in Vermont to be given the appointment in the interests of equity.[81] Two Methodists were nominated also, but Bartlett won on the second ballot, by a close vote and after much debate. It was quite logical that Bartlett's sermon should include a plea for the actual practice of religious liberty as set forth in the principles outlined in the state constitution.[82] Bartlett did not serve as chaplain during the 1825 session, for he had been elected as a representative from Hartland, and propriety dictated that he decline the chaplaincy. Loveland thereupon nominated John E. Palmer of Barre, another Universalist, to fill the position.

Palmer (1783-1873), yet another native of New Hampshire, had been ordained in the ministry of the "Christian Connexion" which he had helped to found. He settled first in Danville, and became a Universalist in 1821. In that year Loveland had first met Palmer, with whom he was greatly impressed.[83] Palmer served several societies in the state, and when he died at the age of ninety was "the oldest Universalist minister on the American Continent."[84] Palmer was elected, even though a Congregationalist was also nominated.

Universalists, in the choice of Bartlett and Palmer by the state legislature, had thus won an important victory in their struggle to achieve acceptance and respectability. This did not mean the cessation of attacks on their denomination; they continued in the press and from orthodox pulpits. Hosea Ballou carried on a verbal feud for several years with Lemuel Haynes, a Negro ex-slave who was possibly the first to preach regularly to white congregations. He preached in Torrington, Connecticut, and for several years in Rutland, Vermont, as a Congregationalist.[85] The product of a racially mixed marriage, Haynes fought during the American Revolution and was a member of the expedition to Ticonderoga in 1777, and married a white woman.

Universalists had overcome most opposition by the mid-nineteenth century and gradually but steadily permeated the entire state of Vermont. Universalists and Unitarians, many with Universalist backgrounds, were to be found not only as farmers and businessmen and in most other occupations, but also in high political office at both the state and national levels. Justin S. Morrill (1810-1898), a United States senator for thirty-two years and sponsor of tariff and land-grant legislation bearing his name, was a Unitarian whose Universalist forbears had settled in Strafford in 1795.[86] Of the 233 members of the Vermont legislature in the 1870-71 session, Universalists were the third most numerous (34), exceeded only by Methodists and Congregationalists.[87]

The first associations organized in Vermont were on a regional rather than on a county basis. In fact, the first one created, the Northern Association, included not only Vermont but parts of New Hampshire and eastern New York, as well as the southern tier of communities in Lower Canada. It was organized at Jericho, Vermont, in 1804, with the assistance of Zebulon Streeter, Hosea Ballou, and Joab Young, representing the New England Convention.[88] Its second and third meetings were held in New Hampshire and New York State respectively. The Franklin Association, organized in 1822, at Bernardston, Massachusetts, originally had jurisdiction not only in Windham County, Vermont, but in Franklin County, Massachusetts, and Cheshire County, New Hampshire. This probably explains the unusually large attendance of clergy at many of its meetings; sixteen were present in 1832, and fifteen societies were in fellowship.[89] The Green Mountain Association was created in 1829, and at first comprised the three counties of Windsor, Rutland, and Bennington. The Lamoille Association, created in 1833, like many others, was recombined into other configurations. The Universalists in Bennington County and Windsor County tried the experiment of separate organizations; but that was excessive fragmentation, and they combined with the Windham Association, organized in 1834, as the Windham and Bennington Association in 1838. The Champlain Association was created in 1833, and the Central Association in 1848, which embraced three counties. The same five associations were in existence in 1870.

As in other states, associations in Vermont combined religious and social functions. They exercised powers of fellowshipping societies, issuing licenses to preach, and ordaining and disciplining of clergy. Kittredge Haven, one of the most important of the nineteenth-century Universalist leaders, was ordained at the meeting of the Northern Association which met in Kingsbury, New York, in 1821.[90] The Northern Association disfellowshipped at least two preachers in the 1820s, one for conduct "unbecoming the Christian, and especially the Christian minister;" the other in "disapprobation of his moral conduct."[91]

It was the Northern Association which, in 1832, recommended the establishment of a state convention, which was to include Lower Canada.[92] Delegates from societies were invited to meet in Barre in

January 1833 to organize it.[93] The meeting was actually held in Montpelier, in the Congregational church. James Ward, from Lennoxville, Lower Canada, was one of the fourteen clergymen present.[94]

The original name was "Convention of Universalists of the State of Vermont and a Portion of Lower Canada." The first meeting of the convention was held in Bethel in August 1833, and at the meeting in 1834 the first in an almost continuous tinkering with the constitution began. In that year the title of the organization was changed to "Vermont State Convention of Universalists." Typical attendance was about twenty "ministering brothers" in the 1830s, and from eight to thirty delegates from the associations. When the General Convention recommended "a better organization of our denomination" the Vermont Convention took it under advisement, and debated "whether they receive the advice of the U.S. Convention or not." It was obvious that Vermonters were going to be as independent as their fellow Universalists in Maine.

Like most state conventions, the Vermont body appointed standing and special committees on such subjects as "the moral reforms of the day" (headed by Eli Ballou for many years), Sunday schools, denominational education, and "the state of the cause within our borders." A missionary society was established in 1852, and Eli Ballou presented in 1861 a proposal to spread Universalism by creating a "General Universalist Church" or "Convention Church" which would welcome all who were sympathetic to Universalism, whether members or not. It was to be a branch of the state convention, and bore an interesting resemblance to the Church of the Larger Fellowship organized in 1944 to serve Unitarians living in areas not served by churches. Such a "Church of the Convention" was actually organized by the Vermont body in 1861, and 123 individuals were elected and given the Right Hand of Fellowship that year. But the innovation had ceased to be attractive by 1864, when only five were elected, and the experiment came to an end.

In 1864 the associations lost their representation in the state convention, and were replaced by one lay delegate from each society or church. This was in keeping with the recommendation of the General Convention that increased centralization be achieved at the state level. The associations were left with no real powers when in 1864 the state convention created its own committee on fellowship, ordination, and discipline, and took over these functions from the associations.

The state convention was poverty-stricken throughout most of its history in the nineteenth century. It had no assured source of funds and was forced to depend on collections taken up at annual meetings, and on volunteer assistance. The commitment to raise $10,000 for the Murray Fund was a real strain, and the pledge was never met, although a Women's Centenary Committee did its best. The convention treasury in 1870 amounted to only $115.72.[95] A levy of 50 cents per year per family was finally established, in 1881, and in the same year the policy was approved of encouraging societies and/or churches to deed their property to the convention. St. Johnsbury was the first to do so, in 1884, but such an arrangement brought in no immediate source of revenue. The permanent fund was less than $2,500 by 1894. Financing missionary activity and requests for aid to parishes and other projects became chronic problems which were never really solved.

Relations with Universalist neighbors across the border had always been a part of official policy on the part of Vermonters. When the Northern Association had been organized in 1804 its jurisdiction extended to the fellowshipping of societies in southern Canada, although few took the step because they were as small and as scattered as many of their counterparts in Vermont. When the constitution of the state convention was revised in 1845, its jurisdiction was extended to include "such ministers residing in Canada East . . . in fellowship with the Northern Association."[96] The convention met in Canada once in the nineteenth century, when it convened at Waterloo, in the Province of Quebec, in 1872. The denominational status of Canadians in Quebec was further clarified in 1868, when the name of the state convention was changed to include that province. The name was retained in 1888 when the Universalist Convention of Vermont and Quebec was incorporated by the state legislature and ratified by the convention the following year. The organization was reincorporated in 1937 as the Vermont and Quebec Universalist Unitarian Convention, anticipating in the title by almost a quarter of a century the merger of the two denominations in 1961.

A Note on Canadian Universalism

The Universalist state and regional organizations in Vermont and Maine in the nineteenth century had the unique distinction of being international in their character, for they claimed jurisdiction over Universalists in parts of southern and eastern Canada. When the Northern Association had been created in 1804, centered in Vermont, it included Universalists in what was then known as Lower Canada. When the Vermont State Convention added Quebec to its title in 1868, the jurisdiction of the old Northern Association was extended to include clergy as well as societies. In 1868 the Maine Convention voted to admit Universalists in the provinces of "Lower Canada" to its fellowship.[97] This rather vague wording caused a certain amount of confusion, for the precise jurisdiction of the Maine organization was not originally made clear. Therefore, a word of explanation seems to be in order regarding terminology and political geography.

That portion of Canada roughly south and east of Hudson Bay had originally been a single ill-defined administrative area usually known as Quebec. In 1791 Quebec had been divided into Upper and Lower Canada. Between 1841 and 1867 the two had been reunited. Lower Canada, known also as Canada East, included the so-called Eastern Townships between the American frontier and the St. Lawrence River, settled largely by Americans after the Revolution. Upper Canada became known as Canada West. By the British North America Act of 1867, Lower Canada became the Province of Quebec, and Upper Canada the Province of Ontario. The two Maritime Provinces of New Brunswick and Nova Scotia became part of the Dominion of Canada the same year, and Prince Edward Island joined the confederation in 1873.

Universalists in Canada were considered of sufficient interest and importance by the 1830s and 1840s to have their communications and reports published occasionally in such papers as the *Trumpet* and the *Universalist Union.* The *Universalist Register* also carried a brief (and not always accurate) statistical report on the "British Provinces." Universalists from Canada often attended Universalist meetings in the northern United States and were always welcomed warmly. Several also served as corresponding secretaries of the Universalist Historical Society in the years immediately after its organization in 1834. There was considerable migration back and forth throughout the nineteenth century, across the "unguarded frontier," particularly in northern New England.

The majority of Universalists in Canada in the early nineteenth century had come from the United States.[98] The first American known to have preached Universalism in Canada was Christopher Huntington, who settled in 1804 with his family in Compton, in Lower Canada.[99] Others served as itinerants, among them James Ward, who lived in Stanstead. In 1834 he was dividing his time between the villages of Stukely and Waterloo and was planning to organize a society in each, in spite of much opposition.[100] Isaiah Boynton, a preacher from Vermont who died at the age of twenty-nine, had visited Stanstead as early as 1829.[101] By 1835 three preachers and five societies were reported in Canada (Stanstead, organized in 1830; Shipton, Ascot, Compton, and Broome).[102] All were close to the international border. Jacob L. Watson, a New Englander, was apparently the first Universalist to be ordained in Lower Canada. The ceremony took place in Shefford in 1836, in an academy operated by the Methodists.[103] The society at Stanstead seems to have had the most stable existence. Ward served there for several years, and a meeting house was constructed in 1842.[104] In 1844 Caleb P. Mallory, a Canadian Universalist then living in Lennoxville, set out to visit every community in the province to identify Universalists.[105] He had been fellowshipped by the Northern

Association (Vermont) in 1832 and ordained at Glover, Vermont, in 1843.[106] Until his death in 1882 he spent much time in Huntingville, which was one of the few wholly Protestant communities in Quebec.[107]

After the name of the Vermont Convention was changed to include Quebec, the Canadian society at Bedford was fellowshipped in 1869.[108] The Vermont and Quebec Universalist Convention voted financial assistance to the society at Coaticook in 1889 and 1890, but refused to render such aid in 1898 because the organization had disappeared and hence was not entitled to fellowship.[109]

Two centers of Universalism had appeared in southeastern Quebec (the Eastern Townships) by 1870. One was the village of Huntingville, where a Universalist meeting house was dedicated in 1845 and where Mallory centered his activities for almost forty years.[110] The other was in Waterloo, where a substantial church building was erected and dedicated in 1871. The use of regional churches was a practical solution to the problems faced by Universalists, who were scattered and lacking in resources.

The attention of American Universalists was first called to their coreligionists in Upper Canada (Canada West) in 1831, when a society was organized at London (Middlesex County).[111] Many were native Americans, and were accused of disloyalty during the Rebellion of 1837. Some were jailed.[112] The only other society known to have been organized before 1840 was at Merrickville, where Mrs. Mary Ann Church preached occasionally; she was a convert to Universalism, and was not in formal fellowship when she was preaching in the late 1830s.[113] There was also itinerant preaching in the 1830s and early 1840s by such Americans as J. Whitney of Rochester, New York.[114]

The most important of the early Universalists in Upper Canada were David Leavitt, who arrived in 1837, and preached all over the province; and A.G. Laurie, the first ordained minister in the area, who made frequent reports to Universalist newspapers in the United States.[115] He was a native of Scotland and held several pastorates in the United States, where he was ordained in 1843. He lived in Simcoe and then in London, while in Canada, between 1843 and 1849, and reconstituted the London society which had lapsed. His last pastorate before his death in 1891 at the age of seventy-five, was in Erie, Pennsylvania.[116]

The first organization of Canadian Universalists beyond the society or individual church level was created in Smithville (Niagara District) in 1844, where Laurie had organized a society that year. George Rogers, an itinerant from Ohio, happened to be visiting in upstate New York, and spent several weeks in Upper Canada, preaching in Sparta, Brantford, Toronto, Hamilton, and Smithville.[117] While in Smithville he attended a meeting to organize an association. He was appointed to draw up a constitution, which was adopted.[118] There were delegates present from three societies (Victoria District, London, and Smithville).

The new organization, the "Christian Universalist Association for Canada West," lasted until 1873.[119] When a disastrous fire reduced much of the town of London in 1845, the Universalist meeting house was spared, but many members of the society lost their homes and other possessions.[120] George Rogers issued a special plea for assistance to them because he had recently visited there and had participated in their activities.

At its meeting in 1845 at Belleville (Victoria District), the association voted to circulate petitions requesting the Provincial Parliament to extend "the same toleration, the same protection, and the same privileges which have been conferred on other denominations."[121] The outlook seemed promising for Universalists, and Leavitt, who had been the moving force in calling the meeting to organize the association and served as its secretary until 1873, held periodic meetings in Belleville in 1845, in rented quarters.[122] Leavitt and a co-worker, J.R.W. Lavelle, were ordained by the association in 1846 and 1848, respectively. Lavelle, who organized the Ontario Universalist Convention in 1877, had become a convert from a Presbyterian background while in New York City, under the influence of Abel C. Thomas. From 1846 until his death in 1898 Lavelle served as a missionary in Ontario.[123] Lavelle assumed the leadership in the province after Laurie returned to the United States in 1849.

The Canadian association in 1846 requested the fellowship of the General Convention in the United States, but without the requirement of subordination regarding discipline.[124] The representatives of the association, David Leavitt and Jonathan Striker, explained that this was not to be interpreted as jealousy or as unwillingness to cooperate, but was necessitated by political and legal considerations. Any "seeming alliance" with an organized body in the United States that exercised superior jurisdiction over a Canadian organization was not advisable. The proposal from the Canadians was unacceptable to the General Convention, so relations were left on an informal basis until 1881. In that year an amendment to the constitution of the General Convention was ratified extending its jurisdiction to the Dominion of Canada. The application for fellowship of what had by then become the Universalist Convention of Ontario was immediately and unanimously granted.[125]

In 1862 Sylvanus Cobb of Massachusetts, whose paper, the *Christian Freeman*, had just been merged with the *Trumpet,* visited several Universalist societies in Canada West, and attended a meeting of the association.[126] The association voted to request fellowship with the New York Convention in 1863, but there is no indication that the plan was carried out.[127] One individual who frequently attended association meetings in Canada West was George Moses, a member of the Delaware tribe and the first native American Indian to enter the Universalist ministry. He organized a society among the Indians in 1864, the first such in the denomination, and lived and preached in Willow Grove, Province of Ontario. He was ordained by the association in 1871.[128]

The first records of American Universalists in New Brunswick go back to the early 1820s, when such men as Joseph Butterfield, J.B. Dods, and Sylvanus Cobb visited Calais, Maine, and crossed the border into neighboring St. Stephen and St. Davids.[129] Oliver Smith of Fredricton, N.B. attended the General Convention in 1835 when it met in Hartford, Connecticut, and was publicly commended for coming.[130] He and Amos Hitchings were present at the convention in 1839 at Portland, Maine, and were made honorary members of the council.[131] Hitchings became in 1840 the first ordained Universalist minister in New Brunswick, and organized a society in St. Davids.[132] T.P. Abell, of Castine, Maine, conducted the ordination ceremony. A society had appeared in St. Stephen by 1842, which also constructed a meeting house.[133] W.C. George served as the pastor.[134] Universalism had been recognized in 1841 "as among the Christian denominations in the Province."[135]

There was occasional preaching elsewhere in New Brunswick. W.S. Clark of Lubec, Maine, preached in Woodcock, Dorchester, and Saint John in 1835, but no society appears to have taken root. Hitchings, a corresponding secretary for the Universalist Historical Society, reported to that body in 1845 indicating the existence of only the two societies at St. Davids and St. Stephen.[136] The meeting house in Milltown (St. Stephen) burned in 1854, but had been replaced by 1857.[137] During the 1850s H.A. Philbrook, who was based in Calais, Maine, also served the Milltown society. He had been ordained in 1858.[138] He also revived the society in St. Davids in 1866 while continuing to hold services both in St. Stephen and at Calais.[139] The meeting house at Milltown was destroyed by a gale in the fall of 1869, leaving only the one at St. Davids, which was remodelled in 1870.[140] Philbrook left Calais in 1870 to assume the pastorate in Shirley, Massachusetts, and was replaced in Calais by Isaac C. Knowlton. Whether he preached in Canada is not recorded. Philbrook by 1878 had been settled in Halifax, Nova Scotia, which by that date was in fellowship with the Maine Convention, as Quebec was with the Vermont Convention.[141] Meanwhile, the society in St. Stephen's parish had long since disappeared. Except for an aborted attempt in Saint John in the late 1880s, it was not until 1911 that churches were organized in New Brunswick (Harvey, York County; and Moore's Mills, St. Stephen) as part of the missionary efforts of Charles H. Pennoyer.

The first Universalist society in Nova Scotia was organized at Pugwash in 1834, with nearly thirty members, by William Delaney. He had been converted to Universalism the previous year by reading the Scriptures.[142] The society organized the first Universalist church in the province, and also constructed and dedicated, in 1835, the first

Universalist meeting house.[143] Delaney requested the fellowship of the General Convention but was told that it would be appropriate for Canadian Universalists to organize their own association or convention. But none was ever organized in the Maritime Provinces. W.S. Clark from Maine preached in Maneada and Amherst in 1835, but nothing apparently came of his efforts.[144] David Wilson, a Canadian from Hope, was also preaching in 1835.[145]

American Universalists were encouraged as early as 1835 to assist in organizing a society in Halifax, but nothing came of the request.[146] The first attempt by residents of Halifax and neighboring Dartmouth "for the purpose of promoting the cause of Universalism" was a fiasco. The public meeting, held in the fall of 1837, was not at all organized, and a number of persons opposing Universalism were present.[147] "The meeting fell into confusion and disorder–and became an entire failure." Although the meeting was not a success, the twenty-six individuals from Halifax and Dartmouth who publicly avowed their Universalism at the meeting at least identified themselves. They met in private homes and at various other locations, created an informal society in 1837, and held services conducted by William F. Teulon. Teulon, a lay preacher, was a London-born physician who had left the Methodist church; he remained until 1841.[148] His successor, Robinson Breare, was also a "Bible convert" from Methodism to Universalism, in 1841. This probably explains at least in part the particular animosity which the Methodists seemed to have exhibited toward Universalists in Halifax. Breare had come to Halifax from England as a missionary for the Wesleyan Association. He served as pastor from 1841 until 1845.

Breare visited the Boston Association in Massachusetts as part of his efforts to raise money for a meeting house.[149] After the First Universalist Church of Halifax was organized in 1843, Breare visited the United States as far south as New York City, and returned with almost $1,000 in donations.[150] He had already made yet another trip to the States earlier in 1843. His predecessor, Teulon, had never been fellowshippped because there had been no organization in Canada authorized to do so. Breare came to the First Universalist Society in Boston to be ordained because there were no facilities in Canada.[151] A meeting house was finally built and dedicated in 1844 after much financial difficulty. The greatest disappointment at the dedication was the failure of any Universalists from the United States to attend.[152] The same complaint that Universalists in eastern Canada were almost completely isolated from those in the United States was made in 1870.[153]

The church in Halifax continued to lead an uneven existence, with pastors changing rapidly. They often came from the States. Among them was Nathaniel Gunnison (1811-1871), a native of New

Hampshire, who served as pastor from 1857 to 1865. He had been ordained in 1837 and had held pastorates in several New England communities.[154] He was apparently very successful in Halifax, for the church prospered during his administration. He might not have resigned if he had not also been Deputy Consul for the United States in Halifax and had not so strongly supported the North during the Civil War. He antagonized many of his parishioners who sided with the Southern Confederacy.

Although there had been considerable activity, much strong leadership, ambitious plans, and great hopes, Universalism, taken as a general movement, did not proper in Canada in the nineteenth century. When the Provincial Censuses (excluding the Maritimes) were taken in 1851, there were over 6,000 Universalists; the number had declined to less than 3,200 by 1891.[155] Many of the same explanatory factors can be listed for the weaknesses in both American and Canadian Universalism in the nineteenth century, some of them exaggerated in Canada: the scattered, uncoordinated and rural character of much of the denomination; the tendency of societies or churches to become moribund or to disappear when exceptional leadership was removed; aversion to, or at least apathy toward, effective organization; inadequate financial support because of unwillingness or inability to provide the necessary resources; the lessening of theological differences among denominations which undermined Universalist distinctiveness over the years.[156]

Even though the General Convention claimed to represent both the United States and "the British Provinces," there was the question of how much communication could be maintained, and of how much actual support could be and was provided, beyond the furnishing of some ministers and occasional words of encouragement. Pleas for funds were answered minimally, if at all, because the organization had a difficult enough time as it was to meet its other commitments. So almost all of the financial aid had to come through the efforts of individuals or token contributions by hard-pressed state conventions bordering on Canada. A plea for funds to help pay off church indebtedness in Waterloo, Province of Quebec, addressed to the General Convention in 1873, brought no assistance. The best that the *Universalist* could do was call the plight of the church to the attention of the denomination.[157] Much of the support for Universalist churches and missionary activity in Canada after 1880 came from the bequest of William West and his family and descendants.[158] The Ontario Convention, which lasted into the twentieth century, outlived most of its original constituency. At the time of the merger of the Universalist and Unitarian denominations in the United States in 1961, the three remaining Universalist congregations in Canada (Olinda in Ontario,

North Hatley in Quebec, and Halifax in Nova Scotia) took the same step with Unitarians in Canada. Another era in the history of Universalism had come to an end or a new beginning.

New Hampshire

Universalism was first preached in New Hampshire almost simultaneously but quite independently in two opposite corners of the state. John Murray was responsible for the introduction of Universalism in the eastern seaport town of Portsmouth, in 1773; and Caleb Rich in the rural communities of Richmond, Jaffrey, and Winchester, in the southwest, about 1778.[159] Rich organized a regional society comprising Universalists in Warwick, Massachusetts, and Richmond and Jaffrey, New Hampshire, in the winter of 1780, but the first society in the state to be actually incorporated was in Portsmouth, in 1793.

The numerous Universalist societies more or less organized in the early nineteenth century were characterized by short lives, informal organization, much reconstitution and combination, and the almost complete absence of full-time preaching. There was often a lapse of a decade or more between the first preaching of Universalism in a community and the appearance of a society. The population between the end of the eighteenth century and 1860 seems to have been in a state of constant flux, and the preachers seldom stayed in one location for long except in a few societies in urban centers such as Portsmouth.

The records of the early societies, again with the exception of Portsmouth, have been either lost or never existed. Therefore any attempt to identify with exactness the dates of establishment of great numbers of societies is difficult if not impossible. New Hampshire Universalists seemed to have had an unusual reluctance to organize, and the number of churches created out of societies was exceptionally small. The ebb and flow of early Universalism can be illustrated by Elias Smith, who in 1800 organized in Portsmouth the "Christian Connexion," which became a forerunner of the Campbellites and Disciples of Christ. Smith wandered in and out of Universalism on at least four occasions.

The most complete record of early Universalism in New Hampshire relates to the society established in 1780 in Portsmouth.[160] John Murray made the first of several trips to Portsmouth in November 1773, when he remained about a week and preached in two different meeting houses. By carefully avoiding any public commitment to Universalism he was warmly received. When the implications of his preaching became clear on the next trip, early in 1775, church doors were generally closed against him. He was welcomed only at the Episcopal church.

Among those converted by Murray was Noah Parker, "an honest and upright mechanic" (a blacksmith). In 1777 five other converts began meeting in private homes, with Parker as the lay preacher, and by 1780 the first society in the state had come into being. The original society acquired sufficient other converts to meet in enlarged quarters. The informal society erected its own meeting house in 1783-84. Between the time of Parker's death in 1787 and 1794, the society was without regular preaching. Efforts were begun as early as 1789 to obtain an act of incorporation from the state legislature, but they were not successful until 1793, when John Langdon, a representative from Portsmouth (not a Universalist) came to the defense of the petitioners and testified to their "respectability and moral worth."[161] A statement of belief and fellowship was adopted in 1794, signed by thirty-eight men. The act of incorporation included an interesting restriction prohibiting the society from levying taxes for the support of a minister, a limitation removed in 1806.

The first pastor was George Richards from Boston, who began his work with the society late in 1793 and was ordained in 1799. He served until his resignation in 1809, when he moved to Philadelphia. He was replaced by Hosea Ballou, who served at an annual salary of $800 and departed for Salem, Massachusetts, in 1815. For the next thirty years five other pastors served, including such well-known individuals as Thomas Farrington King, father of Thomas Starr King. A church of seventy-five members was organized in 1805, probably the first in the state, and was reorganized in 1816. A meeting house was built in 1808, financed by subscriptions, and a Sunday school was established in 1832. By 1840 the Portsmouth society, with 160 families, was one of the largest in the state, as well as the largest one of any denomination in the town.[162]

Early Universalism elsewhere in New Hampshire developed in a completely haphazard manner. By 1800 societies had appeared in Richmond, which was the temporary headquarters of Caleb Rich, who was succeeded in 1791 by David Ballou, an older brother of Hosea Ballou; in Charlestown, where William Farwell was ordained in 1791 and served until 1803; Langdon, in 1791, where Elhanan Winchester had preached many years before; and Chesterfield, organized in 1798.[163] Not one had a stable or uninterrupted existence. There was no settled pastor in Richmond for almost forty years after David Ballou's departure in 1801. An identical situation prevailed in Charlestown, which had no regular pastor between 1803 and 1845. The Langdon society was reorganized in 1819 and two years later was combined with the society in Alstead as the "Langdon and Paper Mill Village Society." There had apparently been legal or other difficulties encountered when the society in Langdon was originally created, for its constitution in 1791 had provided that in case any member of the society was oppressed or obliged to defend himself under the law for his religious opinions, each member of the society would bear part of the expenses, according to his financial ability. It was in the Langdon meeting house that Abner Kneeland had been ordained in 1805. The Chesterfield society temporarily disappeared a few years after it had been created, and was reorganized in 1818.

Probably the experience of the Winchester society can be taken to stand for great numbers of others. Caleb Rich had preached there as early as 1778, but there was no organization at all until after 1810, when Timothy Bigelow arrived. After preaching in neighboring towns as well as in Winchester, he moved to Ohio.[164] A society was actually incorporated in 1819 but soon disappeared for lack of a preacher.[165] Hopes went up again when the part-time services of William S. Balch were obtained in 1828, and the society was reincorporated. But that did not prosper either. For the next twenty years Winchester enjoyed "more or less preaching by various individuals."[166]

By 1800 there were four Universalist preachers in New Hampshire fellowshipped by the New England Convention.[167] The number had risen to nine in 1813.[168] There were never enough clergy to go round, and many societies collapsed because they had no clerical leadership. Reiterated exhortations to conduct services without preachers were usually disregarded. There were less than half a dozen Universalists in Atkinson when Joshua Flagg started preaching there in 1808; by the time T.G. Farnsworth preached in the village in 1818, the number had more than trebled, but he lived in Haverhill, Massachusetts, and preached in Atkinson only one-fourth of the time.[169] When Jacob Wood first preached Universalism in Dover in 1817, there were only two or three Universalists; there were over 150 by 1824, and a society was organized in 1825, but had no settled minister.[170]

The statement was made in 1828 that there were fewer Universalists in New Hampshire in proportion to total population than in any other New England state.[171] But even if new societies were created among those Universalists still unorganized, if there were no preachers available it was difficult at best to maintain them. It was estimated in 1829 that there were 100 societies in the state (probably an exaggeration), with an approximate ratio of one preacher for every twenty societies.[172] Yet Hopkinton was attempting to support two societies in 1844, one having been organized in 1830 and the other in 1841, each with a part-time preacher.[173] When John G. Adams became the pastor in Wentworth in 1833, the demands for his services in various communities added up to seven-quarters of his time, besides Wentworth—a most obvious impossibility.[174]

By the best estimates available, the greatest number of societies reported before 1870 was ninety-six, in 1845.[175] But many existed in name only, as the editor of the *Universalist Register* was frank to admit.

Even if the number of societies were halved, there were only thirty-nine preachers available, and five of them were not in fellowship.[176] Only fifteen churches had been organized by 1845. Universalist momentum perceptibly slowed after 1850. In 1862 there were only twenty-eight ministers in residence, and only seventeen of them had settled pastorates.[177] Three counties had only one settled pastor in each, and three had none at all. By 1870, organized Universalism in New Hampshire had been reduced to twenty-nine societies (parishes) and sixteen clergy.[178] Even the attempts to establish a denominational press in the state had not been successful. Of the four periodicals established between 1832 and 1842, none survived after 1846.[179] They were too localized, located too close to Boston, and were inadequately patronized.

The same unhappy fate befell the three academies established by Universalists in the state. The Unity School with which Alonzo A. Miner had been associated had lasted less than ten years. Lebanon Liberal Institute had closed in 1850, and Mount Caesar Seminary-Swanzey Academy struggled until 1859. An attempt failed to establish an academy in Plymouth in 1855. In 1865 Universalists in the state were "earnestly considering" the question of opening a denominational academy, and two years later the subject was "considerably discussed," but that was as far as the idea ever progressed.[180]

Six associations had been organized in New Hampshire by 1836, and several of these underwent periodic reorganizations and subdivisions. The oldest, the Merrimack River Association, was organized in the summer of 1824 in Westmoreland by four clergymen, only one of whom became a permanent resident of the state. Originally called the "New Hampshire Association," it changed its name after other associations were created. The Rockingham Association, also organized in 1824, was established by clergy from Boston as a "missionary instrumentality."[181] In 1827 a committee was appointed by the (then) New Hampshire Association to confer with the Rockingham Association to consider the expediency of uniting the two, but localism was too prevalent.[182] Adoption of a constitution for the Rockingham Association had to be delayed until after 1827 because the majority of the clergy attending were not even residents of the state.[183] The other associations comprised one or more counties, and underwent frequent changes of jurisdiction. In 1861 the associations lost their powers to the state convention and one by one they disappeared. They had become merely conferences "for moral and spiritual counsel, encouragement, and instruction."[184] By 1870, only three existed (Cheshire, Rockingham, and Sullivan).

The original proposal which resulted in the establishment of the New Hampshire Convention in 1832 had been to organize a combined convention with Vermont. The idea of a "union convention" had been broached by the New Hampshire Association in 1831. The idea was reaffirmed early in 1832, subject to the approval of the clergy and societies in the two states.[185] However, the plan was disapproved by the Rockingham Association, so separate conventions were created.[186] A meeting was convened in Claremont later in the year, and after Universalists were assured that the convention would have no authority over the associations and would provide only information and fellowship, a constitution was adopted.[187] In 1836 the convention assumed exclusive power to grant preaching licenses and to ordain "evangelists."[188] When the constitution was rewritten in 1861, all fellowshipping, ordination, and discipline was reserved to it.[189] The state missionary society organized several years earlier was also merged into the convention in 1861. However, the Sabbath School Convention, created in 1869, maintained a separate existence and met annually immediately preceding the convention. The convention, incorporated in 1865, was "the only recognized ecclesiastical authority in the state." New Hampshire thus followed the organizational pattern found elsewhere.

Connecticut

John Murray was the first to introduce Universalism into Connecticut. On his various trips between New York and Boston, the first in 1772, he preached in at least eight communities in the state. Murray visited Norwich in 1773 and again in 1774. In Norwich he attracted the favorable attention of John Tyler, rector of the Episcopal church, whose six sermons in defense of Universalism were published anonymously in 1798.[190] First published in Boston, the sermons were reprinted several times, including one edition published in Norwich in 1815. Richard Sibbey, a Universalist who had come from Long Island, New York, and had settled in the community of Long Ridge (part of Stamford) during the Revolution, may have been a lay preacher. The Universalist views of Joseph Huntington, Congregational pastor of the church in Coventry from 1763 until his death in 1795, were presented in the posthumously published *Calvinism Improved.*[191] Universalism was preached in Stafford (Tolland County) as early as 1780, when Joshua Flagg visited, and was followed by Edward Turner who held services in a tavern.[192] In 1780 Isaac Foster, pastor of the Congregational society in Strafford, announced his Universalism, and the majority of the congregation followed his lead.[193]

Elhanan Winchester visited Norwich in 1794 and preached there at intervals until 1797.[194] He was followed by Edward Mitchell of New York City. Murray probably visited Hartford in 1781, and between 1796 and his death the following year, Winchester preached there also.

Universalists, few in number and probably at first reluctant to identify themselves, could be found scattered throughout the state in the 1790s and early 1800s, but it is almost impossible to tabulate systematically either their numbers or location. There were sufficient Universalists in Woodstock, Preston, and Wallingford by 1793 to receive invitations to attend the New England Convention in Oxford, Massachusetts.[195] Societies may have been organized as early as the time of the Revolution in Long Ridge, in 1791 in Norwich, in Southington in 1792, in Windsor in 1794, and in Hartford in 1796, but the records are too scanty and the definition of what constituted a society too vague to be certain of any of these dates.

One of the basic explanations for difficulty in piecing the story together was the unusually large amount of opposition which Universalists faced in Connecticut, extending well into the nineteenth century. The hostility that was naturally to be expected toward a sect which preached doctrines contrary to the beliefs of the majority was heightened by the fact that the Congregational church held a tight-fisted monopoly on religion in the state. Universalists were lumped together with atheists, deists, and Unitarians, and no records of their existence were kept by the established church.[196] Congregationalists believing in universal salvation were excommunicated. The Congregational General Conference in Connecticut declared in 1793, in reply to Joseph Huntington's Universalism, that belief in the final salvation of all men was "a censurable heresy."[197] Even the competency of Universalists to take oaths was challenged.

The tide may have begun to turn by the early 1840s. It was reported to the General Convention in 1841 that Universalism in Connecticut was having at least an indirect influence which was greater than statistical measurements indicated. Even the Congregationalists "now regard it as an important recommendation of their pastor that 'he is a very *liveral* man, and seldom *says anything about hell.*' "[198] But even if so, Universalism was far from triumphing. In 1844 J.H. Plumb of Berlin referred to Connecticut as "this land of Calvinistic darkness."[199] As late as 1857 the editor of the *Trumpet* came to a reluctant conclusion: "Connecticut, it must be confessed, is a hard state in which to advance Liberal Christianity—in any of its phases."[200] With only thirty-two societies, and many of them on paper only, and with only sixteen preachers, it was an uphill struggle for Universalists. The Unitarians were in an even worse plight. Within three years, all four of their societies, together with their pastors, had disappeared.

Opposition or no, Universalism persisted and even spread, disorganized and disparaged as it was, especially in rural areas. The chronological gap between the first preaching of Universalism in a community and the appearance of societies was often a wide one; and was even wider between the organization of societies and the establishment of church organizations. Preachers were few and far between. Solomon Glover of Newtown began preaching in 1800 and was reported (erroneously) to have been the only resident clergyman in Connecticut for twenty years.[201] He was indeed the only Connecticut preacher in fellowship with the New England Convention in 1813.[202] The convention did, however, meet once in Newtown, in 1807. Glover died in 1842 at the age of ninety-two, at the time the oldest Universalist preacher in the denomination.[203]

There were ten societies in the state by 1830, with considerable occasional preaching; five settled pastors; and three meeting houses. Universalists gained many recruits from Congregational societies, and often found it advantageous to cooperate with fellow dissenters such as the Baptists. There were sufficient Universalists in Stafford to erect a meeting house in 1814 jointly with the Baptists, who had withdrawn from the Congregational society.[204] The two groups conducted their business as the "New Meeting House Society" and until 1818 hired a Baptist as pastor. In that year the Universalists organized a society of their own, purchased the Baptist interest in the meeting house for $60, and selected Hosea Ballou 2d as their first pastor. He presided, for the three years he was in the community, in what was the only Universalist meeting house in the state at the time. A church was not organized until late in 1847, two years after a new meeting house was constructed.

Between the death of Elhanan Winchester in 1797 and 1821, when Hosea Ballou visited, there was no permanent organization or regular preaching in Hartford. Ballou stirred up sufficient enthusiasm to result in the settlement of Richard Carrique (1821-24), although no society was organized until 1827. There was a sizable accession in 1822 to the informal group when a schism occurred in the Second Congregational Church and sixty members joined the Universalists. They met in the State House until 1824, when their first meeting house was built. The subscription list indicates that the original "ten church pillars" were among the wealthiest men in Hartford and held important civic and political positions.[205] The first settled pastor of the actual society was Menzies Rayner (1827-31), a convert from the Episcopal church. During his pastorate he edited the first Universalist periodical in the state, the *Religious Inquirer,* which continued under a series of editors until 1847. Between 1839 and 1843, the *Universalist* was published simultaneously in Middletown and Hartford, but had to be abandoned because of insufficient support. It was merged with the *Trumpet* in 1843, which thereafter carried a column devoted to Connecticut denominational news. During the same decade (in 1846) a Sunday School Association was organized, with eleven schools initially represented. There were only twelve Sunday schools reported in the state in 1870.[206] The Hartford society over the years constructed two other churches in the center of the city, one in 1860 and the other in 1906. A new church was constructed in West Hartford in 1931, reflecting the westward movement of the urban population.

By 1833 it was estimated that there were ten preachers and about thirty societies in the state.[207] This was probably a grossly exaggerated figure, for only three years earlier only five "principal" societies were listed (Stafford, Hartford, Norwich, Newtown, and Windham).[208] Unorganized Universalists in all likelihood still constituted the majority. Typical was the report of Hosea Ballou when he stopped in Ashford enroute to a meeting in Berlin in 1830. He found "a few believers in Universalism scattered through the towns of Union, Woodstock, Ashford, and Pomfret."[209] When statistical reports were made to the General Convention in 1835 it was frankly admitted that the number of Universalists in Connection was unknown.[210] In 1840, after only four months as pastor in Hartford, John Moore came to the unhappy conclusion that Universalism in Connecticut was about fifteen years behind the rest of New England.[211] There seemed to be a constant removal of clergy to other states. There was always the promise of "a better state of things," but of the forty societies established between 1820 and 1870, the majority had gone out of existence within a few years, mostly in rural communities.[212] When the centennial of the denomination was celebrated in 1870, there were sixteen parishes in the state, of which six were either inactive or without regular pastors.[213] Connecticut Universalists did have one unique distinction as of 1870. The first two women ordained in the denominational ministry both held pastorates in the state. Olympia Brown was serving in Bridgeport and Phebe A. Hanaford in New Haven.

Connecticut was reported in 1843 still to be more completely under Calvinist religious control than any state in the Union. It was "under the domination of an iron-fisted aristocracy . . . in a sort of half-way form, between Presbyterianism and Congregationalism."[214] The same view was expressed in 1852. The religious climate was just not favorable for liberal Christianity to flourish. There were in that year "probably more dead and dying societies of liberal Christians in Connecticut, than in any New England state of its size."[215]

The reports may have been discouraging, but the Universalists did not give up. A missionary society was organized in 1853, incorporated by a special act of the legislature, which required submission of an annual report. The society lasted until 1862, as an auxiliary of the state convention which then absorbed it. Abraham Norwood served as the state missionary agent throughout the life of the society.[216] He died destitute, owing $500 on his home in Meriden, after having eked out an existence for himself and a large family on $200 a year.[217] Two mission stations were established by the state convention. One was in Southington (Hartford County) and was started in 1897, long after the

"First Society of United Brethren" organized in 1829, had disappeared. The mission lasted less than five years. The other was at Stony Creek, Branford (New Haven County) and had become dormant by 1900.

The Women's Universalist Missionary Society of Connecticut was organized in 1869 as part of the effort to raise the Murray Fund for the centennial. A vice president was selected for each state, and Mrs. C.A. Skinner served for Connecticut. After the Connecticut branch of the Woman's Centenary Association was organized in New Haven in 1873, its name was changed in 1899 to the Women's Universalist Missionary Society, and to the Association of Universalist Women of Connecticut in 1940.

The possibility of organizing a state convention was first discussed in 1830.[218] A follow-up meeting was held in New Haven in 1832, when the convention came into existence. A constitution was adopted in 1836 and was revised three years later, in which the decentralized character of Universalism was stressed. The associations, which sent delegates to the convention, were given jurisdiction over fellowshipping, ordination, and ministerial discipline.[219] This arrangement lasted into the twentieth century.

The three associations created in the nineteenth century were the end-product of a recommendation made by the state convention. The first, the Connecticut Association, was organized in 1834 and was intended to cover the entire state. Prior to that date Universalists had been served by, and had participated in, two regional organizations located elsewhere: the Providence Association in Rhode Island and the Southern Association (organized in 1827) which included both southeastern Massachusetts and eastern Connecticut. The Connecticut Association became the Hartford County Association in 1836, although it also included Litchfield County as well.[220] The two other associations, the Quinnebaug and the Southern, were both established in 1836. The Quinnebaug Association covered the eastern counties of the state and the Southern the south-central and southwestern counties.[221]

Typical of most associations when first organized was the Quinnebaug. It had six societies within its jurisdiction in 1837, with Stafford the oldest and most active.[222] Norwich had had a very erratic history, and was without a pastor. The society at Bolton had only twelve members. The Union society had preaching only six times a year. Neither Coventry nor New London was represented at the 1837 meeting, the latter described as having a large but "a little cold and sleepy" society. When the Hartford County Association met in 1839, there was a discussion of whether even three associations might be too many, but the number remained at that figure.[223] The associations were abolished in 1906 and replaced by exclusive representation in the convention from societies, churches, and Sunday schools.

Connecticut Universalists were neither numerous in relation to the total population nor a powerful force in the state, religiously speaking.[224] In the perspective of the Civil War era, Connecticut had always been "hard soil," where getting a foothold had been "a work of toil and patience."[225] But there was still reason for satisfaction that any progress at all had been made by Universalists. By 1864 there were no Unitarian societies known to exist in the entire state, so the whole burden of keeping liberal Christianity alive had fallen on the Universalists. It was the very liberalizing of other denominations in which Connecticut Universalists played a part, that helped explain the declining strength of the denomination in the state by 1870.

Rhode Island

The seeds of Universalism in Rhode Island were planted in 1772 when John Murray visited Newport. While there he was invited to Providence, where he preached in the Beneficent Congregational Church.[226] The first Universalists identified in Providence on the eve of the Revolution were three men and one woman who were expelled from the First Baptist Church for professing belief in universal salvation.[227] When called upon to speak before the congregation and defend themselves, it was the woman, Mrs. Amey Brown, widow of Captain William Brown, who was selected by prearrangement to speak for the group because of her eloquence and knowledge of the Scriptures. Murray made a second visit to Rhode Island in 1773, when he was invited to settle in Newport. It was during this trip that he made the acquaintance of General Nathaniel Greene of Revolutionary War fame. While there, Murray again preached and made several appearances in 1775, in which year he was made a chaplain of the Rhode Island Brigade stationed near Boston.

Universalists were to be found scattered throughout the Rhode Island Colony (which was admitted to the Union in 1790) soon after the Revolution. They were invited to send representatives to the meeting in Oxford, Massachusetts, in 1785, and in 1793 when the New England Convention was organized. Elhanan Winchester had spent some time in Providence.[228] However, no societies were organized for almost half a century after Murray's appearance. Richard Carrique, operating out of Attleboro, Massachusetts, preached occasionally in Providence in 1820-21, followed by Fayette Mace.[229] The first real impulse to organize Rhode Island Universalists came in the 1820s. The First Universalist Society of Providence, which was by far the largest in the state throughout the nineteenth century, was organized by twenty-five men in the spring of 1821, at a meeting in the court house. The society was incorporated with forty members. A stone meeting house costing $19,000 was built and dedicated in 1822. Pews sold at auction brought

$15,000.[230] The building burned in 1825 and was immediately rebuilt at approximately the same cost as the original, and was still in use in 1870. After Mace served as the first pastor for less than a year he was replaced by David Pickering, who was one of the leaders in the Restorationist controversy. Between 1835 and 1868, the society was served by four other pastors: William S. Balch, Henry Bacon, Edwin A. Eaton, and Cyrus H. Fay. The society had become so prosperous by the late 1830s that it outgrew its quarters and a second society was organized in 1840. It met in the Town House, with John N. Parker of Yarmouth Port, Massachusetts, as its first pastor.[231]

A society was organized in Pawtucket, then known as North Providence, in 1827. Two years later one appeared in Woonsocket Falls, on the Massachusetts border. Another was organized near Woonsocket in 1838, at Cumberland Hill. By 1839 there were only four societies in the state, considered "nothing worth boasting about."[232] Only the one first organized in Providence had created a church by that date. Except for Providence, the Rhode Island societies averaged fifty members each in the 1830s and had part-time preaching. The number of societies reached a maximum of twelve in 1860, but with only five preachers available.[233] By 1865 there were only five societies in existence.

Whatever may have been lacking in either numbers or societies, Universalists took an exceptionally active part in tract publication and distribution. A Tract Society met in conjunction with the state convention in the 1850s. This activity was supplemented by a state missionary society which was in operation by 1857 and employed a missionary on a half-time basis. The society was merged with the state convention in 1861. *A Christian Catechism for Instruction in Doctrine and Duty* was published under the auspices of the convention in 1865.[234]

All but the two societies (parishes) in Providence and the one in Pawtucket had disappeared or were inactive by 1870.[235] It was almost entirely the rural societies that had failed to survive. One urban society had existed for a short time in the 1860s with part-time preaching in East Providence, but had closed by 1866. It might be added that the identical phenomenon occurred in neighboring Connecticut, where by 1940 seven of the eight active churches remaining were located in urban centers. Strafford was the single exception.[236] The three clergymen in Rhode Island in 1870 (Massena Goodrich, E.H. Capen, and H.W. Rugg) all held positions of leadership in the denomination.

The predecessor of the Rhode Island Convention of Universalists, organized in 1838, had been the Providence Association. This organization had originated in 1827 at a meeting of a quarterly conference of ministers in Central Falls, when a decision was made to invite the societies in Rhode Island, southern Massachusetts, and eastern Connecticut to form a regional body.[237] The association, under the leadership of David Pickering, declared its independence of the New England Convention in 1829, and the majority of clergy seceded and formed the Massachusetts Association of Universal Restorationists. The remnants of the Providence Association continued to meet until 1836.[238]

The state convention was organized following a meeting in Providence under the leadership of William S. Balch. Among those who attended the first meeting after organization were Hosea Ballou, John G. Adams, and T.B. Thayer.[239] The convention claimed to "possess no right to control, or interfere with the management of Societies in any case whatsoever," and was described in 1845 as "of a merely associational character." The convention was reorganized and incorporated in 1861, using the Massachusetts convention constitution as a model. Decentralization and local autonomy may have been particularly appropriate for a small state of less than 1,300 square miles and only five counties, but it accurately reflected the general philosophy of the denomination.

New York

The history of Universalism in New York State falls into two well-defined geographical segments: The metropolitan area centered in New York City; and the vast interior west of the Hudson River, stretching to Lake Erie, Lake Ontario, and north to the St. Lawrence River and the Canadian border. Universalism in New York City can, in turn be divided into several fairly well defined periods. The first (1770-1796) included the visits of John Murray, the publication of several works that were universalist in spirit if not in name, and the organization of the Society of United Christian Friends in 1796. The second (1796-1829) extended for the life of this society, and was marked by disorganization and near-failure. A third, beginning in 1829 and lasting until T.J. Sawyer's departure from the Orchard Street church in 1845, was the period of solid establishment and expansion.[240]

It was Murray, so far as the sketchy records indicate, who introduced Universalism into the city, which at the time of his first trip there late in 1770, comprised less than 20,000 inhabitants. He was urged to stay during the course of his numerous journeyings thereafter between New England and Philadelphia, but preferred to remain in the Boston area.[241] His first preaching took place in a Baptist meeting house, and on at least two occasions offers were made to construct a house of worship for his use. The extent of his influence in New York is impossible to determine, but in the 1780s and 1790s there were books and pamphlets published in New York propounding the idea of general salvation, written by William Pitt Smith and Joseph Young, both of

Symbol of the General Convention of Universalists adopted in 1870 and used for many years

whom had been physicians during the American Revolution.[242] It was here also that was published Abel Sargent's *Free Universal Magazine* in 1793, the first Universalist periodical published in America.

A group of Methodists who believed in the doctrine of universal salvation, among whom was Edward Mitchell, separated from the main body and organized the United Christian Friends, known as the Duane Street Society, in 1796, with fourteen original members. The society was incorporated in 1800 and in 1803 Mitchell was ordained as their minister.[243] He never formally joined the Universalists after they became a denomination, and remained a trinitarian long after unitarian belief had become prevalent among Universalists. Universalism was also represented by a weekly periodical, the *Gospel Herald* (1820-27), published by Henry Fitz.

A second society of United Christian Friends was incorporated in 1828, known as the Prince Street Society, and constructed a meeting house. Nehemiah Dodge, a convert from the Baptists, was the first pastor and was replaced by the controversial Abner Kneeland. Ill feeling existed between the two societies from the start, the new society being much resented by Mitchell. Bad matters were made worse by Kneeland's infatuation with the ideas of the British social reformer Robert Owen. The Prince Street church was rent asunder by this and other disagreements, and disappeared as soon as its church building was sold after three tumultuous years (1827-29). Mitchell's society disintegrated shortly after his death in 1834. An attempt was made to keep the organization alive when David Pickering became the pastor in 1835. Disaster could have been predicted, for he was a Restorationist of unitarian belief who had broken with the main body of Universalists in

1829. Preaching to trinitarian Universalists was not likely to produce harmony, let alone success.[244]

An effort was made by a few Universalists to rebuild their ruined cause, and in 1829 they organized the First Universalist Society (Grand Street society) and obtained a small building on leased land. After losing the services of Abel C. Thomas, who stayed only a few months, the society was rescued from oblivion by T.J. Sawyer, then a young and inexperienced preacher from New England. He started his ministry in New York in 1830 at an annual salary of $500 and a pitifully small congregation. Only six or eight individuals could be depended on to defray expenses. In 1831 a young journeyman printer named Horace Greeley joined the group and remained until Sawyer left the city in 1845. Not as well known outside of the Universalist bailiwick as Greeley was Philo Price, who threw in his lot with Sawyer in 1831 and began publication of the *Christian Messenger,* with 300 original subscribers.[245] The two served as co-editors. The *Messenger* and its successor, the *Universalist Union,* served as the principal voices of New York Universalism for many years. But even with that assistance, Universalism did not flourish at first. Sawyer estimated that at least one-half of the Universalists in the city were attending "limitarian" churches and a large number of others were associated with one of the two Unitarian churches available in the early 1830s. But he undertook as much missionary activity as he could, and assisted in organizing a society in Brooklyn in 1832.

Sawyer's society leased what became known as the Orchard Street church in 1832, a building constructed about 1828 for the Reformed Dutch Church which had been unable to pay for it. They organized as the "Second Universalist Society in the City of New York" shortly after the move. A Sunday school was opened in 1835 through Sawyer's efforts. On the initiative of two members of the congregation, the Third Universalist Society (Bleecker Street society) was organized. One of the two was Cornelius Harsen, whose son in 1844 created the first fund for the families of deceased or incapacitated clergymen in New York State. The Orchard Street church grew and began to prosper through Sawyer's efforts, and in 1834 it was able to purchase the building it occupied.

The Fourth Universalist Society was organized in 1838, with William Whittaker as pastor. Sawyer was not convinced that it was needed but reluctantly agreed to its establishment. But after taking over the building of the old Mitchell society, by then defunct, Whittaker suddenly renounced his Universalism and was succeeded by Isaac D. Williamson, to be followed by Edwin H. Chapin and Charles H. Eaton. The New York Universalist Missionary Society, organized in 1839, established a preaching station in Manhattan Hall, out of which evolved the Fifth Universalist Society in 1841.[246]

Of the five societies organized between 1796 and 1841, not a one had a continuous pastorate for any length of time. Abel C. Thomas, looking back on those early years in which he himself had been a participant, wondered what would have happened if the Universalists had concentrated in one society and not fragmented their efforts and engaged in internal squabbling.[247] Universalism in New York City, although reasonably well established by the mid-nineteenth century, was also weakened by the refusal of some of the preachers to file a required statement with the New York Association that they accepted the Bible as special revelation.[248] The influence of Abner Kneeland may have been at work here.

One explanation for the period of expansion which did take place after 1830 was the attention called to Universalism by a series of public debates in which Sawyer participated. One was a prolonged written controversy with Edwin F. Hatfield, a Presbyterian clergyman who had been one of Sawyer's classmates at Middlebury College. As soon as the Orchard Street church was filled, as it was by 1842, it was Sawyer's policy to urge families to leave his congregation and to assist other societies not as well populated. Even then, his own society continued to prosper, with 800 members in 1843. It was through his efforts that the entire indebtedness of the church (about $5,000) was paid off.[249] Sawyer resigned from the Orchard Street church in 1845 to take over the presidency of Clinton Liberal Institute. His successor was Otis A. Skinner, who resigned in 1849 to become financial agent for a denominational institution of higher learning which had been proposed in 1849 and which came into existence as Tufts College in 1852.

The Orchard Street church immediately sought the services of Sawyer, their former pastor, but he elected to remain at Clinton. After various attempts to raise sufficient funds either to turn the Institute at Clinton into a college or to establish a theological school on a permanent foundation had failed, Sawyer returned to New York in 1852. He accepted the pastorate of the Fifth Universalist Society which had been established as part of the missionary efforts he had urged on his parishioners during his first residence in New York. But the society disbanded after unsuccessful efforts to buy or build a church uptown, and Sawyer returned to his former parishioners in the Orchard Street church in December 1853. After he threatened to leave unless a new location were found, the society sold its church in 1859 and moved into temporary quarters. But he remained less than two more years, and in 1861 retired to his farm in Clinton.

Universalism in New York City was already being weakened by the 1850s with failure to keep pace with the south-to-north movement of the Manhattan population. Universalists soon found themselves stranded in deteriorating residential neighborhoods or surrounded by industries and business establishments. Typical were the Orchard Street church and the Sixth Universalist Society, organized in 1851.[250] T.B. Thayer also found continued prejudice against Universalists to be an obstacle, and referred to "the pharisees of Brooklyn," where he was serving as pastor in 1846.[251]

Universalism in southern New York State was not confined to the city. Societies had appeared on Long Island by the 1830s. The first meeting house there was constructed at Southold about 1836, and the society was active in 1838 under William Fishbough.[252] A meeting house was erected in Huntington the same year, and one was planned for Babylon. Thomas Miller served the societies in each of these communities.

Universalism was introduced into upstate New York in 1802 by Edwin Ferriss, a preacher in fellowship with the New England Convention when he visited Otsego County. In 1803 he settled with his family in the village of Butternuts, where a society was formed, consisting of twenty-five male members. A church of eight members was organized in 1804 and had a maximum membership of about forty.[253] After Ferriss' departure in 1810 he was succeeded by C. Winslow, who was dismissed after a year as "unsatisfactory." The society disappeared a few years later, although an attempt was made in 1829 to revive it. In 1804 Miles T. Wooley, also in fellowship with the New England Convention, was appointed to assist New York Universalists to organize societies, and likewise established himself in Otsego County (at Hartwick), where a society was formed early in 1805. The individual best known among the pioneer preachers in that area was Nathaniel Stacy (1779-1868) of Massachusetts, who arrived in 1805 and made Brookfield (Otsego County) his headquarters the following year. He was responsible for organizing numerous rural societies, and spent much of his long life as an itinerant, travelling by day and preaching at night.[254]

A fourth pioneer, who left a record of his reminiscences particularly during the 1820s, was Stephen R. Smith (1789-1850), who preached all over upstate New York.[255] He had first heard Universalism preached by Hosea Ballou at Utica in 1808, and in 1811 had decided to become a preacher.[256] Between 1811 and 1817 he travelled through three counties on a circuit of almost 400 miles which took two months to complete. He was also the leading fund-raiser for Clinton Liberal Institute between 1827 and its establishment in 1831.

It was men such as those mentioned who sought to furnish religious services to the hundreds of New Englanders who swept into and across New York State during the great westward migrations of the early nineteenth century. Universalist families were identified in upstate counties as early as 1802; they had migrated from Rhode Island, Connecticut, and New Jersey.[257] Although Universalism had been preached for a decade, it was not until 1815 that the first meeting house was owned and used exclusively by Universalists. It was located near Whitestown (New Hartford, Oneida County), where a society had been organized in 1805 and a church in 1806.[258]

Societies by 1830 outnumbered preachers by four to one.[259] Yet Universalists became an integral part of the exciting religious movements of the 1820s and 1830s in the upstate counties. The mixed religious complexion of Westfield reported by a resident in 1834 was probably not unusual for the time. In a community of 3,000 there were societies of Presbyterians, Episcopalians, Methodists, Baptists, Universalists, Mormons, "besides some Deists and Nothingarians."[260] By 1845 Universalists in New York State had almost as many congregations as the Episcopalians, and twice as many as the Roman Catholics.[261] Universalist preachers were chronically in short supply, the population largely rural, scattered, and constantly on the move; and follow-up visits were frequently impossible. Preachers tried their best to counteract the frenetic religious revivalism that periodically swept the area, and sought to maintain and spread the religious liberalism for which they stood. When George Rogers of Cincinnati visited the state in 1834 he noted "a complete chain of preaching posts" extending from New York City to Utica, which was the axis for Universalism in the northern and western part of the state.[262]

The first formal meeting of Universalist preachers in the state was a rather modest affair by later standards. In 1805 a "general conference" convened in Burlington (Otsego County), with the three preachers then in the state in attendance. This contrasted rather dramatically with the 50 in 1830 and over 110 only nine years later. The increase in the number of societies was equally impressive—from three in 1805 to 150 in 1830 and over 200 in 1839. Most of the early societies were fortunate, however, to hear a preacher as often as once a month, and often consisted of less than ten members.[263] During the same period the number of associations had climbed from one in 1806 to nine in 1830 and fifteen by the end of the decade, and a state convention had been organized. The number of church buildings increased correspondingly, with 110 by 1840.

The number of societies had mushroomed by 1845 to about 250, and meeting houses to 150, almost all of them west of the Hudson River and in the northern part of the state. A.B. Grosh, editor of the *Universalist Register* during the 1840s, reported in exasperation in the 1846 issue that accurate statistics were completely lacking and were "simply guesses at the truth . . . . How many of the societies have died, or meeting houses been blown down or sold, we never learn *fully*."

By the mid-1840s there had also been organized a state Sunday School Association (1842) and an auxiliary body for western New York, created in 1845.[264] A Sunday School Convention for the central part of the state was organized in 1865.[265] The number of denominational periodicals in the state had likewise multiplied with great rapidity by the mid-1840s, and were destined to follow the typical pattern of proliferation followed by consolidation. In 1845 Universalists had a choice of the following weeklies: The *Christian Messenger* (New York City); the *Universalist Union* (the *Messenger* without secular news, and with a smaller format); the *Evangelical Magazine and Gospel Advocate* (Utica); and the *Western Luminary* (Rochester). By 1845 at least five others had come and gone.

The growth above the society level was by no means either steady or harmonious. It testified not only to the pragmatic and rather haphazard character of organizational evolution but also to the jealously-guarded autonomy which frequently dampened the spirit of cooperation that would have fostered an even greater Universalist strength and solidarity that might have developed within the state. As the nineteenth century opened, there existed only one regional body that even nominally embraced New York State; namely the "General Convention of the New England States and others" (the New England Convention) which had no defined limits. By 1813 there were ten preachers in upstate New York fellowshipped by the convention.[266] Sufficient Universalists had settled in the rural portions of the state by 1806 to justify the creation of the Western Association, with a vague jurisdiction extending over all territory west of the Hudson River. This organization, which emerged out of the meeting of the three preachers in Burlington in 1805, was considered at first as a branch "in connexion with" the New England Convention.[267] It was authorized by the New England Convention in 1805 for the purpose of accommodating the ministers and societies that found it impractical or impossible to attend sessions usually held in Massachusetts, New Hampshire, or Vermont. An informal convention was held in Columbus (Chenango County) in the summer of 1807, organized by Nathaniel Stacy.[268] After adjourning from a private home, a small assemblage listened to Hosea Ballou on an open hillside.

This state of affairs continued until 1814, when the Western Association itself began to be divided into a series of associations which could more effectively serve the needs of local constituents. The "Genesee Branch" was formed in 1814 in the western part of the state, and included the entire area lying west of Lake Cayuga. The Black River, Cayuga, and Chenango Associations were organized in 1823, originally designated as branches of the Western Association. The parent association in the 1820s claimed the right to disavow any act of its branches, but had no power to compel acceptance of its own.[269] The maximum discipline that could be imposed was withdrawal of fellowship.

The year 1825 was an eventful one in New York Universalist history. Two more associations (Chautauqua and Hudson River) came into being. And in the same year the Western Association adopted a new constitution and declared itself "The Universalist Convention of the State of New York." This transformation of the original Western Association, which met with much opposition, replaced delegates from societies with exclusively clerical representation from associations. After the formation of the new convention, the territory of the original association became the Central Association and joined the new convention in 1828, after the constitution of the new body was amended to include lay delegates. A "Conventional Association," organized in 1826 to support the new state organization, became the Mohawk Association.

The Genesee and Cayuga Associations categorically refused to join the new convention when it was organized, and passed strong resolutions against it. The Genesee organization in 1826 resolved to remain thereafter "an independent body so far as is necessary to transact its own local concerns, maintaining fellowship with all others." The defiant association expressed its feelings even more decisively the next year by voting unanimously to "disapprove of the New York Convention of Universalists" by going on record that it did "not wish to have a Convention of any kind at present." The recalcitrant Genesee group then proceeded in 1831 to divide itself by setting off its northwestern portion as the Niagara Association. This new entity retained its independence for four years, not becoming a member of the state convention until 1835. The original Genesee body remained its own master for another ten years. When it finally acknowledged in 1845 that state conventions could serve as courts of appeal from associations, it pointedly referred to the fact that such conventions otherwise constituted only "advisory councils."[270] As a parting shot, the Genesee Association resolved "that in our opinion, the respective societies have ability to govern themselves—that associations have the exclusive right of granting letters of fellowship and conferring ordination."

One of the many complications which arose from this refusal to accept any plan that smacked of centralization had to do with the request in 1845 of two widows of Universalist ministers for financial assistance from the trustees of the New York Universalist Relief Fund which had been provided by Cornelius Harsen of New York City and which became available that year. The donor had specified that only those clergymen (or their families, if the clergymen were deceased) would be eligible if they had been in fellowship with the state convention at the time of their death. Not only was it alleged that the two individuals had not been fellowshipped by that body, but one had been so strongly opposed to its creation that he had withdrawn from the old Western Association and had joined the uncooperative Genesee Association to express his disapproval.[271] T.J. Sawyer, one of the trustees of the relief fund who refused to vote in favor of granting the request for aid, prepared a report justifying his stand on the grounds that the family of neither clergyman was eligible to receive benefits from the fund. His report was adopted by the trustees, who unanimously reversed their former decision and rejected the applications in question. A fellow New Yorker, Stephen R. Smith, disagreed completely with the findings in one of the cases, but he was outvoted.[272]

In the meantime other associations had been formed with great rapidity. The St. Lawrence Association had been organized in 1828, followed by the Erie Association in 1833 (reorganized in 1845). Out of the original Genesee Association came the Ontario and Steuben Associations in 1834. The Otsego Association was organized in 1833; the Alleghany and New York Associations were created in 1835. Record keeping was apparently not a major concern in many associations; it seems the Alleghany Association was one of the worst offenders. In 1839 a fruitless effort was made to gather statistics of societies within its jurisdiction, but there was no response. There was not even a record of who had organized it in the first place.[273] Southern New York State had originally been part of the New York and Philadelphia Association, organized in 1829 (at a meeting in New Jersey).[274] The New York Association was carved out of the southern half of the Hudson River Association and included Newark, New Jersey as well as Long Island.[275] In a final burst of activity the Buffalo Association appeared in 1845. In the same year the troublesome Genesee Association was finally fellowshipped by the state convention and the organization of associations was rounded out.

One of the distinguishing characteristics of the New York associations was their exaggerated attitude of independence and their reluctance to relinquish their prerogatives to a state convention. Hence the organization created in 1825 was challenged from the very beginning and almost failed to come into existence at all. When the Western Association announced that it was henceforth to be considered the state convention, other associations at first refused to accept the idea.[276] A meeting of the delegates from other associations completely disregarded the action taken by the Western Association and met in Auburn in 1827 and voted not to establish a convention.[277] It was only after the state convention had met twice and had agreed to admit lay as well as clerical delegates that the convention really began to function. Even then, some of the associations, notably the Genesee, refused to recognize the jurisdiction of the convention. It was not until 1836 that the convention affirmed its right to grant letters of fellowship and to confer ordination. But in the face of determined opposition by the associations, it relinquished to them the right of fellowshipping "as a matter of expediency."[278] As to ordination, it retained the right, but subject to whatever rules had been established by the association in which the candidate resided.

There was also great discussion over whether the meetings of the convention should be rotated around the state or should be held in one centrally located place. Every community vied for an opportunity to have the convention meet on their home ground. Philo Price objected to the practice of "putting the Convention on wheels . . . and trundling it from one extremity of the state to the other, and to all points of the compass."[279] But sectionalism prevailed, and the meetings were rotated. Attendance was often poor, particularly by lay delegates, who were sometimes outnumbered by more than two to one even though they were entitled to equal representation. With a certain lack of logic the laymen then accused the convention of "clerical usurpation."[280] In 1842 the still-uncooperative Genesee Association called for a "jubilee session" of all associations "to consult together on the interests of our common cause."[281] At least one clergyman present interpreted this as an effort "ultimately to do away with the New York State Convention." This obviously did not happen, but it illustrated the particularism which weakened the convention in its early history.

The state of New York by 1870 could claim the largest number of Universalists of any, having exceeded Massachusetts after the Civil War. The number of societies (parishes) had stabilized at about 135, with approximately 90 preachers. The greatest overall strength was to be found in the semi-rural and urban areas of the north and west. The number of active parishes in New York City had settled at four, with all the pastorates filled by men well known throughout the denomination.[282] Of the four, Chapin, pastor of the Fourth Universalist Society and of the Church of the Divine Paternity, dedicated in 1866, was probably the best known both inside and outside the denomination as a writer, orator, and advocate of social reform. Universalists also operated a mission in Harlem, organized in 1869. A Young Men's Universalist Association was organized in 1870 in New York City to assist those moving to the metropolis. New York Universalists had the greatest resources of any state for relief and assistance to disabled or aged clergymen and their families. The principal of the Harsen Fund had grown to $32,000 by 1872.[283]

One of the major papers in the denomination, the *Christian Ambassador,* was published by the state convention.[284] In 1870 Clinton Liberal Institute, the oldest school established by Universalists with a continuous history, was still in operation in what had been the heart of pioneer denominational territory upstate forty years before. St. Lawrence University, its location reflecting, like Clinton's, the strength of Universalism in the northern and western parts of the state, offered both liberal arts and professional education. The sixteen associations which had completed their organization in 1845 still existed in 1870 to serve a state of great size and diverse needs and interests. New York State was without question the "Empire State" of pre-Civil War Universalism, and was to hold that position into the twentieth century.

Chapter 24

MOVING WITH THE FRONTIER: THE MIDWEST

Scarcely had the American Revolution been fought when New Englanders began to pour into the trans-Appalachian area, the region of the Great Lakes, and across to the Mississippi River. They were joined by Americans from the Middle Atlantic and southern states, and by 1800 the converging streams of population had established settlements along the Ohio River, the first in Marietta in 1786, and then in the northeastern corner of the Ohio Territory known as the Western Reserve. Within forty years after Ohio had been admitted to the Union in 1803, the population had moved to areas farther west and had thrust into Indiana, Illinois, Wisconsin, Michigan, Minnesota, and Iowa.

A tumultuous society developed in the Midwest during the first half of the nineteenth century, with a great diversity of peoples from all kinds of backgrounds. Almost every color and shade of the religious spectrum was represented, and fierce sectarianism was the order of the day. Universalism was very much a part of this rapidly moving and constantly changing frontier.

Ohio

The seeds of Universalism in Ohio were planted first in the southeast, in and around Marietta, and in the northeast as migrants crossed upstate New York and Pennsylvania and clustered along the shore of Lake Erie.[1] The first Universalists appeared about 1789 in the oldest settled area of what became Washington, Morgan, Meigs, and Athens Counties, along the Ohio River in Marietta and Belpre. Among them were Major A. Waldo Putnam and his son William Pitt Putnam, lineal descendants of Israel Putnam of Connecticut.[2] Others were Daniel Loring; Colonel N. Cushing, who had defended John Murray when he was attacked in Boston; General James M. Varnum, also a friend of Murray, who became a judge in the Ohio Territory; and Captain Winthrop Sargent, secretary of the Ohio Company, a speculative land venture; he was a member of the family which helped to establish Universalism in Gloucester, Massachusetts.

The first individual known to have appeared in Ohio to preach Universalism was Abel Morgan Sargent (Sarjent). His birthplace is unknown, but he lived in Morgantown, (West) Virginia, and was originally a Freewill Baptist preacher who declared his Universalism about 1790, attended the Philadelphia Convention at several of its meetings, and preached in New Jersey.[3] He was also the publisher of the *Free Universal Magazine.* He first preached in Ohio Territory about 1800 and organized a number of so-called "halcyon" or "Free" churches, some of which became Universalist. The sect seemed to have disappeared after 1807, but churches were organized in western Virginia, Pennsylvania, and Ohio. It produced several early Universalist preachers, among them M. Croy and Aylett Raines; the latter was ordained as a Universalist in 1829.[4]

Sargent was apparently a mystic who claimed to have periodic revelations. He preached a unitarian theology and denied the existence of a physical hell. His ideas were considered sufficiently "peculiar" by other denominations to attract the attention of Methodists and Congregationalists. Sargent began publishing in Cincinnati the *Rational Bible Reformer* in 1825, renamed the *Lamp of Liberty,* of which ten issues had appeared by the close of 1827. After preaching in southeastern Ohio for several years, Sargent retired to Indiana, where he died in 1839.

The first Universalist society in Ohio was organized in Marietta (Washington County) in 1816. It bore the name "First Universalian Religious Society of Marietta" and grew out of a decision to establish a library.[5] It was incorporated in 1822 and two years later voted to support preaching one-fourth of the time. Beginning in 1828 the services of Alpheus Swett were secured on a half-time basis, and by 1843 a meeting house had been erected and a pastor obtained for three-fourths of the time. A church was organized the following year, and a Sunday school was established. Under the provisions of the land granted by the Ohio Company, the rent from certain acreages was to be devoted to the support of religion. The revenue received by each denomination was in proportion to the number of inhabitants of that faith in each district. By 1826 the Universalist subscribers in Marietta received the largest share.[6]

Plans for organizing a society in Belpre, a few miles south of Marietta and across the Ohio River from Parkersburg, (West) Virginia, were made in 1823 but had to be delayed a year because of the death of Daniel Loring, chairman of the planning committee. The society, consisting originally of nineteen males, had no preacher at first, but a church was organized in 1827 under the guidance of Eliphalet Case from New Hampshire. After his departure later the same year, the societies in Marietta and Belpre requested a preacher who would be willing to serve both at a stipend of $600.[7] A meeting house was built in Belpre in 1835 and membership had grown from twenty to sixty-one by 1843.

Universalism spread rapidly in southeastern Ohio in the 1820s and 1830s and there were sufficient churches to result in the creation of the Washington Association in 1833. It was organized in an old mill belonging to William P. Putnam near Belpre and its jurisdiction extended to the southernmost tip of the state, where the Gallia (County) Association was set off in 1845. There were fifteen societies and six churches in the original jurisdiction of the Washington Association, with a total of about 600 members; seven of the societies possessed meeting houses in 1833.

The Western Reserve in northeastern Ohio was also an area of much Universalist settlement in the early nineteenth century. When Connecticut had ceded to the government under the Articles of Confederation in 1780 the western lands claimed under its charter, it reserved a three-million-acre section. The Western Reserve had then been purchased by the Connecticut Land Company in 1795 and its general agent, Moses Cleaveland, laid out and named the city of Cleveland the next year. Universalists from New England moved into the territory as early as 1805, and in 1814 the first preacher settled there. Timothy Bigelow from Winchester, New Hampshire, who had been ordained by the New England Convention, established himself near Ravenna (Portage County). Between the time of his arrival and his death in 1823, the number of Universalists in the area increased from twenty to over 1,500, sufficient to justify the creation of the Northern Ohio Association in 1821. Representatives from eleven churches, sixteen societies, and twenty-two locations without societies attended the organization meeting.[8] Bigelow was responsible for its establishment. A Central Association was created in 1824, and by 1860 a total of seventeen had been established.[9]

In southwestern Ohio Universalism was spread in the 1820s by itinerants like Jonathan Kidwell, one of the more colorful frontier preachers, who travelled all over the rural western counties of the state and into Indiana. Cincinnati became the headquarters of the denomination in the Midwest. It was to that urban center that Universalists looked for leadership and strength, rather than to the rural communities.[10] It was to Cincinnati that preachers came to serve apprenticeships, publish denominational literature, and it was that city which served as a central point from which missionary activity fanned out into the countryside. Early Universalism was, in short, in no sense an exclusively rural and small-town phenomenon.

Plans for the formation of a society in Cincinnati were laid in 1822.[11] There was occasional preaching until J.C. Waldo arrived in 1828. Eliphalet Case had spent a month in the city in 1827, by which time a society had been incorporated and property for a meeting house had been acquired.[12] Thomas Whittemore paid a visit to Cincinnati in 1827 and received an invitation to become the pastor but declined after considering the offer for some time, and returned to Boston.[13] Waldo departed in 1832, and for several years meetings continued but were conducted by laymen. Several clergy, including Linus S. Everett (New York) and Calvin Gardner (Maine) were offered the pastorship but declined.[14] One impatient Universalist in 1834 reported that people were "becoming sick of having damnation always poured down upon them" and begged for a regular preacher.[15] He estimated that five or six societies could easily be formed within a thirty-mile radius of Cincinnati if clergy were available.

In 1835 George Rogers returned to Cincinnati after one of his many tours and revived the society, and a new meeting house was obtained costing over $6,500. But Rogers was on the road more often than in the city, and served less than two years. The society was also weakened in the 1830s and 1840s by the establishment of a Restorationist society under the leadership of Daniel Parker, and of a German Christian Church in 1838. Neither was in fellowship with the Miami Association, which had jurisdiction.[16] In 1842 the Second Universalist Society of Cincinnati was formed, with Enoch M. Pingree as its pastor, and a church was organized in 1848. Multiplicity rather than unity prevailed in Cincinnati and did little to strengthen Universalism there. When the "hard times" associated with the panic and depression of 1857 hit Cincinnati, both the original and second societies were at a low ebb.[17] John A Gurley, who had taken over the pastorate of the First Society on a part-time basis in 1857, offered $1,000 to each society on a matching basis to pay off the considerable indebtedness with which each was encumbered.[18] But only the First Society survived, and the property of the Second Society was sold to the Unitarians.

If societies in Cincinnati had difficulties in organizing and co-operating, part of the deficiency was made up by the multitude of denominational publications which originated in the city and spread Universalism all over the Midwest. Besides a large number of books and tracts, such as George Rogers' autobiography and Pingree's public debates, there was a major newspaper. The *Star in the West* had been started as a monthly in Eaton in 1827 by Jonathan Kidwell and continued as a weekly under the name *Sentinel and Star in the West* in Cincinnati. After a brief sojourn in Philomath, Indiana, it returned to Cincinnati in 1837, where it remained under its original name and a succession of editors until 1880. In that year it became part of the *Star and Covenant.* It was under the editorship of John A. Gurley from 1838 to 1854, and was the leading paper in the area. Its nearest competitor was the *Glad Tidings and Ohio Universalist* (1836-40), published in Columbus; Pittsburgh, Pennsylvania; and later in Akron. It was absorbed by the *Star in the West* in 1841, as was the *Universalist Preacher and Evangelical Repository* (Dayton) at the same time.

A state convention finally emerged in Ohio in 1837 out of a rather haphazard series of *ad hoc* meetings held in various parts of the state extending over a decade. A meeting had taken place in Jacksonburg (Butler County) in the western part of the state in 1826, attended by three clergy and several laymen.[19] A second was held near Franklin (Warren County) in 1827.[20] Still another convened at Mt. Pleasant, near Cincinnati in 1828, and appointed "committees of correspondence" to make contact with other Universalists. The meeting in 1827 was somewhat grandly called the "Convention of Universalists of the Western States," redesignated as the "Western Convention of Universalists" in 1830 and "General Convention of Universalists of the Western States" in 1833. This meant, rather imprecisely, "Indiana, Ohio, and others."[21] But in spite of all the impressive names there was still no state convention. At the meeting in which the Washington Association was organized in 1833, delegates from the other associations called for the establishment of a convention limited to Ohio.[22]

The individual who took the initiative was George Rogers. In 1836 he put his finger on the basic weakness of the denomination in Ohio and in fact in the entire Midwest. It was lack of concerted action.[23] By the 1830s Universalism had, in his view, made no real impact despite the devotion of half a dozen individuals. Why not? It was "an almost total absence of organization in the West, and a prevalent reluctance, on the part of persons professing our faith, to come into any kind of ecclesiastical order. The consequence was, that our people were scattered like sheep without folds or shepherds."[24] Meeting houses were almost non-existent, most preachers in one part of the state had not the least idea of who else might be preaching Universalism elsewhere, too many preachers considered their clerical activities as mere avocations. The time for "unity of action" was at hand, based on better acquaintance with "each other's views, condition, and prospects."[25]

The meeting at which the state convention was organized in 1837 took place in Columbus (Franklin County), in the very center of the state. By the best estimate, there were at the time thirty preachers and almost fifty societies, but no one knew for sure; a goodly number of the clergy were preaching only part-time.[26] As Elmo A. Robinson assessed the situation almost a century later, "early Universalism in Ohio was a propaganda rather than an organization."[27] Judging from the statistics available, measured by the number of preachers, societies, and meeting houses, the greatest expansion took place in the 1840s. Seven associations were organized between 1840 and 1846. A "great excitement" in religion swept through the state in 1842 and Universalist growth was especially noticeable in the southern part of the state.[28] The number of societies, many with churches connected with them, exceeded 100 by 1844.[29]

George H. Emerson from Massachusetts spent eight months in Ohio and Kentucky in 1849. What impressed him most was the constantly fluctuating population, which seemed to be afflicted with a chronic restlessness.[30] This was mirrored in the perpetual coming and going of Universalist preachers throughout the state. Many of the early clergy were recruited from other denominations and their flirtation with Universalism was often brief. When the Northern Ohio Association was organized in 1821, there were ten preachers in the Portage County area alone; of these, three were ex-Baptists, two were from the Methodists, and two had belonged to the Christian denomination.[31] By the time of Bigelow's death in 1823 all but one or two had disappeared. The preaching force was also reduced by retirement or the pressure of secular business. Many were lost to the "Reformers" (the Campbellites) or to the Disciples of Christ.[32]

One of the important stabilizing factors in Ohio Universalism was the creation of the "General Agency of Universalist Churches and Sunday Schools" by the state convention in 1867. The idea of having a general superintendent in each state to oversee and coordinate denominational affairs had been suggested by William H. Ryder at the General Convention which met in Galesburg, Illinois, in 1866.[33] S.P. Carleton served very successfully as the first general agent in Ohio, although one was not appointed on a continuous basis. In 1875 the state superintendent, as the office was then being designated, reported that the major difficulties in the placing of ministers in vacant pastorates were "an excess of the controversial spirit," rapid turnover of personnel, and the desire of churches to secure only "big name" preachers.[34] The office of superintendent went through several changes of title and responsibilities in succeeding decades.

Several specialized organizations subordinate to the state convention were organized in the 1860s. The first conference of ministers in the state was held in 1862, out of which evolved the Ohio Universalist Ministerial Association. A state Sunday School Convention was organized in 1866; nineteen of the twenty-four Sunday schools sent delegates to the organization meeting. The Women's Centenary Association organized in 1869 made canvassing for funds for what became Buchtel College a major part of its activity. After the centennial effort had been completed the Women's Universalist Missionary Association was organized in 1889 and much of the money raised was used to assist churches in both rural and urban communities.

Relations with the General Convention between 1837, when the state convention was organized, and 1870, were generally harmonious. In 1843 Universalists in Akron played host to the first meeting of the General Convention held west of the Alleghenies. Support not only of the General Convention but of the provision for a uniform system of church government was strongly advocated by Enoch M. Pingree, who was based in Louisville, Kentucky, but was active also in the Miami Association in southern Ohio.[35] The state convention heeded Pingree's call and that of the General Convention for tighter and more coherent organization and enforcement of clerical discipline. The associations relinquished their ordination and fellowship functions to the state convention in the 1860s, as did those in most other states at about the same time. There was some opposition in Ohio to the centralizing tendencies evident in the General Convention even before the Civil War and there was some talk of seceding from that body and forming a Western Convention. But the majority of Universalists insisted on cooperating with the General Convention and the closest that Ohio came to turning away from that body was to join the Northwestern Conference, organized in 1860. It included all seven midwestern states and had no ecclesiastical power. Much of its effort was devoted to raising funds for Lombard College in Illinois, and in general missionary activity.

Ohio Universalists set themselves an ambitious goal as their contribution to the centennial of the denomination in 1870. Besides pledging $10,000 for the Murray Fund authorized by the General Convention, Ohio Universalists elected to establish what was tentatively called the "Universalist Centenary School of Ohio." A few schools had been established under Universalist auspices or with their support prior to 1870. One was across the state border in Philomath, Indiana, known as Western Union Seminary (1833-46), of which Jonathan Kidwell was the moving spirit. Madison Liberal Institute (Hamilton County) was incorporated in 1836, as was Sharon Academy (Medina County). As was the case with the Universalist Institute of Ohio City near Cleveland, incorporated in 1839, all had short histories. The most successful of the academies was the Western Liberal Institute organized in Marietta in 1849.

The Universalist Collegiate Association of Ohio was organized in 1857 to establish a denominational college in the state, but the plan failed to produce one. Until after 1870 Ohio Universalists supported and patronized Lombard College. The proposed Centenary School was opened in 1872 as Buchtel College, named in honor of John R. Buchtel, its chief benefactor.

There were 115 Universalist churches in Ohio in 1870.[36] They were concentrated in the four corners of the state and coincided with the largest settlements of New Englanders in the early nineteenth century. The greatest decade of expansion had been the 1840s, when fifty new churches had been organized. This brought the total to 163, the maximum in the history of the denomination within the state. But many disappeared almost immediately and very few survived into the twentieth century. Those created after 1870 were relatively fewer in number but had more prospects of permanence as the population settled in and organizational techniques were refined. In terms of rural-urban distribution, there was a rough balance, although almost every urban church had an uneven and troubled history up to 1870, notably in Cincinnati, the historic center of Universalist activity in the first half of the nineteenth century. Some rural churches such as the one in Eldorado (Preble County), organized in 1849, were still active over a century later.

Indiana

Early Universalism in Indiana was closely associated with the development of the denomination in Ohio, and many of the same personalities were active in both states. Jonathan Kidwell (1799-1855), a native of Kentucky and a convert to Universalism about 1815 through his study of the Bible, was probably the first to preach the doctrine in Indiana.[37] He settled with his family at Sulphur Spring, near Abinton (Wayne County). He formed a preaching circuit in 1826 which covered southern Ohio, northern Kentucky, and much of Indiana. At the time, Kidwell estimated that there were fewer than 200 Universalists in southern Ohio and Indiana; the number had increased to more than 2,000 by 1829. It was Kidwell who first preached Universalism in Indianapolis, in 1829, and appointed agents for the *Star in the West* in a dozen communities in the state.

Aylett Rains, a pioneer itinerant in the Midwest, reported Universalists to be numerous in Indiana by 1827.[38] In 1830 a conference was called at Milton (Wayne County) "for the purpose of taking into consideration the propriety of our brethren organizing themselves into societies."[39] At least four had been organized by the end of the year, although their locations were not identified except for one at Leavenworth (Crawford County) on the Kentucky border. E.B. Mann, who travelled over much of southern and eastern Ohio in the early 1830s, lived in that community.[40] The others were probably at Vevay (Switzerland County) on the Ohio River; Madison (Jefferson County); and Liberty (Union County). All were in the southern and eastern part of the state and undoubtedly reflected the influence of itinerants operating out of Cincinnati.

Preachers were in such short supply that when the "First Association of Universalists in the State of Indiana" was organized at Leavenworth in 1831, only one preacher, E.B. Mann, was present, and he had apparently not been fellowshipped at the time.[41] Laymen from four counties attended, and requested guidance from eastern Universalists on how to proceed. By 1835 Mann had organized five societies, according to his own report, and had sold several hundred dollars worth of Universalist books.[42]

The Cambridge Association (Wayne County) had been organized on the Ohio border soon after 1831, and probably represented an extension of the Western Union Association in southwestern Ohio. There were eleven other associations organized by 1860, but many disappeared or were consolidated with others. The Rogers Association, organized in 1848 and named in honor of the well-known itinerant George Rogers, was the only one which had a continuous existence and for which the records were reasonably complete. It was still serving the southeastern corner of the state in the twentieth century.

The first state convention in Indiana was organized in 1837 in the rural community of Sheets' Mills (Jefferson County) with delegates from the two associations then in existence, and from a society established in Patriot (Switzerland County), and reflected the concentration of Universalists in southeastern Indiana.[43] At the time of its organization, Kidwell and Mann were the only clergymen in the state, and both served as convention officers for many years. The community of Patriot comprised only 400 inhabitants when the Universalists dedicated the only meeting house in 1839, a brick structure boasting not only a tower but a bell.[44]

Much of the time and energy of the Indiana Convention was taken up in the 1840s by a series of feuds between Kidwell, who was accused of holding heretical ideas and was violently opposed to subordination to the General Convention, and Erasmus Manford, George Rogers, Enoch M. Pingree, John A. Gurley, and other Universalists, who were rival newspapermen and supported the General Convention.[45] Kidwell managed to block for several years the fellowshipping of the Indiana Convention with the General Convention. He was expressing on the state level the fierce independence and individualism to be found among many Indiana Universalists.

When a society was organized at Jacks Creek (Green County) in 1842, various resolutions were adopted. The first two read as follows: "That we have certain inalienable rights as christians to exercise a self-government in all matters of faith and practice [and] we come out independently, acknowledge ourselves as Universalists, and exercise those rights we hold in common with other christians."[46] Their theological beliefs were listed at the very end, and consisted of a paraphrase of the Winchester Profession. The Miami Association (Ohio) solicited reactions from the Indiana Convention in 1841 regarding the propriety of petitioning the General Convention to establish some uniform system of government for the denomination. The reply was abrupt and to the point: "The Universalists of the state of Indiana are of age, and consider themselves capable of self-government, and therefore cannot submit to any dictation or control, either on the part of our brethren in the east, or elsewhere."[47]

A rival state convention opposing Kidwell was organized in 1848 and became the one recognized by the General Convention.[48] It was finally incorporated in 1883. The convention supporting Kidwell continued to meet in the southern part of the state until his death in 1855, when its members were invited to affiliate with the new convention.

Sectional consciousness was as evident in Indiana as in the other midwestern states, and a proposal to dissolve the General Convention and divide it into four independent jurisdictions was made by the state convention in 1857. It was reconsidered two years later and was withdrawn; instead of supporting a Western Convention of Universalists, Indiana became a participant in the Northwestern Conference when it was created as a non-legislative body in 1860. The convention's more localized problem was to overcome the chronic shortage of clergy. There were forty-six churches in the state in 1862, and eight associations, but only twenty ministers in fellowship.[49]

In the 1840s Universalist churches appeared in the western part of the state, with Terre Haute (Vigo County) as a sort of headquarters. A church was organized there in 1841, with twelve members, and occupied its first meeting house for twenty-five years.[50] When the second church building was constructed in 1869 at a cost of $10,000, the membership was over 100 and was considered "one of the flourishing religious organizations of the city."[51] The structure was used also as a community center and was purchased by the city in 1896 and served for a time as the public library. Terre Haute was also the publishing and/or distribution headquarters in the 1840s for several denominational papers in the state, including the *Western Universalist and Christian Teacher* (1844-49) and Kidwell's *Independent Universalist* (1846-50).

State missionary activity and the establishment of circuits had become by 1870 the principal state convention and association activities. A state Board of Missions was incorporated in 1863 but its accomplishments were meager and it was dissolved ten years later. A state superintendency was created in 1873 but funds were inadequate to fill the position regularly. A separate Sunday School Convention was organized in 1871, and the first women's organization was created the same year. It was at first a temporary association to raise funds for Smithson College in Logansport, but became permanent in 1879 as a body to raise funds and otherwise assist in denominational projects.

Organized Universalism grew much more slowly and sporadically in the central and northern part of Indiana than in the south. Small societies had appeared by 1838 in Elkhart (Elkhart County) and South

Bend (St. Joseph County) along the Michigan border.[52] William C. Talcot was the only Universalist preacher in northern Indiana in 1842.[53] The missionary activity of the state convention never reached the northern part of the state in an effective way. Instead it was individuals operating independently that seemed to have made the greatest impression. Erasmus Manford, who lived for a time in Lafayette and later in Indianapolis, was in 1841 the first to preach Universalism in Logansport.[54] For several years there was occasional preaching. A society of seventeen members was organized in 1857, and Thomas Gorman became the first resident pastor in 1859. Universalists met in the court house until a brick church was dedicated in 1866. In 1861 the preacher was J.D.H. Corwine, who had made an unsuccessful attempt to turn Kentucky Liberal Institute near Louisville into a college three years before. During his brief pastorate in Logansport he was also the principal of the Logansport Collegiate Institute.[55]

Universalism never became solidly established in Indianapolis until after 1860. There was no public Universalist activity between 1829, when Kidwell had made a brief appearance, and 1838. Abner H. Longley, a native Kentuckian converted by Kidwell, was an itinerant preacher in Ohio and Indiana; he was a surveyor by main occupation. He preached in Indianapolis in 1838. Erasmus Manford preached there occasionally during his numerous visits to Indiana. A society was organized in 1844, but refused to stay alive, and there was no regular pastor for most of its pre-Civil War history. The society was reorganized in 1853 by Benjamin F. Foster, who resigned in 1860. He was described as "the most eminent clergyman of the denomination in Indiana" and was the Grand Secretary of the Order of Odd Fellows in the state.[56] After Foster's departure the congregation "could not harmonize in this world" and a group seceded and formed a separate society, complete with their own meeting house. The rival society, created because of some local disaffection, soon disintegrated and Foster returned to serve the original church, with one brief interlude, from 1861 to 1869. His duties as state librarian demanded his full-time attention. The church became inactive for several years, but received financial assistance from the General Convention in 1872 and 1873 in an effort to prevent it from disappearing.

Educational efforts by Universalists in Indiana in the nineteenth century were first expended on Jonathan Kidwell's Western Union Seminary in Philomath, which closed in 1846. Several Universalist clergymen were connected with private academies such as the one at Logansport in the 1850s. The state convention first expressed an interest in establishing a denominational academy in 1854 and in 1857 had an opportunity to purchase one in Richmond which was declined.[57] A joint effort was made the same year with the Ohio

Convention, the school to be located in Oxford, Ohio, but after much discussion the project was abandoned.

As a member of the Northwestern Conference, Indiana was solicited for funds to assist Lombard College in Illinois, but there was still hope that an institution under denominational sponsorship could be organized within the state. The opportunity seemed to have come with a substantial bequest from Joshua Smithson of Vevay, made known in 1867. Smithson College in Logansport was opened in 1872 but closed less than a decade later, the victim of inadequate support, and lack of both endowment and patronage. No educational institution was permanently established by the denomination in Indiana.

There were about forty churches or societies (parishes) in Indiana, with approximately half that number of clergy, in 1870.[58] Universalists in that state were, at least so far as organization went, never as strong as in the neighboring state of Ohio. It was not because the clergy were less able or less willing to expend effort or to engage in debate as a means of spreading the faith.[59] George Rogers attributed the comparatively slow development in Indiana to the lax discipline and lack of system among Universalists.[60] Numerous individuals who professed Universalist beliefs failed to join or support their own societies or churches. The author of the circular letter distributed by the Western Union Association in 1841 complained that there was "no christian denomination which had so few preachers, according to the number of adherents, as the Universalists—and there is no denomination that offers so little encouragement to their ministering brethren."[61] Universalists attended and/or joined whatever churches happened to be conveniently located, regardless of denomination. Yet their very presence probably helped to spread the religious principles for which they stood, and Universalists especially in rural Indiana held tenaciously to their faith.

Illinois

Aside from a group of Dunkers led by George Wolf who held to their own version of Universalism and had settled in the Illinois Territory as early as 1812, the first preacher in fellowship with the Universalists known to have preached there was A.R. Gardner, who arrived about 1835.[62] He lived in several communities, including Attaloo and Henderson, where he preached on an occasional basis. After a short residence in Iowa City, Iowa, he returned to Illinois and settled in Farmington (Fulton County). In 1837 Aaron Kinney located at Joliet (Will County), where a society was organized but apparently soon disappeared. Kinney was described as "better calculated to found societies than to sustain them." Two other Universalist preachers were reported to have been in the state in 1836.[63]

In the fall of 1836 William Rounsville visited St. Charles (Kane County), and with the exception of about three years in Chicago, remained there. He found, as did many another preacher who settled in the Midwest, that most of the population in the 1830s consisted of emigrants from New England and New York, with some from Kentucky, Ohio, and Tennessee. None was wealthy, but the majority was liberal in social and religious views, and many found Universalism congenial. Several Universalists travelled through Illinois in the 1830s, preaching as they went. One was John A. Gurley, who preached in Peoria, Galena, and Chicago in 1837. There was a great religious mixture in the frontier state in 1839, matched by others in the Midwest at the time. Within a radius of three miles of LaHarpe (Hancock County), there were about 100 families representing almost every Protestant denomination, from fourteen Congregational families to "a number" of Universalists.[64]

Universalists in St. Charles organized a society in 1839 and erected a meeting house in 1842, the first in the state. A small meeting house was soon built in Joliet and another at Canton (Fulton County). Universalism was first preached in Chicago by William Queal in the summer of 1836, when a society was also organized.[65] Queal may have come at the request of one A. Gale, who asked for a preacher that year, and claimed that one-third of the inhabitants were Universalists.[66] However, when Erasmus Manford preached in Chicago in 1839, he recollected that there was no organization and no regular meetings.[67] A lot in Chicago was purchased from the state in the late 1830s but the property was over-appraised at $2,750. After $800 had been paid, the lot was forfeited and returned to the state. Subsequently a law was enacted by which each religious society was to receive a lot by donation. The one acquired by the Universalists was near the center of the city. The society had occasional preaching by a number of itinerant clergymen until 1843. In March of that year W.E. Manley became the settled pastor, and in 1844 a church was erected which, together with its furnishings, was worth $2,500.[68] By 1845 the society consisted of ninety members, and conducted a Sunday school.

Even before more than half a dozen preachers had appeared in the state, a convention was created with only a handful of societies, at a meeting in Canton in the fall of 1837.[69] When first organized, all Universalists in the state were invited to become members, whether clergy or laymen, and whether organized into societies or not.[70] In 1840 the constitution was amended to provide that voting members of the convention would consist of clergymen in the state and delegates from societies and churches in fellowship with it.

The number of associations grew with great rapidity after the convention was organized, and in 1844 delegates from these bodies rather than from societies and churches were provided. The first two associations were the Spoon River and the Fox River, both created in 1841. By 1870 eight others had been organized, and one more was established in 1871. In many ways the associations in Illinois were at first more powerful than the state convention, which relinquished rather than claimed various functions. In 1852 it gave to the associations the licensing and ordination powers which it originally claimed. The functions of the Home Missionary Society, created in 1849, were turned over to the associations in 1853. It was not until 1870 that the convention exercised the powers outlined under the uniform rules established by the General Convention.[71] Universalists in Illinois followed the same practice found in most other states of establishing a Women's Association (1868).

One of the most important methods of spreading Universalism was the "Universalist Mississippi Valley Institute," which was an association for the supplying of denominational literature created by the state convention at the time of its organization in 1837.[72] The *Better Covenant* served as the state newspaper between 1842 and 1847, published at various locations in turn and finally in Chicago, until it was merged with the *Star in the West.* The *Better Covenant* was immediately replaced by the *New Covenant* (1848-83), published in Chicago, and in turn absorbed the *Star in the West* in 1880 and became the *Star and Covenant.* It was sold to the Universalist Publishing House in 1883. *Manford's Monthly Magazine* was also based in Chicago, beginning in 1864. The educational concerns of Illinois Universalists were served by the Illinois Liberal Institute in Galesburg (Knox County), planned in 1851, chartered in 1852, and transformed in 1857 into Lombard University. There was talk among Universalists in the southern part of the state in 1873 of establishing a denominational school to be financed by a joint-stock company with capital of $50,000, but nothing was done.[73]

By 1839 there were thirteen preachers in the state, twelve of whom attended the state convention that year.[74] The convention was fellowshipped by the General Convention in 1842, by which time there were sixteen societies reported in the state.[75] The number had jumped to about thirty by 1843, with an average membership of thirty.[76] This optimistic figure was counterbalanced by several societies which had died, or, as the *Register* reported, had "gone to sleep." The number of preachers changed constantly; in the year 1847 alone the number reported in the state dropped from twenty-nine to twenty-two as they migrated elsewhere or engaged full-time in secular business.[77]

In 1851 William Rounsville, pastor of the society in Peoria (Peoria County), and a resident of the state since 1838, took stock of the denomination in Illinois and did not like what he found. He insisted that eastern Universalists had a distorted and greatly exaggerated conception of the actual strength of Universalism, particularly in northern Illinois, and believed that the prosperity claimed had never been as great in actuality. There were only three preachers who were regularly engaged in denominational work in that area; besides himself, there were only Samuel P. Skinner in Chicago, who was also co-editor of the *New Covenant* and could not devote much of his time to preaching; and S. Park in Poplar Grove (Boone County), near the Wisconsin line.[78] The number of actual preachers in the state was never more than three-fourths of those credited in denominational publications. It was "brethren abroad" as much as Universalists actually on the scene who were responsible for the falsely optimistic picture that was painted.

Part of the difficulty was the lack of full-time preaching; part was the constant migration of clergy; and part was the tone of the preaching. It tended to be more controversial than educational, with excessive concentration on why others were wrong than on why Universalists were right. The impression seemed to be given that Universalism was "a kind of covert infidelity" rather than a Christian denomination with a constructive and positive message. Rounsville's assessment seems to have been borne out by one report of a "protracted meeting" conducted by the American Home Missionary Society at which an elderly man rose and appealed to his neighbors to forgive him for advocating Universalism. He feared that some would become reluctant to embrace Christianity if they adopted Universalist teachings.[79] The difficulty was aggravated by the fact that Universalists came under so much attack that much of the virulence and bitterness they faced forced them to reply in kind. Further, many who toyed with Universalism without really understanding it, deserted when they realized its demands for self-discipline. It was easier to join a "popular" church than to become aware that Universalism was more than "a kind of masked skepticism."

Nonetheless, Universalist preachers in Illinois capitalized on the opposition they faced. After a Baptist preacher had delivered a series of six lectures against Universalism and had "thrust us all into hell, with the hypocrites, and there left us," Rounsville had delivered in 1840 a series of counterattacks of which "much good" was expected to come.[80] It was this very necessity of resorting to polemics about which he was complaining a decade later.

Rounsville's concern about the unstable character of Universalism in Illinois in the early 1850s seems not to have been borne out in the next two decades. The number of societies and churches in the state had reached nearly seventy by 1870, with fifty-six clergy in residence.[81] A large number was concentrated in the Greater Chicago area, and there were three Universalist churches in the city itself. The oldest, St. Paul's, dating from 1836, was for many years under the dynamic leadership of William H. Ryder. The second and third societies were organized in 1858 and 1869, respectively. St. Paul's was completely destroyed in the great fire of 1871. On the Sunday following the conflagration the congregation stood on the ruins of the burned-out church and held services as usual.[82] Ryder immediately toured the East for money to rebuild, and the response was sufficiently generous from all quarters to replace the edifice in 1872. When the Third Society (Murray Chapel) experienced financial difficulty in 1872, Ryder's church offered $2,000 toward the liquidation of a substantial indebtedness.[83]

Chicago served also as the midwestern publishing headquarters of the denomination for many years, and numerous books and tracts were issued through the office of the *New Covenant* in the 1860s, notably while D.P. Livermore and his wife Mary A. Livermore were associated with it (1858-69). The North Western Universalist Publishing House was organized in 1870, with William H. Ryder as its first president. The new organization took over the publishing of the *New Covenant.* During the great fire, only the mailing list was spared; publication was immediately resumed after suspension for only one week.[84] The general vitality of Universalism in Illinois was indicated by the fact that seven of the associations organized after 1840 were still active in 1871, among them the first two to have been organized.

Wisconsin

Universalism was preached in Wisconsin at least a decade before the territory achieved statehood in 1848. The first preacher mentioned in denominational records was L. Harris, who lived west of Racine in Troy (Walworth County). There was occasional preaching in 1842 and 1843 in the Milwaukee area, but it was not until 1846 that a relatively detailed report of Universalism was made by C.F. LeFevre, a corresponding secretary of the Universalist Historical Society. He had arrived in the territory in 1844 and settled in Milwaukee, where he purchased a farm.[86] He discovered that Seth Barnes, then living in Rockford, Illinois, had preached in Milwaukee and that a meeting house had been constructed, the first in the territory. T.S. Bartholomew, a resident of the territory, had organized a society in Racine in 1842 and had a part in organizing the Wisconsin Association at a meeting in Whitewater (Walworth County) in 1844.

By 1846 there were seven societies in the territory, and ten preachers, all but three of them serving part-time. All of the societies were clustered along southern Lake Michigan and in the southern counties adjoining Illinois. The society in Janesville (Rock County) was among the most active, meeting regularly in the courthouse, with F. Whitaker as the pastor until he retired about 1850. He had moved from

Southbridge, Massachusetts, and had the distinction of serving as the chaplain of the territorial legislature in 1846. He had been elected "to the no small astonishment of his opponents," a Presbyterian and an Episcopalian.[87]

The Wisconsin Association was transformed in 1848 into the state convention, and organized a missionary association to supplement the work of the ten preachers in the state. It apparently failed to achieve its purpose, for a new missionary society was created in 1852.[88] No associations were organized until 1857, when three were created. The jurisdictions included in each clearly demonstrate the concentration of Universalists in the south and east. The Northern Association included all territory north and west of the Wisconsin River, an area comprising over three-fourths of the state. The other two associations were almost immediately consolidated into one, known as the Southern Association and in 1858 redivided, with the creation of the Lake Shore Association. It included the majority of societies in the state.

Although less than 2,000 Universalists were reported in Wisconsin in 1871, there were 28 parishes and 22 ministers in residence.[89] Only one of the original societies (Racine) had had a continuous history without at least one major reorganization or reconstitution. The vast majority of the older societies had been reconstructed in the 1860s, among them Milwaukee (1865) and Whitewater (1868). In the same decade, Wisconsin Universalists sponsored one denominational school in the state, Jefferson Liberal Institute (1866-77).

Michigan

New Englanders had poured into Michigan Territory by the hundreds in the 1820s and 1830s, and there was sufficient population to justify statehood in 1837. Among those who migrated westward were many Universalists who organized their first society of forty male members in Bloomfield (Wayne County) near Detroit, in 1829.[90] Another society was created in 1830, in Pontiac (Oakland County).[91] Among the early itinerant preachers were Liscomb Knapp and Pitt Morse; the first settled preachers in full fellowship were T. Wheeler (Macomb County) and Nathaniel Stacy, who preached in Ann Arbor.[92] There were Universalists in St. Clair and Macomb Counties northeast of Detroit by 1833, and they were a source of irritation to preachers working for the American Home Missionary Society. One orthodox missionary reported that "Universalism & Deism [were] the most common and popular errors," and constituted much of the "current of infidelity" so strong in Michigan Territory.[93]

Universalists were indeed in the thick of the fierce denominational competition in these counties, trying to combat revival meetings by organizing societies, lay preaching, and the distribution of denominational literature.[94] The "First Independent Universalist Society" was organized in St. Clair in 1833.[95] A.H. Curtis, residing in Adrian (Lenawee County), organized a society there in 1833 and one in Ann Arbor (Washtenaw County) in 1834, where the first Universalist meeting house in the territory was built.[96]

Associations began to be organized even before the denomination was firmly established or Michigan had obtained statehood. The first, the Central Association, was created in 1836; when it met in 1837, seven clergy and seven lay delegates were present.[97] In 1841 the association was divided into two parts on a north-south line, and the western section became the Kalamazoo River Association. Three more were created eventually, the Southern (1848), Grand River (1857), and the Southwestern (1863). A state convention was organized in 1843 and was fellowshipped by the General Convention the same year.[98] At the time there were twenty-two societies and churches in the state, and thirteen preachers.[99] Several congregations were ministered to on a part-time basis, including some only one-eighth of the time.[100] The state convention was reorganized in 1866 to bring its functions into harmony with the recommendations of the General Convention.[101]

The number of active parishes by 1870 had stabilized at about thirty, not any more than the number reported fifteen years earlier. Constant removals and relocation of preachers had reduced them to about fifteen in 1855, but the number had risen to twenty-two in fellowship by 1870. One reason for the high turnover of clergy was undoubtedly the rigorous life that they were forced to lead. Elmore Case of North Adams (Hillsdale County) wrote a wistful and envious letter to the editor of the *Trumpet* in 1857 in which he wondered if Boston-area ministers realized the hardships experienced by many of their colleagues farther west. He referred to "us poor backwoods pioneers, our hard labors, homely garments, and dusty and toilworn forms, standing up in a log schoolhouse by the road side, to a few friends to preach." Case left the ministry in 1860.[102] But many others remained to face the challenges of a not always hospitable environment.

Michigan Universalists were served briefly by one locally produced publication, the *Primitive Expounder* (1843-52). It was merged with the *Star in the West* in 1852, and a "Michigan Department" was introduced. No denominational school was ever established in the state although plans were made for one in 1860. The citizens of Lyons (Ionia County) pledged $10,000 to establish a college, providing the denomination would raise $20,000.[103] The proposal was discussed at a meeting of the Central Association and immediately discarded. Such a sum would not even properly finance an academy; further, one Universalist institution in the Midwest (Lombard University) was considered sufficient. Sylvanus Cobb, who reported the proposed school to eastern Universalists, suggested that if money were available it should be expended on missionary activity. Whether Michigan Universalists were aware of Cobb's gratuitous advice is not known, but in 1860 they joined the Northwestern Conference, one of the purposes of which was to support missionary work in the Midwest. An academy, Lyons Institute, did operate briefly with some Universalists on its staff, but as a private venture.[104]

Iowa

Among the flood of migrants who streamed into Iowa Territory before statehood in 1846 were Universalists from states farther east. The first societies were created in the centers of frontier population along the Mississippi River and in the first tiers of counties farther west. A.R. Gardner, who migrated from Illinois in the 1830s, was probably the first to preach Universalism in Iowa City (Johnson County), where the first society and meeting house in the territory were to be found. When Iowa City, the seat of government, was laid out, each denomination was allowed to select a lot and hold it, provided a structure was built on it within a prescribed time. Gardner filed a claim on behalf of the Universalists and was immediately challenged by other denominations who took the Universalists to court and attempted to dispossess them.[105] Gardner won the contest in 1841 but the Universalists, "few and feeble" in numbers and resources, were faced with a deadline of mid-1842 on which to make good their claim by constructing a meeting house.

The Universalists immediately sent out an appeal for aid in any form, from cash to nails and shingles. Gardner made a hurried trip east to raise funds, and visited Boston, Philadelphia, and Baltimore in the winter of 1842, after he had obtained a one-year extension of the deadline from the territorial legislature.[106] The extended deadline was met, and the meeting house was dedicated in December 1843. By 1846 the Iowa City socity had seventy members and a flourishing Sunday school, but no preacher.[107]

Two other societies had been created by 1843 and a convention was organized that year, in Iowa City. It immediately plunged into social issues by adopting a resolution disapproving capital punishment.[108] The convention sought fellowship with the General Convention in 1844 but the request was denied because no delegate was present. The rather unusual request that James Shrigley of Maryland serve as the Iowa delegate was denied inasmuch as he was not a resident of the territory.[109]

Early Universalism in Iowa was handicapped by several factors besides chronic opposition from other denominations. Preachers were scarce, and laymen seemed to be more interested in land speculation than in religious affairs. Typical of the difficulties in organizing and maintaining the denomination were the experiences of Universalists in Dubuque.[110] The first attempt to organize a society had been made in 1837 but was abandoned. Universalists gathered informally for many years to hear itinerant preachers and to discuss topics in such denominational publications as the *Better Covenant.* A considerable number of Unitarians resided in the community, and there was talk in 1858 of establishing a society. Many Universalists were willing to "promote any form of liberal Christianity" and join the proposed society. The organization meeting took place that year but it immediately precipitated a lengthy debate over what the name should be. It was at first called the "Society of Liberal Christians," but before the meeting was over the title was changed to the "First Universalist Society of Dubuque," and then to the "Society for Christian Progress." After considering "First Unitarian Society," the meeting, attended by thirty-two men and eight women, voted by written ballot to designate it as a Universalist society.

Joseph S. Dennis, a native of Marblehead, Massachusetts, who had served pastorates in the East, became the minister in 1858 at a guaranteed salary of $2,000. He remained until 1863, when he moved to Chicago to enter the business world. Lombard University in Illinois conferred on him a Master of Arts degree in 1862 in recognition of his services in the denomination.[111] The society was incorporated in 1860 and secured a meeting house in 1862, purchased from the Baptists. Between 1863 and 1870 the society was served by a series of pastors. An attempt to organize a church was first made in 1866 but was not accomplished until 1883. The majority of the congregation saw no reason why they could not remain an informal society and still observe the Christian ordinances without the bother of organizing a church. Many other Iowa Universalists, as those elsewhere, seemed to have felt the same way, for in 1871 there were forty-eight parishes reported but only twenty church organizations in the state.[112] The denomination in Iowa was served by thirty-one ministers that year, including Augusta J. Chapin in Iowa City. She was a delegate from Iowa at the 1870 centennial celebration and was the first woman to serve on the council of the General Convention.

In 1849 the state convention was redesignated as the "State General Association," but in 1850 this bit of semantics was abandoned and again it became the state convention. It was composed, unlike the original convention organized in 1843, of preachers as well as delegates from societies. Each society was entitled to three lay delegates if there were as many as seven members, with an additional delegate for every additional ten members.[113] At the time, there were twelve societies in the state and four fellowshipped preachers. The Iowa City society still possessed the only meeting house. A state missionary association had been organized by 1853 and in 1857 two agents were appointed, one for the northern and one for the southern part of the state. But missionary activity had to be suspended almost immediately because of economic depression.[114]

In the 1850s four associations were organized in the state and five were in existence in 1870. All but two were suspended during the Civil War but were reorganized and expanded after 1865. The Turkey River Association, organized in 1856, was the largest geographically; it included the entire state north of a line running west of Dubuque, where Universalists were fewest in number. The Clayton County Association, in the northeastern part of the state, was organized in 1860 specifically "to aid in building churches in destitute places."[115] An executive board was composed of directors in each township.

Universalists in Iowa had to depend on denominational publications from outside the state. One attempt was made in 1849 in Burlington (Des Moines County) to publish a semi-monthly paper, the *Angelic Messenger,* but it lasted only one year.[116] A decision was made in 1857 to establish a denominational academy under the auspices of the state convention, and an educational convention was held in Iowa City the following year.[117] An "educational board" headed by D.C. Tomlinson was appointed to employ an agent to solicit funds. But Tomlinson returned to the East and no progress was made until after the Civil War. Mitchell Seminary, the result of a donation of land for educational use, was opened in 1872 and closed in 1879 when the public school system had expanded and made the school superfluous.

Minnesota

Minnesota, in which Universalism first appeared in the 1850s, was not at first as rapidly occupied as most of the other midwestern frontier states. Although the first settlements had been made by 1805, it was not until 1858 that the territory was admitted to statehood. Universalism was first preached in the eastern part of what was then Minnesota Territory, in the Minneapolis-St. Paul area, by E.A. Hodston in 1852.[118] The first society was organized in 1853 in St. Anthony's Falls (Hennepin County), which also constructed the first Universalist meeting house in the territory in 1857.[119]

The first news of developments in Minnesota to Universalists in the East came in 1855 by way of a notice in the *Christian Freeman* that a meeting house was being planned and that numerous Universalists had already settled in Minneapolis.[120] By 1857 there were three preachers in the territory. Seth Barnes had arrived in 1855 at St. Anthony's Falls as the first pastor; Moses Goodrich had organized a society in Anoka (Anoka County) by 1857; and J. M. Westfall had arrived from Illinois and settled in Rochester (Olmsted County).[121] There was also preaching in Excelsior, a few miles west of Minneapolis, in 1858.

A state convention (reorganized in 1866) and missionary society were established in 1860, at which time there were three societies in the state, although six preachers were reported.[122] The convention was at first composed of societies only, which numbered ten by 1866, most in large towns rather than in rural communities. By 1870 there were nineteen parishes, with the three largest churches in the urban centers of St. Anthony (North Minneapolis), Minneapolis, and St. Paul. By then a state Sabbath School Convention had been organized, and nine ministers were in residence. The one who attracted the most attention by 1871 was Herman Bisbee, pastor of the St. Anthony church, who was accused of heresy and whose case became a *cause célèbre* in the denomination.

⋆ ⋆ ⋆ ⋆ ⋆

In addition to those states already mentioned, by the opening of the 1870s outposts of Universalism had been established in four more states and one territory. W.S. Bates was in Yankton, Dakota Territory; a state convention had been organized in Kansas in 1869 at Lawrence; plans were under way to build a chapel in Lincoln, Nebraska; and four preachers were at work in Texas. Small as they may have been in numbers, Universalists and Universalism were to be found everywhere in the nation, in some fashion and in some form, when the denominational centennial was celebrated.

Chapter 25

SLOW AND ERRATIC PROGRESS: THE MID-ATLANTIC AND BORDER STATES

Within the four major sections of the nation into which it has been more or less arbitrarily divided for purposes of this study, Universalism had the most diverse and contrasting history in the Middle Atlantic and border states of the seaboard and interior. This reflected to a great extent the heterogeneity and flux of the population, from Philadelphia and environs to the maritime Southern border states of Maryland and Virginia and the Western interior, including Pittsburgh which was in many respects as much as a Western frontier area as Kentucky, Tennessee, and Missouri. Eastern Pennsylvania was an historic center of early Universalism, yet nearby Delaware was the only state east of the Mississippi River in which only one Universalist society is known ever to have been organized. Wilmington was a "missionary station" where John T. Goodrich preached in 1867 and 1868 and organized a society which disappeared after his departure.[1]

Efforts to establish Universalism in the nation's capital were slow to achieve success because of the transient character of so much of the population. There was an unusually noticeable mobility in the Universalist population, both lay and clerical, throughout the Middle Atlantic area which largely disregarded political and geographical boundaries. Universalists in the upper counties of Pennsylvania frequently migrated into equally rural western New York State, and those in western Pennsylvania and the comparable parts of Maryland and Virginia ventured into eastern and southern Ohio as well as into the border states of the South. They were all part of the vast expansion into the interior which populated the Middle West with almost bewildering rapidity in the first half of the nineteenth century.

Pennsylvania

The history of Universalism in Pennsylvania before 1870 can be divided into four well-defined periods: The late eighteenth century, characterized by much activity and organizational effort; a period of quiescence which lasted until the late 1820s; an era of renewed activity and expansion into the interior in the 1830s and 1840s; and a period of stability and slow but relatively steady growth after 1850 as denominational organization matured.[2] The first individuals holding Universalist beliefs in Pennsylvania, although they did not actually preach the doctrine, were to be found among the English and Welsh Baptists in the Philadelphia area and in such pietistic German groups as the Dunkers, the German Seventh Day Baptists, and small Separatist organizations; and in Berks and Montgomery counties in the interior.[3]

A Baptist church had been organized by 1689 among families living along Pennypack Creek, north of Philadelphia. Members of the original Pennypack church, known also as the Lower Dublin Baptist Church, spread south and west. A Baptist church had been organized in Philadelphia in the early eighteenth century, and it was to this church that Elhanan Winchester had been called in 1780 and from which he had been ejected in 1784. Out of this had come a congregation of Universal Baptists in Philadelphia, organized about 1785, and owning a meeting house. Meanwhile, John Murry had made several appearances in Philadelphia and vicinity, beginning in 1771, and had made the acquaintance of Winchester. Sufficient numbers of believers in universal salvation existed by 1790 to hold a convention in Philadelphia, over which Murray had presided.

The Universalist society in Philadelphia, which dated its origin to 1790, obtained in 1796 the services of Thomas Jones, who came from England at Murray's request and who remained in Philadelphia until 1804 when he became the long-time pastor of the Gloucester society in Massachusetts. The society led a very unstable existence for several years after Jones' departure, with a succession of preachers. George Richards, who succeeded Noah Murray in 1809, resigned in 1813 after difficulties with his congregation. He suffered from periodic depression, and after the death of his wife became mentally deranged and hanged himself in 1814 in the hospital to which he had been committed.[4] He was buried in an unmarked grave in the society's cemetery; by a certain irony it was Richards who had been responsible for marking the grave and furnishing the inscription for Elhanan Winchester who had died in Hartford, Connecticut, in 1797.

The meeting house in Philadelphia (later known as the Lombard Street Church) was closed for over three years (1814-16) and had only occasional preaching until Abner Kneeland's arrival in 1818. It finally achieved a measure of stability under Abel C. Thomas, who resigned in 1839 after almost a decade of service. A society consisting of followers of Winchester was organized in 1820 in the section of Philadelphia known as the Northern Liberties. Known as "The Second Independent Church of Christ, called Universalists," it was open to all denominations of Christians. It was never formally fellowshipped.[5] The second

Universalist society (the Callowhill church) was organized in 1822 and dedicated a meeting house the following year.[6] But by the 1840s the church had gone into a period of torpor.

Organized Universalism almost disappeared in the early nineteenth century north and west of Philadelphia. The Philadelphia Convention ceased to meet after 1809 and almost no new societies were created. The attempt to maintain a society at suburban Kensington was unsuccessful, and a fourth, organized in 1842, had only a short life. The constant shifting of population and preachers was offered as the basic cause for failure.[7]

The Church of the Messiah, organized in 1850 by a number of families in the western portion of the city who withdrew from the Lombard Street church, was the most active of all by 1870 under the leadership of E.G. Brooks. A church was organized in Luzerne (Plymouth County, later Luzerne County) in 1802, and was fellowshipped by the Philadelphia Convention that year.[8] Three or four societies appeared in Susquehanna County in the northeastern corner of the state in the early 1820s. Most were established by Charles R. Marsh from Vermont, who published the *Candid Examiner* (Montrose), of which only two volumes ever appeared (1825-26).

It was in Marietta (Lancaster County) that Universalism first obtained a firm hold west of Philadelphia. In 1827 Stephen R. Smith, then pastor of the Callowhill church in Philadelphia, was invited to speak in the community. A society was organized in 1829, known as "The First Society of Universalists in Lancaster" and was made up largely of individuals excluded from a society of United Brethren (Moravian). Leadership was assumed by Jacob Meyers, a German Baptist convert who was ordained in the Lombard Street church in Philadelphia in 1829. He had the advantage of being bilingual, so could easily communicate with inhabitants of German background. He delivered sermons in both English and German at state convention meetings, sometimes also using both languages in the same church services of local societies. He created a circuit covering four counties, and with George Grosh published *Der Frohliche Botschafter (The Messenger of Glad Tidings),* a monthly Universalist journal (1829-38). Several societies resulted from Meyers' efforts. Some of them were virtually family affairs; of the twenty-two members of the Marietta church when it was organized, ten bore the name Grosh.[9] A.B. Grosh, long the editor of the *Universalist Register,* was a member of this extended family. Meyers was so successful that the organization of a German Universalist Association was considered, but was abandoned.[10]

After 1830 Universalism spread rapidly all over the state. Organizing a society was simplicity itself. Typical was one organized in 1830 in Luzerne County, east of the Susquehanna River. "A few of us collected together, drawed up [*sic*] three Articles of Faith and obtained ten signers to it. We met on Sunday, and Mr. Jonathan Parker read several Hymns and a sermon by Kittredge Haven [of Vermont]. Quite a number of orthodox attended, merely out of curiosity, I suppose. We shall continue to have meetings every Sunday, and read some of the best sermons we can procure."[11] There were about twelve societies in the state in 1830, including the two in Philadelphia, and six preachers.[12] A society of eighty members had been organized in Pittsburgh by 1836.[13]

Universalist periodicals appeared in the state in great numbers in the 1830s and 1840s, most of which had the same short existence as the *Candid Examiner.* Stephen R. Smith and Pitt Morse had edited in Philadelphia the *Herald of Salvation* in 1826 which lasted only a year. Smith concluded that Universalists already had "too many religious journals. As a Christian denomination we are neither very numerous nor very wealthy, and yet we are sustaining more publications than any other church in America." Other Universalists in Pennsylvania apparently did not agree with Smith, for there were three denominational papers published in the state in 1833.[14]

The Universalist Publishing Society of Pennsylvania was organized in Philadelphia in 1841, with fifteen charter members, and lasted until 1844.[15] The publishing firm of Gihon, Fairchild & Co. undertook to prepare and distribute at least 500 copies of each publication. They consisted of both tracts and sermons. Each manuscript was read aloud before a vote was taken on whether to publish it. Before the society was dissolved, it was sponsoring as many as 2,500 copies of each publication. Some of the tracts were published in the *Nazarene* (1840-43) rather than separately, and in all, thirty-three titles appeared under the auspices of the society.

Universalists in Pennsylvania without their own meeting houses experienced the same difficulties as elsewhere in finding places to meet. In Lancaster they finally obtained in 1834 the limited use for one year of the German Lutheran Church. Until then they met "in the market house, theater, court house, and woods."[16] Of the twenty societies reported in 1835, only nine had meeting houses, and some of those were shared with other denominations.[17] The number of societies by 1845 had reached forty-four, but with less than twenty meeting houses.[18] The number of societies had dropped by the early 1850s to about forty, which probably accounts for the organization of a state Missionary, Educational, and Tract Association in 1853, incorporated in 1859. It was created largely through the efforts of John Galbraith, a judge and prominent citizen of Erie.[19] The society in Pittsburgh had a difficult time in maintaining itself, and when the missionary association was organized there had been no Universalist preaching for about a decade.[20] Davis Bacon managed to revive the society of sixty members. Even the publication of a monthly denominational paper *(Gospel*

Tidings) was attempted in Pittsburgh for one year (1861).[21] The number of Universalist societies in Pennsylvania by 1870 had stabilized at forty-two, with half that number of ministers.[22] By 1870 Universalism in Philadelphia had seemingly reached a plateau, but in relation to the population of the city was measurably in decline. With 750,000 inhabitants and nearly 500 churches, Philadelphia in the mid-1870s had only three Universalist churches and one Unitarian. Less than 750 adults attended the three Universalist churches (the Lombard Street church, the Church of the Restoration, and the Church of the Messiah). As one Universalist observed in 1874, his friends outside the denomination regarded him "as a sort of natural curiosity. A real, live, flesh and blood Universalist appears . . . . as strange a thing as some of Barnum's wonders."[23]

At the association level, Pennsylvania Universalists were at first served by a temporary regional organization, the New York and Philadelphia Association, created in 1829 and including Universalists in New Jersey also. It held two additional meetings that year but the arrangement was immediately found to be impractical, so a separate Philadelphia Association was created in 1831. In 1834 the Union Association was organized in Reading, and in 1851 the two were combined as the Philadelphia Union Association. The northward and westward expansion of the denomination was recognized by the organization of the Susquehanna Association in 1834 and the Lake Erie Association in 1838. The North Branch Association was carved out of the Susquehanna Association four years later. The western third of the state was represented in the Pittsburgh Association, organized in 1837. It also included at first eastern Ohio and western Virginia. It held its organization meeting in the latter state.[24] It was reorganized in 1859 and its jurisdiction confined to Pennsylvania and what became West Virginia. The Stacy Association was also created in 1859, comprising two counties in the northwestern part of the state adjacent to the New York border. It was named in honor of Nathaniel Stacy, a pioneer preacher in both states.

Some of these administrative divisions represented hopes for the future rather than the realities of the present. When the Union Association was created there were only two clergymen resident in the area of Berks and Lancaster Counties.[25] Universalists were often so scattered in sparsely settled counties that some associations, such as the Susquehanna, held two meetings a year so that all societies could be accommodated.[26] Others, like the Union Association, established circuits to cover as many as fifteen counties.[27] Five of the six associations were still in existence in 1870, the Stacy Association having been incorporated into the Lake Erie Association.

At the meeting in 1831 when the Philadelphia Association was created, plans were made for organizing a state convention.[28] It was established in 1832 at a meeting in Columbia (Lancaster County) held under considerable difficulty. The Universalists were denied the use of the town hall in spite of a petition by eighty Universalist taxpayers.[29] After they assembled in a private home, the building was stoned. They were forced to meet in an academy building in 1836 because they were refused permission to use any church in Chestnut Hill, a suburb of Philadelphia.[30] The Quaker and Dunker influence was evident at the second meeting of the convention; Universalists were discouraged from taking oaths and wearing mourning for the dead.[31] The assembly was told that the only prerequisites for the ministry were good moral character and attachment to the truths of Universalism.

The incorporation of the convention was delayed until 1877 because of state law. An application had been refused by the state supreme court in 1873 under a law enacted in 1855 which placed all religious property under the control of bodies composed of lay members only. The law was modified to allow property to be held by an executive committee, providing the majority were laymen. A new state constitution in 1874 provided that a charter could be obtained from the county where the business was transacted. Compliance with this provision brought to an end the migratory headquarters of the Pennsylvania Convention, which had met all over the state (except in Philadelphia). Philadelphia was fixed as the legal headquarters and the charter was finally secured, although no convention met in the city until 1904.[32] Before 1845 the convention met at least once (in 1841) in New Jersey. The meetings of the convention before 1870, although "both agreeable and profitable" according to Abel C. Thomas, conducted so little business that he omitted its history deliberately in his account of Universalism in the state.[33]

New Jersey

One of the paradoxes of Universalist history at the state level was the failure, comparatively speaking, of the denomination to flourish in the very area where John Murray had landed in 1770. In 1856, when the cornerstone of a new church of the First Universalist Society in Newark was laid, there were only two other denominational meeting houses in the state, one at Hightstown and one in Sussex County, in the northwest corner of the state. Asher Moore, who delivered the principal address, pointed out ruefully that there was "not a free State in this whole Union where there are so few Universalist organizations."[34] This was not quite true, but his point was well taken.

He placed the blame on the lack of a widespread common school system by which the populace would have been enlightened and therefore would have been more receptive to Universalist teachings. He contended that Universalism found "its most congenial soil in the minds of an educated people." He was positive that when every town and village provided a free public school system, Universalism would prosper. This singling out of education as an explanation was not as unlikely as it may seem, for opportunities were severely limited. Fees for public schools were not abolished in New Jersey until 1871. In 1870, in this densely populated state, there were only six Universalist parishes and three ministers in residence. Only three of the parishes had regular preaching (Newark, Hightstown, and Irvington); Irvington did not even own a meeting house.[35]

The first individual known to have preached Universalism in the state after Murray was Nicholas Cox, a Baptist who attended all of the sessions of the Philadelphia Convention, including its first meeting in 1790.[36] He preached in Warren and Sussex Counties in the northern part of the state adjoining Pennsylvania. Cox died in Mansfield (Warren County) in 1826 at the age of eighty-four. Among the first Universalists to subscribe to Abel Sarjent's *Free Universal Magazine* (1793-94) and to buy copies of Relly's hymn book were residents of New Jersey. Another resident, William Worth of Pittsgrove (Penns Grove, Salem County) was a Baptist preacher "tinctured with Universalism" who served as moderator of the first meeting of the Philadelphia Convention. There was also Universalist preaching by Artis Seagrave in the southern county of Cape May before 1790. Numerous societies were reported to exist when the convention met in 1792 but Universalism did not take root after a promising start. Abel C. Thomas placed the entire fault at the door of lack of organization and follow-up. The preachers roamed from one place to another, "now here, now there, with no special charge."[37] Too much depended on the efforts of isolated individuals.

The "Free Universal Church of Christ" was organized in 1793 at New Hanover by some of Murray's converts, and a meeting house was constructed in 1795. Robert Lawrence, a convert from the Methodists, was among those who conducted meetings there, but he was never fellowshipped or ordained. The leadership in constructing the meeting house and keeping the society together had been taken by a woman, Alice Brown, but after her death in 1810 the society disappeared and the meeting house became a haybarn. The first Universalist meeting house in Essex County had been erected in 1828 at Middleville, near Newark, but it had depended on the largesse of one man; when he passed off the scene the church edifice fell into other hands.[38]

Itinerants wandered about the state in the late 1820s but no real start was made until after 1830. Only a week after two orthodox clergymen in Trenton had publicly expressed their gratification that no Universalism had ever been preached in the town, Theophilus Fisk spoke to a large audience in 1828.[39] But he did not remain, and when

Thomas Whittemore inventoried the state of Universalism in New Jersey in 1830 he was able to identify by name only one preacher (William A. Hagadorn), who resided "somewhere in the state."[40]

The greatest attention paid to promoting Universalism in New Jersey after 1830 was at first in Newark, where several clergy preached in 1831, including Menzies Rayner.[41] A society was organized in 1832 and a meeting house was acquired two years later and was occupied for some sixteen years. L.C. Marvin served as the first pastor.[42] In the 1830s the stigma of belonging to the denomination was so great that no woman would be seen in the congregation during daylight hours. By 1870 most of the members of the society were women.

The church building by 1850 was both outgrown and still encumbered with a heavy debt, so the structure was sold and services were held for the next six years in various halls. In this interim period, a second society was organized in 1851 in Newark, although the original one was never large; the new society also constructed its own church. Moore, in his address on the occasion of the dedication of the original society's new building in 1856, made a plea for peaceful coexistence, conciliation, and an end to "jostling against one another" that had precipitated the organization of a rival society. This was not accomplished until 1862, when the union of the two churches was effected, with A. St. John Chambré as pastor and about seventy members.[43]

While Newark Universalists were trying to support two rival congregations, their denomination spread very slowly elsewhere in the state. A society had been organized in Hightstown by 1833 and had acquired a former Baptist church building.[44] George Rogers, visiting from the Midwest, preached sixteen sermons in seven communities in 1834.[45] He reported that in many areas he was the first to preach Universalism. "A sea-serpent could hardly have been a greater *curiosity.*"[46]

A small congregation of Dutch Universalists was discovered in 1837 near Paterson, but they were in fellowship with no organization although within the limits of the New York Association.[47] In 1840 there was but one preacher known in the state, and he was not preaching regularly. The editor of the *Universalist Register* commented in 1841 that "the cause advances but slowly, if at all, in New Jersey," and the next year omitted the state entirely in his statistical summary. The Universalist society in Newark was "few in numbers, and not abundantly blessed with this world's goods."[48] They almost lost their meeting house in 1843 but were saved by a recent convert who bought up the mortgage. The society in Hightstown had become moribund by 1844, and the only forward movement that year was the organization of a society at Camptown, near Newark.[49]

Until 1845 the Universalists of central and southern New Jersey were under the nominal jurisdiction of, first, the New York and

Philadelphia Association which occasionally furnished itinerant preaching, and after 1832 the Pennsylvania Convention. In 1844 a conference was held in Hightstown which recommended the establishment of a state convention.[50] This was accomplished in 1845, in a meeting at Newark, where James Gallager was the pastor. A constitution was adopted and the new organization was fellowshipped by the General Convention the same year.[51] In 1845 there were four preachers in the state, three of whom had settled pastorates (Newark, Hightstown, and Jersey City). J.H. Plumb was the first pastor of the Jersey City society, organized in 1845. He pulled up stakes in 1847 after reporting that "it is rather a sterile soil, and productive of but little but bigotry, religious spite, and strife."[52] Gallager also met much opposition in Newark, but noted that at least it had the merit of advertising Universalism. He moved to Pennsylvania in 1849.[53] There had been a complete turnover of clergy by 1855 and by 1858 only Chambré (Newark) remained in the state.[54] In the latter year the Second Universalist Church and Society summarily and unilaterally dissolved its fellowship with the state convention without either an explanation or a formal request.[55] The state convention by then consisted of little more than its standing clerk, Chambré.

Organized Universalism in New Jersey almost foundered in the late 1850s, but was partially rescued in 1859 when a society was organized in Rahway. In the northwestern part of the state Universalists were still to be found in Sussex County, centered in Branchville. There was even talk of establishing a denominational academy there, to be under the control of the state convention, and $3,000 had been pledged by 1859 by the citizenry.[56] How such a project was to have been supported is a moot question, in view of the fact that in 1869 there were only four preachers and five societies in the entire state.[57] The state convention did organize a missionary society in 1859, and by 1864 the convention had been incorporated, with seven trustees.[58]

One of the reasons behind the decision to charter the convention was a plan to purchase from the Methodists the property on which the original Potter church had stood at Good Luck, where John Murray had first set foot in America. The property had fallen into the hands of the Methodists after Potter's death, and a church had been constructed near the site. The project to acquire the property was to be jointly sponsored by the New Jersey Convention and the General Convention if sufficient funds could be raised. The Murray Grove Association was organized for this purpose in 1866.[59] The hope was either to purchase and remodel the Methodist church building or build a replica of the Potter meeting house. By 1868, about $5,700 had been collected, but general mismanagement left only $300.[60] The state convention then undertook, as part of its contribution to the celebration of the denominational centennial in 1870, to erect an iron fence around the dilapidated Potter grave and to purchase the grove opposite "as an assembling-ground for the pilgrims of the future."[61] The grove, of about one acre, was acquired in 1870 by the convention for $275.[62] As a part of the centennial celebration, the "Universalist Society of Waretown and Good Luck" was organized in 1869 and met, with part-time preaching, in a small wooden structure in Waretown, about five miles from the Murray landing place. A relic of the original Potter meeting house was built into the pulpit.[63]

The Woman's Centenary Association of New Jersey undertook in 1875 to acquire the Potter property or to erect a "summer church" on the recently acquired property, but their efforts were not successful.[64] The second of the two proposed projects became the more practical of the two in the 1870s, but even then there were difficulties. An attempt was made to raise $3,000 to construct a small chapel, and a Potter Memorial Fund was established in 1876 with headquarters in New York City. By mid-1877 most of the materials had been acquired, but the building remained uncompleted for several more months because only about one-half of the funds had been raised and the workmen could not be paid.[65] The Murray Grove Association was reorganized in 1886 at the Potter Memorial Church and in 1909 the Potter home and farm were purchased for $4,000. An adjoining farm with buildings was also acquired, the two totalling over 200 acres. Universalists also obtained unrestricted use of the "old Potter meeting house" during one month each summer, when institutes and other meetings were held. Establishing a denominational shrine was a long and arduous business.

Maryland

Preaching Universalism in the seaboard border state of Maryland in the nineteenth century was a pioneer adventure which took considerable fortitude as well as persistence. The state had a large Roman Catholic population, particularly in the east, but Universalists encountered as much or more opposition from Protestants, especially the German Reformed Church. The denominational experience in Maryland, as in New Jersey, challenges the traditional image of Universalism as a predominantly rural phenomenon. It was in Baltimore that Universalism remained strongest throughout the nineteenth century, and it was largely from that base that rural Universalists were served. Attempts failed to establish the denomination on either the Eastern Shore or in the western part of the state, both overwhelmingly rural.

It was in Baltimore that Universalism was first preached in the state, and it was there that the first society was organized in 1831. This was preceded by itinerant preaching by Paul Dean, Theophilus Fisk, and Lemuel Willis and the efforts of six laymen who had attempted to organize in the 1820s.[66] Otis A. Skinner became the first pastor, in 1831, and a year later a church was organized and boasted a Sunday school, a library, and a choir and singing school.[67] Universalists first occupied leased quarters known as the Branch Tabernacle. The building had been constructed by an eccentric gentleman named Charles Warfield who had planned to establish the "First Philosophical and Evangelical Church of Baltimore" which never materialized.[68] He ousted the Universalists when they refused to adopt the creed which he had prepared. Universalists then built their own church in the center of the city in 1837, an undertaking which placed them heavily in debt.

In 1833 Skinner was joined by his brother Samuel, who assisted him in editing the *Southern Pioneer and Gospel Visitor* (1831-37). Samuel P. Skinner also preached for a short time in 1834 in the New Jerusalem Church in Baltimore which had been made available for Universalist use.[69] Baltimore Universalists had their share of difficulties, financial and otherwise. Just as their new church was opened in 1837 it was badly damaged by a flood; among the items lost was an expensive organ.[70] The indebtedness was so great ($20,000) by 1839 that the church was put up for sheriff's auction.[71] A hastily assembled group managed to buy it back. The Baltimore church enjoyed its greatest period of prosperity before 1870 under the pastorate of James Shrigley, beginning in 1841. The church had 108 members that year, with an average church attendance of 800 in a building that would seat almost 1,000.[72]

Otis A. Skinner did considerable travelling while headquartered in Baltimore between 1831 and his departure in 1835. He visited the peninsula between the Chesapeake and Delaware Bays (the Eastern Shore) and envisioned the establishment of two circuits in the state, one in the east and one in the west, with Baltimore as the focal point.[73] Nothing ever came of the idea. When Erasmus Manford from the Midwest visited Maryland in the 1840s he spent six months in Salisbury in the eastern part of the state and then headed west to Hagerstown, where he had been preceded by Samuel A. Davis who resided briefly in Funkstown.[74] Both men encountered nothing but opposition; Davis had given up and moved to a more promising field in Pittsburgh. Skinner was also responsible for the establishment of a society in Elkton, in the northeastern part of the state. The first Universalist meeting house erected exclusively for Universalists was dedicated at Woodsboro, in the western section of the state, in 1837.[75] The Universalists in Baltimore were still using rented quarters while their church was under construction; it was not completed until later that year.

Societies in rural communities in Maryland never prospered. Several appeared in the records in the 1830s and 1840s but were never heard of again. In spite of these discouraging prospects, there was talk of organizing a state convention as early as 1835, but instead the Southern Convention was created that year as a regional agency, including the state of Virginia.[76] Its activities were devoted primarily to Maryland Universalism, and its basic tasks were to establish circuit preachers and to serve as an ordaining and fellowshipping agency.[77] It apparently lasted only a few years; there were never sufficient societies to form a viable state convention.[78] No more than four societies existed at any one time in the state, and for some periods the Baltimore church was the only one. Associations were of course superfluous. Because of Baltimore's unique situation it was fellowshipped directly by the General Convention, in 1852.[79]

While pastor of the Baltimore church, Shrigley did all in his power to make the denomination known in the city. He was not always successful. In 1845 a large and elegant map of Baltimore was prepared, purporting to show all the important buildings, including churches.[80] Shrigley was dismayed to discover that all were included but his, which was portrayed as a vacant lot. On the other hand, he got along very well with the Roman Catholic clergy and was especially pleased when he was unanimously elected an honorary member of the Calocagathian Society, a literary organization at St. Mary's College, a Roman Catholic institution. He promptly accepted, having already come to the conclusion that "the Catholics are more liberal and tolerant than any Protestant partialist sect in existence."[81]

Shrigley moved from Baltimore in 1850 but returned to Maryland four years later, where he lived in Catonsville, a suburb of Baltimore, and served as a supply pastor. By 1860 the Baltimore society and church were the only ones in the state and were in the midst of selling their building and constructing an even larger and better one.[82] After the disruption of the Civil War, four societies (parishes) existed by 1870, with the Baltimore church heading the list. There were only three clergymen in the state.[83] By 1877 a second church had been organized in the city, and only one society existed, in the rural community of Chesapeake City. The metropolis had triumphed over the countryside.

Washington, D.C.

The District of Columbia was not a propitious place to establish Universalism on a permanent basis, and the history of the denomination there clearly shows it. Although there was a core of permanent residents, a high proportion of the population shifted constantly as governmental and political personnel came and went. Universalist preachers were as transient as the population itself. Theophilus Fisk, in 1827, was the first known to have paid occasional visits, and Otis A. Skinner preached there in 1834.[84] G.T. Flanders organized a society in

1845 and preached in 1846 in both the hall of the House of Representatives, with John Quincy Adams in attendance, and in the Unitarian church, but the society seems to have disappeared shortly thereafter.[85] James Shrigley may have attempted to organize a society in 1853, but if so it did not last.

Serious attention to providing Universalist services in the nation's capital was not given until the late 1860s. In 1866 Shrigley, then in Philadelphia, recommended to the General Convention that $100,000 be raised to erect a church in Washington to serve as a temporary religious home for Universalists who came to the city.[86] Nothing came of his suggestion at the time, although the Philadelphia Union Association suggested the same year that Washington be made a "specific missionary ground."[87] A.B. Grosh resided in Washington in 1866 and was joined in 1867 by W.W. Dean, but neither considered it a permanent home and retained their fellowship elsewhere. Beginning in 1868 the General Convention undertook to supply pastors while Congress was in session.[88] The trustees were skeptical at first about the success of the experiment, so the General Secretary spent two Sundays in Washington to assess the situation.[89] Over 200 individuals attended the first meeting, so a temporary organization was effected, and a Sunday school and Bible class were organized.

Enthusiasm was so great that Grosh and Dean urged that not only a settled ministry be established but that a church edifice suitable for the nation's capital be built as a national symbol of the denomination.[90] Thus was born the idea that took the form of the Universalist National Memorial Church over fifty years later. The original suggestion, made on the eve of the celebration of the denominational centennial in 1870, was not only to provide a fitting way of emphasizing the national character of the denomination but of providing a potential agency for rebuilding the almost destitute ruins of the denomination in the South. The Centenary Committee created by the General Convention considered the suggestion and discarded it. So all references to establishing a memorial church in Washington were stricken from their final report in 1869.[91] The trustees were instructed instead to provide as much assistance to the society in Washington as "the means at their command will warrant." The Murray Universalist Society in Washington was formally organized in May 1869.[92]

There had been immediate and widespread opposition to erecting a memorial church, especially at the proposed figure of $100,000. The *New Covenant* (Chicago) objected strenuously to a church which would be "little more than a monument any way, and we have no surplus funds to devote to monument building."[93] The sectional character of the denomination, in spite of all the professions about national unity, became all too visible. Universalists in Minnesota objected to the entire idea, while the *Universalist,* based on the Atlantic seaboard, supported the project as a symbol of the unity of the denomination as a truly national institution.[94] But Universalists had to be satisfied with far less, for the General Convention agreed to supply the pulpit in Washington for only ten months a year, on a temporary basis, and the building of a church of the dimensions originally recommended was completely out of the question.[95] The convention did agree in 1872 to pledge $1,000 a year to help support a pastor, provided only that the society could raise at least $1,500. The trustees of the General Convention recommended that a lot be purchased on which to build "a temporary chapel at the cheapest possible cost consistent with comfort and good taste."[96]

A.B. Grosh was requested in 1873 to prepare a history of Universalism in Washington, D.C. to be put in the cornerstone of the proposed building.[97] Just ten years later a building was finally provided, in the form of the Murray Universalist Church. It was a "plain Gothic edifice" of brick and stone, constructed at the corner of L and 13th Streets.[98] It was financed from a combination of sources: a special canvass begun in 1880 by the General Convention; the Washington parish; and miscellaneous donations. Alexander Kent, who had become pastor in 1879, served as the agent. The original cost was estimated to be $30,000, including the lot, but the actual total was almost $47,000, including furnishings, the provision of which was a special project of the Woman's Centenary Association.[99]

The cornerstone was laid in 1882 and the building was completed in time to serve as the headquarters of the General Convention meeting in 1883. Although the church building, which was deeded to the convention without any encumbrances, was not as elaborate as the one projected during the centennial, it was much more than the "temporary chapel" recommended in 1872 by the trustees, and a great improvement over the various rented quarters used previously, including Lincoln Hall and the Masonic Temple. But the denomination had to wait until 1930 to dedicate a memorial church on the scale projected in 1868.

Virginia and West Virginia

Nicholas Cox, a native of Philadelphia and a Universal Baptist and pioneer in establishing Universalism in New Jersey, was probably the first to have preached in Virginia, in 1809 and 1810.[100] He had attended all of the sessions of the Philadelphia Convention (1790-1809) and can be classified as one of the earliest missionaries of the faith. Edward Mitchell, then of New York City, preached in Richmond in 1823, and Jabez Price, a layman who died in 1845, was possibly the first to advocate Universalism there.[101] The first call for a Universalist preacher in the state came in 1829; by then there were over eighty subscribers to Universalist periodicals.[102]

There were two parallel movements of population in Virginia in the early nineteenth century, one along the Atlantic seaboard and centered in Richmond, and one in the western part of the state, running in a north-south direction through the Shenandoah Valley (the "Great Valley") into which hundreds of migrants filtered from Pennsylvania, many of them with German pietistic backgrounds. There were many Dunker congregations believing in universal salvation established in the Blue Ridge (western) section of the state, but they preferred to retain that designation rather than the Universalist.[103] The denomination never established a firm foothold in that section of Virginia, although roving preachers appeared for several decades. There was occasional preaching in Lynchburg as early as 1830 but a society was not organized until 1841. A meeting house was constructed two years later, and G.L. Lumsden moved from Accomack County in Virginia to serve as pastor.[104]

Even in eastern Virginia, concentrated in Richmond and vicinity, organized Universalism lived a precarious existence. A society was formed in Richmond in 1830, largely through the efforts of John B. Dods who was then based in Boston but spent ten weeks in Virginia.[105] He elected not to remain, and was replaced by John B. Pitkin, another New Englander. Ambitious plans to construct a church costing $10,000 were projected but by 1833 only $1,600 had been raised when Dods made a second trip to Richmond.[106] Both the formation of the society and plans to build a church were the joint efforts of the few Universalists and Unitarians then in Richmond, and the society originally bore the name "Unitarian Universalist Society of Richmond."[107] A meeting house much more modest than first planned was built in 1833. Pitkin was ordained by Bernard Whitman, a Unitarian clergyman from Waltham, Massachusetts, and Otis A. Skinner, then living in Baltimore.[108] This cooperation of clergy from the two denominations was one of the first of its kind recorded, and struck William A. Drew, editor of the *Christian Intelligencer* (Maine) as a very mysterious proceeding.[109] The name of the society was changed in 1833 to the "First Independent Christian Church." The society emphatically declared that it would be subject to the jurisdiction of no other body.[110] Pitkin died only two years after his installation, and the society experienced one trial and tribulation after another. A succession of preachers stayed only short periods, and the meeting house was closed at several intervals for the next twenty years. One attempt was made to publish a denominational paper in Richmond. In 1842 the *Christian Warrior* was established but only three volumes appeared.[111]

Some linkage was provided with northern Universalism when Jabez

Parker, the leading layman in the Richmond society, was made the corresponding secretary for Virginia when the Universalist Historical Society was organized in 1834.[112] Additional communication with Universalists outside Virginia was also provided when scattered groups in eastern and southeastern parts of the state sent delegates to Baltimore in 1835 to organize the short-lived Southern Convention.[113] A state convention was also organized in 1835 at a meeting in Gloucester County.[114] It was not a very large undertaking, with only two clergymen (Otis A. Skinner and George C. McCune) and a handful of laymen present. The main purpose was to establish circuit preaching, and McCune was ordained for that purpose. The convention was more of a dream of the future than a recognition of organizational strength, for at the time it was created, McCune was the only preacher resident in the state, and Richmond had the only society and meeting house in the state.[115] It was no wonder than when Isaac D. Williamson visited southeastern Virginia in 1839 he found the prospects for Universalism there not very encouraging. Besides the usual opposition, which was in itself bad enough, there was widespread indifference, especially among the middle and upper strata of society.[116] The original convention met no more than two or three times and was replaced in 1844 by a second one, created in Richmond and fellowshipped by the General Convention.[117]

Attempts had been made by Dods and others in the 1830s to establish societies in Williamsburg, Norfolk, and Portsmouth, but with no success at first. In Williamsburg, in spite of the fact that the historic Episcopal church of Bruton Parish had been declared public property and open to all Christian denominations, its use was refused to Universalists in 1831.[118] After Samuel P. Skinner of Baltimore had followed Dods at Williamsburg, there were thought to be sufficient Universalists to support a preacher, but none could be found.[119] Dods also preached in Gloucester, southeast of Richmond, in 1832; and was followed the next year in the Portsmouth area by L.F.W. Andrews, who had moved from Pennsylvania and travelled all over the South in the next few decades.[120] George C. McCune preached on a wide circuit and engaged in public debates in King and Queen County, east of Richmond, in 1834.[121] Otis A. Skinner visited southeastern Virginia the same year.[122]

One isolated cluster of Universalists was organized at Belle Haven (Accomack County), in that portion of the Delmar peninsula belonging to Virginia. Universalism was first preached there in 1839, and a meeting house was erected in 1841, with G.L. Lumsden as the pastor of the society, which had eighteen members in 1842.[123] John C. Burruss, a native Virginian, spent most of his life in Alabama, but visited Belle Haven and took charge of the society in 1844. It met only during warm weather because the interior of the meeting house was unfinished.

Universalism flourished in Virginia in neither urban nor rural areas. There were constant turnovers of preachers in Richmond in the east and at Lynchburg in the west, and rural societies fared no better. There were only five societies in the entire state in 1850, three of them in the urban centers of Richmond, Lynchburg, and Norfolk (organized in 1848).[124] W.R. Chamberlin (1816-1876), a native of New Hampshire, used Abingdon in the southwest corner of the state as a base, and travelled hundreds of miles up and down the Shenandoah Valley between 1848 and 1850.[125] He preached once a month at four designated stations, including log cabins, but in 1850 moved to Cincinnati after he was "nearly starved out." Although there is no record of any societies he may have organized, he did his best as an itinerant, a life which he enjoyed in spite of its hardships and privations. As he wrote in 1849, "our health is good. Our coat worn out–hat most gone–boots split out, &c, but the Lord is with us."[126]

The society in Richmond had to be rebuilt and reorganized constantly. W.N. Barber, who was apparently the first Universalist to serve as a chaplain in a southern legislature (in Virginia), attempted to revive the society in 1852.[127] But he stayed only a year and was replaced by Eliphalet Case, at a starting salary of $800.[128] James Shrigley and A. Bosserman, who between them served from 1858 until 1862, had difficulties because they supported the Union rather than the Southern cause. In fact, Bosserman was arrested for treason because he refused to open his church for a day of prayer and thanksgiving proclaimed by Jefferson Davis, president of the Confederacy, after the Battle of Manassas in 1862.[129]

The Richmond society by 1865 had no pastor, and its church building was used first by the Nazarenes and then by the Methodists before it was eventually sold.[130] Not a single society existed in the state in 1870 and the only preacher was J.L.C. Griffin, who had temporarily given up the ministry and resumed his original profession as a physician in Williamsburg.[131] In 1874 James Shrigley, who had been pastor in Richmond sixteen years earlier, attempted to supply the society on a temporary basis, but all efforts to secure a permanent minister failed, and the society finally went out of existence officially in 1875.[132] It was unable to raise the $1,000 needed to employ a minister.[133]

In that portion of Virginia which became the separate state of West Virginia in 1863, small islands of Universalists were to be found in the 1830s and 1840s, mostly in rural communities in the northern part of the state. The first Universalist meeting house known to have been built in West Virginia was in the countryside near Wheeling. A widow named Radcliff, sometime in the late 1820s or early 1830s, provided a one-acre plot for a meeting house and burial ground.[134] She had lived in the community for over sixty years and was possibly the first white woman in the area. There was occasional preaching in what was known as "Radcliff's meeting house" or as "Grave Creek" as late as 1868.[135] A second meeting house was also provided by a woman. Elizabeth Tomlinson donated both land and money at a crossroads known as Elizabethtown. A church was organized in 1837, of which she was a charter member, and was fellowshipped by the Pittsburgh Association.[136]

A society was organized in Wheeling in 1851.[137] The following year George W. Webster was installed as pastor of the Independent Congregational Church. Although known as a Unitarian church, it served "both branches of the Liberal Church" and the president of the society was "an out and out, in and out, old fashioned Bible Universalist."[138] After the Civil War a state convention was organized at Moundsville (Marshall County) in 1868, and there were three active parishes in the state in which churches had been organized: Fork Ridge (1869), Moundsville (1869), and Wheeling (1871).[139] A society at Philippi (Barbour County), organized by Thomas Jones in 1869, met in a log cabin.[140]

None of the existing societies and churches in the state had a full-time pastor in 1870. The faltering condition of the Universalist cause in West Virginia was summarized by the clerk of the state convention in 1875: "[Universalists] are so scattered and few and crippled by poverty, that not a single preacher is now supported in the State . . . . If we do not get some help from some source, we will go down. We have such hard work to raise money, and are so far from each other."[141] Still, a remnant of Universalists doggedly clung to their faith. There was one preacher in the state in 1913.

Tennessee

The story of Universalism in Tennessee by 1870 can be briefly summarized. It was a frontier state, sparsely populated, and without significant wealth or urban development before the Civil War. Most preachers, except for a few itinerants like George Rogers, were natives or had migrated from the Carolinas, Virginia, Maryland, or Georgia, and were caught up in the waves of westward migration in the 1830s and 1840s. What few Universalists there were lived among a grand mixture of denominations, predominantly Baptists, Methodists, Presbyterians, and Campbellite Christians, all of whom were revival-minded and fundamentalist in their religious outlook.[142] Almost all Universalists in the state who engaged in preaching were laymen who served on a part-time basis; few were ever fellowshipped or ordained. Most obtained their Universalism from itinerants or the reading of denominational literature. The editor of the *Trumpet* received requests from Tennessee for Universalist materials as early as 1829.[143]

Universalism on anything approaching a systematic or permanent basis did not appear in Tennessee until after 1890, and tended to be concentrated in such urban centers as Knoxville, Harriman, and Chattanooga. No associations were ever organized and the closest approximation to a state convention was a conference system centered in Chattanooga in the twentieth century.

George Rogers from Cincinnati was in 1836-37 the first Universalist itinerant preacher to visit the western part of the state.[144] He found more apathy than opposition, and decided that cock-fighting, horse racing, and camp-meeting revivals were the principal occupations outside of farming. He wandered in and out of dozens of hamlets, crossroads taverns, and plantations, speaking wherever the opportunity existed. How many societies he might have organized—if any—is completely unknown.

The oldest society of which there is a record and that had a relatively long life was established in Lauderdale County by James Crook, who had migrated from the eastern part of the state.[145] It was located at a crossroads known as Glimp (or Glimpville) which contemporary cartographers have not deigned to include on their maps. Two ex-Baptists began preaching Universalism in Springfield (Robertson County) near the Kentucky border, about 1841.[146] One, Washington Low, was identified in the first mention of Tennessee in the *Universalist Register* in 1842. Arthur Woodward in Springfield possessed a lending library of Universalist books and served as the agent for denominational periodicals in 1843.[147] Sufficient Universalists had been identified in the Knoxville area in 1842 to request a preacher, and there were at least forty Universalists in adjoining Roane County.[148] But they were too scattered and too lacking in resources to build a church. D.B. Clayton, who became one of the better known itinerants in the South both before and after the Civil War, found in the course of his travels in southwestern Tennessee in 1849 small groups of Universalists in Henderson (Chester County) and Fayetteville (Lincoln County).[149] Most had migrated from South Carolina.

There were a few Universalists known in Nashville by the mid-1840s, but no society was ever organized there. Most Universalists attended the Campbellite Christian Church and occasionally used the meeting house to listen to Universalist itinerants or conduct services led by laymen.[150] There were only four Universalist preachers in the state in 1845, and two of them were itinerants from other states.[151] Universalism was introduced into the bustling Mississippi port city of Memphis in 1844 by George Rogers.[152] A society had been organized by 1845 and Rogers secured for it the services of L.M. Gaylord. A multipurpose brick building was partially constructed in 1846, financed largely by Universalists, with services held in an upper floor. The lower floor and cellar were rented out to various businesses in order to pay for construction.[153] The building eventually became a "Varieties Theatre . . . a low place of amusement."[154] The marble slab identifying it as the "First Universalist Church of Memphis" was belatedly removed.

The major difficulty in maintaining the Memphis society was shared by others. There was a constant succession of preachers. The first remained only "a season" and his successors seldom stayed for more than one year. The society was finally suspended at the end of 1860 until the financial and political turmoil were over.[155] That seems to have been the end of organized Universalism in Memphis.

Between 1850 and 1870 from three to six Universalist preachers resided in the state, scattered from Shelby and Decatur Counties in the west to rural communities bordering Alabama and Georgia on the east. John C. Burruss, based in Alabama, was the first to preach Universalism in Chattanooga in 1857 but no church was organized until the twentieth century.[156] Fayetteville (Lincoln County) near the Alabama border, was the headquarters for several years of Robert E. Neeld and his brother William, converts from the Methodist ministry.[157] In the absence of any appropriate ecclesiastical body to conduct ordination ceremonies, when a church was organized in Fayetteville in 1850 with Allen Fuller of South Carolina present, he merely declared the Neelds to be Universalist preachers. Universalism was strictly a bootstrap operation in the state. In Nashville, J.B. Ferguson, an ex-Campbellite preacher, declared his belief in 1852 in Winchesterian Universalism; i.e., in an intermediate state between death and resurrection.[158] Without either fellowship or ordination, he conducted his own church for several years without benefit of any ecclesiastical authority. Thomas Childs, a convert from the Primitive Baptists and owner of a plantation known as Craigshead in Lincoln County, preached Universalism for twenty years (1850-1870) but he was never ordained by any agency.[159] Tennessee was not a promising field for the propagation of Universalism despite the efforts and persistence of a few hardy souls.

Kentucky

Frontiersmen with Universalist beliefs were to be found in Kentucky as early as 1793, only a year after it had been admitted to statehood. Abel Sarjent's *Free Universal Magazine* (1793-94), published first in New York and then in Baltimore, carried accounts of several individuals excommunicated from Baptist congregations for their restorationist beliefs and were referred to as "Hell Redemptionists."[160]

J. Bailey, a believer in Universalism, reported in 1793 from Lincoln County, in the center of the state, that four churches had been organized and that there were about 200 Universalists in Kentucky.[161] Peter Cartwright, best known as a Methodist circuit preacher, made numerous references, mostly uncomplimentary, to the existence of Universalists in Kentucky in the late eighteenth and early nineteenth centuries. He cited the instance of one James O'Kelly, who left the Methodist church in 1792 and organized his own, out of which came some Universalists.[162]

Cartwright noted with much satisfaction that as a result of the great Cumberland revival which swept over the frontier in 1801 that "Universalism was almost driven from the land."[163] He seems to have been correct, for the sole reference found to Universalism between that date and 1820 was to William Lowe of Simpson County on the Tennessee border. In 1819 he visited Christian County, in the southwestern part of the state, and established a church near Hopkinsville in which he preached occasionally.[164] Known as "Consolation Church," it was reorganized in 1836 by Joab Clark (1807-1882) who lived in the vicinity, near the crossroads known as Woolridge's Store. With the exception of one year in the state legislature, he spent his entire life in the county.[165] He started with a dozen members, and the congregation had increased to ninety by 1868.[166] A society near Lexington (Fayette County) was reported by a circuit preacher in 1826. He knew of only two Universalist preachers in the southern part of the state, one of whom was probably Lowe.[167]

The most numerous body of Universalists known in the state in the late 1820s was in Louisville, which until after 1850 was the unofficial headquarters of the denomination in Kentucky. Among the early preachers were Theophilus Fisk, Jonathan Kidwell, and Josiah C. Waldo.[168] A society was organized in 1827 and contributed, with the Unitarians, to the construction of a union meeting house. Upon its completion, Unitarians refused Universalists the use of it, and the latter had to meet wherever they could; they convened in a tobacco warehouse in 1829. The society fell apart, and numerous attempts by such itinerants as George Rogers were made in the 1830s to revive it. In the absence of any other vehicle for spreading Universalism in Louisville, Nathan Wadsworth opened in 1837 the Kentucky Book Union to circulate and sell denominational literature, and in true frontier fashion financed the operation by forming a stock company with shares at $10 each.[169] He also published the *Louisville Berean and Biblical Interpreter* in 1837. The montly publication lasted one year.

A society with some prospect of permanence was finally organized in Louisville in 1840, with assistance from Universalists in Cincinnati. A former Episcopal church on the Ohio River waterfront was purchased and repaired.[170] The first pastor, W.W. Dean, had left his studies at

Hamilton College, Clinton, New York, to prepare for the ministry under Stephen R. Smith, and had served his apprenticeship in Cincinnati.[171] He left Louisville in 1843 and headed farther west.

The decades of the 1830s and 1840s constituted the period of greatest local activity, but even then the societies were widely scattered and had little or no communication with each other. A society was organized in 1830 in Cynthiana, the seat of Harrison County in the north. Like many other Universalist societies in the South and on the frontier, it owed its existence and its meeting house to the efforts of one individual.[172] Other societies appeared in country locations, but most became what by the 1850s were called "preaching stations." Not one of the five preachers known to have resided in the state outside of Louisville between 1840 and 1843 was even in fellowship.[173] Machinery for licensing was finally established in the state in 1843, when a convention was organized in Louisville. There were eleven societies in the state by then.[174]

George Rogers, travelling about Kentucky in 1836 and 1837, was appalled at the illiteracy and superstition which he found everywhere, and was struck by the poverty in the rural areas.[175] Among the sects he discovered was the "Live-Forevers," who believed in man's eventual rejuvenation. They apparently saw nothing in Universalism any more attractive than what they already possessed in the way of religious belief.

The most dynamic Universalist in Kentucky in the 1840s was Enoch M. Pingree (1816-1849).[176] Born in Littleton, New Hampshire, of a Universalist family, he decided on the ministry in 1835 and after occasional preaching, moved to Cincinnati where he engaged in extensive missionary activity and preached to the Second Universalist Society. He became one of the most accomplished debaters and polemicists in the denomination. According to those who knew him, the rough frontier environment "eventually transformed him."[177] A quiet and reserved New Englander when he arrived, Pingree became a combative and formidable opponent in debate and exhibited "an excited manner of delivery." This was, as an Ohio preacher pointed out, the key to success, for it was "the only style of speaking that succeeds well in Kentucky, where almost every man becomes a 'stump speaker' from his youth."[178]

Pingree assumed the Louisville pastorate in 1843, and the church grew rapidly under his administration. Thanks to his fund-raising efforts, a new brick church was immediately constructed, with a seating capacity of 600.[179] By 1845 the number of church members in Kentucky societies ranged from six in a rural community like one in Shelby County to 102 in Louisville.[180] A second society was organized in Louisville in 1847 but lasted less than a year.[181] Lay support came from William B. Chamberlain of Warsaw (Gallatin County), a physician who offered to donate a library of Universalist books to every society organized during 1844.[182] Only one, in Hancock County, was recorded that year.[183]

Pingree was an unusually capable organizer and administrator and was responsible not only for the creation of the state convention in 1843 but for the three associations organized in the next two years.[184] Most Universalists by the mid-1840s were to be found in the northern counties. When John A. Gurley, editor of the *Star in the West* in Cincinnati, toured Kentucky in 1844 he found almost none in the southern counties.[185] Plans for an association in northern Kentucky had been discussed in 1836 at a meeting held in a rural community in Hardin County, but nothing happened.[186] But as soon as Pingree arrived on the scene he divided the state into three jurisdictions. The Licking River Association was organized in 1844 in the northeast; the Murray Association in the north and central section, including Louisville, in 1845; and the Green River Association the same year, for the southern and western counties. The latter association had disappeared by the mid-1850s, and in 1858 all of the state was divided on a north-south basis between the Licking River and Pingree Associations.[187] Pingree had died in 1849, at the age of thirty-three, and the Universalist cause in the state suffered accordingly. After his death a new association had been organized in 1850 named in his honor. It was revived after being suspended during the Civil War, and in 1875 became the nucleus of a new state convention.

The denomination in Kentucky from 1850 to 1870 made but little progress, although there were occasional meetings which were well attended. The state convention held a mass meeting in 1851 which was described as the largest yet held.[188] An estimated 800 were present, but everything was reported as quiet and orderly, in sharp contrast to those held by other denominations. The society in Louisville fell upon hard times after Pingree's leadership was lost. Isaac D. Williamson served briefly (1852-54); Theodore Clapp, a well-known independent preacher from New Orleans, supplied the church for several years, but died in 1866. He was never fellowshipped in the denomination. The Louisville society disappeared during the Civil War period and sold its church building. The remnants of the congregation merged with the Unitarians in 1870 and put the proceeds from the sale into the Unitarian church.[189]

Many preachers left the state or the denomination after 1845. C.B. Tharp, an ex-Campbellite preacher, resigned his Universalist affiliation in 1849 and returned to his original denomination in a fit of pique.[190] A Universalist neighbor had refused to furnish slaves to work on his property while he was absent on a preaching tour.[191]

There was no denominational paper published in Louisville in the

1850s. Those in the area, the *Star in the West* and the *Gospel Herald* (Indiana) served what few Universalists there were. Two schools were operated by Universalists in Kentucky, but one was a private affair, and the other closed almost as soon as it opened. Nathan Kendall and his sister had operated the Mount Washington Academy (Bullitt County) in 1848.[192] In 1856 the First Universalist Church of Boone County laid plans to operate the Kentucky Liberal Institute near Covington.[193] The coeducational academy opened in 1857 with J.D.H. Corwine as the principal.[194] It was chartered as Union College in 1858, but apparently ceased operation about the same time.[195]

After 1850 the focus of Universalism shifted to rural areas. By the time of the Civil War the only churches "in an organized condition" were to be found in the countryside.[196] It was there that Universalism was revived after 1865. Small churches in Christian, McLean, and Caldwell Counties comprised the Pingree Association in 1868. All of the clergy, few in number, had secular occupations, preached only occasionally, and "somewhat promiscuously."[197] Most of the churches were really nothing more than preaching stations by 1870, with a total of 385 individuals claiming formal membership in the denomination.[198] When the Pingree Association met in 1872 there were representatives from four churches, all in rural locations.[199] Organized Universalism in Kentucky was struggling to survive.

Missouri

It was comparatively easy to migrate from the adjoining states of Tennessee, Kentucky, and Illinois into Missouri in the second quarter of the nineteenth century, or to come from as far away as New England and the Middle Atlantic area, as thousands had done by 1840. Universalists were first known among a colony of Dunkers in Troy (Lincoln County), just west of the Mississippi River and not far from St. Louis. There was a church at least by 1839, when J.P. Fuller was serving as their pastor.[200] Unlike the Dunkers in Pennsylvania and the Shenandoah Valley, those in Missouri were "open and avowed Universalists" and were baptized by immersion. George Rogers preached three times in Troy in 1843, in the courthouse, and found the Universalists small in number and lacking in wealth but "strong in purpose."[201] A high proportion of the population consisted of transplanted Yankees.[202]

A second Universalist society was organized in 1841, this time in St. Louis.[203] N.M. Gaylord, a Dunker, served as the pastor, and had gone to Missouri at the request of John A. Gurley of Cincinnati.[204] A church was organized in St. Louis in 1845 but it failed to hold together until George S. Weaver arrived in 1851, after occasional preaching by Erasmus Manford.[205]

L.C. Marvin became the first preacher in Boonville (Cooper County), in the very center of the state, where a society was organized in 1843.[206] The first Universalist meeting house in the state was dedicated at St. Charles, on the Missouri River, in 1842.[207] It was not until 1850 that the Universalists in Troy erected a meeting house, a substantial brick edifice, but there was no regular preacher at the time.[208] Thomas Abbott was responsible for establishing the first society in the western part of the state, near Kansas City and the Kansas border.[209] Few of the first preachers, almost all of them originally from states farther east and north, remained more than a year or two. Of the five preachers reported in the state in 1850, only one (Gaylord) had resided there eight years before.

Universalists could be counted on to establish denominational papers almost everywhere they went, and those in Missouri were no exception. Marvin in Boonville published the *Faithful Witness,* a semi-monthly, in 1846, but he had neither the resources nor the subscribers to support it; it lasted only one year.[210] Erasmus Manford settled in St. Louis in 1851 and began publication of the *Golden Era,* a monthly which lasted until 1855, when it was merged into what became the *Herald and Era* in Madison, Indiana. Manford then started *Manford's Monthly Magazine,* which was moved to Chicago in 1864 and lasted for another twenty years.

The reluctance of Universalists to organize in Missouri at even the most basic level is illustrated by the fact that throughout most of the 1850s there were seldom more than four societies active at any one time, although there was considerable occasional preaching by as many as nine clergymen. Even though three of the seven preachers in the state lived in St. Louis at the end of the decade, Manford and Weaver were busy editing newspapers or were on the road, and Thomas Abbott attempted to serve the local society. Dunkers continued to swell Universalist ranks from time to time. A German Baptist church led by J.H. Miller joined in 1859.[211] There were Universalists more or less organized in about twelve counties by 1860, so the Northwestern Association was created that year in an attempt to encourage cooperation.[212] It also included counties in Kansas bordering on the Missouri River.

Missouri, as a border state, was badly divided over the issues of slavery and the maintenance of the Union, and Universalism suffered greatly as a result. As was true in other border states such as Virginia, Unionist sentiment was strong among the preachers, so far as the imperfect records indicate. Many projects had to be abandoned because of the unsettled state of affairs. Paul R. Kendall came to Missouri from Illinois in 1859 to open a denominational academy in a village in Platte

County, on the Missouri River a few miles north of Kansas City.[213] But he found himself caught up in the tensions of the time and discarded the idea. He became a recruiting officer for the Union army and was commissioned as a quartermaster. After the Civil War he became principal of Clinton Liberal Institute and president of Smithson College. Universalists in St. Louis had high hopes of building a new church, and toward that end the women in the congregation had collected $2,000 by 1860.[214] But war clouds descended on the city and destroyed all prospects. Half a century later, there were fifteen Universalist families known to reside in St. Louis, and they were without either a pastor or a church building.[215]

An effort was made in Missouri, as in all Southern and border states after the Civil War, to regroup the Universalists who had been dispersed by the conflict. An inventory was taken in 1868 by the General Secretary of the General Convention, with very disappointing results.[216] Nine clergy had been reported in the *Universalist Register* in 1868. Two letters of inquiry were returned unclaimed; L.C. Marvin, one of the first to preach in the state, had long since ceased, and had no information at all; five letters remained unanswered. One clergyman reported preaching on a monthly basis to two societies. A combined Universalist-Unitarian society in the Missouri Valley had adopted the Winchester Profession and called themselves the "Conference of Liberal Christians." It was on the basis of such fragmentary and imperfect knowledge that Universalism had to be rebuilt.

A start was made in 1868 when a state convention was organized at Brookfield (Linn County), and the Northwestern Association was revived in 1869. But the church in St. Louis had disappeared and there was only one full-time clergyman in the state in 1870, Stephen Hull in Brookfield in the northern part of the state.[217] A society had been organized there in 1860. As happened so often in the border and southern states, Universalism in Missouri had become more the story of preaching stations than of flourishing churches and active parishes.

Chapter 26

"A LITTLE BUT DETERMINED BAND:" THE SOUTH

In the spring of 1827, just a matter of weeks before a scattering of Universalists participated in an abortive attempt to organize a Southern Convention in North Carolina (lasting less than a year), William A. Drew, editor of the *Christian Intelligencer* in Gardiner, Maine, commented that "Liberal Christianity has never flourished so well at the South as it has among us at the North."[1] This assessment was quite accurate, if the historical record is to be trusted. Between the late eighteenth century and the Civil War, small footholds were obtained and in many instances retained, but the denomination acquired neither the stature nor numerical strength there that it attained in New England, upstate New York, or parts of the Midwest. It was, and has been, as the circuit preacher George Rogers recorded in his autobiography in 1845, a "neglected region."[2]

When plans were discussed at the General Convention in 1857 to establish a denominational fund to publish newspapers and support colleges, they were projected exclusively on an East-West axis. The South was disregarded.[3] Scholarly research has likewise been meager, and very little attention has been paid to Universalism in the South.[4] Yet Universalism not only did exist in the South as early as the eighteenth century, but was identifiable well into the twentieth. Two of the five state conventions still operating in the mid-1970s had been initially organized long before the Civil War, and had continuous histories since the opening of the twentieth century; and, although comprising only a small handful of active churches tracing their origins back to the 1830s and 1840s, they doggedly survived and, with more or less reluctance, joined forces with the Unitarian Universalist Association in 1961 and thereafter.

Handicapped in the nineteenth century by geography, lack of sufficient clergy, inadequate financial support, indifference and opposition within the region, unwillingness to engage wholeheartedly in the revivalistic activities of many of their fellow Protestants, a growing divergence with their northern brothers over slavery, and eventually by the disruption of civil war, Universalism remained a relatively insignificant factor in the religious life of the South before 1865.

Both Northern and Southern Universalists in the ante-bellum period offered explanations from time to time to account for this situation. A.B. Grosh, editor of the *Universalist Register,* attributed the failure of Universalism to prosper in the South to the sparseness of the population and to "the want of general intelligence among the poorer classes."[5] Without question, Universalists in the South met the same opposition as their brethren elsewhere, from pen, pulpit, and neighbor. A Baptist revival meeting in the South in 1838 was told that "the Atheists, Deists, Infidels, Roman Catholics and Universalists" in the North had joined forces to do away with the use of the Bible.[6]

But the existence of slavery became the culprit and was most frequently cited by nineteenth-century Universalists, especially by those in the North. Thomas J. Sawyer of New York paid tribute in 1847 to those Universalist societies which did exist in the South, but put the blame for their slow progress squarely on slavery.[7] Universalism would make no headway there, according to Sawyer, as long as the majority of Southerners saw "no moral deformity in a system of human slavery," and were therefore ill-fitted to appreciate a religion which taught men "to behold in every human being a neighbor and a brother." At the General Convention held in Galesburg, Illinois, in 1866 (at which no delegate from the South was present), the standing Committee on Education offered the same explanation.[8] Under a slave system which had created a "barbarous" society, with "the operation of laws unequal, civil government flagrantly and shamelessly unjust, and Christianity a name only and a mockery," it was no wonder, readers of the committee's annual report were told, that "our peculiar form of faith never had, and never could have had any general influence." But Universalism's very existence testified to its appeal to some Southerners, and its continued efforts to maintain denominational identity after that date were evidence, if nothing else, of roots planted long in the past.

Southern Universalism before the Civil War derived from four major sources, aside from independent discovery by individual interpretation of the Bible and familiarity with Universalist publications which appeared, by one avenue or another, in even the remotest corners of the region. The earliest sources of Southern Universalism were to be found among the English Baptist splinter groups such as the General Baptists and Seventh Day Baptists who had established churches in Virginia and the Carolinas by the first quarter of the eighteenth century.[9] They believed in an eventual general redemption, and for the most part rejected the Calvinism held by the majority of Baptists. Between about 1750 and 1770, most of the General Baptist churches in the South joined the mainstream of the denomination, due largely to the missionary efforts of the Calvinistic Baptists who operated out of Philadelphia. It was among those who remained believers in eventual general salvation that the seeds of Universalism were planted, particularly in the Carolinas.

A more significant source of Universalism, numerically and in terms of later influence, derived from two streams of German migration which converged in interior sections of the Carolinas in the mid-eighteenth century, including particularly the Dunkards who had moved south and east from the Philadelphia area in the second quarter of the eighteenth century. The third source comprised the northern Universalists, mostly clergymen, who migrated south and remained, and who joined their efforts with their Southern-born colleagues. The fourth contribution to the spread and persistence of Universalism in the South consisted of the families and descendants of the original settlers of that persuasion who eventually fanned out into the then-frontier areas of Tennessee, Georgia, Mississippi, western Florida, and Texas. A high proportion had South Carolina origins.[10]

South Carolina

The first colonies of Protestant Palatinate and Swiss Germans to arrive in the South, beginning in 1709, had settled at New Bern, North Carolina and Charleston, South Carolina. Their descendants gradually moved inland, where they Anglicized their names (or found them changed by their English, Scotch-Irish, or other non-German neighbors), established prosperous but often isolated agricultural communities, and after 1745 were joined by their numerically larger and more distinctively pietistic fellow-Germans from Pennsylvania. Many of the family names of these early settlers from both the coast and from Pennsylvania are to be found in the records of both nineteenth- and twentieth-century Universalist societies; e.g., Grum (Croom), Pfister (Feaster), Kohlman (Coleman), Breuer (Brewer), and Somer (Summer).[11]

Among the numerous German sects which had been attracted to America by William Penn's offer of religious freedom and economic opportunity in the late seventeenth and early eighteenth centuries were the Mennonites, the Moravians, the Schwenkfelders, and the Dunkards. Many of the Mennonites, the first to arrive, settled in what became Lancaster County, Pennsylvania, where Universalism was also being extensively preached by the 1830s and in which two societies had by then been organized.[12] A contingent of Moravians (Evangelical Brethren), who had first settled in Georgia in 1735, moved to

Pennsylvania five years later, and in 1753 had established the Wachovia settlements of Bathabara and Salem, North Carolina. The Schwenkfelders first appeared in Pennsylvania in 1734.

Of all the German groups, it was the Dunkards whose early history in America was most closely associated with Universalist beginnings in the Middle Atlantic region and the South. It was among the Dunkards, whose beginnings in America dated from two migrations (1719 and 1730) totalling fifty families, many of whom settled initially at Germantown, Pennsylvnaia, that George de Benneville had spent much of his life. The Dunkards were commonly called by others Dunkers, Tunkers, Tumblers, Taufers, Tunkards, Dumplers, and Dippers because their distinctive form of baptism consisted of trine immersion, face forward, preferably in a flowing stream. However, they called themselves the Church of the Brethren and were often referred to as the German Baptists or German Baptist Brethren.[13]

Like the Universalists, the Dunkards refused to develop an elaborate creed, emphasized the centrality of the Bible as a guide to belief and behavior, believed in man's general redemption and ultimate salvation (although not generally preached as an article of faith), placed much emphasis on lay preaching with little or no material compensation expected therefor, and made little effort to keep a record of the number of communicants. Elhanan Winchester, in a work published in 1787, expressed great admiration for the sect and preached in several of its churches.[14]

Of the thirty-odd Dunkard churches known to have existed in the United States in 1790, at least ten were to be found in the South, concentrated in South Carolina, and several had become Universalist by then.[15] Dunkards were never so numerous in North Carolina as in the neighboring state; there were three churches with a total of about 100 members in 1770, but only two were known to exist at the time of the outbreak of the Civil War.[16] Small clusters of Dunkards settled in southwestern South Carolina in Fairfield, Newberry, Abbeville, Lexington, Laurens, Anderson, and Saluda counties (then districts), and it is there that Universalists organized the most numerous societies in the state, some persisting into the twentieth century.[17]

The extensive German influence in the early settlements is seen in Lexington District. It was originally known as Saxe-Gotha and was renamed by a patriotic nineteenth-century state legislature in commemoration of the famous skirmish associated with the beginning of the American Revolution.[18] The first Dunkard church of which there is a record to profess Universalism openly was the congregation of Liberty Meeting House, Fairfield District, in 1778. David Martin, the pastor for many years and a native of Pennsylvania, came to doubt the doctrine of eternal punishment and preached Universalism for at least seven years thereafter, until his death at the age of seventy.[19] Instead of disowning him, the congregation followed him into Universalism. Almost simultaneously, and probably independently, Elhanan Winchester, who had moved from Massachusetts to South Carolina in 1774, was becoming "half a convert" to Universalism by the time of his departure from the South in 1779.[20] It was while he had charge of a Baptist church at Welsh Neck, on the Pee Dee River in that colony, that he read Siegvolck's *Everlasting Gospel.*

One of the converts in Martin's congregation, Giles Chapman, a saddler who had migrated from his native Virginia and who wore his beard long as was the custom among Dunkers, had begun preaching Universalism by 1782, and engaged in a far-flung itinerant ministry not only in South Carolina but in adjoining areas of western North Carolina until his death in 1819 at the age of about seventy-five. Described by a Baptist as "an eloquent and gifted preacher," he was reputed to have married more couples than any other clergyman in the vicinity.[21] It was said that he would never take more than $1.00 for conducting the service. John Ham, a Dunkard, was also known to have preached Universalism in both Carolinas, beginning about 1790.[22]

Universalism had appeared in sufficient strength by 1792 to prompt the Presbyterian General Assembly, through the Synod of the Carolinas, to condemn the doctrine officially and to repeat the condemnation two years later.[23] An additional recruit from the same church that had produced Martin and Chapman was Elijah Linch, who in 1797 was the last member of the congregation to join in accordance with the Dunkard ceremony.[24] In 1805 Linch began preaching Universalism, and for many years before his death in 1842, was the only Universalist preacher in the state.[25] One by one, previous Dunkard churches became Universalist; by 1835 there were at least five such societies in the central and western parts of the state.[26]

With the exception of South Carolina, Universalists seldom exploited the possibilities of recruiting Dunkards for the denomination in spite of the fact that the latter were to be found in small numbers in widely scattered areas of the United States in the nineteenth century. Universalists were much pleased in 1833 when one Dunkard preacher in the community of Welch Run, Pennsylvania, declared his Universalism openly; his avowal "was received with manifest applause by all his congregation."[27] In 1837 the itinerant George Rogers spoke to a group of "Tunkers" near Jackson, Tennessee and received a warm welcome.[28] He found in that section of the state (where their neighbor, Davy Crockett, represented them in Congress) that they were not only called Universalists, but used that designation to describe themselves; they saw no advantage in changing their denominational allegiance. The editor of the *Universalist Register* pointed out that by the late 1830s Dunkards not only lived in such western states as Illinois and Missouri, but were "open and avowed Universalists."[29] In fact, he was convinced that there were hundreds of others among the German Baptists who believed in universal salvation but hesitated to proclaim it publicly.[30]

A Universalist informed Hosea Ballou in 1839 that he had attended the annual meeting of the Dunkards in the Midwest held in the vicinity of Quincy, Illinois, with about 800 present.[31] They professed their Universalism openly, and had declined formal fellowship with their Pennsylvania brethren because the latter had refused to do so. As late as 1879, John C. Burruss, editor of the *Universalist Herald*, recommended that the General Convention appoint a committee "to confer with the Dunkard brethren in regard to the feasibility of having them unite with us."[32] No systematic attempt was ever made, however, to tap this potential source of Universalist strength.

Universalism, despite an early start and occasional bursts of activity, did not flourish in South Carolina. The churches, which became small organizations identified with particular families in each area, had but little population upon which to draw for increased membership and their rural isolation tended to give them a static, if not stagnant, character. Further, there was constant opposition to be faced from more orthodox neighbors. Jacob Frieze, then living in Wilmington, North Carolina, made a trip in 1827 into the interior of both that state and South Carolina, and was much discouraged by the hostile reception he encountered.[33] He found all non-Universalist meeting houses closed to him, and had to meet either in the open air or in court houses; private homes were too small because news of his presence in a neighborhood at least provoked curiosity.

One of the major difficulties was the reluctance to organize societies or churches at all. Further, there were often no Universalist preachers in many counties, and even when circuit preaching was provided after 1830, Universalists had to depend on denominational publications and occasional meetings among themselves for spiritual sustenance. Probably in no other section of the nation was lay participation in Universalist concerns greater than in the South, and notably in the Carolinas. Necessity as well as conviction required it.

Until 1827 there was no formal linkage among the ex-Dunkard congregations which became the nucleus of Universalism in South Carolina. In that year, the creation of the Southern Convention in North Carolina encouraged the organization of societies or churches which could be fellowshipped with it.[34] However, nothing was accomplished in South Carolina until 1830, after the Southern Convention had disappeared. In 1830 delegates from congregations in four districts (counties), and one representative from Charleston, organized the South Carolina Convention of Universalists at Hartford meeting house, Newberry District.[35] In the same year, two Universalist societies were organized out of ex-Dunkard congregations—one in

Fairfield District and one in Newberry District. The first was located in the community of Feasterville, founded by Andrew Pfister (Feaster), who had been a German Swiss immigrant from Berne and a Dunkard preacher; he had migrated from Lancaster County, Pennsylvania about 1780, and settled in South Carolina after a brief residence in Georgia. He died in 1821, aged eighty-six. A son, John, frequently served as a lay delegate to state conventions, and built Liberty Church on land which he donated. It was the original congregation of this church, founded by the Dunkards in 1749, that had been converted to Universalism by David Martin, and was the oldest Universalist church in South Carolina.[36]

Joseph W. Summers, originally from Maryland and a Dunkard, was the patriarch of the first Universalist society to be organized in Newberry District, and was elected the first standing clerk of the South Carolina Convention.[37] This society had become Universalist by 1823, when two and one-half acres a few miles south of the village of Newberry were conveyed to four trustees, one of whom was Summers.[38] The network of early family connections in the area is illustrated by the fact that Summers was Giles Chapman's father-in-law.

Although no society had yet been organized in Lexington, Laurens, or Anderson Districts, Universalists in each sent delegates to the organization meeting of the Convention in 1830. Societies were organized in these districts in 1831, 1832, and 1834 respectively. Unlike Universalist practice in most other areas, meeting houses in the South were frequently built or acquired before societies came into being. In South Carolina this was the case with the Fredonia meeting house (Newberry District), built in 1835 and "open to all professing to be Christians"; and the meeting house at Bathabara (Laurens District), where there had originally been a Dunkard congregation. Newberry District had the greatest number of meeting houses before the Civil War. There were four, all within a few miles of each other, and all were in the countryside rather than in the village of Newberry itself, which was the county seat. Only the one at Feasterville was still standing by 1888.[39]

When the South Carolina Convention was organized and a confession of faith adopted, only one ordained minister was present—Elijah Linch of Newberry; he and J.L.E.W. Shecut of Charleston, a physician and a lay preacher, conducted the services.[40] The convention, which managed to meet annually through 1860, expended most of its efforts in securing and retaining a circuit preacher for the loosely organized groups of Universalists and attempting to provide "a living patronage" for him, and urging, usually unsuccessfully, the establishment of societies and the organization of churches.[41]

Allen Fuller's services were obtained, beginning in 1831, to supplement the labors of Elijah Linch, but his compensation was erratic and pledges made were seldom fulfilled in their entirety. Fuller, who at first made the village of Newberry his headquarters, was on the road constantly, attempting to organize new societies or revive dormant ones.[42] Of the various denominations, he found the Baptists most numerous; in fact, in some places it had "become so fashionable to join the Baptist church . . . that almost every individual of a settlement has united with it."[43]

Fuller lived the life of a typical circuit preacher in the ante-bellum South. During one ten-week period in 1834 he found time and energy to travel over 800 miles, and to preach in thirteen places in South Carolina, Georgia, and Alabama.[44] In 1832 he had become "occasional preacher" for a society organized by laymen in Laurens District under the leadership of Joshua Teague, and two years later he preached to the remnants of the original Dunkard group to which David Martin and Giles Chapman had ministered. They had heard no Universalist preaching since the death of Chapman fifteen years before.[45] Fuller frequently preached "under the broad canopy of Heaven," either because he was denied the use of meeting houses of other denominations or, as sometimes happened, no building was sufficiently commodious to hold his listeners.

Thanks to the efforts of L.F.W. Andrews of Alabama, who visited South Carolina in 1834, a society of nineteen members was organized in Anderson District, with a new meeting house which was dedicated when the state convention met there that year.[46] The new society, which attained a maximum membership of thirty-five, did produce one new minister. James Mullikin received a letter of fellowship at the 1834 convention and was ordained by that body four years later; he served in the Anderson District.[47] In 1840 Fuller resigned from his circuit preaching assignment for family reasons and moved to Pickens County, the westernmost county in the state; his new home was a crossroads which was christened "Salubrity" by the post office, and where he served as the first postmaster.[48] However, Fuller continued to be a "travelling preacher" and to serve as the clerk of the state convention until his removal to Alabama in 1851.

While serving as the convention circuit preacher, Fuller met with all kinds of discouragements, from inadequate support to sometimes fruitless attempts to revive societies which showed signs of life when he appeared but disappeared as soon as his visits were over. In 1838 the convention collected in his behalf from four societies the munificent sum of $250 for his services; the societies in Lexington and Laurens Districts had ceased to function that same year, in spite of his efforts to keep them alive.[49] The 1838 convention also had authorized the establishment of thirteen "preaching stations," with the expectation that each would have the services of a clergyman at least four times each year.[50]

South Carolina Universalists attempted to maintain contact with the main body of the denomination in the North, although regular communication was not always maintained. The *Trumpet* in Boston sometimes failed to carry the state convention proceedings, and Universalists in New England and elsewhere either remained uninformed or depended on other denominational papers for news about the South. New England Universalists learned that the South Carolina Convention in 1832 had approved the creation of the General Convention by reading the *Impartialist* (New Hampshire) and the *Christian Intelligencer* (Maine).[51] In 1833 the state convention appointed only three delegates (all laymen) to the newly-created General Convention, explaining that they could not comply with the constitutional provision for ministerial delegates "without borrowing a few clerical brethren from some distant part of the country."[52] None of the lay delegates from the state was able to attend the meeting, which was held in Strafford, Vermont, that year. In 1834 the state convention completely forgot to appoint delegates to the General Convention.[53] In the thirty years of the South Carolina Convention's existence, only three delegates attended meetings of the General Convention, and two of these were already in the North on other business. Even then, South Carolina was the only southern state ever officially represented by a delegate before the Civil War.

Even closer home, difficulties were encountered in securing attendance from various societies. Universalists in Abbeville and Anderson Districts were not represented in the convention until 1833, and even annual rotation of meetings at society locations failed to bring satisfactory attendance. The convention that year, which was held at the Bethabara meeting house in Laurens District, was attended by only eleven delegates besides the two clergymen in the area (Linch and Fuller).[54]

The convention had to contend with other difficulties besides apathy. The population of the state continued to be very much in flux, and Universalists, like their neighbors, were constantly on the move in search of better land or enhanced economic opportunity. They found themselves also competing with other denominations for attendance at the public services conducted in connection with convention meetings. Those held in 1833 were sparsely attended in part because the Baptists had just concluded a "protracted" meeting of seven days, and people were weary of church-going.[55] At the meeting in 1835, held in the Hartford meeting house in Newberry District, only three of the six societies in the convention sent delegates. The best-attended meeting in the history of the convention up to that time occurred in 1839, with no less than five clergy (one a visitor from Georgia) and thirty-two lay delegates present. For the first time in almost a decade, Universalists in Charleston were represented.

Universalists in eastern South Carolina never had more than minimal contact with their brethren in the western part of the state. They were not only separated from their fellow Universalists in the interior by distance–some 170 rugged miles–but they struggled with problems of organization and survival quite different from those at the other end of the state. The emergence of organized Universalism in Charleston had, in fact, a unique history in several respects. Although it had been first preached in Charleston by Richard Clarke, pastor of St. Philips Church (Anglican) between 1754 and 1759, Universalism did not take root for three-quarters of a century.[56] It was the Unitarians who first introduced liberal religion into Charleston on a sustained basis, and when Universalists finally organized, they expressed trinitarian rather than unitarian theology.

The first Universalists had appeared in Charleston about 1789, but were afraid to profess their beliefs publicly.[57] With no clergy to provide leadership, some probably attended existing churches, including the Congregational and, after 1817, the Unitarian.[58] At least a semblance of a society was created in 1824, with a declaration of faith; they called themselves "Bible Universalists."[59] Three years later, in 1827, "three gentlemen privately formed the 'Association of Universalists in Charleston' " and held weekly meetings in the office of one of them, J.L.E.W. Shecut. They published a pamphlet in 1829 in which they designated themselves as the "Primitive Apostolic Church of Trinitarian Universalists in the City of Charleston."[60] This nomenclature was abandoned in 1830, when Paul Dean of Boston visited Charleston and organized "The First Universalist Society" and accepted the office and title of "Bishop."[61] Two years earlier, Dean had ostensibly resigned from the denomination and had become a leader in the Massachusetts Restorationist Association.

The Charleston society was sufficiently active by 1832 to purchase a site in the center of the city on which to build a church.[62] However, the society (the membership of which is unknown) led an uncertain existence for several years, was without a settled pastor for most of the period before the Civil War, and had to depend on occasional preaching by visiting clergy. It was not until 1838 that a building was finally constructed and 1839 that Albert Case's services were obtained to strengthen the faltering society.[63] After 1844 the society again found itself without a regular pastor and in 1856 the church building was sold and later razed.[64] Universalists in Charleston apparently lost their identity as a group after the Civil War; most of the surviving members of the society attended the Unitarian church to which in 1869 they lent their remaining funds.[65] In South Carolina, as elsewhere in the South, it was the rural Universalist societies that were destined to survive the longest, although they never really prospered.

While the Charleston church was falling upon hard times in the 1840s, Universalists farther west were making but modest progress. A small contingent was assembled in Edgefield District in 1841 when John A. Chapman, of a long-standing Universalist family, became the preacher at Coleman's Crossroads after having been fellowshipped by the state convention that year.[66] After Fuller's departure, L.F.W. Andrews served briefly in Feasterville and in 1842 a young preacher, Daniel Bragg Clayton from Spartanburg County, who had been excommunicated by the Baptist church for his Universalism, appeared at the state convention.[67] He was destined to become one of the best known and most widely travelled of the Universalist circuit preachers in the South in the nineteenth century.

Andrews, who eventually settled in Georgia after serving in Alabama for several years, immediately attracted a loyal following while residing in South Carolina and was indirectly responsible for the erection of a meeting house in Abbeville District in 1844. In that year an elderly and wealthy Universalist named Partlow died. His three sons insisted that Andrews conduct the funeral service. Having been refused the use of the nearby Baptist church because Partlow had been a Universalist, the brothers arranged to have their own meeting house built. Within four weeks, the timber was cut and hauled to the mill, the lumber was sawed, and the church built in which a memorial service was conducted.[68] The state convention met there in 1845, at which time Clayton was ordained by Fuller, one of whose sermons Clayton had heard in 1838. It was this experience that had turned him to Universalism and it was Fuller who had assisted him in preparing for the ministry by lending books and offering advice.[69]

But even with the addition of Clayton to the ranks, Universalism failed to hold its own in western South Carolina. Deaths, removals, opposition, apathy, and failure to organize the churches that would have brought more religious discipline, all hindered positive development. Linch's services had been lost by death in 1842, Chapman resigned in 1845 from the fellowship of the state convention, and Clayton moved to Mississippi in 1846.[70] A few lay preachers appeared from time to time, but had little influence. The greatest blow came in 1851, when Fuller moved from the state. E.H. Lake, a native of Massachusetts who had moved south for his health, settled temporarily in Fairfield District but changed his residence to North Carolina after a brief sojourn in the Feasterville community.

At the 1857 convention an attempt was made to raise $800 to finance a circuit preacher.[71] Two years later, the search for both money and a preacher was still in progress, the effort of the previous year having been unsuccessful. Because only $750 had been pledged in 1858, no preacher was obtainable and the pledges were voided.[72] The convention, meeting at the Huntsville church (Laurens District), called for "an entire reconstruction of church organization," considering church discipline "almost imperative" and almost completely lacking at the time. The only immediate concrete result of the plea was the organization of the Huntsville church during the convention out of the group of Universalists residing there.[73]

Very little progress was made from 1859 to the outbreak of the Civil War. John C.C. Feaster was joined by J.L.C. Griffin in 1859 as itinerant preacher in the five counties in the western part of the state, together with S.M. Simons in the Lexington area, but none was financed by the convention.[74] Only one of the five clergymen present at the Feasterville church at the 1860 convention (Griffin) was resident in the state.[75] The eighteen laymen at the convention represented only a half-dozen families, and most of these were from one of the two churches in existence at the time (Feasterville and Huntsville).[76] Both churches became dormant during the Civil War; the Feasterville church was revived in 1872 through the efforts of D.B. Clayton and continued to exist, with occasional preaching, into the 1880s.[77] Another meeting of the convention was scheduled to convene in Feasterville in 1861, but never took place. The South Carolina Convention, as an organization, had come to an end, for it was never revived after the Civil War.

The failure of Universalism to spread in South Carolina before 1865 beyond its basically Dunkard origins and family-oriented societies was due, according to contemporary accounts, not so much to overwhelming opposition as to aversion to organization and religious discipline. At the time of the convention meeting in 1857, there was only one organized Universalist church in the entire state (Feasterville).[78] This situation was blamed at least in part on the refusal or reluctance of those Universalists who had come out of Dunkard congregations to submit to any church discipline at all.[79] In addition, clergy were "too few and too far between," and those that did appear seldom found it possible to support themselves and their families at more than a subsistence level; they either gave up the ministry altogether or migrated to more promising areas.[80] The same story could be writ large for Universalism in the entire South. There was only one newspaper to cover the entire area by 1861; while hundreds of clergymen were active in other portions of the nation, only a dozen or so were to be found in the South in as many states. The high hopes of the 1820s and 1830s had just not been realized.

Georgia

The first known preaching of Universalism in Georgia occurred about 1795, when one Philip Gibbs appeared in the central part of the state (Warren and Hancock Counties).[81] He and his followers were called "Hell-redemptioners" and were held in "great contempt" by their neighbors. Gibbs, who died in 1810, was the author of a pamphlet in the form of a will bequeathing the heritage of the restitution of all men to its readers.[82]

In 1802 two brothers in the same area of central Georgia, John and Thomas Mitchell, left the Methodist church and publicly avowed their Universalist beliefs. The second publication known to have appeared in Georgia announcing the salvation of all men was written by Isaac Eilands, who was living in the vicinity of Milledgeville in 1816. He was known to have been an admirer of John Murray and his ideas.[83] Michael Smith, who had migrated from Lexington, Kentucky to Milledgeville, then the state capital, was preaching Universalism by 1825, and edited a newspaper, the *Star of the South.* Smith also published, while in Milledgeville, a work edited by Russell Canfield of Hartford, Connecticut, entitled *Light of Truth, and the Pleasure of Light,* originally published in Hartford. It was said to have been "a mere plagiarism" of several Universalist authors.[84]

Before the end of the 1820s, Universalist newspapers from other sections of the country were arriving in Georgia, sent to postmasters for distribution and solicitation of subscriptions.[85] Universalists had appeared in sufficient numbers in central Georgia by then to cause concern to Methodist and Baptist preachers there.[86] The editor of the *Star of the South* reported many more Universalists than he had first thought were in the vicinity, and sent a "circular solicitation" to Universalists in the East for ministers to come south.[87] Meanwhile, "a few scattered believers" were found elsewhere in the state by Allen Fuller, who had been employed by the South Carolina Convention in 1831 and who travelled extensively in Georgia the following year.

The decade of the 1830s saw the first permanent results of Universalist activity in Georgia. The first Universalist meeting house in the state was erected in 1834, in Harris County. The building, which was located near the Mulberry Grove Post Office in a settlement known as Mitchell's Mills, was made necessary because the Universalists in the community had been denied the use of the nearby Methodist church. The Methodist preacher complained that Universalists were desecrating the neighborhood by holding meetings in the home of one of the Mitchell family which was within sight of the Methodist church.[88] The new structure was known as a "Republican" meeting house because it was to be free to the use of all denominations. Almost simultaneously, plans were announced to erect or acquire meeting houses in other rural communities. One was projected near Zebulon (Pike County) and another at Monroe (Alton County).[89] In 1835 a Baptist church was purchased at Green Hill (Jones County) and was opened to all.[90] In

Harmony Universalist Church near Senoia (Coweta County), Georgia, built in the nineteenth century and still open for services in the 1970s

most instances, informal groups of Universalists assembled occasionally at these locations and others, and after meeting houses were provided, formally organized themselves into societies; for example, the Mulberry Grove society was not organized until four years after the church was built.[91]

In 1837 a temporary organization of Universalists was created near Senoia (Coweta County), a meeting house was erected there in 1840, and a permanent organization (Harmony Church) was effected in 1843.[92] The original structure was replaced in 1896 on the same site, and was still in occasional use in the 1970s. Universalists in Macon and Houston counties cooperated in the building of Mt. Zion chapel in 1838, and announced plans to form a society.[93] They disregarded the suggestion of L.F.W. Andrews that the meeting house be named "Murray Chapel" in honor of the founder of the denomination.[94] During the same year, a society was organized at Talbotton.[95] There were believed to be sufficient Universalists in the interior of the state before the end of the 1830s to support at least two circuit preachers.[96]

Small clusters of Universalists had appeared in such numbers by 1838 in the interior (western and northern counties) to result not only in the formation of two associations but to justify a state convention the following year. In the summer of 1838 the Chattahoochee Association was organized at the Mulberry Grove church and included parts of Alabama as well as Georgia. Because there were so few resident clergy, it was provided that, regardless of the number of preachers present at its meetings, no quorum was to exist unless an equal number of laymen also attended. Independence from all other ecclesiastical bodies was also provided in the association's constitution. The organization was to be an autonomous and self-sufficient unit. Within a few weeks after the organization of the Chattahoochee Association, the "Northern Association of Universalists in the State of Georgia" was created at a meeting held in a private home in Hall County.[97] Allen Fuller from South Carolina was the only ordained clergyman present; besides one lay preacher, eleven laymen attended.

The new association, which represented Universalists in three counties, recommended that a state convention be organized before the end of the next year, and in fact appointed five delegates in case it was created before the next meeting of the association. Partly as a result of the urging of L.F.W. Andrews, a state convention was organized in conjunction with the meeting of the Chattahoochee Association in Talbotton in the fall of 1839.[98] The state convention continued to meet annually through 1860, with an average of four clergy and fifteen laymen at each meeting; usually at least one preacher from a neighboring state was present. The high point in attendance before the Civil War was in 1857, when twenty-seven individuals (including three clergymen) comprised the council.[99]

At no time before 1861 were there sufficient clergy in the state to take advantage of the Universalist potential or to keep alive or to strengthen some of the scattered societies that did come into being. When the first Universalist meeting house had been dedicated in 1834, there was not a single ordained clergyman resident in the state; Fuller, who conducted the services, was then based in South Carolina. L.F.W. Andrews, who had resigned his pastorate of the Second Universalist Society in Philadelphia in 1832, travelled extensively in the South. While en route to Alabama, he preached in Augusta, Clinton, Monroe, and Milledgeville where, while the legislature was in session in 1833, he spread Universalist ideas among congregations assembled in the Hall of Representatives.[100] He saw great possibilities for a society in Monroe, the county seat of Walton County, which could be used as headquarters for a circuit.[101] At least a dozen preachers could be advantageously settled in the region if they could be induced to come. The greatest obstacle to success, besides lack of clergy, was that believers were so scattered that it was "difficult to collect them together." From his base in Montgomery, Alabama, Andrews travelled through western Georgia in 1834 and preached to Universalists in the Mulberry Grove area en route to the South Carolina Convention, where he met Fuller for the first time.[102]

Willis Atkins, a native of Georgia residing in Alabama, a convert from the Methodist Episcopal Church and a Universalist lay preacher since 1830, was to have been ordained at the Mulberry Grove dedication, but was unable to attend.[103] The first two individuals to be ordained in Georgia were Philo Brownson of Macon and Spencer J. McMorris, a native of South Carolina who had moved to Alabama but itinerated extensively in Georgia where he resided briefly in Columbus.[104] Their ordination took place at the organization meeting of the Chattahoochee Association in 1838.[105] David H. Porter, who had been a lay preacher of the Liberty Society (Habersham County), which had begun to meet in 1838, was ordained at their request by the Northern Association in 1839.[106] Until McMorris returned to Alabama in 1841, he and Porter (then residing in Clarkesville) were the two circuit preachers in the state. They were aided by Brownson who was also busy editing the *Evangelical Universalist* and preaching in twelve counties.[107]

In 1841 C.F.R. Shehane, who had been a Campbellite Baptist preacher about twelve years and was then living in Henry County, avowed his Universalism and became an itinerant operating out of Columbus. Even after he had settled in Alabama and added newspaper editing to his preaching activities, he continued to be actively involved in Georgia Universalism. One preacher, James C. Kendrick of Greenville, served as clerk of the state convention for several years in the 1840s and 1850s. Daniel Bragg Clayton, a native of South Carolina and well known among Universalists in several southern states as an itinerant preacher, appeared briefly in Georgia in 1846 and was immediately asked to locate there. He elected instead to use Mississippi as his base of operations, but attended Georgia State Convention meetings whenever his travels about the South made it possible.[108]

John Durden, a Universalist layman in Morgan County, offered a 100-acre farm, complete with buildings, and a one-year supply of pork and corn to any Universalist preacher who would settle there.[109] The offer is not known to have produced the desired results. Two more clergy were added, however, to Georgia Universalist rolls in 1851, when Shehane ordained James Park and John Fricks in Walker County.[110] Park was from the denomination known as Christians, and Fricks came from a Baptist background. In 1852 William Coleman of Randolph

County, a judge and financial supporter of Universalism, began a career as a lay preacher.[111] The Coleman name was a familiar one in southern Universalist circles in both the nineteenth and twentieth centuries.

For most of the 1840s and 1850s there were no regularly appointed circuit preachers in the state at all. In 1855 B.F. Strain of Waleska (Cherokee County) had agreed to serve on behalf of the state convention on a part-time basis, but he threatened to leave the ministry entirely and was thinking of "going back to the corn field" if he could not be adequately supported. As it was, he had to supplement his meager clerical income by farming.[112] In 1858 J.M.H. Smith of Spalding County was appointed "state missionary" by the convention to assist Strain, and served for two years.[113] Strain did remain faithfully at his post, and in the mid-1870s was still serving as the pastor of three churches and as a missionary in general.[114]

Georgia Universalists before the Civil War made two efforts to support schools. The first took place in 1851, on the initiative of a wealthy layman, P.B. Cox of Griffin, who offered $10,000 toward the establishment of a college to be located there.[115] The charter limited stock subscriptions to $20,000, with the understanding that Cox's gift would be matched by other subscriptions.[116] Over $5,000 had been raised within the year, and Cox announced plans to erect a building to be used as a boarding house.[117] An academic building had been completed by the spring of 1853, and it was announed that the "Southern Liberal Institute" was ready to receive students. Shehane was to serve as general agent.[118] The institution, which was a coeducational secondary school rather than the college originally planned, opened "with fair prospects," under the direction of William Wallace and his wife.[119] There was no direct aid provided by the state convention, but only its blessing.

Five years later, plans were discussed for establishing a Universalist-sponsored school in the South under the direct and official auspices of the Georgia Convention, and Clayton was authorized to serve as an agent to solicit subscriptions on behalf of a committee to raise $15,000.[120] However, there was considerable confusion among the subscribers over the nature of the proposed institution, to be located in Americus, Georgia. Some thought it was to be a "Denominational High School," while others were given to understand that it would be a college. As a result of the misunderstanding, the $6,000 in pledges secured within a three-month period in 1859 were voided the following year. The committee to raise funds, this time specifically for a high school, were reconstituted and directed to start all over again.[121] The project was apparently never carried beyond this stage.

Between 1840 and the Civil War, the number of organized societies and/or churches in Georgia remained almost static. There were only eight in the entire state in 1860, concentrated in the two tiers of western counties. Two of the churches were less than two years old at that date. Friendship Church (Dawson County) had been organized during the state convention which met there in 1859; one had also been organized in Walker County.[122] A society had been organized in 1848 at Plains of Dura (Sumter County) known as New Hope Church.[123] Salem Church (Cherokee County) had been organized in 1855. Burruss had dedicated a new church in Troup County in January of 1850.[124] The maximum number of Universalist meeting houses at any one time was thirteen (in 1860).[125] All of the nine preachers reported in the state in 1860 served on a part-time basis, including L.C. Fambro of Starkville (Lee County), a physician and a convert from the Methodists. In 1860 he announced his availability to preach in the southwestern part of the state.[126]

It was all too familiar a story—too wide a dispersion, with no focal point; inadequate organization; lack of church discipline; too few clergy too stintingly supported; no concrete assistance from a General Convention far away; and inevitable opposition from other denominations on the home front. After a preaching tour in 1838, Philo Brownson described the experience of many travelling preachers when he reported that in Coweta County he had been subjected to much "unprincipled and wilful slander and abuse."[127] However, this factor should not be given undue weight, for every clergyman who put his views on record placed the real responsibility for the lack of growth and the general weakness of the denomination in the state on the Universalists themselves rather than on their enemies. It boiled down to lack of organization and discipline.

Allen Fuller, after many years of experience as a circuit preacher in South Carolina, told the Georgia Convention in 1857 that neither individual example nor temporary enthusiasm stirred up at meetings was the real answer to Universalist problems.[128] The keys to success, he said, were at the local level. Churches had to be organized and church membership and the discipline it entailed were "the proper basis." But Universalists refused to organize in either the numbers or strength that Fuller hoped for, and even when churches were constituted they were likely to be small and their itinerant clergy inadequately supported. Strain considered himself fortunate to collect $250 a year for his services. Judging from the few precise statistics available for those churches created in Georgia before 1861, the largest had only twenty-nine members; some had less than fifteen. It was also pointed out that as long as Universalists confined their efforts to rural areas exclusively, no other result could have been expected.

Not a single society or church in Georgia existed in an urban center before the Civil War. In 1871 Andrews recommended that the General Convention ought to spend "a few thousand dollars" establishing churches in such centers as Atlanta, Macon, Savannah, Augusta, and

Columbus.[129] There had not been sufficient attention to tapping the Universalist potential he was sure existed in such places. But who was to do it? As early as 1838, Andrews had himself received an urgent request to organize a society in Savannah, but had been too busy and replied that he had already spread his efforts too thinly to comply.[130] Philo Brownson had visited Augusta in 1840 and had preached in the Unitarian church there; but his plea for a Universalist clergyman to settle there went unheeded.[131] He had also spoken to large audiences the same year in the town hall in Athens (which he described as "the headquarters of Orthodoxy in Georgia") but there was no one to follow up his efforts.[132] As late as 1875, every one of the ten parishes and the six churches existing within them in the state of Georgia were in the countryside rather than in an urban center.[133] And it was in these rural areas that historic Universalism was to persist the longest.

North Carolina

Two Dunkards, John Ham and John Stanstel, were responsible for the first Universalist preaching in the years between 1780 and 1800 in eastern North Carolina, where most of the earliest Universalist societies in the state were organized.[134] At the meeting of the Kehukee Baptist Association in Halifax County in 1790, three elders were appointed to visit the Flat Swamp church (organized in 1776 in Pitt County) to investigate the theological damage done by "a certain John Stansill," who was propagating the doctrine of Universal Restoration.[135]

No Universalist preacher was known to have resided in the state until 1826, although there were occasional visits by various itinerants. One D.M. Cole was reported to have visited in 1823 or 1824; Abner Kneeland, before his departure from the Universalist faith, visited from Philadelphia in 1825 and preached in Wilmington and vicinity for approximately one month; and a New Englander named William Ives, who peddled dry goods and notions from a Yankee carry-all wagon, spread Universalist ideas during the same decade.[136] In 1826 Jacob Frieze, a native of Rhode Island, settled in Wilmington at the urging of Hosea Ballou, who had received a request for a preacher; Kneeland had also suggested that Frieze's services were needed in the South.[137] After preaching in several communities spread over three counties, and after a brief trip to Boston, Frieze returned to North Carolina in 1827 and remained for a year. He was forced to relinquish his post because of health problems in his family.[138] Although he made another visit to the state in 1845, and in 1857 projected another one, he had to leave the further organization of Universalism there to others.[139]

By the time Frieze returned to the North in 1828 to become the pastor of a society in Rhode Island and to assist in publishing a denominational paper there, he had travelled in at least five counties in North Carolina, had organized five societies, had published a newspaper (the *Liberalist*), and had attempted to organize a Southern Convention.[140] On an extended trip in 1827 which apparently took him also into South Carolina, he travelled over 300 miles and preached to at least twelve congregations, with even more preaching engagements arranged.[141]

The societies which Frieze organized in 1827 were all located in the eastern part of the state and, with the exception of the one he organized at Wilmington (New Hanover County), were all in rural areas in the immediate interior (Onslow, Sampson, and Duplin Counties). The "First Universalist Society of Duplin County, N.C.," which served as a sort of parish headquarters for the county, with monthly preaching at four locations (including Limestone), held its first meeting in the summer of 1827 at the court house in Kenansville.[142] Two of the other societies were located at Richlands (Onslow County) and Clinton (Sampson County), with the fifth probably at Chinquapin (Duplin County) or vicinity; a Universalist meeting house was known to have existed in the Chinquapin community at the time.[143] All of the societies had constructed or acquired meeting houses by 1827 except at Kenansville, which did not build one until more than thirty years later.[144] Universalists were to be found by the 1830s also in Edenton (Chowan County) and Halifax (Halifax County) in the northeastern corner of the state.

None of the societies which Frieze organized had a continuous history, although the decendants of many of the first members appeared in those which were later organized or underwent sporadic revival. Between 1829 and 1834, there was no settled minister in the state at all, and Universalists had to depend either on their own efforts or on the ministrations of itinerants who occasionally appeared. Time after time, pleas for one or more preachers from the North were published in denominational papers. A North Carolinian reported in 1831 that "half the people of this state are Universalists" and those that avowed such religious beliefs publicly were "the most respectable, and intelligent of our citizens."[145] A Universalist in New Bern wrote a long letter to the editor of the *Trumpet* extolling the virtues of that seaport town as the location for a clergyman.[146] But tangible results were disappointing. One A.J. Maurice appeared briefly in Wilmington in 1829 to succeed Frieze, but was reported to have done "vast injury to the cause."[147] Both he and the society at Wilmington disappeared.

A few New England clergymen, as a result of the earlier pleas for help, did visit eastern North Carolina for short periods. Among them was J.B. Dods of Taunton, Massachusetts, who in 1832-33 engaged in a public debate with a Baptist preacher in Edenton, and attracted much attention.[148] He also visited New Bern briefly the following year.[149]

L.F.W. Andrews, en route to Augusta, Georgia, visited Edenton for about a week in the fall of 1833, and preached several times.[150] In 1834 Menzies Rayner also paid a brief visit, preaching in Edenton and Elizabeth City and neighboring communities, and reported that Universalists in Edenton could easily support a preacher part-time.[151] Rayner was critical of the Baptists and Methodists (whom he considered the most vociferously opposed to Universalism), with their "noise and uproar–groaning, shouting, clapping hands . . . [where] every thing goes by excitement, and upon high-pressure principles." One of the leading Universalist laymen in Edenton at the time was Jonathan Council, who was excommunicated by the Baptists. He served as local agent for Universalist newspapers, including the *Southern Pioneer,* to which he was also a frequent contributor.

The situation looked more promising by 1835. A society had been organized in 1834 at Red Hill (Sampson County) near Clinton, with twenty-six members.[152] It was probably organized out of what had previously been a Baptist church, when the pastor, Luther Rice, was converted to Universalism and the majority of the congregation followed him; they retained possession of the existing church building.[153] The chronic problem of lack of clergy seemed to have been alleviated by 1835, for John Parsons of Portsmouth, New Hampshire, visited the state that year and decided to stay. He established himself at Trenton (Jones County) where Frieze had earlier visited. Parsons made a 200-mile tour in the winter of 1835-36 and found four of the five societies established by Frieze still in existence.[154]

Among his projected activities was to have been the revival of the convention organized in 1827. Unfortunately for the Universalist cause in the state, Parsons decided to return north for reasons of health. He was much discouraged by the weakened state of the cause, blaming the situation in part on the activities of the aforementioned Maurice and one Henry Hawley, whom Parsons described as "unworthy individuals [who] passed themselves off for Universalist preachers."[155]

Between 1836 and 1846, organized Universalism virtually disappeared from the state. There was no mention of either societies or preachers in the *Universalist Register* between 1837 and 1844, although the society at Red Hill is known to have existed for at least part of the decade ending in 1846. There was probably no one in the state in a position to make an accurate report. Although there were Universalists in the Edenton-Halifax area, apparently no society was formally organized. It seems that lack of clergy was the principal reason, for on his visit to Edenton in 1832-33, Dods had been assured that a meeting house would be built if the services of a preacher could be obtained.[156] The most prominent Universalist layman in that vicinity was G.C. Marchant, a physician who served for many years as corresponding secretary for the Universalist Historical Society for North Carolina, beginning in 1834. He had heard Dods debate in Edenton, and afterwards engaged in an extended correspondence with him over theological questions through the columns of the *Trumpet.*[157] Marchant was also the local agent for some Universalist papers, including the *Southern Evangelist.*[158]

The individual most responsible for keeping Universalism alive in eastern North Carolina in the late 1840s and early 1850s was John C. Burruss, who had been ordained in his native state of Virginia in 1844 and had settled in Kinston (Lenoir County), North Carolina, before moving to Alabama in 1849.[159] He moved to North Carolina in 1846 at the solicitation of Jacob Frieze, who had returned briefly to the state and realized that no societies or meeting houses at all were reported for 1845.[160] Burruss organized a church in Sampson County of nineteen members (probably Red Hill) and identified seventeen union or "free" meeting houses in which Universalists met occasionally. Included was one at Hallsville, where he organized a society of ten members in 1848.[161] He was probably responsible also for organizing the church in Richlands (Onslow County) in July 1849.[162] He somehow managed to travel through ten counties during his three-year residence in the state.

Before his departure for Alabama in the fall of 1849, Burruss was also responsible for reconstituting the convention of 1827, except in this instance on a state rather than a regional basis. It was reorganized in 1846 at a meeting in the Limestone community near Kenansville, and met until the outbreak of the Civil War.[163] It was at Limestone Chapel that Burruss also organized a church in 1846, in connection with which the first Universalist baptisms in the state (by immersion) took place.[164] It was also in Limestone that the state convention met for at least three years.

For almost two years after Burruss' departure, there was no ordained Universalist minister in North Carolina. Only one meeting house was known to belong to Universalists in 1850—Richlands Chapel (Onslow County)—which had been dedicated in the summer of 1849 when a church was organized at the same time.[165] A layman, John M. Francks, one of Jacob Frieze's converts, was the chief benefactor. William S. Balch of New York City visited North Carolina in 1851 and preached several times. He reported that almost the entire town of Swansboro, both black and white, turned out to hear him.[166] Five years later, John Stebbins Lee, then principal of the Green Mountain Liberal Institute in South Woodstock, Vermont, spent several weeks in eastern North Carolina. He visited numerous communities, including Swansboro, and preached at Richlands, where he stayed at Francks' home.[167] He decided not to preach at New Bern, for he found only one professed Universalist in the town.

By 1850 two lay preachers had appeared—Henry Swinson (Snow Hill, Greene County) and William S. Matthews (Clinton, Sampson

County). Both men served for several years as clerks of the state convention.[168] Matthews was a schoolteacher who had begun preaching Universalism in 1849.[169] Swinson, who died in 1859, had been a Baptist preacher for twenty-five years before his conversion to Universalism in 1849. He had been excommunicated for his alleged heresy by an ecclesiastical council which met in the Bear Marsh Baptist church (Duplin County) where he had ministered for several years.[170] After the excommunication had taken place, Swinson was then given an opportunity to speak. He delivered "a powerful and eloquent argument in defense of his new faith" which so impressed Sylvanus Cobb, editor of the Boston-based *Christian Freeman,* that he reproduced the entire address on the front page of his paper.[171]

Five Universalist clergy resided in North Carolina in 1852, including two new local lay preachers—John K. Taylor (Snow Hill) and William Griffin (New Bern). One of the five was Hope Bain, who moved to the state from Virginia in 1851. He had been born in Aberdeen, Scotland, the son of a British naval officer, and had served in a company of volunteers in Maryland during the War of 1812.[172] He had been reared as a Presbyterian, but had become a Universalist in 1847, and while serving as a schoolteacher was ordained at Norfolk, Virginia, the following year. Burruss had assisted in the ceremony.[173] Bain lived at first in Warsaw (Duplin County) and from 1854 until his death in 1876, made Goldsboro (Wayne County) his home.[174] Although he was a Unionist throughout the Civil War and hence was not always popular, he remained at his post. For the twenty-five years of his ministry in North Carolina he was on several occasions the only resident minister of the denomination in the entire state, and furnished the only continuity for Universalism there. Before 1861 he preached in no less than twenty counties. He frequently travelled on foot; he could not afford a horse or buggy on the total stipend of $300 which he received in 1859 (at the age of sixty-five), and on which he was attempting to support a wife and three children.[175]

Even with Bain's arrival, Universalism experienced no significant growth in the state. Now and then a new meeting house was added—for example at Lisbon (Greene County) in 1852 and at Red Hill in 1856; a few lay preachers appeared, and as promptly disappeared. Porter Thomas spent a month travelling in six counties in 1857 and deplored the lack of organization he found in the state.[176] The situation did look more promising that year, in at least one respect, for E.H. Lake arrived from South Carolina and settled at first at Kenansville. When he became a circuit preacher for four societies he purchased a small house and a 100-acre farm in Magnolia.[177] Lake was a native of Massachusetts who had served in various New England pastorates and had moved south for his health. The fact that he was a Yankee did not work to his advantage in a period of growing sectional tension. Nonetheless he did his best to spread Universalist ideas, and travelled extensively in the state. In 1857 he delivered a series of sermons in the courthouse in Elizabeth City (where he found all churches closed to him) and sold Universalist works.[178] He also expended part of his efforts with Universalists in neighboring Virginia. The North Carolina Convention had agreed to pay him $800 a year for his services as a circuit preacher, but by the fall of 1858, one-third of his salary had actually been paid by Universalists in Portsmouth and Norfolk.[179]

On the eve of the Civil War, the prospects for Universalism in North Carolina were far from encouraging, measured both by comparison with other denominations and internally. In 1860, with a total adult white population of slightly less than 300,000 in the state, of the approximately half of that number who were presumed to belong to churches, about 80 per cent were Methodists and Baptists.[180] The Roman Catholics, who ranked tenth among the ten leading groups, could claim more congregations (a total of seven, with 350 members) than the Universalists, who were listed together with a scattering of Jews and Deists as too small in number to justify the popular opposition and prejudice that existed against them. There were, in fact, only six organized Universalist societies in the state that year. One, at Red Hill, had just created a church in connection with its society, with a membership of twenty-five.[181] There were but two ministers in North Carolina in 1860—Hope Bain (Goldsboro) and E.H. Lake (Magnolia)—and one lay preacher (J.L.C. Griffin, M.D.), who had just arrived. Although there were twenty-six meeting houses used by Universalists, only four were owned by them, including one at Kenansville which had not yet been completed.[182]

Small and weak as organized Universalism was in the state in the early 1860s, an effort was made to establish an educational institution under denominational auspices comparable to what Georgia Universalists had attempted a few years before and what Universalists had been able to accomplish on a much larger scale in the North and Midwest. Until 1860 the only academy in the eastern part of the state which Universalists claimed to be non-sectarian was a private school in Swansboro (Onslow County).[183] A Universalist layman, Lucius A. Spencer, had arrived in 1857 to take charge of it. The institution apparently foundered, for an effort was soon thereafter made to establish a school under official Universalist patronage. The impetus came from Lake. When an academy building became available in Magnolia in 1860, he urged Universalists to acquire it and open a school where the religious views of the students would not be "molested."[184]

He spoke from unhappy first-hand experience, for his own children had been expelled from a school because he was a Universalist minister, and he had had to enroll them elsewhere, with higher tuition and board costs than he could afford.[185] Arrangements were thereafter made to acquire the available property for $2,500 (less than half of the cost of original construction) and several "benevolent gentlemen" undertook to raise the necessary funds. Plans had so far progressed by the winter of 1860-61 that a prospectus could be issued announcing the opening of the "Magnolia Male & Female Seminary" on 1 February 1861.

James L.C. Griffin, a physician and ordained Universalist clergyman, agreed to serve as the principal. He was a native of Virginia, a graduate of the College of William and Mary, and received his medical training at the University of Pennsylvania. After having served briefly as a Methodist preacher following his conversion at a revival meeting in Virginia, he became a Universalist in 1844, and led the life of a roving teacher, preacher, and doctor in several southern states.[186] After one year (1857) on the faculty of Lombard University, the Universalist institution in Illinois, he returned to the South as an itinerant preacher.

The "Female Department" of the proposed seminary was to have been operated by Miss Ella F. Lake, at the residence of her ministerial father. There is no evidence that the academy building was actually acquired or ever opened, although Griffin may have conducted a school briefly in his home. Lack of funds and the approach of sectional conflict can be offered as explanations for the failure of the school to materialize. Griffin returned briefly to his native Virginia and after the Civil War moved to western Florida.[187]

Burruss had admonished Lake publicly for preaching with such fervor and vehemence that the North Carolina clergyman was endangering his health.[188] Lake literally "wore himself out" on behalf of Universalism, and died in 1862 at the age of forty-two in Richmond, Virginia, while on a visit.[189] Nonetheless, he had somehow found time to engage in numerous debates, write several pamphlets, and produce two books besides fulfilling his pastoral responsibilities. When Universalists in North Carolina struggled after the Civil War to rebuild the remnants of the denomination there, only Hope Bain remained in the eastern part of the state to carry on the task.

Alabama

It was Universalist laymen from South Carolina who probably first represented the denomination in Alabama.[190] Members of the prolific and influential Coleman family had already migrated from Feasterville, South Carolina, and settled in 1812 in what was then a part of Mississippi Territory, out of which the state of Alabama was carved in 1819. They settled in the Brewton area in the extreme south, which in the 1970s remained one of the small centers of Universalism in the state. A society was probably organized there as early as the 1820s at Lewis Station (near Brewton). In 1827 northern Universalists were informed that preachers were needed for both Georgia and Alabama.[191] It was in the decade of the 1830s that Universalism took root in parts of the state, when societies were organized in both rural areas and in small-town centers concentrated in the east-central counties. In this decade a family-organized church appeared in Renfroe (Talladega County), headed by John Hubbard.[192] Churches were organized in 1834 at Mt. Olympus and at nearby Montgomery.

The pioneer Universalist clergyman largely responsible for establishing the denomination in Alabama was Willis Atkins. A native of Georgia, he was originally a Methodist, and after moving to Alabama had become a prosperous planter. He had donated land and otherwise aided the Methodists in providing a meeting house near his home north of Montgomery.[193] However, when he became a Universalist after having read works by Elhanan Winchester and Hosea Ballou, he found the Methodist church closed to him; so he constructed his own nearby and in 1830 became a lay preacher in Montgomery County.[194] He was ordained in 1834 at the Universalist church in Montgomery, with Allen Fuller and L.F.W. Andrews officiating.[195] The meeting house constructed by Atkins was the first Universalist edifice in the state, and was dedicated in mid-1834, one month before the Universalist society of Mt. Olympus was organized to occupy it.[196]

The second individual prominent in early Alabama Universalism was L.F.W. Andrews (1802-1875) who, until the time of his death, had appeared in almost every southern state as a missionary and denominational newspaper publisher. He had arrived in Montgomery in the winter of 1833 and within a few weeks had organized a church there. Atkins had already laid the groundwork with his preaching, and as early as 1832 subscriptions had been solicited to construct a church.[197] With this promising beginning, Andrews agreed to stay for one year and to use Montgomery as his headquarters for itinerant activities.

Both the Montgomery church organization and meeting house were interesting examples of ecumenical cooperation. The organization was a joint venture of Universalists and Unitarians, and was known officially as the "First Unitarian Universalist Society of Mongtomery" when it was created with thirty members.[198] The church building, completed at the same time the society was created, was equipped with a steeple and bell (unusual for southern Universalist churches), and furnished with an organ which had been financed in large part by $300 contributed by a Roman Catholic.[199] When George Rogers visited Montgomery in 1837 he was impressed not only by the structure but by the fact that not a one of the major contributors actually lived in town, but on plantations in the vicinity.[200] The lack of a sizeable Universalist population within the city was undoubtedly a factor explaining the dormancy of the society by 1839.[201]

By 1840 at least six societies had been organized in the state, including one in Wetumpka (Elmore County), north of Montgomery, and at Lafayette. Itinerants like Rogers and Andrews had preached in these locations in 1837 and 1839, respectively.[202] Like so many Universalist societies, the one in Lafayette had to depend on services conducted by laymen, interspersed with occasional and usually infrequent visits by clergymen such as S.J. McMorris. Even his ministrations were lost when he moved to Mississippi in 1841, although he later returned to reside in Wetumpka.[203] The few Universalists in Mobile followed the same policy as their contemporaries in Montgomery, and cooperated with other denominations in order to survive. Until 1844, when a society was organized in Mobile, Universalists heard preaching by Andrews (1834) and H.F. Sterns, a visitor from New Hampshire the same year.[204] But they were neither numerous nor strong enough to establish their own organization. After James Freeman Clarke organized a Unitarian society in 1836, some Universalists attended.[205] In the early 1840s Universalists joined with Unitarians and other Protestant denominations in conducting non-sectarian services for seamen in a rented hall.[206] This was an outgrowth of a Unitarian effort in 1838, when a Seaman's Friend Society was organized.

The immediate occasion for the organization of a society in Mobile was the appearance in 1843 of Isaac D. Williamson, a Vermonter who had served various societies in New England and New York State and who went south for his health. His arrival followed a meeting of Universalists in Mobile who had determined to secure a pastor and had even appointed a committee to make a trip north to interview possible candidates.[207] Williamson immediately went into action and engaged in a debate with one Jefferson Hamilton, a Methodist, by way of a series of sermons published in 1844 in pamphlet form.[208] The society began to prosper in 1844 under Williamson's leadership, and he remained the balance of the year, not returning to the North until the summer of 1845.[209] The small chapel being used for services proved to be totally inadequate, so a church built in 1836 by the Unitarians and then leased by the Presbyterians, was purchased.[210] However, the Universalists lost the building because of a defect in the title, and the society faltered and disappeared after Williamson left Alabama.

It was in rural areas and small towns in Alabama that Universalism managed to survive in the 1840s and 1850s. Even then, the denomination made but little headway before the Civil War. C.F.R. Shehane made a 200-mile trip into the northern part of the state in 1845 and found that many Universalists had not bothered to form societies but had joined the numerous Baptist and Methodist churches instead.[211] Among the Universalists he identified was the granddaughter of "the celebrated Patrick Henry;" she was living in Athens (Limestone County). There were never more than ten Universalist preachers known to be active at any one time in the entire state between 1845 and 1860, and many of them had not been ordained or even licensed. As one correspondent wrote from Huntsville in 1855, Universalism in Alabama was about as far advanced as it had been in New England half a century earlier.[212]

Occasionally, special inducements were offered to lure preachers to various communities. One Universalist in Butler County, in the southern part of the state, offered besides eighty acres of first-rate land, to build a house and equip a preacher with livestock.[213] John P. Myers, a convert from the Methodist Episcopal ministry and a resident of the county, answered the call.[214] But he left both the ministry and the denomination a decade later.[215] Sometimes the hopes for additional clergy misfired. In 1853 the only denominational paper in the state at the time, the *Universalist Herald,* ran a notice that two clergymen of the "right stamp" were needed as itinerants in Alabama.[216] Maxey B. Newell, who had preached Universalism for fourteen years, announced that he was moving from Virginia to Alabama to become a travelling preacher; but he took over the pastorate in Charleston, South Carolina, instead.[217] Major James Cooper, a Universalist layman in Tallapoosa County, opened his home for religious discussions by members of any denomination who cared to come.[218] He and his neighbors built a church in 1849 near his residence, and monthly meetings were held by Shehane for the twelve to fifteen who attended.

In 1850 a church was organized and a meeting house constructed in the hamlet of Plantersville (Dallas County). Small societies (for which records are scanty or non-existent) also appeared in the 1840s and 1850s in small settlements in the northern part of the state.[219] In 1853 J.M.H. Smith of Huntsville (Madison County), who served as a preacher in the area beginning in the early 1850s, claimed to be the only public advocate of Universalism in all of northern Alabama.[220] Not one of the six churches in the town would open its doors to Universalists. Preachers continued to appear in the central part of the state from time to time in the 1850s, such as one at Selma (Dallas County) conducted in 1852 by J.E. Hargrove.[221] But both the names of many of the preachers and those of their residences have been buried in obscurity. When the Civil War broke out, there were only six Universalist preachers known to be living in the state; even then some, like the veteran McMorris, were on the road much of the time travelling in Georgia and Florida.

One Universalist society which did flourish both before and after the Civil War was at Camp Hill (Tallapoosa County). Established by the Harper and Slaughter families in 1845, it was organized by Shehane in 1847 as part of his rounds as an itinerant. In the century between 1846 and 1946, 550 individuals had joined the church, which had a maximum of 250 members at any one time.[222] John J. Slaughter, a convert to Universalism through the efforts of his wife (a member of the Harper family) had moved to Camp Hill about 1830. Services were held irregularly for many years when such individuals as D.B. Clayton, Isaac D. Williamson, and Shehane chanced to pay a visit in the course of their travels. Meetings were held originally in a frame building that had once been a Negro Baptist church.

The community of Notasulga (Macon County) was known after the middle of the nineteenth century not so much for the importance of its Universalist society as for the prominence of one of its clergymen and long-time members—John C. Burruss (1821-1910). His name became synonymous not only with Alabama Universalism but with southern Universalism in general. For over sixty years he served the denominational cause in the state as a preacher, newspaper publisher, bookseller, and, much to the embarrassment and irritation of many northern Universalists, as an outspoken defender of Negro slavery.[223] When Burruss, a native of Virginia, arrived in 1849 from North Carolina, he was only twenty-eight, but had been ordained five years earlier in Richmond, Virginia, and had already accumulated considerable experience as an organizer of Universalist churches in Virginia and North Carolina, and as an itinerant. Throughout his career he was reluctant to organize mere societies, insisting that Universalism was more likely to endure and to attract desirable members if the discipline of formal church organization were applied.[224] Before the end of his long career he had organized churches in seven southern state, had preached in the Midwest, and had received an honorary Doctor of Divinity degree from Buchtel College (Ohio) in 1879, in partial recognition of his services to the denomination.

Immediately upon settling in Notasulga, Burruss plunged into Universalist activities. He played a major part in organizing the Universalist church in Notasulga in 1850. Almost simultaneously, a meeting house was constructed on land comprising part of the Burruss property. The white frame building was equipped with a steeple and "a fine mellow toned bell" donated by Major Thomas Cowles of Montgomery.[225] Almon Gage, a former lawyer in Rochester, New York who had entered the Universalist ministry in 1847, served briefly as the pastor.[226] Burruss not only served the church for many years, but travelled incessantly, preaching and attending denominational meetings all over the South whenever he could fit them into his busy schedule. He served as pastor of the flourishing Camp Hill church on a part-time basis for some thirty-one years; it was due largely to his efforts that the church became the largest Universalist organization in the state both before and after 1865.

Burruss even found time to serve as mentor for prospective young ministers. One such was Bliss B. Arms, who studied under Burruss for a year in 1853 and served for many years on various circuits in Alabama as well as in northern Florida.[227] Described by a contemporary as "a theologian every inch," Burruss took delight in participating in public religious debates, many of which were published in either book or pamphlet form, or in his *Universalist Herald.* Typical of the titles he gave to his debates was a rejoinder which he delivered to an attack on Unversalism by a Campbellite preacher; "Error Battered, and its Foundations Shattered with a Volley of Hot Shot from Mount Zion. Being a reply to Rev. John T. Walsh's Discourses, entitled 'Universalism Exposed from the Inner Tample,' preached in Kinston, N.C., April 12th, 1857."[228] One project Burruss planned but never carried out was to have been a history of Universalism in the South.[229] It surely would have made interesting as well as informative reading.

It was on the recommendation of Burruss and McMorris in 1857 that a state convention was organized in Alabama the following year. It was not so much the urging of the General Convention of the denomination as local circumstances that prompted the move. Burruss pointed to the success of the southern Methodists, who showed the organizational ability, training, and discipline which he believed the Universalists lacked.[230] The convention was organized at Liberty Church at Camp Hill in the summer of 1858 and immediately received fellowship in the General Convention of Southern Universalists by ratifying its constitution.[231] Six clergymen and thirty laymen attended, six of whom were baptized by immersion in a ceremony conducted by Burruss. He also became the standing clerk of the convention and later its president. The convention met again in 1860, with four clergymen and twenty-five laymen present, and a meeting was scheduled for the following year but apparently was never convened. At the 1860 meeting it was voted to publish the proceedings only in the *Universalist Herald* and not bother to notify denominational papers in either the West or the North. The South, they felt, had been too often ignored and this was one way to retaliate.[232]

Alabama Universalists did try after the Civil War to regroup their scattered forces, and organized a new state convention in 1870. Five years later there were nine Universalist churches in Alabama, with a total of 230 members; three church buildings; and eight preachers.[233] But, as the editor of the *Universalist Register* asked rhetorically, "what are those few preachers compared to the broad extent of the State, embracing a territory nearly as large as the six New England States?" There was obviously much work yet to be done.

Mississippi

The story of Universalism in Mississippi before the Civil War repeated the same pattern to be found in most other states of the South; namely, isolated pockets of believers in universal salvation scattered over a rural landscape, largely without organization, and depending on roving preachers who were small in number and often based in other states.[234] It should be pointed out that, in a state with no large metropolitan centers even after the Civil War, well over half of the Universalist churches were organized in the county seats, which were usually the largest communities in the state and served as political and religious as well as commercial headquarters.

The first known Universalist to reside in Mississippi between 1798 and 1817, when it achieved statehood, was Winthrop Sargent of Gloucester, Massachusetts, the first territorial governor. Sargent, brother of Judith Sargent who married John Murray, resided in Natchez. Although the area was occasionally visited by travelling preachers, no church was organized there before the Civil War. The first church of which there is a record was located in the northern part of the state at Spring Hill (Benton County), a community no longer to be found on the map. The early inhabitants included Universalists who had migrated from South Carolina, starting about 1800. George Rogers, in the course of his far-flung missionary travels, visited in the area in 1837, in the heart of what was still Chickasaw Indian country, and preached for several weeks.[235] While roaming about the countryside, Rogers stayed at an inn where he discovered a copy of John Murray's autobiography on a mantelpiece. Rogers noted with satifaction that "these heretical prints insinuate themselves every where." In one community he preached to "at least two hundred" individuals. D.B. Clayton, who for many years was the only Universalist preacher in the state, visited the community of Spring Hill from time to time, beginning in the 1840s and operating out of his residence in Red Banks, in adjoining Marshall County. There was a church in Holly Springs (Marshall County) to which Rogers preached in the 1830s, and Clayton in the 1840s and 1850s.

Other groups of Universalists had appeared in the state by the 1830s, including members of the Coleman, Lynch, and Halfacre families from Newberry District, South Carolina. They settled at various locations in Choctaw and Winston Counties. Liberty Church was built on the Coleman plantation near the county seat of Louisville (Winston County) in 1846. Clayton made his first visit there in 1850.[236] A new Liberty Church was dedicated in 1859, also located on land donated by the Colemans, with between twenty and thirty members.[237] The widespread use of the term "Liberty" in the official names of Universalist churches in the South was explained by an individual present at the dedication. It stood for liberty and freedom of conscience in religious belief, and it signified the fact that other denominations or organizations were "at liberty" to use their facilities when they were not being used by Universalists. This practice was in sharp contrast to the policies of other denominations, as the Universalists had all too often discovered by unhappy experience. There are but few instances of such actual use in local church records, although Masonic groups sometimes met in southern Universalist meeting houses.

Daniel Bragg Clayton (1817-1906) was the leading Universalist preacher in Mississippi in the mid-nineteenth century, and played much the same role as Burruss in Alabama. Born in 1817 and reared in Spartanburg District, South Carolina, and with a limited formal education completed in his teens, Clayton came from a long line of Baptist clergymen and laymen and was himself baptized into that faith during a frontier revival.[238] His introduction to Universalism came in 1837 and 1838, when he was given a copy of the *Evangelical Magazine and Gospel Advocate* (Utica, New York) and heard a sermon by Allen Fuller, an itinerant Universalist clergyman. When, through Fuller's influence, he decided to enter the ministry, he was excommunicated from the Baptist church (an experience shared by his wife several years later). He trained for the ministry with Fuller's aid, taught school, and preached his second sermon from a stump outside a Baptist meeting house between services. He became a circuit preacher and was ordained in 1845; his first circuit was five churches, at an annual salary totalling $250 contributed by the churches.

Like Burruss, Rogers, and many another pioneer preacher, Clayton delighted in public debate. Almost immediately after his arrival in Mississippi in 1846 he had "one little theological tilt" with a Cumberland Presbyterian.[239] One of his more ambitious endeavors was participation in 1848 in a six-day debate (four hours a day) with a Campbellite preacher. But it was also a lonely life for him professionally during his early days in Mississippi, for at the time of this debate he knew of no other Universalist preacher within 300 miles. His travels were by no means confined to Mississippi. In 1846 he journeyed for two months in neighboring Georgia, delivering sermons and discourses to whomever might listen. But for seventeen years his headquarters remained in northern Mississippi, from which he fared forth innumerable times. He tried his hand unsuccessfully at politics by running for a county office as a Democrat at a Whig stronghold. In the course of his travels all over Mississippi in which he preached in village and country churches, he was impressed by the fact that a majority of the Universalists represented the wealthier and most important citizenry in many communities. His impressions have been borne out by later scholarship.[240]

Clayton's travels became an integral part of his life style. In 1849 and 1850 he traversed over 1,200 miles, his preaching carrying him into Tennessee as well as Alabama and Georgia. In the early 1850s he lived briefly in Aberdeen (Monroe County), Mississippi, where he was an associate in a newspaper and printing office, and reduced his preaching to part-time. After a month of itinerating in North Carolina and a brief tour in the army of the Confederacy during the Civil War, he moved to Feasterville, South Carolina, in 1863, and engaged in mercantile affairs; occasional preaching extended over several states, including Texas. He recorded preaching in fifty-five different places spread over six states in the one year of 1874. The year 1880 found him residing in Atlanta, Georgia, where he published the *Atlanta Universalist.* Before his death in Columbia, South Carolina, in 1906, full of years and affectionate appreciation among Universalists (including an honorary degree from Lombard College in 1897), he had probably covered, with one exception, more territory than any other missionary preacher in the denomination; had engaged in more debates (thereby spreading Universalist ideas); and had introduced the liberal faith to more individuals than any among his contemporaries. The exception was his co-worker, Quillen Hamilton Shinn (1845-1907), who became the epitomé of the post-Civil War Universalist missionary.[241]

Other preachers besides Clayton who provided ministerial services in Mississippi in the 1840s and 1850s were S.J. McMorris, who spent much of his time in Alabama; and E.H. Lake, a native of Massachusetts who served as a missionary in the South for over a decade, and was residing in Magnolia, North Carolina, when he died in 1862. B.F. Strain also served briefly in Mississippi before returning to Georgia on the eve of the Civil War, and his son, A.G. Strain, served for many years as minister of the Liberty Church as well as at other places in the state.

Another branch of the Coleman family established itself at Sharon (Madison County) and had established a church, probably in the 1830s. The minister for several years (1852-1860) was J.L.C. Griffin, a native Virginian, physician and teacher, and a convert to Universalism in 1844.[242] Other small churches were organized between 1835 and 1860 in such localities as Scooba and DeKalb (Kemper County), and Richland (Holmes County). Typical of the family churches so prevalent among southern Universalists was one at Falling Spring (Clarke County), probably organized in the 1830s and populated largely by the family and descendants of Marmeduke Gardner from Barnwell District, South Carolina.[243] A grandson and namesake began preaching Universalism in 1848 in Quitman (Clarke County) and organized a twenty-three member church there the following year.[244] He moved to Texas in the 1850s and became a pioneer Universalist preacher in that state. A church was organized at Lodi (Montgomery County), probably in the 1840s; both McMorris and Clayton preached there a decade later. The somewhat inaccurately (and ambitiously) designated "First Universalist Church of Mississippi" was organized in Brandon (Rankin County) in 1842, with six charter members.[245] The *Universalist Union* (published in New York City) was the only denominational paper they had ever seen. They had no regular preacher and had to depend on visits from itinerants. R.B. Stroud, a Baptist preacher turned Universalist, organized a small church at Fort Bayou (Jackson County) in 1850. Following southern custom, ten of the fifteen original members were baptized by immersion.[246]

Other family churches appeared in rural settlements like Egypt (Chicksaw County) as well as at various locations in Pontotoc County which have long since disappeared from the map. The great majority of such churches became casualties of the Civil War, but some were reorganized or otherwise reborn in the late nineteenth and early twentieth centuries, largely through the energetic missionary endeavors of Burruss, Clayton, and Shinn. Several clusters of Universalists still active in the 1970s in and near Ellisville (Jones County) traced their origins back to the late 1850s. Among the twentieth-century products were the Burruss Memorial Church in the countryside, and "Our Home" Universalist Church, organized in Ellisville.[247] The church was so named because Orange Sherwood Herrington, a convert to Universalism in 1905, insisted that a church be established even if it had to meet in his home.[248] This was the case until a small wooden edifice was constructed in 1906, later replaced by a small brick church. The first service in the original church was held in 1907.[249] At its height (ca. 1933), "Our Home" church claimed 155 members, the largest Universalist congregation in the state. Although the Burruss Memorial Church and the Ellisville church were less than ten miles apart, there was no more than friendly rivalry. Kinship ties explained the relative harmony.

On the eve of the Civil War, there were only four Universalist preachers residing in the state—Griffin, Clayton, John W. Day (who settled in Banner, Calhoun County), and T.H. Rush, an ex-Methodist preacher until 1854, who lived in DeKalb.[250] He had been converted to Universalism after hearing a sermon by E.H. Lake.[251] However, Rush's services to Mississippi Universalists were lost after 1860 when he moved to Arkansas to help establish his son on a frontier farm.[252] When a state convention was organized at Liberty Church in Winston County in 1859, only two of the six ministers present even lived in the state.[253] The other four (including McMorris and Burruss) were from Alabama. Almost all of the twenty-eight lay delegates were from the immediate vicinity.[254]

The newly formed convention ratified the constitution of the General Convention of Southern Universalists except for the clause making it subordinate to the General Convention of the denomination. The state convention met only once more (in 1860), at the same church where the organization meeting had taken place. Only two clergy were present, and the number of lay delegates had dropped to sixteen.[255] A post-Civil War state organization (known as a "conference" rather than as a convention) was not organized until 1904. Reestablishing Universalism in Mississippi after 1865 on a strong basis was a long and not very successful effort, although valiant attemps were made.

Florida

While Universalist preachers were providing itinerant services in much of the southern parts of Georgia, Alabama, and Mississippi in the 1850s and early 1860s, some ventured as far south and east as the sparsely settled area of the western panhandle of northern Florida. Among them were S.J. McMorris, M.B. Newell, John C. Burruss, E.B. Arms, and E.H. Lake. Arms made his temporary headquarters in Pensacola. Lake, who made the trip to Florida in 1861 ostensibly to improve his health, located briefly in Tallahassee and preached as far east as Jacksonville.[256] He was true to his word that he was "willing to travel from one end of [the] state to the other . . . . All I ask is that you defray my travelling expenses."[257]

Universalists had actually appeared in Florida even before statehood had been achieved in 1845. Half a dozen Universalist families requested the services of a preacher in 1844 in the community of Almaranta (located probably in what became a county bordering on Alabama; the name is no longer to be found on a map).[258] By 1850 a meeting house had been erected.[259] At about the same time, Joshua S. Vann, an unfellowshipped convert from the Calvinist ministry, appeared in Campbellton (Jackson County), and is considered to have been the first Universalist preacher to reside in the state.[260] Another preacher, W.J. Green, a convert from the Campbellite Baptists, likewise resided in northwestern Florida (at Alligator) and conducted a society until his death in 1856.[261]

Small centers of Universalism in the 1850s were to be found in Walton County, where in 1860 the First Universalist Church of West Florida was dedicated and a church formed at McDade's Pond.[262] On that occasion J.H.D. Cawthorn was ordained by Burruss. But Universalism, never much more than a name in Florida in pre-Civil War days, did not show signs of growth until after 1870, thanks to the efforts of the Cawthorn family and the missionary labors of Quillen Hamilton Shinn.

Louisiana

Louisiana probably represents the most unusual denominational situation of all the southern states before the Civil War, with the configuration in New Orleans unique and set apart from Universalism elsewhere within state borders. Outside of that city, there were, with one possible exception, no Universalist societies at all before 1870, and what few (approximately five) that did exist between then and about 1910 were small and struggled to survive.[263] In 1870 there was only one Universalist clergyman (George H. Deere) in residence in the entire state (New Orleans). He was one of the successors of Theodore Clapp, whose church had no ecclesiastical connection with any denomination.[264] In the case of New Orleans, liberal religionists of all shades received their spiritual sustenance from Clapp, who for thirty years, beginning in 1822, preached as an independent, refusing formal association with either Unitarianism or Universalism although sympathetic to both. As the editor of the *Universalist Register* reported in 1849, Clapp preached Universalism "boldly, eloquently, and effectively."

Perhaps Clapp found it the better part of wisdom not to declare his religious preferences openly or officially, for in the winter of 1823 one D.M. Cole had arrived in New Orleans and had announced that he would preach in favor of Universalism.[265] He was forbidden by the mayor to meet anywhere in the city, and was forced to hold services (including one on Christmas Day) on a vessel in the Mississippi River. It was estimated at the time that there were between 200 and 300 Universalists (all white) in the area. After Cole's departure, 110 individuals petitioned without success to use the local court house for religious services.[266] They were likewise unsuccessful in raising funds to construct a meeting house and therefore began to attend Clapp's non-denominational church.[267] George Rogers was among the Universalists who spoke from Clapp's pulpit (in 1842). Clapp resigned his pastorate in 1856 because of declining health and was replaced briefly by two Universalists—Edwin C. Bolles, for two years; and Charles B. Thomas, who returned to the North in 1861 with the outbreak of hostilities between North and South.

Only a few Universalists were known to live in other parts of Louisiana before the Civil War. Many had migrated either from New England or from settlements in South Carolina where Universalism had been established. Itinerant preachers such as Rogers, McMorris, and Almon Gage appeared from time to time, visiting such communities as Clinton (East Feliciana Parish), and Baton Rouge (East Baton Rouge Parish). Rogers, after spending a month in southeastern Louisiana in 1842, took a dim view of Universalist prospects for permanency there. The population was in a constant state of movement, and was too engrossed with "sordid interests" to pay much attention to religion.[268] The one Universalist church probably organized before 1870 was in Downsville (Union Parish) in the northwestern corner of the state.[269] P.H. Roberts a preacher from Georgia, was conducting regular services in the 1850s and continued until about 1872, when the organization disappeared. In 1870 a society of ten members was organized by Shehane near Minden (Webster Parish), and a church building was provided by Mrs. Sarah Miller, whose husband had been born in South Carolina and was a Universalist.[270] The society lasted until 1882. With the exception of short-lived societies in northwestern Louisiana like one at Summerfield (Claiborne Parish), organized Universalism died out almost completely and for many years there were no entries at all for the state in the *Universalist Register.*

Even in New Orleans, where the greatest number of Universalists was to be found, Clapp's church continued to be as much Unitarian as Universalist. In 1874 an abortive effort was made to change the official designation of the church to "The First Universalist Parish of New Orleans," provided the Universalists would commit themselves to assist in extinguishing a debt of $25,000.[271] Although the name was never changed to the one suggested, the church continued to be owned jointly by the Unitarians and Universalists, with Unitarians occupying the pulpit.[272] In historical perspective, it appeared that Louisiana was not destined to be a center of Universalist activity. The Unitarians there met very much the same fate.[273]

Regional Cooperation

The first attempt to make Southern Universalists aware of each other's existence and to bring them into closer communication by cutting across state lines was the organization of the Southern Convention of Universalists at Kenansville, North Carolina, in June 1827. Under the leadership of Jacob Frieze of Rhode Island, who had settled at Wilmington, North Carolina, the previous year at the instigation of Hosea Ballou, the convention was organized in a private home by sixteen delegates representing four societies in as many counties in the state.[274] When Frieze prepared a printed circular letter, as instructed, it included a "Salutation to Posterity," a constitution, and a Confession of Faith, and the names of fifty-seven men besides himself who had eventually signed the document, including all of the delegates.[275] Although almost all of the signatories were from existing societies in the state, there were included also "the names of a few, who first dared to come forward in the face of persecution" and affix their signature.

The new organization, considering itself "a sovereign and independent body," apparently held only one session thereafter. In accordance with the constitution, which called for two meetings a year, a second session was held in October 1827 at Richlands, North Carolina, with sixteen present. Although it voted to meet quarterly thereafter, with the next meeting scheduled for Clinton, North Carolina, there was no record that it ever reconvened.[276] In spite of its ambitious title, the convention was probably intended to serve primarily as a state convention, although one was not formally organized in the state until the 1840s.[277]

The next effort at regional cooperation took place in another part of the South. A proposal was made in 1834 to form a "Southern Evangelical Association" of Universalists, embracing parts of Alabama and Georgia.[278] Four years later, the Chattahoochee Association was formed to serve this purpose.[279] Representing six counties in Georgia and two adjacent counties in Alabama, the association was given advisory powers only, except for enforcing clerical discipline; its main purpose was to seek support for circuit preaching.

It was not until 1858, however, that an organization was created that included the entire Lower South. The General Southern Convention was created at a meeting in Fairfield District, South Carolina. It was the outgrowth of a long-felt need to bring the scattered Universalist leadership in that section into closer contact. Furthermore, the General Convention was usually held in locations too far away for Southerners to attend. Because distances were so great and financial resources so limited, it was arranged that the Southern Convention meetings, which would rotate among the five states represented at the first meeting, would be held the two days preceding the state convention, and at the same place in the host state. In accordance with this plan, the 1859 convention met in Georgia, and in 1860 in North Carolina. The 1859 meeting took place in Friendship Church, Dawson County, Georgia; and the North Carolina meeting was held in Dr. Williams' church, Pitt County.[280] The meeting for 1861 (never held) was to have convened in Montgomery, Alabama, prior to that of the state convention.[281]

The continuing isolation and dispersion of Universalists within the South was reason alone for organizing a regional convention. Yet it was designed to serve another less constructive purpose in terms of Universalist national unity. Its creation reflected a growing sentiment in the South by the late 1850s for an organization separate from that of the General Convention. The growing isolation of southern Universalists from their northern colleagues and the heightening tensions between North and South in general were evident from the very beginning of the General Southern Convention. Before it had been organized, Henry Summer, a prominent layman in Newberry District, South Carolina, attempted to assure Universalists both north and south that such a move would not mean withdrawal from connection with Universalists in the North.[282] Yet the trend of events dictated otherwise.

Although representatives from states in the Middle Atlantic area and New England were invited to the first meeting (in 1858), none appeared. At the South Carolina Convention, which met immediately afterwards, Universalists were told that the existence of the new convention was not to be interpreted as a severance of connections with the General Convention.[283] When the decision was made by the General Convention in 1859 to solicit from the various state conventions suggestions for reorganizing the structure of the denomination, the committee appointed to carry it out did not bother to contact those in the South.[284] The reasons given were that South Carolina had been the only Southern state to have ever sent delegates to a General Convention meeting; and a Southern Convention had been organized which had made no effort whatsoever to communicate with the General Convention or to exhibit any desire to be "really connected with it." The creation of the General Southern Convention was based on the need for strengthening Universalism in the South, with the clear implication that neither Universalists in the North in general nor the General Convention in particular had any real appreciation of that section's problems or any desire to assist.

The growing urge to declare independence from northern Universalism was expressed most clearly when the constitution drawn up for the General Southern Convention was considered by the state conventions. It explicitly provided that it was to be subordinate to the General Convention. The South Carolina Convention duly ratified the document, but the Georgia Convention reacted otherwise.[285] After eliciting "considerable discussion pro and con," the convention constitution was ratified except for the provision for subordination.[286] One of the first official acts of the delegates to the Mississippi State Convention after its creation in 1859 was to resolve "that we regard the General Southern Convention as an independent body, neither *superior* nor *inferior* to the United States Convention of Universalists, but we consider it, its *equal,* and ask co-operation with it as such."[287]

That same year, the South Carolina Convention had a change of heart. Under the dominating leadership of Alabama Universalist newspaper editor John C. Burruss (who attended every convention meeting in the South he could fit into a busy schedule, regardless of where it met), another resolution was substituted for that of 1858. It provided that "in view of the aggressive spirit of many of our Northern brethren, relative to the institution of slavery, we as a State Convention, *expunge* that portion of the General Southern Convention [constitution] which places it in subordination to the United States Convention."[288] The regional organization was also referred to frequently by Burruss in his *Universalist Herald* as the "General Convention of Universalists–South." The section of the constitution of the General Southern Convention referring to subordination to the General Convention of the United States was stricken out at its meeting in 1859.[289]

The efforts to establish an effective vehicle for regional cooperation among southern Universalists were, in perspective, not very successful, even allowing for the disruptiveness of civil war. The same handful of faithful preachers put in an appearance at the three meetings held before 1861. Distances were too great, other demands were too pressing, and money to travel too hard to come by to permit the lay attendance always hoped for and called for. Universalists in the pre-Civil War South were too few and too dispersed to create and maintain a flourishing organization. Meetings were so sparsely attended that the clerk of the 1859 Convention called it "a poor farce."[290] Five clergymen were present that year, representing four states; and one from the fifth (North Carolina) received fellowship and was licensed to preach (Rodrick Norton). But all of the twelve lay delegates were from Georgia, where the convention met. The clerk (J.M.H. Smith, one of the two ministers from Georgia) came to the conclusion that if attendance were not improved, the convention should be abolished as not worth the time and effort. At the last meeting of the convention (in 1860), of the six clergymen present, only four of the seven then active in the South were able to attend.[291] The number of lay delegates was not recorded.

In 1858, while on a visit to Boston, E.H. Lake, who had for many years preached in the South and particularly in North Carolina, wrote his southern cohorts: "Thank God, Universalism knows no South—nor North—but breaks over all enclosures, and embraces the world."[292] Yet Universalists in the South preceding the outbreak of the Civil War were no more able to transcend their sectional loyalties than their northern counterparts nor their fellow Protestants below the Mason-Dixon Line. The General Southern Convention, so far as it expressed Southern views, supported the Southern cause. It even expressed a preference for patronage of the adamantly pro-southern *Universalist Herald* over northern denominational newspapers.[293] At the 1860 Convention, attendants on J.M.H. Smith's sermon were urged to preach the Gospel according to Christ—"not according to [Theodore] Parker, or [William Lloyd] Garrison, . . . not according to Fanny Wright or Uncle Tom's Cabin." Religious liberalism and political and social conservatism went hand-in-hand. A plea was also made to support the regional convention; after all, the "Northern Church" had its "General Conventional Organization," and the South had its own. For better or worse, most Southern Universalists were following the path dictated by sectional allegiance.[294]

SECTION VIII

Retrospect and Prospect

Chapter 27

UNIVERSALIST-UNITARIAN MERGER: FROM ANTAGONISM TO COEXISTENCE

Relations with other Denominations

"Universalism made its appearance in America as an 'offbrand' religion. Its theology, judged by the prevailing orthodoxies, was heresy and was treated as such by its opponents. Universalists won a place for themselves only against the most stubborn opposition . . . . They were a people set apart. They built a sect with a faith, a discipline and bonds of fellowship peculiar to themselves."[1] Thus in a few sentences Clinton Lee Scott, a clergyman and historian of the denomination, writing in the 1950s, summed up the situation in the perspective of time. It was, said one nineteenth-century Universalist (A.B. Grosh) a "liberality of feeling" that led Universalists "to tolerate a diversity of religious opinions in their denomination, almost as great as can be found in all the opposing sects united."[2]

It is abundantly clear from the historical record that the Universalist challenge to orthodoxy brought attacks from all quarters. In 1775, four years before the first Universalist society had even been organized in Gloucester, Massachusetts, the potential threat which the nascent faith represented had already been voiced by Andrew Croswell of Boston. The title of his pamphlet is self-explanatory: *Mr. Murray unmask'd. In which among other things is shewn that his Doctrine of Universal Salvation is inimical to Virtue, and productive of all manner of Wickedness; and that the Christians of all Denominations ought to be on their guard against it* . . . . Even clearer in its message was the warning issued, also in pamphlet form, a year later by John Cleaveland, pastor of the Second Church in Ipswich, Massachusetts: *An attempt to nip in the bud the unscriptural doctrine of Universal Salvation, and some other dangerous errors connected with it, which a certain Stranger who calls himself John Murray, has of late been endeavoring to spread in the First Parish of Gloucester, to draw away disciples after him* . . . . But Cleaveland's efforts proved fruitless, and Universalism not only survived but, as a new sect, found itself of necessity coexisting with and competing against other faiths in a new nation characterized by increasing religious pluralism. But Universalism, said one of its leading early defenders, would eventually triumph because it was "the cause of *the people* against a sectarian aristocracy."[3]

Opposition to Universalism on theological grounds was expressed early and frequently, not only by individual clergymen of all denominations, but by official ecclesiastical bodies as well. One of the first to excoriate the group proclaiming "Universal Salvation and the finite duration of Hell Torments" as "a dangerous opinion" was the Presbyterian Synod of New York and Philadelphia, in 1787.[4] The Synod was constrained "to declare their utter abhorrence of such doctrines as they apprehend to be subversive of the fundamental principles of religion and morality." The General Assembly of the Presbyterian church decreed in 1792 that believers in such ideas were to be refused admission to its churches; the prohibition was reaffirmed two years later. An almost endless array of similar examples exist. But rather than further documenting the long tradition of opposition to Universalism, it would be more instructive to inquire into the attitudes of Universalists toward other sects, faiths, and denominations.

There is little evidence that Universalists before the Civil War had more than minimal contacts with Jews in America, and only scattered references were made to what was a fractional minority of the population until after 1870. Most mention of Jews was confined to Biblical exegesis, with special attention to the Old Testament. When Jews were referred to at all by Universalists (or the reverse) in a nineteenth-century context, the theological similarities rather than differences between Judaism and Universalism were emphasized. Sylvanus Cobb, in a lengthy editorial in his newspaper in the 1840s, expressed amazement that the Jews had managed to survive over so many centuries as "a separate race," in spite of many dispersions, the fact that they were "everywhere insulted," and existed without a country to call their own.[5] James Shrigley, pastor of the Universalist society in Baltimore in the 1840s, thought Universalists should be aware that Jews and Universalists had an affinity.[6] Neither believed in endless punishment, the Jews relying on the Old Testament and the Universalists on the New Testament as well. Thomas Whittemore saw fit in the late 1850s to cite an article in a Jewish publication (the *Israelite*) calling attention to the similarity of beliefs between the two faiths —denial of the doctrine of the Trinity, common adherence to "the final salvation of all men without distinction of creed," and the rejection of future punishment and enless hell-fire.[7] But for most Universalists, the Jews were apparently outside their experience and hence the scantiness of references to them.

Universalists had considerably more to say about another religious minority, the Roman Catholics, who were becoming more and more visible during the 1830s and 1840s as a part of a dramatic influx of immigrants from northern and western Europe, and in particular the Irish. Many native Americans became uneasy about the fact that "too many foreigners [were] pouring into this country, who had no sympathy with our feelings, our habits, our religion, or our system of government."[8] Two tangible results came out of the burst of new arrivals. One was a phenomenal increase of Roman Catholics among the population, notably in the cities of the East and the frontier areas of the Midwest; the other was an upsurge in parochial schools at the very time that the concept of public education was beginning to take hold in earnest. The fact that Protestant as well as Catholic children attended religiously operated schools became a cause for much alarm among non-Catholics. George W. Quinby, Ohio correspondent briefly for the *Trumpet* in the 1850s, reported that the more than 30,000 Roman Catholics in Cincinnati posed a serious threat to the public school system; the fact that two were serving on the city school board meant that they held the balance of political power in that body.[9]

One church-operated school which attracted attention throughout the East was located in Charlestown, Massachusetts, and was conducted by the sisters of an Ursuline convent. Growing tension between Catholics and Protestants, fired by hysteria and rumors and counter-rumors over the threat of "popery," was climaxed by the burning of the convent by a mob in the late summer of 1834.[10]

Universalists shared with other Protestants the increasing concern over rising Catholic numbers and influence. They made crystal clear their dislike of Roman Catholic theology and practice, although Universalists usually attempted (not always successfully) to make a distinction between the Church as an institution and its individual members. But the term "popery" and others associated with it conjured up all kinds of dire imaginings connected with unknown forces of evil. Hosea Ballou referred to "the dense cloud of popish darkness."[11] Universalists were told that "the Papal religion is spreading with a fearful rapidity in the United States .... [with] dangerous tendencies."[12]

The editors of the two leading eastern denominational papers may be considered representative spokesmen. The basic anti-Catholicism of both Thomas Whittemore and Sylvanus Cobb showed through their conscious efforts to at least counsel moderation and toleration. Whittemore, however, used a somewhat different approach from that of his journalistic colleague. Although he might have agreed at heart with the justice of the Protestant attacks on the alleged dangers of Catholicism, Whittemore accused the "orthodox" Protestant denominations of demonstrating almost every evil of which they were complaining in regard to Roman Catholics. Whittemore singled out for special condemnation the lack of toleration by Protestants of other groups than their own.[13]

When the Baptist Educational Association expressed alarm about the virtual takeover of some areas in the Midwest (particularly the Mississippi Valley), and the establishment of numerous parochial schools, Whittemore admitted the same concern but warned that fellow Protestants were frequently establishing and maintaining the same kind of sectarian educational institutions about which they were complaining.[14] He saw little to choose, as between Catholic and Protestant partialism, except that the latter was less given to secrecy. On balance, it made orthodox Protestantism merely the lesser of two evils.[15]

Like most responsible citizens, Whittemore was shocked and horrified by the burning of the Charlestown convent. It was an "outrage [that] admits of no justification—such violations of law, and of every principle of moral justice, cannot be too severely reprimanded."[16] But above all else he distrusted the aura of secrecy that was alleged to surround Roman Catholicism. He disagreed with the report of the committee of Bostonians which investigated the burning of the Ursuline convent and blamed the episode on religious intolerance. It was, rather, that the convent stood beyond the law and that the general public had never been properly informed as to what goings-on took place behind its closed doors.[17] Hosea Ballou 2d gently chided Universalists in general and Whittemore in particular for being taken in by stories of atrocities and for exaggerating the threat of Catholicism.

> I should be extremely sorry to see Suspicion and Rumor, which have never been famed for the most scrupulous accuracy, let loose to inflame popular passion, and especially to aggravate a heinous wrong already inflicted, and patiently endured .... It would be easy ... to inflame the natural propensities of a Protestant community against the Catholic, by dwelling on the cruelities and vices that marked former ages. There are spots in our history, blacker than pen can make; and we know that for the time being, there are passages too in the history of Protestants as black. Let not this be forgotten....[18]

But Whittemore insisted that such institutions as convents had to be put under civil supervision.[19] He expressed his absolute opposition to a new convent established in Charleston, South Carolina. "We think Protestants should not countenance them in any way."[20]

Numerous unsuccessful attempts were made over many years to obtain compensation from the state legislature for the loss suffered by the destruction of the convent. George H. Emerson, as late as 1852, regretted that the public authorities still refused "to remunerate the Catholics for the illegal and disgraceful destruction of their property."[21] Compensation would have been not only simple justice but the politic thing to do; otherwise the Catholics might become martyrs because of "legislative persecution." Whittemore disagreed. Unfortunate as destruction of *any* property by a mob might be, the legislature had never followed a policy of reimbursement for private loss. Unless a rule providing compensation for all such acts were provided, Roman Catholics deserved no special consideration.

Whittemore was not averse to casting aspersions on Roman Catholics himself, and to making acid remarks about their hierarchy and its policies. John England (1786-1842), Roman Catholic bishop of Chrleston, South Carolina, obtained a papal dispensation to permit communicants in the United States to eat meat on Fridays under certain conditions. Whittemore commented that "probably His Holiness found his people getting into the Protestant faith on this point and seeing they were determined to have their own way, concluded he might as well *let* them have it."[22] Under the heading "Wonderful Condescension" he noted that some parishioners would "be very much obliged" if the bishop would "furnish the *meat,* as well as the liberty to eat it."[23] But Whittemore categorically refused to join any organized crusade or political party aimed at attacking Roman Catholics.[24] Much as he might have disliked Catholicism, he had too much faith in the free institutions of which the nation boasted and too much pride as a citizen to indulge in such activities. James Shrigley of Baltimore took much the same stand. A group of militant Protestant clergymen in that city attempted to organize a movement to suppress Catholicism.[25] When he refused to have any part of it, he and Universalists in general were vociferously attacked from numerous pulpits.

Like Whittemore, Sylvanus Cobb was exercised over the rapid spread of Roman Catholicism and its potential threat to the "American way of life." He insisted that his apprehension was based on "the Catholic system, with its essential political monarchy and spiritual wickedness," and not on dislike of individual Roman Catholics.[26] In the same way, he tried not to condemn all Irish indiscriminately, but to make a distinction between the "low and degraded class of Irish amongst us" who flocked to the cities and filled the alms-houses and penitentiaries and prisons, and those who made their own way, especially as farmers.[27] The greatest misfortune was that individuals were "held by the iron grasp of the priesthood" and were not allowed to inquire into religion for themselves. Cobb was opposed to parochial schools because they isolated Roman Catholic youth from the mainstream of Americans and hence should in no manner receive public aid. He agreed with Whittemore that, deplorable as the burning of the Charlestown convent had been, no indemnification should be provided by the state.[28]

Cobb, distrustful of Roman Catholics at best, and an active abolitionist, roundly condemned the *Boston Pilot,* a Roman Catholic organ, for approving the return of a fugitive slave to the South in 1854. This showed clearly "the pro-slavery position of the Catholic fraternity."[29] Thomas B. Thayer delivered a strongly anti-Catholic sermon at the Universalist General Convention in Philadelphia in the same year. He considered the Catholic church even more "radically opposed to the spirit and genius of our republican institutions" than slavery—"the most thorough, unyielding, and dangerous depotism on this earth."[30] Cobb wholeheartedly concurred, and reprinted the sermon in full on the front page of his paper. Universalists had to be on guard against "the wily machinations of the Papal Jesuitical legions at work among us . . . [creating] a separate nation within a nation."

Among the Roman Catholic clerical orders it was the Jesuits who came in for particular criticism. They were not only considered intransigent for their attitude toward Protestants but were among the leading teaching orders and were hence considered a special threat to the rise of public education. They were signled out in a feature article in the *Trumpet* entitled "Offensive Principles of the Papists."[31] Jesuits, said Whittemore, were the special enemies of the public school system and were "seeking to bring this country under bondage" by establishing parochial schools.[32] One of the signal triumphs of Universalists in their verbal jousts with Jesuits was the conversion of one of their number to Universalism in 1851. J.C. Pitrat, a French-born member of the faculty of the University of Paris and an anti-monarchist during the Revolution of 1848, edited an anti-clerical paper before his immigration to the United States.[33] He was the first Roman Catholic priest known to have become a Universalist. He wrote a polemical work entitled *Jesuitism Unveiled* and after migrating to America, joined the Second Universalist Society in Cincinnati in 1851 and delivered a sermon on human brotherhood the same day. He was naturally much in demand as a speaker among Universalists.

Henry W. Bellows, a leading Unitarian clergyman and advocate of closer ties with Universalism, injected a jarring note into inter-denominational relations in 1859 when he called for a "New Catholic Church." He presumably meant by this not only a grand spiritual awakening but the restoration of ritual, with mystical overtones, that had been lost by Protestants. E.G. Brooks, secretary of the Committee on the State of the Church for the Universalist General Convention, reacted immediately. He saw some merit in Bellows' idea of spiritual regeneration, in spite of the Unitarian clergyman's "finical notions and rhetorical swells."[34] But he disagreed vigorously with Bellows' attempt to fit Protestantism "into the old forms of the Romish Church. The Church of the future is to be a Protestant Church, and not a rejuvenated Roman Catholic Church, with the Pope left out."

The heightened presence of Roman Catholicism most certainly put the Universalist profession of toleration for all religious bodies to a test, and complete consistency was not always achieved. One might raise an eyebrow at a statement made by C.D. Stuart following a visit to Maryland in 1844. After noting the high percentage of Catholics in that state, he observed that Catholicism there was "so tolerant that it can hardly be distinguished from real Universalism."[35]

But it was not with Roman Catholics that the Universalists had the most contact, but with fellow Protestants. The trials and tribulations, defeats and victories of Universalists in their various relationships were to be measured basically within the context of the Protestant majority which comprised the American religious configuration before 1870. It should be recorded, however, that Universalists spoke with unanimity against one non-Catholic group. Mormonism, born in 1830 in the "burned over" area of upstate New York, where Universalists competed vigorously for recognition and for the religious allegiance of the inhabitants, was unhesitatingly condemned. Philo Price, a denominational newspaper editor in New York State, had no use for either the new sect or for its founder, Joseph Smith. Mormonism was not even a true Christian religion, in Price's estimation; it had merely appropriated (and misrepresented) Biblical ideas in a "very wicked attempt to impose upon the credulity of the ignorant."[36] Smith was "a thorough going scoundrel too lazy to dig, and too ignorant to succeed in any honest calling without the labor of his hands." Whittemore referred to the Mormons as "these deluded people."[37]

After the Mormons overflowed the confines of New York State and headed west, Jonathan Kidwell, the iconoclastic Indiana Universalist, offered to engage in a written debate with any Mormon elder, including Sidney Rigdon, one of their leaders. Having failed to elicit a reply to his challenge, Kidwell wrote a series of blistering articles on the subject.[38] The Book of Mormon was "a base imposture" which stood "convicted by its own internal evidence," including contradictions to doctrines preached by some of the elders themselves. Needless to say, Kidwell likewise considered the leaders "a set of base imposters." Another Universalist (unidentified) considered Mormonism as "a compound of superstition and error, and their pretensions to supernatural powers blasphemous."[39]

Sylvanus Cobb, like other Universalists, was skeptical of the claims of the Mormons and considered Joseph Smith a charlatan who operated a "great scheme of trickery and delusion."[40] The polygamy practiced by the Mormons in Utah was "but a self-constituted and self-legalized system of licentiousness .... a terrible sore in the body politic."[41] However, Cobb insisted that the Mormons were entitled to freedom of conscience and should not be persecuted. As another Universalist expressed it, "This is a free country, and they have the same right to their opinion which others have."[42] There is no indication that Universalists engaged in actual confrontations with the Mormons of which they had such a low opinion. On the other hand, contacts with such "orthodox" and "partialist" denominations as Congregationalists,

Episcopalians, Methodists, Baptists, and Presbyterians were both frequent and at times unpleasant.

It is difficult and even dangerous to generalize about the attitudes toward and treatment of most other Protestant denominations by Universalists, for much depended on not only individual experience but the human equation in terms of personality differences and local circumstances. It is probably safe to assume that almost all Protestant groups were lumped together by Universalists as Calvinist ("orthodox" or "partialist" in some degree) and therefore not to be considered theologically sound. But hatred *per se* of other denominations, or systematic attacks on them seemed to have been quite lacking among Universalists. Criticism was another matter, but even then most other faiths failed to receive from Universalists the degree and intensity of censure that they meted out to Universalists.

A high proportion of Universalist effort, particularly in the early days, was expended on defense against allegations by other denominations. When counter-attack was called for, it usually came promptly and effectively (at least according to the Universalist version). When the Restorationist struggle had begun to surface among eastern Universalists in the early 1820s, other denominations gleefully noted that they were contending among themselves. Editor Samuel C. Loveland of the *Christian Repository* (Vermont) reminded critics of Universalism of the numerous varieties of Baptists, Methodists, and Congregationalists (including Unitarian). Divisions in the ranks were in no sense unique to Universalists.[43]

Except for an understandable tendency to be defensive, the strategies and tactics employed by Universalists to maintain and spread their faith were much the same as those of other denominations—"doctrinal" sermons, newspaper editorials, tracts, public debates (both oral and written)—whether in settled and urban areas, or on the ever-expanding and changing frontier. In at least two respects, however, the Universalists departed from the general practices of other denominations: They opened their pulpits and meeting houses to those of other faiths from the very beginning; and they held meetings of all kinds "to which Christians of all denominations were most cordially invited."[44] None of these tactics, regardless of the motives which prompted their use, was an unalloyed success, but the very rebuffs Universalists often received merely strengthened their determination. Unfortunately for the Universalists, however, they most often found themselves merely talking or writing to and for each other rather than for the larger audience which might have bolstered their cause.

One of the earliest examples of the opening of Universalists pulpits to outsiders occurred in 1793, when Ezekial Cooper of Maryland, a Methodist Episcopalian, spoke in John Murray's church in Boston.[45]

James Shrigley, pastor of the Baltimore Universalist society, allowed E.W.R. Allen, minister of the Methodist Episcopal church in Oriskany, New York, not only to speak in his church but to solicit donations to aid in extinguishing a church debt.[46] Shrigley was naturally criticized for such an unusual action, but vigorously defended himself by reminding his own congregation as well as Universalists elsewhere that "we were *all brethren,* members of one great family; and that as christians we were duty bound to do all that we could to help each other," regardless of denomination or creed. He went on to point out that when the Methodists were building their first house of worship in Boston, John Murray's congregation had been among the contributors and that Murray himself, an ex-Methodist, had also made a donation. The Baltimore incident was made even more interesting by the fact that the visiting minister had been refused permission to take up collections in churches of his own denomination in Baltimore.

Universalists usually made a point of granting permission to visitors to speak at their meetings. Associations and other organized groups sometimes invited clergy from other denominations to participate even in the deliberations of their legislative councils, as did the Black River Association (New York) in 1838.[47] But this practice sometimes backfired. When such permission was granted to Deacon Daniel Galpin of the Congregational church in Berlin, Connecticut, at a meeting of the Southern Association (New England) he used the opportunity to conduct a verbal attack on Universalism which lasted an entire morning.[48]

Universalists had particular difficulty in securing accommodations not only for regular services but for special meetings, including annual conventions. This was occasionally due to lack of advance planning, but more often because of the opposition to their use of either religious or secular facilities because Universalists were not a religiously acceptable body. Sometimes a change of heart on the part of church wardens, clergy, trustees, or other officials resulted in refusals to use church buildings. Time and again Universalists found even courthouses or school buildings closed to them, even after prior permission had been obtained. Such was the case when the New England Convention met in Woodstock, Vermont, in 1799 and was unexpectedly met at the door of the courthouse by the local sheriff, complete with drawn sword.[49] But the verbal powers of Hosea Ballou, one of the three preachers present, prevailed, and the sheriff was reported to have retreated in shame and confusion. On another occasion Ballou was prevented from preaching in a church in the Massachusetts village of Mattapoiset on the ground that the religion he represented was "subversive of Christianity."[50]

Sometimes legal technicalities of great complexity were involved in the use of church facilities. After Thomas Whittemore began a series of discourses in a public hall in Malden, Massachusetts, in 1826, the quarters became inadequate to hold the overflow audiences, and the use of the more commodious First Parish Church (Congregational) was requested and immediately denied by the pastor because Whittemore was a Universalist.[51] But a controversy ensued over who had authority to grant or deny permission—the pastor, the trustees, or the parish collectively. After legal counsel was consulted, the parish made the decision to allow Whittemore the use of the building. How much time elapsed before a decision was reached was not recorded, but at least three votes were taken. The failure of Universalists to secure the use of churches of other denominations could also be a direct benefit. Upon the Baptist's refusal of their building in Hudson, New Hampshire, Universalists promptly erected an awning on the common facing the church and after hearing a sermon announced plans for "the speedy erection of a meeting house."[52]

Formal cooperation of Universalists with the organizations and agencies of other denominations was almost totally lacking, even when the initiative came from outside of Universalist circles. As has been pointed out, Universalists were reluctant to join forces with other groups advocating such reforms as temperance and abolition. Their fear of associating with "sectarian" groups of almost any kind led them to an almost perversely independent course which tended often to weaken their efforts, sympathetic as they might have been to both the aims and methods of others. The American Bible Society, organized in New York City in 1816 as one of the earliest interdenominational efforts, had as its main goal the distribution of copies of the Scriptures. They solicited subscriptions and support from a wide range of sources. A few Universalists subscribed as individuals, but Thomas Whittemore advised against participation. It appeared to him to be only a vehicle for disseminating "orthodoxy."[53] Universalists in Portsmouth, New Hampshire, declined to assist in distribution of Bibles, on the ground that Universalists were already adequately equipped, and produced statistics to prove it.[54] A representative of the American Bible Society spoke to the Maine State Convention in 1858 requesting support from "all denominations of Christians," but no official action was taken. Over a decade later a motion was made in a meeting of that same body to approve in principle an American Bible Society project to circulate the Scriptures "without note or comment" and to cooperate with other denominations to assist in distribution, but the suspicious northern-tier New Englanders indefinitely postponed action on the proposal.

Universalists did cooperate at times in local interdenominational projects such as the buying of shares and the contributing of books to the General Theological Library in Boston, organized as a subscription library in 1860. But the shares were purchased by individual Universalists and not by any one group. It was the denominational publishing house that donated books.[55] Cooperation and a "spirit of Christian brotherhood" in relation to others did exist, but usually on a strictly informal and often quite personal level. When Stephen R. Smith needed a place to preach in upstate New York in the 1820s, he found the Methodists uniformly willing to open at least their homes to Universalist meetings.[56]

When they had unhappy experiences with members of other denominations, Universalists were usually careful to identify the religious affiliation of the offender, but in only one known instance (the Mormons) did they issue a blanket condemnation. George Rogers, in his frontier travels, found Dutch Reformed clergymen particularly unreceptive to Universalism, and envied the Methodists because they could use emotionalism and the orthodox hell-fire and damnation approach, while he had to arouse "the reasoning facilities of men" and could not promise, as could the Methodists, "an exclusive freehold in Paradise."[57] Whittemore had a distinct dislike of Methodists, but this was due mainly to their presumed propensity for hiring preachers of dubious moral character.[58]

All too often overlooked in the midst of inter-denominational quarrels and bickering were the many instances of cooperation and fraternal expression at the local level, from pulpit exchanges to meeting house construction and dedication. The initiative came both from Universalists and from other denominations. At the raising of a Universalist meeting house in Turner, Maine, in 1825, representatives from all the churches in the vicinity were invited, and a Congregational minister delivered the prayer.[59] Joint ownership of a meeting house by two or more denominations ("union houses") was not uncommon in the nineteenth century, notably in rural areas and in small towns which could not support more than one church edifice. Universalists were part owners and/or users of scores of such buildings in all sections of the nation where they settled, and more or less elaborate schedules for use were worked out among the cooperating denominations. Typical were the meeting houses in Wendell, New Hampshire owned "principally" by the Freewill Baptists and Universalists and dedicated in an ecumenical service in 1833; and the meeting house in Hartford (Cortland County), New York, financed equally by three denominations (Universalists, Methodists, and Presbyterians).[60] Teachers and pupils of four Protestant Sabbath Schools in Framingham, Massachusetts, held joint services to celebrate the anniversary of American independence in 1836. A Universalist delivered the main address.[61]

Interdenominational cooperation did not always work out as harmoniously as planned. A union meeting house, owned principally by Universalists and partly by Methodists, was to have been dedicated jointly in Lee, New York, in 1834. But the Methodist contingent failed to appear, and the Universalists concluded that their erstwhile religious colleagues were "too holy to associate with sinners" and left the entire ceremony to the Universalists on that account.[62] In the early 1840s the Universalists, Methodists, and Unitarians conducted a series of "union meetings" in East Cambridge, Massachusetts, with clergy of the three denominations conducting services in each other's churches.[63] Relations among denominations were by no means a story of unrelieved antagonisms.

It was with the Unitarians that there rested the greatest potential for maximum cooperation. On the surface, it might have appeared that the two denominations had sufficient mutual interests and even identities to have gone a step farther and combined forces, and even to have merged. This was actually considered a possibility by both denominations more than once before 1870. But theological as well as socio-economic factors and a host of other considerations prevented such an eventuality for almost a century after the Universalists celebrated their first century. The love-hate relationship which existed between the two liberal religious bodies for the first 100 years of Universalism deserves fairly detailed consideration.

From Antagonism to Coexistence

Before an attempt is made to tell the tangled, often ambiguous, and sometimes contradictory story of relations between Universalists and Unitarians up through 1870, certain caveats should be entered and certain explanations should be offered. The eventual outcome is already known to many, and the temptation to anticipate the twentieth-century union of the two denominations which did take place must be strongly resisted. The ostensible similarities of the two groups as "twin heresies" in the nineteenth century, noted by not only those within both denominations but by many outside observers, actually concealed deep differences of theology, class configuration, philosophy, behavior, and attitudes which cannot be easily overlooked or minimized. Some twentieth-century church historians have tended to make the two denominations almost interchangeable in the nineteenth century. As has been pointed out earlier in this study, belief regarding the unitarian nature of the Deity, the basic tenet of Unitarianism, had been clearly and forcefully enunciated by Hosea Ballou in his *Treatise on Atonement* in 1805, twenty years before the American Unitarian Association had been organized. Writing in the 1960s, Winthrop S. Hudson noted that under Ballou's leadership "the Universalists adopted an anti-trinitarian position and, except for social status, became indistinguishable from the Unitarians."[64]

In 1820 Barzillai Streeter, a Universalist, had raised the question, in "An Appeal to Unitarians," of what, aside from belief in the unity of

God, distinguished the Unitarians from Universalists and most other Protestant sects.[65] This inquiry may have seemed naive or simplistic, but it is true that Universalism and Unitarianism were frequently linked in the identification of both individuals and religious societies, some examples of which have been previously cited. One of the Universalists who had served as pastor of the Hartford, Connecticut, society (H.B. Soule) called attention to the fact that when it had been chartered in 1824, it had one of the longest cognomens in the denomination: "The Independent Congregational Unitarian Universalist Society of Hartford."[66] An English immigrant who had been a Free Will Baptist, became a "Unitarian Universalist" in 1845, and ministered to a small society in Manlius (Onondaga County), New York. A Universalist in 1820 had concluded that many Unitarians were mere "Universalists in disguise."[67] Still another decided that Henry Ware, Professor of Divinity at Harvard in 1821, was expressing Universalist views regarding the limited state of future punishment.[68] Samuel C. Loveland, editor of the *Christian Repository* (Vermont) acknowledged that he was happily surprised to meet with so many Universalist ideas in the *Unitarian Miscellany*.[69]

James G. McAdam, a Scottish immigrant serving as a part-time lay Unitarian preacher in upstate New York in the 1830s, discovered, much to his delight, that American Universalists were already unitarians in their theology.[70] He promptly suggested that the two denominations unite. Josiah C. Waldo, preaching in a dozen towns in Ohio in the 1820s, found that the vast majority of adherents were "Unitarian Universalists."[71] William A. Drew, Universalist editor of the *Christian Intelligencer* (Maine) was one of the first to use the term "liberal Christianity" to link the two denominations, and announced a policy of supporting "all the friends of that cause, whether Universalists or Unitarians."[72]

In 1823, two years before Unitarians became a denomination, a Universalist observed that the principles of Unitarianism tended so much toward Universalism that he "sometimes thought that the former was only another name for the latter. Indeed I have often wondered why Unitarians did not marshall themselves under the latter term, as this would serve to lessen the great number of denominations which christians have assumed, which is a very perplexing evil."[73] Still another Universalist suggested in the mid-1820s that if Unitarian and Calvinist ministers, in the Boston area at least, had been willing to exchange pulpits with Universalists, the Universalists would "not be driven to establish and maintain separate congregations."[74] By their refusal to cooperate even in this small way, and by treating Universalists "as though we were heathens rather than christians," Unitarians and Calvinists were contributing to an unfortunate further splintering of Christianity. But these more or less random examples in no sense made historically inevitable the merger of the two denominations, especially in the pre-Civil War period.

It should be noted also that there was no *ex cathedra* or in any sense official stance taken by either Universalists or Unitarians as duly constituted religious bodies until after the mid-1860s; even then the results were tentative and exploratory rather than definitive, and produced greater cooperation and good will rather than any serious attempt at amalgamation. Nor was there ever appointed or elected a single individual to serve as the official representative for either denomination although some assumed or aspired to that role. Thomas Whittemore was one of these. A belligerently defensive Universalist, he probably did more within the denomination to keep the two groups apart, inadvertently or otherwise, than any other person. Harry W. Bellows, equally influential as an unofficial spokesman among Unitarians, was one of the first to predict that the two faiths would eventually become one body. This singling out of two individuals should in no way be interpreted to mean that it was the Unitarians who first offered the olive branch or that the Universalists were the recalcitrants. The evidence is overwhelmingly clear that both groups were divided within themselves over what the nature and extent of interdenominational relationships were, or should be, and that there were innumerable instances of friendship, collaboration, and harmony as well as antagonism, separateness, and discord. Much of the image projected on one denomination by members of the other emerged out of personal experience or individual prejudice or proclivity, and not out of superior omniscience, access to inside information, or privileged position. There was the inevitable, although not necessarily appropriate, tendency to generalize from all too limited information, and to paste on an entire religious body a label which fitted only a small segment of it. In short, both Universalists and Unitarians sometimes failed to recognize or acknowledge one of the basic features which they shared—their individuality and their commitment to diversity within their own ranks.

"Professing little reverence for human creeds, having no common standard but the Bible, and allowing, in the fullest extent, freedom of thought and the liberty of every Christian to interpret the records of divine revelation for himself, they look for diversity of opinion as the necessary result. They see not, they say, how this is to be avoided without a violation of the grand Protestant principle of individual faith and liberty." These words could easily have been written by a nineteenth-century Universalist. In fact, they came in the mid-1840s from the pen of a Unitarian pastor in Dedham, Massachusetts, Alvan Lamson, in an article on "Unitarian Congregationalism" prepared to enlighten the general public.[75]

Although there was a discernible evolution over the decades from the undisguised polemics of the early nineteenth century to a softening of historic antagonisms by the 1860s, the process was slow, erratic, and incomplete, and never a matter of complete consensus on either side. Further, it is impossible to identify with any precision any neatly compartmentalized stages in this evolution, complete with dates and turning-points. There were pulpit exchanges between Universalists and Unitarians long before 1825. Stephen R. Smith (Universalist) and I.B. Pierce (Unitarian) exchanged in 1822, and Pierce, intending to be helpful, urged Universalists to change their name to "Universalist Congregationalist or Independent" in order to achieve respectability.[76] On the other side of the coin, Moses Ballou, almost forty years later, and after a quarter of a century of contact with Unitarians as a Universalist clergyman, thought that "there is no sect on earth which would more glady destroy us, than the Unitarians, if it had but the power to do so."[77]

The reasons offered by Universalists for joining forces with or for remaining separate from Unitarians were recurrent and almost endlessly repetitive. Once stated, they appeared time and time again in various contexts. This author could have sorted them out arbitrarily and classified them into neat pigeonholes. But that would have isolated and fragmented them and possibly might have distorted the historical record. Hence direct quotation as well as paraphrase has been used liberally, and many arguments for or against closer relations between Universalists and Unitarians have often been given more than once because they were part of the reasoning used to make a larger point. It is principally for this reason also that a generally chronological rather than topical pattern has been followed here.[78]

One of the most frequently cited instances of early antagonism between Unitarians and Universalists occurred in 1824, on the occasion of the building of a Universalist meeting house in Chatham (Barnstable County), Massachusetts. News of its construction prompted David Reed, the founder and editor of the *Christian Register* (Unitarian) to write a blistering editorial in which he referred to Universalism as "this miserable, false and unspeakably pernicious system."[79] Being a religion "without sanctions, it lays no restraint on their vicious propensities and passions, and their impure and depraved habits." It allowed individuals to hope they would be saved in their sins; this permitted them, in turn, "to be slaves to their own lusts and impurities so long as the poor remnant of their mortal strength lasts them." Reed, it should be pointed out, was not referring to all Universalists, but only "to that class . . . who admit of no future punishment." These poor creatures were "miserably deluded;" in their zeal to reject Calvinism, some Universalists had "become blind to the defects in their own system." The editorial, without mentioning his name, was aimed specifically at Hosea Ballou, "an able and popular man" who was attempting to spread "the doctrine that the sufferings of iniquity end with the present life, and that all men at death become sharers of the happiness of heaven." This referred explicitly to the "death and glory" principle associated with Ballou's theory and not to the Restorationist or ultimate "Restitution of all things" doctrine adhered to by many Universalists and Universalist-Unitarians such as Thomas Starr King.

Ballou was quick to reply to Reed's strong language.[80] Universalists, particularly those who did not believe in future punishment, had not, said Ballou, over-reacted to the rigidities of Calvinism and gone to the other extreme. In fact, numerous and highly respected people sincerely believed in some variety of Calvinism. There was no justification for the editor of the *Christian Register* to have issued a blanket condemnation of Calvinism, calling it "repugnant to reason and scripture, and dishonorary of God." Ballou was even more irritated by the ambivalence and lack of commitment by Unitarians to a positive set of beliefs beyond the nature of the Deity than to blasts against Calvinism and even against some varieties of Universalism. In 1825 he wrote an open letter to the Unitarians challenging them to take the next step and declare their belief in Universalism.[81] Ballou thought it was high time that they "come out boldly from under those rags, which can no longer hide you, and own the truth and the whole truth." Unitarianism had "already made a noise in throwing off the superstition of the trinity, and why should you now be afraid to take another bold step." That "bold step" was to declare unequivocally the belief in universal salvation. This the Unitarians refused to do. They contented themselves instead, as Ballou had expressed it earlier (in 1822), with lumping together the doctrine of universal salvation and the Calvinistic doctrine of election and reprobation, and condemning them both as false.[82]

Ballou also introduced some of the non-theological reasons for disliking Unitarians that were to reappear frequently, although not always worded the same way. Unitarians, said Ballou, were snobbish, insisting as they did that "in the future world, people will take rank according to their attainments in this life."[83] This ran counter to the Universalist promise of salvation for all, without regard to previous station. Massena Goodrich shared with Ballou his criticism of Unitarians and was even more specific about the future abode appropriate for that privileged group. "An aristocratic heaven, where the parlor, at least, should be reserved for the wealthy, learned, and fashionable of earth, would come nearer their ideal of a desirable state of things."[84]

In a sermon delivered to the Second Universalist Society in Boston in 1829 entitled "Commendation and Reproof of Unitarians," Ballou drew up a balance-sheet.[85] The positive attributes outnumbered the negative ones by a score of seven to four. The Unitarians were reproved for refusing to acknowledge themselves as Universalists, in spite of the fact that their principles led them inexorably to such a position. They avoided discussion of their doctrines in the pulpit and indulged "in speculations about a future state of rewards and punishments." Unitarians were chided for "the satisfaction with which they contemplate their exaltation over their fellow men in the future state, and the scorn with which they regard the system which places all men in equally favorable circumstances." Finally, Unitarians were inconsistent because they argued that differences of opinion should not prevent pulpit exchanges, and complained that the orthodox would not exchange pulpits with them, yet Unitarians were just as unwilling to exchange with Universalists.

Friction between the two denominations was to be found most markedly before 1840 at the individual society and church level. Some of the ill-feeling was over trivial and petty matters, but even then gave some indication that relatively peaceful coexistence was still in the future. Squabbles over the use of meeting houses were frequent and sometimes acrimonious. If the protestations of Universalists are to be taken at face value, it was usually they who found themselves locked out of Unitarian churches rather than the reverse. Universalists in Cambridge, Massachusetts, were particularly incensed in 1828 when they were not only denied the use of Unitarian facilities but watched the latter deliberately schedule evening meetings at the same time as the Universalists.[86] After the Unitarians had made an attempt to prevent the use by Universalists of the First Parish Church (Congregational) in Malden, Massachusetts, one Universalist wrote bitterly that "there are no greater enemies to the prosperity of the Universalists than are the Unitarians."[87] But other instances can be found of the "Christian liberality" on the part of Unitarians which Universalists felt was so lacking. When the First Universalist Society in Boston voted to raze "their ancient house of worship" in 1838 and build a new structure, the pastors of both neighboring Unitarian societies volunteered the use of their churches at any hour of any Sunday when not being used by Unitarians.[88]

Universalists complained time after time that when Unitarians were in the minority in a community they cultivated Universalist sympathy and support, but when they had achieved their goals, they abandoned and rebuffed Universalists. Universalists in Concord, New Hampshire, were much upset in 1829 when the Unitarian minister solicited funds from Universalists for building a meeting house and used the argument that there was no real difference between the two groups.[89] After money had been raised with Universalist assistance, the minister announced that Unitarians believed in eternal punishment and hence were not Universalists in belief at all and that Universalists were not displayed great friendship for the local Universalists it was discovered that the Unitarians, the smallest of the three Protestant societies in the community, were attempting to expel the Calvinist Congregationalists from the jointly-used meeting house and were merely seeking Universalist assistance for that one purpose. In actuality, said one Universalist, Unitarian antagonism toward Universalists ran too strong and too deep for even such momentary cooperation. "Unitarians have no more desire for the spread of Universalism than they have for that of Popery."[90] In 1830 the Universalists in Chelmsford, Massachusetts, who had for many years been members of the local Unitarian church, seceded and formed their own society because the Unitarians refused to allow Universalists in the pulpit, even on an exchange basis.[91]

Universalists often explained such uncharitable acts in terms of Unitarian jealousy and fear of growing Universalist numbers and influence. Universalist editors periodically reported the comparative statistical strength of the two denominations, and were triumphant when the Universalists usually turned out in fact to be in the majority. George Rogers, itinerating in Alabama in the late 1830s, talked with the Unitarian minister in Mobile, who was having difficulty in keeping his small flock from disintegrating. After telling him that the Unitarians would have greater success if they "proclaimed their doctrines boldly," Rogers explained why Universalists were making more progress than the Unitarians, even though Universalists had "less learning than you; less wealth; less age; a less respectable history."[92] It was "simply because we address outselves to the common sense of the people."

Some Universalists by the 1830s and 1840s began to detect closer and more cordial relations with Unitarians than previously, and some Universalists played an important part in bringing them about. Elbridge Gerry Brooks, one of the most accomplished orators in the denomination, delivered a laudatory sermon in 1842 on the occasion of the death of William Ellery Channing.[93] He was eulogized as a reformer, a philanthropist, and a Christian. Channing had been openly hostile to the Universalist movement, and when Hosea Ballou had moved to Boston he was offered no ministerial courtesies or fellowship. It was reported that Channing treated him as though he were a leper.[94]

Stephen R. Smith, from the vantage point of upstate New York, thought he discerned greater respect on the part of the Unitarians for Universalists, and accounted for it by the rapid growth of Universalism and its increasing influence and respectability.[95] He was heartened to see increased pulpit exchanges and a slightly more favorable attitude on the part of Unitarians toward the idea of universal salvation, but he took a very cautious stand nonetheless. He saw no way in which the denominations could "come together on equal terms," and union was impossible under any other circumstances. Unitarians still had too many traits and characteristics unacceptable to Universalists. Unitarians persisted in studiously suppressing their own views although "a few of the dominant sects have looked upon Unitarianism as a convenient name to cover much secret infidelity." Smith resented the fact that

Unitarianism had "assumed that it embodied all the learning, refinement and respectability of the two sects; and that all of the weight of public odium, was on the side of Universalism." Even pulpit exchanges and growing cordiality among a few clergymen were still only "ministerial courtesies" and not official denominational acts. The Massachusetts State Convention reported to the General Convention in 1834 that sentiment against Universalists was on the decline but there were still "three classes of opponents—the orthodox, the unitarians, and infidels."[96]

Looking at Universalism and Unitarianism from the outside in the 1830s and early 1840s, the orthodox *Quarterly Christian Spectator* made the judgment that the latter had no really popular appeal because it was "too refined, too literary, too negative and sceptical, to produce an impression on the multitude." On the other hand, even if they had not achieved respectability, the Universalists were becoming "a much more formidable adversary of truth and righteousness, than any other heresy."[97] For one thing, Universalism had "none of the aristocratic refinement of Unitarianism."

When the final volume of the first edition of the *Encyclopedia Americana* appeared in 1833 (including the last portion of the alphabet), Thomas Whittemore immediately checked the write-ups of Unitarianism and Universalism. He was exceedingly unhappy with what he found.[98] The Unitarians rated ten columns, including mention of several denominations (Congregational, Christian, and Reformed Baptist) which had Unitarians among their members; but not one sentence about the approximately 800 Universalist congregations holding an identical view. To make bad matters worse, the Universalists rated less than one-third of a column, and the description was not only sketchy but inaccurate, and did not mention a single individual or a one of the more than twenty denominational publications then available.

Robert Baird, author of a survey of religion in America published in the early 1840s, made generalizations about both the Universalists and the Unitarians which probably made them both cringe (if they read the work at all). Hosea Ballou's ideas had

> done something to diffuse Unitarian opinions among Universalists . . . . [and] the Unitarians have, to a great extent, and it is believed generally, embraced the doctrine of the final salvation of all men. There is, therefore, no doctrinal distinction between the two sects. As Unitarianism is esteemed the more genteel religion of the two, Universalists are under a strong temptation to change their name, and call themselves Unitarians.[99]

Of all the Universalists who expressed themselves regarding Unitarians, it was Thomas Whittemore who had the most to say. Almost from the day in 1829 when he became the sole editor of the *Universalist Magazine* until shortly before his pen was stilled by death in 1861, Whittemore became the most strident voice in behalf of Universalism and the most articulate opponent of Unitarianism. His first barrage was fired in 1829, when he outlined the differences between the two denominations. It was a simple "all or nothing" alternative that he proposed; there was no middle ground. "The fact is, a man is a Unitarian who believes in the unity of God, and he is a Universalist if he believes in the salvation of all men, and if he holds to both these doctrines, he is a Unitarian Universalist or, if the expression be thought a better one, he is a Universalist Unitarian."[100]

In pungent, often homely and colorful, and always vigorous language, he downplayed the similarities with Universalists and underlined the shortcomings of Unitarians as he saw them. He was by no means always consistent in this respect. At one time he would praise and admire Unitarians for their intellectual and educational accomplishments and at another, when he felt envious or was particularly upset by their attitudes, behavior, or actions, would lambaste them for their artistocratic tendencies and secretive ways. The single theme of the history of American Unitarianism which he published in five installments in 1845 was that the denomination had been propagated in a covert manner.[101]

He was so negative and so harsh in his treatment of Unitarians in general that he was sometimes accused by fellow Universalists of driving a wedge between the two denominations. After all, said one such critic of Whittemore, Universalism and Unitarianism were actually "the two grand divisions of the great reform party in religion," both aiming at the same goal of diffusing "the great doctrine of *one Universal Father*."[102] Another Universalist who thought Whittemore was entirely too severe in his treatment of Unitarians, was almost defiant in their defense. "I love the Unitarians next to my own denomination. And hope and believe the time is not distant when we shall be one with them in name and interest, as we are now one in general religious sentiment."[103]

Whittemore stoutly denied that he was trying to keep the two denominations apart.[104] But in spite of his frequent professions about brotherhood and love for humanity, when it came to Unitarians he usually made an exception, whether he would admit it or not. He did verbal battle with almost any and every Unitarian spokesman, feuded with the editors of Unitarian newspapers (especially the *Christian Register*), distrusted the motives of most Unitarians, innocent and well meaning as they might have been. When the number of pulpit exchanges between Universalists and Unitarians notably increased after 1835, Whittemore greeted the trend with skepticism rather than with pleasure.[105] Even though the initiative might have come from the Universalists, he was positive that the Unitarians who participated had questionable motives.

Whittemore catalogued repeatedly all of the points on which he disagreed with Unitarians. The list was a long one. His first-expressed and endlessly reiterated complaint in 1829 was that the Unitarians refused "to declare their sentiments." Almost a quarter of a century later, he was voicing the same complaint. In 1852 he put the matter with his customary directness: "Our objections to Unitarianism are not so much for what it says, as for what it refuses to say, and its sins are rather of omission, than commission. There is in it a silence, an indefiniteness upon the subject of human destiny which renders it defective, feeble, and inefficient."[106] He had no patience with New England divines whose Unitarianism consisted of "taking a precise half-way course, between the doctrines of endless misery and Universalism."[107]

But there were other objections built into and related to Unitarianism. In an editorial in 1830 referring to "the present fashionable, indefinable, intactible [*sic*] something called Unitarianism," Whittemore found in a New England Unitarian, "neither one thing nor another. He is neither cold nor hot, up nor down. He endeavors to preserve a careful balance between orthodoxy and Universalism .... Unitarianism is in a flourishing condition whenever the beam is exactly horizontal."

Then there was the virtual monopoly held by Unitarians in Massachusetts in higher education (by which Whittemore actually meant Harvard and its divinity school). Adin Ballou reacted much the same way as did Whittemore to the elevated position of Harvard, although not as vociferously. He, like Whittemore, had received but little formal education (at the common school level) and the relatively sophisticated intellectual world of the Unitarians was beyond his experience. Ballou noted that the Unitarians were almost all well educated, while the Universalists, by Unitarian standards, were unlearned and ignorant and "little better than barbarians when compared with the graduates of Harvard College, and other polished literati."[108] Unitarians, so far as Ballou had observed, disliked Universalists to a degree amounting "almost to contemptuous disgust."

When Ballou was installed as pastor of the First Parish Church (Unitarian Congregational) in Mendon, Massachusetts, in 1832 he commented that it "required no little moral courage" on the part of Unitarian Bernard Whitman to deliver the sermon for a ceremony arranged for a person who had been formally a Universalist less than two years before. Whitman later told Ballou that he (Whitman) was accused by a colleague of having been a party to promoting the ministerial careers of unlearned men. In 1833 Whitman assisted in the ordination of J.B. Pitkin, a Universalist in Richmond, Virginia, an editor of the *Southern Pioneer.*[109] W.S. Balch, editor of the *Impartialist* (Universalist), who printed the account of the ordination, expressed the hope that such interdenominational good fellowship would someday exist also in New England.

Whittemore also called attention to the preponderance of Unitarians in state governmental circles in the 1830s. All but one member of the state Supreme Judicial Court in 1831 was a Unitarian (the lone exception was an Episcopalian), and Governor Lincoln was described as a "high-toned Unitarian."[110] Whittemore did not spell out the political affiliations or party allegiance of specific individuals, but he implied that most Unitarians had been Federalists (later Whigs), while he made it clear that the majority of Universalists were anti-Federalists, Jeffersonian Republicans, and in the 1830s, Jacksonian Democrats.[111] They were as anti-aristocratic in political sentiment as they were democratic in the religious realm. While the debate over separation of church and state (accomplished in 1833) was in progress in the Massachusetts Senate in 1831, it was Unitarians (some of whom Whittemore listed by name) who had voted for indefinite postponement of the bill to amend Article III of the state constitution. So much for the boasted "liberality" of Unitarians, said Whittemore.[112]

As for possible Universalist-Unitarian collaboration, Whittemore asserted that "we know perfectly well . . . that Universalists . . . have no desire for a union of the two denominations. We do not believe, if it were put to a vote in any Universalist Convention or Association, that it would be decided the two denominations ought to unite and become one."[113] Whittemore was not averse to resorting to near-caricature or at least the creation of stereotypes, when describing Unitarians, or to making gratituous uncomplimentary remarks if the opportunity could be found. He described Unitarian preachers as "too much like clerical *dandies,* pressed into shape with buckram, clad in glossy black, peering through gold-mounted spectacles, saying well learned prayers, and reading polished discourses."[114] He predicted dire consequences for the First Congregational Church in Richmond, Virginia, which had been built by Universalists but had been taken over by Unitarians and dedicated in 1833. "Nothing will so quickly run a society down in the southern states, as to have it cursed with the policy of New England Unitarianism."[115] Whittemore was not immune from the use of sarcasm. He pointed out that in the neighborhood of Boston, Unitarians claimed "to be the *rich* and *fashionable* part of [the] community."[116] He conceded that some of them probably were, and advised socially conscious visitors to take seats in a Unitarian house of worship. They would have, even if they did not get "the joy-giving hope of the Gospel, at least, the glorious consolation of being fashionable."

Whittemore felt that one of the reasons for the friction and ill-feeling exhibited by Unitarians toward Universalists was ignorance of Universalism; namely, failure to realize that "a very large majority" of Universalists had "long ago" rejected both trinitarianism and the so-called orthodox version of the Atonement. He argued that, at base, "no two denominations in Christendom agree more nearly in sentiment." What had happened to perpetuate and even to intensify friction, and to make Universalists accustomed to regard Unitarians as, in one sense at least, the same as the orthodox, was their attempt to stop the spread of Universalism. It was, in short, a "spirit of competition and rivalship" rather than theology *per se* that divided them.[117] Some twenty years later, however, Whittemore had changed his mind. He had come to the conclusion by 1849 that theologically an "unbridgable chasm" separated Unitarians and Universalists. It centered around the refusal of Unitarians to recognize the certainty of man's ultimate salvation by divine plan.[118] The Unitarians would admit of no "grand design;" all was left uncertain, for they did not believe in "the overruling providence of God."

Other Universalists provided additional support for some of Whittemore's arguments about the deficiencies of Unitarianism, but usually in milder and more closely reasoned language than he used. Henry Bacon, long-time editor of the *Ladies' Repository,* contributed to the Rhode Island Universalist Tract Society a four-page discussion in which he argued that there were two basic theological distinctions that kept the two denominations apart.[119] According to him, all "moral freedom" (free will) in man was ultimately "under the control of the Sovereignty of God." For a Universalist, restoration to holiness and happiness was a certainty; to the Unitarian, a contingency, dependent on "the liberty of the human will." The Unitarian was, in effect, exalting freedom of the will—human agency—above divine sovereignty. By so doing, Unitarians were injecting an element of uncertainty that did not exist in the minds of Universalists. Universalists too believed in "moral freedom," but within the limit imposed by divine agency; e.g., "the absolutely certain triumph of good over evil, truth over error." The divine law of love overrode all contingencies.

A second basic difference keeping Unitarians and Universalists apart was, in Bacon's view, the matter of emphasis on priorities. Ultimate salvation—or "restoration"—might be achieved, said Unitarians, but it was in no sense the central message or distinguishing feature of the Gospels. Such a teaching should therefore not find a prominent place in preaching, but should occupy a subordinate place in the Christian scheme. Universalists argued the reverse; universal salvation was *the*—not "a" Bible doctrine. Unitarians did not go far enough. Like Universalists, they rejected the doctrines of the Trinity, vicarious atonement, election and reprobation, and total depravity. But Unitarians refused to take the final and climactic step by adding another truth. Unitarians failed to see in the doctrine of ultimate holiness and happiness of all men the moral efficacy and regenerating power claimed by Universalists. Universalists in turn argued that the Unitarian emphasis on the fatherhood of God without linking it to universal redemption left the schema incomplete.

Sylvanus Cobb had "high regard for the people, in general, composing the Unitarian sect" which was to be congratulated and thanked for rejecting the "cruel dogmas of Calvinism" and for expending "much learning and eloquence on the beauties of *one God in unity.*"[120] But he too had reservations. Unitarianism was "cold and lifeless, devoid of any principle of confidence and sentimental devotion towards God." The Deity had not, as the Unitarians implied, retired from the scene after having created the world, and left his handiwork to take care of itself. Unitarianism lacked the conception of an active and continuous government of God holding out the promise of salvation. The denomination's refusal to carry the divine plan for the moral destiny of man to its logical (Universalist) conclusion was the greatest stumbling-block to possible union.[121] Furthermore, Unitarian clergymen were by the 1850s minimizing the value of the Scriptures and were delivering little more than "mere moral, or literary, or scientific essays" more appropriate for the Lyceum circuit than the pulpit.[122] Unfortunately Cobb was beginning to see the same tendency among some Universalist clergy. He would not accept what seemed to amount to no more than a system of "ethical philosophy" which resulted in "nothingarian indifference [and] nodding assent to all shades of opinion."[123]

James Shrigley in 1844 saw no advantage in a union with Unitarians. Judging from his experience over many years in Baltimore, he concluded that the Roman Catholics were "much more liberal in their sentiments, and nearer Universalism than American Unitarianism ever was."[124] He wrote in exasperation: "from American Unitarianism, '*good* Lord deliver us.' "[125]

Universalist criticism of Unitarians continued to be voiced in the early 1840s and early 1850s, but there was also much talk of increased cooperation and harmony, and some of the asperities had begun to lose their sharpness. A.S. Kendall of Groton, Massachusetts had nothing but good to say of Unitarians; he not only preached from their pulpits on invitation but had been made the superintendent of the local Unitarian Sunday School in 1845.[126] He hoped "to make the breach which now exists between us and the Unitarian denomination still smaller." Philo Price, editor of the *Universalist Union,* detected a new note of cordiality for Universalists among Unitarians.[127] This was as it should be, in Price's estimation, for by their very nature both denominations were promoters of religious liberty. On the Unitarian side, C.W. Upham, editor of the *Christian Register,* greeted with enthusiastic approval the

Universalist policy of encouraging free discussion, and cited as examples two articles which had appeared in the *Universalist Quarterly* which took opposite sides on the question of future retribution. Upham hailed Universalists as "fellow travellers with us in the road to truth."

John M. Austin, Universalist editor of the *Christian Ambassador,* was so sanguine about the desirability of closer cooperation with Unitarians that Whittemore accused him of deserting the Universalist cause.[128] This occurred after Austin had rebuked Whittemore severely for making war needlessly on the Unitarians. It was not only uncalled-for but self-defeating. It was no way to present a united front against orthodoxy.

The eventual union of the Unitarians and Universalists was raised in the late 1840s as a distinct possibility by Henry W. Bellows (1814-1882), who for over forty years (from 1838 until his death) was a prominent Unitarian clergyman in New York City and was the founder of the *Christian Inquirer* (1846). In 1847 he made a tour of the interior of the state and returned with a warm and sympathetic report on "our Universalist friends."[129] He found the Unitarians and Universalists in many places "drawing towards each other and confessing that, however high the walls might be in other sections of the country, they could not find any fence strong enough to keep them apart." The "Ultra Universalism" associated with the earlier Restorationist controversy had by then "next to no existence anywhere." Bellows pointed out that for many decades Universalist theology had been in a state of transition and clarification but had finally settled into a very acceptable pattern. In fact, Bellows was quick to say that "the idea of God's infinite and unrestrained love," the heart of Universalist belief, "was and is a noble and most important idea at the bottom of their system."

Bellows wrote that, in historical perspective, Universalism was "the protest of the common people against the intolerable errors of Calvinism." With "a blunt and courageous force, they turned the Calvinistic system against itself, and made it destroy its own curse." Universalism had done "a great and good work by protesting against all the harsh and tyrannical views of God and his government which prevailed." Universalists had likewise come to a unitarian position regarding the nature of God. Then what divided the two denominations theologically? It was the debate over the final restoration of all to God's favor. The Universalists had made this an article of faith; the Unitarians, who considered the issue much less important, were divided. But Bellows could not see any fundamental points of Christian doctrine on which there was radical disagreement as between the two groups. The real difference, theologically, seemed to be in emphasis—a matter or degree rather than of kind. Bellows considered eventual union of the two denominations inevitable, but only on the basis of "actual agreement, not from any compromises of sentiment on either part." Each had made its way independently of the other; it was to be a union of equals, not a case of one having been swallowed up by the other.

Bellows noted also the contrasting historical origins of the two denominations—Unitarianism with scholastic associations and growing out of "exegetical criticism;" Universalism, with popular associations and growing out of "the irrepressible disgust of the common people for the terrors of Calvinism." Because Universalism was a basically democratic movement, with its strength lying among "the common people," the comparatively uneducated Universalist clergy reflected its origins. It spread faster than clergy could be provided, and "embraced a public who did not demand learning or taste in its clergy." This had been the case with most other rapidly-growing denominations, and Bellows cited the Methodists as an example. But times were changing, and Universalists were now demanding not only an educated ministry but were seriously considering the establishment of colleges as well as theological schools. The educated Universalist clergy ("and there are men in their ranks that would do credit to any sect") had come to realize that the days of "mere protest" were over, and that a more sophisticated and "more moralized and devotional system" was needed. Bellows somewhat smugly pointed out that the Unitarians had long since gone through the same phase in their thinking; the Universalists were merely catching up with their fellow religious liberals.

Then what were the barriers to such union? It was more than a denominational distinction, in the organized sense. Most Unitarians had, in actuality, mistakenly or not, made as great a distinction from Universalism as from orthodoxy. Universalism had been merely another term for irreligion. It was partly a matter of self-preservation; it would be folly to associate with a denomination so under a cloud as Universalism, and would threaten the very existence of Unitarianism so far as it was an organized body of believers. Bellows admitted that Unitarians in the past had not been "wholly free from the charge of having conciliated powerful orthodoxy by condemning Universalism in the days of its feebleness." But the greatest barrier was social distinction. Recruitment from different classes in society, in Bellows' view, had "undoubtedly done more to keep us apart than all other things. Unitarians have looked down upon Universalists, and Universalists have felt a social jealousy of Unitarians." This situation was, of course, most evident where Unitarians and Universalists occupied the same ground. Bellows felt that inherited social distinction was beginning to disappear, and should disappear. There ought to be greater pulpit exchange so that each others' faith could be better understood.

Whittemore greeted Bellows' article with grudging approval, although he detected a note of condescension which irked him, and he begged to differ on some points.[130] He believed that Bellows was premature in sensing that Universalists were "verging more and more" toward Unitarians and chided the latter for their persistent and studied refusal to acknowledge Hosea Ballou's pioneer contribution to strengthening Unitarian theology. Whittemore admitted that, doctrinally speaking, Universalists were more closely related to Unitarians than to any other body of Christians. It was the contrasts in other respects that Whittemore emphasized. Using an analogy derived from nature, he contrasted the spontaneous appearance and spread of Universalism like vegetation in sunny climes with the "elegant green-house plant" of Unitarianism, "nurtured at first privately, shown to but few, and that wilts and shrivels in the open air."

Whittemore repeated the point he had made innumerable times before, and alluded to by Bellows, that "Unitarianism is the liberal Christianity of the aristocracy,—Universalism of the common people." Unitarians continued to be aloof, with a demeanor of "cold indifference." Whittemore had seen no sign that most Unitarians were as cordial as Bellows, and was not nearly as sure as the Unitarian about the possibility of an eventual merging of the two denominations. Whittemore was positive that if such were ever effected, the Universalists would probably be the losers, partly because they would somehow be expected to modify substantially or even abandon their treasured conceptions of divine benevolence and a divine plan for ultimate human happiness.

Whittemore had been particularly incensed when Bellows' communication to the *Christian Inquirer* reporting his trip in 1847 had been reprinted in the *Christian Register* and the extensive section dealing with the Universalists had been omitted. Whittemore accused the editor of "cowardly calculating bigotry" and of deliberately fomenting discord between Unitarians and Universalists.[131] The editor admitted that the letter had been abridged to accommodate the printer, and had left out the paragraphs referring to Universalism on the ground that they would not be of much interest to readers of his paper.[132]

The editor of the *Christian Register* reprinted the letter in its entirety in the next issue, but not before he had reproached Whittemore for his constant attacks on the Unitarians—"his sarcasms and taunts . . . violent hemorrhage of abuse . . . railing and censure." All of this had "done more, and yet does more, to keep Unitarians from friendly intercourse with Universalists than all other causes put together." As to any possibility of union, the editor of the *Register* saw no need for considering it. The ideal was denominational distinctiveness accompanied by fraternal cooperation in such broad objects as moral reform and such local arrangements as pulpit exchange.

Whittemore, who reprinted the entire correspondence, remained unconvinced that relations were improving.[133] He looked in vain for any sign that Unitarians in general approved the course suggested by

Bellows.[134] But he did sometimes think that he saw grounds for hope where individual Unitarians were concerned. When A.A. Livermore became editor of the *Christian Inquirer* in 1858 and issued a hearty welcome to Universalists, Whittemore was much pleased.[135] He was even more optimistic when Livermore made his beliefs public in the *Inquirer* in 1859. He apparently had "the spirit of a Universalist" even though he called himself a Unitarian.[136]

There seemed to be in the 1850s more mention of possible union than before. Even the secular press was offering free advice on the desirability of fusion. The *New York Evening Mirror* called attention to an article in a Unitarian publication in Philadelphia advocating union.[137] The idea was supported by the editor of the *Mirror* on the ground that the only significant factor that kept Universalists and Unitarians apart appeared to be social rather than theological differences. He cited frequent pulpit exchanges and the example of Thomas Starr King—"one of the most talented and brilliant divines and thinkers of the Universalist persuasion, preaching regularly to a Unitarian congregation in Boston." The editor issued a call for all liberal-minded Christians "to fuse into one grand Christian church."

Austin, the editor of the *Christian Ambassador,* possibly recalling Whittemore's earlier attacks on him for being too pro-Unitarian, was not so sure. Although he acknowledged that this seemed to be the current of public opinion, he doubted it would ever happen, either in the 1850s or later. He was not himself enthusiastic about either the possibility or desirability of such a union. The two denominations could probably do more for the cause of both religious truth and liberal Christianity as separate organizations. But there was no reason why Universalists could not live harmoniously with Unitarians and cooperate "in all good works."

Many Universalists expressed their approval of union in principle, but almost always had reservations about how equal the union would be in practice. E.G. Brooks favored the idea, but only on the basis of complete equality. Concessions could not be "like the handle of a pitcher—all on one side."[138] John A. Gurley, speaking as a newspaper editor from the Midwest, basically disliked Unitarians. Union, if it could take place at all, would have to be on the basis of "*equality* and mutual *toleration*" only; and he thought this most unlikely.[139] There were numerous instances of local cooperation between Universalists and Unitarians in the West reported by the *New Covenant,* published in Chicago, which also noted a general sharing of social position, community leadership, wealth, and influence—a feature thought to be generally lacking in the more conservative and more class-conscious East.[140]

It was estimated that in the 1850s Universalist societies and preachers in the Midwest outnumbered the Unitarians by about five to one and four to one, respectively. Even then, the ministers outside urban centers were likely to be Unitarians even though half or more of their congregations might be Universalists. Such societies were usually listed as Unitarian in official records and hence gave a distorted picture of comparative strength of the two denominations, at least according to Universalist representatives. L.B. Mason, a Universalist, reported in 1856 that there was "not a single Universalist society in the West, where the Unitarians, as a body, have united to aid them in the establishment of a Universalist house and Universalist preaching." Universalists tolerated such arrangements as long as nothing was said against their doctrines from the pulpit, but in effect were helping to maintain Unitarianism rather than the reverse. Erasmus Manford, Universalist preacher, editor, and publisher in the Midwest, referring to the struggle to maintain the Universalist cause in St. Louis during the Civil War, noted that the Unitarian church offered neither sympathy nor cooperation. It "stood off cold as an iceberg."[141] He believed that Unitarians wanted the two denominations to unite, but only Unitarians could be dominant. "We would be fine fellows if we allowed ourselves to be swallowed, head and heel, without kicking." Mary A. Livermore, then in Chicago, suggested a more positive approach in 1862 to inter-denominational relations. She proposed that the four congregations of liberal Christians in the city—two Universalist and two Unitarian—hold monthly Sabbath School joint meetings and otherwise "take measures for a more general diffusion of liberal religious principles among the rising generation."[142]

The *Christian Inquirer* devoted an article in 1857 to relations between Universalists and Unitarians, calling for increased cordiality rather than amalgamation.[143] The author deplored the "mutual distrust and recrimination" that seemed to exist between the two denominations. This represented a lack of "common sense as well as of Christian charity." After all, the two groups were both "branches of the one tree of Liberal Christianity." Universalism was "more the child of the heart." The first appeared among scholars, learned men, and "the aristocratic classes of society," while Universalism was "the offspring of the people at large, and was deeply rooted in the democratic elements of the community."

While Channing was addressing the elite in Boston, Hosea Ballou was making the circuit of rural and small-town upper New England, preaching to farmers and mechanics. Unitarianism was "timid, fastidious, cautious, prudent, deprecating; Universalism was bold, combative, presumptuous, aggressive." But regardless of their differences—or possibly because of them—they complemented rather than competed with each other. Both had a mission "to uphold a new and better Church, the Church of the New World." There was no need for formal fusion. Both groups were "too proud and individual and peculiar to lose their characteristics;" but there was no reason why they could not "cordially cooperate, . . . respect and not backbite or scorn each other." They could join in public worship in communities where both groups were small, and exchange pulpits. Unitarians could learn much from "Universalist democracy" while Universalists could profit from the "careful learning and the earnest humanitarian views of religion taught by the Unitarian divines." In short, "head and heart ought to work together–philosophy and republicanism." All would thus serve to strengthen one great Christian church. Even Thomas Whittemore could find no grounds on which to carp at this rendition of coexistence and joint purpose.[144]

A.B. Grosh used almost the same language as did the writer in the *Inquirer*–the comparison between the "heart" and the "head"–to distinguish the two denominations.[145] He likewise detected a more positive attitude toward Universalists in the early 1860s, especially in the West, with the rise of a new generation which had not experienced the religious tumult and divisiveness of earlier days. He predicted that "a few years more of assimilating progress" might even result in making of Universalists and Unitarians "*one* great, liberal denomination." J.O. Skinner, corresponding secretary of the New Hampshire State Convention, observed with approval that in 1862 the pastors of over fifteen Universalist societies in the state had reported pulpit exchanges with as many Unitarians. He saw "no good reason for cultivating and nursing any petty jealousies and prejudices arising from old and obsolete controversies."[146] Eventual union was both possible and desirable in his view. It would be achieved neither immediately nor by passing resolutions, but by a natural, spontaneous growth of good will.

In December 1863 James Freeman Clarke, pastor of the Hollis Street Church (Unitarian) in Boston, delivered the first of a series on "The Positive Doctrines of Liberal Christianity." He singled out three for special consideration: The inherent worth of man; the infinite love of God; and the immanence of the divine "in nature, in history, in the soul of man."[147] He acknowledged that it was Universalists who were largely responsible for contributing the second doctrine, representing as they did "the democracy of Christianity." Nathan Gunnison, pastor of the Universalist church in Halifax, Nova Scotia, in 1864, sensed the new mood that seemed to be overtaking both Universalists and Unitarians. "I trust the day is not far distant when the Unitarians and Universalists will be but branches of one Liberal Church, working together in harmony and good fellowship."

Perhaps the antagonisms and distrust which had for so long marred relations between the two denominations had actually given way to coexistence. The even brighter possibility of formal cooperation might be in store for the future.

Chapter 28

UNIVERSALIST-UNITARIAN MERGER: GESTURES OF FRATERNITY

Theodore Clapp and Thomas Starr King

If one were to seek two individuals personifying, symbolizing, or even serving as epitomes of the relations between Universalism and Unitarianism in mid-nineteenth-century America, they could be found in the persons of Theodore Clapp (1792-1866) and Thomas Starr King (1824-1864). Their lives and careers contrasted sharply in several respects, but both men were committed theologically to liberal Christianity. Although Clapp, unlike King, was never associated formally with either the Universalist or Unitarian denominations during their lifetime, both served as bridges between the two religious bodies.

For thirty-five years Theodore Clapp, a controversial and colorful rebel from a New England Calvinist religious background, held the pastorate of what became a unique non-denominational church which attracted great attention and which became the center of pre-Civil War religious liberalism in the cosmopolitan and rapidly-changing metropolis of New Orleans. Theologically, he foreshadowed by a century the eclecticism and humanism which was to become associated with much of the Unitarian Universalism of the mid-twentieth century. Rejecting all formal creeds and dogmas, opening his pulpit to clergy of all religious persuasions, refusing after 1833 to bind himself to any denomination, he found Unitarianism and Universalism the most congenial of all beliefs. He served, in a way, as a link between the two groups at a time when there was growing talk of possible union. Clapp corresponded extensively with both Unitarians and Universalists and urged them to join forces to extirpate the remnants of Calvinism and create a truly liberal Christian commonwealth. In turn, both Unitarians and Universalists claimed him as one of their own. In spite of his refusal to be associated formally with any one denomination, his name was carried for many years in the yearbook of the American Unitarian Association, beginning with its first issue in 1846.[1]

Theodore Clapp was born in Easthampton (Hampshire County), in western Massachusetts, on 29 March 1792.[2] After a year at Williams

College he transferred to Yale, and after one brief interruption, was graduated in 1814. He then studied at the Andover Theological Seminary for one year (1816) and in 1817 was licensed to preach by the Hampshire Association of Congregational Ministers. He immediately accepted an invitation to serve as a tutor in a family near Lexington, Kentucky. In the course of his year's stay, he became acquainted (or at least met) such notables as Henry Clay, the politician, and Horace Holley, the president of Transylvania University, as well as members of the prominent Breckenridge family. He moved to Louisville, Kentucky in 1819, and continued as a teacher. He also preached occasionally, following the popular style of speaking extemporaneously. He found it expedient to burn the three sermons he had written out and delivered while in New England, and for the remainder of his life in the ministry he spoke without notes. His pulpit oratory became as well known as his unorthodox religious ideas.

Clapp was invited in the fall of 1821 to fill the pulpit of what became the First Presbyterian Church in New Orleans, one of the two Protestant churches in the city. The offer came after two of the church's trustees visiting a fashionable resort on the Ohio River heard him deliver an extemporaneous sermon one Sunday. He accepted without enthusiasm, for he had planned to return to Massachusetts as soon as his teaching duties had been completed. He reluctantly agreed to go to New Orleans, with the understanding that he would remain there no longer than three months. He was still in New Orleans over thirty years later.

The church to which Clapp was invited had been organized in 1818 as the result of an earlier effort to establish a Congregational church in New Orleans. Its pastor was Sylvester Larned, who had been a classmate of Clapp's at Williams College and whom Clapp encountered in Lexington, Kentucky in 1819.[3] An impressive church building had been built the same year, and opened on the national holiday of 4 July. When Clapp arrived in 1822, there was an indebtedness of $45,000 which he insisted be liquidated before he would accept the pastorate. This was promptly achieved by the combination of a legislatively approved lottery and the purchase of the building by a wealthy Jewish merchant and philanthropist from Newport, Rhode Island, one Judah Touro. He generously turned over to Clapp the proceeds from pew rentals, and kept the church in repair. After the church was destroyed by fire in 1851 and no Protestant church would allow Clapp to use its facilities, Touro purchased another building until a new one could be erected. The new structure was commodious, with 118 pews on the lower floor and a gallery which could accommodate about 400. Into this gallery flocked persons of every description, attracted by word of Clapp's oratorial abilities and religious views. They came in such numbers, from such diverse backgrounds, that his place of worship

Theodore Clapp (1792-1866), who preached for thirty-five years in a non-denominational church in New Orleans

became known as "the Strangers' church." It was commonly reported that no planter or merchant visiting the city on business would leave without going both to the theatre and to one of "Parson" Clapp's services.[4]

Clapp fitted comfortably into the easy-going and tolerant society of New Orleans and made friends wherever he went, with a charm and an outgoing personality that attracted even his theological enemies.[5] He sufficiently impressed the president of the board of trustees of the short-lived College of Orleans, who heard some of his sermons, to offer Clapp the presidency in 1824.[6] The institution, opened in 1805 with a combination of municipal, state, and private support, closed its doors in 1826.[7] Clapp was one of the trustees of the Touro Free Library Society, and an associate member of the Physio-Medical Society. His relations with the Roman Catholic majority in New Orleans were exceptionally harmonious throughout his residence there. He both preached and practiced brotherhood, toleration, and understanding, and believed that Roman Catholic concern for the poor and the unfortunate was "infinitely superior to any Protestant denomination." Although he was receiving a generous salary of $5,000 a year at the end of his ministerial career and lived very comfortably, he saved nothing. All beyond his own needs went to relieve the destitute and distressed; his popularity extended to every level of society.

Clapp also attracted attention because of the humanitarian services he rendered during the numerous epidemics of yellow fever and cholera which swept over the city. Between his arrival in 1822 and 1849, there were thirteen onslaughts of yellow fever, and another serious outbreak in 1853.[8] There were three Asiatic cholera epidemics of major proportions, in 1832, 1833, and 1849. Clapp left vivid descriptions of the epidemics in several chapters of his autobiography. Throughout these holocausts, in which literally thousands died, Clapp seemed to have led a charmed life. He attributed his good fortune in part to "regular habits," including total abstinence from alcoholic beverages. After having passed unscathed through three yellow fever epidemics, Clapp did suffer a mild case of the disease in 1828, but was out making his rounds again in less than a week. He visited the sick and dying, conducted funerals by the dozens, and lost two of his six children in one epidemic. He was the only Protestant clergyman who remained in the city through the years 1832 and 1833 and worked side by side with the Roman Catholic priests, for whom he had great admiration. All but three or four of the congregation to which he had originally preached had perished by 1833.

Clapp, who had been reared in a strictly orthodox Puritan household, arrived in New Orleans as a New School Presbyterian, probably influenced by his training at Andover.[9] According to him, he had soon rebelled against the strict Presbyterianism adopted by the

New Orleans church in 1823, and felt that there was too much emphasis on the catechism and profession of faith, and too little on the Bible. He told northern religious liberals that he knew nothing at the time of either Unitarianism or Universalism, beyond possible random pamphlets which came his way after he arrived in New Orleans, and that he had seen no systematic writings of either denomination until after 1835. He insisted in his correspondence with Whittemore and others, and reaffirmed in his autobiography, that his own study of Scriptures had led him by the 1830s to reject both the doctrine of the Trinity and belief in endless punishment because authority for neither was to be found in the New Testament.

Judging from the evidence available, Clapp's transition from Calvinism to Unitarian Universalism was a slow and deliberate process which began about 1824. According to his own account, his congregation remained uninformed of his change of religious views until he delivered a sermon in mid-1834, when he announced that he could no longer subscribe to such Presbyterian doctrines as election, vicarious atonement, original sin, and endless punishment. He went on to deny the doctrine of the Trinity, to enunciate his belief in universal salvation, and to describe a God of love and benevolence—all basic Universalist teachings.[10]

However, in terms of chronology this was strictly an *ex post facto* performance by Clapp. He apparently never hesitated to exhibit his intellectual and religious independence, for he had found himself in difficulty with a portion of his New Orleans congregation almost immediately after his arrival in New Orleans.

As early as 1826 an attempt was made to prepare a formal case against Clapp. He was accused before the Mississippi Presbytery (which had jurisdiction) on three specifications: teaching "false doctrines"; neglecting the proper religious instruction of children and failure to hold prayer meetings; and allowing social festivities to be held by Blacks (both slave and free) at the College of Orleans over which he had presided briefly. The last two charges were dropped, but doubts about his theological views remained, and for the next six years there were repeated reviews of his beliefs as complaints about his lack of orthodoxy continued to be made. His case was finally settled in 1833, when he was excluded from the local Presbytery. The only detailed account of his "heresy" trial known to exist was one he himself wrote and published anonymously the following year.[11] Regardless of the merits of Clapp's case, he determined in 1833 never again to affiliate himself formally with any denomination whatever; in this he was faithful to his self-imposed pledge.

The majority of Clapp's congregation followed him rather than remain within Presbyterianism, and retained the church building. A new Presbyterian church was organized, and had occupied another structure by 1835. Clapp's popularity suffered no diminution after his unhappy experience with the Presbyterians, for seats in his church were "sought after at any price, and a vast increase of men and money" came to his support.[12] He opened the doors of his church to speakers on all kinds of topics and to numerous visiting clergymen, including Universalists. There were lectures on astronomy, phrenology, and other popular subjects. School programs were held there, at one of which "all the members of the Legislature were present."[13] Before the Medical College of New Orleans, which opened in 1835 and eventually became the Tulane University Medical School, occupied its own buildings, many of its lectures were delivered in the church. The first commencement exercises of the medical school were also held there, and one of the founders of the institution was a member of Clapp's congregation.

The Clapp church was incorporated in 1833 as the "First Congregational Church in the City and Parish of New Orleans" and when the charter expired in 1853 it was redesignated as the "First Congregational Unitarian Church," referred to usually as simply "the Unitarian Church."[14] Clapp literally conducted the church as a one-man operation. There was no Bible class, no Sunday school, no committee structure or auxiliary organizations, and no affiliation of any kind with any other religious body. Clapp *was* the church, and attracted overflow congregations at his single Sunday-morning services. After a fire destroyed the original church building in 1851 and an elaborate Gothic-style structure replaced it in 1855, both the words "Congregational" and "Unitarian" were dropped from the church name in favor of the non-sectarian "Church of the Messiah." Clapp even dispensed with a formal dedication of the new structure, and merely appeared at the appointed time to deliver the sermon.

In May 1856 Clapp finally bowed to the demands of chronic poor health, and reluctantly resigned his pastorate. He spent the remainder of his life based in Louisville, Kentucky, where he wrote his autobiography and a work in which he discussed his theological beliefs.[15] His request that he be interred in New Orleans was honored, for after his death at the age of seventy-four on 17 May 1866, his remains were returned in 1867 to the city where he had spent most of his days.

Universalists first became aware of Theodore Clapp about the time of his final break with the Presbyterians in 1833, and while he was in the process of completing his transition to religious liberalism. The first actual contacts came through Southern Universalists and were reported first in Southern denominational journals. It was not until 1838 that his name began to be known in the North. From then until his death in 1866, Clapp's relations with both Unitarians and Universalists became more and more cordial and his name was cited with more and more frequency in the newspapers of the two denominations. The high point of his contact came in the late 1840s. Clapp openly described himself as both a Unitarian and a Universalist in 1848.[16] The Universalist General Convention in 1849 was delighted that he had made a "manly and generous avowal" of his Universalism, and invited him to deliver the occasonal sermon at the next annual meeting, to be held in Buffalo, New York.[17] He journeyed as far north as New York City, where he visited several Universalist clergymen, including W.S. Balch, who was much impressed by Clapp.[18] Clapp was unable to attend the convention, however, because of the illness and death of his father, and his place was taken by Balch.[19] Clapp later made other trips to the North, including New England. In 1855 he spent the summer at the Connecticut home of P.T. Barnum while recuperating from an illness.[20] Two years later he visited the Midwest; while in Chicago he preached in St. Paul's Church (Universalist), where W.W. King served as pastor.[21] Clapp also spent considerable time offering free advice to both denominations on how to achieve a closer and more effective relationship.

L.F.W. Andrews, who spent much of his ministerial career in the South, was the first Universalist known to have recorded his impressions of Clapp. Andrews spoke in Clapp's church in 1834, and reported that the New Orleans pastor did not appear to be as liberal in his religious ideas as he had been led to expect.[22] Clapp, who began a correspondence with Andrews after the latter's visit, told him that he was in no way opposed to Universalism, but was strictly unsectarian in his approach to Christianity. He had "all the creeds to be found in Christendom" in his New Orleans congregation and had no intention of making them "Presbyterians, Methodists, Baptists, Unitarians, or Universalists."[23] Andrews thereupon lent Clapp a number of Universalist books and reported that Clapp had left "a general impression on his audience that he was a Universalist in sentiment."[24] This was confirmed by a member of Clapp's congregation, who noted that Clapp, after having perused the books Andrews had lent him, had become "quite liberal of late."[25]

George Rogers, one of Universalism's most tireless and best known itinerant preachers, preached many times in Clapp's church and became well acquainted with him. Rogers emphasized Clapp's reluctance to identify himself with any sect or denomination, but noted that Clapp was especially sympathetic to Universalist ideas and even offered $500 towards construction of a Universalist church in New Orleans if there were sufficient interest and support for one.[26] John A. Gurley, editor of the *Star in the West* in Cincinnati, who visited Clapp in 1838, considered him an avowed Universalist.[27] Isaac D. Williamson, while wintering in Mobile, Alabama, received a cordial invitation in 1844 to visit Clapp and speak from his pulpit. Clapp wrote him that he was anxious to "fraternize" with Universalist clergymen because Clapp "fully and perfectly agrees with us in regard to the final destiny of man."[28] G.H. Emerson, who reviewed Clapp's *Theological Views* (published in 1859), commented that although the pastor from New Orleans had obtained "occasional help" from both Unitarian and Universalist publications, he presented a systematic theology which was not only "emphatically his own" but bore a "close affinity" to the views held generally by New England Universalists.[29]

Clapp had himself gone a step further in expressing his commitment to Universalism. When he moved to Louisville, Kentucky, after his retirement from his New Orleans ministry in 1856, he regularly attended the Universalist church presided over by W.W. Curry. Clapp was much impressed by Curry and referred to the excellent manner in which he presented "the great principles and leading facts essential to our faith."[30] Clapp's Unitarian Universalism was unequivocally expressed in 1858 in a letter to Whittemore on the occasion of the latter's receipt of the honorary degree of Doctor of Divinity from Tufts College. Clapp paid a double tribute to the men who had expressly influenced his religious ideas: William Ellery Channing, representing Unitarianism and Thomas Whittemore, representing Universalism.[31] Clapp claimed to have read all of Whittemore's books as well as the *Trumpet* and professed to prefer Whittemore's style of writing over Channing's because it was simpler and more direct than that of the Unitarian. Whether Clapp could have made an equivalent response to Channing is a moot question, in view of the fact that Channing had passed off the scene over a decade earlier.

From 1838 onward, Clapp was claimed by the denomination as a Universalist. He was listed as an unaffiliated Universalist preacher in the *Register* from 1839 until his death, and was for many years identified as "the only preacher known to preach Universalism openly" in Louisiana. Richard Eddy, in his history of the denomination, noted that after Clapp had publicly renounced the doctrine of endless punishment, he and "the great majority of his congregation, adopted the Universalist belief."[32] Eddy also called attention to the fact that Edwin C. Bolles, a Universalist clergyman, succeeded Clapp after the latter's retirement.

Transcriptions of Clapp's sermons were often reprinted in both the *Trumpet* and the *Christian Freeman.*[33] In 1849 the editors of each paper reprinted an extended discussion between Clapp and the editor of the *Christian Register* (Unitarian) over the doctrine of eternal punishment, and Clapp corresponded with both Whittemore and Cobb on the subject. Clapp, who by then subscribed to the papers of both denominations, had nothing but compliments for the Universalists and, with one exception, for the Unitarians. Both had done admirable work, he wrote, for the cause of true religious liberalism. If only the Unitarians would join with the Universalists in rejecting "the horrid doctrine of endless misery" (which he understood the Universalists had already rejected), the two denominations could do even more good work, and much more effectively, by presenting a united front.[34] Clapp could not understand why Unitarians were so reluctant to commit themselves. During his many years in New Orleans, he had yet to find a single Unitarian who subscribed to the doctrine.[35]

Enthusiasm for Clapp among Universalists, and for the work he was doing in the religiously conservative South, remained high in spite of his refusal to compromise a whit of his independence by formally joining the denomination. Their cordiality was tempered in only one major respect: Clapp supported slavery and refused to sympathize with or support the abolitionist cause. He gave his reasons quite frankly in 1849, and devoted his Thanksgiving sermon in 1850 to the subject.[36] After admitting that slavery in the abstract was an evil, he argued that when the realities of the situation were faced, the institution had to be defended in the South for both the good of the slave and for public order. Furthermore, he found in the New Testament no clear prohibition of slavery. Slavery, he said, was a man-made institution. If one were opposed to it, he could say so, and was free to do what he could to bring about a change in the laws allowing and protecting it. In the meantime, Clapp announced that as long as he was a resident of Louisiana, where slavery was permitted, he would duly render obedience to the laws of the state and was bound by Christian principle to submit. He found no "higher law" that would justify emancipation on either religious or moral grounds. Sectional loyalty had again transcended the Universalist principle of human brotherhood which Clapp had professed for so many years.

Quite different because of his total loyalty to the American nation as historically conceived was Thomas Starr King, Clapp's younger contemporary. Starr King (as he was generally known) became such a fervent supporter of American nationalism during the Civil War that he has been often credited with almost single-handedly preventing the secession of California and allying it with the Union. King was born in New York City on 17 December 1824, the son of Thomas Farrington King (1798-1839).[37] The father was a Universalist minister with Restorationist sympathies who died at the age of forty-two after having served several churches, the last one in Charlestown, Massachusetts, between 1835 and 1839. He left but little in the way of worldly wealth for his family. His fifteen-year-old son, one of six children, received only a "desultory" education, and became the head of the family and supported them with a variety of teaching and clerical jobs. Of scholarly bent from the first, he spent much of his free time mastering several foreign languages and read widely and deeply in both European and American philosophical and religious literature, including Biblical criticism. He was much influenced as a youth by the works of William Ellery Channing.

King served briefly (1842-43) as principal of a grammar school in Medford, in the Greater Boston area. It was through Hosea Ballou 2d, then pastor of the Universalist society in Medford and a member of the local school committee, that he obtained the appointment.[38] It was Ballou who provided for King a systematic course of study for the ministry—the only approach to a formal theological education that he ever received. However, it was toward the Unitarian rather than the Universalist ministry that he leaned. Even in 1843, while studying with Ballou, he attended the local Unitarian church, and explained the reason for his preference. He believed that Unitarians, as a group, were doing more for the cause of liberal Christianity, in spite of all their vagueness about the final restoration of all men, than Universalists like Whittemore with their dogmatic stance about the certainty of ultimate happiness and holiness for all.[39] Much of King's Universalist-Unitarian belief can be traced, respectively, to the influence of Hosea Ballou 2d, a lifetime friend; and to the Unitarian divine, James Walker (1794-1874), minister for twenty-one years of the so-called "Harvard" church in Charlestown, and later president of Harvard College, Walker's alma mater. What ripened into a long personal acquaintance started when King heard Walker deliver a series of lectures on natural theology at the Lowell Institute which the young man carefully recorded.

King preached his first sermon at Woburn in 1845, two years after he had resigned from his school position in Medford and had become a clerk in the Charlestown Navy Yard at double his previous salary. His annual stipend as a schoolteacher had been $500.[40] Regarding his limited formal education, he once described himself facetiously as a "graduate of the Boston Navy Yard."[41] After serving briefly as a substitute preacher in Boston, he accepted in 1846 the pastorate of the Universalist church in Charlestown which his father had served. Succeeding Edwin H. Chapin, King remained in Charlestown only two years. His reputation as an effective minister spread rapidly and invitations from other churches began to arrive. He declined an offer from the Second Unitarian Church (Church of the Messiah) in New York City, of which Orville Dewey had been pastor; but King refused in part because one of the conditions had been that he first spend a year at the Harvard Divinity School. He likewise declined an offer from the Fourth Universalist Society in the same city. He resigned from the Charlestown church in 1848, primarily because he considered his position rather incongruous. He had been a mere boy when his father had served there, and the older generation in the church had difficulty in realizing that he had become "a grown man" in spite of his youthful appearance and lively demeanor. He felt that a stranger would be a

Thomas Starr King (1825-1864), a leading Universalist-Unitarian; Congressional Hall of Statuary, Washington, D.C.

much more appropriate choice and could wield much greater influence than himself.

The offer which he finally accepted was at the Hollis Street Unitarian Church in Boston, founded in 1732 and being rent asunder with dissension over the issues of abolition and temperance. After first declining, King accepted a renewed offer in 1848 and in the fall of that year took on the challenging assignment which the church represented. Four of the thirty-nine pastors and delegates at the installation ceremony were Universalists, including Hosea Ballou 2d who was unquestionably pleased to hear King confirm his belief in the assurance of universal salvation.[42] King's Boston home immediately became a social and intellectual center for both Unitarian and Universalist clergymen, and was frequented as well by theological students and others who sought his aid and hospitality. In 1850, only two years after assuming the Hollis Street position, he had attracted sufficient attention to receive an honorary Master of Arts degree from the Harvard which he had never attended. Two Universalists, T.J. Sawyer and Lucius R. Paige, received similar recognition from Harvard that year, with an honorary Doctor of Divinity and Master of Arts respectively.[43]

In the eleven years of his ministry at the Boston church King was credited not only with literally saving it from dissolution but with rebuilding and unifying it in the face of all the political turmoil of the day. He made it clear that he would speak on the religious implications of such burning issues as slavery and abolition (as he frequently did, in a forthright manner). He likewise had a clear understanding with the parish committee that if he gave offense he would tender his resignation. One of his most noteworthy sermons, portraying both his considerable oratorical powers and his hatred of slavery, was delivered in 1857 after the Supreme Court sanctioned slavery in the Dred Scott case.[44] Even though his congregation represented many shades of opinion on political issues, King's resignation was never called for.

The young minister's busy and highly successful early career was made even more demanding by his frequent appearances as a lecturer on lyceum platforms both in the Boston area and outside—literally from Maine to Missouri. He was, according to Edward Everett Hale, "born to be a great orator."[45] King's reputation as a powerful speaker spread early and far. He had delivered his first public address at a 4th of July celebration in 1845, in Medford, and in the following year had greatly impressed the audience of the Mercantile Library Association of Boston. In 1847 he had attracted public attention with his patriotic address delivered in Charlestown on Bunker Hill Day (17 June) on the principles behind the American Revolution.[46] The subjects usually reflected his own interests and his wide reading; among the most popular of his presentations was a lecture on Goethe. He summered for many years in Gorham, New Hampshire, preferring the mountains to the seashore after sampling them both. He became so fascinated with and enamored of the New Hampshire mountains that he produced in 1859 a popular guidebook entitled *The White Hills.* His appreciation of, and enthusiasm for, nature remained undiminished throughout his life. Almost as soon as he arrived in California in 1860 he visited the Yosemite area on the west slope of the Sierra Nevada. He was among the first to inform Easterners of its natural wonders by way of a series of eight articles which appeared in the *Boston Evening Transcript* (1 December 1860 - 9 February 1861).[47] Yosemite comprised part of California's first state park, created in 1864, and became a national park in 1890.

The strong sense of duty which seemed always to characterize King's choice of activities was put to the test when he was approached to take over the faltering First Unitarian Society in San Francisco which had been organized in 1850. The opportunities he saw for furthering the cause of liberal religion on the West Coast and the urging of Henry W. Bellows, an influential Unitarian, finally convinced him that his departure from Boston was the best course to follow. He also had a very personal motive in moving to California: He hoped that the western climate might restore the state of his health, which had always been precarious and was already declining.[48] He was painfully aware that his father had suffered from debilitation as early as the age of thirty-six and died prematurely.

King's congregation, reluctant to accept his resignation, gave him a purse of $2,000 and granted him a fifteen-month "vacation," with the understanding that the pastorate would be held for him if he chose to return. He delivered what became his farewell address in the spring of 1860 but did not submit his formal resignation until the fall of 1861. He sailed from New York, where he was feted before departure at a breakfast and reception arranged by Unitarian clergymen in the city. The poet William Cullen Bryant presided over an assemblage of 250. King was criticized by some Universalists for making an extemporaneous speech in which he paid tribute to Unitarian clergy without mentioning Universalists.[49]

Twenty-four hours after his arrival on the West Coast, King delivered his first sermon, composed on board ship. Within a year the Unitarian society had been reorganized and revitalized, and plans for a new and larger building were undertaken. The cornerstone of the costly and elaborate Gothic stone structure which he considered his monument was laid in the winter of 1862 and dedicated early in 1864. He preached in the new church in January of that year, just a few weeks before his death. With 218 pews, the church could accommodate nearly 1,500 persons. Even then, the demand for seats exceeded the number available. King himself contributed the $3,500 expended on the custom-designed organ. He raised the funds by delivering a series of six lectures on leading American poets.[50] Pews were not sold to individuals, as was customary, but were rented, the building having been financed by subscriptions. Pews were secured for $20,000 annually (in gold).[51]

King found himself almost immediately in demand as a lecturer, and his popularity grew as rapidly in the West as it had in the East. His oratorical talents, his extraordinary command of language, his emphasis on individualism, were all given free rein in the fluid, restless, and open society to be found in San Francisco, and unquestionably added to his instant popularity.[52] The San Francisco correspondent of the *New York Times* (an Episcopalian) noted that, although King was a "heretic" in his religious views, he had "done more than any dozen men in the State to educate us into the love of that liberty that our flag used to intimate before it was disgraced."[53] According to the *New York Tribune,* by 1861 King was not only the most influential advocate of the Union in the state, but had the largest Protestant congregation in California.[54] There were, in fact, so many demands on his time and energies that he had little opportunity to prepare new sermons but used many delivered earlier in Boston.[55] The sermons which he did compose in California were usually dictated, while the speeches delivered on the lecture circuit were frequently extemporaneous, with much improvisation to fit the particular occasion. He spoke to temperance societies, Masonic groups, and even at a high school dedication.[56] He did find time, however, to keep up a vigorous correspondence with friends and colleagues back East, including his old mentor, Hosea Ballou 2d. King wrote him in 1861 that "there ought to be a strong Universalist church here, and will be, I hope, before a great while."[57]

The actual number of Universalists in and about San Francisco when King arrived is not known, but there were undoubtedly a few. As reported in the *Universalist Register,* King's congregation was "largely composed of Universalists" although the church was officially Unitarian.[58] King himself made no reference to the presence of Universalists in his church although he did mention Alpheus Bull, one of the first Universalist preachers in California; he accompanied King on his first visit to Yosemite.[59]

By the time King arrived in San Francisco, two Universalist societies had already come and gone in that city, and a scattering of Universalists had appeared elsewhere in California even before it achieved statehood in 1850.[60] Four preachers had already arrived in what was then known as "Upper California" and there were others who had expressed their intention "to start for this modern Ophir."[61] One of the latter was T.J. Sawyer of New York. Disgruntled because he did not consider his efforts on behalf of Universalism in that state adequately appreciated, he thought of moving to California in 1852 but did not do so.[62]

Alpheus Bull from Lafayette, Indiana, who had been fellowshipped in 1847, moved to San Francisco in 1848 and preached occasionally while acquiring wealth in mining and business enterprises. E.F. Quinby, who arrived from Maine in 1849, returned to the East in 1852 and died in Norway, Maine, shortly thereafter.[63] Jonathan C. Phelps set out from Grafton, New Hampshire, in the winter of 1849 with the hope of establishing a Universalist society in San Francisco.[64] But it was another Universalist (Josiah Upson) who actually created the first society in 1853. A native New Englander, a graduate of Yale University and the Ohio Medical College, he had become a preacher at the Second Universalist Society in Cincinnati.[65] He headed for California in 1850, ostensibly for his health. He immediately created controversy. There was a question of how much his compensation should be; he finally offered to preach without pay for six months.[66] There was also considerable doubt about the acceptability of his theological views and the fact that he disclaimed fellowship with any church although he claimed to be a Universalist. But some of his ideas "respecting the tenets of the Universalist Church [were] peculiar to himself." He argued in behalf of non-denominational religion, refused to celebrate the Lord's Supper, and was suspected of holding rationalist views similar to those of Theodore Parker.[67] He resigned after less than a year and returned shortly thereafter to Ohio; his health was again said to be impaired. To make matters worse, his ill-starred society was unable to procure a suitable building and had to settle for the Music Hall.[68] As part of the arrangement, the Universalists were required to use the services of a musical group known as the "Pacific Troupe" which served as a choir. The fee was $250 each time the hall (and accompanying choir) were used. Shortly after the society collapsed in 1854, Alpheus Bull, who had in the meantime moved from Sacramento to San Francisco, attempted to revive it, but the society refused to remain alive.

The first of the pioneer preachers to appear in Northern California after 1850, and claiming to be a Universalist, was Abraham Coryell Edmunds (1827-1879). Edmunds, a native of Whitby (York County), Canada, lived a diversified life as a traveller, publisher and newspaper editor, preacher, and ardent exponent of phrenology. He claimed to have travelled on foot from Michigan to California in 1850, a journey which took "a little over six months."[69] He was not in fellowship with any denomination when he started preaching Universalism in Nevada City in 1856.[70] After moving to Marysville in 1857, where a society was organized, he began publication of the *Star of the Pacific* as a Universalist monthly (later semi-monthly, published in Sacramento and then Petaluma) which lasted until 1862, when Edmunds enlisted in the Union Army.[71] In 1863, by which time he had moved to Oregon, the announcement was made that he and his wife would revive the publication under the title *Herald of Reform*, intended for Universalists in both California and Oregon.[72] After moving to Oregon he edited and/or published almost a dozen short-lived journals and newspapers in which he supported the Union vociferously, as well as abolitionism, temperance, and the rights of labor. He was an admitted religious controversialist and during his preaching of over a decade he engaged in numerous public debates. He insisted that he was bound by no religious creed or "net work of theology," but whatever he may have lacked in orthodoxy he made up by activity. He was reported to have travelled, in 270 days in 1861, no less than 5,124 miles, of which 2,652 were on foot, and to have preached 127 discourses and held two discussions, one lasting seven days.[73]

Between 1857 and 1860, five societies or churches had been organized in California, but none had anything approaching a continuous history. A society had been created in Sacramento in 1857, with forty members, but had no regular minister and was supplied on a part-time basis by Edmunds.[74] The first Universalist meeting house known to have been built in California was in Shasta County, in the community of Piety Hill (known also as Horsetown and later as Igo).[75] When a lay preacher, B.M. Parker, arrived in 1858, eight Universalist families resided there. A meeting house was constructed in the fall of 1860, with capacity for 100 persons, and was dedicated by Edmunds. But the society disappeared shortly after Parker's departure in 1862.

The Sacramento Association was organized in 1858, when four societies were in existence. A state convention was created in 1860, at which time Edmunds and D. Van Alstine were appointed to serve as missionaries and to collect funds for the cause.[76] When King arrived in San Francisco in 1860 there was not only no Universalist society there, but only four Universalist preachers known to be in the state. Not a one had been ordained or was serving in a full-time capacity. Judging from the sparse and sometimes unreliable information made available to Universalists in the East, others came and went with bewildering rapidity. Typical was J.M. Peebles, who in 1862 was reported to be preaching Universalism in Sacramento "to a congregation of no denomination."[77] He had been installed as pastor of the Universalist church in Baltimore, Maryland, as a "Unitarian Universalist" in 1856 in an ecumenical service, but had remained there only a year.[78] Of all the transient Universalist preachers who appeared (and disappeared) during King's brief life in California, Alpheus Bull was the only one he mentioned.[79] It was no wonder that "a man of more than ordinary talent" was required to preach liberal Christianity on the West Coast. This was the role that King was destined to play for both Universalists and Unitarians in California. His wish, expressed to Hosea Ballou 2d, to see a Universalist organization in San Francisco, was not realized until 1873, when a church of seventy-five members was formed.[80]

King joined one of the local Masonic lodges in 1861, and immediately rose to prominence in the order, having been installed in 1862 as Grand Orator of the Grand Lodge of California—a position which he held until his death two years later.[81] King moved easily in the circles of men of prominence. He maintained a close friendship with John C. Fremont, who had been one of California's first United Stares senators and in 1856 the first presidential candidate of the newly organized Republican Party. King likewise served on the board of trustees of the College of California in Oakland which later became the nucleus of the University of California in Berkeley. It was to King that was given the honor of flashing the first words along the transcontinental telegraph line that connected San Francisco with the eastern seaboard in 1861.[82] It was the same line which first brought to Easterners news of King's death three years later.

But the event which made King "the foremost citizen of California" was the outbreak of the Civil War. There was serious doubt about the state's loyalty to the Union, partly because a high proportion of the population was originally from the South. King placed all of his oratorical talents at the disposal of the Unionist element, and helped, as a member of the "Home Guard," to combat secessionist tendencies. He appeared on the lecture circuit beginning in February, 1861, with speeches opposing secession. His orations on George Washington and Daniel Webster drew large and appreciative audiences. A few weeks after the war commenced, he announced in a sermon to his parishioners his strong stand for the Union. Patriotic sermons, lectures, and addresses became King's trademark, and there was talk of nominating him for the United States Senate. However, interested as he was in political affairs, he refused to be considered. He would "swim to Australia before taking a political post."[83] He did not hesitate to castigate publicly local politicians who were lukewarm in their enthusiasm for the Union. Instead of entering the political arena, he divided his energies between parish affairs and securing funds for the United States Sanitary Commission to aid sick and wounded soldiers. Over $200,000 was raised in San Francisco alone. King spoke on behalf of the commission not only in California, but in Oregon, Nevada, and Washington Territories, and even in Vancouver, Canada. While in Portland, Oregon in 1862, in true ecumenical fashion he spoke from many pulpits on request. He delivered an address for the benefit of the local Presbyterian church and preached to the Methodists. King was the first Unitarian ever to have officiated in that state.[84]

Starr King died on 4 March 1864, the victim of diphtheria and exhaustion of a frail physical frame worn out from over-exertion. He had, in his brief sojourn in California, achieved such renown and attracted so much favorable attention that most of the state went into mourning with his passing. Flags were flown at half mast all over San

Francisco and on the ships in its harbor; bells were tolled, and business houses were closed. In the years that followed, King was memorialized in numerous ways. A bronze statue of King executed by Daniel C. French (responsible for the famous Minuteman in Concord, Massachusetts), was erected in Golden Gate Park in 1892. A public school in San Francisco was named in his honor, as were at least two Masonic lodges. His portrait was placed in the state capital in Sacramento. Mountain peaks in Yosemite and in New Hampshire carry his name. King was immortalized likewise when a representation was unveiled in 1931 in Statuary Hall in the nation's capital. King shared, fittingly, the honor of this tribute with Father Junipero Serra, the Roman Catholic missionary priest. California became the only state in the Union to commemorate two clergymen.[85] A replica of King's statue in Washington was placed in the Government Center of Yosemite National Park in 1951. Within denominational circles, it was appropriate that the Pacific Unitarian School for the Ministry in Berkeley (opened in 1904) was renamed the Starr King School for the Ministry in 1941.

It was likewise fitting, when news of King's death in 1864 reached the Boston area, that a commemorative service was held in the local Unitarian church by Universalists in Charlestown whose own church was undergoing repairs. A similar service was held in the Hollis Street (Unitarian) church which King had served for twelve years. The two major addresses paying tribute to King were delivered, respectively, by Edwin H. Chapin (Universalist) and Edward Everett Hale (Unitarian).

King was no narrow sectarian. He seldom mentioned in either his sermons or in his private correspondence even the names of the two denominational heritages which he represented. It was King who helped lend increasing currency in the 1860s to the term "liberal Christianity" to embrace both Universalism and Unitarianism. His religious philosophy was summed up in a statement made when he was thirty-five: "My great ambition in life is to serve the cause of Christianity as represented by the noblest souls of all the liberal Christian parties."[86] His own far-ranging intellectual and religious interests were reflected in his emphasis on the interaction of the individual and society. As he put it, "Eclecticism is the motto on the banner of the nineteenth century."[87] He took the same broad view of the reciprocity between faith and reason. As he wrote to a friend in 1844, reason was "the very essence of faith, else faith is a blind idolatry. The true faith is the self-renunciation of reason where reason finds that it can know no farther."[88] It was this kind of incisive thought-pattern, couched in flowing rhetoric, that helped make King's reputation as a speaker and writer. His intellectual sophistication set him on a plane high above Theodore Clapp.

Typical of King's Universalism-Unitarianism was his attendance at the annual Unitarian festival in Faneuil Hall in 1858, followed a week later by his appearance at a Unversalist festival at the same location. In a speech made on the latter occasion he told his audience that both Unitarians and Universalists were "called by Providence to serve the same ends."[89] He was saddened at the needless jealousy and strife which he detected between the two denominations, for they were the "twin-truths" of liberal Christianity. They ought, he said, "to be indissolubly united, even if they keep separate names, like the Siamese twins."[90] He saw his own role as "a small fibre in the ligament that should join them." He cared not whether he was called a Universalist or a Unitarian, for he was both.

King delivered the closing lecture as part of a series in 1858 by seven Boston clergymen on the creeds and goals of the denominations they represented. T.B. Thayer spoke for the Universalists and Orville Dewey for the Unitarians.[91] It is significant that King claimed to represent neither denomination, but instead spoke on the broader topic of "Spiritual Christianity." He told his audience that a truly liberal religion would transcend all sects and embrace all: "Trinitarian and Unitarian, Calvinist and Arminian, Partialist and Universalist."[92] They all had a common denominator, and each had something to contribute to a world-wide fellowship.

King consistently emphasized the congeniality of both sides of the liberal Christian coin. When he announced his resignation to the Charlestown society in 1848 he made it clear that his decision in no way signalled any change in his theological views. He insisted that his firm belief in "the cardinal principles of Universalism" remained unshaken, and that his change in pulpits would in no way weaken his attachment to Universalism. His acceptance of the call to the Hollis Street church elicited the same response. He knew of no "Peculiarity of belief which ought to prevent his acceptance." He had long ago, he explained, embraced and preached "the distinctive feature" of Unitarian theology. Only the name, not the faith, separated Unitarians and Universalists.[93] It was King who, in his speech to Universalists in Faneuil Hall in 1858, contributed the often-quoted aphorism to the effect that Universalists believed that God was too good to damn them forever, while Unitarians believed that they were too good to be damned.[94] King added, half jokingly, that the reason the two denominations had not united long ago was that they were really "too near of kin to be married."

King's refusal to acknowledge any deep or fundamental difference between Unitarians and Universalists upset some Universalists. T.J. Greenwood was very disturbed in 1856 because King, with professed Universalist sympathies, was preaching in the Hollis Street church. King apparently stood "midway between the two denominations . . . a Universalist in faith, and feeling, and fellowship, but ministering to a Unitarian society, *not in fellowship with Universalists.*"[95] No matter what King's motives might have been in accepting the Unitarian offer, Greenwood considered such behavior a detriment to Universalism. Without a doubt, Thomas Whittemore was King's most outspoken critic. Suspicious of Unitarians in any case, and hypersensitive to any aspersion or slight, real or imagined, cast on Universalism, he never really trusted King or his theology. According to Whittemore's interpretation, King was at heart ambivalent, at best, about the certainty of man's eventual holiness and happiness. That automatically put him outside the pale of true Universalism.

In 1853 King precipitated a theological controversy which reverberated for several weeks in the columns of the *Trumpet* and cast much doubt in the minds of some Universalists about his real commitment to their principles. In an article entitled "What Must We Do to be Saved?" King argued forcefully that death did not bring automatic or immediate salvation.[96] "The gospel is not a plan of salvation from future woe. Its privileges and blessings cannot be represented as tickets to introduce us into paradise through the avenue of death." Christ came to save man from the miseries of sin on earth, and it was a man's character that determined the dimensions of one's heaven or degree of salvation. Ideal character could be achieved only by a Christ-like life on earth. Redemption was an internal matter: "We get the heaven *we earn.*" Working for ultimate salvation was a continuous process, calling for effort and discipline on the part of man; this might not always be achieved. King, as a strong believer in immortality of the soul, therefore refused to rule out the possibility of punishment after physical death.

King was attacked from so many quarters that he replied at length not only in the *Trumpet* but in a second article.[97] Whittemore objected strenuously to the prominence given the role of the human will by King and the subordination of the role of the divine will. The resulting indefiniteness about man's destiny, so characteristic of Unitarian thinking in Whittemore's eyes, placed King poles apart from such true-blue Universalists as Hosea Ballou and even King's own father.[98]

In 1858 Whittemore wrote a detailed review of two of King's published sermons.[99] Whittemore took serious issue with King on several points and insisted that the Hollis Street pastor had done Universalism more harm than good.[100] Whittemore's principal criticism was that King, in spite of the unambiguous title of the sermons, left the doctrine of eternal punishment and the fate of the human soul "floating about, on the sea of uncertainty." King had carefully avoided an unequivocal assertion of the basic tenet of Universalism. After reviewing King's career, Whittemore was convinced that, even though ordained as a Universalist (in the same pulpit in Charlestown from which his father had preached), King was not a true believer. He had never preached "boldly and decidedly the doctrine of the final holiness and happiness of all men." At first King seemed not to have been "tainted," like some others of the Unitarian clergy, with rationalism. But, unfortunately, King had "embraced Universalism as a philosophy, rather than as a revelation." King's reservations about future punishment which Whittemore detected, and his reputation as a learned speaker, were what apparently made him attractive to Unitarians.

As to specifics, Whittemore chastised King for admitting his failure to find any clear statement in the four gospels supporting the doctrine of ultimate salvation of all souls. Whittemore then cited over a dozen proofs that such a doctrine *could* be found. Whittemore was also alarmed that King emphasized the fragmentary and even contradictory nature of the gospels, taken as a unit. This, by Whittemore's reading, weakened reverence for the Bible. King also denigrated Christ's character by putting excessive stress on his poetic and mystical tendencies, his indefinite language, and his extensive use of imagery. King was, in short, teetering dangerously on the brink of infidelity.

Whittemore in effect read King out of the denomination in 1859, claiming that he had no right to speak for Universalists; the young minister had "joined the Unitarian party" because King cast doubt on the distinguishing feature of Universalist belief.[101] As might have been expected, Whittemore was greatly insensed because the farewell breakfast given by the "liberal Christians" of New York City in King's honor before his departure for California in 1860 had included no official invitation to Universalists.[102] Whittemore considered this but one more instance of Unitarian haughtiness and self-righteousness.

Thomas B. Thayer was among those Universalists who were at first distressed when King made his denominational change, but came to realize the implications and ultimate value of the "larger faith" which King preached and exemplified. After Thayer became editor of the *Universalist Quarterly* the year of King's death (1864), he published Frothingham's memoir of King and paid tribute in an editorial to the adopted Californian as a "true Christian and patriot."[103] Thayer, much more of a theologian than Whittemore and with a considerably broader religious perspective, had a much clearer perception of King's vision of a liberal Christianity which would break down the barriers of religious provincialism and bring to man's consciousness the true meaning of the word "universalism."

From Coexistence to Gestures of Fraternity

However tragic the experience of the Civil War era might have been in most respects, it had a salutory effect on Universalist-Unitarian relations. Joint efforts through the United States Sanitary Commission under the leadership of Unitarian Henry W. Bellows brought members of the two denominations closer together as Universalists like Mary A. Livermore achieved national recognition with their humanitarian activities. The removal of the strident anti-Unitarian voice of Thomas Whittemore from the columns of the *Trumpet* after 1861 undoubtedly played a part in promoting more harmonious relations. After he relinquished control of the paper, almost no mention was made of Unitarianism at all by either Sylvanus Cobb, who served briefly as the theological editor, or by General Editor George H. Emerson. There seemed also to be a lessening of inter-denominational hostilities over theological differences. In 1865 Samuel J. May, a prominent Unitarian, heartily commended Universalists for their persistent and largely successful effort in opposing the doctrine of endless punishment.[104]

The editor of the *Universalist* (the successor to the *Trumpet*) believed that the chief point of controversy over the universality of salvation had begun to fade away. The new issue, affecting Unitarians more vitally than Universalists, although still of concern to them, seemed to be the challenge to the authoritative character of Biblically-centered Christianity by a growing radical (rationalist) movement preponderantly among the younger generation of Unitarian clergy. This took the loosely-organized form of the Free Religious Association, created in 1867.[105] There is no evidence that the organization made any special appeal to or had any impact on the main body of Universalists, although it did cause a brief flurry in one Universalist church in Boston. Rowland Connor from Concord, New Hampshire, was employed as associate pastor at A.A. Miner's School Street church (the Second Universalist Society) in January 1867. After he had served little more than six months, Connor joined in a call for a meeting of the Free Religious Association, served as its secretary when it convened in Horticultural Hall, and delivered an address supporting the idea of a "religion of humanity." Theology, he said, was to be subordinated to social conscience, for man came first in the cosmic order of things; God was a secondary consideration. The majority of Miner's congregation were scandalized by Connor's ideas and voted to dismiss him; his theological views were considered completely antagonistic to Universalist teachings as Miner interpreted them and as his congregation understood them.

A minority of Miner's congregation who supported Connor seceded from the church and formed an independent society known as the "Fraternal Association of Universalists." To make matters worse, when they organized they adopted the Winchester Profession of Faith "in spirit only."[106] Miner immediately preached a series of sermons on Universalist beliefs, including one on the Profession, challenging Connor's interpretation that it meant no more than the practice of the Golden Rule. The indignant pastor pointedly remarked that Universalists had "never claimed to be so intensely liberal as to believe in nothing at all."[107]

The annual meeting of the Massachusetts Convention in 1867 was a tumultous affair, for the Committee on Fellowship refused to recognize either Connor or his new society, and the case was brought to the floor of the convention, where Connor was given an opportunity to present his ideas and defend himself.[108] He insisted that he believed in Universalist principles but denied the plenary inspiration and infallibility of the Bible, rejected miracles unless verified by natural law, and refused to accept the idea of the physical resurrection of Christ. The convention, predictably, refused to fellowship Connor, by a vote of 16 to 95.

Most of the dissident members who had followed Connor out of the church returned after discovering that they had been "misled." Miner and his parish were chastised in the local press for "bigotry and narrowness" in dismissing the young minister. But as Miner saw it, the episode was of great benefit to the denomination. "From that day on, the classifying of Universalists with infidels, atheists, deists, sceptics, and drunkards, entirely ceased. The work of an unfriendly press accomplished in a month what our whole church could not have done in twenty years."[109]

A Universalist speculated in the 1950s that the Free Religious Association might have been "a means of bringing the Universalists and Unitarians together . . . [and] could have meant the formation of a new denomination."[110] However appealing some of its ideas were to proponents of liberal religion of a later day, the scientific humanist propagated by the Association had little popular appeal in the nineteenth century. It had begun to decline by 1880 and by 1900 had disappeared as an identifiable organization.

Of basic significance to Universalist-Unitarian relations in the 1860s was a new mood that captured the imagination of Unitarians. The value of organized effort during the Civil War was recognized by a burst of activity by the American Unitarian Association, particularly in the field of missionary endeavor and the demonstration of a greater ecumenical spirit than had hitherto prevailed. This "denominational awakening," so described by George W. Cooke, an historian of Unitarianism, was ushered in by a special meeting of the Association in the Hollis Street Church in Boston in December 1864.[111] At the well-attended and enthusiastic two-day meeting a call was issued for raising the unprecedented sum of $100,000, and a special meeting was called in New York City to complete the drive already begun. One organizational innovation was the official representation of Unitarian churches for the first time in the history of the denomination. Prior to 1865 the Association had never been more than "an organization of contributing individuals."[112] The upshot of the meeting was the creation in the spring of 1865 of the National Conference of Unitarian Churches. It was to meet annually and serve as an advisory body to the Association.[113] As indicated by the original title, the conference was intended to consist of delegates and other individuals of that denomination only. But a year later, after much discussion and difference of opinion, the title was amended to include "other Christian Churches." The name was changed to appeal to "liberal spirits in other denominations."

One by-product of the new National Conference was the appearance of informal local and regional conferences in many parts of the nation.[114] One such conference was held in Syracuse, New York, early in 1867. Six Unitarian and thirteen Universalist churches were represented.[115] One Universalist representative asked for a clarification of the intended makeup of the conference because he had been reproached by several of his fellow clergymen for having allegedly deserted his denomination by attending. This provoked a discussion of Universalist-Unitarian relations which lasted a substantial part of two days. The Universalists present were assured that Unitarians had "been guided always by the sincerest desire to be friendly and brotherly towards the Universalist denomination." It was acknowledged by Unitarians that the Universalists had "always been before us in missionary zeal and in denominational activity"; but in their sweep of the country many societies had faltered or collapsed, and it was logical that the other major branch of liberal religion should attempt to revive them if the Universalists were unsuccessful. Unitarians called for a broader view by Universalists and less sensitivity and less narrow competitiveness of spirit.

Charles Lowe, secretary of the American Unitarian Association at the time of the Syracuse conference, was present and used the relations of Universalists and Unitarians as the main theme of a sermon delivered during the conference.[116] Like Henry W. Bellows, James Freeman Clarke, and Samuel J. May, he was a strong supporter of closing the gap between the two denominations. In fact, Lowe saw "nothing in the differences of belief or of methods or of principle between us and the Universalists to prevent our uniting at once, cordially and heartily, in one organization, that should entirely efface the lines that now divide us." He insisted that "the doctrine of God's paternal character," for which he gave Universalists full credit, was "of much more importance to unite us, than all our differences to divide." It was "almost an accident" that they were two denominations rather than one. But the time for union was not yet. Independent, but coordinated, action had to suffice for the time being. The two branches of "the Liberal Church,—with our different methods and different habits and different machinery, are for a while working as two bodies instead of one . . . . By and by, we will be ONE army." So the conference in Syracuse concluded that "in the present condition of things we must continue to act as two denominations, because the majority of both are not yet prepared for the union." It was therefore appropriate that every new liberal society should assume the name Unitarian or Universalist instead of any compromise between the two, such as "Independent."

Most important, so far as it affected Universalists, was the growing recognition given to Universalist and Unitarian relations in the national meetings of each denomination. There had been isolated instances of individuals of one denomination who appeared at meetings of the other, but these had had no official sponsorship. G.W. Webster, a Unitarian minister in Wheeling, (West) Virginia, appeared at the Universalist General Convention in 1853 and had attempted unsuccessfully to obtain simultaneous Universalist fellowship. His aim was to obtain Christian union on other than a doctrinal basis.[117] He was instructed to apply to a local association or state convention for fellowship if he wished to become a delegate.

The first proposal from an official body of either denomination that had to do with possible union came from the Unitarians in 1865. At the initial meeting of their National Conference, Samuel J. May offered a resolution in favor of appointing a committee to consider the subject. Instead, the committee to which his recommendation was referred offered a generalized resolution (which was passed) calling for greater fellowship and cooperation with all Christians. A committee of three (May, Clarke, and Robert Collyer) was appointed to promote such an end. The committee did confer with members of several denominations, including Universalists, and it was the committee who recommended that the name of the new Unitarian organization be broadened to include others of liberal persuasion. Reports from the committee, and a similar one which succeeded it in 1868, indicated a uniformly cordial reception at meetings of other denominations they attended; but they encountered simultaneously a reluctance to make any commitment to formal cooperation with the National Conference as an organized body.

Universalist reaction to May's resolution ranged from noncommittal to negative. It was apparently not taken seriously. Friendly relations and cooperation in supporting the religious truths shared by the two denominations were as far as most would go.[118] May's resolution was interpreted as "very fair and honorable" in intent, but the idea of joining forces with a denomination harboring a radical wing that showed a marked lack of respect for both Christ and the Bible was completely repugnant to the great majority of Universalists.

While the Unitarians were calling for increased harmony in inter-denominational relations in 1865, the Universalists were still intent on following their own course of action. At their 1865 meeting, the Committee on the State of the Church had offered a projection of the future role of the denomination. They saw great possibilities for Universalists to fill in the liberal religious gap between Unitarianism, with its policy of "indifference and latitudinarianism with respect to any fundamentals of Christian faith; and Congregationalism, with its renewed orthodoxy expressed at a recent meeting of its National Council."[119] Universalism, occupying a position between these two extremes, had "the grandest Providential opportunity for Christian work ever offered to any people."

Meanwhile the news of what had happened at the Unitarian meeting in 1865 had been received and considered. The reply at the General Convention in 1866 was to adopt a resolution (offered by J.J. Twiss) recognizing the Unitarian denomination as "engaged in a work kindred to our own."[120] Universalists extended to the Unitarian church "our cordial sympathy in its efforts to promote the spread of liberal Christianity in our country," and expressed the willingness of Universalists to cooperate with it, "in all practicable ways, for the Christianizing of the world."

Of at least symbolic significance at the centennial celebration of Universalism in 1870 was the presence of two invited guests—Edward Everett Hale and Charles Lowe, representing the National Conference of Unitarian and other Christian Churches. Edward Everett Hale (1822-1909) was a well-known Unitarian clergyman who from 1856 until his death had been associated with the South Congregational Church (Unitarian) in Boston, and after retiring from the active ministry was to become chaplain of the United States Senate. Hale was considered to be a "most ardent and enthusiastic proclaimer and defender of Unitarianism."[121] Charles Lowe (1828-1874), likewise a clergyman in the Boston area, was secretary of the American Unitarian Association at the time of the Universalist centennial.[122]

Hale served as spokesman for the two-man committee. After bringing greetings acknowledging briefly the services of Universalist theologians and philanthropists "to all Christendom," and excoriating the Roman Catholic Church for (among other things) misappropriating or misusing the word "catholic" ("universal"), Hale made haste to point out that he was not present "to suggest, even by an innuendo, any consolidation or any fusion of the bodies here represented."[123] He did recognize "the happy and friendly relation" which existed between "the two leading liberal bodies of America." But each group had "a history of its own, with martyrdoms of its own, with traditions of its own." These should not be sacrificed for "a mock fusion." The ultimate success of America was based on the standards and principles of Universalism and Unitarianism rather than on the doctrine of Calvinism and the Roman Catholic Church. Beyond these generalities he would not go.

One small step was taken in 1870 as the two denominations edged

Church of the Unity (1868-1961) in Springfield, Mass., designed by Henry Hobson Richardson

warily toward each other. In response to an invitation from the National Unitarian Conference, James M. Pullman and A. St. John Chambré were appointed by the General Convention to attend their next meeting. Their only instructions were to "present the fraternal greetings of the Universalist body."[124]

This was where matters stood a century after American Universalism had been planted by John Murray and slightly less than half a century after Unitarianism had assumed denominational form. They had at least learned how to live with one another, uneasy as their coexistence seemed to be at times. Thomas Whittemore, in 1852, had compared the two denominations to "two vessels bound to the same port, but dreading a contact, they have steered their courses near each other, maintaining all the while a careful distance."[125] Moses Ballou, as a fellow Universalist, put the matter thus in 1860: "Let them go their own way, and we will go ours.–The world is wide enough for all of us, and there is enough for us all to do."[126]

There was indeed much for all to do. For Universalists the immediate task was to prepare for the celebration of the centenary of the denomination in 1870. G.H. Demarest, like many other Universalists, was in a retrospective mood as the centennial year approached. He put his thoughts to paper in an article intended to provide some historical perspective.[127] One of the points he emphasized early in the article was the shift over the years from antagonism to friendship in Universalist-Unitarian relations, a tendency which he viewed with complete approval. He was particularly conscious of Universalist roots, for in January of 1870 he had prepared for the Universalist Publishing House a special centenary edition of the life of John Murray. To make the denominational associations with the past come alive, he had included, besides a likeness of Murray, sketches of the Potter meeting house, the first Universalist church in America (in Gloucester), the first Universalist church in Boston, and Murray's grave in Mount Auburn cemetery in Cambridge.

Demarest identified two themes in the history of American Universalism over its first 100 years: "An Idea, and a body of Christians." The Idea was "the universal, unchangeable, illimitable love of Almighty God." The "body of Christians" in 1870 comprised about 900 societies or churches, with 600 ministers.[128] The first Universalist meeting house, a simple frame building, had been erected in 1780; twenty years later there were but five. In 1800 there had been but twenty Universalist preachers, so small a number that they could easily be called by name. They spread the gospel of salvation to any who would listen, in open fields or groves of trees, or "in whatever cottage, or barn, or shop, or mill, or school house, or other public building would give them hospitality."

By 1870 the dozens of preachers had been replaced by hundreds of ministers and pastors, often conducting their services in impressive stone edifices. By 1870 two generations of preachers had come and gone and those who had known the second generation at first hand were beginning themselves to pass off the scene. The names of Murray and Winchester had become little more than traditions. It was to preserve the names and memories of the pioneers in the denomination that prompted E.G. Brooks to begin the preparation of a series of biographies of early Universalists, the first of which appeared in 1870. Hosea Ballou's was the first.[129] It was time for the denomination to pause and to see where it had been, where it was, and where it was to go.

Chapter 29

UNIVERSALISM AT MID-POINT: THE DENOMINATIONAL CENTENNIAL

Preparing the Way

As the year 1870 approached, there were unusual stirrings among Universalists. The 100th anniversary of John Murray's arrival on American shores was about to take place, and it was agreed and expected that appropriate observances would be forthcoming. It was logical that the General Convention should undertake the planning and oversight of this significant event in the history of American Universalism.

The first tangible step was taken at the annual meeting in September 1867, held in Baltimore, Maryland. Five of the most prominent Universalists representing as many states were appointed "to take into consideration the Centennial Anniversary of the Denomination" and were to report the next year.[1] But the committee took no action, and had nothing to report in 1868. The second attempt was more successful. On Alonzo A. Miner's initiative, a thirteen-person committee was created in 1868 and given "full power . . . to determine the time, objects, and methods of observing the Centenary." The names of only two of the original committee (Israel Washburn and Richard Eddy) appeared on the reconstituted list. Mrs. Mary A. Livermore was the only woman appointed to serve.

In 1869 at its meeting in Buffalo, the General Convention approved the report of the Centenary Committee and thereby committed the denomination to the most elaborate and challenging program in its history. It centered about what had been called in 1866 by the Committee on the State of the Church, the most urgent needs of Universalism: "*members* and *money.*" And of these, the greater was money. Every one of the six objects of the centennial observance spelled out by the Centenary Committee had to do with finances, and the overall goal called for the raising of the staggering sum of $1,000,000. All contributions made in 1869 and 1870 in support of the objectives listed were to be counted as part of this grand total, to be known as the "Centennial Offering."

Specifically, the objectives were: A concerted effort on the part of all Universalist entities to pay off indebtedness; the erection of new church buildings and the improvement of existing ones; increased support for denominational educational institutions; missionary work "wherever called for"; and a special memorial offering of $200,000, to be known as the Murray Centenary Fund. The fund was intended to commemorate the anniversary of the first sermon preached by Murray at Good Luck (later Murray Grove), New Jersey, on 30 September 1770. The income was to be used for the aid of theological students, the distribution of Universalist literature, church extension and "the missionary cause."

How was all of this to be achieved? Six recommendations were made, starting with the widest possible publicity, to be provided by the denominational press. Every parish, Sunday school, association, conference, and state convention, as well as the General Convention, was urged to make the centennial "a subject of special consideration" by whatever means were available. Clergy were expected to call attention to the celebration and to devote the first Sunday in June 1870 to the holding of special services in their churches and Sunday schools. Mass meetings, including speakers, were to be arranged in all major metropolitan centers and reports were expected at the centennial meeting of the General Convention. So that every Universalist family could be assured of participation, "missionary boxes" were to be placed in each home. This proposal had come in 1867 from D.L. Holden, an officer of the Leather Manufacturers' National Bank in New York City in response to a request for money-raising suggestions from the General Secretary.[2] But the creation of a special memorial fund became the focus of most attention and the source of the greatest misgivings. How could such a large sum be raised in view of the less than generous record of giving in the past?

The root of the idea of creating a fund for "a general missionary work" can be traced back to 1865, when the trustees of the General Convention had issued a "Statement and Appeal" calling for the raising of $100,000, to be used "to inaugurate judicious missionary enterprise, in the name of the whole church."[3] It was for this purpose that the decision to incorporate had been made (accomplished in 1866). The fund proposed in 1865 was to be used primarily for evangelism, and the establishment and strengthening of societies, especially in the West, Northwest, and South.

The goal may have seemed unattainable to some Universalists, but it certainly had not seemed so to E.G. Brooks, a great champion of an aggressive ecclesiastical policy. He had written the annual report for the Committee on the State of the Church for the 1865 General Convention meeting. In the course of an extended argument for greater generosity in denominational giving, he pointedly referred to the success of the Unitarians, who with less than half the numerical strength of the Universalists, had raised $220,000 within that very year; and to the Orthodox Congregationalists who would probably achieve with ease their annual goal of $750,000.[4] Brooks conceded that Universalists did not have the wealth claimed by Unitarians or some of "the older and larger sects." But he saw no reason why Universalists could not raise "at least $100,000" that same year of 1865. The convention, he thought, should take steps then and there to provide at least $50,000; if the delegates adjourned without doing so, Universalists would need to hang their heads "in an utter loss of self-respect, and this country will have reason to point at us with the finger of disgust." The convention disregarded Brooks' warning, for not a cent was pledged at the beginning to create a general fund. Even a year later, when the first annual report of the permanent treasurer was made under the revised constitution of 1865, the total assets comprising the missionary fund and a one-per-cent levy on societies amounted to less than $10,000.[5]

The record of giving by 1868 was even more discouraging. Less than $6,000 was contributed to the missionary fund that year, and only forty societies added less than $350 to the general fund. The treasurer (E.W. Crowell) pointed to the success of the Methodists in raising over $8,000,000 and blamed the Universalist failure in part on the fact that their organization was disjointed and fragmented. Unless a radical change were made, the denomination would remain "powerless either to raise large sums of money, or to carry on any of those great religious movements called for by the age in which we live."[6] It was painfully clear that something had to be done, and soon, to create a permanent fund independent of the uncertain and totally inadequate local contributions. The denomination therefore had two financial challenges to meet: the creation of an adequate permanent fund, and the raising of a special fund as part of the centennial, earmarked for specified purposes.

The immediate move to create a "Murray Centenary Fund," designated as such, had been made at the meeting of the General Convention in 1868, but was delayed a year until a committee could be created to place the fund-raising in the broader context of plans for the centennial year. The Centenary Committee in 1869 naturally assigned first priority to the creation of the Murray Fund, to be used for the purposes enumerated. But when it suggested a formula by which state conventions could assign quotas within their jurisdictions, the committee reminded the conventions (in italics for emphasis) that the proposed Murray Fund was *"over and above all other offerings."* The regular expenses of the General Convention, including the reimbursement of its permanent secretary's expenses, still had to be met.

There was one development at the 1869 convention that helped to alleviate the gloom that seemed to have settled over its deliberations over the Murray Fund. A new resourcc, not yet even partially tapped in the first century of the denomination's history in any systematic or official way, came to the attention of the General Convention in rather dramatic fashion. That resource comprised the thousands of Universalist women who had faithfully served the denomination in many unheralded ways, but who had never played a role commensurate with their talents because they had never been called upon to do so. The centennial gave them that opportunity.

The Woman's Centenary Aid Association

The groundwork for what became the Woman's Centenary Aid Association had been laid in the winter of 1867 when E.G. Brooks, the General Secretary of the convention, had issued a special plea for assistance addressed "to the women of the unorganized portions of the Universalist denomination" to raise funds for educational and missionary purposes.[7] Special attention was urged to the eastern and midwestern states, and within a year a women's executive committee had been organized in the Midwest and Northwest, headed by Mrs. Mary Livermore. The work of what became the Woman's Centenary Aid Association represented one of the more successful of the activities associated with the anniversary of the denomination and brought the women to the forefront for the first time.

The Association was organized in a matter of hours in a basement Sunday school room of one of the churches in which the council of the General Convention was meeting in Buffalo in September 1869.[8] While their husbands were busy in the main auditorium of the church discussing the feasibility of creating the Murray Fund, the women who had accompanied them to the meeting were likewise busy. After electing a temporary chairman (Mrs. D.C. Tomlinson) and a secretary (Mrs. F.J.M. Whitcomb), they talked at some length about how they could contribute to the centennial celebration. Mrs. Caroline A. Soule opened the discussion and was followed by others who addressed the assemblage, including women who "never before had ventured to utter aloud their thoughts, save in the home and social circle."

Learning that a meeting was in progress, Mrs. Tomlinson's husband was delegated by the council to inquire as to its nature. When told that they were considering ways of furthering the centennial effort, he spoke words of encouragement. Within two hours, during the morning of the last day of the General Convention, the decision was made to organize an association of women. Their special project was to be the soliciting of funds for the "Murray Centenary Offering," and was reflected in the first name suggested—the "Ladies' Murray Centennial Association." Mrs. Soule addressed the council and guests, and within minutes $273 was collected. The Murray Fund had become more than an idea. With the approbation of the council to encourage them, during the concluding hours of the convention sessions the women prepared and adopted a constitution, elected officers, and outlined plans for accomplishing their purpose. The setting of an exect sum to be raised was left for further discussion.

Mrs. Caroline A. Soule (1824-1903), elected as the first president of the Woman's Centenary Association, was a natural choice, for she had already made some of her literary, leadership, and religious qualities visible. An honors graduate of the Albany Female Academy (New York), she was for a time principal of the female department of Clinton Liberal Institute, where she met her future husband, Henry Birdsall Soule, who served briefly as principal of the male department. After his death in 1852 she published a widely circulated memoir of his life. She served as associate editor of the *Ladies' Repository*; as editor of the *Guiding Star* and the *Myrtle,* Sunday school papers; and was a regular contributor to several annuals edited and published by Universalists, including the *Rose of Sharon* and the *Lily of the Valley.* She also engaged in preaching and became one of the ordained women in the Universalist ministry.

The organization that was born in the fall of 1869 at the meeting in Buffalo was indeed a novel and significant one for the denomination at the time, as the founders themselves recognized. It represented not only an important effort in furthering the goals of the denomination as it closed its first century but marked "the grand uprising" of the women of the church. It signified the beginning of the end of women's role of "mute spectators" of denominational affairs and gave them a sense of involvement never before experienced. For the first time, Universalist women from all over the country had, in the years that followed, an organization in which they could associate and through which they could contribute. The foundation laid in 1869 made possible the first meeting of the Association on a truly national level at the centennial convocation at Gloucester in 1870. The intent had been made clear at the organization meeting in 1869, for twenty-three vice-presidents had been elected, representing Universalists in as many states.

The women's organization lost no time in getting its activities under way. Branches were quickly established all over the nation. The first to respond with money was the Illinois contingent, which raised and transmitted to the secretary of the General Convention the sum of $500. This constituted the net profits from an entertainment held in St. Paul's Church in Chicago. After the 1869 meeting, $200 in addition was donated to the women of the Buffalo Universalist Church which had been destroyed by fire. The net contribution of the Woman's Centenary Aid Association to the Murray Fund, presented appropriately at the 1870 General Convention, and with mathematical precision, was

$35,000.53. Expenses amounted to less than $775. Nearly 13,000 women had become members by the close of the centennial year, their individual gifts ranging from $1 to $1,000. Meetings had been held in major cities in 1869-70, culminating in the grand convocation at Gloucester.

The immediate mission of the organization had been accomplished with gratifying success within the space of only one year. The original plan had been to dissolve the Association at the centenary meeting, but because the reports were not yet complete it was voted to continue for one more year, under the same name and with the same officers. The 1870 General Convention readily agreed. The Association accordingly met in Philadelphia in 1871 to hear a resumé of its work before disbanding. But the enthusiasm and fellowship generated by two years of effort, and the financial success that had been achieved, resulted in a vote to reorganize on a permanent basis with the name "Woman's Centenary Association" (WCA). A constitution was adopted which became the basis for its government for eleven years. Between 1871 and 1891 the WCA had but two presidents—Mrs. Soule, who served until 1880; and Mrs. M. Louise Thomas. The organization met annually at the same time and place as the General Convention, and could claim a distinction that went far beyond Universalist circles. It was the first national organization of church women to be created on a permanent basis by any denomination in the United States for specific purposes independent of the ongoing work of its governing body. The Universalist community itself officially took cognizance of the Association when Mrs. George B. Marsh of Chicago was elected as a trustee of the General Convention.

The WCA undertook a wide variety of activities. Among them were assistance to weak parishes, churches, and Sunday schools; financial aid to students preparing for the ministry (originally intended for women but later broadened); help to sick and disabled ministers and the families of deceased clergy; distribution of denominational literature; and the undertaking of both home and foreign missionary projects. All major decisions were made by vote of the entire Association at its annual meetings, direction and coordination being furnished by an executive committee. In 1872 it created a department of special gifts for those wishing to contribute to specific individuals, institutions, or organizations. During the next year Mrs. Soule embarked on field work which yielded $25,000. The Illinois branch contributed $5,000 toward the construction of a women's dormitory at Lombard College. Another donation, the largest received in 1873, was $10,000 made by her husband in memory of Mrs. Chloe Pierce of Sharpsville, Pennsylvania. It was to be used toward the endowment of $20,000 of a professorship for women at Buchtel College in Ohio. Although the pledges were not all collected because of the national financial crisis of 1873, $6,000 was raised through the efforts of the WCA to supplement the Pierce gift. The next largest contribution came from Miss Harriet H. Fay, who made a gift of $3,000 for the purchase of an organ for the Universalist church in Washington, D.C.

The first annual meeting of the WCA was held in Cincinnati, Ohio, in 1872. Almost $1,400 had been raised during the year, with nineteen states represented. The first gift by the Association was a Bible for the parish in Lincoln, Nebraska, the money for which had been raised by the Pennsylvania branch. Aside from a small gift to S.J. McMorris, who was trying to rebuild Universalism in the post-Civil War South, the most important expenditure was a gift to Jefferson Liberal Institute (Wisconsin). But this was only the beginning. By the end of Mrs. Thomas' presidency in 1891, the Association had raised a quarter of a million dollars for missionary work alone, not counting contributions from time to time to other denominational needs, including the general treasury. As Mrs. Soule wrote in 1886, "the possibilities of the WOMAN'S CENTENARY ASSOCIATION are of the grandest character." Its potential for service was realized many times over in succeeding years.

When the centennial-born Association voted in 1871 to continue as an organization, one of its projects was to take responsibility for providing tracts to explain and spread Universalism. In 1873 the executive committee voted to devote all of the funds except those needed for operating expenses to the preparation and dissemination of denominational literature. A publications committee was created, under the leadership of Mrs. Thomas, and in one year had produced twelve tracts. Within the next fifteen years the number of titles, in multiple copies, had risen to sixty-eight, representing over 5,000,000 printed pages.[9] Written by eight clergymen, including Mrs. Soule, the tracts were sent "to almost every part of the inhabited earth." Over two-thirds were distributed free of charge, including those made available at railroad stations in Philadelphia while the centennial celebration of the nation was in progress in 1876. In addition, hundreds of copies of denominational books, pamphlets, and newspapers were broadcast by the Association.

In order to increase its scope and strengthen its organization, the Association was incorporated in Washington, D.C., under special act of Congress in September 1873. By then, friction had begun to develop between the organization and the General Convention. The women's group had been reorganized in 1871 as an independent agency, with both the money they raised and the projects they sponsored to be completely under their control. Criticism of this seemingly centrifugal tendency by an autonomous organization came to a climax at the annual meetings in 1874, but the problem was amicably settled with a victory for the Association. The president was admitted to the floor of the General Convention after assuring those present that the Association was devotedly loyal to the General Convention and had the welfare of the entire denomination at heart. President Soule also convinced the delegates that the intent of the Association was to work cooperatively rather than competitively.

Still searching for the most effective means of increasing "the pecuniary returns" as well as strengthening its organization, the Association in 1874 created the office of General Superintendent and put Mrs. Soule into the field. For nine months she travelled from Maine to Missouri, working on behalf of any activity that would further denominational interests. Her journeying was cut short in January 1875 by illness, and she embarked for Europe for a much-needed respite from an extremely arduous regimen. It was while on that trip that she spent six months visiting Universalists in Scotland which resulted in her assignment as a missionary there from 1878 to 1882.[10]

Mrs. Soule had expressed the wish, as first president of the WCA, that both the work and the name of the organization would last at least a century. Although the name was changed, its historic functions not only were continued but expanded. In 1882 a new charter and a new set of bylaws were adopted, to be in effect for twenty years. When that time had elapsed, the name was changed (in 1905) to the Women's National Missionary Association of the Universalist Church, which coincided with its undertaking of the Universalist mission in Japan already organized under the auspices of the General Convention. In 1939 the organization became the Association of Universalist Women (AUW), and in 1963, two years after the consolidation of the Universalist Church of America and the American Unitarian Association, another change was made. It was voted to unite the AUW with the Alliance of Unitarian Women to form the Unitarian Universalist Women's Federation. The organization that had contributed so much to the Universalist denomination for almost a century could now face challenges and opportunities shared with a new partner.

"Once in a Hundred Years:" The Gloucester Celebration

The three days of 20-22 September 1870 were indeed a time of triumph and celebration as thousands of Universalists crowded into the fishing community of Gloucester, Massachusetts, northeast of Boston, where John Murray had held the first settled pastorate in the history of American Universalism. Delegates from twenty-one of the thirty-five states, districts and territories of the nation flooded into the seaport town, and were joined by others as the General Convention of Universalists in the United States of America was called to order at

10:00 A.M. on Tuesday, 20 September, in the Universalist church by the president, J.G. Bartholomew of New York.[11]

Elaborate preparations had been made for this special occasion, including five hymns written and used in the celebration. Mother Nature cooperated with "fair and perfect" weather—a continuation of the driest season known in the area for fifty years. Special police hired to maintain law and order reported "an extraordinary reign of sobriety and quiet" prevailing, an unusual circumstance in view of the fact that an estimated maximum of 12,000 people attended; there were 242 Universalist clergymen registered. This assemblage was considered by the press to have been the largest religious gathering in the nation's history. Over 100 tents were provided in a level area adjacent to the Atlantic seashore, housing not only individuals but assemblies and organizations of various kinds. The tent assigned to the Universalist Publishing House served as the headquarters of the sprawling camp which had mushroomed. About 2,000 families were housed by residents of the community and vicinity. There were some minor irritations. The Eastern Railroad which then serviced Boston and Gloucester had failed to make the special provisions requested. Some of the trains to the convention took up to three hours or more and as many as one-third of the passengers were forced to stand for the entire trip. Even though the main tent had a seating capacity of 5,000, as many as 7,000 attempted to jam into it. By the afternoon of the first day, it had been decided that in order to accommodate the vast assemblage, an open-air meeting beside the main tent was the only solution.

The events of the convention were covered by reporters from a dozen papers, including the *New York Times,* Horace Greeley's *New York Tribune,* the *Springfield Republican,* and the Boston press. One event which attracted unusual attention occurred just before the official proceedings commenced. H.F. Ballou of Vermont exhibited what was said to have been the last cloak worn by John Murray and dramatically called upon someone to fill it. Other linkages with the Universalist past were provided by numerous special commemorative events. Services were held outside the building which had been erected in 1780 and had served until 1805 as the first Universalist meeting house in Gloucester. After it had been replaced by a new structure, the original building in which Murray had preached had been bought in 1815, moved to a location about two miles from the town, and in 1870 was being used as a hay barn and stable on the farm of Edward H. Pearce. After a memorial service there, conducted by Abel C. Thomas of Philadelphia, hundreds of Universalists visited the grave of Thomas Jones, Murray's successor in Gloucester who had served there for over forty years until his death in 1846. The communion set imported from

England by Murray for the use of his Gloucester congregation and in 1870 possessed by the Watertown (Massachusetts) Universalist Church, was used for a special celebration of the Lord's Supper. An ecumenical atmosphere prevailed at the two memorial services, for local Methodists had donated flowers for the ceremony at the Murray meeting house, and the Baptists had done likewise at the Jones graveside.

After the organizational details of the council had been routinely taken care of on the morning of the first day, under the presiding hand of Sidney Perham, Governor-elect of Maine, and the historic Universalist church having proved completely inadequate to contain the 3,000 people who appeared, the next session was held outdoors. After referring annual and special reports to appropriate committees for review and recommendation, the delegates discussed proposals for an amended constitution. This was temporarily interrupted to hear Alonzo A. Miner deliver the keynote sermon of the convention. Throughout the proceedings, delegates and others in attendance also heard addresses and sermons of varying lengths, interspersed among the business sessions.

The evening session of the second day was spent in an article-by-article discussion of the amended constitution, with several amendments to the amendments introduced. The same fate befell the amended bylaws, which were the main order of business for the following morning. A set of Rules of Order was adopted thereafter, without amendment; but a model plan for the organization of a state convention was altered on the floor, as was a similar set of recommendations for organizing a church. The proposed "Laws for securing a uniform system of Fellowship, Government and Discipline" were likewise amended by the delegates in several respects. Some sections were recommitted for further study.

The last formal session, on the evening of the last day, was an understandably short one. The weary delegates dispensed with the reading of most of the minutes of previous sessions, and declined to consider a resolution offered by Eli Ballou of Vermont on the evils of war and the importance of settling all international disputes by arbitration. Action on the resolution was postponed for a year. The last important item of business was the appointment of J.M. Pullman and A. St. John Chambré to attend the forthcoming National Unitarian Conference which had relayed cordial fraternal greetings to the Universalists as they celebrated their centennial.

Conspicuously missing from most of the numerous reports dealing with fund-raising were references to the South. Likewise absent from the deliberations were representatives from the Southern states. Neither lay nor clerical delegates were present from the Carolinas, Georgia, Florida, Mississippi, or Alabama. Where state conventions had existed at all before the Civil War, they had at least temporarily disappeared.

Tent City of the Universalist Centennial Convention, Gloucester, Massachusetts, September 1870

There were two lay delegates from the newly created state of West Virginia, but none from the parent state. Among the border states, only Maryland was represented; even then, the two delegates (both from Baltimore, one layman and one clergyman) had their credentials challenged.

The barebones of the official minutes of the General Convention in 1870 give but little indication of the excitement of the occasion, and of the differences as well as the agreements which came out of the series of sessions. A review of the committee reports and the comments of participants shed much light on how far the Universalists had come and how much farther they had yet to go before all of their dreams and expectations were realized. One source of embarrassment to the Committee on the State of the Church was the almost complete lack of information on the actual numerical strength of the denomination. After acknowledging that there were "no statistics worth the name," the committee skirted the problem by explaining that "the life and growth of the Church is not to be estimated by numbers, but by the more real, though perhaps less tangible evidence of spiritual activity and Christian fruit."

Miner's Centenary Sermon was naturally a high point of the convention. It was a lengthy preroration, in which he reviewed in considerable detail the history of the universalist concept and Universalist institutional and theological development from Judeo-Christian origins in ancient times to 1870, all within less than three hours. In his prefatory remarks he alluded to the findings of modern science, which he considered no threat to faith or the immanence of God, for science and the material world were finite. The "higher truths" involving man's soul, his immortality, and his "blessed destiny" were still to be found in the word of God and revealed through Christ. Miner's faith in divine revelation remained unshaken, as did his conviction that the Universalist mission would, in the coming century, be realized in "the thorough leavening of the civilized world."

E.H. Chapin, who gave the Communion meditation at a special service celebrating the Lord's Supper, attended by "an immense congregation" (estimated at seven thousand), devoted much time to the meaning of what was taking place. He expressed regret that what was intended to be a bond of union among all Christians had instead become a subject of controversy and divisiveness. Whatever the form or the interpretation, it was the idea of remembrance of Christ that was important, and the spiritual benefit to the participant, whether a simple memorial (as Universalists interpreted it) or partaking of the miraculous. He went beyond the confines of denominationalism to welcome all to "the Lord's table," Unviversalist or not; they were all welcome in the Church of Christ Universal, of which the particular church which he represented was but one part.

A mass meeting heard Israel Washburn of Maine review briefly his conception of the historically unique role that Universalism had played as "a positive form of Christianity," and call attention to the providential appearance of John Murray on the eve of the American Revolution. Out of the latter had come fundamental principles of government "identical with those of Universalism." Liberty and equality in the political realm had been matched by democracy in the religious realm.

Many who spoke during the convention had their special interests and concerns uppermost, such as Richmond Fisk, Jr., president of St. Lawrence University; William R. Shipman of Tufts College; and John R. Buchtel, the philanthropist business man from Ohio, who all spoke on the importance of denominational education and its support, present and future. Mary A. Livermore devoted a major part of an address at a mass meeting to the contribution of women to the denomination and more particularly to their money-raising efforts during the centennial. J. Smith Dodge, a clergyman from Connecticut, reviewed the history and importance of the Sunday school movement. William H. Ryder of Chicago gave what he termed a "practical talk" on the uses to which funds being raised should be put. They coincided with the final decisions regarding the allocations of the Murray Fund. Henry B. Metcalf, as a layman and successful businessman, stressed the importance of the "Missionary Army" and the missionary boxes not only as money-raising devices but as ways to heighten the sense of involvement of the rank and file in the denomination.

The Woman's Centenary Aid Association met, with an overflow attendance, in the Universalist church while the main convention was in session. The Association heard addresses by, among others, Mrs. Ada Bowles, of the First Universalist Parish of Cambridge, Massachusetts; Miss Augusta J. Chapin of Iowa, on her missionary work in the West; and Mrs. Mary A. Livermore and her activities on behalf of the denomination. It was she who recommended at the 1870 meeting that after the Association was disbanded, a permanent organization of Universalist women be established. During their principal session, presided over by Mrs. Soule, the Association set as an initial target the sum of $10,000 as their contribution to the Murray Fund, and established branches in every state.

Much of the space and attention in the various reports to the General Convention in 1870 was naturally devoted to finances and particularly to the progress of the Murray Fund. The "Committee on the Missionary Army" which had charge of preparing and distributing missionary boxes reported that 30,000 had been prepared, of which 25,500 had been sent throughout the country, 10,000 of them in the New England states. They were wryly described by Henry B. Metcalf, a Universalist businessman, as "invented in the wilds of New Jersey and manufactured in the immaculate city of New York, at a cost somewhat less than is demanded for a tolerable cigar." Over 10,000 boxes had been returned by the fall of 1870, averaging $1.02 each. The total credited to the Murray Fund from this source was $10,380.81, and was considered a "very satisfactory" source of revenue. The Murray Fund also received $23,827.46 from other sources. One hopeful sign was that a total of $129,000 had been pledged to the Murray Fund by twelve state conventions, largely through the efforts of Asa Saxe, the General Secretary, who had visited eight states and the District of Columbia and had seen to the appointment of financial agents in all states. Before the end of 1870, four states had already made good their pledges, but it was clear that completion of the Murray Fund had to be the top priority for 1871. By the time of the Gloucester meeting, Massachusetts Universalists had made the largest pledge of any state ($12,000). The state raising the largest amount above its quota was Minnesota which, "with the true Prussian energy . . . in the space of three weeks, ended the Centenary Campaign in a blaze of glory." The largest individual contribution in the name of the centennial was the gift of $31,000 by John Buchtel, which was donated for a college to be established in Ohio and which was soon to bear his name.

One unsuccessful attempt was made at the 1870 convention to divert the Murray Fund from its original purposes. A resolution was offered by Horace Greeley to the effect that the fund "should be sacredly devoted to the foundation of a Universalist Publishing House after the general plan of the Methodist Book Concern." The Committee of Investment to which the Murray Fund was entrusted reported unfavorably on such a proposal. Worthy as Greeley's plans might have been, it would have been directly contrary to the purposes endorsed by the 1869 General Convention (aid to theological students, distribution of Universalist literature, church extension, and the missionary cause). The Woman's Centenary Aid Association had already taken on the responsibility of distributing denominational materials, and any other use of the income would have been considered a breach of faith. Furthermore, the General Convention had either committed itself already to aid existing publishing ventures, or had such plans on the drawing board.

One of the goals established in 1869 had been the paying off of indebtedness. Ironically, the General Convention itself unhappily claimed the largest amount—$17,000, for which the Murray Fund was not available. The board of trustees had noted rather caustically in 1870 that, in its preoccupation with plans for the centennial observance, the council of the General Convention had overlooked the fact that money was needed to carry out existing commitments. Hence it had become necessary to borrow $15,000 to supplement the meagre $2,500 in the treasury. Numerous pleas were made at the centennial meetings to remedy this situation, and a call was made for spontaneous donations and pledges from the floor. P.T. Barnum led off with $100, and before the sessions were over a total of $2,800 had been either received or promised. But even though the chronic deficit in convention finances remained as a cloud over its existence as Universalism entered its second century, the new General Secretary, Asa Saxe, was determinedly hopeful. He was positive that the denomination had sufficient resources to justify "an announcement to all the world, that we are here, and have come to stay."

Much of the three-day Gloucester gathering was spent on an examination of the ecclesiastical structure of Universalism as it stood a century after John Murray's arrival. In part the sessions were retrospective, and in part they were a projection into an unknown future. The keynote was struck in the report of the Committee on the State of the Church. In assessing the first 100 years, the most striking feature seemed to have been "a tendency to organize." For some three generations, common beliefs and the need to defend unpopular theological views had been the only real ties binding the denomination together. But after a century of growing and maturing, the Universalists as a body had made their way sufficiently (at least in the eyes of the committee) to recognize the need for greater consolidation than had heretofore prevailed. The scattered strength of the denomination needed more focus and more direction. The same sentiments had been expressed repeatedly at previous sessions. The watchwords of the 1865 General Convention after the conclusion of the Civil War had been "Union and Consolidation," reflecting in denominational terms the goal of the recently divided nation. Delegates were told by the Committee on the State of the Church that one of the lessons of the conflict was the error of states' rights—"simply the political side of an extreme congregationalism."[12]

No clearer indication of the new mood could be found than in the new constitution adopted by Universalists, with minor editorial revisions, at the centennial session. Most of the changes, as compared with the 1865 document, might have seemed cosmetic rather than basic; but the goals of tightening the reins of power and streamlining the entire organization were confirmed and made more explicit than ever before. The 1870 constitution represented the culmination of literally years of discussion, debate (and disagreement) which went back, so far as the immediate past was concerned, exactly a decade. In 1860 the Committee on Organization had called attention to the need for expanded powers of the General Convention as "a practical working body."[13] A partial answer to the problem of ineffectual central authority and fragmented control had been provided with the revised constitution adopted in 1865 and the incorporation of the board of trustees the following year.

The new constitution of "The Universalist General Convention" was based on the assumption that, from the centenary year onward, Universalists would no longer speak of themselves as a denomination but as "THE UNIVERSALIST CHURCH." In the constitution itself, the term "parish" was substituted for "society" in order to emphasize the basically religious character of the "primary bodies" in the organization. Associations were no longer considered part of the "ecclesiastical system." Only three levels of organization were recognized by the constitution: the parish, the state convention (as representative of parishes), and the General Convention itself. Associations were left as strictly local organizations, without formal status. An attempt led by the standing committee on Sunday schools to have that part of the church's constituency officially incorporated into the organizational structure was rejected.

With a revised set of bylaws in 1870, together with rules of order, a model constitution and bylaws for state conventions, and guidelines for organizing a parish and a church, Universalists were now equipped with the sort of system that so many had found wanting or deficient earlier. The General Convention likewise adopted a set of "Laws for Securing a Uniform System of Fellowship, Government and Discipline." The elaborate system of standing committees provided in the 1865 bylaw was abolished as "wholly unnecessary." The trustees were expected to touch on such matters as the state of the church, education, and the like, in their annual reports.

The Centennial Year was a logical time to review the adequacy and status of the Winchester Profession of Faith of 1803 which had been adopted when Universalism was still very much on the defensive. With this in mind, J.G. Adams prepared an article on the subject which was published in the spring of 1870.[14] He found the Profession to be still a thoroughly admirable document and considered it "a model creed, for one so short." It needed no alteration.

Almost simultaneously an editorial appeared in the *Ladies' Repository* reviewing the frequently-expressed need for "a new article of faith."[15] The writer pointed out that the Profession had been in effect forced upon Universalists by both theological disagreements within the ranks and by the necessity of preparing some such statement in order to obtain a charter as a religious body. What Walter Ferriss and others responsible for drafting the declaration had done was to produce a document that seemed "to say as little as possible." Beyond stating the distinguishing article of faith of Universalists—the ultimate salvation of all men—the Profession merely reaffirmed fundamental truths accepted by all Christians. It was therefore a document as remarkable for what it omitted as for what it included. There was no mention of "two underlying premises of our whole system of faith—the fatherhood of God and the brotherhood of man." Hence it came close to being "all things to all men."

Had the time come, asked the author of the editorial, to formulate a more definite statement of belief "which shall express the salient points . . . and place us in a juster because more definite position before the world."? The answer was "no." What the writer called for was not a new profession at all, but a spiritual awakening of an intensely personal nature which would make truly meaningful the "external truths" represented by any creed. This could not be easily verbalized, but was essential to any truly vital religion. When the time came at the centennial meeting to consider the Winchester Profession, the General Convention stood firm on adherence to the Profession as originally adopted. It was not only included in the constitution of 1870 but was repeated in the "Laws." There was no official recognition of latitudinarian interpretation by way of a "liberty clause." The ambiguous statement in the 1865 constitution that provided "an expressed or implied assent to the Confession" for fellowship was reworded to specify "expressed assent" only.

Taken as a unit, the constitution of 1870, at least in the view of the five men responsible for drafting it, constituted "a more perfect body of method and law" than had yet been devised by or for the newly designated Universalist Church. It was surely no slip of the pen that the new rules and regulations were referred to as the "General Canon Law." Few of the founding fathers would have recognized or could have foreseen the relatively complex institution that had been built around a simple declaration of faith less than seventy years before. As G.W. Skinner of Quincy, Massachusetts, and Alonzo A. Miner of Boston kept reiterating, Universalism was "no longer a loose denominational organization," a sort of religious undercurrent. It was now a full-fledged church, firmly embedded in the mainstream of the American religious tradition.

Israel Washburn carried the point even farther. He predicted that historic necessity and the logic of events would make Universalism "the American Church of the future . . . .Paternity, brotherhood, equality of destiny,—the doctrine we have taught,—all are hastening to teach. It is the Universalist Church which has made this possible."[16] The work of the church, Washburn told the centennial gathering, was "before the world." On the whole, it had been well done. But as Universalism stood "at the gateway of another century, a different and perhaps more difficult labor confronts it." Universalists were to have, as a separate and independent religious body, almost exactly 100 years to accept and meet the challenge which Washburn hinted at but did not spell out.

Appendix A
John Murray's Writings

As early as 1785 John Murray had dropped a broad hint that someone should collect his letters on "a variety of subjects"; they might, he thought, be particularly useful if anyone saw fit, after his death, to attack him or his ideas. By such a circumstance, "encouragement may be given for printing Memoirs and Letters of the late Mr. John Murray, &c, &c." The hint was not acted on, so Murray proceeded to carry the project himself. The result was a three-volume collection, published as *Letters, and Sketches of Sermons,* which appeared almost thirty years later.[1] Murray was in declining health associated with advanced years at the time, so he hastened to gather the materials not only to share them with others but to derive from the sale of the volumes whatever funds he could with which to replenish a personal treasury greatly depleted by medical expenses.

The first volume consists of thirteen items, mostly sermons; the second, of sixty-four items, mostly letters and fragments on miscellaneous matters; and the third, of sketches of sermons and commentaries, particularly on Biblical passages. In a prefatory note in the last volume, written in the summer of 1800, Murray indicated that he would leave to his wife the task of collecting the notes and making them available to the public. Mrs. Murray, who survived her husband by five years, faithfully complied with his wishes. She left at her death a large and valuable collection of manuscripts, correspondence, and other papers, including Murray's diaries, on which his autobiography was based, and letters from George and Martha Washington, General Nathaniel Greene, and many others. These materials, stored for many years in an unoccupied building on a plantation near Natchez, Mississippi, deteriorated to such an extent because of heat, humidity, and mildew, that none of the originals survived. Fortunately, some, including the sources discussed here, had been previously put into print or used extensively before their destruction.

The letters and other materials in the section of the *Life* prepared by Mrs. Murray (Chapters 7-9) must be used with caution. She had apparently not received the assistance she expected when she undertook to continue her husband's narrative, and was rather overwhelmed with the task before her. She followed the practice of occasionally changing the wording in her late husband's correspondence, and she frequently omitted considerable material without any indication that elisions had been made; for example, in the letter of 26 September 1785 to Noah

Parker reporting the Oxford meeting, she not only made minor changes of wording, but omitted the central portion of the letter which sheds much light on the growing rift between Murray and Winchester.[2]

The notes were assembled in no discernible order, and were for the most part undated; in the case of the letters, very few of the recipients were identified. No correspondence addressed to him was included.[3] Murray knew his Scriptures so well that he made few notations until late in life. He had not only a good memory but considered himself "designed rather for a speaker than a scribe." His writings might therefore have been much more voluminous, especially if he had had access to the periodical press which flowered within the Universalist denomination soon after his death. Publication of the *Universalist Magazine,* the weekly newspaper with the longest continuous existence, commenced in 1819, only four years after Murray's death.

The original edition of his autobiography was published in 1816 in Boston by Munroe and Francis. Murray had completed the story, divided into six chapters, only through the winter of 1774, so his widow continued the narrative in three additional chapters, the concluding one of which includes interesting interpretations of some of Murray's basic religious ideas.

Interest in the man and his work, and steady growth of the denomination, were sufficient to necessitate several reprints and new editions, with variant titles, by the 1840s. A second edition (actually a second printing identical with the first) was published in 1827 in Boston by Bowen and Cushing, the publishers of the *Universalist Magazine.* The third edition carried both the name and imprint of an editor, as did a stereotype edition in 1832.[4] In the 1833 edition, Linus S. Everett, a Universalist clergyman, provided not only "notes and remarks" but "other improvements"; among the latter were the addition of several sentences in italics to one of the concluding paragraphs, and two final sentences which updated the story by referring to a surviving daughter who served as "the prop, and consolation of her WIDOWED MOTHER." Everett also added editorial footnotes, references to Scripture, and passages from Thomas Whittemore's *Modern History of Universalism* which had been published two years before the third edition appeared. In a three-page Appendix, Everett reported with great enthusiasm the steady growth of the denomination.

Almost simultaneously with the appearance of the 1833 edition by Marsh, Capen, & Lyon, yet another was announced. This one, published by the *Trumpet* office, was prepared by Whittemore, the indefatigable editor of the successor to the *Universalist Magazine.* Infighting immediately broke out. The firm which had been publishing the Everett edition complained that Whittemore's edition was "unauthorized," for he had published his without prior consultation and "without any good reason." Whittemore, in a peppery rejoinder, pointed out that Marsh, Capen, & Lyon had never bothered to consult *him* when they had published earlier editions. Further, Murray's autobiography was the common property of Universalists everywhere, and the monopoly of no one person or publisher. There were no heirs, and no copyright in force, so there were no legal obstacles to an unlimited number of editions or printings if demand justified them. The disgruntled publishers, irked by the competition represented by Whittemore, had to face another irritation, for Whittemore offered his edition at the bargain price of 50 cents, even though enlarged by documentation not provided before. Ostensibly, Whittemore's reduced price was intended to encourage an enlarged readership. The first two editions had sold for $1.50 and $1.25 ($1.00 in boards) respectively; the third "authorized" edition was reduced to 75 cents to meet Whittemore's competition. Such a maneuver on his part was labelled an "injustice" and lacking "Christian Spirit."[5] When the next edition appeared, the name of the firm of Marsh, Capen, & Lyon was conspicuously missing from the title page.

The Whittemore edition was in many ways the most valuable of all, for it was extensively annotated by a man who could and did add important supplementary information based on first-hand knowledge. For example, he furnished many of the complete names and dates that were "sadly wanting" in the original autobiography. Besides including in an Appendix several excerpts from Murray's *Letters and Sketches* pertinent to his biography, Whittemore published for the first time documents in his possession bearing on the earliest history of Universalism in the American colonies. Included are the instrument drawn up in 1779 forming the first Universalist society (Gloucester); the correspondence and minutes of the Second Universalist Society in Oxford, Massachusetts; and a sketch of the history of the First Universalist Society in Boston (1785-1830). Whittemore also added a commentary comparing the views of Murray and Elhanan Winchester, and provided an index for the first time.

The timing of the Whittemore edition was also especially appropriate. All members of the Murray family—widow, daughter, and granddaughter—had died by 1833; as Whittemore wrote in the Preface, "and not a descendant of Mr. Murray is on the earth." The opening chapter in the history of American Universalism had come to a close.

Only four months after Whittemore's edition appeared (1833), a printing of the original work (designated the fifth edition) was prepared by Everett and published by Abel Tompkins of Boston as the first in a series with the general title "The Universalist Library." An Appendix consisted of an evaluation of Murray by Everett and various Universalist ministers (including A.B. Grosh, one of the best-known Universalist editors); excerpts from Murray's *Letters and Sketches;* and most of the documents printed by Whittemore. In 1844 the last of the numbered Everett editions (the eighth) appeared; it was reprinted twice by Abel Tompkins—in 1854 and 1858. In 1842 Zepheniah Baker, proprietor of the *Gospel Messenger* in Providence, Rhode Island, announced plans to edit and publish extracts from Murray's autobiography and letters, together with an introductory essay on Murray's character, the work to be entitled "The Beauties of Murray."[6] Reactions to the proposal were so negative, with two complete editions of the *Life* already on the market, that the project was abandoned. Baker did, however, publish a pocket-sized edition of the *Life,* at 33 cents, in 1846.

All editions of Murray's autobiography had gone out of print by the late 1860s; in fact, the plates of the Everett edition had been broken up and sold for scrap type-metal. In 1869, on the eve of the centennial of Murray's arrival in America, Gerherdus L. Demarest, another Universalist clergyman and author, prepared a new edition, issued by the Universalist Publishing House in Boston. Demarest used the Whittemore edition as the basis for his own, although he omitted some of the earlier editor's notes, as well as several documents which Demarest deemed inappropriate, too space-consuming, or not directly relevant. There was sufficient demand for the work in the centennial year of Murray's landing in America to justify a second printing in 1870. There was only one more reprint, by the Universalist Publishing House, in 1896.

Separately published writings by Murray include *Some Hints Relative to the Forming of a Christian Church* (1791) and a 96-page collection of sermons delivered in Boston under the title *Universalism Vindicated* (1798, republished in 1810). As was the case with the sermons of many other clergymen, especially in his day, many of Murray's discourses were printed, after delivery, in pamphlet form. The earliest extant is "The Substance of a Thanksgiving Sermon delivered at the Universal [*sic*] Meeting House in Boston, Feb. 19, 1795," and published that year. Very few original letters by Murray are known to exist.[7] In 1866 Demarest, who was to be responsible for the 1869 edition of the *Life,* obtained a packet of thirty-two letters from the son of Robert Redding of Falmouth, England, whom Murray had met while there in 1788, and with whom he corresponded until Redding's death in 1807.[8] No critical edition of either Murray's autobiography or his letters had yet appeared when the bicentennial of his arrival in America was celebrated, beginning in 1970.[9]

Appendix B

Hosea Ballou's *Treatise on Atonement*

The *Treatise on Atonement,* first published in 1805, had gone through fifteen editions and/or reprintings by 1959. The original work was published in Randolph, Vermont, printed by Sereno Wright, and was an octavo volume of 216 pages. The uncopyrighted work next appeared in 1811 as an unauthorized reprinting at Bennington, Vermont, sometimes referred to as the "surreptitious edition." This printing was identical to the original edition except that a correction appended to the last page was incorporated into the text of the pirated edition and the book comprised 313 pages because of the larger type used. A list of seventy-seven subscribers was included, indicating that an effort had been made in advance to finance the edition. The person responsible for this edition was Ebenezer Walbridge; the printer was William Haswell. According to Whittemore, the printer had been admonished for having taken the liberty of reprinting the book without permission. He had defended his action by saying that "Such a book is unlike other books,—it belongs to all the world,—no restriction ought to be put upon its publication or its sale."[1]

The second authorized edition appeared in Portsmouth, New Hampshire, in 1812, and was printed at the Oracle Press. Ballou was at the time living in that city, and made the arrangements himself. This time Ballou protected himself by filing a statement of authorship as provided by existing Congressional copyright laws (1790), and followed the same policy for those subsequent editions for which he was responsible.

There were apparently two printings of the third edition, one by Caleb P. Bailey in Gardiner, Maine, in 1827, and the other by C. Spaulding in Hallowell, Maine, in 1828.[2] The 1828 edition included an important introductory letter from Ballou dated 1827 and addressed to the publisher. The author pointed out that he had not had the opportunity to give the work "a general revision," and had left the text unchanged. However, Ballou called attention to the fact that if such a revision were undertaken he would make a few minor alterations and "some particular application of certain passages of scripture, which, undoubtedly, would receive some modifications." But he held fast to his major ideas, and reaffirmed his unitarianism; he was more firmly convinced than ever of "the entire dependence of Christ on God." His earlier strong inclination "to believe that the scriptures did not teach that either sin or its punishment would exist in man's future state" had by 1827 become a certainty.

The closest to an actual revised edition was published in 1832, following a German-language edition prepared by John Golly and printed by Jacob Grosh in Marietta, Pennsylvania, in 1829. Published in Boston by Marsh, Capen, and Lyon, the 1832 edition (designated the fourth), became the basis for most later so-called "editions," which were in reality only reprintings.[3] To compound the problem, the 1832 edition carried an "Author's Preface to the Fifth Edition," which was reprinted in most later appearances of the work.[4] In this edition, Ballou did actually make a few changes. These related to such matters as the pre-existence of Christ (which he now doubted), man's existence before taking corporeal form (likewise doubted), and the application and reinterpretation of some passages in the Scriptures.[5] He had also come to the definite conclusion by 1832 that sin was confined to the mortal state; future retribution did not exist.

Stylistically, Ballou left the original work unchanged, awkward phraseology and all. Hosea Ballou 2d, whose inclinations were much more scholarly than those of his great-uncle, and whose writing was considerably more polished, considered Ballou's style "often barbarous."[6] This deficiency, however, did little to diminish Hosea Ballou 2d's high estimate of the book or lessen his appreciation of the important contributions of its author.

The *Treatise* was next issued in Utica, New York, in 1840 by Orren Hutchinson, of the firm of Grosh and Hutchinson which also published the *Universalist Register* and other denominational literature. In spite of the fact that the edition was identical to that of 1832—a stereotype reprinting from the 1832 plates—it was labelled the sixth edition on the title page. Five printings of what were all listed as the sixth edition appeared in 1844, 1848, 1853, 1854, and 1860. They were all published by Abel Tompkins in Boston, and had identical pagination. For reasons unknown, Ballou's explanatory letter of 1827 was omitted, although the letter to the reader accompanying the original edition was included. The 1854 printing was also listed as the third volume of "Ballou's Select Works," which had been published in 1832 and totalled five volumes.

Between 1832 and 1882, only reprints of the fourth edition had actually appeared, in spite of their identification as "editions." After the lapse of exactly half a century, in the latter year another truly new edition appeared, the format of which was followed in all later issuances of the work. In 1882 the Universalist Publishing House offered what was listed as the fourth edition, disregarding the earlier numbering. Alonzo A. Miner, who was responsible for preparing this edition, restored Ballou's letter prepared for the third (1828) edition and made another significant change. Ballou had written the *Treatise* without marking any divisions except for paragraphing. Miner, for the first time, divided the work into parts (three), which were subdivided into chapters (ten). He also created appropriate short titles for each division and chapter, out of which he created a table of contents. Ballou had been so orderly and logical in the presentation of his thoughts that Miner was able to divide the work without doing violence either to Ballou's wording or to his original sequence.

The next appearance of the *Treatise* was in 1902, again issued by the Universalist Publishing House. By counting every known edition or printing, it was issued as the fourteenth edition. Ballou's prefaces to the original (1805) and 1832 editions (but not the 1828), as well as a list of all the known editions, comprised an appendix. John Coleman Adams wrote a seventeen-page introduction in which he identified the *Treatise* as "one of the great books of American theology," and "the first American book to anticipate all the essential points of . . . liberal theology." In Adams' estimation, Ballou's great contribution was to formulate for the first time basic Universalist principles into "something like an orderly and coherent system." Adams was also responsible for several editorial and mechanical changes in the 1902 edition. Using the 1832 edition as a base, Adams omitted Ballou's overly generous use of italics, and restored the person pronoun "I" which had disappeared from earlier editions. He also inserted numbered paragraph sub-titles (226 in all) in bold-face type "as a help to the reader in following the author's argument," and prepared a six-page index.

The fifteenth edition of the *Treatise* was published in 1959, more than 150 years after the book had been first offered as the tentative thoughts of a rural New Englander who thought seriously about the religious and spiritual destiny of mankind. It was issued in paperback by the Universalist Publishing House, with an introduction by Gordon B. McKeeman, then pastor of St. Paul's Universalist Church in Palmer, Massachusetts. Republished less than two years before the consolidation of the Universalist and Unitarian denominations, the *Treatise* was intended not only as a reminder to Universalists of their theological heritage, but as a work relevant to all men in a troubled mid-twentieth century.

Appendix C
Universalist Historical Society Officers, 1954-1978

President

Albert F. Ziegler (1954)
Emerson H. Lalone (1955-58)
William A. DeWolfe (1958-63)
David H. McPherson (1964-66)
(Mrs) Richard (Helen) Goundry (1966-70)
Theodore Webb (1970-72)
Carl Seaburg (1972-76)
Christopher Gist Raible (1976-78)

Vice-President

Francis C. Anderson (1954-58)
Robert S. Wolley (1958-59)
David H. Cole (1959)
Ernest A. Thorsell (1960-63)
Alan F. Sawyer, Sr. (1964-68)
Melvin C. Van de Workeen (1968-72)
(Mrs) Benjamin (Laura) Hersey (1972-76)
(Mrs.) Sinclair (Cate) Hitchings (1976-78)

Secretary

Melvin C. Van de Workeen (1954-58)
Alan L. Seaburg (1959-61); Resident Secretary (1962-63)
Davis H. McPherson (1959-61) (Recording Secretary)
Dorothy Spoerl (1961-63)
Peter Lee Scott (interim, 1964); 1964-66)
Carl Seaburg (1966-70)
Wyman Rousseau (1970-74)
Charles W. Grady (1975-76)
Ms. Allison Brayton (1976-78)

Treasurer

Robert Cummins (1954-58)
Harry M. Sherman (1958-63)
Melvin C. Van de Workeen (1964-66)
Charles Vickery (1966-70)
Richard Woodman (1970-74)
Eugene Adams (1975-78)

Notes

Chapter 1: ENGLISH BACKGROUNDS AND AMERICAN BEGINNINGS

1. Virtually all information about the early life of John Murray before his arrival in America, and much of his career and personal and family life thereafter, must of necessity be based on only two principal sources: An unfinished autobiography which he composed apparently at the solicitation of his second wife, Judith Sargent Stevens Murray; and a series of sermons, letters, and miscellaneous notes. (*Records of the Life of the Rev. John Murray ... written by Himself, to which is added, a Brief Continuation to the Closing Scene, by a Friend* [Mrs. Judith Murray], first published in 1816; and *Letters, and Sketches of Sermons.* 3 vols. (1812-13).) For additional bibliographical data and a history of these publications, see Appendix A. Unless otherwise indicated, the biographical materials included here have been based on the 1833 (Whittemore) and 1869 editions of the *Life.* Most of the specific dates have had to be derived from other sources, for they are conspicuously missing from Murray's own writings. There are perils built into any autobiography. Besides the fallibilities of human memory, there is always the temptation, conscious or otherwise, to justify, defend, or exonerate, and to add wisdom gained from hindsight. There is no reason to be particularly skeptical of Murray's reminiscences beyond these general cautions, but it should also be remembered that the sentimentality (including copious shedding of tears), elaborate reconstructions of extended conversations, and a tendency toward verbosity and overblown language which are all to be found in Murray's work, were part of the literary baggage and techniques of eighteenth- and early-nineteenth century literature and should be taken into account accordingly. Anyone raising an eyebrow about the accuracy of some of the detail in Murray's autobiography should bear in mind that he, unlike many of his contemporaries and successors (such as his American colleague, Hosea Ballou), kept a journal on which to base his autobiography. Many passages in this work are also almost verbatim transcriptions from his correspondence and notes which have survived.

2. Murray gave no dates for either his marriage or the death of his child or of his first wife. Richard Eddy, in his study of Murray's second wife, indicates only that Murray had originally married "early in life." *Universalist Quarterly* 18 n.s. (April 1881): 194.

3. The original London edition was published in 1759, and the first American edition (Boston) in 1779; it was reprinted in Providence, Rhode Island, in 1782 as a result of Murray's efforts.

4. The record of Relly's life, about which much remains unknown, has been reconstructed by Wayne K. Clymer, "The Life and Thought of James Relly," *Church History* 11 (September 1942): 193-216. See also Geoffrey Rowell, "History of Univer-

salist Societies in Britain, 1750-1850," *Journal of Ecclesiastical History* 22 (January 1971): 35-56; he does not cite Clymer's essay.

5. The manuscript is in the Andover-Harvard Theological Library. There are also Murray materials relating to Relly in the New York Historical Society.

6. The inlet is not to be found on a modern map, for it had filled in with sand by the early 1830s and had become part of the beach.

7. Frederick A. Bisbee, *From Good Luck to Gloucester: The Book of the Pilgrimage* (Boston: Murray Press, 1920).

8. *John Murray's Landfall: A Romance and a Foregleam* (New York: G.P. Putnam's Sons, 1911).

9. The most detailed study of Thomas Potter was begun by Thomas Butler (1871-1945), a Universalist clergyman in Philadelphia who spent many of his later years after leaving the staff of the *Philadelphia Evening Call* in genealogical studies and in probing various aspects of the history of American Universalism. He had completed only six of a projected twenty-chapter manuscript entitled "Thomas Potter of Good Luck" when he died. The six chapters were published serially in scattered issues of the *Pennsylvania Universalist* 16-18 (1945-1947). Butler's notebooks and scrapbooks were deposited in the library of the Historical Society of Pennsylvania (Philadelphia), of which he was a member; the typescript drafts of the first six chapters are in the Andover-Harvard Theological Library.

10. *Trumpet and Universalist Magazine* 14 (27 October 1832): 70.

11. Abel C. Thomas, *Autobiography* (Boston: J.M. Usher, 1852), p. 120.

12. *Trumpet* 19 (24 June 1837): 1. The meeting house, still standing in the early 1830s, had been willed to Murray by Potter "for the use of all denominations," but because of complications in probating Potter's will, was put up for sale and purchased by the Methodists. Whittemore edition, *Life* (1833), pp. 121-23 n. The original edifice was taken down about 1842 and a larger structure erected very near the same site; some of the material taken from the old building was incorporated into the new one. Abel C. Thomas, *A Century of Universalism in Philadelphia and New York* . . . (Philadelphia: Published by the author, 1872), p. 251 n. A sketch of the original Potter church was made by C.F. LeFevre during a visit in 1834 and was reproduced in the Demarest edition of Murray's autobiography.

13. The exact date, used by such early historians of Universalism as Thomas, was confirmed from external evidence by Richard Eddy, *Universalism in America.* 2 vols. (Boston: Universalist Publishing House, 1884, 1886) 1: 137 n.

14. The date of 1773 recorded in his autobiography was an error. See Thomas, *Century of Universalism,* p. 258 n.

15. *An Inquiry concerning the future state of those who die in their sins* . . . (Newport, R.I., n.p.) According to Thomas Whittemore, it was Hopkins' "wounded pride" after his conversation with Murray that prompted him to write the 194-page pamphlet attacking universalism. His followers were referred to as Hopkinsians. Whittemore edition, *Life,* pp. 143-44 n.

16. Franklin Bowditch Dexter (ed.), *The Literary Diary of Ezra Stiles, D.D., LL.D.* 3 vols. (New York: Charles Scribner's Sons, 1901) 1: 289-90, 400, 421; 2: 382.

17. See Thomas, *Century of Universalism,* pp. 258-59, 269-70; for a biog-

raphy of "Damnation" Murray, see the *Universalist* 51 (4 December 1869): [3].

18. Justin Winsor (ed.), *Memorial History of Boston.* 4 vols. (Boston: James R. Osgood & Co., 1881) 2: 236; Samuel Adams Drake, *Old Landmarks and Historic Personages of Boston* (Boston: James R. Osgood & Co., 1873), p. 64.

19. For the religious background, see E.S. Gaustad, *The Great Awakening in New England* (New York: Harper, 1957).

20. Varnum's letter to Murray regarding the chaplaincy, dated 24 May 1775, is included in the Whittemore edition of the *Life* (p. 184) but was omitted in most later editions.

21. Broadside, Massachusetts Historical Society, cited by Eddy, *Universalism* 1: 148.

22. Letter No. 24, *Letters and Sketches of Sermons* 2: 140.

23. Quoted in *Christian Freeman* 9 (31 March 1848): 189.

24. *Trumpet* 27 (13 December 1845): 102.

25. *Letters and Sketches* 3: 372-73.

26. The letter is reproduced in Richard Eddy, *Universalism in Gloucester, Massachusetts* (Gloucester, Mass.: Proctor Brothers, 1892), Appendix A, pp. 105-106.

27. Stiles to Forbes, 24 December 1777, in Eddy, *Gloucester,* pp. 162-65.

Chapter 2: THE CREATION OF THE FIRST RELIGIOUS SOCIETIES

1. The action of the First Parish church, transcribed from its records, comprises Appendix C of Richard Eddy, *Universalism in Gloucester* (Gloucester, Mass.: Proctor Bros., 1892), pp. 111-17.

2. There are extracts of the "Articles of Association" in the various editions of the *Life.* The complete instrument is reproduced in the Appendix of Whittemore's edition (Note A, pp. 239-41) and Eddy, *Gloucester,* Appendix G, pp. 154-56. For a detailed narrative history of the "Independent Christian Society," from its beginnings to 1860, see John J. Babson, *History of the Town of Gloucester, Cape Ann, including the Town of Rockport* (Gloucester, Mass.: Proctor Bros., 1860; reprint, 350th Anniversary Edition (Gloucester, Mass.: Peter Smith, 1972), Chapters XXIII, XXVII.

3. Whittemore edition, *Life,* p. 325 n, citing *Journal of Convention, 1779-1780.* Likewise, the final wording of the article providing that "every denomination of Christians shall be equally under the protection of the laws" was, as originally proposed, much more restrictive. Two alternative versions were rejected: "every denomination of Christians, *whose avowed principles are not inconsistent with the peace and safety of society*" and "*except such whose principles are repugnant to the Constitution.*" Quoted in Whittemore edition, *Life,* pp. 325-26 n, where the passages were italicized.

4. Both pamphlets were reprinted in the Appendix in Eddy, *Universalism in Gloucester.*

5. These individuals were fully identified by Eddy, who also furnished brief biographies, ibid., Appendix D, pp. 118-29.

6. Reproduced in ibid., Appendix I, pp. 177-85.

7. Quoted in the *Universalist* 46 (3 December 1864): [1]. This aspersion

on Murray's character was printed without comment by Reuben A. Guild, librarian of Brown University, when he published a biography of Manning in 1864. It so incensed John Greenleaf Adams, at the time pastor of the Second Universalist Church in Providence, Rhode Island, that he delivered a lecture entitled "Vindiction of John Murray" in which he took Guild to task for publishing the extract "without contradiction, apology, or explanation." The lecture was published in the *Providence Journal* and reprinted in the *Universalist* 46 (3 December 1864): [1].

8. The document was reproduced in Eddy, *Universalism in Gloucester*, Appendix F, pp. 130-31.

9. Whittemore edition, *Life*, p. 193 n; Letter No. 43, in *Letters and Sketches* 2: 351; *Life*, pp. 330-31.

10. See *Province Laws*, 1728-29, Chap. 4; 1729-30, Chap. 6; Nathan Dane, *A General Abridgement and Digest of American Law* (Boston: Cummings, Hilliard & Co., 1823) 2: 330.

11. See, for example, Anson Phelps Stokes, *Church and State in the United States*. 3 vols. (New York: Harper, 1950) 1; 745; Jacob C. Meyer, *Church and State in Massachusetts from 1740 to 1833* (Cleveland, Ohio: Western Reserve University Press, 1930), especially Chapter IV.

12. *Massachusetts Acts*, 1800, Chap. 87, Sec. 4.

13. See William McLoughlin, *New England Dissent, 1630-1833: The Baptists and the Separation of Church and State*. 2 vols. (Cambridge: Harvard University Press, 1971).

14. One of the most comprehensive treatments of the whole subject is Leo Pfeffer, *Church, State, and Freedom* (Boston: Beacon Press, rev. ed., 1967).

15. For the Oxford meeting, and for a summary of Murray's theological views, see below.

16. The resolution is printed in the Whittemore edition of the *Life*, pp. 200-201; see *Massachusetts Resolves*, 1787, Chap. 87.

17. See 6 *Massachusetts Reports* 401. The act of incorporation is reproduced in Eddy, *Universalism in Gloucester*, Appendix 0, pp. 198-200.

18. *Massachusetts Special Laws*, 1792, Chap. 18.

19. The episode was recorded in Abigail Adams' diary of her return voyage to America, 30 March-1 May 1788, reproduced in L.H. Butterfield (ed.), *Diary and Autobiography of John Adams*. 4 vols. (Cambridge: Belknap Press of Harvard University Press, 1961): 4.

20. The complete account of the proceedings, taken from the church records, is in Eddy, *Universalism in Gloucester*, Appendix L, pp. 191-93.

21. See Richard Eddy, "Mrs. Judith Murray," *Universalist Quarterly* 18 n.s. (April 1881): 194-213; 19 April 1882): 140-51; Vena B. Field, *Constantia: A Study of the Life and Work of Judith Sargent Murray, 1751-1820*, (University of Maine Studies, 2d series, No. 17. Orono: University of Maine, 1931).

22. Both letters are reproduced in the Whittemore edition of the *Life*, pp. 207-208.

23. Murray left an undated account of a nostalgic visit to the late home and grave of Thomas Potter, his first American friend, who had died in 1782. *Letters and Sketches* 1: 334-41. Whittemore assumed that the visit was made in the summer of 1790, but other Universalist historians offered more convincing evidence that the visit was probably made to Good Luck in the summer of 1783, when he had had his first meeting with Elhanan Win-

chester in Philadelphia. Eddy, *Universalism* 1: 196; Hosea Ballou 2d, "Dogmatic and Religious History of Universalism in America," *Universalist Quarterly* 5 (January 1848): 79-103.

24. See Justin Winsor (ed.), *Memorial History of Boston* 1: xxvi, 511; 3: 485.

25. The story was printed in the *New England Magazine* (August 1835) and, for obvious reasons, reprinted widely in Universalist publications; e.g., *Universalist* 46 (11 March 1865): [1].

26. For an account of Jones and the church during his tenure, see Eddy, *Universalism in Gloucester,* pp. 36-62; Babson. *History of the Town of Gloucester,* Chapter XXVII. In 1806 a church was organized in connection with the Gloucester society by adoption of a covenant and articles of faith.

27. Records, General Convention (1835), pp. 28-29.

28. Ibid., (1837), pp. 75-76.

Chapter 3: ESTABLISHING A THEOLOGICAL BASE

1. *Hell's Ramparts Fell* (Boston: Universalist Publishing House, 1941), p. 86.

2. *Modern History of Universalism* (Boston: Published by the author, 1830), p. 305.

3. "Dogmatic History," p. 79.

4. See Ernest Cassara, *Universalism in America: A Documentary History* (Boston: Beacon Press and Universalist Historical Society, 1971), especially pp. 6-7, 47. The most detailed and most amply documented history of the first thirty years of American Universalism since Eddy's work, emphasizing both instutional and theological development, is Paul I. Chestnut, "The Universalist Movement in America, 1770-1803" (unpublished doctoral dissertation, Duke University, 1973; Ann Arbor, Mich.: University Microfilms, 1974).

5. For de Benneville, see Albert D. Bell, *The Life and Times of George de Benneville,* (Boston: Universalist Church of America, 1953); David A. Johnson, "George de Benneville and the Heritage of the Radical Reformation," *Annual Journal of the Universalist Historical Society* 8 (1969-70): 25-43; "The Life and Trance of Dr. George de Benneville," retranslated and edited by Ernest Cassara, with the assistance of Alan Seaburg, ibid., 2 (1960-61): 71-87. For Winchester, see Edwin Martin Stone, *Biography of Reverend Elhanan Winchester* (Boston: H.H. Brewster, 1836); Charles White McGehee, "Elhanan Winchester: A Decision for Universal Restoration," *Annual Journal of the Universalist Historical Society* 1 (1959): 43-58; Joseph R. Sweeny, "Elhanan Winchester and the Universal Baptists" (unpublished doctoral dissertation, University of Pennsylvania, 1969). For Rush, see Nathan G. Goodman, *Benjamin Rush: Physician and Citizen, 1746-1813* (Philadelphia: University of Pennsylvania Press, 1934); David F. Hawke, *Benjamin Rush, Revolutionary Gadfly* (Indianapolis: Bobbs-Merrill, 1971); and Donald J. D'Elia, "Benjamin Rush: Philosopher of the American Revolution," *Transactions of the American Philosophical Society* 6 n.s., Part 5 (1974), which gives much attention to the evolution of Rush's religious thought.

6. See Charlotte Irwin, "The Pietist Origins of American Universalism" (unpublished master's thesis, Tufts University, 1966).

7. Rowell, "Universalist Societies in Britain," p. 39.

8. See Preface, *The Universal Resto-*

ration, 2d ed. (London, 1792).

9. See D'Elia, "Benjamin Rush," pp. 9 ff.

10. See Edwin M. Stone, *Biography of Rev. Elhanan Winchester,* pp. 183-99.

11. Rush to Richard Price, 2 June 1787, *Letters of Benjamin Rush,* edited by L.H. Butterfield. 2 vols. (Princeton, N.J.: Princeton University Press, for the American Philosophical Society, 1951) 1: 419.

12. Rush to Griffith Evans, 4 March 1796, ibid., 2: 773.

13. See, for example, the admirable summary by Williams, "American Universalism," especially pp. 6-8 and notes.

14. James H. Allen & Richard Eddy, *A History of the Unitarians and Universalists in the United States* (New York: The Christian Literature Co., 1894), Chapter IV. The history of Universalism comprises pp. 251-493 of the volume.

15. Unless otherwise indicated, all references to Murray's theological ideas are derived from his three-volume *Letters and Sketches* or the *Life.*

16. William S. Balch, "Reflections on the Life and Character of Elder Rich," *Universalist Union* 4 (15 June 1839): 252.

17. Demarest edition, *Life* (1869), p. 338 n.

18. Eddy, "Judith Murray," p. 212.

19. Eddy, *Universalism* 2: 60-61.

20. *Trumpet and Universalist Magazine* 17 (4 June 1836): 197.

21. See *The Winchester Centennial, 1803-1903* (Boston: Universalist Publishing House, 1903).

1803-1903 (Boston: Universalist Publishing House, 1903.

22. Records, General Convention (1803), p. 75.

23. Walter Ferriss, "Book of Sketches, Records, &c . . . [1804-1806], Andover-Harvard Theological Library.

24. *Familiar Conversations . . .* (Philadelphia: Gihon, Fairchild, & Co., 1833), p. 6 n.

25. *Trumpet* 17 (4 June 1836): 197.

26. Ferriss, "Sketches, [n.p.]

27. *Memoirs of the Life of Nathaniel Stacy* (Columbus, Pa.: Published for the author by Abner Vedder, 1850), pp. 94, 95-96.

28. Ferriss, "Sketches," [n.p.]

29. "Appeal," in Eddy, *Universalism in Gloucester,* Appendix G, pp. 134-35.

30. *The Evangelists' Manual: or a Guide to Trinitarian Universalists* (Charleston, S.C., 1829).

31. *Trumpet* 11 (8 May 1830): 179.

32. *Impartialist* 1 (19 January 1833): 78.

33. Proceedings, Southern General Convention, *Southern Pioneer* 5 (9 July 1836): 401.

34. Thomas Butler, "Universalism in Pennsylvania" (typescript) 1 [n.p., n.d.], quoting from convention records.

35. *Universalist Magazine* 3 (18 May 1822): 186-87.

36. *Universalist* 46 (3, 10 September 1864): [2], [2].

37. *The Universalist Centennial* (Boston: Universalist Publishing House, 1870), p. 35.

Chapter 4: EVOLUTION OF A STRUCTURE

1. *Universalist Register and Almanac,* 1836, p. 6.

2. *Trumpet* 14 (5 January 1833): 112.

3. *Southern Pioneer* 5 (21 November 1835): 124.

4. *Impartialist* 2 (4 January 1834): 62.

5. *Evangelical Universalist* 1 (7 April 1838): 1.

6. Stephen R. Smith, *Historical Sketches and Incidents* .... 2 vols. (Buffalo: Steele's Press; James Leavitt, 1843, 1848) 2: 109.

7. Eddy, *Universalism* 1: 97-99.

8. See Smith, *Historical Sketches.*

9. Eddy, *Universalism* 2: 345.

10. Records, General Convention (1811, 1813) 1: 144, 163.

11. *Universalist Register,* 1838, p. 28.

12. *The Universalist Church of America: A Short History* (Boston: Universalist Historical Society, 1957), p. 28.

13. *Christian Intelligencer* 8 (12 September 1828): 146.

14. *Trumpet* 10 (2 May 1829): 175.

15. *Letters and Sketches* 3: 336-38.

16. Ibid., p. 347.

17. See Clymer, "James Relly," pp. 211-12.

18. Note A, Appendix, Whittemore edition, *Life,* pp. 239-40.

19. *Universalist Watchman* 2 (16 April 1831): 202-203.

20. Proceedings, *Universalist Herald* 11 (16 October 1857): 89.

21. *Impartialist* 1 (20 October 1832): 26.

22. *Trumpet* 13 (14 January 1832): 114.

23. Records, Washington Association of Universalists, Ohio State Historical Society.

24. Records, Camp Hill Church.

25. *Impartialist* 1 (12 January 1833): 74.

26. *Register,* 1839, pp. 29-31.

27. Records, Maine State Convention (1836).

28. Records, Piscataquis Association (1846).

29. Records, Somerset Association (1839).

30. Ibid. (1848)

31. Records, Maine State Convention (1872).

32. *Trumpet* 10 (15 August 1828): 26-27.

33. Ibid. (26 July, 1 November 1828): 15, 70; 12 (5 March 1831): 142.

34. Smith, *Historical Sketches* 1: 15-16.

35. *Trumpet* 14 (29 September 1832): 54.

36. Extract from Proceedings, ibid., 16 (6 June 1835): 198.

37. Records, Somerset Association (Maine) (1848).

38. Records, General Convention (1844) 1: 524, 543-44.

39. Records, Pennsylvania State Convention (1868, 1871).

40. *Trumpet* 11 (12 June 1830): 198.

41. *Universalist Register,* 1840, p. 17.

42. See Whittemore, *Modern History;* Hosea Ballou 2d, "Dogmatic History"; and Eddy, *Universalism* 1: 168-72. All drew heavily on a memoir written by Rich, published in 1827, six years after his death.

43. Eddy, *Universalism* 1: 178-79.

44. Reproduced in ibid., 1: 207-208.

45. For the beginnings of organized Universalism in southern Massachu-

setts, see Anson Titus, "Reminiscences of Early American Universalism," *Universalist Quarterly* 18 n.s. (October 1881): 431-40.

46. See Abel C. Thomas, *A Century of Universalism* .... (Philadelphia: published by the author, 1872, pp. 32-33.

47. Eddy, *Universalism* 2: 344, 464-72.

48. Thomas, *Century of Universalism*, pp. 68-71.

49. Eddy, *Universalism* 2: 345. For numerous other examples of variant designations in this one state alone, see Work Projects Administration, *An Inventory of Universalist Archives in Massachusetts* (Boston: Historical Records Survey, 1942).

50. Records, New England Convention (1821), pp. 250-51.

51. Eddy, *Universalism* 2: 344-45.

52. Daniel B. Clayton, *Forty-Seven Years in the Universalist Ministry* (Columbia, S.C.: privately printed, 1889), p. 276.

53. Richard J. Purcell, *Connecticut in Transition, 1775-1818* (Washington, D.C.: American Historical Association, 1918; Middletown, Conn.: Wesleyan University Press, 1963), p. 59.

54. *Universalist Register*, 1836, pp. 6, 8.

55. Ibid., p. 8.

56. See William S. Balch, "Random Sketches," *Universalist Union* 4 (25 May 1839): 229 n.

57. Whittemore edition, *Life*, Appendix, Note B, pp. 241-43. The other Massachusetts societies represented besides Oxford and Gloucester were Boston, Milford, and Bellingham. There was also one delegate from Providence, Rhode Island.

58. Whittemore, *Modern History*, p. 362.

59. Whittemore, *Early Days*, p. 344.

60. *Trumpet* 14 (1 September 1832): 39.

61. *Universalist Register*, 1836, p. 10.

62. *Trumpet* 16 (14 March 1835): 151.

63. Eddy, "Mrs. Judith Murray," p. 206. For the most detailed and scholarly history of the three earliest attempts to organize Universalism (1785, 1790, and 1793), based on a thorough analysis of existing documentation, see Eddy's series of articles in the *Universalist Quarterly* 11 n.s. (July 1874): 328-44; 12 n.s. (January 1875): 5-21; (April 1875): 201-16; (July 1875): 310-23; (October 1875): 444-58.

64. Eddy, *Universalism* 2: 191.

65. "The Universalist General Convention from Nascence to Conjugation," *Annual Journal of the Universalist Historical Society* 8 (1969-70): 48; portions of this article were reprinted in Chapter 3 of his *American Universalism* (New York: Exposition Press, 1970).

66. "Universalism," in Rupp, *Original History*, pp. 726-27.

67. *Trumpet* 14 (1 September 1832): 38; Whittemore, *Early Days*, pp. 344-45.

68. Whittemore, *Early Days*, p. 344.

69. Whittemore, *Modern History*, pp. 366-68.

70. Eddy, *Universalism* 1: 419.

71. Thomas, *Century of Universalism*, pp. 146-47.

72. *Universalist Register*, 1836, p. 8.

73. Proceedings, *Southern Pioneer* 3 (23 November 1833): 22; *Trumpet* 20 (17 November 1838): 89-90.

74. Proceedings, Constitution, and Circular Letter, *Southern Pioneer* 4 (23 May 1835): 224-25.

75. Ibid., 4 (21 March 1835): 166.

76. *Southern Evangelist* 2 (1 October

1835): 3.

77. *Southern Pioneer* 5(10 October 1835): 79.

78. Proceedings, ibid., 5 (9 July 1836): 401.

79. Proceedings, Georgia State Convention, *Universalist Herald* 11 (16 October 1857): 89.

80. Eddy, *Universalism* 2: 362.

81. Ibid., p. 363.

82. *Universalist Magazine* 7 (16 July 1825): 14.

83. Proceedings, ibid., 9 (24 November 1827): 89.

84. *Universalist Register,* 1840, pp. 27-28.

85. Extract from Proceedings, Genesee Association (1835), *Southern Pioneer* 5 (15 September 1835): 55.

Chapter 5: TOWARDS A NATIONAL ORGANIZATION

1. The original "Convention Book," comprising the records of the organization from 1789 through 1807, was donated to the Universalist Historical Society in 1839, only five years after the latter had been created, by Abel C. Thomas of Philadelphia. When he prepared his *Century of Universalism,* published in 1872, Thomas had apparently forgotten his earlier gift, for he reported that the original book of records had been lost. *Century of Universalism,* p. 34 n. The ledger was mutilated when Thomas acquired it, the pages containing minutes of the meetings of 1799, 1808, and 1809 having been cut out. Thomas in *Universalist Union* 3 (15 September 1838): 357. None of the documents prepared at the meeting were included in the record book, presumably because they were authorized to be printed, and appeared in pamphlet form. It was not until 1833 that they were made available to the Universalist public, when they were reprinted in the *Trumpet* 6 (10 August 1833): 28. An abstract of the manuscript minutes was also published in the *Universalist Union* shortly afterward. The first circular, the Articles of Faith, and the list of recommendations, were also reproduced. See also Eddy, *Universalism* 1: 294-301.

2. Eddy, *Universalism* 1: 296.

3. For biographical sketches of the clergymen who attended, see Thomas, *Century of Universalism,* pp. 40-61.

4. Eddy, *Universalism* 1: 303.

5. See, for example, Murray to Rush, 11 July, 22 November 1791, *Miscellaneous Correspondence of Benjamin Rush,* Vol. 22; Historical Society of Pennsylvania.

6. Eddy, *Universalism* 2: 121; Thomas, *Century of Universalism,* p. 60.

7. See Eddy, *Universalism* 2: 121-24.

8. Thomas, *Century of Universalism,* p. 48.

9. Ibid, p. 71.

10. Eddy, *Universalism* 1: 382-84.

11. *Memoirs of the Life of Rev. Nathaniel Stacy* (Columbus, Pa.: published for the author by Abner Vedder, 1850), p. 55.

12. Records, New England Convention (1797) 1: 16-17.

13. Eddy, *Universalism* 2: 44-47.

14. Ernest Cassara, *Hosea Ballou* (Boston: Universalist Historical Society and Beacon Press, 1961), pp. 20, 44; Whittemore, *Life of Ballou* 1: 106.

15. Records, New England Conven-

tion (1801) 1: 41.

16. Eddy, *Universalism* 2: 13 n.

17. Records, New England Convention (1801) 1: 37-38.

18. Ibid. (1803) 1: 62.

19. Ibid. (1802) 1: 48.

20. Ibid. (1803) 1: 62, 68.

21. Ibid. (1810) 1: 136.

22. Eddy, *Universalism* 1: 19, 36.

23. Stacy, *Memoirs,* p. 94.

24. *Vermont Laws,* 1797, Chap. 51, Sec. 4.

25. Ibid., 1801, Chap. 11, Sec. 2.

26. Ibid., 1800, Chap. 1, Sec. 4.

27. Balch, "Random Sketches," pp. 337-40.

28. The wording of the one-sentence certificate is reproduced in Otis F.R. Waite, *History of the Town of Claremont, New Hampshire* (p. 85), cited in Charles B. Kinney, Jr., *Church and State: The Struggle for Separation in New Hampshire, 1630-1900* (New York: Columbia University Press, 1955), p. 95.

29. See Eddy, *Universalism* 2: 18-36; William McLoughlin, *New England Dissent, 1630-1833.* 2 vols. (Cambridge: Harvard University Press, 1971) 2: 870-71. McLoughlin's discussion is based directly on the relevant court records. According to him, the earlier case was possibly argued by William Plumer, who became governor of the state in 1812 and who championed the separation of church and state.

30. 1 *New Hampshire Reports,* pp. 36-37, quoted in Kinney, *Church and State,* p. 95.

31. Records, New England Convention (1802) 1: 48.

32. Kinney, *Church and State,* p. 96.

33. Ibid., pp. 107 ff.

34. *Universalist Quarterly* 5 (January 1848): 103.

35. Records, New England Convention (1816) 1: 194.

36. *Universalist Magazine* 1 (4 December 1819): 89-90.

37. Records, General Convention (1856) 2: 151.

38. Ibid. (1839) 1: 453.

39. Records, New England Convention (1821) 1: 252.

40. Proceedings, *Universalist Magazine* 7 (19 November 1825): 85-86.

41. Records, New England Convention (1827).

42. *Trumpet* 10 (4 October 1828): 54.

43. Records, Maine Convention (1830).

44. Records, New York Convention (1830).

45. Proceedings, *Universalist Magazine* 7 (15 October 1825): 66-67.

46. Circular Letter, New England Convention (1831), *Trumpet* 13 (17 September 1831): 47.

47. *Trumpet* 11 (26 September 1829): 50.

48. In 1830 a group known as the "Western Convention of Universalists" existed, and was in reality a regional organization which included Indiana, Ohio, "and others," and was an outgrowth of a meeting held in 1826.

49. Proceedings, *Trumpet* 13 (15 October 1831): 62.

50. *Trumpet* 14 (29 September 1832): 54.

51. Proceedings, ibid., 14 (13 October 1832): 62.

52. Ibid., 14 (29 September 1832): 54.

53. Ibid., 15 (2 November 1833): 74.

54. Records, New England Convention (1832).

55. Proceedings, South Carolina Con-

vention, *Trumpet* 14 (26 January 1833): 122.

56. Abstract of Proceedings, ibid., 14 (14 July 1832): 14.

57. Ibid., 15 (28 September 1833): 54.

Chapter 6: MODIFYING AND REFINING THE THEOLOGICAL BASE

1. See the biography by Ernest Cassara, *Hosea Ballou: The Challenge to Orthodoxy* (Boston: Universalist Historical Society and Beacon Press, 1961). For a briefer treatment by the same author, emphasizing Ballou's theology, see *Hosea Ballou and the Rise of American Religious Liberalism* (Boston: Universalist Historical Society, 1958). The most detailed study of Hosea Ballou is a four-volume biography by a contemporary: Thomas Whittemore, *Life of Rev. Hosea Ballou, with Accounts of his Writings, and Biographical Sketches of his Seniors and Contemporaries in the Universalist Ministry* (Boston: J.M. Usher, 1854-55). For evaluations of this and other full-length biographies published prior to his own, see Cassara, *Ballou,* pp. 177-78; for a balanced shorter account, see E.G. Brooks, "Biographical Sketches—Hosea Ballou," *Universalist Quarterly* 7 (1870): 389-420. Hosea Ballou had a namesake (a great-nephew) who also had a prominent part in early American Universalism and is referred to frequently in this study. The younger Ballou (1796-1861) joined his great-uncle as his teaching assistant in 1813 in a private school in Portsmouth, New Hampshire, conducted by the elder Ballou. From that time on, the younger man added "2d" to his name to avoid confusion. All of Hosea Ballou 2d's surviving correspondence and all of the books in his extensive private library carry this signature. He refused to use the Roman numeral "II," preferring the rendition with an Arabic number. See Hosea Starr Ballou, *Hosea Ballou 2d, D.D., First President of Tufts College: His Origin, Life, and Letters* (Boston: E.P. Guild & Co., 1896), pp. 55-56. There was another namesake of Hosea Ballou, Hosea Ballou 3d (1800-1880), a farmer and a son of Nathan Ballou, a brother of the elder Ballou. See *Christian Leader* 62 (16 December 1880): 8.

2. Hosea Ballou 2d, "Rise and Prevalence of Unitarian Views among the Universalists," *Universalist Quarterly* 5 (October 1848): 371; this was the second part of an article dealing with the history of Universalism in America; see ibid., 5 (January 1848): 79-103.

3. "Unitarian Views," p. 370.

4. Ibid., p. 375.

5. Ballou to Whittemore, 25 November 1829, Whittemore, *Modern History,* pp. 433-38 n. This retrospective note by Ballou was obtained by Thomas Whittemore in 1829. Ballou kept no journal and in spite of much importuning, refused to write an autobiography. His youngest son, Maturin Murray Ballou, and Whittemore, Ballou's former ministerial student, did extract from him some recorded reminiscences. Ballou had "an unconquerable aversion to writing about himself," arguing that his pulpit activities and his ideas were available in his sermons and writings, and that his family would have knowledge of his private life. *Universalist Miscellany* 5 (April 1848): 405.

6. See Cassara, *Ballou,* especially Chapter 5; see also Carol Morris, "A Comparison of Ethan Allen's *Reason the Only Oracle of Man* and Hosea

Ballou's *A Treatise on Atonement,*" *Journal of the Universalist Historical Society* 2 (1960-61): 34-69.

7. *A Literary Correspondence between Joel Foster, A.M., Minister in New Salem, and Hosea Ballou, an itinerant preacher of the sect called Universalists* (Northampton, Mass., 1799).

8. Proceedings, General Convention (1860), pp. 2-3.

9. Records, General Convention (1852) 2: 108.

10. *Universalist and Ladies' Repository* 5 (15 March 1837): 361-62.

11. Whittemore, *Life of Ballou* 1: 226.

12. *The Universalist Centennial* (Boston: Universalist Publishing House, 1870), p. 35.

13. All quotations are from the original (1805) edition, including his italics.

14. Prefatory "Letter to the Reader," p. iv.

15. See his *Examination of the Doctrine of Future Retribution, on the Principles of Morals, Analogy, and the Scriptures,* published in 1834.

16. For examples, see Whittemore, *Life of Ballou* 1: 191-92 n. The various editions of the *Treatise on Atonement* are discussed in Appendix B of the present work.

17. Hosea Ballou 2d, "Unitarian Views," p. 384.

18. Ibid., p. 393.

19. Ibid.

20. *Modern History,* p. 432.

21. See Conrad Wright, *The Beginnings of Unitarianism in America* (Boston: Starr King Press, 1955; Earl M. Wilbur, *A History of Unitarianism.* 2 vols. (Cambridge: Harvard University Press, 1958).

22. *Trumpet* 10 (22 November 1828): 82.

23. Eddy, *Universalism* 1: 93.

24. *Salvation for All Men . . .,* published anonymously as a pamphlet in Boston in 1792 and in London in 1784 as *The Mystery Hid from Ages and Generations, or, The Salvation of all Men.*

25. See Wright, *Beginnings of Unitarianism,* pp. 200 ff.

26. *The Early Days of Thomas Whittemore . . .* (Boston: J.M. Usher, 1859), pp. 230-31.

27. Eddy, *Universalism* 2: 132-37, 260-342. For the most recent study, see Kenneth M. Johnson, "The Doctrine of Universal Salvation and the Restorationist Controversy in Early Nineteenth Century New England." PhD dissertation, University of Ottawa, 1978.

28. Unless otherwise indicated, the material in this section is based on Eddy, the *Universalist Magazine,* and the *Gospel Visitant.*

29. Quoted in Eddy, *Universalism* 1: 337-38.

30. Hosea Ballou to Thomas Whittemore, 25 November 1829, Whittemore, *Modern History,* p. 437 n.

31. See *Universalist Magazine* 4 (1822): 126.

32. Cited in Eddy, *Universalism* 2: 269.

33. *Christian Repository* 3 (December 1822): 240.

34. See *Trumpet* 14 (27 April 1833): 174.

35. *Christian Repository* 4 (December 1822; August 1823).

36. *Universalist Magazine* 6 (31 July 1824): 23-24.

37. *Christian Repository* 8 (December 1827): 184.

38. *Modern History,* pp. 439-41 n.

39. Ibid., p. 435.

40. Eddy, *Universalism* 2: 328.

41. "Notice to the Public," *Trumpet* 13 (17 September 1831): 46.

42. Ibid., 12 (29 January 1831): 122.

43. Ibid., 12 (14 May 1831): 182.

44. Ibid., 12 (18 June 1831): 202.

45. Ibid., 20 (15 September 1838): 50.

46. Ibid., 13 (17 September 1831): 46.

47. Quoted in the *Impartialist* 1 (19 January 1833): 78.

48. Eddy, *Universalism* 2: 333-34.

49. *Autobiography of Adin Ballou, 1803-1890,* completed and edited by William S. Heywood (Lowell, Mass.: Vox Populi Press, Thompson and Hill, 1896), p. 333.

50. *An Original History of the Religious Denominations at present existing in the United States ....* (Philadelphia: J.Y. Humphreys, 1844), Preface, and pp. 637-55.

51. "Universalism," in Rupp, *Original History*, p. 719.

52. See *Southern Pioneer* 2 (20 July 1833): 158-59.

53. *Christian Ambassador,* quoted in Eddy, *Universalism* 2: 314-15.

54. *Gospel Banner* 8 (1 July 1843): 194.

55. J.G. Adams, *Memoir of Thomas Whittemore, D.D.* (Boston: Universalist Publishing House, 1878), p. 250.

56. Proceedings, Vermont State Convention (1871), p. 185; (1872), p. 194.

57. Eddy, *Universalism* 2: 340-42.

58. Quoted in Adams, *Memoir of Whittemore,* p. 343.

59. *Trumpet* 42 (22 January 1860).

60. *Practical Christian* 20 (14 April 1860); *Autobiography*, p. 424.

61. *Universalist* 52 (25 February 1871): [1].

62. Scott, *Universalist Church of America,* p. 39; Benjamin B. Hersey, "Universalism, What It Is," *Proceedings of the Unitarian Historical Society* 11 (Part 1) (1956): 20.

63. His participation in the entire controversy is detailed in Chapters X-XVI (pp. 170-317) of his autobiography.

64. *Universalist Register,* 1891, p. 97.

65. *Trumpet* 38 (22 November 1856): 98-99.

66. Grosh, "Universalism," in Rupp, *Original History*, p. 727.

67. Extract from Proceedings, *Universalist Miscellany* 5 (December 1847): 242-43.

68. Ibid., 5 (January 1848): 281.

69. Otis A. Skinner, ibid.

70. *Christian Freeman* 10 (21 July 1848): 46.

71. *Trumpet* 29 (8 April 1848): 170.

72. *Universalist Register,* 1875, p. 124.

73. *Trumpet* 29 (1 January 1848): 113-14; *Christian Freeman* 10 (16 June 1848): 26.

74. Adams, *Memoir of Whittemore,* p. 177.

75. Records, General Convention (1848), pp. 75-76.

76. "Universalism and Rationalism," *Universalist Miscellany* 5 (April 1848): 384-88.

77. *Universalist Union* 5 (26 September 1840): 710.

78. *Christian Freeman* 18 (15 August 1856): 62.

79. Records, Vermont State Convention (1860) 1: 118.

80. Records, Ohio State Convention (1884).

81. "Dogmatic and Religious History of Universalism in America," *Universalist Quarterly* 5 (January 1848): 79-103.

82. Ibid., 8 (April 1851): 186 ff.

83. See Octavius Brooks Frothingham, *Transcendentalism in New England: A History* (New York: Putnam, 1876).

84. *Christian Freeman* 3 (6 August 1841): 54.

85. Ibid., 10 (3 November 1848): 106.

86. *Trumpet* 23 (26 June 1841): 3.

87. Ibid., 28 (8 August 1846): 30.

88. Quoted in ibid., 20 (2 October 1847): 62.

89. *Story of My Life* (Hartford, Conn.: A.D. Worthington & Co., (1897), pp. 378-79.

90. "Views of Rev. Theodore Parker," *Universalist Miscellany* 2 (April 1845): 367-80.

91. Proceedings, *Trumpet* 28 (12 September 1846): 50.

92. Extract from Proceedings, *Universalist Miscellany* 6 (July 1848): 38.

93. *Universalist Union* 7 (1 October 1842): 731.

94. George Huntston Williams, "American Universalism: A Bicentennial Historical Essay," *Journal of the Universalist Historical Society* 9 (1971): 12.

95. Thayer, *Theology of Universalism* (Boston: Universalist Publishing House, 1862), pp. iii-iv.

96. First Report of the Board of Trustees, General Convention (1866), p. 12.

Chapter 7: BECOMING A CHURCH: THE UNIVERSALIST GENERAL CONVENTION

1. T.J. Sawyer to Editor, *Trumpet* 16 (23 May 1835): 189-90; *Universalist Union* 1 (27 August 1836): 335.

2. Records, General Convention (1846) 2: 55.

3. In the 1970s the same call for biennial meetings was being debated and defeated at the annual meeting of the Unitarian Universalist Association.

4. Circular Letter, General Convention (1850) 2: 92.

5. Records, General Convention (1852) 2: 108.

6. *Universalist Union* 1 (1 October 1836): 373.

7. Records, General Convention (1837) 1: 78.

8. Proceedings, *Trumpet* 16 (4 October 1834): 59.

9. Records, General Convention (1835) 1: 18.

10. *Southern Evangelist* 2 (1 October 1835): 3.

11. Records, General Convention (1841) 1: 468.

12. Proceedings, General Convention (1858), pp. 19-20.

13. Records, General Convention (1838) 1: 443.

14. Circular, *Trumpet* 23 (11 September 1841): 47.

15. Extract from Proceedings, *Universalist Union* 7 (23 July 1842): 567.

16. For abundant evidence that Universalist clergymen, especially on the frontier, were not alone in requiring surveillance and even disciplinary action for infractions of various behavioral norms, see Warren W. Sweet, "The Churches as Moral Courts of the Frontier," *Church History* 2 (March 1933): 3-21.

17. *Universalist Union* 3 (29 December 1821): 105-106.

18. Proceedings, *Trumpet* 11 (26 June, 1830): 206; 12 (17 July 1830): 10.

19. Proceedings, ibid., 12 (18 June 1831): 204.

20. Proceedings, Vermont State Con-

vention (1840), pp. 31-32.

21. Ibid., p. 33.

22. Proceedings, *Universalist Union* 5 (1 August 1840): 582.

23. Smith, *Sketches* 2: 23.

24. Extract from Proceedings, *Christian Freeman* 21 (15 July 1859): 42-43.

25. Proceedings, *Universalist Union* 5 (11 July 1840): 531-32.

26. Ibid., 5 (10 October 1840): 745-46.

27. Proceedings, ibid., 6 (10 July 1841): 535.

28. *Christian Freeman* 6 (9 August 1844): 58.

29. Records, Maine Convention (1844).

30. Smith, *Sketches* 2: 76-78.

31. *Trumpet* 24 (2 July 1842): 7; *Universalist Union* 7 (6 August 1842): 601-602.

32. *Universalist Union* 7 (23 July 1842): 567.

33. Proceedings, ibid., 1 (22 October 1836): 395.

34. Ibid., 1 (16 January 1836): 77.

35. Proceedings, ibid., 1 (22 October 1836): 395.

36. Circular Letter, Connecticut State Convention, ibid., 1 (29 October 1836): 402-403.

37. Ibid., 2 (1 April 1837): 165-66.

38. Ibid., 1 (29 October 1836): 406-407.

39. Records, General Convention (1836), p. 46.

40. Proceedings, *Universalist Union* 6 (30 October 1841): 794.

41. Ibid., 7 (23 July 1842): 568.

42. Extract from Proceedings, ibid., 7 (12 November 1842): 824.

43. Summary of Proceedings, ibid., 7 (16 July 1842): 554-55.

44. Proceedings, ibid., 8 (11 November 1843): 833.

45. Ibid., 8 (21 October 1843): 783-84.

46. Records, General Convention (1842) 1: 480-81.

47. Rogers, *Memoranda*, pp. 367-68; *Universalist Union* 8 (7 October 1843): 754.

48. Records, General Convention (1843) 1: 502.

49. All quotations which follow, unless otherwise indicated, are taken from the minutes of the General Convention (1844), pp. 508-19.

50. It might be noted parenthetically that when the centennial of Murray's birth was recognized by special services in Boston in 1841, the speakers carefully avoided any discussion either of his theology or of his part in organizing the denomination. Instead, they emphasized the contrast between the opposition he had faced and the progress that had been made since his arrival in America. *Christian Freeman* 3 (31 December 1841): 136.

51. Proceedings, *Trumpet* 26 (22 June 1844): 4.

52. *Philomath Encyclopedia* 7 (April 1845): 86 ff.

53. Ibid., 7 (October 1845): 382.

54. Circular Address, Proceedings, ibid., 7 (August 1845): 279.

55. Proceedings, ibid., 7 (April 1845): 78.

56. They are reproduced in ibid., 7 (October 1845): 360-62.

57. Ibid., pp. 344-45.

58. Records, General Convention (1847) 2: 65.

59. Ibid., (1848) 2: 75-76.

60. Ibid., (1850) 2: 87.

61. Ibid., (1853) 2: 119.

62. Ibid., (1854) 2: 128-29.

63. Ibid., (1852) 2: 105-106.

64. Proceedings (1858), pp. 29-31.

65. Ibid., (1859), pp. 10-11.

66. Ibid., (1860), pp. 9-10.

67. Records, General Convention (1843) 1: 502-503.

68. Ibid., (1858), pp. 15-17.

69. Ibid., p. 22.

70. Ibid., (1859), pp. 36, 37.

71. Ibid., pp. 20 ff.

72. Report, Committee on Organization, Proceedings (1860), p. 47.

73. Proceedings (1861), p. 11.

74. Report of the Committee on Church Organization, Proceedings (1860), p. 13.

75. Proceedings (1861), p. 7.

76. Report of Committee on Organization, Proceedings (1860), p. 36.

77. E.G. Brooks, "Historical Sketch," Massachusetts State Convention (1859), pp. 3-7.

78. Proceedings, Special Meeting, Massachusetts State Convention (1858), p. 8.

79. Appendix, Proceedings, General Convention (1861), p. 25.

80. Appendix, Report of Committee on Organization, Proceedings (1862), p. 12.

81. Appendix B, Report of Committee on Organization, Proceedings (1863), pp. 10-30.

82. Ibid., p. 33.

83. Proceedings, *Trumpet* 46 (1 October 1864): [1].

84. Summary of Proceedings, Vermont State Convention, ibid., 46 (3 September 1864): [2].

85. Proceedings, Vermont State Convention (1846) 1: 54.

86. Ibid., (1864) 1: 145.

87. Proceedings, General Convention (1865), p. 3.

88. The Act of Incorporation was included in the first annual report of the Board of Trustees, appended to the proceedings of the General Convention (1866), pp. 11-21.

89. Proceedings, General Convention (1870), pp. 54, 61.

90. *Universalist Quarterly* 22 n.s. (January 1885): 116.

91. *In Memoriam. Israel Washburn, Jr.* ([n.p.], 1884).

Chapter 8: "THE PROMINENT HERESY OF OUR TIMES"

1. Hosea Ballou 2d, "Dogmatic and Religious History of Universalism in America," *Universalist Quarterly* 5 (January 1848): 102-103. The preachers were Elhanan Winchester (Pennsylvania), John Murray (Massachusetts), Caleb Rich (Massachusetts), Zephaniah Lathe (Massachusetts), Noah Parker (New Hampshire), Adam Streeter (Rhode Island), Thomas Barnes (Vermont), and Moses Winchester (Pennsylvania), half-brother of Elhanan Winchester. The societies were located in Oxford, Gloucester, and Boston, Massachusetts; Portsmouth, New Hampshire; Philadelphia, Pennsylvania; and probably Providence, Rhode Island.

2. Quoted in the *Trumpet* 15 (17 May 1834): 186. The heading of this chapter is derived from a similar quotation, to be found in ibid., 11 (24 April 1830): 170.

3. Quoted in ibid., 25 (2 March 1844): 146.

4. Minutes, General Convention 1 (1835): 27.

5. 1 n.s. (January, July 1833): 61-76, 276-83.

6. *Trumpet* 16 (27 September 1834): 54.

7. Ibid., 20 (3 November 1838): 78.

8. Circular Letter, General Convention (1850) 2: 87.

9. Records, ibid., (1851) 2: 98.

10. Ballou, "Dogmatic History," p. 103. Richard Eddy was more generous in his estimate, listing thirty by name. *Universalism* 1: 544.

11. *Universalist Union* 5 (18 January 1840): 131.

12. See Elmo Arnold Robinson, *American Universalism* (New York: Exposition Press, 1970), especially p. 48; and George Huntston Williams, "American Universalism: A Bicentennial Historical Essay," *Journal of the Universalist Historical Society* 9 (1971): 3, 4.

13. See Thomas Whittemore, *Expositor* 1 n.s. (January 1833): 63 ff.

14. When the fourth United States census was taken in 1820, less than eight per cent of the population lived in incorporated places of 2,500 or more inhabitants. By the same definition, less than twenty per cent lived in urban areas as late as 1860, and not until well into the twentieth century was the rural-urban percentage reversed. Universalists were to be found in both population categories from their very first appearance. Their uniqueness lay elsewhere than in their demography. For a graphical representation of the numbers and geographical distribution of Universalist churches in 1820, 1850, and 1860, and a comparison of the number of Unitarian and Universalist churches, 1830-1850, see Edwin S. Gaustad, *Historical Atlas of Religion in America* (New York: Harper & Row, 1962), Figures 31-33, 42, 107-110 (pp. 43, 44, 54, 129-31).

15. *Universalism* 2: 479.

16. Gaustad, *Historical Atlas,* p. 43.

17. Smith to William Worrall (Glasgow, Scotland), *Universalist Magazine* 4 (11 January 1823): 115; Smith, *Sketches* 2: 207-208.

18. *Universalist Magazine* 6 (27 November 1824): 89; *Trumpet* 11 (27 February 1830): 138.

19. *Trumpet* 14 (6 October 1832): 58.

20. Ibid., 17 (30 January 1836): 126.

21. Circular Letter, General Convention (1835), p. 29.

22. *Impartialist* 1 (17 November 1832): 43.

23. *Christian Visitant* (New York) 1 (January 1832): 2 n.

24. Ballou, *Expositor* 3 n.s. (March 1839): 78.

25. *Trumpet* 15 (4 January 1834): 109-110.

26. Ibid., 14 (19 January 1833): 119.

27. Ibid., 14 (17 November 1832): 82.

28. Cited in ibid., 16 (5 July 1834): 6.

29. *The Religious Creeds and Statistics of every Christian Denomination in the United States and British Provinces* (Boston: John Hayward, 1836), p. 151.

30. *Trumpet* 18 (3 September 1836): 42.

31. *Religious Creeds,* Appendix, Note "W," p. 150.

32. *Trumpet* 18 (13 October 1836): 67. Whittemore did not indicate the source of his information. The Baptists claimed the largest number (4,300,000), with the Swedenborgians ranking seventeenth, with 4,000 members. Philo Price, editor of the *Universalist Union* in New York City, using Hayward's statistics for 1836 as a base, estimated a Universalist "population" of 750,000 two years later. *Universalist Union* 3 (20 January 1838): 81-82.

33. *Expositor* 3 n.s. (January 1839): 77.

34. *Register,* 1841, p. 72; *Trumpet* 16 (13 September 1834): 46.

35. *Register,* 1838, p. 19; 1839, p. 29.

36. Ibid., 1841, pp. 59-61.

37. *Trumpet* 14 (16 February 1833): 134; 17 (17 January 1836): 118.

38. *Religion in America* (New York: Harper & Bros., 1844), p. 282.

39. *Trumpet* 20 (2 October 1847): 62.

40. Ibid., 25 (9 March 1844): 150.

41. *The Seventh Census of the United States: 1850* (Washington, D.C.: Robert Armstrong, 1853), pp. lvii-lix. Two notes regarding these statistics should be borne in mind: Neither the total number of members of any denomination nor the number of church attendants was included in the census reports; and the information was compiled independently of any statistics published by the respective denominations. A comparison with the information provided in the *Universalist Register* for 1850 reveals a major discrepancy. No less than 1,055 churches or societies were reported (p. 57). This was probably a grossly inaccurate figure, the editor admitting that the list needed "some pruning." No statistics as to the value of church property or the number of individuals who could be accommodated ("sittings") were published by the denomination until 1871, but even then they were considered "too scanty and imperfect to be used to advantage." *Register,* 1871, p. 114.

42. *Universalist Register,* 1850, p. 60.

43. Timothy L. Smith, *Revivalism and Social Reform in Mid-Nineteenth Century America* (Nashville, Tenn.: Abingdon Press, 1957), p. 21, citing Joseph Belcher, *The Religious Denominations in the United States* (1857).

44. *Statistics of the United States: 1860: 3 [Mortality, and Miscellaneous Statistics]* (Washington, D.C.: Government Printing Office, 1866): 501, 502.

45. The statistics summarized here are derived from the *Register* for 1861, which reflected, unless otherwise indicated, the state of the denomination as of August 1860.

46. *Expositor* 3 n.s. (March 1839): 77 ff.

47. *Universalism* 2: 482.

48. Benjamin B. Hersey, "Universalism, What It Is," *Proceedings of the Unitarian Historical Society* 11 (Part 1) (1956): 10.

49. *Christian Repository* 3 (June 1822): 1-3.

50. Transcript of Proceedings, *Universalist Magazine* 2 (24 February 1821): 137.

51. Ibid., 2 (2 December 1820): 90.

52. *Trumpet* 15 (22 February 1834): 138-39.

53. *Magazine and Advocate,* reprinted in the *Trumpet* 16 (11 October 1834): 62.

54. Baird, *Religion in America,* pp. 269, 276, 277, 282.

55. A systematic and comprehensive study of the interchanges between Universalists and members of other denominations, and the public image of Universalism as reflected in polemical literature, are desiderata at this time. Attention has been called to this by Williams, "American Universalism," p. 29 n. The editor of the *Universalist Register* occasionally carried listings of all public debates in which Universalists were involved, and many which were published (through 1886) are listed in Eddy's comprehensive bibliography (*Universalism* 2: 485-589). Denominational newspapers are a prime source for such information, including debates which were reported in varying detail but were never published separately, or in their entirety.

56. See, for example, Eddy, *Universalism* 2: 481.

57. Note A, Appendix, Whittemore edition, *Life*, p. 239.

58. *Universalist Magazine* 2 (6 January 1821): 111.

59. *Trumpet* 10 (18 April 1829): 166.

60. Ibid., 10 (28 February 1829): 139.

61. Ibid., 16 (19 July 1834): 14.

62. For the background of disestablishment in 1833, see Susan M. Reed, *Church and State in Massachusetts, 1691-1740* (Urbana, Ill.: University of Illinois Press, 1914); Jacob Meyer, *Church and State in Massachusetts from 1740 to 1833* (Cleveland, Ohio: Western Reserve University Press, 1930); John D. Cushing, "Notes on Disestablishment in Massachusetts, 1780-1833," *William and Mary Quarterly* 26 (April 1969): 169-90. The most detailed coverage, emphasizing the role of the Baptists but with more attention to the contributions of the Universalists than any other work, is to be found in William G. McLoughlin, *New England Dissent, 1630-1833.* 2 vols. (Cambridge: Harvard University Press, 1971), especially Vol. 2. McLoughlin considers Meyer's treatment "skimpy and superficial throughout" (2: 1293).

63. The relevant documentation based on the court records is in Cushing, "Disestablishment," pp. 173-81, and notes.

64. McLoughlin, *New England Dissent* 2: 1158, 1235.

65. *Trumpet* 12 (21 May 1831): 187.

66. *Universalist Magazine* 2 (30 December 1820): 107.

67. *Trumpet* 12 (4, 11 June 1831): 194, 198.

68. McLoughlin, *New England Dissent* 2: 1216, 1245 ff.

69. See J.G. Adams, *Memoir of Thomas Whittemore, D.D.* (Boston: Universalist Publishing House, 1878), pp. 49-53.

70. *Trumpet* 12 (25 June 1831): 206.

71. Ibid., 13 (15 October 1831): 63.

72. Ibid., 15 (10 August 1833): 26.

73. Ibid., 10 (12 July 1828): 6. For a discussion of the strained relations between the Baptists and the Universalists, see McLoughlin, *New England Dissent* 2: 1233-1234.

74. Ibid., 2: 1229; compare the detailed treatment given by McLoughlin (especially Chapters 62 and 63) with Meyer, *Church and State in Massachusetts,* in which the Universalists receive only passing mention, and Whittemore and his role are ignored completely.

75. *Trumpet* 12 (11 December 1830): 94.

76. George E. Ellis, *The Puritan Age and Rule in the Colony of Massachusetts Bay, 1629-1685* (Boston: Houghton Mifflin Co., 1888), p. 160.

77. The sermons were reproduced in the *Trumpet* 10 (16 May 1829): 182-83.

78. Ibid., 14 (14 July, 4 August 1832): 10, 22.

79. Ibid., 12 (18 June 1831): 202.

80. Ibid.

81. Ibid., 16 (27 December 1834): 106.

82. Ibid., 11 (19 June 1830): 202.

83. *Christian Intelligencer* 12 (18 January 1833): 10.

84. Records, Maine Convention (1853).

85. Leo Pfeffer, *Church, State, and Freedom* (Boston: Beacon Press. rev. ed., 1967), p. 257.

86. *Universalist Magazine* 9 (22 September 1827): 56.

87. Ibid., 9 (24 November 1827): 96.

88. *Trumpet* 10 (18, 25 October; 15, 29 November; 20 December 1828):

61, 69, 77, 85, 97.

89. Eddy, *Universalism* 2: 515.

90. *Trumpet* 12 (15 January 1831): 114.

91. Ibid., 11 (12, 19 June 1830): 198, 202.

92. Quoted in Albert Post, *Popular Freethought in America, 1825-1850* (New York: Columbia University Press, 1943), pp. 214-15.

93. *Trumpet* 11 (19 June 1830): 202.

94. Ibid., 17 (20 February 1836): 138.

95. The petition was reproduced in the *Universalist Union* 3 (16 December 1837): 45.

96. Proceedings, Pennsylvania State Convention, ibid., 6 (26 June 1841): 502, 504.

97. The letter was reproduced in the *Christian Freeman* 3 (4 June 1841): 18.

98. Thomas, *Autobiography,* pp. 231, 234.

99. Daniel Bragg Clayton, *Forty-Seven Years in the Universalist Ministry* (Columbia, S.C.: privately printed, 1889), pp. 355-56.

100. Shaw *v* Moore. The majority opinion was reproduced in the *Christian Freeman* 18 (27 February 1857): 173.

101. *Trumpet* 23 (31 July 1841): 22.

102. Clayton, *Forty-Seven Years,* pp. 356-58; *Trumpet* 23 (22 January 1842): 122.

103. Quoted in *Southern Pioneer* 3 (27 September 1834): 198-99; *Southern Evangelist* 1 (August 1834): [3].

104. *Southern Evangelist* 1 (September 1834): [2].

105. Quoted in *Southern Pioneer* 3 (27 September 1834): 199.

Chapter 9: UNIVERSALISM AND INFIDELITY: DENOMINATIONAL DEFECTIONS

1. Brownson's religious autobiography, up to his conversion to Roman Catholicism in 1844, is detailed in *The Convert; or, Leaves from My Experience,* published in 1857 and reprinted in Henry F. Brownson (comp.), *The Works of Orestes A. Brownson* (Detroit, Mich.: Thorndike Nourse, 1884) 5: 1-200. This is the edition utilized here. His conversion to and subsequent rejection of Universalism are discussed in Chapters III and IV of *The Convert.* For a full-scale biography, see Arthur M. Schlesinger, Jr., *Orestes A. Brownson: A Pilgrim's Progress* (Boston: Little, Brown Co., 1930). Brownson's religious history has attracted much attention from scholars. Representative works are George K. Malone, *The True Church: A Study of the Apologetics of Orestes Augustus Brownson* (Mundelein, Ill.: St. Mary of the Lake Seminary, 1957); Per Sveino, *Orestes A. Brownson's Road to Catholicism* (New York: Humanities Press, 1970); and the study by William J. Gilmore.

2. Brownson's strictures were so acerbic that the *Princeton Review,* organ of the "old school" Presbyterians, published (January 1858) an attack on *The Convert,* which in turn produced an extended and lively rejoinder in *Brownson's Quarterly Review* (April 1858), reprinted in the *Works of Orestes Brownson* 5: 200-240.

3. Proceedings, New England Convention, *Universalist Magazine* 7 (25 October 1825): 66.

4. A semi-monthly Universalist newspaper published there prior to

merger with the *Utica Magazine;* the enlarged paper became the *Evangelical Magazine and Gospel Advocate.*

5. The creed was reproduced in *The Convert* (pp. 43-44), and was initially published on 27 June 1829.

6. *Trumpet* 11 (21 November 1829): 82.

7. Proceedings, ibid., 12 (2 October 1830): 54.

8. Quoted in ibid., 12 (26 March 1831): 154.

9. Ballou, *Autobiography,* p. 254.

10. *Trumpet* 18 (24 December 1836): 106.

11. Ibid., 15 (8 February 1834): 130.

12. *Christian Freeman* 6 (6 December 1844): 126.

13. Ibid., 7 (9 January 1846): 145.

14. *Trumpet* 13 (2 July 1831): 2.

15. Ibid., 29 (3 June 1848): 202.

16. Ibid., 31 (15 December 1849): 106.

17. Quoted in *Christian Freeman* 15 (10 February 1854): 162.

18. An interesting brief discussion of Brownson's contribution to Catholic liberalism is to be found in James D. Hunt's "Orestes A. Brownson: Our Man in the Catholic Church," *Unitarian Universalist Christian* 25 (Autumn 1969-Winter 1970): 38-42.

19. Considerable literature exists about Kneeland, especially regarding his trials for alleged blasphemy. The most thorough study is Roderick S. French, "The Trials of Abner Kneeland: A Study in the Rejection of Democratic Secular Humanism" (unpublished doctoral dissertation, George Washington University, 1971; Ann Arbor, Mich.: University Microfilms, 1972). The definitive collection of relevant materials is Leonard W. Levy (ed.), *Blasphemy in Massachusetts: Freedom of Conscience and the Abner Kneeland Case: A Documentary Record* (New York: DaCapo Press, 1973). See also Harry M. Sherman, "Abner Kneeland: Religious Pioneer" (unpublished BD thesis, Crane Theological School, Tufts College, 1953); and Henry S. Commager, "The Blasphemy of Abner Kneeland," *New England Quarterly* 8 (March 1935): 29-41.

20. *Life of Hosea Ballou* 1: 275.

21. Miner, "Century of Universalism," p. 491.

22. Prefatory Note, *A Refutation of the Unmerciful Doctrine of Endless Misery* (Manlius, N.Y.: L. Kellogg, 1816), pp. 6-8.

23. Thomas, *Century of Universalism,* pp. 72-75, 79, 145-46.

24. *Trumpet* 28 (29 May 1847): 198-99.

25. Thomas, *Century of Universalism,* p. 78.

26. See Albert Post, *Popular Freethought in America, 1825-1850.*

27. Records, New England Convention (1814) 1: 175-76.

28. Ibid., (1816) 1: 194.

29. Smith, *Sketches* 1: 150.

30. Proceedings, *Christian Intelligencer* 7 (26 October 1827): 170.

31. Proceedings, ibid., 9 (6 February, 6 March 1829): 22, 38.

32. Records, Penobscot Association, Maine Historical Society, Portland, Me.

33. *Trumpet* 10 (28 February 1829): 138.

34. Kneeland to Whittemore, ibid., 10 (14 March 1829): 147.

35. Thomas, *Century of Universalism,* p. 72.

36. Proceedings, *Trumpet* 10 (30 May 1829): 190.

37. *An Appeal to Universalists, on the Subject of Excommunication, or the Withdrawing of Fellowship, on Account of Diversity of Opinion* (New

York: George H. Evans, 1829).

38. *Trumpet* 11 (4 July 1829): 2.

39. Ibid., 11 (3 October 1829): 54.

40. See Ballou's *Series of Letters in Defense of Divine Revelation; in Reply to Rev. Abner Kneeland's Serious Inquiry into the Authenticity of the Same . . . .* (Boston: 1820).

41. Cassara, *Ballou,* p. 52.

42. *Trumpet* 11 (21 November 1829): 81-82.

43. Proceedings, ibid., 12 (2 October 1830): 54.

44. Ibid., 28 (29 May 1847): 198-99.

45. See, for example, ibid., 12 (8 January, 26 March 1831): 110, 153.

46. Ibid., 12 (26 March 1831): 153.

47. Ibid., 15 (10 August, 28 December 1833): 26, 106.

48. Ibid., 15 (28 December 1833): 106.

49. The letter, dated 24 May 1833 at Hebron, New Hampshire, was reproduced in ibid., 15 (22 February 1834): 138.

50. Ibid., 15 (8 February 1834): 130.

51. Commonwealth of Massachusetts *v* Kneeland, 20 Pickering 206.

52. Chapter 8, *Massachusetts Statutes,* 1782; Chapter 130, par. 15, *Revised Statutes,* Commonwealth of Massachusetts.

53. Chapter 272, Sec. 36, *General Laws,* Commonwealth of Massachusetts, 1921, 2: 2767.

54. The petition was reproduced in W.H. Channing, *The Life of William Ellery Channing* (Boston: American Unitarian Association, 1880), pp. 504-505.

55. Post, *Popular Freethought,* pp. 217-18; for an extreme statement of the threat which Kneeland ("the hoary-headed apostle of Satan") purportedly represented, written prior to Kneeland's conviction, see Samuel Gridley Howe, "Atheism in New England," *New England Magazine* 7 (December 1834): 500-509; 8 (January 1835): 53-62.

56. *Trumpet* 15 (18 January 1834): 119; 17 (15 August 1835): 30.

57. Ibid., 20 (30 June 1838): 6.

58. *Evangelical Universalist* 1 (19 May 1838): 3.

59. Thomas, *Century of Universalism,* p. 280.

60. *Trumpet* 20 (1 June 1839): 197.

61. Cited in Levy, *Blasphemy in Massachusetts,* pp. xix-xx.

62. *Trumpet* 21 (17 August 1839): 35.

63. Post, *Popular Freethought,* p. 107.

64. Reproduced in the *Trumpet* 20 (6 April 1839): 166.

65. *Memoirs,* pp. 88 ff.

66. Sherman, "Kneeland," p. 8.

67. *Memoirs,* p. 90.

68. Ibid.; Whittemore, *Trumpet* 20 (1 June 1839): 197.

69. *Autobiography,* pp. 170-71.

70. W.S. Balch, *Universalist Union* 8 (12 August 1843): 630-31.

71. *Trumpet* 20 (1 June 1839): 197.

72. *Christian Intelligencer* 9 (27 February 1829): 34.

73. *Trumpet* 11 (27 February 1830): 138; *Universalist Register,* 1838, p. 27.

74. For example, see Post, *Popular Freethought,* p. 195.

75. *Expositor and Universalist Review* 3 n.s. (September 1839): 361.

76. *Trumpet* 21 (14 December 1839): 99.

77. See *Christian Freeman* 2 (12 March 1841): 1-2, for a documentary record of his tangled relations with the Salem society.

78. A.B. Grosh, *Universalist Register,* 1842, pp. 44, 52.

79. Ibid., 1843, p. 52.

80. For a biographical sketch of Elias Smith, see *Christian Freeman* 8 (21 August 1846): 65.

81. *Trumpet* 28 (15 August 1846): 33; Eddy, *Universalism* 2: 13-14.

82. Hosea Starr Ballou, *Hosea Ballou 2d, D.D.* (Boston: E.P. Guild & Co., 1896), pp. 225-26.

83. See Donald Watt, *From Heresy toward Truth: The Story of Universalism in Greater Hartford and Connecticut, 1821-1971* (West Hartford: The Universalist Church of West Hartford, Connecticut, 1971), pp. 52 ff.

84. Smith detailed the reasons for his first renunciation of Universalism in the *Religious Inquirer* (Hartford, Connecticut), reprinted in the *Trumpet* 16 (6 June 1836): 199.

85. For a summary of his religious career up to 1850, see Thomas, *Autobiography*, pp. 280-81; *Christian Freeman* 12 (26 July 1850): 50.

86. *Trumpet* 32 (14 December 1850): 106.

87. *Christian Freeman* 13 (20 June 1851): 30; 14 (27 August 1852): 66.

88. Ibid., 14 (27 August 1852): 66.

89. Ibid., 15 (31 March 1854): 190.

90. Ibid., 18 (20 June 1856): 30.

91. *Christian Leader* 60 (13 November 1879): 4, 5.

92. *Christian Freeman* 21 (12 August 1859): 58.

93. Ibid., 15 (21 October 1853): 99.

94. Ibid., 21 (12 August 1859): 58.

95. For the attack on Ballou, see *Universalism Examined*, p. 315; *Universalist Miscellany* 4 (1847): 479.

96. *Universalist Register*, 1842, p. 52.

97. Quoted from the *Christian Warrior* (29 October 1842) in Browne, p. 88.

98. *Universalist Register*, 1842, p. 43.

99. *Universalist Union* 5 (15 August 1840): 614-16.

100. The correspondence was reproduced in ibid.

101. *Universalist Quarterly* 6 (October 1849): 424-25.

Chapter 10: UNIVERSALISM AND THE CHALLENGE OF SOCIAL AND RELIGIOUS UNORTHODOXY

1. For a discussion of the religious context of many of these movements, see Edwin S. Gaustad (ed.), *The Rise of Adventism* (New York: Harper & Row, 1974), in which there are scattered references to Universalist participation.

2. "Fourierism, and Similar Schemes," *Universalist Quarterly* 2 (January 1845): 52-76. The two pamphlets reviewed were Parke Godwin and others, *A Popular View of the Doctrines of Charles Fourier* (New York: J.S. Redfield, 1844); and the fourth edition of Albert Brisbane's *Concise Exposition of the Doctrine of Association* . . . . (New York: J.S. Redfield, 1843).

3. *Universalist Quarterly* 2 (April 1845): 136-47.

4. Ibid., 4 (April 1847): 147.

5. Ibid., 9 (July 1852): 326-27.

6. *Trumpet* 12 (13 February-26 March 1831): 125, 133, 137, 141, 145, 149, 153. The articles were collected later the same year as a 44-page pamphlet, published by B.B. Mussey of Boston, with a new title: *An Exposure of the Principles of the "Free Inquirers."*

7. For a history of the Free Inquirers, see Post, *Popular Freethought in America*.

8. See John F.C. Harrison, *Robert Owen and the Owenites in Britain and*

America: The Quest for the New Moral World (London: Routledge and Kegan Paul, 1969).

9. For Owen's ideas, see Richard W. Leopold, *Robert Dale Owen: A Biography* (Cambridge: Harvard University Press, 1940). Everett had little to say about Robert L. Jennings, who was not as well known as the others. Jennings, a one-time Universalist preacher, was a member of the original governing committee of New Harmony and was also associated with the utopian Franklin Community in New York State. Harrison, *Robert Owen*, p. 107.

10. This was a repeat performance for Owen, for he had already defended himself in the *Free Inquirer* against Menzies Rayner, Universalist editor of the *Religious Inquirer* in Hartford, who had accused Owen of "atheistic bigotry"; and against Benjamin Ferriss, a Hicksite Quaker. Leopold, *Robert Dale Owen*, p. 74.

11. The controversy is detailed in the *Trumpet* 13 (7, 14 January 1832): 109-10, 113-14.

12. See the *Gospel Advocate* 5 (23 June 1827): 198.

13. Cross, *Burned-over District*, p. 332.

14. For the central role played by Kidwell in midwestern Universalism, see David A. Johnson, *To Preach and Fight* (Tucson, Ariz.: Philomath Press, 1973).

15. *Philomath Encyclopedia* 1 (January-June 1837); reprinted in ibid., 6 (February-April 1844).

16. Ibid., 1 (January 1837): 246-47.

17. Ibid., 6 (February, March 1844): 284, 339.

18. See Whittemore, *Modern History*, pp. 429-30; Elmo A. Robinson, "Universalism in Indiana," *Indiana Magazine of History* 13 (1917-18): 1-19; and David A. Johnson, "Beginnings of Universalism in Louisville," *Filson Club History Quarterly* 43 (April 1969): 173-83.

19. Whittemore, *Modern History*, pp. 429-30.

20. *Philomath Encyclopedia* 1 (June 1836): 5.

21. Ibid., 5 (December 1842): 578.

22. Ibid., 7 (February 1844): 279 ff.

23. Ibid., 4 (September 1840): 3; 5 (July 1842): 334.

24. Advertisement, ibid., 4 (September 1840).

25. Ibid., 1 (April 1837): 393.

26. Ibid., 4 (July 1841): 516.

27. Ibid., 5 (April 1842): 189-92; *Trumpet* 28 (23 January 1847): 126.

28. Preface, *Alpha and Omega, being a Disquisition on the Pentateuch and a Key to Revelation* (1843), cited by Robinson, "Universalism," p. 15; *Trumpet* 32 (12 February 1842): 134. Most of the book first appeared serially in the *Philomath Encyclopedia*.

29. *Philomath Encyclopedia* 6 (December 1843): 193.

30. Ibid., 7 (October 1845): 353 n.

31. Quoted in ibid., 4 (September 1840): 5 n.

32. *Christian Freeman* 9 (23 July 1847): 46.

33. *Philomath Encyclopedia* 4 (April 1842): 176 ff.

34. Proceedings, Western Union Association, ibid., 5 (June 1842): 324.

35. Ibid., 4 (April 1842): 189.

36. Ibid., 5 (December 1842): 549.

37. Ibid., 6 (June 1842): 276.

38. *Trumpet* 15 (29 March 1834): 158.

39. Proceedings, ibid., 15 (16 November 1833): 82.

40. *Atlas of Union County, Indiana* (Chicago: J.H. Beers, 1884), p. 48.

Much interesting detail about the founding of Philomath is to be found in this source. See also Eddy, *Universalism* 2: 424-25.

41. Prospectus, *Philomath Encyclopedia* 1 (June 1836): 48.

42. *Atlas,* p. 57.

43. *Philomath Encyclopedia* 1 (June 1837): 528.

44. Robinson, "Universalism," p. 30.

45. Proceedings, *Philomath Encyclopedia* 7 (August 1845): 277.

46. *Atlas,* p. 47.

47. Ibid.; *Universalist Register,* 1885, pp. 17, 18.

48. Robinson, "Universalism," p. 30.

49. *Universalist Union* 10 (8 February 1845): 198-99.

50. See his *Primitive Christianity and its Corruptions.* 3 vols. (Boston and Lowell, Mass., 1870, 1900). The second and third volumes, the last comprising lectures delivered at Hopedale in 1871 and 1872, were published posthumously, edited by William S. Heywood.

51. Williams, "American Universalism," p. 35.

52. The literature by and about Adin Ballou is extensive, for he wrote on many subjects, and the Hopedale Community has attracted much attention. Indispensable to a study of Ballou and his ideas is his autobiography, published posthumously as the *Autobiography of Adin Ballou, 1803-1890 . . .* (Lowell, Mass.: The Vox Populi Press, Thompson & Hill, 1896), based on a detailed diary, and carried by Ballou to mid-1890 and completed by William S. Heywood; and Adin Ballou, *History of the Hopedale Community, from its inception to its virtual submergence in the Hopedale Parish* (Lowell, Mass.: The Vox Populi Press, Thompson & Hill, 1897), also edited by William S. Heywood. The manuscript prepared by Ballou was dated 5 August 1876. A comprehensive microfilm collection of the materials relevant to the Hopedale Community has been prepared, in six reels; see Jack T. Ericson (ed.), "Hopedale Community Collection, 1821-1938: A Guide to the Microfilm Edition" (Glen Rock, N.J.: Microfilming Corporation of America, 1976). Ballou also wrote numerous tracts on slavery, non-resistance, his conceptions of Christianity, and prepared an elaborate genealogy of the Ballou family. Among numerous interpretations of Ballou and his work, see Barbara L. Faulkner, "Adin Ballou and the Hopedale Community" (unpublished PhD dissertation, Boston University, 1965; Ann Arbor, Mich.: University Microfilms); and Jerry V. Caswell, " 'A New Civilization Radically Higher than the Old:' Adin Ballou's Search for Social Perfection," *Journal of the Universalist Historical Society* 7 (1967-68): 70-96.

53. *Universalist Register,* 1891, pp. 96-97.

54. Ballou, *Hopedale Community,* p. 2.

55. Eddy, in his bibliography of Universalist periodicals (*Universalism* 2: 595) erroneously listed the publication as having lasted only one year (1843). It was described in the *Universalist Register* (1844, p. 47) as a journal advocating "anti-slavery principle and action."

56. *Practical Christian* 1 (1 April 1840): 4.

57. Ibid., 1 (15 September 1840): 38.

58. Ibid., 3 (4 February 1843): 74.

59. *Universalist Quarterly* 12 (April 1855): 213.

60. The constitution, a detailed explanation of it by Ballou, and the proceedings of the first community

were reproduced in the *Practical Christian* 1 (15 February 1841): 77-80; see also 2 (16, 30 October, 13 November 1841): 45-46, 50-51, 53-54.

61. *Practical Christian* 2 (16 October 1841): 47.

62. Ibid., 2 (19 February 1842): 82.

63. Ibid., 2 (18 September 1841): 38.

64. Resolves and Bylaws, Fraternal Community No. 1, ibid., 2 (2 October 1841): 42.

65. Proceedings, ibid., 2 (22 January 1842): 74.

66. The sermon was reproduced in ibid., 3 (25 June 1842): 9-10.

67. Ibid., 3 (11 June 1842): 7.

68. For a detailed description of the matured principles on which the community was based, see Ballou's *Practical Christian Socialism* (Hopedale, Mass.: published by the author, 1854).

69. *Christian Freeman* 8 (7 August 1846): 57.

70. *Practical Christian* 2 (27 November 1841): 58.

71. Ibid., 2 (25 December 1841): 67.

72. Ibid., 2 (22 January 1842): 74.

73. *Universalist Quarterly* 12 (April 1855): 210.

74. Ballou, *Hopedale Community,* p. 339.

75. Ibid., pp. 350-51.

76. Preface, *Autobiography,* p. vii.

77. *Evidence from Scripture and History of the Second Coming of Christ, about the year 1843* (Troy, N.Y.: E. Gates). For a sympathetic analysis of Miller and his work, see Francis D. Nichol, *The Midnight Cry* (Washington, D.C.: *Review and Herald* Publishing Association, 1944).

78. Adams, *Memoir of Whittemore,* p. 103.

79. *Trumpet* 21 (8 February 1840): 129.

80. The lectures were reproduced in the *Christian Freeman* 1 (21 February 1840): 169-70.

81. *Trumpet* 34 (9 October 1852): 69.

82. *Philomath Encyclopedia* 5 (December 1842): 568-71.

83. Cross, *Burned-over District,* p. 287.

84. *Universalist Quarterly* 9 (July 1852): 326-27.

85. *Mediums of the 19th Century,* 2 vols. (New Hyde Park, N.Y.: University Books, 1963) 1: 217.

86. *Religion in America* (New York: Charles Scribner's Sons, 1965), p. 197.

87. *Trumpet* 11 (13 February 1830): 131; 14 (7 July 1832): 7.

88. Proceedings, *Christian Freeman* 10 (16 June 1848): 26; *Universalist Miscellany* 6 (August 1848): 76.

89. For authoritative works on spiritualism, see Podmore, *Mediums of the 19th Century,* a reprint of a work originally published in London in 1902 under the title *Modern Spiritualism: A History and a Criticism;* Slater Brown, *The Heydey of Spiritualism* (New York: Hawthorn Books, 1970), a perceptive and balanced popular account from which much of the material presented here has been drawn; and Howard Kerr, *Mediums and Spirit-Rappers and Roaring Radicals . . . 1850-1900* (Urbana, Ill.: University of Illinois, 1972).

90. *An Exposition of Views Respecting the Principal Facts, Causes and Peculiarities involved in Spirit Manifestations; Together with Interesting Phenomenal Statements and Communications* (Boston: Bela Marsh, 1852).

91. Lewis Perry, *Radical Abolitionism: Anarchy and the Government of God in Antislavery Thought* (Ithaca, N.Y.: Cornell University Press, 1973), pp. 217-18.

92. *Trumpet* 34 (13 November 1852): 88.

93. See Sig Synnestvedt, biographical introduction, *The Essential Swedenborg* (New York: Twayne Publishers, 1970).

94. *Ladies' Repository* 22 (December 1853): 238. Fernald's edition, published in Boston by Crosby and Nichols, became the standard source for many years and was the basis for a new and enlarged edition prepared by Samuel M. Warren, published in 1875 and reprinted as recently as 1974 under the imprimatur of the Swedenborg Foundation (New York).

95. For a clear and readable summary of Swedenborg's ideas, see Brown, *Heydey of Spiritualism,* Chapter 4.

96. Thomas, *Century of Universalism,* p. 120.

97. *Lectures on Clairmativeness; or, Human Magnetism* (New York, 1845), cited by Brown, *Heydey of Spiritualism,* pp. 76-77, 253. Podmore attributed the pamphlet to Davis and was consequently unable to find it listed among his collected works. *Mediums of the 19th Century,* p. 167 n.

98. See Brown, *Heydey of Spiritualism,* pp. 87, 89-91.

99. Podmore, *Mediums of the 19th Century,* p. 171.

100. *Trumpet* 22 (18 July 1840): 15.

101. See his *Twelve Discourses on Government: purporting to have been delivered in Boston, Mass., December 1853, by Thomas Jefferson of the Spirit-World; through John M. Spear, Medium* (Hopedale, Mass.: Community Press, 1853); and *Twenty Years on the Wing. Brief Narrative of my travels and labors as a missionary sent forth and sustained by the Association of Beneficents in spirit land* (Boston: William White & Co., 1873). The "Association of Beneficents" referred to in the title was claimed by the author to include, among others, the spirits of Benjamin Rush; John Howard, a prominent British philanthropist and prison reformer; Benjamin Franklin; and Thomas Jefferson.

102. *Christian Freeman* 14 (23, 30 July 1852): 45, 49-50.

103. The details of the machine, its purpose, and its fate, are summarized by Brown, *Heydey of Spiritualism,* Chapter 11. The New Motive Power is discussed in a work edited by A.E. Newton entitled *The Educator: being Suggestions, Theoretical and Practical, designed to promote man-culture and integral reform, with a view to the ultimate establishment of a divine social state on earth. Comprised in a series of revealments from organized associations in the spirit-life, through John Murray Spear* (Boston: Office of Practical Spiritualists; printed by Hobart & Robbins, 1857). Among the Universalists associated with Spear in this attempt to translate spiritualist ideas into a new life for humanity was Charles Hammond of Rochester, N.Y., who had been a clergyman from 1829 until 1849, before he became a spiritualist lecturer, author, and the first "writing medium." *Universalist Register,* 1860, p. 40; Cross, *Burned-over District,* p. 346. It was as a result of a séance in which he and Spear had participated that the New Motive Power machine had been constructed.

104. *Trumpet* 24 (31 December 1842): 111.

105. Ibid., 22 (29 May 1841): 195.

106. Quoted in Adams, *Memoir of Whittemore,* p. 173.

107. *Trumpet* 33 (23 August 1851): 42.

108. Quoted in Adams, *Memoir of Whittemore,* pp. 212-13.

109. He had several works on spiritualism and related subjects in his

extensive private library which was donated to Tufts College by his widow in 1877. Many, including Hewitt's *Messages from the Superior State,* were the gift to Whittemore from the Boston publisher, Bela Marsh, who specialized in works on spiritualism.

110. *Christian Freeman* 14 (31 December 1852): 138.

111. Ibid., 22 (19 April 1861): 202.

112. Harrison, *Robert Owen and the Owenites,* p. 251.

113. *Trumpet* 34 (27 November 1852): 98.

114. Proceedings, Vermont State Convention (1871), p. 186.

Chapter 11: "ONE SADDLE AND BAGS": THE PREACHER ON THE ROAD AND AT HOME

1. Records, Milford (Mass.) Universalist Society, quoted in Anson Titus, Jr., *Universalist Quarterly* 18 (October 1881): 436.

2. William Warren Sweet, the church historian, in a series of volumes published over a quarter of a century beginning in 1930, probably did more than any other individual to call attention to the role of the travelling preacher and to make the institution almost synonymous with not only the western frontier but with the Methodists and Baptists. See, besides his general works on the history of American religion, the series of source collections which he edited, entitled *Religion on the American Frontier, 1783-1860,* which includes volumes on the Baptists (1931), the Presbyterians (1936), the Congregationalists (1939), and the Methodists (1946). See also his earlier work, *Circuit-Rider Days in Indiana* (1916).

3. *Religious History of the United States* (New Haven: Yale University Press, 1972), p. 483.

4. *Sketches* 1: 91-93.

5. Ibid., 1: 161-62.

6. Clayton, *Forty-Seven Years in the Universalist Ministry*, p. 242.

7. Unless otherwise indicated, the material concerning Rogers is drawn from his 400-page autobiographical *Memoranda* (Cincinnati: John A. Gurley, 1845), published the year before his death.

8. Thomas, *Autobiography,* p. 77.

9. Proceedings, Universalist Convention of Western Canada, *Trumpet* 26 (7 September 1844): 47.

10. Thomas, *Autobiography,* p. 354.

11. *Trumpet* 28 (22 August 1846): 37.

12. John A. Gurley, *Star in the West,* quoted in ibid., 28 (1 August 1846): 26.

13. Thomas, *Autobiography,* p. 356.

14. See, for example, the one delivered by John Greenleaf Adams in Malden, Mass., and reproduced in the *Trumpet* 28 (8 August 1846): 29.

15. Thomas, *Autobiography,* p. 79.

16. *Trumpet* 16 (16 May 1835): 186.

17. Ibid., 18 (18 March 1837): 154.

18. Ibid., 21 (3 August 1839): 26.

19. J.G. Forman (Akron, Ohio), in ibid., 27 (22 December 1845): 105.

20. Ibid., 27 (11 October 1845): 66.

21. *Universalist Quarterly* 3 (April 1846): 217.

22. *Universalist Register,* 1839, p. 29.

23. Rogers, *Memoranda,* p. 332.

24. *Evangelical Universalist* 1 (3 April 1839): 6.

25. *Memoranda,* pp. 396-97.

26. An analysis of the data in the WPA Inventory of Universalist Churches in Massachusetts published

in 1942 indicates that all but one of these (Mansfield) became Universalist before 1850, with the largest number of change-overs in the years between 1820 and 1840.

27. *Universalist Magazine* 5 (17 January 1824): 117-18.

28. *Universalist Union* 3 (14 April 1838): 182-83.

29. Proceedings, *Universalist Magazine* 4 (11 January 1823): 113.

30. Reprinted in the *Trumpet* 24 (7 January 1843): 114.

31. Thomas, *Century of Universalism*, pp. 40 ff.

32. McLoughlin, *New England Dissent* 2: 718-19, 721.

33. Smith, *Sketches* 2: 242-43.

34. Ibid., 2: 147.

35. Ibid., 2: 100-101.

36. Proceedings, General Convention (1837) 2: 77-78.

37. Ibid., (1852) 2: 106-107.

38. Ibid., (1853) 2: 115-16.

39. *Trumpet* 23 (15 February 1851): 142.

40. *Universalist Quarterly* 10 (July 1853): 275-93.

41. *Trumpet* 20 (4 May 1839): 182.

42. Ibid., 25 (24 February 1844): 144.

43. Ibid., 21 (4 April 1840): 161.

44. *Universalist Miscellany* 2 (June 1845): 482.

45. *Universalist Register*, 1840, p. 18.

46. Proceedings, Vermont State Convention (August 1857) 1: 101.

47. *Universalist* 46 (22 October 1864): [2].

48. *Sketches* 1: 137 ff.

49. Ibid., 1: 78.

50. *Christian Freeman* 11 (29 March 1850): 189.

51. *Autobiography*, p. 103.

52. *Christian Freeman* 10 (6 December 1848): 126.

53. Records, Somerset Association (1848).

54. *Trumpet* 11 (24 April 1830): 171; 15 (14 August 1833): 34.

55. Ibid., 22 (25 May 1850): 197.

56. Charles Brooks (comp.), *A Statement of Facts from each religious denomination in New England, respecting Ministers' salaries* (Boston: John Wilson & Son, 1854).

57. It is almost impossible to make meaningful comparisons for the 1850s between ministerial salaries and other nonmanual occupations. Insufficient data are available for professional service occupations prior to 1870. Statistical Abstract Supplement, U.S. Bureau of the Census, *Historical Statistics of the United States, Colonial Times to 1957* (Washington, D.C.: Government Printing Office, 1960), p. 74. The approximate annual income of a skilled workman (e.g., a carpenter) in Massachusetts in 1860, based on a six-day work week, was $530. *Statistics of the United States in 1860 . . . . The Eighth Census.* 4 vols. (Washington, D.C.: Government Printing Office, 1866) 4: 512. The first annual report of the Massachusetts Bureau of Statistics of Labor was not published until 1869.

58. *Christian Freeman* 15 (25 November 1853): 117.

59. Ibid., 16 (17 November 1854): 113.

60. Ibid., 16 (25 August 1854): 65.

61. Report of the State Superintendent, Proceedings, Vermont Convention (1906).

62. *Christian Freeman* 15 (6 May 1853): 2; 17 (11 May 1855): 6.

63. *Autobiography*, p. 268.

64. For an account of one such festivity, held in honor of A.B. Grosh and

his family, see *Christian Freeman* 2 (12 March 1841): 2.

65. *Story of My Life*, pp. 430-32.

66. *Christian Freeman* 16 (4 September 1854): 74.

67. *Universalist* 46 (25 March 1865): [3].

68. Proceedings, *Universalist Magazine* 7 (25 October 1825): 66.

69. Records, New England Convention (1827).

70. Proceedings, *Trumpet* 13 (16 June 1832): 202; 14 (12 January, 16 February, 2 March 1833): 115, 134, 143.

71. Circular Letter, *Universalist Union* 1 (9 July 1836): 277; see, for example, Proceedings, Chenango Association, ibid., 1 (8 October 1836): 379.

72. Proceedings, ibid., 2 (10, 24 June 1837): 243, 261.

73. *Universalist Register*, 1845, p. 49.

74. *Universalist Union* 10 (30 August 1845): 666.

75. Report of Trustees of the New York Universalist Relief Fund, ibid., 10 (14 June 1845): 483.

76. Ibid., 10 (16 August 1845): 636.

77. Eddy, *Universalism* 2: 391.

78. Records, Maine Convention (1853, 1867).

79. Appendix, Proceedings, General Convention (1863), p. 31.

80. Report of the Centenary Committee, Proceedings, General Convention (1869), p. 30.

81. Report of the Board of Trustees, Proceedings, General Convention (1870), p. 18.

82. *Universalist Register*, 1901, p. 61. Universalists in New York State were ineligible to receive assistance from this fund because they were already provided for through the Harsen bequest.

Chapter 12: EXTENDING DENOMINATIONAL ACTIVITIES

1. *Religious History of New England* (Cambridge: Harvard University Press, 1917), p. 319.

2. *Universalist Magazine* 1 (25 March 1820): 155.

3. Records, New England Convention (1809) 1: 129, 130.

4. *Universalist Magazine* 1 (25 March 1820): 155. County designations have been included in this study not only as an aid in locating communities but in accordance with nineteenth-century church records which frequently identified the county rather than the specific town or community. This was particularly appropriate and even necessary for societies and churches organized in rural areas outside of incorporated towns and other centers of population. Most early associations and other regional bodies also followed county lines in marking out their jurisdictions. Historically, the county was a much more important political and geographical unit in the South and in the Midwest than in New England and elsewhere, but in the interests of consistency the designation has been included for all sections.

5. *Sketches* 1: 179-80.

6. *Universalist Magazine* 4 (19 April 1823): 171-72.

7. Ibid., 8 (17 March 1827): 155.

8. Ibid., 9 (15 December 1827): 103.

9. *Universalist Register*, 1838, p. 30.

10. *Trumpet* 11 (20 February 1830): 133.

11. Ibid., 12 (2 April 1831): 158.

12. *Christian Intelligencer* 12 (15

February 1833): 26.

13. *Universalist Union* 4 (26 October 1839): 407.

14. *Christian Messenger,* quoted in the *Trumpet* 14 (30 March 1833): 159.

15. Ibid., 23 (3 May 1851): 185.

16. *Universalist Union* 7 (29 October 1842): 787-88.

17. *Philomath Encyclopedia* 7 (August 1845): 285-86.

18. *Gospel Anchor,* quoted in the *Trumpet* 14 (6 April 1833): 162-63.

19. *Christian Intelligencer* 12 (January, February 1833); Records, Maine State Convention (1834).

20. *Philomath Encyclopedia* 3 (September 1839): 428.

21. Summary of Proceedings, *Trumpet* 16 (12 July 1834): 10.

22. Records, Maine State Convention (1835).

23. *Universalist Union* 1 (8 October 1836): 382.

24. *Philomath Encyclopedia* 5 (December 1842): 579-80.

25. Ibid., 7 (August 1845): 285-86.

26. Quoted in the *Trumpet* 23 (29 March 1851): 166.

27. Ibid., 22 (10 April 1841): 166; *Universalist Union* 7 (9 April 1842): 325-26.

28. Proceedings, Connecticut Convention, *Universalist Union* 7 (10 September 1842): 677-78; 8 (25 February 1843): 234.

29. Ibid., 8 (24 December 1842): 86-87.

30. *Trumpet* 19 (12 December 1846): 103.

31. Proceedings, ibid., 19 (6 March 1847): 151.

32. Ibid., 19 (15 January 1848): 124.

33. Ibid., 23 (24 May 1851): 198.

34. Ibid., 23 (15 February 1851): 143.

35. Proceedings, *Christian Freeman* 14 (4 June 1842): 18.

36. Ibid., 16 (9 June 1854): 22.

37. Ibid., 15 (11 November 1853): 109.

38. Extract from Proceedings, *Trumpet* 16 (5 July 1834): 6.

39. This discussion is based on the Vermont State Convention records and the detailed account to be found in Edith MacDonald, *Rebellion in the Mountains: The Story of Universalism and Unitarianism in Vermont* (Concord, N.H.: New Hampshire-Vermont District of the Unitarian Universalist Association, 1976), Part One.

40. *Universalist Quarterly* 6 (January 1849): 110-11.

41. *Christian Freeman* 10 (5 January 1849): 142.

42. Proceedings, General Convention (1859), p. 12.

43. Ibid., (1865), p. 4.

44. The first trustees (two clergymen and two laymen) were, respectively, E.G. Brooks, G.L. Demarest, James Cushing, Jr., and Quentin McAdam.

45. Report of the Board of Trustees, General Convention (1866), pp. 12-15.

46. Appendix, Proceedings, General Convention (1866), pp. 23-25.

47. Appendix A, Proceedings, ibid., (1867), pp. 9-10.

48. Appendix A, Proceedings, ibid., (1868), p. 11.

49. Proceedings, New England Convention, *Universalist Magazine* 7 (25 October 1825): 66.

50. Ibid., 9 (31 May 1828): 198.

51. *Trumpet* 10 (11 April 1829): 164.

52. Extract from Proceedings, ibid., 11 (4 July 1829): 2.

53. Ibid., 22 (27 June 1840): 2.

54. Most of the numerous pamphlets

are included in the bibliography of Universalist publications compiled by Eddy, *Universalism* 2: 485-599. Extensive collections of the tracts are to be found in the Andover-Harvard Theological Library of the Harvard Divinity School, and the Division of Special Collections, Wessell Library, Tufts University.

55. Summary of Proceedings, *Universalist Union* 7 (16 July 1842): 554.

56. Proceedings, *Christian Freeman* 6 (31 May 1844): 18.

57. *Universalist Miscellany* 4 (November 1846): 199-200.

58. Proceedings, *Christian Freeman* 9 (4 June 1847): 18.

59. Proceedings, *Trumpet* 22 (1 June 1850): 203.

60. Records, General Convention (1855) 2: 142-43.

61. *Universalist Magazine* 8 (1 July 1826): 7.

62. Circular Letter, New York Association (1845), *Universalist Union* 10 (18 October 1845): 785.

63. *Universalist Register,* 1842, pp. 57-58.

64. Extract from Proceedings, *Christian Freeman* 22 (9 November 1860): 110.

65. Proceedings, General Convention (1870), p. 31.

66. For examples of the literature on revivalism, see William Warren Sweet, *Revivalism in America: Its Origin, Growth and Decline* (New York: Charles Scribner's Sons, 1944), and for more detailed consideration, his three-volume *Religion on the American Frontier* (1931-39); Bernard A. Weisberger, *They Gathered at the River: The Story of the Great Revivalists and their Impact upon Religion in America* (Boston: Little, Brown, 1958); C.A. Johnson, *The Frontier Camp Meeting* (Dallas, Texas: Southern Methodist University Press, 1955); and William G. McLoughlin, Jr., *Modern Revivalism: Charles Grandison Finney to Billy Graham* (New York: Ronald Press, 1959).

67. See his *Lectures on Revivals of Religion,* edited by William G. McLoughlin (Cambridge: Belknap Press of Harvard University Press, 1960); and the *Memoirs of Rev. Charles G. Finney, Written by Himself* (New York: A.S. Barnes & Co., 1876).

68. See Whitney R. Cross, *The Burned-over District: The Social and Intellectual History of Enthusiastic Religion in Western New York, 1800-1850* (Ithaca, N.Y.: Cornell University Press, 1950), especially Chapter 9.

69. For examples, see Finney, *Memoirs,* pp. 68-70, 98.

70. Ibid., p. 106.

71. Ibid., pp. 49-51; see also McLoughlin, *Modern Revivalism,* pp. 24-25.

72. *Trumpet* 11 (3 October 1829): 58-59.

73. *Christian Freeman* 19 (8 May 1857): 6.

74. Quoted in Adams, *Memoir of Thomas Whittemore,* p. 287.

75. Thomas, *Century of Universalism,* p. 207.

76. *Universalist Magazine* 8 (12 May 1827): 188.

77. *Trumpet* 11 (24 October 1829): 66.

78. Ibid., 19 (7 October 1837): 61.

79. *Universalist Union* 7 (20 November 1841): 10-11.

80. *Trumpet* 11 (16 January 1830): 114.

81. *Southern Pioneer* 1 (December 1831): 46.

82. *Trumpet* 12 (19 March 1831): 150.

83. Ibid., 15 (7 December 1833): 95.

84. Ibid., 15 (15 March 1834): 150.

85. Ibid., 22 (4 July 1840): 7.

86. Adams, *Memoir of Thomas Whittemore,* p. 121.

87. *Universalist Quarterly* 4 n.s. (November 1840): 394, 396.

88. Proceedings, *Trumpet* 14 (26 January 1833): 122.

89. *Evangelical Universalist* 2 (28 August 1839): 140-41.

90. Ibid., 2 (11 September 1839): 156.

91. The eight-page pamphlet is undated, unpaginated, and without the name of a printer. There is a copy in the Divison of Special Collections, Wessell Library, Tufts University.

92. *Trumpet* 16 (21 March 1835): 153.

93. *Southern Pioneer* 5 (14 May 1836): 337.

94. Proceedings, *Universalist Union* 7 (10 October 1842): 726.

95. *Trumpet* 17 (26 March 1836): 158, 160.

96. *Universalist Union* 1 (12 March, 16 July 1836): 141, 285.

97. *Southern Pioneer* 5 (2 April 1836): 277.

98. *Philomath Encyclopedia* 3 (September 1839): 414.

99. *Universalist Union* 1 (26 March 1836): 157-58.

100. See the examples gathered from contemporary sources cited in Paul I. Chestnut, "The Universalist Movement in America, 1770-1803" (unpublished PhD dissertation, Duke University, 1974; Ann Arbor, Mich.: University Microfilms, 1974), especially pp. 228-29.

101. Adams, *Memoir of Thomas Whittemore,* pp. 127 ff.

102. *Autobiography,* p. 347.

103. *Universalist Union* 9 (2 December 1843): 38.

104. *Memoranda,* p. 370.

105. *Southern Pioneer* 4 (16 May 1835): 220.

106. Cross, *Burned-over District,* pp. 17-18, 43-44.

107. Albert Post, *Popular Freethought in America, 1825-1850,* p. 27.

108. *Memoirs of the Life of Nathaniel Stacy,* pp. 116-17.

109. Cross, *Burned-over District,* p. 324.

110. McLoughlin, *Modern Revivalism,* p. 139.

111. *Universalist Register,* 1841, p. 66.

112. Smith, *Sketches* 1: 201 ff.

113. *Christian Freeman* 19 (7 August 1857): 58.

114. *Universalist Miscellany* 5 (May 1848): 444-45.

115. Extracts from Proceedings, *Christian Freeman* 19 (10 July 1857): 42; 20 (9 July 1858): 38.

116. The sermon was reproduced in ibid., 19 (26 March 1858): 191.

117. McLoughlin, *Modern Revivalism,* pp. 7-8.

118. *Universalist Herald* 18 (1 June 1871): 186.

119. Proceedings, Washington Association (August 1875).

120. McLoughlin, *Modern Revivalism,* p. 220.

121. Eddy, *Universalism* 2: 408; for a detailed study, see his "Universalist Origin of American Sunday Schools," *Universalist Quarterly* 19 n.s. (October 1882): 448-59.

122. Ibid., 23 n.s. (October 1886): 503, 504.

123. See Thomas, *Century of Universalism,* pp. 135-38.

124. *Columbian Centinel,* 20 April 1791, cited in Carl Seaburg, "Universalism in the Early *Centinel,*" p. 13.

125. Undated fragment, *Letters* 2: 416.

126. Eddy, *Universalism in Gloucester,* p. 221.

127. Records, New England Convention (1794) 1: 5.

128. Ibid., (1797) 1: 15-16.

129. *Christian Intelligencer* 8 (20 June 1828): 97.

130. Records, Maine State Convention (1831).

131. *Universalist Register,* 1839, p. 24.

132. *Christian Freeman* 16 (18 August 1854): 62.

133. Proceedings, General Convention (1858), pp. 41-42.

134. Ibid., (1861), pp. 21-22.

135. See, for example, the *Register* for 1840, pp. 28-29.

136. Ibid., 1845, p. 37.

137. Report of the Sunday School Committee, Proceedings, General Convention (1870), p. 52.

138. Ibid., (1861), pp. 21-22.

139. *Trumpet* 22 (5 June 1841): 198; Seventh Annual Report, Universalist Sabbath School Association, *Christian Freeman* 6 (1 November 1844): 105.

140. Appendix B, Proceedings, General Convention (1861), p. 20.

141. *Universalist Register,* 1862, p. 49; 1872, p. 161.

142. Report of the Sunday School Committee, Proceedings, General Convention (1870), p. 48.

143. Ibid., p. 23.

144. Records, Maine State Convention (1846, 1848).

145. Ibid., (1864).

146. *Universalist Register,* 1844, p. 43.

147. Proceedings, Vermont State Convention (1869), p. 176.

148. MacDonald, *Rebellion in the Mountains,* p. 97.

149. Records, General Convention (1844) 1: 507, 526-27.

150. Proceedings, General Convention (1858), pp. 39-40.

151. Ibid., (1860), p. 7.

152. Ibid., (1870), p. 44.

153. Report on Revision of Constitution, Proceedings, ibid., (1870), p. 55.

154. Report of the Sunday School Committee, Proceedings, ibid., p. 51.

155. According to his recollections, recorded in a letter dated 28 May 1887, the ceremony was first observed in 1863. He also acknowledged that the Methodists might have introduced it earlier than the Universalists. Transcript in Universalist Historical Society files.

156. *Christian Freeman* 21 (13 May, 3 June 1859): 6, 18.

157. Proceedings, Massachusetts Sabbath School Association, ibid., 21 (17 June 1859): 27.

158. *Christian Freeman* 21 (24 June 1859): 30.

Chapter 13: THE NEWSPAPER PRESS

1. Eddy, *Universalism in America* 2: 485-599.

2. For a brief history of Universalist serials, see Alan Seaburg, "Remembering Publishing History: Universalist Periodicals," *Unitarian Universalist World* 2 (15 April 1971): 2.

3. *Universalist Union* 3 (18 November 1837): 15.

4. *Trumpet* 28 (29 August 1846): 42.

5. Extract from Proceedings, *Christian Freeman* 10 (11 August 1848): 58; *Trumpet* 32 (20 July 1850): 22.

6. *Universalist Union* 8 (19 August 1843): 645-47.

7. Ibid., 8 (5 November 1843): 811.

8. *Christian Intelligencer* 12 (8 February 1833): 24; *Southern Pioneer and Gospel Visiter* 2 (16 February 1833): 65-66.

9. *Trumpet* 38 (7 February 1857): 142.

10. Ibid., 28 (15 August 1846): 33; 38 (7 February 1857): 142.

11. Ibid., 23 (3 May 1851): 186.

12. *Universalist Magazine* 9 (3 May 1828): 183.

13. *Trumpet* 34 (15 January 1853): 125.

14. *The Early Days of Thomas Whittemore. An Autobiography extending from A.D. 1800 to A.D. 1825* (Boston: James P. Usher, 1859), Preface (pp. 4-5). Unless otherwise indicated, the biographical information on Whittemore up to 1852 was derived from the autobiography and from an article written by T.J. Sawyer which first appeared in the *Universalist Miscellany* (February 1849) and was reprinted in the *Trumpet* 34 (25 December 1852): 109-10, with annotations and updated material furnished by Whittemore. For a laudatory biography, emphasizing the post-1825 period, see John G. Adams, *Memoir of Thomas Whittemore* (Boston: Universalist Publishing House, 1878).

15. *Universalist Magazine* 2 (23 June 1821): 207.

16. The letter was reproduced in ibid., 3 (13 October 1821): 62.

17. *Modern History of Universalism*, p. 183.

18. Whittemore published a revised and expanded volume in 1860, on the eve of his death; it was to have been the first of a two-volume set, the second of which was to have been a history of American Universalism.

19. *Trumpet* 12 (1 January 1831): 110.

20. Whittemore's attitudes toward and involvement in both religious and social issues during his career are discussed elsewhere.

21. Adams, *Whittemore*, p. 54.

22. *Universalist and Ladies' Repository* 5 (15 April 1837): 433-34.

23. Ibid., p. 433.

24. See, for example, his editorial in the *Trumpet* 34 (2 April 1853): 170.

25. Ibid., 15 (20 November 1833): 90.

26. Adams, *Whittemore*, pp. 282-83.

27. *Trumpet* 10 (5 July 1828): 2.

28. Ibid., 10 (2 August 1828): 19; 29 (5 February 1848): 135.

29. Ibid., 12 (6 November 1830): 74.

30. Ibid., 10 (25 April 1829): 171.

31. A picture of the "Salamander Safe" graced the frontispiece of the *Universalist Union* 4 (1838-39).

32. *Trumpet* 21 (26 October 1839): 70.

33. *Trumpet* 10 (20 June 1829): 203.

34. Ibid., 14 (8 September 1832): 42.

35. Ibid., 14 (8 December 1832): 94.

36. Ibid., 18 (19, 26 November 1836): 87, 91.

37. Ibid., 15 (29 March 1834): 158.

38. *Universalist Magazine* (1819-28); *Dialogical Instructor* (1828); *Spirit of the Pilgrims and Messenger of Reconciliation* (1828-29); *Star in the East and New Hampshire Universalist* (1834-42); [*Connecticut*] *Universalist* (1839-43); *Nazarene* (1840-42); and *Star of Bethlehem* (1840-42).

39. Russell Streeter, in the *Universalist Watchman* (Vermont), *Trumpet* 25 (13 January 1844): 118.

40. Ibid., 24 (8 November 1851): 86.

41. Ibid., 10 (20 September 1828): 51.

42. Ibid., 12 (1 January 1831): 110.

43. Ibid., 13 (14 April 1832): 166.

44. Report, General Convention (1836), p. 56.

45. *Christian Freeman* 14 (16 July 1852): 42.

46. *Ladies' Repository* 18 (April 1850): 400.

47. A.J. Patterson, quoted in Adams, *Whittemore,* pp. 29-30 n.

48. *Trumpet* 39 (16 January 1858): 130.

49. *Autobiography of the First Forty-One Years of the Life of Sylvanus Cobb, D.D., to which is added a Memoir by his eldest son, Sylvanus Cobb, Jr.* (Boston: Universalist Publishing House, 1867), p. 282.

50. *Trumpet* 20 (2 March 1839): 147.

51. *Autobiography,* pp. 359-60.

52. Ibid., pp. 314-15.

53. *Universalist Union* 4 (9 March 1839): 143.

54. Ibid., 7 (11 June 1842): 472.

55. *Universalist Register,* 1846, p. 24.

56. *Christian Freeman* 1 (22 November 1839): 118.

57. Cobb, *Autobiography,* p. 283.

58. *Trumpet* 20 (27 April 1839): 178.

59. *Christian Freeman* 4 (30 September 1842): 86.

60. *Autobiography,* pp. 371-72.

61. *Christian Freeman* 5 (12 April 1844): 198.

62. Ibid., 1 (27 March 1840): 155.

63. Ibid., 5 (19 May 1843): 10.

64. Ibid., 2 (18 December 1840): 2.

65. Ibid., 7 (2 May 1845): 2.

66. Ibid., 7 (21 November 1845): 118.

67. Ibid., 5 (25 August 1843): 66.

68. *Ladies' Repository* 18 (April 1850): 400.

69. Quoted in the *Christian Freeman* 9 (24 March 1848): 186.

70. *Trumpet* 38 (30 May 1857): 206; *Trumpet and Christian Freeman* 1 (26 April 1862): 1, 3.

71. *Christian Freeman* 23 (10 May 1861): 6.

72. Report, Trustees of the Publishing House, General Convention (1861), p. 27.

73. *Christian Freeman* 23 (18 April 1862): 202. These two papers actually maintained a separate existence for several more years. The *Repository* was sold to the *Universalist* in 1870 and the *Banner* was merged into the *Universalist Leader* in 1897.

74. *Christian Freeman* 22 (5 April 1861): 194.

75. *Autobiography,* pp. 501-502.

76. Ibid., p. 503.

77. *Universalist* 46 (14 May 1864): [2].

78. Scrapbooks in the possession of Mrs. Martha Hardwick Swann, Notasulga, Alabama. It was Mrs. Swann and her late mother, Mrs. Hardwick, who kindly made available to the author not only the scrapbooks but other valuable documents and information about John C. Burruss, who edited the *Universalist Herald* for over forty years and was Mrs. Swann's great-grandfather.

79. "History of Universalism in Georgia," *Universalist Herald* 13 n.s. (1 April 1879); see also Whittemore, *Modern History,* pp. 423-24; Eddy, *Universalism* 2: 370.

80. There were no agents listed for either North Carolina or Mississippi; organized Universalism in neither state was able to maintain a continuous existence until after 1830.

81. The present author was unable to locate copies of either of Smith's

papers. The editor of the *Universalist Herald* possessed the one volume of the *Star of the South,* which had been donated by a Universalist living in South Carolina.

82. The paper was printed at the press of the *Wilmington Herald.* Information concerning this paper is to be found principally in letters from Frieze published in the *Universalist Magazine* and its successor, the *Trumpet and Universalist Magazine* (with continuous volume numbering); see also Whittemore, *Modern History,* p. 423. No complete file of the paper is known to exist. A microfilm copy of one original issue (in the Henry E. Huntington Library, San Marino, Cal.) was located in the North Carolina Department of Archives and History, Raleigh.

83. *Southern Pioneer* 1 (October 1831): 23.

84. The secondary title was consistently spelled thus throughout the first four volumes, for reasons unknown.

85. *Trumpet* 18 (18 March 1837): 154.

86. The unhappy story of the last year of the paper is told in the *Universalist Union* 2 (1 April 1837): 167.

87. Proceedings, ibid., 2 (3 June 1837): 239.

88. Andrews, who for a time was one of the corresponding editors of the Universalist Historical Society, donated copies of these volumes to the Society's library. Fuller served in 1835 as the corresponding editor of the *Evangelist* for South Carolina.

89. *Southern Evangelist* 2 (16 November 1835): 3.

90. Ibid., 1 (October 1834): 3; 2 (15 September 1835): 4.

91. Ibid., 1 (October 1834): 3.

92. *Universalist Union* 1 (23 July 1836): 295.

93. Ibid., 2 (22 April, 15 July 1837): 190, 285-87; *Trumpet* 18 (29 April, 10 June 1837): 178, 202.

94. *Trumpet* 19 (3 February 1838): 130.

95. His letter of resignation was reproduced in the *Trumpet* 20 (11 August 1838): 30.

96. Prospectus, *Evangelical Universalist* 1 (7 April 1838): 1, 3.

97. Ibid., 1 (7 April, 12 December 1838): 3, 8.

98. *Trumpet* 19 (26 May 1838): 194; *Evangelical Universalist* 2 (12 February 1840): 326.

99. Prospectus, *Evangelical Universalist* 2 (18 March 1840): 366. For a discussion of Universalist attitudes and actions regarding slavery and its abolition, see Chapters 21, 22.

100. *Universalist Register,* 1841, p. 70; 1843, pp. 62-63.

101. Ibid., 1844, p. 63; 1845, p. 58.

102. Ibid., 1843, p. 63; Eddy, *Universalism* 2: 595.

103. *Trumpet* 24 (11 February 1843): 134.

104. Ibid., 26 (22 February 1845): 143.

105. Ibid., 27 (28 February 1846): 146; Eddy, *Universalism* 2: 596.

106. *Trumpet* 25 (2 March 1844): 146.

107. Ibid., 27 (28 February 1846): 146.

108. The most complete file of the *Herald* known to exist was donated by Burruss' great-granddaughter, Mrs. Martha Hardwick Swann, to the Auburn University Library Archives (Alabama). Another extensive file of the paper, not as complete, is located in the State Department of Archives and History, Montgomery, Alabama. The pre-Civil War issues were not paginated

in the original, but numbers were later inserted and are indicated here. When he began the eleventh volume of the *Herald* in 1857, Burruss, the editor, discovered to his chagrin that he did not himself have a complete set of his own newspaper, and issued a plea for copies of the two preceding volumes "in the interests of posterity." *Universalist Herald* 11 (9 May 1857).

109. *Christian Freeman* 11 (8 March 1850): 178.

110. *Universalist Register*, 1851, p. 56.

111. *Trumpet* 32 (29 March 1851): 166.

112. *Universalist Herald* 13 n.s. (1 April 1879): 4.

113. Ibid., 11 (16 October 1857): 89.

114. "History of Universalism in Georgia," ibid., 13 n.s. (1 April 1879): 4. An unsuccessful search for a file of the *Progressionist* was made by the author; the collection donated by the Universalist Historical Society to the Andover-Harvard Theological Library contained only one issue.

115. Proceedings, *Universalist Herald* 11 (16 October 1857): 89.

116. Ibid., 13 n.s. (1 April 1879): 4.

117. Ibid.

118. For the last four months in 1859 the paper carried the combined title, but resumed its own name on 1 January 1860.

119. Proceedings, Georgia State Convention, *Universalist Herald* 13 (11 November 1859): 445. A Universalist paper with the identical title had been published for one year (1843-44) in Barnstable, Mass., before it merged with another publication.

120. Proceedings, Georgia State Convention, *Universalist Herald* 13 (11 November 1859): 446-47.

121. Ibid., 14 (1 March 1861): 558.

122. For note of the fire, see ibid., 18 n.s. (1 November 1870): 142.

123. Clayton, *Forty-Seven Years*, pp. 314-15.

124. Ibid., pp. 326, 332.

125. *Universalist Herald* 15 n.s. (1 May 1867): 17.

126. Program, 12th Annual Induction Program, 4 October 1975, Alabama Press Association, furnished through the courtesy of Mrs. Martha Hardwick Swann.

127. *Universalist Herald* 11 (2 October 1857): 86.

Chapter 14: HYMNOLOGY, LITERARY CULTURE, AND SCHOLARSHIP

1. Proceedings, Vermont Convention (1845) 1: 49.

2. *Trumpet* 29 (9 October 1847): 66

3. Proceedings, Ohio State Convention (1892).

4. Records, Franklin Association (Maine) (1899).

5. Records, Washington Association (Ohio) (1870).

6. Extract from Proceedings, *Christian Freeman* 10 (28 July 1848): 50.

7. Many Universalist churches celebrating anniversaries reproduced or followed their original order of services. See, for example, the 125th anniversary program of the First Universalist Church in 1956 in Medford, Mass., and others in the files of individual churches in the Andover-Harvard Theological Library.

8. See the *Columbian Centinel* for 23, 26 December 1789.

9. *Trumpet* 19 (6 January 1838): 114.

10. *Story of My Life*, p. 385.

11. Sylvanus Cobb, *Autobiography*,

pp. 443-45.

12. Seaburg, *"Centinel,"* pp. 18-19.

13. *Universalist Magazine* 3 (20 October 1821): 67.

14. *Trumpet* 27 (3 January 1846): 115.

15. Thomas, *Century of Universalism*, pp. 218-19.

16. *Southern Evangelist* 1 (July 1834): [2].

17. *Early Days of Thomas Whittemore*, pp. 123-24, 132.

18. Adams, *Memoir of Thomas Whittemore*, pp. 85-87, 119.

19. The indispensable reference for hymnology is Henry Wilder Foote, "Catalogue of American Universalist Hymn Writers and Hymns" (typescript, Cambridge, Mass., 1959); this thirty-five page article was prepared for a proposed Dictionary of American Hymnology, and includes both an annotated list of American Universalist hymn books arranged in chronological order through 1937, when the first joint Universalist-Unitarian hymnal was produced; and brief biographical sketches of the hymn writers. This work has been drawn upon for this study; some Universalist hymnbooks and editions which did not come to Foote's attention have been included here. It should be pointed out that Universalists had participated in the preparation of the *Beacon Song and Service Book* published by the Beacon Press (Boston) in 1935. A second important source is a two-part article by Whittemore outlining the history of denominational hymnology up to 1846, containing details not available elsewhere, which appeared in the *Trumpet* 28 (5, 12 September 1846): 46, 50.

20. *Trumpet* 28 (5 September 1846): 46.

21. Burlington, N.J.: Isaac Collins, 1776.

22. Eddy, *Universalism* 1: 163.

23. Thomas, *Century of Universalism*, pp. 140-41.

24. Philadelphia: Thomas Dobson.

25. Eddy, "Universalist Conventions and Creeds," *Universalist Quarterly* 12 (April 1875): 203-204 n.

26. Boston: J. Thomas & E.T. Andrews.

27. *Trumpet* 29 (2 October 1847): 62.

28. Ibid., 18 (27 May 1837): 194.

29. Records, New England Convention (1805) 1: 98; (1806) 1: 104; (1807) 1: 111.

30. *Trumpet* 28 (5 September 1846): 46.

31. Boston, Samuel T. Armstrong.

32. Records, New England Convention (1817) 1: 202.

33. Boston: Munroe & Francis.

34. *Universalist Magazine* 2 (5 May 1821): 179.

35. Hudson, N.Y.: A. Stoddard.

36. Providence, R.I.: Marshall & Brown.

37. *Trumpet* 28 (5 September 1846): 46.

38. Boston: Charles Crocker.

39. *Trumpet* 10 (3 January 1829): 10.

40. Boston: Marsh & Capen.

41. *Trumpet* 16 (20 December 1834): 102.

42. Ibid., 28 (12 September 1846): 50.

43. Ibid., 17 (13 February 1836): 135.

44. Boston: B.B. Mussey.

45. *Trumpet* 18 (27 May 1837): 194.

46. New York: Philo Price.

47. *Universalist Union* 3 (25 November 1837): 22.

48. Cincinnati: R.P. Brooks.

49. Cincinnati: J.A. Gurley.

50. *Memoranda,* p. 359.

51. Boston: Abel Tompkins.

52. *Universalist Register,* 1864, p. 53.

53. Boston: Abel Tompkins.

54. *Christian Freeman* 20 (18 June 1858): 27. The work was originally published by G. Collins (Philadelphia) and in 1858 was transferred to Henry Lyons (New York).

55. Appendix G, Proceedings, General Convention (1860), pp. 27-28.

56. Boston: Universalist Publishing House.

57. Boston: J.M. Usher.

58. *Christian Freeman* 22 (1 February 1861): 158.

59. *Universalist* 47 (23 September 1865): [2].

60. *Universalist Register,* 1867, p. 100.

61. Ibid., 1868, p. 100.

62. Charles Follen Lee, "Faith and Song," *Universalist Quarterly* 26 n.s. (July 1889): 319. For other indications of Universalist interest in music, particularly congregational singing, see Thomas S. Lathrop, "Hymns as a Basis of Christian Union," ibid., 27 n.s. (January 1890): 59-69; and S.P. Smith, "Sacred Song as an Element of Worship," ibid., 25 n.s. (October 1888): 424-36.

63. *Universalist Register,* 1846, p. 34.

64. Frank Luther Mott, *History of American Magazines,* 4 vols. (Cambridge: Harvard University Press, 1938-1957); see especially Vol. 2.

65. *Universalist Register,* 1841, pp. 40-41.

66. *Universalist Union* 4 (1838-39), Frontispiece.

67. *Universalist Miscellany* 1 (November 1843): 176.

68. *Ladies' Repository* 19 (October 1850): 157-58.

69. *Universalist Quarterly* 7 (October 1850): 421-22.

70. *Universalist* (1832-34); *Universalist and Ladies' Repository* (1834-42); *Ladies' Repository: A Universalist Monthly Magazine for the Home Circle* (1843-72); *Ladies' Repository: A Religious and Literary Magazine for the Home Circle* (1873); and the *Repository: A Magazine for the Christian Home* (1874). Mott, in identifying the publication (2: 57), overlooked the final volume.

71. *Southern Pioneer* 3 (7 December 1833): 31.

72. *Trumpet* 18 (20 April 1837): 180.

73. *Universalist Union* 11 (20 December 1845): 85.

74. *Ladies' Repository* 26 (July 1857): 36-37.

75. Ibid., 29 (June 1861): 579.

76. Mrs. Sawyer served three years (1862-64); Mrs. Sara A. Nowell for one year (1865); Mrs. Phebe A. Hanaford from 1866 to 1868; and Mrs. Henrietta A. Bingham from 1869 to 1874; the last two issues were prepared by Mrs. E.M. Bruce, who had become co-editor because of Mrs. Bingham's declining health.

77. *Repository* 51 (January 1874): 72-73.

78. Ibid., 52 (December 1874): 470-73.

79. *Autobiography,* pp. 181-82.

80. See Hannah Josephson, *The Golden Threads; New England's Mill Girls and Magnates* (New York: Duell, Sloan, and Pearce, 1949); see also Harriet H. Robinson, *Loom and Spindle; or, Life Among the Early Mill Girls, with a Sketch of "The Lowell Offering" and Some of its Contributors* (New York: T.Y. Crowell, 1898); revised edition, including corrections by the author (Kailua, Hawaii: Press

Pacifica, 1976).

81. Robinson, *Loom and Spindle,* p. 62.

82. Thomas, *Autogiography,* p. 266.

83. This newspaper and its name had a tangled history after 1841. The editors sold the subscription list to the *Trumpet* in 1842 after Eliphalet Case, the proprietor of the *Star,* moved to Portland, Me. *Trumpet* 23 (16, 30 April 1842): 170, 178. But the paper was continued under the same name by a variety of editors until 1846, when it became part of a complex reshuffling of papers, all of which were absorbed by the *Christian Freeman* in 1847.

84. See Jeannine Dobbs, "America's First All Women's Magazine," *The New England Galaxy* 19 (Fall 1977): 44-48.

85. Robinson, *Loom and Spindle,* p. 78.

86. *Autobiography,* p. 267.

87. *Loom and Spindle,* pp. 13-14. Judging from the biographical sketches of the principal contributors to the *Lowell Offering* prepared by Mrs. Robinson (Chapter 8), the young ladies represented a broad cross-section of religious affiliations.

88. *Loom and Spindle,* pp. 64-65.

89. Preface, *Lowell Offering* (Lowell, Mass.: Powers & Bagley, 1840).

90. *Autobiography,* p. 285.

91. *Trumpet* 23 (9 April 1842): 166.

92. Quoted in *Loom and Spindle,* p. 67; for other reactions to the *Lowell Offering,* see ibid., pp. 68 ff.

93. London: C. Knight & Co., 1844. The most recent collection is *The Lowell Offering: Writings by New England Mill Women (1840-1845),* edited by Benita Eisler (Philadelphia: Lippincott, 1978).

94. *Universalist Quarterly* 28 n.s. (October 1891): 454.

95. *To-Day* 3 (January 1896): 48.

96. Ibid., 1 (September 1894): [411].

97. Edward Bellamy, "Progress of Nationalism in the United States," *North American Review* 154 (June 1892): 742.

98. *Trumpet* 11 (6 March 1830): 143.

99. Ibid., 12 (10 July 1830): 7.

100. Ibid., 13 (14 April 1832): 166; *Universalist* 1 (8 September 1832): 130-31.

101. *Trumpet* 14 (13 October 1832): 62; Records, Vermont Convention (1833) 1: 4.

102. Quoted in the *Trumpet* 14 (29 December 1832): 106.

103. Ibid., 14 (11 May 1833): 182; 15 (8 February 1834): 139.

104. Ibid., 15 (4 January 1833): 110; 18 (8 October 1836): 61.

105. *Universalist Union* 2 (19 August 1837): 322.

106. Ibid., 7 (20 November 1841): 8; *Universalist Register,* 1839, p. 28.

107. *Trumpet* 20 (16 March 1839): 155.

108. Ibid., 23 (2, 16 October 1841): 58, 66; *Universalist Union* 6 (9 October 1841): 749.

109. *Universalist Union* 7 (20 November 1841): 8-9.

110. *Trumpet* 32 (18 January 1851): 126.

111. Anson Titus, *Universalist Leader* 22 n.s. (4 January 1919): 9.

112. *Universalist* 46 (31 December 1864): [3].

113. *Universalist Quarterly* 23 n.s. (October 1886): 512.

114. Eddy, *Universalism* 2: 476.

115. Proceedings, General Convention (1859), p. 5.

116. *Ladies' Repository* 18 (April 1850): 400.

117. Report of the Committee on a Publishing House, Proceedings, General Convention (1860), pp. 8-9.

118. Proceedings, *Trumpet* 46 (1 October 1864): [1].

119. Cobb, *Autobiography*, p. 498.

120. Quoted in Eddy, *Universalism* 2: 476.

121. Proceedings, Massachusetts State Convention (1863), pp. 23-24.

122. *Universalist* 46 (28 May 1864): [2].

123. A.A. Miner, "Centenary Sermon," Proceedings, General Convention (1870), p. 109.

124. Proceedings, General Convention (1870), p. 6.

125. Eddy, *Universalism* 2: 478.

126. Miner, "Century of Universalism," in Winsor (ed.), *Memorial History of Boston* 3: 507.

127. Eddy, *Universalism* 2: 479.

128. *Trumpet* 19 (7 November 1846): 82.

129. Ibid., 15 (12 April 1834): 168.

130. The proceedings of the first meeting, as well as most subsequent sessions, were published in the *Trumpet* and other denominational papers, at the request of the Society. They were also published occasionally as part of the records of the General Convention. Unless otherwise indicated, the information presented here is derived from the Society's record books (1834-1975), miscellaneous ledgers, and the files of various secretaries. The minutes of several of the early sessions were not transcribed until 1899.

131. It is rather difficult to determine the exact number of individuals who personally affixed their names at the first meeting, as the secretary inserted many of the dates at later times; they are listed in the record book in only rough chronological order. After 1913 the practice of signing the constitution and/or bylaws was abandoned. Even before 1914 many names were written in by the secretary rather than by autograph.

132. An extended correspondence concerning this matter was published in the *Universalist Union* 4 (23 February 1839): 125-26.

133. *Trumpet* 16 (27 September 1834): 54.

134. *Universalist Union* 4 (25 May 1839): 228-29.

135. See ibid., 2 (26 November 1836): 17-18; *Trumpet* 18 (10 December 1836): 97.

136. *Trumpet* 29 (16 October 1847): 70.

137. Ibid., 20 (25 September 1847): 58.

138. Ibid., 19 (21 November 1846): 90.

139. The donors were Cyrus Buttrick of Boston and his brother Abiel. Ibid., 19 (5, 12 December 1846): 98, 102.

140. This notation is included in the record book, and no minutes are extant for this period.

141. *Trumpet* 31 (11 December 1852): 105.

142. Records, General Convention (1855), p. 141.

143. Ibid., (1858), pp. 27-28.

144. Ballou to Sawyer, 17 April 1861, Tufts University Archives.

145. At least one list, published in 1838, included several items not included in Eddy's bibliography prepared in the 1880s.

146. The mail ballot was sent to thirty-two individuals, twenty of whom were listed as active in the Society; neither the number nor names of those attending the June meeting was recorded in the minutes.

147. For details of the reactivation of the Society, see Melvin C. Van de Workeen, "The Universalist Historical Society," *Universalist Leader* 136 (September, October 1954): 201-203, 227-28.

148. See particularly the annotated copy from Emerson Lalone's library in the Andover-Harvard Theological Library.

149. *Universalist Leader* 139 (January 1958): 23.

150. The years 1960-61, 1964-65, 1967-68, and 1969-70 were combined issues, and five years elapsed between the appearance of the ninth and tenth volumes (1971, 1976). It was therefore appropriate that the word "Annual" which had appeared as part of the title of the first two volumes be abandoned with the seventh volume in 1967-68.

151. For a list of the officers of the Society, 1954-1976, see Appendix C.

Chapter 15: NON-SECTARIAN EDUCATION IN THEORY AND PRACTICE: ACADEMIES AND SEMINARIES

1. Proceedings, General Convention (1870), p. 37.

2. Quoted in Albert I. Spanton (ed.), *Fifty Years of Buchtel, 1870-1920* (Akron, Ohio, 1922), p. 5.

3. Dorothy Kendall Cleaveland Salisbury, "They Builded Better Than They Knew" (Boston: Association of Universalist Women, 1957), p. 1.

4. For its application to Massachusetts, see Sherman M. Smith, *The Relation of the State to Religious Education in Massachusetts* (Syracuse, N.Y.: Syracuse Union Bookstore, 1926), especially Chapter 1.

5. The Plan of Government was reproduced in the *Trumpet* 15 (10 August 1933): 28.

6. For a more detailed discussion of this subject, with special reference to Massachusetts, see Russell E. Miller, "Universalism and Sectarian Education before 1860," *Annual Journal of the Universalist Historical Society* 3 (1962): 30-53.

7. *Trumpet* 22 (18 September 1841): 50.

8. Ibid., 16 (3 January 1835): 112.

9. *Christian Freeman* 10 (9 March 1849): 177.

10. *Universalist Expositor* 2 (November 1831): 133 ff.

11. *Trumpet* 43 (21 September 1861): 66.

12. *Universalist Union* 9 (6 April 1844): 328-29.

13. Proceedings, Vermont State Convention (1875) 2: 11.

14. *Universalist Magazine* 1 (11 December 1819): 93.

15. *Universalist Expositor* 2 (September 1831): 131.

16. *Trumpet* 16 (5 July 1834): 5.

17. Charles B. Kinney, Jr., *Church and State: The Struggle for Separation in New Hampshire, 1630-1900* (New York: Teachers College, Columbia University, 1955), p. 160 n.

18. *Universalist Magazine* 8 (20 September 1826): 58.

19. *Trumpet* 15 (7 December 1833): 93.

20. Ibid., 15 (24 May 1834): 189.

21. *Impartialist* 1 (20 July 1833): 182.

22. *Christian Freeman* 18 (27 March 1857): 190.

23. *Trumpet* 18 (27 May 1837): 193.

24. Ibid., 22 (28 July 1849): 26.

25. Records, New England Convention (1814) 1: 175.

26. Ibid., (1815) 1: 185.

27. General Epistle, Proceedings, New England Convention, *Universalist Magazine* 1 (4 December 1819): 90.

28. Proceedings, ibid., p. 89.

29. Minutes, Board of Trustees, 11 August 1819, ibid., 1 (11 September 1819): 43.

30. Ibid., 1 (11 December 1819): 93.

31. Ibid., pp. 93-94; (11 March 1820): 148.

32. Eddy, *Universalism* 2: 414.

33. *Universalist Magazine* 1 (18 March 1820): 150-51.

34. Ibid., 1 (11 March 1820): 148.

35. *Trumpet* 22 (29 May 1841): 195.

36. *Universalist Magazine* 7 (6 August 1825): 28.

37. *Trumpet* 11 (26 September 1829): 51.

38. Ibid., 11 (3 October 1829): 53.

39. Ibid., 11 (20 March 1830): 151.

40. Ibid., 20 (20 October, 24 November 1838): 71, 94.

41. Eddy, *Universalism* 2: 431; *Universalism in Gloucester,* pp. 59-60.

42. *Trumpet* 20 (2 February, 23 March 1839): 132, 157-58.

43. Ibid., 20 (2 March 1839): 147; 21 (6 July 1839): 10.

44. Ibid., 21 (24 August 1839): 38.

45. Ibid., 21 (5 October 1839): 62, 63.

46. Ibid., 21 (23 May 1840): 191.

47. *Christian Freeman* 5 (22 March 1844): 187.

48. *Trumpet* 26 (29 March 1845): 163.

49. Ibid., 24 (20 May 1843): 191. Wait's name was variously spelled "Waitt" and "Waite." A printed report card of the academy carried the spelling as "Waitt."

50. *Universalist Register,* 1840, p. 25; 1841, p. 46. This writer is indebted to the Rev. Richard Woodman, pastor of the Unitarian Universalist Church of Reading, Mass., for furnishing the biographical information about Wait.

51. *Trumpet* 24 (27 May 1843): 195.

52. Ibid., 25 (2 September 1843): 43.

53. Ibid., 24 (27 May 1843).

54. Ibid., 25 (24 June 1843): 3.

55. Ibid., 25 (9 September 1843): 47.

56. Records, General Convention (1844), p. 529.

57. *Trumpet* 25 (9 September 1843): 47.

58. Ibid., 25 (9 March 1844).

59. Ibid., 26 (22 June 1844): 4.

60. Proceedings, Trustees of Reading Seminary, ibid., 27 (7 February 1846): 135.

61. Ibid., 27 (21 February 1846): 143.

62. Ibid., 28 (27 June 1846): 7.

63. Ibid., 28 (28 November 1846): 95.

64. Ibid., 28 (10 October 1846): 67.

65. Ibid., 30 (24 June 1848): 7; *Christian Freeman* 10 (14 July 1848): 42.

66. *Trumpet* 31 (1, 8 September 1849): 47, 51.

67. Ibid., 31 (15 September 1849): 55.

68. Ibid., 35 (30 July 1853): 31.

69. Obituary, *Reading Chronicle* (Massachusetts), 10 April 1884.

70. Information on the history of the academy building in its later years was furnished through the courtesy of Miss Ruth A. Woodbury of the Wakefield Historical Society.

71. Proceedings, Massachusetts State Convention (1863), p. 28; (1864), p. 28.

72. The act of incorporation was reproduced in the Proceedings, ibid., (1865), pp. 23-24.

73. Cobb, *Autobiography,* pp. 216-17.

74. *Universalist Register,* 1870, p. 64.

75. Annual Report, Executive Committee, Massachusetts State Convention (1866), p. 12.

76. Ibid., (1869), p. 21.

77. *Universalist Register,* 1872, p. 111.

78. Ibid., 1878, p. 75.

79. Eddy, *Universalism* 2: 416.

80. *Trumpet* 13 (2 July 1831): 2.

81. Proceedings, ibid., 12 (4 June 1831): 194.

82. *Universalist Union* 6 (9 October 1841): 742.

83. Ibid., 1 (12 March 1836): 138.

84. *Universalist Register,* 1852, p. 45.

85. *Universalist Union* 7 (20 October 1842): 793.

86. T.J. Sawyer, *Memoir of Rev. Stephen R. Smith* (Boston: Abel Tompkins, 1852), pp. 285-86.

87. *Universalist Union* 1 (13 August 1836): 315.

88. *Trumpet* 15 (27 July 1833): 20.

89. Ibid., 17 (29 August 1835): 38.

90. *Universalist Union* 1 (12 March 1836): 138.

91. *Universalist Expositor* 1 n.s. (July 1833): 281.

92. Rogers, *Memoranda,* p. 164.

93. *Trumpet* 15 (27 July 1833): 20.

94. Ibid., 17 (29 August 1835): 38.

95. *Universalist Register,* 1842, p. 54.

96. Ibid., 1844, p. 52.

97. The constitution and bylaws were reproduced in the *Universalist Union* 1 (12 March 1836): 137-38.

98. Ibid., 6 (11 September 1841): 682.

99. *Trumpet* 23 (21 August 1841): 36.

100. Ibid., 20 (29 September 1838): 58; 22 (10 October 1840): 62.

101. *Christian Freeman* 4 (20 January 1843): 150.

102. Proceedings, *Universalist Union* 6 (11 September 1841): 680.

103. Ibid., 7 (18 June 1842): 486.

104. Ibid., 6 (11 September 1841): 681.

105. Ibid., 10 (16 November 1844): 5.

106. Ibid., 9 (10 August 1844): 624.

107. Proceedings, ibid., 10 (4 June 1845): 482.

108. Proceedings and Constitution, ibid., 10 (9 August 1845): 615.

109. Ibid., 10 (30 August 1845): 669.

110. *Universalist Register,* 1848, p. 53.

111. *Universalist Union* 10 (23 August 1845): 651.

112. *Trumpet* 27 (6 September 1845): 46.

113. Records, General Convention (1846), pp. 56-57.

114. Extract from Proceedings, *Christian Freeman* 11 (3 August 1849): 54.

115. *Trumpet* 31 (28 July 1849): 25.

116. Ibid., 31 (7 July 1849): 14.

117. Ibid., 31 (11 August 1849): 34.

118. Ibid., 31 (15 December 1849): 107.

119. *Christian Freeman* 12 (14 February 1851): 166.

120. Ibid., 11 (1 February 1850): 158.

121. Ibid., 13 (9 January 1853): 146; *Trumpet* 32 (10 May 1851): 190.

122. *Christian Freeman* 13 (20 February 1852): 171.

123. *Universalist Register,* 1853, p. 43.

124. Ibid., 1856, p. 43.

125. Report of the Committee on Education, Proceedings, General Convention (1859), p. 13.

126. *Christian Freeman* 19 (12 February 1858): 166.

127. Ibid., 20 (11 February 1859): 163.

128. *Universalist Register*, 1860, p. 35.

129. Appendix F, Proceedings, General Convention (1860), p. 50.

130. Report, Committee on Education, ibid., (1865), p. 57.

131. Ibid., (1867), p. 47.

132. Ibid.

133. *Universalist Register*, 1877, p. 73.

134. Ibid., 1889, pp. 73-74.

135. Salisbury, "They Builded Better Than They Knew," p. 2; *Universalist Register*, 1903, p. 88.

136. Proceedings, General Convention (1866), p. 34.

137. *Universalist Union* 5 (12 September 1840): 688.

138. Adams, *Fifty Notable Years*, p. 240; *Universalist Register*, 1869, pp. 34, 35.

139. Proceedings, *Trumpet* 12 (20 November 1830): 83.

140. Records, Maine Convention (1831).

141. *Christian Intelligencer* 12 (8 March, 5 April 1833): 38, 54.

142. *Universalist Register*, 1840, p. 19.

143. *Trumpet* 22 (26 September 1840): 54.

144. Ibid., 25 (9 December 1843): 98.

145. Extract from Proceedings, *Christian Freeman* 20 (9 July 1858): 38; 21 (5 August 1859): 55.

146. Report, Committee on Education, Proceedings, General Convention (1862), pp. 20-21.

147. Ibid., (1863), p. 42; (1865), pp. 55-56; (1867), p. 45.

148. Records, Maine Convention (1868).

149. *Universalist Union* 3 (23 December 1837): 54.

150. *Trumpet* 23 (4 December 1841): 94; 28 (12 December 1846): 103.

151. Report, Committee on Education, Proceedings, General Convention (1868), p. 84.

152. *Trumpet* 16 (11 January 1834): 114; *Impartialist* 2 (11 January 1834): 66.

153. For a brief biographical sketch of Partridge, see William A. Ellis (comp.), *Norwich University* (Concord, N.H.: Rumford Press, 1898), pp. 99-104.

154. *Impartialist* 2 (1 March 1834): 95.

155. Reprint from *Universalist Watchman*, in the *Trumpet* 17 (28 June 1834) 4.

156. *Impartialist* 2 (11 January 1834): 66.

157. Partridge to William Bell, ibid., 2 (25 January 1834): 75.

158. Ibid., 2 (1 March 1834): 95.

159. Ibid., 2 (12 April 1834): 117.

160. Ibid., 2 (3 May 1834): 131.

161. *Trumpet* 16 (8 March 1834): 145; 17 (28 June 1834): 4.

162. Proceedings, New Hampshire Convention, *Trumpet* 17 (12 July 1834: 10; Records, Vermont Convention (1834) 1: 7, 8.

163. Proceedings, *Impartialist* 2 (5, 12 July 1834): 166, 171; *Trumpet* 17 (28 June 1834): 4.

164. The charter was reproduced in Ellis, *Norwich University*, pp. 474-76.

165. *Impartialist* 2 (22 March 1834): 106.

166. *Evangelical Universalist* 1 (25 August 1838): 5.

167. Ibid., 2 (11 December 1839): 255.

168. *Impartialist* 2 (1 March 1834): 94.

169. *Trumpet* 17 (29 November 1834): 90.

170. Ellis, *Norwich University*, p. 8.

171. *Trumpet* 17 (11 July 1835): 11.

172. Ibid., 23 (31 August 1850): 47.

173. There are biographical sketches or reminiscences in Ellis, *Norwich University*. Alonzo A. Miner was erroneously listed as a graduate, complete with a biographical sketch apparently copied from the one appearing in a history of Tufts College published in 1896. Edith MacDonald identified more than fifteen Universalists who attended the institution. *Rebellion in the Mountains*, p. 77.

174. *Trumpet* 23 (31 August 1850): 47.

175. Proceedings, Vermont Convention (1836) 1: 15, 16.

176. Eddy, *Universalism* 2: 434; *Trumpet* 31 (23 June 1849): 5.

177. *Trumpet* 29 (7 August 1847): 31.

178. *Christian Freeman* 9 (26 November 1847): 122.

179. *Trumpet* 30 (25 November 1848): 92.

180. Proceedings, Vermont Convention (1849) 1: 62.

181. *Trumpet* 31 (23 June 1849): 5.

182. *Christian Freeman* 13 (9 April 1852): 198.

183. Ibid., 15 (2 December 1853): 123.

184. Ibid., 16 (8 December 1854): 127.

185. *Ladies' Repository* 24 (February 1856): 318.

186. *Trumpet* 41 (26 November 1859): 103.

187. MacDonald, *Rebellion in the Mountains*, p. 81.

188. *Universalist* 46 (19 November 1864): [1].

189. Report, Committee on Education, Proceedings, General Convention (1866, 1867), pp. 35, 45-46.

190. Ibid., (1865), p. 55.

191. Eddy, *Universalism* 2: 437; *Universalist Register*, 1862, p. 24.

192. MacDonald, *Rebellion in the Mountains*, p. 82.

193. Report, Committee on Education, Proceedings, General Convention (1868), p. 85.

194. *Universalist Register*, 1872, p. 109.

195. *Centennial*, p. 15.

196. Records, Vermont Convention (1863) 1: 137.

197. The committee on location comprised Alonzo A. Miner (Boston, Mass.), G.W. Bailey (Lebanon, N.H.), and Eliphalet Trask (Springfield, Mass.).

198. *Universalist* 46 (3 September 1864): [2].

199. Ibid., 46 (29 April 1865): [2].

200. Eddy, *Universalism* 2: 442; Report, Committee on Education, *Centennial*, p. 14.

201. *Universalist Register*, 1875. p. 101.

202. For further details of architecture and construction, down to almost every brick and cornice, see "Historical Sketch and Circular of the Green Mountain Central Institute," published as part of the first catalogue in 1870. Unless indicated otherwise, the information on Goddard Seminary through 1880 was derived from the school bulletins.

203. *Trumpet* 19 (6 January 1838): 115.

204. Ibid., 19 (20 January 1838): 123.

205. Eddy, *Universalism* 2: 428.

206. *Star of Bethlehem*, cited in *Trumpet* 23 (24 July 1841): 17.

207. *Trumpet* 18 (24 December 1836): 106.

208. Ibid., 19 (25 November 1837): 91.

209. Ibid., 22 (6 February, 20 March

1841): 131, 155.

210. Ibid., 23 (4 December 1841): 94; *Universalist Register,* 1842, p. 47.

211. *Trumpet* 23 (31 July 1841): 23; 24 (29 October 1842): 74.

212. *Universalist Register,* 1842, p. 47.

213. *Trumpet* 23 (24 July 1841): 17.

214. Ibid., 23 (8 January, 5 February 1842): 116, 132.

215. Ibid., 23 (5 March 1842): 147; 24 (17 December 1842): 102.

216. Ibid., 24 (6 August 1842): 27; 26 (30 November 1844): 95.

217. *Christian Freeman* 9 (29 October 1847): 101.

218. Eddy, *Universalism* 2: 432.

219. *Trumpet* 26 (10 August 1844): 29.

220. Ibid., 28 (19 September 1846): 55.

221. Proceedings, *Christian Freeman* 9 (15 October 1847): 94.

222. *Trumpet* 38 (21 June 1856): 10.

223. Eddy, *Universalism* 2: 433.

224. *Christian Freeman* 16 (12 February 1855): 146; 17 (18 May 1855): 11.

225. The Act of Incorporation was reproduced in the *Philomath Encyclopedia* 5 (January 1842): 17-19.

226. Extract from Proceedings, Washington Association (Ohio), *Trumpet* 17 (2 August 1834): 22.

227. *Impartialist* 1 (16 February 1833): 94-95.

228. *Philomath Encyclopedia* 1 (June 1836): 40-41.

229. *Sentinel and Star in the West,* cited in the *Impartialist* 1 (16 February 1833): 94-95; *Christian Intelligencer* 12 (29 March 1833): 50.

230. *Trumpet* 14 (9 February 1833): 130.

231. Extract from Proceedings, *Trumpet* 17 (5 July 1834): 6.

232. Eddy, *Universalism* 2: 424.

233. *Philomath Encyclopedia* 2 (June 1837): 288.

234. Ibid., 1 (August 1836): 51.

235. Ibid., 1 (June 1836): 25.

236. Ibid., 1 (August 1836): 83-84.

237. Ibid., 1 (June 1836): 44.

238. Ibid., 3 (September 1839): 432.

239. Minutes, Board of Trustees, ibid., 1 (June 1837): 527.

240. Proceedings, Western Union Association, ibid., p. 514.

241. E.M. Pingree, quoted in ibid., 5 (January 1842): 13.

242. Ibid., pp. 13-19.

243. Eddy, *Universalism* 2: 431.

244. The "Ohio City" referred to was a part of what is today Greater Cleveland, and should not be confused with the twentieth-century town of Ohio City in northwestern Ohio, on the Indiana border.

245. Eddy, *Universalism* 2: 429-30.

246. See, for example, the *Universalist Union* 3 (6 October 1838): 375.

247. *Universalist Register,* 1844, p. 57.

248. George Sumner Weaver, *Autobiography* (Albany, N.Y.: privately printed, 1965), p. 39. The autobiography was edited, with an epilogue, by Dorothy Cleaveland Salisbury, author of a brief history of Universalist schools and colleges; numerous members of her family were associated with various Universalist educational institutions.

249. Salisbury, "They Builded Better Than They Knew," p. 3.

250. Eddy, *Universalism* 2: 436.

251. Report, Committee on Education, Proceedings, General Convention (1868), p. 87.

252. *Universalist Register,* 1876, p. 87.

253. Report, Committee on Education, Proceedings, General Convention (1866), pp. 35-36; Report, *Centennial,*

p. 14.

254. *Universalist Register,* 1873, p. 114.

255. Other educational interests of Universalists in the post-Civil War period, including the Southern Industrial Institute, established in 1898, will be considered in the second volume of this study.

256. *Universalist Register,* 1871, p. 98.

257. Ibid., 1876, p. 88.

258. Eddy, *Universalism* 2: 445.

Chapter 16: THE HIGHER LEARNING: THEOLOGICAL OR LITERARY?

1. Edith MacDonald, *Rebellion in the Mountains,* p. 220, writing of early Universalism in Vermont and suggesting a generational approach.

2. Smith, *Sketches* 1: 142 ff.

3. *Christian Freeman* 23 (14 March 1862): 182.

4. Quoted in Eddy, *Sawyer,* p. 37.

5. General Circular, New England Convention, *Universalist Magazine* 1 (4 December 1819): 90.

6. *Memoirs,* pp. 265-66.

7. Proceedings, *Universalist Magazine* 8 (1 July 1826): 7-8.

8. Ibid., 9 (3 November 1827): 77-79.

9. *Universalist Expositor* 2 (July, November 1831): 14-32, 142.

10. *Trumpet* 13 (17 September 1831): 46.

11. Proceedings, ibid., 14 (2 November 1833): 74.

12. Ibid., 15 (31 August 1833): 39.

13. Proceedings, ibid., 15 (12 October 1833): 62; 16 (18 October 1834): 66.

14. *Universalist Union* 1 (14 September 1836): 366.

15. *Southern Evangelist* 1 (September 1834): [1].

16. Proceedings, General Convention (1835), p. 28.

17. Proceedings, *Universalist Union* 1 (4 June 1836): 235.

18. Proceedings, ibid., 1 (14 November 1835): 3.

19. Proceedings, ibid., 1 (21 November 1835): 11.

20. *Trumpet* 17 (2, 16 April 1836): 163, 170.

21. Proceedings, *Southern Pioneer* 5 (7 May 1836): 317.

22. Extract from Proceedings, *Trumpet* 18 (2 July 1836): 7.

23. Quoted in the *Universalist Union* 1 (2 July 1836): 269.

24. Circular Letter, Proceedings, General Convention (1836), p. 49.

25. Proceedings, *Universalist Union* 1 (21 May 1836): 217.

26. Proceedings, *Trumpet* 18 (24 September 1836): 55.

27. Proceedings, ibid., 19 (24 June 1837): 4.

28. Proceedings, *Universalist Union* 1 (22 October 1836): 397.

29. Ibid., 3 (28 July 1838): 302.

30. *Trumpet* 20 (30 May 1839): 161.

31. *Universalist Miscellany* 6 (September 1848): 109.

32. *Christian Freeman* 1 (6 March 1840): 177-78.

33. *Trumpet* 21 (2 May 1840): 170.

34. *Universalist Expositor* 3 n.s. (September 1839): 351-61.

35. *Trumpet* 20 (1 September 1838): 42.

36. Ibid., 29 (8 April 1848): 170.

37. Quoted in ibid., 20 (8 December 1838): 98.

38. *Universalist Expositor* 3 n.s. (1839): 104.

39. *Universalist Union* 5 (21 December 1839): (4 January 1840): 72, 104.

40. *Trumpet* 20 (16 March 1839): 153.

41. Proceedings, ibid., 21 (22 June 1839): 4.

42. Ballou, *Hosea Ballou 2d,* p. 255.

43. Unless otherwise indicated, the information concerning the seminary was derived from the minutes of the trustees.

44. *Universalist Expositor* 1 n.s. (July 1833): 281.

45. *Christian Freeman* 2 (15 January 1841): [2].

46. Reproduced in the *Trumpet* 23 (24 July 1841): 17.

47. Ibid., 22 (17 April 1841): 170.

48. Ibid., 23 (16 October 1841): 66.

49. Ibid., 23 (11 September 1841): 46.

50. Ibid., 23 (16 October 1841): 66.

51. Proceedings, Pennsylvania State Convention, *Universalist Union* 6 (26 June 1841): 502; Proceedings, Massachusetts State Convention, *Trumpet* 23 (31 July 1841): 21.

52. Proceedings, General Convention (1841), p. 473.

53. *Trumpet* 20 (22 December 1838): 105.

54. Proceedings, Special Meeting of the Trustees, Walnut Hill Seminary, ibid., 23 (17 July 1841): 15.

55. Ibid., 23 (14 August 1841): 29.

56. Ibid., 23 (11, 18 September 1841): 45, 52.

57. The fullest biography is Richard Eddy, *The Life of Thomas J. Sawyer, S.T.D., LL.D. and of Caroline M. Sawyer* (Boston: Universalist Publishing House, 1900); it is of particular value for its extensive excerpts from Sawyer's correspondence, sermons, and other writings.

58. For tributes to Sawyer and his work, see ibid., pp. 393 ff.

59. Extract from Proceedings, ibid., p. 182.

60. Quoted in ibid., p. 165.

61. Ibid., pp. 196, 200.

62. The most comprehensive biography, including much correspondence, is Hosea Starr Ballou, *Hosea Ballou 2d, D.D., First President of Tufts College: His Origin, Life and Letters* (Boston: E.P. Guild & Co., 1896). Much of the voluminous correspondence between Sawyer and Ballou, the gift of the biographer, is deposited in the Tufts University Archives. Unless otherwise indicated, all biographical data included here were drawn from the Ballou volume and from the correspondence.

63. The library comprises part of the Special Collections of the Tufts University Library.

64. E.G. Brooks, "Hosea Ballou 2d," *Universalist Quarterly* 15 n.s. (October 1878): 398.

65. *Universalist Miscellany* 6 (February 1849): 283.

66. Eddy, *Universalism* 2: 136-37.

67. Records, New England Convention (1816) 1: 193.

68. Proceedings, New England Convention, *Universalist Magazine* 1 (4 December 1819): 89; 2 (16 September 1820): 48.

69. *Christian Intelligencer* 7 (19 January 1827): 10.

70. Eddy, *Universalism* 2: 192.

71. *Universalist Quarterly* 22 n.s. (April 1885): 222.

72. Whittemore, *Modern History of Universalism* (1830) was in process of revision and enlargement at the time of his death in 1861; only the first volume of a projected two volumes was completed and published in 1860.

73. For a detailed summary by Ballou of his book, see *Universalist*

Expositor 2 n.s. (May 1838): 184-209.

74. *Trumpet* 20 (1 June 1839): 198. The total number of volumes printed is unknown.

75. For a bibliography of Ballou's contributions to the *Universalist Expositor* and its successor, the *Universalist Quarterly,* see Ballou, *Ballou,* pp. 153-57.

76. *Trumpet* 24 (11 March 1843): 150.

77. See "Course of Biblical and Theological Study," *Expositor and Universalist Review* 5 (September 1839): 351-61; see also Ballou, *Ballou,* pp. 216-18.

78. For biographical sketches of some of Ballou's students who became prominent in the denomination, see Ballou, *Ballou,* Chapter 11; for a complete listing, see Eddy, *Universalism* 2: 198.

79. *Expositor* 5 (March 1839): 77-104.

80. The proceedings were published in most Universalist papers; e.g., *Christian Freeman* 3 (8 October 1841): 90.

81. Ballou to Sawyer, 31 July 1845.

82. Ballou, *Ballou,* p. 261.

83. Proceedings, General Convention (1845), p. 545.

84. Ibid., (1846) 2: 53.

85. *Universalist Union* 10 (2 August 1845): 610.

86. Proceedings, New York State Convention, *Universalist Union* 11 (13 June 1846): 482-83.

87. *Trumpet* 28 (4 July 1846): 11.

88. Proceedings, *Trumpet* 28 (10 October 1846): 67.

89. Ballou to Sawyer, 16 March 1847.

90. *Christian Freeman* 8 (23 April 1847): 206.

91. For the proceedings, see the *Christian Freeman* 9 (13 August 1847): 58.

92. The sermon was reproduced in the *Christian Freeman* 9 (24 September 1847): 85-86.

93. *Trumpet* 29 (25 September 1847): 58.

Chapter 17: THE HIGHER LEARNING: COLLEGES AND UNIVERSITIES

1. Their post-1870 histories are chronicled in the second volume of this study. For histories of Tufts see Alaric B. Start (ed.), *History of Tufts College. Published by the Class of 1897* (Tufts College, Mass., 1896); it is particularly valuable for the biographical sketches of its early presidents and faculty; and Russell E. Miller, *Light on the Hill: A History of Tufts College, 1852-1952* (Boston: Beacon Press, 1966).

2. *Trumpet* 32 (24 May 1851): 198.

3. Ibid., 32 (27 July 1850): 25.

4. Eddy, *Sawyer,* pp. 175-76.

5. Ballou to Sawyer, 31 December 1849, Tufts University Archives.

6. Ibid., 23 August 1851.

7. *Christian Freeman* 13 (5 September 1851): 74.

8. Trustee Minutes 1 (18 September 1851): 18-19.

9. *Acts and Resolves,* General Court of Massachusetts, 1852, Chapter 141.

10. Ibid., 1850, Chapter 102.

11. The section containing the reference to the Tufts Institution of Learning was later expunged.

12. Ballou to Sawyer, 18 July 1848.

13. Ballou, *Hosea Ballou 2d,* p. 278 n.

14. *Christian Freeman* 16 (4 August 1854): 54.

15. Ibid., 17 (1 September 1855): 70.

16. Proceedings, General Convention (1859), pp. 13-15.

17. *Christian Freeman* 18 (5 September 1856): 74.

18. For the most extensive of several biographies, see George H. Emerson, *Life of Alonzo Ames Miner, S.T.D., LL.D.* (Boston: Universalist Publishing House, 1896); see also the biographical sketch by Anson Titus in *To-Day* 2 (March 1895): 122-26.

19. *Trumpet* 21 (29 June 1839): 6.

20. Titus, "Miner," pp. 124-25.

21. Miner, "Century of Universalism" Winsor, *Memorial History of Boston* 3: 500.

22. *Universalist* 47 (30 September 1865): [2].

23. For the transcriptions of the hearings, see the *Universalist* 48 (23 March 1867): [1].

24. *Trumpet* 37 (6 October 1855): 70.

25. *Christian Freeman* 19 (21 August 1857): 66.

26. Report of the Committee on Education, General Convention (1863), p. 39.

27. *Universalist* 48 (4 August 1860): [1].

28. *Christian Freeman* 14 (13 August 1852): 59.

29. Boston correspondent of the *New York Times,* quoted in the *Trumpet* 36 (12 August 1854): 38.

30. *Christian Freeman* 13 (5 September 1851): 74.

31. Eddy, *Sawyer,* pp. 216-17.

32. See a brief history of the custom by David Hicks MacPherson, "The Meaning of Children's Sunday" (unpublished pamphlet, March 1977), available in the Andover-Harvard Theological Library.

33. Emerson, *Miner,* p. 390.

34. For a collaborative history of St. Lawrence, see Louis H. Pink and Rutherford E. Delmage (eds.), *Candle in the Wilderness: A Centennial History of the St. Lawrence University* (New York: Appleton-Century-Crofts, 1957); for a history of the theological school, see the essay by Emerson H. Lalone (Chapter 3, pp. 22-62).

35. Extract from Proceedings, *Christian Freeman* 11 (3 August 1849): 54.

36. Extract from Proceedings, ibid., 12 (30 August 1850): 71.

37. Ibid., 12 (7 February 1851): 162; *Trumpet* 32 (8 February 1851): 138.

38. *Trumpet* 32 (15 February 1851): 142.

39. *Universalist Quarterly* 11 (October 1854): 349-64.

40. *Christian Freeman* 16 (9 March 1855): 177.

41. Ibid., 17 (28 March 1856): 190.

42. Lalone, "Theological School," Pink and Delmage, *St. Lawrence University*, p. 27.

43. Pink and Delmage, *St. Lawrence University,* p. 11.

44. *Trumpet* 38 (5 July 1856): 18.

45. Report, Committee on Education, Proceedings, General Convention (1859), pp. 16-17.

46. *Christian Freeman* 21 (30 March 1860): 189.

47. *Trumpet* 43 (21 September 1861): 66.

48. See, for example, the *Universalist Register,* 1870, p. 68.

49. *Trumpet* 38 (25 October 1856): 82.

50. Proceedings, ibid., 38 (11 October 1856): 75.

51. For a biography of Fisher, see George H. Emerson, *Memoir of Ebenezer Fisher, D.D.* (Boston: Universalist Publishing House, 1880).

52. *Christian Freeman* 21 (30 March 1860): 189.

53. Proceedings, General Convention (1860), pp. 53-54.

54. *Christian Freeman* 23 (10 May 1861): 5; for a detailed account of the first Commencement, see the *Trumpet* 42 (11 May 1861): 197.

55. *Trumpet* 44 (6 September, 8 November 1862): 79, 114.

56. *Universalist* 46 (30 July 1864): [2].

57. Ibid., 46 (15 October 1864): [1].

58. Proceedings, General Convention (1864), p. [7].

59. One such, delivered by A. St. John Chambré of Stoughton, Mass., reproduced in the *Universalist* 46 (19 November 1864): [1].

60. *Universalist Register,* 1868, p. 73; 1870, p. 70.

61. *Universalist* 47 (26 August 1865): [2].

62. For her experiences as a theological student, see her autobiography, edited and completed by her daughter Gwendolyn B. Willis, published in the *Annual Journal of the Universalist Historical Society* 4 (1963); for additional information, see also below.

63. Proceedings, Massachusetts State Convention (1865), p. 21; Proceedings, General Convention (1865), pp. 57-58.

64. *Universalist Register,* 1859, p. 40; 1860, p. 37.

65. Pink and Delmage, *St. Lawrence University,* p. 14.

66. *Christian Freeman* 18 (13 June 1856): 26.

67. Report, Board of Trustees, General Convention (1870), p. 17.

68. The trustees of the theological school were listed separately in the *Universalist Register* for 1869.

69. *Universalist* 47 (30 December 1865): [3].

70. *Universalist Register,* 1866, p. 23.

71. Report, Committee on Education, Proceedings, General Convention (1866, 1867), pp. 38, 48.

72. Pink and Delmage, *St. Lawrence University,* p. 237.

73. *Universalist Register,* 1871, p. 89.

74. Ibid., 1871, p. 98.

75. The most comprehensive history of the institution, written as an undergraduate thesis, has never been published; see Arthur Swanson, "A History of Lombard College, 1851-1930" (Macomb, Ill.: Western Illinois State College, 1955), used with the kind permission of the author; a copy is available in the Andover-Harvard Theological Library. The bulk of the documentation on Lombard is in the library of Knox College. Swanson also made extensive use of local newspapers and included rosters of both officers (1900-1930) and faculty members (1852-1930). See also Arthur Calvin Walton, "Annals of Lombard College: Some Important Events in its History," *Lombard Directory* [n.d., n.p.], furnished to the author through the courtesy of Dorothy T. Spoerl, and used extensively in this work. For the reminiscences of Carl Sandburg, a native of Galesburg and one of the school's most famous students (a nongraduate, 1898-1902), see his *Always the Young Strangers* (New York: Harcourt, Brace, 1952, 1953). Sandburg was editor of the school literary magazine in 1901-1902; he was awarded an honorary degree in 1923. Lombard University was also described from year to year in the *Universalist Register,* together with other institutions conducted by the denomination. Separate accounts of each school were begun in 1867 and often include information not available elsewhere.

76. Proceedings, Spoon River Associ-

ation (Illinois) (1841), [n.p.], Andover-Harvard Theological Library.

77. *Universalist Register,* 1871, p. 86.

78. Emerson, *Miner,* p. 392 n.

79. *Christian Freeman* 15 (21 October 1853): 98.

80. Ibid., 16 (19 January 1855): 150; 17 (28 May 1855): 14.

81. *Universalist Register,* 1867, pp. 67-68.

82. Weaver, *Autobiography,* p. 49.

83. *Trumpet* 36 (19 May 1855): 198.

84. Report, Committee on Education, Proceedings, General Convention (1859), p. 15; *Universalist Register,* 1867, p. 67.

85. *Christian Freeman* 23 (2 August 1861): 54.

86. Eddy, *Universalism* 2: 466.

87. Report, Committee on Education, General Convention (1863), p. 40.

88. Proceedings, ibid., (1861, 1862), pp. 10-11, 17-18.

89. Report, Committee on Education, ibid., (1866), p. 37.

90. Manford, *Twenty-five Years,* p. 354.

91. Proceedings, General Convention (1864), [n.p.].

92. *Universalist* 46 (19 November 1864): [1].

93. Proceedings, Washington Association (Ohio) (1866), [n.p.], Ohio State Historical Library.

94. Report of Northwestern Conference, Proceedings, General Convention (1868), p. 60.

95. Eddy, *Universalism* 2: 466.

96. Ibid., 2: 463.

97. The circumstances under which the Unitarians took over the institution are related in greater detail in the second volume of this study.

98. Report, Committee on Education, Proceedings, General Convention (1866), p. 38.

99. *Universalist* 50 (4 July 1868): [2].

100. Swanson, "Lombard College," p. 59.

101. The definitive history is George W. Knepper, *New Lamps for Old: One Hundred Years of Urban Higher Education at the University of Akron* (Akron, Ohio: University of Akron, 1970). Unless otherwise indicated, the account presented here was derived from this source and from various records of the Ohio Universalist Convention (1869-1895) in the Ohio State Historical Library; other records of the convention (1865-1880, 1896-1922) are in the Andover-Harvard Theological Library.

102. Report of Financial Secretary, Proceedings, Trustees of the Ohio State Convention, 27 January 1870.

103. Address at Gloucester Centennial, *Centennial,* p. 47.

104. The highest elevation (1,550 feet) is Campbell Hill (Logan County), in the west-central part of the state.

105. Eddy, *Universalism* 2: 473.

106. Records, Washington Association (Ohio), August 1872.

107. Weaver, *Autobiography,* p. 68.

108. *Ladies' Repository* 50 (July 1873): 68-69.

109. *Universalist Register,* 1882, p. 73.

110. Records, Ohio State Convention (1891).

111. *To-Day* 2 (March 1895): 126-31.

112. The exact wording of the resolutions relevant to this is to be found in Knepper, *University of Akron,* p. 103.

113. For a biography of Smithson, see Perret Dufour, *The Swiss Settlement of Switzerland County, Indiana* (Indianapolis: Indiana Historical Commission, 1925); see also the *Universalist*

Register, 1868, pp. 83-84. For a history of Smithson College, see James H. Smart, *The Indiana Schools and the Men who have Worked in Them* (Cincinnati: Wilson, Hinkle & Co., 1876). The Indiana State Library (Indianapolis) possesses the most complete collection of circulars, catalogues, and other literature relating to the school, and was used by courtesy of that library.

114. Dufour, *Switzerland County,* pp. 88-89.

115. Julia LeClerc Knox, "Stories That Old Houses Tell," *Indiana Magazine of History* 29 (June 1933): 122-27.

116. Eddy, *Universalism* 2: 474.

117. Report, Committee on Education, Proceedings, General Convention (1867), p. 49.

118. Report, Northwestern Conference, General Convention (1868), p. 60.

119. John Z. Powell (ed.), *History of Cass County, Indiana* (Chicago: Lewis Publishing Co., 1913), pp. 94-95.

120. Circular, Smithson College (1871), Indiana State Library.

121. Thomas B. Helm (ed.), *History of Cass County, Indiana* (Chicago: Brant & Fuller, 1886), pp. 379-81.

122. *Universalist Register,* 1873, p. 106.

123. The *Register* for 1872, pp. 100-101, includes a detailed description of the building.

124. Circular, Smithson College (1871).

125. Ibid.

126. Smart, *Indiana Schools,* p. 160; Dufour, *Switzerland County,* pp. 148, 171.

127. Circular, Smithson College (1871).

128. Report, Committee on Education, *Centennial,* p. 14.

129. *Universalist Register,* 1876, p. 77.

130. Weaver, *Autobiography,* p. 73.

131. Program, First Annual Commencement, Indiana State Library.

132. Helm, *Cass County,* pp. 379-81.

133. *Indiana Magazine of History* 29 (June 1933): 123 n.

134. Powell, *Cass County,* pp. 94-95.

135. Proceedings, *Centennial,* pp. 15-17.

136. *Universalist Register,* 1871, p. 113.

137. Ibid., 1871, p. 98.

Chapter 18: BETTERING THE LOT OF HUMANITY

1. See Arthur M. Schlesinger, Jr., *The Age of Jackson* (Boston: Little, Brown, 1945); Alice Felt Tyler, *Freedom's Ferment: Phases of American Social History from the Colonial Period to the Outbreak of the Civil War* (New York: Harper, 1944); Henry Steele Commager, *The Era of Reform, 1830-1860* (Princeton, N.J.: D. Van Nostrand, 1960); David Brion Davis (ed.), *Ante-Bellum Reform* (New York: Harper & Row, 1967); C.S. Griffin, *The Ferment of Reform, 1830-1860* (New York: Crowell, 1967).

2. The discourse, "A Plea for Charity," was published as a sixteen-page pamphlet by Abel Tompkins in Boston.

3. *The Philosophy of Reform . . .* (New York: C.L. Stickney, 1843), p. 31.

4. *Trumpet* 28 (27 June 1846): 7.

5. For a brief discussion of Universalist social action, see Emerson H. Lalone, *And Thy Neighbor as Thyself* (Boston: Universalist Publishing House, 1939; enlarged edition, 1959).

6. Proceedings, *Trumpet* 28 (20

June 1846): 3.

7. Ibid., 29 (12 June 1847): 207.

8. Proceedings, *Christian Freeman* 21 (10 June 1859): 22.

9. A detailed account of this meeting, as of all subsequent ones, is to be found in both the *Trumpet* and the *Christian Freeman.*

10. Proceedings, *Christian Freeman* 19 (5 June 1857): 22.

11. Ibid., 23 (7 June 1861): 22.

12. Proceedings, General Convention (1858), p. 34.

13. *Prisoners' Friend* 9 (September 1856): 16; the address was also published as an eight-page pamphlet.

14. *Christian Freeman* 3 (24 December 1841): 133.

15. *Trumpet* 26 (25 January 1845): 127.

16. Ibid., 32 (25 January 1851): 130.

17. *Prisoners' Friend* 5 (December 1852): 186.

18. *Christian Freeman* 15 (28 April 1854): 207.

19. Much insight into Spear's activities and ideas can be derived from the diary which he kept between 1841 and 1849, located in the Boston Public Library; there is a copy in the Andover-Harvard Theological Library.

20. One of the most scholarly accounts of the American prison system before the Civil War, based on primary sources, and carrying the story up to the time that Spear became involved, is Orlando F. Lewis, *The Development of American Prisons and Prison Customs, 1776-1845* (New York: Prison Association of New York, 1922) and it has been drawn upon in this study. For a general treatment of the entire subject, see Blake McKelvey, *American Prisons: A Study in American Social History prior to 1915* (Chicago: University of Chicago, 1936; reprint, Montclair, New Jersey: Patterson Smith, 1968).

21. For a discussion of Rush's ideas on penal reform, see Lewis, *American Prisons,* pp. 19-24.

22. For a nineteenth-century account based on the records then existing, see Gideon Haynes, *Pictures from Prison Life. An Historical Sketch of the Massachusetts State Prison* (Boston: Lee & Shepard, 1869).

23. Lewis, *American Prisons,* p. 75.

24. *Trumpet* 29 (3 July 1847): 10.

25. *Prisoners' Friend* 9 n.s. (December 1856-January 1857): 94.

26. See, for example, Spear's account of a trip made into southern Massachusetts and Rhode Island in 1856 in the *Prisoners' Friend* 9 n.s. (September 1856): 24-28; (March 1857): 151.

27. Ibid., 4 n.s. (July 1852): 502.

28. Ibid., 4 n.s. (January 1852): 216 ff.

29. "History of the *Prisoners' Friend,*" ibid., 1 n.s. (September 1848): 3.

30. *Trumpet* 26 (5 April 1845): 167.

31. *Prisoners' Friend* 1 n.s. (September 1848): 2.

32. Ibid., 9 n.s. (April-May 1857): 203.

33. Ibid., 5 n.s. (March 1853): 326 n.

34. *Trumpet* 28 (24 April 1847): 178.

35. *Prisoners' Friend* 1 n.s. (July 1849): 501.

36. Ibid., 1 n.s. (March 1849): 304-305. The article was accompanied by one of the few engravings known to exist of Barnum's famous home near Bridgeport.

37. Ibid., 3 n.s. (December 1850): 181-82.

38. Records, General Convention (1835), p. 18.

39. Proceedings, *Christian Freeman*

12 (14 June 1850): 26-27.

40. Records, General Convention (1854) 2: 136.

41. Proceedings, General Convention (1858), pp. 24, 39.

42. Proceedings, Vermont Convention (1859) 1: 114.

43. Proceedings, *Trumpet* 40 (5 June 1858): 2.

44. *Christian Freeman* 5 (11 August 1843): 57.

45. *Prisoners' Friend* 6 n.s. (January 1854): 215.

46. Ibid., 5 n.s. (April 1853): 383-84.

47. Ibid., 9 n.s. (October 1856): 51-52.

48. *Trumpet* 29 (3 July 1847): 10.

49. *Prisoners' Friend* 9 n.s. (October 1856): 73.

50. Hartford, Conn.: B. Sperry, 1833.

51. *Prisoners' Friend* 2 n.s. (September 1849): 2.

52. *Universalist Union* 10 (14 December 1844): 69 ff.

53. *Universalist Miscellany* 5 (July 1847): 5-18.

54. Cincinnati: G.W. Quinby, 1856.

55. Philip English Mackey, "An All-Star Debate on Capital Punishment, Boston, 1854," *Essex Institute Historical Collections* 110 (July 1974): 191 n.

56. For brief treatments of the subject, see Louis Filler, "Movements to Abolish the Death Penalty in the United States," *Annals of the American Academy of Political and Social Science* 284 (November 1952): 124-36; David Brion Davis, "The Movement to Abolish Capital Punishment in America, 1787-1861," *American Historical Review* 63 (October 1957): 23-46; and Elizabeth Ann Tuttle, *The Crusade Against Capital Punishment* (Austin: University of Texas, 1959).

57. Cited by Chestnut, "Universalist Movement," p. 219.

58. Filler, "Death Penalty," p. 125.

59. *Trumpet* 12 (14 August 1830): 26.

60. Extract from Proceedings, Pennsylvania State Convention (1842), quoted in Butler, "Universalism in Pennsylvania," [n.p.].

61. "Legislation on Capital Punishment in the United States," *Prisoners' Friend* 6 n.s. (January 1854): 196; see also "Legislative History of Capital Punishment in Massachusetts," in *House Document* 2575 (1959).

62. *Trumpet* 12 (4 December 1830): 90.

63. *Autobiography*, p. 437.

64. *Trumpet* 16 (6, 13 June 1835): 200, 204.

65. Ibid., 17 (16 April 1836): 170.

66. *Prisoners' Friend* 1 n.s. (March 1849): 313-14.

67. *Trumpet* 24 (4 February 1843): 130.

68. The sermon was reproduced in ibid., 16 (7 February 1835): 129-30.

69. *Southern Pioneer* 3 (4 January 1834): 46.

70. *Southern Evangelist* 1 (August 1834): [3].

71. Manford, *Twenty-five Years*, pp. 78-80.

72. *Philomath Encyclopedia* 6 (June 1844): 484.

73. Records, Spoon River Association (Illinois) (1841).

74. Proceedings, *Philomath Encyclopedia* 5 (August 1842): 383.

75. Proceedings, General Convention (1835), p. 19.

76. Ibid., (1836), p. 47.

77. Proceedings, *Christian Freeman* 1 (28 February 1840): 175.

78. Ibid., 9 (17 September 1847): 78.

79. Records, Maine Convention (1844).

80. *Universalist Miscellany* 3 (August 1845): 84.

81. Ibid., 3 (March 1846): 360.

82. *Trumpet* 17 (11 June 1836): 204.

83. Ibid., 15 (2 November 1833): 74.

84. *Prisoners' Friend* 1 n.s. (March 1849): 313.

85. Ibid., 1 n.s. (May 1849): 400-401, 411.

86. For a graphic description of Spear's final interview with Goode, and of the execution, see ibid., 1 n.s. (July 1849): 502 ff.

87. Ibid., 3 n.s. (July 1851): 524.

88. *Trumpet* 26 (4 January 1845): 113.

89. Spear's experiences were detailed in a series of articles in the *Prisoners' Friend* 3 n.s. (February-July 1851; 4 n.s. (January 1852): and 6 n.s. (September 1853). He left the operation of his periodical in the hands of his brother, John Murray Spear, and Benjamin H. Greene of Boston.

90. *Prisoners' Friend* 4 n.s. (January 1852): 216 ff.

91. *Christian Freeman* 4 (16 December 1842): 129.

92. *Trumpet* 24 (26 November 1842): 90.

93. See, for example, Proceedings, Vermont Convention (1845) 1: 51; (1851) 1: 73; (1881) 2: 45.

94. Philip English Mackey, "Reverend George Barrell Cheever: Yankee Reformer as Champion of the Gallows," *Proceedings of the American Antiquarian Society* (October 1972): 323-42.

95. *Christian Freeman* 4 (20 January 1843): 150.

96. Proceedings, *Universalist Union* 7 (24 September 1842): 710.

97. Ibid., 8 (14 January 1843): 129-30.

98. Proceedings, ibid., 10 (18 October 1845): 779.

99. Ibid., 10 (8 February 1845): 201.

100. *Trumpet* 27 (27 December 1845): 111.

101. They were treason, murder, armed robbery, rape, arson (in certain cases), burglary (in certain cases), and wilfully allowing or consenting to the escape of a prisoner sentenced to death. For citations, see "Legislative History" and the *Trumpet* 32 (21 September 1850): 58.

102. Spear's involvement is discussed in detail in the *Prisoners' Friend* 2 n.s. (October 1850) and numerous other articles.

103. Proceedings, Old Colony Association, *Trumpet* 32 (26 October 1850): 79.

104. *Prisoners' Friend* 4 n.s. (April 1852): 379.

105. *Massachusetts Statutes,* 1852, Chapter 274.

106. This episode and its consequences are detailed in Mackey, "All-Star Debate."

107. The author of this study is indebted to Mackey, cited above, for this reference to Miner's participation. Miner's biographer, George H. Emerson, made no mention of this, but in his discussion of Miner's services outside the denomination, concentrated instead on his abolitionist and temperance activities.

108. Proceedings, *Christian Freeman* 19 (5 June 1857): 22.

109. *Prisoners' Friend* 9 n.s. (September 1856): 26-27.

110. *Christian Freeman* 15 (7 December 1853): 125.

111. See Merle E. Curti, *The American*

Peace Crusade, 1815-1860 (Durham, N.C.: Duke University Press, 1929; reprint, New York: Octagon Books, 1965; and Peter Brock, *Pacifism in the United States: From the Colonial Era to the First World War* (Princeton, N.J.: Princeton University Press, 1968).

112. *Universalist Magazine* 3 (12 January 1822): 115.

113. The sermon was reproduced in the *Trumpet* 15 (29 March 1834): 157.

114. Proceedings, General Convention (1870), p. 15.

115. Records, Somerset Association (1843).

116. *Christian Freeman* 5 (13 October 1843): 94.

117. Proceedings, ibid., 6 (17 January 1845): 150.

118. Ibid., 7 (16 May 1845): 14.

119. Proceedings, *Trumpet* 27 (13 September 1845): 50.

120. *Christian Freeman* 4 (17 February 1843): 166.

121. Ibid., 8 (27 November 1846): 121.

122. Proceedings, ibid., 8 (25 September 1846): 86.

123. Ibid., 10 (16 June 1848): 26.

124. The work, written by A.A. Livermore, a clergyman in Keene, N.H., was entitled *The War with Mexico Reviewed* (Boston: William Crosby & H.P. Nichols).

125. *Universalist Quarterly* 7 (April 1850): 212-14.

126. *Trumpet* 28 (1 May 1847): 182.

127. *Prisoners' Friend* 4 n.s. (October 1851): 58-62.

128. Proceedings, *Christian Freeman* 14 (4 June 1852): 18.

129. Proceedings, ibid., 15 (4 June 1853): 18.

130. Proceedings, ibid., 17 (15 June 1855): 26.

131. Curti, *Peace Crusade*, p. 87.

132. Philadelphia: J. Miller McKim. Excerpts from this work have been widely reprinted; see, for example, *American Radical Thought: The Libertarian Tradition* (Lexington, Mass.: D.C. Heath, 1970, edited by Henry J. Silverman), pp. 148-52.

133. Boston: Non-resistance Society, 1839. Ballou also published at the press of the Hopedale Community in 1860 *A Discourse on Christian Non-Resistance in Extreme Cases.* See also "War—Personal Injury," *Universalist Quarterly* 3 (April 1846): 221-46. For the relation of Ballou's ideas about non-resistance to Perfectionism, see Jerry V. Caswell, " 'A New Civilization Radically Higher Than the Old:' Adin Ballou's Search for Social Perfection," *Journal of the Universalist Historical Society* 7 (1967-68): 70-101.

134. *Trumpet* 12 (12 February 1831): 130.

135. Ibid., 31 (8 September 1849): 50.

136. For a detailed history of the Non-Resistance Society and for a summary of Ballou's ideas, see Brock, *Pacifism*, especially pp. 590-604; see also Perry, *Radical Abolitionism*, pp. 130 ff.

137. *Autobiography*, pp. 109-110.

138. *Practical Christian* 1 (1 April 1840): 4.

139. Brock, *Pacifism*, p. 590.

140. *Practical Christian* 3 (7 January 1843): 65-66.

141. See Perry, *Radical Abolitionism*, pp. 3-4; Brock, *Pacifism*, pp. 613-15.

Chapter 19: FROM TEMPERANCE TO TOTAL ABSTINENCE

1. The literature on the subject published in the United States, both scholarly and polemical, is nothing short of staggering. For a general survey of the entire subject, see Richard Eddy, *Alcohol in History: An Account of Intemperance in All Ages* (New York: The National Temperance Society and Publication House, 1887). For the movement in the United States, see John A. Krout, *The Origins of Prohibition* (New York: A.A. Knopf, 1925; reprint, New York: Russell & Russell, 1967); the most detailed chronology, including legislation, is Ernest H. Cherrington, *The Evolution of Prohibition in the United States of America* (Westerville, Ohio: American Issue Press, 1920; reprint, Montclair, N.J.: Patterson Smith, 1969); Joseph R. Gusfield, *Symbolic Crusade: Status Politics and the American Temperance Movement* (Urbana, Ill.: University of Illinois Press, 1963) is a sociological analysis; Norman H. Clark, *Deliver Us From Evil: An Interpretation of American Prohibition* (New York: W.W. Norton, 1976) represents an interdisciplinary approach.

2. Emerson, *Miner*, pp. 433-34.

3. Cherrington, *Prohibition*, p. 14.

4. Ibid., p. 51.

5. Eddy, *Alcohol in History*, p. 279; Murray to Rush, 11 July 1791, Miscellaneous Correspondence of Benjamin Rush, Vol. 22, Item 84, Historical Society of Pennsylvania.

6. *Christian Leader* 66 (24 September 1885): [1].

7. Miscellaneous Correspondence, Vol. 22.

8. Cherrington, *Prohibition*, p. 54.

9. *Universalist Quarterly* 24 n.s. (July 1887): 379-80.

10. The paper, "A Century of Temperance in the Universalist Church," was reproduced in the *Christian Leader* 66 (24 September 1885): [1].

11. *Sketches* 2: 24.

12. *Christian Intelligencer* 8 (22 August 1828): 134.

13. *Trumpet* 10 (6 June 1829): 194.

14. Smith, *Sketches* 1: 217-18.

15. Proceedings, *Trumpet* 11 (3 October 1829): 53.

16. Eddy, *Alcohol in History*, pp. 280-81; *Universalist Quarterly* 1 n.s. (January 1864): 146.

17. See George Faber Clark, *History of the Temperance Reform in Massachusetts, 1813-1883* (Boston: Clarke & Carruth, 1888).

18. Eddy, *Alcohol in History*, p. 284.

19. *Trumpet* 11 (13 March 1830): 146.

20. Ibid., 11 (20 March 1830): 151.

21. Eddy, *Alcohol in History*, p. 285.

22. Records, Maine Convention (1830).

23. Cherrington, *Prohibition*, p. 104.

24. *Christian Intelligencer* 12 (1 February 1833): 18.

25. *Autobiography*, pp. 227-28.

26. Cherrington, *Prohibition*, pp. 59, 83.

27. Eddy, *Universalism in Gloucester*, pp. 76-77.

28. *Autobiography*, pp. 219 ff.

29. *Trumpet* 14 (27 April 1833): 174.

30. Proceedings, *Impartialist* 1 (20 July 1833): 182.

31. *Trumpet* 14 (16 March 1833): 159.

32. Ibid., 15 (3 August 1833): 22.

33. Quoted in the *Impartialist* 1 (17 August 1833): 198.

34. *Christian Intelligencer* 12 (8 March 1833): 38.

35. See, for example, the *Impartialist* 1 (17 August 1833): 198; *Trumpet* 17 (3 October 1835): 58; *Southern Pioneer* 5 (2 January 1836): 172; *Christian Freeman* 2 (11 December 1840): [3].

36. Cherrington, *Prohibition*, p. 105.

37. See, for example, Proceedings, Hudson River Association (New York), *Universalist Union* 4 (26 October 1839): 406.

38. Proceedings, ibid., 2 (26 November 1836): 19.

39. *Trumpet* 23 (25 September 1841): 54.

40. *Southern Pioneer* 2 (22 June 1833): 142.

41. Eddy, "Century of Temperance."

42. *Southern Evangelist* 1 (June 1834): [1-2].

43. Ibid., 1 (October 1834): [1].

44. *Universalist Union* 7 (4 June 1842): 457.

45. *Trumpet* 15 (15 March 1834): 162.

46. Manford, *Twenty-five Years*, pp. 77-78.

47. *Impartialist* 2 (2 August 1834): 183.

48. Proceedings, Vermont Convention (1834) 1: 8; (1836) 1: 17.

49. Proceedings, *Trumpet* 18 (12 November 1836): 83.

50. Ibid., 18 (29 October 1836): 75.

51. Ibid., 18 (5 November 1836): 78.

52. *Evangelical Universalist* 2 (11 December 1839): 256.

53. Proceedings, *Universalist Union* 6 (16 October 1841): 760-61.

54. *Trumpet* 17 (3 October 1835): 58.

55. *Autobiography*, p. 347.

56. Ibid., pp. 250-51.

57. Ibid., pp. 348-49.

58. Ibid., pp. 249-51.

59. For a detailed history of the Boston branch, see David Harrisson, Jr., *A Voice from the Washington Home* (Boston: Redding & Co., 1860).

60. Proceedings, *Universalist Union* 7 (10 September 1842): 677-78.

61. The correspondence was reproduced in the *Trumpet* 24 (28 January 1843): 126; 26 (3 August 1844): 26.

62. Harrisson, *Washingtonian Home*, p. 108.

63. Ibid., pp. 216-17.

64. *Trumpet* 24 (1 April 1843): 163.

65. *Christian Freeman* 11 (10 August 1849): 58.

66. *Universalist Miscellany* 6 (October 1848): 145.

67. Eddy, "Century of Temperance."

68. Extract from Proceedings, *Christian Freeman* 3 (8 October 1841): 90.

69. Eddy, "Century of Temperance."

70. Proceedings, *Universalist Union* 7 (12 November 1842): 820-21.

71. Records, General Convention (1842), p. 480.

72. Extract from Proceedings, *Trumpet* 26 (30 November 1844): 94.

73. *Christian Freeman* 5 (8 March 1844): 177.

74. Ibid., 15 (2 December 1853): 122.

75. Adams, *Memoir of Whittemore*, p. 122.

76. *Trumpet* 24 (29 October, 24 December 1842): 74, 106.

77. Cherrington, *Prohibition*, p. 122.

78. *Christian Freeman* 10 (9 February 1849): 162; 15 (23 September 1853): 82.

79. It appeared in the 1851 (fifteenth) edition of *Hymns for Christian Devotion*, edited by Adams and Chapin.

80. *Christian Freeman* 11 (15 March 1850): 182.

81. *Story of My Life,* p. 377.

82. Ibid., p. 400.

83. *Christian Freeman* 13 (17 November 1851): 114; 14 (9 July 1852): 38.

84. Proceedings, *Christian Freeman* 14 (4 June 1852): 18.

85. Records, General Convention (1853) 2: 114; (1854) 2: 136.

86. Cherrington, *Prohibition,* pp. 142-43.

87. Proceedings, Massachusetts Convention (1866), p. 18.

88. Emerson, *Miner,* p. 450.

89. Ibid., p. 437.

90. A transcription of the speech appeared in the *Universalist* 48 (2 March 1867): [1].

91. Extract from Proceedings, ibid., 50 (19 December 1868): [2].

92. Emerson, *Miner,* p. 124.

93. *Trumpet* 15 (17 May 1834): 185, 186.

94. Ibid., 24 (25 June 1842): 1.

95. *Christian Freeman* 5 (1 March 1844): 174-75.

96. Ibid., 16 (2 March 1855): 174.

97. *Universalist* 50 (14 November 1868): [2].

98. Ibid., 52 (5 February, 6 August 1870): [1], [1].

99. Records, General Convention (1842), pp. 481-82.

100. Eddy, "Century of Temperance."

101. Proceedings, Massachusetts Convention (1868), p. 25; (1869), p. 5.

102. Extract from Proceedings, *Universalist* 51 (15 May 1869): [2].

103. *Christian Leader* 66 (8 January 1885): 5.

104. *Universalist Register,* 1907, p. 105.

105. Ibid., 1905, p. 108.

106. Records, Ohio State Convention (June 1881).

Chapter 20: 'GOD BLESS AND MAKE US GRATEFUL FOR OUR WOMEN!'

1. Quoted in John G. Adams, *Fifty Notable Years,* p. 81.

2. Eleanor Flexner, *Century of Struggle: The Woman's Rights Movement in the United States* (Cambridge: Harvard University Press, 1959; revised edition, 1975), p. 15. This is one of the most scholarly accounts to appear on the eve of the "women's liberation" movement which began in the 1960s. The extensive bibliographical essay in the first edition was not included in the revised edition, but was supplemented by reference to major works published since 1959.

3. Quoted in Eddy, "Mrs. Judith Murray," *Universalist Quarterly* 18 n.s. (April 1881): 205; see also her collected works, the *Gleaner* (1798), especially 1: 167-68; 3: 196 ff.

4. Flexner, *Century of Struggle,* p. 17.

5. *Daughters of America; or, Women of the Century* (Boston: B.B. Russell, 1883). Published originally in 1876 in recognition of the centennial of American independence, it was revised and extended in 1882 and was arranged topically, according to the activity or profession with which each woman was primarily associated. Over twenty-five Universalist women were included, with entries ranging from mere mention of a name to several pages.

6. *Our Woman Workers* (Chicago: *Star and Covenant* Office).

7. The 1897 edition was republished in 1972 in two volumes under the title *American Women: A Comprehensive*

Encyclopedia (New York: Somerset Publishers) and in 1974 as *American Women: 1500 Biographies with Over 1400 Portraits* (Detroit, Michigan: Gale Research Co.). John G. Adams devoted one brief chapter to "The Universalist Church and its Women" (pp. 79-83) in his *Fifty Notable Years;* in the last of nine chapters devoted to biographical sketches of deceased ministers, he appended sketches of three women ministers (Elvira J. Powers, Fanny Upham Roberts, and Prudy LeClerc Haskell). For brief and appreciative sketches of fifteen Universalist women, arranged in chronological order, see Laura S. Hersey, *"By Their Works"—Biographical Sketches of Universalist Women* (Boston: The Association of Universalist Women, 1954). For biographical sketches of ordained Universalist women ministers deceased at the date of publication, see Catherine F. Hitchings, "Universalist and Unitarian Women Ministers," *Journal of the Universalist Historical Society* 10 (1975). This is an invaluable reference work and has been drawn upon by the present author both for information and for verification of data from other sources.

8. The law was reproduced in the *Universalist Union* 7 (22 October 1842): 772.

9. Eddy, *Universalism in Gloucester,* p. 50.

10. Smith, *Sketches* 2: 9-11.

11. Records, Maine Convention (1836).

12. Circular, *Trumpet* 15 (14 December 1833): 100.

13. *Memoranda,* p. 214.

14. Ibid., pp. 59-60.

15. *Trumpet* 18 (10 September 1836): 46.

16. MacDonald, *Rebellion in the Mountains,* p. 24; Proceedings, Vermont Convention (1855) 1: 95.

17. Extract from Proceedings, *Christian Freeman* 18 (25 July 1856): 50.

18. *Trumpet* 19 (28 April 1838): 177.

19. Ibid., 17 (31 October 1835): 74.

20. Record Book, Historical Society of Pennsylvania.

21. Proceedings, *Trumpet* 28 (5 June 1847): 203.

22. Proceedings, *Universalist Union* 1 (22 October 1836): 397.

23. *Impartialist* 1 (16 February, 16 March 1833): 94, 110-11.

24. Prospectus, *Universalist* 2 (2 November 1833): 184.

25. *Christian Intelligencer* 12 (15 March 1833): 42.

26. *Southern Pioneer* 5 (7 November 1835): 108-109.

27. Manford, *Twenty-five Years,* p. 282.

28. Ibid., pp. 282-83.

29. *Universalist Miscellany* 1 (August-November 1843).

30. *Trumpet* 32 (21 December 1850): 111.

31. *Prisoners' Friend* 2 n.s. (July 1850): 514-16.

32. Ibid., 3 n.s. (December 1850, April 1851): 185-86, 344.

33. Ibid., 3 n.s. (April 1851): 359 ff.

34. Ibid., pp. 365-66.

35. *Ladies' Repository* 19 (January 1851): 256-59.

36. "Woman and her Work," ibid., 26 (June 1858): 474-75.

37. *Christian Freeman* 1 (31 May 1839): 18.

38. Ibid., 12 (22 November, 27 December 1850): 118, 137, 138.

39. Ibid., 21 (18 November 1859): 114.

40. *Trumpet* 32 (9 November 1850): 86.

41. Ibid., 32 (29 March 1851): 166.

42. *Prisoners' Friend* 5 (May 1853): 387-98.

43. *Christian Freeman* 21 (12 October 1859): 93.

44. Proceedings, ibid., 14 (12 July 1852): 34.

45. Proceedings, General Convention (1863), p. 8.

46. *Christian Freeman* 15 (21 October 1853): 98.

47. Livermore, *Story of My Life,* p. 608.

48. Proceedings, *Christian Freeman* 15 (17 June 1853): 26; 16 (14 July 1854): 42; 17 (22 June 1855): 30.

49. Ibid., 18 (5 September 1856): 74.

50. Ibid., 16 (14 July 1854): 42.

51. Ibid., 17 (1 February 1856): 158.

52. Ibid., 18 (10 April 1857): 197.

53. *Trumpet* 36 (9 September 1854): 54.

54. Livermore, *Story of My Life,* p. 608.

55. *Christian Freeman* 16 (4 August 1854): 53.

56. Report, Committee on Education, General Convention (1863), p. 40.

57. *Ladies' Repository* 44 (December 1870): 472.

58. *Universalist* 52 (4 March 1871): [1].

59. J.P. Weston to A.A. Miner, 10 June 1873; Secretary's File B, Trustee Records, Tufts College.

60. *Ladies' Repository* 48 (August 1872): 153.

61. Ibid., 46 (October 1871): 232-33.

62. Proceedings, *Universalist* 55 (1 November 1873): [2].

63. Proceedings, ibid., 56 (31 October 1874): [2].

64. Boston: James R. Osgood & Co., 1873.

65. *Repository* 51 (February 1874): 149-51.

66. Julia Ward Howe (ed.), *Sex and Education: A Reply to Dr. E.H. Clarke's "Sex in Education"* (Boston: Roberts Brothers, 1874).

67. Report from Lombard University, Howe, *Sex and Education,* pp. 201-202.

68. *Repository* 51 (April 1874): 310.

69. Howe, *Sex and Education,* pp. 197-99.

70. *Universalist* 48 (31 August 1867): [2].

71. Howe, *Sex and Education,* p. 198.

72. *Repository* 51 (February 1874): 81-86.

73. *Evangelical Universalist* 1 (8 September 1838): 7. Statistical summaries did not begin to appear in the *Register* until 1840.

74. This report was made by Phebe A. Hanaford, one of the four, in the *Ladies' Repository* 40 (November 1868): 388, 392-93.

75. *Universalist* 52 (20 August 1870): [2].

76. *Fifty Notable Years,* p. 254.

77. Hitchings, "Universalist Ministers," p. 6.

78. Adams, *Fifty Notable Years,* p. 254 n.; Hanaford, *Daughters of America,* p. 425.

79. Stacy, *Memoirs,* p. 223.

80. Smith, *Sketches* 1: 32.

81. Stacy, *Memoirs,* pp. 227-28.

82. Hanson, *Our Woman Workers,* p. 23.

83. *Trumpet* 34 (27 November 1852): 97.

84. *Christian Freeman* 19 (12 June 1857): 27.

85. Hanson, *Our Woman Workers,* p. 426.

86. *Christian Freeman* 20 (16 July 1858): 42.

87. Ibid., 20 (28 May 1858): 14.

88. Ibid., 20 (10 September 1858): 74.

89. *Trumpet* 40 (30 October 1858): 86.

90. *Christian Freeman* 19 (12 June 1857): 27.

91. *Trumpet* 38 (18 April 1857): 182.

92. *Trumpet* 40 (30 October 1858): 86.

93. Ibid., 40 (11 December 1858): 110.

94. Ibid., 40 (4 December 1858): 106. Whittemore was here referring to the costume introduced by Elizabeth Smith Miller and popularized briefly by Amelia Jenks Bloomer in the nineteenth century.

95. Ibid., 40 (1 January 1859): 122.

96. Quoted in Adams, *Memoir of Whittemore,* p. 323.

97. *Trumpet* 40 (21 August 1858): 46.

98. Ibid., 40 (25 September 1858): 65.

99. *Universalist Register,* 1861, pp. 41, 43.

100. *Christian Freeman* 20 (30 July 1858): 50.

101. Proceedings, General Convention (1858), pp. 36, 39.

102. *Christian Freeman* 20 (8 April 1859): 195.

103. *Trumpet* 41 (21 April 1860): 186; *Universalist Register,* 1861, p. 38.

104. *Universalist Register,* 1867, p. 34.

105. Hanson, *Our Woman Workers,* p. 426.

106. *Trumpet* 41 (2 July, 6 August, 10 September 1859): 18, 37, 56.

107. *Universalist Register,* 1872, pp. 156-57. In E.R. Hanson, *Our Woman Workers,* she was identified as "Elmina" Powers (p. 394) and listed as "Ermina" Powers in the index (p. 500).

108. See her autobiography, *Glances and Glimpses; or, Fifty Years Social, including Twenty Years' Professional Life* (Boston: John P. Jewett & Co., 1856).

109. *Trumpet* 40 (9 April 1859): 178.

110. Address of Mary A. Livermore, *Centennial,* p. 55.

111. *Trumpet* 41 (17 September 1859): 62.

112. Hanaford, *Daughters of America,* pp. 536-37.

113. *Universalist* 50 (29 August 1868): [3].

114. *Story of My Life,* p. 407.

115. Hitchings, "Universalist Ministers," p. 30. Unless otherwise indicated, all biographical data for ordained Universalist women ministers referred to in the present study were derived from this source. For Brown, see also the entire issue of the *Annual Journal of the Universalist Historical Society* 4 (1963).

116. For a biographical sketch, see Hitchings, "Universalist Ministers," pp. 155-56.

117. *Christian Freeman* 16 (24 November 1854): 118.

118. Hanson, *Our Woman Workers,* p. 428.

119. *Universalist* 51 (1 May 1869): [3].

120. Ibid., 51 (12 June 1869): [3].

121. *Annual Journal of the Universalist Historical Society,* p. 33.

122. *Universalist* 46 (16 July 1864): [2].

123. Ibid., 46 (23 September 1865): [2].

124. Hanaford, *Daughters of America,* p. 426.

125. Hanson, *Our Woman Workers,* p. 431.

126. *Universalist Register,* 1906, pp. 102-103.

127. Hanaford, *Daughters of America,* p. 427.

128. For an account of the ordination and installation, see the *Ladies' Repository* 39 (April 1868): 308.

129. Hanson, *Our Woman Workers,* p. 453.

130. *Universalist* 48 (26 January 1867): [3].

131. *Daughters of America,* pp. 428-29.

132. The two ordained by 1870 in addition to those mentioned were Prudy LeClerc Haskell (1869) and Marianna Thompson Folsom (1870).

133. For her activities as a missionary, see the second volume of this study.

134. *Repository* 51 (February 1874): 128.

135. *Universalist* 50 (21 November 1868): [3].

136. Ibid., 50 (26 December 1868): [2-3].

137. The individual arguing in favor of women in the ministry was Daniel P. Livermore, a Universalist clergyman who later wrote extensively in favor of women's suffrage. His wife, Mary A. Livermore, was one of the best known denominational leaders and social reformers in the nineteenth century.

138. *Universalist* 51 (26 March 1870): [2].

139. Ibid., 52 (23 July 1870): [2].

140. Ibid., 52 (9 July 1870): [1].

141. *Twenty-five Years,* p. 233.

142. *Woman's Record; or, Sketches of all Distinguished Women, from "the beginning" till A.D. 1850* (New York: Harper & Bros.); in the second edition, revised and updated, published in 1860, she changed the part of the title referring to "the beginning" to "the Creation" and carried her coverage up to 1854.

143. *Fifty Notable Years,* pp. 79 ff.

144. Hanaford, *Daughters of America,* p. 238.

145. Ibid., pp. 670-71.

146. *Universalist* 51 (8 May 1869): [2].

147. While preaching in New Jersey in the 1870s her salary was $2,500, among the more substantial stipends then being paid.

148. *Ladies' Repository* 38 (October 1867): 308.

149. *Universalist* 59 (29 December 1877): [2].

150. *Ladies' Repository* 40 (November 1868): 345 n.

151. Ibid., 38 (October 1867): 308.

152. Hale, *Woman's Record,* p. 886.

153. Eddy, *Sawyer,* p. 307.

154. *Memoir and Writings of Mrs. Julia H. Scott* (Boston: Abel Tompkins).

155. See *Poetry and Prose, by Mrs. Charlotte A. Jerauld, with a Memoir by Henry Bacon* (Boston: Abel Tompkins, 1860).

156. *Universalist Miscellany* 1 (February 1844): 283; (July 1844): 40.

157. See Hanson, *Our Woman Workers,* pp. 80-105, for glowing biographies of each; see also *Selections from the Writings of Mrs. Mayo, with a Memoir (and portrait), by her Husband* (Boston: Abel Tompkins, 1849).

158. Proceedings, General Convention (1848) 2: 72.

159. Eddy, *Sawyer,* pp. 294-95, 298 ff.

160. Ibid., p. 295.

161. *Woman's Record,* p. 836.

162. For examples of Mrs. Sawyer's prose and poetry, see Eddy, *Sawyer,*

pp. 325 ff; Hanson, *Our Woman Workers,* pp. 150-54.

163. *Ladies' Repository* 38 (July 1867): 4.

164. *Twenty-five Years,* pp. 76-77. See Mary Clemner Ames, *A Memorial of Alice and Phoebe Cary, with some of their Later Poems* (New York: Hurd & Houghton, 1873, 1874); and *Ladies' Repository* 46 (July, September 1871): 1-9, 228-30.

165. Hale, *Woman's Record,* p. 827. Mrs. Dodd was mentioned in neither Mrs. Hanaford's *Daughters of America* nor Mrs. Hanson's *Our Woman Workers.*

166. Hartford, Conn.: Case, Tiffany and Burnham, 1844; Boston: [n.p.], 1846.

167. Adams, *Fifty Notable Years,* p. 80.

168. Hanson, *Our Woman Workers,* p. 120.

169. Hitchings, "Universalist Women," pp. 32-33.

170. *Ladies' Repository* 38 (October 1867): 308.

171. *Universalist* 50 (28 November 1868): [2].

172. Hanaford, *Daughters of America,* pp. 407-408.

173. *Gospel Peace* .... (New Haven, Conn.: Stafford Company, 1871).

174. *Universalist* 53 (11 November 1871): [2].

175. Ibid., (18 November 1871): [2].

176. *Repository* 51 (February 1874): 128-30.

177. Unless otherwise indicated all biographical data were derived from her autobiography, *The Story of My Life* (1897), previously cited. See also: Edward T. James and others (eds.), *Notable American Women, 1607-1950* (Cambridge: Belknap Press of the Harvard University Press, 1971) 2: 410-13; Julia Ward Howe (ed.), *Representative Women of New England* (Boston: New England Historical Publishing Co., 1904), pp. 430-32; L.P. Brockett & Mary C. Vaughn, *Woman's Work in the Civil War* (Philadelphia: Zeigler, McCurdy & Co., 1867), pp. 577-89; Hanson, *Our Woman Workers,* pp. 120-44; and the biographical sketch by J.S. Dennis in the *Ladies' Repository* 39 (January 1868): 1-7.

178. Hartford, Conn.: A.D. Worthington & Co.

179. "Personal Reminiscences of President Lincoln," *Ladies' Repository* 39 (January 1868): 40-52.

180. Hanson, *Our Woman Workers,* p. 128.

181. *Ladies' Repository* 34 (September 1865): 171-72.

182. *Universalist* 52 (4 June 1870): [2].

183. Ibid., 51 (16 April 1870): [2].

184. Ibid., 52 (25 June 1870): [1].

185. *Woman Suffrage defended by irrefutable arguments, and all objections to Woman's Enfranchisement carefully examined and completely answered* (Boston: Lee & Shepard, 1885); *Arguments against Woman Suffrage by H.M. Dexter, D.D. carefully examined and completely answered* (Boston: Cupples, Upham & Co., 1886).

186. *Ladies' Repository* 45 (January 1871): 72-73.

187. *Universalist* 50 (28 November 1868): [2].

188. Ibid., 52 (30 July 1870): [1].

189. Ibid., 55 (26 July 1873): [2].

190. Flexner, *Century of Struggle,* pp. 156-57.

191. *Universalist* 55 (4 October 1873): [2].

192. She furnished the *Universalist* with an advance copy which was published in that paper (55 (20 December

1873): [1]).

193. Attention to the distortion of Mrs. Livermore's language was called by the writer of an editorial in the *Ladies' Repository* 48 (July 1872): 71.

194. Hanson, *Our Woman Workers*, p. 131; for some insight into how she went about raising money, see the address which she delivered at the General Convention in Providence, R.I., reproduced in the *Ladies' Repository* 39 (November 1868): 388-91.

195. "Preface," *Story of My Life*, p. xi.

Chapter 21: "WE ARE ALL BRETHREN": UNIVERSALISTS AND THE ABOLITION OF SLAVERY

1. *Universalist Miscellany* 3 (February 1846): 319.

2. For the broad context and events of the struggle over the abolition of slavery, about which a vast and sometimes contradictory literature exists, (and in which little or no mention is made of the role of the Universalists), see Louis Filler, *The Crusade Against Slavery, 1830-1860* (New York: Harper & Bros., 1960); Dwight Lowell Dumond, *Antislavery: The Crusade for Freedom in America* (Ann Arbor: University of Michigan Press, 1961; Carleton Mabee, *Black Freedom: The Nonviolent Abolitionists from 1830 through the Civil War* (New York: Macmillan, 1970).

3. Timothy L. Smith, *Revivalism and Social Reform in Mid-Nineteenth Century America* (Nashville, Tenn.: Abingdon Press, 1957), p. 190.

4. For a provocative discussion of this aspect of the subject, see Robert W. Fogel and Stanley L. Engerman, *Time on the Cross.* 2 vols. (Boston: Little, Brown, 1974), especially Vol. 1, *The Economics of American Negro Slavery;* for a rebuttal, see Paul A. David and others, *Reckoning with Slavery* (New York: Oxford University Press, 1976).

5. See, for example, the *Christian Freeman* 2 (23 October 1840): 100; 3 (7 January 1842): 141.

6. See Aileen S. Kraditor, *Means and Ends in American Abolitionism: Garrison and his Critics on Strategy and Tactics, 1834-1850* (New York: Pantheon Books, 1969).

7. *Universalist Miscellany* 2 (August 1844): 79-80.

8. *Universalist Union* 7 (11 June 1842): 472.

9. *Christian Freeman* 2 (9 October 1840): 93.

10. For a reprint, see *The Selected Writings of Benjamin Rush,* edited by Dagobert D. Runes (New York: Philosophical Library, 1947); excerpts are included in Cassara, *Universalism in America: A Documentary History*, pp. 175-80.

11. Dumond, *Antislavery,* pp. 20, 46-47.

12. Preface, *The Universal Restoration* (Philadelphia, 1843; 1st ed., 1792).

13. *History of the Rise, Progress, & Accomplishment of the Abolition of the African Slave-Trade, by the British Parliament.* 2 vols. (London: Longman, Hurst, Rees, and Orme, 1808) 1: 186-87, 191. The first American edition was also published in 1808 (Philadelphia: James P. Parke). Numerous subsequent editions, with variant titles, were published, including a one-volume abridgement in 1816 and another two-volume edition in 1830.

14. Ibid., p. 187 n.

15. *Christian Freeman* 2 (23 April 1841): 1-3.

16. *Practical Christian* 2 (12 June 1841): 10-11.

17. Ballou, *Autobiography,* p. 228.

18. Eddy, *Universalism in Gloucester,* p. 188.

19. Quoted in ibid., p. 52.

20. Whittemore, *Modern History,* p. 382.

21. Thomas, *Century of Universalism,* p. 64 n.

22. Carl Seaburg, "Universalism in the Early *Centinel,*" unpublished manuscript, [n.d.], p. 26.

23. John Hope Franklin, *From Slavery to Freedom: A History of Negro Americans.* 3d ed. (New York: Knopf, 1967), p. 164.

24. *Trumpet* 14 (6 April 1833): 163; *William Lloyd Garrison, 1805-1879: The Story of his Life told by his Children.* 4 vols. (New York: Century Co., 1885) 1: 419, 425.

25. *Second Annual Report of the Board of Managers of the New-England Anti-Slavery Society* (Boston: Garrison & Knapp, 1834), p. 11.

26. He was erroneously listed in the *Trumpet* as president of the American Anti-Slavery Society, which was organized in Philadelphia later the same year.

27. *Universalist Magazine* 5 (29 May 1824): 196.

28. See, for example, *Universalist Magazine* 9 (12 April 1828): 172.

29. *Impartialist* 1 (27 July 1833): 186.

30. *Trumpet* 15 (5 April 1834): 163.

31. Dumond, *Antislavery,* p. 328.

32. *Trumpet* 13 (19 November 1831): 82.

33. Ibid., 18 (15 October 1836): 67.

34. Ibid., 21 (29 June 1839): 8.

35. *Impartialist* 1 (11 May 1833): 141.

36. See Early Lee Fox, *The American Colonization Society, 1817-1840* (Baltimore: The Johns Hopkins Press, 1919).

37. *Universalist* 1 (30 March 1833): 365.

38. *Impartialist* 1 (11 May 1833): 141.

39. Ibid., 1 (19 August 1833): 197.

40. *Christian Freeman* 16 (26 January 1855): 154.

41. Ibid., 16 (22 December 1854).

42. Ibid., 22 (18 January 1861): 150.

43. Proceedings, General Convention (1861), p. 9.

44. Filler, *Crusade Against Slavery,* p. 67.

45. Ibid., pp. 66-67.

46. Proceedings and Constitution, American Abolition Society, *Christian Freeman* 1 (14 June 1839): 28.

47. Dumond, *Antislavery,* p. 175.

48. Mabee, *Black Freedom,* p. 231.

49. Ibid., p. 222.

50. *Christian Freeman* 5 (26 April 1844): 206.

51. Records, Maine Convention (1836).

52. Proceedings, Second Universalist Anti-Slavery Convention (1841), *Christian Freeman* 3 (29 October 1841): 101.

53. Extract from Proceedings, ibid., 3 (29 October 1841): 102.

54. *Trumpet* 18 (12 November 1836): 83.

55. Ibid., 19 (16 June 1838): 206.

56. Ibid., 23 (23 October 1841): 71.

57. Ibid., 26 (13 July, 19 October 1844): 14, 71.

58. *Christian Freeman* 3 (4, 11 June 1841): 18, 22.

59. *Universalist and Ladies' Repository* 7 (July 1838): 78.

60. Extract from Proceedings, *Trumpet* 20 (23 June 1838): 4.

61. Proceedings, ibid., 21 (22 June 1839): 4.

62. Proceedings, ibid., 21 (20 June 1840): 206.

63. *Christian Freeman* 2 (12 June 1840): 26.

64. Ibid., 4 (6 January 1843): 142.

65. Ibid., 1 (1 November 1839): 106.

66. Ibid., 1 (8 November 1839): 110.

67. Ibid., 5 (12 May 1843): 5. The account was published originally in an 1823 issue of the *Gospel Advocate* (then published in Buffalo, N.Y.) and reprinted the same year in the *Religious Inquirer* (Hartford, Conn.).

68. *Christian Freeman* 2 (28 August 1840): 70.

69. Proceedings, ibid., 1 (28 February 1840): 175.

70. Proceedings, ibid., 2 (28 August 1840): 70.

71. Ibid., 2 (11 September 1840): 78-79.

72. Ibid., 2 (25 September 1840): 86.

73. Ibid., 3 (25 June 1841): 29.

74. Ibid., 2 (25 September 1840): 86.

75. Ibid., 4 (25 November 1842): 118.

76. Ibid., 3 (21 May 1841): 10.

77. Ibid., 3 (4 June 1841): 18.

78. Proceedings, ibid., 3 (22 October 1841): 99.

79. Ibid., 1 (21 February 1840): 170.

80. Ibid., 2 (23 October 1840): 100.

81. Proceedings, First Universalist Anti-Slavery Convention, ibid., 2 (4, 11, 18 December 1840): 126-27, 129-31, 134-35. The proceedings were also published as a forty-six page pamphlet.

82. *Christian Freeman* 1 (17 May 1839): 10.

83. Proceedings, ibid., 3 (29 October, 5 November 1841): 101, 105.

84. *Southern Universalist,* quoted in ibid., 3 (10 October 1841): 86.

85. See Benjamin Quarles, *Frederick Douglass* (Washington, D.C.: Associated Publishers, 1948) and the same author's *Black Abolitionists* (New York: Oxford University Press, 1969).

86. *Narrative of the Life of Frederick Douglass, an American Slave, written by Himself,* edited by Benjamin Quarles (Cambridge: Belknap Press of Harvard University Press, 1960), pp. 85-86, 124.

87. *Christian Freeman* 3 (12 November 1841): 110.

88. *Southern Evangelist* 2 (15 September 1835): [3].

89. Ibid., 2 (16 November 1835): [3].

90. *Evangelical Universalist* 1 (30 June 1838): 7; 9 June 1838): 7.

91. *Universalist Union* 2 (15 April 1837): 183.

92. *Evangelical Universalist* 1 (15 September 1838): 6-7.

93. Quoted in *Christian Freeman* 1 (21 June 1839): 30.

94. *Evangelical Universalist* 2 (19 June 1839): 62.

95. Ibid., 2 (2 October 1839): 182.

96. *Christian Freeman* 1 (25 October 1839): 102.

97. *Trumpet* 25 (13 July 1843): 14.

98. *Christian Freeman* 4 (10 June 1842): 22.

99. *Evangelical Universalist* 2 (18 December 1839): 259.

100. Proceedings, *Trumpet* 27 (13 September 1845): 51.

101. *Evangelical Universalist* 2 (4 December 1839): 242.

102. *Christian Freeman* 3 (13 August 1841): 58.

103. *Trumpet* 24 (11 February 1843): 134.

104. *Christian Freeman* 4 (17 February 1843): 166.

105. *Trumpet* 24 (25 March 1843): 159.

106. *Christian Freeman* 4 (24 March 1843): 186.

107. *Gospel Messenger,* quoted in ibid., 7 (27 February 1846): 174.

108. *Christian Freeman* 16 (28 February 1855): 170.

109. *Universalist* 46 (20 July 1864): [2].

110. *Christian Freeman* 16 (23 March 1855): 186.

111. Ibid., 16 (30 March 1855): 190.

112. Quoted in ibid., 16 (6 April 1855): 194.

113. Ibid., 17 (6 July 1855): 38.

114. Ibid., 17 (25 January 1856): 154.

115. Ibid., 19 (22 January 1858): 154.

116. *Universalist Herald,* cited in ibid., 23 (10 May 1861): 6.

117. Clayton, *Forty-Seven Years in the Universalist Ministry,* pp. 220-21.

118. *Southern Pioneer* 5 (12 September 1835): 47.

119. Ibid., 5 (29 August 1835): 30.

120. *Christian Freeman* 5 (19 January 1844): 149-50.

121. Ibid., 5 (1 March 1844): 173-74.

122. *Memoranda,* p. 348.

123. *Universalist Union* 7 (28 May 1842): 434.

124. *Memoranda,* p. 355.

125. Ibid., p. 353.

126. *Christian Freeman* 15 (2 September 1853): 70.

127. *Memoranda,* p. 318.

128. *Universalist Union* 2 (15 July 1837): 284.

129. *Memoranda,* pp. 218-19.

130. *Universalist Union* 4 (27 April 1839): 198.

131. *Trumpet* 34 (27 November 1852): 98.

132. *Universalist Miscellany* 10 (25 January, 15 March, 1845): 163-66, 273-77.

133. *Universalist Herald* 12 (5 February 1858); 143.

134. *Christian Freeman* 16 (16 March 1855): 182.

135. *Philomath Encyclopedia* 6 (August 1843): 52-53.

136. Ibid., 6 (May 1844): 433.

137. Ibid., 6 (December 1843): 213.

138. Interviews by the author with a number of Universalists in Alabama, Georgia, and Mississippi in the winter of 1970 confirmed the fact that many of their immediate ancestors had been slaveholders.

139. *Christian Freeman* 12 (7 June 1850): 22.

140. Ibid., 10 (16 February 1849): 166.

141. *The Story of My Life or the Sunshine and Shadow of Seventy Years* (Hartford, Conn.: A.D. Worthington & Co., 1897), Chapters 9-21 (pp. 143-365).

Chapter 22: BRETHREN ONCE MORE

1. Proceedings, *Christian Freeman* 4 (2 December 1842): 121-22.

2. See William G. Hawkins, *Lunsford Lane; or, Another Helper from North Carolina* (Boston: Crosby & Nichols, 1863), based on a narrative prepared by Lane in 1842 and the author's acquaintance with Lane; see also Quarles, *Black Abolitionists.*

3. Address delivered before the Universalist Anti-Slavery Convention, 13 December 1841; *Christian Freeman* 3 (26 November 1841): 117-18.

4. *Trumpet* 24 (12 November 1842): 82.

5. *Christian Freeman* 4 (11 November 1842): 108.

6. Proceedings, ibid., 4 (27 January 1843): 155.

7. Extract from Proceedings, *Trumpet* 24 (6 May 1843): 183.

8. Extract from Proceedings, *Christian Freeman* 4 (30 September 1842): 86.

9. Proceedings, Vermont Convention (1842) 1: 38-39.

10. Proceedings, ibid., (1838) 1: 24-25.

11. *Christian Freeman* 4 (16 December 1842): 129.

12. Ibid., 5 (16 June 1843): 27.

13. Proceedings, ibid., 5 (23 June 1843): 31.

14. Ibid., 5 (14 July 1843): 41.

15. Ibid., 4 (30 September 1842): 86.

16. Records, General Convention (1843), pp. 501-502.

17. The resolutions are reproduced in Cassara (ed.), *Universalism in America*, pp. 189-90.

18. *Christian Freeman* 5 (6 October 1843): 90.

19. Ibid., 5 (13 October 1843): 94.

20. Ibid., 5 (27 October 1843): 101.

21. See Mabee, *Black Freedom*, Chapter 14, for the effect of the non-violent abolitionist agitation on most of the churches; the Universalists are not discussed.

22. *Universalist Miscellany* 3 (July 1845): 43-44.

23. *Christian Freeman* 5 (10 November 1843): 110.

24. Proceedings, General Convention (1865), p. 43.

25. Proceedings, *Christian Freeman* 6 (26 July 1844): 50.

26. *Universalist Union* 9 (9 December 1843): 54.

27. Proceedings, *Trumpet* 26 (22 June 1844): 4.

28. *Christian Freeman* 6 (21 June 1844): 29.

29. Proceedings, *Trumpet* 26 (7 September 1844): 47.

30. Quoted in *Christian Freeman* 5 (9 February 1844): 161.

31. Ibid., 7 (16 May 1845): 9.

32. The proceedings of this *ad hoc* meeting were kept separate from the official minutes, and were reported in detail in the *Trumpet* 27 (27 September 1845): 58-59; and the *Christian Freeman* 7 (26 September, 3 October 1845): 85-86, 90.

33. *Christian Freeman* 7 (13 February 1846): 164.

34. Ibid., 7 (9 January 1846): 145.

35. Ibid., 7 (17 April 1846): 201-202.

36. *Trumpet* 27 (7 March 1846): 150.

37. Ibid., 27 (17 January 1846): 124.

38. Ibid., 27 (21 February 1846): 143.

39. Ibid., 27 (7 February 1846): 134.

40. Ibid., 27 (28 February 1846): 145.

41. Ibid., 27 (28 February 1846): 146.

42. Quoted by Bacon in ibid.

43. Ibid., 27 (21 February 1846): 143.

44. *Christian Freeman* 8 (5 June 1846): 21.

45. *Philomath Encyclopedia* 7 (October 1845): 366-74.

46. *Narrative of William Wells Brown, a Fugitive Slave,* was published in Boston in 1847; his novel, *Clotel; or the President's Daughter,* appeared in 1853; *Christian Freeman* 11 (3 August 1849): 54.

47. *Prisoners' Friend* 4 (March 1852): 324-26.

48. *Christian Freeman* 5 (26 April 1844): 206.

49. *Universalist Quarterly* 5 (July 1848): 321 ff.

50. Proceedings, *Trumpet* 32 (8 June 1850): 206.

51. *Christian Freeman* 13 (4 July 1851): 38.

52. Ibid., 12 (28 June 1850): 33.

53. *Universalist Quarterly* 8 (January 1851): 56-68.

54. *Prisoners' Friend* 4 (March 1852): 326.

55. *Trumpet* 32 (19 October 1850): 74.

56. Proceedings, ibid., 32 (26 October 1850): 79.

57. Ibid., 32 (18 January 1851): 126.

58. Proceedings, *Christian Freeman* 12 (15 November 1850): 114.

59. Ibid., 12 (11 October 1850): 93.

60. *Universalist Quarterly* 8 (April 1851): 169-85.

61. Proceedings, *Christian Freeman* 13 (20 June 1851): 30.

62. Proceedings, ibid., 15 (17 June 1853): 26.

63. Ibid., 14 (17 September 1852): 79; Records, Vermont Convention (1851) 1: 73.

64. *Christian Freeman* 15 (24 June 1853): 30.

65. Ibid., 16 (16 June 1854): 26.

66. Ibid., 16 (2 June 1854): 18.

67. *Trumpet* 36 (10 June 1854): 3.

68. Ibid., 36 (24 June, 1 July 1854): 10, 12; 13, 14.

69. Ibid., 36 (8 July 1854): 18.

70. For the origin of the party, including eyewitness accounts and the part played by Washburn, see Henry Wilson, *History of the Rise and Fall of the Slave Power in America.* 3 vols. Fifth edition. (Boston: Houghton Mifflin, 1884) 2: 406-18.

71. See his speech of 7 April 1854, *Congressional Globe, Containing the Debates and Proceedings, 1833-1873.* 109 vols. (Washington, D.C.: Blair and Rives and others, editors and publishers, 1834-1873) 31: 492-500; for other examples of Washburn's active career as a United States Congressman, see his speech of 4 January 1854 urging annexation of the Sandwich Islands; his address on the contested election in Kansas, delivered 14 March 1856; and his discussion of the Republican Party (10 January 1859). All of these speeches were published separately in pamphlet form as well as in the *Congressional Globe.* Washburn's papers, consisting of 300 items and comprising for the most part correspondence concerned with public issues, are located in the Manuscript Division of the Library of Congress, and cover the years between 1838 and 1908.

72. *Universalist Quarterly* 11 (July 1854): 269-70.

73. For additional biographical information, see *In Memoriam: Israel Washburn, Jr.* (Portland, Me.: Privately printed, 1884).

74. *Trumpet* 34 (4 December 1852): 102.

75. Extract from Proceedings, ibid., 36 (1 July 1854): 13.

76. Proceedings, ibid., 36 (24 June 1854): 11.

77. Proceedings, *Christian Freeman* 16 (16 June 1854): 26.

78. Ibid., 16 (23 June 1854): 31.

79. Records, General Convention (1854) 2: 136.

80. Extract from Proceedings, *Christian Freeman* 16 (30 June 1854): 34.

81. Extract from Proceedings, ibid., 18 (3 October 1856): 90.

82. Ibid., 18 (26 December 1856): 138.

83. Proceedings, *Trumpet* 32 (26 October 1850): 79.

84. Quoted in ibid., 32 (4 January 1851): 118.

85. *Universalist Herald* 11 (17 July 1857): 38.

86. Ibid., 15 (1 June 1867): 22.

87. Quoted in *Christian Freeman* 16 (8 December 1854): 126.

88. *Gospel Herald,* quoted in the *Trumpet* 36 (9 December 1854): 105.

89. Records, Maine Convention (1855).

90. Extract from Proceedings, *Christian Freeman* 18 (26 December 1856): 138.

91. Ibid., 16 (1 September 1854): 69.

92. Mary A. Livermore, *Story of My Life,* pp. 454-56.

93. Proceedings, *Christian Freeman* 18 (6 June 1856): 22.

94. Ibid., 18 (11 July 1856): 42.

95. Ibid., 18 (13, 20 June 1856): 26, 30.

96. Ibid., 18 (4 July 1856): 38.

97. Ibid., 18 (6 June 1856): 23.

98. Quoted in Adams, *Memoir of Whittemore,* p. 282.

99. Proceedings, *Christian Freeman* 19 (5, 19 June, 10 July 1857): 22, 31, 42.

100. Proceedings, ibid., 20 (4 June 1858): 18.

101. Ibid., 21 (16 December 1859): 180.

102. Ibid., 22 (28 December 1860): 138.

103. Ibid., 15 (24 June 1853): 29-30.

104. Proceedings, *Universalist* 46 (9 July 1864): [2].

105. Ibid., 46 (20 July 1864): [2].

106. *Universalist Herald* 14 (30 November 1860): 522.

107. *Universalist Register,* 1863, p. 57.

108. Records, Maine Convention (1861).

109. Butler, "Universalism in Pennsylvania," [n.p.].

110. Proceedings, General Convention (1861), pp. 7-8.

111. Ibid., (1863), p. 6.

112. *Fifty Notable Years,* p. 70.

113. *Christian Freeman* 7 (20 March 1846): 186.

114. Proceedings, Vermont State Convention (1862, 1864) 1: 134, 146; Records, Maine Convention (1862).

115. Appendix, Proceedings, General Convention (1865), p. 45.

116. For details of the riot, see J.G. Randall and David Donald, *The Civil War and Reconstruction.* 2nd ed. (Boston: D.C. Heath, 1961), pp. 195-96.

117. Appendix, Proceedings, General Convention (1865), p. 54.

118. Ibid., pp. 48-49, 51-52.

119. *Christian Freeman* 22 (1 March 1861): 174; 23 (17 May 1861): 10.

120. Appendix, Proceedings, General Convention (1865), p. 54.

121. Ibid., p. 53.

122. Proceedings, Massachusetts Convention (1864), pp. 11-13.

123. *The Story of My Life,* p. 472; for a detailed account of her experiences and activities, and of the contribution of others to "the womanly side of the war," see *My Story of the War,* published in 1888.

124. There is considerable literature both by and about Clara Barton; see, for example, Ishbel Ross, *Angel of the Battlefield* (New York: Harper & Bros., 1956); Blanche C. Williams, *Clara Barton* (Philadelphia: Lippincott, 1941): and Robert S. Wolley, "Clara Barton: A Biographical Sketch of Compulsion," *Annual Journal of the Universalist Historical Society* 1 (1959): 11-31.

125. Wolley, "Clara Barton," p. 26.

126. See, for example, the resolutions adopted in 1864 and reproduced in the *Universalist* 46 (1 October 1864): [1]. There were no printed copies of the proceedings published that year.

127. Proceedings, General Convention (1865), p. 9.

128. Appendix, Proceedings, General Convention (1865), p. 46.

129. *Universalist* 46 (6 August 1864); [1].

130. Ibid., 29 (October 1864).

131. Records, Maine Convention (1864).

132. Records, Vermont State Convention (1868) 1: 171.

133. Appendix, Proceedings, General Convention (1865), p. 47.

134. Ibid., (1866), p. 9.

135. *Story of My Life,* p. 488.

136. *Universalist* 46 (15 April 1865): [2].

137. *Universalist Herald* 15 (1 April-15 July 1867).

Chapter 23: THE HEART OF UNIVERSALISM: NEW ENGLAND AND NEW YORK

1. These generalizations are based on statistics reported in the *Universalist Register* for the years indicated.

2. These statistics are derived from the *Inventory of Universalist Archives in Massachusetts* (Boston: Historical Records Survey, Works Projects Administration, 1942). p. 52. Thanks to this Depression-born project, the documentation regarding Massachusetts Universalism is more detailed and more complete than for any other New England state. This inventory was the first of a projected series to have been published for all denominations in Massachusetts as well as other states. The series was never completed because of the Second World War. This particular volume was compiled with the cooperation and assistance of Alfred S. Cole, then librarian of the Universalist Historical Society and a member at the time of the faculty of the Tufts School of Religion; Lee S. McCollester, then dean emeritus of the School of Religion; and numerous Universalist clergy and lay persons who searched out and made available local church records. The inventory includes a brief historical sketch of the denomination; a history of each society and/or church; a guide to churches and other denominational organizations; a bibliography; and indexes to names, locations, and chronology of churches and their ministers.

3. Proceedings, *Trumpet* 15 (3 May 1834): 178.

4. Records, New England Convention (1816) 1: 192.

5. Summary of Proceedings, *Trumpet* 15 (29 June 1833): 2.

6. Proceedings, *Universalist Magazine* 3 (29 December 1821, 22 June 1822): 106-107, 207.

7. Proceedings, ibid., 5 (20 December 1823): 103-104.

8. Circular Letter, *Trumpet* 12 (11 September 1830): 42; Records, New England Convention (1835), p. 21.

9. *Trumpet* 10 (28 March 1829): 154.

10. Records, New England Convention (1835), p. 21.

11. *Trumpet* 17 (30 January 1836): 126.

12. Ibid., 21 (6 July 1839): 10.

13. Proceedings, ibid., 26 (14 September 1844): 51.

14. *Christian Freeman* 15 (25 No-

vember 1853): 117.

15. For the most detailed statistical report made before the Civil War on the state of Universalism within the Boston Association, see ibid., 16 (17 November 1854): 113.

16. Proceedings, *Trumpet* 13 (16 June 1832): 202.

17. Proceedings, Old Colony Association, ibid., 14 (3 November 1832): 74; Circular, ibid., 15 (14 December 1833): 99.

18. Ibid., 15 (14 December 1833): 99.

19. Ibid., 15 (4 June 1834): 202.

20. Extract from Proceedings, ibid., 16 (13 June 1835): 202.

21. See, for example, Proceedings, ibid., 17 (11 June 1836): 202; 24 (17 June 1843): 206.

22. Proceedings, Massachusetts Convention (1865), pp. 22; (1867), p. 35.

23. Executive Committee Reports, ibid., (1860, 1861), pp. 5, 7.

24. See, for example, Proceedings, ibid., (1867), pp. 30-31.

25. Adams, *Memoir of Whittemore,* pp. 334, 336-37.

26. See, for example, the secretary's report for 1862; Proceedings, ibid., pp. 9-13.

27. Ibid., (1867), pp. 6-7.

28. Proceedings, ibid., (1868), p. 9.

29. Proceedings, ibid., (1869), p. 13.

30. Proceedings, ibid., p. 16.

31. Proceedings, ibid., (1866), pp. 17-18.

32. Proceedings, ibid., (1867), p. 10.

33. Proceedings, ibid., p. 9.

34. Proceedings, ibid., (1869), pp. 19-20.

35. Ibid., (1870), p. 17; (1871), p. 7.

36. *Gospel Banner* 19 (2 July 1853).

37. *Christian Intelligencer* 9 (26 June; 3, 17 July; 25 September 1829); see also Anson Titus, "Universalism in Maine prior to 1820," *Universalist Quarterly* 22 n.s. (October 1885): 430-53. Unless indicated otherwise, the information on the early history of Maine Universalism presented here is based on these sources. Harold C. Perham (ed.), *The Maine Book on Universalism* (Norway, Me.: Printed by the *Advertiser-Democrat,* 1953), is a collection of numerous short essays, including much historical information and illustrated histories of societies and churches.

38. Eddy, *Universalism* 1: 515.

39. For sketches of early Universalist lay people in this and surrounding communities, see Titus, "Universalism in Maine," pp. 448-52.

40. Eddy, *Universalism* 2: 378.

41. For an account of his life, see *Memoir of the Rev. Thomas Barnes, written and compiled by his Daughter, Mrs. Levisa Buck, and edited by Rev. George Bates* (Portland, Me.: S.H. Colesworthy, 1856); see also *Christian Intelligencer* 4 (June 1824).

42. *Universalist Register,* 1836, p. 20.

43. *Trumpet* 10 (20 December 1828): 98.

44. The petitions are transcribed in Titus, "Universalism in Maine," pp. 437-39 n.

45. *Gospel Banner,* quoted in *Christian Freeman* 22 (29 March 1861); 189.

46. *Christian Intelligencer* 8 (26 December 1828): 206.

47. Whittemore, *Modern History,* pp. 392, 393.

48. *Trumpet* 12 (28 August 1830): 34.

49. Records, New England Convention (1835), p. 20.

50. *Trumpet* 12 (28 August 1830): 33.

51. *Christian Freeman* 5 (11 August

1843): 57.

52. *Universalist Expositor* 1 n.s. (January 1833): 69; Records, General Convention (1835), p. 21. The *Christian Intelligencer* was discontinued in 1837. The *Christian Pilot* was merged in 1836 with the *Gospel Banner,* which lasted until 1886.

53. *Universalist Register,* 1830, p. 18; 1841, p. 56.

54. Ibid., 1842, pp. 45-47.

55. Ibid., 1840, p. 15.

56. Cited in the *Trumpet* 25 (15 June 1844): 205.

57. Drew wrote a detailed account of the origins of each in a series of articles in the *Christian Intelligencer* 9 (26 June-25 September 1829): 101 ff.

58. *Universalist Register,* 1841, p. 15.

59. Derived from reports in ibid.

60. Records, Piscataquis Association (1844).

61. Records, Penobscot Association (1846).

62. Records, Somerset Association (1849).

63. Records, Franklin Association (1880).

64. Records, Eastern Association (1828).

65. Proceedings, *Trumpet* 11 (11 July 1829): 6; Records, Maine Convention (1831).

66. Proceedings, *Christian Freeman* 6 (26 July 1844): 50.

67. Ibid., 22 (22 March 1861): 186; Records, Maine Convention (1859-61).

68. Report of Missionary Committee, Records, Maine Convention (1870).

69. *Universalist Register,* 1872, p. 51.

70. Whittemore, *Modern History,* p. 396.

71. This information is based on Eddy, *Universalism;* and Edith Fox MacDonald's *Rebellion in the Mountains: The Story of Universalism and Unitarianism in Vermont* (Concord, N.H.: New Hampshire-Vermont District of the Unitarian Universalist Association, 1976). This indispensable reference work was compiled at the request of the Vermont and Quebec Universalist Unitarian Convention, and has been drawn upon extensively by this author. See also Mary Grace Canfield, "Early Universalism in Vermont and the Connecticut Valley" (unpublished typescript, [n.d.], Andover-Harvard Theological Library).

72. *Trumpet* 39 (8 May 1858): 194.

73. *Universalist Expositor* 1 n.s. (January 1833): 69-70.

74. *Universalist Register,* 1840, p. 24; 1841, pp. 57, 58.

75. *Universalist* 52 (21 May 1870): [2]. The date given in Eddy, *Universalism* 2: 592, of 1874, is an error.

76. *Universalist Register,* 1871, p. 68; Report of the Sunday School Committee, *Centennial,* p. 24.

77. Unless otherwise indicated, the material presented here was derived from a sketch by Kittredge Haven, long-time pastor of the society, reproduced in the *Trumpet* 41 (26 November 1859): 101. For the general historical setting of Universalism up to the middle of the nineteenth century, see David Ludlum, *Social Ferment in Vermont, 1791-1850* (New York: Columbia University Press, 1939).

78. MacDonald, *Rebellion in the Mountains,* pp. 154-55.

79. Eddy, *Sawyer,* pp. 33-34.

80. The incident is detailed in William Gribbin, "Vermont's Universalist Controversy of 1824," *Vermont History. Proceedings of the Vermont Historical Society* 41 (Spring 1973): 82-94.

81. *Christian Intelligencer* 4 (29 January 1825).

82. Robert Bartlett, *A Sermon delivered on the Day of General Election, at Montpelier, October 13, 1825, before the Legislature of Vermont* (Montpelier, Vt.: E.P. Walton, 1825).

83. *Christian Repository* 1 (September 1821): 75.

84. Records, Vermont Convention (1873) 2: 3.

85. See the *Trumpet* 19 (2 September 1837): 42; and Timothy M. Cooley, *Sketches of the Life and Character of the Rev. Lemuel Haynes, A.M.* (New York: Harper, 1837).

86. For biographical data on more than fifty Universalist and Unitarian lay persons and their families in Vermont, see MacDonald, *Rebellion in the Mountains*, pp. 189-201.

87. *Universalist* 52 (5 November 1870): [3].

88. Eddy, *Universalism* 2: 54.

89. *Impartialist* 1 (1 September 1832): 2.

90. Proceedings, *Universalist Magazine* 3 (8 December 1821): 93-94. For brief biographical sketches of some 325 Vermont clergymen, with much information not available elsewhere, see MacDonald, *Rebellion in the Mountains*, Part III (pp. 122-88).

91. Proceedings, *Universalist Magazine* 4 (21 December 1822): 103; *Trumpet* 10 (1 November 1828): 69.

92. Proceedings, *Trumpet* 14 (3 November 1832): 74.

93. *Impartialist* 1 (3 November 1832): 34.

94. A typescript of the convention minutes (1833-1909), in loose-leaf notebooks, was kindly made available to the author by Mrs. Edith Fox MacDonald. For further information on the records of the convention, see *Rebellion in the Mountains*, pp. 210 ff. The first constitution of the convention was not included in the original records, but was reproduced in the *Impartialist* 1 (9 February 1833); 90-91, and in MacDonald.

95. Records, Vermont Convention (1870) 1: 183.

96. Ibid., (1845) 1: 47.

97. Records, Maine Convention (1868).

98. The author acknowledges the generosity of Rev. Phillip Hewett, minister of the Unitarian Church of Vancouver, B.C., who has shared the results of his research dealing with Canadian Universalism, part of his larger study of the history of Unitarianism in Canada.

99. MacDonald, *Rebellion in the Mountains*, p. 150; see also pp. 117-21 for further information on societies in Lower Canada (Canada East).

100. *Trumpet* 15 (12 April 1834): 166.

101. Ibid., 11 (13 February 1830): 131.

102. *Impartialist* 1 (22 December 1832): 62.

103. *Trumpet* 18 (10 September 1836): 46.

104. *Universalist Register*, 1843, p. 64.

105. *Impartialist* 1 (3 November 1832): 34; *Universalist Union* 10 (14 December 1844): 80.

106. MacDonald, *Rebellion in the Mountains*, p. 155.

107. Records, Vermont Convention (1862) 1: 145 ff.

108. Ibid., (1869) 1: 176.

109. Ibid., (1889, 1890, 1898) 2: 120, 123; 3: 2.

110. Hewett, "History of Unitarianism in Canada" (typescript), p. 80.

111. *Trumpet* 22 (26 November 1831): 86.

112. Hewett, "Unitarianism," p. 75.

113. *Universalist Register*, 1839, p. 21; 1840, p. 36.

114. Ibid., 1843, p. 63.

115. *Universalist Union* 8 (19 August 1843): 637-38.

116. *Universalist Register,* 1892, p. 95.

117. Rogers, *Memoranda,* pp. 383-86.

118. Proceedings, *Trumpet* 26 (7 September 1844): 47. The constitution was reproduced in the *Universalist Union* 10 (8 November 1845): 823-25.

119. The single volume of records is located in the Andover-Harvard Theological Library. The *Universalist Register* at first mistakenly identified the organization as a "convention" but corrected the error in the 1847 issue.

120. *Trumpet* 27 (20 December 1845): 107.

121. Extract from Proceedings, ibid.,

122. Ibid., 27 (29 November 1845): 94.

123. *Universalist Register,* 1899, p. 100.

124. Records, General Convention (1846), pp. 54-55.

125. Proceedings, ibid., (1881), pp. 3, 4.

126. *Trumpet and Christian Freeman* 44 (21, 28 June, 5 July 1862): 34, 38, 42.

127. Proceedings, ibid., 45 (27 June 1863): 39.

128. *Universalist Register,* 1871, p. 76; 1872, p. 121.

129. Cobb, *Autobiography,* pp. 177-78 n.

130. Records, General Convention 27 (22 November 1845): 90.

(1835), p. 20.

131. Ibid., (1839), p. 453.

132. *Trumpet* 22 (21 November 1840): 87.

133. *Universalist Register,* 1843, p. 64.

134. *Universalist Union* 10 (4 October 1845): 745.

135. *Universalist Register,* 1842, p. 62.

136. *Universalist Union* 10 (4 October 1845): 745.

137. *Universalist Register,* 1858, p. 57.

138. The *Universalist Register* did not identify him with the Canadian society until 1861, but he was reported as preaching in Canada as early as 1859.

139. Ibid., 1867, pp. 16, 57.

140. Ibid., 1871, p. 46.

141. Ibid., 1879, p. 10.

142. *Trumpet* 15 (24 May 1834): 190.

143. Ibid., 16 (1 November 1834): 74.

144. Ibid., 17 (22 August 1835): 36.

145. *Universalist Register,* 1836, p. 46.

146. *Trumpet* 16 (16 May 1835): 186.

147. Record Book No. 1 (1843-1861), First Universalist Church of Halifax; the records of the church were made available to the author in 1974 through the courtesy of the pastor, the Rev. Frederick Gillis.

148. *Universalist Union* 11 (29 November 1845): 41.

149. *Christian Freeman* 4 (11 November 1842): 110, 111.

150. *Universalist Union* 8 (15 April 1843): 356.

151. *Trumpet* 24 (28 January 1843): 126.

152. *Christian Freeman* 5 (26 January 1844): 155.

153. *Universalist* 53 (5 August 1871): [2].

154. *Universalist Register,* 1872, pp. 153-55.

155. Hewett, "Unitarianism," p. 85; n. 29.

156. These are all discussed briefly in Hewett, in their Canadian context.

157. *Universalist* 55 (29 November 1873): [3].

158. *Christian Leader* 63 (6 October 1881): 8.

159. For brief histories of Universalism in New Hampshire, see Clinton

Lee Scott, "Universalism in New Hampshire," *Annual Journal of the Universalist Historical Society* (1959): 1-10; J.F. Witherell (comp.), *New Hampshire Historical Register, containing Denominational Statistics for the Year 1844* (Concord, N.H.: *Balm of Gilead* Office, 1844), which contains historical sketches of many societies; and Asa M. Bradley's typescript notes on Universalist societies, based on Witherell but updated into the 1920s; Andover-Harvard Theological Library.

160. See A.J. Patterson, "A Hundred Years: An Historical Discourse delivered at the Centennial Celebration in Portsmouth, N.H., Nov. 16, 1873," *Universalist Quarterly* 11 n.s. (January 1874): 70-96. An earlier history of the Portsmouth society (1773-1848) had been compiled by Thomas Whittemore and was published in the *Universalist Miscellany* 6 (September 1848): 91-106; it was reprinted in the *Trumpet* 31 (11 May 1850): 189-90.

161. Witherell, *New Hampshire Register.*

162. *Trumpet* 15 (12 April 1834): 166; *Universalist Register,* 1840, p. 20.

163. This information was derived from Witherell, *New Hampshire Register,* which includes the most complete information on the early societies.

164. *Christian Repository* 4 (February 1824): 242-43.

165. *Trumpet* 10 (22 November 1828): 82.

166. Witherell, *New Hampshire Register,* p. 56.

167. Eddy, *Universalism* 1: 543.

168. *Trumpet* 39 (8 May 1858): 194.

169. Ibid., 10 (13 September 1828): 42.

170. Witherell, *New Hampshire Register,* pp. 35-36; *Universalist Magazine* 6 (3 July 1824): 8.

171. *Trumpet* 10 (13 September 1828): 42.

172. Circular, New Hampshire Association, ibid., 10 (6 June 1829): 194.

173. Witherell, *New Hampshire Register,* p. 40.

174. *Trumpet* 14 (23 February 1833): 138.

175. *Universalist Register,* 1846, pp. 31-32.

176. Witherell, *New Hampshire Register,* pp. 57-58.

177. Report of Corresponding Secretary, New Hampshire Convention, *Trumpet* 44 (19 July 1862): 49.

178. *Universalist Register,* 1871, pp. 47-48.

179. *Impartialist* (Claremont, 1832-35); *Star in the East and New Hampshire Universalist* (1834-37); *Universalist Family Visitor* (1841-42); *Balm of Gilead and Practical Universalist* (1842-46).

180. *Universalist Register,* 1866, p. 11; Report of Committee on Education, General Convention (1867), p. 45.

181. Cobb, *Autobiography,* p. 216.

182. Proceedings, *Universalist Magazine* 9 (7 July 1827): 12.

183. Proceedings, ibid., 9 (8 September 1827): 46-47.

184. *Universalist Register,* 1866, p. 10.

185. Proceedings, *Trumpet* 13 (17 September 1831): 47; (16 June 1832): 202-203.

186. Proceedings, *Impartialist* 1 (15 September 1832): 6.

187. Ibid., 1 (3 November 1832): 34-35.

188. Proceedings, *Trumpet* 18 (9 July 1836): 11.

189. The new constitution was reproduced in the *Christian Freeman* 23 (15 July 1861): 43.

190. *Universal Damnation and Salva-*

tion, clearly proved by the Scriptures of the Old and New Testament.

191. *Universalist* 46 (22 October 1864): [3].

192. *Trumpet* 35 (25 February 1854): 151.

193. The most detailed and authoritative collection of materials on Connecticut Universalism is the unpublished "Inventory of Universalist Church Records in Connecticut," prepared by the Works Projects Administration in 1940. An undated, unpaginated typescript copy is in the Andover-Harvard Theological Library, and has been utilized in this study. See also Donald Watt, *From Heresy toward Truth: The Story of Universalism in Greater Hartford and Connecticut, 1821-1971,* prepared under the auspices of the Universalist Church of West Hartford, Conn. and published in 1971. For the historical setting of Universalism in the state, see Richard Purcell, *Connecticut in Transition, 1775-1818* (Washington, D.C.: American Historical Association, 1918; Middletown, Conn.: Wesleyan University Press, 1963); and Charles R. Keller, *The Second Great Awakening in Connecticut* (New Haven: Yale University Press, 1942).

194. See R.O. Williams, *A Historical Sketch of Universalism in Norwich, Connecticut* (Norwich, Conn.: George W. Conklin, 1844).

195. Whittemore, *Modern History,* p. 368.

196. Purcell, *Connecticut in Transition,* pp. 59-60.

197. Keller, *Second Great Awakening,* pp. 21-22.

198. Records, General Convention (1841), p. 469.

199. *Universalist Union* 9 (3 February 1844): 186.

200. *Trumpet* 38 (24 January 1857): 135.

201. Eddy, *Universalism* 1: 543.

202. *Trumpet* 39 (8 May 1858): 194.

203. *Universalist Union* 7 (13 August 1842): 624.

204. *Trumpet* 35 (25 February 1854): 151.

205. Watt, *Heresy toward Truth,* pp. 15-17.

206. Report of Sunday School Committee, *Centennial,* p. 24.

207. *Universalist Expositor* 1 n.s. (January 1833): 71.

208. Whittemore, *Modern History,* p. 406.

209. *Trumpet* 11 (19 June 1830): 202.

210. Records, General Convention (1835), pp. 23-27.

211. *Universalist Union* 5 (2 May 1840): 375.

212. This generalization is based on an analysis of the societies listed in the "Inventory."

213. *Universalist Register,* 1871, p. 21.

214. *Trumpet* 25 (6 January 1844): 114.

215. *Christian Freeman* 14 (15 October 1852): 94.

216. *Universalist* 46 (1 October 1864): [3].

217. Ibid., 46 (25 March 1865): [3].

218. *Trumpet* 12 (30 October 1830): 70.

219. Proceedings, *Universalist Union* 4 (14 September 1839): 355.

220. Ibid., 1 (21 May 1836): 217.

221. Proceedings, ibid., 1 (3 July 1836): 271; 2 (26 November, 3 December 1836): 19, 27.

222. Circular Letter, ibid., 2 (28 October 1837): 403.

223. Ibid., 4 (25 May 1839): 231. For reasons unknown, the Hartford County Association was not listed in the *Universalist Register* after 1870.

224. Norris G. Osborn, *History of Connecticut in Monograph Form* 3: 385-86, cited in "Inventory."

225. *Universalist* 46 (3 September 1864): [3].

226. The most detailed information on the early history of the Providence society is included in an historical address delivered by the pastor, Elmer H. Capen, on the occasion of the celebration of the society's semi-centennial in 1871; *Universalist* 52 (22 April 1871): [2].

227. *Trumpet* 24 (26 November 1842): 92.

228. Eddy, *Universalism* 1: 206; 2: 397.

229. Whittemore, *Modern History*, p. 403.

230. *Universalist Magazine* 4 (30 November 1822): 91.

231. *Universalist Union* 5 (9 May 1840): 292; *Trumpet* 22 (20 March 1841): 155.

232. Circular Letter, Rhode Island Convention, *Trumpet* 20 (25 May 1839): 196.

233. *Universalist Register*, 1862, p. 29.

234. Ibid., 1866, p. 19.

235. Ibid., 1871, p. 64.

236. "Inventory."

237. *Universalist Magazine* 9 (17 November 1827): 87.

238. Eddy, *Universalism* 2: 332.

239. *Trumpet* 19 (7, 21 April 1838): 167, 174; for the proceedings and Circular Letter, see ibid., 19 (2 June 1838): 200.

240. This tripartite division of the early history was used by Sawyer in an unpublished sermon delivered in 1845 when he began his sixteenth year in New York City. For extracts from the sermon, see Eddy, *Sawyer*, pp. 43 ff.

241. *Letters and Sketches* 2: 400.

242. Eddy, *Sawyer*, pp. 47-48. Eddy drew much of the material on early New York Universalism from an historical sketch which appeared in the *Christian Messenger*. There is also considerable material in Abel C. Thomas, *Century of Universalism.*

243. Thomas, *Century of Universalism*, pp. 267-69.

244. Eddy, *Sawyer*, p. 56 n.

245. *Universalist Union* 10 (2 August 1845): 600.

246. Ibid., 10 (10 May 1845): 409.

247. *Century of Universalism*, p. 275.

248. Ibid., p. 314. Thomas listed five by name.

249. Eddy, *Sawyer*, pp. 150-51.

250. Thomas, *Century of Universalism*, pp. 317-19.

251. *Trumpet* 28 (23 January 1847): 127.

252. Report of New York Association, *Universalist Union* 4 (8 December 1838): 38.

253. *Trumpet* 10 (6 June 1829): 196.

254. Smith, *Sketches* 1: 58. Stacy's autobiography comprises one of the best personalized accounts of upstate New York Universalism in the nineteenth century; see *Memoirs of the Life of Nathaniel Stacy* . . . (Columbus, Penna.: Published for the author by Abner Vedder, 1850).

255. See his *Historical Sketches and Incidents, illustrative of the Establishment and Progress of Universalism in the State of New York.* 2 vols. (Buffalo, N.Y.: Steele's Press, 1843; James S. Leavitt, 1848).

256. Ibid., 1: 21 ff.

257. Eddy, *Universalism* 2: 38.

258. *Trumpet* 11 (23 January 1830): 119.

259. Whittemore, *Modern History*, pp. 409-10.

260. *Trumpet* 16 (13 September 1834): 46-47.

261. Cross, *Burned Over District,* p. 18, citing state census returns.

262. *Trumpet* 15 (10 May 1834): 184.

263. Smith, *Sketches* 1: 25, 94-95.

264. *Universalist Register,* 1844, p. 52; 1846, p. 40.

265. Ibid., 1866, p. 21.

266. *Trumpet* 39 (8 May 1858): 194.

267. Ibid., 11 (18 July 1829): 12.

268. *Christian Freeman* 7 (30 May 1845): 17.

269. Smith, *Sketches* 2: 186.

270. Abstract of Proceedings, 18 June 1845, *Universalist Union* 10 (26 July 1845): 583.

271. Ibid., p. 580.

272. Ibid., 10 (16 August 1845): 634.

273. Ibid., 4 (10 August 1839): 318.

274. *Trumpet* 11 (13 February 1830): 130.

275. Extract from Proceedings, *Trumpet* 17 (27 June 1835): 2; *Universalist Union* 2 (2 September 1837): 341.

276. The first constitution of the convention was reproduced in the *Universalist Magazine* 7 (16 July 1825): 14.

277. Proceedings, ibid., 9 (24 November 1827): 89.

278. Extract from Proceedings, *Trumpet* 17 (11 June 1836): 202.

279. *Universalist Union* 9 (15 June 1844): 484.

280. Proceedings, ibid., 2 (3, 10 June 1837): 243, 246.

281. Proceedings, ibid., 7 (9 July 1842): 539.

282. E.C. Sweetser, E.H. Chapin, Isaac M. Atwood, and J.M. Pullman.

283. Thomas, *Century of Universalism,* pp. 339-40.

284. In 1851 three papers being published in New York City had been merged; the *Ambassador* was renamed the *Christian Leader* in 1867 and was merged with the *Universalist,* published in Boston under the auspices of the denominational publishing house, in 1879.

Chapter 24: MOVING WITH THE FRONTIER: THE MIDWEST

1. The history of Universalism in Ohio has been exceptionally well documented. A Committee on Historical Research was created in 1917 by the Ohio State Convention and arranged for the deposit in the Ohio State Historical Library not only of its proceedings but of numerous other Universalist materials. Other documents relating to Ohio Universalism are in the Andover-Harvard Theological Library. A history of Universalism in the state was prepared by the historical committee under the chairmanship of Elmo Arnold Robinson and was published by the Ohio Universalist Convention in 1923 under the title *The Universalist Church in Ohio.* The work is particularly valuable for information on local church history and biographical notes of ministers who served in the state.

2. Much of the material presented here was drawn from an article by M.L. Edwards, Jr., entitled "Early History of Universalism in Ohio," which appeared in the *Trumpet* 28 (24 April 1847): 177; the article was prepared for the Universalist Historical Society.

3. The question has been raised about whether there might have been two individuals with the same or similar names operating in different locations. What is known of the chronology indicates that it was probably the same person, although this cannot be stated definitively. See Eddy, *Universalism* 1: 384, 417-18; Robinson, *American Universalism,* pp. 29-30 and his *Universalist Church in Ohio,* pp.

12-17.

4. Johnson, "Universalism in Louisville," p. 175; Robinson, *Universalist Church in Ohio,* p. 16 n.

5. *Trumpet* 28 (24 April 1847): 177.

6. Robinson, *Universalist Church in Ohio,* pp. 17-18.

7. *Universalist Magazine* 9 (28 July 1827): 22.

8. Proceedings, *Universalist Magazine* 3 (15 December 1821): 100.

9. For a listing, with explanatory notes and diagrams, see Robinson, *Universalist Church in Ohio,* pp. 83-84, 273, 275.

10. This point is emphasized by David Johnson, *To Preach and Fight,* p. 75.

11. *Universalist Magazine* 4 (24 August 1822): 35.

12. Ibid., 9 (1 September 1827): 42.

13. Ibid., 9 (12 January 1828): 120.

14. *Trumpet* 10 (19 July 1828): 10; 16 (26 July 1834): 18.

15. Ibid., 16 (26 July 1834): 18.

16. *Universalist Register,* 1845, p. 51.

17. *Universalist Herald* 11 (9, 15 May 1857): 4, 6.

18. Ibid., 11 (26 June 1857): 29.

19. *Universalist Magazine* 8 (24 February 1827): 143.

20. *Trumpet* 10 (2 August 1828): 18.

21. *Universalist Register,* 1836, p. 18.

22. Proceedings, *Trumpet* 15 (7 September 1833): 42.

23. Ibid., 17 (12 March 1836): 150.

24. *Memoranda,* p. 393.

25. *Trumpet* 17 (12 March 1836): 150.

26. Ibid., 20 (17 November 1838): 89-90; *Universalist Register,* 1838, pp. 20-22.

27. *Universalist Church in Ohio,* p. 68.

28. *Universalist Register,* 1843, p. 60.

29. Ibid., 1845, p. 53.

30. *Trumpet* 31 (23 June 1849): 5.

31. *Universalist Magazine* 4 (10 August 1822): 27.

32. Robinson, *Universalist Church in Ohio,* p. 53.

33. *Universalist* 48 (17, 24 August 1867): [2].

34. Robinson, *Universalist Church in Ohio,* p. 98.

35. Ibid., pp. 133-34.

36. The statistics and other information given here were derived from material gathered in tabular and graphical form in ibid., pp. 139-40, 271, 273.

37. James A. Stoner, "Before and after Winchester," *The Winchester Centennial, 1803-1903* (Boston and Chicago: Universalist Publishing House, 1903), p. 124. Stoner prepared this paper as a contribution to the centennial of the Winchester Profession of Faith on behalf of the Indiana State Convention. At the time he was preaching on a circuit near Indianapolis, including the Oaklandon church which was still active in the 1970s. See also Elmo Arnold Robinson, "Universalism in Indiana," *Indiana Magazine of History* 13 (1917-18): 1-19, 157-88. The documents dealing with Indiana Universalism are widely scattered, but the most extensive collection is in the Indiana State Library, Indianapolis.

38. *Universalist Magazine* 8 (17 March 1827): 155.

39. Quoted in Robinson, "Universalism in Indiana," p. 5.

40. *Southern Pioneer* 4 (16 May 1835): 217.

41. *Trumpet* 12 (21 May 1831): 186; 14 (20 April 1833): 170.

42. Ibid., 17 (10 October 1835): 62.

43. The constitution was reproduced in the *Philomath Encyclopedia* 6 (April 1844): 412-15.

44. *Universalist Union* 4 (24 August 1839): 335.

45. For details of the controversy, see Robinson, "Universalism in Indiana," pp. 15-19.

46. Proceedings, *Philomath Encyclopedia* 5 (June 1842): 286.

47. Proceedings, ibid., 4 (August 1841): 565-66.

48. Records, General Convention (1848) 2: 71.

49. Robinson, "Universalism in Indiana," pp. 20-21.

50. H.C. Bradsby, *History of Vigo County, Indiana, with Biographical Sketches* (Chicago: S.B. Nelson & Co., 1891), p. 599.

51. C.C. Oakey, *Greater Terre Haute and Vigo County* (Chicago: Lewis Publishing Co., 1908), pp. 337, 352.

52. *Universalist Register,* 1839, pp. 21, 27.

53. *Philomath Encyclopedia* 5 (August 1842): 344.

54. Powell, *Cass County,* pp. 430-31.

55. Helm, *Cass County,* pp. 424-25.

56. Jacob P. Dunn, *Greater Indianapolis* (Chicago: Lewis Publishing Co., 1910), pp. 89 ff.

57. Robinson, "Universalism in Indiana," p. 31.

58. *Universalist Register,* 1871, p. 29.

59. See Robinson, "Universalism in Indiana," p. 39, for a record of debates in which Universalists participated between 1829 and 1899.

60. *Memoranda,* pp. 394-95.

61. Proceedings, *Philomath Encyclopedia* 4 (July 1841): 511.

62. Unless otherwise indicated, the information on early Universalism in the state was derived from William Rounsville, "Rise and Progress of Universalism in Illinois," *Ladies' Repository* 19 (January 1851): 244-46; also printed in the *Trumpet* 32 (4 January 1851): 117.

63. *Universalist Register,* 1837, p. 26; *Trumpet* 19 (15 August 1837): 25.

64. Sweet, *Religion on the American Frontier* 3: 174 n.

65. *Trumpet* 26 (12 April 1845): 170.

66. *Universalist Union* 1 (2 April 1836): 167.

67. *Twenty-five Years,* p. 74.

68. *Trumpet* 26 (12 April 1845): 170.

69. Proceedings, ibid., 19 (17 February 1838): 140; *Universalist Union* 4 (12 January 1839): 75.

70. Eddy, *Universalism* 2: 372.

71. Ibid., p. 373.

72. *Universalist Register,* 1839, p. 24.

73. *Universalist* 55 (4 April 1874): [2].

74. *Universalist Register,* 1840, p. 34.

75. Ibid., 1843, p. 62; Records, General Convention (1842), p. 480.

76. *Universalist Register,* 1844, pp. 60-61; 1845, pp. 56-57.

77. Ibid., 1848, p. 67.

78. *Ladies' Repository* 19 (January 1851): 244-46.

79. Sweet, *Religion on the American Frontier* 3: 265-66.

80. *Universalist Union* 5 (13 June 1840): 472-73.

81. *Universalist Register,* 1871, p. 27.

82. *Universalist* 53 (28 October, 4 November 1871): [2, 3], [1].

83. Ibid., 53 (9 March 1872): [2].

84. *Universalist Register,* 1872, p. 91.

85. Ibid.

86. He sent identical reports to the *Universalist Union* 11 (18 July 1846): 566-67; and the *Trumpet* 28 (15 August 1846): 33.

87. *Trumpet* 28 (13 March 1847): 154.

88. *Universalist Register,* 1849, p. 57; 1853, p. 52.

89. Ibid., 1872, pp. 85-86.

90. *Christian Intelligencer* 9 (13 March 1829): 42.

91. Eddy, *Universalism* 2: 384-85.

92. *Universalist Register,* 1848, pp. 63-64.

93. Sweet, *Religion on the American Frontier* 3: 312-13, 315.

94. *Trumpet* 15 (28 December 1833): 107.

95. *Impartialist* 2 (4 January 1834): 62.

96. *Trumpet* 15 (5 April 1834): 162; 16 (22 November 1834): 86.

97. Proceedings, *Universalist Union* 2 (15 July 1837): 283.

98. Records, General Convention (1843), p. 490.

99. Twenty-two preachers were listed in the *Universalist Register* that year, but many were actually laymen; one or two actually belonged to other denominations but were listed because they openly preached universal salvation.

100. *Universalist Register,* 1841, p. 68.

101. Ibid., 1867, p. 46.

102. *Trumpet* 39 (13 June 1857): 5; *Universalist Register,* 1861, p. 46.

103. *Christian Freeman* 22 (24 August 1860): 65, 66.

104. Ibid., 1861, p. 37.

105. *Universalist Union* 7 (8 January 1842): 123.

106. Ibid., 8 (4 February 1843): 185; *Trumpet* 25 (1 July 1843): 7.

107. *Universalist Register,* 1847, pp. 57-58. The most detailed study of Iowa Universalism is Elva Louise Tucker, "The History of the Universalist Church in Iowa, 1843-1943" (unpublished master's thesis, Iowa City: State University of Iowa, 1944).

108. Extract from Proceedings, *Universalist Union* 9 (17 February 1844): 217. The convention records (1843-1925) are in the Andover-Harvard Theological Library.

109. Records, General Convention (1844), pp. 506-507.

110. Record Book and History, 1858-1893, First Universalist Society; Meadville/Lombard Theological School.

111. *Universalist Register,* 1863, p. 551.

112. Ibid., 1872, p. 45.

113. Ibid., 1850, p. 57; 1851, p. 54.

114. Ibid., 1854, p. 51; 1858, p. 48; 1860, pp. 50, 51.

115. Ibid., 1861, p. 51.

116. *Christian Freeman* 11 (10 August 1849): 58; Eddy, *Universalism* 2: 597.

117. Proceedings, Universalist Educational Convention, *Christian Freeman* 19 (29 January 1858): 159-60.

118. Eddy, *Universalism* 2: 385.

119. *Universalist Register,* 1871, p. 60. The community was later incorporated into Minneapolis.

120. *Christian Freeman* 17 (14 December 1855): 130.

121. *Universalist Register,* 1858, p. 48.

122. Ibid., 1861, pp. 50-51.

Chapter 25: SLOW AND ERRATIC PROGRESS: THE MID-ATLANTIC AND BORDER STATES

1. *Universalist Register,* 1868, p. 41; 1869, p. 41.

2. The bulk of the records of Pennsylvania Universalism were deposited in 1935 in the Historical Society of Pennsylvania by Thomas Butler, the

official historian of the Pennsylvania Convention. They comprise approximately fifty volumes and include church, association, and convention records from 1810 to 1934. In addition, there is much material relevant to early Universalism in the papers of Benjamin Rush, originally a part of the collections of the Library Company of Philadelphia and transferred to the Historical Society library. Included is considerable correspondence of Elhanan Winchester and John Murray. Butler undertook to collect and transcribe everything concerning the history of Universalism in Pennsylvania. The project was never completed but he deposited what material he had assembled in the form of loose-leaf, unpaginated scrapbooks labelled "Universalism in Pennsylvania." See also Abel C. Thomas, *Century of Universalism*.

3. Unless otherwise indicated, the information on early Philadelphia Universalism was derived from the Butler notebooks.

4. Thomas Whittemore published a biography of Richards in the *Trumpet* 29 (11, 18 September; 2 October 1847); 50, 54, 62.

5. *Universalist Magazine* 3 (6 April 1822): 163; 4 (14 September 1822): 47; Whittemore, *Modern History*, pp. 415-16.

6. Thomas, *Autobiography*, p. 151.

7. Thomas, *Century of Universalism*, pp. 125-26.

8. Records, Philadelphia Convention (1802) [n.p.]. Following local practice, the term "society" was seldom used in rural Pennsylvania, and like those in the South, were called "churches" in spite of the informality of their structure. Most Universalist records, however, continued to refer to them as "societies."

9. *Trumpet* 10 (14 March 1829): 146.

10. Ibid., 14 (29 December 1832): 106.

11. Ibid., 12 (8 January 1831): 110.

12. Whittemore, *Modern History*, p. 419.

13. *Universalist Register*, 1839, p. 25.

14. Butler, "Universalism in Pennsylvania," [n.p.]; *Universalist Expositor* 1 n.s. (January 1833): 72.

15. Record Book, 1841-44, Historical Society of Pennsylvania.

16. *Trumpet* 16 (27 December 1834): 106.

17. *Universalist Register*, 1836, p. 43.

18. Ibid., 1846, p. 49.

19. Ibid., 1855, p. 45; 1861, p. 41.

20. *Universalist Herald* 11 (7 August 1857): 51.

21. *Universalist Register*, 1862, p. 35.

22. Ibid., 1871, p. 63.

23. *Universalist* 56 (14 November 1874): [3].

24. Proceedings, *Universalist Union* 2 (5 August 1837): 307.

25. Proceedings, *Trumpet* 16 (29 November 1834): 90.

26. Ibid., 24 (3 December 1842): 94.

27. Ibid., 28 (24, 31 October 1846): 73, 77.

28. Ibid., 13 (5 November 1831): 74.

29. Proceedings, *Southern Pioneer* 1 (July 1832): 199-202.

30. Proceedings and Circular Letter, *Universalist Union* 1 (4 June 1836): 238.

31. Butler, "Universalism in Pennsylvania," [n.p.].

32. The information on the state convention charter was derived from the Butler notebooks.

33. *Century of Universalism*, p. 147.

34. *Trumpet* 38 (2 August 1856): 33.

35. *Universalist Register*, 1871, p. 48.

36. For early Universalism in New

Jersey, see Thomas, *Century of Universalism*, pp. 41-42.

37. Ibid., pp. 187-89.

38. *Trumpet* 38 (2 August 1856): 33.

39. Ibid., 10 (6 December 1828): 90.

40. Whittemore, *Modern History*, pp. 412-13.

41. *Trumpet* 12 (9 April 1831): 162.

42. *Universalist* 51 (23 April 1870: [3].

43. *Universalist Register*, 1863, p. 45.

44. *Trumpet* 14 (20 April 1833): 170.

45. Ibid., 15 (10 May 1834): 184.

46. *Memoranda*, p. 167.

47. *Universalist Union* 2 (2 September 1837): 341.

48. Ibid., 8 (21 October 1843): 787.

49. Ibid., 9 (4 May 1844): 393.

50. Ibid., 9 (2 November 1844): 807.

51. The constitution was reproduced in ibid., 10 (12 July, 9 August 1845): 562, 614-15; Records, General Convention (1845), p. 540.

52. *Trumpet* 28 (23 January 1847): 127.

53. *Universalist Register*, 1850, p. 49.

54. Ibid., 1856, p. 45; 1859, p. 43.

55. Proceedings, New Jersey Convention (1858), *Trumpet* 29 May 1858): 207.

56. Summary of Proceedings, *Christian Freeman* 21 (27 May 1859): 14.

57. *Universalist Register*, 1861, p. 41.

58. Ibid., 1865, p. 14.

59. *Universalist* 48 (21 September 1867): [3].

60. Ibid., 50 (7 November 1868): [2].

61. Ibid., 52 (23 July 1870): [3].

62. Ibid., 52 (10 September 1870): [3].

63. Ibid., 52 (11 June 1870): [3].

64. Ibid., 52 (2 October 1875): [3].

65. Ibid., 59 (5 May 1877): [3].

66. *Trumpet* 13 (23 July 1831): 14; 32 (20 July 1850): 22-23.

67. *Southern Pioneer* 1 (October 1831): 22-23; (October 1832): 141.

68. Ibid., 5 (4 June 1836): 359.

69. *Trumpet* 16 (15 November 1834): 82.

70. Ibid., 19 (1 July 1837): 6.

71. *Universalist Union* 4 (23 March, 4 May 1839): 158, 206.

72. *Trumpet* 23 (23 October 1841): 72.

73. *Southern Pioneer* 2 (6 July 1833): 150.

74. Manford, *Twenty-five Years*, pp. 22-25.

75. *Universalist Union* 2 (15 April 1837): 183.

76. *Southern Pioneer* 4 (23 May, 6 June 1835): 224, 242-43.

77. Ibid., 5 (7 May 1836): 316-17.

78. Records, General Convention (1841), pp. 470-71.

79. Ibid., (1852), p. 104.

80. *Universalist Union* 11 (20 December 1845): 86.

81. Ibid., 11 (27 December 1845): 103.

82. *Universalist Register*, 1862, p. 45.

83. Ibid., 1871, p. 36.

84. Eddy, *Universalism* 2: 369; *Southern Pioneer* 3 (2 August 1834): 166.

85. *Trumpet* 28 (5 September 1846): 46.

86. *Universalist* 48 (19 May 1866): [3].

87. Ibid., 55 (11 October 1873): [3].

88. *Universalist Register*, 1869, p. 41.

89. Report of Trustees, General Convention (1868), pp. 13-16.

90. Ibid., pp. 14-15.

91. Proceedings, ibid., (1869), pp. 7, 8.

92. *Universalist* 51 (12 June 1869): [3].

93. Ibid., 51 (10 July 1869): [2].

94. Ibid., 50 (27 February 1869): [1].

95. Report of Trustees, *Centennial,* p. 51.

96. Abstract of Minutes, Board of Trustees, 10 April 1872, *Universalist* 53 (27 April 1872): [2].

97. Ibid., 55 (11 October 1873): [3].

98. For a detailed architectural description, with illustrations, see the *Christian Leader* 64 (27 July 1882): 1.

99. Ibid., 63 (15 December 1881): 2.

100. Thomas, *Century of Universalism,* p. 41.

101. *Universalist Union* 4 (4 May 1839): 203; *Trumpet* 27 (23 August 1845): 38.

102. *Trumpet* 11 (25 July 1829): 14.

103. Ibid., 11 (5 September 1829): 39.

104. *Universalist Register,* 1842, p. 61; Whittemore, *Modern History,* p. 420; *Trumpet* 24 (1 April 1843): 163; 25 (16 December 1843): 103.

105. *Trumpet* 12 (2 October 1830): 54.

106. Ibid., 14 (13 April 1833): 166.

107. Ibid., 40 (27 November 1858): 103.

108. Ibid., 14 (9 February 1833): 130.

109. *Christian Intelligencer* 12 (15 February 1833): 26.

110. *Southern Pioneer* 2 (23 February, 26 May 1833): 71, 124.

111. Eddy, *Universalism* 2: 595.

112. Proceedings, Universalist Historical Society (1834).

113. *Southern Pioneer* 4 (11 April 1835): 186-87.

114. Proceedings, ibid., 5 (25 July 1835): 4-5.

115. *Universalist Register,* 1836, p. 45.

116. *Universalist Union* 4 (13 July 1839): 285-86.

117. *Universalist* 57 (11 December 1875): [2]; Records, General Convention (1844), p. 506.

118. *Southern Pioneer* 2 (20 July 1833): 155.

119. Ibid., 2 (3 August 1833): 168.

120. Ibid., 3 (7 December 1833): 30.

121. *Trumpet* 16 (29 November 1834): 90.

122. *Southern Pioneer* 3 (2, 16 August 1834): 166, 174-75.

123. *Trumpet* 27 (8 November 1845): 83; *Universalist Union* 7 (11 June 1842): 480.

124. *Trumpet* 30 (2 September 1848): 46.

125. Some of the accounts of his experiences were published in the *Universalist* 58 (3 June, 26 August 1876): [1], [2].

126. *Trumpet* 31 (23 June 1849): 5.

127. Ibid., 33 (29 May 1852): 202.

128. Ibid., 34 (13 November 1852): 89.

129. *Christian Freeman* 23 (21 March, 11 April 1862): 186, 198.

130. *Universalist* 47 (3 May, 3 June 1865): [2], [1]; Report on the State of the Church, General Convention (1868), p. 55.

131. *Universalist Register,* 1871, p. 65.

132. *Universalist* 56 (21 November 1874): [2].

133. Ibid., 56 (13 February 1875): [3].

134. Rogers, *Memoranda,* p. 180.

135. *Universalist Register,* 1869, p. 42.

136. Proceedings, *Universalist Union* 2 (5 August 1837): 307.

137. *Universalist Register,* 1853, p. 53.

138. *Trumpet* 34 (20 November 1852): 95.

139. *Universalist Register,* 1873, p. 73.

140. Ibid., 1874, p. 67.

141. Ibid., 1876, p. 61.

142. This generalization is based on a history of Universalism in eastern Tennessee prepared by William Hale, a Universalist physician in Kingsport, Tenn. (Sullivan County), and published serially in the *Universalist Herald* in 1879-80.

143. *Trumpet* 10 (11 April 1829): 164.

144. *Memoranda,* pp. 195 ff.

145. C. Wayman McCarty, "Universalist Church in the Mid-South," p. 108.

146. *Trumpet* 22 (29 May 1841): 195.

147. Rogers, *Memoranda,* pp. 373-74.

148. *Universalist Union* 7 (8 October 1842): 745-46.

149. Clayton, *Forty-Seven Years in the Universalist Ministry,* pp. 171 ff.

150. *Universalist Union* 10 (21 June 1845): 500.

151. *Universalist Register,* 1846, p. 57.

152. *Trumpet* 26 (11 January 1845): 118.

153. *Trumpet* 28 (22 August 1846): 38.

154. Clayton, *Forty-Seven Years,* pp. 144-45.

155. *Christian Freeman* 22 (18 January 1861): 150.

156. *Universalist Herald* 11 (16 October 1857): 90.

157. *Christian Freeman* 11 (22 March 1850): 186.

158. Ibid., 14 (3 September 1852): 70.

159. *Universalist Register,* 1871, p. 65; 1872, p. 81.

160. See David A. Johnson, "Beginnings of Universalism in Louisville," *Filson Club History Quarterly* 43 (1969): 173-83; Eddy, *Universalism* 1: 409-10.

161. His letter was reproduced in the *Christian Intelligencer* 12 (15 February 1833): 28.

162. *Autobiography of Peter Cartwright, the Backwoods Preacher,* edited by W.P. Strickland (New York & Cincinnati: The Methodist Book Concern, [1856]; numerous reprints), pp. 39-40.

163. Ibid., p. 48.

164. Eddy, *Universalism* 2: 231.

165. *Universalist Register,* 1883, p. 86.

166. State Report, Proceedings, General Convention (1868), p. 54.

167. *Universalist Magazine* 8 (17 March 1827): 155.

168. Johnson, "Universalism in Louisville," pp. 176-77.

169. *Universalist Union* 3 (25 November 1837): 22.

170. Johnson, "Universalism in Louisville," p. 178.

171. *Universalist Union* 7 (28 May 1842): 433.

172. *Trumpet* 12 (13 November 1830): 79.

173. *Universalist Register,* 1842-44.

174. State Report, Proceedings, General Convention (1844): 531.

175. *Memoranda,* p. 189.

176. See Henry Jewell, *Life and Writings of Rev. Enoch M. Pingree* (Cincinnati: Longeley & Bro., 1850).

177. Thomas, *Autobiography,* p. 337.

178. *Trumpet* 27 (20 December 1845): 105.

179. Johnson, "Universalism in Louisville," p. 181.

180. *Universalist Register,* 1846, p. 57.

181. Ibid., 1847, pp. 58-59; 1848, p. 68; *Universalist Miscellany* 5 (August 1847): 84.

182. Records, General Convention (1844), p. 531; Rogers, *Memoranda,* p. 395.

183. *Universalist Register,* 1845, p. 57.

184. The constitution of the Kentucky State Convention of Universalists was reproduced in the *Universalist Union* 8 (17 June 1843): 502.

185. *Christian Freeman* 6 (27 December 1844): 138.

186. *Trumpet* 18 (22 October 1836): 74.

187. *Universalist Register,* 1859, p. 52.

188. *Trumpet* 33 (27 September 1851): 61.

189. Johnson, "Universalism in Louisville," p. 183; *Universalist Register,* 1872, p. 47.

190. *Christian Freeman* 10 (12 January 1849): 146; *Universalist Register,* 1850, p. 57.

191. *Trumpet* 30 (3 February 1849): 134.

192. Weaver, *Autobiography,* p. 114.

193. *Christian Freeman* 18 (2 January 1857): 142.

194. *Universalist Herald* 11 (21 August 1857): 58.

195. This should not be confused with Union College, Barbourville (Knox County), operated by the Methodists.

196. *Universalist Register,* 1865, p. 21.

197. State Report, Proceedings, General Convention (1868), p. 54.

198. *Universalist Register,* 1872, p. 47.

199. Ibid., 1873, p. 40.

200. Ibid., 1840, p. 35.

201. *Memoranda,* p. 372.

202. *Universalist Union* 7 (28 May 1842): 433.

203. *Universalist Register,* 1842, p. 61.

204. *Trumpet* 23 (9 April 1842): 166.

205. Manford, *Twenty-five Years,* p. 246.

206. *Universalist Register,* 1844, p. 62.

207. *Trumpet* 24 (2 July 1842): 6.

208. *Christian Freeman* 12 (16 August 1850): 62.

209. *Universalist Register,* 1847, p. 58.

210. Eddy, *Universalism* 2: 596.

211. *Universalist Register,* 1860, p. 51.

212. Ibid., 1861, p. 52.

213. Salisbury, "They Builded Better Than They Knew," p. 5.

214. *Christian Freeman* 21 (17 February 1860): 166.

215. *Universalist Register,* 1911, p. 65.

216. State Report, Proceedings, General Convention (1868), pp. 53-54.

217. *Universalist Register,* 1871, p. 45.

Chapter 26: "A LITTLE BUT DETERMINED BAND": UNIVERSALISM IN THE SOUTH BEFORE THE CIVIL WAR

1. *Christian Intelligencer* 7 (11 May 1827): 74. The quotation comprising part of the title of this chapter was taken from the "Remarks" accompanying the minutes of the Chattahoochee Association of Universalists which met in Talbotton, Ga. in November 1839; the minutes were printed in the *Evangelical Universalist* 2 (13 November 1839): 230.

2. *Memoranda,* p. 262.

3. Records, General Convention (1857), pp. 170-71.

4. Clinton Lee Scott, Richard Eddy, and Elmo Robinson, to cite only three historians of the denomination, have given that section only passing mention, or have attributed whatever success has been achieved to northern missionary efforts. A few studies have been made in recent years, but have been limited in scope; among them are C. Wayman McCarty, "A History of the Universalist Church in the Mid-South" (master's thesis, Mississippi State University, 1964); and Earl Wallace Cory, "Unitarians and Univer-

salists of the Southeastern United States during the Nineteenth Century" (Ph.D. dissertation, University of Georgia, 1970; Ann Arbor, Mich. University Microfilms, 1971). A geographical limit has likewise been somewhat arbitrarily placed on the definition of the term "South" for this portion of the present study. With the exception of Louisiana, the treatment of the trans-Mississippi South has been deferred for later consideration. The author visited all of the churches in both North Carolina and Georgia Conventions between 1970 and 1973, as well as the one remaining Universalist Church in Newberry, S.C. and churches in Mississippi and Alabama, and can testify to their continued, if modest, existence at that time.

5. *Universalist Register,* 1846, p. 20.

6. *Evangelical Universalist* 1 (22 September 1838): 7.

7. Annual Report, Universalist Historical Society (1847), Proceedings, pp. 104-105.

8. Records, General Convention (1866), p. 33.

9. See David Benedict, *A General History of the Baptist Denomination in America.* 2 vols. (Boston, 1813); George Paschal, *History of the North Carolina Baptists.* 2 vols. (Raleigh, N.C., 1930).

10. McCarty, "Universalist Church in Mid-South," p. 98.

11. For a detailed history of both German groups to about 1850, see Gotthardt D. Bernheim, *History of the German Settlements and of the Lutheran Church in North and South Carolina* (Philadelphia: The Lutheran Bookstore, 1872; reprint, Spartanburg, S.C.: The Reprint Co., 1972).

12. Report accompanying Proceedings, Union Association of Universalists, *Trumpet* 16 (29 November 1834): 90.

13. The earliest authoritative history of the Baptists, and most frequently cited by historians, was written by Morgan Edwards, at the time a Fellow at Rhode Island College and overseer of the Baptist church in Philadelphia. His work, *Materials toward a History of the American Baptists,* was published in 1770. David Benedict was pastor of the Baptist church in Pawtucket, R.I., when he wrote his two-volume history of that denomination, published in 1813; he drew heavily on Edwards' work, which he updated. See also Martin G. Brumbaugh, *A History of the German Baptist Brethren in Europe and America* (1899); reprint, New York: AMS Press, 1971).

14. Eddy, *Universalism* 2: 35-41, includes a brief discussion of the Dunkards, and indicates their connection with Universalism. There is an extended quotation from Winchester illustrating his sympathetic attitude toward the Dunkards in Rupp's *Original History of . . . Religious Denominations* (1844), p. 94; although no source was given, it was probably from Winchester's *The Face of Moses Unveiled by the Gospel; or Evangelical Truths discovered in the Law,* which was published in Philadelphia in 1787.

15. Benedict, *Baptist Denomination* 2: 434-35; Leah Townsend, *South Carolina Baptists* (Florence, S.C., 1935), pp. 167 ff.

16. Benedict, *Baptist Denomination;* Guion G. Johnson, *Ante-Bellum North Carolina: A Social History* (Chapel Hill: University of North Carolina Press, 1937), p. 342.

17. McCarty identified nine original Dunkard-Universalist churches in South Carolina. "Universalist Church in Mid-South," Appendix A, p. 127.

18. Bernheim, *German Settlements,* p. 129.

19. The earliest account of Universal-

ism in South Carolina appeared in the *Liberalist* (published in Wilmington, N.C.) in 1827; it was reproduced in the *Universalist Magazine* 9 (8 September 1827): 47-48; see also Benedict, *Baptist Denomination* 2: 434. Whittemore dated Universalist preaching in South Carolina from "about 1780." *Modern History*, p. 421.

20. Autobiographical Preface, *The Universal Restoration*, quoted in Eddy, *Universalism* 1: 219 ff.

21. *Christian Freeman* 22 (16 November 1860): 113.

22. *Universalist Herald* 18 (15 March 1871): 170.

23. Eddy, *Universalism* 1: 101-102; 2: 38.

24. *Universalist Magazine* 9 (8 September 1827): 47-48.

25. *Evangelical Universalist* 1 (20 October 1838): 7; D.B. Clayton, *Forty-Seven Years in the Universalist Ministry* (Columbia, S.C.: Privately printed, 1889), p. 91.

26. *Universalist Register*, 1836, p. 45.

27. *Southern Pioneer* 3 (4 January 1834): 43.

28. *Memoranda*, pp. 202-203.

29. *Universalist Register*, 1840, p. 35.

30. Ibid., 1841, p. 44.

31. *Trumpet* 20 (8 June 1839): 202.

32. *Universalist Herald* 13 n.s. (15 August 1879): 202.

33. *Universalist Magazine* 9 (20 October 1827): 71-72.

34. Ibid., 9 (11 August 1827): 30-31.

35. *Trumpet* 12 (22 January 1831): 118.

36. Julian S. Bolick, *Sketchbook of Fairfield* [n.d.], pp. 266-67, furnished the author through the courtesy of Mrs. Iona Williams McLaurin, Charleston, S.C.

37. John B. O'Neall, *The Annals of Newberry, Historical, Biographical, and Anecdotal* (Charleston, S.C.: S.G. Courtenay & Co., 1859), pp. 76-77; *Trumpet* 12 (22 January 1831): 118.

38. Thomas H. Pope, *The History of Newberry County, South Carolina* (Columbia: University of South Carolina Press, 1973) 1: 82 n.

39. Clayton, *Forty-Seven Years*, pp. 91, 276.

40. Proceedings, *Trumpet* 12 (12 January 1831): 118.

41. Ibid., 14 (26 January 1833): 121.

42. His itineraries were published in the *Evangelical Universalist* and its successor, the *Southern Evangelist*.

43. *Southern Pioneer* 1 (May 1832): 161.

44. *Trumpet* 16 (11 April 1835): 166.

45. Ibid., 14 (3 November 1832): 75; *Southern Evangelist* 1 (June 1834): 4.

46. Proceedings, *Southern Evangelist* 1 (15 November 1834): 2-3.

47. Proceedings, *Evangelical Universalist* 1 (25 August 1838): 3.

48. Ibid., 2 (22 January 1840): 303.

49. Ibid., 1 (28 November 1838): 7; *Universalist Register*, 1839, p. 27.

50. Proceedings, *Evangelical Universalist* 1 (25 August, 5 December 1838): 3, 3.

51. *Impartialist* 1 (19 January 1833): 78; *Christian Intelligencer* 12 (18 January 1833): 10.

52. Circular Letter, *Trumpet* 15 (14 December 1833): 100.

53. Proceedings, *Southern Evangelist* 1 (17 November 1834): 2.

54. Proceedings and Circular Letter, *Trumpet* 15 (14 December 1833): 100.

55. Circular Letter, ibid.

56. Ibid., 17 (21 May 1836): 190; see also Whittemore, *Modern History*, pp. 310-12.

57. *Trumpet* 11 (8 May 1830): 179.

58. No records exist for the early history of either church, except for a ledger recording the sale of pews. Most of the records prior to 1844 had been deposited in the state capital and were destroyed when Columbia was burned during the Civil War. A review by the author of the existing records for the nineteenth century for both St. Phillips Episcopal Church and the Congregational church indicated no Universalists who identified themselves as such on the membership rolls. For Unitarianism, see George H. Gibson, "Unitarian Congregations in the Ante-Bellum South," *Proceedings of the Unitarian Historical Society* 12 (Part II, 1959): 53-78; Cory, *Unitarians and Universalists,* Chapter 1; and the records of the Charleston Unitarian Church.

59. *Trumpet* 11 (8 May 1830): 179; see also Eddy, *Universalism* 2: 398.

60. Ibid.; Eddy, *Universalism* 2: 517-18, cites the pamphlet in his bibliography of Universalist publications.

61. L.F.W. Andrews, *Southern Pioneer* 3 (7 December 1833): 27.

62. *Trumpet* 14 (3 November 1832): 75. According to Andrews, one motive behind the decision was to counterbalance the Unitarian church. *Southern Evangelist* 2 (August 1835): 3.

63. *Evangelical Universalist* 2 (1 May 1839): 6. In 1839 the state convention donated $47.05 to support the church. Ibid., 2 (11 September 1839): 159.

64. *Universalist Register,* 1857, p. 56; Elias Bull, archivist of the Charleston Unitarian Church, interview with the author, 8 April 1971.

65. Vestry records, Unitarian Church of Charleston, S.C. 1 (3 May 1869): 67.

66. *Universalist Register,* 1842. p. 61; Records, General Convention (1841), p. 470; John A. Chapman, *History of Edgefield County from the Earliest Settlements to 1897* (Newberry, S.C.: Elbert H. Aull, 1897).

67. *Universalist Register,* 1843, p. 62; Clayton, *Forty-Seven Years,* pp. 60 ff.

68. Clayton, *Forty-Seven Years,* p. 91.

69. Ibid., pp. 52 ff.

70. *Universalist Register,* 1846, p. 58; Clayton, *Forty-Seven Years,* pp. 137 ff.

71. Proceedings, *Universalist Herald* 11 (4 December 1857): 118.

72. Ibid., 13 (21 October 1859): 433.

73. There were seventeen in the original congregation; eight were added during the convention. Proceedings, ibid. The meeting house at Huntsville, to which Universalists had contributed when it was constructed in 1835, was shared with other denominations.

74. *Universalist Herald* 13 (23 December 1859): 462.

75. Abstract of Proceedings, ibid., 14 (31 August 1860): 486.

76. *Universalist Register,* 1861, p. 54.

77. Clayton, *Forty-Seven Years,* pp. 272-73, 276.

78. Circular Letter, South Carolina Convention, *Universalist Herald* 11 (4 September 1857): 65.

79. Records, General Convention, 1839, p. 460.

80. *Universalist Herald* 18 (1 July 1870): 121; *Evangelical Universalist* 2 (1 January 1840): 276.

81. "History of Universalism in Georgia," *Universalist Herald* 12 n.s. (1 April 1879): 2; Allen Green to T.J. Sawyer, 30 June 1836, *Universalist Union* 1 (13 August 1836): 317. Green was the corresponding secretary of the Universalist Historical Society for Georgia at the time, and resided at Green Hill (Jones County), where a small group of Universalists resided.

82. Extracts from Gibbs' pamphlet were published by L.F.W. Andrews in the *Southern Evangelist* 1 (30 October 1834): 3.

83. Portions of his pamphlet, "Thirteen Questions and Answers on the Faith of Universal Redemption," were reprinted in ibid.; the editor, L.F.W. Andrews, identified the author as Isaiah Eisland. *Southern Pioneer* 3 (15 March 1834): 88.

84. Whittemore, *Modern History,* p. 424.

85. *Universalist Union* 1 (13 August 1836): 317.

86. *Southern Pioneer* 4 (6 June 1835): 249.

87. *Universalist Magazine* 8 (25 November 1826): 90; 9 (25 August 1827): 39.

88. *Southern Evangelist* 1 (September 1834): 3.

89. Ibid., 1 (May, September 1834): 2, 3; 2 (15 May 1835): 2.

90. Ibid., 2 (1 June 1835): 3.

91. *Evangelical Universalist* 1 (16 June 1838): 4.

92. "Centennial Magazine, 1865-1965," *Newnan* (Georgia) *Times-Herald* (December 1965).

93. *Evangelical Universalist* 1 (19 December 1838): 7.

94. Ibid., 1 (25 August 1838): 5.

95. Proceedings, ibid., 1 (28 July 1838): 3.

96. *Universalist Union* 1 (13 August 1836): 317.

97. Proceedings and Circular Letter, *Evangelical Universalist* 1 (5 December 1838): 4.

98. Various dates for the organization of the Georgia Convention have been assigned, from 1838 to 1842. The proceedings of the organization meeting in 1839 were reproduced in ibid., 2 (13 November 1839): 231.

99. Proceedings, *Universalist Herald* 11 (16 October 1857): 89.

100. *Southern Pioneer* 3 (4 January 1834): 46.

101. Ibid., 3 (1 February 1834): 62.

102. *Southern Evangelist* 1 (September 1834): 2.

103. Atkins to Thomas Whittemore, *Trumpet* 13 (14 January 1832): 114; 16 (1 November, 13 December 1834): 74, 98.

104. *Southern Pioneer* 3 (15 February 1834): 71.

105. Proceedings, *Evangelical Universalist* 1 (14 July 1838): 7.

106. Ibid., 2 (7 August 1839): 119.

107. Ibid., 2 (12 February 1840): 327; Brownson to editor, *Trumpet* 19 (28 April 1838): 180.

108. Clayton, *Forty-Seven Years,* pp. 128, 131, 136, 176.

109. *Christian Freeman* 11 (1 February 1850): 158.

110. *Universalist Herald,* cited in ibid., 13 (25 July 1851): 50.

111. Ibid., 14 (14 May 1852): 6.

112. Proceedings, Georgia State Convention, *Universalist Herald* 11 (16 October 1857): 89; Strain to editor, ibid., (28 August 1857, 20 January 1858): 63, 138-39.

113. Proceedings, ibid., 13 (11 November 1860): 445.

114. Proceedings, Georgia State Convention, ibid., 9 n.s. (15 October 1875): 577.

115. *Christian Freeman* 13 (19 December 1851): 134.

116. Ibid., 15 (20 May 1853): 10.

117. Ibid., 13 (2 January 1852): 142.

118. *Universalist Register,* 1854, p. 53.

119. Ibid., 1855, p. 53.

120. Proceedings, Georgia State Convention, *Universalist Herald* 12 (1 October 1858): 262.

121. Proceedings, Georgia State Convention, ibid., 13 (11 November 1859): 445; 14 (9 November 1860): 512.

122. Proceedings, ibid., 13 (11 November 1859): 445; *Universalist Register*, 1861, pp. 54-55.

123. The name of the rural community was later shortened simply to "Plains" and in the mid-1970s became famous as the home of the 39th President of the United States; by then, the Universalist society had long since disappeared.

124. *Christian Freeman* 11 (8 March 1850): 178.

125. *Universalist Register*, 1861, pp. 54-55.

126. *Christian Freeman* 22 (4 January 1861): 142.

127. *Evangelical Universalist* 1 (28 July 1838): 7.

128. *Universalist Herald* 11 (11 September, 16 October 1857): 73, 89.

129. *Universalist Register*, 1872, p. 38.

130. *Evangelical Universalist* 1 (1 September 1838): 7.

131. Ibid., 2 (26 February 1840): 342.

132. Ibid., 2 (4 March 1840): 350.

133. *Universalist Register*, 1875, p. 38.

134. Jacob Frieze, "History of Universalism in North Carolina," *Universalist Magazine* 9 (11 August 1827): 30-31, reproduced from the *Liberalist* (Wilmington, North Carolina). The most comprehensive collection of materials dealing with the history of Universalism in the state, particularly valuable for information since 1865, is John E. Williams and others, *History of Universalism in North Carolina*, issued under the auspices of the state convention in 1968.

135. Joseph Biggs, *A Concise History of the Kehukee Baptist Association* (Tarboro, N.C.: George Howard, 1834), pp. 85, 276.

136. Whittemore, *Modern History*, p. 422; Thomas, *Century of Universalism*, p. 79; Clayton, *Forty-Seven Years*, p. 354.

137. *Universalist Magazine* 8 (2 September 1826): 43; 9 (11 August 1827): 30-31.

138. Frieze to editor, *Christian Intelligencer* 8 (8 December 1828): 194.

139. *Universalist Herald* 11 (11 December 1857): 122.

140. *Universalist Magazine* 9 (11 August 1827): 30-31; *Trumpet* 10 (29 November 1828): 86.

141. *Universalist Magazine* 8 (12 May 1827): 188.

142. Proceedings, ibid., 9 (11 August 1827): 32.

143. There were several other societies organized in the same county during the nineteenth century. The precise location of most of the first societies was given neither in the proceedings of the 1827 meeting nor in Frieze's reports; the determination has therefore had to be made from other sources, part of which is tradition and recollection rather than solid evidence.

144. *Universalist Herald* 12 (15 January 1858): 130.

145. *Trumpet* 13 (31 December 1831): 107.

146. Ibid., 16 (5 July 1834): 6.

147. *Universalist Union* 1 (14 November 1835): 7.

148. *Trumpet* 14 (12 January 1833): 114.

149. Ibid., 16 (26 July 1834): 18.

150. *Southern Pioneer* 3 (7 December 1833): 31.

151. Raynor to editor, *Trumpet* 16 (3, 24 January 1835): 111, 122. Raynor's trip is detailed in a letter to Otis A. Skinner, editor of the *Southern Pioneer* 4 (7 February 1835): 116-17.

152. *Trumpet* 16 (6 September 1834): 42; *Southern Pioneer* 3 (27 September

1834): 199.

153. Williams, *Universalism in North Carolina,* p. 139.

154. Parsons to editor, *Universalist Union* 1 (14 November 1835, 30 January 1836): 7, 91.

155. *Universalist Union* 1 (27 August 1836): 354. This may have been the same Hawley who had been disavowed in 1834 by Otis A. Skinner, editor of the *Southern Pioneer,* because of his "obscenity of language, intemperance, and gambling." *Southern Pioneer* 3 (29 March 1834): 94.

156. *Trumpet* 14 (7 July 1832): 7; 15 (12 April 1834): 167.

157. Proceedings, Universalist Historical Society, 1834; reprinted in the *Trumpet* 16 (25 April 1835): 176.

158. *Southern Evangelist* 2 (16 November 1835): 4.

159. See Martha Hardwick Swann, "John Crenshaw Burruss," *Alabama Historical Quarterly* 18 (Summer 1956): 137-41.

160. Eddy, *Universalism* 2: 392; *Universalist Register,* 1846, p. 58.

161. *Universalist Miscellany* 5 (November 1847): 203; *Universalist Register,* 1848, p. 70; 1849, p. 58.

162. *Christian Freeman* 11 (6 July 1849): 38.

163. The *Universalist Register,* 1848, p. 70, erroneously listed the date of reorganization as 1844. The proceedings of the North Carolina Convention were carried in the *Universalist Herald* until it suspended publication in 1861. William Farrior of Hallsville was the first standing clerk, serving several years.

164. Williams, *Universalism in North Carolina,* p. 127.

165. *Christian Freeman* 11 (6 July 1849): 38.

166. Ibid., 12 (14 February 1851): 166.

167. Ibid., 17 (14 March 1856): 182.

168. *Universalist Register,* 1861, p. 54.

169. *Christian Freeman* 11 (8 March 1850): 178.

170. Ibid., 11 (1 February 1850): 158.

171. Ibid., 11 (8 February 1850): 161.

172. *Universalist Register,* 1877, pp. 116-17.

173. Scrapbooks in possession of Mrs. Fannie Hardwick, Notasulga, Alabama; *Trumpet* 21 (2 September 1848): 46.

174. Extracts from his diary are reproduced, in a combination of direct quotation and paraphrase, in Williams, *Universalism in North Carolina,* pp. 57-78.

175. *Trumpet* 32 (10 December 1859): 110.

176. *Universalist Herald* 11 (11 December 1857): 122.

177. Clayton, *Forty-Seven Years,* pp. 217, 218; *Universalist Register,* 1864, p. 19.

178. *Trumpet* 30 (8 August 1857): 39.

179. Circular Letter, North Carolina Convention, *Universalist Herald* 12 (29 October 1858): 279.

180. Guion Griffis Johnson, *Ante-Bellum North Carolina: A Social History* (Chapel Hill: University of North Carolina Press, 1937), p. 369.

181. *Universalist Register,* 1861, p. 54.

182. Ibid.; *Universalist Herald* 18 (15 May 1870): 110.

183. *Universalist Herald* 11 (22 May 1857): 10.

184. Ibid., 14 (18 January 1861): 539.

185. Ibid., 14 (11 January 1861): 533.

186. *Trumpet* 23 (7 December 1850): 102; *Universalist Register,* 1880, p. 85.

187. There was no reference to the school in any of the reports of the Committee on Education of the General Convention which attempted a comprehensive annual inventory of schools, beginning in 1858. For infor-

mation on Griffin, see the *Universalist Register,* 1880, p. 85; Williams, *Universalism in North Carolina,* pp. 20-21; Clayton, *Forty-Seven Years,* pp. 352-53.

188. *Universalist Herald* 15 (1 March 1867): 2.

189. Ibid.

190. For a history of Universalism in this state, emphasizing the local and family-centered character of the denomination there, see McCarty, "Universalist Church in Mid-South," Chapter 2. Much of his information was based on interviews. Through the kind generosity of L.C. Prater of Camp Hill, Ala., the present author was able to visit several Universalist churches in Alabama and Mississippi in the winter of 1970-71, and to examine many of the surviving church records.

191. *Universalist Magazine* 9 (25 August 1827): 39.

192. McCarty, "Universalist Church in Mid-South," pp. 53-54.

193. *Southern Evangelist* 1 (May 1834): [4].

194. *Trumpet* 13 (14 January 1832): 114.

195. *Southern Evangelist* 1 (17 November 1834): [3].

196. Ibid., 1 (June 1834): [3-4].

197. *Trumpet* 14 (13 October 1832): 63.

198. *Southern Evangelist* 1 (June 1834): [3]. This was one of the earliest recorded uses of the combined name.

199. *Southern Pioneer* 3 (15 February, 1 March 1834): 71, 78.

200. *Memoranda,* pp. 216, 217.

201. *Evangelical Universalist* 1 (3 April 1839): 6.

202. Ibid.; Rogers, *Memoranda,* pp. 219-20.

203. *Trumpet* 16 (1 November 1834): 74; *Universalist Register,* 1842, p. 61; 1846, p. 58.

204. *Southern Pioneer* 3 (26 April 1834): 105; *Trumpet* 16 (1 November 1834): 75.

205. McCarty, "Universalist Church in Mid-South," p. 117.

206. *Trumpet* 28 (19 December 1846): 105-106.

207. Ibid., 25 (8 July 1843): 10.

208. Ibid., 26 (22 June 1844): 2.

209. *Universalist Register,* 1846, p. 58.

210. *Christian Freeman* 5 (8 March 1844): 178.

211. *Trumpet* 26 (24 May 1845): 194.

212. *Christian Freeman* 16 (23 March 1855): 186.

213. Ibid., 11 (29 June 1849): 341.

214. *Trumpet* 31 (17 January 1850): 126.

215. *Universalist Herald* 14 (12 October 1860): 502.

216. *Christian Freeman* 15 (23 December 1853): 134.

217. Ibid., 14 (7 January, 18 March 1853): 142, 182.

218. *Trumpet* 30 (26 May 1849): 197.

219. Some are identified in McCarty, "Universalist Church in Mid-South," p. 49.

220. *Trumpet* 35 (7 January 1854): 122.

221. *Universalist Register,* 1853, p. 54.

222. Information about this society, particularly for the post-Civil War period, was derived largely from a manuscript history, newspaper clippings, and church records kindly made available to the author by L.C. Prater, retired pastor of the church.

223. The most detailed and authoritative account of Burruss is by his great-granddaughter, Martha Hardwick Swann, in the *Alabama Historical Quarterly* 18 (Summer 1956): 137-41.

224. These remarks, reported in the *Christian Freeman* 9 (5 November 1847): 110, were made after Burruss had established a church in Sampson County, N.C., in 1847.

225. *Christian Freeman* 12 (2 August 1850): 54; *Trumpet* 32 (5 October 1850): 66.

226. *Universalist Miscellany* 5 (December 1847): 243; *Universalist Register,* 1852, pp. 55-56.

227. *Christian Freeman* 15 (2 September 1853): 70; McCarty, "Universalist Church in Mid-South," pp. 13-14.

228. *Universalist Herald* 11 (9 May 1857): 1-2.

229. *Universalist Register,* 1859, p. 54.

230. *Universalist Herald* 11 (21 August 1857): 58.

231. The proceedings, constitution, and circular letter of the state convention were published in ibid., 12 (27 August 1858): 241.

232. Ibid., 14 (12 October 1860): 502.

233. *Universalist Register,* 1876, p. 21.

234. As is the case with Alabama, the most comprehensive study of antebellum Universalism in Mississippi is C. Wayman McCarty's "History of the Universalist Church in the Mid-South;" see Chapter 3 of his work.

235. *Memoranda,* p. 206.

236. Clayton, *Forty-Seven Years in the Universalist Ministry,* p. 272.

237. *Southern Universalist,* cited in the *Trumpet* 41 (10 September 1859): 58.

238. Unless otherwise indicated, the information about Clayton is derived from his autobiography, completed in 1888 when he was seventy years of age.

239. *Trumpet* 28 (17 April 1847): 174.

240. See McCarty, "Universalist Church in Mid-South," p. 120.

241. His life and contributions are discussed in the second volume of this work.

242. *Universalist Register,* 1880, p. 85.

243. McCarty, "Universalist Church in Mid-South," p. 77.

244. *Universalist Miscellany* 6 (October 1848): 148; *Universalist Register,* 1850, p. 59.

245. *Universalist Union* 7 (29 October 1842): 792.

246. *Christian Freeman* 12 (28 February 1851): 174.

247. The records of the Burruss Memorial Church were destroyed in a fire at the farm home in which the secretary's files were kept. The records of the "Our Home" church were made available to the author through the generosity of Mrs. Oleta Herrington Vance.

248. McCarty, "Universalist Church in Mid-South," p. 93.

249. Church records 3 (1907): 104.

250. *Universalist Herald* 11 (4 September 1857): 66.

251. *Christian Freeman* 17 (8 February 1856): 162.

252. *Universalist Herald* 18 (1 May 1870): 106.

253. Proceedings, ibid., 13 (12 August 1859): 298-99.

254. For a detailed account of the organization meeting, see the *Trumpet* 41 (10 September 1859): 57.

255. Proceedings, *Universalist Herald* 14 (5 October 1860): 498.

256. *Christian Freeman* 23 (3 May 1861): 2.

257. *Universalist Herald* 14 (1 March 1861): 558.

258. *Universalist Union* 9 (3 February 1844): 192.

259. *Christian Freeman* 11 (15 March 1850): 182.

260. Ibid., 12 (31 May 1850): 18; the

community was listed for several years as "Camilton" in the *Universalist Register.*

261. *Universalist Register,* 1858, p. 51.

262. *Christian Freeman* 22 (28 December 1860): 139; 25 January 1861): 154.

263. Their histories are given in McCarty, "Universalist Church in Mid-South," pp. 98 ff.

264. *Universalist Register,* 1874, p. 38.

265. The episode is detailed in Whittemore, *Modern History,* pp. 424-25.

266. The petition was reproduced in the *Universalist Magazine* 5 (27 March 1824): 158.

267. Rogers, *Memoranda,* p. 249; *Universalist Union* 7 (28 May 1842): 434.

268. *Universalist Union* 7 (28 May 1842): 434.

269. McCarty, "Universalist Church in Mid-South," p. 100.

270. Ibid., p. 101; *Universalist Register,* 1872, p. 48.

271. *Universalist Register,* 1875, p. 47.

272. Ibid., 1878, p. 18.

273. See the brief chapter on the Unitarians in McCarty, "Universalist Church in Mid-South," pp. 112-19.

274. Proceedings, *Universalist Magazine* 9 (14 July 1827): 14-15.

275. A facsimile of the circular letter was reproduced in Williams, *Universalism in North Carolina.*

276. Proceedings, *Universalist Magazine* 9 (15 December 1827): 103.

277. *Universalist Register,* 1848, p. 70.

278. *Trumpet* 16 (1 November 1834): 74.

279. The proceedings of the organization meeting, which took place at the Mulberry Grove Universalist church (Harris County) in Georgia in July, and of the next meeting in Lafayette, Ala., in November of the same year, together with the circular letter and the constitution, were printed in the *Evangelical Universalist* 1 (14, 21 July; 14, 28 November 1838).

280. The proceedings of each were published in the *Universalist Herald.*

281. Proceedings, General Southern Convention, ibid., 14 (16 November 1860): 517.

282. Ibid., 12 (15 January 1857): 129.

283. Circular Letter, ibid., 12 (27 August 1858): 241.

284. Report, Committee on Organization, Proceedings, General Convention (1860), p. 34.

285. Proceedings, South Carolina Convention, *Universalist Herald* 12 (20 August 1858): 237.

286. Summary of Proceedings, ibid., 12 (1 October 1858): 262.

287. Ibid., 13 (12 August 1859): 399.

288. Proceedings, South Carolina Convention, ibid., 13 (13 October 1859): 433.

289. Proceedings, ibid., 13 (2 December 1859): 464.

290. Postscript to Proceedings, ibid.

291. Proceedings, ibid., 14 (16 November 1860): 517.

292. Ibid., 12 (22 January 1858): 135.

293. Ibid., 14 (16 November 1860): 517.

294. Remarks accompanying Proceedings, ibid.

Chapter 27: UNIVERSALIST-UNITARIAN MERGER: FROM ANTAGONISM TO COEXISTENCE

1. Scott, *Universalist Church,* p. 105.

2. Rupp, *Original History,* p. 725.

3. *Trumpet* 14 (14 July 1832): 10.

4. Eddy, "Universalist Conventions and Creeds," *Universalist Quarterly* 12 (July 1875): 321 n.

5. *Christian Freeman* 4 (13 January 1843): 145.

6. Ibid., 5 (15 September 1843): 78.

7. *Trumpet* 39 (6 February 1858): 142.

8. *Trumpet* 16 (24 January 1835): 123.

9. Ibid., 34 (2 April 1853): 171.

10. For an account of the wave of anti-Catholicism which swept over America before the Civil War, see Ray A. Billington, *The Protestant Crusade, 1800-1860* (New York: Macmillan, 1938).

11. *Trumpet* 15 (28 December 1833): 106.

12. Ibid., 16 (3 January 1835): 111.

13. Ibid., 11 (16 January 1830): 114.

14. Ibid., 15 (15 March 1834): 150.

15. Adams, *Memoir of Thomas Whittemore*, pp. 214-15.

16. *Trumpet* 16 (16 August 1834): 31.

17. Ibid., 16 (11 October 1834): 63.

18. Ibid., 16 (1 November 1834): 76.

19. Ibid., 16 (30 August 1834): 38.

20. Ibid., 16 (10 January 1835): 114.

21. Ibid., 34 (12 June 1852): 2.

22. Ibid., 15 (9 November 1833): 78.

23. Ibid., 15 (8 March 1834): 146.

24. Ibid., 25 (24 June 1843): 2.

25. Ibid., 24 (27 May 1843): 193.

26. *Christian Freeman* 5 (18 August 1843): 62.

27. Ibid., 7 (30 May 1843): 18.

28. Ibid., 5 (19 May 1843): 10.

29. Ibid., 16 (30 June 1854): 34.

30. Ibid., 16 (6 October 1854): 89.

31. *Trumpet* 16 (20 December 1834): 102.

32. Ibid., 40 (2 April 1859): 174.

33. Ibid., 33 (14 June 1851): 2.

34. Proceedings, General Convention (1859), p. 30.

35. *Universalist Union* 9 (12 October 1844): 757.

36. Ibid., 3 (5 May 1838): 205.

37. *Trumpet* 39 (16 January 1858): 130.

38. *Philomath Encyclopedia* 5 (April 1842): 146-52.

39. *Universalist Miscellany* 2 (August 1844): 77.

40. *Christian Freeman* 7 (13 June 1845): 25.

41. Ibid., 16 (22 December 1854): 134.

42. *Universalist Miscellany* 2 (August 1844): 77.

43. *Christian Repository* 4 (August 1823): 76-78.

44. *Trumpet* 18 (24 December 1836): 106.

45. Carl Seaburg, "Universalism in the early *Centinel*," p. 16A.

46. *Universalist Union* 10 (15 February 1845): 214-15.

47. Proceedings, ibid., 3 (21 July 1838): 291.

48. Proceedings, *Trumpet* 11 (26 June 1830): 206.

49. Stacy, *Memoirs*, p. 57.

50. *Universalist Magazine* 1 (27 May 1820): 191.

51. Ibid., 8 (24 March 1827): 158-60.

52. *Trumpet* 12 (11 September 1830): 42.

53. Ibid., 11 (15 August 1829): 24-25.

54. Ibid., 11 (11 June 1830): 198; Records, Maine Convention (1858).

55. *Trumpet* 44 (13 December 1862): 135; 45 (13 June 1863): 31.

56. Smith, *Sketches* 1: 189.

57. *Memoranda,* pp. 121, 123.

58. *Trumpet* 15 (17 August 1833): 30.

59. *Universalist Magazine* 6 (18 June 1825): 206.

60. *Trumpet* 15 (14, 28 December 1833): 98, 107.

61. Ibid., 18 (23 July 1834): 17.

62. Ibid., 16 (19 July 1834): 18.

63. Ibid., 24 (25 June 1842): 2.

64. *Religion in America,* p. 162.

65. *Universalist Magazine* 2 (21 October 1820): 66.

66. *Trumpet* 32 (8 March 1851): 154.

67. *Universalist Magazine* 2 (18 November 1820): 81.

68. Ibid., 2 (10 March 1821): 147.

69. *Christian Repository* 2 (June 1821): 29.

70. *Universalist Union* 1 (22 October 1836): 397.

71. Whittemore, *Modern History,* p. 441 n.

72. *Christian Intelligencer* 7 (5 January 1827): 2.

73. *Universalist Magazine* 4 (12 April 1823): 165.

74. Ibid., 7 (18 March 1826): 154.

75. Rupp, *Original History,* pp. 703-18.

76. Smith, *Sketches* 2: 188-89.

77. *Christian Ambassador* 10 (21 April 1860): 62; the statement was italicized for emphasis.

78. By far the best source for tracing historically the relations between Universalists and Unitarians is the denominational press. Systematic studies have been confined almost exclusively to twentieth-century development. The three most important such works are unpublished theses or dissertations, and were all written when discussion of consolidation was about to result in concrete action. All three devote only a few paragraphs or pages to the pre-1870 period. See Charles N. Vickery, "A Century of Attempted Rapprochement between the Universalist Church of America and the American Unitarian Association" (STB thesis, Crane Theological School, Tufts College, June 1945); Joseph L. Sullivan, "The Universalist Church and the Unitarian Moves [*sic*] Again toward Merger" (doctoral dissertation, Central School of Religion of Indianapolis [1956]; and Peter Lee Scott, "A History of the Attempts of the Universalist and Unitarian Denominations to Unite" (BD thesis, St. Lawrence University Theological School, 1957). The present author is indebted to all three of these works for calling attention to sources which might otherwise have been overlooked. Alfred S. Cole (1893-1977), long interested in the historical aspects of relations between Unitarians and Universalists, and himself an advocate of merger, made many contributions to the history of Universalism as a scholar and as an officer and librarian for many years of the Universalist Historical Society. While pastor of the Unitarian church in Lebanon, N.H. (1955-66) he prepared for local distribution a mimeographed booklet of excerpts from both Universalist and Unitarian publications to provide background for the merger that was then imminent. He kindly furnished a copy to the author. One of Cole's most pertinent works was *Our Liberal Heritage* (Boston: Beacon Press, 1951), originally prepared as a publication of the Department of Education of the Universalist Church of America. See also the brief treatments of the subject in Scott, *Universalist Church of America,* Chapter 15; and Robinson, *American Universalism,* pp. 168-81.

79. *Christian Register* 3 (21 May

1824): 162. The extended excerpt from this editorial given in Eddy, *Universalism* 2: 480, has often been quoted. It should be pointed out that Eddy failed to indicate either the context in which it was written, or the identity of the author. By omitting part of the quotation, Eddy also failed to clarify an important distinction among Universalists made by the author of the editorial.

80. *Universalist Magazine* 5 (5 June 1824): 197-98.

81. Ibid., 6 (14 May 1825): 187.

82. Ibid., 3 (1 June 1822): 194.

83. Ibid., 9 (10 November 1827): 83.

84. *Trumpet* 37 (16 February 1856): 147.

85. Ibid., 11 (12 December 1829): 94.

86. Ibid., 10 (2 August 1828): 18.

87. *Universalist Magazine* 8 (24 March 1827): 158.

88. *Trumpet* 19 (16 June 1838): 206.

89. Ibid., 10 (20 June 1829): 202.

90. *Universalist Magazine* 8 (11 November 1825): 83-84.

91. *Trumpet* 11 (6 February 1830): 127.

92. *Memoranda,* p. 283.

93. Reproduced in the *Christian Freeman* 4 (28 October 1842): 101.

94. *Trumpet* 42 (15 September 1860): 62.

95. Smith, *Sketches* 2: 194-96.

96. *Trumpet* 16 (27 September 1834): 54.

97. Quoted in the *Universalist Expositor* 1 n.s. (July 1833): 276-77.

98. *Trumpet* 14 (19 January 1833): 119.

99. *Religion in America,* pp. 276-77.

100. *Trumpet* 11 (7 November 1829): 74.

101. Ibid., 26 (1-29 February 1845).

102. *Universalist Union* 5 (29 February 1840): 228-29.

103. *Trumpet* 27 (6 September 1845): 45-46.

104. Ibid., 29 (16 October 1847): 70.

105. Ibid., 21 (11 January 1840): 114.

106. Ibid., 35 (11 September 1852): 54.

107. Ibid., 13 (21 April 1832): 170.

108. *Autobiography,* pp. 218-19.

109. *Impartialist* 1 (16 February 1833): 94.

110. *Trumpet* 12 (2 April 1831): 158.

111. Ibid., 11 (1 May 1830): 174; 12 (10 July 1832): 6.

112. Ibid., 13 (2 July 1831): 2.

113. Ibid., 13 (24 December 1831): 102.

114. Ibid., 14 (30 March 1833): 158.

115. Ibid., 14 (26 January 1833): 122.

116. Ibid., 16 (3 January 1835): 110.

117. Ibid., 10 (22 November 1828): 82.

118. Ibid., 31 (15 September 1849): 54.

119. Tract No. 20, "Unitarians and Universalists;" substantially the same article appeared in the *Ladies' Repository* 18 (September 1849): 81-87.

120. *Christian Freeman* 4 (27 January 1843): 154.

121. Ibid., 10 (8 September 1848): 74.

122. Ibid., 14 (16 July 1852): 42.

123. Ibid., 17 (18 April 1856): 202.

124. *Universalist Union* 9 (22 June 1844): 506.

125. *Trumpet* 26 (9 November 1844): 81.

126. Ibid., 27 (22 November 1845): 91.

127. *Universalist Union* 10 (23 August 1845): 649.

128. *Trumpet* 33 (8 November 1851): 86.

129. The trip was reported in detail in the *Christian Register,* and substantial portions were reprinted in the *Trumpet* 29 (9 October 1847): 65.

130. Ibid., p. 66.

131. Ibid., 29 (25 September 1847): 59.

132. *Christian Register* 26 (2 October 1847): 158.

133. *Trumpet* 29 (16 October 1847): 70.

134. Ibid., 29 (23 October 1847): 74; 8 January 1848): 118.

135. Ibid., 40 (4 December 1858): 106.

136. Ibid., 41 (16 July 1859): 26.

137. Cited in the *Christian Ambassador* 27 (28 June 1856): 102.

138. *Trumpet* 32 (2 November 1850): 81.

139. *Star in the West,* cited in ibid., 33 (10 January 1852): 122.

140. *Trumpet* 42 (7 July 1860): 23.

141. *Twenty-Five Years in the West,* p. 304.

142. *New Covenant,* quoted in the *Trumpet* 44 (2 August 1862): 57.

143. *Christian Inquirer* 11 (16 May 1857): [2]; part of the article was reprinted in ibid., 38 (23 May 1857): 202.

144. *Trumpet* 38 (23 May 1857): 202.

145. Ibid., 44 (14 June 1862): 29.

146. Ibid., 44 (19 July 1862): 49.

147. Ibid., 45 (10 December 1863): 138.

Chapter 28: UNIVERSALIST-UNITARIAN MERGER: GESTURES OF FRATERNITY

1. Henry Wilder Foote, "Theodore Clapp," *Proceedings of the Unitarian Historical Society* 3: Part II (1934): 13-39.

2. The principal source for Clapp's life and career is his 419-page *Autobiographical Sketches and Recollections, during a Thirty-five Years' Residence in New Orleans* (Boston: Phillips, Sampson & Co., 1857); for selections from the autobiography, and a valuable brief biography, see John Duffy (ed.), *Parson Clapp of the Strangers' Church of New Orleans* (Baton Rouge: Louisiana State University Press, 1957). Of the numerous biographical sketches, one of the most useful and revealing for the period up to 1849 was published by Thomas Whittemore in the *Trumpet* 22 (8 September 1849): 49, and has been drawn upon in this study. Whittemore's sketch was based on extensive correspondence between Clapp, Whittemore, and other Universalists, much of which was reproduced over several years in both the *Trumpet* and the *Christian Freeman,* as well as in such Unitarian journals as the *New York Christian Inquirer* and the *Christian Register;* see also *Christian Freeman* 16 (29 December 1854): 137.

3. Duffy, *Parson Clapp,* pp. 10-11.

4. *Trumpet* 31 (8 September 1849): 49.

5. See Duffy, *Parson Clapp,* pp. 34-36.

6. *Trumpet* 31 (8 September 1849): 49; Whittemore referred to the institution as "Louisiana College."

7. Duffy, *Parson Clapp,* pp. 36-37.

8. See John Duffy, *Sword of Pestilence: The New Orleans Yellow Fever Epidemic of 1853* (Baton Rouge: Louisiana State University Press, 1966.)

9. *Trumpet* 31 (8 September 1849): 49.

10. Duffy, in his biographical sketch,

ignores completely Clapp's interest in, sympathy for, and involvement with Universalism and Universalists, and refers to him throughout as a Unitarian. The only reference to Universalism in his essay is included in a quotation from Clapp's autobiography (Duffy, *Parson Clapp,* p. 15). The only reference to an individual Universalist is a footnote mention of Whittemore, who is identified only as a "clergyman, author, journalist, and financier, ... one of the great liberal preachers who dabbled in a number of reform movements" (p. 184).

11. "A Report on the Trial of the Rev. Theodore Clapp before the Mississippi Presbytery at Their Sessions in May and December 1832." According to Duffy, who gives a detailed analysis of the trial and Clapp's expulsion (pp. 17 ff), based on Clapp's account, the original records of the Mississippi Presbytery for that period no longer exist. Duffy gives sufficient evidence of inconsistencies, discrepancies, and contradictions in Clapp's testimony between 1828 and 1832 to cast some doubt on Clapp's credibility. As Duffy is careful to point out, Clapp omitted all mention of his unpleasantness with the Presbytery in his autobiography.

12. *New Orleans Advertiser,* quoted in the *Trumpet* 14 (2 March 1833): 144.

13. Quoted by Duffy, *Parson Clapp,* p. 37.

14. Ibid., p. 39. For histories of the church after 1833, see John F.C. Waldo, "Historical Sketch of the First Unitarian Church of New Orleans, La." (New Orleans: [n.p.], 1907); and "Theodore Clapp, A Discourse delivered at the One Hundredth Anniversary of the First Unitarian Church of New Orleans, February 26, 1933" (Boston: [n.p., n.d.].

15. *Theological Views, comprising the Substance of Teachings during a Ministry of Thirty-five Years, in New Orleans* (Boston: A. Tompkins, 1859); see also Chapter 11 of his autobiography.

16. *Trumpet* 29 (29 April 1848): 182.

17. Records, General Convention (1849), p. 85.

18. *Trumpet* 32 (19 October 1850): 74.

19. *Christian Freeman* 12 (11 October, 1 November 1850): 94, 106.

20. Ibid., 17 (8 June 1855): 22.

21. *Trumpet* 39 (31 October 1857): 86.

22. *Southern Pioneer* 3 (26 April 1834): 105.

23. Clapp to Andrews, 28 February 1834, ibid., 3 (26 April 1834): 106.

24. Ibid., 3 (19 July 1834): 159.

25. *Southern Evangelist* 1 (May 1834): [2].

26. *Universalist Union* 4 (15 June 1839): 249-50.

27. *Trumpet* 19 (26 May 1838): 194.

28. *Christian Freeman* 5 (8 March 1844): 179.

29. *Universalist Quarterly* 26 (January 1859): 94.

30. Clapp to editor, *Star in the West,* quoted in the *Trumpet* 39 (6 March 1858): 158.

31. *Trumpet* 40 (14 August 1858): 42.

32. Eddy, *Universalism* 2: 377.

33. See, for example, *Trumpet* 29 (29 April 1848): 182; *Christian Freeman* 12 (21 February 1851): 170; 16 (23 March 1855): 183.

34. Clapp to Whittemore, *Trumpet* 31 (16 June 1849): 1.

35. *Christian Freeman* 11 (29 June 1849): 34.

36. *Trumpet* 31 (8 September 1849):

49; *Christian Freeman* 12 (21 February 1851): 170; see also numerous references to slavery in his autobiography.

37. For biographies of the father, see the obituary in the *Trumpet* 21 (21 September 1839): 54; A.C. Thomas, *Century of Universalism,* p. 334; and J.H. Adams, *Fifty Notable Years,* pp. 129-30. There are numerous biographies of Thomas Starr King, of which two are basic: Richard Frothingham, *A Tribute to Thomas Starr King* (Boston: Ticknor and Fields, 1865), who had access to over seventy letters exchanged between King and a close friend, Randolph Ryer of New York City, between 1841 and 1864, many of which are reproduced in their entirety; and a memoir written by Edwin P. Whipple which served as a preface to an edition of some of King's sermons originally published in 1877 under the title *Christianity and Humanity* (Boston: Houghton Mifflin), and later reprinted. The most comprehensive biography, written by a close acquaintance, is Charles W. Wendte's *Thomas Starr King: Patriot and Preacher* (Boston: Beacon Press, 1921). Hal Curtis' *Starr King: Patriot and Mason* (San Francisco: Crane Printing Co., 1951) emphasizes King's secular activities. See also William Day Simonds, *Starr King in California* (San Francisco: Paul Elder & Co., 1917) and Arnold Crompton, *Apostle of Liberty: Starr King in California* (Boston: Beacon Press, 1950). For a full bibliography, see Elmo A. Robinson, "The Universalist Connections of Thomas Starr King," *Annual Journal of the Universalist Historical Society* 5 (1964-65): 3-29, which also includes considerable biographical information on the father's career culled from the denominational press.

38. Frothingham, *Tribute,* pp. 41-42.

39. Ibid., pp. 48-49.

40. *Christian Freeman* 21 (13 April 1860): 198.

41. Quoted in Curtis, *Starr King,* p. 5.

42. Frothingham, *Tribute,* pp. 107-108.

43. *Christian Freeman* 12 (26 July 1850): 50.

44. The sermon was reproduced in Whipple's edition of King's sermons, pp. 224-41.

45. *Unitarian Review* 29 (April 1888): 309.

46. Frothingham, *Tribute,* pp. 91-92.

47. Curtis, *Starr King,* p. 9.

48. Frothingham, *Tribute,* p. 194.

49. Ibid., p. 163 n.

50. Whipple, "Preface," p. li.

51. Frothingham, *Tribute,* p. 213.

52. Whipple, "Preface," pp. xlv-xlvii.

53. Quoted in *Christian Freeman* 23 (24 May 1861): 14.

54. Cited in ibid., 23 (20 September 1861): 82.

55. Of the twenty-two sermons reproduced in Whipple's collection, sixteen had been delivered originally in the East. Most of these were repeated at least once in San Francisco. Whipple, "Preface," p. xliii.

56. Frothingham, *Tribute,* p. 181.

57. Ibid., p. 191.

58. *Universalist Register,* 1862, p. 48; substantially the same reference was made in the three succeeding issues. See also the *Trumpet* 45 (12 March 1864): 186.

59. Robinson, "King," pp. 17-18.

60. The facts available regarding early California Universalism are scanty and sometimes contradictory. Asa M. Bradley's unpublished "History of Universalism on the Pacific Coast" (typescript) prepared in 1910, largely a reminiscence and highly personalized, must be used with caution, but has

considerable primary material not available elsewhere. Information has been pieced together by the present author largely from contemporary denominational publications.

61. *Universalist Register,* 1850, p. 59.

62. *Christian Freeman* 13 (12 March 1852): 182.

63. *Universalist Register,* 1854, p. 37.

64. *Christian Freeman* 11 (14 December 1849): 130.

65. Robinson, "King," p. 17.

66. *Christian Freeman* 16 (5 January 1855): 142.

67. Ibid., 15 (7 April 1854): 194.

68. *Trumpet* 35 (10 December 1853): 106.

69. Much of the information about Edmunds was derived from material collected by George N. Belknap, university historian of the University of Oregon, including an autobiographical sketch by Edmunds published in 1873. See also *The Western Life Boat and Journal of Biography* 1 (1873): 203.

70. *Universalist Register,* 1857, p. 57.

71. Ibid., 1863, p. 56.

72. *Trumpet* 44 (14 March 1863): 186.

73. *Universalist Register,* 1862, p. 48.

74. *Christian Freeman* 19 (25 December 1857): 139.

75. Bradley, "Pacific Coast," p. 4.

76. Extract from Proceedings, *Christian Freeman* 22 (16 November 1860): 114.

77. *Universalist Register,* 1862, p. 48.

78. *Christian Freeman* 17 (7 March 1856): 178.

79. Robinson, "King," pp. 17-18.

80. *Universalist Register,* 1874, p. 27.

81. See Curtis, *Starr King,* pp. 27-28.

82. *Trumpet* 45 (12 March 1864): 186.

83. Quoted in Frothingham, *Tribute,* p. 203.

84. *Trumpet* 44 (27 September 1862): 90.

85. Curtis, *Starr King,* p. 39.

86. Frothingham, *Tribute,* p. 47.

87. Ibid., p. 62.

88. Ibid.

89. Frothingham, *Tribute,* pp. 119-21.

90. *Trumpet* 40 (5 June 1858): 3.

91. *The Pitts-Street Chapel Lectures* (Boston: J.P. Jewett & Co., 1858).

92. Quoted in Wendte, *Thomas Starr King,* p. 108.

93. Frothingham, *Tribute,* p. 102 n.

94. There are several variant wordings of this statement, depending on which transcription of his speech is accepted. The wording to be found in Frothingham (p. 121) and reported also in the *Trumpet* 40 (5 June 1858): 3, is suggested as probably the most accurate. King himself ascribed the statement to an unidentified Universalist layman.

95. *Trumpet* 38 (27 December 1856): 119.

96. *Universalist Quarterly* 10 (January 1853): 73-88.

97. *Trumpet* 34 (16 April 1853): 177; "Agencies of Salvation," *Universalist Quarterly* 10 (July 1853): 293-317.

98. *Trumpet* 34 (16 April 1853): 178.

99. *The Doctrine of Endless Punishment for the Sins of this Life, Unchristian and Unreasonable* (Boston: Crosby, Nichols & Co., 1858).

100. *Universalist Quarterly* 15 (October 1858): 373-400.

101. *Trumpet* 40 (26 February 1859): 154.

102. Ibid., 41 (28 April 1860): 190.

103. *Universalist Quarterly* 1 n.s. (July 1864): 390-91; see 343-83 for Frothingham's biographical sketch, which also accompanied a collection of

King's contributions to Universalist periodicals entitled *Patriotism and Other Papers* (Boston: Tompkins & Co., 1864).

104. *Universalist* 46 (15 April 1865): [2].

105. See Stow Persons, *Free Religion: An American Faith* (New Haven: Yale University Press, 1947); and Sydney E. Ahlstrom, "Francis Ellingwood Abbot and the Free Religious Association," *Proceedings of the Unitarian Historical Society* 17, Part II (1973-1975): 1-21. For an unsympathetic account of its early history by a Universalist clergyman, see A.D. Mayo, "Free Religion in the West," *Universalist Quarterly* 8 n.s. (October 1871): 389-412.

106. *Universalist* 48 (31 August 1867): [2].

107. Miner's sermon was reproduced in ibid., 48 (28 September 1867): [1].

108. The discussions were not recorded in the official minutes, but were transcribed in full in ibid., 48 (26 October 1867): [2].

109. Seventy-fifth Anniversary Discourse, quoted in George H. Emerson, *Life of Alonzo Ames Miner, S.T.D., LL.D.* (Boston: Universalist Publishing House, 1896), p. 209.

110. Scott, "Attempts . . . to Unite," p. 14.

111. *Unitarianism in America,* Chapter 8.

112. Wilbur, *Our Unitarian Heritage,* p. 447.

113. For information on the creation and role of the National Conference and its leadership, see Conrad Wright, "Henry W. Bellows and the Organization of the National Conference," *Proceedings of the Unitarian Historical Society* 15, Part II (1965): 17-46; for a tribute to Bellows' organizing ability from a Universalist, see the *Universalist* 47 (17 February 1866): [2]. For its official reports, see the *Monthly Journal of the American Unitarian Association.*

114. See Cooke, *Unitarianism in America,* Appendix A, for a chronological listing.

115. *Monthly Journal* 8 (March 1867): 51-60.

116. The bulk of the sermon was reproduced in ibid., pp. 58-60.

117. Records, General Convention (1853) 2: 113-14, 119-20.

118. *Universalist* 46 (15 April 1865): [2].

119. Proceedings, General Convention (1865), pp. 37-38.

120. Ibid., (1866), p. 7.

121. *Unitarian Year Book* (1 July 1909), pp. 163-64.

122. See Samuel A. Eliot (ed.), *Heralds of a Liberal Faith* (Boston: American Unitarian Association, 1910) 3: 228-32.

123. *Universalist Centennial,* p. 69.

124. Proceedings, General Convention (1870), p. 15.

125. *Trumpet* 33 (24 January 1852): 130.

126. *Christian Ambassador* 10 (21 April 1860): 62.

127. "The Murray Centenary," *Universalist Quarterly* 7 n.s. (April 1870): 133-55.

128. T.B. Thayer, editor of the *Universalist Quarterly* at the time, estimated that there were 1,000,000 Universalists in America in 1870, comprising 200,000 families. Ibid., 7 n.s. (January 1870): 124 n.

129. Ibid., 7 n.s. (October 1870): 389-420.

Chapter 29: UNIVERSALISM AT MID-POINT: THE DENOMINATIONAL CENTENNIAL

1. Proceedings, General Convention (1867), p. 7. The committee consisted of Israel Washburn (Maine), William H. Ryder (Illinois), Thomas A. Goddard (Massachusetts), Richard Eddy (Pennsylvania), and Horace Greeley (New York).

2. Proceedings, General Convention (1868), pp. 60-61.

3. The full statement appeared as part of the Appendix to the Proceedings of the General Convention for 1866, pp. 21-22.

4. Proceedings, General Convention (1865), p. 39.

5. Report of the Permanent Treasurer, Appendix C, Proceedings, General Convention (1866), pp. 26-28.

6. Treasurer's Report, Appendix, Proceedings, General Convention (1868), p. 11.

7. Appendix, Proceedings, General Convention (1868), pp. 35-36.

8. The history of the Association up to 1886, together with some of the tracts it prepared, was published in *Centenary Voices; or, a part of the work of the women of the Universalist Church from its Centenary Year to the Present Time* (Philadelphia: Woman's Centenary Association, 1886), and was drawn upon for this account. See also Ida M. Folsom, *A Brief History of the Work of Universalist Women, 1869-1955* (Boston: The Association of Universalist Women, 1955). She had access to the files of the Association which for many years were stored in a Boston bank and later became part of the collection of the Andover-Harvard Theological Library.

9. They are listed by author and title in Eddy, *Universalism* 2: 578.

10. For details of the foreign and domestic missionary activity of the denomination after 1870, including the work of the WCA, see the second volume of this study.

11. The fullest record of the three-day meeting was published as *The Universalist Centennial* (Boston: Universalist Publishing House, 1870), a 111-page book including accounts of all the conferences and preaching services, council proceedings, several special reports, the major sermons, hymns, and addresses, and reprints of the coverage by four secular newspapers and two denominational journals—the *Christian Register* (Unitarian) and the *Universalist.* The caption "Once in a Hundred Years" was used by the latter in its 1 October issue to introduce a feature article on the celebration. The official minutes and reports of committees were also printed separately, together with Alonzo A. Miner's Centenary Sermon. Unless otherwise indicated, all references in this section were derived from the Centennial volume and the official proceedings.

12. Proceedings, General Convention (1865), p. 38.

13. Proceedings, General Convention (1860), p. 45.

14. "The Winchester Confession," *Ladies' Repository* 43 (April 1870): 241-45. Adams used the term "Profession" in the article itself.

15. *Ladies' Repository* 43 (March 1870): 225-28. The authorship is unknown, for it was the policy of the Universalist Publishing House, which was responsible for the magazine, not to publish signed editorials. Mrs. Henrietta A. Bingham was the editor in 1870 but not necessarily the author of the editorial.

16. *In Memoriam,* quoted in the *Universalist Quarterly* 22 n.s. (January 1885): 117.

NOTES TO APPENDIX A

1. The volumes were published by Joshua Belcher in Boston (Vols. I and II, 1812; Vol. III, 1813).

2. The present writer used Murray's rendition of his own correspondence wherever possible, including the *Letters and Sketches* for letters written prior to publication in 1813.

3. Many of the letters were dated by external and internal evidence by Hosea Ballou 2d; see his "Dogmatic History."

4. Boston: Marsh, Capen & Lyon, and Waitt & Dow, 1831.

5. *Christian Intelligencer* 13 (17 May 1833): 78-79.

6. *Universalist Union* 7 (7 May 1842): 392.

7. The Andover-Harvard Theological Library contains only nine items in his handwriting, and copies of twenty-four letters, from scattered sources.

8. The letters were published either in whole or in part, with explanatory notes by Demarest, in the *Universalist Quarterly* 4 n.s. (July 1867): 312-32; 5 (January, October 1868): 25-47, 462-76; 6 (1869): 25-36, 419-30; 8 (1871): 222-31; and 9 (1872): 385-405. The location of the originals, only a few of which were included in Murray's *Letters and Sketches,* is unknown. Extracts from some of those published by Demarest were also printed in the *Ladies' Repository* 14 (November 1845): 191-92.

9. See George Huntston Williams, "American Universalism: A Bicentennial Historical Essay," *Journal of the Universalist Historical Society* 9 (1971): 5 n.

NOTES TO APPENDIX B

1. Whittemore, *Life of Ballou* 1: 235-36; he gave no source or authority for this quotation.

2. The Bailey printing is included in a chronology of the various editions listed in the 1902 edition, but no copy of it has been located.

3. Cassara, in his biography of Ballou, lists only the first four editions in his bibliography, presumably for this reason. *Ballou,* p. 183.

4. In this preface, Ballou referred to four editions through which the *Treatise* had already passed; no edition designated as the "fifth" has been located.

5. See Cassara, *Ballou,* pp. 133-35, and Whittemore, *Life of Ballou* 1: 235-36 n. Whittemore quotes Russell Streeter, who noted that "the *fanciful* notions concerning the *creation* and *formation* of man" in the original edition had been omitted. *Universalist Watchman* (April 1849).

6. Pencilled annotation dated October 1847, in Hosea Ballou 2d's personal copy of the 1812 (Portsmouth) edition, Tufts University Library. At the time the notation was made, he was probably preparing the article on the history of American Universalism which appeared in two installments in the *Universalist Quarterly* in 1848. Hosea Ballou 2d apparently possessed only the 1805 and 1812 editions, and for some curious and unexplicable reason he noted in 1848 that the *Treatise* had "never been revised and corrected, though it ought to be." *Universalist Quarterly* 5 (October 1848): 375 n. It is difficult to understand why he neglected to mention the 1832 edition, including not only Ballou's preface but the actual revisions. Perhaps his conception of what constituted a "revision" differed significantly from that held by others.

Selected Bibliography

Sources Consulted and Cited

COLLECTIONS AND DEPOSITORIES

Department of Special Collections and Archives, Nils Y. Wessell Library, Tufts University, Medford, Massachusetts

Historical Society of Pennsylvania, Philadelphia, Pennsylvania

Indiana State Historical Library, Indianapolis, Indiana

Maine Historical Society, Portland, Maine

Meadville/Lombard Theological School, University of Chicago, Chicago, Illinois

North Carolina Department of Archives and History, Raleigh, North Carolina

Northeast District, Unitarian Universalist Association, Portland, Maine

Ohio State Historical Library, Columbus, Ohio

Records, Georgia State Universalist Convention

Records, Local Societies, Churches, and Associations (see footnotes)

Records, Vermont and Quebec Universalist Unitarian Convention

State Department of Archives and History, Montgomery, Alabama

Universalist Convention of North Carolina

Universalist Historical Society Collection, Andover-Harvard Theological Library, Harvard Divinity School, Cambridge, Massachusetts

Vermont Historical Library, Montpelier, Vermont

DENOMINATIONAL NEWSPAPERS, MAGAZINES, AND JOURNALS

Christian Freeman and Family Visiter [*sic*]

Christian Intelligencer

Christian Leader

Christian Register (Unitarian)

Evangelical Universalist

Expositor and Universalist Review

Gospel Banner

Gospel Visitant

Impartialist

Journal of the Universalist Historical Society

Ladies' Repository

Lily of the Valley

Lowell Offering

Monthly Journal of the American Unitarian Association

Philomath Encyclopedia
Practical Christian
Prisoners' Friend
Rose of Sharon
Southern Evangelist
Southern Pioneer and Gospel Visiter [*sic*]
Star in the West
To-Day
Trumpet and Christian Freeman
Trumpet and Universalist Magazine
Unitarian Review
Unitarian Universalist World
Unitarian Year Book
Universalist
Universalist Expositor
Universalist Herald
Universalist Leader
Universalist Magazine
Universalist Miscellany
Universalist Quarterly and General Review
Universalist Register
Universalist Union
Universalist Watchman and Christian Repository

DENOMINATIONAL HISTORY

Adams, John Coleman. "Hosea Ballou and the Larger Hope," *Pioneers of Religious Liberty in America, being the Great and Thursday Lectures delivered in Boston in Nineteen Hundred and Three.* Boston: American Unitarian Association, 1903.

_____. "The Universalists," *Religious History of New England.* Cambridge, Mass.: Harvard University Press, 1917.

Adams, John Greenleaf. *Fifty Notable Years: Views of the Ministry of Christian Universalism during the last Half-Century, with Biographical Sketches.* Boston: Universalist Publishing House, 1882.

_____. *Memoir of Thomas Whittemore, D.D.* Boston: Universalist Publishing House, 1878.

Ahlstrom, Sydney E. "Francis Ellingwood Abbot and the Free Religious Association," *Proceedings of the Unitarian Historical Society* 17 (Part 2, 1973-75): 1-21.

Ballou, Adin. *Autobiography of Adin Ballou, 1803-1890, containing an elaborate record and narrative of his life from infancy to old age, with appendixes, completed and edited by his son-in-law, William S. Heywood.* Lowell, Mass.: Vox Populi Press, Thompson & Hill, 1896.

_____. *History of the Hopedale Community, from its inception to its virtual submergence in the Hopedale Parish,* edited by William S. Heywood. Lowell, Mass.: Vox Populi Press, Thompson & Hill, 1897.

Ballou, Hosea. *A Treatise on Atonement; in which the finite nature of Sin is argued, its causes and consequences as such; the necessity and nature of Atonement, and its glorious consequences in the final Reconciliation of All Men to Holiness and Happiness.* Randolph, Vt.: Sereno Wright, 1805.

Ballou, Hosea 2d. *The Ancient History of Universalism: from the time of the Apostles to its Condemnation in the Fifth General Council, A.D. 553. With an appendix tracing the doctrine down to the Era of the Reformation.* Boston: Marsh and Capen, 1829.

_____. "Dogmatic and Religious History of Universalism in America," *Universalist Quarterly and General Review* 5 (January 1848): 79-103.

_____. "Review of the Denomination of Universalists in the United States," *Expositor and Universalist Review* 3 n.s. (1839): 77-104.

_____. "Rise and Prevalence of Unitarian Views among the Universalists," *Universalist Quarterly and General Review* 5 (October 1848): 370-95.

Ballou, Hosea Starr. *Hosea Ballou, 2d., D.D., First President of Tufts College: His Origin, Life, and Letters.* Boston: H.P. Guild & Co., 1896.

Bell, Albert D. *The Life and Times of Dr. George de Benneville.* Boston: Universalist Church of America, 1953.

Barry, J.S. "Early History of Universalism in New England," *Universalist Quarterly and General Review* 1 n.s. (April 1864): 162-71.

Bisbee, Frederick A. *From Good Luck to Gloucester: The Book of the Pilgrimage.* Boston: Murray Press, 1920.

Bradley, Asa Mayo. "History of Universalism on the Pacific Coast." Typescript, 1910. Andover-Harvard Theological Library.

Brooks, Elbridge Gerry. *Our New Departure; or, the Methods and Work of the Universalist Church as it enters on its second century.* Boston: Universalist Publishing House, 1874.

Brown, Olympia. "An Autobiography." Edited and completed by Gwendolen B. Willis, 1960. *Annual Journal of the Universalist Historical Society* 4 (1963): 1-76.

Brownson, Orestes A. *The Works of Orestes A. Brownson,* collected and arranged by Henry F. Brownson. 20 vols. Detroit, Mich.: Thorndike Nourse, 1882-1907.

Butler, Thomas. "Universalism in Pennsylvania." Typescript, n.d. Historical Society of Pennsylvania.

Canfield, Mary Grace. "Early Universalism in Vermont and the Connecticut Valley." Typescript, 1941. Andover-Harvard Theological Library.

Cassara, Ernest. *Hosea Ballou: The Challenge to Orthodoxy.* Boston: Universalist Historical Society and Beacon Press, 1961.

_____. (ed.). *Universalism in America: A Documentary History.* Boston: Beacon Press, 1971.

Caswell, Jerry V. " 'A New Civilization Radically Higher Than the Old:' Adin Ballou's Search for Social Perfection," *Journal of the Universalist Historical Society* 7 (1967-68): 70-96.

Centenary Voices; or a Part of the Work of the Women of the Universalist Church, from its Centenary Year to the Present Time. Philadelphia: Woman's Centenary Association, 1886.

Channing, W.H. *The Life of William Ellery Channing.* Boston: American Unitarian Association, 1880.

Chapin, Edwin Hubbell. *The Philosophy of Reform: A Lecture delivered before the Berean Institute, in the Broadway Tabernacle, New-York, Jan. 20, 1843; with four discourses, upon the same general topic, delivered in New-York and Brooklyn.* New York: C.L. Stickney, 1843.

Chestnut, Paul Iver. "The Universalist Movement in America, 1770-1803," Ph.D. dissertation, Duke University, 1974; Ann Arbor: University Microfilms, 1974.

Clayton, Daniel Bragg. *Forty-Seven Years in the Universalist Ministry.* Columbia, S.C.: privately printed, 1889.

Clymer, Wayne K. "The Life and Thought of James Relly," *Church History* 11 (1942): 193-216.

Cobb, Sylvanus. *Autobiography of the First Forty-one Years,* edited by Sylvanus Cobb, Jr. Boston: Universalist Publishing House, 1867.

Cole, Alfred S. *Our Liberal Heritage.* Boston: Beacon Press, 1951.

Collier, Charles A., Jr. "Aspects in the Growth of American Universalism." Honors thesis, Harvard College, 1952.

"Constantia" [Judith Sargent Murray]. *The Gleaner, A Miscellaneous Production.* 3 vols. Boston: I. Thomas and E.T. Andrews, 1798.

Commager, Henry S. "The Blasphemy of Abner Kneeland," *New England Quarterly* 8 (March 1935): 29-41.

Cooke, George Willis. *Unitarianism in America.* Boston: American Unitarian Association, 1902.

Cory, Earl Wallace. "Unitarians and Universalists of the Southeastern United States during the Nineteenth Century," PhD dissertation, University of Georgia, 1970; Ann Arbor, Mich.: University Microfilms, 1971.

Crompton, Arnold. *Apostle of Liberty:* [Thomas] *Starr King in California.* Boston: Beacon Press, 1950.

Curtis, Hal. *Starr King: Patriot and Mason.* San Francisco: Crane Printing Co., 1951.

de Benneville, George. "A True and remarkable account of the Life and Trance of George de Benneville," edited by Ernest Cassara, with the assistance of Alan Seaburg, *Annual Journal of the Universalist Historical Society* 2 (1960-61): 71-87.

Demarest, G.L. (ed.) "John Murray [Letters]," *Universalist Quarterly and General Review* 4 n.s. (1867): 312-32; 5 (1868): 25-47, 462-76; 6 (1869): 25-36, 419-30; 8 (1871): 222-31; 9 (1872): 385-405.

Dodge, Henry Nehemiah. *John Murray's Landfall: A Romance and a Foregleam.* New York: G.P. Putnam's Sons, 1911.

Duffy, John (ed.). *Parson Clapp of the Strangers' Church of New Orleans.* Baton Rouge, La.: Louisiana State University Press, 1957.

Eddy, Richard. "History of Universalism," Allen, Joseph Henry and Eddy, Richard, *A History of the Unitarians and Universalists in the United States* (New York:

Christian Literature Co., 1894), pp. 251-493.

_____. "Mrs. Judith Murray," *Universalist Quarterly and General Review* 18 n.s. (April 1881): 194-213; 19 n.s. (April 1882): 140-51.

_____. *The Life of Thomas J. Sawyer, S.T.D., LL.D. and of Caroline M. Sawyer.* Boston: Universalist Publishing House, 1900.

_____. *Universalism in America: A History.* 2 vols. Boston: Universalist Publishing House, 1884-1886.

_____. *Universalism in Gloucester, Massachusetts, an Historical Discourse on the One Hundredth Anniversary of the First Sermon of Rev. John Murray in that Town, delivered in the Independent Christian Church, November 3, by Richard Eddy, D.D., then pastor of the church, with Addresses on the same occasion, notes and Appendix.* Gloucester, Mass.: Proctor Bros., 1892.

_____. "Universalist Conventions and Creeds," *Universalist Quarterly and General Review* 11 n.s. (1874): 328-44; 12 (1875): 5-21, 201-16, 310-23; 444-58; 13 (1876): 149-77; 14 (1877): 162-79; 15 (1878): 34-46; 17 (1880): 389-400.

_____. "The Universalist Origin of American Sunday Schools," *Universalist Quarterly and General Review* 19 n.s. (October 1882): 448-59.

Eisler, Benita (ed.). *The Lowell Offering: Writings by New England Mill Women (1840-1845).* Philadelphia: Lippincott, 1977.

Eliot, Samuel A. (ed.). *Heralds of a Liberal Faith.* Boston: American Unitarian Association, 1910.

Ellis, William A. (comp.). *Norwich University.* Concord, N.H.: Rumford Press, 1898.

Emerson, George H. *Life of Alonzo Ames Miner, S.T.D., LL.D.* Boston: Universalist Publishing House, 1896.

_____. *Memoir of Ebenezer Fisher, D.D.* Boston: Universalist Publishing House, 1880.

Faulkner, Barbara L. "Adin Ballou and the Hopedale Community," PhD dissertation, Boston University, 1965; Ann Arbor, Mich.: University Microfilms, 1966.

Field, Vena B. *Constantia: A Study of the Life and Work of Judith Sargent Murray, 1751-1820.* University of Maine Studies, 2d series, no. 17. Orono: University of Maine, 1931.

Folsom, Ida M. (ed.). *A Brief History of the Work of Universalist Women, 1869-1955.* Boston: The Association of Universalist Women, 1955.

Foote, Henry Wilder. "Catalogue of American Universalist hymn writers and hymns," Cambridge, Mass.: Hymn Society of America, 1959.

_____. "Theodore Clapp," *Proceedings of the Unitarian Historical Society* 3 (Part 2, 1934): 13-39.

French, Roderick Stuart, "The Trials of Abner Kneeland: A Study in the Rejection of Democratic Secular Humanism," PhD dissertation, George Washington University, 1971; Ann Arbor, Mich.: University Microfilms, 1972.

Frothingham, Richard. *A Tribute to Thomas Starr King.* Boston: Ticknor and Fields, 1865.

Gribbin, William, "Vermont's Universalist Controversy of 1824," *Vermont History: The Proceedings of the Vermont Historical Society* 41 (Spring 1973): 82-94.

Grosh, A.B. "Universalists," Rupp, I. Daniel (comp.), *An Original History of the Religious Denominations at Present existing in the United States.* (Philadelphia: J.Y. Humphreys, 1844), pp. 719-34.

Hanson, E.R. *Our Woman Workers. Biographical Sketches of Women eminent in the Universalist Church for literary, philanthropic and Christian work.* Chicago: *Star and Covenant* Office, 1882.

Hersey, Benjamin B. "Universalism, What It Is," *Proceedings of the Unitarian Historical Society* 11 (Part 1, 1956): 5-26.

Hersey, Laura S. *"By Their Works"–Biographical Sketches of Universalist Women.* Boston: The Association of Universalist Women, 1954.

Hewett, Phillip. History of Unitarianism in Canada. Typescript, 1977.

Hitchings, Catherine F. "Universalist and Unitarian Women Ministers," *Journal of the Universalist Historical Society* 10 (1975): 3-165.

Hunt, James D. "Orestes A. Brownson: Our Man in the Catholic Church," *Unitarian Universalist Christian* 15 (August 1969-Winter 1970): 38-42.

In Memoriam: Israel Washburn, Jr. Portland, Maine: privately printed, 1884.

Irwin, Charlotte. "Pietist Origins of American Universalism," Master's thesis, Tufts University, 1966.

Johnson, David A. "Beginnings of Universalism in Louisville," *Filson Club History Quarterly* 43 (April 1969): 173-83.

——. "George de Benneville and the Heritage of the Radical Reformation," *Journal of the Universalist Historical Society* 8 (1969-70): 25-43.

——. *To Preach and Fight: Universalism in the Queen City of the West (Cincinnati), 1800-1849.* Tucson, Arizona: Philomath Press, 1973.

Johnson, Kenneth M. "The Doctrine of Universal Salvation and the Restorationist Controversy in Early Nineteenth Century New England." PhD dissertation, University of Ottowa, 1978.

King, Thomas Starr. *Christianity and Humanity: A Series of Sermons.* Edited, with a memoir, by Edwin P. Whipple. Boston: J.R. Osgood & Co., 1877; 6th ed. Boston: Houghton Mifflin, 1882.

Kneeland, Abner. *An Appeal to Universalists, on the Subject of Excommunication, or the Withdrawing of Fellowship, on Account of Diversity of Opinion.* New York: George H. Evans, 1829.

Knepper, George W. *New Lamps for Old: One Hundred Years of Urban Higher Education at the University of Akron.* Akron, Ohio: University of Akron, 1970.

Lalone, Emerson. *And Thy Neighbor as Thyself: A Story of Universalist Social Action.* Boston: Universalist Publishing House, 1939; encl. ed., 1959.

Levy, Leonard W. (ed.). *Blasphemy in Massachusetts: Freedom of Conscience and the Abner Kneeland Case: A Documentary Record.* New York: DaCapo Press, 1973.

Livermore, Mary A. *The Story of My Life; or the Sunshine and Shadow of Seventy Years.* Hartford, Conn.: A.D. Worthington & Co., 1897.

MacDonald, Edith Fox. *Rebellion in the Mountains: The Story of Universalism and Unitarianism in Vermont.* Concord, N.H.: New Hampshire-Vermont District of the Unitarian Universalist Association for the Vermont and Quebec Universalist and Unitarian Convention, 1976.

MacPherson, David Hicks. "The Meaning of Children's Sunday," n.p. March 1977. Andover-Harvard Theological Library.

Manford, Erasmus. *Twenty-five Years in the West.* Chicago: published by the author, 1867; rev. ed., Chicago: Mrs. H.B. Manford, 1875.

McCarty, G. Wayne, "A History of the Universalist Church in the Mid-South," Master's thesis, Mississippi State University, 1964.

McGehee, Charles White. "Elhanan Winchester: A Decision for Universal Restoration," *Annual Journal of the Universalist Historical Society* 1 (1959): 43-58.

Miller, Russell E. "Hosea Ballou 2d: Scholar and Educator," *Annual Journal of the Universalist Historical Society* 1 (1959): 59-79.

——. *Light on the Hill: A History of Tufts College, 1852-1952.* Boston: Beacon Press, 1966.

Miner, Alonzo Ames. "Century of Universalism," Winsor, Justin (ed.), *Memorial History of Boston, including Suffolk County, Massachusetts, 1630-1880.* 4 vols. Boston: James R. Osgood & Co., 1880-81.

Morris, Carol. "A Comparison of Ethan Allen's *Reason the Only Oracle of Man* and Hosea Ballou's *A Treatise on Atonement,*" *Annual Journal of the Universalist Historical Society* 2 (1960-61): 34-69.

Murray, John. *Letters and Sketches of Sermons.* 3 vols. Boston: Joshua Belcher, 1812-13.

——. *Records of the Life of the Rev. John Murray; Late Minister of the Reconciliation, and Senior Pastor of the Universalists, congregated in Boston, written by Himself, to which is added, a Brief Continuation to the Closing Scene, by a Friend* [Mrs. Judith Sargent Murray]. Boston: Munroe and Francis, 1816.

New Hampshire Universalist Register, containing Denominational Statistics for the Year 1844. Compiled by J.F. Witherell. Concord, N.H.: *Balm of Gilead* Office, 1844.

Perham, Harold (ed.). *The Maine Book on Universalism.* Norway, Maine: Printed by the *Advertiser-Democrat,* 1953.

Pink, Louis Heaton (ed.). *Candle in the Wilderness: A Centennial History of St. Lawrence University.* New York: Appleton-Crofts, 1957.

Relly, James. *Union: or a Treatise of the Consanguinity and Affinity between Christ and His Church.* London, 1759; first American edition, Boston, 1779.

Robinson, Elmo Arnold. *American Universalism: Its Origin, Organization and Heritage.* New York: Exposition Press, 1970.

——. "Universalism in Indiana," *Indiana Magazine of History* 13 (1917-18): 1-19, 157-88.

——. *The Universalist Church in Ohio.* [n.p.]: Ohio Universalist Convention, 1923.

——. "The Universalist Connections of Thomas Starr King," *Annual Journal of the Universalist Historical Society* 5 (1964-65): 3-29.

——. "The Universalist General Convention from Nascence to Conjugation," *Journal of the Universalist Historical Society* 8 (1969-70): 44-93.

Rogers, George. *Memoranda of the Experience, Labors, and Travels of an Universalist Preacher, written by Himself.* Cincinnati: John A. Gurley, 1845.

Rowell, Geoffrey. "The Origins and History of the Universalist Societies in Britain, 1750-1850," *Journal of Ecclesiastical History* 22 (January 1971): 35-56.

Salisbury, Dorothy Kendall Cleaveland. "They Builded Better Than They Knew: The Universalist Church and its Concern for Education." Boston: Association of Universalist Women, 1957.

Sawyer, Thomas J. *Memoir of Rev. Stephen R. Smith.* Boston: Abel Tompkins, 1852.

Schlesinger, Arthur M., Jr. *Orestes A. Brownson: A Pilgrim's Progress.* Boston: Little, Brown, 1930.

Scott, Clinton Lee. "Universalism in New Hampshire: An Address," *Annual Journal of the Universalist Historical Society* 1 (1959): 1-10.

——. *The Universalist Church of America: A Short History.* Boston: Universalist Historical Society, 1957.

Scott, Peter Lee. "A History of the Attempts of the Universalist and Unitarian Denominations to Unite," B.D. thesis, St. Lawrence University Theological School, 1957.

Seaburg, Alan. "Recent Scholarship in American Universalism: A Bibliographical Essay," *Church History* 41 (December 1972): 513-23.

——. "Remembering Publishing History: Universalist Periodicals," *Unitarian Universalist World* 2 (15 April 1971): 2.

Seaburg, Carl. "Universalism in the Early *Centinel*: Some Newspaper Notes on Murray and Universalism." Typescript, n.d.

Sherman, Harry M. "Abner Kneeland: Religious Pioneer," B.D. thesis, Tufts College School of Religion, 1953.

Simonds, William Day. *Starr King in California.* San Francisco: Paul Elder & Co., 1917.

Skinner, Clarence R. and Cole, Alfred S. *Hell's Ramparts Fell.* Boston: Universalist Publishing House, 1941.

Smith, Stephen Rensselaer. *Historical Sketches and Incidents, illustrative of the Establishment and Progress of Universalism in the State of New York.* 2 vols. Buffalo: Steele's Press, 1843; James S. Leavitt, 1848.

Spear, Charles. Diary, 1841-49. Typescript, Andover-Harvard Theological Library.

Spear, John Murray. *Messages from the Superior State: communicated by John Murray through John M. Spear, in the Summer of 1852; carefully prepared for publication, with a Sketch of the Author's earthly life, and a brief Description of the Spiritual Experience of the Medium.* By S.C. Hewitt. Boston: Bela Marsh, 1852.

Stacy, Nathaniel. *Memoirs of the Life of Nathaniel Stacy, Preacher of the Gospel of Universal Grace.* Columbus, Penna.: Abner Vedder, 1850.

Start, Alaric B. (ed.). *History of Tufts College; published by the Class of 1897.* Tufts College, Mass., 1896.

Stone, Edwin Martin. *Biography of Elhanan Winchester.* Boston: H.H. Brewster, 1836.

Sullivan, Joseph Ladd. "The Universalist Church and the Unitarian Church Moves [*sic*] Again toward Merger," doctoral dissertation, Central School of Religion of Indianapolis, Indiana, [1957].

Swann, Martha Hardwick. "John Crenshaw Burruss," *Alabama Historical Quarterly* 18 (Summer, 1956): 137-41.

Swanson, James Arthur. "A History of Lombard College, 1851-1930," undergraduate paper, Western Illinois State College, 1955.

Sweeny, Joseph R. "Elhanan Winchester and the Universal Baptists," PhD dissertation, University of Pennsylvania, 1969.

Thayer, Thomas Baldwin. *Theology of Universalism.* Boston: Universalist Publishing House, 1862.

Thomas, Abel C. *Autobiography of Rev. Abel C. Thomas; including Recollections of Persons, Incidents, and Places.* Boston: James M. Usher, 1852.

_____. *A Century of Universalism in Philadelphia and New-York, with Sketches of its History in Reading, Hightstown, Brooklyn and elsewhere.* Philadelphia: published by the author, 1872.

Titus, Anson. "Alonzo Ames Miner, S.T.D., LL.D.," *To-Day* 2 (March 1895): 122-26.

_____. "Reminiscences of Early American Universalism," *Universalist Quarterly and General Review* 18 n.s. (October 1881): 431-40; 22 n.s. (October 1885): 442-46.

Tucker, Elva Louise. "The History of the Universalist Church in Iowa," Master's thesis, State University of Iowa, 1944.

The Universalist Centennial held in Gloucester, Massachusetts, September 20th, 21st, & 22nd, 1870. Boston: Universalist Publishing House, 1870.

Vickery, Charles Nelson. "A Century of Attempted Rapprochement between the Universalist Church of America and the American Unitarian Association," S.T.B. thesis, Crane Theological School, Tufts College (University), 1945.

Watt, Donald. *From Heresy Toward Truth: The Story of Universalism in Greater Hartford and Connecticut, 1821-1971.* West Hartford, Conn.: The Universalist Church of West Hartford, 1971.

Weaver, George Sumner. *Autobiography of George Sumner Weaver, D.D.: A Sketch of a Busy Life.* Edited by Ernest L. Robinson. Albany, N.Y.: privately printed, [1965].

Wendte, Charles W. *Thomas Starr King: Patriot and Preacher.* Boston: Beacon Press, 1921.

Whittemore, Thomas. *The Early Days of Thomas Whittemore. An Autobiography extending from A.D. 1800 to A.D. 1825.* Boston: James M. Usher, 1859.

_____. *Life of Rev. Hosea Ballou, with Accounts of his writings, and biographical sketches of his seniors and contemporaries in the Universalist Ministry.* 4 vols. Boston: James M. Usher, 1854-55.

_____. *The Modern History of Universalism, from the Era of the Reformation to the Present Time.* Boston: published by the author, 1830.

_____. "State of the Doctrine and Denomination of Universalists," *Expositor and Universalist Review* 1 n.s. (January, July 1833): 61-76, 276-83.

Wilbur, Earl Morse. *A History of Unitarianism.* 2 vols. Cambridge, Mass.: Harvard University Press, 1945-1952.

Williams, George Huntston. "American Universalism: A Bicentennial Historical Essay," *Journal of the Universalist Historical Society* 9 (1971): 1-94.

Williams, John E. & others. *A History of Universalism in North Carolina.* [n.p.]:

Universalist Convention of North Carolina, 1968.

Winchester, Elhanan. *The Reigning Abominations, especially the Slave Trade, considered as Causes of Lamentations; being the Substance of a Discourse delivered in Fairfax, Virginia, December 30, 1774, and now published with several additions.* London, 1788.

_____. *Reverend Elhanan Winchester: Biography and Letters.* Edited by Edwin S. Gaustad. New York: Arno Press, 1972.

_____. *The Universal Restoration: exhibited in Four Dialogues between a Minister and His Friend.* Philadelphia, 1792, 1843.

The Winchester Centennial, 1803-1903. Historical Sketch of the Universalist Profession of Belief adopted at Winchester, N.H., September 22, 1803, with the Addresses and Sermons at the Commemorative Services held in Winchester [N.H.], *Rome City, Ind., and Washington, D.C. September and October 1903.* Boston: Universalist Publishing House, 1903.

Wolley, Robert S. "Clara Barton, A Biographical Sketch of Compulsion," *Annual Journal of the Universalist Historical Society* 1 (1959): 11-31.

Work Projects Administration. *An Inventory of Universalist Archives in Massachusetts.* Boston: Historical Records Survey, 1942.

_____. "An Inventory of Universalist Church Records in Connecticut," [n.p., typescript, 1940].

Wright, C. Conrad. *The Beginnings of Unitarianism in America.* Boston: Starr King Press, 1955.

_____. "Henry W. Bellows and the Organization of the National Conference," *Proceedings of the Unitarian Historical Society* 15 (Part 2, 1965): 17-46.

GENERAL REFERENCES

Ahlstrom, Sydney E. *A Religious History of the American People.* New Haven: Yale University Press, 1972.

Babson, John J. *History of the Town of Gloucester, Cape Ann, including the Town of Rockport.* Gloucester, Mass.: Proctor Bros., 1860. 350th Anniversary edition, Gloucester, Mass.: Peter Smith, 1972.

Baird, Robert. *Religion in America; or, an Account of the origin, progress, relation to the State, and present condition of the Evangelical churches in the United States, with notices of the Unevangelical Denominations.* New York: Harper & Bros., 1844.

Benedict, David. *A General History of the Baptist Denomination in America.* 2 vols. Boston, 1813.

Bernheim, Gotthardt D. *History of the German Settlements and of the Lutheran Church in North and South Carolina.* Philadelphia: Lutheran Book Store, 1872; Spartanburg, S.C.: The Reprint Co., 1972.

Biggs, Joseph. *A Concise History of the Kehukee Baptist Association.* Tarboro, N.C.: George Howard, 1834.

Brock, Peter. *Pacifism in the United States: From the Colonial Era to the First*

World War. Princeton, N.J.: Princeton University Press, 1968.

Brockett, L.P. and Vaughn, Mary C. *Woman's Work in the Civil War: A Record of Heroism, Patriotism, and Patience.* Philadelphia: Zeigler, McCurdy & Co., 1867.

Brooks, Charles (comp.). *A Statement of Facts from each religious denomination in New England, respecting Ministers' Salaries.* Boston: John Wilson & Son, 1854.

Brown, Slater. *The Heyday of Spiritualism.* New York: Hawthorn Books, 1970.

Cartwright, Peter. *Autobiography of Peter Cartwright, the Backwoods Preacher.* New York & Cincinnati: The Methodist Book Concern, [1856].

Cherrington, Ernest H. *The Evolution of Prohibition in the United States of America.* Westerville, Ohio: American Issue Press, 1920.

Clarke, Edward H. *Sex in Education; or, A Fair Chance for the Girls.* Boston: James R. Osgood & Co., 1873.

Clarkson, Thomas. *History of the Rise, Progress, & Accomplishment of the Abolition of the African Slave-Trade, by the British Parliament.* 2 vols. London: Longman, Hurst, Rees, and Orme, 1808. Philadelphia: James P. Parke, 1808.

Cross, Whitney R. *The Burned Over District: The Social and Intellectual History of Enthusiastic Religion in Western New York, 1800-1850.* Ithaca, N.Y.: Cornell University Press, 1950.

Curti, Merle. *The American Peace Crusade, 1815-1860.* Durham, N.C.: Duke University Press, 1929.

Cushing, John D. "Notes on Disestablishment in Massachusetts, 1780-1833," *William and Mary Quarterly* 26 (April 1969): 169-90.

Davis, David Brion. "The Movement to Abolish Capital Punishment in America, 1787-1861," *American Historical Review* 63 (October 1957): 23-46.

Dobbs, Jeannine. "America's First All Women's Magazine," *New England Galaxy* 19 (Fall 1977): 44-48.

Dumond, Dwight Lowell. *Antislavery: The Crusade for Freedom in America.* Ann Arbor: University of Michigan Press, 1961.

Eddy, Richard. *Alcohol in History: An Account of Intemperance in all Ages; together with a history of the various methods employed for its removal.* New York: The National Temperance Society and Publication House, 1887.

Filler, Louis. *The Crusade Against Slavery, 1830-1860.* New York: Harper & Bros., 1960.

_____. "Movements to Abolish the Death Penalty in the United States," *Annals of the American Academy of Political and Social Science* 284 (November 1952): 124-36.

Finney, Charles Grandison. *Lectures on Revivals of Religion.* Edited by William G. McLoughlin. Cambridge, Mass.: Belknap Press of the Harvard University Press, 1960.

_____. *Memoirs of Rev. Charles G. Finney, written by Himself.* New York: A.S. Barnes & Co., 1876.

Flexner, Eleanor. *Century of Struggle: The Woman's Rights Movement in the United States.* Cambridge, Mass.: Harvard University Press, 1959; rev. ed., 1975.

Franklin, John Hope. *From Slavery to Freedom: A History of Negro Americans.* 3d ed. New York: Knopf, 1967.

Frothingham, Octavius Brooks. *Transcendentalism in New England.* New York: Putnam, 1876.

Gaustad, Edwin S. *The Great Awakening in New England.* New York: Harper, 1957.

——. *Historical Atlas of Religion in America.* New York: Harper & Row, 1962.

Hale, Sarah Josepha. *Woman's Record; or, Sketches of all Distinguished Women, from "the beginning" till A.D. 1850.* New York: Harper & Bros., 1853; 2d ed., 1860.

Hanaford, Phebe A. *Daughters of America; or, Women of the Century.* Boston: B.B. Russell, 1883.

Harrison, John F.C. *Robert Owen and the Owenites in Britain and America: The Quest for the New Moral World.* London: Routledge and Kegan Paul, 1969.

Harrisson, David, Jr. *A Voice from the Washingtonian Home.* Boston: Redding & Co., 1860.

Hayward, John. *The Religious Creeds and Statistics of every Christian Denomination in the United States and British Provinces.* Boston: John Hayward, 1836.

Howe, Julia Ward (ed.). *Representative Women of New England.* Boston: New England Historical Publishing Co., 1904.

——. *Sex and Education: A Reply to Dr. E.H. Clarke's "Sex in Education."* Boston: Roberts Brothers, 1874.

Howe, Samuel Gridley. "Atheism in New England," *New England Magazine* 7 (December 1834): 500-509; 8 (January 1835): 53-62.

Hudson, Winthrop S. *Religion in America.* New York: Charles Scribner's Sons, 1965.

James, Edward & others. *Notable American Women, 1607-1950.* 3 vols. Cambridge, Mass.: Belknap Press of the Harvard University Press, 1971.

Johnson, Guion Griffis. *Ante-Bellum North Carolina: A Social History.* Chapel Hill: University of North Carolina Press, 1937.

Josephson, Hannah. *The Golden Threads: New England's Mill Girls and Magnates.* New York: Duell, Sloan and Pearce, 1949.

Keller, Charles R. *The Second Great Awakening in Connecticut.* New Haven: Yale University Press, 1942.

Kerr, Howard. *Mediums, and Spirit-Rappers, and Roaring Radicals: Spiritualism in American Literature, 1850-1900.* Urbana: University of Illinois Press, 1972.

Kinney, Charles B., Jr. *Church and State: The Struggle for Separation in New Hampshire, 1630-1900.* New York: Teachers College, Columbia University, 1955.

Leopold, Richard W. *Robert Dale Owen: A Biography.* Cambridge, Mass.: Harvard University Press, 1940.

Lewis, Orlando F. *The Development of American Prisons and Prison Customs, 1776-1845.* New York: Prison Association of New York, 1922.

Mabee, Carleton. *Black Freedom: The Nonviolent Abolitionists from 1830 through the Civil War.* New York: Macmillan, 1970.

Mackey, Philip English. "An All-Star Debate on Capital Punishment, Boston, 1854," *Essex Institute Historical Collections* 110 (July 1974): 181-99.

——. "Reverend George Barrell Cheever: Yankee Reformer as Champion of the

Gallows," *Proceedings of the American Antiquarian Society* 82 (October 1972): 323-42.

McKelvey, Blake. *American Prisons: A Study in American Social History prior to 1915*. Chicago: University of Chicago Press, 1936.

McLoughlin, William G., Jr. *Modern Revivalism: Charles Grandison Finney to Billy Graham*. New York: Ronald Press, 1959.

——. *New England Dissent, 1630-1833: The Baptists and the Separation of Church and State*. 2 vols. Cambridge, Mass.: Harvard University Press, 1971.

Meyer, Jacob C. *Church and State in Massachusetts from 1740 to 1833: A Chapter in the History of the Development of Individual Freedom*. Cleveland, Ohio: Western Reserve University Press, 1930.

Mott, Frank Luther. *A History of American Magazines*. 4 vols. Cambridge, Mass.: Harvard University Press, 1938-57.

Narrative of the Life of Frederick Douglass, an American Slave, written by Himself. Edited by Benjamin Quarles. Cambridge, Mass.: Belknap Press of the Harvard University Press, 1960.

O'Neall, John B. *The Annals of Newberry* [South Carolina], *Historical, Biographical, and Anecdotal.* 2 vols. Charleston, S.C.: S.G. Courtenay & Co., 1859.

Perry, Lewis. *Radical Abolitionism: Anarchy and the Government of God in Antislavery Thought.* Ithaca: Cornell University Press, 1973.

Pfeffer, Leo. *Church, State, and Freedom.* Boston: Beacon Press, rev. ed., 1967.

Podmore, Frank, *Mediums of the 19th Century*. 2 vols. Reprint of *Modern Spiritualism* (1902). New Hyde Park, N.Y.: University Books, 1963.

Pope, Thomas H. *The History of Newberry County, South Carolina.* Vol. 1: 1749-1860. Columbia: University of South Carolina Press, 1973.

Post, Albert. *Popular Freethought in America, 1825-1850.* New York: Columbia University Press, 1943.

Purcell, Richard J. *Connecticut in Transition: 1775-1818.* Washington, D.C.: American Historical Association, 1918; rev. ed., Middletown, Conn.: Wesleyan University Press, 1963.

Quinby, George Washington. *The Gallows, the Prison, and the Poor-House.* Cincinnati: G.W. Quinby, 1856.

Randall, J.G. and Donald, David. *The Civil War and Reconstruction.* 2d ed. Boston: D.C. Heath, 1961.

Reed, Susan M. *Church and State in Massachusetts, 1691-1740.* Urbana: University of Illinois Press, 1914.

Robinson, Harriet H. *Loom and Spindle; or, Life Among the Early Mill Girls, with a Sketch of "The Lowell Offering" and Some of its Contributors.* New York: T.Y. Crowell, 1898; rev. ed., including corrections by the author, Kailua, Hawaii: Press Pacifica, 1976.

Rush, Benjamin. *Letters of Benjamin Rush.* 2 vols. Edited by L.H. Butterfield. Princeton, N.J.: Princeton University Press, 1951.

——. *The Selected Writings of Benjamin Rush.* Edited by Dagobert D. Runes. New York: Philosophical Library, 1947.

Smith, Sherman M. *The Relation of the State to Religious Education in Massachusetts.* Syracuse, N.Y.: Syracuse Union Bookstore, 1926.

Smith, Timothy L. *Revivalism and Social Reform in Mid-Nineteenth America.* Nashville, Tenn.: Abingdon Press, 1957.

Stiles, Ezra. *The Literary Diary of Ezra Stiles, D.D., LL.D.* 3 vols. Edited by Franklin Bowditch Dexter. New York: Charles Scribner's Sons, 1901.

Stokes, Anson Phelps. *Church and State in the United States.* 3 vols. New York: Harper, 1950.

Swedenborg, Emanuel. *Compendium of the Theological and Spiritual Writings of Emanuel Swedenborg.* [Compiled by Woodbury M. Fernald.] Boston: Crosby & Nichols, 1853.

Sweet, William Warren. "The Churches as Moral Courts of the Frontier," *Church History* 2 (March 1933): 3-21.

———. *Religion on the American Frontier, 1783-1860.* 4 vols. Chicago: University of Chicago Press, 1946.

———. *Revivalism in America: Its Origin, Growth and Decline.* New York: Scribner's Sons, 1944.

Townsend, Leah. *South Carolina Baptists, 1670-1805.* Florence, S.C., 1935; Baltimore, Md.: Genealogical Publishing Co., 1974.

Tuttle, Elizabeth Ann. *The Crusade against Capital Punishment.* Austin: University of Texas Press, 1959.

William Lloyd Garrison, 1805-1879: The Story of His Life told by his Children. 4 vols. New York: Century Co., 1885.

Wilson, Henry. *History of the Rise and Fall of the Slave Power in America.* 3 vols. 5th ed. Boston: Houghton Mifflin, 1884.

Index

C

D

G

M

Q

R

S

T

U

V

W

Y

Z